W9-CHV-992

STRATEGIC MARKETING

THE IRWIN SERIES IN MARKETING

Gilbert A. Churchill, Jr., Consulting Editor
University of Wisconsin, Madison

Alreck & Settle
The Survey Research Handbook, 1/e

Arens & Bovee
Contemporary Advertising, 5/e

Belch & Belch
Introduction to Advertising and Promotion: An Integrated Marketing Communications Approach, 2/e

Bernhardt & Kinnear
Cases in Marketing Management, 6/e

Bonoma & Kosnik
Marketing Management: A Strategic Approach, 1/e

Boyd & Walker
Marketing Management: A Strategic Approach, 1/e

Boyd, Westfall & Stasch
Marketing Research: Text and Cases, 7/e

Burstiner
Basic Retailing, 2/e

Cadotte
The Market Place: A Strategic Marketing Simulation, 1/e

Cateora
International Marketing, 8/e

Churchill, Ford & Walker
Sales Force Management, 4/e

Cole
Consumer and Commercial Credit Management, 9/e

Cravens
Strategic Marketing, 4/e

Cravens & Lamb
Strategic Marketing Management Cases, 4/e

Crawford
New Products Management, 4/e

Dillon, Madden & Firtle
Essentials of Marketing Research, 1/e

Dillon, Madden & Firtle
Marketing Research in a Marketing Environment, 3/e

Engel, Warshaw & Kinnear
Promotional Strategy, 8/e

Faria, Nulsen & Roussos
Compete, 4/e

Futrell
ABC's of Selling, 4/e

Futrell
Fundamentals of Selling, 4/e

Hawkins, Best & Coney
Consumer Behavior, 5/e

Kerin, Hartley, Rudelius & Berkowitz
Marketing, 4/e

Lambert & Stock
Strategic Logistics Management, 3/e

Lehmann
Market Research and Analysis, 3/e

Lehmann & Winer
Analysis for Marketing Planning, 3/e

Lehmann & Winer
Product Management, 1/e

Levy & Weitz
Retailing Managment, 1/e

Mason, Mayer & Wilkinson
Modern Retailing, 6/e

Mason, Mayer & Ezell
Retailing, 5/e

Mason & Perreault
The Marketing Game!, 2/e

McCarthy & Perreault
Basic Marketing: A Global-Managerial Approach, 11/e

McCarthy & Perreault
Essentials of Marketing: A Global-Managerial Approach, 6/e

Patton
Sales Sim, 1/e

Peter & Donnelly
A Preface to Marketing Management, 6/e

Peter & Donnelly
Marketing Management: Knowledge and Skills, 3/e

Peter & Olson
Consumer Behavior and Marketing Strategy, 3/e

Peter & Olson
Understanding Consumer Behavior, 1/e

Quelch & Farris
Cases in Advertising and Promotion Management, 4/e

Quelch, Dolan & Kosnik
Marketing Management: Text & Cases, 1/e

Smith & Quelch
Ethics in Marketing, 1/e

Stanton, Buskirk & Spiro
Management of a Sales Force, 8/e

Thompson & Stappenbeck
The Marketing Strategy Game, 1/e

Walker, Boyd & Larréché
Marketing Strategy: Planning and Implementation, 1/e

Weitz, Castleberry & Tanner
Selling: Building Partnerships, 1/e

STRATEGIC MARKETING

David W. Cravens
M. J. Neeley School of Business
Texas Christian University

Fourth Edition

IRWIN
Burr Ridge, Illinois
Boston, Massachusetts
Sydney, Australia

Senior sponsoring editor: *Stephen M. Patterson*
Editorial coordinator: *Lynn Nordbrock*
Marketing manager: *Scott J. Timian*
Project editor: *Karen J. Nelson*
Production manager: *Ann Cassady*
Designer: *Larry J. Cope*
Art coordinator: *Heather Burbridge*
Compositor: *University Graphics, Inc.*
Typeface: *10/12 Times Roman*
Printer: *R. R. Donnelley & Sons Company*
Cover Illustration: *Sally Wern Comport*

Library of Congress Cataloging-in-Publication Data

Cravens, David W.
Strategic marketing / David W. Cravens.—4th ed.
p. cm.—(The Irwin series in marketing)
Includes bibliographical references and indexes.
ISBN 0-256-12212-1 ISBN 0-256-15612-1 (International Edition)
1. Marketing—Decision making. 2. Marketing—Management.
3. Marketing—Management—Case studies. I. Title. II. Series.
HF5415.135.C72 1994
658.8′02—dc20 93–15608

Printed in the United States of America
3 4 5 6 7 8 9 0 DOC 0 9 8 7 6 5 4

To Sue and Karen

Preface

Marketing strategy plays a key role in the successful performance of businesses in a wide array of industries throughout the world. The escalating importance of customer satisfaction, diversity in the marketplace, rapidly changing technology, and global competitive challenges requires effective marketing strategies for sustaining a competitive edge. Although the changes confronting managers in the 1980s were unprecedented, the 1990s display even greater diversity and turbulence. *Strategic Marketing* examines the concepts and processes for gaining competitive advantage in the marketplace.

THE MARKETING ORGANIZATION

As the world moves toward the 21st century, the core role of strategic marketing in business performance is demonstrated in the market-driven strategies of successful organizations competing in a wide array of product and market situations. Several aspects of the rapidly changing competitive environment are apparent:

- Marketing strategy is an essential process for gaining competitive advantage, requiring the active participation of all major business functions in the organization.
- Restructuring of the traditional organization into flexible, multifunc-

tional team units is reforming the traditional hierarchical organization.

- These changes in how organizations are designed place new priorities on relationships with customers, suppliers, marketing channel members, and competitors.
- Strategies for competing are increasingly made up of interorganizational strategic alliances, often global in scope.
- The environmental and ethical aspects of business practice are critical concerns, requiring active involvement by marketing managers and staff.
- Total quality management (TQM) is a competitive reality and is altering many conventional business practices.
- Mass customization of manufacturing processes makes it possible to satisfy diverse customer needs at attractive prices.

Managing effectively in a constantly changing business environment is a requirement for success. Developing and implementing dynamic business and marketing strategies that are adaptable to changing conditions are essential in the 1990s. These challenges mandate that organizations develop the skills essential to anticipating and responding to the constantly changing needs of customers and markets.

Market diversity and new forms of competition create impressive growth and performance for those firms in which management applies strategic marketing concepts and analyses when developing and implementing business strategy. The marketing challenge is apparent in a variety of industries in the United States and around the world. Strategic marketing is essential to companies' survival and growth in the rapidly changing business environment of the 1990s. Organizations' strategies are influenced by complex forces in the marketplace. Analyzing market behavior and adjusting strategies to changing conditions require a hands-on approach to marketing planning and strategy implementation. Because of the frequent need to alter strategies for goods and services and markets, decision-based planning is critical. Penetrating financial analysis is an essential skill of the marketing professional. Seat-of-the-pants approaches to marketing strategy are poorly focused and often ineffective in the current environment.

Strategic Marketing is a complete examination of marketing strategy using a combination of the text and case materials. It is designed for use by undergraduates in capstone courses in marketing strategy and management and in the MBA marketing core and advanced strategy courses.

NEW AND EXPANDED SCOPE

Competing in any market today requires a global perspective. This emphasis is expanded in the fourth edition. The shrinking time and access boundaries of global markets establish new competitive requirements. This issue is far too important to restrict to a single chapter. The global dimensions of marketing strategy are integrated throughout the chapters of the book and also considered in various cases.

Several contemporary strategy topics are integrated throughout the text. These include relationship marketing, strategic alliances, competitive benchmarketing, total quality management, and new organizational forms. Competitive advantage is a major dimension that spans the entire book.

THE TEXT

Strategic Marketing examines the key issues and variables in selecting a strategy. It has become increasingly apparent that instructors desire more emphasis on marketing strategy that incorporates business strategy issues. Importantly, discussions with various instructors indicate a desire to provide a strategy perspective and emphasis that extends beyond the traditional focus on managing the marketing mix. Emphasis on services as well as products is expanded in the fourth edition.

The book is designed around a marketing planning approach with a clear emphasis on how to do strategic analysis and planning. The text is divided into five parts. The first part examines business and marketing strategies. Part II discusses marketing situation analysis. Part III covers designing marketing strategy. Part IV considers marketing program development. Finally, Part V discusses implementing and managing marketing strategy. Numerous how-to guides are provided throughout the book to assist the reader in applying the analysis and planning approaches developed in the text.

THE CASES

Three fourths of the cases are new to the fourth edition. Short, application-focused cases are placed at the end of each part of the book. These cases are useful in applying the concepts and methods discussed in the chapters. The cases can be used for class discussion, assignments, formal presentations, and examinations. The cases span a wide variety of business environments, both domestic and international. They include goods and services; organizations at different distribution channel levels; and small, medium, and large enterprises.

A group of comprehensive cases is located in Part VI of the book. These cases have been carefully selected to offer students a variety of marketing strategy application opportunities. Each case examines several important strategy issues. The cases represent several different competitive situations for consumer and business products and domestic and international markets.

CHANGES IN THE FOURTH EDITION

The basic design of *Strategic Marketing* from prior editions is retained in the fourth edition. Nevertheless, the revision incorporates many significant changes and additions and new examples. Every chapter has been revised to include new material and expanded treatment of important topics.

A new chapter is included on Strategic Partnerships (Chapter 3). It considers the escalating use of strategic alliances and other collaborative relationships. Marketing planning is covered in Chapter 4 rather than at the end of the book. The marketing information system chapter is also repositioned to Chapter 8. Current marketing topics including market diversity, flexible organizations, teamwork, technology, databases, and market trends are discussed in several chapters. A series of application Features is new to this addition. One Feature is located in each chapter.

Every chapter has been revised to incorporate new concepts and examples, improve readability and flow, and generate reader interest and involvement. Topical coverage is expanded (or reduced), where appropriate, to better position the book for teaching and learning in the rapidly changing business environment of the 1990s. Financial analysis guidelines are in the Chapter 4 Appendix and sales forecasting materials are in the Chapter 5 Appendix.

INSTRUCTOR'S MANUAL

A complete and expanded teaching-learning package is available in the Instructor's Manual. It includes course planning suggestions, answers to end-of-chapter questions, instructor's notes for cases, a multiple-choice question bank, and a complete set of transparency masters.

This edition of the manual has been substantially revised and expanded to improve its effectiveness in course planning, case discussion, and examination preparation. Detailed notes concerning the use of the cases is provided, including epilogues when available.

The text, cases, and instructor's manual offer considerable flexibility in course design, depending on the instructor's objectives and the course in which the book is used.

ACKNOWLEDGMENTS

The book benefits from the contributions and experiences of many people and organizations. Business executives and colleagues at universities throughout the United States, Europe, and Asia have influenced the development of *Strategic Marketing.* While space does not permit thanking each person, a sincere note of appreciation is extended to all. I shall identify several whose assistance was particularly important. A special note of appreciation is extended to consulting editor Gilbert A. Churchill, Jr., University of Wisconsin.

A special thank you is extended to the many reviewers of prior editions and to colleagues who have offered many suggestions and ideas. Throughout the development of the fourth edition, a number of reviewers made many important suggestions for improving the book. I appreciate very much the assistance of the following professors: Nick Brockunier, University of Maryland; Gary Frankwick, Oklahoma State University; Lynn J. Loudenback, New Mexico State University; Carlos Rodriguez, Pennsylvania State University; and Mark Spriggs, University of Oregon.

I am indebted to the case authors who gave me permission to use their cases. Each author is specifically identified at the beginning of each case. Karen S. Cravens, University of Tulsa, prepared Chapter 8. Her contribution is also very much appreciated.

A special note of thanks is due to the management and professional staff of Richard D. Irwin, Inc. for their support and encouragement on this and prior editions of *Strategic Marketing.* John Black, as publisher, has provided an important editorial leadership role. As senior sponsoring editor, Steve Patterson, and his assistant, Lynn Nordbrock, have been a constant source of valuable assistance and encouragement. Scott Timian provided important marketing direction for the project. Ann Cassady and Karen Nelson guided the book through the various stages of production while Larry Cope polished the design.

Many students provided various kinds of support that were essential to completing the revision. In particular, I appreciate the excellent contributions to this edition made by Dennis M. Maloney, Suzanne Holmes, Kristen Kraker, and Paul Lauritano. I also appreciate the helpful comments and suggestions of many students in my classes.

I greatly appreciate the support and encouragement provided by Dean H. Kirk Downey and William C. Moncrief, chair of the Marketing Department. Special thanks are due to Sue Cravens, Billie Hara, and Mary Tidwell for typing the manuscript and for their assistance in other aspects of the project. Finally I want to express appreciation to Eunice West and her late husband, James L. West, for the endowment that supports my position and enables me to work on projects like this book.

David W. Cravens

Contents in Brief

Contents

CASES FOR PART II

PART III

CHAPTER 10
Marketing Strategies for Different Market and Competitive Environments 323

CHAPTER 11
Planning for New Products 356

CASES FOR PART III

PART IV

MARKETING PROGRAM DEVELOPMENT 413

CHAPTER 12
Product, Branding and Customer Service Strategies 415

CHAPTER 13
Distribution Strategy 444

CASES FOR PART IV

PART V

MARKETING ORGANIZATION AND CONTROL *557*

CASES FOR PART V

PART VI

PART

I

BUSINESS AND MARKETING STRATEGIES

CHAPTER

1

The Marketing Organization

Successfully competing in today's ever-changing global business environment requires market-driven strategies that respond to customers' needs and wants. Peter Drucker defined the marketing organization's characteristics 40 years ago:[1] The marketing organization understands buyers' needs and wants and effectively combines and directs the skills and resources of the *entire* organization to provide high levels of satisfaction to its customers. "That model of competing, which links R&D, technology, innovation, production, and finance—integrated through marketing's drive to own a market—is the approach that all competitors will take to succeed in the 1990s."[2] Rather than a specialized function within the organization, marketing is the way the company does business. Marketing includes all of the various actions of the organization that are aimed at achieving customer satisfaction.

The turnaround of Detroit Diesel Corporation provides an impressive example of how management's vision, a customer focus, and organizational teamwork can transform a company into a powerful competitor.[3] Former auto racer Roger Penske bought control of the company from General Motors Corporation in 1988. Penske changed Detroit Diesel's operating philosophy and style: The company became a customer-focused, market-driven organization, with the entire work force striving enthusiastically to satisfy customers. An important contributor to the turnaround was a successful new engine design; the only personnel change in the profitable turnaround was the elimination of 440 corporate staff jobs. The result? Under Penske's leadership the diesel engine maker's market share increased from 3 percent in 1987 to 23 percent in 1991, with sales in the $1.26 billion range. Cummins Engine Company, with a market position nearly three times that of the next largest competitor in the heavy-duty diesel engine market, lost a large portion of its market share to Detroit Diesel.

This chapter—and this book—begins with an examination of the competitive business environment of the 1990s. Then we will look closely at the process of achieving a customer focus and analyze the escalating impact of technology on business and marketing decisions. Several considerations important in deciding how a company should compete are presented. Finally, the characteristics of the marketing organization are described in detail.

THE COMPETITIVE ENVIRONMENT

As the world catapults toward the 21st century, companies are drastically altering their business and marketing strategies to get closer to their customers, counter competitive threats, and strengthen competitive advantages. While changes confronting managers in the 1980s were unprecedented, the 1990s apparently will display even greater diversity and turbulence.[4] Challenges to management include escalating international competition, political and economic upheaval, the dominance of the customer, and increasing market complexity.

Within the competitive environment, the nature and scope of market diversity require description. We will also examine important global competitive challenges and discuss the realities of competing in a constantly changing business environment.

Market Diversity: Dimensions of Change

Anticipating market change and acting quickly to take advantage of opportunity while avoiding threats is a key success requirement in an era of great market diversity. Buyers' needs vary, so the targeting of buyers within a specific market is more narrowly focused today than in the past. The automobile market offers a good example of selective targeting. In 1965 the sales of GM's Chevrolet Impala model were 1.5 million units; in 1987 Chevrolet's best-selling Celebrity model had sales of about 300,000 units. GM's largest-selling model in 1987 garnered only one fifth the sales of the high-volume car in 1965. This change in buyers' preferences is even more dramatic considering that total automobile sales were much higher in 1987 than in 1965.

Today's buyers want more than just transportation. More than ever, image, style, price, features, and other product attributes segment buyers in the automobile market. Such a complex marketplace makes customer segment–focused strategies essential. A major problem with GM's brands in the 1980s was that they all looked alike. The company's production-driven corporate culture lost sight of the customer and failed to recognize that market dynamics had changed the competitive arena.

In an interesting analysis of future trends, the book *Megatrends 2000* identified several major changes expected in the 1990s.[5] Changes of significance to the competitive environment include the escalating importance of the global economy, the movement toward similar global life-styles counteracted by pressures for individualism among countries, cultures, and individuals. Another anticipated trend—already under way—is the movement toward free-market systems in socialist countries. We can also expect the privatization of the welfare state, an expanded leadership role for women, the economic growth of the Pacific Rim, and the emergence of a major era of biotechnology.

The preferences of purchasers of consumer goods and services are changing in various ways. These shifts are partially explained by the movement of people through the different stages of the life cycle. For example, the baby boom generation of the U.S. population will start reaching age 65 in 2010. Exhibit 1–1 charts projected population age group changes from 1990 to 2010. As these demographic shifts occur, buyers' needs and preferences change:[6]

- Much of the U.S. population growth of 41 million people to more than 282 million in 2010, will be due to immigration, which will help to internationalize the United States.
- Convenience will be an increasingly key focus of the food business.
- An older, more ethnic society will challenge companies to create new products and services.
- Health care for the elderly will offer enormous potential for business.
- Service-related industries will continue to expand as the baby boomers seek convenience and avoid housekeeping tasks.
- Luxury travel will expand, with nearly half of U.S. households earning over $35,000 by 2000.

Many other changes are impacting buyers in the marketplace. As they create market diversity, they make the task of identifying and meeting customers' needs and wants ever more complex.

Global Competitive Challenges

The various trends mentioned above create a global business challenge centering on two important competitive issues. First, companies with the skills and resources for competing beyond their domestic markets have major

EXHIBIT 1–1 Projected Changes in the U.S. Population by Age Group

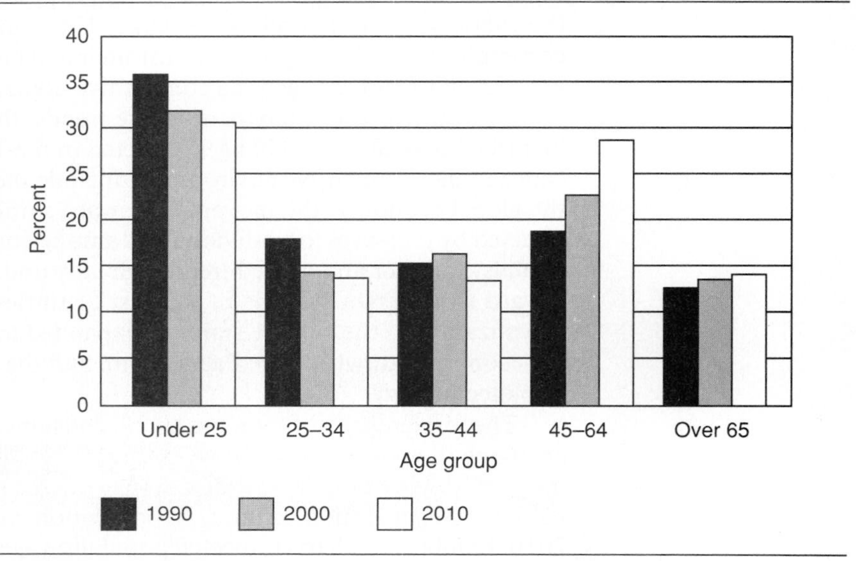

Source: U.S. Census Bureau.

opportunities for growth. Importantly, these opportunities are not restricted to industry giants. Second, maintaining a competitive position in the domestic market requires knowledge of key competitors in the global marketplace. The successful competitor in domestic markets keeps informed of foreign competitors' strategies and strengths.

Surprisingly many U.S. managers do not recognize the global challenge confronting them.[7] A survey of 1,500 managers found that only 35 percent of the Americans thought "experience outside the headquarters' country" was very important, compared with 74 percent of foreign counterparts. Only 18 percent of American managers considered the 1992 unification of Europe "substantial," contrasted with 34 percent of Latins, 52 percent of Japanese, and 55 percent of Europeans. Researchers conducting the study observed that the results indicate a broad "parochialism" expected in 1980 but surprising nearly a decade later.

New Era of Competition. Whether or not corporate managements recognize the fact, new market arenas are rapidly developing throughout the world. The Pacific Rim countries, western Europe, eastern Europe, and other regions offer promising markets and new sources of competition as they change and develop. The competitive battle among the world's major airlines illustrates the new era of competition that is developing.[8] As shown in Exhibit 1–2, global passenger traffic is expected to experience strong

EXHIBIT 1–2 Global Air Passenger Mile Projections

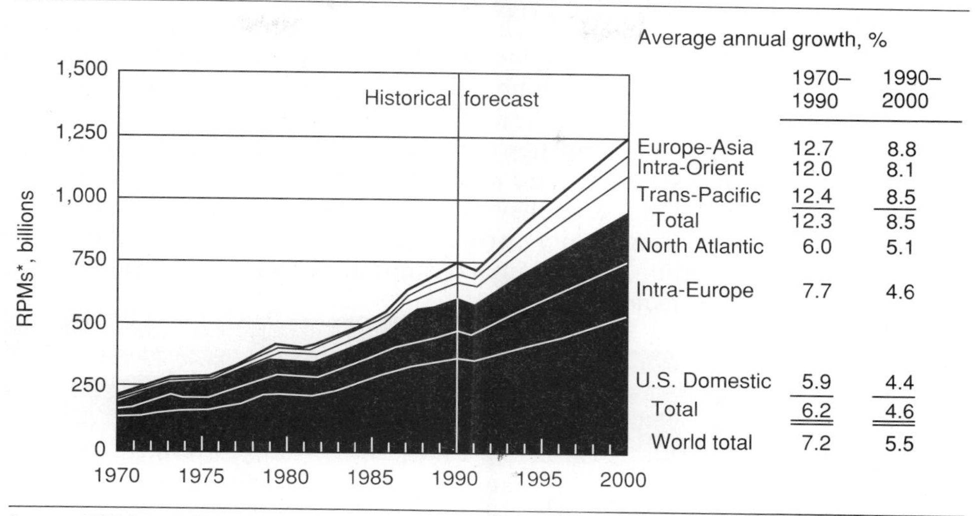

Source: *1992 Current Market Outlook* (Seattle: Boeing Commercial Airplane Group, February 1992), p. 2.34.
*RPM = Revenue Passenger Miles.

growth during the 1990s. Traffic should be much higher than the 1990 level by 2000. Europe's borders are more open than in the past. Passenger growth in Asia is very favorable. The U.S. domestic competitive situation has stabilized through industry consolidation and the failure of some carriers such as PanAm and Braniff. Industry experts predict the following competitive advantages will be important to airlines in the 1990s:

- Availability of airport gates and landing rights.
- Possession of real estate and a focused infrastructure in the financial capitals of the world (for example, London, Tokyo, New York, and Chicago).
- Operation of effective hub-and-spoke systems (e.g., feeder routes between cities such as St. Louis and major international cities such as Chicago).
- Ability to quickly respond to changing market conditions such as adding or eliminating routes.
- Access to government help in obtaining route authority and airport gates.

Of U.S. airlines, American Airlines, Delta, and United are favorably positioned to become global megacarriers. Other carriers are likely to form multicompany strategic alliances and/or to focus on specific customer segments.

The unification of Europe in 1992 exemplifies the changes occurring in markets throughout the world. The elimination of trade barriers in the 12 participating European countries requires major alterations of business and marketing strategies. These changes affect both the organizations within the 12-nation group and other nations' firms that want to compete in the unified market.

Competing in this huge market will require managers in countries outside Europe to reshape business and marketing strategies. Among the strategic issues they face is the need to evaluate whether to obtain a European Community partner. Other issues to be resolved include trade protection, advertising constraints, product design variations, and distribution requirements.

Requirements for competing globally are both different and more demanding than competing domestically. Differences in customs, languages, currency, and trade practices create risks and uncertainty for new market entrants. The social and political changes that occurred in eastern Europe in 1989 are illustrative. Almost overnight, access to these countries was possible and major social, political, and economic reforms were initiated.

Strategies for Competing Globally. The expanding importance and altered scope of international markets require that companies evaluate alternative strategies for competing in existing markets and entering new markets. An increasingly important organizational form is the global or transnational corporation. Such corporations see the world as their competitive arena. The *global corporation*

> manufactures, conducts research, raises capital, and buys supplies wherever it can do the job best. It keeps in touch with technology and market trends all around the world. National boundaries and regulations tend to be irrelevant, or a mere hindrance. Corporate headquarters might be anywhere.[9]

This strategy is appropriate for large corporations that must, to survive and grow, compete in North America, Europe, and the Pacific Rim countries. (Organizations that serve selected market segments with differentiated products or services can be more effective using focused strategies.) The global industry structures developing in tires, brewing, household appliances, computers, and chemicals comprise a few large firms and several smaller companies concentrating on one or a few market segments. Industry characteristics, the nature and scope of competition, and the unique competitive advantages of an organization are important factors in determining the benefits of global strategies.

Another organizational concept for competing in global markets, the *strategic alliance,* can be an attractive option. British Airways and U.S. Air proposed an alliance strategy in 1992 for competing in the global air transportation market. The carriers would coordinate marketing, scheduling, and operations. The major U.S. carriers voiced concerns to the government about the alliance. The relationship would give British Airways open access to U.S. airports. American, Delta, and United asked the U.S. Transportation Department to negotiate for open access to airports in the United Kingdom.

Expanding Role of Government. Governments affect the business environment by trade negotiations and protection, deregulation of industries, antitrust actions (e.g., the breakup of AT&T), support of research, the creation of incentives for investment, and the spin-off of government enterprises into private ownership. Governments of many countries act in various areas to support domestic corporations. The role of western Europe's governments in shaping policies for Europe 1992 clearly illustrates this involvement.

Many governments participate in shaping business policy and strategies. Japanese government officials play a dominant role in the economic sector. The president of the United States, through the secretary of commerce and other key staff members, is active in a wide variety of international business and finance areas. (Conversely, in some countries, private industry leaders influence government policy. For example, Deutsche Bank has a major influence on government industrial policy in Germany.)

Regional trade coalitions among the governments of several countries provide important evidence of governmental involvement in global business. Examples include Unified Europe, the Asian Pacific Tariff Union, and the North American Free Trade Agreement (NAFTA). These coalitions present countries that are not part of a trade union with complex choices as to where (and when) to focus their cooperative efforts. For instance, should a country attempt to gain membership or instead negotiate for special trade rights?

Viewing Change as an Opportunity

Good managers in the contemporary business environment recognize constant change as normal. Successful companies in the 1990s must, then, develop effective management systems to compete within this dynamic business arena. Executives must design and implement strategies that do more than cope; they must capitalize on the rapid change. "The winners of tomorrow will deal *proactively* with chaos, will look at the chaos per se as the source of market advantage, not as a problem to be got around."[10] Successful business and marketing strategies require:

1. Scanning and understanding customer, supplier, demographic, and technological trends.
2. Establishing more adaptive and flexible organization practices.
3. Setting a vision that forms a direction for the organization.

4. Encouraging a strategic unity between the organization and its external stakeholders by involving customers and suppliers in organization practices.[11]

Such strategies must be directed at constantly changing customer targets. Market awareness, organizational flexibility, strategic vision, and external relationships are important strategic capabilities in these turbulent markets.

THE CUSTOMER FOCUS

Many companies are (1) making customer satisfaction a top priority, (2) improving customer communications and knowledge, (3) strengthening service support and field linkages, and (4) implementing a customer-oriented philosophy.[12] Achieving high levels of customer satisfaction requires understanding the buyer's requirements and developing the commitment of everyone in the organization to meeting these needs. Management must build an organizational culture dedicated to understanding and meeting the needs of customers.

Factors Impacting Customer Satisfaction

Successful companies satisfy their customers. Stated another way, unhappy customers negatively affect the business. U.S. companies with excellent reputations for customer satisfaction include American Airlines, L. L. Bean, Hewlett-Packard, Marriott, and Rubbermaid. Many other companies throughout the world are very successful at keeping their customers happy. The strong performance of Japanese companies in the global market for automobiles certainly makes the point. Honda's success with the Acura Legend in the European-dominated luxury import segment of the car market demonstrates the value of high-quality products designed to satisfy buyers' preferences. Now, since Honda's pioneering entry into this market segment, Lexus, Infiniti, and other Japanese luxury brands offer strong competition to Mercedes-Benz, BMW, and other European brands.

Satisfying customers requires close monitoring of their needs and wants. Management's objective is to identify the product and supporting service attributes that buyers consider important when purchasing and using products. The level of customer satisfaction is influenced by the company's delivery system, the performance of the product or service, the image of the company/product/brand, the price-value relationship perceived by the customer, the level of employee performance, and competitors' advantages and weaknesses.[13]

Delivery System. Moving a product from the producer to the consumer or business end-user often involves a distribution channel of suppliers, manufacturers, and intermediaries. To end up with a satisfied customer, this network must function as an integrated and coordinated unit, with all members understanding and responding to customer needs and wants. For example, the time span between placing an order and receiving the item can be important, even crucial to industrial buyers of component parts. To strengthen supplier-producer relationships, many manufacturers are drastically reducing the number of suppliers from which they purchase goods and services and establishing close working relationships with those they keep.

Product/Service Performance. Performance and reliability are important influences on customer satisfaction with a product or service. The market success of Japanese automobile producers has resulted from the high quality of their products. Within only two years of entering the luxury European-style segment in the United States, the Honda Acura Legend gained first place in sales and customer satisfaction. Obviously, product quality can provide a major competitive advantage.

Image. A favorable image of a firm or its brand is widely acknowledged by business executives as a competitive advantage because it affects the customer's level of satisfaction in a positive way. Companies spend millions of dollars to promote a good image of their brands in existing and potential buyers. When buyers have a favorable experience with a product, brand image is developed or reinforced. Over time, brand value (equity) is built. Certain brand names, such as Rubbermaid in kitchenware and Kodak in photo supplies, are powerful customer franchises. Although not shown as an asset in corporate financial statements, the value of an established brand or name is a major asset of a company.

Price-Value Relationship. Buyers want the value offered by a brand to be worth its price. That is a favorable price-value relationship. One of the objectives for the Toyota Lexus and Nissan Infiniti luxury automobiles is to convince buyers that the cars offer value comparable to that of BMW and Mercedes-Benz models but at lower prices. A company may promote its brand as a unique value that is worth the price. Alternatively, management may decide to compete on a low-price basis among brands that buyers already consider to be of equivalent value.

Employee Performance. The performance of the product and delivery system depends on how well the entire organization functions as a customer-satisfaction process. Everyone in the organization affects customers—favorably or unfavorably. Businesses have discovered that awareness of customer needs and training help employees meet these responsibilities. So, many companies, such as Hewlett-Packard and Monsanto, are training their entire work force on product-quality improvement. Awareness of the customer is being integrated into the corporate culture.

Competition. Competitors' weaknesses and strengths also influence customer satisfaction and offer opportunities to gain competitive advantage.

Analyzing both the customer and the competition is important. Specific competitors may be better (or worse) at meeting the needs of specific customer groups (market segments). Finding gaps between buyers' needs and competitors' offerings provides opportunities for improving customer satisfaction. Also, companies study competitors' products to identify ways to improve their own.

Factors specific to a particular industry or company can be determined in each of the above types of influence. The product attributes that affect satisfaction often vary among classes of buyers, so identifying customers with similar needs aids customer-satisfaction analysis. Satisfaction should be compared with prior performance, industry benchmarks, and/or key competitor performance.

Finding Competitive Advantage

The marketing concept is an important guide to competitive advantage. Essentially, the marketing concept is simple: If people do not want or need what you are marketing, they will not buy it. This applies to computers, toothpaste, industrial cranes, and any other product or service. This simple, yet critical, logic lies at the heart of business success. It also applies to not-for-profit organizations. The marketing concept consists of three cornerstone elements:

- Start with the customer's needs and wants as the foundation of business purpose. Identify these needs and wants and then decide which ones to try to satisfy.
- Next, determine how the organization will satisfy these needs and wants. Customer satisfaction is the responsibility of all members of the enterprise, not just those assigned to the marketing function.
- Finally, use the enterprise's efforts to deliver customer satisfaction and obtain competitive advantage for the organization.

While the marketing concept's message is not new and its commonsense logic is clear, a surprising number of businesses have never put the concept into practice. The problem is perhaps even more critical in the public sector. Consider, for example, the futile efforts of the U.S. Treasury more than a decade ago to force people to use a coin that did not correspond to their needs and wants. The Susan B. Anthony dollar was a disaster in the marketplace and a major cost to taxpayers. Nearly 800 million coins were minted, although only one third of the coins were placed in circulation. Today, the Anthony dollar has virtually disappeared. Its problem was that it looked like a quarter; retailers, consumers, and financial institutions did not want the hassles of distinguishing between the two coins.

To repeat, understanding customers' needs and wants is critical to influencing their satisfaction. And satisfaction affects how well a company competes in the marketplace. We know that unhappy customers tell twice as many people about bad experiences as happy customers tell about good ones.[14] Research findings also indicate that if a customer complaint is resolved, the chances of repurchase are about six times higher than if the customer does not complain. So companies place 800 numbers on product packages to encourage customers to obtain product and service information and voice complaints.

Satisfied customers are a major asset; they create sustainable competitive advantage for an organization. When the costs of obtaining a new customer and developing a favorable long-term relationship are totaled, the investment is often substantial. Moreover, a satisfied customer will continue to purchase the preferred brand if it offers value over competing brands. Thus, building customer equity is important.

Customer-Driven Business Strategies

Putting the philosophy of the marketing concept into action requires the efforts of everyone in the organization, not just those assigned specific sales and marketing responsibilities. The requirements for developing a customer-oriented organization include:

- Instilling customer-oriented values and beliefs supported by top management.
- Integrating market and customer focus into the strategic planning process.
- Developing strong marketing managers and programs.
- Creating market-based measures of performance.
- Developing customer commitment throughout the organization.[15]

Note how closely these requirements correspond to the actions top management took in Detroit Diesel's turnaround discussed in the chapter opener.

ESCALATING INFLUENCE OF TECHNOLOGY

Technology is important to all companies, not just those competing with high-technology products: "So pervasive is technology today that it is virtually meaningless to make distinctions between technology and nontechnology businesses and industries: there are *only* technology companies."[16] We will look first at several important characteristics of technology, then at the critical role of innovation in the organization. As in other aspects of business, product-service quality is involved, so we will discuss that area and examine the importance of information technology. Finally, technology is crucial to the environmental responsibility of business firms, which we will consider.

Important Characteristics

Technology influences a company's competitive position. The demands of creating new technologies require huge investments by corporations. Also, technology accelerates the life cycles of products and provides a wide range of alternatives for buyers.

Competitive Advantage. Because high-quality products and services favorably affect customer satisfaction, gaining technological superiority that can be used to meet buyers' needs and wants creates a competitive edge for a company. Gaining and keeping competitive advantage through superior technology is clearly important, perhaps essential in today's global business environment. Technology generates new products that play a pivotal role in business strategy.

The rapidly changing competitive environment requires continuous attention to new-product development. Said one manager: "The marketplace will demand customized products and immediate delivery. This will force managers to make swift product-design and marketing decisions that now often take months and reams of reports."[17] The Minnesota Mining and Manufacturing Company's strategy for competing in foreign markets is illustrative.[18] Employing a modest level of investment, 3M begins to compete in a market with one product. Examples include reflective traffic sign sheeting in Russia and scouring pads in Hungary. New products are added one at a time, and local participation (e.g., workers and managers) helps to compress market entry time.

High Cost. Creating new technology is very expensive. The financial demands of developing and commercializing technology require a major financial commitment by a company. In fact, the cost of resources and skills needed for new technology is becoming increasingly prohibitive for a single organization. In several industries, corporations are forming strategic alliances for technology and product development.

New technology is a central feature of Gillette's Sensor razor, introduced in 1990. The financial stakes were high: The innovative shaving process offered by Sensor required more than $200 million to develop and start manufacturing, plus another $110 million in advertising during the introductory year. Thus, the business challenge that confronted the Sensor project was described as formidable:

> To substantially increase Gillette's profits, Sensor must perform a marketing miracle: halt a 15-year trend toward inexpensive disposable razors. At double the cost of shaving using disposables, Sensor will be a hard sell.[19]

Sensor was a tremendous success, exceeding management's forecasts of revenues and profits. The technology used to develop Sensor proved to be a superior competitive advantage over existing brands.

Short Life Cycles. Products, like people, grow old and may eventually become obsolete. New technology compresses the life cycles of products. Word-processing equipment eliminated the need for office typewriters, and personal computers replaced word-processing equipment. Maintaining a competitive edge requires the continuous development of new products. In extreme situations, new technology may destroy the advantage of existing technology. For example, plain-paper printing technologies eroded the competitive position of the thermal process in the fax market during the early 1990s; the plain-paper machines also offered suppliers higher profit margins than the thermal paper machines.

Range of Choices. Technology has created a huge array of choices for buyers. According to Marketing Intelligence Service, more than 15,000 new consumer products were introduced in 1991.[20] Many were extensions of existing brands rather than new-to-the-world products. Whether new products or improvements, they presented buyers with a wide range of choices in the marketplace. New technology continues to fuel these choices. For example, in 1991 AT&T introduced a new videophone targeted to the consumer market. The phone was priced at $1,500 per unit.

Innovation Process. New technology is essential to corporate survival and growth. "Above all the innovative company organizes itself to abandon the old, the obsolete, the no longer productive."[21] The customer-satisfaction chain shown in Exhibit 1–3 illustrates how various business functions need to work together in producing customer satisfaction.[22] Moving this array of activities and functions toward the common goal of customer satisfaction requires (1) an understanding of the product and service characteristics that customers want and need and (2) effective coordination and interaction among the various business functions.

Analyzing Customer Needs. Relying only on managers' perceptions of customer needs carries great risk in today's complex marketplace. The problems experienced by Western Union in the 1980s show the dangers of not recognizing changes in customer requirements and not identifying new forms of competition (e.g., facsimile transmission). Staying in close contact with the marketplace is critically important. Regular measurement of customer satisfaction may indicate that buyer needs or preferences are changing. Evaluation activities should involve all personnel in contact with customers, because an important part of the monitoring task is identifying buyers' future needs. Within the organization, marketing professionals should be continuously evaluating the changing requirements of end-users and channel members.

The Innovative Company. Innovative companies display several important characteristics.[23] One is the stated objective of creating new value and new satisfaction for the customer. Also, innovation extends beyond the

EXHIBIT 1–3 Customer Satisfaction Chain

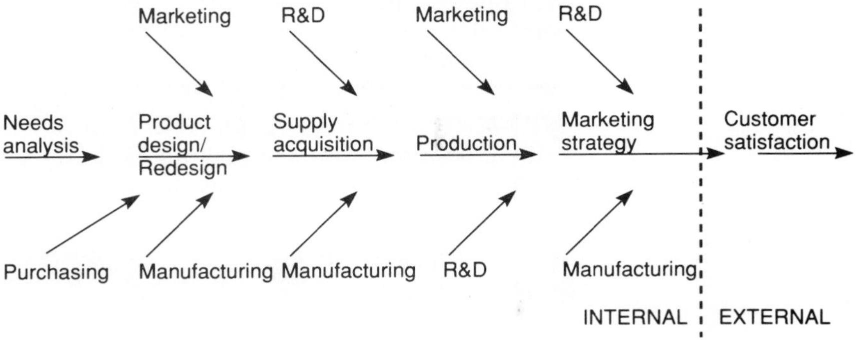

Marketing R&D Marketing R&D

Needs analysis → Product design/Redesign → Supply acquisition → Production → Marketing strategy → Customer satisfaction →

Purchasing Manufacturing Manufacturing R&D Manufacturing

INTERNAL | EXTERNAL

research and development (R&D) laboratory to include changes in all organizational areas. Abandoning obsolete and no-longer-productive products and services is a normal process of the innovative business. It recognizes that regular evaluation of existing products is essential and that expenditures for innovation do not always yield commercial successes. The objective is to generate a stream of new products or services sufficient to maintain the vitality of the organization.

Exhibit 1–4 compares major recipients of U.S. patents. Many patents were granted to foreign firms, and U.S. companies lost the three top positions to Japanese firms during the decade ending in 1987. (These data provide further evidence of the global scope of competition, mentioned earlier, that exists in many markets.) Does the patent record suggest that Japanese manufacturers are more inventive than their U.S. rivals? Would analysis show that U.S. corporations do not spend enough on research and development or instead do not spend effectively?

Product and Service Quality

The topic of product quality has made national headlines as a critical competitive issue confronting U.S. firms.[24] Quality has traditionally been seen as a manufacturing responsibility. However, the application of product quality-improvement concepts and methods is important to improving the performance of all business functions.[25] The theory and techniques of statistical process control offer a promising analytical approach for increasing the productivity and effectiveness of manufacturing, research and development, finance, distribution, and marketing processes.[26] Strategies to improve quality are being implemented by many companies such as Campbell's Soup, Hewlett-Packard, IBM, and Ford.

EXHIBIT 1–4 Top Ten Corporations Receiving U.S. Patents

1987		*1978*		*1978–1987*	
Canon	847	GE	820	GE	7,504
Hitachi	845	Westinghouse Electric	488	Hitachi	5,333
Toshiba	823	IBM	450	IBM	4,952
GE	779*	Bayer	434	RCA	4,336
U.S. Philips	687	RCA	424	Toshiba	4,228
Westinghouse Electric	652	Xerox	418	AT&T	4,213
IBM	591	Siemens	412	U.S. Philips	4,127
Siemens	539	Hitachi	388	Siemens	4,099
Mitsubishi Denki	518	Du Pont	386	Westinghouse Electric	3,953
RCA	504*	AT&T	370	Bayer	3,878

*General Electric acquired RCA in 1986, but their patents are listed separately.
Source: *The Wall Street Journal,* October 4, 1988, p. 84.

Adopting quality improvement as a business strategy imposes three key requirements on management and the work force.[27] First, a major overhaul in corporate culture may be necessary. Second, because total quality management requires close teamwork across business functions, implementing such a strategy may require a radical shift in management philosophy at all levels of the organization. Third, success demands an ongoing commitment by management and the work force.

Quality-improvement programs extend beyond the production line to include all business functions; thus, order processing becomes a quality-improvement task. Actions taken to improve quality must relate to customers' perceptions of quality. Each should be guided by customer needs and wants.

Information Technology

Information systems reduce processing time, improve communications, and aid decision making. They offer an important technology advantage that many organizations do not fully utilize.[28] Information systems will become more critical in the future, connecting cooperating organizations, suppliers, and customers. For example, vertical integration of the independent organizations, from suppliers to end-user customers, into a single organization offers few advantages when the cooperating organizations can establish effective information links. Firms with information systems can gain many of the same coordination and control benefits of vertical integration without the need to own the other companies.

The J. C. Penney Company, a leader in the use of computerized information for planning and control, has developed an impressive array of information and decision support systems.[29] The company:

- Includes suppliers in the electronic data interchange system.
- Uses bar-code tags on merchandise to input data into the inventory tracking and control system.
- Uses the bar-code data bank for new management applications in sales and trend analysis.
- Uses image-processing to transmit images of products to customers across a satellite television network.

Penney shares information with its suppliers through electronic data exchange.

Environmental Responsibility

Technology gives organizations the means to create satisfaction for customers and advantage for themselves. Unfortunately, the products developed from new technology may also lead to important concerns about protecting the physical environment and the well-being of consumers. Reducing litter, recycling wastes, and protecting people and the environment against products and contaminations that may endanger them are critically important concerns. The term *green marketing* is often used to highlight the importance of protecting the environment and reducing environmental waste.

Environmental concerns are global in scope, although countries vary in their level of concern and the priorities they place on the issues. The actions taken by the German government illustrate the importance of environmental concerns. A packaging law enacted in 1991 requires that by 1995, 80 percent of packaging waste must be collected.[30] This unprecedented law requires that 90 percent of glass and metals and 80 percent of paper, board, plastics, and laminates must be recycled; incineration is not allowed. Other European Community countries are also enacting stricter environmental laws. Clearly environmental responsibility will expand in importance in the future.

DECIDING HOW TO COMPETE

The watch industry in Switzerland and the United States experienced major competitve problems in the 1970s because manufacturers in these countries did not develop quartz crystal technology or strategies for competing in global markets. Hattori Seiko Company and other Asian competitors gained significant positions in the market. The Swiss Corporation for Microelectronics & Watchmaking Industries (SMH) is an impressive example of how one company's strategic vision for reviving the Swiss watchmaking industry enabled it to compete with Hattori Seiko for the title of the world's number

Courtesy of Omega Corporation

one watchmaker.[31] SMH's watch brands include Omega, Longines, Rado, Tissot, Certina, Mido, Hamilton, Balmain, Swatch, Flik Flak, and Endura. The company also competes in telecommunications, lasers, and other high-technology products.

We will cite SMH's strategy for regaining competitive advantage in the global watch industry throughout this discussion of deciding how to compete. First, we examine the critical responsibility of management vision in selecting a competitive strategy.

Strategic Vision

Selecting a strategy to compete successfully in today's turbulent and highly competitive global economy presents a complex management challenge. Chief executives in many companies, like SMH, are drastically altering their business and marketing strategies to improve their competitive advantage. For example, over one half of the Fortune 500 companies restructured during the 1980s.[32] To cope with market turbulence, management may decide to downsize, reposition, concentrate on a market niche, alter the business portfolio, or establish strategic alliances with other companies. General Electric's portfolio of businesses is less than one fifth of the former total. The common denominator in GE's remaining businesses is that each holds a strong market position and a sustainable competitive advantage.

Strategic vision involves decisions about *where* to compete, *when* to compete, and *how* to compete. It may also involve deciding not to compete. These decisions require knowledge of market needs and trends, competition, and competitive advantages of the organization. Rapidly changing markets and competitive threats demand high levels of executive skill in charting the course of an organization through a constantly changing business environment. Assessing that environment and deciding the future product and market direction of the corporation are critical to the performance of the enterprise. Top management must anticipate and deal proactively with future threats and opportunities; it must select the product and market areas in which the corporation can compete best and then develop market-driven strategies for gaining competitive advantage.

Failure to develop strategic responses to changes in the business environment negatively impacts corporate performance. The evidence against complacency is overwhelming:

> For two decades, the Made in America label has been vanishing as overseas manufacturers dominate entire industries. While U.S. manufacturers in 1969 produced 82 percent of the nation's television sets, 88 percent of its cars and 90 percent of machine tools, last year (1988) they made hardly any TVs, and gave up half the domestic machine-tool market and 30 percent of the auto market. Even in a new industry like semiconductors, this country's world market share has shrunk to 15 percent from 85 percent in 1980.[33]

SMH's management was not complacent in deciding how the company should compete in the watch industry. The strategy implemented by management included a portfolio of watch brands covering a range of prices from inexpensive to expensive. Several issues are involved in selecting business strategies. They include creating competitive advantage, improving organizational effectiveness, and building relationships with other companies.

Creating Competitive Advantage

Companies obtain competitive advantage by offering superior value to the customer through (1) lower prices than competitors for equivalent benefits or (2) unique benefits that more than offset a higher price.[34] Several important considerations enter into achieving customer satisfaction and gaining competitive advantage:[35]

1. The process should be customer focused.
2. Analysis of needs/wants (requirements) should look at subgroups of buyers with similar needs/wants (market segments).
3. Opportunities for advantage occur when gaps exist between what customers want and competitors' efforts to satisfy them.
4. Opportunities are identified by finding specific product/service attributes for which buyers' requirements are not being satisfied.
5. Customer satisfaction analysis should identify the best opportunities for the organization to create superior value.

SMH achieves competitive advantage in the watch market with both value and cost strategies. Its expensive brands offer unique value derived from high quality and prestigious image. Meanwhile management has lowered costs through automated production processes.[36] For example, the Swatch watch sells today at a price very similar to its price a decade ago. Swatch sales exceeded 100 million units in 1992.

Organizational Effectiveness

Determining the types of executives likely to be effective strategic decision makers is difficult. Study of managerial actions in successful corporations provides some general guidelines.[37] These managers are very good at deciding where and when to compete. The way they manage business processes enables them to outperform the competition in producing and marketing the product or service. Finally, successful managers effectively direct the entire value-added system—suppliers, internal operations, intermediaries, and customers.

Although several factors contribute to the effectiveness of an organization, competitive advantage is a core requirement. "Chief executives must take the lead in moving their institutions toward strategic management by designing organizations and developing management systems that look forward and look out."[38] Several elements are influencing change in organization structure. The relationships between business functions such as manufacturing, marketing, research and development, finance, and human resources are becoming more integrated in many companies. Teams of people from different functions are working together to design new products and improve customer service. Causes of these changes include (1) a turbulent business environment that is global in scope and (2) the availability of an impressive array of information technology that can be used to improve effectiveness.

Organizational change occurred in a wide range of companies in the 1980s. Many companies reduced the size of professional staff and the number of management levels. "Holding up the latest ideal in organizational design, the flat organization, many companies have already cut the layers of management between the chief executive and front-line supervisors from a dozen to six or fewer."[39] Such changes drastically alter the span of control of managers and require new management and control systems. For example, information technology performs many of the functions traditionally handled by middle-level managers. The increased scope of management also requires executives to have a better understanding of work functions than in the past.

SMH's chief executive, Nicolas G. Hayek, implemented several actions to turn around the poor performance of Switzerland's two largest watchmakers (which combined in 1983 to create SMH).[40] He streamlined operations, replaced weak managers, strengthened marketing capabilities, and achieved direct control of distribution. When the banks financing SMH wanted out of the watch business, insiders took over the company with support from investors. The inexpensive Swatch line was introduced and production costs reduced to facilitate a low-price strategy. Efforts continue toward producing quality at the lowest cost. Innovation generates a regular stream of new products.

Relationships with Other Organizations

Businesses competing in the 21st century will make greater use of collaborative relationships among companies. These partnerships are essential in gaining access to markets, providing needed financial resources, obtaining new technology, sharing risks, and gaining other skills and resources beyond the capacity of a single corporation. Strategic alliances can expand competitive advantage by combining the capabilities of organizations. These complex relationships also pose challenges to management, since the alliance requires sharing responsibilities and performance of functions. Partnerships enable firms to move quickly to enter new product and market areas without having to develop internal capabilities or invest in a complete acquisition of another company. The speed and resource advantages possible make the alliance more adaptable to change than other, more formal relationships (discussed in Chapter 3).

THE MARKETING ORGANIZATION

How does a company turn itself into a *marketing organization?* As stated above, the process begins with top management's awareness of the customer's importance and its commitment to becoming a customer-focused organization. Don't all chief executive officers (CEOs) place a high priority on the customer? Surprisingly, in a survey of CEOs' concerns and priorities, their primary functional preoccupation was in financial planning.[41] Only 7 to 14 percent of the respondents indicated considerable involvement in customer relations, production/manufacturing, new-product development, and research and development, compared to 46 percent for financial planning.

These findings suggest that many CEOs are much more concerned with the finance function than with customers, products, and operations. If so, this may explain why many U.S. companies have lost their competitive edge: The relentless pursuit of customer satisfaction is a prerequisite to financial performance, and an organizational focus on the customer has to start at the top of the organization.

The Customer-Focused Organization

The earlier discussion of the customer satisfaction chain (Exhibit 1–3), emphasizes aligning the entire organization toward customer satisfaction. In a rapidly changing environment where speed is essential, that total alignment requires the use of multifunctional teams. Many business activities—new-product planning, product-quality improvement, monitoring customer satisfaction, processing customer orders—require the participation of several business functions. The use of functional teams encourages the various business specialists to cooperate toward a common goal. Both evaluation of results and rewards focus on the project or program outcome.

The Cryovac division of W. R. Grace & Company, a producer of plastic packaging and storage materials, forms teams of managers and staff from various functions to develop strategic and operational plans for each of its major business areas. Management also encourages interaction and teamwork between functions by moving managers into two or more business areas—manufacturing and marketing, for example—during their careers. Some companies include suppliers and customers in their multidepartment teams.

Building relationships with customers, suppliers, and distributors and between functions within the organization is essential in becoming a customer-focused organization. An important concept guiding this process is the "internal customer." For example, the supply-acquisition and production functions are the customers of the product design function. Interfunctional units must work together toward customer satisfaction. It is important that everyone in the organization recognize the external and internal customers and understand their needs and wants.

Strategic Targeting

Strategic targeting identifies the external customer group(s) that the organization decides to serve. To respond to the variations in customer requirements in many markets, targeting one or more subgroups of buyers is essential. The earlier discussion of the diversity in buyers' preferences in the automobile market serves the point. Market segments are subgroups of buyers within a market. Buyers' needs and wants and their responsiveness to marketing efforts are similar within a segment and different between segments. For example, the Swiss watchmaker, SMH, appeals to several market segments with its different brands of watches.

Variations in buyers' needs and wants present opportunities rather than threats. They enable businesses to design product offerings to meet the preferences of various customer groups. Companies can concentrate on meeting certain needs more effectively than competitors do. Having the customer as the organization's strategic focus requires that top management select the product and market scope of the firm. To do this, management must understand customer needs and wants and target the segment(s) offering the strongest competitive advantage and potential favorable performance.

Equally important, management must develop a total organizational commitment to customer satisfaction. For success, the entire organization needs to work together as a team to identify segment requirements and achieve goals. The chief marketing executive and staff must be involved in the planning. Their strategic role is to assemble the company's market-influencing capabilities into an integrated strategy. Also, making the distribution network part of a customer-driven team of cooperating organizations is essential to successful implementation of customer-focused strategies.

Targeting all buyers in a market is not a typical strategy for most firms. Even those that decide to serve an entire market divide it into segments and develop strategies for each segment.

Dell Computer quickly gained a position in the personal computer market by selectively targeting business buyers of computers. Michael Dell founded the firm in 1984; 1992 sales were $2 billion. Dell's targeting strategy was to sell PCs by mail at competitive prices, supporting the marketing effort with a 30-day money-back guarantee, a one-year warranty, and guaranteed 24-hour on-site service.[42] These service features gave the company important competitive advantages over other mail-order suppliers of PCs.

Role of the Marketing Function

The responsibility of marketing is to assist top management in selecting one or more groups of buyers the organization will serve and in combining the organization's customer-influencing capabilities into a coordinated

EXHIBIT 1–5 Attributes of Market-Driven Behavior

Market-Driven Businesses	*Internally Oriented Businesses*
Segment by customer applications and economic benefits received by the customer	Segment by product
Know the factors that influence customer-buying decisions; focus on a package of values that includes product performance, price, service, applications	Assume that price and product performance/technology are the keys to most sales
Invest in market research and systematic collection of sales reports to track market changes and modify strategy	Rely on anecdotes and have difficulty disciplining the sales force to provide useful reports
Treat marketing investments in the same way as R&D investments	View marketing as a cost center with little of the value associated with an investment
Communicate with the market as a segment	Communicate with customers as a mass market
Talk about customer needs, share, applications, and segments	Talk about price performance, volume, and backlogs in orders
Track product, customer, and segment P&Ls and hold junior managers responsible for them	Focus on volume, product margins, and cost allocations among divisions; junior managers not held accountable due to the "political" nature of allocations
See channels as extensions of sales force and partners in serving users	Think of distribution channels as conduits
Know the strategy, assumptions, cost structure, and objectives of major competitors	Know competitive product features
Management reviews spend as much time on marketing and competitive strategy issues as on R&D, sales, and human resources	Marketing not reviewed outside of budget time

set of actions. The American Marketing Association defines *marketing* as:

> the process of planning and executing the conception, pricing, promotion, and distribution of ideas, goods, and services to create exchanges that satisfy individual and organizational objectives.[43]

AMA's definition highlights several important points about marketing's role in the organization. The marketing-management process consists of analysis, planning, implementation, and management of the firm's customer-influencing capabilities (products, pricing, promotion, and distribution). The concept of a product is broad, including goods, services, and ideas. The marketing process should result in an exchange between the parties (buyers and sellers) that satisfies the objectives of both. Finally, this concept of marketing portrays the process as an enterprise-spanning responsibility rather than a specialized function of the organization.

Exhibit 1–5 compares the attributes of market-driven and internally oriented organizations. Note the major emphasis in the market-driven attributes on strategic customer targeting and building a customer-focused organization. A market-driven perspective offers a more promising basis for competing in the contemporary business environment than an internally oriented focus does.

SUMMARY

Several key issues are involved in designing market-driven business and marketing strategies. In the constantly changing business arena, managers need to understand the dynamics of the marketplace and view change as an opportunity rather than a threat. The expanding global business challenge offers both opportunities and requirements for competing in domestic and international markets. Achieving customer satisfaction is critical to gaining sustainable competitive advantage. In finding strategies for competitive advantage, several considerations are important: the key role of strategic vision in guiding the enterprise, the role of organizational effectiveness in business strategy, and use of information systems to gain strategic advantage. Also important are product and service innovation and the need for total involvement of the organization in the process of becoming a marketing organization. Customer satisfaction is the responsibility of the entire work force.

Satisfying customers is the focus of marketing. Adoption of the marketing concept provides a logical basis for achieving this objective. The marketing concept has three cornerstones: (1) start with the customer's needs and wants as the foundation of business purpose, (2) develop the organization's approach to satisfying these needs and wants, and (3) meet the organization's objectives by delivering customer satisfaction. To succeed, management must select the needs and wants the organization is best suited to satisfy, develop an effective corporate marketing effort, and perform sound marketing planning and implementation. Sustainable competitive advantage comes as a consequence of high levels of customer satisfaction.

Strategic Marketing examines marketing decisions, analyses, and issues, emphasizing an organizational rather than functional perspective. The book offers value to students, marketing professionals, and other executives interested in marketing strategy. With an emphasis on integrating corporate and marketing strategic planning, it provides action guidelines for strategic marketing planning. Wide use is made in the book of how-to-do-it guides to analysis and planning. The book also explores various techniques and methods used in corporate and marketing strategic analysis and planning, illustrating how they are used in business analysis and screening, product-market analysis, segmentation, product positioning, new-product planning, price analysis, financial planning, and many other application areas. The cases in each part of the book offer an opportunity to apply the concepts and methods discussed in that section.

Often we can learn as much by analyzing mistakes as we do by studying the successes of business firms. To that end, the book examines the corporate and marketing strategies of a variety of companies. They illustrate both successful and unsuccessful decisions involving consumer and industrial product and service firms. The objective of these examinations is neither praise nor criticism of any company's management. Rather, these experiences enhance the study of how to develop successful strategies for capitalizing upon opportunities and avoiding threats.

QUESTIONS FOR REVIEW AND DISCUSSION

1. Discuss some of the reasons why managing in an environment of constant change will be necessary in the future.
2. Explain how a company may achieve a competitive advantage.
3. Discuss the relationship between the customer-satisfaction chain and customer satisfaction.
4. Why is product/service innovation important in achieving customer satisfaction?
5. Explain the use of the marketing concept as a guiding philosophy for a social service organization, giving particular attention to user needs and wants.
6. Identify and discuss the problems a company may encounter if management does not decide how to compete and then implement strategic plans for gaining a competitive advantage.
7. Suppose you have been appointed to the top marketing post of a corporation and the president has asked you to explain the strategic role of marketing to the board of directors. What will you include in your presentation?
8. Discuss the importance of strategic vision for competing in today's business environment.
9. Why is a global perspective important for the top management of any company, regardless of where it competes?
10. Discuss the issues that are important in transforming a company into a marketing organization.

NOTES

1. Peter F. Drucker, *The Practice of Management* (New York: Harper & Row, 1954).
2. Regis McKenna, "Marketing Is Everything," *Harvard Business Review,* January–February 1991, p. 72.
3. The illustration is based on Joseph B. White, "Revved Up: How Detroit Diesel Out from GM, Turned Around Fast," *The Wall Street Journal,* August 16, 1991, pp. A1 and A5.
4. Fred G. Steingraber, "Managing in the 1990s," *Business Horizons,* January–February 1990, pp. 50–61.
5. John Naisbitt and Patricia Aburdene, *Megatrends 2000* (New York: William Morrow, 1990).
6. Thomas R. King, "Catering to the Mature Baby-Boom Generation," *The Wall Street Journal,* Centennial Edition, 1989, p. A7.
7. Jolie Soloman, "Managing," *The Wall Street Journal,* July 12, 1989, p. B1.
8. This illustration is based on Asra Q.

Nomani, "Global Dogfight: World's Major Airlines Scramble to Get Ready for Competitive Battle," *The Wall Street Journal,* January 14, 1992, pp. A1 and A9.
9. Jeremy Main, "How to Go Global—and Why," *Fortune,* August 28, 1989, p. 70.
10. Tom Peters, *Thriving on Chaos* (New York: Knopf, 1987), p. xii.
11. David Ulrich and Margarethe F. Wiersema, "Gaining Strategic and Organizational Capability in a Turbulent Business Environment," *Academy of Management Executive* 3, no. 2 (May 1989), p. 122.
12. Earl L. Bailey, "Getting Closer to the Customer," Research Bulletin No. 229 (New York: Conference Board, 1989).
13. Larry Gulledge, "Measure Satisfaction, Performance to Meet Customers' Expectations," *Marketing News,* March 14, 1988, pp. 34–35.
14. Patricia Sellers, "How to Handle Customers' Gripes," *Fortune,* October 24, 1988, pp. 88–89.
15. Frederick E. Webster, Jr., "The Rediscovery of the Marketing Concept," *Business Horizons,* May–June 1988, p. 37.
16. McKenna, "Marketing Is Everything," p. 65.
17. Ann Barry as quoted in Carol Hymowitz, "Day in the Life of Tomorrow's Manager," *The Wall Street Journal,* March 20, 1989, p. B1.
18. Robert Ross, "Success Abroad," *The Wall Street Journal,* March 29, 1992, pp. A1, A10.
19. Lawrence Ingrassia, "Face-Off: A Recovering Gillette Hopes for Vindication in a High-Tech Razor," *The Wall Street Journal,* September 29, 1989, p. A1.
20. Laura Bird, "Marketing," *The Wall Street Journal,* January 13, 1992, p. B2.
21. Peter F. Drucker, "The Innovative Company," *The Wall Street Journal,* February 26, 1982, p. 8.
22. The following discussion is from David W. Cravens, "The Marketing of Quality," *Incentive,* November 1988, p. 28.
23. The following discussion is based on Drucker, "The Innovative Company," p. 8.
24. "Special Report: Quality," *Business Week,* June 8, 1987, pp. 130–40.
25. W. Edwards Deming, *Out of the Crisis* (Cambridge: Massachusetts Institute of Technology, Center for Advanced Engineering Study, 1986).
26. David W. Cravens, Charles W. Holland, Charles W. Lamb, Jr., and William C. Moncrief, "Marketing's Role in Product and Service Quality," *Industrial Marketing Management,* Fall 1988, pp. 285–304.
27. "Special Report: Quality," *Business Week.*
28. Jeremy Main, "The Winning Organization," *Fortune,* September 26, 1988, pp. 51–52.
29. Philip J. Gill, "J. C. Penney Pursues the Ultimate System with Creative Applications," *ComputerWorld Premier 100,* September 11, 1989, pp. 82–83.
30. "A Wall of Waste," *Economist,* November 30, 1991, p. 73.
31. The illustration is based on Margaret Studer, "SMH Leads a Revival of Swiss Watchmaking Industry," *The Wall Street Journal,* January 20, 1992, p. B4.
32. Walter Kiechel III, "Corporate Strategy for the 1990s," *Fortune,* February 29, 1988, p. 34.
33. Timothy D. Schellhardt and Carol Hymowitz, "U.S. Manufacturers Gird for Competition," *The Wall Street Journal,* May 2, 1989, p. A2.
34. Michael E. Porter, *Competitive Advantage* (New York: Free Press, 1985), p. 3.
35. This discussion is based on Porter, *Competitive Advantage,* and George S. Day and Robin Wensley, "Assessing Advantage: A Framework for Diagnosing Competitive Superiority," *Journal of Marketing,* April 1988, pp. 1–20.
36. Studer, "SMH Leads a Revival," p. B4.

37. Frederick W. Gluck, "A Fresh Look at Strategic Planning," *Journal of Business Strategy,* Fall 1985, pp. 16–17.
38. Ibid.
39. Brian Dumaine, "What the Leaders of Tomorrow See," *Fortune,* July 3, 1989, p. 50.
40. Studer, "SMH Leads a Revival," p. B4.
41. Richard T. Hise and Stephan W. McDaniel, "American Competitiveness and the CEO—Who's Minding the Shop?" *Sloan Management Review,* Winter 1988, pp. 49–55.
42. Andy Zipser, "Can Dell, CompuAdd Broaden Niches?" *The Wall Street Journal,* January 5, 1990, pp. B1 and B6.
43. American Marketing Association definition of *marketing,* 1985.

CHAPTER

2

Business Strategy and Competitive Advantage

The changing patterns of global competition require continually analyzing important forces and altering business and marketing strategies to take advantage of opportunities and to avoid threats. Demanding buyers, fast-moving technologies, intense global competition, deregulation, and social change create new challenges and opportunities for executives in a wide range of businesses. As discussed in Chapter 1, developing strategies in this environment of constant change is a key corporate success requirement.

Increasingly, companies are concentrating on the business areas and markets where their competitive advantage is greatest. Benetton Group S.P.A., the Italian casual wear producer, has a new strategy for growth in the 1990s.[1] After experiencing explosive growth, in the late 1980s management halted the expansion program and cut margins, due primarily to weak demand in the United States. Benetton's growth priorities in the 1990s are shifting to Latin America, eastern Europe, and Asia. Emphasis is placed on upgrading the quality and expanding the range of goods in its core markets in western Europe (70% of sales), and the United States (10% of sales). Benetton lost market position in the late 1980s in the United States because of strong competition from The Limited and The Gap, conflicts with its retailers, adverse customer reaction to its controversial socially active "United Colors of Benetton" advertising campaign, and the termination of many licensing agreements with retailers. The Benetton corporate structure is quite flexible, enabling management to quickly adapt its strategies to new competitive challenges. This capability is important in the fast changing world of fashion. Benetton has a design team and administrative offices in Ponzano Veneto, Italy. Most of its manufacturing is subcontracted to over 400 producers. All of the more than 6,000 retail stores throughout the world are licensed to independent owners, who agree to purchase apparel from Benetton in return for using its name for the retail shop. Management will add 1,000 new boutiques during the early 1990s, including 200 stores in Japan. The social issues advertising campaign pushed the brand into a strong global position. A 1992 print ad showing a photograph of a dying AIDS victim created new critics and widespread attention throughout the world.

This chapter considers how strategy is formulated for the entire business. Marketing strategy is guided by the decisions top management makes about how, when, and where to compete. Because of this close relationship it is important for us to examine the major aspects of designing and implementing business strategy.

We begin the chapter with a look at the nature and scope of global competition. A discussion of the sources of competitive advantage and the requirements for achieving advantage follows. Next, several key features of business strategy are considered. Finally, analysis and strategy selection are discussed.

CHANGING PATTERNS OF GLOBAL COMPETITION

Strategic refocusing is the continuing process of an organization taking advantage of opportunities and avoiding threats created by the turbulent business environment.[2] Management may alter the basic mission and scope of the enterprise, the products or services offered, the geographic scope of operations, and the customers or market segments targeted by the company.[3] Management may change how activities are performed and even the corporate culture. The General Electric Company's major shifts in its business portfolio in the late 1980s are illustrative. Management refocused the company on a few business areas such as jet engines, where GE has a dominant market position. Many other product groups such as appliances and consumer electronics products were sold. Corporate strategies may involve expanding, downsizing, or otherwise changing the nature of business operations.

Analyzing the Forces of Change

The perspective adopted in this book is that "organizations can and do implement a variety of strategies designed to modify existing environmental conditions."[4] Examples of proactive strategies include deciding in what product markets to compete, mergers, strategic alliances, promotional programs, activities designed to reduce competition, contractual relationships, political lobbying to influence legislation, and structural changes. An organization can influence its environment, recognizing there are external forces whose impact may be unavoidable.

A major study conducted by the Conference Board of 64 Canadian, European, Japanese, and United States corporations documents the widespread global trend toward strategic refocusing.[5] A related survey of 271 companies headquartered in 34 countries found that 61 percent of managers expect their business will broaden in scope, 26 percent forecast a shift in focus, and 13 percent anticipate a narrowing of business scope.[6] Constant change is expected across a wide range of organizations and business environments during the 1990s. These changes occur because of shifts in customer needs and wants, industry consolidation, new patterns of competition, distribution trends, and various changes in the global business environment. Not surprisingly, market-related changes are the most common restructuring influences.

Various changes in the international and domestic environment create opportunities and threats that require strategic actions. These influences include public policy changes (e.g., deregulation), social forces, technology advances, and economic performance. One of the most exciting examples of environmental change occurred in eastern Europe in 1989. Countries in the Eastern bloc like Poland and Hungary experienced dramatic reforms that are likely to create tremendous political and economic impacts during the 1990s. These countries are moving toward more democratic political systems and more free-market economies. The potential implications include opening new markets, the development of powerful economic forces, and shifting expenditures of the United States and other countries away from defense.

Strategic Responses

An organization's responses to the changing patterns of global competition may include: (1) adjusting the size of the business, (2) changing product and/or market scope, or (3) creating new working relationships with other organizations. We describe several examples of changes in business strategy.

Rapid Growth/Retrenchment. Reducing or rapidly expanding the number of employees of a company or business unit while retaining the existing product mix and market scope is one form of strategic change. This action alters the size rather than the scope of the organization. Size adjustments may require a new organizational structure and the redeployment of people.

Industry consolidation affects the size of the organizations involved. Consolidation has occurred in kitchen appliance, manufacturing, air transportation, energy, and wholesaling industries. For example, Vallen Corporation, the leading firm in safety equipment distribution, is expanding its nationwide channel network by opening branches and acquiring other safety equipment distributors.

Changing the Product Mix. Altering a company's mix of products may affect business operations, marketing strategy, and selling strategy. Product expansion strategies may be achieved through internal development or by acquisition. Benetton's expansion of its retail lines is illustrative. The company's new shops offer an expanded range of goods, including household accessories such as towels and bed linens, cosmetics, shoes, and eyeglasses.[7] In early 1991, Benetton launched two joint ventures in Japan for the marketing of shoes and accessories. The logo on shops was also restyled to emphasize racial harmony, as reflected in Benetton's advertising.

Altering Market Scope. Some firms change market focus using the same product mix. Illustrative actions include expanding into new international markets, altering geographic scope, and targeting new customer groups. An example is Tandy Corporation, which targeted its personal computer line at the business market in the mid-1980s. Tandy's prior targets consisted of consumer and small business buyers served through retail stores. It was necessary to train and deploy a marketing and sales organization to serve organizational buyers. Larger commercial buyers required direct contact by field salespeople.

The unification of Europe in 1992 has caused the United States and Japan to change market scope. The elimination of many intra-European trade barriers offers a competitive advantage to the companies whose nations are members of the EC. U.S. and Asian competitors must redesign their strategies and organizations to compete effectively in this new market environment. The 12 European partners are repositioning through mergers and cooperative arrangements.

The accompanying Global Feature describes Lufthansa's strategy for competing in the air travel market. The German carrier's losses in 1992 are expected to be three times as high as the 1991 losses. Reducing costs and expanding its global market access are major pressures confronting Lufthansa in the 1990s.

Repositioning. Turbulent market pressures may cause management to reposition the company, business, or product with the target customers. The purpose of repositioning is to change how customers and prospects perceive an organization and its brands. Changes in the product mix, distribution, price, and promotion are used to influence buyers' positioning of companies, products, and brands. For example, the pork industry promotes the meat as a healthy alternative to "the other white meat."

Diversification. Despite the poor performance record of many diversification strategies, some corporations continue to expand into new product and market areas.[8] Strategies may include expansion into product and market areas related to the core business or into unrelated products and markets. Diversification requires performing all business functions in a new organization. The firm's existing organizational structure normally cannot serve

GLOBAL FEATURE Lufthansa's Strategy for Competing in the Air Travel Market

A major challenge for Germany's Lufthansa A.G. is deciding how to compete in the increasingly competitive global airline market. Lufthansa ranks 11th out of the top 20 global carriers based on passenger traffic. Top management began to implement several actions in 1992 designed to strengthen company performance.

- Using a customer-focused strategy, the company reorganized the airline, charter services, hotels, catering, and cargo operations.
- Strategic alliances are being established with American and Asian carriers to gain access to their domestic feeder networks. The carrier has a strong alliance with Air France.
- Directed by a new vice president for customer service, the airline's services are being improved to make them comparable to high-rated global carriers.
- Lufthansa is strengthening its position in eastern Europe aided by the liquidation of East German Interflug. The carrier has services to Russia.

Fleet expansion, modernization, and high personnel costs have placed heavy financial demands on the company. Lufthansa had a loss of 426 million marks for 1991. A critical avenue to improving competitive advantage is cutting costs. Its costs are high compared to competitors. The five-year investment program totals 10 billion marks ($6.27 billion based on 1992 exchange rates). Lufthansa's strongest competitive position is in Europe. It faces aggressive competition from the major U.S. carriers in the 1990s (American, United, and Delta).

Source: Brian Coleman, "Lufthansa's New Chairman Is Planning to Restructure Carrier, Seek Alliances," *The Wall Street Journal,* November 8, 1991, B3.

the needs of a diversification unit. Because of this, a typical practice is to acquire a business already serving in the product/market area targeted for diversification.

Strategic Partnering. Cooperative arrangements between two or more independent companies are intended to create a competitive advantage for the partners. The complexity and costs of new technology, gaining access to new markets, and the sharing of risks provide impetus for intercompany alliances. Corporate strategies increasingly involve collaborative relationships because one company cannot supply the necessary array of resources to compete on its own. Relationships between companies are discussed in Chapter 3.

What Is a Business Strategy?

"Strategy is the means an organization uses to achieve its objectives."[9] Strategy implements management's concept of business scope, mission, purpose, and objectives. The major components of corporate strategy and several key issues related to each component are shown in Exhibit 2–1. The issues highlight important questions that management must answer in charting the course of the enterprise. Management's skills and vision in addressing these issues are critical to the performance of the corporation. Essential to cor-

EXHIBIT 2–1 Corporate Strategy Components and Issues

Strategy Component	*Key Issues*
Scope, mission, and intent	• What business(es) should the firm be in? • What customer needs, market segments, and/or technologies should be focused on? • What is the firm's enduring strategic purpose or intent?
Objectives	• What performance dimensions should the firm's business units and employees focus on? • What is the target level of performance to be achieved on each dimension? • What is the time frame in which each target should be attained?
Development strategy	• How can the firm achieve a desired level of growth over time? • Can the desired growth be attained by expanding the firm's current businesses? • Will the company have to diversify into new businesses or product-markets to achieve its future growth objectives?
Resource allocation	• How should the firm's limited financial resources be allocated across its businesses to produce the highest returns? • Of the alternative strategies that each business might pursue, which will produce the greatest returns for the dollars invested?
Sources of synergy	• What competencies, knowledge, and customer-based intangibles (e.g., brand recognition, reputation) might be developed and shared across the firm's businesses? • What operational resources, facilities, or functions (e.g., plants, R&D, salesforce, etc.) might the firm's businesses share to increase their efficiency?

Source: Orville C. Walker, Jr., Harper W. Boyd, Jr., and Jean-Claude Larréché, *Marketing Strategy* (Homewood, IL: Richard D. Irwin, 1992), p. 38.

porate success is matching the competitive advantage of the organization with opportunities to achieve long-term customer satisfaction. We now consider this important influence on business strategy and performance.

COMPETITIVE ADVANTAGE

Jack Welch, chairman of the General Electric Company, emphasizes the reality of advantage: "If you don't have a competitive advantage, don't compete."[10] Most authorities agree that there is a strong relationship between business performance and competitive advantage.

A discussion of the concept of competitive advantage, how competitive position is analyzed how to sustain competitive advantage, and how market-entry barriers create advantage, provides insights into this important strategic concept.

EXHIBIT 2–2 The Elements of Competitive Advantage

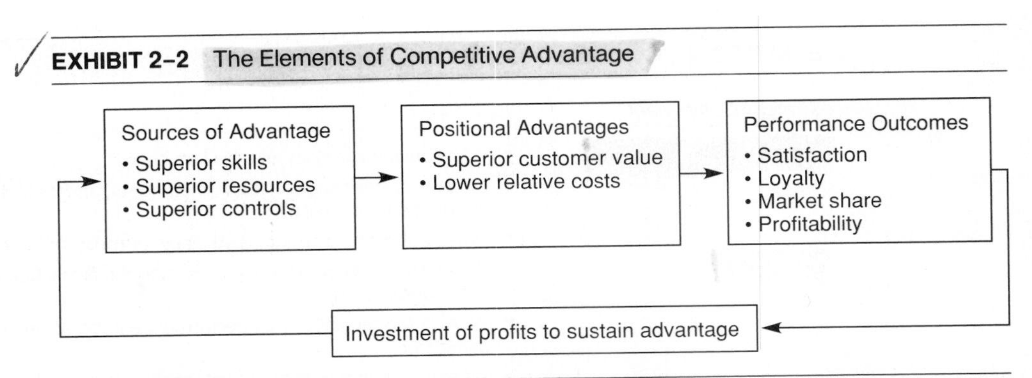

Source: George S. Day and Robin Wensley, "Assessing Advantage: A Framework for Diagnosing Competitive Superiority," *Journal of Marketing*, April 1988, p. 30.

The Concept of Competitive Advantage

Day and Wensley suggest viewing competitive advantage as a dynamic process rather than an outcome.[11] The process shown in Exhibit 2–2 includes sources of advantage, positional advantages, and performance outcomes and investment of profits to sustain advantage. Each element is described, including its role in the advantage process.

Sources of Advantage. Competitive advantage analysis shows the differences among competitors or uniqueness, in the case of a firm holding a monopoly position. The sources of advantage are superior skills, resources, and controls.[12]

Superior skills enable an organization to select and implement strategies that will differentiate the organization from its competition. Skills include technical, managerial, and operational capabilities. For example, knowledge of customers' needs and requirements helps a company to use its capabilities to satisfy its customers. Research and development expertise is another skill.

Superior resources are the enabling dimensions of advantage. Examples include strong distribution networks, production capability, marketing power (experienced salesforce), technology, and natural resources. De Beers' control of 85 percent of the world supply of uncut diamonds is illustrative. This monopoly position enables the company to control the flow and prices of diamonds throughout the world.

Superior controls include capabilities in monitoring and analyzing business processes and results. For example, superior cost controls constrain costs and identify areas where management assessment and action are needed. Control systems also provide performance benchmarks. Monitoring efforts should extend beyond internal operations to include customers, competition, and distribution networks. Companies with powerful computerized information systems like The Limited (women's apparel), Dillard's (department stores), and Frito-Lay (snack foods) have superior controls.

Positional Advantages. As discussed in Chapter 1, positional advantage results from cost leadership or differentiation that gives customers superior value.[13] Lower costs enable a firm to offer superior value by pricing an equivalent product at a lower price than its competitors. Differentiated product features that match buyers' preferences yield unique benefits that more than offset a higher price. An important factor in seeking advantage is deciding where and how to compete. For example, the decision of Home Depot's management to serve do-it-yourself home improvement needs (rather than professionals) enabled the firm to target a market segment, offering buyers low prices and salespeople that assist them in selecting hardware, plumbing, and electrical items.

Performance Outcomes. When the organization's skills, resources, and controls are used to gain value and/or cost advantage, these positional advantages lead to favorable performance outcomes (customer satisfaction, brand loyalty, market share, and profitability) as shown in Exhibit 2–2. Competitive advantage is a moving target, so management must use a portion of profits to sustain advantage. For example, highly successful Tootsie Roll Industries annually uses a substantial portion of profits to improve production operations and reduce the costs of producing its popular candy products.

Advantage Analysis

Determining the organization's competitive advantage or identifying a new opportunity to gain advantage may require analysis of customers and competition. Several techniques for customer- and competitor-oriented advantage analysis are discussed.

Customer-Oriented Analysis. This activity includes determining who is the customer, identifying the values they are seeking, comparing the organization's performance to its competition, and identifying why customers consider one firm superior to another.[14] Analysis may be necessary at several levels, including the business unit (discussed later in the chapter), the industry, market segment, and product category. Methods of customer analysis are discussed in Chapters 5 and 6.

Competitor-Centered Analysis. Two techniques useful in competitor analysis are value-chain analysis and benchmarking. "The value chain desegregates a firm into its strategically relevant activities in order to understand the behavior of costs and the existing and potential sources of differ-

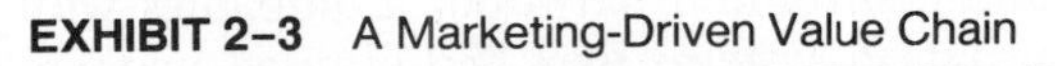

EXHIBIT 2–3 A Marketing-Driven Value Chain

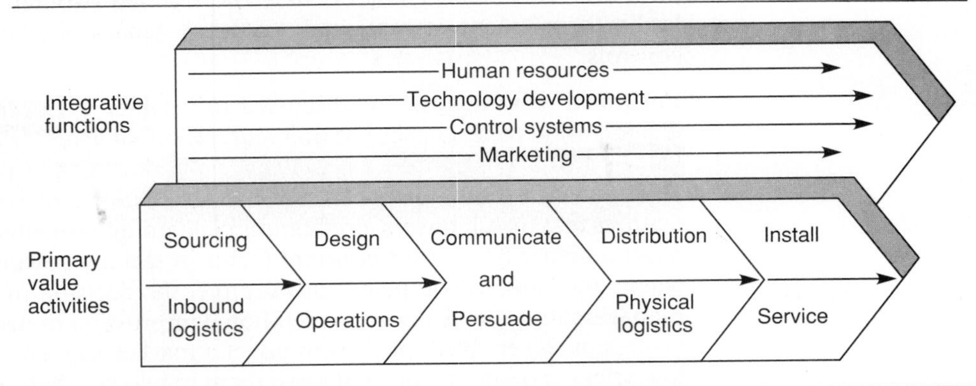

Reprinted with the permission of The Free Press, a Division of Macmillan, Inc. from MARKET DRIVEN STRATEGY: Processes for Creating Value by George S. Day. Copyright © 1990 by George S. Day.

entiation."[15] The activities that an organization performs to design, produce, market, deliver, and support its products or services represents its value chain. A marketing-driven value chain is shown in Exhibit 2–3. A producer is part of a value system composed of its suppliers and distribution network (e.g., distributors, dealers, retailers). Competitive advantage occurs when the organization performs value-chain activities (e.g., marketing and sales technology development, production) at lower costs or better than competing firms. Value-chain analysis examines each key activity to determine competitive advantage.

"Benchmarking is the process of continually comparing a company's performance on critical customer requirements against the best in the industry (direct competitors) or the class (companies recognized for superiority in performing certain functions) in order to determine which areas should be targeted for improvement."[16] This competitor analysis tool places attention on the entire value chain rather than only completed products. Benchmarking was developed by Xerox in 1979 to compare the manufacturing cost and features of their copying machines to competitors' products. Several other American companies began using benchmarking in the 1980s.

Sustaining Competitive Advantage

"For a producer to enjoy a competitive advantage in a product/market segment, the difference or differences between him and his competitors must be felt in the market place; that is, they must be reflected in some *product/delivery attribute* that is a *key buying criterion* for the market."[17] A capability gap is the difference between a firm's position and that of its strongest competitor for a buying criterion. Competitive advantage occurs when an organization's capability exceeds the strongest competitor for a buying criterion that is important to buyers. Competitive advantage is gained by finding an aspect of differentiation that targeted customers will perceive as a superior value and that cannot be easily duplicated by the competition. Capability gaps fall into these categories:[18]

- **Business system gaps** result by performing individual functions better than competitors and the difficulty of competitors to eliminate the gap. L. L. Bean, in mail-order retailing, achieves fast and accurate delivery of orders, creating high levels of customer satisfaction.
- **Position gaps** occur because of prior decisions, actions, and circumstances. The development of Rubbermaid's strong brand image is illustrative. The image was built during a long time span.
- **Regulatory/legal gaps** are provided through special treatment of a firm by government. Examples include patents, quotas, operating licenses, import quotas, and consumer safety laws. Landing rights at airports for commercial airlines are illustrative.
- **Organizational or managerial quality gaps** are the consequence of an organization's ability to consistently innovate and adapt more quickly and effectively than the competition. The Limited, in women's apparel retailing, can identify new clothing trends, produce the clothing, and move it to retail stores much faster than its competitors.

Competitors are always trying to reduce (or eliminate) capability gaps. Advantage is sustained by striving for continuous improvement in the value offered to buyers and/or reducing the costs of providing the product or service. New products that meet buyers' needs better than existing products create advantage. For example, the rapid adoption of fax services by business users virtually eliminated Western Union's wire services advantage.

Competitive advantage is an important challenge in all business and strategic marketing decisions. The topic is integrated into many of the chapters of this book. Our present objective is to provide a frame of reference by defining the concept, identifying sources of advantage, showing how to measure advantage, and indicating key considerations in sustaining competitive advantage.

Market-Entry Barriers

The firm(s) serving the market often have an inherent advantage over others planning to enter the market.[19] This edge results from the market-entry barriers that the new entrant will encounter. Considering the nature and significance of entry barriers in a product-market is important to both actual and potential competitors. There are three strategic issues concerning entry bar-

EXHIBIT 2–4 Market Entry Barriers

Concept	*Definition*
Cost advantages of incumbents	The advantages include the decline in unit cost of a product as the absolute volume of production per period increases as well as the reduction in unit cost resulting from product know-how, design characteristics, favorable access to raw materials, favorable locations, government subsidies, and learning or experience curve.
Product differentiation of incumbents	Established firms have brand identification and customer loyalties stemming from past advertising, customer service, product differences, or simply being first into the market.
Capital requirements	The need to invest large financial resources to enter a market and compete in that market.
Customer switching costs	One-time costs to the buyer due to switching from one supplier to another (i.e., employee retraining costs, cost of new ancillary equipment, need for new technical help, product redesign, etc.).
Access to distribution channels	The extent to which logical distribution channels for a product are already served by the established firms in the market.
Government policy	The extent to which government limits or forecloses entry into industries with such controls as licensing requirements and limits access to raw materials (i.e., regulated industries and Environmental Protection Agency laws).

Source: Fahri Karakaya and Michael J. Stahl, "Barriers to Entry and Market Entry Decisions in Consumer and Industrial Goods Markets," *Journal of Marketing,* April 1989, p. 85.

riers: (1) identifying the barriers and their relative importance, (2) estimating the effect of the barriers on entry at different stages of product-market maturity, and (3) examining how entry barriers vary in different product-markets (e.g., consumer and industrial products).

Entry Barriers. Six barriers are shown in Exhibit 2–4 with accompanying definitions.[20] A variety of specific barriers can be identified within the six areas, as suggested by Exhibit 2–4. For example, cost advantage may be achieved through volume production, design efficiency, and experience.

The results of one study placing a sample of Fortune 500 executives in a simulated business environment found that respondents considered all of the six barriers in Exhibit 2–4 relevant.[21] Cost advantages were perceived as the most important entry barrier, with capital requirements second and product differentiation third. No distinct relative importance pattern was found for the remaining three factors.

Early versus Late Market Entry. The market pioneer (first to enter) often gains a sustainable competitive advantage over firms entering the market later.[22] Entering the market first does not assure the pioneer of a favorable market and profit position. Initial entry offers an opportunity for rewards but is also risky. The successful pioneer must select and implement strategies for sustaining competitive advantage.

Entry Barriers in Different Product-Markets. Research indicates that the importance of the six entry barriers varies across consumer and industrial markets.[23] All of the barriers except capital requirements are different for industrial and consumer markets. Product differentiation and access to distribution channels are more influential in early entry for consumer markets. Variation in the importance of entry barriers appears to be influenced by product-market characteristics. The relative importance of barriers may also differ within consumer and industrial markets.

BUSINESS STRATEGY

Business strategy is overviewed earlier in the chapter (Exhibit 2–1). We turn now to a more complete look at business strategy. Developing strategies for sustainable competitive advantage, implementing them, and changing the strategies to respond to new environmental requirements is a continuing process. It begins by defining the mission of the business. Management monitors the market and competitive situation the corporation faces. The corporate mission may, over time, be changed because of problems or opportunities identified by monitoring. An important part of the strategic planning process in a firm made up of more than one business area (e.g., different products and/or markets) is the periodic analysis of the portfolio of business units. These units often have different objectives and strategies, offering various opportunities and requirements. For example, the Justin Company competes in the cowboy boot and construction brick markets. The strategy for each unit indicates how the unit will fulfill its assigned role in the corporation. Underlying each unit's strategic plan are functional strategies for marketing, finance, and operations. Strategies are then implemented and managed.

Deciding Corporate Mission

The corporate mission defines the nature and scope of a business and provides important guidelines for managing the corporation. Management initially establishes the firm's operations and adjusts these decisions as necessary over time. Strategic choices about where the firm is going in the future—choices that take into account company capabilities, resources, opportunities, and problems—establish the mission of the enterprise.

Early in the strategy-development process management defines the mission of the corporation. The mission is reviewed and updated as shifts in the strategic direction of the enterprise occur over time. The mission statement sets several important guidelines for business operations:

1. The reason for the company's existence and its responsibilities to stockholders, employees, society, and various other stakeholders.
2. The customer needs that are satisfied by the firm's products or services (areas of product and market involvement).
3. The extent of specialization within each product-market area.
4. The amount and types of product-market diversification desired by management.
5. Management's performance expectations for the company.
6. Other general guidelines for overall business strategy, such as technologies to be used and the role of research and development in the corporation.

The guidelines used to prepare and revise the mission statement for a telecommunications company are shown in Exhibit 2–5. This company develops mission statements for each major level of the corporation. The composition (e.g., group, business unit) of a corporation is discussed shortly.

Factors Affecting Mission. Several factors help determine the nature and scope of the business mission. Among these factors are the following:

Benefits provided to the customer.

Technologies used (to perform particular customer functions).

Customer segments served (market targets).

Level in the distribution system (level of participation in the sequence of stages in the value-added system from raw materials to the end-user).[24]

An illustration shows how these factors contribute to business definition. Durr-Fillauer Medical, Inc. distributes pharmaceuticals, drugstore sundries, medical products, and orthopedic devices to hospitals, drugstores, nursing homes, physician offices, and laboratories.[25] The company also manufactures, fabricates, and distributes components for artificial limbs and braces. The customer benefits consist of supplying various medical products and offering assistance in product use; the technologies used are distribution capabilities, such as transportation, storage, and information systems; the customer segments consist of hospitals, physicians, and other medical facilities; and distribution is at the wholesale level (and the manufacturing level for limb and brace components). Durr-Fillauer's 1992 sales exceeded $1 billion and net profit after taxes was about $20 million.

A key influence on the mission decision is what management wants the business to be. Acknowledging the constraining nature of capabilities, resources, opportunities, and problems, management has a lot of flexibility

EXHIBIT 2–5 Mission Statement—A Telecommunications Company

The purpose of the mission statement is to express the underlying design, aim, purpose and thrust of a business entity based on the situation analysis and discussion with upper management. Each business unit, group, functional department and the company as a whole has a mission, so each should have a written mission statement. This statement should be available for review in the conference documents, but should not be covered in detail in the conference unless changes have been or should be made. This statement, as well as the rest of the business plan, should be viewed as a contract with executive management that should not be changed without their approval.

The mission statement is the first and most general component of a business plan. It should describe the parameters of the business, providing general direction on the role of the business and its scope of operations.

The mission statement has two parts:

- **Guiding concept**—a single, short statement of the inspirational goal of the business. It should be something that all employees can grasp as the essence of their culture, yet describe the value being provided to the customer. Examples include AT&T's focus on telephone service quality and IBM's focus on computing innovation.
- **Mission**—about a half-page that tells *what* you want to be. The points that should be covered vary with the level in the hierarchy of the company since the role and scope are different for each level. The following are brief topic outlines for each of the three major levels.

Mission Statement Profiles

Corporate	**Group**	**Business Unit**
Guiding Concept **Mission** Scope of operations — Maximizing shareholder value — Value provided to customer — Industries/major markets — Geographic areas Corporate center role (value provided to corporation) — Portfolio management — Resource allocation — Synergy management — Corporate development — Executive management development Social policies	**Guiding Concept** **Mission** Scope of operations — Markets — Position targeted in markets — Geographic areas Group role (value provided to corporation and BU's) — Fulfillment of role in corporate portfolio — Portfolio management — Synergy management — Resource allocation — Group development	**Guiding Concept** **Mission** Scope of operations — Markets/segments served — Customer needs filled — Products provided — Functions performed (manufacture, distribute, service, etc.) — Position targeted in markets — Geographic areas Business unit role (value provided to group and corporation) — Fulfillment of role in group portfolio — Market development — Business/product development — Distribution development — Resource management — Operations management

Source: Rochelle O'Connor, *Facing Strategic Issues: New Planning Guides and Practices,* Report No. 867 (New York: The Conference Board, Inc., 1985), p. 35.

in selecting the mission as well as changing it in the future. Sometimes the priorities and preferences of the CEO or the board of directors may override factual evidence in selecting the business mission. For example, many of the diversifications pursued by companies in the 1970s were not sound decisions, and the strategic errors resulted in the restructuring and downsizing of many companies during the 1980s.

Corporate Objectives. Objectives should also be set so that the performance of the enterprise can be gauged. Corporate objectives are often established in the following areas: *marketing, innovation, resources, productivity, social responsibility,* and *finance.*[26] Examples include growth and market-share expectations, improving product quality, employee training and development, new-product targets, return on invested capital, earnings growth rates, debt limits, energy reduction objectives, and pollution standards. Objectives are set at several levels in an organization beginning with those indicating the enterprise's overall performance targets.

Corporate Development Alternatives

Several possible directions of growth may be taken from the core (initial) business of the corporation. The major corporate development options are shown in Exhibit 2–6. There are, of course, many specific combinations of these options. Success often leads to expanding into related areas and sometimes entirely new product-market areas. A brief look at each alternative provides an overview of corporate expansion activities.

Core Business. The initial venture of an enterprise is the core business, as bakery products are for Sara Lee or cowboy boots are for the Justin Company. Many firms start out serving one product-market. The product or service offered may be a single product or line or products. This strategy, when it involves a single product-market, offers the advantages of specialization but has the risks of being dependent on one set of customer needs. As the corporation grows and prospers, management often decides to move into other product and market areas, as shown in Exhibit 2–6. For example, Sara Lee expanded into underwear, leisure wear, and Coach leather goods. Reducing dependence on the core business is a major factor in corporate development. Of course, financial resources are necessary to expand into related or new areas. Sara Lee's food business generates the cash needed to expand into other consumer goods lines.

New Markets for Existing Products. One way to expand away from serving a single product-market is to serve other customer groups by using the same product or a similar product. Northern Indiana Public Service Company, for example, supplies electricity and natural gas to both commercial and household customers. For many companies, expanding into new markets is a natural way to expand operations. This strategy reduces the risks of depending on a single market, yet it allows the use of existing technical and

EXHIBIT 2–6 Corporate Development Options

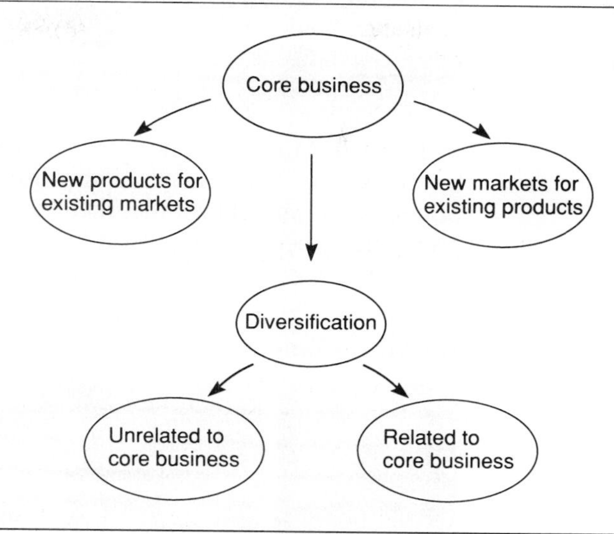

production capabilities. When deciding to pursue this strategy, management must have the resources for expansion and must develop a marketing strategy for the new customer group(s).

New Products for Existing Markets. Another strategy for shifting away from dependence on one product is to expand the product mix offered to the firm's target market. In the 1980s Maytag, the washer and dryer manufacturer, added to its appliance offering by acquiring lines of ranges and ovens and refrigerators and freezers. Use of common distribution channels, promotional support, and research and development are among the possible advantages of this strategy. New products can be developed internally, although acquisition may be faster. Resources are necessary to support either alternative. By following this strategy the company is subject to the market changes in a particular product-market area, such as kitchen appliances.

Diversification. Finally, many firms select diversification for corporate development. Diversification is movement into a new product and market area by internal development or acquisition. This option is often the riskiest and costliest of all those shown in Exhibit 2–6. Yet it may be an attractive avenue for growth if the firm's existing product-market areas face slow growth, if resources for diversification are available, and if good choices are made. Unfortunately, the success record for diversification has been dismal.[27] A comprehensive study of the diversification records of 33 large U.S.

companies during the 1950–1986 period found that most of the firms had (1) disposed of many of their acquisitions and (2) dissipated instead of created shareholder value. Successful diversification appears to be closely related to industry attractiveness, favorable cost-of-entry, and the opportunity for improving competitive advantage.[28]

Movement beyond the core business is not unusual as businesses grow and mature. More than one of the options shown in Exhibit 2–6 may be used by a company. Several factors may influence the rate and direction of corporate development activities including available resources, management's preferences, pending opportunities and threats, and the desire to reduce total dependence of the corporation on a single product-market area.

Business Composition

Defining the composition of a business is essential in both corporate and marketing strategic planning. In single-product firms, such as Tootsie Roll Industries (candy products), it is easy to determine the composition of the business. In many other firms it is useful to separate the business into parts to facilitate strategic analyses and planning. When firms are serving multiple markets with different products, grouping similar business areas together aids decision making. The Westinghouse Electric Corporation business portfolio is shown in Exhibit 2–7. Some of Westinghouse's traditional businesses have been reduced in scope or eliminated. For example, the company no longer competes in consumer products. Profit margins improved during the last half of the 1980s, but Westinghouse experienced serious financial problems in the early 1990s because of real estate write-offs in the financial services unit, the defense expenditure slowdown, and the 1991–1992 recession. Westinghouse's problems attest to the complexity of effectively managing a portfolio of diversified businesses.

Business Segment, Group, or Division. These terms often identify the major areas of business of a diversified corporation. Each segment, group, or division often contains a mix of related products (or services), although a single product can be assigned such a designation. Note that the term *segment* does not correspond to a market segment (subgroup of end-users in a product-market), which is discussed throughout the book. Most large corporations break out their financial reports into business or industry segments according to the guidelines of the Financial Accounting Standards Board. Some firms may establish subgroups of related products within a business segment that are targeted to different customer groups.

Strategic Business Unit. A business segment, group, or division is often too large in terms of product and market composition for use in strategic analysis and planning, so it is divided into more specific strategic units. One of the most popular names for these units is the *strategic business unit* (SBU). Typically SBUs display product and customer group similarities. A

EXHIBIT 2–7 Westinghouse's Restructuring

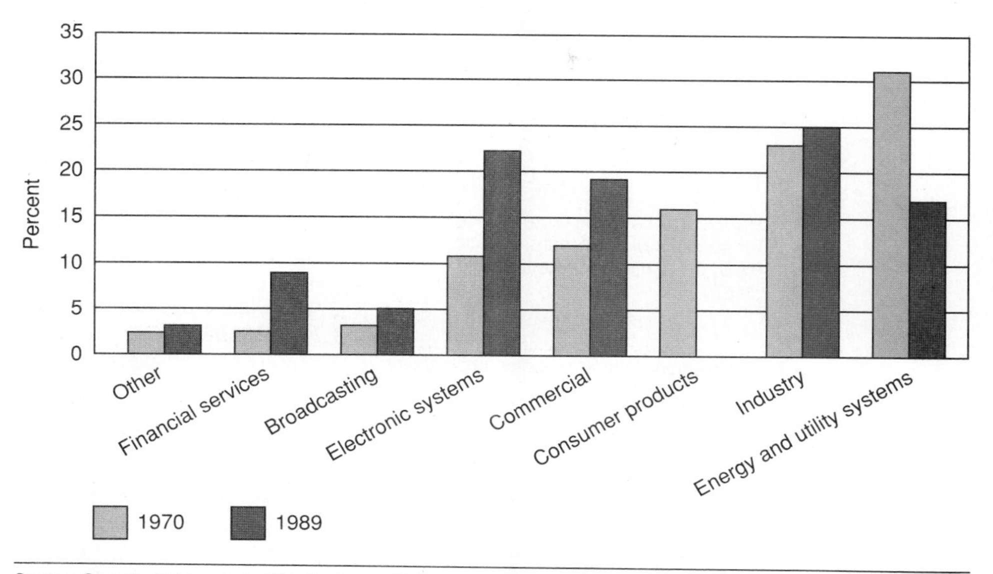

Source: Gregory Stricharchuk, "Westinghouse Relies on Ruthlessly Rational Pruning," *The Wall Street Journal,* January 24, 1990, p. A4.

strategic business unit is a single product or brand, a line of products, or a mix of related products that meets a common market need or a group of related needs, and the unit's management is responsible for all (or most) of the basic business functions. The characteristics of the ideal SBU are profiled in Exhibit 2–8. The SBU has its own strategy rather than a shared strategy with another business area. It is a cohesive organizational unit that is separately managed and can produce sales and profit results.

An SBU may itself comprise a portfolio rather than being a single homogeneous unit. In a large study of business portfolio planning in corporations, many of the participants indicated that they consider an SBU as a group of product-market segments that occupy very different market attractiveness and business strength positions and strategic missions.[29] The SBU may cut across market segments with different characteristics and opportunities. Creating an SBU for each segment would result in too many SBUs in companies targeting several segments.

An important issue is whether the use of SBUs to guide strategy and organization enhances corporate performance. AMR Corporation, parent of American Airlines, is widely recognized as a well-managed transportation

EXHIBIT 2–8 Characteristics of the Ideal Strategic Business Unit

Characteristic	*Rationale*
• Serves a homogeneous set of markets with a limited number of related technologies	Minimizing the diversity of a business unit's product-market entries enables the unit's manager to do a better job of formulating and implementing a coherent and internally consistent business strategy.
• Serves a unique set of product-markets	No other SBU within the firm should compete for the same set of customers with similar products. This enables the firm to avoid duplication of effort and helps maximize economies of scale within its SBUs.
• Has control over the factors necessary for successful performance, such as R&D, production, marketing, and distribution	This is not to say that an SBU should never share resources, such as a manufacturing plant or a salesforce, with one or more business units; but the SBU should have authority to determine how its share of the joint resource will be used to effectively carry out its strategy.
• Has responsibility for its own profitability	Because top management cannot keep an eye on every decision and action taken by all its SBUs, the success of an SBU and its managers must be judged by monitoring its performance over time. Thus, the SBU's managers should have control over the factors that affect performance, and then be held accountable for the outcomes.

Source: Orville C. Walker, Jr., Harper W. Boyd, Jr., and Jean-Claude Larréché, *Marketing Strategy* (Homewood, IL: Richard D. Irwin, 1992), p. 76.

services company. American's information technology business is an interesting example of the use of strategic business units. SABRE is divided into three business areas: (1) the SABRE Computer Services Division provides support for American Airlines; (2) the SABRE Travel Information Network markets reservations, ticketing, and other services to travel agencies and corporations; and (3) AMR Information Services, Inc. has seven strategic business units that market information services to other airlines, hotel and car rental companies, freight shippers, and telemarketers and provide technical training and data-entry services.[30]

Corporate Strategy

Top management sets the guidelines for long-term strategic planning of the corporation. In a business that has two or more strategic business units, decisions must be made at two levels. Corporate management must first decide what business areas to pursue and then establish priorities for allocating resources to each SBU. Decision makers within each SBU determine the appropriate strategies for implementing the corporate strategy and getting the results that management expects. Corporate-level management may assist the SBUs in achieving their objectives.

Corporate strategy and resources should help an SBU to compete more effectively than if the unit operates on a completely independent basis. "To remain competitive, corporations must provide their business units with low-cost capital, outstanding executives, corporate R&D, centralized marketing where appropriate and other resources in the corporate arsenal."[31] Corporate resources and synergies help the SBU establish its competitive advantage. The strategic focus and priorities of corporate strategy guide SBU strategies. Finally, top management's expectations for the corporation indicate the results expected from an SBU, including both financial and nonfinancial objectives. When viewed in this context, the SBUs become the action centers of the corporation.

STRATEGIC ANALYSIS AND STRATEGY SELECTION

The corporate strategy defines the business portfolio of an organization and how it will compete in a given business.[32] The strategy is a set of decisions indicating objectives, plans for achieving the objectives, and the businesses where the company is to compete. Strategy may also spell out the organization's role in society, its responsibilities to the stakeholders (employees, stockholders, etc.), ethical guidelines, and environmental priorities.

Selecting a strategy for an organization requires deciding the environments in which to compete (corporate-level strategies) and how to compete within those environments (business-level strategies).[33] Performance is due to a combination of the strategy choices and how well the strategy is implemented.

Assessing Situational Advantage

Several factors may influence the strategy choice and performance process. Examples include the attractiveness of the market, the intensity of competition, and the competitive advantage(s) of the organization. Researchers, consultants, and managers have devoted extensive efforts to develop situational classifications for generic business strategies. A generic strategy would apply to any organization encountering the same situational factors. The generic strategies form a simplified classification system. These strategies offer several important advantages in guiding strategy selection:[34]

1. They combine separate, situation-specific strategies, capturing their major commonalities so that they facilitate the understanding of broad strategic patterns.
2. They guide corporate-level decisions concerning business portfolio management and resource allocation.
3. They assist business-level strategy development by suggesting priorities and providing broad guidelines for action.

Importantly, the generic strategies are not complete strategies. Instead, their value is in indicating the type of strategy (e.g., downsizing) that is appropriate for the situation. The generic strategy suggests what should be accomplished (e.g., growth). Management must determine how to achieve the strategy. Strategic classification models and generic strategy guidelines are useful in setting business-unit priorities and suggesting general strategy guidelines. Combining this information with more specific customer and competitor analysis, strategic plans are developed for each business unit in the corporate portfolio.

Strategy Classification Models

A classification model is a scheme for placing business units into strategy categories (e.g., growth, retrenchment) using two or more contingency factors as the basis of classification. Several classification schemes are available for guiding business strategy analysis and choice. A brief review of the more popular models highlights how they are used in strategy analysis.

Portfolio Investment Models. These classification models position a corporation's business units on two-way grids based on market attractiveness and business strength. For example, attractiveness can be measured by the estimated future growth rate of the market. Relative market share compared to the market leader is one gauge of business strength. The objective of the analysis is to determine how to allocate resources to each of the business units in the corporate portfolio. Two examples of these models are the Boston Consulting Group (BCG) growth-share matrix and the General Electric/McKinsey screening grid.

these models relate more to resource allocation See Exh. 2-1

A company with several business units or products can analyze its portfolio by plotting each SBU or product on a two-way matrix as shown in Exhibit 2–9. Market share and market growth rate values are used to position each SBU or product on the grid. The names shown in each quadrant, "cash cow," "star," "dog," and "problem child," were popular with strategic planners in the 1980s to denote the attractiveness of each position and its cash needs. An illustrative diagnosis is that a company with a low market share in a mature, slow-growth market is likely to be attempting an unprofitable battle if it decides to try to gain a market share against entrenched competitors. The other positions vary in their cash needs, with a cash cow generating more cash than is needed and the problem child and star both requiring additional cash.

Although the BCG growth-share matrix helped establish the concept of business portfolio analysis, companies have moved beyond using only market growth and market-share measures for positioning SBUs or products on grids. The evaluation of several factors may be necessary to fully understand a company's strengths and weaknesses.

An example of a GE-type screening grid is shown in Exhibit 2–10. Unlike the BCG grid, it uses multiple measures of attractiveness and busi-

EXHIBIT 2–9 Balancing the Product Portfolio

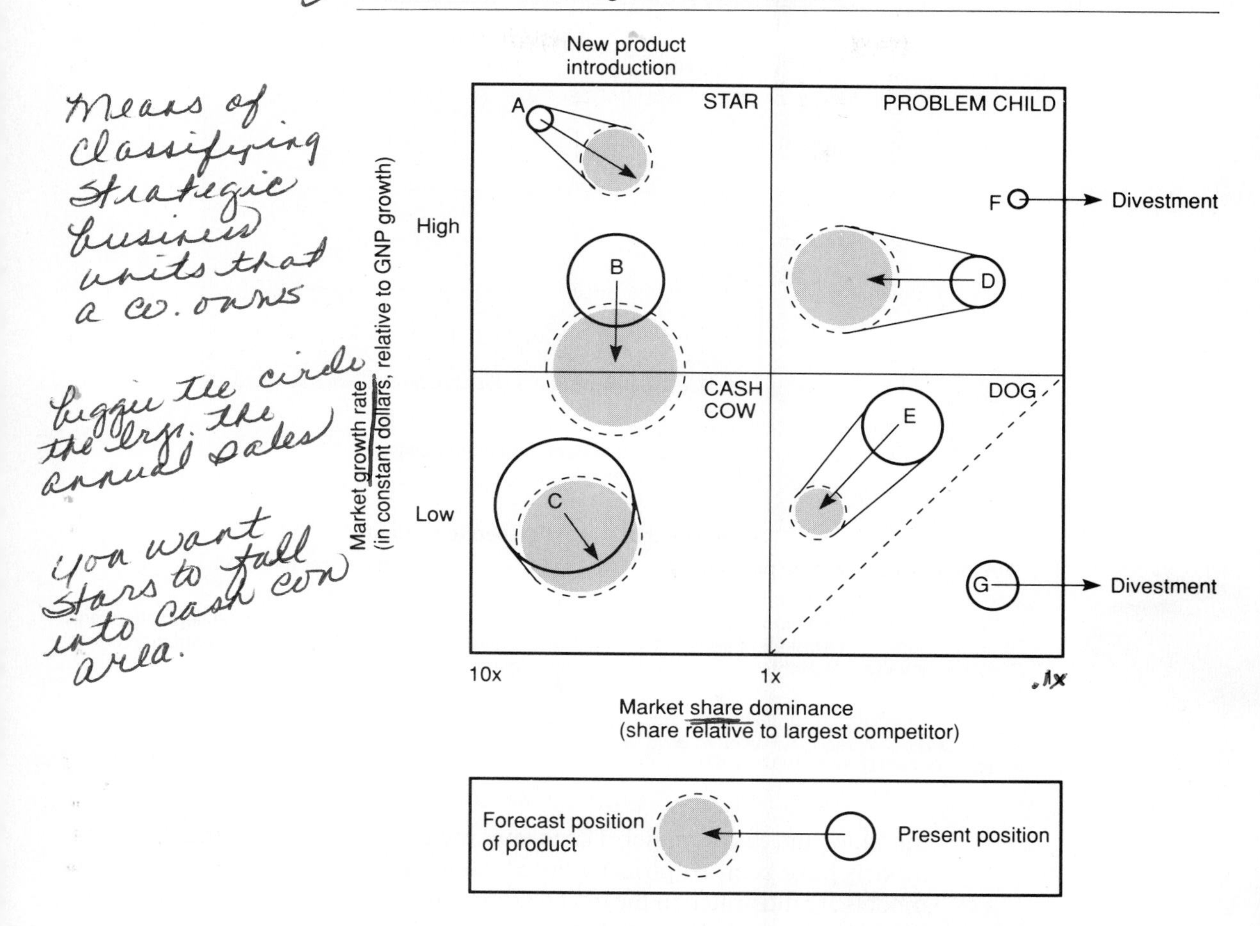

Diameter of circle is proportional to product's contribution to total company sales volume.
Source: George S. Day, "Diagnosing the Product Portfolio," *Journal of Marketing,* April 1977, p. 34.

ness strength. SBUs can be plotted as circles on the Exhibit 2–10 grid, using diameters proportional to the SBU's contribution to total company sales. Those units that fall into the high-high categories are in a desirable zone for investing/growing the business, whereas a low-low positioning indicates harvesting or divesting the unit. The assumption is that return on investment will be high in a high-high category, and so on.[35]

Comprehensive Models. These models provide a full strategic description.[36] Variables included relate to strategic position, strategic change, and their interactions. Examples include the Galbraith and Schendel model and

EXHIBIT 2–10 The Industry Attractiveness–Business Position Matrix

Business's competitive position	Industry attractiveness: High	Medium	Low
High	1	1	2
Medium	1	2	3
Low	2	3	3

1 Invest / grow
2 Selective investment / maintain position
3 Harvest / divest

Variables that might be used to evaluate:

Business's competitive position		Industry attractiveness	
Size	Distribution	Size	Profitability
Growth	Technology	Growth	Technological sophistication
Relative share	Marketing skills	Competitive intensity	Government regulations
Customer loyalty	Patents	Price levels	
Margins			

Source: Orville C. Walker, Jr., Harper W. Boyd, Jr., and Jean-Claude Larréché, *Marketing Strategy* (Homewood, IL: Richard D. Irwin, 1992), p. 57.

the Miles and Snow model. The former includes 26 strategic variables. Both models have been empirically tested. Generic strategy guidelines for these models are illustrated in the next section, which also considers the guidelines offered by several other models.

Generic Strategies

Several generic strategies are offered by the various classification models. The strategies are compared in Exhibit 2–11 on the basis of the stages of product-market evolution and/or the corporate life cycle (see two left-hand columns). Note that several of the strategies shown in the 3rd through the 12th columns are similar. In an effort to synthesize the different classifications, Herbert and Deresky propose four generic strategies (right column): *develop, stabilize, turnaround,* and *harvest.*[37] Their classification scheme has the following features:

1. It is based on common (or overlapping) variables and characteristics of strategic types in other models.

EXHIBIT 2–11 Comparison of Generic Strategies

Corporate Life Cycle (James)	*Product/ Market Evolution*	*Glueck*	*Hoffer and Schendel*	*Galbraith and Schendel Consumer Products*	*Galbraith and Schendel Industrial Products*	*BCG*	*Buzzell Gale and Sultan GE/Shell McKinsey*	*Wissema*	*Miles and Snow*	*Burns and Stalker*	*Proposed*
Emergence	Introduction		Share increase	Builder	Growth			Explosion	Prospector	Organic	
		Growth				"Stars"	Build				Develop
Growth	Growth		Growth increase					Expansion			
Maturity	Maturity	Stability	Profit	Cashout		"Cash cows"	Hold	Continuous growth	Defender	Mechanistic	
		(combination)		Continuity	Maintenance				(analyzer)		Stabilize
			Market concentration/ Asset reduction	Niche	Niche			Consolidation			
Regeneration			Turnaround	Climber							Turnaround
Decline	Decline	Retrench	Liquidate or divest	Harvest	Low commitment	"Dogs"	Harvest	Slip contraction			Harvest

Source: Theodore T. Herbert and Helen Deresky, "Generic Strategies: An Empirical Investigation of Typology Validity and Strategy Content," *Strategic Management Journal* 8 (1987), p. 137.

2. It proposes strategies that are independent of other strategies, environmental situations, or organizational or product-development stages. Thus, a *harvest* strategy could occur within a rapidly *developing* business.
3. It encompasses/explains major and common types of generic strategies and their characteristics.
4. It has been tested using data from a sample of companies. Consistent and interrelated findings were found in the research results.[38]

The Develop Strategy. Organizations using the develop strategy tend to be relatively new businesses, firms with rapidly changing technology and product line, or companies entering new product-markets because of unfavorable conditions in the existing business arena. Develop strategies seek long-term growth via new product and/or market development. Firms in this category pursue market leadership strategies. Apple Computer's pioneering entry strategy in the personal computer market is an example of the develop strategy.

The Stabilize Strategy. Companies that want to stabilize are found in mature, stable industries (e.g., textiles, chemicals). In markets where buyers' needs are relatively similar, management's strategies emphasize cost leadership. In differentiated markets, market segmentation (or focus) strategies or some type of specialization are employed. The strategy typically emphasizes high-quality products and service and close contact with customers. In the tire industry, Goodyear follows this strategy.

The Turnaround Strategy. Turnarounds involve survival and rebuilding. Emphasis may be on improving cash flow and reducing costs or refocusing the organization. Downsizing and other forms of restructuring may occur. The cost strategy involves actions to increase efficiency, where refocusing may include reorganization, diversification, and acquisitions (or mergers). The Detroit Diesel Corporation turnaround masterminded by Roger Penske illustrates this generic strategy (Chapter 1).

The Harvest Strategy. A business adopting a harvest strategy is a candidate for removal from the corporate portfolio. The factors influencing the decision to harvest the business include poor financial performance, lack of compatibility with the core business, lack of competitive advantage, and lack of fit with the future direction of the corporation. General Electric's sale of its small appliance business to Black & Decker is an example of a harvest strategy.

Generic strategies do not provide specific guides to action. Instead, they indicate direction or end results (e.g., harvest). They offer broad guides to action. Specific action plans must be developed by management. We conclude this section with a look at the Profit Impact of Marketing Strategies (PIMS) methods and a discussion of the contents of strategic business plans.

PIMS Research

The Profit Impact of Marketing Strategies (PIMS) program is a computerized data bank of strategy information collected from more than 3,000 businesses. Multiple regression models describe the relationship between measures of profit (e.g., return on investment) and predictors such as research and development expenditures. The Strategic Planning Institute (SPI) has built an extensive data bank of strategic information about business performance and various factors related to performance.

The PIMS analyses extend beyond generic strategy considerations to include assessments of specific strategies (e.g., recommended changes in research and development expenditures) and financial performance relationships. Diagnostic analysis of PIMS data provides prescriptive guidelines for future strategic decisions. The variables used in the PIMS model also identify the relevant strategic factors.

Overview of the PIMS Program. The data obtained from each participating company consists of about 100 items on each business. As a part of the input data, the firm must supply its assumptions about the "most likely" future rates of change of sales, prices, materials costs, wage rates, and equipment costs. This is done for short-term (1–4 years) and long-term (5–10 years). The unit of analysis in the PIMS studies is described as follows:

> The unit of observation in PIMS is a business. Each business is a division, product line, or other profit center within its parent company, selling a distinct set of products and/or services to an identifiable group of customers, in competition with a well-defined set of competitors, and for which meaningful separation can be made of revenues, operating costs, investments, and strategic plans.[39]

The PIMS model identifies nine major strategic influences on profitability and net cash flow. In approximate order of importance, they are investment intensity, productivity, market position, growth of served market, product/service quality, innovation/differentiation, vertical integration, cost push, and current strategic effort.[40] Many of the influences on profitability and net cash flow are positive. Investment intensity has a negative effect. The effects of cost push and current strategic effort are more complex.

The nine influences account for up to 80 percent of the observed variation in profitability across the businesses in the database. "These factors are incorporated into a set of profit-predicting models that assign to each factor its proper weight, judging from the experiences reflected in the database. The models also indicate how the impact of each profit-determining factor is conditioned by other factors."[41]

Output Reports for PIMS Users. The PIMS analyses include both diagnostic and prescriptive information. The four major reports supplied to the participating firm are as follows:

> The "Par" Report specifies the return on investment that is normal (or "par") for the business, given the characteristics of its market, competition, position, technology, and cost structure. . . .
>
> The Strategy Analysis Report is a computational pretest of several possible strategic moves in the business. It indicates the normal short- and long-term consequences of each such move, judging by the experience of other businesses making a similar move, from a similar starting point and in a similar business environment. It specifies the profit (or loss) likely to be achieved by such projected changes, along with the associated investment and cash flow. . . .
>
> The Optimum Strategy Report nominates that combination of several strategic moves that promises to give optimal results for the business, also judging by the experiences of other businesses under similar circumstances. . . .
>
> Report on "Look-Alikes" (ROLA) provides managers with a way to discover effective tactics for accomplishing their strategic objectives (for example, increasing profitability or cash flow, gaining market share, improving productivity or product quality). ROLA retrieves from the database businesses that are strategically similar to the business being analyzed (its "look-alikes") and reports a large number of the strategic and operating characteristics that helped them to attain the specified objective.[42]

The PIMS reports can be used in several ways to assist in analyzing business performance and formulating future strategies.

Critical Assessment of the PIMS Approach. One of the major strengths of PIMS is that several logical strategic factors are shown to be related to profitability (ROI) and cash flow, using a large cross section of businesses. The opportunity for analyzing what-if questions is an important feature of the PIMS model. The PIMS analysis is systematic and not subject to the judgments of particular individuals in the firm. The data, of course, are supplied by the firm and can be inaccurate or incorrectly reported. Completion of the PIMS forms may be beneficial to the executive(s) answering them because, in order to answer the questions, one needs to make a comprehensive analysis of business operations. PIMS also has important limitations. It is historical in orientation, so there is no way to be sure that past relationships will hold in the future.

Its limitations acknowledged, PIMS research has the distinction of being one of the few efforts (the only one of comparable scope) to conduct empirical research in the area of corporate strategy, which for so long has been guided primarily by wisdom, simple rules of thumb, and management experience and judgment.

Developing the Strategic Plan for Each Business

The objective of strategic analysis is to: (1) diagnose the SBU's strengths and limitations, and (2) identify alternative strategic actions for maintaining or improving performance. Management decides what priority to place on

EXHIBIT 2–12 Plan Outline—A High-Technology Products Manufacturer

I. Management Summary
II. Business Definition
  — Mission
  — Purpose
  — Role
III. Progress Report
  — Comparison of key financial and market indicators
  — Progress made on major strategies
IV. Market and Customer Analysis
  — Potential versus served market
  — Market segmentation
V. Competitive Analysis
  — Description of three major competitors
  — Analysis of competitors' strategies
VI. Objectives, Strategies, and Programs
  — Key objectives
  — Major strategies to accomplish the objectives
  — Action programs to implement strategies
  — Major assumptions and contingency programs
  — Market share matrix
VII. Financial Projections
  — Financial projections statement
  — Personnel projections

Source: Rochelle O'Connor, *Facing Strategic Issues: New Planning Guides and Practices,* Report No. 87 (New York: The Conference Board, Inc., 1985), p. 32.

each business unit regarding resource allocation and implements a strategy to meet the objectives for the SBU. The strategic plan indicates the action agenda for the business. An example of a plan outline is shown in Exhibit 2–12. The "major strategies" shown in Part VI of the plan include the major strategic actions planned for business development, marketing, quality, product and technology, human resources, manufacturing/facilities, and finance.

The situation assessment provides a basis for establishing the SBU's mission, setting objectives, and determining the strategy to use to meet these objectives. The SBU's strategy indicates market target priorities, available resources, financial constraints, and other strategic guidelines needed to develop functional plans. Depending on the size and diversity of the SBU, the functional plans may either be included in the SBU plan or developed separately.

The strategy checklist used by a packaging manufacturer to assist business units in developing strategic plans is shown in Exhibit 2–13. Note the questions raised concerning environmental change, competitive advantage, market position and structure, product-market maturity, organizational effectiveness, resources, risks, and contingencies. Several potential strategy mistakes are also highlighted.

EXHIBIT 2–13 Strategy Checklist—A Packaging Manufacturer

A. *Is the strategy consistent with the environment?*

1. Does your strategy address the critical issues?
2. Does the plan include creative thinking as opposed to being "more of the same"?
3. Have you evaluated the possible impact on your strategies of technological developments by your SBU, by your customers, competitors, suppliers and, especially, by those outside your industry?
4. Have you included the impact of cyclicality, if any, in your forecasts?
5. Have you given attention to how broader social and political trends might have an impact on total industry opportunities and threats?

B. *Market, customer, and competitor analysis*

1. Are you satisfied that the SBU's served market is defined properly?
2. Have you examined the possibility of a change in the industry structure, i.e., the basic competitive nature and economics of the industry?
3. Does the plan reflect an assessment of the possible methods of segmenting the market?
4. Does the plan, to your satisfaction, describe how the SBU will successfully differentiate itself from its key competitors?
5. If you are planning to initiate a new strategy, does it represent the course that competitors would least expect?
6. Have you given adequate attention to probable competitive response to your planned strategic moves?
7. Does your strategy leave you vulnerable to the power of one major competitor, customer, or supplier?
8. If the strategy is an imitation of the strategy of your most successful competitor, have the differences between your strengths and weaknesses and his been considered in determining the probable success of your strategy?
9. Is the timing of your implementation appropriate in light of what is known about market conditions?
10. How valid and complete is the information on which your strategy is based?
11. Does your strategy fit a niche in the market which is now filled by others? Is this niche likely to remain open to you for a long enough time to recover your capital investment plus earning an adequate return?
12. Have you given consideration to pricing as part of your total strategy? Given the rate of inflation in your costs, what differential rate of inflation will be necessary in your selling prices and what will the impact be?
13. Have the real reasons why customers buy from you been discovered? Are they likely to change in the future?
14. Have you identified your major competitors, determined who their major customers are and the competitive advantage this suggests?
15. Has the cost structure of each major competitor been estimated? What relative strengths and weaknesses does this suggest?

C. *Does the strategy fit the stage of the product life cycle?*

1. Does the strategy fit the life cycle of the product(s) involved (development, growth, shakeout, maturity, saturation)?
2. Does your strategy involve the production of a new product, the use of a new technology, and/or the entry into a new market? If so, have you really assessed the risks and the requirements for successful implementation?

D. *Is the strategy consistent with your internal policies, styles of management, philosophy, and operating procedures?*

1. Is your strategy explicit and understood by all those responsible for executing it?
2. Is your strategy consistent with the objectives and policies of your organization?
3. Are your supporting objectives and strategies consistent with your strategic intention?
4. Are all supporting objectives and strategies mutually consistent?
5. Does the strategy exploit your strengths and avoid your major weaknesses? Does it concentrate your strengths against your competitors' weaknesses?
6. Is your organizational structure consistent with your strategy?
7. Is the strategy consistent with the objectives and strategies of the corporation?

E. *Is the strategy in line with your resources?*

1. *Capital*
   a. Is your cash flow consistent with the strategic intention assigned to this SBU in the past?
   b. Does your strategy embody the concept of economy—are you planning to succeed at any cost or at the minimum cost?
   c. Have full considerations been given to the financial consequences on this SBU, if the requested capital allocations are made?
   d. Have all the investment requirements necessary to support successful implementation of your strategy been included in the financial projection for the SBU?
2. *Technology*
   a. Do you have, or will you have, adequate technology to permit realization of the strategy?
   b. Does your strategy result in the identification of solvable problems?
   c. Has an evaluation of potential new technologies (substitutes) been conducted?
3. *Manpower*
   a. Do you have, or will you have, the sufficient manpower to realize your strategy?
4. *Supplies*
   a. Have you considered future supply (materials and energy) constraints and possible alternate sources, both in general and by geographic region?
   b. Has the impact of future cost increases in materials and energy been included in forecasted constant-dollar margins?
   c. Are you satisfied that proper action plans have been developed so that future, adverse supplier pricing actions can be mitigated as much as practicable?

F. *Are the risks in pursuing the strategy acceptable?*

1. Do you have too much capital and management tied into this strategy in light of the SBU's matrix position?
2. To what extent is the success of your strategy dependent upon displacing a well-established competitor?
3. Is the payback period acceptable in light of potential environmental change?
4. Does the strategy take you too far from your current products, markets, and capabilities? Is it the right risk for you?
5. Has the strategy been tested with appropriate risk analysis, such as sensitivity analysis?

G. *Contingency plans*

1. Have you developed alternative plans for achieving your strategic intention in light of changing circumstances and differing competitive response?

EXHIBIT 2–13 (concluded)

2. Will the contingency plans allow you to keep the initiative or are they merely an across-the-board cutback (retreat)?

H. Some frequent strategy mistakes

1. Betting on long shots.
2. Trying for a "turnaround" in an unpromising situation.
3. Not believing your good luck and thereby failing to capitalize on competitors' errors.
4. Wounding a competitor without seriously crippling him.
5. Precipitating a collapse while attempting to harvest the business.
6. Excessive marketing and R&D when the SBU is weak, and insufficient marketing and R&D when strong.
7. Risking major trouble for little prospective gain.
8. Inadequate attention to the history of the SBU and the industry it is in, especially with respect to defining the limits of the possible.
9. Confronting a competitor on his own ground and on his own terms.
10. Biting off more than you can chew. Don't exhaust the confidence of your organization in a vain effort.
11. Failure to develop a strategy that is flexible and adaptable to changing circumstances.
12. Persisting in the same competitive strategy, with additional resources, in spite of initial failure.
13. Forgetting that business strategy represents the means to an economic end and that economic objectives must govern business strategy.
14. Preoccupation with developing tactical efficiency at the expense of strategic thinking.
15. Failure to consciously choose the competitor whom you wish to challenge.
16. Failure to reexamine an apparently stable environment and thereby mistakenly perceive a strategic challenge as merely a tactical challenge.
17. Failure to recognize an opportunity presented by a changing environment.

Source: Rochelle O'Connor, *Facing Strategic Issues: New Planning Guides and Practices,* Report No. 87 (New York: The Conference Board, Inc., 1985), pp. 44–46.

SUMMARY

Our discussion of the changing patterns of global competition highlights the importance of coping with change in the dynamic competitive arena. Factors creating market turbulence include changes in customer needs, industry structure, distribution trends, and environmental influences. These factors often require shifts in business strategy. Gaining and keeping a competitive advantage is essential to achieving high performance. Advantage is a moving target in the turbulent and rapidly changing marketplace. The primary sources of competitive advantage are superior skills, superior resources, and superior controls. These sources of advantage are used to gain value and cost positional advantage. Sustaining competitive advantage requires creating capability gaps relative to competitors. Strategic planning guides the business in managing the forces of change and maintaining a competitive edge.

Strategy formulation for the corporation includes: (1) defining the corporate mission and setting objectives, (2) forming strategic business units, and (3) establishing strategy guidelines for long-term strategic planning of the corporation and its business units. Top management decides what corporate strategies will move the firm toward its objectives. After implementing the strategy, management decides how the strategy is progressing and what adjustments are needed. Successfully executing these steps requires penetrating and insightful analyses. Strategic planning is essential to corporate survival and performance.

The corporate mission statement defines the nature and scope of the business and provides essential strategic direction for the corporation. The firm's objectives indicate the performance desired by management. If management decides to move away from the core business, several paths of corporate development are possible, including expansion into new products and/or markets as well as diversification. Strategic analysis begins by assessing the situational advantage of each business in the corporate portfolio. Several classification models assist in deciding what generic strategy to select for each business in the corporate portfolio. Four broad generic strategies are described: develop, stabilize, turnaround, and harvest strategies. The generic strategy provides a strategic focus for developing a specific action plan. PIMS analyses are used to further diagnose business strategy and identify future actions for consideration by management.

The SBU strategies are guided by corporate strategy guidelines. The process begins by considering each business unit's market opportunity, position against competition, financial situation and projections, and strengths and weaknesses. The planning models provide useful frameworks for situation analysis. The situation analysis shows the strategy alternatives for the SBU. Management then selects a strategy and develops a strategic plan. The plan is implemented and managed.

QUESTIONS FOR REVIEW AND DISCUSSION

1. One important part of a corporate/business unit situation assessment is the identification and evaluation of competitors. Finding potential competitors is a key problem in preparing such a situation assessment. Suggest several ways to determine potential competitors of a company.

2. Top management of companies probably devoted more time to reviewing (and sometimes changing) their corporate mission in the 1980s than in any other period in the past. Discuss the major reasons for this increased concern with the business mission.

3. What advantages do you see in defining a corporate mission in a very specific way? Are there any disadvantages to clearly describing the corporate purpose?

4. Discuss the major issues that top management should consider in deciding whether or not to expand business operations beyond the core business.

5. Discuss the environmental factors that should be assessed on a regular basis by

a large retail corporation like the Dayton Hudson Corporation.

6. What are the advantages of combining two or more strategic business units into a division or group, compared to keeping the planning units as separate organizational units?
7. Discuss what you consider to be the major issues in trying to divide a corporation into strategic business units, indicating for each problem suggestions for overcoming it.
8. What are the major advantages in using one of the product-market grid methods for strategic analysis of a firm's planning units?
9. Is there any value to a single product-market firm in using one of the strategic analysis methods? Discuss.
10. What considerations may be important in deciding between the use of specific products and lines of products as the unit of analysis in strategic planning?
11. Some strategic planners suggest that databases, such as the one developed for the PIMS analysis, should be based on data collected from the industry of which a firm is a part rather than being made up of a broad cross section of firms and industries. Discuss.
12. Why might top management decide *not* to adopt a formal method of strategic analysis, and rely instead upon management's judgment and experience as the basis of deciding how to allocate resources to business units?
13. Discuss the importance of finding a competitive advantage. Indicate how a company of your choice has accomplished this objective.
14. Explain how a company can gain and sustain competitive advantage.

NOTES

1. Guy Collins, "Benetton Weaves Strategy for Growth," *The Wall Street Journal,* February 4, 1991, p. A7A; and Teri Agins, "Shrinkage of Stores and Customers in U.S. Causes Italy's Benetton to Alter Its Tactics," *The Wall Street Journal,* June 24, 1992, pp. B1, B10.
2. The material in this section is drawn from David W. Cravens, Raymond W. LaForge, and Thomas N. Ingram, "Selling Strategy Dynamics: Restructuring in Turbulent Markets," working paper, June 14, 1989.
3. James K. Brown, *Refocusing the Company's Business,* Report No. 873 (New York: The Conference Board, Inc., 1985), p. 1.
4. Carl P. Zeithaml and Valarie A. Zeithaml, "Environmental Management: Revising the Marketing Perspective," *Journal of Business,* Spring 1984, p. 48.
5. Brown, *Refocusing the Company's Business.*
6. Harold Stieglitz, *Chief Executives View Their Jobs: Today and Tomorrow,* Report No. 871 (New York: The Conference Board, Inc., 1985).
7. Collins, "Benetton Weaves Strategy," p. A7A.
8. Michael E. Porter, "From Competitive Advantage to Corporate Strategy," *Harvard Business Review,* May–June 1987, pp. 43–59.
9. Roger A. Kerin, Vijay Mahajan, and P. Rajan Varadarajan, *Strategic Market Planning* (Boston: Allyn and Bacon, 1990), p. 6.
10. As quoted in Stratford P. Sherman, "The Mind of Jack Welch," *Fortune,* March 27, 1989, p. 50.
11. The discussion in this section is based on George S. Day and Robin Wensley, "Assessing Advantage: A Framework for Diagnosing Competitive Superiority," *Journal of Marketing,* April 1988, pp. 1–20.

12. George S. Day, *Market Driven Strategy* (New York: The Free Press, 1990), pp. 128–31.
13. Michael E. Porter, *Competitive Advantage* (New York: The Free Press, 1985), p. 3.
14. Day, *Market Driven Strategy,* pp. 138–47.
15. Porter, *Competitive Advantage,* p. 33.
16. Ernst & Young Quality Improvement Consulting Group, *Total Quality* (Homewood, IL: Business One Irwin, 1990), p. 50.
17. Kevin P. Coyne, "Sustainable Competitive Advantage—What It Is, What It Isn't," *Business Horizons,* January–February 1986, p. 55.
18. The following discussion is based on ibid., pp. 57–58.
19. Michael Porter, "Industry Structure and Competitive Strategy: Keys to Profitability," *Financial Analysts Journal,* July–August, 1980, pp. 30–41.
20. Ibid.
21. Ibid.
22. See, for example, ibid., and William T. Robinson, "Sources of Market Pioneer Advantages: The Case of Industrial Goods Industries," *Journal of Marketing Research,* February 1988, pp. 87–94.
23. Karakaya and Stahl, "Barriers to Entry," pp. 80–91.
24. George S. Day, *Strategic Market Planning* (St. Paul, MN: West Publishing, 1984), pp. 18–22.
25. Durr-Fillauer Medical, Inc., *1988 Annual Report.*
26. Peter F. Drucker, *Management* (New York: Harper & Row, 1974), p. 100.
27. Michael E. Porter, "From Competitive Advantage to Corporate Strategy," *Harvard Business Review,* May–June 1987, pp. 43–59.
28. Ibid., 46.
29. Philippe Haspeslagh, "Portfolio Planning: Uses and Limits," *Harvard Business Review,* January–February 1982, p. 65.
30. David A. Ludlum, "Is Service Keeping Airline Aloft Despite AMR's New Competition?" *Computer World Premier 100,* September 11, 1989, pp. 20–21.
31. This discussion is based on Boris Yavitz and William H. Newman, "What the Corporation Should Provide Its Business Units," *Journal of Business Strategy* 3, no. 1 (Summer 1982), p. 14.
32. Kenneth R. Andrews, *The Concept of Corporate Strategy* (Homewood, IL: Richard D. Irwin, 1980).
33. Theodore T. Herbert and Helen Deresky, "Generic Strategies: An Empirical Investigation of Typology Validity and Strategy Content," *Strategic Management Journal* (1987), pp. 135–47.
34. Ibid., p. 135.
35. Derek F. Abell and John S. Hammond, *Strategic Market Planning* (Englewood Cliffs, NJ: Prentice Hall, 1979), pp. 374–75.
36. Herbert and Deresky, "Generic Strategies," pp. 136–37.
37. Ibid., pp. 136–38.
38. The following description is drawn from ibid., pp. 141–44. More extensive discussion is provided in the source.
39. *The PIMS Program* (Cambridge, MA: Strategic Planning Institute, 1980), p. 8.
40. *The PIMSETTER on Business Strategy,* no. 1 (Cambridge, MA: Strategic Planning Institute, 1977), pp. 3–5.
41. *The PIMS Program,* p. 10.
42. Ibid., pp. 11–12.

CHAPTER

3

Strategic Partnerships

Strategic relationships between independent organizations occur for several reasons. The objective may be to gain access to markets, reduce the risks generated by rapid environmental change, share complementary skills, or obtain resources beyond those available to a single enterprise. These relationships are not recent innovations, but they are escalating in importance because of the environmental complexity and risks of a global economy, and the skill and resource limitations of a single organization.[1] Strategic alliances, joint ventures, and supplier-producer collaborations are examples of cooperative relationships between independent firms. Gaining competitive advantage increasingly demands cooperative relationships to access technology, expand resources, improve productivity and quality, and penetrate new markets.

Strategic partnerships among companies are illustrated by the Japanese *keiretsu* companies. These conglomerate-type industrial groups display a wide range of relationships, as shown in Exhibit 3–1. The Mitsubishi Group includes over 100 independent companies, each with its own board of directors. Leadership of *keiretsu* is provided by Mitsubishi Bank and Mitsubishi Heavy Industries. "The building of long-term relationships is a crucial part of the business environment in Japan."[2] The *keiretsu* companies provide the skills and resources for entering new industries and sustaining a competitive edge in existing markets.

EXHIBIT 3–1 Complexity of *Keiretsu:* The Mitsubishi Group

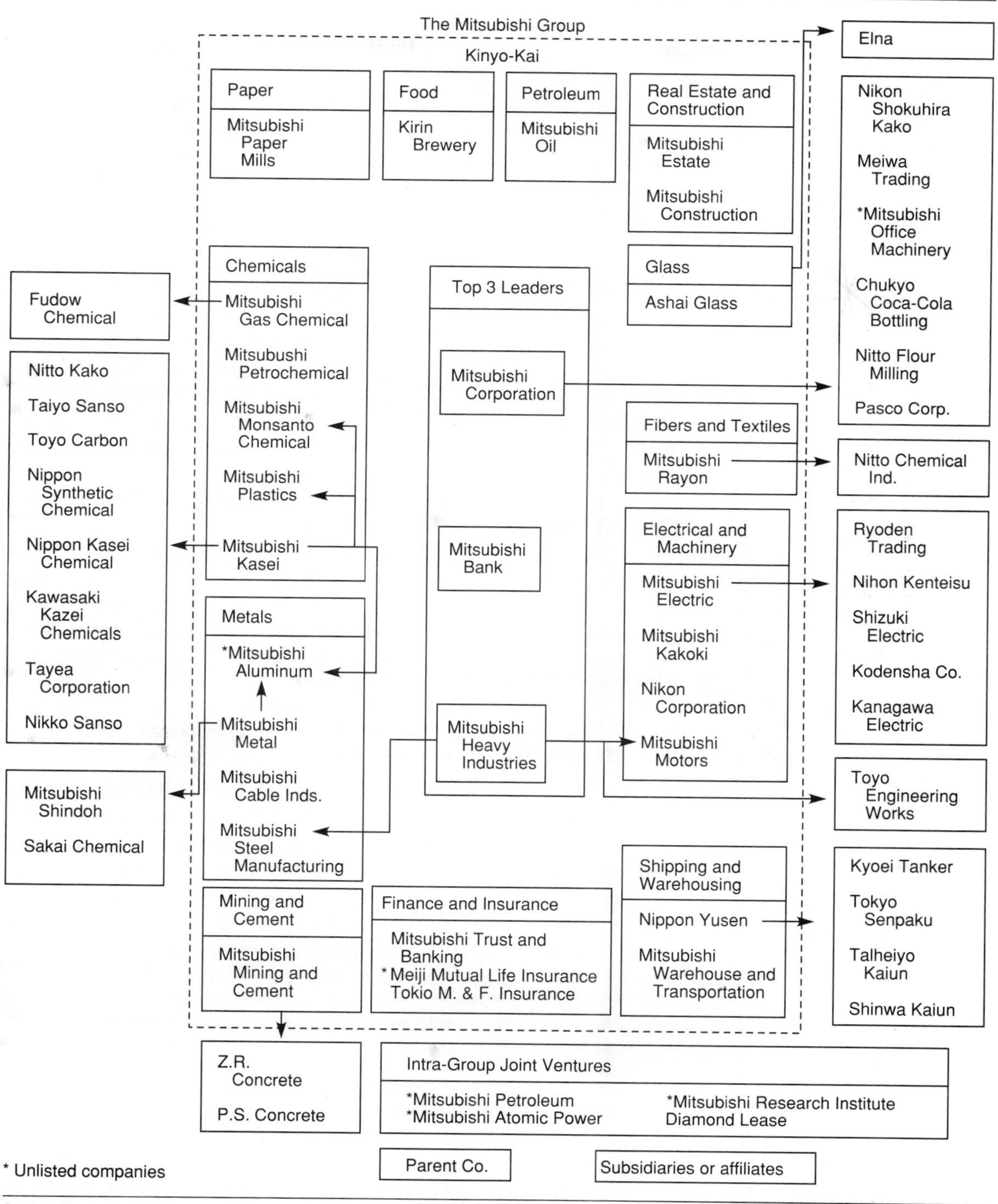

Source: Timothy M. Collins and Thomas L. Doorley, *Teaming Up for the 90s* (Homewood, IL: Business One Irwin, 1991), p. 290.

Often, business and marketing strategies involve more than a single organization. In this chapter we examine the nature and scope of the strategic relationships among organizations. First, we consider the rationale for these relationships. Next, we look at important relationship concepts, followed by a look at different kinds of relationships among organizations. Finally, the chapter examines several considerations that are important in developing effective interorganizational relationships.

WHAT DRIVES INTERORGANIZATIONAL RELATIONSHIPS?

In the past, companies established relationships to achieve tactical objectives such as selling in minor overseas markets.[3] Today strategic relationships among organizations consider the elements of overall competitive strength—technology, costs, and marketing. Unlike the tactical relationships, the effectiveness of these strategic agreements among companies can affect the long-term performance of the business.

Several forces create a need to establish cooperative strategic relationships with other organizations. These forces include the diversity, turbulence, and riskiness of the global business environment; the escalating complexity of technology; the existence of large resource requirements; the need to gain access to global markets; and the availability of an impressive array of information technology for coordinating intercompany operations. These forces fall into two broad categories: (1) environmental turbulence and diversity and (2) skill and resource gaps.[4]

Environmental Turbulence and Diversity

Since the global business environment is examined in several chapters, the present discussion is brief. Diversity refers to differences between the elements in the environment, including people, organizations, and social forces affecting resources.[5] Interlinked global markets create important challenges for companies.

Coping with diversity involves both the internal organization and its relationships with other organizations. Environmental diversity reduces the capacity of an organization to respond quickly to customer needs and new-product development.[6] Organizations meet this challenge by: (1) altering their internal organization structures and (2) establishing strategic relationships with other organizations.

Environmental diversity makes it difficult to link buyers and the goods and services that meet buyers' needs and wants in the marketplace. Because of this difficulty, companies are teaming up to meet the requirements of fragmented markets and complex technologies. These strategies may involve supplier and producer collaboration, strategic alliances between competitors, joint ventures between industry members, and network organizations that coordinate partnerships and alliances with many other organizations.[7] Examples of these organization forms are discussed in the next section.

The business environment creates risks for organizations that are unable to make rapid changes. Turbulence is caused by technological innovation/obsolescence stimulated by the pace of growth in knowledge and its proliferation.[8] One response to turbulence and risk is to establish flexible relationships with other organizations, thus avoiding ownership investments in sources of supply, production, and distribution. Ownership of the entire value-added system may be less effective and more risky in a turbulent environment. The Strategy Feature describes relationships among several companies in various industries from the huge original equipment manufacturer (OEM) market.

Companies may coordinate an independent network of suppliers, producers, and distributors. For example, as we saw in Chapter 2, Benetton, the global casual wear company, contracts much of its production to producers throughout the world. All of Benetton's retailers are independent dealers. The Benetton core organization coordinates and directs the global production and distribution system, using its powerful information capabilities. The computer network monitors sales and sends incoming orders to the factories. Similar strategies involving networks of participating organizations are employed by Casio in electronics, Nike in athletic shoes, and the Bombay Company in furniture and fixtures.

Skill and Resource Gaps

During the last two decades, expenditures for research and development have grown three times faster than spending on capital assets.[9] The skills and resource requirements of technologies in many industries often surpass the capabilities of a single organization. Thus, the sharing of complementary technologies and risks are important drivers for strategic partnerships. In addition to technology, financial constraints, access to markets, and availability of information systems encourage establishing relationships among independent organizations.

Increasing Complexity of Technology. Technology constraints impact industry giants as well as smaller firms. Small companies with specialized competitive strengths are able to achieve impressive bargaining power with larger firms because of their high levels of competence in specialized technology areas and their ability to substantially compress development time. The partnerships between large and small pharmaceutical companies are illustrative. The small firm gains financial support, while the large firm gets access to specialized technology. For example, Glaxo Holdings, PLC, the British company, has collaborative agreements with a small U.S. company developing a novel treatment for diabetes and with a biotechnology company involved in genetics research.[10] These cooperative relationships allow

STRATEGY FEATURE Organizational Relationships

Whose Product Is It Anyway?

The original-equipment-manufacturer market is unglamorous but enormous. Whenever a company lacks the expertise or size to make a product on its own, it buys the product from a so-called OEM and affixes its own logo.

In the computer business, that means American Telephone & Telegraph Co. sells under the AT&T label personal computers made by Intel Corp., and Digital Equipment Corp. sells personal computers made by Tandy Corp. Both AT&T and Digital had failed—expensively—in attempts to crack the PC market. Both felt the need to offer a complete product line, which must include PCs, but both decided it would be cheaper and easier to buy them rather than try again to develop their own.

Other OEM arrangements: Supermarkets may want to sell their own brand of orange juice but don't want to be in the orange-growing business, or a department store may want to carry its own line of tools but doesn't want to go into tool making. From the point of view of the manufacturer, General Electric Co.—as one example—sells refrigerators to distributors wanting to carry a private line.

One downside to the OEM business is that markups tend to be small. Every company in the process is having to take just a piece of the markup that would ordinarily have gone to the manufacturer alone. In addition, the OEM supplier can be stuck with the risk. If the economy slows and a store cuts its orders, the OEM supplier is the one that must somehow support the manufacturing capacity that is idled.

Source: Paul B. Carroll, "Reprogramming Itself, IBM Now Wants to Become a Big Supplier of Little Parts," *The Wall Street Journal,* May 15, 1991, p. B1.

Laser Printer Makers . . .

First quarter 1991 market share of low-end laser printer manufacturers, in percent

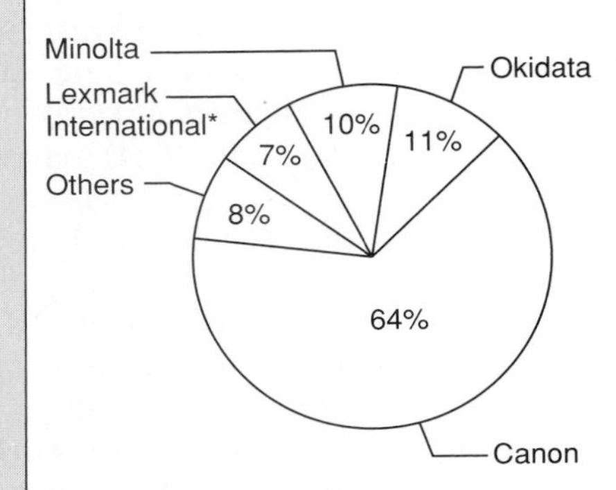

*Formerly a division of IBM

And Marketers

First quarter 1991 market share of low-end laser printer sellers, in percent and their manufacturers

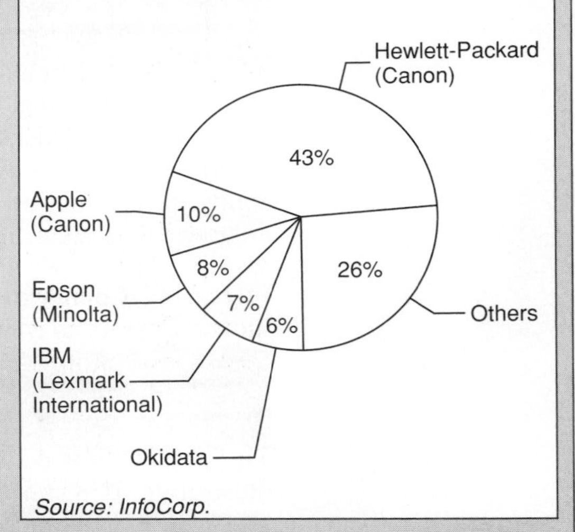

Source: InfoCorp.

large pharmaceutical companies to access smaller partners that have expertise in emerging research areas, thus accelerating the process of moving new drugs to the marketplace.

Access to technology and other skills, specialization advantages, and the opportunity to enhance product value are important motivations for establishing relationships among organizations. These relationships may be vertical between suppliers and producers or horizontal across industry members.

Financial Constraints. The financial needs for competing in global markets are often greater than the capacity of a single organization. As a result, many companies must seek partners to obtain the resources essential for competing in many industries or to spread the risk of financial loss with another firm.

McDonnell Douglas, the aerospace company, illustrates the limitations of a single company trying to compete in the global market for large commercial aircraft. The company's top management announced that to compete in the 1990s with new aircraft designs, management would establish partnerships with other companies. The alliances would involve both financial support and the subcontracting of production. Asian partners were targeted to provide market access to the rapidly growing Asian market for commercial aircraft. Management's objective was to sell ownership in the company for an estimated $2 billion. McDonnell Douglas would retain the core technology, coordinate production, and direct marketing operations. Interestingly, by early 1993, management had been unable to recruit partners.

Access to Markets. Organizational relationships are also important in gaining access to markets. The McDonnell Douglas strategy for obtaining access to Asian purchasers of commercial aircraft is illustrative. Products have traditionally been distributed through marketing intermediaries such as wholesalers and retailers in order to access end-user markets. These vertical channels of distribution are important in linking supply and demand. During the 1980s several horizontal relationships were established between competing firms to access global markets and domestic market segments not served by the cooperating firms. These cooperative marketing agreements expand the traditional channel of distribution coverage and gain the advantage of market knowledge in international markets.

International strategic alliances are used by many companies competing throughout the world.[11] For example, Fanuc, the leading Japanese computer numerical controls and robot producer, typically works with a local partner to market its high-technology products. Many other cooperative arrangements provide companies access to markets. Some are between competing firms, such as the research and marketing alliance between IBM and Apple computers.

Information Technology. Information technology makes establishing organizational relationships feasible in terms of time, cost, and effectiveness. Advances in information technology provide an important resource for improving the effectiveness of both internal and interorganizational communications:

> Advances in information technology and telecommunications have removed many of the communications barriers that prevented companies from drawing on overseas technical resources. Indeed, the ability to transmit documents and even complex design drawings instantaneously from one part of the globe to another by electronic mail means that it is often more efficient to collaborate globally in product development.[12]

Information systems enable organizations to effectively communicate even though the collaborating firms are widely dispersed geographically. The use of information systems for marketing analysis, planning, and control is discussed in Chapter 8, and examples are shown in several chapters.

TYPES OF ORGANIZATIONAL RELATIONSHIPS

A useful way to examine organizational relationships is to consider whether the tie between firms is vertical or horizontal, as shown in Exhibit 3–2. The symbols used in the diagram refer to manufacturer (M), wholesaler (W), retailer (R), and end-user (EU). An organization may participate in both vertical and horizontal relationships. We first look at vertical relationships among organizations, then strategic alliances and joint ventures. Evolving global relationships among organizations are examined in a subsequent section.

Vertical Relationships

A typical method for moving products through various stages in the value-added process is the linking of suppliers, manufacturers, distributors, and consumer and business end-users of goods and services into vertical channels. Functional specialization and efficiency create the need for different types of organizations. For example, wholesalers stock products in inventory and deploy them when needed to retailers, thus reducing the delays of ordering direct from manufacturers. We look at customer-supplier and distribution channel relationships to provide insights into vertical relationships between companies.

Customer-Supplier Relationships. The suppliers and buyers of a vast array of raw materials, parts and components, equipment, and services (e.g., consulting, maintenance) are linked together in vertical channels of distribution. The relationships between the supplier and customer range from trans-

EXHIBIT 3–2 Illustrative Interorganizational Relationships

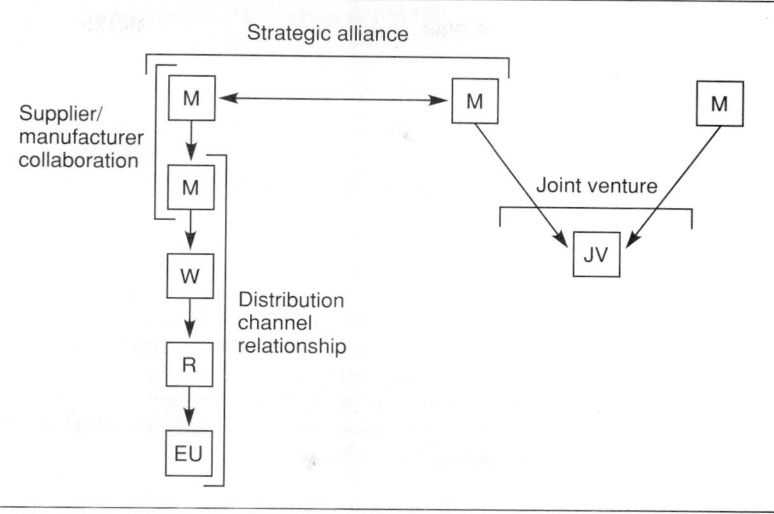

Source: This diagram is adapted from an example suggested by David Wilson, Penn State University.

actional to highly collaborative partnerships.[13] The transactional working relationship is the simple exchange of basic products at competitive prices. In contrast, collaborative association is much more interactive and adaptive in nature. The partners build strong social, economic, service, and technical relationships over a long time horizon.

Collaborative relations include shared activities such as product and process design, applications assistance, long-term supply contracts, and just-in-time inventory programs.[14] The amount of collaboration may vary substantially among industries. Moreover, in a given competitive situation, a firm may pursue different degrees of collaboration across its customer base. Some supplier-customer relationships are transactional, but the same supplier may seek collaborative relationships with other customers.

Collaborative relationships between suppliers and their customers are widely advocated by business authorities. These partnerships are important aspects of total quality management (TQM) programs. Nevertheless, the decision of a supplier to develop a strong collaborative partnership should include assessment of these factors:[15]

1. **Philosophy of Doing Business.** The partners' approach to business should be compatible. For example, if one firm has adopted a TQM philosophy and the other partner does not place a high priority on TQM, conflicts are likely to develop in the working relationship.

2. **Relative Dependence of the Partners.** The collaborative relations are more likely to be successful if the dependence is important and equivalent between the two organizations.
3. **Technological Edge Contributions.** The buyer may represent an opportunity for a supplier to improve its product or process because of the customer's leading-edge application of the supplier's product or service. For example, collaborative codesign of industrial equipment can contribute to the supplier's competitive advantage.

These same criteria can be evaluated from the customer's perspective to assess the value and limitations of establishing a strong cooperative relationship. If such a tie is not advisable, the firms can still operate in a transactional buyer-seller relationship.

In the United States, producers are drastically reducing the number of suppliers, as shown in Exhibit 3–3. TQM philosophy advocates working with one supplier rather than several suppliers of the same materials or parts. The objective is to build a strong collaborative relationship between the supplier and producer.

Adaptation between two organizations is an essential part of a collaborative relationship. Understanding the adaptation process is important for several reasons:[16]

1. Considerable investments may be required of one or both firms.
2. The adaptation may be essential to conducting business with a specific customer or for the customer in securing needed products from the supplier.
3. These interfirm investments often cannot be transferred to other business relationships.
4. The relationship may have important consequences for the long-term competitiveness of both firms.

Thus, evaluating the extent to which a company should enter into a collaborative relationship is an important issue for both partners.

Distribution Channel Relationships. Vertical relationships also occur between producers and marketing intermediaries (e.g., wholesalers and retailers) as shown in Exhibit 3–2. These channels provide the producer access to consumer and organizational end-users. Channel relationships vary from highly collaborative to transactional ties. A strong collaborative relationship exists in a vertical marketing system (VMS).[17] These systems are managed by one of the channel members such as a retailer, distributor, or producer. The VMS may be owned by a channel firm, linked together contractually (e.g., a franchise system), or held together by the power and influence of the firm administering the channel relationships.

The theory related to power and dependence suggests that "in working relationships, a firm adapts to a counterpart to the degree that it is dependent

EXHIBIT 3–3 Diminishing Suppliers

Many companies are cutting back the number of suppliers they use and demanding higher quality from those they keep.

	*Number of Suppliers**		
	Current	*Previous*†	*% Change*
Xerox	500	5,000	−90%
Motorola	3,000	10,000	−70
Digital Equipment	3,000	9,000	−67
General Motors	5,500	10,000	−45
Ford Motor	1,000	1,800	−44
Texas Instruments	14,000	22,000	−36
Rainbird	380	520	−27
Allied-Signal Aerospace	6,000	7,500	−20

*Companies have different ways of counting their supplier base. For example, some count only direct manufacturing suppliers, while others count service and support suppliers.

†Number of suppliers firm had prior to starting reduction programs.

Source: John R. Emshwiller, "Suppliers Struggle to Improve Quality as Big Firms Slash Their Vendor Roles," *The Wall Street Journal,* August 16, 1991, p. B1.

on that counterpart."[18] This may result in supplier dependence or customer dependence. Illustrative aspects of dependence include the importance of the customer, buyer concentration, supplier importance, supplier market share, and product complexity.

A conventional (non-VMS) distribution channel has no center of power and has a transactional rather than collaborative linkage. The participants function on an independent basis, completing the necessary buying and selling transactions between each other. Distribution channel strategy is discussed in Chapter 12.

Strategic Alliances

A strategic alliance between two organizations is an agreement to cooperate to achieve one or more common strategic objectives. The relationship is horizontal in scope (Exhibit 3–2). While the term *alliance* is sometimes used to designate supplier-producer partnerships, it is used here to identify collaborative relationships between companies at the same level in the distribution channel. The alliance relationship is intended to be long-term and strategically important to both parties. The following discussion assumes an alliance between two parties, recognizing that a company may establish several alliances.

Each organization's contribution to the alliance is intended to complement the partner's contribution. The alliance requires each participant to yield some of its independence: "Alliances mean sharing control."[19] The rationale for the relationship may be to gain access to markets, utilize existing distribution channels, share technology development costs, or obtain specific skills or resources.

The alliance is not a merger between two independent organizations, although the termination of an alliance may lead to an acquisition of one partner by the other partner. It is different from a joint venture launched by two firms or a formal contractual relationship between organizations. Moreover, the alliance extends beyond purchasing stock in another company. Instead, it is a commitment to actively participate on a common project or program that is strategic in scope. One of the major purposes of global alliances is to gain access to markets.

General Electric's jet engine partnership with Snecma, the French government-controlled aerospace company, is an example of a successful long-term strategic alliance.[20] Formed in 1974 to help GE sell aircraft engines in Europe, the alliance was successful for both partners. The GE-French partnership obtained orders and purchase commitments for more than $11 billion in 1989. The relationship illustrates several of the challenges and requirements for success in strategic partnerships.

- GE's personnel must resolve cultural, linguistic, logistical, and foreign-exchange problems.
- Investment and revenue are shared on an equal basis by GE and Snecma.
- The two partners delegate broad responsibilities to their senior engineering executives.
- GE is responsible for system design and most of the complex engine technology.
- Snecma concentrates on fans, boosters, low-pressure turbines, and related work.
- Snecma's marketing role is expanding, although, until the early 1990s, GE was responsible for most of the marketing activities.

The GE-Snecma partnership is a model of a well-structured alliance. It has several important characteristics of successful alliances. First, we discuss the success record of alliances. Next, several uses of alliances are described. Finally, alliance success requirements are examined.

Success of Alliances. The competitive realities of surviving and prospering in the complex and rapidly changing business environment encourage companies to form strategic alliances in many different industries. The record of success of alliances is not particularly favorable, although there are some notable successes such as the GE-Snecma jet engine alliance. While the alliance is a promising strategy for enhancing the competitive advantage of the partners, several failures have occurred because of the complexity of managing these relationships.

One of the more visible alliances in the 1980s that did not work out was the partnership between AT&T and Olivetti & Company, the Italian office equipment producer.[21] It was a cooperative marketing agreement for AT&T to sell Olivetti's personal computers in the United States and for Olivetti to market AT&T computers and telephone-switching machines in Europe. Unfortunately, computers and telecommunications did not fit together very well in a coordinated marketing effort. Compounding the situation were major cultural differences and decision-making conflicts.

Successful alliance outcomes are difficult to achieve because of:[22]

1. Shifting strategic requirements resulting from changing conditions and market and technology uncertainties.
2. The lack of clear decision-making responsibility.
3. Conflicts concerning objectives, cultural differences, and styles of making decisions.
4. The decline of long-term interest and commitment by one of the alliance partners.

The GE-Snecma alliance shows how these problems can be overcome, whereas the AT&T-Olivetti partnership shows how failure to resolve key issues threatens the success of the alliance.

Kinds of Alliances. The alliance typically involves one or more marketing, research and development, operations (manufacturing), and financial relationships between the partners. Capabilities may be exchanged or shared. In addition to functions performed by the partners, other aspects of alliances may include market coverage and effectively matching the specific characteristics of the partners.

The alliance helps each partner to obtain business and technical skills and experience that are not available internally. One partner contributes unique capabilities to the other organization in return for needed skills and experience. The rationale of the alliance is that both parties benefit from sharing complementary functional responsibilities rather than independently performing them.

The partners may differ according to size, functional specialization, resource capabilities, culture, and other characteristics. For example, one issue is whether or not the partners should be the same size. The concern is that the small firm may be at a disadvantage in an alliance with a large company. Experts suggest that defining the objectives of the alliance and the equivalency of the contribution of each partner to the mutual objectives are more important in establishing the bargaining position of the partners than are size, amount of resources, and other characteristics of the partners.[23]

Alliance Success Requirements. The success of the alliance may depend heavily on effectively matching the capabilities of the participating organizations and on achieving the full commitment of each partner to the alliance. The benefits and the trade-offs in the alliance must be favorable for each of the partners. The contribution of one partner should fill a gap in the other partner's capabilities. In the GE-Snecma alliance, GE gained market access and knowledge of Airbus operations while Snecma obtained technical skills and experience in engine design and production. Both benefited from the financial success of the venture.

One important concern in the alliance relationship is that the partner may gain access to confidential technology and other competitive advantages. While this issue is important, the essential consideration is assessing the relationship's risks and rewards and the integrity of the alliance partner. A strong bond of trust between the partners exists in most successful relationships. The purpose of the alliance is for each partner to contribute something distinctive rather than to transfer core skills wholesale to the partner.[24] It is important for management in each organization to evaluate the advisability and risks concerning the transfer of skills and technologies to the partner.

Joint Ventures

These relationships are agreements between two or more firms to establish a separate entity (Exhibit 3–2). Joint ventures may be used to develop a new market opportunity, access an international market, share costs and financial risks, gain a share of local manufacturing profits, or acquire knowledge or technology for the core business.[25] While joint ventures are similar to strategic alliances, the ventures differ in several ways. They result in the creation of a new organization. Environmental turbulence and risk set the rationale for the venture more so than a major skill/resource gap, although both pressures may be present.

IBM's strategy to form a joint venture for sending videos, software, and other information to homes and businesses illustrates the motivation for these relationships.[26] This strategy is heavily influenced by the huge financial losses (billions of dollars) incurred by IBM and other companies in attempting to send games, shopping, and other services on phone lines into households. Thus, reducing risk is a major driver of IBM's decision to launch a joint venture for this project.

A study of cooperative research joint ventures among competitors in Japan provides some interesting findings concerning power and dependence in organizational relationships:[27]

1. Cooperative research is likely to be more successful for projects involving applied rather than basic research.
2. Research and development (R&D) costs are reduced and the chances of project success increased when the partners provide complementary skills and resources.
3. Large firms have a greater incentive to cooperate, although they

favor small partners (thus limiting the loss of revenues from the venture's results).

4. Small firms, if they possess the necessary skills and resources, prefer to conduct their own R&D. (Thus, power and dependence may be an important driver of establishing the relationship.)
5. Because of the hesitancy of small firms to cooperate with large companies, relationships may be more likely to occur among large competitors.

Not surprisingly, this research indicates that competitive relationships offer potential for conflict among the participants.

GLOBAL RELATIONSHIPS AMONG ORGANIZATIONS

Several traditional organizational forms are used to compete in global markets. One is the multinational corporation that may compete in several countries, often using a separate organization in each country. We focus the present discussion on organizational forms that involve relationships with other organizations. Strategies for competing in global markets are examined in Chapter 10.

Several examples of the use of joint ventures and strategic alliances to compete in international markets are discussed earlier in the chapter. The expanded use of cooperative agreements by companies in the United States, Japan, and the European Community is shown by Exhibit 3–4. The growth of such agreements increased more than five times during the decade covered in the chart.

The need to develop more flexible organizational concepts for competing in rapidly changing global markets is illustrated by two types of organizations: (1) the network corporation and (2) the Japanese form of trading company.[28] We also discuss the strategic role of government in global relationships among organizations.

The Network Corporation. This kind of organization consists of a core corporation that coordinates activities and functions between sources of supply and end-users of the product. The network, or hollow corporation, has a relatively small work force, relying instead on independent suppliers often located at several places throughout the world. The organizations are linked by a sophisticated information system. The core company may be vertically integrated at the retail level or, instead, may utilize an independent distribution system. A successful example of the network organization form is Dell Computer.

One organization of the network manages the various partnerships and alliances. This network organization coordinates R&D, finance, global strategy, manufacturing, information systems, marketing, and the management of relationships.[29] The primary organizing concept is a small network con-

EXHIBIT 3–4 Cooperative Agreements, 1978–1989

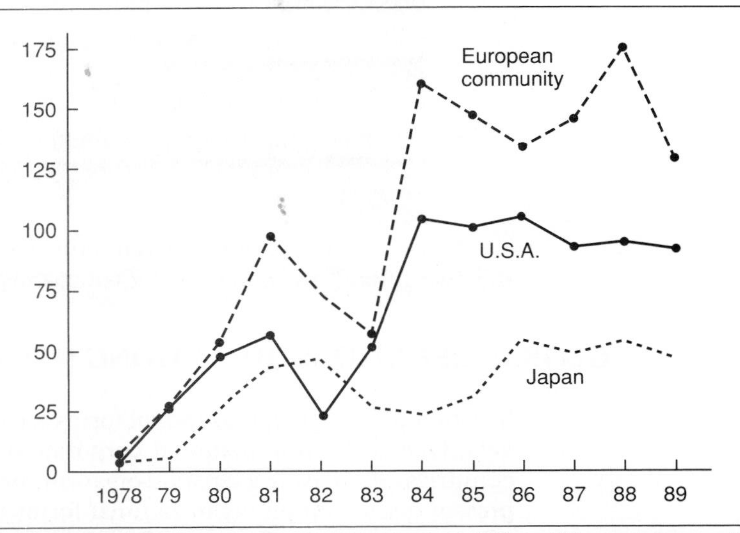

Source: INSEAD (Fontainbleu, France). Reproduced in Timothy M. Collins and Thomas L. Doorley, *Teaming Up for the 90s* (Homewood, IL: Business One Irwin, 1991), p. 4.

trol center that uses independent specialists to perform various functions. Thus, the priority is placed on "buying" rather than "producing" and on "partnership" rather than "ownership." The network organization must define the skills and resources it will use to develop new knowledge and skills. For example, a core competency of the network organization may be designing, managing, and controlling partnerships with customers, suppliers, distributors, and other specialists.

The Calyx & Corolla Company (C&C) works with a network of suppliers in its business of marketing fresh, perishable flowers through catalogs. C&C's 1990 revenues reached $10 million. The company has partnerships with 25 growers who cut and package fresh flowers. The growers ship direct to the customer by Federal Express delivery service. At the center of C&C's flexible organization is a powerful computer network linking C&C orders with Federal Express. The network of cooperating organizations is shown in Exhibit 3–5. Larger growers are on-line with the system, whereas the smaller growers receive orders via Federal Express delivery service. C&C supplies growers with packaging, cellophane, packing tissue, and other materials used in wrapping the flowers. Flower purchasers select items from a colorful catalog offering a wide array of cut and other flower arrangements. Orders are placed using an 800 number. Since the orders are assembled by the growers and shipped direct to the customer, the flowers are often fresher than those available from local flower shops.

EXHIBIT 3–5 Calyx & Corolla's Flexible Organization

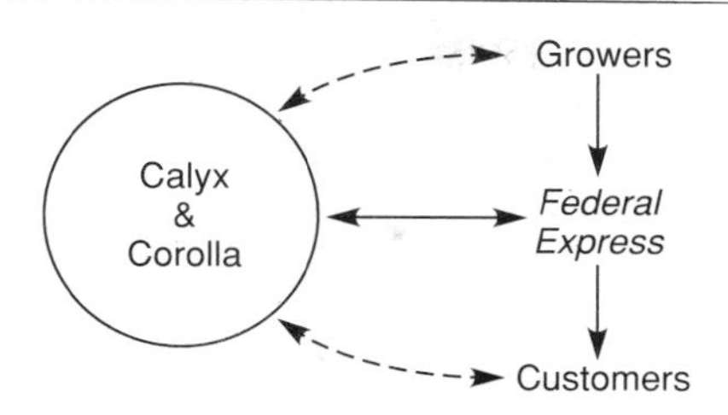

Trading Companies. The use of trading companies dates far back into history in Asia. Since they share certain of the characteristics of network organizations, a look at this organization form provides additional insights into interorganizational relationships. The Japanese have been very successful in developing and coordinating extensive global operations and information management.[30] These *sogo shosha* concentrated primarily on commodity products, worked most directly with suppliers, and maintained a strong national (rather than global) perspective. An example of a trading company's network of relationships is shown in Exhibit 3–6. This trading company functions as an intermediary organization for the steel industry by developing sources of supply and demand.

The skills and experience developed by Japanese companies through the *sogo shosha* provide these companies an important competitive advantage in developing other forms of flexible organizations, like the network company discussed above. Japan's needs for natural resources were important influences on the development of trading companies. Today, these giant organizations are active in helping emerging countries such as China and Vietnam develop their markets.

The Strategic Role of Government

While the role of the government in the United States is largely one of facilitating and regulating free enterprise, the governments in several other countries play a more active role with business organizations. For example, the Japanese government encouraged the development of the *sogo shosha.* In considering the role of government, we look at three types of relationships between government and private industry: (1) the single-nation partnership, (2) the multiple-nation partnership, and (3) the government corporation.

Single-Nation Partnership. A country's government may form a partnership with one or a group of companies to develop an industry or achieve some other national objective. Japan has successfully used this method of creating a national competitive advantage in a targeted industry in several

EXHIBIT 3–6 How Japanese Trading Companies Contribute to Trade Development

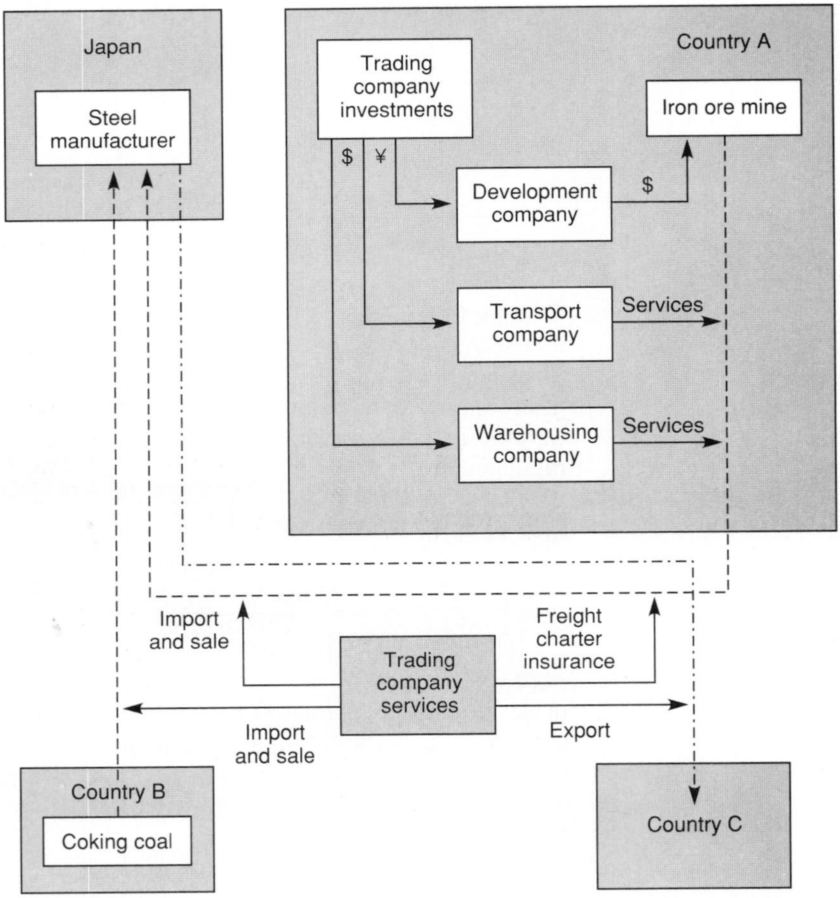

Source: "The Role of Trading Companies in International Commerce" (Tokyo: Japan External Trade Organization, 1983), pp. 15–16. Courtesy of JETRO (Japan External Trade Organization).

instances.[31] For example, the Japanese Ministry of International Trade and Industry (MITI) performs a coordinating role in industry development. MITI resources and personnel establish alliances among companies, provide planning and technical assistance, and sponsor research. Government policy helped Japan build its competitive advantage by encouraging demand in new industries, fostering intraindustry competition, and identifying and encouraging the development of emerging technologies.

Multiple-Nation Partnerships. Regional cooperation among nations may lead companies to form consortium relationships in selected industries. For example, Airbus Industrie is a consortium of English, French, German, and Spanish aerospace companies. Airbus Industrie members have received more than $12 billion in loans from the governments of the participating companies.[32] Airbus Industrie has reported profits in only 1 of the last 20 years. Boeing and McDonnell Douglas dominated the industry until government subsidies and multination sharing of skills and resources enabled Airbus to gain second place in the worldwide market for large commercial aircraft in the early 1990s.

Government Corporations. Several nations operate government-owned corporations. In recent years a trend toward privatization of these corporations has occurred in the United Kingdom, Australia, Mexico, and other countries. Nevertheless, government-supported corporations continue to compete in various global industries, including air transportation, chemicals, computers, and consumer electronics. Examples include Air France, Rhone-Poulenc (a French chemical company), and Thompson (a French electronics company). Not surprisingly, competitors often are critical of government organizations because of their unfair advantage resulting from government financial support.

Government Legislation. Antitrust laws in the United States prohibit certain kinds of cooperation among direct competitors in an industry. The intense global competition and loss of competitiveness in many industries seem to be changing the traditional view of lone-wolf competition among companies. While the antitrust laws are in place, there may be more flexibility by government agencies in interpreting whether collaboration among firms in an industry is an antitrust issue.

DEVELOPING EFFECTIVE RELATIONSHIPS BETWEEN ORGANIZATIONS

It is apparent from the prior discussion that developing effective collaborative partnerships between independent organizations is complex. The purpose of the present discussion is to provide further insights into the process of developing effective relationships between independent organizations. The objective of the cooperative relationship is first considered, followed by a discussion of several relationship guidelines.

Objective of the Relationship

Several major strategic objectives are considered to illustrate how strategic relationships are used to achieve the objectives.[33] In some situations both an internal (single organization) strategy and collaborative action may be used for the same purpose.

Identifying and Obtaining New Technologies and Competencies. This objective is a continuing challenge for many companies because of the increasing complexity of technology and the short time span between identifying and commercializing new technologies. Failure to identify and monitor important telecommunications technologies was a key factor in the serious competitive problems of Western Union during the 1980s.

There are several ways to locate and exploit external sources of research and development:

- Collaboration with university departments and other research institutions.
- Precompetitive collaborative R&D to spread research resources more widely.
- Corporate venturing—making systematic investments in emerging companies to gain a window on the technologies and market applications of the future.
- Joint ventures and other forms of strategic partnership that enable a company to acquire new competencies by "borrowing" from a company with a leadership position.[34]

Japanese companies aggressively pursue all these strategies, whereas U.S. companies rely more heavily on internal R&D. However, the future trend is toward expanded use of external research and development collaboration by U.S. and other companies throughout the world.

Developing New Markets and Building Market Position. Alliances and other collaborative relationships may be effective alternatives for a single company interested in developing a market. This strategy requires finding potential partners that have strong marketing capabilities, and/or market position. Collaboration may be used to enter a new product market or to expand a position in a market already served.

Increasingly, major corporations are pursuing collaborative strategies in research and development and in gaining market access. General Electric has a corporate objective of globalization, which requires participation in each major market in the world:

> This requires several different forms of participation: trading technology for market access; trading market access for technology; and trading market access for market access. This "share to gain" becomes a way of life.[35]

GE's globalization objective has led to forming over 100 collaborative relationships.[36]

Market Selectivity Strategies. Competing in mature markets often involves either market domination or market selectivity strategies. Competition in these markets is characterized by a small core of major firms and several smaller competitors that concentrate their efforts in market segments. Firms with small market position need to adopt strategies that enable them to compete in market segments where they have unique strengths and/or the segments are not of interest to large competitors. Cooperative relationships may be appropriate for these firms. The possible avenues for relationships include purchasing components to be processed and marketed to one or a few market segments, subcontracting to industry leaders, and providing distribution services to industry leaders.

The high entry barriers in producing semiconductors encourage the formation of strategic alliances.[37] Partnerships are essential in developing niche markets in this industry. Alliances are being formed between small U.S. firms that have specialized design expertise and Japanese, Korean, Taiwanese, and European companies with large-scale electronics manufacturing capabilities. The alliances make possible market entry for the design specialists. The cost of moving a complex new chip design to commercialization is an estimated $1 billion.

Restructuring and Cost-Reduction Strategies. The realities of competing in international markets often require companies to restructure and/or reduce product costs. Restructuring may result in forming cooperative relationships with other organizations. Cost reduction requirements may encourage the firm to locate low-cost sources of supply. Many producers in Europe, Japan, and the United States establish relationships with companies in newly industrialized countries such as Korea, Taiwan, and Singapore. These collaborative relationships enable companies to reduce plant investment and product costs.

Relationship Management Guidelines

While collaborative relationships are increasingly necessary, the available concepts and methods for managing these partnerships are limited. Contemporary business management skills and experience apply primarily to a single organization rather than offering guidelines for managing interorganizational relationships. However, the experience that companies have gained in managing distribution-channel relationships provides a useful, although incomplete, set of guidelines. To expand the existing base of management knowledge, Collins and Doorley conducted a major global study of strategic partnerships.[38] Companies in North America, Europe, Japan, and Korea participated in the study. The research identified the eight key guidelines for strategic-partnership management shown in Exhibit 3–7. A brief discussion of each guideline follows.

Planning. Comprehensive planning is critical when combining the skills and resources of two independent organizations to achieve one or more strategic objectives. The objectives must be specified, alternative strategies for achieving the objectives evaluated, and decisions made concerning how the relationship will be structured and managed. To determine the feasibility and attractiveness of the proposed relationship, the initiating partner may want to evaluate several potential partners before selecting one.

EXHIBIT 3–7 Success Guidelines for Strategic Partnership Management

1. The critical importance of planning.
2. Balance trust with self-interest.
3. Anticipate conflicts.
4. Establish strategic leadership.
5. Provide flexibility.
6. Accommodate cultural differences.
7. Orchestrate technology transfer.
8. Learn from partner's strengths.

Source: Timothy M. Collins and Thomas L. Doorley, *Teaming Up for the 90s* (Homewood, IL: Business One Irwin, 1991), pp. 101–2.

Trust and Self-Interest. Authorities generally agree that successful partnerships involve trust and respect between the partners and a willingness to share with each other on various self-interest issues. Confrontational relationships are not likely to be successful. Prior informal experience may be useful in showing whether participants can cooperate on a more formalized strategic project.

Trust is enhanced by meaningful communication between the partners.[39] The process of building trust leads to better communication. Thus, building and sustaining partnership relationships require both communication and the accumulation of trust between the organizations. Trust, in turn, leads to better cooperation among the partners.

Conflicts. Realizing that conflicts will occur is an important aspect of the relationship. The partners must respond when conflicts occur and work proactively to resolve the issues:

> Even firms in successful partnerships would readily acknowledge that disagreements are inevitable. Rather than allowing these conflicts to run their course capriciously, however, adroit partner firms develop mediating mechanisms to diffuse and settle their differences rapidly.[40]

Mechanisms for conflict resolution include training the personnel that are involved in relationships, establishing a council or interorganizational committee, and appointing a mutually acceptable ombudsman to resolve problems.

Leadership Structure. "Failure to create an effective leadership structure can be fatal; it makes coordination difficult and expensive, slows down development, and can seriously erode the decision-making process."[41] Strategic leadership of the partnership can be achieved by (1) developing an independent leadership structure or (2) assigning the responsibility to one of the partners. The former may involve recruiting a project director from outside. The latter option is probably the more feasible of the two in many instances.

Flexibility. Recognizing the interdependence of the partners is essential in building successful relationships. Each organization has different objectives and priorities. "Management must be predominantly by persuasion and influence, with a willingness to adapt as circumstances change."[42] Relationships change over time. The partnership must be flexible in order to adjust to changing conditions and partnership requirements.

Cultural Differences. Strategic relationships between companies from different nations are influenced by cultural differences. Both partners must accept these realities. If partners fail to respond to the cultural variations, the relationship may be adversely affected. These differences may be related to stage of industrial development, political system, religion, economic issues, and corporate culture.

Technology Transfer. When the partnership involves both developing technology and transferring the technology to commercial applications, special attention must be given to implementation. Important issues include organizational problems, identifying a commercial sponsor, appointing a team to achieve the transfer, and building transfer mechanisms into the plan. Planners, marketers, and production people are important participants in the transfer process.

Learning from Partner's Strengths. Finally, the opportunity for an organization to expand its skills and experience should be exploited. Japanese companies are particularly effective in taking advantage of this opportunity. One objective of the partnership should be to learn the skills of the cooperating firm, as well as completing a specific project or program.[43] Surprisingly, U.S. companies often fail to capitalize on this opportunity in their interorganizational relationships. Japanese companies view cooperative ventures as another form of competition enabling them to transfer acquired skills to other parts of the business.

This concludes our look at the use of cooperative partnerships between independent organizations to achieve various strategic objectives. These strategies promise to expand in importance during the 1990s.

SUMMARY

The competitive realities of surviving and prospering in a complex and rapidly changing business environment encourage teaming up with other companies. Cooperative strategic relationships between independent companies are escalating in importance. The major drivers of interorganizational relationships are environmental turbulence and diversity, and skill and resource gaps. The increasing complexity of technology, financial constraints, the need to access markets, and the availability of information technology all contribute to skill and resource gaps.

Relationships between organizations range from transactional exchange to collaborative partnerships. These relationships may be vertical or horizontal in scope. Vertical relationships may involve collaboration between suppliers and producers and distribution channel linkages among firms. Horizontal partnerships may involve competitors and other industry members. These horizontal forms include strategic alliances and joint ventures.

Collaborative relationships are complex and may generate conflicts. Many horizontal relationships have not been particularly successful, even though the number of these partnerships is growing throughout the world. Trust between the partners is critical to building a positive relationship.

Global relationships among organizations may include conventional organizational forms, alliances, joint ventures, network corporations, and trading companies. Governments in several countries play a proactive role in organizational relationships through coordination, financial support, and government corporations.

Several objectives may be achieved by strategic relationships, including accessing new technologies, developing new markets, building market position, implementing market selectivity strategies, and pursuing restructuring and cost-reduction strategies. The requirements for successfully managing interorganizational relationships include planning, balancing trust and self-interest, recognizing conflicts, defining leadership structure, achieving flexibility, adjusting to cultural differences, facilitating technology transfers, and learning from partners' strengths.

QUESTIONS FOR REVIEW AND DISCUSSION

1. Discuss the major factors that encourage the formation of strategic partnerships between companies.
2. Compare and contrast vertical and horizontal strategic relationships between independent companies.
3. Discuss the similarities and differences between strategic alliances and joint ventures.
4. A German electronics company and a Japanese electronics company are discussing the formation of a strategic alliance to market the other firm's products in their respective countries. What are the important issues in making this relationship successful for both partners?
5. Establishing successful interorganizational relationships is difficult, according to authorities. Will the success record improve in the future as more companies pursue this strategy?
6. Are vertical relationships more likely to be successful than horizontal relationships? Discuss.
7. Suppose you are seeking a Japanese strategic alliance partner to market your French pharmaceutical products in Asia. What characteristics are important in selecting a good partner?
8. Discuss how alliances may enable foreign companies to reduce the negative reaction that is anticipated if they tried to purchase companies in other countries.
9. Discuss how government may participate in helping domestic companies develop their competitive advantages in an industry such as aerospace products.

NOTES

1. David W. Cravens, Shannon H. Shipp, and Karen S. Cravens, "Analysis of Cooperative Interorganizational Relationships, Strategic Alliance Formation, and Strategic Alliance Effectiveness," *Journal of Strategic Marketing,* March 1993.
2. Timothy M. Collins and Thomas L. Doorley, *Teaming Up for the 90s* (Homewood, IL: Business One Irwin, 1991), p. 292.
3. Ibid., p. 5.
4. Cravens, Shipp, and Cravens, "Analysis of Cooperative Interorganizational Relationships."
5. Ravi S. Achrol, "Evolution of the Marketing Organization: New Forms for the Turbulent Environments," *Journal of Marketing,* October 1991, pp. 78–79.
6. Ibid.
7. Frederick E. Webster, Jr., "The Changing Role of Marketing in the Organization," *Journal of Marketing,* October 1992, pp. 1–17.
8. Achrol, "Evolution of the Marketing Organization," p. 81.
9. Collins and Doorley, *Teaming Up for the 90s,* p. 5.
10. Udayan Gupta and Jeffrey A. Tannenbaum, "Small Drug Firms Break Through with Research Deals," *The Wall Street Journal,* December 2, 1991, p. 32.
11. Collins and Doorley, *Teaming Up for the 90s,* p. 8.
12. Ibid.
13. The following discussion is based on James C. Anderson and James A. Narus, "Partnering as a Focused Market Strategy," *California Management Review,* Spring 1991, pp. 96–97.
14. Ibid.
15. Anderson and Narus, "Partnering as a Focused Market Strategy," pp. 100–103.
16. Lars Hallen, Jan Johanson, and Nazeem Seyed-Mohamed, "Interfirm Adaptation in Business Relationships," *Journal of Marketing,* April 1991, p. 30.
17. Bert C. McCammon, Jr., "Perspectives for Distribution Programming," in *Vertical Marketing Systems,* ed. Louis P. Bucklin (Glenview, IL: Scott, Foresman, 1970), p. 43.
18. Hallen et al., "Interfirm Adaptation in Business Relationships," pp. 31–32.
19. Kenichi Ohmae, *The Borderless World* (New York: Harper Business, 1990), p. 114.
20. This illustration is based on Bernard Wysocki, Jr., "Global Reach: Cross-Border Alliances Become Favorite Way to Crack New Markets," *The Wall Street Journal,* March 26, 1990, pp. A1 and A5.
21. Wysocki, "Global Reach," p. A2.
22. George S. Day, *Market Driven Strategy* (New York: The Free Press, 1990), pp. 275–76.
23. Udayan Gupta, "Tough Economic Times Can Make Strategic Bedfellows," *The Wall Street Journal,* November 23, 1990, p. B2.
24. Gary Hamel, Yves L. Doz, and C. K. Prahalad, "Collaborate with Your Competitors—and Win," *Harvard Business Review,* January–February 1989, pp. 135–36.
25. Collins and Doorley, *Teaming Up for the 90s,* pp. 205–9.
26. Michael W. Miller, "IBM Commits More than $100 Million on Venture to Relay Video, Other Data," *The Wall Street Journal,* September 16, 1992, pp. B1, B5.
27. Deepak K. Sinha and Michael A. Cusumano, "Complementary Resources and Cooperative Research: A Model of Research Joint Ventures Among Competitors," *Management Science,* September 1991, pp. 1091–1106.
28. Achrol, "Evolution of the Marketing Organization," pp. 84–85; and Webster, "The Changing Role of Marketing," pp. 8–9.
29. Webster, "The Changing Role of Marketing," pp. 8–9.

30. Achrol, "Evolution of the Marketing Organization," p. 84.
31. Michael E. Porter, *The Competitive Advantage of Nations* (New York: The Free Press, 1990), pp. 414–16.
32. David W. Cravens, H. Kirk Downey, and Paul Lauritano, "Global Competition in the Commercial Aircraft Industry: Positioning for Advantage by the Triad Nations," *Columbia Journal of World Business,* Winter 1992, pp. 46–58.
33. The following discussion is based on Collins and Doorley, *Teaming Up for the 90s,* Chapter 3.
34. Ibid., p. 30.
35. General Electric Company, *Operating Objectives to Meet the Challenges of the 90s* (Fairfield, CT: General Electric Company, March 14, 1988).
36. Day, *Market Driven Strategy,* p. 273.
37. William B. Scott, "Global Alliances Spur Development of Niche Market Semiconductors," *Aviation Week and Space Technology,* September 9, 1991, pp. 70–71.
38. The following discussion is drawn from Collins and Doorley, *Teaming Up for the 90s,* Chapter 5.
39. James C. Anderson and James A. Narus, "A Model of Distributor Firm and Manufacturer Firm Working Partnerships," *Journal of Marketing,* January 1990, p. 45.
40. Ibid., p. 56.
41. Collins and Doorley, *Teaming Up for the 90s,* p. 108.
42. Ibid., p. 110.
43. Wysocki, "Global Reach," pp. A1 and A5.

CHAPTER

4

Marketing Strategy and Planning

An understanding of business strategy and competitive advantage is important for marketing strategy development. Marketing professionals are involved in the business planning process in three important ways: (1) they participate in strategic analysis and planning; (2) they serve with other functional managers as members of the business unit strategy team; and (3) they develop and implement strategic marketing plans for the markets served by the organization. "Marketing as culture, a basic set of values and beliefs about the central importance of the customer that guide the organization (as articulated by the marketing concept), is primarily the responsibility of the corporate and SBU-level managers."[1]

Du Pont's successful European marketing strategy for its elastic fiber, Lycra, shows the close relationship between business and marketing strategies. Management's plan is to concentrate on developing, producing, and marketing products with distinct technological competitive advantages.[2] Besides Lycra, Du Pont produces and markets Nomex flame-retardant fibers, extrastrong Kevlar used for bullet-proofing, Arylon polymers for auto interiors, and chemicals used to purify water and make paint pigments. Du Pont's factories and marketing operations extend throughout Europe. The company's strategy for Lycra illustrates its pan-European strategy. Lycra production and sales in Europe are coordinated from Geneva, Switzerland. Lycra applications include incorporating the material into cotton T-shirts, men's wool jackets, women's hosiery, and into the edges of disposable diapers. Du Pont has a 60 percent share of the world market for spandex fibers even though its Lycra patent expired several years ago. The fiber has a strong brand image throughout the world, making market entry by look-alike fibers difficult. Lycra accounts for 10 percent of Du Pont's worldwide operating income on sales of $900 million.

Du Pont's Lycra illustrates several key elements of marketing strategy, including targeting different user applications, producing distinctive products, developing aggressive marketing programs, building strong brand image, and establishing global distribution networks. In this chapter we examine the nature and scope of marketing strategy. It overviews the rest of the book. The chapter begins with a discussion of how business strategy and strategic marketing are related. Next, it presents the process for developing, implementing, and managing marketing strategy. The remainder of the chapter describes and illustrates each stage of the strategy process. The stages include (1) marketing situation analysis, (2) designing marketing strategies, (3) marketing program development, and (4) strategy implementation and management. The chapter concludes with a discussion of preparing the marketing plan.

THE ROLE AND SCOPE OF MARKETING

In gaining a complete view of marketing, it is useful to consider it from both corporate and SBU perspectives. We view marketing as a core part of the entire business as well as a function.

Marketing from a Corporate Perspective

The chief marketing executive's strategic planning responsibilities include: (1) participating in corporate and business strategy formulation and (2) developing marketing strategies that follow business unit priorities. Since these two areas are closely interrelated, it is important to examine marketing's role and functions in both areas to gain more insight into marketing's responsibilities and contributions. Peter F. Drucker describes this role:

> Marketing is so basic that it cannot be considered a separate function (i.e., a separate skill or work) within the business, on a par with others such as manufacturing or personnel. Marketing requires separate work, and a distinct group of activities. But it is, first, a central dimension of the entire business. It is the whole business seen from the point of view of its final result, that is, from the customer's point of view.[3]

Frederick E. Webster describes the role of the marketing manager:

> At the corporate level, marketing managers have a critical role to play as advocates for the customer and for a set of values and beliefs that put the customer

> first in the firm's decision making, and to communicate the value proposition as part of that culture throughout the organization, both internally and in its multiple relationships and alliances.[4]

This role includes assessing market attractiveness in the markets available to the firm, providing a customer orientation, and communicating the firm's specific value advantages.

Business Unit Strategies

Before work can start on marketing strategy, management's objectives and plans for each SBU must be clearly understood. Our discussion in Chapter 2 (business composition, strategic analysis of SBUs, and the selection of an SBU strategy and objectives for each unit) considers these decisions and activities. Chapter 3 looks at strategic partnerships between organizations. An understanding of business purpose, scope, objectives, and strategy is essential to making strategic marketing decisions consistent with the corporate and business unit plan of action.

Top management is concerned with two major issues. First, based on an assessment of the SBU's business strength and attractiveness in each product-market, what broad strategy will the unit pursue and what financial resources will be made available to carry out the strategy? Will the unit be managed for cash flow, growth, or earnings? Second, what are the specific expectations of top management regarding sales, market share, profit contribution, and other aspects of performance? These guidelines provide the basis for developing the SBU and marketing strategies.

Marketing strategy at the business unit level is focused on market segmentation, targeting, and positioning to determine how the SBU will compete.[5] The central issue is deciding how the business will compete in its product-market area(s). Segmentation, targeting, and positioning are core strategy considerations.

A comparison of corporate/business unit and marketing strategy issues and actions is shown in Exhibit 4–1. The unit of analysis and strategy development from the corporate and business unit perspective is the SBU. The market target provides the strategic focus for marketing strategy. The SBU typically comprises two or more market targets.

Strategic Marketing Activities

Marketing strategy is defined as the analysis, strategy development, and implementation activities in:

> Selecting market target strategies for the product-markets in each business unit, setting marketing objectives, and developing, implementing, and managing the marketing program positioning strategies designed to meet the needs of the customers in each market target.

EXHIBIT 4–1 Illustrative Comparison of Business and Marketing Strategies

	Corporation/Business Units	*Marketing*
• Perspective	Organizational and/or competitive focus, often with a heavy industry orientation	Customer and/or product focus, often with a heavy end-user orientation
• Decisions	• Mission determination • Allocation of business resources to business units • Acquisition/diversification • Elimination of business units • Product development and management • Selection and implementation of SBU strategies	• Identification of market opportunities • Choice of target market(s) • Marketing program positioning strategy • Product, distribution, price, and promotion strategies
• Strategic focus	• How to gain and keep strategic advantage • How to determine business strategies • How to organize the business for planning/control	• How to divide product/markets into segments • What segment(s) to serve • How to position for each segment
• Information needs	• Financial performance • Business opportunity assessment • Market performance and forecasts • Competitors' strategies and performance	• Financial performance by market target and product type • Customer/prospect description and requirements • Market position and forecasts • Competitors' marketing strategies and performance

Strategic marketing is a market-driven process of strategy development, taking into account a constantly changing business environment and the need to achieve high levels of customer satisfaction. Strategic marketing focuses on financial performance rather than the traditional concern about increasing sales. Marketing strategy builds competitive advantage by combining the customer-influencing strategies of the business into an integrated array of market-focused actions.[6] Strategic marketing links the organization with the environment and views marketing as a responsibility of the entire business rather than a specialized function.

Because of marketing's boundary orientation between the organization and its customers, channel members, and competition, it is central to the business strategy planning process.[7] Strategic marketing provides the expertise for environmental monitoring, for deciding what customer groups to serve, for setting product specifications, and for selecting which competitors to position against. Successfully integrating multifunctional strategies is critical to providing high levels of customer satisfaction. Customer preferences for product attributes must be transformed into product design and production guidelines. Success in achieving high quality products and services

EXHIBIT 4–2 Strategic Marketing Process

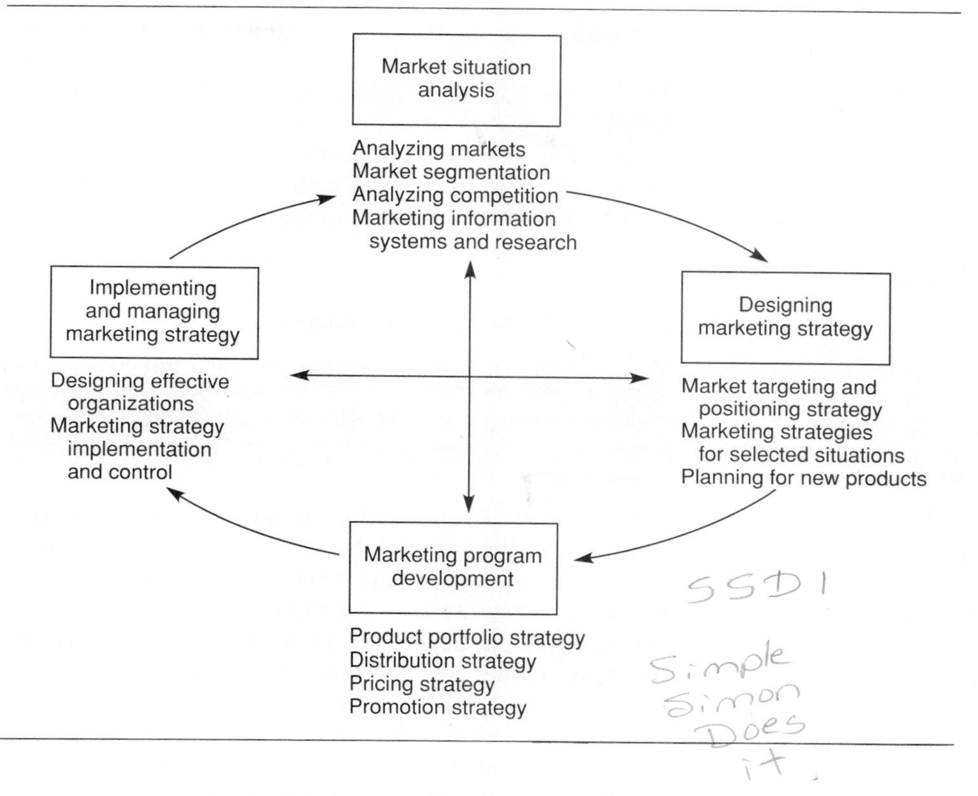

requires finding out which attributes of product and service quality drive customer satisfaction.

The analysis, planning, implementation and management process that we follow in this book is illustrated in Exhibit 4–2. The activities correspond to Parts II through V of the book. The situation analysis considers market structure and analysis, market segmentation, competitor analysis, and information systems and research. Marketing strategy design examines customer targeting, positioning analysis, strategy selection for different competitive situations, and new product strategy. Marketing program development consists of product, distribution, price, and promotion strategies designed and implemented to meet the needs of targeted buyers. Strategy implementation and management considers organizational effectiveness and marketing strategy implementation and control. Each aspect of the strategy process is overviewed in the rest of the chapter. This process and the activities included in each stage provide a framework for examining and applying strategic marketing.

MARKETING SITUATION ANALYSIS

The marketing situation analysis is the first step in the design of a new strategy or examining an existing strategy. The situation analysis is conducted on a regular basis after the strategy is implemented to determine necessary strategy changes. A situation summary is often included at the beginning of a marketing plan. The situation assessment typically includes market definition and analysis, market segmentation, and competitor analysis. Marketing research and information systems generate the information for the situation analysis.

Market Definition and Analysis

Markets should be defined so that the right buyers and competition are analyzed. For a market to exist, there must be people with particular needs and wants and one or more products that can satisfy these needs. Also, the buyers must be both willing and able to purchase a product that satisfies their needs and wants.

As an illustration, the market for products that prevent blood clots is described in Exhibit 4–3. The current method of treatment to prevent blood clots in the arteries of patients at risk of heart attack or stroke is taking aspirin or heparin.[8] Neither of these drugs is as potent as desired by physicians. A major need exists for a super aspirin, which is currently in the experimental stage of development. Both the lifesaving and market potential of super aspirin is very promising. Industry analysts forecast a market of $1 billion a year by 2000 if the super aspirin can be successfully developed.

A product-market is a specific product (or line of related products) that can satisfy a set of needs and wants for the people (or organizations) willing and able to purchase it. The term *product* refers to either a physical product or an intangible service. This definition matches people or organizations with a particular set of similar needs and wants to a product category that can satisfy those needs and wants.

Analyzing product-markets and forecasting how they will change in the future are vital to business and marketing planning. Decisions to enter new product-markets, how to serve existing product-markets, and when to exit from unattractive product-markets are critical strategic marketing choices. Analyzing product-markets includes the following activities:

1. Identifying new product-markets that offer opportunities for a company.
2. Evaluating existing product-markets to guide strategies.
3. Scanning the environment and forecasting future trends in product-markets.

EXHIBIT 4–3 Market for Clot Blockers (annual market for clot blockers, in thousands)

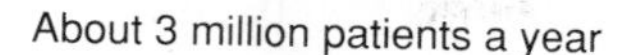

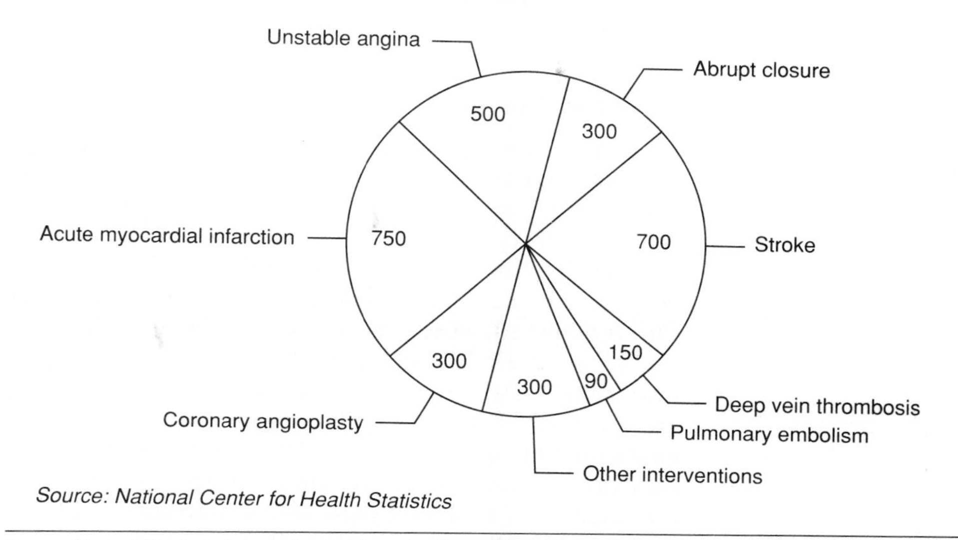

Source: Michael Waldholz, "Super Aspirin's Promise Exemplifies Value of Biotech," *The Wall Street Journal,* February 27, 1992, p. B3.

Market Segmentation

Segmentation analysis considers the nature and extent of diversity of buyers' needs and wants in a market. It offers an opportunity for an organization to selectively match its business capabilities to the requirements of one or more groups of buyers. The objective in segmentation is to find differences in needs and wants and to identify the segments within the product-market of interest. Each segment contains buyers with similar needs and wants for the product category of interest to management. The subgroups reflect the various characteristics of people, the reasons they buy or use certain products, and their preferences for certain brands of products. Likewise, segments of industrial product-markets may be formed according to the type of industry, the uses for the product, frequency of product purchase, and various other factors.

Each segment may vary considerably from the average characteristics of the entire product-market. The similarities of buyers' needs within a segment enable more effective targeting of the marketing program. In consumer markets, factors such as age, income, and life-style are often linked to purchasing patterns for automobiles, foods, financial services, and other products. In segmenting medical services, the type of medical problem may identify a possible basis of segmentation. For example, in the treatment of glaucoma the specific properties of drugs offered by different companies vary in terms of effectiveness, side effects, ocular discomfort, price, and other characteristics. These characteristics may be useful to segment the market.

Analyzing Competition

Evaluation of competitors' strategies, strengths, limitations, and plans is also a key aspect of the situation analysis. It is important to identify both existing and potential competitors. Typically, a few of the firms in the industry comprise the organization's key competitors. Competitor analysis includes defining the competitive arena, analyzing the strategic group, and describing and evaluating each key competitor. The analyses should show the competition's important strengths and weaknesses.

An interesting market size analysis and competitor identification for the Caribbean cruise market is shown in Exhibit 4–4. The cruise ship companies are targeting various potential user groups with their marketing efforts. Revenues for 1991 increased nearly 10 percent to $6 billion. The top 4 companies, out of a total of 32, account for nearly 60 percent of the market. The domination of a market by a few competitors is characteristic of many mature markets.

Marketing Information Systems and Research

Effective management information systems offer an important competitive advantage by alerting companies to problems and opportunities. Information systems improve organizational effectiveness. Exciting advances in information technology streamline organizational designs and compress the time span between decisions and results.

Information and Marketing Strategy. "The information processing requirements of enterprises are expanding as their competitive environments become more dynamic and volatile."[9] Environmental turbulence requires flexible and adaptable strategies. Relevant and timely information improves strategic analysis and decision making. The efficient processing of various kinds of information, such as customer orders, places major demands on the modern organization. Good information systems can reduce costs, improve customer satisfaction, and improve organizational effectiveness. These systems can also improve operating relationships between cooperating, independent organizations.

Information Technology. The hardware and software technology that is available offers an impressive array of information processing, analysis, and communication capabilities. Included are both computers and telecommunications. Large reductions in equipment costs make available cost-

EXHIBIT 4–4 Caribbean Cruise Market Size and Competition

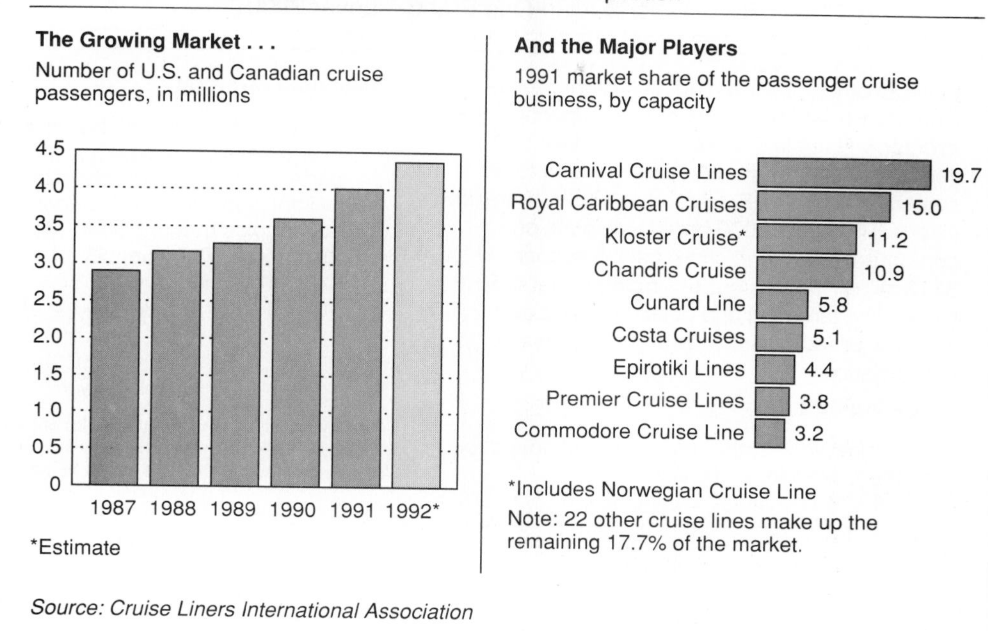

Source: Laurie M. Grossman, "Cruise Lines Enjoy Smooth Sailing Despite Recession," *The Wall Street Journal,* February 10, 1992, p. B4.

effective opportunities for data storage, analysis, and transmission. Information technology has changed the economic cost-benefit balance in favor of making major expansions in the information-processing capabilities of organizations. For example, Volkswagen AG has an international satellite network that links its operations in Germany, Brazil, and Canada. The company also has a satellite and submarine-cable network for product-related services and communication.[10]

MARKETING STRATEGY DESIGN

The situation analysis identifies opportunities and threats in the business environment and the organization's strengths and weaknesses. This information plays a key role in designing marketing strategy, which includes market targeting and positioning analysis, marketing strategy choice, and developing and positioning new products. The Strategy Feature describes the market targeting and positioning strategies employed for the successful new soap brand, Lever 2000.

STRATEGY FEATURE Lever's All-in-One Brand—Lever 2000

Lever Brothers, a New York unit of the Anglo-Dutch Unilever Group, has been competing with Procter & Gamble in the soap market for 100 years. In 1991, for the first time, Lever's toilet-soap market share ($) exceeded P&G's share (see insert). The Lever 2000 brand was a major contributor to Lever's share gain. It accounted for $113 million in sales out of a market total of $1.6 billion. The targeting and positioning of Lever 2000 were major factors in the brand's successful performance.

Targeting Strategy

- Entire family rather than different soaps for men, women, and children.

Positioning Strategy

- Positioned as "the mildest antibacterial soap ever created," "a soap for 2000 body parts." Heavy use of advertising ($25 million), sampling, and coupons to convince households that one soap will meet all of their needs. Premium priced compared to Ivory and Dove.

Source: Valerie Reitman, "Buoyant Sales of Lever 2000 Soap Bring Sinking Sensation to Procter and Gamble," *The Wall Street Journal*, March 19, 1992, pp. B1 and B8.

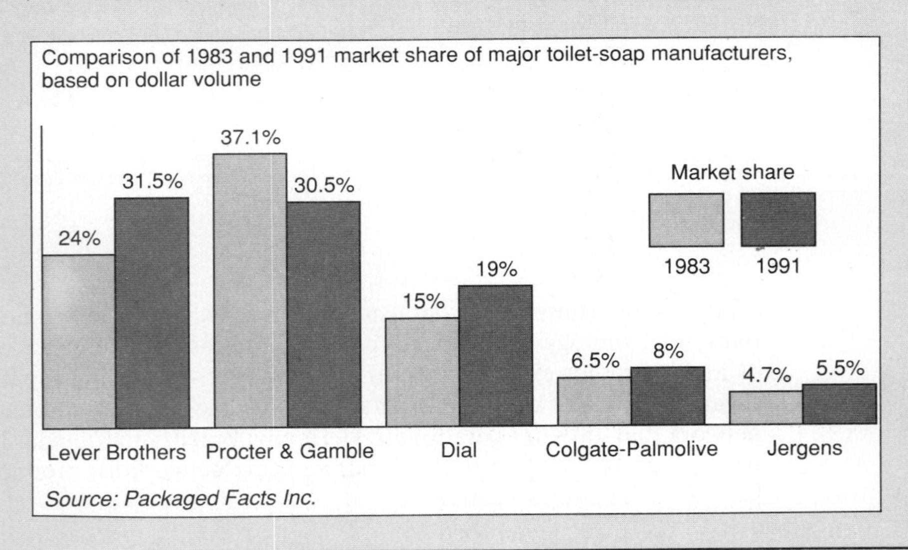

Source: Packaged Facts Inc.

Market Targeting and Positioning Strategy

Marketing advantage is influenced by several situational factors, including industry characteristics, type of firm (e.g., size), extent of differentiation in buyers' needs, and the specific competitive advantage(s) of the company designing the marketing strategy. The essential issue is deciding how, when, and where to compete, given a firm's environment. For example, a marketing strategy for the leading firm in a new industry differs in several important ways from that of a small firm in a mature industry.

Market Target Strategy. Market targeting selects the people (or organizations) that management wishes to serve in the product-market. When buyers' needs and wants vary, the market target is usually one or more segments of the product-market. Once the company's product-markets are identified and their relative importance to the firm determined, management selects the targeting strategy. This decision is the focal point of marketing strategy, since targeting guides the setting of objectives and developing a positioning strategy. The options range from targeting most of the segments to targeting one or a few segments in a product-market. The targeting strategy may be influenced by the market's maturity, the diversity of buyers' needs and preferences, the firm's size compared to competition, corporate resources and priorities, and the size of market position required to achieve favorable financial results.

The targeting and positioning strategies used by ConAgra Incorporated for the Healthy Choice frozen food line helped the new brand successfully enter the market in the early 1990s. The low-calorie, low-cholesterol, low-sodium frozen food line introduced in 1989 quickly gained a strong market position.[11] Frozen food is a very competitive supermarket category because freezer space in stores is limited. Healthy Choice was introduced into the stagnant male-oriented frozen dinner segment of the market. It was positioned as a "health product." This positioning was successful even though it conflicts with conventional marketing guidelines: The female-oriented frozen food is the rapid-growth segment, and "health" positioning had been used to describe poor-tasting, low-calorie brands. The strategy apparently worked because the health issue is of great concern to men and the taste of Healthy Choice is appealing to consumers who tried the brand. The new line of frozen foods gained an impressive 25 percent market share in the $700 million frozen dinner market. The line was extended in the early 1990s to include breakfast items, deli meats, and soups. By 1992 intense price, new products, and promotion actions of the competition eroded Healthy Choice's position in the frozen dinner market, demonstrating the realities of competing against experienced food marketers.

Positioning Strategy. The marketing program positioning strategy is the combination of product, channel of distribution, price, and promotion strategies a firm uses to position itself against its key competitors in meeting the needs and wants of the market target. This strategy is also called the "marketing mix" or the "marketing program." The positioning strategy provides the unifying concept for deciding the role and strategy of each component of the mix. Improving health is the positioning concept used for Healthy Choice frozen dinners. The positioning concept indicates how management would like the buyers in the market target to view the firm's marketing mix.

The Toyota Motor Corporation's Lexus 400, introduced in 1989, was positioned as a high-performance European-style luxury automobile offering the quality assurance of Japanese manufacturing. It was introduced to offer a reasonably priced and better performing alternative to Mercedes and BMW models priced $15,000 to $30,000 higher than Lexus. Toyota's key competitive advantage was luxury value at a competitive price. When the Lexus was introduced, European competitors were experiencing slow sales because of the high prices of their cars. Lexus became a very successful new brand.

The first step in developing a positioning strategy is deciding what is to be accomplished for each market target. Marketing objectives are established at several levels in an organization. The corporate objectives—for which the marketing function is partially responsible—indicate overall performance targets (e.g., growth, profit, customer satisfaction, employee development, and other broad objectives). Specific objectives are set for each market target. Objectives form a hierarchy ranging from very broad corporate objectives to the specific sales objectives of salespersons.

Positioning strategy should take into account:

1. The criteria or benefits the buyer considers when purchasing a product, including the relative importance of the criteria.
2. How the firm is differentiated from its competition.
3. The limitations of competing products regarding important buyer needs and wants.

The positioning concept indicates how the firm or its brand would like to be perceived in the eyes and minds of the market target customers. Positioning is stated in terms of some reference basis, usually competition. Strategy development includes product, distribution, price, and promotion strategies. These strategy components make up a team of actions that both complement and reinforce each other.

Notice, for example, the Toyota Lexus advertisement. This is one of the ads Toyota used to introduce the car in the United States. The message and photograph encourage targeted buyers to associate Lexus with the luxury sedan market segment. Since Toyota's other lines are in the medium-price range, positioning Lexus into the segment served by BMW and other luxury imports is important to gaining a market position.

Decisions about products, distribution channels, price, advertising, and personal selling should create a cohesive marketing program aimed at meeting the needs and wants of customers in the firm's target market. The marketing program combines the firm's marketing capabilities into a package of actions intended to position the firm against its competition to compete for the customers that make up its market target.

Marketing Strategy Selection

Selecting a marketing strategy takes into account the situational and competitive factors an organization encounters. For example, when management is developing a strategy for entering a new market, it can benefit from

Advertisement Introducing Toyota's Lexus

Introducing The Lexus LS400. It's Not A Car, It's An Invention.

Some cars are called "new" more by virtue of their date of release than by their degree of innovation. Not so the Lexus LS 400 luxury sedan.

If this sounds like so much advertising hyperbole, consider the fact that the automobile you see before you has a long list of patents pending.

Next, consider that it's armed with a Four-Cam, 32-valve, 250-horsepower V8 engine.

For a luxury sedan to have this much muscle is impressive by itself.

But the 1400 engineers from Toyota didn't stop to be impressed.

Instead they insisted on wedding this kind of power to an astonishing level of efficiency. Indeed, the Lexus LS 400 is projected to be one of the only 250-horsepower luxury sedans able to avoid the stigma, as well as the cost, of the U.S. gas guzzler tax.*

In fact, no single aspect of the LS 400's performance comes at the expense of another.

For example, while the LS 400 can zip from zero to 60 mph in only 7.9 seconds,** our engineers asked themselves what is the good of such swift acceleration if it becomes unusable in foul weather?

Their answer was an engineering breakthrough called TRAC, otherwise known as our new optional Traction Control System.

TRAC can actually sense when the rear drive wheels are beginning to slip on slick surfaces. Within milliseconds, TRAC can limit the wheelspin by throttling back the engine and pulsing the rear brakes.

As for the four vented disc brakes themselves, they're activated by one of the world's most advanced Anti-lock Braking Systems, capable of sensing different levels of traction.

The same degree of ingenuity was reserved for the car's interior as well.

Lavished in California Walnut and optional leather trim and seats, the cabin also features as standard equipment what may be the first power tilt steering wheel in America that combines the comfort of an adjustable telescopic column with the prudence of an airbag Supplemental Restraint System.

And to the right of this same remarkable column you'll find something else of note.

The ignition switch.

To acquire the key for it and to arrange a test drive, call 800-USA-LEXUS for the dealer nearest you.

You'll find that when it comes to new and better ways to serve you, he's as inventive as our engineers.

LEXUS
The Relentless Pursuit Of Perfection.

Courtesy of Lexus

study of the strategic issues and strategy guidelines pertaining to new market-entry situations. Other kinds of strategy situations include product life-cycle strategies, strategies for fragmented markets, global strategies, and strategies for small firms.

A useful basis of analysis is to classify the marketing strategy situation into emerging, growth, mature, declining, or global stages of product-market evolution. Using this classification, strategy analysis considers market structure, segmentation, industry/competitor analysis, competitive advantage, targeting, and positioning.

New-Product Strategies

New products are needed to replace old products with declining sales and profits. Strategies for developing and positioning new market entries involve all functions of the business. Closely coordinated new-product planning processes are essential to satisfy customer requirements and produce products with high quality and competitive prices.

Listening to the customer is critical to identifying the important product features that influence customer satisfaction. The new-product planning process starts by identifying gaps in customer satisfaction. The differences between existing product attributes and those desired by customers offer opportunities for new and improved products. A leader in product innovation is Minnesota Mining and Manufacturing. The company has a reputation of developing products faster and better than most companies.[12] The new-product success guidelines 3M follows include: (1) keeping business units small, (2) encouraging experimentation and risk taking, (3) motivating and rewarding innovators, (4) staying close to the customer, (5) sharing technology with other firms, and (6) avoiding killing the projects of staff advocates.

MARKETING PROGRAM DEVELOPMENT

Market targeting and program positioning strategies for new and existing products guide the design of strategies for each part of the marketing mix. Product, distribution, price, and promotion strategies are combined to form the positioning strategy selected for each market target. The relationship of the positioning components to the market target is shown in Exhibit 4–5.

Management must determine the role of each mix component. This involves identifying the functions unique to each component as well as deciding the roles of the mix components that can perform the same functions. The interactive effects of the mix components is also evaluated. For example, advertising and personal selling combined may have a stronger effect on customer response than either by itself, even if the total expenditures are the same. These mix allocation decisions determine how and to

EXHIBIT 4–5 Positioning Strategy Development

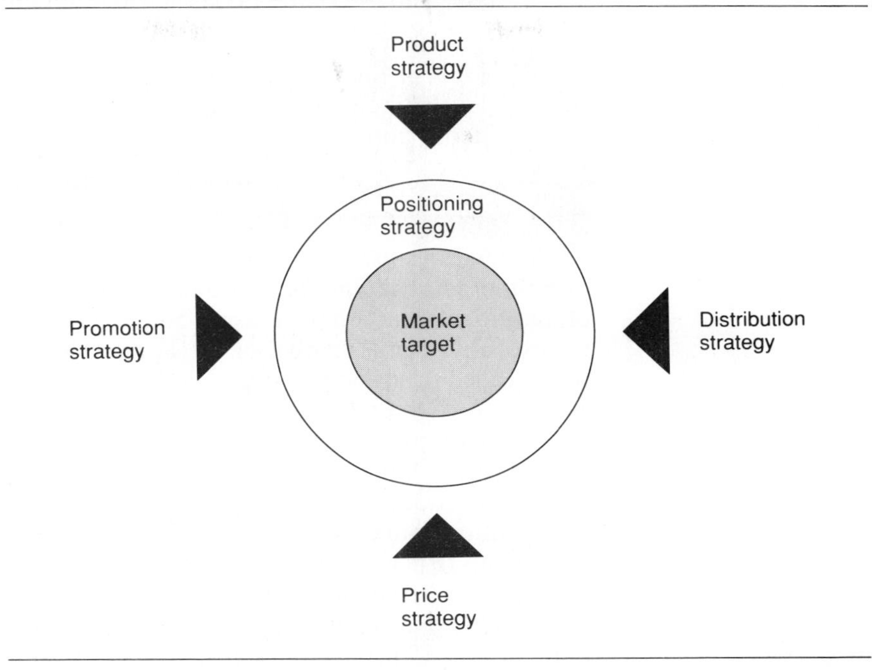

what extent each mix component is to be used in the positioning strategy. Marketing management must also select the most cost-effective way to perform each mix component function. Such decisions establish the composition and characteristics of the positioning strategy.

These operating-level marketing mix decisions implement the business strategy.[13] The objective is to allocate financial, human, and production resources to markets, customers, and products as effectively and efficiently as possible. A core dimension of these functional strategies is responding well to customer needs and building long-term customer relationships.

Product/Service Strategy

To select a product strategy, the firm needs the following information on current and anticipated performance of the products (services) in the business unit:

1. Consumer evaluation of the company's products, particularly their strengths and weaknesses vis-à-vis competition (that is, product positioning by market segment information).

2. "Objective" information on actual and anticipated product performance on relevant criteria such as sales, profits, and market share.[14]

This information helps management formulate strategies for each product in the mix or line. Products are typically the focal point for positioning strategy development, particularly when companies or business units adopt organizational approaches emphasizing product or brand management. Product strategy includes: (1) developing plans for new products, (2) managing programs for successful products, and (3) selecting strategies for problem products (e.g., to reduce costs or improve the product).

The writing instrument market shows how product strategy may change over time. The ballpoint pen virtually eliminated the competitive advantage of traditional fountain pens nearly 50 years ago. Today, the fountain pen is the executive status symbol of the 1990s. The German Montblanc brand spearheaded the trend toward expensive pens. Montblanc has an estimated 50 percent of the market for pens priced over $100.[15] Parker Pen has the second place position in the market. A. T. Cross introduced its Signature line in 1991. Since only about 10 percent of households with annual incomes over $50,000 use a fountain pen on a daily basis, there is a large opportunity for market penetration. Sales of fountain pens in 1991 were $79 million, up 16 percent from the previous year. The chance to tap this market potential has stimulated aggressive efforts by Montblanc, Parker, Waterman, and Cross. Advertising expenditures of these companies totaled $12 million, over 15 percent of industry sales in 1991.

Distribution, Price, and Promotion Strategies

One of the major challenges in managing the marketing mix is combining the components effectively. Product, distribution, price, and promotion strategies need to be integrated into a coordinated plan of action. Each component helps to influence buyers in their positioning of products. If the activities of these mix components are not coordinated, the actions may conflict and resources may be wasted. For example, if advertising messages for a company's brand stress quality and performance, but salespeople emphasize low prices, buyers will be confused and brand image may be affected.

Distribution Strategy. Contact with target market buyers is made on a direct basis using the firm's sales force or, instead, through a distribution network of marketing intermediaries (e.g., wholesalers, retailers, or dealers). Distribution channels are increasingly essential in linking producers with end-user household and business markets. Distribution channel decisions by producers concern the type of channel organizations to use, the extent of channel management performed by the firm, and the intensity of distribution appropriate for the product or service. The choice of distribution channels influences buyers' positioning of the brand. For example, Rolex watches are available through a limited number of retailers with prestigious images. Such retailers help to reinforce the brand's image.

Pricing Strategy. Price also helps to position a product or service. Customer reaction to alternative prices, the cost of the product, the prices of the competition, and various legal and ethical factors establish the extent of flexibility management has in setting prices. Price strategy selects the role of price in the positioning strategy, including the desired positioning of the product or brand as well as the margins necessary to satisfy and motivate distribution channel participants. Price may be used as an active (visible) component of marketing strategy or, instead, marketing emphasis may be on other marketing mix components (e.g., product quality).

Promotion Strategy. Advertising, sales promotion, the sales force, and public relations strategies all help the organization to communicate with its customers, cooperating organizations, the public, and other target audiences. Promotion strategies perform essential roles in positioning products in the eyes and minds of buyers. Promotion informs, reminds, and persuades buyers and others who influence the purchasing process. Hundreds of billions of dollars are spent annually on promotion activities. This mandates planning and executing promotion decisions as effectively and efficiently as possible.

Targeting and Positioning Strategy Illustration

The Cooper Tire and Rubber Company is an interesting example of a mid-sized company competing successfully against large global competitors like Michelin, Goodyear, and Bridgestone. Cooper and Goodyear are the only two publicly owned U.S. tire companies left in the market.[16] Cooper's sales are about one twelfth the size of Goodyear's sales. The firm does not compete for original equipment sales to automobile producers. Instead, management targets the replacement market, distributing tires through a strong dealer network. The company cultivates its dealers rather than spending large amounts on consumer advertising. The Cooper brand's association with its dealers helps to position the brand. Tight cost control is practiced. Management's product strategy is to duplicate the successful tires of the leading original equipment manufacturers within a few years after introduction. The firm expands plant capacity to meet demand for its tires. Its strengths acknowledged, Cooper's management has a continuing challenge in competing successfully against the international giants.

IMPLEMENTING AND MANAGING MARKETING STRATEGY

Selecting the customers to target and the positioning strategy for each target moves marketing strategy development to the action stage (Exhibit 4–2). This stage considers the design of the marketing organization and implementation and control of the strategy.

Designing the Marketing Organization

An effective organization design selects people and assigns them work responsibilities in a way that is best for accomplishing the firm's marketing strategy. Deciding how to assemble people into organizational units and assigning responsibility to the various elements that make up marketing strategy impact strategy performance. Organizational structures and processes must be matched to the different types of business and marketing strategies that are developed and implemented. Environmental turbulence affects organizational effectiveness, creating new organizational design requirements. The marketing organization has to be flexible to respond to changing conditions and strategy needs. Organizational design needs to be evaluated on a regular basis to assess its adequacy and to identify necessary changes.

Implementation and Control

Marketing strategy implementation and control includes three important management activities: (1) preparing the marketing plan and budget; (2) implementing the plan; and (3) managing and controlling the strategy.

Marketing Plan and Budget. The marketing plan typically includes a situation analysis summary; a market target description and strategic evaluation; overall objectives and specific objectives for each market target; a marketing program positioning strategy; specific strategies for product, distribution, price, promotion, marketing research, and coordination with other business functions; forecasts and budgets; and contingency plans. The preparation of the marketing plan is discussed in the next section.

Implementation Strategy. The marketing plan should specifically include action guidelines concerning the activities to be implemented, who does what, the dates and location of implementation, and how implementation will be accomplished. Several factors contribute to implementation effectiveness, including the implementation skills of the people involved, organizational design, incentives, and the effectiveness of communication within the organization and externally.

Evaluation of Marketing Performance. Marketing strategy is a continuing process of making decisions, implementing them, and gauging their effectiveness over time. Planning is adaptive rather than an activity that fixes actions. In terms of its time requirements, strategic evaluation is far more demanding than planning. To be meaningful and effective, plans must contain commitments. Evaluation and control are concerned with tracking performance and, when necessary, altering plans to keep performance on track. Strategic evaluation also includes looking for new opportunities and potential threats in the future. It is the connecting link in the strategic marketing planning process shown in Exhibit 4–2. By serving as both the last stage and the first stage (evaluation before taking action) in the planning process, strategic evaluation assures that strategy is an ongoing activity.

PREPARING THE MARKETING PLAN AND BUDGET

The marketing plan performs an essential implementation and control role, indicating what the strategic actions are expected to accomplish and how they are to be accomplished. Marketing plans vary widely among organizations in scope and detail. Nevertheless, all plans should be based on analyses of the product-market and segments, industry and competitive structure, and competitive advantage. Several important planning considerations provide a checklist for plan preparation.

Planning Relationships and Frequency

Plans are developed, implemented, evaluated, and adjusted to keep the marketing strategy on target. Since the strategy typically spans beyond one year, implementation is aided by developing an annual plan to manage short-term marketing activities. Planning is really a series of annual plans guided by the marketing strategy.

The frequency of planning activities varies by company and marketing activity. Market targeting and positioning strategies are normally not changed significantly during the annual planning period. Tactical changes in product, distribution, price, and promotion strategies may be included in the annual plan. For example, the aggressive response of competitors to Healthy Choice's successful market entry required changes in ConAgra's marketing plan.

Planning Considerations

Suppose that a new product is to be introduced into the national market next year. The plan for the introduction should include expected results, targets, actions, responsibilities, schedules, and dates. The plan indicates details and deadlines, production plans, a market introduction program, advertising and merchandising actions, employee training, and other information necessary to launching the product. The plan needs to answer a series of questions—what, when, where, who, how, and why—for each action targeted for completion during the short-term planning period.

Responsibility for Preparing Plans. Normally a marketing executive is responsible for preparing the marketing plan. Some companies combine the business unit's plan and the marketing plan into a single document. Planning responsibilities based on a survey completed by 223 executives are shown in Exhibit 4–6. The planning process often involves several people and functions. For example, a product or market manager may prepare the formal plan for his/her area of responsibility, coordinating and receiving inputs from advertising, marketing research, sales, and other marketing specialists. Coordination with other business functions (R&D, finance, operations) is also important. The product group manager will then consolidate the plans of each product manager, and the chief marketing executive will

EXHIBIT 4–6 Responsibility for Preparing Plans

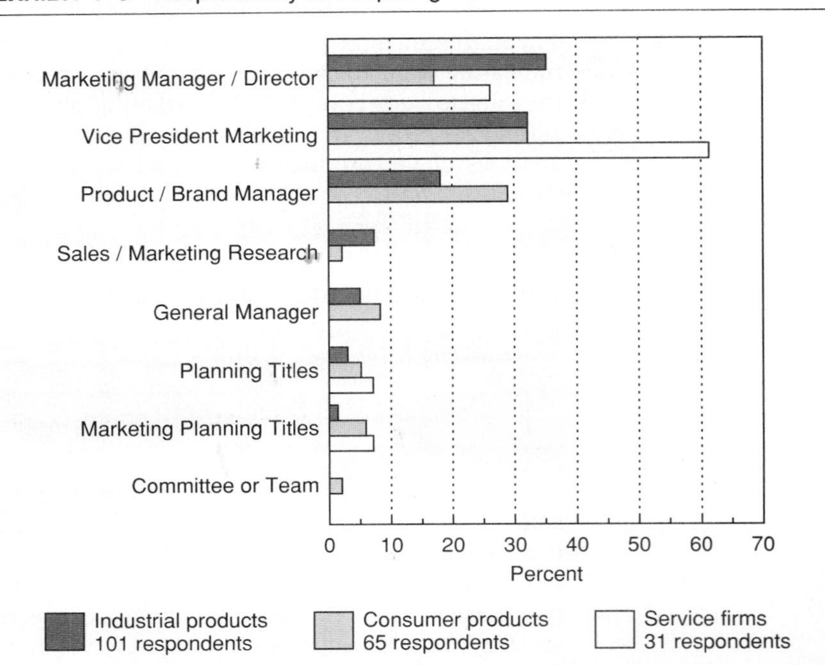

Source: Howard Sutton, *The Marketing Plan in the 1990s* (New York: The Conference Board, Inc., 1990), p. 16.

review and consolidate the plans covering all marketing operations, creating a master plan.

Planning Unit. The choice of the planning unit may vary because of the product-market portfolio of the organization or SBU. Some firms plan and manage by individual products or brands. Others work with product lines, market targets, or specific customers. The planning unit may reflect how marketing activities and responsibilities are organized. The market target is a useful basis for planning regardless of how the plan is aggregated. Focusing on the target helps to keep the customer in the center of the planning process.

Preparing the Marketing Plan

The Conference Board has several examples of plan formats in its report on marketing planning.[17] Formats and contents depend on the size of the organization, managerial responsibility for planning, product and market scope, and other situational factors. An outline of a typical marketing plan is shown in Exhibit 4–7. A discussion of the major parts of the planning outline illus-

EXHIBIT 4–7 Outline for Preparing an Annual Marketing Plan

Strategic Situation Summary
A summary of the strategic situation for the planning unit (business unit, market segment, product line, etc.).

Market Target(s) Description
Define and describe each market target, including customer profiles, customer preferences and buying habits, size and growth estimates, distribution channels, analysis of key competitors, and guidelines for positioning strategy.

Objectives for the Market Target(s)
Set objectives for the market target (such as market position, sales, and profits). Also state objectives for each component of the marketing program. Indicate how each objective will be measured.

Marketing Program Positioning Strategy
State how management wants the firm to be positioned relative to competition in the eyes and mind of the buyer.

A. *Product Strategy*
Set strategy for new products, product improvements, and product deletions.
B. *Distribution Strategy*
Indicate the strategy to be used for each distribution channel, including role of middlemen, assistance and support provided, and specific activities planned.
C. *Price Strategy*
Specify the role of price in the marketing strategy and the planned actions regarding price.
D. *Promotion Strategy*
Indicate the planned strategy and actions for advertising, publicity, personal selling, and sales promotion.
E. *Marketing Research*
Identify information needs and planned projects, objectives, estimated costs, and timetable.
F. *Coordination with Other Business Functions*
Specify the responsibilities and activities of other departments that have an important influence upon the planned marketing strategy.

Forecasts and Budgets
Forecast sales and profit for the marketing plan and set the budget for accomplishing the forecast.

Contingency Plans
Indicate planned actions if events differ from those assumed in the plan.

trates the nature and scope of the planning process. The market target is used as the planning unit.

Strategic Situation Summary. This part of the plan includes the market definition and its important characteristics, size estimates, and growth projections. Market segmentation analysis selects the segments to be targeted. The competitor analysis indicates the key competitors (actual and potential), their strengths and weaknesses, probable future actions, and the organization's competitive advantage(s) in each segment of interest. The summary should be brief. Supporting information for the summary is sometimes placed in an appendix or into a separate analysis.

Describing the Market Target. This part of the plan includes a clear definition of each target, size and growth rate, description of end-users, positioning strategy guidelines, and other available information useful in planning and implementation. When two or more targets are involved, management should indicate priorities to aid in resource allocation.

Objectives for the Market Target(s). This part of the plan spells out what the marketing strategy is expected to accomplish during the year. Some objectives may extend beyond one year into the future. They should be stated for each market target. Objectives may be financial, market position, or customer satisfaction achievements. Where possible the objectives are quantified. Objectives are also included for each component of the marketing program. These are usually included in the positioning strategy portion of the plan. The mix component objectives often indicate intermediate results that move the strategy toward the market target objectives. For example, an illustrative advertising objective is increasing market target awareness of a brand by some specified amount.

Marketing Program Positioning Strategy. The positioning statement indicates how the targeted customers and prospects perceive the firm or brand. Specific strategies for product, distribution, price, and promotion are explained in this part of the plan. Actions to be taken, responsibilities, time schedules, and other implementation information are included at this point in the plan.

Planning and implementation responsibilities often involve more than one person or department. An executive or planning team may be assigned the responsibility for each market target and each marketing mix component. Product and geographical responsibilities are also allocated to people in some organizations. The responsibilities and coordination requirements need to be indicated for marketing units and other business functions. Importantly, the planning process should encourage participation from all of the areas responsible for implementing the plan. For example, plans developed by product or brand managers often are implemented by salespeople. The success of the plan in these instances may depend on how well the sales force is motivated to execute the plan.

Contingency plans may be included in the positioning section of the annual plan or in a separate section. The contingencies indicate possible actions if the anticipated planning environment is different from what actually occurs. It is difficult to always forecast future events. The plan should discuss how the marketing strategy will be changed if the future is different than anticipated. Actions planned for major contingencies should be included. Companies often use planning meetings during the planning period to discuss contingencies that affect the original plans.

Forecasting and Budgeting. Marketing financial planning includes forecasting revenues and profits and estimating the costs necessary to carry out the marketing plan (see the appendix to Chapter 4 for details). The executives responsible for market target, product, geographical area, or other units may prepare the forecast. Large companies may have forecasting specialists. Comparative data on sales, profits, and expenses for prior years is a useful link of the plan to previous results. If plans are developed for several similar organizational units such as products, the budgets may be combined at a higher organization level.

Schlissel and Giacalone suggest a strategic marketing budgeting approach that identifies, at each organizational level in the firm, the quantitative amount of task performance required from each resource unit to achieve a specific objective.[18] Objectives and tasks are determined at each organizational level and delegated for implementation to the level below. The approach encourages involvement in the planning and budgeting process by the entire marketing team. Evaluation and control are aided by the numerical statements of objectives and task performance.

Marketing Planning by Sonesta Hotels. The planning outline used by Sonesta Hotels is shown in Exhibit 4–8. The planning procedure is developed around market segments. Attention is given to each of the marketing program (mix) components.

SUMMARY

Marketing strategy is the analysis, planning, implementation, and control process designed to satisfy customer needs and wants. It starts with an undertanding of the corporate mission and objectives and the strategy of each strategic business unit. The strategic marketing planning process is shown in Exhibit 4–2. The first part comprises product-market analysis, market segmentation, competition analysis, and information systems. These analyses guide the choice of marketing strategy. Market definition establishes the overall competitive arena. Market segmentation finds possible customer groups for targeting by business. Competitor analysis looks at the strengths, weaknesses, and strategies of key competitors. Information systems and marketing research supply information for analysis and decision making.

Designing marketing strategies comprises the second stage in strategy development. The company's selection of the people (or organizations) to be targeted is guided by the situation analysis. The market target decision indicates the buyer groups whose needs are to be satisfied by the marketing program positioning strategy. The positioning strategy indicates how the firm will position itself against its key competitors in meeting the needs of the buyers in the market target. Strategy selection considers the situational and competitive factors in the product-market that is targeted. New-product strategies are essential to generate a continuing stream of new entries to replace mature products that are eliminated.

The third phase of the strategy process is concerned with designing the marketing program. Specific marketing mix strategies for products, distribution, price, and promotion are developed to implement the positioning strategy management has selected. The programming task is to achieve a

EXHIBIT 4–8 Sonesta Hotels: Marketing Plan Outline

Note: Please keep the plan concise—Maximum of 20 pages plus summary pages. Include title page and table of contents. Number all pages.

I. *Introduction.* Set the stage for the plan. Specifically identify marketing objectives such as "increase average rate," "more group business," "greater occupancy," or "penetrate new markets." Identify particular problems.

II. *Marketing Position.* Begin with a single statement that presents a consumer benefit in a way that distinguishes us from the competition.

III. *The Product.* Identify all facility and service changes that occurred in 1989 and are planned for 1990.

IV. *Marketplace Overview.* Briefly describe what is occurring in your marketplace that might impact on your business or marketing strategy, such as the economy, the competitive situation, etc.

V. *The Competition.* Briefly identify your primary competition (three or fewer) specifying number of rooms, what is new in their facilities, and marketing and pricing strategy.

VI. *Marketing Data*

   A. Identify top five geographic areas for transient business, with percentages of total room nights compared to the previous year.

   B. Briefly describe the guests at your hotel, considering age, sex, occupation, what they want, why they come, etc.

   C. Identify market segments with percentage of business achieved in each segment in current years (actual and projected) and project for next year.

VII. *Strategy by Market Segment*

   A. Group

      1. *Objectives:* Identify what you specifically wish to achieve in this segment. (For example, more high-rated business, more weekend business, larger groups.)

      2. *Strategy:* Identify how sales, advertising and public relations will work together to reach the objectives.

      3. *Sales Activities:* Divide by specific market segments.

         a. Corporate
         b. Association
         c. Incentives
         d. Travel agent
         e. Tours
         f. Other

         Under each category include a narrative description of specific sales activities geared toward each market segment, including geographically targeted areas, travel plans, group site inspections, correspondence, telephone solicitation and trade shows. Be specific on action plans, and designate responsibility and target months.

      4. *Sales Materials:* Identify all items, so they will be budgeted.

      5. *Direct Mail:* Briefly describe the direct mail program planned, including objectives, message and content. Identify whether we will use existing material or create a new piece?

      6. *Research:* Indicate any research projects you plan to conduct in 1990 identifying what you wish to learn.

   B. Transient (The format here should be the same as group throughout)

      1. *Objective*

      2. *Strategy*

EXHIBIT 4–8 (concluded)

3. *Sales Activities:* Divide by specific market segments.
    a. Consumer (rack rate)
    b. Corporate (prime and other)
    c. Travel agent: business, leisure, consortia
    d. Wholesale/Airline/Tour (foreign and domestic)
    e. Packages (specify names of packages)
    f. Government/Military/Education
    g. Special interest/Other
4. *Sales Materials*
5. *Direct Mail*
6. *Research*

C. Other Sonesta Hotels

D. Local/Food and Beverage
1. *Objectives*
2. *Strategy*
3. *Sales Activities:* Divide by specific market segments.
    a. Restaurant and Lounge, external promotion
    b. Restaurant and Lounge, internal promotion
    c. Catering
    d. Community Relation/Other
4. *Sales Materials* (e.g., banquet menus, signage, etc.)
5. *Direct Mail*
6. *Research*

VIII. *Advertising*

A. Subdivide advertising by market segment and campaign, paralleling the sales activities (group, transient, F&B).

B. Describe objectives of each advertising campaign identifying whether it should be promotional (immediate bookings) or image (longer-term awareness).

C. Briefly describe contents of advertising identifying key benefit to promote.

D. Identify target media by location and type (e.g., newspaper, magazine, radio, etc.).

E. Indicate percent of the advertising budget to be allocated to each market segment.

IX. *Public Relations*

A. Describe objectives of public relations as it supports the sales and marketing priorities.

B. Write a brief statement on overall goals by market segment paralleling the sales activities. Identify what proportion of your effort will be spent on each segment.

X. *Summary:* Close the plan with general statement concerning the major challenges you will face in upcoming year and how you will overcome these challenges.

Source: Howard Sutton, *The Marketing Plan in the 1990s* (New York: The Conference Board, Inc., 1990), pp. 34–35.

coordinated combination of the marketing mix components that will accomplish the market target objectives in a cost-effective manner.

Finally, in the last phase of the process, strategy implementation and management of marketing strategy are examined. These activities focus on evaluating and improving organizational effectiveness and marketing strategy implementation and control. This is the action phase of marketing strategy.

The marketing plan is the basis for communicating decisions, actions, responsibilities, deadlines, and forecasts and budgets. Strategic marketing is a continuing process of making decisions, implementing them, and evaluating and managing the marketing strategy.

QUESTIONS FOR REVIEW AND DISCUSSION

1. The topical areas included in marketing plans are very similar, even though they are developed for firms in different industries, size categories, and channel levels. Considering the wide differences in organizations, why are the planning areas so similar?
2. The situation analysis is the first step in developing a marketing plan. Prepare an outline of the questions you would use to conduct a situation analysis for a regional supermarket chain.
3. As marketing manager you have been asked by the chief executive of your firm to develop specific objectives for the marketing function. What information do you need before preparing these objectives?
4. While markets and products are the primary determinants of marketing strategy, both are influenced by environmental forces. Discuss some examples of the effects of environmental forces in the 1980s that necessitated changes in the markets or products of various firms.
5. Does the list of frequent flyers enrolled by American Airlines or Delta Airlines constitute a market target?
6. Discuss the issues that are important in positioning the Toyota Lexus.
7. Why is the coordination and integration of marketing mix components very important?
8. What is involved in marketing strategy implementation and management? How do these activities vary between firms in different industries?
9. Indicate the strategic planning role and functions you feel the chief marketing executive and staff should be responsible for in a company (or division). Support your arguments, showing why these responsibilities should be assigned to marketing.
10. Develop an outline showing what you would include in the marketing plan for a new product.

NOTES

1. Frederick E. Webster, Jr., "The Changing Role of Marketing in the Corporation," *Journal of Marketing,* October 1992, p. 10.
2. This illustration is based on Scott McMurray, "Du Pont Weaves Pattern to Fit Europe," *The Wall Street Journal,* November 12, 1991, p. A6.

3. Peter F. Drucker, *Management: Tasks, Responsibilities, Practices* (New York: Harper & Row, 1974), p. 63.
4. Webster, "The Changing Role of Marketing," p. 11.
5. Ibid.
6. David W. Cravens, "Developing Marketing Strategies for Competitive Advantage," in *Handbook of Business Strategy 1988/89,* ed. H. E. Glass (New York: Warren, Gorham & Lamont, 1989), p. 16-1-19.
7. George S. Day, *Strategic Market Planning* (St. Paul: West Publishing, 1984), p. 3.
8. Michael Waldholz, "Super Aspirin's Promise Exemplifies Value of Biotech," *The Wall Street Journal,* February 27, 1992, p. B3.
9. John Child, "Information Technology, Organization, and the Response to Strategic Challenges," *California Management Review,* Fall 1987, p. 33.
10. Ibid., pp. 43–44.
11. This example is based on D. John Loden, *Megabrands* (Homewood, IL: Business One Irwin, 1992), pp. 184–85.
12. *Business Week,* "Masters of Innovation," April 10, 1989, pp. 58–63.
13. Webster, "The Changing Role of Marketing," p. 13.
14. Yoram Wind and Henry J. Claycamp, "Planning Product Line Strategy: A Matrix Approach," *Journal of Marketing,* January 1976, p. 2.
15. Joshua Levine, "Pen Wars," *Forbes,* January 6, 1992, pp. 88–89.
16. This example is based on Ralph E. Winter, "Mid-Sized Cooper Tire Treads Warily But Thrives in World Ruled by Giants," *The Wall Street Journal,* August 22, 1988, p. 34.
17. David S. Hopkins, *The Marketing Plan* (New York: The Conference Board, Inc., 1981). See also Howard Sutton, *The Marketing Plan in the 1990s* (New York: The Conference Board, Inc., 1990).
18. Martin R. Schlissel and Joseph A. Giacalone, "Budgeting the Strategic Marketing Plan," *Managerial Planning,* January–February 1982, pp. 25–29.

APPENDIX 4A

Financial Analysis for Marketing Planning and Control

Several kinds of financial analyses are needed for marketing analysis, planning, and control activities. Such analyses represent an important part of case preparation activities. In some instances it will be necessary to review and interpret financial information provided in the cases. In other instances, analyses may be prepared to support specific recommendations. The methods covered in this appendix represent a group of tools and techniques for use in marketing financial analysis. Throughout the discussion, it is assumed that accounting and finance fundamentals are understood.

UNIT OF FINANCIAL ANALYSIS

Various units of analysis that can be used in marketing financial analysis are shown in Exhibit 4A–1. Two factors often influence the choice of a unit of analysis: (1) the purpose of the analysis and (2) the costs and availability of the information needed to perform the analysis.

EXHIBIT 4A–1 Alternative Units for Financial Analysis

Market	*Product/Service*	*Organization*
Market	Industry	Company
Total market	Product mix	Segment/division/unit
Market niche(s)	Product line	Marketing department
Geographic area(s)	Specific product	Sales unit
Customer groups	Brand	Region
Individual customers	Model	District branch
		Office/store
		Salesperson

FINANCIAL SITUATION ANALYSIS

Financial measures can be used to help assess the present situation. One of the most common and best ways to quantify the financial situation of a firm is through ratio analysis. These ratios should be analyzed over a period of at least three years to discern trends.

Key Financial Ratios

Financial information will be more useful to management if it is prepared so that comparisons can be made. James Van Horne comments upon this need:

> To evaluate a firm's financial condition and performance, the financial analyst needs certain yardsticks. The yardstick frequently used is a ratio or index, relating two pieces of financial data to each other. Analysis and interpretation of various ratios should give an experienced and skilled analyst a better understanding of the financial condition and performance of the firm than he would obtain from analysis of the financial data alone.[1]

As we examine the financial analysis model in the next section, note how the ratio or index provides a useful frame of reference. Typically, ratios are used to compare historical and/or future trends within the firm, or to compare a firm or business unit with an industry or other firms.

Several financial ratios often used to measure business performance are shown in Exhibit 4A–2. Note that these ratios are primarily useful as a means of comparing:

1. Ratio values for several time periods for a particular business.
2. A firm to its key competitors.
3. A firm to an industry or business standard.

There are several sources of ratio data.[2] These include data services such as Dun & Bradstreet, Robert Morris Associates' *Annual Statement Studies,* industry and trade associations, government agencies, and investment advisory services.

[1]James C. Van Horne, *Fundamental of Financial Management,* 4th ed. (Englewood Cliffs, NJ: Prentice Hall, 1980), pp. 103–4.

[2]A useful guide to ratio analysis is provided in Richard Sanzo, *Ratio Analysis for Small Business* (Washington, DC: Small Business Administration, 1977).

EXHIBIT 4A–2 Summary of Key Financial Ratios

Ratio	*How Calculated*	*What It Shows*
Profitability ratios:		
1. Gross profit margin	(Sales − Cost of good sold) / Sales	An indication of the total margin available to cover operating expenses and yield a profit.
2. Operating profit margin	Profits before taxes and before interest / Sales	An indication of the firm's profitability from current operations without regard to the interest charges accruing from the capital structure.
3. Net profit margin (or return on sales)	Profits after taxes / Sales	Shows after-tax profits per dollar of sales. Subpar profit margins indicate that the firm's sales prices are relatively low or that its costs are relatively high or both.
4. Return on total assets	Profits after taxes / Total assets or (Profits after taxes + Interest) / Total assets	A measure of the return on total investment in the enterprise. It is sometimes desirable to add interest to after-tax profits to form the numerator of the ratio, since total assets are financed by creditors as well as by stockholders; hence it is accurate to measure the productivity of assets by the returns provided to both classes of investors.
5. Return on stockholders' equity (or return on net worth)	Profits after taxes / Total stockholders' equity	A measure of the rate of return on stockholders' investment in the enterprise.
6. Return on common equity	(Profits after taxes − Preferred stock dividends) / (Total stockholders' equity − Par value of preferred stock)	A measure of the rate of return on the investment which the owners of common stock have made in the enterprise.
7. Earnings per share	(Profits after taxes − Preferred stock dividends) / Number of shares of common stock outstanding	Shows the earnings available to the owners of common stock.
Liquidity ratios:		
1. Current ratio	Current assets / Current liabilities	Indicates the extent to which the claims of short-term creditors are covered by assets that are expected to be converted to cash in a period roughly corresponding to the maturity of the liabilities.
2. Quick ratio (or acid-test ratio)	(Current assets − Inventory) / Current liabilities	A measure of the firm's ability to pay off short-term obligations without relying upon the sale of its inventories.
3. Cash ratio	Cash & Marketable securities / Current liabilities	An indicator of how long the company can go without further inflow of funds.
4. Inventory to net working capital	Inventory / (Current assets − Current liabilities)	A measure of the extent to which the firm's working capital is tied up in inventory.

EXHIBIT 4A–2 (concluded)

Ratio	*How Calculated*	*What It Shows*
Leverage ratios:		
1. Debt to assets ratio	$\frac{\text{Total debt}}{\text{Total assets}}$	Measures the extent to which borrowed funds have been used to finance the firm's operations.
2. Debt to equity ratio	$\frac{\text{Total debt}}{\text{Total stockholders' equity}}$	Provides another measure of the funds provided the creditors versus the funds provided by owners.
3. Long-term debt to equity ratio	$\frac{\text{Long-term debt}}{\text{Total stockholders' equity}}$	A widely used measure of the balance between debt and equity in the firm's overall capital structure.
4. Times-interest-earned (or coverage ratios)	$\frac{\text{Profits before interest and taxes}}{\text{Total interest charges}}$	Measures the extent to which earnings can decline without the firm's becoming unable to meet its annual interest costs.
5. Fixed-charge coverage	$\frac{\text{Profits before taxes and interest} + \text{Lease obligations}}{\text{Total interest charges} + \text{Lease obligations}}$	A more inclusive indication of the firm's ability to meet all of its fixed-charge obligations.
Activity ratios:		
1. Inventory turnover	$\frac{\text{Cost of Goods Sold}}{\text{Inventory}}$	When compared to industry averages, it provides an indication of whether a company has excessive inventory or perhaps inadequate inventory.
2. Fixed-assets turnover*	$\frac{\text{Sales}}{\text{Fixed assets}}$	A measure of the sales productivity and utilization of plant and equipment.
3. Total-assets turnover	$\frac{\text{Sales}}{\text{Total assets}}$	A measure of the utilization of all the firm's assets; a ratio below the industry average indicates the company is not generating a sufficient volume of business given the size of its asset investment.
4. Accounts receivable turnover	$\frac{\text{Annual credit sales}}{\text{Accounts receivable}}$	A measure of the average length of time it takes the firm to collect the sales made on credit.
5. Average collection period	$\frac{\text{Accounts receivable}}{\text{Total sales} \div 365}$ or $\frac{\text{Accounts receivable}}{\text{Average daily sales}}$	Indicates the average length of time the firm must wait after making a sale before it receives payment.

*The manager should also keep in mind the fixed charges associated with noncapitalized lease obligations.

Source: Adapted from Arthur A. Thompson, Jr., and A. J. Strickland III, *Strategy and Policy,* 4th ed. (Homewood, IL: Richard D. Irwin, 1987), pp. 270–71.

EXHIBIT 4A–3 Illustrative Contribution Margin Analysis for Product X ($000)

Sales	$300
Less: Variable manufacturing costs	100
Other variable costs traceable to product X	50
Equals: Contribution margin	150
Less: Fixed costs directly traceable to product X	100
Equals: Product net income	$ 50

Other ways to gauge productivity of marketing activities include sales per square feet of retail floor space, occupancy rates of hotels and office buildings, and sales per salesperson.

Contribution Analysis

When the performance of products, market segments, and other marketing units is being analyzed, management should examine the unit's profit contribution. Contribution margin is equal to sales (revenue) less variable costs. Thus, contribution margin represents the amount of money available to cover fixed costs, and contribution margin less fixed costs is net income. An illustration of contribution margin analysis is given in Exhibit 4A–3. In this example, product X is generating positive contribution margin. If product X were eliminated, $50,000 of product net income would be lost, and the remaining products would have to cover fixed costs not directly traceable to them. If the product is retained, the $50,000 can be used to contribute to other fixed costs and/or net income.

FINANCIAL ANALYSIS MODEL

The model shown in Exhibit 4A–4 provides a useful guide for examining financial performance and identifying possible problem areas. The model combines several important financial ratios into one equation. Let's examine the model, moving from left to right. Profit margin multiplied by asset turnover yields return on assets. Moreover, assuming that the performance target is return on net worth (or return on equity), the product of return on assets and financial leverage determines performance. Increasing either ratio will increase net worth. The values of these ratios will vary considerably from one industry to another. In grocery wholesaling, for example, profit margins are typically very low, whereas asset turnover is very high. Through efficient management and high turnover, a wholesaler can stack up impressive returns on net worth. Furthermore, space productivity measures are obtained for individual departments in retail stores that offer more than one line such as department stores. The measures selected depend on the particular characteristics of the business.

EXHIBIT 4A–4 Financial Analysis Model

Profit margin		Asset turnover		Return on assets		Financial leverage		Return on net worth
↓		↓		↓		↓		↓
$\frac{\text{Net profits (after taxes)}}{\text{Net sales}}$	×	$\frac{\text{Net sales}}{\text{Total assets}}$	→	$\frac{\text{Net profits (after taxes)}}{\text{Total assets}}$	×	$\frac{\text{Total assets}}{\text{Net worth}}$	=	$\frac{\text{Net profits (after taxes)}}{\text{Net worth}}$

EVALUATING ALTERNATIVES

As we move through the discussion of financial analysis, it is important to recognize the type of costs being used in the analysis. Using accounting terminology, costs can be designated as fixed or variable. A cost is *fixed* if it remains constant over the observation period, even though the volume of activity varies. In contrast, a *variable* cost is an expense that varies with sales over the observation period. Costs are designated as mixed or semivariable in instances when they contain both fixed and variable components.

Break-Even Analysis[3]

This technique is used to examine the relationship between sales and costs. An illustration is given in Exhibit 4A–5. Using sales and cost information, it is easy to determine from a break-even analysis how many units of a product must be sold in order to break even, or cover total costs. In this example 65,000 units at sales of $120,000 are equal to total costs of $120,000. Any additional units sold will produce a profit. The break-even point can be calculated in this manner:

$$\text{Break-even units} = \frac{\text{Fixed costs}}{\text{Price per unit} - \text{Variable cost per unit}}$$

Price in the illustration shown in Exhibit 4A–5 is $1.846 per unit, and variable cost is $0.769 per unit. With fixed costs of $70,000, this results in the break-even calculation:

$$\text{BE units} = \frac{\$70{,}000}{\$1.846 - \$0.769} = 65{,}000 \text{ units}$$

This analysis is not a forecast. Rather it indicates how many units of a product at a given price and cost must be sold in order to break even. Some important assumptions that underlie the above break-even analysis include the use of constant fixed costs and one price.

[3]This illustration is drawn from David W. Cravens, Gerald E. Hills, and Robert B. Woodruff, *Marketing Decision Making: Concepts and Strategy,* rev. ed. (Homewood, IL: Richard D. Irwin, 1980), pp. 335–36.

EXHIBIT 4A–5 Illustrative Break-Even Analysis

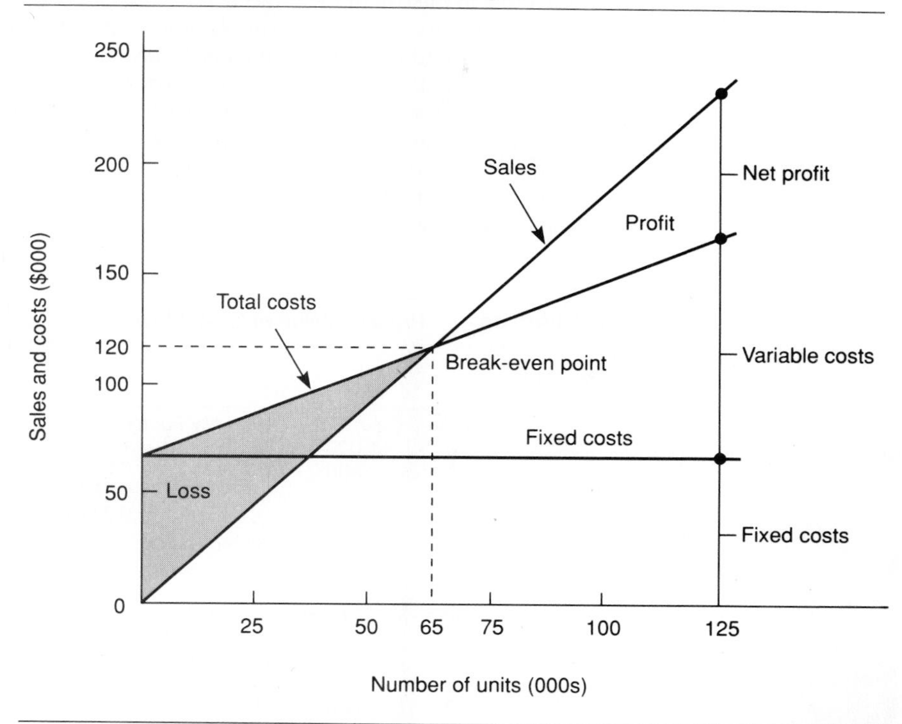

EXHIBIT 4A–6 Cash Flow Comparison ($000s)

	Project X	*Project Y*
Start-Up Costs	⟨1,000⟩	⟨1,000⟩
Year 1	500	300
Year 2	500	400
Year 3	200	600

In addition to break-even analysis, several other financial tools are used to evaluate alternatives. Net present value of cash flow analysis and return on investment are among the most useful. For example, assume there are two projects with the cash flows shown in Exhibit 4A–6.

Though return on investment is widely used, it is limited in its inability to consider the time value of money. This is pointed out in Exhibit 4A–7. Return on investment for *both* projects X and Y is 10 percent. However, a dollar today is worth more than a dollar given in three years. Therefore, when assessing cash flows of a project or investment, future cash flows must be discounted back to the present at a rate comparable to the risk of the project.

Discounting cash flows is a simple process. Assume the firm is considering projects X and Y, and its cost of capital is 12 percent. Additionally, assume that both projects carry risk comparable to the normal business risk. Under these circumstances, the analyst should discount the cash flows back to the present at the cost of capital, 12 percent. Present value factors can be looked up, or computed using the formula $1/(1 + i)n$, where i equals our discounting rate per time period and n equals the number of compounding periods. In this example, the present value of cash flows would be as follows:

EXHIBIT 4A–7 Present Value of Cash Flows

Project X

Time	*Cash Flow*	*PV Factor*	*NPV of Cash Flow*
0	⟨1,000⟩	$1/(1 + .12)^0 = 1$	⟨1,000⟩
1	500	$1/(1 + .12)^1 = 0.8929$	= 446.45
2	500	$1/(1 + .12)^2 = 0.7972$	= 398.60
3	300	$1/(1 + .12)^3 = 0.7118$	= 213.54
		Present value	+ 58.59

Project Y

Time	*Cash Flow*	*PV Factor*	*NPV of Cash Flow*
0	⟨1,000⟩	$1/(1 + .12)^0 = 1$	⟨1,000⟩
1	300	$1/(1 + .12)^1 = 0.8929$	= 267.87
2	400	$1/(1 + .12)^2 = 0.7972$	= 318.88
3	600	$1/(1 + .12)^3 = 0.7118$	= 427.08
		Net present value	+ 13.83

Because both projects have a positive net present value, both are good. However, if they are mutually exclusive, the project should be selected with the highest net present value.

FINANCIAL PLANNING

Financial planning involves two major activities: (1) forecasting revenues and (2) budgeting (estimating future expenses). The actual financial analyses and forecasts included in the strategic marketing plan vary considerably from firm to firm. In addition, internal financial reporting and budgeting procedures vary widely among companies. Therefore, consider this approach as one example rather than the norm.

The choice of the financial information to be used for marketing planning and control will depend on its relationship with the corporate or business unit strategic plan. Another important consideration is the selection of performance measures to be used in gauging marketing performance. The objective is to indicate the range of possibilities and to suggest some of the more frequently used financial analyses.

Pro forma income statements can be very useful when projecting performance and budgeting. Usually, this is done on a spreadsheet so that assumptions can be altered rapidly. Usually, only a few assumptions need be made. For example, sales growth rates can be projected from past trends and adjusted for new information. From this starting point, cost of goods can be determined as a percent of sales. Operating expenses can also be determined as a percent of sales based on past relationships, and the effective tax rate as a percent of earnings before taxes. However, past relationships may not hold in the future. It may be necessary to analyze possible divergence from past relationships.

Cases for Part I

CASE 1–1 Autodesk Inc.

When Carol Bartz was named the new chairman and chief executive of Autodesk Inc. last month, the talk focused on her being the first woman outsider ever brought in to run a major high-tech company. But that obscured the larger issue: Whether an unruly clique of programmers at one of America's most strangely run big companies will make her its latest managerial victim.

Autodesk? If the name barely registers, you're not alone—even though, remarkably, the London Business School last year calculated that Autodesk was by one measure the most profitable company of the 1980s, based on the school's survey of 2,000 public companies worldwide.

Though the world's sixth largest PC software company, Autodesk is hardly a household name for a couple of reasons. One is that it dominates a niche: software that allows relatively inexpensive personal computers to produce powerful models for engineers, architects, and other professional designers.

The other reason is Autodesk's founding genius, John Walker, a reclusive programmer who doesn't allow the company to distribute his picture or publish it in its annual report. In a rare interview granted for this article, a prickly Mr. Walker insisted that a reporter sit in front of a video camera, declared that Autodesk claimed a copyright on the ensuing discussion, and debated the meaning of each question.

Just as Microsoft Corp., the world's largest software supplier, is an extension of the personality of William Gates III, Autodesk is largely a creature of Mr. Walker. Like Mr. Gates, Mr. Walker is superb at identifying computer trends and spreading his vision to the troops. But unlike Mr. Gates, Mr. Walker, 42, never really wanted to run his company. "I'm an engineer, I'm a programmer, I'm a technologist," he says. "I have no interest in running a large U.S. public company, and I never have. It was a means to an end to accomplish the technological work I wished to achieve."

He relinquished the top spot in 1986 to Alvar Green, formerly Autodesk's chief financial officer, to return to programming. But the real power still rested with Mr. Walker, Autodesk's biggest shareholder, and an elite group of programmers called "Core," who had either helped Mr. Walker found the company in 1982 or led its most important projects.

Core members are contentious, eccentric freethinkers who have had a way of devouring professional managers. They have often attacked each other and company executives, usually by sending "flame mail"—biting electronic letters. The outbursts sometimes have led to changes, and sometimes brought work to a halt. "The whole company is a theocracy of hackers," says Charles M. Foundyller, president of Daratech Inc., a market research firm in Cambridge, Mass.

A year ago, Mr. Walker issued the ultimate in flame mail, a 44-page letter brutally attacking Mr. Green for allegedly trying to bolster short-term profits by neglecting investment in new products and marketing. Mr. Green later decided to resign, but stayed on until the selection of Ms. Bartz, 43, who formerly ran worldwide field operations for Sun Microsystems Inc.

She is regarded as a canny pick, particularly because she has experience managing rapid growth. She's also a tough manager who got her first big promotion at Sun when she convinced top management that she could do a better job than her boss, who was on vacation. "I am not coming [to Autodesk] as a dictator," she says. "But I am not a consensus manager in the extreme. I do not believe the best decision is a group grope."

That, however, is largely how Autodesk has been managed until now. It was founded by Mr. Walker and a dozen programmer pals just as International Business Machines Corp. revolutionized the computer industry with its original PC. Mr. Walker saw Autodesk as a diversified supplier of PC software with a can't-miss future. "We should consider ourselves extremely lucky to be in this business at this time in history," Mr. Walker wrote in 1982, egging on his cofounders. "I cannot imagine any scenario other than the total collapse of society in which the sales of microcomputer application software will not grow by a factor of 10 in the next five years."

Actually, Autodesk's own sales did better than that, jumping nearly tenfold to $9.8 million in the fiscal year ending Jan. 31, 1985, only its second full year of operation. Sales reached $100 million, another factor of 10, four years later; for the year ended Jan. 31, it earned $57.8 million on revenues of $284.9 million.

Mr. Walker didn't invent the program that drove all this phenomenal success. Instead, Autodesk's hit product proved to be a computer-aided-design (CAD) program that Mr. Walker purchased from an outside programmer named Michael Riddle. The program, which became AutoCad, did for designers of buildings, interiors and machines what VisiCalc's spreadsheet did for the accountant: It made the personal computer an essential tool, where once pencil and paper reigned.

Mr. Walker quickly grasped the promise of AutoCad when Mr. Riddle gave him a presentation in 1982. "When I showed him the program, he was quiet for 45 minutes. It was the first time he's ever been quiet [with me]," says Mr. Riddle. Then, "he says, 'You've got a fortune here.'" Before long, Autodesk dropped virtually all of its other work to concentrate on AutoCad. The program, which now sells for about $3,500, was a runaway success, cutting deeply into the sales of computer companies that blended software and hardware into systems that might cost 10 times the price of a PC with AutoCad, and yet afford only somewhat better performance.

While established CAD leaders ignored the threat from the PC, Autodesk began to entrench itself with customers. The company signed up dealers by the hundreds; many were architects and draftsmen themselves who sold it to their colleagues. And Mr. Walker created an AutoCad language so that consultants or customers could take the program and modify it to handle specific tasks. Today, thousands of AutoCad applications exist.

Mr. Walker gave Mr. Riddle an extraordinarily generous royalty agreement that eventually amounted to more than $10 million. The payment may be a record for an outside programmer in the PC business, but Mr. Walker has always operated by a different set of rules. He doesn't care a whit about office decorum or hierarchy, so Autodesk was always casual and libertarian, even by techie standards.

"I realized this was a different place when at my first staff meeting, I was licked by a dog," says one manager. But within this unstructured setting, Mr. Walker for the first four years ruled by charisma, relentless memo writing and sheer force of will.

Mr. Walker has unusual interests, which he imposed on Autodesk. When he grew intrigued with outer space, Autodesk invested in a company that salvages used fuel tanks from the Space Shuttle with the idea of sending them back into orbit, carrying the concept of recycling about as far as it can go. When he grew enamored of cellular automata and chaos theory, arcane fields at the intersection of computing, mathematics and biology, the company released a family of products based on those concepts that are essentially video games for brainy adults.

While Mr. Walker is intensely private about his personal life, he has had no qualms about airing Autodesk's dirty laundry—or effusively describing his technical ideas. He published a book containing scores of confidential Autodesk memos, many written by himself. And he once unsuccessfully tried to interest journalist Hunter Thompson in chronicling the company's rise. An obsessive writer who often revises a memo dozens of times before releasing it, he also has written a manuscript for a diet book, based on his experience of losing (and keeping off) about 100 pounds.

He is prone to making unexpected pronouncements. In a rare public appearance in March, Mr. Walker interrupted the description of a new product with this observation: "We are living on a small blue sphere in an endless black void."

Besides programming, Mr. Walker wrote press releases and ad copy and even pitched the product at trade shows in the company's early years. But wearing so many hats frayed his nerves. He began to show increasing impatience with co-workers. "The only way he knows how to deal with people is to bluster," says Mr. Riddle, who argued with him about the technical direction of AutoCad.

These fits of impatience dovetailed with Mr. Walker's continuing suspicion of professional managers, shared by other members of Core. In early 1986, he forced out John G. Ford, Jr., the vice president for marketing and sales, who built the dealer network that many observers say is still Autodesk's most valuable asset. Neither Mr. Walker nor Mr. Ford will comment.

Despite Mr. Walker's rough edges, employees were, and still are, drawn to him the way kids admire the baddest boy in class. He "is the cult hero of Autodesk," says Joe Oakey, who directs the company's charitable foundation. "He could stand up before a [company] meeting and say I hate you, and everyone would cheer."

It was also in 1986 that Mr. Walker tired of management and handed daily responsibilities to Mr. Green. Two years later, he resigned as chairman to devote himself fully to writing software from his nearby home. But he still held a huge stake in the company. (He currently owns 869,000 shares—less than 4 percent of the shares outstanding, but still worth more than $30 million.)

Mr. Green was ill-suited to ride herd on the rambunctious Core. Trained in finance, Mr. Green didn't even keep a computer on his desk, so he missed the electronic chatter that went on behind his back. When he needed to send an electronic message—the preferred means of discourse at Autodesk—he asked his secretary to do it.

Meanwhile, disputes kept breaking out among programmers and managers, usually about the technical direction of the company. "Over time, Autodesk became almost unmanageable," says Mr. Foundyller, the analyst. "Why? Autodesk was run very democratically. People met. They discussed things. Many flowers bloomed. But nobody harvested."

Sometimes, the paralysis was relatively innocuous, as when employees voted to delay the company's move into a new office complex because they preferred an alternative site opposed by management.

Other times, disagreements led to debates over how to lessen the company's dependence on its AutoCad cash-cow—or even whether the company should try to diversify. The need for consensus led to many organizational quirks. Last year, for instance, the critical AutoCad division was assigned two general managers—one from the business side and one from Core—because neither was believed to have the experience to run it alone. Ms. Bartz has already changed that, appointing a new head of the division to whom the former cogeneral managers report.

The most bitter disputes arose between programmers and the company's marketing and sales executives. "A tremendous schism" has existed for years between the two sides, says Mark Macgillivray, who has consulted for Autodesk on marketing issues. Core members and other programmers have simply refused to work on certain new products because they found them boring. Sometimes these are products that customers are clamoring for, such as a more memory-efficient version of AutoCad, which "the techies fought us tooth and nail on," recalls one marketing executive.

At many software companies, a product manager balances the interests of sales, which wants to satisfy customer demand for certain product features, and the interests of engineers, who push certain features because they are possible. At Autodesk, when products were being conceived "it became very difficult to get features agreed to," says Tim Cox, who was a product manager for two years until departing last November. "The problem we kept running into—everything needed to be the programming group's idea."

Indeed, opposing Core was tantamount to "attempting to butcher the sacred cow," says Roger Clay, who left Autodesk last year to form a software company.

For a long time, the financial results didn't reflect the conflict. From 1986 to 1990, net income nearly quintupled and sales jumped more than five-fold. But in the fourth quarter of fiscal 1991 ended Jan. 31, earnings fell about 25 percent below expectations on an unexpected slow-down in growth. The stock fell 22 percent in a single day. Financial analysts blamed Mr. Green for not keeping them informed, and Mr. Walker blamed him, too—for catering too much to analysts. He asserted that Mr. Green kept profit margins high at the expense of much-needed investments in new products and marketing, which "is how a company dies from making too much money," he said in his memorable broadside in April 1991, entitled "The Final Days."

Writing from his new home in Neuchâtel, Switzerland, where he had recently moved to find more seclusion, Mr. Walker observed that it pained him "watching Autodesk squander everything I've been working 16 hours a day for since 1982." He accused Mr. Green of "taking [his] marching orders from the accounting rules rather than the real world" and said he "was so appalled by what I heard at one management meeting that I vowed never to attend another managment meeting and I never have."

The memo was regarded as overwrought by some of Mr. Walker's own Core associates. "That letter caused me a lot of pain to read," says Gregory P. Lutz, one of two Core programmers on the board of directors. "He was right about a lot of things and I hadn't done anything about it. [But] I thought some of it was unfair and a little exaggerated."

Moreover, the broadside didn't mention that Mr. Walker himself had left the company and picked Mr. Green as his successor. "When somebody like [Mr. Walker] isn't there, it leaves a vacuum," observes Microsoft's chief, Mr. Gates. "People are free to do what they want. It's just a damn shame that he hasn't chosen to stay in management or even within the mainstream of software development at the company."

But Mr. Walker's pungent analysis (termed "just brilliant" by Mr. Gates) succeeded in getting everyone's attention at Autodesk. "It was like when you fire a shotgun in an aviary," recalls Mr. Walker of the letter's effect. "It caused everybody to say: What is our strategy? What are we doing out there?"

Mr. Green dutifully decided to do most of what Mr. Walker wanted: invest more in marketing and advertising of new products Mr. Walker said were being "abandoned" after introduction; push harder on a new version of AutoCad for Windows, Microsoft's emerging standard for controlling PC software; and back forays into new areas such as software tools for do-it-yourself designers and scientists. But Mr. Walker's attack destroyed the credibility of Mr. Green, who in October disclosed plans to resign as chairman and chief executive.

Mr. Green defends his record and downplays Mr. Walker's memo as a factor in his demise, saying he intended for some time to step down. But he adds that Mr. Walker "perpetually" criticized him. "To a great degree, he was right," Mr. Greens says of Mr. Walker's memo, adding that "John's batting average is pretty high" when it comes to picking strategies.

Mr. Green protests that it never was clear to anyone how best to diversify Autodesk's revenue. He concedes that he approved the company's issuance of an extraordinary $1.50 a share special dividend because retained profits were mounting so rapidly. "We were asked by people, 'Don't you have anything better to do with your cash,'" recalls Mr. Green. "Well, no we didn't."

To get a closer look at operations—and to help select a new chief executive—Mr. Walker invited himself back to Autodesk this year for three months as "manager of technology."

The timing of Ms. Bartz's ascension to the top job appears auspicious. There are signs that managers and programmers are starting to cooperate better. In March, for instance, Core and other AutoCad development teams for the first time agreed to compile a single to-do list required to complete the next version, which is due out by midyear. The list, which used to be kept in the heads of various developers, consists of 7,000 items. Each is assigned a completion deadline and the name of a person responsible for it.

Moreover, new products are starting to flow. In March, the company removed one monkey from its back by shipping its first Windows version of AutoCad. Autodesk also introduced its first scientific product in March, a

EXHIBIT 1

Autodesk Rules Its Market . . .

Estimated 1991 market share in PC-based computer-aided-design software

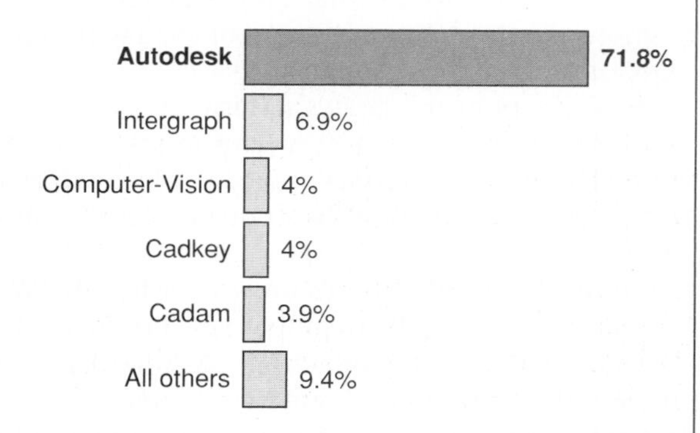

Source: Datatech Inc.

But Profits Have Stalled

Net income in millions of dollars: years end Jan. 31

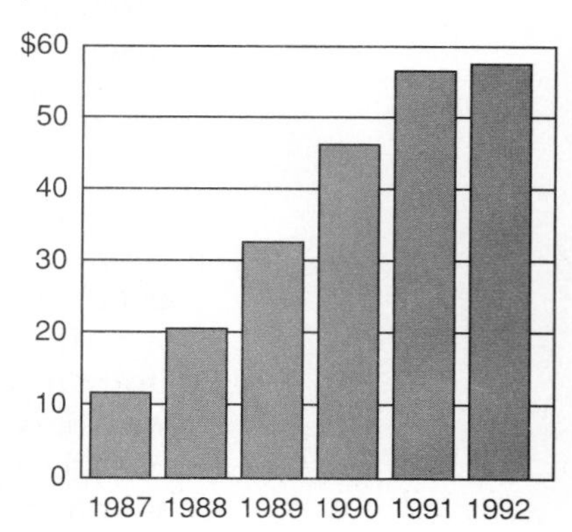

program called HyperChem that allows chemists to create molecular models. The scientific market is "the hidden iceberg in software," says Joel Voelz, the product manager. All together, Autodesk expects to release 25 new products in the fiscal year ending next January 31.

"Very few [public companies] have been encouraged to report disappointing short-term results to make the investments that are necessary to adapt to a changing market," Mr. Walker says. "Autodesk had that problem. Autodesk doesn't have that problem any more."

Indeed, last week, Autodesk reported that first-quarter profit fell 41 percent, citing heavy investment in new products. But investors seem willing to give Autodesk some time: The stock, which is trading at about half of its year-ago all-time high, went up on the news.

Another point in Ms. Bartz's favor: Mr. Walker seems content for the moment. He returned to Switzerland on April 16, but not before pledging his "total and unqualified" support for Ms. Bartz and promising that neither he nor other Core members will "step in and prevent change at the last minute," as has occurred in the past.

"It seems as if John and I are having a love-in," says Ms. Bartz. But she also pointedly notes that Mr. Walker is so talented, "he could have many careers," even one as a writer. "I admire John's amazing writing skills," she says.

Source: G. Pascal Zachary, "Tech Shop: Theocracy of Hackers," *The Wall Street Journal,* May 28, 1992, pp. A1, A14. Reprinted by permission of THE WALL STREET JOURNAL.

CASE 1–2 Telefonos de Mexico S.A.

In Mexico, even $1.76 billion may not buy you a quick dial tone.

That was the price Mexican magnate Carlos Slim and his U.S. and French partners paid for control of the spectacularly inefficient telephone monopoly Telefonos de Mexico S.A. Yet on a recent afternoon the receptionist at Mr. Slim's headquarters had to endure an aggravation common to millions of their countrymen: a phone line on the blink.

All right, so there are still kinks to be worked out before Telmex becomes a world-class telecommunications company.

Mr. Slim and his partners, Southwestern Bell Corp. and France Telecom Inc., knew to expect a bit of a struggle when they bought into Telmex in December 1990. Though Mexico is the world's 13th largest economy, it ranks 83rd in the world in phone lines per capita. The average wait for a new line is three years. The typical lag for repairs is several months. And even figures like these don't convey the depth of the problems. Most Telmex pay phones operate for free because repair crews can't keep up with vandals. Lines are so often crossed the befuddled dialers commonly open a conversation by asking *Adonde hablo?*—Where am I speaking?

But even as Mexican consumers have been complaining bitterly about Telmex, investors have been loving it. While complaints against Telmex were soaring 230 percent last year, its stock price was climbing 237 percent. Some conservative U.S. mutual funds were among the big buyers.

Maybe they knew something. For despite the immensity of the challenge, Mr. Slim's Telmex turnaround appears to be off to a promising start, telecommunications specialists say. Even though 1991 was considered a transitional year, the new owners managed to reduce costs by hundreds of millions of dollars. They installed a record number of new lines.

And they improved at least some of the service. Mr. Slim, finally finding a line in his office that works, dials the number for reporting service problems and—after a moment of suspense—the call goes through. "Our operator picked up in eight seconds," he says, checking his watch. "That wouldn't have happened a year ago." When asked to fill out Mr. Slim's first-year report card, an analyst at Nomura Securities, Joanne Smith, gives him an A.

For investors, Telmex is a play on a country that's coming on strong. "Buying Telmex is very much buying Mexico," says Raul Solis, director general of Mexico's Banco International, which helped plan the 1990 Telmex privatization. And buying Mexico, a nation of 80 million rebounding after a decade of economic stagnation, is very much in fashion. A record $5 billion in foreign capital flowed into Mexican stocks last year, more than half of that money into Telmex.

Robert Lamons, a retired military officer from Lawton, Oklahoma, took note of Telmex after hearing that there were only five phone lines for every 100 Mexicans, half the phone density of the former Soviet Union. "I thought, 'Now there's a company that's going to grow,'" he says. Indeed it has; Telmex is expected to report that 1991 profit rose about 60 percent to around $1.8 billion as revenue grew about 30 percent to $5 billion. The stock Mr. Lamons bought last summer has more than doubled. (There are two ways to trade Telmex in the U.S.: The New York Stock exchange lists American depositary shares that each represent 20 "L" shares with limited voting rights; quoted on the Nasdaq are Telmex ADRs that each represent one full voting "A" share.)

Many telecommunications analysts think there's more to come. Telmex outshines the U.S. Bell holding companies in nearly every measure of growth potential, says analyst Jack Grubman, who wrote a glowing Telmex report for PaineWebber Inc. in November ("the right company in the right country at the right time"). He sees earnings growing 25 percent annually for five years, far faster than at the regional Bells. The Mexican government concession requires Telmex to increase lines by 12 percent a year through 1994, Mr. Grubman notes, adding that favorable regulation preserves the company's monopoly through 1996 and allows it flexibility on rate increases.

If the government has been kind to Telmex, it's paid off. Through the sale of the Telmex stake to Mr. Slim's group and a later public offering of Telmex shares, Mexico has earned a total of $4.8 billion. The government still holds a 9.5 percent interest, worth $2.5 billion.

Southwestern Bell also has a warm place in its heart for Telmex. Its $953 million investment in 10 percent of Telmex has a current market value of $2.85 billion.

For Mr. Slim, sturdy as a lineman and rarely without a big cigar, the task is to make service soar the way the stock price has. The 51-year-old entrepreneur learned his first lessons in business from his father, a Lebanese immigrant who ran a general store in Mexico City. The father taught his eight-year-old son to use an accounting ledger to keep track of every peso of his allowance. Maybe that explains the keen eye for a good buy that Mr. Slim displayed during the Mexican debt crisis of the 1980s. While most businessmen were bailing out of Mexico, Mr. Slim built what's now Mexico's biggest business empire, ranging from mines to tire factories to cafeterias.

"Companies were absurdly undervalued," he says. "This country has endured worse crises than that of the 1980s, and it has always survived." Mexican history is a passion for Mr. Slim, who has a valuable collection of books on the Spanish Conquest and the Mexican Revolution.

He and his U.S. and French partners are hoping that Telmex's customers will take the long view when considering the company's service problems. Notes John H. Atterbury, president of Southwestern Bell's Mexican operations: "Telmex didn't get this bad overnight, and it's not going to get better tomorrow."

Telmex was a more or less typically ineffective Third World utility until the 1980s, when it was racked by a natural disaster and a manmade one. The 1985 Mexico City earthquake severely damaged the Telmex network. Meanwhile, Mexico's debt depression kept the government from making the huge investments needed to upgrade Telmex. In 1989, President Carlos Salinas de Gortari said the only way to make Telmex work was to privatize it.

In winning the controlling interest in Telmex, Mr. Slim's group narrowly outbid a consortium that included GTE Corp. Mr. Slim pledged to invest $13 billion over six years to double the number of phone lines. But he warned: "One must have patience."

He didn't realize how much patience would be needed until he got a good look inside. The first order of business was replacing Telmex's outdated analog technology with digital, which carries vastly more information. But the new managers encountered a mind-bending problem: For about a third of the lines in the system, Telmex lacked accurate information about how they were connected to the main network. "Before you can change lines you have to know where they run," says Mr. Atterbury. So Telmex is undertaking the laborious process of checking every line.

The new owners discovered that purchasing had been conducted in a similarly haphazard fashion. An audit found $300 million of equipment scattered in 105 Telmex warehouses throughout the country. The warehouses are being consolidated into just six equipment storage centers.

Mr. Slim's group had the opposite problem with maintenance centers: They were too centralized. All of the repair crews in Mexico City, which has 20 million residents, were crammed into 11 buildings. In one center there were 300 repair trucks—and one exit. It took an hour and a half each morning simply to roll all of the trucks onto the street. The new management built four maintenance centers last year and will add 14 more this year. They will have multiple exits.

One of the most burdensome legacies was an agreement to buy hundreds of millions of dollars worth of equipment over five years from local affiliates of Stockholm-based Telefon AB L.M. Ericsson and Paris-based Alcatel N.V. According to PaineWebber's Mr. Grubman, Telmex's suppliers were charging the company three times what the Bell companies pay for switches and other basic equipment. When Mr. Slim sought to renegotiate the agreement, he ignited a battle that dragged on all last year. "They were tough, tough, negotiations," says Rodrigo Calderon, an executive at Alcatel. "The new Telmex is not an easy client."

Unable to get the suppliers to budge after months of bargaining, Mr.

Slim played hardball: He threatened to defer all of the purchases Telmex was obligated to make under the five-year agreement until the final year. Facing the prospect of four lean years, the suppliers agreed to lower Telmex's equipment rates by $250 million in 1992. To ensure that Ericsson's and Alcatel's prices stay competitive, Telmex has brought in American Telephone & Telegraph Co. as a third supplier.

"In a remarkably brief time, Slim has succeeded in giving Telmex a much more business-like management culture," says Jorge Arredondo, an Ericsson executive.

Having spent last year doing that, Mr. Slim now hopes to concentrate on building up the network. Juan Antonio Perez Simon, director general, says line growth for 1992 should reach 14 percent, well above the government's mandate. Telmex is expanding pay phone service by putting lines in mom and pop stores, where the presence of the store owners discourages vandals. Construction of an 8,000-mile fiber optic line connecting 54 cities is ahead of schedule.

Operators, who for years labored at 1940s vintage switchboards, are switching to computerized systems that enable them to handle 50 calls an hour, instead of the current 15. "We're shipping these to a museum," says Emma Rosa Hernandez, a supervisor, pointing to the old ones.

Technology won't solve all of Telmex's service problems. Even after it replaced the switchboards, management had to haggle with the balky telephone workers' union to reassign the people needed to run the new computers. That points to the biggest potential problem with the Telmex privatization: The owners and equipment may be new, but the workers are all too familiar. To prevent the powerful 45,000-member phone workers' union from blocking the privatization, the government specified in its concession that Telmex's new owner couldn't make layoffs.

Telmex has nearly twice as many employees per line as the average Bell company. Productivity has always been substandard. Repair crews have traditionally sold their services to the highest bidder. Telmex linemen for years refused to use cable protected with rainproof jelly, because it was slippery to handle.

To offer employees an incentive to work harder, the privatization scheme gave the union a 4.4 percent stake in Telmex. It's still early, but there are signs that more of a work ethic is finally emerging within the work force. The union has disavowed several workers fired for corruption. Linemen have agreed to give the waterproof cable a trial. One operator has decorated her new computer terminal with a card that says: "Be understanding of people's mistakes and they will be understanding of yours."

In the wake of the privatization, however, Telmex customers are no longer so understanding. "People expected service to improve dramatically overnight," sighs Mr. Slim. It hasn't. Last summer's unusually heavy rains left the phone network as fouled up as it had been in years.

The combination of high expectations and high water accounted for last year's 230 percent increase in complaints about Telmex to the attorney general, a government ombudsman for the consumer. One typically unsatisfied customer is Marcelino Hernandez. He tells a Telmex lawyer and an arbitrator for the attorney general that he's been overbilled for 90,000 pesos ($30). The Telmex attorney suggests Mr. Hernandez has made a mathematical error. But the customer has his records, and the arbitrator quickly rules in his favor. "The new Telmex—hah," says Mr. Hernandez, stalking out.

Antonio Arrona Lopez, the Telmex lawyer, is resigned to dealing with people who'd like to reach out and throttle him. "Every day they cuss at you and call you a thief," he says. He loses 80 percent of his cases, which would get him fired from most corporate legal departments. "But that's a pretty good record," he says, "considering I'm defending Telmex."

Source: Matt Moffett, "Rewiring a Nation: Telmex is Off to a Promising Start in Mexico," *The Wall Street Journal,* February 19, 1992, pp. A1, A15. Reprinted by permission of THE WALL STREET JOURNAL.

CASE 1–3 Euro Disney

A few days before this Sunday's grand opening of Euro Disney, hundreds of French visitors invited to a preopening party gazed, perplexed, at what was placed before them.

It was a heaping plate of spareribs. The visitors were at the Buffalo Bill Wild West Show, a cavernous theater featuring a panoply of "Le Far West," including 20 imported live buffaloes. And Disney deliberately didn't provide silverware.

"There was a moment of consternation," recalls Robert Fitzpatrick, Euro Disney's president. "Then they just kind of said, 'The hell with it,' and dug in." One problem: the guests couldn't master the art of gnawing ribs and applauding at the same time. So Disney will provide more napkins—and teach visitors to stamp their feet.

For all the grumbling about "cultural imperialism," France is swallowing its pride and embracing Mickey and his pals in a very big way. The $3.9 billion Euro Disney theme park and resort complex, built on sugar-beet and sunflower fields 20 miles east of Paris, is one of Europe's largest construction projects. At a time when other grandiose real-estate schemes are collapsing, the park marks an extraordinary triumph of commerce over ideology. For it is the French state that is assuming the bulk of the financial risk—far more than even Disney itself.

The U.S. company has put up a paltry $160 million of its own capital to fund the project, an investment whose value has swelled to $2.4 billion after a popular stock offering in Europe. French national and local authorities, by comparison, are providing about $800 million in low-interest loans and pouring at least that much again into infrastructure. Two freeway exits recently were completed, a suburban train line connecting to the Paris Metro is just steps from the park's entrance, and a high-speed rail line will open in 1994. The French government was so eager to please Disney that it even provided cheap land and gave Disney a tax break on ticket sales.

"We've had less problems in France than we had in Long Beach," says Walt Disney Co. Chairman Michael Eisner. Disney recently walked away from a possible $3 billion theme park in Long Beach, Calif., leaving city official in a crossfire of recrimination about the loss. The park here moved from design to opening in six years.

Some French intellectuals continue to be outraged. "I wish with all my heart that rebels would set fire to Disneyland," thundered one in the French newspaper *Le Figaro,* which this week devoted a special supplement to anti-Disney outpourings. Mickey Mouse, sniffed another, "is stifling individualism and transforming children into consumers."

But the Socialist government, long the darling of the very same intellectuals who are denouncing the project, is battling a 10 percent unemployment rate. It knows Disney will create tens of thousands of badly needed jobs, both on and off the site, and attract many other investors to the depressed outskirts of Paris. International Business Machines Corporation and Banque National de Paris are among those already building in the area. One of the new buildings going up is a factory that will employ 400 outside workers to wash the 50 tons of laundry a day generated by Euro Disney's 14,000 employees.

Thousands of Europeans are spending this week of preopening festivities swarming over the park and resort complex, happily scarfing down fast food, snapping up pricey Disney merchandise and gazing in wonderment, oblivious to a chilling wind. And rather than charging onto rides as they might at the U.S. parks, the visitors meander and gape at what Disney designers call "layering."

And the layering, in this country of actual Gothic and medieval embellishment, is remarkable. Disney's "Imagineering" design unit has seemingly textured every bit of walkway with brickwork and tilework. Empty spaces are stuffed with props. Euro Disney is so extravagantly detailed that in many ways it makes Disney's parks in Florida and California look like penny arcades.

The lavishness must be hard to swallow for the notoriously cost-conscious Mr. Eisner, but as the largest project in his eight-year reign at Disney, Euro Disney reflects his quest to emulate Walt Disney himself and replicate what he calls Mr. Disney's "maniacal sense of detail." He personally ordered the installation of 35 fireplaces in hotel lobbies and restaurants, ordered a

$200,000 staircase removed two weeks ago for blocking a view, and assembled a staff of architects that designed oddities like a salad bar in the bed of an old pickup truck.

"When Walt went beyond the carnival to create Disneyland, he made a big step because [the attractions] told a story" says Mickey Steinberg, executive vice president of Imagineering. "This is a more sophisticated story."

And Europeans are responding, despite recession. "We believe it's a market that's going to be incredibly successful this year," says Jane Shaw, head of marketing for the British tour operator Airtours. It already has sold 70 percent of its allocated Disney tickets and hotel space for the year.

Disney expects 11 million visitors in the park's first year. The break-even point is estimated at between seven million and eight million. One worry had been that Euro Disney would cannibalize the flow of European tourists to Walt Disney World in Florida, but European travel agents say their customers still are eagerly signing up for Florida, lured by cheap dollars and the promise of sunshine.

Disney owns 49 percent of Euro Disneyland SCA, the operating company for the park, through a complex arrangement that leaves 51 percent publicly traded in Europe. Disney is expected to get a major financial boost in the next few years from its interest here.

One analyst, Margo L. Vignola of Salomon Brothers, estimates that the park will pull in three million to four million more visitors than the 11 million the company expects the first year. At that level, she says, in the first six months Euro Disneyland SCA would contribute $75.5 million, or 27 cents a share, to Disney's net income for the fiscal year ending September 30. She projects total net income this year for Walt Disney of $864.5 million, or $6.50 a share.

In fiscal 1993, the first full year of Euro Disneyland operations, Ms. Vignola estimates that Disney's operating income from the park will be $145 million—about 13 percent of the total operating income worldwide from theme park and resort operations, which is by far the largest segment at Walt Disney Co. By fiscal 1994, she figures Euro Disney operations will contribute 96 cents a share to Disney net income.

Disney's chief concern here is the weather. "People walk around Disney World in Florida with humidity and temperature in the 90s and they walk into an air-conditioned ride and say, 'This is the greatest,'" says Mr. Eisner. "Here, when it's raining and miserable, I hope they'll walk into one of these lobbies with the fireplace going and say the same thing. For all I know, it could be snowing Sunday."

The key to attendance growth is getting people to come to the park in the winter months, when fixed costs still are high, says John Forsgren, Euro Disney's chief financial officer. Despite the weather, Disney chose this site over sunnier Spain because of its proximity to Paris, the tourist capital of Europe. Many European tour operators are selling packages that combine visits to both. And while the idea of using a Euro Disney hotel as a home base from which to visit the City of Light seems bizarre, hotel prices—though steep—are competitive with those in Paris.

"When people come to Disney, we hope they might find an afternoon off to visit Paris," Samir Naessany, a French banker closely involved in financing the project, says with a wry smile (Exhibit 1).

Mr. Eisner admits to one other nagging worry: politics. Disney has already had a taste of that. A few of its major contractors kicked up a fuss earlier this year, complaining that they weren't being paid for extra work. Most of the disputes have since been settled. But Communist labor unions are threatening "a surprise" for the opening, probably a strike by subway workers.

Still, the French are clearly on Disney's side, and part of Disney's secret is Mr. Fitzpatrick, whose job it is to mollify the French. Urbane, married to a Frenchwoman and fluent in the language, Mr. Fitzpatrick previously ran the California Institute of the Arts and the 1984 Los Angeles Olympic Festival. While Disney executives in the U.S. play hardball, negotiating and litigating mercilessly, Mr. Fitzpatrick wines and dines the French establishment, and even pals around with the very intellectuals who are savaging Disney.

Mr. Eisner himself made periodic visits to the continent, dragged employees around Europe, rode roller coasters in existing parks and visited public places like Tivoli Gardens in Copenhagen. After a trip to Strasbourg and its cathedral's famous clock, Mr. Eisner set Disney designers working on a Mickey Mouse clock to rival it. The clock now tops the centerpiece hotel.

Everywhere is what, in Imagineering-speak, is called "museumlike interface." There are no blank walls or empty spaces, to avoid "no-man's lands with no meaning," sayd Tony Baxter, Imagineering's senior vice president for creative development. Disney won't say so, but the reference is to the company's gargantuan and sometimes impersonal Disney World. Built after Walt Disney died, it since has undergone what Disney calls "retrofitting." Says Mr. Baxter: "The French demanded more depth and sophistication. They regard America as on the shallow side."

But Euro Disney is determinedly American in theme, and Mr. Eisner hewed the line on traditional Disney values. There's an alcohol ban in the park despite an attitude among Frenchmen that wine with a meal is a God-given right. When designers presented a plan for Main Street U.S.A. based on scenes of 1920s America, because research indicated Europeans loved the Prohibition Era, Mr. Eisner decreed that images of gangsters and speak-easies were too negative. Main Street, though made more ornate and Victorian than Walt Disney's idealized Midwestern small town, remains Main Street.

The familiar Disney Tomorrowland, with its dated images of the space-age 1950s, has been jettisoned entirely, replaced by a gleaming wood-and-brass complex called Discoveryland, based on themes of Jules Verne and Leonardo da Vinci. Mr. Eisner ordered $8 million to $10 million in extras

EXHIBIT 1

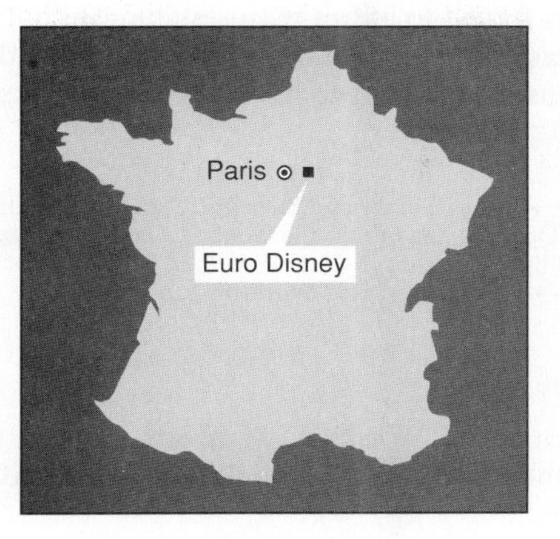

The Euro Disney Resort

5,000	Acres in size
12,000	Employees
6	Hotels (with 5,184 rooms)
10	Themed restaurants
414	Cabins
181	Camping sites

to the "Visionarium" exhibit, a 360-degree movie about French culture required by the French in their original contact.

The designers strived to avoid competing with the nearby European reality of actual medieval towns, cathedrals, and chateaux. While Disneyland's castle is based on Germany's Neuschwanstein and Disney World's is based on a Loire Valley chateau, Euro Disney's Le Chateau de la Belle au Bois Dormant—as the French insisted that Sleeping Beauty be called—is more cartoonlike, with stained glass windows built by English craftsman and depicting Disney characters. Fanciful trees grow inside and a beanstalk is out back.

"Otherwise," says Imagineering President Martin Sklar, "we'd be bringing coals to Newcastle."

Despite talk of cultural differences, the only real cultural difference, Mr. Eisner joked at a news conference last year, is "we'll be taking out French francs." And although some analysts are cautioning that the stock price of both Walt Disney Co. and Euro Disney already contain all the Euro-optimism they can absorb, Disney has built-in management incentive fees that steeply escalate as certain cash flow targets are reached.

Other sources of funding at Euro Disney are the park's 12 corporate sponsors, and Disney is paying them back in kind. The "Autopolis" ride, where kids drive cars, features coupes emblazoned with the "Hot Wheels" logo. Mattel Inc., sponsor of the ride, is grateful for the boost to one of its biggest toy lines. And Disney isn't missing opportunities to advertise itself: "The Little Mermaid" and "Beauty and the Beast" attractions are planned, and Adventureland boasts "L'Echoppe d'Aladin," foreshadowing this year's upcoming animated feature, *Aladdin.*

Children all over Europe are primed to consume. Even one of the intellectuals who contributed to Le Figaro's Disney-bashing broadsheet this week was forced to admit with resignation that his 10-year-old son "swears by Michael Jackson." And at Euro Disney, under the name "Captain EO," Disney just so happens to have a Michael Jackson attraction waiting.

Source: Richard Turner and Peter Gumbel, "Major Attraction: As Euro Disney Braces for Its Grand Opening, the French Go Goofy," *The Wall Street Journal,* April 10, 1992, pp. A1, 8. Reprinted by permission of THE WALL STREET JOURNAL.

Epilogue

Euro Disney S.C.A. is fighting an uphill battle to turn a profit at the Magic Kindgom theme park and hotel resort it opened to great fanfare in April outside Paris.

But start-up problems in Europe haven't halted parent Walt Disney Co.'s plans for worldwide expansion. Lobbying business and civic leaders for support of Disney's proposed $3 billion addition to its Anaheim, Calif., theme park, chairman Michael D. Eisner said the company will build a second theme park in Tokyo called "Disney Sea."

Disney had wanted to build a "Disney Sea" theme park as part of a $3 billion "Port Disney" entertainment complex in Long Beach, Calif., but nixed the idea after encountering a thicket of regulatory and environmental concerns. Instead, Disney opted for the $3 billion expansion at nearby Disneyland, with the addition of several hotels and a second, world's fair–styled theme park called "Westcot." But it remains to be seen whether Disney can get the substantial governmental funds it is seeking for public improvements, as well as clear regulatory and environmental hurdles needed for its "Disneyland Resort" project.

The company has long talked of building a second theme park next to Tokyo Disneyland, which it built 10 years ago for Oriental Land Co., but until Mr. Eisner's comments the prospects had seemed slim. Oriental Land earlier this year rejected Disney's proposal for a movie studio and theme park patterned after its Disney-MGM Studies in Florida.

Disney said its original plans for Disney Sea, which was to have been an ocean-themed amusement and marine-life park adjacent to the Port of Long Beach, are currently being adapted for Tokyo. Disney President Frank Wells said the company is currently in negotiations with Oriental Land, which owns Tokyo Disneyland, and that the Japanese company has shown "enthusiasm" for the project. But it will likely be another 6 to 12 months before Disney has anything more definitive, Mr. Wells said.

Disney's eagerness to build yet another foreign theme park comes despite the headaches it has encountered with Euro Disney. Euro Disney

S.C.A., which is 49 percent owned by Walt Disney, reported a net loss of 188 million francs ($35 million) for fiscal 1992 ended September 30, and says it expects to have a loss again in fiscal 1993.

Having failed to draw the crowds it budgeted for during its first months of operations, Euro Disney now faces the dual challenge of dismal winter weather and an economic slowdown in Europe. Company officials, however, say they are confident that their recipe is a fundamentally successful one, and they are trying to fine-tune their staffing and other arrangements to enhance profitability. They have also postponed or amended some expansion plans because of the soft real estate market in France.

The Euro Disney loss didn't drag down results of the parent company however, which yesterday posted a 29 percent increase in net income for the fourth quarter ended September 30 to $223.7 million, or 42 cents a share, on a 21 percent rise in revenue to $2.08 billion. For the year, the parent company's net income rose 28 percent to $816.7 million, or $1.52 a share, from $636.6 million, or $1.20 a share, while revenue climbed 23 percent to a record $7.5 billion from $6.1 billion. Earnings were bolstered by increases in attendance and spending at Disney's domestic theme parks and its strong slate of films and home videos.

Disney actually earned an $11 million profit on its Euro Disney investment for the year, with the losses at the European company offset by royalties and noncash income the parent company received from Euro Disney. But Disney warned that Euro Disney's contribution to its profits will be "negative" in 1993, since it has opted to defer the management fees it receives from Euro Disney for two years.

That decision results in an extraordinary gain of 109 million francs to Euro Disney for 1992. Under the original fee structure, Euro Disney had been expected to pay 3 percent of its gross revenue annually to Disney for the first five years. Instead, it will now start paying the deferred amount in 1994—estimated by officials at 300 million francs ($56 million)—and only if the company is profitable by then.

The agreement is a sop to Disney's European shareholders, who own 51 percent of the stock and have watched with anguish as the price has tumbled from its high of 164 francs last March to its close on the Paris Bourse Thursday at 68 francs, just above its all-time low and below its original issue price. Some European-based analysts who dislike the stock have argued that Euro Disney seems to owe greater allegiance to its U.S. parent than to its majority European shareholders.

"The deferment is a very good gesture that shows confidence in the future and will help the situation of smaller shareholders," said Philippe Bourguignon, Euro Disney's director general.

He acknowledged that the plunging stock price is just one of several difficulties that have beset the company since it opened the doors of its theme park in April. Despite heavy publicity and an attendance record that would

EXHIBIT 2 Euro Disney Investment Roller Coaster

A Falling Stock Price

Monthly stock price, in French francs

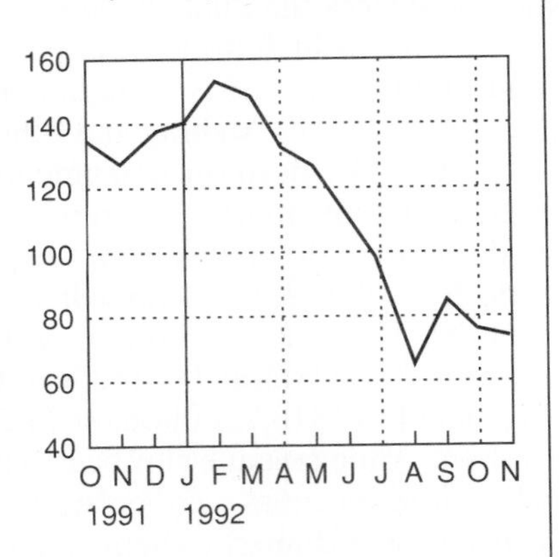

Source: Datastream International

Few French Visitors

Percentage of each nationality of the seven million visitors between April and Sept. 30, 1992

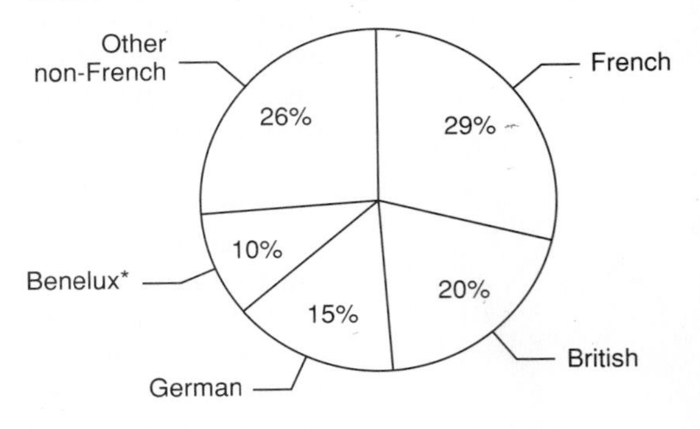

*Includes Belgium, Netherlands and Luxembourg

Source: Euro Disney

be the envy of its European rivals, Euro Disney has had trouble boosting its attendance figures to the expected level. In the period to the end of September, almost seven million visitors came to gape and ride on attractions including Sleeping Beauty's Castle and the Big Thunder Mountain Railroad. But the company had banked on 11 million visitors in the first 12 months, a target that now seems unrealistic. Hotel occupany during the same period was also lower than expected, averaging about 74 percent.

Management's biggest disappointment has been the fickle French, who were supposed to provide the core of visitors. French nationals were still the biggest single group, accounting for 29 percent of visits, but many fewer came than envisaged. Indeed, more people came from Britain and Germany combined. Some French apparently were scared off initially by fears of traffic jams and huge crowds—fears that Disney's own publicity blitz did nothing to ease (Exhibit 2).

The company is now trying to find new ways to draw crowds during the winter. It has been putting up Christmas trees and arranging numerous seasonal attractions such as Santa Claus and teams of reindeer. It is also organizing a new TV and radio publicity campaign, and wooing schools, corporations, and other groups.

Staffing is one way it hopes to improve matters. Euro Disney is seeking to deploy more part-time seasonal staff and to change schedules for the 12,000 permanent employees in order to cope better with the peaks and troughs of attendance. Officials are also trying to fine-tune sales of merchandise and food at the park after disappointing figures they blame partly on initial staffing methods.

Europe's economic woes cast a dark shadow over the future, however. Finance director John Forsgren said that the higher-than-anticipated level of French interest rates cost the company about 200 million francs. Both Germany and France are currently in a marked economic slowdown, and the currency turmoil in Europe this September that led to a sharp devaluation of the British pound, the Italian lira, and the Spanish peseta against the franc will make trips more expensive for some of the park's most enthusiastic visitors. Still, Mr. Bourguignon said that Euro Disney hadn't so far noticed any substantial fall in attendance from British, Spanish, or Italian visitors.

Largely because of the troubled economic picture, some analysts in Europe are pessimistic about the company. "If you're a shareholder it's pretty dismal," said Nigel Reed at Paribas Capital Markets in London, who this month issued a damning report and a sell recommendation on the stock. "It's dead money for a year until things pick up."

Euro Disney itself is reacting to the economic downturn by postponing or amending some of its expansion plans. A planned second theme park that would include a Disney-MGM Studios and water attractions is still planned, but an exact date is being negotiated with French authorities and hasn't yet been fixed. But Euro Disney executives say they are pulling back from some earlier plans to build several more hotels as well as constructing office and residential projects at the site, 25 miles east of Paris.

The sluggish world-wide economy isn't hurting other operations of the parent company, based in Burbank, Calif. Operating income of the company's filmed entertainment segment rose 21 percent to $121.6 million for the fourth quarter, and 60 percent for the year to $508.2 million, driven by the box office success of Disney's *Beauty and the Beast, Sister Act,* and *The Hand That Rocks The Cradle,* and home video sales of *Fantasia* and *101 Dalmations.* Overall income from theme parks and resorts rose 44 percent for the quarter to $213.9 million, and 18 percent for the year to $644 million. The company's consumer products segment showed an 18 percent increase in income for the quarter to a record $60.4 million, and a 23 percent increase for the year to $283 million.

"Disney had record earnings for any film studio in 1992, and 1993 is going to be even better," said Morgan Stanley analyst Alan Kassan. "Euro Disney is the only thorn in their side."

Source: Peter Gumbel and David J. Jefferson, "Disney Continues Drive to Expand World-Wide," *The Wall Street Journal,* November 20, 1992, p. B3. Reprinted by permission of THE WALL STREET JOURNAL.

CASE 1–4 Southwest Airlines

Wally Mills is watching the clock.

At 3:15 P.M., Southwest Airlines Flight 944 from San Diego lands, on time, at Sky Harbor International Airport here. By 3:30, Mr. Mills, a rotund crew leader, and six other Southwest ramp agents must have this plane turned around and on its way to El Paso, Texas. "I think of this as a game," says Mr. Mills. "I like to play against the [gate agents] up there working with the people to see if we can beat them."

With Indy pit-stop precision, workers attach the push-back gear to the Boeing 737, unload the Phoenix bags, load the ones for El Paso, restock the galleys, and pump aboard 4,600 pounds of fuel. A last-minute bag costs the ramp crew the race with the gate agents, who have boarded 49 passengers. Then Mr. Mills puts on a headset and prepares to direct the jet away from the gate. It is 3:29.

Mr. Mills and his team have done in less than 15 minutes what other airlines, on average, need triple the time to do. That kind of hustle isn't a fluke at Southwest: 80 percent of its 1,300 flights a day get into the air as quickly as Flight 944.

"It all boils down to Herb's corporate philosophy," says Southwest pilot Roy Martin, invoking company Chairman Herb Kelleher. "Those airplanes aren't making any money while they're sitting on the ground."

In an industry decimated by nearly three years of steep losses—about $7.5 billion in red ink, in all—Southwest has a singular distinction: It makes money. In fact, the Dallas-based carrier has been profitable for all but the first 2 of its 21 years. Last week other airlines began reporting the extent to which they were ravaged by the recession and the summer's fare war, with Delta Air Lines posting a $106.7 million loss, for instance, and American parent AMR Corp. an $85 million deficit. Only Southwest showed a third-quarter profit—up 71 percent from a year earlier to $26.9 million.

How does Southwest do it? For starters, its managers have always been financially conservative, eschewing the airline acquisitions—and debt—of the past decade. Its costs are the industry's lowest, primarily because of a classic no-frills approach to service. Drawn by bargain fares, many customers are loyal to the carrier, sometimes passing up hometown airlines or even driving hours to fly Southwest. And as competitors falter, especially here in Phoenix, in Chicago, and in California, Southwest swoops in to pick up market share.

On top of this, Southwest has a highly motivated, productive work force—and one of the most fun-loving. Its flight attendants have been known to sing safety regulations to the tune of the *William Tell* Overture and to hide in overhead luggage bins to surprise passengers. The company's top government-affairs lawyers—all men—recently threw a lunchtime luau for the headquarters staff, wearing grass skirts and coconut-shell "bras" for the occasion. Mr. Kelleher, the 61-year-old chairman, is an indefatigable prankster who arm-wrestled another chief executive earlier this year to settle a dispute over an advertising slogan. He likes to impersonate Elvis.

If you've never heard of Southwest, it's probably because you live in one of the 35 states it doesn't serve. The seventh largest U.S. carrier, with annual revenue last year of $1.31 billion, Southwest has just 2.6 percent of the nation's air-travel market. It flies only as far east as Cleveland, and its route map is dominated by a series of short hops. Travel agents won't find Southwest in any of the big reservations computers because it deems booking fees too costly. They have to get in touch with the airline.

Yet within the beleaguered airline industry, tiny Southwest has become the carrier to emulate. And as airlines try to copy various aspects of its service, even some passengers who have never flown Southwest will find their air-travel experiences changing because of the maverick's success.

"We're taking much of what Southwest is doing correctly and applying it to putting [our carrier] together," says John Anderson, who this year helped launch Kiwi Airlines in Newark, N.J. Robert Crandall, chairman of AMR and American Airlines, the nation's largest carrier, has ordered up studies on whether American should convert some flights to Southwest's bare-bones style. "Airlines of that ilk have a big-time future," he predicts.

For the passenger, flying Southwest is an entirely democratic affair. There is no first class. Seats aren't assigned. Gate agents issue reusable numbered plastic cards on a first-come, first-aboard basis. And because meals are expensive and Southwest flights are so short—55 minutes, on average—expect only peanuts and drinks (with vanilla wafers or peanut butter cookies on longer flights). Shunning meal service is the primary way Southwest keeps its ground time to a minimum.

Even with this proletarian approach, Southwest carries more than two thirds of the passengers flying within Texas, the second largest market outside the West Coast. In California, where Southwest has become a dominant player, some San Jose residents drive an hour north to board Southwest's Oakland flights, skipping the local airport where American has a hub. Similarly, so many Atlantans were forgoing Delta's huge base there and driving 150 miles to Birmingham, Ala., to fly Southwest that an entrepreneur started a van service between the two airports.

"Sure you get herded on the plane, and sure you only get peanuts and a drink," says Richard Spears, vice president of a Tulsa, Okla., oil research firm. "But Southwest does everything they can to get you to the right place on time, and that's most important." Indeed, Mr. Kelleher boasts of the eight times that Southwest has won the industry's triple crown—a given month's best on-time performance, lowest customer complaints, and fewest lost bags. No other airline, he notes, has won it even once.

Mr. Spears figures it's only because of Southwest that he can keep his office in Tulsa rather than Houston, where most of his clients are. "So long as Herb keeps his prices low and his planes exactly on-time," he says, "I can promise I'll be a regular."

The efficient, low-fare, high-frequency service that Mr. Spears likes would be a lot harder to achieve if Southwest didn't have such low operating costs. Its 140-plane fleet includes just one kind of aircraft—fuel-efficient Boeing 737s—keeping maintenance costs down. (Southwest recently placed a $1.2 billion order for 34 new Boeing 737s for delivery starting in 1995.)

Despite its aggressive growth, Southwest's debt, at 49 percent of equity, is the lowest among U.S. carriers. Southwest also has the industry's highest Standard & Poor's credit rating, A-minus.

The airline spends an average $43,707 a year on salary and benefits for each unionized worker, compared with Delta's $56,816 and the industry average of $45,692, according to Airline Economics Inc. Yet workers have been known to complain when they thought they weren't busy enough. Maintenance supervisors in Kansas City felt so underworked in 1985 that four of them formed the "Boredom Club," petitioning management to increase flights from three a day.

"We had two to three hours between flights, and you can only clean so much," says Kay Porter, a charter member who now works in Southwest's training department. The Boredom Club has disbanded now that Southwest has 37 flights a day into Kansas City.

Employees say they're willing to work hard because they feel appreciated and are encouraged to have fun. An orientation video for new employees is done in rap. Flight attendants have bunny costumes for Easter and wear turkey outfits on Thanksgiving and reindeer antlers at Christmas. As the official carrier to SeaWorld in San Antonio, Southwest has three planes painted to resemble Shamu, the whale.

It was flight attendant Raelene Chilcoat who used to hide in overhead bins and pop out as passengers tried to stow bags. She says she stopped after an elderly passenger grabbed his chest and called for oxygen.

By leading from the front lines, Mr. Kelleher has forged *esprit de corps* among his troops. Ms. Chilcoat recalls one crowded flight with Mr. Kelleher aboard in which the chairman put ice in the glasses while she took drink orders. In explaining the company's placid labor relations, union head Tom Burnett, who represents Southwest mechanics and cleaners, says: "Lemme put it this way. How many CEOs do you know who come in to the cleaners break room at 3 A.M. on a Sunday passing out doughnuts or putting on a pair of overalls to clean a plane?"

Debi Marchovik, a Southwest flight attendant for six years, sums up what motivates a lot of airline's employees: "You don't want to let Herb down."

Although he is 61, questions about Mr. Kelleher's retirement or a successor are generally shrugged off at Southwest. Senior management has a tradition of longevity; Jack Vidal, vice president of maintenance, is 74. Mr.

Kelleher addresses the issue with a quick "I'm immortal" before adding, more seriously, "There's plenty of life after Herb Kelleher for Southwest Airlines."

A bigger concern is that the company's recent growth spurts might change things for the worse for employees and passengers. Currently, even with 11,500 workers, Mr. Kelleher still attaches the right name to the right face most of the time. Judy Haggart, a six-year employee in the marketing department, says Mr. Kelleher asks about her son Andrew by name. But some worry that Mr. Kelleher's personal, laugh-a-minute management style won't work as well if Southwest grows too big. The airline is so concerned that it has formed a team of 44 employees from various locations to devise ways of keeping Southwest intimate.

"You have to take into account that you're getting bigger," Mr. Kelleher says, fidgeting as usual and puffing on an ever-present Barclay. "You modify your tactics, but you don't change your strategy or your basic approach."

Southwest's approach is the byproduct of a monumental legal battle that it lost but turned to its advantage. In 1974 the carrier avoided a forced move from Dallas's Love Field to the new Dallas/Fort Worth International Airport, 30 minutes farther from downtown. But in 1978, competitors sought to have Congress bar flights from Love Field to anywhere outside Texas. The airline finally was able to wangle a compromise, now known as the Wright Amendment, that allowed flights from Love Field to the four states contiguous to Texas. Thus was born the strategy of short flights that's been a key to the carrier's success.

"As long as they stick to the formula they know and the moderate pace of expansion they have planned," says Ed Greenslet, an airline consultant, "I don't think there's any inherent reason why it runs out of room to work."

In a couple of markets, Southwest has found itself growing a lot faster than planned. In Phoenix, America West Airlines cut back service, trying to conserve cash after its Chapter 11 bankrtupcy filing last year. Southwest picked up the slack, as it did also in Chicago when Midway Airlines folded last November. In California, several big airlines abandoned the Los Angeles-San Francisco run after Southwest forced ticket prices down with a $59 one-way fare on routes to airports near those cities. Before Southwest arrived, fares had been as high as $186 one way.

Cities outside Southwest's route system beg for service. Sacramento Metropolitan Airport sent two county supervisors, the president of the chamber of commerce, and the airport director to Dallas early last year to beseech Mr. Kelleher to initiate service. A few months later, he did. The airline got 51 such requests in 1991.

On many routes, Southwest's fares are so low they compete with the bus, and can even coax people out of their cars. In June, Southwest started flights between Chicago and Columbus, Ohio, at $49 one way, $39 with restrictions. During last summer's fare wars, Southwest executives joked that they'd have to *raise* fares to match competitors.

Southwest officials don't joke much about a proposed high-speed train in Texas, however. The airline opposes the train, which it says would strike at the heart of its route system with an unfair advantage—government subsidies. "We just don't want to fight with a transportation company that has billions of dollars of government money invested in it, and access to more," Mr. Kelleher says. He has offered to drop his opposition if rail proponents vow to never take public money. "That's a fair fight," he says.

Mr. Kelleher, a New Jersey-born graduate of New York University law school, moved to San Antonio in 1961 with his Texas-born wife. (They met as students at Wesleyan University.) In 1966, Southwest founder Rollin King hired Mr. Kelleher as outside counsel, and he joined the board and bought an early stake in the airline. Southwest flew its first flight in 1971, and Mr. Kelleher was named president in 1978.

He currently owns 1.9 percent of the stock, worth $21.8 million. Nevertheless, several years ago an ad campaign exhorted, "Fly Southwest: Herb needs the money."

Source: Bridget O'Brian, "Flying on the Cheap: Southwest Airlines Is a Rare Air Carrier: It Still Makes Money," *The Wall Street Journal,* October 26, 1992, pp. A1, 7. Reprinted by permission of The Wall Street Journal.

PART

II

MARKETING SITUATION ANALYSIS

CHAPTER

5

Defining and Analyzing Markets

A broad view of the whole market is important, even when our interest is centered only on one or a few segments in the market. Mapping the entire market is necessary to understand and anticipate market changes and competitive threats. "Equipped with this map, a company can be in a position to examine all of the players serving the arena and anticipate what changes may occur between and among the segments of the map."[1] Defining markets and evaluating the opportunities they offer for sales and profits provide essential information for market targeting and positioning decisions. Market analysis (1) identifies promising business opportunities, (2) evaluates existing and potential competition, (3) guides the choice of which buyers to target, and (4) indicates the customer requirements to be satisfied by the marketing positioning strategy. Rapid change, global competition, and the diversity of buyers' needs and wants in many markets require the constant attention of market watchers to see the shifting requirements of buyers, evaluate changes in competitive positioning, and recognize opportunities for new products and services.

Markets change because of shifts in buyers' needs, new technologies, socioeconomic forces, and competitive actions. These changes create new opportunities and threats for the firms that serve the market. As an example, digital electronics is transforming the market structure of four major industries: computers, consumer electronics, communications, and entertainment.[2] The ability to convert information, sound, video, text, and images into digital form enables the use of a common base of electronic equipment.

EXHIBIT 5–1 1991 U.S. Consumer Electronics Market

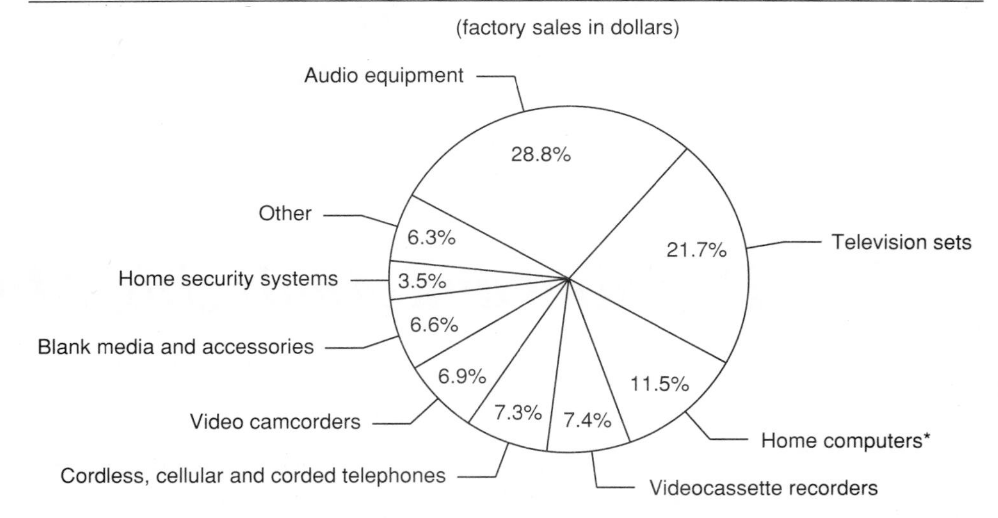

*Computers selling for less than $3,000 purchased by consumers for use in the home

Source: Electronic Industries Association

Source: "Technology," *The Wall Street Journal,* October 21, 1991, p. R15.

These integrated electronic capabilities offer an exciting potential for consumers. For example, an information appliance can be developed to perform multiple functions, such as telecommunications, computing, and visual display. The composition of the U.S. consumer electronics market is shown in Exhibit 5–1. The blurring of product-market boundaries among the industries involved creates an array of competitive challenges, including setting electronic standards, deciding where (and how) to compete, and establishing collaborative relationships between industries and companies.

We begin with a discussion of how to define product-markets and determine market boundaries. Next, the chapter describes several important characteristics of markets. A step-by-step process for market opportunity analysis follows. Finally, the relationships between market analysis, customer segments, and targeting are discussed.

DEFINING PRODUCT-MARKETS

Markets can be defined in many different ways, and they are constantly changing, creating new marketing situations. For example, even though athletic shoes perform a basic footwear function, many variations occur according to:[3]

- Specific *functions* provided: walking, running, jumping, exercise, and competing in various sports.
- Shoe and materials *technology:* sole design, sole air inflation, and space shoe material.
- Design *type:* shoes for tennis, aerobics, basketball, and other uses.
- Prices, quality, materials, and features.
- Sales to individual consumers, athletic teams, government, and other organizations.
- Private brand sales (Kmart, Sears, Penney's, and others).
- Sales in specific geographic areas (nations, regions, states, and large cities).

The many options for defining the market for athletic shoes highlight the importance of creating a market definition that can be applied to any market situation. The market should be defined so that it is strategically relevant for the organization. Thus, the definitional boundaries should include appropriate customer, product, and competitor dimensions.

Matching Needs with Product Benefits

The term *product-market* recognizes that markets exist only when there are buyers with needs and products available to satisfy the needs. Intuitively, it is easy to grasp the concept of a product-market, although there are differences in how managers define the term. Markets are groups of people who have the *ability* and *willingness* to buy something because they have a need for it.[4] Ability and willingness indicate that there is a demand for a particular product or service. People with needs and wants buy the benefits of a product or service. A product-market matches people with needs—needs that lead to a demand for a product or service—to the product benefits that satisfy those needs. Unless the product benefits are available, there is no market—only people with needs. Likewise, there must be people who have a demand for what a given product can do for them. Thus, a product-market combines the benefits of a product with the needs that lead people to express a demand for that product. Markets are defined in terms of need substitutability among different products and brands as well as in terms of the different ways in which people choose to satisfy their needs. "A product-market is the set of products judged to be substitutes within those usage situations in which similar patterns of benefits are sought by groups of customers."[5]

Both customer needs and how these needs are met change. By understanding how a firm's specific products are positioned within more general product-markets, management can monitor and evaluate changes to determine whether alternate targeting and positioning strategies and product offerings are needed. In defining a product-market, it is essential to establish boundaries that contain all of the relevant product categories that are competing for the same needs. The approach to product-market definition and analysis discussed later in the chapter encourages this perspective.

Alternative Product-Market Boundaries

While the general idea of a product-market is widely accepted, there are different ways to define a product-market. These issues can be resolved by recognizing that: (1) terms such as *generic, product type,* and *brand* may convey different meanings to managers; and (2) the size and scope of product-markets vary according to how buyers' needs and products are specified.

Generic Product-Market. This market includes a broad group of products that satisfy a general, yet similar, need. For example, several classes or types of products can be combined to form a generic product-market for consumer electronics. Audio equipment, TVs, and the other products shown in Exhibit 5–1 fall into this generic category. Note that the term generic is sometimes used in retailing to designate nonbranded versions of a specific product like paper towels.

The starting point in product-market definition is to determine the particular customer need or want that a group of products satisfies, such as housing. Since people with a similar need may not satisfy it in the same manner, generic product-markets are often heterogeneous, that is, they comprise different end-user groups. The generic product-market is a group of product types that satisfy the generic need. Included in the housing generic product-market are apartments, single-family homes, condominiums, and other forms of housing.

Product-Type Product-Market. The boundary at this level includes all brands of a particular product type or class, such as apartments. The product type is a product category or product classification that offers a specific set of benefits intended to satisfy a customer's need or want in a specific way. Thus, two different technologies that satisfy a particular need or want are different product-type product-markets. Since all of the brands in a specific product category may not compete with each other, it contains user groups with dissimilar needs (for example, people who want luxury apartments and those who desire economy apartments). Thus, product classes such as people's needs for apartments often contain market segments made up of subgroups in the product-market.

Product Variants. Differences in products within a product-type (class) product-market may exist, creating subcategories.[6] The product category "cereal," for example, has several variations, including natural, nutritional, presweetened, and regular cereals. Each variant can be designated as a product-market. Variants of coffee include ground and instant coffee, with caffeine-containing and decaffeinated varieties for each. The product-variant distinction is important as a level of analysis, providing there is limited substitution of different variants by the end-user. Large, mature product-markets may have more than one product variant level.

Competition among Brands. A subset of brands from a product-type or variant product-market may compete with each other. Brands from other product-markets that satisfy the same needs may also be competitors. Thus, a product or brand may compete in more than one product-market, which results in overlapping markets.[7] Brand level competition is discussed in Chapter 6, since it is a market segmentation issue.

Determining Product-Market Boundaries

We need to consider how broad the generic product-market definition should be. For example, defining the relevant product-market as the market served by a specific product, such as microwave ovens, excludes potentially useful information about how kitchen appliances satisfy the overall generic need for cooking food. Judgment is often involved in establishing product-market boundaries. The study of industry practices, management experience, and a thoughtful analysis of product uses will assist in defining a logical generic product-market and the product-type and variant markets within the generic product-market. In both industrial and consumer markets, the focus should be on the end-user of the product or service—the person or organization that consumes the product.

A look at the eating-away-from-home product-market highlights some of the issues encountered when trying to establish product-market boundaries. A generic product-market can be formed in several ways, using one or a combination of the categories shown in Exhibit 5–2. The important consideration is to avoid a generic definition that is either too narrow or too broad. For most purposes the entire block shown in Exhibit 5–2 is too broad, whereas one cell may be too restrictive if, by using it, competing products and brands are excluded.

Industry classifications often consist of one product type and thus are too restrictive for use in a generic definition. For example, defining product-market structure by focusing only on frozen foods eliminates from consideration competing and complementary products. Because of the interrelationships of people's needs and wants, competing products and services do not always fall into well-defined categories. An illustrative product-market structure for cereals is shown in Exhibit 5–3.

Considerations in Forming Product-Markets

The considerations that influence forming product-market boundaries include market definition alternatives, the purpose of the analysis, and the changes in market boundaries over time.

Market Definition Alternatives. Should the product-market definition start with a strategic business unit (SBU) and attempt to break it down into specific product-markets? Or, instead, should a product-market structure be developed for a firm's product that considers applications, use situations, and product alternatives? A third possibility is to start by defining the generic

EXHIBIT 5–2 Characteristics of People's Generic Needs for Food and Beverages

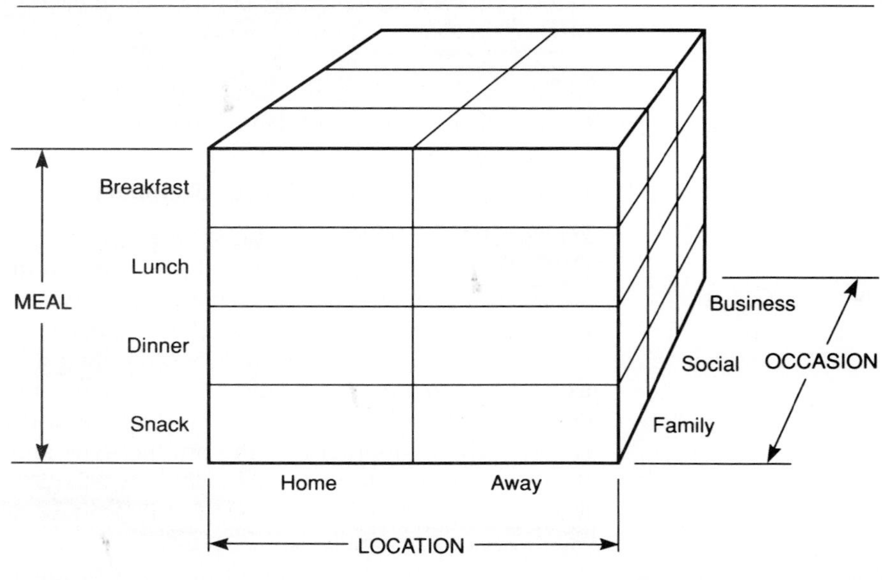

product-market and then determining the specific product-market categories that compete with each other. Each viewpoint may be useful, depending on the purpose of the analysis.

Caution should always be exercised in assuming that an existing industry classification scheme properly defines product-market boundaries. Industry-based definitions may not include different needs and alternative ways of meeting the needs. Industry classifications typically have a product rather than user orientation. Nevertheless, since industry associations, trade publications, and government agencies, generate much information about products and markets, these sources should be used in the market analysis.

Purpose of Analysis. Another consideration is the purpose of the product-market analysis. If management is deciding whether or not to exit from an SBU, primary emphasis may be on financial performance and competitive position. Detailed analysis of product-market structure may not be necessary. Alternatively, if the firm is trying to find an attractive market segment to target in a product-market, comprehensive analysis is necessary. For example, when different products can satisfy the same need, the product-market boundaries should contain all relevant products and brands. Product-market boundaries should be formed in a manner that will be of strategic

EXHIBIT 5–3 Illustrative Product-Market Structure

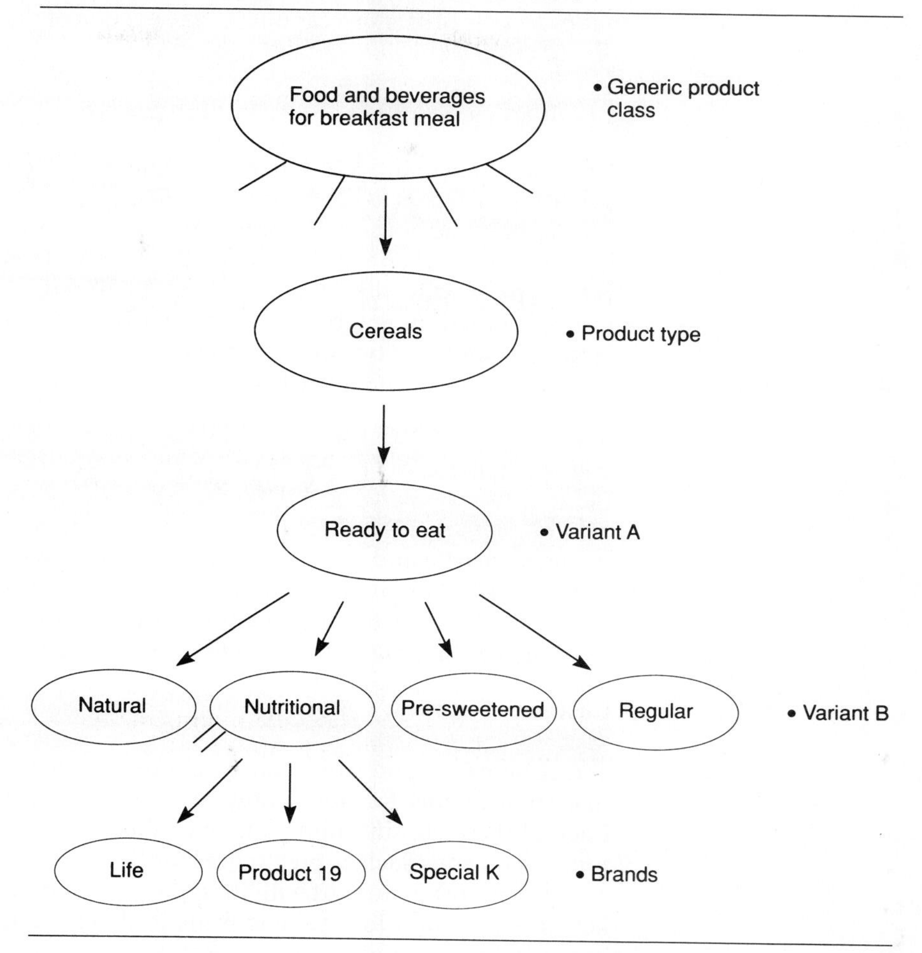

value, allowing management to capitalize on existing and potential opportunities and to help avoid possible threats.

Changing Structure of Markets. Finally, product-market boundaries may change as new technologies become available and new competition emerges. As products mature and substitutes become available, the market structure changes. Consider, for example, the influence of deregulation of financial services in the 1980s. New service alternatives modified the groups of competing firms. Bankers became brokers, and retailers offered financial services. Consumers had many new service alternatives that were previously not available because of government regulation.

Factors Affecting Market Complexity

Three aspects of markets capture a large portion of the variation in the scope of markets: (1) the *functions,* or uses, of the product by the customer; (2) the *technology* used in the product to provide the desired function; and (3) the *customer segment* using the product to perform a particular function.[8]

Customer Function. This dimension considers the function the product or service performs. It is the benefit provided to the customer. Thus, the function satisfies the needs of the customers. Functions relate to the types of use situations each user encounters.[9] In the case of athletic shoes, the function is the type of body movement of the person wearing the shoes. Importantly, multiple functions and benefits may be involved. The teenager living in the large city who buys two or three pairs of sneakers a month is meeting more than a body-movement need.

Technology. A customer function may be satisfied by products that use different technologies. The technology consists of the materials and designs incorporated into products. In the case of a service, the technology relates to how the service is rendered. For example, a surgeon may close a skin opening using needle and thread or, instead, a surgical stapler. Gas and electric utilities use different energy sources for heating, cooling, and other functions. The broader the product-market definition, the wider the range of technologies that may be used to perform the customer function.

Customer Segment. This dimension recognizes the diversity of the needs of customers for a particular product such as automobiles. The same model and color of a brand won't satisfy all buyers' needs and wants. Two broad market segments for automobile use are households and organizations. Each of these classifications can be further divided into more specific customer segments, such as preferences for European-style luxury sedans.

It is important to start with the end-user customer when defining a market. It is common for business firms to designate those who purchase an organization's products as their customers. Products move through various stages in the production and distribution process from the supply of raw materials to the final purchase by the consumer or organizational end-user. The end-user is the customer on which market definition and analysis should be focused:

> Purchases by end-users determine the market opportunity enjoyed by all firms—manufacturers and resellers. Therefore, all companies in a channel should be involved in planning and coordinating marketing strategies to generate sales from end-users. Considering end-users as markets is the best way to ensure this involvement.[10]

It is also important to define the stages in the value-added system from the raw material stage to the final uses of the product or service.[11] Analysis of the complete value-added system helps to understand how organizations cooperate to meet end-user needs and wants.

A company's marketing efforts may be directed toward more than one level in the value-added system. For example, a major producer of vegetable seeds uses its sales force to call on seed dealers and commercial vegetable growers. The seed producer does not direct its marketing activities to consumers of vegetables. However, the producer monitors vegetable consumption trends to guide its seed development, production, and marketing activities.

Differences in Product-Market Complexity. Some product-markets have clearly defined boundaries. For example, the market for large commercial aircraft can be defined in a straightforward manner. Companies like Boeing use very accurate methods for forecasting air-passenger travel demand throughout the world (see appendix). There are only three producers of large commercial aircraft and less than 100 purchasers of these aircraft. In contrast, the product-market for financial services is complex and the market boundaries are blurred. Consumer, business, and institutional end-users have a wide range of needs and wants and available products. For example, a loan may be obtained from a bank, broker, retirement fund, insurance company, or pawnshop.

MARKET OPPORTUNITY ANALYSIS

Defining and analyzing product-markets underlies most, if not all, of the strategic decisions made in a business. Analyzing market opportunity follows the steps shown in Exhibit 5–4.[12] After determining the product-market boundaries and structure, information on various aspects of the market is collected and examined. First, it is important to study the people or organizations that are the end-users in the product-market at each level (generic, product type, and variant). These market profiles of customers are useful in evaluating opportunities and guiding market targeting and positioning strategies. Next, identification and analysis of the firms that market products and services at each product-market level aid strategy development. Industry and key competitor analysis considers the firms that compete with the company performing the market opportunity analysis. Thus, industry analysis for a producer would include the producers that make up the industry. The analysis should also include firms operating at all stages in the value-added system such as suppliers, manufacturers, distributors, and retailers. The next step is a comprehensive assessment of the major competitors. The key competitor analysis should include both actual and potential competitors. Competitor analysis helps management decide what target-markets to select and which positioning strategy to use. Finally, management is interested in forecasting the size of each product-market and the rate of future growth.

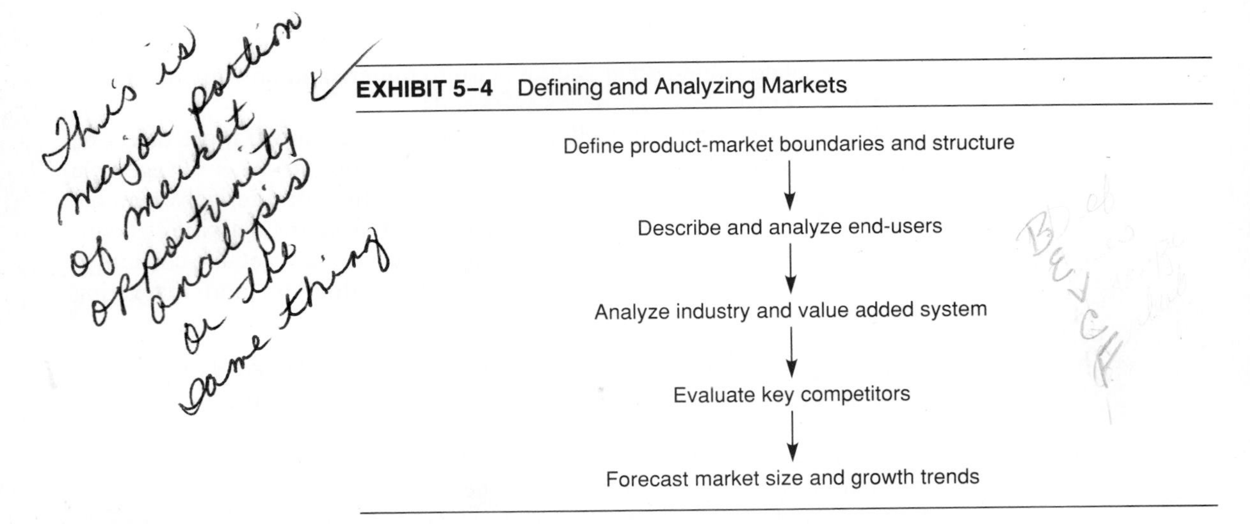

EXHIBIT 5–4 Defining and Analyzing Markets

Forecasts are needed one to three years in the future for detailed business planning, and longer-term projections are required in strategic planning.

Defining Product-Market Boundaries and Structure

A company's brands of products compete with its competitors' brands in generic, product-type, and product variant product-markets. Market definition and analysis provide important information for developing effective business and marketing strategies. The analyses also alert management to new competition. Considering only the company's brands and its direct competitors may not indicate potential competitive threats or opportunities.

Guidelines for Definition. It is helpful to identify the scope of product-markets, market size and composition, and the brand and/or product categories competing for the needs and wants of specific end-user groups. Suppose the management of a kitchen appliance firm wants to expand its mix of products. The present line of laundry and dishwashing products meets a generic need for the kitchen functions of cleaning. Other kitchen functions include heating and cooling of foods. A logical expansion would be to move into a closely related product type to gain the advantages of common distribution channels, manufacturing, advertising, and research and development. The Maytag Company illustrates this situation with its line of washers, dryers, and dishwashers. In the 1980s Maytag's management acquired several companies, expanding from a specialty producer into a full line of kitchen appliances including refrigerators, stoves, and microwave ovens.

A product-market structure can be defined by following the steps shown in Exhibit 5–5. Let's see how it is used in evaluating possible opportunities in the kitchen function product-market. In this application the generic need

EXHIBIT 5–5 Breaking Out Product-Market Boundaries

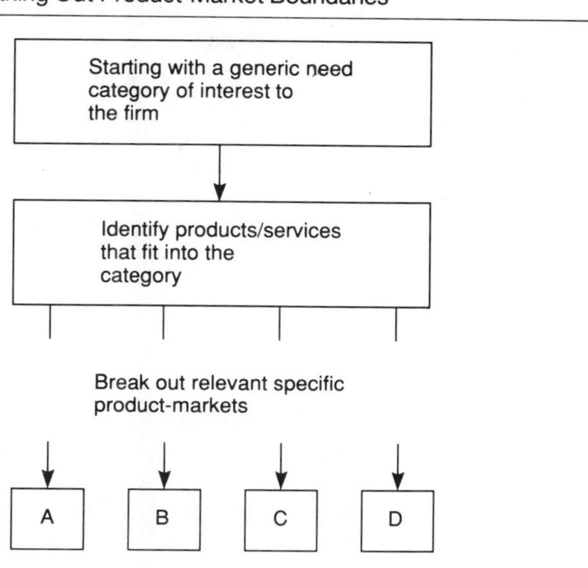

is performing various kitchen functions. The products that fit into the generic category perform the kitchen functions. The breakout of products into specific product-markets (e.g., A, B, C, and D) includes equipment for washing and drying clothing, appliances for cooling food, cooking appliances, and dishwashers. Management can analyze the buyers in various specific product-markets and the different brands competing in these product-markets. The process of defining the product-market structure begins by identifying the generic need (function) satisfied by the product of interest to management. Need identification is the basis for selecting the products that can satisfy the need.

Strengths and Limitations of Hierarchical Analysis. The approach outlined in Exhibit 5–5 defines the product-market levels using a hierarchical (structured) framework. The structured generic approach draws from management judgment and experience and from available information on products and markets. Research methods can be used with the structured approach. In complex product markets it may be necessary to form arenas of competing products and brands from a pool of many products and uses.[13] Research analysis may be essential in defining and analyzing these market structures. Preference mapping can be used for this purpose. This technique is discussed and illustrated in Chapter 6.

An illustrative product-structure for analyzing the fast-food market is shown in Exhibit 5–6. A fast-food restaurant chain such as McDonald's

EXHIBIT 5–6 Illustrative Fast-Food Product-Market Structure

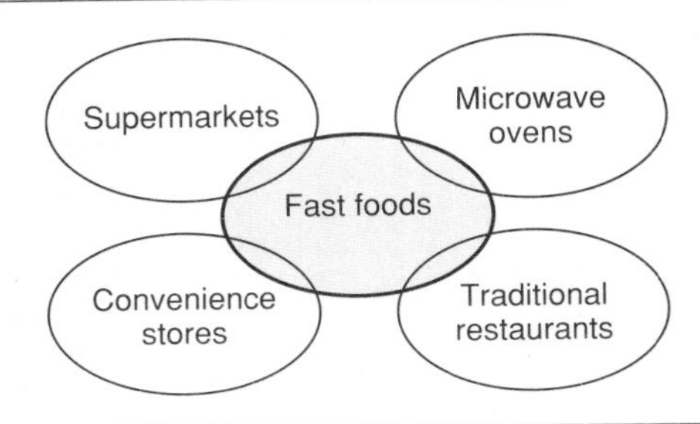

needs to include more than its regular customers and direct competitors in the market opportunity analysis. For example, microwave oven preparation of foods has affected fast-food patronage. The money saved by home food preparation enables families to eat out in a traditional restaurant such as Olive Garden. Thus, it is essential to analyze market behavior and trends in the markets shown in Exhibit 5–6. Competition may come from microwave food preparation, traditional restaurants, convenience stores, and supermarket delis.

The structured approach links families of product-markets into a hierarchy that can be systematically examined at increasingly more specific levels. We assume when using this method that the generic product-market is defined so that it contains all competing specific product-market categories. The structured approach may fail to identify a relevant product category, particularly in a complex or changing product-market situation. Thus, if not used with care, the hierarchical approach may be too rigid in some instances.

Describing and Analyzing End-Users

Profiles of buyers are developed for the generic, product-type, and product-variant levels of the product-market. Buyers are identified, descriptions are developed, purchase decision criteria are determined, and environmental influences (e.g., interest rate trends) on buyers are evaluated. Profiling the market segments within a product-market is discussed in Chapter 6.

Identifying and Describing Buyers. Typically, demographic and socioeconomic characteristics are used to identify buyers in product-markets. Various characteristics, such as family size, age, income, geographical location, sex, and occupation, are often useful in identifying buyers in consumer markets. Illustrative factors used to identify end-users in business markets include type of industry, size, location, and product application. Many published sources of information are available for use in identifying and describ-

EXHIBIT 5–7 Six Types of Supermarket Customers

Customer Type	*Description*
Avid shoppers	Traditional supermarket customers who cook practically all family meals, shop frequently, and look for bargains (slightly more than 25% of total).
Kitchen strangers	Childless men and women who find cooking an inconvenience and rely instead on take-out food and restaurants (about 20% of total).
Constrained shoppers	Low income families and individuals who buy little but basic food needs (less than 20% of total).
Hurried shoppers	Busy people who mostly eat at home but look for shopping and cooking shortcuts (less than 20% of total).
Unfettered shoppers	Primarily older working people whose kids have flown the nest, leaving them with more disposable income to spend on food (about 13% of total).
Kitchen birds	Mainly very old people who are light eaters (about 6% of total).

Source: Alan L. Otten, "People Patterns," *The Wall Street Journal,* June 13, 1989, p. B1.

ing customers. Some examples include U.S. Census data, trade association publications, and studies by advertising media (TV, radio, magazines). When experience and existing information do not clearly identify buyers, research studies may be necessary to locate and describe customers and prospects.

A research study of supermarket customers highlights the differences among buyers in the generic product-market for foods.[14] The study was conducted for the Coca-Cola Retailing Research Council. The findings indicate that changes in cooking and eating habits have created six types of supermarket customers. Each group has different shopping needs and attitudes, as described in Exhibit 5–7. The information for the study was obtained from focus groups (small-group interviews), consumer surveys, trade journal reports, and retailers' experiences.

How Buyers Make Choices. Often, simply describing buyers is not adequate for targeting and positioning decisions. Determining *why* people buy offers important insights for marketing strategy. When considering how customers decide what to buy, it is useful to analyze how they move through the sequence of steps leading to a decision to purchase a particular brand. Buyers normally follow a decision process. They begin by recognizing a need; next, they seek information; then, they identify and evaluate alternative products; and finally, they choose a brand. Of course, this process varies by product and situation. Some decisions that are repetitive and for which a buyer has past experience tend to be routine. One part of studying buyer decision processes is finding out what criteria people use in making decisions. For example, how important is the brand name of a product?

Environmental Influences. The final step in building customer profiles is to identify external factors that influence buyers. Environmental influences include the government, social change, economic shifts, technology, and other macroenvironmental factors that alter buyers' needs and wants. Typically, these factors are not controlled by either the buyer or the firms that market the product. However, substantial changes in these uncontrollable influences can have a major impact on customers. Therefore, it is important to identify the relevant external influences on a product-market and to estimate their future impact. During the past decade, various changes in market opportunities occurred as a result of uncontrollable environmental factors. Illustrations include the shifts in age-group composition, changes in tax laws affecting investments, automobile purchases, and variations in interest rates. Consider, for example, the population trends for the 50 states in the United States from 1990 to 2000. As shown in Exhibit 5–8 some states will experience high growth rates while others will decline in size.

Building Customer Profiles. The profiling process starts with the generic product-market. Exhibit 5–7 shows some examples of the information often included in the customer profile. Of course, a complete profile provides much more detail. The product-type and variant profiles are similar to the generic profiles, although they are more specific concerning customer characteristics (needs and wants, use situations, activities and interests, opinions, purchase processes and choice criteria, and uncontrollable influences on buying decisions). Baby boomers will be important buyers in many consumer markets in the 1990s. An interesting comparison of 1988 and 2000 market shares for baby boomer spending is shown in the Market Feature.

The key marketing strategy issue is deciding which buyers to target within generic, product-type, and product-variant markets. The profiles help marketing management make these decisions. More comprehensive analyses are often undertaken through market segmentation analysis, which is discussed in Chapter 6.

Industry and Value-Added System Analyses

Normally, the analysis is conducted from the point of view of a particular firm. For example, a department store chain such as Dayton-Hudson should include other retailers in its industry analysis. This analysis looks at two kinds of information: (1) a study of the industry, and (2) an analysis of the distribution channels that link together the various organizations in the value-added system serving end-users. The industry study is a horizontal analysis covering similar types of firms (e.g., department stores), whereas the distribution channel analysis focuses on the vertical value-added system of firms that supply materials and/or parts, produce products (and services), and distribute the products to end-users.

EXHIBIT 5–8 Projected Percent Change in State Populations: 1990 to 2000

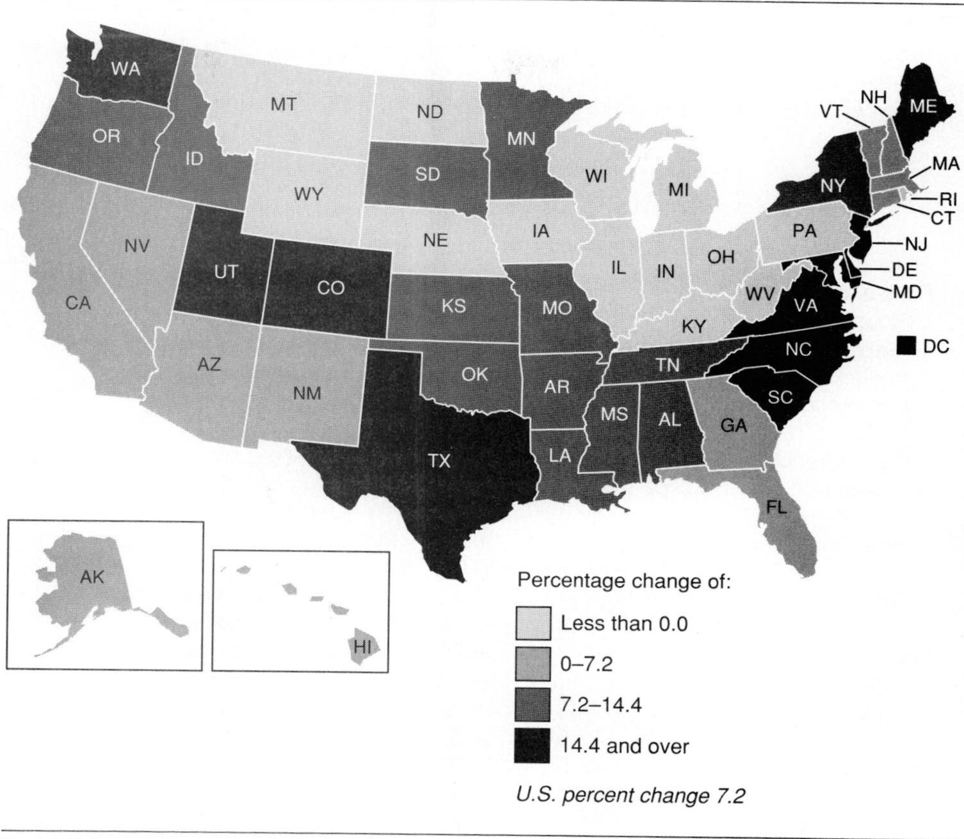

Source: U.S. Department of Commerce, Bureau of Census.

Industry Analysis. The information needed for an industry analysis includes: (1) industry characteristics and trends, such as sales, number of firms, and growth rates; and (2) operating practices of the firms in the industry, including product mix, service provided, barriers to entry, and geographical scope (see Chapter 7).

The first step in the analysis includes identifying the companies that compose the industry and developing descriptive information on the industry and its members. It is necessary to examine industry structure beyond domestic market boundaries, since international industry developments may affect regional, national, and international markets. For example, the Free Trade Agreement between Canada and the United States created a

MARKET FEATURE Consumer Spending Power Shifting to Middle-Aged Householders

The baby boomers will dominate many consumer markets in the 1990s. The householders age 35 to 54 will rise from 38 percent of all households in 1990 to 44 percent in the year 2000.

Percent of all category expenditures accounted for by householders age 35 to 54 in 1988 and 2000:

	market share 1988	market share 2000
All food	44.3%	54.1%
Food at home	42.9	52.1
Flour	38.5	47.1
Prepared flour mixes	39.3	48.8
Poultry	43.1	52.3
Dairy products	42.6	51.9
Butter	38.9	47.7
Canned/packaged prepared foods except soup/frozen	40.0	50.6
Baby food	20.4	30.1
Cola	47.6	57.8
Other carbonated drinks	47.4	57.4
Coffee	40.8	48.9
Food away from home	46.2	56.7
Meals at restaurants, carryouts, other	45.2	55.8
Alcoholic beverages	38.5	49.6
Housing	44.5	54.0
Shelter	45.4	55.3
Owned dwellings	50.9	59.7
Maintenance and repair services	38.5	44.8
Maintenance and repair commodities	45.0	53.6
Rented Dwellings	33.2	44.1
Other lodging	53.6	62.3
Utilities, fuels, public services	42.1	51.0

	market share 1988	market share 2000
Household services	40.9%	49.6%
Baby-sitting	34.3	46.1
Day-care centers, nursery, preschool	44.6	56.1
Dry cleaning and laundering	37.1	47.7
Appliance rental	32.8	43.8
Housekeeping supplies	41.7	50.8
House furnishings, equipment	45.7	55.7
Furniture	47.1	57.6
Sofas	42.4	53.3
Living-room chairs	38.8	47.9
Living-room tables	44.5	55.3
Kitchen and dining-room furniture	56.6	67.0
Infants' furniture	32.1	43.6
Outdoor furniture	59.3	67.7
Major appliances	42.1	51.0
Washing machines and dryers	45.6	55.6
Sewing machines	53.0	63.4
Small appliances and misc. housewares	50.3	59.6
Clocks	47.9	59.5
Lamps and lighting fixtures	44.9	56.9
Power and hand tools	46.7	58.2
Luggage	50.1	60.2

Source: Margaret Ambry, "More Meat in the Middle," *American Demographics*, June 1991, p. 60. Based on market share projections from the Bureau of Labor Statistics 1988 Consumer Expenditure Survey. Household projections for 2000 are from the Census Bureau. Author's calculations from *Consumer Power*.

wave of cross-border consolidations. The two countries before free trade were the world's largest trading partners, conducting some $150 billion in trade each year with one another.[15] Further changes in industry structure and composition will continue in the 1990s. Similar consolidations are occurring in Europe as firms strengthen their competitive advantage for competing in unified Europe.

Industry definition is determined by the organization conducting the market analysis. Thus, an automobile producer should base the analysis on the industry comprising automobile producers. The industry identification is based on product similarity, location at the same level in the channel of distribution (e.g., manufacturer, distributor, retailer) and geographical scope. The industry analysis should include:[16]

- Industry size, growth, and composition.
- Typical marketing practices.
- Industry changes that are anticipated.
- Industry strengths and weaknesses.

Analysis of the Value-Added System. A study of supplier and distribution channels is important in understanding and serving product-markets. While in some instances producers go directly to their end-users, many work with other organizations through distribution channels. The extent of vertical integration by competitors backward (supply) and forward toward end-users is also useful information. Alternative channels that access end-user customers should be included in the channel analysis. By looking at other distribution approaches, management can identify important patterns and trends in serving end-users. Distribution analysis can also uncover new market opportunities that are not served by present channels of distribution. Finally, information from various distribution levels can help in forecasting the end-user demand.

Analysis of the Key Competitors

Competition between brands may occur throughout the product-market structure. Brand competition is the most direct type of competition (e.g., Life, Product 19, Special K). Competition also may occur between variants (brands of natural and regular cereal) and brands of product types (cereal and pastries). While the most intense competition is at the brand level, the other types of competition may be important. For example, microwave oven food preparation in the home has negatively impacted sales in fast-food outlets.

Since a company does not normally compete on a direct basis with all firms in an industry, it is necessary to identify which firms are the key competitors. Also, if specific customer needs can be satisfied by product types from other industries, these firms should be included in the analysis. An analysis of the key competitors often covers the following areas:

- Estimated overall business strength of each key competitor.
- Present market share and past trends.
- Financial strengths and performance.
- Management capabilities (and limitations).
- Technical and operating advantages (e.g., patents, low production costs, new products).
- Description and assessment of strengths and limitations of marketing strategy.

Analysis of the structure of competition in product-markets is useful in defining markets and developing positioning strategies. Identification of strategic groups helps to find firms that are pursuing similar strategies.

Regular monitoring of what the competition is doing is important. Information should be obtained and evaluated on a regular basis. A step-by-step approach to identifying and analyzing competitors is discussed in Chapter 7.

Market Size Estimation

An important part of the market opportunity analysis is estimating the present and potential size of the market. Market size is usually measured by dollar sales and/or unit sales for a defined product-market and specified time period. Other size measures include the number of buyers, average purchase quantity, and frequency of purchase. Three measures of market size are often used: *market potential, sales forecast,* and *market share.*

Market Potential. This is an estimate of the maximum amount of product sales that can be obtained from a defined product-market during a specified time period. It includes the total potential for sales by all firms serving the product-market. Potential represents an upper limit of sales that can be achieved by all firms for a generic, product-type, or product-variant product-market. Often, actual industry sales fall somewhat below market potential because imbalances in the production and distribution systems are unable to completely meet the needs of all buyers who are both *willing* and *able* to purchase the product during the period of interest.

Sales Forecast. This estimate indicates what expected sales (rather than potential sales) are likely to be for a defined product-market during a specified time period. The industry sales forecast is the total volume of sales expected by all firms serving the product market. A forecast can be made for total sales at any product-market level and for specific subsets of the product-market (e.g., market segments). A sales forecast can also be made for a particular firm.

EXHIBIT 5–9 Product-Market Forecast Relationships (areas denote sales in $s)

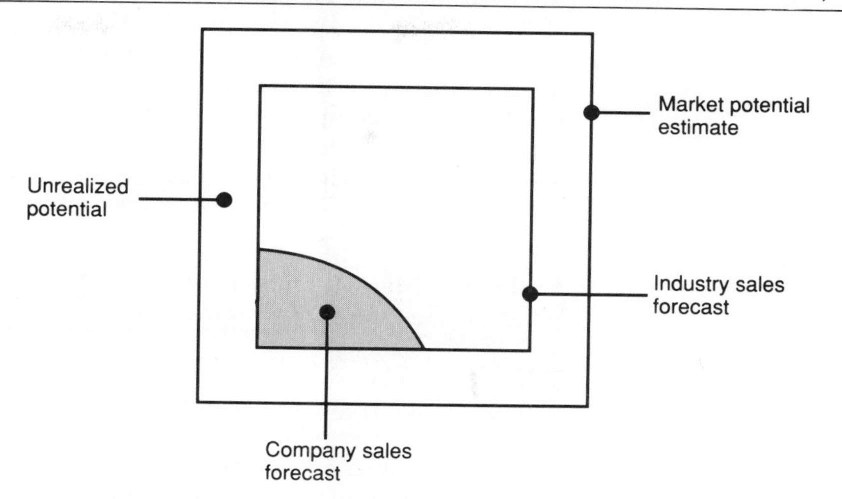

Market Share. Company sales divided by total sales of all firms for a specified product-market determines the market share of a particular firm. Market share is calculated on the basis of actual sales or forecasted sales. Market share can be used to forecast future company sales and to compare actual market position among competing brands of a product.

The relationships among the different estimates are shown in Exhibit 5–9. The area enclosed by the outside boundary of the diagram is the market potential estimate. The next largest area is the industry sales forecast. The difference between potential and the industry forecast is the amount of unrealized potential. The shaded area is the company sales forecast, and dividing this area by the industry sales forecast yields the market share forecast. Comparison of competitor and industry sales results and forecasts with company sales information should be made with caution. Sales and forecasts may vary due to differences in product-market definition, product type, time period, and other factors.

Forecasting Difficulties. Estimating future market size is difficult because sales are influenced by several factors, including the number of buyers willing and able to purchase a product; various uncontrollable influences on market demand; the marketing efforts of the organization; and competitors' marketing activities. Forecasts are needed when deploying marketing resources, scheduling production, and projecting financial requirements. The use of computerized information systems by retailers provides important information on geographical and product sales. These systems establish important databases for sales forecasting.

The forecasts made by Adolph Coors Company for its low-priced beer, Keystone, illustrate the difficulties in making accurate estimates. The sales of Keystone in the last four months of 1989 were 60 percent higher than Coors forecasted.[17] Although the company would not release sales data, industry analysts' estimates of sales ranged from 800,000 to 1 million barrels. Coors used computer-simulated forecasting models for the new brand, which did not take into account the effects of reductions in advertising in 1989 by Stroh and Heileman because of financial problems. The faulty forecast of Keystone sales created severe pressures on Coors' production capabilities.

Evaluating Market Opportunity. A large difference between market potential and forecasted sales in a market indicates an opportunity for market entry by a potential competitor or market expansion by an existing competitor. A rapid growth trend of a market is also a very important indicator of opportunity. High-growth markets are typically viewed as more attractive than mature or declining markets. Nevertheless, high-growth markets may also represent high risks because of the intensity of competition, inadequate distribution, resource requirements, and other risks.[18]

One of the most important requirements in preparing forecasts is to specify exactly what is being forecasted (defined product-markets), the time period involved, and the geographical area. Otherwise, comparisons of sales and market share with those of competing firms will not be meaningful. Several operational problems may occur in forecasting as a result of differences in measures of sales (e.g., dollars versus units), problems in defining the relevant market, leads and lags in distribution channels, promotional pricing practices, and the handling of intracompany transfers.[19] Several other forecasting guidelines are provided in the appendix to Chapter 5.

Since a company's sales depend, in part, on its marketing plans, forecasts and marketing strategy are closely interrelated. Forecasting involves "what if" analyses. Alternative positioning strategies (product, distribution, price, and promotion) must be evaluated for their estimated effects on sales. It is important to consider both estimated sales and planned marketing expenditures in determining the forecast. Also important is the variation in production (and distribution) costs for alternative sales forecasts. The impact of different sales forecasts must be evaluated from a total business perspective. These forecasts affect production planning, human resource needs, and financial requirements.

Geographical Scope of Markets

Markets range from a city to the world. Management's interest in the market may be local, regional, national, international, or global. The important issue is to establish the geographic scope of the analysis, taking into account both the locations of buyers and the market focus of the organization. In some instances these views of the market may be identical. If management's focus is narrower than the natural market boundaries, the market opportunity analysis should be of sufficient scope to identify potential competitors in the firm's market area.

The market for Hispanic foods in the United States has some interesting geographical characteristics. Ten metropolitan markets account for nearly three fourths of the Hispanic population in the United States. The total population is estimated to exceed 30 million by 2000, compared to less than 10 million in 1970.[20] The largest is Los Angeles, followed by New York, Miami, Chicago, and San Antonio. The Hispanic market for foods is influenced by the consumer's country of origin. New York food preferences are different from those of Hispanics in the Southwest. Goya Foods, Inc. dominates the Hispanic food market, concentrating its market position on the East Coast and the Midwest. The company is also expanding its marketing efforts to Mexican-Americans. The tastes and preferences of the Hispanic population also affect the total population, as shown by the fact that sales of salsa products pushed ahead of catsup in 1991.

Consumer and Organizational Markets

The steps in defining and analyzing markets (Exhibit 5–4) can be followed to study both consumer and organizational end-user markets. Analysis of sales opportunities at intermediate levels of the value-added system should start from the end-user markets that determine intermediate level sales. The demand for sales to distribution channel organizations is derived from end-user demand for products and services. For example, Burlington Northern Railroad markets its intermodal services through brokers and trucking firms to end-user manufacturing companies. The demand for the railroad's services is determined by the transportation needs of the manufacturers.

A distinction is often made between business marketing and consumer marketing. Yet there may be more similarities than differences between industrial and consumer buyers. Fern and Brown argue convincingly that marketing professionals should avoid creating a dichotomy between the two areas.[21] They suggest that commonalities between the two types of buyers provide a potentially more useful frame of reference. The bases of comparison they recommend include buying center size, buyer's knowledge, frequency of purchase, and market concentration.

MARKET ANALYSIS, CUSTOMER SEGMENTS, AND TARGETING

The market opportunity analysis provides a framework for evaluating the markets in which the organization's brands now compete or are expected to compete in the future. Defining and analyzing a product-market accomplishes the following objectives:

1. It describes the broad customer/competitor arena of interest to a company.

2. It shows the market boundaries for guiding more comprehensive customer segment analysis.
3. It may identify one or more broad customer segments that can be targeted by the firm (Exhibit 5–7 is illustrative).

The chapter concludes by discussing the relationships among customer segments, segment requirements, competitive advantage, and market size forecasts.[22]

Customer Segments

The product attributes end-users prefer in most product-markets are diverse. Typically, subsets of brands in a product-market compete against each other. Brands may also compete across two or more product-market boundaries (for example, a foreign vacation versus an automobile purchase). The market opportunity analysis is an essential first step in customer segment analysis. The objective of segmentation is to identify groups of buyers within the product-market that have similar requirements. The customer segments are possible market targets for a company.

Exhibit 5–10 illustrates ways to segment the hotel lodging product-market. An additional breakdown can be made on the basis of business and household travelers. These categories may be further distinguished by individual customer and group customer segments. Groups may include conventions, corporate meetings, and tour groups. Several possible segment cells can be distinguished. Consider, for example, Marriott's Courtyard hotel chain. These hotels fall into the midpriced category and are targeted primarily to frequent business travelers who fly to destinations, are in the 40-plus age range, and are in a high-income group.

We examine market segmentation in Chapter 6. Market definition and analysis supplies essential information for guiding segmentation efforts.

Segment Requirements

A successful marketing strategy results from matching customer requirements with products or services that satisfy buyers' expectations. The market analysis should identify the needs of customers. This is the purpose of the customer profile. When the product-market contains buyers with different needs, each segment of interest to an organization should be examined to identify its customer requirements and evaluate targeting opportunities.

Various customer segments may exist in a product-market such as hotel lodging services (Exhibit 5–10). The customers in each segment often have specific needs and wants that differ from those of customers in other segments. Marriott's decision to target the midpriced business segment with its Courtyard chain was the result of extensive analysis of the needs of buyers in this segment. Customer and competitor research determined that travelers would respond to hotels offering attractive facilities, quiet atmosphere,

EXHIBIT 5–10 Product-Market Segment Dimensions for Hotel Lodging Services

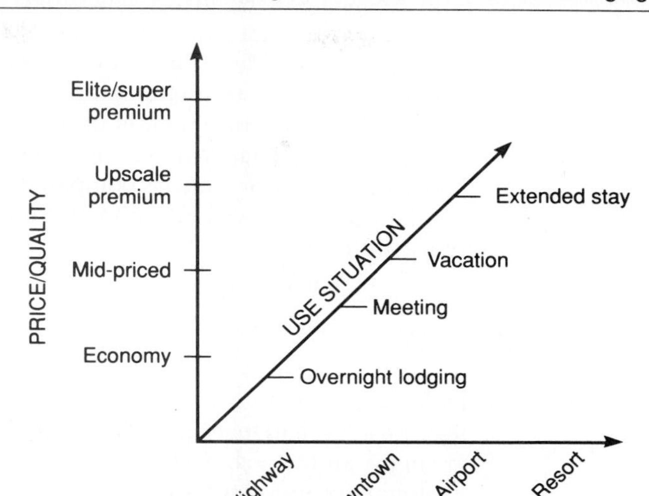

quality service, large rooms, and convenient locations. The Courtyard hotels are designed to appeal to individual and small-group travelers rather than large conference groups. Courtyard's rooms are comparable to Marriott's upscale premium rooms, but the properties do not have extensive conference facilities and services.

Competitive Advantage

The purpose of targeting one or more customer segments is to gain a competitive advantage by achieving a high level of customer satisfaction in each targeted segment. The stronger the competitive advantage of a company, the better opportunity there is for market position and profits. Evaluation of competitive strengths and weaknesses provides the basis for deciding *where* to compete.

Marriott's management decided to enter the medium-priced segment of the individual business traveler market because their studies indicated that the competition was not effectively serving the segment. Holiday Inn, Howard Johnson, and Ramada Inn were vulnerable to a strong competitor offering high-quality service, good locations, and competitive prices. These firms had allowed their facilities to deteriorate. Marriott has a reputation for achieving high customer satisfaction and profitable performance. This segment was attractive to Marriott because of the slow growth and strong competition forecast for its upscale/premium market segment.

Sales forecasts of target markets are needed so that management can estimate the financial attractiveness of both new and existing market opportunities. The market potential and growth estimates gauge the overall attractiveness of the market. The sales forecast for the company's brand in combination with cost estimates provides a basis for profit projections. The decision to enter a new market or to exit from an existing market depends heavily on financial analyses and projections. Alternate market targets under consideration can be compared using sales and profit projections. Similar projections of key competitors are also useful in evaluating market opportunities.

SUMMARY

Defining and analyzing product-markets is essential to making sound strategic business and marketing decisions. The uses of product-market analyses are many and varied. An important aspect of market definition and analysis is moving beyond a product focus by incorporating market needs into the analysts' viewpoint.

This chapter examines the nature and scope of product-market structure. By using different levels of aggregation (generic, product type, and product variant), products and brands are positioned within more aggregate categories, thus helping to better understand customers, product interrelationships, industry structure, distribution approaches, and key competitors. This approach to product-market analysis offers a consistent guide to needed information, regardless of the type of product-market being analyzed. Analyzing market opportunity includes (1) defining product-markets, (2) describing and analyzing end-users, (3) conducting industry and value-added system analyses, (4) evaluating key competitors, and (5) estimating market size and growth rates.

This hierarchical approach to product-market definition has possible deficiencies. Product-market boundaries are highly dependent on how the generic product-market is defined. Analysis and interpretation will be difficult if the definition is too broad or if market boundaries are blurred. At the other extreme, very narrow product-market boundaries may exclude relevant competing product categories. This approach may also encourage a product or supply orientation unless customer needs are the focal point of the definition process.

An important part of product-market analysis is forecasting sales. The forecasts often used in product-market analysis include estimates of market potential, sales forecasts of total sales by firms competing in the product-market, and a sales forecast for the firm of interest. This information is needed for various purposes and is prepared for different units of analysis, such as type of product, brands, and geographical areas. The forecasting approach and techniques should be matched to the organization's needs. Forecasting methods are examined in the appendix.

Market structure definition and analysis establish an important foundation for market segment identification and analysis of competitive advantage. Typically, an organization targets one or more market segments within a product-market. A product-market must be studied to determine if customer segments are present within the market. Methods of segmenting markets are discussed in Chapter 6.

QUESTIONS FOR REVIEW AND DISCUSSION

1. Discuss the important issues that should be considered in defining the product-market for a totally new product.
2. Under what product and market conditions is the consumer more likely to make an important contribution to product-market definition?
3. What recommendations can you make to the management of a company competing in a rapid growth market to help it identify new competitive threats early enough so that counterstrategies can be developed?
4. There are some dangers in concentrating product-market analysis only on a firm's specific brand and those brands that compete directly with a firm's brand. Discuss.
5. Using the approach to product-market definition and analysis discussed in the chapter, select a brand and describe the generic, product type, and brand product-markets of which the brand is a part.
6. For the brand selected in question 5, indicate the kinds of information needed to conduct a complete product-market analysis. Suggest sources for obtaining each type of information.
7. Discuss the conditions that might favor the use of a research method for product-market definition and analysis.
8. Many of the popular forecasting techniques draw from past experience and historical data. Discuss some of the more important problems that may occur in using these methods.

NOTES

1. William E. Rothschild, "Surprise and Competitive Advantage," *The Journal of Business Strategy,* Winter 1984, p. 10.
2. G. Pascal Zachary, "Blurred Borders: Industries Find Growth of Digital Electronics Brings in Competitors," *The Wall Street Journal,* February 18, 1992, pp. A1 and A8.
3. The idea for this illustration is based on George S. Day, *Strategic Marketing Planning: The Pursuit of Competitive Advantage* (St. Paul, MN: West Publishing, 1984), p. 72.
4. This discussion is based upon suggestions provided by Professor Robert B. Woodruff of the University of Tennessee, Knoxville.
5. Rajendra K. Srivastava, Mark I. Alpert, and Allan D. Shocker, "A Customer-Oriented Approach for Determining Market Structures," *Journal of Marketing,* Spring 1984, p. 32.

6. Day, *Strategic Marketing Planning,* p. 75.
7. Srivastava, Alpert, and Shocker, "A Customer-Oriented Approach for Determining Market Structures," pp. 32–33.
8. Derek F. Abell, *Defining the Business: The Starting Point of Strategic Planning* (Englewood Cliffs, NJ: Prentice-Hall), 1980.
9. George S. Day, "Strategic Market Analysis: A Contingency Perspective" (Working Paper, University of Toronto, July 1979).
10. David W. Cravens, Gerald E. Hills, and Robert B. Woodruff, *Marketing Management* (Homewood, IL: Richard D. Irwin, 1987), p. 98.
11. Day, *Strategic Marketing Planning,* pp. 77–78.
12. Cravens, Hills, and Woodruff, *Marketing Management,* pp. 100–20.
13. Srivastava, Alpert, and Shocker, "A Customer-Oriented Approach for Determining Market Structures," pp. 32–45.
14. Alan L. Otten, "People Patterns," *The Wall Street Journal,* June 13, 1989, p. B1.
15. "The North American Shakeout Arrives Ahead of Schedule," *Business Week,* April 17, 1989, pp. 34–35.
16. Cravens, Hills, and Woodruff, *Marketing Management,* pp. 110–11.
17. Marj Charlier, "Keystone Is Heady Success, Coors Says, Citing Fantasy Ads, Rival Beers' Woes," *The Wall Street Journal,* February 2, 1990, p. B3.
18. David A. Aaker and George S. Day, "The Perils of High-Growth Markets," *Strategic Management Journal* 7 (1986), pp. 409–21.
19. Bernard Catry and Michel Chevalier, "Market Share Strategy and the Product Life Cycle," *Journal of Marketing,* October 1974, p. 29.
20. Alfredo Corchado, "Campbell Soup Is Seeking To Be Numero Uno Where Goya Reigns," *The Wall Street Journal,* March 28, 1988, p. 18.
21. Edward F. Fern and James R. Brown, "The Industrial/Consumer Marketing Dichotomy: A Case of Insufficient Justification," *Journal of Marketing,* Spring 1984, pp. 68–77.
22. The following discussion is drawn from Cravens, Hills, and Woodruff, pp. 116–20.

APPENDIX 5A

Forecasting Guidelines

The steps in developing sales forecasts consist of: (1) defining the forecasting problem, (2) identifying appropriate forecasting techniques, (3) evaluating and choosing a technique, and (4) implementing the forecasting system. A brief review of each step indicates important issues and considerations.[1]

Defining the Forecasting Problem

The requirements the forecasting method should satisfy and the output required must be decided. Illustrative requirements include the time horizon, level of accu-

[1]The following discussion is based on Lawrence R. Small, *Sales Forecasting in Canada* (Ottawa: The Conference Board of Canada, 1980), pp. 3–7.

racy desired, the uses to be made of the forecast results, and the degree of disaggregation (nation, state, local), including product/market detail, units of measurement, and time increments to be covered.

Identify, Evaluate, and Select Forecasting Technique(s)

Since several forecasting methods are available, each with certain features and limitations, the user's needs, resources, and available data should be matched with the appropriate techniques. Companies may incorporate two or more techniques into the forecasting process. Typically, one technique is used as the primary basis of forecasting, whereas the other technique is used to check the validity of the primary forecasting method. Also, techniques offer different outputs. Some are effective in obtaining aggregate forecasts, and others are used to estimate sales for disaggregated units of analysis (e.g., products). An overview of the major forecasting techniques is provided in the next section.

Implementation

Many firms begin with very informal forecasting approaches based on projections of past experience coupled with a subjective assessment of the future market environment. As the forecasting needs increase, more formalized methods are developed. Factors that often affect the choice of a forecasting system include the type of corporate planning process used, the volatility and complexity of markets, the number of products and markets, and the organizational units that have forecasting needs.

FORECASTING TECHNIQUES

The major approaches used to prepare forecasts are briefly described. Forecasting techniques generally follow two basic avenues. The first involves making direct estimates of brand sales. The second forecasts brand sales as a product of several components (e.g., industry sales and market share).[2] Several methods used for forecasting sales are described below:

Judgmental Forecasting. A common approach relies on a jury of executive opinion to obtain sounder forecasts than might be made by a single estimator. To put the results in better perspective, the jury members are usually given background information on past sales, and their estimates are sometimes weighted in proportion to their convictions about the likelihood of specific sales levels being realized.

Sales Force Estimates. The sales personnel of some firms—field representatives, managers, or distributors—are considered better positioned than anyone else to estimate the short-term outlook for sales in their assigned areas.

Users' Expectations. Although the dispersion of product users in many markets (or the cost of reaching them) would make such an approach impractical, some manufacturers serving industrial markets find it possible to poll product

[2]Vithala R. Rao and James E. Cox, Jr., *Sales Forecasting Methods: A Survey of Recent Developments* (Cambridge, MA: Marketing Science Institute, 1978), p. 17.

users about their future plans, then use this information in developing their own forecasts.

Traditional Time-Series Analysis. In a familiar approach, the historical sales series may be broken down into its components—trends and cyclical and seasonal variations, including irregular variations—which are then projected. Time-series analysis has the advantage of being easy to understand and apply. But there is a danger in relying on strictly mechanized projections of previously identified patterns.

Advanced Time-Series Analysis. For short-term forecasting purposes, several advanced time-series methods have been generating new interest and acceptance. Most rely on a moving average of the data series as their starting point, and requisite computer software facilitates their use. The methods include variants of exponential smoothing, adaptive filtering, Box Jenkins models, and the state-space technique. All assume that future movements of a sales series can be determined solely from the study of its past movements. However, certain of these methods have the alternative advantage of being able to take into account external variables as well.

Econometric Methods. The econometric approach provides a mathematical simplification or "model" of measurable relationships between changes in the series being forecast and changes in other related factors. Such models are employed most often in the prediction of overall market demand, thus requiring a separate estimate of a company's own share. Increased interest in this approach reflects a growing concern over macroeconomic events as well as a preference for spelling out assumptions that underlie forecasts.

Input-Output Analysis. When developing forecasts for intermediate or commodity products, some firms are finding it advantageous to employ input-output measures within comprehensive forecasting systems that begin with macroeconomic considerations and end with estimates of industry sales. Still other methodologies must be employed in such systems, and specialists are required for the correct application and interpretation of input-output analysis.

New-Product Forecasting. New products pose special problems that are hard for the forecaster to circumvent. A sales forecast for a new product may rest upon any of several bases, including results of marketing research investigations, assumptions about analogous situations in the past, or assumptions about the rate at which users of such products or services will substitute the new item for ones they are presently buying.[3]

Several advantages and limitations of the various forecasting techniques are highlighted in Exhibit 5A–1. A more comprehensive discussion of forecasting techniques is provided by David M. Georgoff and Robert Murdick, "Managers' Guide to Forecasting," *Harvard Business Review,* January–February 1986, pp. 110–20.

---

[3]David L. Hurwood, Elliott S. Grossman, and Earl L. Bailey, *Sales Forecasting* (New York: The Conference Board, Inc., 1978), pp. i–ii.

EXHIBIT 5A–1 Summary of Advantages and Disadvantages of Various Forecasting Techniques

Sales Forecasting Method	*Advantages*	*Disadvantages*
User expectations	1. Forecast estimates obtained directly from buyers 2. Projected product usage information can be greatly detailed 3. Insightful method aids planning marketing strategy 4. Useful for new product forecasting	1. Potential customers must be few and well defined 2. Does not work well for consumer goods 3. Depends on the accuracy of user's estimates 4. Expensive, time-consuming, labor intensive
Sales force composite	1. Involves the people (sales personnel) who will be held responsible for the results 2. Is fairly accurate 3. Aids in controlling and directing the sales effort 4. Forecast is available for individual sales territories	1. Estimators (sales personnel) have a vested interest and therefore may be biased 2. Elaborate schemes sometimes necessary to counteract bias 3. If estimates are biased, process to correct the data can be expensive
Jury of executive opinion	1. Easily done, very quick 2. Does not require elaborate statistics 3. Utilizes "collected wisdom" of the top people 4. Useful for new or innovative products	1. Produces aggregate forecasts 2. Expensive 3. Disperses responsibility for the forecast 4. Group dynamics operate
Delphi technique	1. Minimizes effects of group dynamics	1. Can be expensive and time-consuming
Market test	1. Provides ultimate test of consumers' reactions to the product 2. Allows the assessment of the effectiveness of the total marketing program 3. Useful for new and innovative products	1. Lets competitors know what firm is doing 2. Invites competitive reaction 3. Expensive and time-consuming to set up 4. Often takes a long time to accurately assess level of initial and repeat demand
Time-series analysis	1. Utilizes historical data 2. Objective, inexpensive	1. Not useful for new or innovative products 2. Factors for trend, cyclical, seasonal, or product life-cycle phase must be accurately assessed and included 3. Technical skill and good judgment required
Statistical demand analysis	1. Great intuitive appeal 2. Requires quantification of assumptions underlying the estimates 3. Allows management to check results 4. Uncovers hidden factors affecting sales 5. Method is objective	1. Factors affecting sales must remain constant and be accurately identified to produce an accurate estimate 2. Requires technical skill and expertise 3. Some managers reluctant to use method due to the sophistication

Source: Adapted from Gilbert A. Churchill, Jr., Neil M. Ford, and Orville C. Walker, *Sales Force Management,* 4th ed. (Homewood, IL: Richard D. Irwin, 1993), pp. 204–5.

Sales Forecast Illustration

The annual forecast of world market demand and airplane supply requirements prepared by the Boeing Commercial Airplane Group is an interesting example of the use of forecasting methods. Copies of the *Current Market Outlook* report can be obtained from the company. The forecasting approach and how the forecasts are used are described in Exhibit 5A–2.

EXHIBIT 5A–2 How Boeing Forecasts Aircraft Demand

A long-range forecast is developed annually at Boeing to determine the outlook for world air travel and cargo growth and the consequent commercial jet airplane requirements to meet this demand plus replacement of retired airplanes. It consists of the following:

- Air travel market forecasts (by econometric model*) based on—
  Changes in the cost of air travel.
  Changes in the income of the travel population.
- Airplane retirement assumptions.
- Forecasts for commercial jet airplanes.
  Airplane deliveries in dollars.
  Airplane deliveries in units.
  Categorization by range and size.

The forecasts are used within the Boeing business planning process to develop—

- Financial and production planning.
- Competitor analyses.
- Work force and inventory requirements.
- Resource allocations.
- New-product evaluations.

The market forecasts reflect the Boeing goal of producing a reasonable outlook for the future of the commercial jet aviation industry. The "balanced" single-line forecast is provided with the expectation that future results will have an equal chance of being higher or lower and will fluctuate around this forecast. There are no "cycles"† in the forecast. Internal planning is driven by this forecast, tempered by other forecasts involving risk and opportunities (i.e., evaluation of upside and downside potential), and melded with the near-term order base and sales forecasts.
This document provides a summary of the baseline market forecast prepared by Boeing. It is separated into three major sections.

- The world market demand involving growth in air travel and cargo plus replacement of retired airplanes.
- The airplane supply requirement.
- The manufacturer's position in the industry.

---

*Boeing models are based on the interrelationships between variables that represent the forces believed to drive the commercial jet aviation industry. Airplane deliveries predicted by the forecast process are based on judgments about reasonable future values for variables in the models and are constrained to match industry requirements.

†Cycles, by definition, mean regularly sequenced phenomena. The Boeing view is that unique circumstances caused the major adverse changes in the historical market and that such events are random and, therefore, not predictable (e.g., energy crises, wars). Even economic growth is hardly cyclical. Good monetary and fiscal policies can prevent major economic disruptions. Only two major world recessions have occurred in the jet era, and they were begun by energy crises.

Source: *Current Market Outlook,* Boeing Commercial Airplane Group, February 1992, p. 1.1.

Portions of Boeing's product delivery forecast are shown in Exhibit 5A–3. It is one of many passenger demand and aircraft supply forecasts included in the Boeing report. The report is a penetrating analysis of the commercial aircraft industry. It highlights the importance of forecasting in this industry, where new aircraft designs require several years.

EXHIBIT 5A–3 Product Delivery Forecast

World Commercial Jet Airplane Deliveries

- Total commercial jet airplane delivery requirements are forecast to amount to $380 billion through the year 2000 (1992 dollars) and $857 billion through the year 2010. This is nearly the same level as forecast in last year's *Current Market Outlook.*
- Non-U.S. airlines' future share of the market is 64%, up from 62%, from 1970 through 1990.
- 65% of demand through the year 2000 will come from growth and 35% from replacement. Through 2010, 73% of the demand is for growth and 27% for replacement because two thirds of the fleet retirements are assumed to occur through the year 2000.
- Delivery dollars will average $45 billion per year through the year 2010, 150% higher than the 1970 to 1991 average of $18 billion.
- The Asia/Pacific area will show the greatest percentage gain.
- The U.S. market will maintain its position as the largest market.
- The total backlog of orders and firm options is expected to surpass the ASM capacity required in the mid-1990s. This reflects airline and leasing company strategy to protect upside potential requirements.

World Annual Commercial Airplane Deliveries

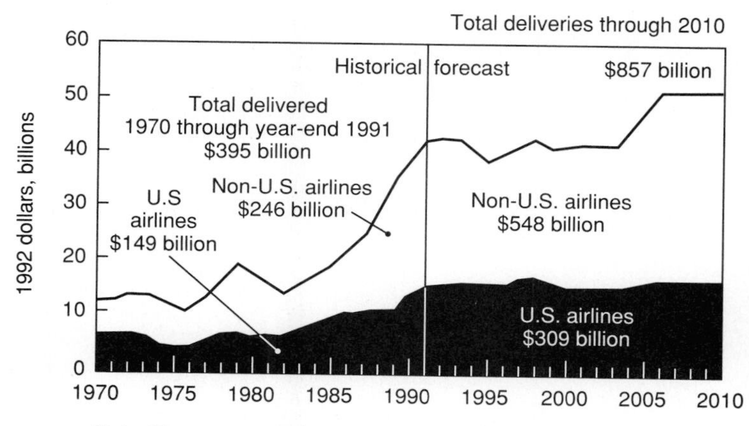

Note: Three-year moving average.

EXHIBIT 5A–3 *(continued)*

Share for Airlines by Geographic Area (1992) delivery dollars)

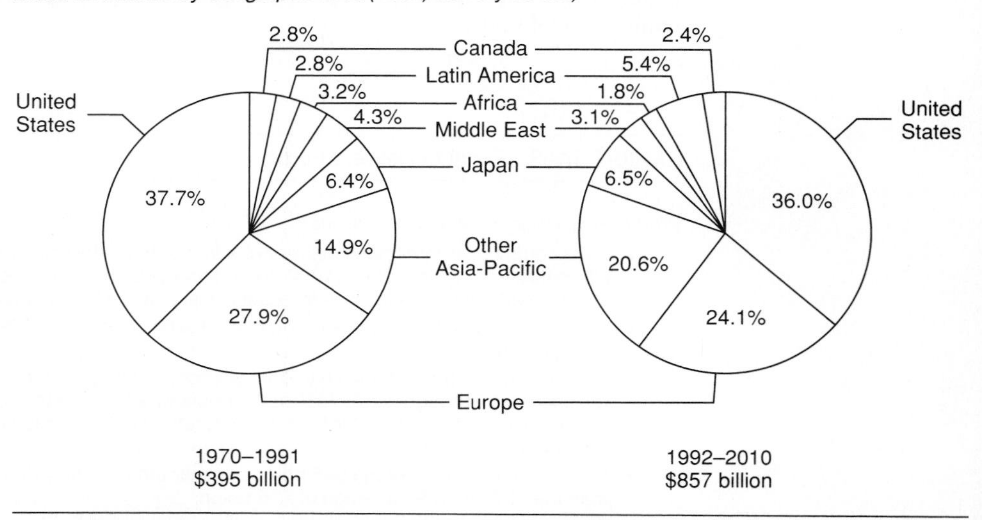

Source: *Current Market Outlook,* Boeing Commercial Airplane Group, February 1992, pp. 304, 305.

CHAPTER

6

Market Segmentation

Understanding how buyers' needs and wants vary guides marketing strategy design. Buyers often display different preferences and priorities for products. They demand products and services that satisfy their needs at competitive prices. Buyers vary according to how they use products, the needs and preferences that the products satisfy, and their consumption patterns. These differences create market segments. Market segmentation is the process of identifying and analyzing the buyers in a product-market with similar response characteristics (e.g., frequency of purchase).

Consider segmenting the market for paper. One way to segment it is according to how the paper is used. The uses of paper include newspapers, magazines, books, announcements, letters, and other applications. Crane & Company, a firm competing in this market, is the primary supplier of paper for printing currency.[1] This segment of the high-quality paper market comprises a single customer—the U.S. Treasury. The company's commitment to making quality products has protected its competitive advantage in this segment since 1879. In 1991 Crane introduced a new currency paper with a polyester thread that distinguishes currency from counterfeit bills. The other three quarters of Crane's $143 million in sales includes fine writing papers and other high-quality paper products.

Market segmentation is a process for examining differences among the buyers in a product market. We begin the chapter with a discussion of segmentation, targeting, and positioning, then consider the purpose of segmentation and the variables used to identify market segments. The next chapter discusses the methods for forming market segments, and describes the process of analyzing market segments. Finally, several new directions in segmentation are considered.

SEGMENTATION, TARGETING, AND POSITIONING

Market segmentation, market targeting strategy, and positioning strategy are closely interrelated. *Market segmentation* is the process of placing the customers in a product-market into subgroups so that the buyers in a segment will respond similarly to a particular marketing positioning strategy. Response similarities are indicated by the amount and frequency of purchase, loyalty to a particular brand, and other measures of responsiveness. Thus, segmentation is an identification process aimed at finding subgroups of buyers within a total market. The opportunity for segmentation occurs when differences in buyers' demand (response) functions allow market demand to be disaggregated into segments, each with a distinct demand function.[2] The term "market niche" is sometimes used to identify a market segment.

Segmentation identifies customer groups within a product-market, each containing buyers with similar preferences toward specific product attributes. Each segment is a possible market target for the organizations competing in the market. Segmentation offers a company an opportunity to effectively match its products or services to buyers' requirements. Customer satisfaction can be improved using a segment focus. Segmentation may occur at the generic, product type, and product variant levels of market structure.

Market targeting is the process of evaluating and selecting each segment that a company decides to serve. It may target one, a few, or several segments. For example, the high-quality paper segment for printing currency is one of Crane's market targets.

As discussed in Chapter 4, a *positioning strategy* is the combination of marketing actions management takes to meet the needs and wants of each market target. The strategy comprises product(s) and supporting services, distribution, pricing, and promotion components. Management's choices about how to influence target buyers to favorably position the product in their eyes and minds help in designing the positioning strategy. For example, Crane seeks to position its currency paper as a high-quality paper that can effectively meet the functional requirements of paper currency. The polyester thread included in the paper design to aid counterfeit detection is part of Crane's positioning strategy.

Market segmentation lays the groundwork for market targeting and positioning strategies. The skills and insights used in segmenting a product-market may give a company important competitive advantages by identifying buyer groups that will respond favorably to the firm's marketing efforts. Faulty segmentation reduces the effectiveness of targeting and positioning decisions.

SEGMENTATION AND COMPETITIVE ADVANTAGE

The reality that makes segmentation analysis so critical is that the buyers in many markets are different. The following excerpt from the Massachusetts Institute of Technology study of competitiveness highlights how segmentation impacts business performance:

> All of the successful firms that we observed are making a concerted effort to develop closer ties to their customers. These ties enable companies to pick up more differentiated signals from the market and thus to respond to different segments of demand. They also increase the likelihood of rapid response to shifts in the market.[3]

We now consider (1) targeting practices, (2) competitive advantage opportunities through segmentation, and (3) choosing the level of the market to be segmented.

Targeting Practices

Companies typically appeal to only a portion of the people or organizations in a product-market, regardless of the breadth of the market targeting strategy used. Management may choose one specific segment to target, such as the Crane's targeting of the U.S. Treasury, or several segments. Alternatively, although a specific segment strategy is not used, the marketing program management selects positions the firm in the product-market to appeal to a particular subgroup within the market. Segment identification and targeting are obviously preferred. Finding a segment by chance does not provide management the opportunity to evaluate the financial and competitive advantages of different segments. When segmentation is employed, it should be by design, and the underlying analyses should lead to the selection of one or more promising target opportunity. Targeting is discussed in Chapter 9.

Segmentation and Competitive Advantage

While broad comparisons of competitive advantage can be made for an entire product-market, more penetrating insights about advantage and market opportunity are gained from market segment analyses. Examining specific market segments helps to (1) identify how to attain a closer match between buyers' preferences and the organization's capabilities, and (2) identify the organization's strengths (and weaknesses) compared to the key competitors in each segment.

Matching Preferences with Capabilities. Customer preferences can be better satisfied within a segment rather than the total market. Consider, for example, customers' needs for banking services. The banking needs of business and institutional customers vary considerably. Even within the business sector, users' needs vary by size and type of business, financial strengths, and other banking requirements. For example, using a segment-level strategy to meet customer needs helps First Business Bank perform well. Targeting companies with annual sales between $3 million and $100 million, the Los Angeles bank has a customer-focused array of services including sending couriers to pick up deposits.[4] The bank's performance has been impressive, with low loan losses and high return on equity, return on assets, and growth.

Competitive Advantage Analysis. The companies that compete in a market often have different strengths and weaknesses. Segment analysis guides actions to improve targeting and positioning advantages over competitors. Segment information helps management design effective marketing programs. First Business Bank's management recognized that the major banks in the Los Angeles market put their attention on big companies and were not adequately meeting the needs and requirements of midsize companies.[5] The gap between these customers' expectations and the actual service performance of the major banks gave First Business Bank a competitive edge. Actions were implemented to meet these needs. Founded in 1981, the bank has an objective of $1 billion in assets by 1995.

Selecting the Market to be Segmented

Market segmentation may occur at any of the product-market levels shown in Exhibit 6–1. Generic-level segmentation is illustrated by the supermarket shopper types discussed in Chapter 5 (see Exhibit 5–7) that purchase health and beauty aids. Product-type segmentation is shown by the price, quality, and features of shaving equipment. Product variant segmentation considers the segments within a product-variant category such as electric razors.

An important consideration in defining the market to be segmented is estimating the variation in buyers' needs and requirements at alternative product-market levels and identifying the types of buyers included in the market. In the First Business Bank application, management defined the product-market to be segmented as banking services for business organizations in the Los Angeles metropolitan area. Segmenting the generic product-market for financial services was too broad in scope for the bank's needs. The market definition selected by management excluded buyers (e.g., consumers) that were not of primary interest to management while including companies with different financial service needs.

EXHIBIT 6–1 Identifying the Health and Beauty Supplies Product-Market to be Segmented

Level of Competition	*Product Definition*	*Illustrative Competitors*	*Need/Want Satisfied*
Generic	Health and beauty aids	Consumer products companies	Enhancement of health and beauty
Product type	Shaving equipment	Gillette, Remington, Bic	Shaving
Product variant	Electric razors	Braun, Norelco, Remington, Panasonic	Electric shaving

IDENTIFYING MARKET SEGMENTS

Once the market to be segmented is defined, one or more variables are selected to identify segments. For example, company size was used by First Business Bank to segment the market. First, we discuss the purpose of segmentation variables, followed by a look at the variables that can be used in segmentation analyses.

Purpose of Segmentation Variables

Segmentation variables perform two important functions. The basis variable(s) is used to divide a product-market into segments. The second function is to describe or profile the segments. These variables discriminate among the segments of the product-market.[6] In practice, the distinction between the two functions is often not apparent since the same variable(s) may be used for both purposes. For example, the basis of segmentation may be company size and financial performance, as in the case of First Business Bank. The same variables also provide descriptive information about each segment.

The variables shown in Exhibit 6–2 indicate the wide range of segment bases and descriptors. Demographic and psychographic (life-style and personality) characteristics of consumers and descriptive variables for organizational buyers are of interest, since this information is available from the U.S. Census reports and other published sources. The use-situation variables consider how the buyer uses the product, such as purchasing a meal away from home for the purpose of entertainment. Variables measuring buyers' needs and preferences include attitudes, brand awareness, and brand preference. Purchase-behavior variables describe brand use and consumption (e.g., size and frequency of purchase). A closer examination of these variables highlights their uses, features, and other considerations important in segmenting markets.

EXHIBIT 6–2 Variables for Dividing Product-Markets into Segments

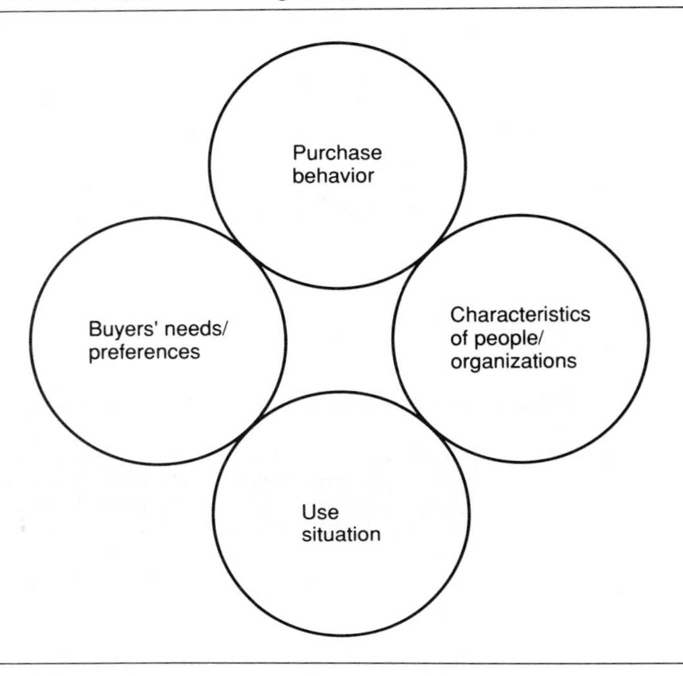

Characteristics of People and Organizations

Consumer Markets. The characteristics of people fall into two major categories: (1) geographic and demographic, and (2) psychographic (life-style and personality). Demographics are more useful in describing consumer segments than in identifying them. Nevertheless, these variables are popular because available data often relate demographics to the other segmentation variables shown in Exhibit 6–2. Geographic location is useful for segmenting certain kinds of product-markets. For example, there are regional differences in the popularity of transportation vehicles. In several states the most popular vehicle is a pickup truck. The "truck belt" runs from the upper Midwest south through Texas and the Gulf Coast states. The Ford brand is dominant in the northern half of the truck belt and Chevrolet leads in the southern half.

Demographic variables describe buyers according to their age, income, education, occupation, and many other factors. Demographic information helps to describe groups of buyers such as heavy users of a product or brand. Demographics used in combination with buyer behavior information are useful in segmenting markets, selecting distribution channels, designing advertising strategies, and other decisions on marketing strategy.

Life-style variables indicate what people do (activities), their interests, their opinions, and their buying behavior. Life-style characteristics extend beyond demographics and offer a more penetrating description of the consumer.[7] Profiles are developed using life-style characteristics. This information is used to segment markets, position products, and guide the design of advertising messages.

Personality information may be of value in gaining a better understanding of buyers. "Personality is more deep-seated than life-style since personality variables reflect consistent, enduring patterns of behavior."[8] Unfortunately, marketing research results show a weak relationship between personality variables and purchase behavior. One problem is that the personality measures used have not been related to marketing behavior. Nevertheless, some success has been achieved.

Organizational Markets. Several characteristics help in segmenting business markets. The type of industry (vertical market) is related to purchase behavior for certain types of products. For example, automobile producers purchase steel, paint, and other raw materials. This form of segmentation enables suppliers to specialize their efforts and satisfy customer needs. Industries may also be geographically concentrated, such as petrochemical processing located along the Gulf Coast of the United States. These concentrations occur because of the availability of labor and material suppliers, transportation costs, and other factors.

Variables for segmenting organizational markets include size of the company, the stage of industry development, and the stage of the value-added system (e.g., producer, distributor, retailer). Organizational segmentation is aided by first examining (1) the extent of market concentration, and (2) the degree of product customization.[9] Concentration considers the number of customers and their relative buying power. Product customization determines the extent to which the supplier must tailor the product to each organizational buyer. If one or both of these factors indicate quite a bit of diversity, segmentation opportunities may exist.

Use-Situation Segmentation

Markets can be segmented based on how the product is used. As an illustration, people may decide to dine away from home on different occasions. The meal may occur during a business meeting, a family occasion, or while on a shopping trip. Needs and preferences vary according to these occasions. Peter R. Dickson identifies several use situations that create market segment opportunities:

> Examples of situation segmentation can be found in the design of furniture, appliances, china, bicycles, motorcycles, automobiles, and camping equipment. Some lounge suites are designed for small apartments, others for beachside holiday homes and yet others for executive suites and lounge bars. Color TVs are

SEGMENTATION FEATURE Clorox Segments the Home Cleaning Product-Market

Clorox found in the mid-1970s that many of its liquid bleach customers were using the product to remove mildew stains from bathroom surfaces. No other firm had a cleaner that performed well in this use situation. Clorox's management decided to develop a new product focused exclusively on mildew removal.

Tilex was introduced in 1979 at a premium price. It was targeted to people seeking a fast and effective way to clean bathroom tile. The name helped to position the brand in the new segment. Today, Tilex has a dominant and profitable position in the segment it created.

Source: D. John Loden, *Megabrands* (Homewood, IL: Business One Irwin, 1992), pp. 185–87.

designed as feature furniture pieces for family rooms and as robust portables for trailers and bedrooms. Special refrigerators are designed for trailers and basement bars. Expensive china is designed for entertaining guests, while cheap, robust Corelle dinnerware is designed for everyday family use. There are commuting motorcycles, dirt motorcycles, farm motorcycles, and highway cruisers. Pickups and four-wheel-drive station wagons are primarily designed for different usage situations than a VW Rabbit or Rolls Royce. Camping gear is designed to be adaptable, but specialist equipment is designed for use in tropical and/or very cold climates and situations where space and weight are at a premium. The clothing and footwear market has long been person-situation segmented to accommodate not only differing sex and size but also differing weather conditions, physical activities, and social role-playing.[10]

People often find new uses for existing products. Baking soda has several uses other than as a baking additive. It is used to remove odors from refrigerators and microwave ovens and as a basic ingredient for toothpaste. The Segmentation Feature describes how Clorox found a household cleaning segment and developed Tilex to meet its needs.

Buyers' Needs and Preferences

Needs and preferences that are specific to products and brands can be used as segmentation bases and descriptors, such as brand loyalty status, benefits sought, and proneness to make a deal. Buyers may be attracted to different brands because of the benefits offered by a brand. For example, Jerome Schulman, a chemist, developed Shane toothpaste to meet the needs of people with bleeding gums and sensitive teeth.[11] The aloe-based brand is premium priced. Shane does not have a multimillion-dollar advertising budget or the endorsement of the American Dental Association. Its segment is small in comparison to the total toothpaste market. Sales of Shane approached $1 million two years after introduction. The product was available in 15 states after an initial rollout in Chicago.

Consumer Needs. Needs motivate people to act. Understanding how buyers satisfy their needs provides guidelines for marketing actions. Consumers attempt to match their needs with the products that satisfy their needs. People have a variety of needs, including basic physiological needs (food, rest, and sex); the need for safety; the need for relationships with other people (friendship); and personal satisfaction needs.[12] Measurement of the nature and intensity of a need is important in (1) determining how well a particular brand may satisfy the need, and/or (2) indicating what change in the brand may be necessary to provide a better solution to the buyer's needs.

An interesting example of segmentation based on needs is the growing desire of consumers for food that is both good-tasting and convenient.[13] Food companies are adding value to products and making them easier to use by tailoring them to the needs of working women, smaller households, and singles. These firms are increasing their profits by helping people solve the problems of food preparation. Studies by the food industry indicate that shoppers from almost every age and income bracket are not as concerned about economizing on food as their counterparts of previous decades were. Many buyers want food that is easy and quick to prepare. Interestingly, the pride of preparation and creativity that prevailed in past decades has given way to a desire to reduce effort while maintaining quality. Buyers are willing to pay for convenience. For example, chicken sells in the supermarket for less than $1 a pound, whereas chicken cordon bleu and breaded breast fillets are priced at $4 a pound or more.

Attitudes. Buyers' attitudes toward brands are important because experience and research findings indicate that such attitudes do influence behavior. Attitudes are enduring systems of favorable or unfavorable evaluations about brands.[14] They reflect the buyer's overall liking or preference for a brand. Attitudes may develop from personal experience, interactions with other buyers, or by marketing efforts such as advertising and personal selling.

Attitude information is useful in a marketing strategy development. A strategy may be designed either to respond to established attitudes or, instead, to attempt to change an attitude. In a given situation, relevant attitudes should be identified and measured to indicate how brands compare. If important attitude influences on buyer behavior are identified and a firm's brand is measured against these attitudes, management may be able to improve the brand's position by using this information. Attitudes are often difficult to change, but firms may be able to do so if buyers' perceptions about the brand are incorrect. For example, if the trade-in value of an automobile is important to buyers in a targeted segment and a company learns through market research that its brand (which actually has a high trade-in value) is perceived as having a low trade-in value, advertising can communicate this information to buyers.

Perceptions. "Perception is defined as the process by which an individual selects, organizes, and interprets information inputs to create a meaningful picture of the world."[15] Perceptions are how buyers select, organize, and interpret marketing stimuli, such as advertising, personal selling, price, and the product. Perceptions form attitudes. Buyers are selective in the information they process. As an illustration of selective perception, some advertising messages may not be received by viewers because of the large number of messages vying for their attention. Or a salesperson's conversation may be misunderstood or not received fully because the buyer is trying to decide if the purchase is really necessary while the salesperson is talking.

People often perceive things differently. Business executives are interested in how their products, salespeople, stores, and companies are perceived. Perception is important strategically in helping management to evaluate the current positioning strategy and in making changes in this positioning strategy. Perception mapping is a useful research technique for showing how brands are perceived by buyers according to various criteria. A set of attributes can be reduced through computer analyses to form two-dimensional maps showing consumer perceptions of brands. We discuss preference mapping for segmentation later in the chapter.

Purchase Behavior

Consumption variables such as the size and frequency of a purchase may be useful in segmenting consumer and business markets. Marketers of industrial products often classify customers and prospects into categories on the basis of the volume of the purchase. For example, a specialty chemical producer concentrates its marketing efforts on chemical users that purchase at least $80,000 of chemicals each year. The firm further segments the market on the basis of how the customer uses the chemical.

Since buying decisions vary in importance and complexity, it is useful to classify them to better understand their characteristics, the products to which they apply, and the marketing strategy implications of each type of purchase behavior. Buyer decisions can be classified according to the extent to which the buyer is involved in the decision and whether it is a decision-making process or an action based on habit.[16] A high-involvement decision may be infrequent, expensive, risky, and important to the consumer's ego and social needs. The decision situation may be simple or complex, depending on whether multiple brands or a single brand are considered. The classification is shown in Exhibit 6–3, based on the amount of involvement and the decision-making situations.

These categories are very broad, since the involvement and decision dimensions cover a range of situations. Nevertheless, the four types of buyer behavior provide a useful way to compare and contrast buying situations. Also, a situation may vary from individual to individual. For example, a high-involvement purchase for one person may not be such for another person.

EXHIBIT 6–3 Four Types of Buyer Behavior

	Type of Purchase Decision	
	High-Involvement	*Low-Involvement*
Decision making (information search, consideration of alternatives)	Complex decision making (medical services, autos, financial planning services, diamonds)	Impulse purchasing (cereals, snacks)
Habit (little or no information search, consideration of only one brand)	Brand loyalty (perfume, cigarettes, beverages)	Inertia (light bulbs, soaps, paper towels)

Source: Adapted from Henry Assael, *Marketing Management* (Boston: PWS–Kent Publishing, 1985), p. 127.

EXHIBIT 6–4 Illustrative Segmentation Bases and Descriptors

	Consumer Markets	*Industrial/Organizational Markets*
Characteristics of people/organizations	Age, gender, race Income Family size Life-cycle stage Geographical location Life-style	Type of industry Size Geographical location Corporate culture Stage of development Producer/intermediary
Use situation	Occasion Importance of purchase Prior experience with product User status	Application Purchasing procedure New task, modified rebuy, straight rebuy
Buyers' needs/preferences	Brand loyalty status Brand preference Benefits sought Quality Proneness to make a deal	Performance requirements Brand preferences Desired features Service requirements
Purchase behavior	Size of purchase Frequency of purchase	Volume Frequency of purchase

Exhibit 6–4 summarizes the various segmentation variables. It indicates segmentation bases and descriptors for consumer and organizational markets. As we examine the methods used to form segments, the role of these variables in segment determination and analysis is illustrated.

FORMING SEGMENTS

As we shall see shortly, the segmentation variables play an essential role in the segmentation process. The requirements for segmentation are discussed first, and then the methods of segment formation are examined.

Requirements for Segmentation

An important question is deciding if it is worthwhile to segment a product-market. Five criteria are useful for evaluating a particular segmentation scheme.[17]

Response Differences. Identifying the responsiveness of people in the product-market to different marketing program positioning strategies is central to segment identification. Variability in demand functions across the buyers in a product-market creates segments. Suppose the customers in a product-market are placed into four groups, each a potential segment. If each group responds (e.g., amount or frequency of purchase) in the same way as all other groups to any marketing mix strategy, then the groups are not market segments. If segments actually exist in this illustration, there must be differences in the responsiveness of the groups to marketing actions such as pricing. Management may simply feel—through experience and judgment—that response differences exist and that dividing the market (by age, income, industry type, and so on) will separate buyers into similar response categories. The presence of real segments requires actual response differences between the segments. After meeting this condition, the other requirements come into play.

Identifiable Segments. It must be feasible to identify the customer groups that actually display response differences. Finding the correct groups may be difficult because it is not always obvious which variables are appropriate for dividing the market into segments. For example, variations in purchase volume may occur in a market. However, it may not be possible to identify a descriptive profile for the different response groups in the market. While it is usually feasible to find descriptive differences among the buyers in a product-market, these variations must be matched to response differences.

Actionable Segments. An organization must be able to aim a marketing program strategy at each segment selected as a market target. Ideally, the targeting effort should focus on the segment of interest and not be wasted on nonsegment buyers. In some situations, promotional efforts for one product or brand may actually attract (cannibalize) customers from another sequent targeted by the same organization using a different brand.

Cost/Benefits of Segmentation. In terms of revenues generated and costs incurred, segmentation must be worth doing. Frederick W. Winter comments on evaluating the benefits of segmentation:

> Market segmentation is the recognition that groups or subsegments differ with respect to properties which suggest that different marketing mixes might be used to appeal to the different groups. These subsegments may then be aggregated if the reduction in cost exceeds the reduction in benefits (revenues). This aggregation is based on the fact that both subsegments respond most to the same marketing mix.[18]

Stability over Time. Finally, the segments must show adequate stability over time so that the firm's efforts will have enough time to succeed. If buyer's needs are changing rapidly, a group with similar response patterns at one point could display quite different patterns several months later. The time period may be too short to justify using a segmentation strategy.

The five above-listed criteria are useful in evaluating a proposed segmentation scheme. For example, if the basis for forming segments does not identify different groups, each with a similar responsiveness within and a variation between groups, then dividing the product-market is of doubtful value. The ultimate criterion, of course, is performance. If a segmentation scheme leads to improved performance (profitability and customer satisfaction) in a product-market, then it is worthwhile.

On occasion the distinction between product differentiation and market segmentation is not clear. *Product differentiation* is a product offering of an organization perceived by the buyer to differ from the competition on any physical or nonphysical product characteristic, including price.[19] Using a product differentiation strategy, a firm may target an entire market or one (or more) segments. Competing firms may differentiate their product offerings in trying to gain competitive advantage with the same group of targeted buyers.

Segments are formed by (1) grouping customers using descriptive characteristics and then comparing response differences across the groups, or (2) creating groups based on response differences (e.g., frequency of purchase) and working backward to see if the groups can be identified based on differences in their characteristics.[20] We examine each approach to show how it is used to identify segments.

Customer Group Identification

After a product-market is defined, it may be possible to identify promising segments, using management judgment in combination with the available information and/or marketing research data.

It is necessary to select one or more of the characteristics of people or organizations as the basis of segmentation. These candidate segments are examined using (1) management judgment and experience, or (2) supporting statistical analyses. The objective is to find differences in responsiveness among the customer groups. We look at each method to show how segments are determined.

Experience and Available Information. In many product-markets management's knowledge of customer needs is a useful guide to segmentation. For example, both experience and analysis of published information are often useful in segmenting business markets. Business segment variables include type of industry, size of purchase, and product application. Recall the use of company size to segment the market for commercial banking services by First Business Bank. Company records may contain information for analyzing the existing customer base. Published data such as industry mailing lists can be used to identify potential market segments. These groups are then analyzed to determine if they respond differently.

Cross-Classification Analyses. Another method of forming segments is to identify customer groups using descriptive characteristics and compare response rates (e.g., sales) by placing the information in table form. Customer groups form the rows and response categories form the columns. Review of industry publications and other published information may identify ways to break up a product-market into segments. Standardized information services such as Information Resources Inc. and Nielsen collect and publish consumer panel data on a regular basis (see Chapter 8). These data provide a wide range of consumer characteristics, advertising media usage, and other information analyzed by product and brand usage. The panel data are generated from a large sample of households throughout the United States.

A wide array of information is available for use in forming population subgroups within product-markets. The analyst can use many sources, as well as management's insights and hunches regarding the market. The essential concern is whether a segmentation scheme establishes customer groups that display different product and brand responsiveness. The more evidence of meaningful differences, the better chance that useful segments exist. Cross-classification has some real advantages in cost and ease of use. There may be a strong basis for choosing a segmenting scheme that uses this approach. This occurs more often in business and organizational markets where management has a good knowledge of user needs because there are fewer users than there are in consumer product-markets. Alternatively, this approach may be a first step in a more comprehensive type of analysis.

Database Segmentation. The availability of computerized databases offers a wide range of segmentation analysis capabilities. This type of analysis is particularly useful in consumer market segmentation. These databases are organized by geography and buyers' descriptive characteristics. They can be used to identify customer groups, design effective marketing programs, and improve the effectiveness of existing programs. The number of available databases is rapidly expanding, the costs are declining, and the information systems are becoming user-friendly. Several marketing research firms offer database services.

AID Analysis. This technique divides a sample of people into categories. Groupings are determined using variables (e.g., income) that achieve the largest discrimination for the response variable (e.g., usage rate). By analyzing a sample of buyers from a product-market, potential segments are identified. An application of the analysis to determine segments in the long-distance telephone market is shown in Exhibit 6–5A.[21] AT&T analyzed a sample of 1,750 consumers to examine heavy and light long-distance callers. Exhibit 6–5B shows the five segments identified in the AID analysis. Demographic and use-situation (type of equipment) data identified the segments. Interestingly, while the heavy-user segment (1) accounted for 29 percent of the dollar billing on calls, it was only 15 percent of the sample.

The intuitive logic underlying these methods is appealing. By identifying customer groups using descriptive characteristics and then comparing them to a measure of customer responsiveness to a marketing mix such as product usage rate (e.g., number of packages of soap per week), potential segments can be identified. If similar response rates are found within a segment and differences in response exist between segments, then promising segments are identified. Segments do not always emerge from these analyses. In some product-markets distinct segments may not exist. In others, the segment interrelationships may be so complex that an analysis of these predetermined groupings will not identify useful segments.

Forming Groups Based on Response Differences

An alternative to selecting customer groups based on descriptive characteristics is to identify groups of buyers by using response differences to form the segments. A look at a segmentation analysis for the packaging division of Signode Corporation illustrates how this method is used.[22] The products consist of steel strappings for various packaging applications. An analysis of the customer base identified the segments shown in Exhibit 6–6. Hierarchical cluster analysis formed the segments using 12 variables concerning price and service trade-offs and buying power. The study included 161 of Signode's national accounts. Measures of the variables were obtained from sales records, sales managers, and sales representatives. Note how the segments vary in responsiveness based on relative price and relative service.

These approaches draw more extensively from buyer behavior information than the customer segment identification techniques discussed earlier. Note, for example, the information on customer responsiveness to marketing-mix variables (Exhibit 6–6). We now look at additional applications to more fully explore the potential of the customer response approaches.

Cluster Analysis. This method identified the segments shown in Exhibit 6–6. Cluster analysis groups people according to the similarity of their answers to questions such as brand preferences on product attributes. The objective of cluster analysis is to identify groupings in which the similarity within a group is high and the variation among groups is as great as possible. Each group is a potential segment. A life-style segmentation study of the snack-food market illustrates how cluster analysis is used in consumer mar-

EXHIBIT 6–5 Illustrative Segmentation for Long-Distance Telephone Service

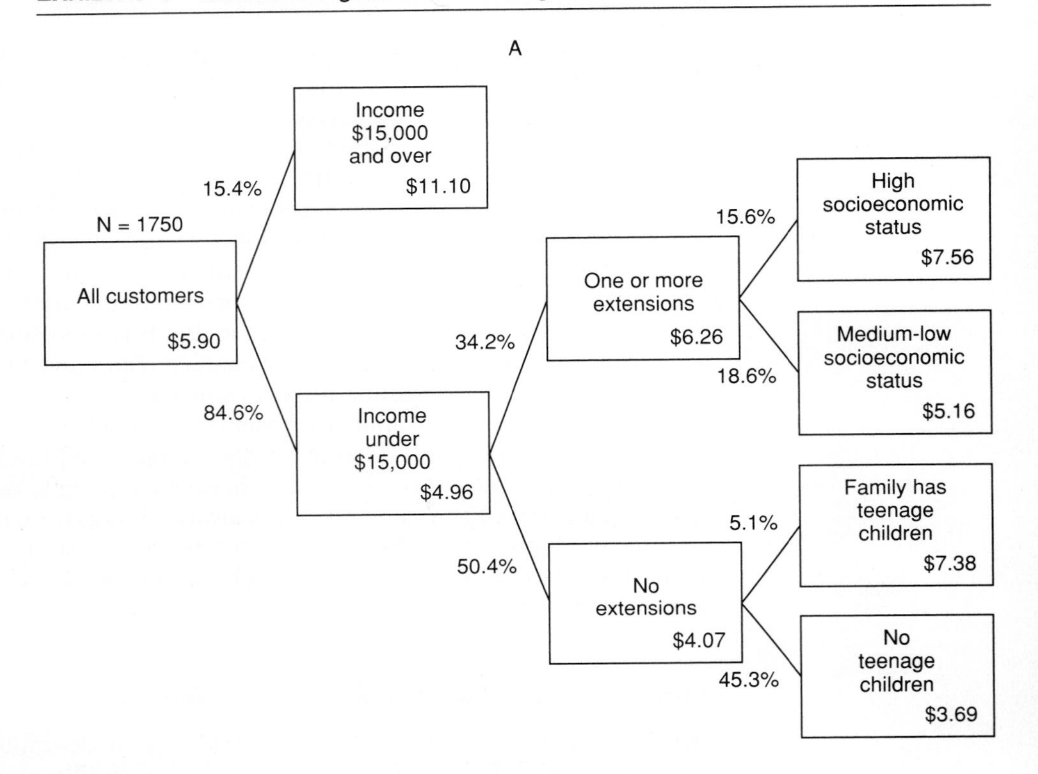

B

Five segments produced by the final output of the AID analysis

Segment profile	*Average long-distance bill*	*Percent of sample*	*Percent of total long-distance billing accounted for by segment*
1. Income $15,000 and over.	$11.10	15.4 %	29.0 %
2. Income less than $15,000, one or more extensions, higher socioeconomic status based on education and occupation.	7.56	15.6	20.1
3. Same as #2, but medium-to-low socioeconomic status.	5.16	18.6	16.2
4. Income under $15,000, no extensions and family has teenage children.	7.38	5.1	6.4
5. Same as #4, but no teenage children.	3.69	45.3	28.3

Source: Henry Assael and A. Marvin Roscoe, Jr., "Approaches to Market Segmentation Analysis," *Journal of Marketing,* October 1976, p. 70.

EXHIBIT 6–6 Segment Profile of Steel Strapping Customers

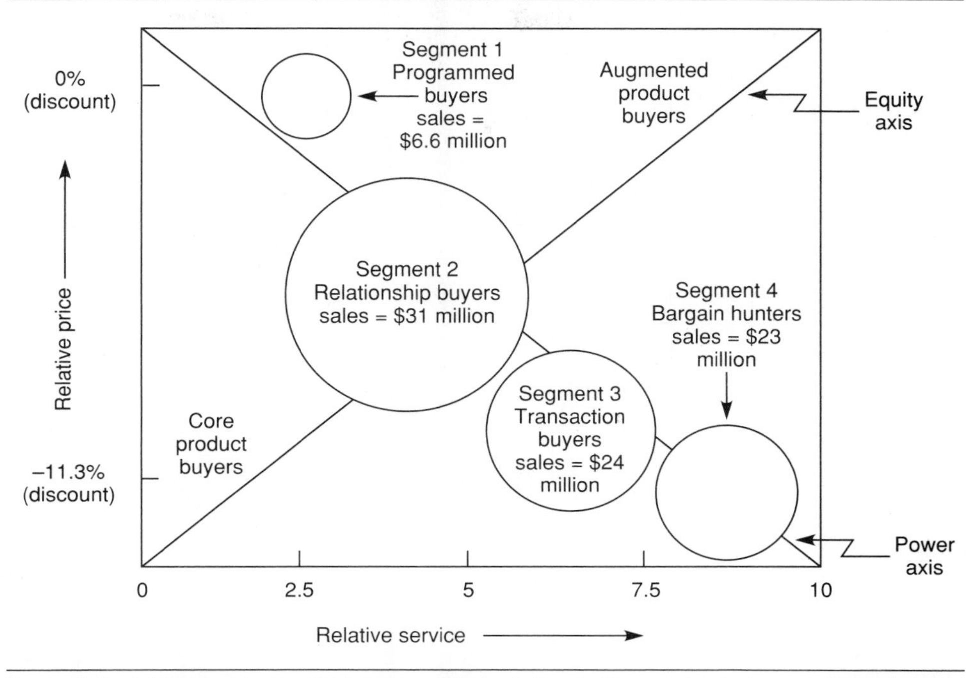

Source: V. Kasturi Rangan, Rowland T. Moriarty, and Gordon S. Swartz, "Segmenting Customers in Mature Industrial Markets," *Journal of Marketing*, October 1992, p. 79.

ket segmentation.[23] Using a sample of 1,500 snack-food users, information on several life-style characteristics and benefits sought in snack foods was collected and analyzed. A summary of the results of the study is shown in Exhibit 6–7. Six potential segments are shown. Comparisons of the groups indicate several differences that are useful in market targeting and marketing program development. Note the variation in the type of snacks the members of each segment usually eat. Also, demographic characteristics vary substantially across segments.

Perceptual Maps. Another promising segmentation method uses consumer research data to construct perceptual maps for products and brands. The analyses are useful in selecting market-target strategies and deciding how to position a product or brand to serve the chosen market target.

While the end result of perceptual mapping is simple to understand, its execution is demanding in terms of research skills. Although approaches vary, the following steps are typically included:

1. Selection of the product-market area to be examined.

EXHIBIT 6–7 Life-Style Segmentation of the Snack-Food Market

	Nutritional Snackers	*Weight Watchers*	*Guilty Snackers*	*Party Snackers*	*Indiscriminate Snackers*	*Economical Snackers*
Percentage of snackers	22%	14%	9%	15%	15%	18%
Life-style characteristics	Self-assured Controlled	Outdoor types Influential Venturesome	High anxiety Isolate	Sociable	Hedonistic	Self-assured Price-oriented
Benefits sought	Nutritious No artificial ingredients Natural snack	Low calorie Quick energy	Low calorie Good tasting	Good to serve guests Proud to serve Goes well with beverage	Good tasting Satisfies hunger	Low price Best value
Consumption level of snacks	Light	Light	Heavy	Average	Heavy	Average
Type of snacks usually eaten	Fruits Vegetables Cheese	Yogurt Vegetables	Yogurt Cookies Crackers Candy	Nuts Potato chips Crackers Pretzels	Candy Ice cream Cookies Potato chips Pretzels Popcorn	No specific products
Demographics	Better educated Have younger children	Younger Single	Younger or older Females Lower socio-economic group	Middle-aged Nonurban	Teens	Larger families Better educated

Source: Henry Assael, *Consumer and Marketing Action,* 2nd ed. (Boston: PWS—Kent Publishing, 1984), p. 262.

2. Determination of the brands that compete in the product-market.
3. Collection of consumer perceptions about attributes for the available brands (and an ideal brand) obtained from a sample of people.
4. Analysis of data to form one, two, or more composite attribute dimensions, each independent of the other.
5. Preparation of a map (two-dimensional X and Y grid) of attributes on which are positioned consumer perceptions of competing brands.
6. Plotting of consumers with similar ideal preferences to see if subgroups (potential segments) will form.
7. Evaluation of how well the solution corresponds to the data that are analyzed.
8. Interpretation of the results as to market-target and product-positioning strategies.

An example of a consumer perception map is shown in Exhibit 6–8. Because of the technical requirements for applying the research approach, marketing research skills and experience are essential. Nevertheless, the potential value of a properly designed and executed study can be significant.

Suppose the mapping as indicated in Exhibit 6–8 is a good representation of preferences. If your brand is C, what are the strategic implications of the analysis? Group V is a logical market target for your firm, and III may represent a secondary market target. To appeal most effectively to group V, you will probably need to change somewhat group V consumers' price perceptions of brand C. Offering another brand less expensive than C to appeal to group IV is another possible action. Of course, it is necessary to study the research results in much greater depth than this brief examination of Exhibit 6–8. Our objective is to show how the results might be used.

Perceptual mapping, like many of the research methods used for segment identification, is expensive and represents a technical challenge. When used and interpreted properly, these methods are powerful tools for analyzing product-market structure to identify possible market targets and positioning concepts. Of course, many issues have to be considered in specific applications, such as the choice of attributes, identification of relevant products and brands, sampling design, and evaluating the strength of results.

Segmentation Application

A segmentation study of the antihistamine product-market illustrates another application of analysis.[24] Attributes were identified using a panel of pharmacists. The 47 potentially relevant product features they identified for allergic rhinitis (AR) were rated for importance by 10 actual AR sufferers. They were also asked to identify any missing attributes. This information was used to determine these attribute categories: onset (speed) of action, dryness, prescription status, interaction with other drugs, effectiveness of relief,

EXHIBIT 6–8 An Illustrative Consumer Perception Map

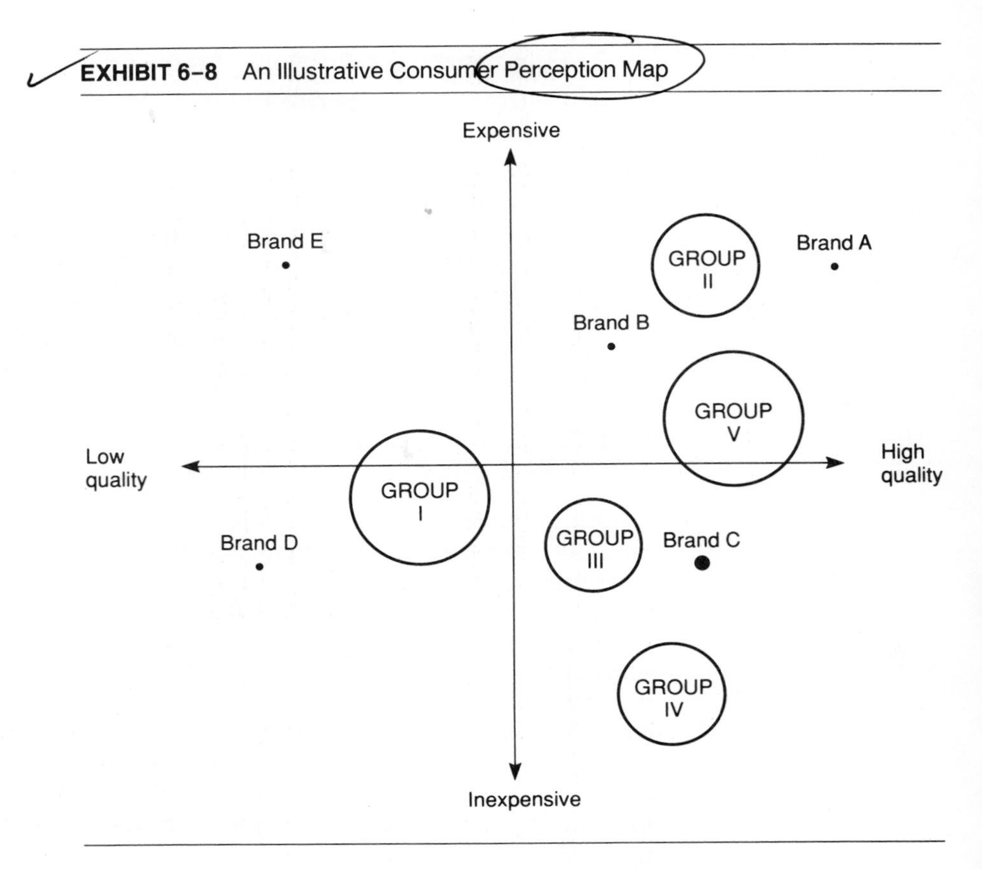

duration of dosage, and extent of drowsiness. Two or three levels of each category were indicated (i.e., yes or no concerning dryness effect). Sixteen hypothetical product profiles were developed and three actual drug products were used to check the validity of the model. A sample of 168 recent users of antihistamines yielded the cluster analysis results shown in Exhibits 6–9 and 6–10. The dependent variable used to form clusters was contingent value (the maximum price the respondent would be willing to pay).

A comparison of clusters 1 and 5 highlights several differences across the seven attribute categories. The larger the attribute value (part-worth) in Exhibit 6–9, the more important is the attribute category for that cluster. For example, cluster 1 has a strong preference for an over-the-counter (OTC) product (level 2) and an all-day duration (level 1). Interaction does not appear to be a concern for these individuals. They show preferences for relief and low drowsiness.

The study results also highlight a potential problem in segment analysis. The descriptive profiles in Exhibit 6–10 indicate the characteristics and pur-

EXHIBIT 6–9 Antihistamine Attribute Values for Selected Conjoint Solutions*

		Q-Type FA Transformed Contingent Valuation					
				Cluster			
Attribute	*Level*	*1 (n = 31)*	*2 (n = 25)*	*3 (n = 34)*	*4 (n = 41)*	*5 (n = 12)*	*Levels*
Onset	1	.393	.236	.000	.779	.380	1. 30 minutes
	2	.000	.000	.042	.000	.000	2. 90 minutes
Dryness	1	.000	.000	.000	.000	.000	1. Yes, the product causes some dryness of the mouth, nose, and eyes
	2	.078	.386	.490	.445	.236	2. No, the product has no dryness effect
Rx status	1	.000	.000	.000	.090	.000	1. Yes, one needs a prescription to buy product
	2	.611	.226	.280	.000	.150	2. No, one can buy product without prescription
Interaction	1	.000	.000	.000	.000	.000	1. Yes, the product worsens intoxication for one who has taken alcohol or tranquilizers
	2	.111	.272	.400	.264	.195	2. No, the product has no effect on alcohol or tranquilizers
Relief	1	.000	.000	.000	.000	.302	1. 4 persons in 10 reported good to excellent relief of allergic rhinitis symptoms (similar to placebo)
	2	.724	1.277	.778	.609	.177	2. 6 persons in 10 reported good to excellent relief
	3	.596	1.785	.993	1.025	.000	3. 7 persons in 10 reported good to excellent relief
Duration	1	.871	.206	.077	.434	.473	1. Product is taken once daily
	2	.511	.392	.310	.586	.380	2. Product is taken two times daily
	3	.000	.000	.000	.000	.000	3. Product is taken four times daily
Drowsiness	1	.618	.000	1.576	.539	1.662	1. 1 person in 10 reported some drowsiness after taking product (similar to placebo)
	2	.455	.216	.878	.737	1.032	2. 3 persons in 10 reported drowsiness
	3	.115	.087	.303	.143	.270	3. 4 persons in 10 reported drowsiness
	4	.000	.022	.000	.000	.000	4. 6 persons in 10 reported drowsiness

*Part-worths for selected conjoint solutions (standardized within each respondent).

Source: Gregory Reardon and Dev S. Pathak, "Segmenting the Antihistamine Market: An Investigation of Consumer Preferences," *Journal of Health Care Marketing*, September 1990, p. 29.

EXHIBIT 6–10 Cluster Member Characteristics

		Cluster				
	n	*1*	*2*	*3*	*4*	*5*
% female	143	52	44	62	73	75
Mean age (years)	143	35	37	36	38	39
% with asthma[a]	143	10	20	21	10	17
Annual family income	140					
% less than $25,000		29	28	24	34	8
% $25,000–50,000		39	36	29	51	58
% over $50,000		32	36	47	15	33
Education	143					
% high school graduate		26	24	18	22	25
% college graduate		23	24	24	15	17
% postgraduate college educated		52	52	59	63	58
Mean AR severity rating	137	3.5	3.2	3.2	3.3	3.2
% perennial sufferers	142	32	52	49	46	58
% visited M.D. in past year[b]	143	13	36	41	49	75
Mean cost of illness ($)	138	43	147	194	184	316
Mean drug cost ($)	87	28	48	75	78	124
WTP to avoid AR ($)	141	100	175	352	302	253

[a]Chi square value is not significant at α = .05; however, it may not be a valid statistic as 40% of cells have expected counts of fewer than five because of the lower prevalence of subjects with asthma.

[b]Chi square value for null hypothesis of independence is significant for this characteristic at α = .05. All other characteristics are not significant at α = .05 according to corresponding (chi square of *F*) statistical tests.

Source: Gregory Reardon and Dev S. Pathak, "Segmenting the Antihistamine Market: An Investigation of Consumer Preferences," *Journal of Health Care Marketing,* September 1990, p. 29.

chase behavior of the five groups.[25] The only statistically significant difference between groups is the percentage of individuals who visited an M.D. in the previous year. The lack of differences in the other characteristics is the result of substantial within-group variation. This inability to relate preferences to descriptive characteristics is one of the difficulties in segmentation. In order to access segments, descriptive profiles are needed. The characteristics in this study portray more similarities than differences between segment groups. It is possible that other variables such as disease history or psychographic and life-style measures would result in segment profiles that better describe the groups.

Selecting a Segmentation Method

The choice of a segmentation method depends on such factors as the maturity of the market, the competitive structure, and the organization's experience in the market. The more comprehensive the segmentation analysis, the higher the costs of segment identification, reaching the highest level when field research studies are involved. It is important to make maximum use of available knowledge about the product-market in combination with the analysis of existing information. An essential first step in segmentation is analyzing the existing customer base to identify groups of buyers with different response behavior (e.g., frequent purchase versus occasional purchase). In some instances this will provide a sufficient basis for segment formation. If not, experience and existing information are often helpful in guiding the design of customer research studies.

The five segmentation criteria discussed earlier help to evaluate potential segments. Deciding if the criteria are satisfied rests with management after examining response differences among the segments. The segmentation plan should satisfy the responsiveness criterion plus the other criteria (end-users are identifiable, they are accessible via the marketing program, the segment(s) is economically viable, and the segment is stable over time). After implementation of the scheme, the organization should continue to evaluate the segmentation approach. Improvements in segment identification may be possible over time.

Consideration should be made of the trade-off between the costs of developing a better segmentation scheme and the benefits gained. For example, instead of using one variable to segment, a combination of two or three variables might be used. The costs of a more insightful segmentation scheme include the analysis time and the complexity of strategy development. The potential benefits include better determination of response differences, which enable the design of more effective marketing-mix strategies.

The competitive advantage gained by finding (or developing) a new market segment can be very important. Segment strategies are consistently adopted by a wide range of small companies with excellent performance records. For example, a segment focus provided Neutrogena an opportunity to differentiate the brand from existing soap brands. In 1967 Neutrogena's sales were $3 million, compared to 1991 sales of over $225 million and $25 million in profit. Initially targeting the premium-priced soap segment is an important reason for the company's strong sales and profit performance for a quarter of a century. The company's product lines include soaps, specialty skin-care products, and hair-care products.

STRATEGIC ANALYSIS OF MARKET SEGMENTS

Each market segment of interest is analyzed in depth to determine its potential attractiveness as a market target. Exhibit 6–11 shows the major areas of analysis. A discussion of each area follows.

Customer Analysis

Customer Profiles. When forming segments, it is important to find out as much as possible about the customers in each segment. Factors such as those used in dividing product-markets into segments are also helpful in describ-

EXHIBIT 6–11 Analyzing Market Segments

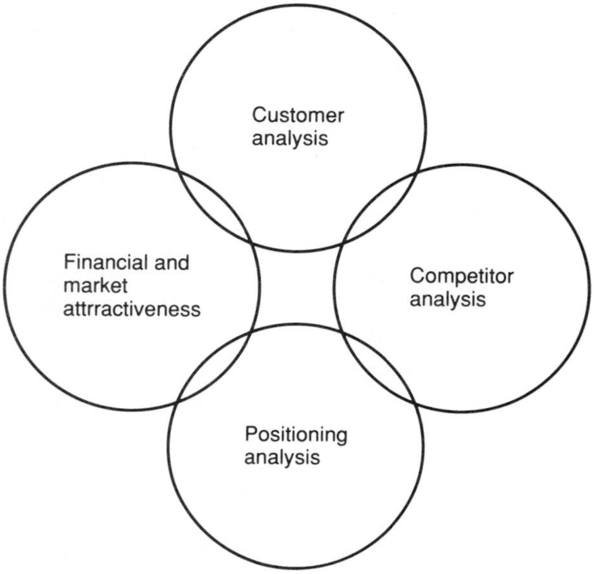

Customer analysis

Financial and market attrractiveness

Competitor analysis

Positioning analysis

ing the people in the same segments. The discussion of customer profiles in Chapter 5 indicates the information needed to profile a product-market. Similar information is used in the segment profile, although it is more comprehensive than the product-market profile.

The profiling objective is to find descriptive characteristics that are highly correlated to the segmentation-basis variables. Standardized information services are available for some product-markets, including foods, health and beauty aids, and pharmaceuticals. Large markets and many competitors make it profitable for marketing research firms to collect and analyze data useful to the firms serving the market.

Information Resources, Inc., a Chicago-based research supplier, has combined computerized information processing with customer research methods to generate useful information for market segmentation. Its Behavior Scan system electronically tracks total grocery store sales and individual household purchase behavior through complete universal product code (UPC) scanner coverage. People in the 2,500 household samples in each of several metropolitan markets covered by the service carry special ID cards and are individually tracked via scanner in grocery stores and drugstores. An example of the type of information generated is given in Exhibit 6–12. Note how the information is used to form age-group segments. The firm publishes

EXHIBIT 6–12 Analysis of Age of Soap Purchasers

Demographics

Q. Within which demographic segments is Ivory Liquid share strongest? Weakest? How do I go about building the weaker segments?

A. With respect to age of female household head, Ivory Liquid performance differs dramatically.

Age of female head

<30	30-39	40-49	50 +
18.6%	21.3%	25.4%	28.7%

Ivory liquid share

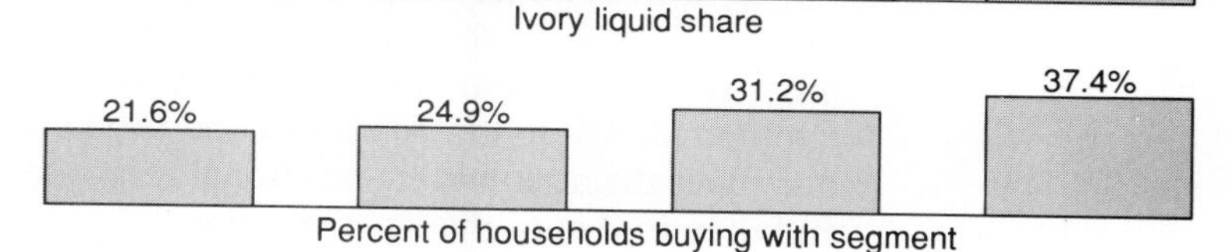

Percent of households buying with segment

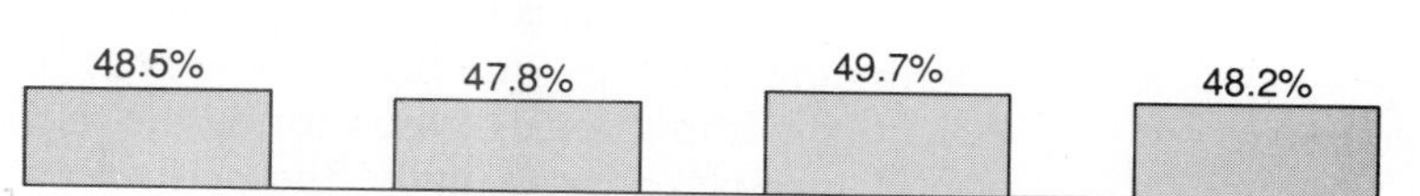

Loyalty to ivory among buyers

The relatively weaker performance among younger households traces to fewer buyers. Among those who *did* buy, loyalty was similar in all segments.

To build a share, promotions (perhaps high-value coupons) and/or advertising aimed at trial generation among younger female household heads should be considered.

This analysis can, of course, include a fill range of additional demographic variables.

The above data are entirely fictional. Brand names are used only to add an element of reality. Any similarity to actual brand data is entirely coincidental.

Source: *The Marketing Fact Book®* (Chicago: Information Resources, 1986), p. 10.

The Marketing Fact Book, which has consumer purchase data on all product categories. Its database can be used for follow-up, in-depth analyses to meet the needs of specific companies.

Analyzing Customer Satisfaction. "Attaining customer satisfaction is the goal of all marketing activities and indicates that these activities have been conducted successfully."[26] Customer satisfaction is measured by comparing customer *expectations* about the product and supporting services with the *performance* of the product and supporting services.[27] Some researches indicate that *prior experience* may be a better basis of comparison than *expectations.*[28]

Customer satisfaction depends on the perceived performance of a product and supporting services and the standards that customers use to evaluate that performance.[29] The customer's standards complicate the relationship between organizational product specifications (e.g., product attribute tolerances) and satisfaction. Standards may involve something other than prepurchase expectations such as the perceived performance of competing products. Importantly, the standards are likely to vary across market segments.

Defining and monitoring customer satisfaction is a challenging task, involving far more than a simple tracking of satisfaction. Determining segment-specific standards is essential when buyers' needs and wants are differentiated. These standards can and probably do change over time. Additionally, satisfaction is an emotional response to a performance evaluation and therefore may change over time.

Customer satisfaction does not have a simple, one-to-one relationship with other purchase/use processes such as customer complaints. This highlights the importance of monitoring the relevant dimensions of quality the customer perceives. Finally, the performance attributes that lead to customer satisfaction may not correspond exactly to those that influence the initial purchase decision. While there may be substantial overlap, unique attributes of satisfaction may exist. For example, the safety of an automobile may not be an important brand-selection criterion. But later, if the buyer learns that his or her car is unsafe, then dissatisfaction is quite likely to occur. The concerns expressed by Audi 5000 owners in the late 1980s about sudden acceleration are illustrative. Investigations found no evidence of faulty performance. However, Audi's sales in the United States drastically declined after the incidents were widely publicized.

Analysis of Competitive Advantage

Since analyzing competition is discussed in Chapter 7, we briefly consider the information needed about competitors. Market-segment analysis looks at the set of key competitors currently active in the segment market plus any potential segment entrants.

The scope of the market segment determines the competitive arena for segment-level analysis. In complex market structures, definition of the competitive arena may require detailed analysis. The competing firms are described and evaluated to highlight their strengths and weaknesses. Information useful in the competitor analysis includes business scope and objectives; market position; market target(s) and customer base; positioning strategy; financial, technical, and operating strengths; management experience and capabilities; and special competitive advantages (e.g., patents). It is also important to anticipate the future strategies of key competitors.

Value-chain analysis can be used to examine competitive advantage at the segment level. Chapter 2 has a framework for advantage analysis and discusses the value-chain concept. A complete assessment of the nature and intensity of competition in the segment is important in determining whether to enter (or exit from) the segment and how to compete in the segment. Porter recommends analysis of five forces to determine segment attractiveness.[30] First, the scope and intensity of competition that currently exists in the segment is evaluated. Second, the threat of new competitors entering the segment is examined. Third, the potential for substitute products becoming available to buyers in the segment is considered. For example, Western Union's management did not recognize the competitive threat of facsimile communication. Fourth, if the bargaining power of buyers is very strong, firms serving the market may be at a disadvantage. Fifth, a similar strong bargaining position of suppliers may create an unfavorable position for the firms the suppliers serve.

Positioning Analysis

We discuss developing a positioning strategy for each of the firm's market targets in Chapter 9. The issue is briefly considered now since segment analysis involves some preliminary choices about positioning strategy. One objective of segment analysis is to obtain guidelines for developing the positioning strategy.

Flexibility exists in selecting how to position the firm (or brand) with its customers and against its competition in a segment. Positioning analysis shows how to combine product, distribution, pricing, and promotion strategies to favorably position the brand with buyers in the segment. For example, positioning guidelines for different steel strapping market segments are shown in Exhibit 6–6. Similarly, promotion strategy guidelines for potential younger buyers of Ivory liquid soap are suggested by the analysis in Exhibit 6–12. The positioning strategy selected should meet the needs and requirements of the targeted buyers at a cost that yields a profitable margin for the organization.

Estimating Financial and Market Attractiveness

The financial and market attractiveness of each segment needs to be evaluated. Included are specific estimates of revenue, cost, and segment profit contribution over the planning horizon. Market attractiveness can be mea-

EXHIBIT 6–13 Segment Financial and Market Attractiveness

Estimated ($ millions)	Segment		
	X	Y	Z
Sales*	10	16	5
Variable costs*	4	9	3
Contribution margin*	6	7	2
Market share†	60%	30%	10%
Total segment sales	17	53	50
Segment position:			
Business strength	High	Medium	Low
Attractiveness‡	Medium	Low	High

*For a two-year period.

†Percent of total sales in the segment.

‡Based upon a five-year projection.

sured by market growth-rate projections and attractiveness assessments made by management.

Financial analysis estimates sales and costs for each segment of interest. Using this information, the segment's estimated profit contribution can be determined. Since accurate forecasting is difficult if the projections are too far into the future, detailed projections typically extend two to five years ahead. Both the segment's competitive position evaluation and the financial forecasts are considered in comparing segments. In all instances the risks and returns associated with serving a particular segment should be considered. Flows of revenues and costs can be weighted to take into account risks and the time value of revenues and expenditures.

An illustrative segment analysis is shown in Exhibit 6–13. A two-year period is used for estimating sales, costs, contribution margin, and market share. Depending on the forecasting difficulty, estimates for a longer time period can be used. When appropriate, estimates can be expressed as present values of future revenues and costs. Business strength in Exhibit 6–13 refers to the present position. Alternatively, it can be expressed as the present position and an estimated future position, based upon plans for increasing business strength. Attractiveness is typically evaluated for some future time period. In the illustration a five-year projection is used.

The example shows how segment opportunities are ranked according to their overall attractiveness. The analysis can be expanded to include additional information such as profiles of key competitors. The rankings are admittedly subjective since decision makers will vary in their weighting of estimated financial position, business strength, and segment attractiveness. Place yourself in the role of a segment evaluator. Using the information in Exhibit 6–13, rank segments X, Y, and Z as to their overall importance as market targets. Unless management is ready to allocate a major chunk of resources to segment Z to build business strength, it appears to be a candidate for the last-place position. Yet Z displays some attractive characteristics. The segment has the most favorable market attractiveness of the three, and its estimated total sales are nearly equal to Y's for the next two years. The big problem with Z is its business strength. The key question is whether Z's market share can be increased. If not, X looks like a good prospect for top rating, followed by Y and then Z. Of course, management may decide to go after all three segments.

SEGMENTATION IN THE CHANGING ENVIRONMENT OF THE 1990s

The rapidly changing global business environment impacts the preferences of buyers in many ways. One important effect of these changes is that segmentation is more complex and more important. For example, the European Community (EC) of 12 nations established in 1992 offers important opportunities for market consolidation. Yet the differences in language, culture, priorities, and economic position among the 12 EC countries generate some interesting segmentation issues. The process of economic unification causes buyers' needs and preferences to become more similar, although changes will not occur immediately. Some products, such as Coca-Cola, Rolex watches, and Levis, are already positioned into global segments. Product standardization and marketing communications will develop pan-European positions for other products. Products like food and beer may continue to hold strong domestic and regional positions for many years.

Global pressures from both buyers and competitors to satisfy the differences in buyers' preferences require improved segment identification. Combining two or more national markets offers the advantage of creating more precise (homogeneous) segments large enough for a company to target economically. For example, the combined population of France (56 million), Italy (57 million), and Spain (39 million) is 152 million. Thus, a segment that spans all three countries has much greater market potential than a single-country segment.

Macro/Microsegmentation

Two-stage segmentation is useful in some product-markets. The first stage creates macrosegments, each of which is further segmented into microsegments. As an example, the telecommunications product-market of business users can be segmented first by type of industry (e.g., financial services); then the industry segments can be further segmented using variables such as size, product needs, geographic location, and other relevant microsegmentation variables.

When macrogroupings are identified in a market, they can be further analyzed to determine if microdifferences are present. Consider for example, the away-from-home lodging market. Price and quality provide an initial basis for segmenting the market. Macrosegments consist of premium-, medium-, and budget-price/quality categories. Each of these segments can be further segmented using variables such as geographic region, location (downtown, airport, and resort), use situation, special features, and other factors. The key objective is to find customer groups with similar needs and preferences. An organization's competitive advantage may be stronger in certain microsegments.

Geographic Segmentation

Geography is sometimes useful in combining or synthesizing a variety of segmentation variables. Differences in demand response occur in different geographic regions within a country for foods, automobiles, and other products. Differences in cultures, climates, histories, and resources influence such consumer activities as media usage, shopping areas, products, and services.[31]

The European Community displays some distinct geographical differences. The northern countries are more industrialized than those in the south. Preferences and consumption patterns of buyers are changing more rapidly in the southern region of the EC than they are in the north. Differences in food preferences are particularly significant between the two regions.

Single/Multiple Product Segments

Segments may exist for more than a single product/brand offering. For example, Neutrogena Corporation initially produced the popular and very profitable translucent glycerine soap. The company now offers a full line of soaps, lotions, shampoos and conditioners. Neutrogena's market segment consists of buyers willing to pay premium prices for pure and healthy personal care products. Segmentation analysis should consider segments for product lines as well as individual products.

Segmentation Dynamics

An opportunity may exist to alter the "demand functions of a set of consumers such that they will become similar and constitute a unique market segment."[32] Segment development requires the existence of a differentiated product or the implementation of a differentiation strategy. Neutrogena created a new segment for body soap with pure and healthy characteristics. Laptop computers developed into a separate personal computer market with segments within the market.

Mass Customization

Mass customization is the capability to produce customized products while achieving the cost benefits of mass production. Technology, such as computer-aided design software, makes producing customized products a reality (see Case 1–1, Autodesk, Inc.). This capability to satisfy buyers' diverse needs offers exciting microsegmentation opportunities for a variety of products. It also highlights the importance of close coordination of marketing and other business functions such as design and manufacturing.

SUMMARY

Market segmentation is a requirement for competing in many product-markets. "Segmenting the marketplace is one of the most important strategic moves that can be made by high-tech companies, industrial firms, and firms that sell services to other businesses."[33] Buyers differ in their preferences for products and services. Finding out what these preferences are and grouping buyers with similar needs is an essential part of marketing strategy development. Market segmentation is an opportunity for a small firm to focus on buyers where the company's strengths are most favorable. Large firms seeking to establish or protect a dominant market position can often do so by targeting multiple segments.

Segmentation of a product-market requires that there are response differences between segments and that the segments are identifiable and stable over time. Also, the benefits of segmentation should exceed the costs. Segmenting a market involves identifying the basis of segmentation, forming segments, describing each segment, and analyzing and evaluating the segment(s) of interest. The variables useful as bases for forming and describing segments include the characteristics of people and organizations, use situation, buyers' needs and preferences, and purchase behavior.

Segments can be formed by identifying customer groups using the characteristics of people or organizations. The groups are analyzed to determine if the response profiles are different across the candidate segments. Alternatively, customer response information can be used to form customer groupings, then the descriptive characteristics of the groups analyzed to find out if segments can be identified. Several examples of segment formation are discussed to illustrate the methods available for this purpose.

Segment analysis and evaluation should identify the segments in a product-market and show the strengths and limitations of each segment as a potential market target for the organization. Segment analysis includes customer descriptions and satisfaction analysis, evaluating existing and potential competitors and competitive advantage, marketing program positioning analysis, and financial and market attractiveness. Segment analysis is important in evaluating customer satisfaction, finding new-product opportunities, selecting market targets, and designing positioning strategies. A good segmentation strategy creates an important competitive edge for an organization.

QUESTIONS FOR REVIEW AND DISCUSSION

1. Competing in the unified European Community market raises some interesting market-segment questions. Discuss the segmentation issues regarding the 12-country market.
2. Why are there marketing strategy advantages in using demographic characteristics to break out product-markets into segments?
3. The real test of a segment formation scheme occurs after it has been tried and the results evaluated. Are there ways to evaluate alternative segmenting schemes without actually trying them?
4. Suggest ways of obtaining the information needed to conduct a market-segment analysis.
5. Why may it become necessary for companies to change their market segmentation identification over time?
6. "Market segmentation is a strategy that is primarily suitable for use in U.S. markets." Discuss.
7. Is it necessary to use a unique positioning strategy for each market segment an organization targets?
8. Under what circumstances may it not be possible to break up a product-market into segments? What are the dangers of using an incorrect segment-formation scheme?
9. What are some of the advantages in using mass customization technology to satisfy the needs of buyers?

NOTES

1. Linda Killian, "Crane's Progress," *Forbes,* August 19, 1991, p. 44.
2. Peter R. Dickson and James L. Ginter, "Market Segmentation, Product Differentiation, and Marketing Strategy," *Journal of Marketing,* April 1987, pp. 1–10.
3. Michael Dertouzos, Richard Lester, and Robert Solow, *Made in America* (Cambridge, Mass.: MIT Commission on Industrial Productivity, 1989).
4. John H. Taylor, "Niche Player," *Forbes,* April 1, 1991, p. 70.
5. Ibid.
6. Gary L. Lilien and Philip Kotler, *Marketing Decision Making* (New York: Harper & Row, 1983), p. 291.
7. Henry Assael, *Consumer Behavior and Marketing Action,* 2nd ed. (Boston: PWS–Kent Publishing, 1984), p. 225.
8. Ibid., p. 266.
9. Jay L. Laughlin and Charles R. Taylor, "An Approach to Industrial Market Segmentation," *Industrial Marketing Management* 20 (1991), pp. 127–36.
10. Peter R. Dickson, "Person-Situation: Segmentation's Missing Link," *Journal of Marketing,* Fall 1982, p. 57.
11. Teresa H. Barker, "Selling a $6 Smile," *Advertising Age,* April 9, 1984, pp. M-4 and M5.
12. A. H. Maslow, "Theory of Human Motivation," *Psychology Review,* July 1943, pp. 43–45.

13. Betsy Morris, "How Much Will People Pay to Save a Few Minutes of Cooking? Plenty," *The Wall Street Journal,* July 25, 1985, p. 23.
14. Assael, *Consumer Behavior and Marketing Action,* p. 650.
15. Bernard Berelson and Gary A. Steiner, *Human Behavior: An Inventory of Scientific Findings* (New York: Harcourt Brace Jovanovich, 1964), p. 88.
16. Henry Assael, *Marketing Management* (Boston: PWS–Kent Publishing, 1985), pp. 126–27.
17. David W. Cravens, Gerald E. Hills, and Robert B. Woodruff, *Marketing Management* (Homewood, Ill.: Richard D. Irwin, 1987), pp. 297–300.
18. Frederick W. Winter, "A Cost-Benefit Approach to Market Segmentation," *Journal of Marketing,* Fall 1979, pp. 103–11.
19. Dickson and Ginter, "Market Segmentation," p. 4.
20. George S. Day, *Market Driven Strategy* (New York: The Free Press, 1990), pp. 101–4.
21. Assael, *Consumer Behavior and Marketing Action,* pp. 261–62.
22. Henry Assael and A. Marvin Roscoe, Jr., "Approaches to Market Segmentation Analysis," *Journal of Marketing,* October 1976, pp. 67–76.
23. V. Kasturi Rangan, Rowland T. Moriarity, and Gordon S. Swartz, "Segmenting Customers in Mature Industrial Markets," *Journal of Marketing,* October 1992, pp. 72–82.
24. Gregory Reardon and Dev S. Pathak, "Segmenting the Antihistamine Market: An Investigation of Consumer Preferences," *Journal of Health Care Marketing,* September 1990, pp. 23–33.
25. Ibid.
26. C. W. Park and Gerald Zaltman, *Marketing Management* (Hinsdale, IL: Dryden Press, 1987), p. 196.
27. A. Parasuraman, Valarie A. Zeithaml, and Leonard L. Berry, "A Conceptual Model of Service Quality and Its Implications for Future Research," *Journal of Marketing,* Fall 1985, pp. 41–50.
28. Robert B. Woodruff, Ernest R. Cadotte, and Roger L. Jenkins, "Modeling Consumer Satisfaction Processes Using Experienced-Based Norms," *Journal of Marketing Research,* August 1983, pp. 296–304.
29. The following discussion of customer satisfaction is based on discussions with Robert B. Woodruff, the University of Tennessee, Knoxville.
30. Michael E. Porter, *Competitive Advantage* (New York: The Free Press, 1985), pp. 4–8.
31. Lynn R. Kahle, "The Nine Nations of North America and the Value Basis of Geographic Segmentation," *Journal of Marketing,* April 1986, pp. 37–47.
32. Dickson and Ginter, "Market Segmentation," p. 4.
33. James D. Hlavacek and B. C. Ames, "Segmenting Industrial and High-Tech Markets," *Journal of Business Strategy,* Fall 1986, p. 39.

CHAPTER

7

Analyzing Competition

Successful companies study their competitors as closely as they do their customers. Analyzing and evaluating competition helps management decide where to compete and how to position against the competition in each market target.

The dangers of ignoring your competition are illustrated by the experience of the Schwinn Bicycle Company. During several generations the company's products forged a strong reputation with consumers.[1] Surprisingly, management did not see the new competitive threats that developed in the 1980s. The firm's annual sales of bicycles were constant during the 1980s at 900,000 units. Yet, industry sales escalated from 6.7 million bikes in 1982 to 12.6 million in 1987. The rapid sales growth of the mountain bike was a major contributor. Schwinn's management made several mistakes, including not taking the competition seriously. The company relied too heavily on the famous Schwinn name and was slow to innovate. Competitive advantage slipped away. Production was moved abroad to control costs, but this led to quality problems. Schwinn was also slow to respond to changing consumer tastes. Its market share fell from 25 percent in the 1960s to 8 percent today. Dealers have been attracted to competing brands. Monitoring existing and potential competitors and changing consumer preferences would have alerted Schwinn's management to new market needs and competitive threats. Schwinn's loss of market position negatively impacted the firm's sales and profits. The company filed for bankruptcy under Chapter 11 in late 1992.

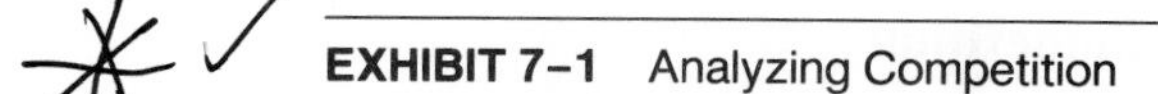

EXHIBIT 7–1 Analyzing Competition

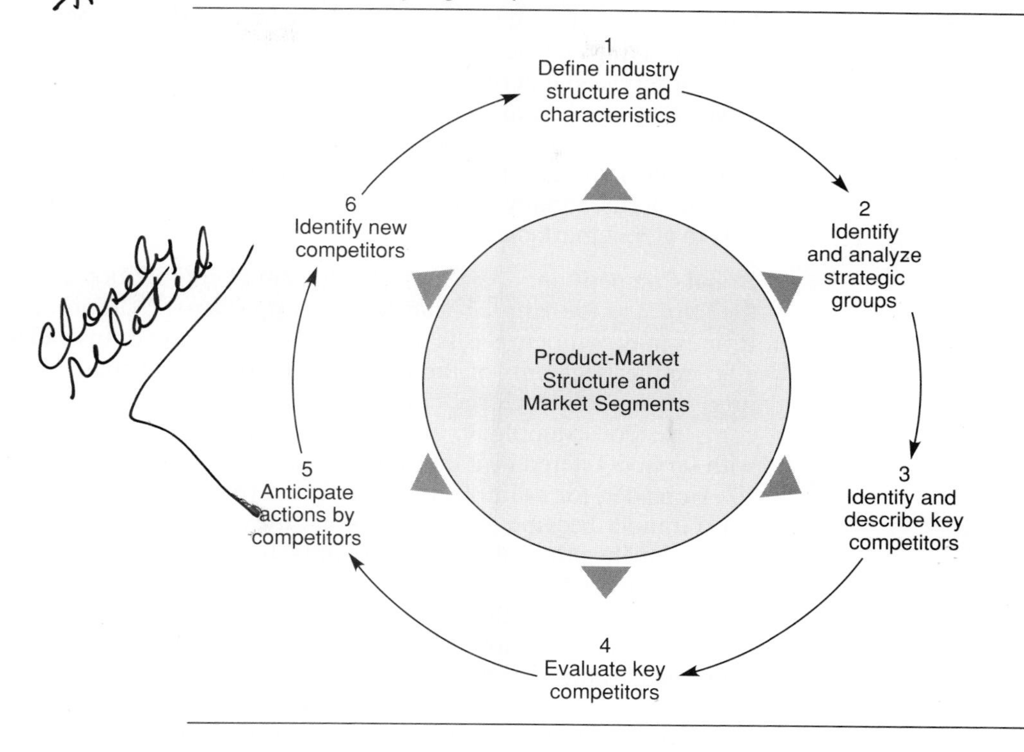

Analyzing competition follows the six steps shown in Exhibit 7–1. We begin by considering how to define the industry structure in which an organization competes and describe the characteristics of the industry. In step two, the strategic groups of companies competing in the industry are identified and analyzed. Steps three and four identify, describe, and evaluate the organization's key competitors. Steps five and six consider competitors' future actions and identify new competitors that may enter the market. Finally, the use of competitor intelligence systems is discussed.

DEFINING THE COMPETITIVE ARENA

Competitor analysis begins by identifying the industry structure in which the organization competes and describing its characteristics. The competitive arena identifies actual and potential competitors. Competition often includes more than the firms that are direct competitors, like Coke and Pepsi.

Sources of Competition

Understanding product-market structure and market segments is essential for identifying competitors and guiding analyses (Exhibit 7–1). The products (or services) that offer solutions to the same customers' needs or wants targeted by the organization's brand are competitors. Besides brand competition, there is also competition between product types and variants that satisfy the same generic need. Competition also occurs between different generic needs. Finally, competition varies geographically, from local markets to global markets.

Brand Competition. The most direct form of competition occurs between the brands in the same product-type and product-variant product-markets. Brands may compete across the total product-market or instead within specific market segments of the product-type or variant market. In complex product-market structures, brands from different product-type markets may compete. For example, financial services offered by a bank may compete with services offered by a mutual fund provider.

Consider, for example, the granola bar (product-variant) product-market. Granola became a substitute for candy bars. Developed in the mid-1970s as a "healthy" alternative to candy, by 1985, granola bars were a $438 million market dominated by Quaker Oats (50% share), General Mills (23% share), and several other brands with very small market shares.[2] Interestingly, the differentiation of granola bars from candy bars that was initially achieved became very blurred by the mid-1980s. Granola bar makers began adding sweet items. Candy bars were stressing the same attributes used to position granola bars. Thus, the competitive arena includes both granola and candy bars. The two leading granola brands were marketed by food processors instead of candy producers. Competition came from a different, although related, industry.

Product-Type and Variant Competition. This form of competition involves two or more product types or variants. The eventual head-on competition between the granola and candy bar product variants is an example of this kind of competition. Different technologies may compete in performing the same function. Thus, cameras using photographic film may compete with other image-recording devices such as videocassette cameras. Plastics may compete with ceramic materials.

Competition between different product types for the same need may alter the competitive arena by attracting new industries into the market. There is always the possible threat of a substitute product becoming available from a new form of competition. For example, word processing using personal computers has virtually eliminated the use of conventional typewriters in offices. High-quality, inexpensive 35 millimeter photographs and one-hour photo processing have negatively impacted Polaroid's market for instant photography. These examples highlight the importance of continuous assessment of potential substitute products for a firm's product(s).

Generic Competition. People have many needs and wants to satisfy. This creates competition for the limited resources available to consumers and organizations. While these forms of competition may not be direct and as intense as brand competition, they are nevertheless relevant in defining the competitive arena. An understanding of buyers' priorities in satisfying their needs is useful in determining where generic competition may occur.

Geographic Competition. Looking at the geographic scope of actual and potential competition is also important. Competition may be global, multinational, national, regional, or metropolitan in scope. Competitors typically do not fit neatly into specific geographic areas. Companies operating in regional or national markets must be alert to competition from companies competing over a broader geographical scope.

The different levels of competition for diet colas are shown in Exhibit 7–2. The product form (variant) is the most direct form of competition. Nevertheless, soft drinks also compete for buyers, as do various beverages. A complete understanding of the competitive arena helps to guide strategy design and implementation. Since competition often occurs within specific industries, an examination of industry structure is important in defining the competitive arena.

Industry Structure and Characteristics

Four aspects of industry structure offer useful insights for defining competitive boundaries. First, the industry form (classification of industries) indicates the size and number of competitors in the industry. Second, analysis of the industry environment provides useful indications of industry characteristics. Third, considering how an industry fits into its value-added system is helpful in evaluating competitive advantage. Finally, study of the competitive forces affecting the industry highlights its important competitive characteristics. These phases of industry structure definition and analysis are shown in Exhibit 7–3. For the purpose of discussion we assume that the industry of interest is made up of producers.

Industry Form. The industry classifications of monopoly, oligopoly, monopolistic competition, and pure competition developed in economics are useful in understanding competition in markets:

Monopoly This industry form consists of one firm. Buyers have no brand choices. The monopolist has extensive market power unless regulated by government. De Beers holds a near monopoly position in the distribution of diamonds. Public utilities are granted monopolies in geographical areas.

Oligopoly This industry form is dominated by a few very large firms. Through their actions (e.g., pricing and product innovation) these firms provide leadership for the rest of the industry. Oligopoly occurs in many

EXHIBIT 7–2 Example of Levels of Competition

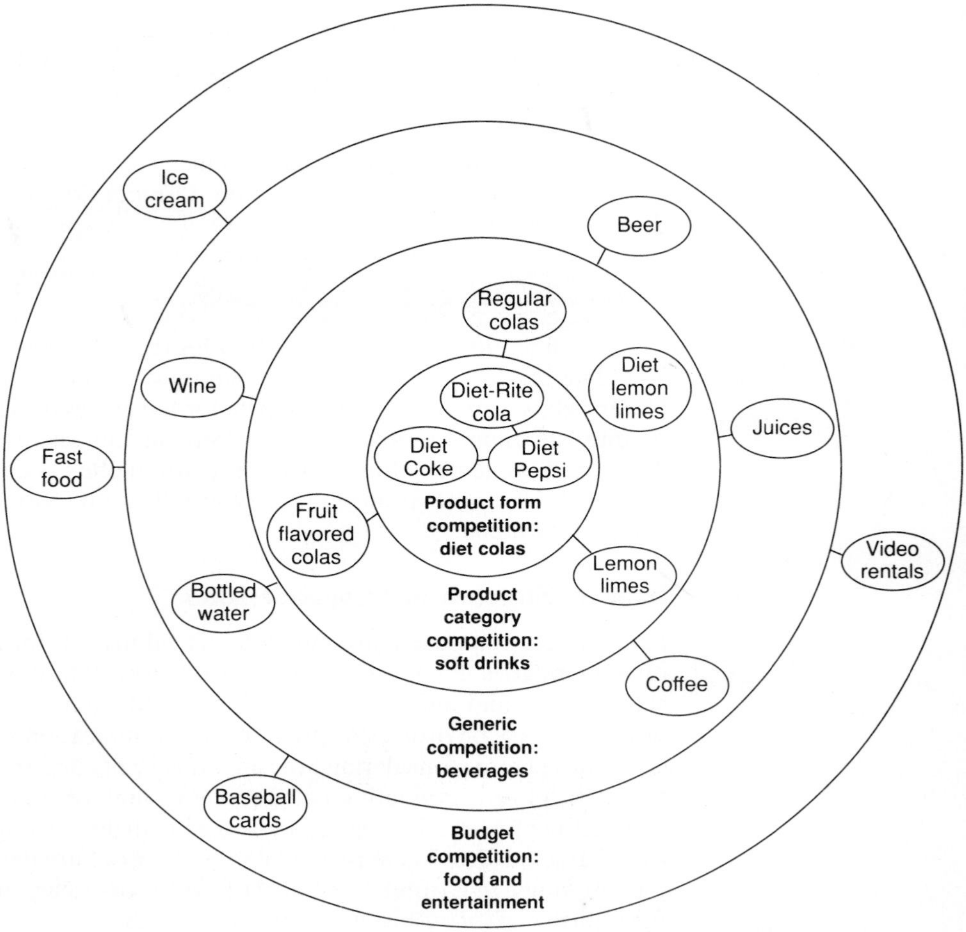

Source: Donald R. Lehmann and Russell S. Winer, *Analysis for Marketing Planning,* 2nd ed. (Homewood, Ill.: Richard D. Irwin, Inc., © 1991), p. 22.

mature industries in developed countries. Steel, beverages, and appliances are illustrative industries.

Monopolistic competition This industry form consists of many small organizations whose products are differentiated. This enables each firm to dominate a small portion of the market. Examples include restaurants, real estate agencies, and domestic cleaning services.

EXHIBIT 7–3 Defining Industry Structure and Characteristics

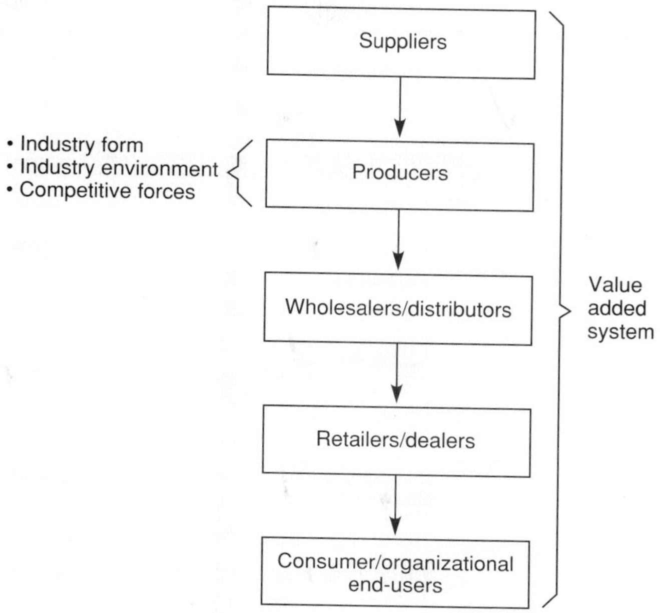

Pure competition This form is made up of many very small competitors whose products are very similar. No single firm has control over pricing.

The industry form is useful for predicting price behavior and other competitive actions such as industry consolidation, acquisition, and marketing actions. Determining the extent of product differentiation, relative positions of firms, and financial performance is useful in evaluating competitive opportunities and threats.

The distribution of company size in many industries is highly skewed, consisting of a few large companies and many smaller ones. Analysis of the Profit Impact of Marketing Strategy (PIMS) data for 1,218 businesses indicates that "sales of a given product category are highly concentrated among a few leading competitors, and that when competitors are ranked by size, each one is considerably larger than the next on the list."[3] Also, there is a tendency for the large-market-share businesses to lose share as the market evolves. The skewed distribution appears to be a "natural" market structure.

Determining the industry form is a logical starting point in defining the structure of an industry. This classification identifies the number and size of competing firms. Another structural characteristic is the degree of differentiation that exists among the industry members on the basis of the market served and the positioning strategy of each firm. The former considers market segmentation, and the latter may include product differentiation as well as differentiation of other components of the marketing mix.

Industry Environment. Michael E. Porter suggests that the industry environment is influenced by the extent of concentration of its firms, the stage of its maturity, and its exposure to international competition. Five generic environments describe the range of industry structures.[4]

Emerging These industries are newly formed or reformed, created by various factors such as a new technology, the changing needs of buyers, and the identification of unmet needs by suppliers.

Fragmented In this type of industry, no company has a strong position regarding market share or influence. Typically, a large number of relatively small firms make up the industry. There are many fragmented industries in the United States and other countries.

Transitional These industries are shifting from rapid growth to maturity, as represented by the product life cycles of the products in the industry. The personal computer industry is in the transitional stage.

Declining In this type of industry, real sales are declining. This industry category is not cyclical, where sales rise and fall over time. Rather, a declining industry is actually fading away instead of experiencing a temporary decline.

Global Firms in this category compete on a global basis. Examples include automobiles, tires, consumer electronics, and steel.

The five industry categories are neither exhaustive nor mutually exclusive. Moreover, changing environmental and industry conditions may alter an industry classification.

The stages of the life cycles of the products in the industry offer useful insights about the industry environment. Porter's generic environments are closely related to the product life cycle (PLC) stages. The examination of competition during the product life cycle and at different product-market levels provides insights into different types and intensities of competition. Products, like people, move through life cycles. The discussion of product-market levels and structure in Chapters 5 and 6 identify the life cycle to be analyzed. The PLC of the product type or product variant can be analyzed. Life-cycle analysis may also focus on a market segment within a product-market.

The life cycle of a typical product is shown in Exhibit 7–4. Sales begin at the time of introduction and increase over the pattern shown. Profits initially lag sales, since expenses often exceed sales during the initial stage of the product life cycle as a result of heavy introductory expenses. Industry

EXHIBIT 7–4 Life Cycle of a Typical Product

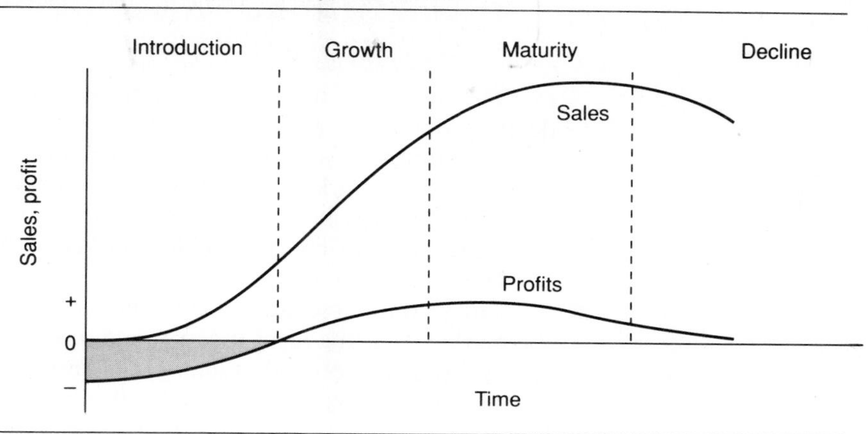

sales and profits decline after the product reaches the maturity stage. Often profits fall off before sales. Product-market evolution is discussed in Chapter 10, and PLC analysis is considered in Chapter 12.

Value-Added System Analysis. In Chapter 3 we looked at the relationships among organizations. Value-added system analysis builds on this discussion. It is concerned with determining where the industry of interest fits into the value-added system. For example, does the industry comprise suppliers, producers, wholesalers, distributors, or retailers/dealers (Exhibit 7–3)? It is important to identify the value-added chain of the company conducting the competitor analysis and the value-added chains of competing firms.

Analysis of the system considers important trends (e.g., supplier consolidation), relative power of organizations at different levels in the system, and possible changes in the system. It is important to identify different value-added systems used in the industry to move materials and supplies to producers and producers' products to consumer and organizational end-users. These variations in value-added systems may indicate potential opportunities or threats for the organization conducting the competitor analysis. Analysis of distribution systems for moving goods and services through distribution channels is discussed in Chapter 13.

Competitive Forces. Porter proposes a useful framework for examining competitive forces in the value-added system. The traditional view of competition is expanded by recognizing five competitive forces that determine industry performance:

1. Rivalry among existing firms.
2. Threat of new entrants.

3. Threat of substitute products.
4. Bargaining power of suppliers.
5. Bargaining power of buyers.[5]

The first force recognizes that active competition among firms helps determine industry performance. This is the most direct and intense form of competition. Rivalry may occur within a market segment or across an entire product-market. The nature and scope of competition may vary according to the type of industry structure. For example, competition in an emerging industry consists of the market pioneer and a few other early entrants.

The second force highlights the possibility of new competitors entering the market. Existing firms may try to discourage new competition through aggressive expansion and other types of entry barriers. The widespread corporate restructuring of the 1980s drastically altered many competitive structures, with companies moving in and out of the markets.[6] The changes in telecommunications and financial services are illustrative. Regional Bell companies are now competitors of AT&T, which also competes in the computer industry. The baby Bells were originally part of the AT&T business portfolio.

The third force consists of the potential impact of substitutes. New technologies that satisfy the same customer need are important sources of competition. Including alternative technologies in the definition of product-market structure should identify substitute forms of competition. Western Union's failure to recognize the competitive threat posed by fax machines is an example of the dangers of defining competitive boundaries too narrowly.

The fourth force is the power that suppliers may have on the producers of an industry. For example, the high costs of labor and aircraft exert a major impact on the commercial airline industry. Companies may pursue vertical integration strategies to reduce the bargaining power of suppliers. By purchasing its suppliers the organization establishes control over suppliers. The emphasis on quality improvement by many producers is strengthening cooperation between suppliers and their customers and reducing the number of suppliers servicing manufacturers (Chapter 3).

Finally, buyers may use their purchasing power on their suppliers. Wal-Mart, for example, has a strong influence on the suppliers of its array of products. A major consequence of Porter's view of competition is that the competitive arena may be altered as a result of the impact of the five forces on the industry. For example, in the case of diamonds, all five forces are at low or negligible levels of intensity because of De Beers's global control of diamond distribution. In contrast, where low barriers of entry exist, the number of firms may increase, leading to greater rivalry among competitors. Strategies of individual firms can also influence the five forces.

The five competitive forces also highlight the existence of vertical and horizontal types of competition. Horizontal competition consists of rivalry among firms in the same industry, such as personal computer producers. Vertical competition involves rivalry among and within distribution channels. The intensity of vertical competition is related, in part, to the bargaining power of suppliers and buyers. The location (level) of an organization in its distribution channel and the extent of its control over the channel may affect the marketing strategy. For example, the marketing strategy for an Ethan Allen furniture dealer consists essentially of implementing the producer's strategy. Individual members of corporate-owned or corporate-controlled channels have limited control over marketing strategy formulation. Thus, an important competitive issue is whether or not a firm controls its channel of distribution. This issue is considered in Chapter 13.

STRATEGIC GROUP ANALYSIS

The firms in an industry can sometimes be placed into groups whose members are similar in the strategies they employ. The concept of strategic groups helps focus competitor analysis on the firms that are similar to each other. Thus, a strategic group is the set of firms in an industry that use a common strategy that is defined using key strategic dimensions.[7] While strategic groups do not occur in all industries, the existence of two or more strategic groups is a more typical pattern.

Strategic group analysis is useful in determining how to compete, comparing performance, and anticipating the future strategies of key competitors. The formation of strategic groups is particularly important when the industry has many competitors.[8] These groupings make competitor analysis more feasible and usable. Since the firms in a strategic group respond to and are affected by industry developments in similar ways, group analysis should provide useful strategic insights. Strategic grouping includes choosing the specific dimensions of strategy for identifying the groups and selecting a method for forming the strategic group(s).

Selecting Dimensions for Group Formation

One approach to describe the strategies of industry members is identifying the companies with similar combinations of strategic *scope* and *resource* commitments.[9] Scope considers the market segments served, the product/service mix, and the geographic reach of a firm's strategy. Resource commitments are the business-level deployments of cash, people, and materials. Exhibit 7–5 illustrates the use of these strategic variables in an analysis of the pharmaceutical industry. The scope variables focus on market and product involvement while the resource variables consider both the amount and

EXHIBIT 7–5 Variables Describing Strategy in the U.S. Pharmaceutical Industry

Strategy Dimension	*Measure*
Scope Commitments:	
Range of market segments	
1. Breadth of scope	1. (Rx sales in 3 largest therapeutic categories)/(Total domestic Rx sales)
2. Commitment to ambulatory care market	2. % drugstore sales in total domestic drug sales
Types of products	
3. Commitment to the ethical drug market	3. % Rx sales in total domestic drug sales
Commitment to the generic drug market	
4. Branded generics	4. % branded generic Rx sales in total domestic Rx sales
5. Commodity generics	5. % commodity generic Rx sales in total domestic Rx sales
6. Commitment to the maintenance drug market	6. % maintenance drug sales in total domestic Rx sales
Geographic scope	
7. Spatial reach	7. % total firm sales generated abroad
Resource Commitments:	
Research and development commitments	
8. Current R&D spending	8. (Total firm R&D)/(Worldwide health care sales)
9. R&D capital stock	9. (Cumulative number of NDAs submitted)/(Cumulative number of INDs submitted)
10. R&D orientation	10. (Cumulative number of NCEs approved)/(Cumulative number of NDAs submitted)
Marketing commitments	
11. Product strategy	11. (Cumulative number of NCEs introduced)/(Cumulative number of all products introduced)
Promotion strategy	
12. Promotion to the medical profession	12. (Total domestic professional promotion)/(Total Rx sales)
13. Advertising to the consumer	13. (Total domestic PTY drug advertising)/(Total domestic Rx sales)
14. Distribution strategy	14. % total domestic drug sales shipped directly to drugstores and hospitals
Size	
15. Scale of drug operations	15. Ln (Total domestic drug sales)

Source: Karen O. Cool and Dan Schendel, "Strategic Group Formation and Performance: The Case of the U.S. Pharmaceutical Industry, 1963–1982," *Management Science*, September 1987, p. 1110.

allocation of resources. Several of the variables are components of marketing strategy.

The purpose of the strategic variables is to capture the variation in strategies across the firms in the industry of interest. Porter recommends using the following strategic factors in strategic group analysis.[10]

extent of product-market specialization (segment focus versus coverage of the entire market)

brand image (leading brands, minor brands, private-label brands)

push versus pull channel strategy (promotion directed at value system companies or end-users)

channel of distribution strategy (intensive, selective, or exclusive distribution)

product quality level (good, better, best)

technological leadership (leader versus follower)

extent of vertical integration (extent of ownership of the value-added system by one company)

cost advantage (relative cost positions of industry members)

supporting services (information systems, applications support, product repair, etc.)

price position (low, medium, high relative prices)

financial and operating leverage (cash flow, debt, profits, etc.)

corporate structure (centralized, diversified)

relationship to home and host government

The objective is to select the key strategic dimensions that are useful in forming the strategic group(s). The dimensions selected should portray how the strategies of the industry members differ.

Mapping Strategic Groups

A strategic map may be based on management judgment or determined by analytical methods. As an example of strategic group formation consider the watch industry. Two strategic dimensions that are useful in showing the differences in the strategies of industry members are (1) relative price/quality, and (2) the intensity of distribution in the marketplace. Price/quality considers the price level of a company's brand compared to the industry average. Distribution intensity concerns how widely a brand is available in the retail distribution network. The Rolex and Casio brands fall into distinctly different strategic groups. Casio and Timex appear more similar in their strategies along the two strategic dimensions. More than two dimensions may be needed to capture the differences (and similarities) across the watch industry. Style could be used as a third dimension.

EXHIBIT 7–6 Descriptive Profile of One Strategic Group in the Pharmaceutical Industry (22 firms in 1982)

1963–1969	*1970–1974*	*1975–1979*	*1980–1982*
Abbott	Abbott	Abbott	Abbott
Lederle	American Home*	American Home	American Home
Eli Lilly & Co.	Lederle	Bristol-Myers*	Bristol-Myers
Merck**	Eli Lilly & Co.	Lederle**	Pfizer*
Squibb	Squibb	Warner-Lambert	Smith Kline*
Upjohn	Warner-Lambert*		Warner-Lambert
—large firms	—expanded into nonprescription market segments	—more movement toward nonprescription market segments	—the earlier profile maintained
—R&D intensive	—some decrease in R&D intensity	—increased consumer advertising	
—prescription drugs		—still less R&D emphasis	
—product innovation		—fewer original drugs	
—multiple market segments			
—wide product mix			

*New member

**Will exit next period

Source: Adopted from Karen O. Cool and Dan Schendel, "Strategic Group Formation and Performance: The Case of the U.S. Pharmaceutical Industry, 1963–1982," *Management Science*, September 1987, pp. 1114–17.

A strategic group analysis of the pharmaceutical industry using the strategy dimensions shown in Exhibit 7–5 resulted in four to six strategic groups, depending on the time period analyzed from 1963 to 1982.[11] Importantly, both group composition and strategies changed over time. The 1982 analysis included 22 industry members and six strategic groups were identified. A comparison of group membership and the strategy profile for one of the groups is shown in Exhibit 7–6.

Judgmental Grids. Two-dimensional plots can be used to position industry members on key strategic dimensions. For example, relative price/quality and distribution intensity could be used to create a grid for the watch industry. A map is prepared showing the relative positions of the firms. Those organizations that cluster together form a potential strategic group. The selection of strategic dimensions is based on management's assessment of the relevance of each strategic factor. The positioning on the map may be classification categories or values (e.g., price/industry average price), depending on the measure used.

Choosing good grid dimensions is important since only two of several strategic factors can be used. The two dimensions must be good proxies for the strategies industry members' use. Combining the strategic impact of several factors into the two dimensions must be subjectively determined by management. Porter indicates that the best strategic variables to use as axes are those that *determine the key mobility barriers* in the industry.[12] For example, trip distance and landing slots are useful in separating commuter, regional, and national airlines into strategic groups.

Multivariate Analysis. The difficulty of selecting the best two strategic factors for mapping can be overcome by using multivariate analysis methods. They are more powerful than the two-way plots since they can incorporate several strategic variables. These techniques provide a composite, multidimensional strategic comparison. The strategic groups identified in the pharmaceutical study discussed earlier were determined using multivariate analysis of variance techniques (see Exhibits 7–5 and 7–6).

Multidimensional scaling methods are useful in developing strategic maps.[13] The preference maps discussed in Chapter 6 are examples of this technique. These methods can be used to generate intraindustry maps showing the positioning of companies against performance criteria and various strategy variables. These two-dimensional maps transform several strategic dimensions into a spatial representation of intraindustry competitive strategy. The mapping technique is useful when there are many competitors in the industry.

Using Strategic Group Analysis

The strategic group concept provides a business-level focus, suggests marketing strategy insights, and offers a basis for performance comparisons.

Business-Level Focus. As illustrated by the pharmaceutical industry example, strategic group formation has a business-level focus rather than identifying competitive sets within market segments. More microlevel competitive analyses are possible, although they may not identify the overall strategic orientation of a company. The segment strategies of a company are likely to vary across the segments that are targeted. Thus, strategic mapping is most useful at the business unit or corporate levels.

Mapping Dimensions. Many of the potential mapping dimensions are marketing strategy components. This highlights the importance of close coordination of business and marketing strategies. It is also clear that multiple dimensions of strategy can provide useful insights into strategy analysis. Strategy dimensions include situational, scope, resource, and performance variables.

Strategy versus Performance. Strategic grouping is useful in comparing the performance of firms within an industry. Identifying strategic groups offers better comparisons of performance than if a total industry perspective is used. However, caution should be exercised in assuming that a competitor is correctly positioned in a particular strategic group. Management may be following a strategy that is inappropriate for the particular contingencies confronting the firm. We examine this issue in Chapter 10.

IDENTIFYING, DESCRIBING, AND EVALUATING COMPETITORS

Strategic group analysis helps identify the key competitors in an industry. The firms in an organization's strategic group are its key competitors. Competitor analysis is conducted for these firms and other companies that management may consider important in strategy analysis (for example, potential group entrants). The importance companies place on competitor analysis is apparent from a Conference Board survey of the strategic priorities and practices of 214 companies in various size groups covering manufacturing, distribution, and service industries:

> The use of competitive intelligence, competitor analysis, and new techniques for gaining a competitive edge has been a major factor in developing strategies over the past five years, according to the survey results. This is exemplified by a large insurance company's planning director, who remarks: "We now watch with varying degrees of interest about 200 competitors, most of which were never considered competitors four years ago. We used to watch about five companies."[14]

Nearly half of the surveyed firms have revised their competitive intelligence procedures compared to the prior five years. They place much greater emphasis on monitoring, analyzing, and evaluating competitors and specific industry environments. It is clear from this study and many other sources that competitor analysis is a high-priority activity in many corporations.

In this section we consider two major aspects of competitor analysis: (1) the development of a descriptive profile of the competitor; and (2) an evaluation of the competitor's strengths and weaknesses (Exhibit 7–1).

Describing the Competitor

A *key competitor* is a firm going after the same market target as the firm conducting the analysis. American, Delta, and United Airlines are key competitors on many U.S. routes. Key competitors are often brands that compete in the same product-market or segment(s) within the market. Different product types that satisfy the same need or want may also actively compete against each other. For example, when U.S. Surgical Corporation entered the market for surgical skin closures with its line of surgical stapling equipment in the early 1970s, the stapler was a competitive threat to needle and

EXHIBIT 7–7 Information Needed for Describing Key Competitors

- Business scope and objectives
- Management experience, capabilities, and weaknesses
- Market position and trends
- Market target(s) and customer base
- Marketing program positioning strategy
- Financial, technical, and operating capabilities
- Key competitive advantages (e.g., access to resources, patents)

suture suppliers. There were no other surgical stapler manufacturers at that time. (See Case 3–2, U.S. Surgical Corporation.)

A checklist of information included in a competitor profile is shown in Exhibit 7–7. Sources of information include annual reports, industry studies by government and private organizations, business magazines and newspapers, trade publications, company reports by financial analysts (e.g., *Value Line Investment Survey*), government reports, standardized data services (e.g., MRCA and Nielsen), databases, suppliers, customers, and salespeople. Financial analysts' research reports are very useful as a first step in competitor description.

It is important to gain as much knowledge as possible about the background, experience, and qualifications of key executives of each major competitor. This information includes the executives' performance records, their particular areas of expertise, and the types of firms where they were previously employed. These analyses are often helpful in suggesting the future strategies a key competitor may follow. Business and industry publications and newspapers are useful sources of this information for executives who work in large firms. Other sources include suppliers, customers, and marketing channel organizations.

The descriptive profile of a competitor includes a historical picture of management's marketing decisions. Past decisions show the pattern of changes in marketing strategy and tactics as management responded to changing market conditions. Analysis of these decisions should attempt to match them with specific changes taking place in markets or with competition. An experienced marketer can then develop a feel for the management style of the key competitor by looking for patterns or consistencies in these decisions.

Strategic group analysis may suggest shifts in the strategies of competitors over time. Note, for example, the changes in strategic group composition for the pharmaceutical industry from 1963 to 1982 (see Exhibit 7–6). The group analyses indicate key strategy dimensions and how each competitor is positioned against a dimension.

EXHIBIT 7–8 Evaluation of the Competition

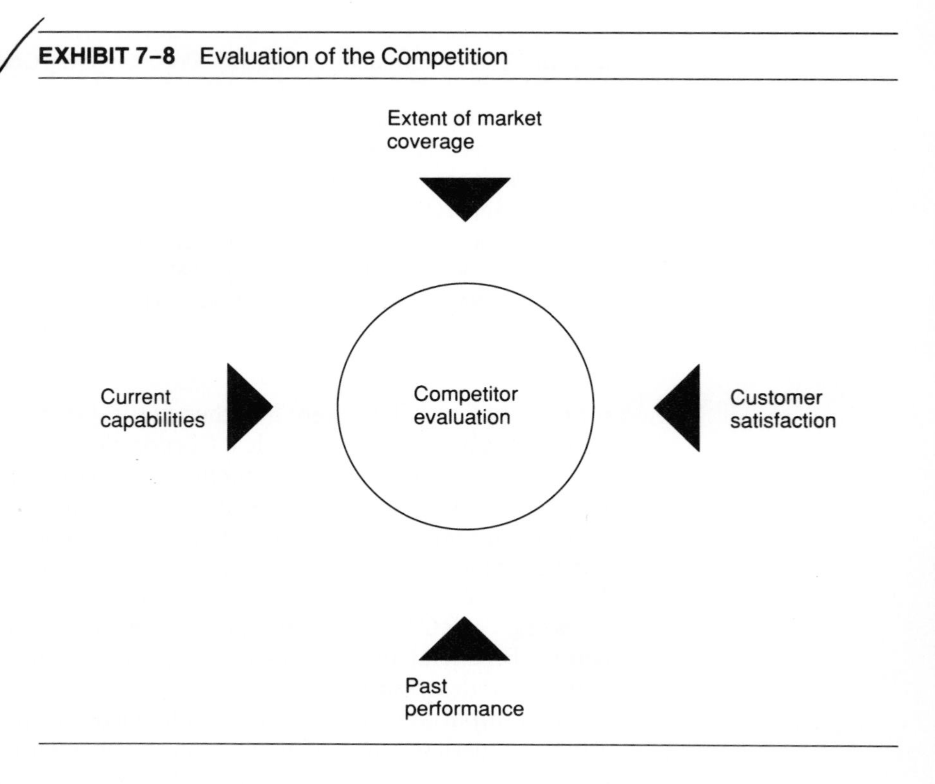

Evaluating the Competitor

Although competitor description and evaluation are interrelated, it is useful to separate the two activities. Evaluation determines the strengths and weaknesses of each competitor in the four areas shown in Exhibit 7–8. When management evaluates the extent of market coverage, customer satisfaction, past performance, and current capabilities, this provides a basis for estimating the competitor's future actions.

Extent of Market Coverage. This evaluation should center on the market segments targeted by the competitor and the competitor's actual and relative market-share position. Relative market position is measured by comparing the share of the firm against the competitor with the highest market share in the segment. All segments in the product-market that could be targeted by the firm should be included in the competitor evaluation. Consider, for example, the brand positioning map shown in Exhibit 7–9. The map is used by Chrysler Corporation to evaluate possible positioning opportunities. The upper-right quadrant offers a possible position for Chrysler and other U.S. automobile manufacturers. Honda introduced the Acura Legend in 1986 to compete in this quadrant. A few years later Toyota introduced the very suc-

EXHIBIT 7–9 Analyzing Market Coverage for Automobile Brands

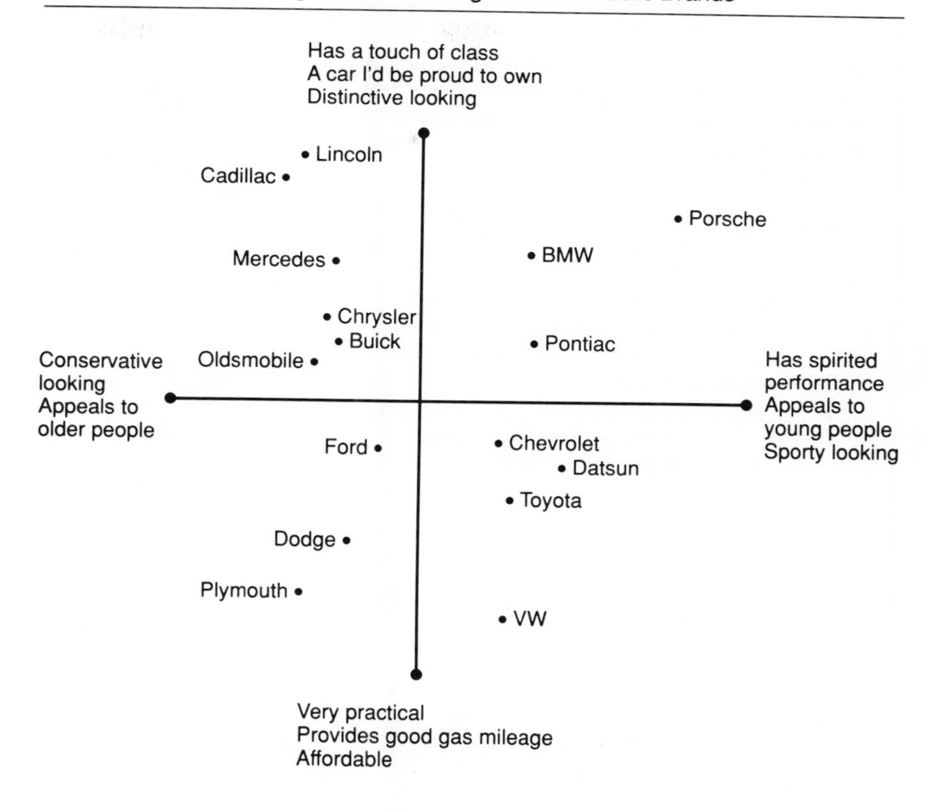

Source: John Koten, "Car Makers Use 'Image' Map as Tool to Position Products," March 22, 1984. Reprinted by permission of *The Wall Street Journal*, © 1984. Dow Jones & Company, Inc. All Rights Reserved Worldwide.

cessful Lexus 400. This analysis suggests segments where competitors are not providing market coverage and alerts a firm to potential new competition.

The *Market Share Reporter* is an annual compilation of reported market-share data on companies, products, and services.[15] It has more than 2,000 entries and draws from various data sources. As an example, the market-share breakdown for nail polish producers in 1989 was as follows (the company's leading brand in parentheses):

P&G/Noxell (Cover Girl)	29%
Unilever (Cutex)	16%
Schering-Plough (Maybelline)	15%
Del Labs (Sally Hansen)	10%

INDUSTRY FEATURE Cereal Giants Battle over Market Share

The ready-to-eat cereal market illustrates the intense competitive battles for market share that occur in many consumer markets. Kellogg holds the top position in this $7.5 billion-a-year market (see chart).

- Kellogg and General Mills are using aggressive advertising, sales promotion, and pricing strategies and tactics, making it tough for the small competitors.
- Kellogg spent an estimated $100 million *more* on marketing in the third quarter of 1991 compared to 1990.
- Holding a market share of 1 percent ($75 million in sales) is significant with profit margins at 20 percent or more.
- Cereals are important for supermarkets since cereals are the second-largest-selling branded food item after soft drinks.
- The name-brand cereals also compete against the retailer's private-label products, offered at substantially lower prices (e.g., $1.69 versus $3.26).
- A stream of new products is introduced to target market segments and maintain market momentum.

Source: Richard Gibson, "Cereal Giants Battle over Market Share," *The Wall Street Journal,* December 16, 1991, pp. B1, 4.

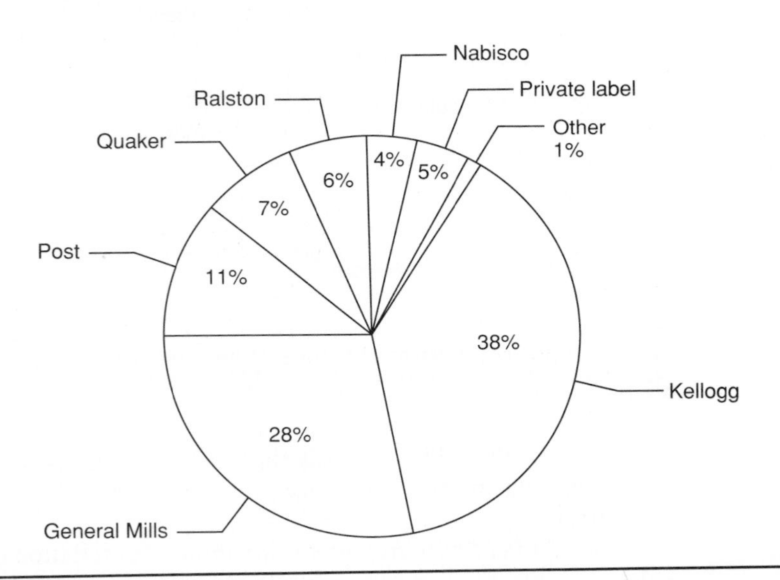

Revlon (Revlon)	7%
Cosmair (L'Oreal)	6%
All others	17%

The Industry Feature examines market share in the ready-to-eat cereal market.

Customer Satisfaction. Value and/or cost advantages build customers' satisfaction with the product or service. The Day and Wensley framework for assessing advantage separates competitive superiority into customer-focused and competitor-centered dimensions of superiority.[16] Positional advantages over competition are achieved by providing superior customer value. Toyota's successful entry into the European-style luxury sedan segment was the result of the superior value provided by the Lexus 400 at a cost lower than comparable BMW and Mercedes models. The brand achieved a top rating by consumers in the first two years after introduction.

The starting point in assessing how well competitors meet customer needs is finding out what criteria buyers use to rate each supplier. Two aspects of customer satisfaction are important. First, buyers have ideal preferences about the attributes of a supplier or product. For example, a consumer may have an ideal amount of chocolate that she or he prefers in ice cream. This provides an important reference point in attribute comparisons between brands. Second, customers have preferences concerning alternative brands. The amount of chocolate in brand A is preferred to the amount in brand B.

Customer-focused measures of customer satisfaction are more useful than relying on management judgments of satisfaction. Measurement methods include customer comparisons of attributes of the firm versus its competitors, customer satisfaction surveys, loyalty measures, and the relative market share of end-user segments.[17] Preference maps like the one shown in Exhibit 7–9 are useful in comparing the competing brands for attributes that are important determinants of customer satisfaction.

Past Performance. An analysis of each key competitor's past sales and financial performance indicates how well the competitor has performed on a historical basis. A typical period of analysis is a few years. Performance information may include sales, market share, net profit, net profit margin, cash flow, and debt. Additionally, for specific types of businesses other performance information may be useful. For example, sales per square foot is often used to compare the performance of retail companies.

Suppose you are interested in evaluating the performance of NCR Corporation. As shown in Exhibit 7–10, NCR has a strong market position in the finance and retail industries.[18] Its domination of these market segments is an important competitive advantage. NCR was acquired by AT&T in 1991. The acquisition was a good strategic fit for AT&T, enabling the firm to gain a critical mass in computers. The partnership also strengthened NCR's position in the very competitive computer market. Of course, more complete analysis is needed to fully evaluate NCR. The information shown in Exhibit 7–10 is illustrative of many sources of competitor intelligence available from published sources such as *The Wall Street Journal.*

Current Capabilities. Determining market coverage, customer satisfaction, and past performance provide useful information about competitors. Using this information, you can develop an overall evaluation of the key competitor's strengths and weaknesses. Additionally, the summary assess-

EXHIBIT 7–10 Illustrative Analysis of NCR Corporation

NCR's Diverse Product Line . . .

Segments' shares of 1989 revenue of $5.96 billion

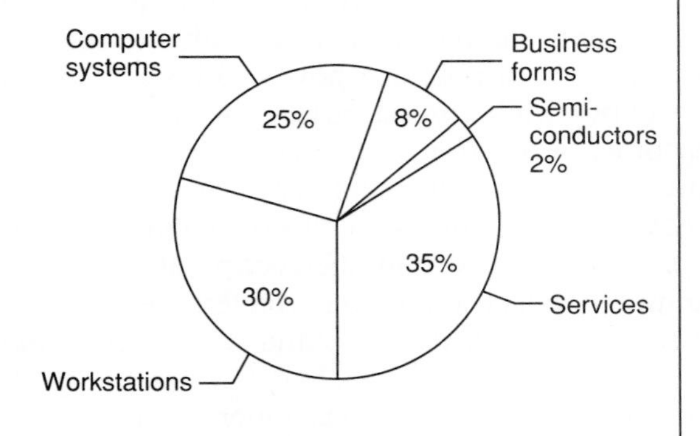

Is Big in Two Key Industries . . .

NCR's sales by industry vs. computer industry average

	NCR	Industry
Finance	39%	10%
Retail	23	13
Government	9	8
Manufacturing	8	21
Wholesale	4	7
Professional	4	8
Education	2	8
Other	11	25

Source: Dean Witter

Productivity Has Risen . . .

Revenue per employee in thousands of dollars

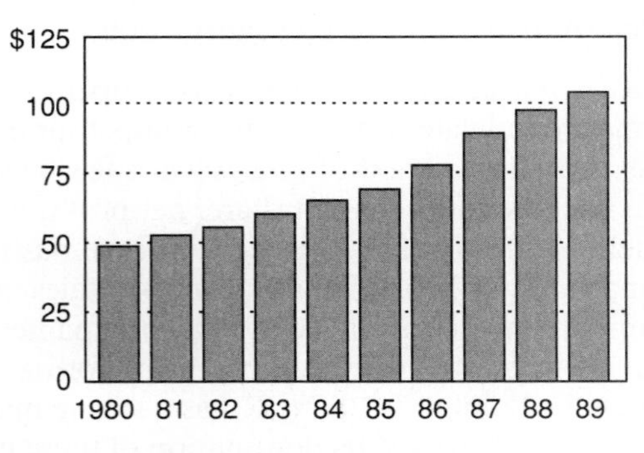

Source: Prudential-Bache Securities

While Its Stock Beat the Industry

NCR vs. DJ computer group; Dec. 1984 = 100

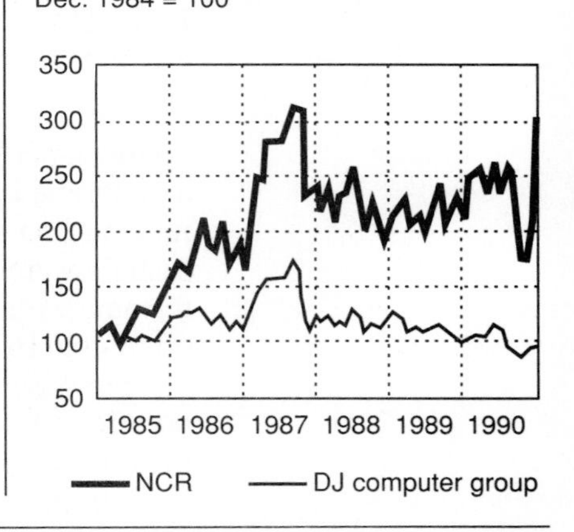

Source: John J. Keller, "Calculated Offer," *The Wall Street Journal,* December 4, 1990, p. A6. Reprinted by permission of The Wall Street Journal, © 1990. Dow Jones & Company, Inc. All Rights Reserved Worldwide.

ment of current capabilities includes information on the competitor's management capabilities and limitations, technical and operating advantages and weaknesses, marketing strategy, and other key strengths and limitations. Since competitors often have different strengths and weaknesses, it is important to highlight these differences. A checklist for evaluating competitor strengths and weaknesses is shown in Exhibit 7–11.

EXHIBIT 7–11 Areas of Evaluation of Competitor Strengths and Weaknesses

- Sales and market position in segments served
- Strategic group position
- Level of customer satisfaction
- Business approach (price, quality, service, aggressiveness)
- Financial performance (current and historical)
  —net profit/sales ratio
  —return on investment
  —number of employees
  —facilities
- Financial resources and leverage
- Cost position relative to key competitors
- Relative product quality
- Innovativeness
- Product portfolio
- Management capabilities
- Marketing strategy and effectiveness
- Methods of distribution
- Summary of key strengths and weaknesses

ANTICIPATING COMPETITORS' ACTIONS

The final steps in competitor analysis consider what each key competitor will do in the future and identify potential competitors. Both the strategic group analysis and competitor evaluation analyses are helpful in estimating future trends. The analysis of industry structure and competitive forces identifies potential competitors.

Estimating Future Strategies

Competitors' future strategies may simply follow the general directions that they have established in the past, particularly if no major external influences require changing their strategies. Nevertheless, assuming an existing strategy will continue to be effective is not wise. Competitors' current actions may signal probable future actions.

A brief analysis of Sara Lee Corporation is illustrative.[19] As shown in Exhibit 7–12, Sara Lee's growth and performance during the 1980s were very favorable. Importantly, there were indications that management had implemented a clearly defined global strategy. The strategy is to find a non-durable consumer product needed by large segments of the population and to pursue a leading (megabrand) market-share position. Sara Lee uses a brand extension strategy of adding products to an established brand name.

EXHIBIT 7–12 Descriptive Profile of Sara Lee Corporation

Sales and Profits by Segment

Annual sales in billions of dollars

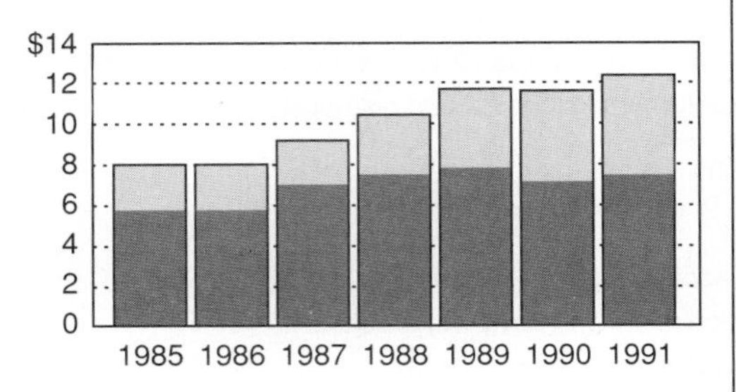

Annual operating profit in billions of dollars

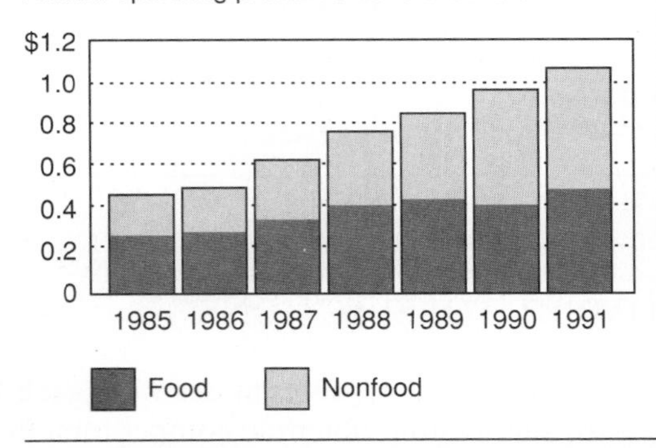

The Fundamentals

	1991	1990
Sales ($ billions)	$12.4	$11.6
Net income ($ millions)	$535.8	$470.0
Earnings per share	$2.15	$1.91

Some Major Sara Lee Brands:

Packaged meats: Ball Park, Hillshire Farm, Mr. Turkey.

Baked goods: Chef Pierre, Sara Lee.

Coffee and tea: Douwe Egberts, Pickwick, Van Nelle.

Hosiery: Dim, Hanes, L'eggs, Sheer Energy, Underalls.

Activewear: Beefy-T, Champion, Hanes Her Way.

Underwear and intimate apparel: Bali, Dim, Hanes, Playtex.

Household, personal-care items: Kiwi, Sanex.

Source: Richard Gibson, "Sara Lee Mulls Purchases to Satisfy Hunger for Growth," *The Wall Street Journal,* April 14, 1992, p. B4. Reprinted by permission of The Wall Street Journal.

Management sticks to basic products such as underwear, socks, and shoe polish. Sara Lee is the largest producer of pantyhose in the world and Hanes is its leading brand. Sara Lee's strategy for the future is apparent: building a powerful portfolio of megabrands that span multiple product lines and political boundaries. Sara Lee was the top performer among the 100 largest U.S. corporations in the 1980s. The company has a strong management and a clearly defined strategy that is very effective. The company produces products for every retail channel (e.g., drugstores, supermarkets, mass-merchandise outlets, department stores, and specialty retailers). Sara Lee is aggressively building market position in Europe.

Identifying New Competitors

New competitors often come from three major sources: (1) companies competing in related product-market; (2) companies with related technologies; and/or (3) companies targeting similar customer groups. Market entry by a new competitor is more likely under these conditions:

- High profit margins are being achieved by market incumbents.
- Future growth opportunities in the market are attractive.
- No major market-entry barriers are present.
- Competition is limited to one of a few competitors.
- Gaining an equivalent (or better) competitive advantage over the existing firm(s) serving the market is feasible.

If one or more of these conditions is present in a competitive situation, new competition will probably appear.

The entry of new competitors can sometimes be predicted with a reasonable degree of certainty. We illustrate this situation by examining a completely new product (surgical staplers) and an established product (nonaspirin).

U.S. Surgical Corporation was the market pioneer for surgical stapling products. By the late 1970s its sales reached $50 million, accounting for about 10 percent of the total wound-closure market.[20] In view of the firm's rapid growth, lack of direct competitors, and the potential opportunity for surgical stapling to capture a substantial portion of the market, it was not surprising that Johnson & Johnson's Ethicon subsidiary entered the market with a disposable stapler in 1978. The disposable feature became very attractive for certain types of surgery, and Ethicon captured a large portion of U.S. Surgical's stapler market share. This caused U.S. Surgical to initiate a major new-product development program that cost $100 million over a four-year period.

During the mid-1970s Tylenol held most of the nonaspirin pain relief market. Tylenol's profit margins were very large, and the marketing costs were relatively low for a consumer product. No consumer advertising had been used to promote Tylenol. Instead, promotion efforts had been concentrated in medical and dental professional publications and sales force contacts with doctors. Because of the large market opportunity, the attractive profit margins, the market dominance by one firm, and the ease of product duplication, the entry of a new competitor was likely to occur. Datril entered the market with an aggressive advertising campaign and prices substantially below Tylenol's. Tylenol's management reduced its prices to meet Datril's. Interestingly, a decade later Tylenol dominated the market. Even the cyanide deaths in 1983, which were attributed to tampering with Tylenol packages, failed to topple Tylenol from its strong market position.

COMPETITOR INTELLIGENCE SYSTEMS

Many of the Fortune 500 companies have well-developed competition intelligence systems. This activity is also a high priority in smaller firms:

> For years, Labconco Corp. never paid much attention to the competition. The Kansas City, Mo., based medical equipment manufacturer considered its marketing strategy adequate—it kept abreast of competitors' new products, price lists and anything that came along in the mail. . . .
>
> Increasingly, smaller firms are tapping secrets of competitors through more sophisticated, systematic ways—via seminars, in-house staff, private consultants and a field of databases whose growth has exploded in the past decade.[21]

Companies are developing intelligence systems to help monitor existing competitors and to spot new competitors. Various techniques are used, including searching large computer databases, conducting customer surveys, conducting interviews with suppliers and other marketing channel participants, hiring competitors' personnel, and studying competitors' products. The databases available for competitor analysis are impressive:

> Electronic databases, which store information to be retrieved by computer, are proliferating. Some 2,000 are now available. One, called Economic Information Systems, published by a subsidiary of Control Data Corp., lists the names and locations of industrial facilities along with estimates of each plant's dollar volume of output, number of employees, and the share of market that its production represents. Another database, called Investext, published by Business Research Corp. of Brighton, Massachusetts, gives subscribers the full text of research reports on companies by security analysts and investment bankers.[22]

Developing an effective competitor intelligence system involves three important actions. First, a system for collecting, analyzing, and interpreting information on competitors is developed and implemented. Second, responsibility needs to be assigned for coordinating information collection and analysis. Finally, the use of benchmarking techniques to study competition is becoming popular.

Information Collection and Analysis

This chapter outlines an approach for identifying the information needed to monitor competition. A wide array of information is available. The real challenge is designing a system for obtaining the information and putting it into a form useful for competitor analysis. The fragments of information must be combined into a useful format describing the competitive arena and each key competitor.

A sophisticated computerized system is not essential, although such systems may be appropriate for large corporations. Many computerized databases can be accessed at very reasonable costs, making them available for small and medium-size companies. Decision makers must identify what information is needed, where it can be obtained, and how to obtain it.

Assigning Responsibility

It is important to assign specific responsibility for coordinating competitor intelligence activities. Motorola Inc. centers its competitor intelligence function in the firm's corporate strategy office.[23] The system serves all business units in the corporation. Capabilities include a data management system that taps a variety of sources such as newspapers, books, industry studies, government reports, on-line data services, and marketing reports. The system also uses consulting reports, technical analysis, and competitor reports.

Several of the companies surveyed by The Conference Board, Inc. delegate the responsibility for monitoring the competition to business units instead of the former practice of assigning the responsibility to the corporate planning department.[24] The business units are closer to the competitive arena than the corporate group.

Competitor analysis is often included in marketing plans. The person (team) responsible for planning may also coordinate competitor intelligence activities. For example, a large pharmaceutical company provides a complete competitor analysis in the marketing plan. The product manager is responsible for obtaining, analyzing, and interpreting competitor intelligence information. The marketing plan includes a description of the competitor's products, its mission statement (for the product category), product positioning concept, advertising and sales promotion strategy, sales force resources and qualifications, current promotion activity, and anticipated future products.

Benchmarking

The practice of studying how other companies design their products and produce them is a useful way to obtain new ideas and improve work processes. As discussed in Chapter 2, benchmarking is an important form of competitor analysis. These activities include companies in other industries. For example, an industrial parts distributor may gain useful information by studying how L. L. Bean processes its mail orders for apparel and camping equipment.

Mellon Bank in Pittsburgh used benchmarking studies to reduce customer credit card complaints by nearly 60 percent.[25] A team of eight people benchmarked seven companies, including other credit card services, an airline, and a competing bank. The study, conducted on a part-time basis by the team members, covered five months. One of the improvements included better accessing of document information using improved software.

Information systems design and management are discussed in Chapter 8. The material is useful in designing competitor intelligence systems.

SUMMARY

Identifying the important competitors and evaluating their strategies are necessary in designing effective marketing strategies. It is vital to know what the competition is doing and what they are likely to do in the future. Competitor analysis provides information that is helpful in deciding when to enter a new market or to exit from an existing market. An understanding of competitors' weaknesses suggests avenues for gaining competitive advantage.

Competition occurs in various forms. Head-on, brand-to-brand competition is the most direct type of competition. Competition may also occur between different product types or variants. The scarcity of buyers' resources also creates competition between generic needs. Finally, geographic variations occur in the competition arena. Strong regional brands of products may offer tough competition for national brands.

This chapter discusses the information needed in the analysis of competition and identifies methods useful in the analysis process. The starting point is defining the competitive arena (Exhibit 7–1). This includes identifying the sources of competition faced by the organization and describing the industry structure and characteristics. Industry structure is described by determining the industry form, analyzing the industry environment, studying the value-added system, and evaluating competitive forces affecting the industry. The competitive arena can be examined in greater depth through strategic group analysis, which focuses on the industry members whose strategies are similar to the organization performing the competitor analysis.

Competitor analysis continues by examining in depth each key competitor and potential competitor management considers important. Competitor analysis includes: (1) describing the competitor, (2) evaluating the competitor, and (3) anticipating the future actions of competitors. It is also important to identify possible new competitors. Competitor analysis is an ongoing activity and requires coordinated information collection and analysis. Increasingly, corporations and business units are using competitor intelligence systems for this purpose.

Competitor identification, analysis, and evaluation has several purposes.[26] Study of the competition helps management to avoid surprises and to identify threats and opportunities. Knowledge of competitor strengths and weaknesses helps firms gain competitive advantage by decreasing reaction time. Planning activities benefit from an understanding of the competitive arena. Finally, competitor analysis enables management to understand its own company better.

QUESTIONS FOR REVIEW AND DISCUSSION

1. In the mid-1980s fast-food industry experts predicted a shakeout of small firms. Identify several key strategic factors affecting the marketing strategy of a small fast-food chain.
2. Select an industry and describe its characteristics, participants, and structure.
3. What are some of the limitations in using the product life cycle as a basis for analyzing the competitive situation in an industry?
4. A competitive analysis of the 7UP soft-drink brand is being conducted. Management plans to position the brand against its key competitors. Should the competitors consist of only other noncola drinks?
5. Identify important strategic dimensions that could be used to analyze strategic groups in the airline passenger transportation industry.
6. Outline an approach to competitor evaluation, assuming you are preparing the analysis for a regional bank holding company.
7. Discuss how a small company (less than $1 million in sales) should analyze its competition.
8. Describe how benchmarking is used to improve a company's competitive advantage.

NOTES

1. This example is based on Timothy L. O'Brien, "Beleaguered Schwinn Seeks Partner to Regain Its Luster," *The Wall Street Journal,* May 20, 1992, p. B2.
2. Julie Franz, "Survivors Fight for Granola-Bar Market," *Advertising Age,* February 17, 1986, pp. 4 and 52.
3. Robert D. Buzzell, "Are There 'Natural' Market Structures," *Journal of Marketing,* Winter 1981, pp. 42–51.
4. Michael E. Porter, *Competitive Strategy* (New York: Free Press, 1980), Chapter 9.
5. Michael E. Porter, *Competitive Advantage* (New York: Free Press, 1985), p. 5.
6. William E. Rothschild, "Who Are Your Competitors?" *Journal of Business Strategy,* May/June 1988, p. 10.
7. Porter, *Competitive Strategy,* p. 129.
8. David A. Aaker, *Strategic Market Management,* 3rd ed. (New York: John Wiley & Sons, 1992), p. 66.
9. Karen O. Cool and Dan Schendel, "Strategic Group Formation and Performance: The Case of the U.S. Pharmaceutical Industry, 1963–1982," *Management Science,* September 1987, p. 1106.
10. Porter, *Competitive Strategy,* pp. 127–29.
11. Cool and Schendel, "Strategic Group Formation," pp. 1114–17.
12. Porter, *Competitive Strategy,* p. 152.
13. Diana Day, Wayne S. DeSarbo, and Terence A. Oliva, "Strategy Maps: A Spatial Representation of Intra-Industry Competitive Strategy," *Management Science,* December 1987, pp. 1534–51.

14. Rochelle O'Connor, *Facing Strategic Issues: New Planning Guides and Practices,* Report No. 867 (New York: The Conference Board, Inc., 1985), p. 9.
15. Arsen J. Darnay, *Market Share Reporter* (Detroit: Gale Research Inc., 1991), p. 200.
16. George S. Day and Robin Wensley, "Assessing Advantage: A Framework for Diagnosing Competitive Superiority, *Journal of Marketing,* April 1988, pp. 1–20.
17. Ibid., pp. 12–16.
18. This illustration is drawn from John J. Keller, "Calculated Offer," *The Wall Street Journal,* December 4, 1990, pp. A1 and A6.
19. This illustration is drawn from Richard Gibson, "Sara Lee Mulls Purchases to Satisfy Hunger for Growth," *The Wall Street Journal,* April 14, 1992, p. B4.
20. Robert Teitelman, "Case Study," *Forbes,* May 7, 1984, pp. 142, 144.
21. Mark Robichaux, "'Competitor Intelligence': A Grapevine to Rivals' Secrets," *The Wall Street Journal,* April 12, 1989, p. B2.
22. Steven Flax, "How to Snoop on Your Competitors," *Fortune,* May 14, 1984, p. 30.
23. "Company Sees Benefits in Centralizing its System of Competitor Intelligence," *Marketing News,* September 12, 1986, p. 39.
24. O'Connor, *Facing Strategic Issues,* pp. 9–10.
25. Jeremy Main, "How to Steal the Best Ideas Around," *Fortune,* October 19, 1992, pp. 104, 106.
26. Howard Sutton, *Competitive Intelligence,* Report No. 913 (New York: The Conference Board, Inc., 1988).

CHAPTER

8

Marketing Research and Information Systems

Management faces a continuing challenge in obtaining information about markets, competition, and marketing performance. Information is analyzed and actions taken to realize opportunities and avoid threats. Information is vital to the strategic process. Well-designed marketing information systems create a strong competitive advantage. Decision makers may possess miraculous skills and may achieve fantastic results, but their efforts are wasted without relevant and timely information. As strategic planning is the key to the long-term survival of the firm, then information plays the pivotal role. Management must concentrate on the acquisition, management, and utilization of information as a separate process worthy of considerable attention. Computers dominate the control of information, coping with a constantly changing and turbulent business environment. Marketing managers need to be aware of the volatility of information technology and be alert to the opportunities for improving competitive advantage with information.

Information plays a vital role in decision making at Frito-Lay, a subsidiary of PepsiCo Inc.[1] Responding to the diversity of buyers' wants, the leading chip maker sells 85 varieties of potato chips. Frito-Lay relentlessly studies consumers preferences, conducting nearly 500,000 interviews a year.

This chapter was prepared by Karen S. Cravens, School of Accounting, University of Tulsa.

Quality control closely monitors chip thickness, since marketing research indicates that consumers complain if their chips are 8/1,000ths of an inch too thick or thin. Over 6,000 taste tests are conducted each year to gain feedback from consumers on new flavors that are being evaluated. Package colors are tested to make sure consumer reactions are favorable. Frito-Lay's 10,000-person sales force is part of the information system, sending headquarters inventory data and competitors' new-product information with their hand-held computers.

Computerized information systems are essential for competing in the rapidly changing business environment. For example, the strategic use of computer systems is indispensable in retailing, helping to reduce labor costs, manage inventory, track styling trends, mark down slow-to-move products, and replace conventional mail with electronic communications.[2] These systems compress response time, reduce costs, and improve decision making. Electronic ordering from suppliers is used by many firms including Kmart Corporation, Wal-Mart, and JCPenney Company. During the late 1980s, Kmart spent $300 million for computerized, laser-scanning registers that automatically reorder merchandise when stocks are low. Wal-Mart orders electronically from over 500 suppliers, reducing order delivery time from three weeks to nine days.

In this chapter we examine the use of research and information systems for marketing analysis, planning, and control. First, we consider how information capability creates competitive advantage. Next, we discuss the various sources of information. The chapter then looks at information methods and capabilities, which include marketing information systems, decision support systems, expert systems, and strategic intelligence. Next, we discuss the escalating use of database marketing. Finally, we consider several important issues concerning information management.

INFORMATION AND COMPETITIVE ADVANTAGE

The strategic use of information systems by Frito-Lay shows how competitive advantage is gained from the effective use of information-processing technology. We examine information advantage followed by a discussion of how information supports marketing decision making.

How Information Creates Competitive Advantage

Information capabilities enhance competitive advantage in four important ways: (1) the rapid transfer and processing of information provide a speed advantage; (2) efficiencies in the use of information systems reduce operating costs; (3) better decisions result from the use of relevant and timely information; and (4) innovative uses of information systems create new opportunities.

Speed Advantage. In the fast-moving business environment, computerized information systems enable firms to reduce the time necessary to accomplish tasks. L. L. Bean outperforms many other direct-mail retailers by delivering orders more rapidly than competitors. Frito-Lay's sales force uses hand-held computers to track the movement of all snack items within 24 hours of the sale, and salespeople save time using computers instead of writing reports. Shell Chemical Company uses an electronic software system to assist sales personnel with individual productivity and companywide communications.[3] The sales force is equipped with laptop computers that store information to manage customer accounts, keep track of expenses, capture and report daily sales information, access data for sales calls, and communicate with others via electronic mail. Shell calls this capability the "Sales Force Automation System."

Customers also benefit from increased efficiency, since billing information and inventory tracking data can be accessed more quickly. Firms answer customer queries on-line and immediately respond to a complaint. For many firms with broad portfolios of product lines and items, knowing the availability of an item can assure a sale. Salespeople who can respond immediately to questions about product availability for an order offer an important convenience to customers. Such responsiveness assists in creating an advantage over competitors. For example, Wal-Mart's electronic ordering system has reduced average inventory investment by about 17 percent for some products.[4] Doing things faster translates to efficiencies that create a competitive advantage. Wal-Mart's speed in reordering and, thus, restocking allows better customer service while reducing the level of inventory investment.

Cost Advantage. Computerized information systems are critical to the operations of supermarkets. These systems implement pricing decisions, control inventory, reduce checkout errors, and measure the performance of products. Electronic systems offer important cost advantages when processing large volumes of information on a continuing basis. Examples include travel reservations, financial transactions, ordering of routine supplies, and telephone processing of orders. Texas A&M University uses this technology to register 40,000 students for classes by touch-tone telephones. Each student accesses the system individually and receives immediate confirmation of course availability. The system informs the student of courses that have reached the maximum enrollment and allows alternate selections. The student may select various fee options, such as athletic tickets and meal plans, and add the cost of these services to the tuition bill. Once the registration is complete, a bill is sent to the student along with a written confirmation of the semester schedule. Universities exemplify the advantages for large corporations, yet the availability of electronic equipment and software at reasonable prices offers important cost advantages to small companies as well. Merely computerizing accounts receivable and accounts payable information may facilitate the collection of delinquent accounts and provide for the payment of bills within a discount period. This is an example of a cost advantage from placing existing information in a more useful format.

Decision-Making Advantage. An effective information system enables decision makers to make better decisions by identifying relevant information and providing analyses of the factors that impact the decision area. The processing of a large volume of information and/or analysis of several variables is not feasible without the aid of an information system. Simple electronic spreadsheet analysis illustrates the most basic of information systems, while American Airline's SABRE reservation system is an example of a complex, sophisticated system. SABRE provides an important competitive advantage, enabling management to make effective decisions concerning pricing, routing, staffing, and other scheduling issues. The Technology Feature describes American Airlines' SMARTS system for analyzing competitive activity and targeting selling effort to travel agencies.

Information systems that help to allocate resources provide the most dramatic examples of decision-making opportunities. In manufacturing, planners can have access to up-to-date production cost and sales figures, using this information to select the optimal mix of materials for production. Critical needs are identified immediately, and resources are shifted to take advantage of sales opportunities resulting from changes in demand or to adjust for shortages resulting from supplier constraints.

In the natural gas industry, a price change of a penny can significantly affect the marketing and supply of natural gas. With information systems, wholesalers can immediately assess their transportation network and financial situation and determine whether or not they should react to specific price changes. Distribution managers can see if they have the capability to transport units of the product to a customer providing they decide to react to a favorable price change. The information system allows for the most efficient allocation of available resources. This analysis capability is very important for sales of commodities that may require immediate delivery.

Innovation Opportunities. Firms may spot opportunities for growth and expansion through the use of an information system. New products and services can be developed, existing products and services can be modified, and new markets or new customer groups can be identified.[5] These capabilities may be the objective of the system or merely benefits derived from systems designed for other purposes. Marketing executives may create innovation opportunities with information derived from any type of system.

The information system itself may also be marketed as a product. The SABRE reservation system is an important source of revenue for American Airlines through fees paid by travel agencies and other airlines. Mrs. Fields' Cookies uses a management-information and decision-support system to obtain sales performance data from 650 stores, schedule store work activities, manage inventory levels, guide employment decisions, and train new employees.[6] The system has drastically reduced the number of headquarters

TECHNOLOGY FEATURE Sales Management and Response Tracking System (SMARTS)

American Airline's powerful sales management information system enables salespeople to compare their past performance for travel agency sales against sales of tickets on all airlines in the market.

How it Works

1. Travel agent books client's flight on computer reservation system.
2. American tracks records of bookings on its SABRE reservation system.
3. American purchases records of bookings on all other reservation systems.
4. American SMARTS computers analyze bookings made by all travel agents, comparing records against desired criteria.
5. American salespeople visit travel agents who are selling less than the company's goals, sometimes offering incentives to sell more flights on American.

Features

- On the 15th of every month sales reps receive, via their GRID laptop computers, last month's ticket sales performance of every agency and travel agent in their assigned territories. Comparisons are provided for previous months and years.
- Analyses are provided by trip routing for each carrier.
- SMARTS enables quick response to changes in the marketplace such as increased marketing activity.
- The system's decision-support capabilities are being expanded and improved on a continuous basis.

Source: Dan Reed, "American's Got SMARTS," *Fort Worth Star-Telegram,* November 24, 1991, pp. F1–2.

staff needed to monitor the operations of the retail chain. The company is marketing the MIS software to other retailers at a price per retail unit of about $12,000.

The information system often makes management aware of situations that provide opportunities. Analyzing sales reports by ZIP codes may point out deficiencies where salespeople are assigned. Data of this type are easily captured by an information system. The system can highlight geographic areas that may require additional salespeople or that may already be saturated. As illustrated by Frito-Lay, information systems that capture various types of consumer preference and demographic data may identify a potential product or a market segment responsive to purchasing complementary product lines. Information systems allow firms to capture more information about their customers, suppliers, and competitors. This capability provides the potential for growth based on informed decisions and a more complete representation of the competitive environment. Also, firms can respond much more quickly to competitors' actions and take advantage of situations in the marketplace.

AT&T has an electronic directory that is a collection of databases designed to assist with competitive intelligence.[7] Employees at all levels in the organization input information into the system. Newspaper and periodical items are also collected from print and electronic sources. A competitive digest is issued to top management daily, and the system is always available for inquiry or special requests. This is an integrated system combining knowledge from a multitude of sources in an organized and standardized manner. It provides a complete analysis of the competitors for AT&T's 70 product lines. Competitors can be analyzed, highlighting growth opportunities or strategies for maintaining market position.

Information, Analysis, and Action

Analysis of the information that is needed is the starting point in planning for and acquiring information. The importance of information for decision making is discussed throughout the book. Information must be collected and evaluated for marketing decisions and linked to the entire strategy of the firm.

Because of the costs of acquiring, processing, and analyzing information, the potential benefits of needed information should be compared to costs. Normally, information falls into two categories: (1) information regularly supplied to marketing management from internal and external sources, and (2) information obtained as needed for a particular problem or situation. Examples of the former are sales costs analyses, market share measurements, and customer satisfaction surveys. Information from the latter category includes new-product concept tests, brand preference studies, and studies of advertising effectiveness.

Several types of marketing information are shown in Exhibit 8–1. The major differences among the types of information are indicated by the degree to which the information assists in decision making and the extent to which customized information is involved. A description of each type of information follows:

Marketing research studies These studies consist of customized information collected and analyzed for a particular research problem. The information may be obtained through surveys and/or published sources.

Standardized information services This information is available from outside vendors on a subscription or single-purchase basis. The services collect and analyze information that is sold to several customers such as prescription sales for drugs marketed to pharmaceutical firms.

Management information systems (MIS) These computerized systems supply information for a variety of purposes such as order processing, invoicing, customer analysis, and product performance. The information in these systems may include both internal and external data.

Database systems This special form of MIS includes information from internal and external sources that is computerized and used for customer and product analyses, mailing lists, identifying sales prospects, and other marketing applications.

EXHIBIT 8–1 Types of Marketing Information

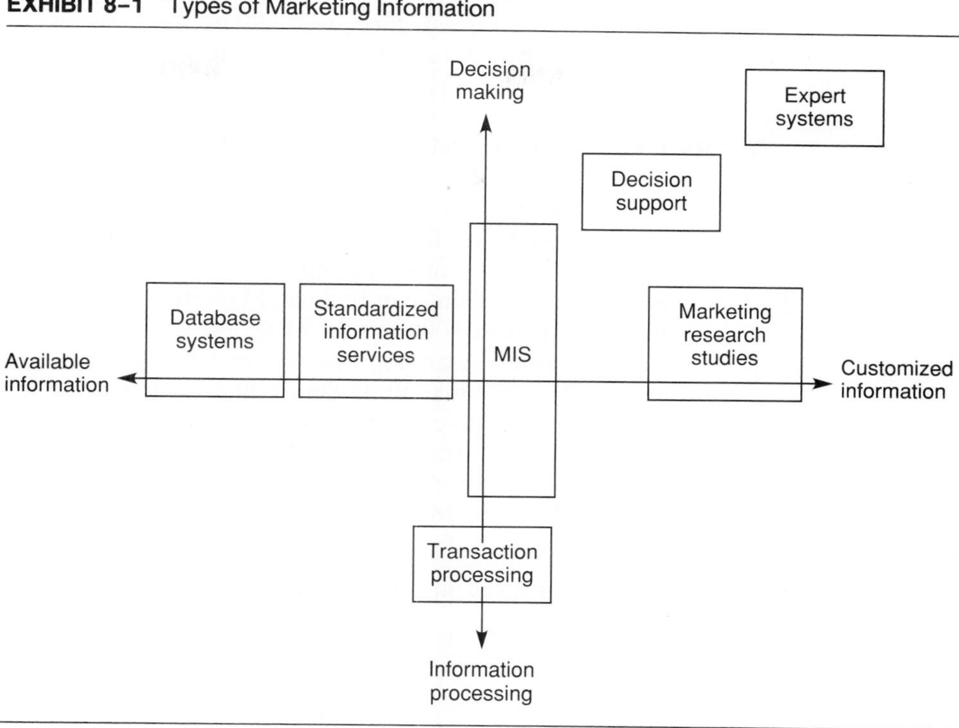

Decision-support systems These computerized systems provide decision-making assistance to managers and staff. Their capabilities are more advanced than a MIS.

Expert systems These systems are designed to replace human decision making for selected situations that can be programmed on computers.

The firm's complete information needs should be considered before committing to major marketing information systems. Most firms benefit from a routine and complete evaluation of their information situation. Cooperation among departments can save the firm countless employee-hours and dollars. Far too often a department launches an expensive information-gathering project only to discover later that another department already had the type of information sought.

In the remainder of the chapter, we examine the methods of acquiring and processing information for use in marketing decision making. The objective is to demonstrate how the various information capabilities assist decision makers in strategic and operating decisions. A good marketing information management strategy takes into account the interrelationship of these capabilities. Information planners also recognize the need to integrate the firm's strategy into the marketing information network.

MARKETING RESEARCH INFORMATION

Marketing research information is obtained from internal records, trade contacts, published information, and many other sources. An example of a research study is shown in Exhibit 8–2. It is a proposed test of the effectiveness of an advertising commercial. Marketing research studies range in cost from less than $10,000 to over $100,000.

Marketing research is "the systematic gathering, recording, processing, and analyzing of marketing data, which—when interpreted—will help the marketing executive to uncover opportunities and to reduce risks in decision making."[8] Strategies for obtaining marketing research information include collecting existing information, using standardized research services, and conducting special research studies.

Collecting Existing Information

The internal information system of the firm affects the extent and ease of collection of existing information. The nature and scope of the information and the information system network will vary greatly from firm to firm and among industries. Given the present technology and the affordability of much of the necessary equipment and software, many firms have extensive internal information systems, or at least the capability to implement such systems.

Most firms do not make a concentrated effort to inform all decision makers of the extent and variety of the information capabilities of the internal system. Therefore, decision makers may have to make their own determination of the potential for the existing system as a marketing information source. A minor change such as modifying the format of an existing report within the system may lead to improved decision making. A sales report grouped by product line may be more informative when also sorted by geographic region. Decision makers may not be aware that the information system contains detailed product-cost data. Incorporating these cost data into pricing strategy analysis can yield increased profits.

There is considerable value and potential in using the information in the organization's current system. This is essential for the strategic mission of the firm, as well as for efficient use of assets. Information is a resource that must be consciously managed.[9] Management should structure the information system to capture this resource and control its use. Information is not a by-product of activities of the firm. It is a scarce, valuable resource that affects the firm's future success or failure. Management may not have con-

EXHIBIT 8–2 Off-Air Test Marketing Research Project Proposal

Brand: Colgate.

Project: Copy Test: "Midnight Delight."

Background and Purpose: A new commercial has been developed—"Midnight Delight." Brand Group is interested in determining its effectiveness. The objectives of this study will be to determine

- Brand recall.
- Copy recall.
- Purchase intent shifts.
- Comparison with previous copy testing results.

Research Method: This research will be conducted using central location mall facilities in Boston, Atlanta, Milwaukee, and San Francisco. Each commercial will be viewed by 200 past-30-week toothpaste users as follows:

		Age Group	*Number of Respondents*
Males	50%	8–11	30
Females	50%	12–17	50
		18–24	25
		25–34	25
		34–49	10
		50+	10
			150

Information to be Obtained:

- Brand recall.
- Copy recall.
- Pre- and postpurchase intentions.

Action Standard: This study, which is being done for information purposes, will be used in conjunction with previous copy testing results.

Cost and Timing: The cost for one commercial will be $6,500 ± 10%. The following schedule will be established:

Field work	3 weeks
Top-line reports	1 week
Final report	3 weeks
Total	7 weeks

Supplier: Leggett Lustig Firtle, Inc.

Source: William R. Dillon, Thomas J. Madden, and Neil H. Firtle, *Marketing Research in a Marketing Environment,* 2nd ed. (Homewood, Ill.: Richard D. Irwin, 1990), p. 698.

trol over the actions of competitors or consumers, but an effective information system provides a way to react.

The product mix and the nature of business operations influence what type of internal marketing information system is appropriate in a particular firm. High-volume sales transactions such as those for banks, groceries, drugs, and other low-unit-price consumer products require computerized tracking and analysis capabilities. In contrast, a producer of low volume, high-cost products such as ships, steam turbines, aircraft, or other large industrial equipment may have less need for this type of system. Instead, systems for these firms may concentrate on the tracking and allocation of costs and materials and on scheduling. Manufacturers have different information requirements than retailers or wholesalers. The size and complexity of the firm also influences the composition of the information system.

The costs and benefits of the information must be evaluated for both short-term and long-term planning. Incremental efforts and expenditures in the early stages of creating an internal information system may avoid future costly modifications. Achieving long-term performance may require temporary losses to finance a system. It is critical to consider a long-term perspective in evaluating information system decisions. In the late 1970s, B. Dalton Bookseller, the retail bookstore chain, developed an impressive control system for strategic planning. It consisted of a computerized book-tracking system that codes each order and monitors the information in a database. As a result, managers can call up weekly sales reports, by title and topic, for every outlet, city, or region, and use the data to restock fast sellers, drop slow movers, and choose new books to buy. Competitors acknowledge that the system is a major advantage for B. Dalton.[10] Clearly the system required a substantial financial outlay that was difficult to justify for the short term. Implementation of a new system often disrupts operations. Yet, B. Dalton was able to overcome these short-term problems in order to achieve this longer-term competitive advantage.

Standardized Information Services

A wide variety of marketing information is available for purchase in special publications and on a subscription basis. In some instances, the information may be free. Suppliers include government agencies, universities, private research firms, industry and trade organizations, and consultants. A key advantage to standardized information is that the costs of collection and analysis are shared by many users. The major limitation is that the information may not correspond well with the user's needs. Such services offer substantial cost advantages, and many are quite inexpensive (for example, data distributed by the U.S. Department of Census). Many services allow on-line access to data, enabling subscribers to automatically input external information into their own information systems.

Dun & Bradstreet's portfolio of standardized information services meet a wide range of decision-making needs. Some examples follow:[11]

> The A. C. Nielsen subsidiary collects information on audience ratings of TV shows. Decisions to continue or drop shows often depend on these ratings.
>
> The Petroleum Information Corporation unit supplies information on drilling and production for firms interested in oil and gas exploration activities.

EXHIBIT 8–3 Nielsen Food and Drug Retail Index System

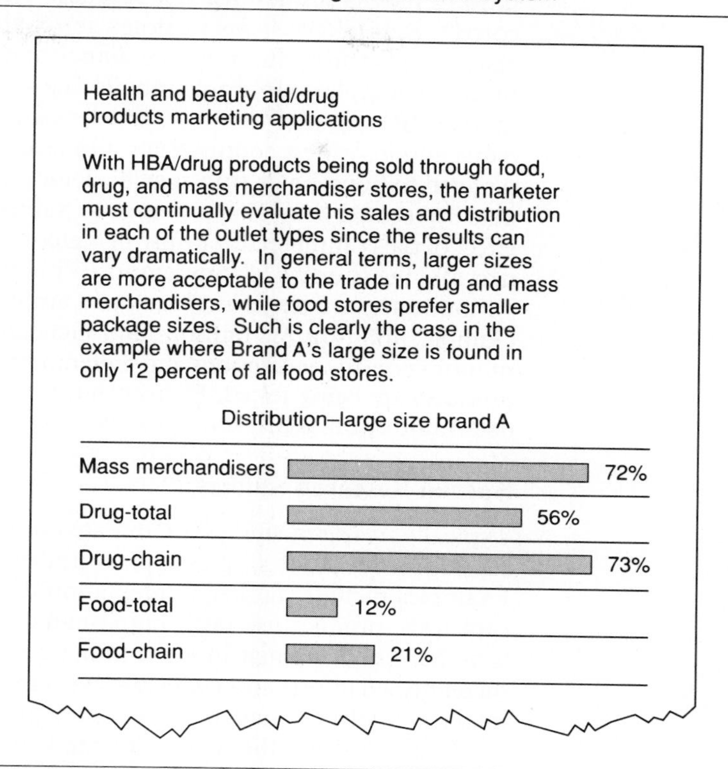

Health and beauty aid/drug
products marketing applications
With HBA/drug products being sold through food, drug, and mass merchandiser stores, the marketer must continually evaluate his sales and distribution in each of the outlet types since the results can vary dramatically. In general terms, larger sizes are more acceptable to the trade in drug and mass merchandisers, while food stores prefer smaller package sizes. Such is clearly the case in the example where Brand A's large size is found in only 12 percent of all food stores.
Distribution–large size brand A
Mass merchandisers
72%
Drug-total
56%
Drug-chain
73%
Food-total
12%
Food-chain
21%

Source: A. C. Nielsen Company.

Moody's Investors Service supplies over 15 million different pieces of information on more than 22,000 companies worldwide and 28,000 local and state governments.

Nielsen's food and drug data are vital to marketing decisions in these markets.

Using the large data banks collected and organized by D&B, many different analyses can be made, depending on a company's strategic marketing information needs. The cost of the information for use by one company would be prohibitive. By sharing the database, a wide range of company information needs can be met. An example from one of A. C. Nielsen's food and drug information reports is shown in Exhibit 8–3.

The research firm Information Resources, Inc. (IRI) uses electronic retail store scanning systems to record purchases by people participating on consumer panels.[12] Previously, these purchases were recorded by the consumer in diaries that yielded many discrepancies. In one situation, only one third of the diaries that listed a purchase of Kellogg's Frosted Flakes were correct. Scanning systems in stores automatically record consumers' purchases, eliminating the need for diaries and providing accurate data. IRI installs a complete electronic monitoring system in each city used as a test market. IRI can also monitor the television programs watched by participants and insert test commercials into programming. Commercials can be targeted to households with specific demographic characteristics, since this data is recorded for all participants. Subsequent purchases measure the effect of the commercial. The use of coupons can be monitored to test products and the strength of competitors. With this network, IRI can respond to various queries from clients such as Campbell Soup Company, Procter & Gamble, Johnson & Johnson, and General Foods Corporation. IRI can monitor consumer reactions and preferences without alerting them to which products are being tested. Firms can introduce advertising campaigns and determine optimal marketing strategies.

Special Research Studies

Typically, research studies are initiated in response to problems or special situations. Several examples of these studies are discussed in other chapters. Examples include market segmentation determination, new-product concept tests, product use tests, brand-name research, and advertising recall tests. Studies may range in scope from exploratory research based primarily on published information to field surveys involving personal, phone, or mail interviews with respondents who represent target populations.

In deciding whether to employ marketing research and when interpreting the results, several considerations are important.

Defining the Problem. Care must be exercised in formulating the research problem. Management should indicate exactly what information is needed to solve the problem. If this cannot be done, exploratory research should be conducted to help define the research problem and determine the objectives. Caution should be exercised to avoid defining a symptom rather than the decision situation.

Understanding the Limitations of the Research. Most studies are unable to do everything that the user wishes to accomplish and also stay within the available budget. Priorities for the information needed should be indicated. Also, obtaining certain information may not be feasible. For example, measuring the impact of advertising on profits may not be possible because of the influence of many other factors on profits.

Quality of the Research. There are many challenges to obtaining sound research results. The available evidence indicates that some studies are not well designed and implemented and may contain biased results. Factors that affect the quality of study results include the experience of the study personnel, the size of the sample, the wording of questions, and how the data are analyzed. This example highlights the difficulties in achieving reliable results:[13]

> A Gallup poll sponsored by the disposable diaper industry asked: "It is estimated that disposable diapers account for less than 2 percent of the trash in today's landfills. In contrast, beverage containers, third-class mail, and yard waste are estimated to account for about 21 percent of trash in landfills. Given this, in your opinion, would it be fair to ban disposable diapers?"

Not surprisingly, given the wording of the question, 84 percent of the respondents answered no to the question.

Evaluating and Selecting Suppliers. Typically, research studies are not conducted by the user. Several experienced marketing research consultants are available. When selecting a supplier, it is important to talk with two or three prior clients to determine their satisfaction with the research firm. It is also important to identify consultants who are experienced in conducting the particular type of research needed by the user. For example, certain firms specialize in conducting advertising recall studies. Some research firms concentrate in specific industries.

Costs. Research studies are expensive. As an example, a proposal for a major market tracking study is described in Exhibit 8–4. Although telephone interviews are much less expensive than personal interviews, the tracking study is nevertheless very expensive. The factors that affect study costs include sample size, the length of the questionnaire, and how the information will be obtained. The complexity of the study objectives also increases the professional capabilities of research personnel.

COMPUTERIZED INFORMATION SYSTEMS

There are many types of information systems within the organization. Manual systems are also used and may provide crucial information. Yet, for purposes of this chapter, attention is focused on computerized information systems. "Strategic systems are those that change the goals, products, services, or environmental relationships of organizations."[14] These information systems alter the way in which a firm does business with competitors, suppliers, and customers. Since the scope of strategic planning is so broad, information generated by the system is invaluable in strategic marketing planning. The system may provide information to assist decision makers with strategic planning or may actually prepare a plan and formulate decisions. Management information systems, database systems, and decision-support systems can be used as strategic systems.

EXHIBIT 8–4 Market Tracking Proposal

Brand: Skweeky Kleen Bar Soap.

Project: Bar Soap National Tracking Study.

Background and Purpose: The Bar Soap Brand Group has requested that a continuous tracking study be conducted in 1990. This study will be a continuation of the 1989 tracking study.

The objectives of this study will be

1. To determine track changes in brand awareness and use since the introduction of new products.
2. To determine changes in volume contribution within the market.
3. To analyze consumer perceptions and to measure changes in those perceptions among various market segments.

Research Method: The 1990 study will be conducted during the course of the year, and monthly waves of interviewing will begin in January. This monthly tracking system was also used in 1989.

As in previous studies, interviewing will be conducted by WATS telephone from a central location. Telephone numbers will be selected via strict probability methods from all working exchanges and numbers in the continental United States. Respondents will be randomly selected within households. A total of 2,400 past-30-day bar soap users will be interviewed (200 per month for the 12 months of January through December 1989).

The basic questionnaire will follow the format used in the 1989 study, and will include the following question areas:

- Brand awareness (unaided and aided).
- Brand use (ever, past 30 days, most often).
- Number of bars used past 30 days.
- Brand ratings for brands ever used, but not past 30 days.
- Importance of product attributes.
- Other diagnostic question areas (to vary).

Management Information Systems

Management information systems provide raw data to decision makers. The system collects data on the transactions of the firm and may include competitor and environmental information. The decision makers (and systems analysts) are responsible for extracting the data relevant for a decision and in the appropriate format to facilitate the process. The system can provide information for decisions at all levels of the organization. Yet, lower and middle-level managers use the system most often for operating decisions. The system may generate routine reports for frequent operating decisions, such as weekly sales by product, or may be queried for nonroutine decisions on an as-needed basis. Nonroutine decisions may consist of tracking the

EXHIBIT 8–4 Continued

Timing and Cost: Field work will be conducted monthly, beginning in January. Top line reports on brand awareness and use will be provided monthly, whereas more complete reports will be reported quarterly and when all the interviews are completed. The specific timing will be

Interview Date	*Number of Interviews*	*Timing of Monthly Top-Lines*	*Timing of Quarterly Top-Lines*	*Final Report*
January	200	2/13	—	—
February	200	3/13	—	—
March	200	4/10	—	—
1st quarter	600	—	5/15	—
April	200	5/8	—	—
May	200	6/12	—	—
June	200	7/15	—	—
2nd quarter	600	—	8/14	—
July	200	8/11	—	—
August	200	9/11	—	—
September	200	10/12	—	—
3rd quarter	600	—	11/13	—
October	200	11/9	—	—
November	200	12/11	—	—
December	200	1/13	—	—
4th quarter	600	—	1/23	—
Total	2,400			3/25

The cost of this study will be $100,000 ± 10%.

Supplier: Burke Marketing Research.

Source: William R. Dillon, Thomas J. Madden, and Neil H. Firtle, *Marketing Research in a Marketing Environment,* 2nd ed. (Homewood, Ill.: Richard D. Irwin, 1990), pp. 716–17.

sales performance of a particular employee over several months, determining the number of customer returns for a particular good, or locating all customers or suppliers within a given geographic area. The basic MIS collects data and allows for retrieval and manipulation of format in an organized manner. Typically, the MIS does not interact in the decision-making process. More advanced MIS capabilities provide decision analysis capabilities.

Consider this MIS application. A sophisticated marketing information system enables a major airline to focus on the needs of specific market segments.[15] The system determines mileage awards for frequent flyers and provides a reservation support database, organized by market segments. The company's top 3 percent of customers account for 50 percent of sales. These key accounts are highlighted on all service screens and reports. Reservations agents are alerted that a person is an important customer. The frequent flyers receive a variety of special services, including overbooking on full flights and first-class upgrades.

Database Systems

Databases are a form of MIS. Some database systems offer capabilities similar to decision-support systems. The use of computerized databases escalated during the 1980s, motivated by hardware and software technology. The information in the systems includes internal data on customers and purchased data on customers and prospects. The customer and prospect information contained in databases can be used to generate mailing lists and prospect lists for salespeople and to identify market segments. These segments offer a direct communications channel with customers and prospects.

These systems offer powerful capabilities for identifying and communicating with customers. The database information enables companies to target individuals or small microsegments of people. The systems are very useful in sales and sales management support and for direct marketing programs. Database marketing has three main benefits: (1) strategic advantage through the more effective use of marketing information internally; (2) improvement in the use of customer and market information; and (3) a basis for developing long-term customer relationships.[16] The systems can be applied to mail-order marketing, telemarketing, and support of personal selling activities. A major objective of database marketing is to find and develop strong relationships with the customer base that accounts for a large portion of a firm's annual sales.

The components of database systems include relational databases, personal computers, electronic publishing media, and voice systems.[17] The intent of database marketing is effectively using a computerized customer database to facilitate a significant and profitable communication with customers. The system includes a database, analytical capabilities, a strategy and structure for using the system, procedures for deploying system capabilities, and controls for managing the database.

Decision-Support Systems

A decision-support system (DSS) assists in the decision-making process using the information captured by the MIS. The marketing decision-support system (MDSS) integrates data that are not easily found, assimilated, formated or readily manipulated with software and hardware into a decision-making process that provides the marketing decision maker with assistance when needed.[18] The MDSS allows the user flexibility in applications and in format. A MDSS can be used for various levels of decision making ranging from determining reorder points for inventory to launching a new product.

The components of the MDSS consist of the database, the display, the models, and the analysis capabilities.[19]

Database. Various kinds of information are included in the database such as standardized marketing information produced by Nielsen and other research suppliers, sales and cost data, and internal information such as product sales, advertising data, and price information. The design and updating of the database are vital to the effectiveness of MDSS. The information should be relevant and organized to correspond to the units of analysis used in the system.

Display. This component of the MDSS enables the user to communicate with the database. Marketing managers and their staff need to interact with the database:

> They must be able to extract, manipulate, and display data easily and quickly. Required capabilities range from simple ad hoc retrieval to more formal reports that track market status and product performance. Also needed are exception reports that flag problem areas. Many presentations should have graphics integrated with other materials.[20]

Models. This component of the MDSS provides mathematical and computational representations of variables and their interrelationships. For example, a sales force deployment model would include an effort-to-sales response function model and a deployment algorithm for use in analyzing selling effort allocation alternatives. The decision-support models are useful in analysis, planning, and control.

Analysis. This capability includes a portfolio of analysis methods such as regression analysis, factor analysis, time series, and preference mapping. Software such as Lotus 1-2-3 may also be included in the system. Analysis may be performed on a data set to study relationships, identify trends, prepare forecasts, and examine the impact of alternative decision rules.

MDSS may operate autonomously or instead may require interaction with the decision maker during the process. There may be several points before a recommendation is formed where the decision maker must respond to queries to refine the scenario. Thus, an interactive MDSS requires more assistance from the decision maker and has more room for variation than an autonomous MDSS. The system is dependent on the quality and accuracy of the information and assumptions that are used in the system. The process should be viewed as a tool to assist in decision making, not a final product in itself.

Ideally, the experience and instincts of management are built into the model. But often information is missing, and the decision maker has the best grasp of the entire situation. The most complete decisions incorporate the recommendation of the MDSS, but do not solely rely upon them. However, a DSS often serves to create or support a consensus, and evidence exists that a DSS does yield favorable decision-making performance when it is properly designed and applied to appropriate decision situations. Evaluations of DSS effectiveness show mixed results.[21] In a controlled laboratory test using senior undergraduate students enrolled in a business policy course, researchers found that groups using the DSS made significantly better decisions than their non-DSS counterparts. Thus, there is supporting evidence of the value of DSS. Nevertheless, further evaluation is needed to better define the conditions and applications where success is likely to occur.

The concept of the MDSS as a tool is most apparent when considering strategic decisions rather than operating decisions. Clear, concise answers may not always be possible, yet the system is a very valuable tool in the process. Consider the following:

> A DSS developed by William Luther analyzes key success factors in the marketplace and makes comparisons with competitors. This system is called a Strategic Planning Model, and is most useful for smaller companies. Managers input their definition of key success factors by means of a standardized questionnaire format. Comparisons are made between the firm and competitors for these factors. The factors can be weighted for importance, and multiple situations can be considered. The model makes projections and recommendations of strategies.[22]

In using this system it is important that managers identify key success factors; otherwise, the model will lose a great deal of credibility. When properly applied it provides a useful framework for decision makers, recognizing that it is not a complete replica of the decision-making situation.

ARTIFICIAL INTELLIGENCE AND EXPERT SYSTEMS

The expert system is a more advanced form of decision support that uses artificial intelligence. These systems combine computer capabilities with software programming to duplicate human reasoning processes. Typical applications replace routine decision making such as providing directory assistance to telephone users. First, the concept of artificial intelligence is examined, followed by a discussion of the design of expert systems.

Artificial Intelligence

Artificial intelligence is the information and human thought processes used to develop computer-based systems that function like human decision makers.[23] These expert systems are based on human decision-making patterns, knowledge, and past decision-making results. The use of the artificial intelligence requires that human decision-making patterns be expressed in written form. Machines (hardware and software) must be capable of performing the humanlike processes. The processes must be programmable.

An expert system application is more likely to be successful when the decision area is: (1) knowledge intensive (e.g., generating new-product ideas); (2) semistructured rather than well structured or highly unstructured; (3) knowledge about the problem is incomplete; and (4) user interaction with the computer system is necessary.[24] Expert systems are more appropriate for tasks that require logic and reasoning and are semistructured such as planning rather than creating advertising concepts.

Expert systems are capable of performing several more advanced functions than DSS. Desirable capabilities include:[25]

1. Drawing conclusions or making recommendations based on data inputs.
2. Providing user-friendly support to decision-makers who are not computer literate.
3. Training novices or further educating experienced decision makers by providing insights, recommendations, and judgments.
4. Allowing users to ask questions.
5. Integrating new information into the analysis process.
6. Facilitating modification of rules or procedures.

Designing Expert Systems

The design of an expert system is an extensive process beginning with defining the problem and determining that it represents a suitable expert system application. The expert system may be custom designed for a particular company decision situation. Alternatively, expert system software can be purchased from a commercial developer for use by several companies. The trade-offs between the custom and standardized systems are higher costs for the custom systems but better applicability to the company situation.

Texas Instruments uses an expert system to forecast sales, incorporating book-to-bill ratios, distributor inventory levels, various business indicators, and forecasting "rules-of-thumb" gained from producing 100 forecasts during a 12-year time span.[26] The expert system generates forecasts, analyzes them, considers fluctuations in the book-to-bill ratio, and examines other significant trends. The new system overcomes problems experienced in meeting delivery schedules for Texas Instruments' computerized industrial controls.

An example of an expert system is shown in Exhibit 8–5. This system was developed to provide guidelines to individuals or teams preparing for international marketing negotiations.[27] The main components of the system are the *knowlege base* and the *inference engine.* The user has various options to interact with the system through the user interface.

MCI Communications Corporation uses a personal computer-based expert system to assist its salespeople in prospect selection, account analysis, and selling strategy selection.[28] The system informs the sales representative how much a prospect is spending on long-distance services, the key purchase

EXHIBIT 8–5 Components of an Expert System

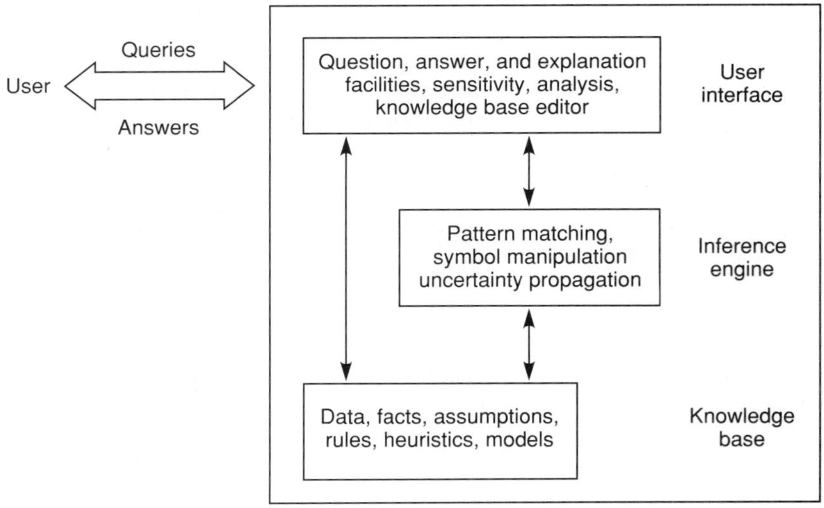

User
Queries
Answers

Question, answer, and explanation facilities, sensitivity, analysis, knowledge base editor — User interface

Pattern matching, symbol manipulation uncertainty propagation — Inference engine

Data, facts, assumptions, rules, heuristics, models — Knowledge base

Source: Arvind Rangaswamy, Jehoshua Eliashberg, Raymond R. Burke, and Jerry Wind, "Developing Marketing Expert Systems: An Application to International Negotiations," *Journal of Marketing,* October 1989, p. 26.

decision maker in the organization, and other information about the business. The system qualifies new prospects by supplying contact lists according to screening criteria such as monthly expenditures on telecommunications. The database supporting the system uses reports from external information sources.

ISSUES IN MANAGING INFORMATION

The rapidly changing technologies available for processing and analyzing information create several important issues in using and managing marketing information. These issues include the impact of information technology on organizations, shared systems, invasion of privacy, and corporate intelligence.

Information Technology and Organizations

Information technology is changing organizations in several ways. Closer links can be established between channel-of-distribution organizations. Order processing time can be reduced through computer and telecommunications links. Organization structures can be simplified and made more effective through the use of information and decision-support systems. The mail-order flower retailer, Calyx & Corolla, uses the Federal Express computer network to link growers and delivery services with customers (see Chapter 3). The company's small team of employees is able to process large numbers of orders using sophisticated information technology.

Information technology will have a widespread impact on organizations in the 1990s. One of the challenges is to not be overwhelmed by too much information. Software for putting information into usable formats will enable users to meet their needs without experiencing information overload. Importantly, managers will be required to use computers in their day-to-day analysis and decision-making activities: "The most radical change will be the computer's move from the sidelines to a central role, where it promises to redefine the nature of work, transform the role of managers, even alter the way corporations are organized."[29]

Shared Information Systems

The development of computerized information systems shared by two or more independent organizations creates several important management and coordination issues. Examples include airline reservation systems, vendor/producer ordering and order status, computer networks between strategic alliance partners, and distribution channel information systems. These shared systems create several legal, ethical, and competitive issues:

- The dependency and power relationships resulting from joint system usage. For example, American Airlines' influence on travel agents is a continuing concern to its competitors.
- The protection of proprietary information such as sales, pricing, and profit information for the customer base served by the information system. Extensive access to the system increases the danger of theft of valuable information.
- Developing training programs for system users. Information networks serving distribution organizations and end-users require training and instructional materials for users. For example, American Airlines conducts workshops to train travel agents in the use of the reservations and ticketing system.
- Selecting methods for allocating systems costs to users. For example, end-users may be unwilling to pay for services even though the services lower the buyers' operating costs. System development and operating costs may need to be included in product or service costs.
- Establishing policies for entering and exiting the system by a participant. For example, what recourse does a retailer have if a wholesaler decides to stop operating a financial management information service for its retailers?

Recognizing these concerns in the use of shared systems, they nevertheless offer competitive advantages for both the system manager and users. Participating firms must evaluate the advantages and limitations of the system relationship. The trend is clearly toward greater use of shared information systems.

Invasion of Privacy

The exciting advances in information technology raise some important concerns about the invasion of privacy of individuals. For example, telecommunications companies offer their business customers an automatic phone number identification service.[30] The phone number of someone calling the business can be matched to the firm's computerized database to retrieve and display the caller's name, credit history, income, marital status, family size, and purchasing history. Such database systems eliminate the anonymity of the caller, reveal unlisted phone numbers, and pose other threats to individual privacy. They also offer an advantage by enabling the call recipient to reject calls from sources they wish to avoid such as obscene callers, aggressive salespeople, and calls from unrecognized sources. Number identification services and other uses of information in databases raise important ethical questions about the right of an organization to release information about the people in its data bank to another organization. The provision of phone number information by the telecommunications company to its business customers is illustrative. For example, hundreds of businesses purchase lists of everyone who calls their 800 or 900 numbers from long-distance companies.[31] This list can be obtained on tape for loading onto a computer database. The information can be combined with other information already in the database.

Information technology, such as the number identification services, offers buyers important advantages by improving services. Companies can offer faster and more complete responses to customer inquiries by quickly displaying information about the caller. These systems also send security and fire protection agencies information that can reduce response time in emergencies.

Corporate Intelligence

Business intelligence activities expanded significantly during the last decade. These activities lack the structure and methodological rigor of formal research and analysis, but nevertheless represent an important source of strategic information. For example, the following corporate intelligence activities are undertaken to assess the impact of federal decisions on business operations:

> Directly or indirectly, corporations deploy hundreds (thousands by some estimates) of agents with widely divergent backgrounds and contrasting methods of operation. Here will be a Ph.D. preparing a scholarly analysis of long-range policy trends, based on private talks with government specialists. There will be a

young free-lance lawyer with a phone-answering machine for an office, hustling to make it, not so much as a lawyer, but as a Washington operator. Here will be a former newspaper reporter worming advance information or an unreleased document out of a carefully cultivated source—but for a private client now, not the reading public. And, of course the high-prestige types—large law firms, well-established information-gathering companies, and the official Washington representatives (often bearing a vice president's title) of the nation's major corporations.[32]

The turbulent business environment of the 1980s created a new wave of consultants. Hundreds of companies pay trend spotters like the Naisbitt Group (Megatrends) retainer fees ranging from $10,000 to $30,000 a year to help management predict the future.[33] While these environmental impact assessments are far from infallible, corporations seem to find the information worth the price. For example, as a result of the Naisbitt Group's reports of the elderly's growing political and economic influence, Southwestern Bell spent nearly $100 million to launch its Silver Pages directory of businesses catering to the elderly. Others use trend-setters to stimulate management thinking and identify important issues.

The value of intelligence consultants lies in the fact that they monitor the environment on a full-time basis, while busy managers do not have the time to do so. Corporations can obtain important insights and assessments when they carefully evaluate the inputs from trend spotters and don't rely on them solely. The usefulness (and cost) of the consultant should be evaluated on a continuing basis.

SUMMARY

Information performs a vital strategic role in an organization. Information capability creates a sustainable competitive advantage by improving the speed of decision making, reducing the costs of repetitive operations, improving decision-making results, and identifying innovation opportunities. Marketing information capabilities include marketing research, marketing information systems, database systems, decision-support systems, and expert systems.

Research information supports marketing analysis and decision making. This information may be obtained from internal sources, standardized information services, and special research studies. The information may be used to solve existing problems, evaluate potential actions such as new-product introductions, and as inputs to computerized data banks.

Computerized information systems include management information systems, database systems, decision support systems, and expert systems. These systems include capabilities for information processing, analysis, routine decision making, and decision recommendations for complex decision situations. The vast array of information processing and telecommunications technology available offers many opportunities to enhance the competitive advantage of companies. The most advanced system form is the expert system. These systems are designed using human decision-making patterns, knowledge, and past experience.

Several key information management issues are examined. Information technology is changing organizations in various ways. Information alliances between two or more organizations create issues concerning dependency and power. Another issue is the invasion of privacy that is possible using advanced information technology. The chapter concluded with a look at the use of strategic intelligence activities by companies.

The development of useful computerized information systems is a key success requirement for competing in the rapidly changing and shrinking global business environment. Marketing decision-making results are improved by the use of effective information systems. Importantly, gaining information advantage requires more than technology. The systems demand creative (and cost-effective) design that focuses on decision-making information needs.

QUESTIONS FOR REVIEW AND DISCUSSION

1. Discuss how an organization's marketing information skills and resources contribute to its competitive advantage.
2. The development of electronic information systems is very expensive. How can large investments in information capability be justified when they reduce the availability of funds for new-product development?
3. Compare and contrast the use of standardized information services as an alternative to special research studies for tracking the performance of a new packaged food product.
4. Discuss the probable impact of cable television on marketing research methods during the next decade as this medium penetrates an increasing number of U.S. households.
5. What should be the role of industry trade associations in the development and distribution of standardized information services? What legal/ethical problems could develop in using trade groups as information sources?
6. Comment on the usefulness and limitations of test-market data as a source of marketing information.
7. Suppose the management of a retail wallpaper chain is considering a research study to measure household awareness of the retail chain, reactions to various aspects of wallpaper purchase and use, and identification of competing firms. How could management estimate the benefits of such a study in order to determine if the study should be conducted?
8. Are there similarities between marketing strategic intelligence and the operations of the U.S. Central Intelligence Agency? Do companies ever employ business spies?
9. Discuss how manufacturers of U.S. and Swiss watches could have used a strategic marketing intelligence program to help avoid the problems that several firms in the industry encountered in the 1970s.
10. Discuss the strategic implications for small independents and regional chains of the expanding strategic use of information technology by large retailers.

NOTES

1. Robert Johnson, "In the Chips," *The Wall Street Journal,* March 22, 1992, pp. B1, B2.
2. Hank Gilman, "The Technology Edge: In Their Drive for Competitive Advantage, Retail Chains Make Strategic Use of Computers," *The Wall Street Journal,* September 16, 1985, pp. C55, C63.
3. "Computer-Based Sales Support: Shell Chemical's System," *The Conference Board's Management Briefing: Marketing,* April/May 1989, p. 4.
4. Gilman, "The Technology Edge," pp. C55, C63.
5. For a complete discussion see Kenneth C. Laudon and Jane Price Laudon, *Management Information Systems* (New York: Macmillan, 1988), Chapter 3.
6. Michelle-Laque Johnson, "Computer Program Helps Keep Mrs. Fields' H. Q. Lean," *Investor's Daily,* January 30, 1990, p. 8.
7. Blaine E. Davis and Martin Stark, "American Telephone & Telephone Co: A Network of Experts," in Howard Sutton, *Competitive Intelligence,* Report No. 913 (New York: The Conference Board, Inc., 1988), pp. 22–24.
8. William R. Dillon, Thomas J. Madden, and Neil H. Firtle, *Marketing Research in a Marketing Environment,* 2nd ed. (Homewood, Ill.: Richard D. Irwin, 1990), p. 828.
9. Laudon and Laudon, *Management Information Systems,* p. 235.
10. "Waldenbooks: Countering B. Dalton by Aping Its Computer Operations," *Business Week,* October 8, 1979, p. 116.
11. Johnnie L. Roberts, "Credibility Gap," *The Wall Street Journal,* October 5, 1989, pp. A1 and A16.
12. This illustration is based on Michael Days, "Wired Consumers," *The Wall Street Journal,* January 23, 1986, p. 3.
13. Cynthis Crossen, "Margin of Error," *The Wall Street Journal,* November 11, 1991, p. A1.
14. Laudon and Laudon, *Management Information Systems,* p. 62.
15. Michael Miron, John Cecil, Kevin Bradicich, and Gene Hall, "The Myths and Realities of Competitive Advantage," *DATAMATION,* October 1, 1988, p. 76.
16. Keith Fletcher, Colin Wheeter, and Julia Wright, "The Role and Status of U.K. Database Marketing," *Quarterly Review of Marketing,* Autumn 1990, pp. 7–14.
17. Bob Shaw and Merlin Stone, "Competitive Superiority through Database Marketing," *Long Range Planning,* October 1988, pp. 24–40.
18. John D. C. Little and Michael Cassettari, *Decision Support Systems for Marketing Managers* (New York: AMA, 1984), p. 7.
19. Ibid., pp. 12–15.
20. Ibid., p. 14.
21. A discussion of DSS effectiveness is provided in Ramesh Sharda, Steve H. Barr, and James C. McDonnell, "Decision Support System Effectiveness: A Review and an Empirical Test," *Management Science* 34, no. 2 (February 1988), pp. 139–59.
22. Illustration from Robert J. Mockler, "Computer Information Systems and Strategic Corporate Planning," *Business Horizons,* May/June, 1987, p. 35.
23. Laudon and Laudon, *Management Information Systems,* Chapter 17.
24. Arvind Rangaswamy, Jehoshua Eliashberg, Raymond R. Burke, and Jerry Wind, "Developing Marketing Expert Systems: An Application to International Negotiations," *Journal of Marketing,* October 1989, pp. 33–34.
25. Diane Lynn Kastiel, "Computerized Consultants," *Business Marketing,* March 1987, p. 60.
26. Ibid., p. 52.
27. Rangaswamy et al, "Developing Marketing Expert Systems," pp. 25–26.
28. Amy Bernstein, "MCI Wins Marketing Game with 'Expert' IS Strategy," *Com-*

puterworld Premier 100, September 11, 1989, p. 18.

29. Joel Dreyfuss, "Catching the Computer Wave," *Fortune,* September 26, 1988, p. 78.
30. This discussion is based on Mary Lu Carnevale and Julie Amparano Lopez, "Party Line," *The Wall Street Journal,* November 28, 1989, pp. A1 and A9.
31. Ibid.
32. Roscoe C. Barn, "Corporate CIA," *Barron's,* March 19, 1979, p. 4.
33. Myron Magnet, "Who Needs a Trend Spotter?" *Fortune,* December 9, 1985, pp. 51, 52, 54, 56.

Cases for Part II

CASE 2–1 Tupperware

The Tupperware Lady is not what she used to be. Most nights of the week, Jamie Dreier doesn't get home until long after her husband and three children are in bed. Instead of eating leftovers stored in her Tupperware Freezer Mates, she usually grabs a burger at McDonald's on the fly. People think "party, party, fun, fun, fun," she says. "It's not like that. It's a job."

It's a job that has grown increasingly tough as Tupperware, once as American as apple pie, has gone the way of the apple pie. The product was a perfect fit for the 1950s. Many women were full-time, frugal homemakers. The new plastic kitchenware stretched leftovers forever. The Tupperware party, the only occasion to buy Tupperware since it isn't sold in stores, was a suburban ritual—a coffee klatch with a commercial twist. Orders poured forth as women marveled that Rice Krispies, preserved in Tupperware, would still snap, crackle and pop a year later.

But the one thing Tupperware hasn't been able to preserve is a way of life. Tupperware aficionados—those who still cook—still rave about their lettuce crispers, Bacon Keepers and more than a hundred other items that are known for their high quality and a price to match. Nuclear families, however, have all but melted down. Women by the millions are in the work force; takeout food and restaurant meals have for some households made leftovers a thing of the past. And Tupperware sales have gone stale.

Yesterday, Tupperware announced a second-quarter loss in its domestic business, providing the biggest sore spot for Premark International Inc., its parent. Although Tupperware is doing well overseas, its domestic side is a shambles. Tupperware U.S. sales fell 33 percent in the quarter to $61.5 million from a year before. (The company won't disclose the size of its loss.) The quarter also saw a 20 percent decline in the number of active U.S. dealers to 23,328. A quarter of active dealers have dropped out since 1986, and competitor Rubbermaid is making off with much of the business.

"Tupperware U.S. remains a serious concern," said Warren L. Batts, Premark's chairman and chief executive officer. "The disappointing loss in this business has detracted from our progress elsewhere, and we expect [Tupperware] sales to continue slipping in the third quarter."

Other companies' fortunes, too, have been linked to the home and to women's place in it. Some have adapted to the times. Pillsbury, now a division of Grand Metropolitan PLC, was once primarily a miller of flour. As baking from scratch declined, Pillsbury pushed cake mixes, then Poppin' Fresh dough, then the microwaveable pancake. And it acquired Burger King. Procter & Gamble Co. trumpeted Ivory Snow for washing dirty diapers. When disposable diapers came along, P&G came out with Pampers.

Others haven't coped so well. Singer Co., with sewing in decline, tried to teach sewing in its stores. But sewing never came back, and Singer spun off the business.

Tupperware, too, has consistently been behind the curve in recognizing and adapting to change, according to some marketing experts. "The correct response in marketing is to let the market change you," says Al Ries, a marketing strategiest in Greenwich, Connecticut. "You can't force the market to act your way. People have changed and don't want to do it Tupperware's way."

Allan R. Nagle, president of Tupperware Worldwide, concedes that it is tougher to reach women nowadays. "We're trying a variety of things to make our product more accessible to women in concert with our sales organization," he says.

In the 1940s Earl Tupper, an inventor in Massachusetts, discerned that women had a problem. The refrigerator, which had replaced the icebox after World War I, wilted food and stole its flavor. Paper packaging and glass bowls often leaked or broke. So, out of a chunk of black polyethylene slag, Mr. Tupper crafted his first lightweight, unbreakable plastic bowls and airtight lids.

Innovative as the product was, women weren't buying it, wary of plastic and baffled by Tupperware lids. The product languished until frustrated distributors hit on the Tupperware party as a sales device.

It brilliantly played on the housewife status system of the day and on keeping up with the Joneses in household technology. Women, often 9 or 10 at a time, would don their silk stockings and cotton housedresses to eat pineapple upside-down cake and sip tea from china cups. They delighted in silly games. (When the Tupperware lady called out "lipstick," the first to fish one out of her purse might win a bud vase.)

Guests bought Tupperware, the hostess got a gift, and the Tupperware lady made some mad money. "Mr. Tupper called it polyethylene, we call it a miracle," Brownie Wise, one of the very first Tupperware ladies, would say, promising that a salad stored in Tupperware "would lose none of its sassiness."

The 1960s and 1970s were the salad days for Tupperware. Sales nearly doubled every five years. Tupperware dealers increased steadily in number. About the only thing the Tupperware ladies had to worry about was scheduling conflicts when there was something really good on television. Given Tupperware's success, Rubbermaid Inc. had also begun selling plastic bowls through home parties. But Tupperware's biggest competition seemed to be the reused Cool Whip container and the empty Pringles's potato-chip can.

Then, along about 1980, the year Tupperware's parent Dart Industries Inc. merged with Kraft Inc., Tupperware ladies noticed things changing. Divorces had become more common. More customers were single, childless, and working outside the home. Rubbermaid, seeing the same trends, called off its parties and moved its wares into grocery stores.

But Tupperware still preferred to look on the bright side. "Working women had more money to spend," says Diane Trillo, a veteran Tupperware lady. "Women at home had only their husband's money." More women seeking work, Tupperware believed, meant more prospective Tupperware dealers. In fact, the company took some of the credit for women's new freedom. "This was the quiet revolution launched by Tupperware . . . a revolution in the lives of housewives from all walks of life all over the country which continues to this day all over the world," a company history boasts.

But by the mid-1980s, Tupperware had become worried. There were fewer married couples with children, fewer children per family, more women in the work force. "Two thirds of Tupperware's potential customers are stranded from the product," the company fretted in 1986.

Its solution: to push dealers like Mrs. Dreier even harder. The energetic Mrs. Dreier is a far cry from the traditional Tupperware lady. She dresses in short skirts, subsists on fast food, dabs lipstick on in her minivan and is happiest doing three things at once. A wooden sign by her front door says, "Mom's Busy . . . Take a Number." She wouldn't be caught dead singing "Burp That Seal," to the tune of "Five Foot Two, Eyes of Blue"—an old Tupperware ritual.

Although her kitchen is full of Tupperware ($1,000 worth of the stuff by her estimate), she doesn't always have time to organize it. While leftover chicken and half an onion sit snugly in their respective Tupperware containers, random stalks of celery, bags of carrots and ice cream cones do not. Naked bags of waffles and chicken nuggets are there risking freezer burn.

One recent evening, with only an hour to feed the kids and change clothes for a Tupperware party, she ordered a pizza. "I didn't defrost anything," she says. "I haven't had time to go to the store. It's been a busy day."

It wasn't until Mrs. Dreier quit her accounting job eight years ago, had her first two children and needed the money to help pay the mortgage that she even thought of Tupperware. "I had never been to a Tupperware party," she says, and she didn't own any of its wares. "I wasn't interested in the least."

Now she is an unusually hard-working Tupperware lady, often holding five parties a week. In a recent week she put in at least one 11-hour day. She gave three evening parties, racked up more than 100 miles, picked up order forms, dropped off defective products, sorted bowls, mailed catalogs and wooed customers. "I want to be their Tupperware lady 10 years from now," she says. Last year, she earned $35,000, which according to the company is twice what its average manager makes. She also gets to drive a company Chevrolet Lumina minivan.

Mrs. Dreier's toughest job is selling to busy people such as herself. One of those is Eileen Rios, a file clerk and mother of two, who didn't show up for her first party last month. The second time around, 8 of the 11 women invited were no-shows (a common problem these days). Mrs. Rios and three relatives ordered $106.80 in Tupperware (of which Mrs. Dreier gets about 25% in commission, after expenses). The whole affair took nearly three hours, and Mrs. Dreier got home to her children, ages 6, 8 and 10, at 10 o'clock.

She considered the night a success because two of the women (men rarely attend) agreed to play host to their own parties. Mrs. Rios is even considering signing on as a Tupperware dealer. "It pays to be patient," Mrs. Dreier says.

With Tupperware's encouragement, sellers like Mrs. Dreier are trying every possible twist on Tupperware parties. They hold them in offices, in parks, even in parking lots. (At these "tailgate" affairs, Tupperware ladies actually solicit total strangers to play host to parties.) They hold "stop and shops" so women can just drop in, "classes" so they can feel they're bettering themselves, and "custom-kitchen" parties—orgies of cabinet-organizing.

A big part of Tupperware's turnaround strategy is new products. Two years ago, it hired designer Morison Cousins, famous for his rendition of the Dixie cup holder, to make its products look less frumpy. Mrs. Dreier dutifully pitches Modular Mates, which defend against cabinet clutter, TupperWave, which microwaves an entire dinner in 30 minutes, and the Earth Pack, a set of containers in a washable green lunch bag. She has varying success, since many people resist microwave cooking and many prefer a Ziploc bag to washing out an Earth Pack.

Her job might be a lot easier if it weren't for one thing: Most American women—55 percent by Tupperware's estimate—either have no idea how to find Tupperware or no desire to go to a Tupperware party. Some 40 percent

EXHIBIT 1 Changing U.S. Life Styles Have Hurt Tupperware

A Decline in Nuclear Families . . .

Share of U.S. households with two parents and at least one child

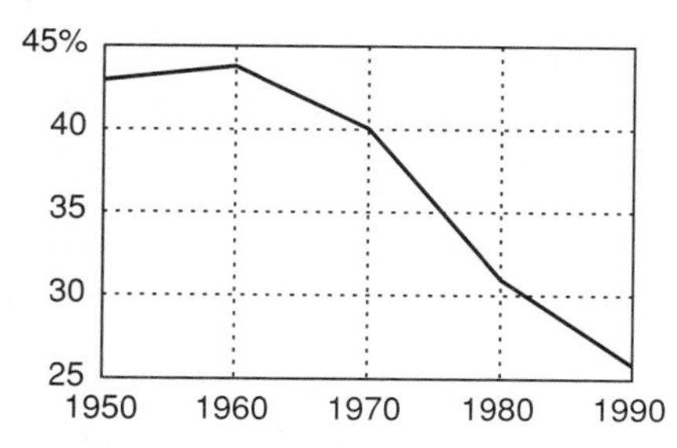

Source: U.S. Census Population Survey

And More Women in the Workforce . . .

Labor force participation of women with children under six years old

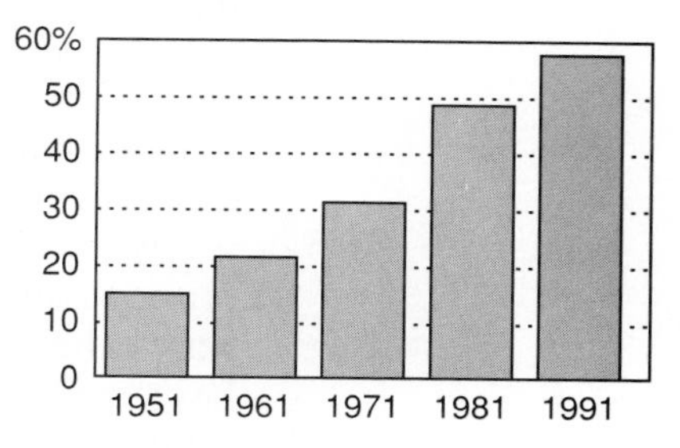

Source: Bureau of Labor Statistics

Have Meant Declining Sales . . .

U.S. sales in millions of dollars

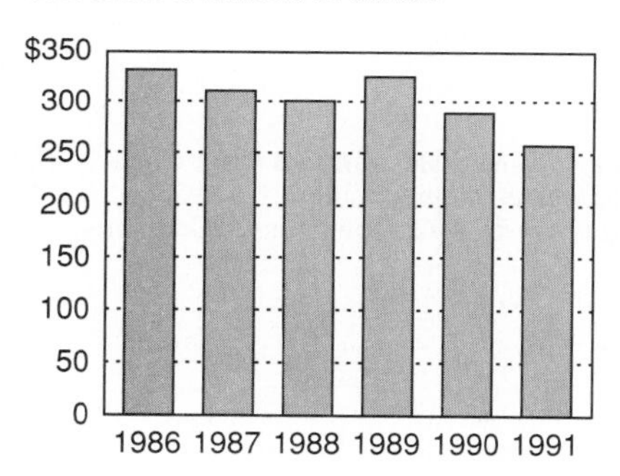

And Fewer Dealers

U.S. active dealers in thousands

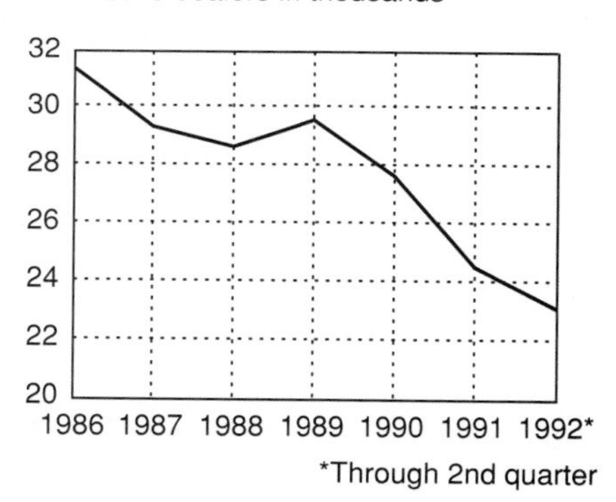

*Through 2nd quarter

of Tupperware's sales are from people who skip the parties but send orders along with friends who attend [see trends in Exhibit 1].

At a General Electric office just down the street from Mrs. Dreier's local Tupperware warehouse, Alice Stetson, a 25-year-old financial specialist, says she "never heard that people have those [parties] anymore. I heard about it happening in the 1950s and 1960s." A GE co-worker, Theresa Swift, says she much prefers her volleyball and dance classes to a Tupperware party. "It doesn't seem enjoyable, and I don't have the time," she says.

By being in supermarkets, Rubbermaid *does* reach such people. Its market share has risen to between 30 percent and 40 percent (of units sold) from about 5 percent or 10 percent in 1984, even as Tupperware's share has slipped to between 40 percent and 45 percent, from 59 percent of the food-storage container market, according to industry estimates.

Tupperware still isn't considering any such marketing move, however. "To wipe away our existing distribution and replace it would be a pretty traumatic exercise," says Tupperware's Mr. Nagle. "I don't see a beneficial trade-off."

Tupperware nearly issued a mail-order catalog four years ago but backed off when its dealers rebelled. It has experimented over the past five years with a delivery service so customers don't have to pick up their purchases from party hostesses.

Now the company is again gingerly experimenting with a catalog. But, for now, the mailing list will include only the names submitted by Tupperware ladies—namely, past Tupperware hostesses. The effort may eventually be expanded, Mr. Nagle says, but, he insists, "we're not going to do anything to jeopardize" the Tupperware sales force. The company plans television advertising to recruit new dealers later this year.

But mostly the company is hoping that the 1990s will see the resurgence of the Tupperware party, which, Mr. Nagle predicts, "will become more in vogue than in the '80s because of the greater propensity of women and families to spend more time at home."

Source: Laurie M. Grossman, "Going Stale: Families Have Changed But Tupperware Keeps Holding Its Parties," *The Wall Street Journal,* July 21, 1992, pp. A1, A3. Reprinted by permission of *The Wall Street Journal.*

CASE 2–2 Yaohan International Group

After taking over the helm at Japan's Yaohan International Group from his father, Kazuo Wada faced up to a problem all too familiar to many American executives hoping to branch into Japan: The country's sky-high rents and complex distribution system were impeding the retail chain's expansion.

So, in the 1970s, Mr. Wada targeted Southeast Asia, where an economic boom was just beginning. And three years ago, Yaohan, seeking to raise its profile in the Southeast Asian business community and to reduce its taxes, moved its headquarters to Hong Kong just after the Tiananmen Square incident had scared many foreign investors away from here.

Now, Yaohan—which is still thought of as a Japanese company—is Japan's biggest retailer overseas and a key player in Southeast Asia, with major operations in Singapore, Thailand, Taiwan and Malaysia.

In a way, that is surprising. Yaohan is no giant at home. With 93 general-merchandise stores scattered in towns near its Japanese headquarters in Numazu, in central Japan, it ranks as only the country's 59th-largest retailer. It hasn't a single outlet in Tokyo.

But in Hong Kong, Yaohan is one of the colony's biggest retail chains. Its four stores here have been so successful selling middle-priced clothing, television sets, and pots and pans that Yaohan plans to open three more outlets this year. In addition, Yaohan was one of the first foreign retailers, apart from a few Japanese department stores catering to Japanese tourists, to open suburban stores not only in Hong Kong but also in Singapore and Kuala Lumpur, the capital of Malaysia. And the company has gone so far afield as to plunge into such untapped markets as Brunei, and it's sowing seeds in China.

Now, Yaohan chalks up 40 percent of its sales outside Japan, from 26 stores and some Hong Kong restaurants, game centers and handbag stores. After lifting worldwide sales 24 percent to 321.1 billion yen (currently equivalent to $2.6 billion) in the year ended March 31, it is aiming at sales of 800 billion yen in five years, with overseas volume tripling to 400 billion yen.

"We want to be an international retail conglomerate," says Mr. Wada, Yaohan's 63-year-old chairman, as he maps out global strategy on a huge video screen. "Hong Kong will be the base to supervise operations in the rest of the world."

The rest of the world includes America, where Yaohan already has some outlets. The company runs eight general-merchandise stores in the U.S., including a huge one in Edgewater, N.J. It plans 12 more stores in the next three years in such cities as Atlanta and Houston.

However, it is Southeast Asia, the world's fastest-growing consumer market, that is attracting Yaohan and Japanese rivals. Overall retail sales are expected to soar 20 percent in Hong Kong and South Korea this year and rise strongly in other Asian nations—while staying flat in the U.S., Europe and even Japan. In Hong Kong last year, the 11 big Japanese retailers selling here accounted for nearly half of the colony's US$17.7 billion in retail sales. Like Yaohan, some of these companies reacted to the Japanese barriers—which turn many American retailers away from Asia altogether—by deciding to look for more open markets in neighboring countries.

American merchants, Mr. Wada says, could probably make money here, too, if they would enter the Southeast Asian market. But they haven't. Most U.S. retailers only buy or manufacture merchandise in the region. Just about the only U.S. chain, apart from franchise operations such as McDonald's Corp., that sells in Hong Kong is Toys "R" Us Inc.

"The perception in America," says Richard Thalheimer, chairman of Sharper Image Corp., "is that the only consumers in that area are in Japan" and that a country such as Singapore has just "a lot of workers." He says Sharper Image is negotiating with investors about licensing stores in Hong Kong, Taiwan and Singapore. "Local business people are better acquainted with regulatory concerns, including liability issues," he adds.

American retailers offer a variety of reasons for generally staying out. Woolworth Corp., perhaps the most adventurous U.S. retailer, is concentrating on Europe, where it expects to open 100 of its Foot Locker stores this year. "We aren't precluding the Pacific Rim from future plans, but we want to do one thing at a time and do it right," a spokeswoman says.

A spokesman for R.H. Macy & Co. comments, "Retailing is such a regional industry," with consumer tastes in national markets differing widely. For example, he says, Macy's shoes may not sell well in Southeast Asia because Asians have smaller feet, and manufacturing those smaller sizes would require a lot of extra effort. At Wal-Mart Stores Inc., a spokeswoman says the company sees enough "potential to grow inside the U.S." and hasn't any plans to invest in Asia.

One of the few U.S. retailers to go after the Asian market is Sears, Roebuck & Co. In the 1970s, it tried to sell its refrigerators and household appliances to Japan's emerging middle class. But Sears, operating in a corner of Tokyo's Seibu Department Store, had trouble selling its appliances because they were too big for tiny Japanese homes. Now, a spokesman says Sears' moves in Asia are limited to auto-repair ventures with Japanese retailers.

Moreover, many American retailing companies are in such bad financial shape that they can't expand anywhere.

Yaohan doesn't have that problem. It had net income of five billion yen ($40.7 million) in the March 31 year. Of its four operating units, Yaohan Japan Co. is the biggest; its stock is traded on the Tokyo Stock Exchange. The other publicly traded unit is Yaohan H.K., listed in Hong Kong.

Mr. Wada works hard to fit into the Southeast Asian business community. He has bought a fancy guest house atop Hong Kong's scenic Victoria Peak, three villas with private beaches and a large cruiser as "social venues" for mingling with Chinese business leaders—even though he doesn't speak Chinese and Japanese rivals dislike lavish displays of wealth.

People close to him say he keeps a tight rein on Yaohan, summoning directors world-wide to twice-a-month board meetings. A voting machine attached to each seat encourages executives to express their views while allowing privacy. He also pushes staffers to convert to his religious sect, Seicho no Ie, which literally means "House of Growth." In his recently published biography, he concedes, "I'm viewed as sort of an odd fish."

Yaohan stores' attraction isn't glamour or originality. Yaohan's sprawling 14,000-square-meter store in Hong Kong's Shatin suburb offers everything from groceries to sneakers to casual clothes until as late as 10 P.M.—convenient for shoppers used to scurrying from stall to stall in crowded outdoor markets. "You can buy everything you need in this store," says Christina Chan, a 28-year-old saleswoman who often shops there on her way home from work.

Yaohan's huge food section, which fills the basement of the four-story building, is especially popular. The individually wrapped vegetables, neatly stacked on brightly lit shelves, contrast sharply with the street markets. In the store's aisles, saleswomen stand hawking samples of such Japanese delicacies as raw fish. And busy housewives like new products such as packages of peeled, chopped and ready-to-cook ingredients for Chinese winter melon soup.

The store also highlights the now popular Japanese mystique by announcing "new-arrival" dresses from Tokyo. But it also modifies Japanese culture if that is what customers want. Finding that Hong Kong shoppers enjoy the Japanese delicacy of broiled eel, Yaohan's restaurant corner includes it in everything from fried rice to a bowl of noodles—an appalling combination to Japanese gourmets.

That kind of flexibility marks a big difference from most Western retailers, which tend to sell the same products abroad as back home and try to maintain a consistent image in overseas stores. Even Marks & Spencer PLC, a British clothing chain with four profitable stores in Hong Kong, offers the same fashion line worldwide and devotes many of its racks to underwear in sizes too large for most Hong Kong consumers, some people complain. "The stores are for Europeans," concludes one annoyed shopper.

Marks & Spencer disagrees. "Our stores in Hong Kong carry appropriate merchandise in terms of styling and size," a spokeswoman says in London.

Meanwhile, Yaohan's success is luring Japanese competitors to Hong Kong. Across the mall from Yaohan's Shatin store is a two-year-old outlet belonging to Seiyu, another Japanese general-merchandise chain. Jusco Ltd., a Tokyo-based chain, is striving to catch up by opening 14 general-merchandise stores in Asia, four of them in Hong Kong.

"General-merchandise stores are the mainstream in Southeast Asia in the future," says Tatsuichi Yamaguchi, general manager of Jusco's Hong Kong subsidiary. Jusco is also expanding in the U.S. through its Talbots women's wear chain, which it acquired three years ago.

So influential are the Japanese retailers that they are even setting the standards for local competitors. Wing On Department Stores, Hong Kong's biggest local chain, recently formed a joint-venture company with Seiyu because it figured it needed Japanese brands and display techniques. And the Japanese dominance in Asia is so strong that most shopping centers are starting to look like Japanese malls, with at least one large Japanese outlet as the key tenant. Hong Kong stores recently began placing on their showcases porcelain cats, a Japanese symbol for thriving business.

And although such symbols of America as McDonald's and Pizza Hut restaurants are commonplace, Hong Kong consumers are increasingly looking to Japan for fashion and product trends. Compared with clothes from Europe or the U.S., "I think I will prefer Japanese design because the design is better," says Belinda Tai, a 19-year-old student.

Some analysts worry that Yaohan may be expanding too rapidly, especially in Hong Kong real estate. They note that its first overseas stores, in Brazil, failed in the wake of the 1970s oil shocks. But the company is skillful in applying knowledge gained in one place to another. After building an American-style department store in Handa in central Japan, it is linking up with two Hong Kong companies to set up a huge shopping center in Sapporo, in northern Japan. And although Japanese retailers probably won't soon launch a major foray into the U.S., where general-merchandise stores are ailing, observers expect it to eventually use its expertise in some way to expand there.

Source: Yumiko Ono, "Surging Market: A Japanese Retailer Finds Southeast Asia Is the Place to Grow," *The Wall Street Journal,* September 4, 1991, pp. A1, A4.

CASE 2–3 Gillette Co.

Several mornings a week, Alfred M. Zeien performs an odd ritual. After lathering his face, he shaves with two razors—one for each side of his face.

Then he runs his fingers over his cheeks to check the closeness of the shave. "That's the only way to really compare shaves," declares Mr. Zeien, chairman and chief executive officer of Gillette Co., who tests both his company's razors and competitors'.

Gillette is a company obsessed with shaving. How many whiskers on the average man's face? Thirty thousand, by Gillette's count. How fast do men's whiskers grow? By 15/1,000ths of an inch a day, or 5½ inches a year. Dry beard hair, Gillette has determined, is about as tough as copper wire of the same thickness.

"We spend more time than you can imagine studying facial hair growth—which is quite different from the growth of other hair on your head—because that's the way to improve your product," explains the very clean-shaven Mr. Zeien, who keeps a drawerful of experimental Gillette blades in his office for trying out.

In the annals of American business, few companies have dominated an industry so much and for so long as this one. "Gillette was the lead brand in 1923 and is the lead brand in 1992," says Jack Trout, a marketing consultant. And not by a little: Its 64 percent share of the U.S. wet-shaving market (in dollars) compares with 13 percent at No. 2 Schick, a unit of Warner-Lambert Co.

But Gillette is one of America's noteworthy corporate successes not just because it has done so well, but also because it once blundered so remarkably—and came back.

In 1962, a small foreign company, Wilkinson Sword Ltd., introduced the first coated stainless steel blade, cutting sharply into Gillette's market share. Swallowing its pride, Gillette came out with its own stainless steel blade.

Humbled, Gillette used the experience to learn lessons many companies don't learn until too late: Never take a rival for granted, no matter how small. Don't concede market niches to competitors, because niches have a way of growing. And don't dally in bringing out new products for fear of cannibalizing old ones; if you don't bring them out, a competitor may.

"Every American corporation of any great size or importance was founded on a core business. Why didn't certain of those companies survive, or [survive] only in a diminished way? They took their eye off the core business," contends Milton Glass, Gillette's vice president of finance. "Gillette has never done that. Each morning Gillette executives face south, to south Boston"—home of its biggest plant, which churns out nearly 2 billion blades a year—"and bow to our razor-blade business. Everything else is secondary."

Gillette so dominates shaving worldwide that its name has come to mean a razor blade in some countries. It is the leader in Europe with a 70 percent market share and in Latin America with 80 percent. Indeed, for every blade it sells at home, it sells five abroad, a figure likely to grow as joint ventures expand sales in China, Russia, and India.

Retaining its dominance in razors also has meant spending hundreds of millions of dollars to develop the innovative twin-blade Trac II razor in 1972, the pivoting-head Atra in 1977, and the hugely successful Sensor, with independently suspended blades, in 1989. It also meant rushing out—albeit reluctantly—a disposable razor in 1976 to fend off French rival Societé Bic SA, even though the cheap throwaways cut into sales of higher-profit Gillette products.

While shaving will account for only a bit more than one third of Gillette's $5 billion in sales this year, razors will ring up nearly two thirds of profits of $500 million—attesting to the manufacturing efficiencies and profit margins that go with its dominance [Exhibit 1].

Gillette's performance in other businesses—deodorants, pens, cosmetics—is decidedly mixed. Braun electric shavers and small electric appliances and Oral-B toothbrushes, bought when they were small companies, have grown rapidly under Gillette. While Braun isn't dominant in electric razors, it is a major player, enabling Gillette to hedge its bet by being in a business that holds a steady 30 percent share of the shaving market.

But Right Guard deodorant, once the leading brand, has been surpassed by rivals. Bic clobbered Gillette in disposable lighters, prompting Gillette to sell its Cricket business. And in writing instruments, Gillette's Paper Mate and other brands produce only so-so profits and growth. Efforts to diversify into everything from hearing aids to eyewear have flopped.

Those problems, combined with the growing market share of low-margin disposable razors, slowed Gillette's sales and earnings growth in the 1980s. Corporate raiders launched hostile takeover bids, criticizing manage-

EXHIBIT 1 Gillette: On the Cutting Edge

A Dominant Market Share . . .
Gillette's share of dollar sales of the U.S. wet shaving market

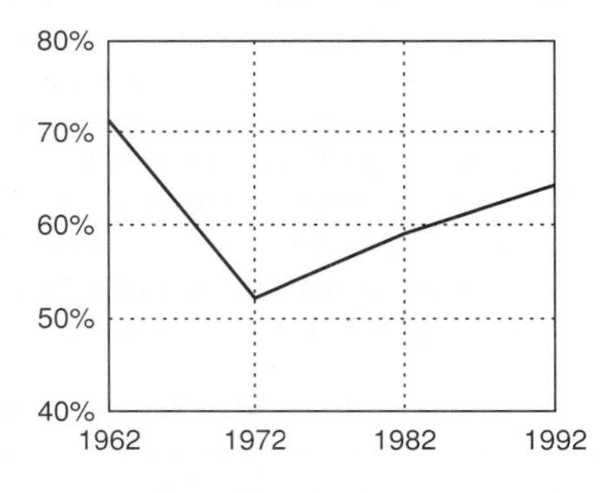

In Its Core Business . . .
Sales in 1991, by business line

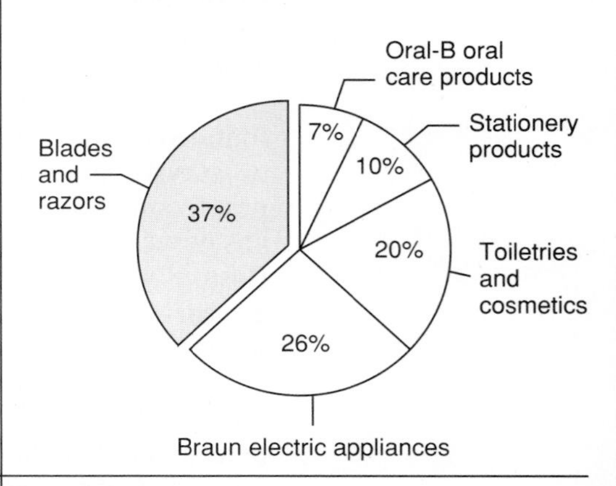

Leads to Rising Profits . . .
Net income, in millions of dollars

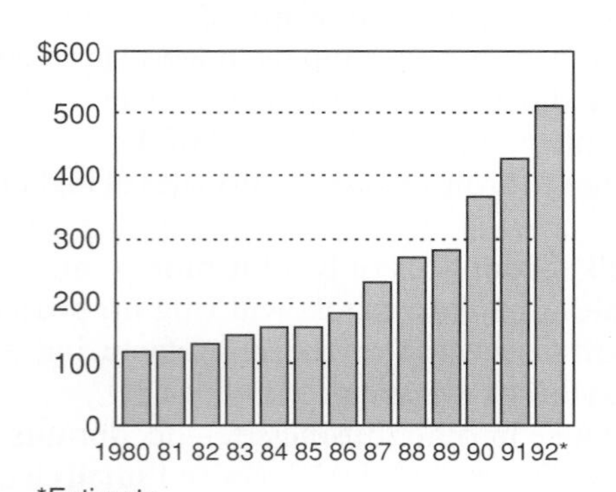

*Estimate
Source: Gillette

And a Soaring Stock
Year-end closing stock prices, adjusted for splits

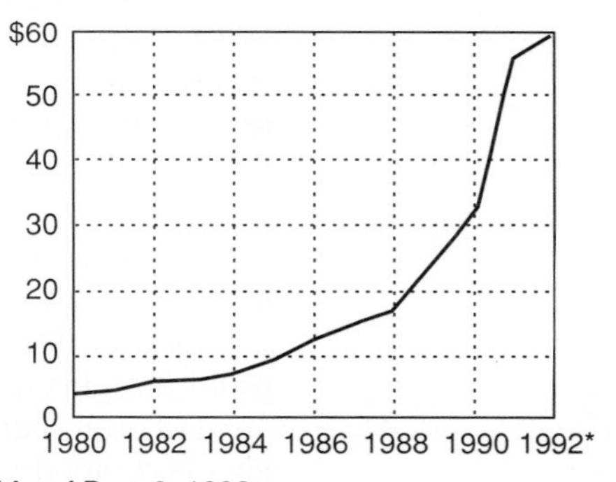

*As of Dec. 9, 1992

ment as lethargic, while some dissident shareholders waged a proxy battle to oust some directors.

Although ultimately unsuccessful, those attacks moved Gillette management to act. The company slashed its bloated staff by 8 percent. And to stem the growth of throwaway razors, Gillette tried a risky strategy—positioning its new Sensor as an alternative to lower-priced disposables. It worked.

Mustaches and beards are rare among Gillette managers, and not only because of a corporate fondness for clean-shaven cheeks. Gillette is a conservative company that expects slavish devotion from its managers, many of whom are 30- and 40-year veterans. Indeed, the only time Gillette ever reached outside for a top executive was in the early 1970s, when it hired marketing whiz Edward Gelsthorpe as president. Known as "Cranapple Ed"—for introducing the Ocean Spray cranberry and apple juice drink—he lasted just 15 months at Gillette. He won't comment, but insiders say he simply didn't fit in.

Those who aren't passionate about Gillette need not apply. A business-school graduate, assured of a position with Gillette after several interviews, was asked in a final meeting whether she had any qualms. Half in jest, she said, "Well, I'm not sure I want to spend the rest of my life worrying about underarms." She didn't get the job.

Nowhere is the obsession more evident than at the South Boston manufacturing and research plant. Here, some 200 volunteers from various departments come to work unshaven each day. They troop to the second floor and enter small booths with a sink and mirror, where they take instructions from technicians on the other side of a small window: try this blade or that shaving cream or this aftershave, then answer questionnaires. Besides men's faces, the research includes the legs of women volunteers; women account for 29 percent of razor sales in the U.S.

"We bleed so you'll get a good shave at home. This is my 27th year. I came here my first week. Haven't missed a day of shaving," says George Turchinetz, manager of the prototype model shop, proudly noting that he is a "preferred" tester because he is "real fussy."

For a close look at the mechanics of shaving, Gillette uses a boroscope—a video camera attached to a blade cartridge using fiber optics. Magnifying the film hundreds of times, researchers can precisely determine how twin blades catch the whiskers, pull them out of the follicles and cut them. Sometimes they collect debris after test shaves and measure the angle of the cut whiskers; the flatter the angle, the less force it took to cut the hair.

"We test the blade edge, the blade guard, the angle of the blades, the balance of the razor, the length, the heft, the width," explains Donald Chaulk, vice president of the shaving technology laboratory. "What happens to the chemistry of the skin? What happens to the hair when you pull it? What happens to the follicle? We own the face. We know more about shaving than anybody. I don't think obsession is too strong a word."

He pauses. "I've got to be careful. I don't want to sound crazy."

Despite the conservatism of Gillette, its research and development effort is a testament to risk taking. At any given time, Gillette has up to 20 experimental razors in development. One promising prototype has been in the works for four years—and won't be ready for eight more. "We're spending more than $1 million a year on that project, knowing we can't launch till 2000 or 2001," says Mr. Zeien, the chairman. "That's assuming we'll overcome the technical barriers, and we're not sure we can."

To understand the Gillette of 1992, it's important to understand the Gillette of 1962. Gillette's U.S. market share had just reached its highest point ever—72 percent. The company had long been a power overseas as well, having gone abroad in 1905, only a decade after King C. Gillette invented the first safety razor.

"We have," an executive boasted to Forbes magazine in 1962, "no complaints on how things are going."

They soon would. Wilkinson Sword—which forged the famous swords for British cavalry at the height of the Empire, but by the 1960s made mostly garden tools—decided to get into blades. Its Super Sword-Edge stainless steel blade, coated with a thin chemical film to protect the edge, lasted up to 12 shaves, or two or three times as many as Gillette's own coated Super Blue Blade, made of softer carbon steel.

Gillette was stunned. "They were the talk of the town," recalls shaving-division vice president Scott Roberts, then a salesman in New York. "Our leadership was threatened."

Gillette knew stainless steel was harder than carbon steel. It also knew about stainless blade coatings—in fact, Wilkinson later had to license technology for making its coated blade from Gillette, which had a patent. But making a stainless blade would have made much of Gillette's manufacturing equipment obsolete.

It was tempted to do what many big companies do: Ignore its rival, hoping the market niche would remain small, or improve its existing carbon-blade technology. Eventually, Gillette decided it had no choice and introduced a stainless blade in late 1963. By then, two other small players had introduced stainless blades, and Gillette's U.S. market share had begun a precipitous drop that would bottom out at around 50 percent.

In retrospect, Gillette was lucky Wilkinson didn't have the firepower to exploit its weakness. "I had nightmares thinking that someone at Procter & Gamble would shave with [a stainless blade] and decide to get in the business or buy out Wilkinson," confesses William G. Salatich, a retired Gillette executive. (Unable to duplicate the breakthrough it made with stainless blades, Wilkinson has become a minor player in most countries; Gillette, in fact, bought Wilkinson's blade business outside Europe and the United States several years ago.)

Though short-lived, the debacle galvanized Gillette in a way a lesser threat wouldn't have. Russell B. Adams Jr., author of a corporate biography for the company, says, "It has become part of the myth and folklore: "This is what happens to you if you're not up there keeping ahead of the market.'"

Indeed, the ordeal prepared Gillette for the next major challenge to its razor and blade business.

Only a few years after Gillette had reasserted itself with the twin-blade Trac II, Bic sold its first inexpensive disposables in Greece in 1974. Again there was skepticism about the product because it offered a worse shave, not a better one. "We'd get samples and I would try them and wonder why anybody would compromise their shave to save a little money," remembers Mr. Scott, the Gillette vice president.

Moreover, why come out with a new razor that cost more to make (because disposables had a handle and blade, as opposed to a cartridge that fit on an existing razor) but sold for less? Especially when it might take sales from more profitable brands. It was similar to the issue Detroit would face when the Japanese invaded the United States with small cars.

"There was sizable debate whether we should or shouldn't make a disposable," says Robert E. Ray, a former overseas manager who now is a management consultant. "If you sit down with pencil and paper, you conclude, 'This ain't such a hot idea, we're going to make less money.' But after a while you didn't have to be rocket scientist to figure out that consumers wanted disposables."

A short while. Bic took a 10 percent market share in Greece almost overnight, then moved into Austria and Italy. With the 1960s disaster in mind, Gillette began a crash program to develop a disposable. Gillette rolled out its Good News disposable—using the Trac II twin-blade technology, compared with Bic's single blade—nationwide in April 1976, months before Bic introduced its razor regionally.

Says former president Stephen Griffin: "We were giving up profitability, but we had to do that to maintain our customers."

"Gillette did exactly the right thing," says Mr. Trout, the marketing guru. "Guys who say they don't like the world to change, guess what—it changes underneath them. That's what kills companies."

Nonetheless, Bic has proven to be a formidable competitor. By forcing Gillette into disposables, Bic contributed to Gillette's problems in the 1980s. Gillette initially thought disposables might get 10 percent of the market. In fact, by the late 1980s disposables had a share of nearly 50 percent in dollars and some 60 percent in units.

While it held a narrow lead over Bic in units and a wide lead in dollars in disposables (Gillette's are priced higher), its profit margins were being squeezed.

The answer came from Gillette's R&D labs. One of the savvy developments of Gillette researchers over the past 20 years has been to design razors that are hard for competitors to make. In the days of the double-edge blade, it was easy for others to make blades that fit Gillette's razors; Trac II and other twin-blade razors changed that. Rivals generally come out with cartridges compatible with new Gillette razors, but only after a lag.

The idea for a razor with twin blades that move independently—the Sensor—originated in Gillette's British labs in the late 1970s. Perfecting it, and figuring out how to make it by the billions, would take a decade and more than $200 million.

Some Gillette managers wanted to use the technology on disposables. But John W. Symons, a now-retired Gillette executive, argued that it offered such a superior shave that it could command a premium price, thus reversing the growth of disposables and increasing profit margins at the same time. Otherwise, he contends, "Our great brand would become a commodity business." Gillette stopped advertising disposables, and —in a huge bet—put nearly all its marketing money on Sensor.

To the astonishment of many, both inside and outside Gillette, the strategy worked. Since Sensor was introduced in 1989, the market share of disposables in dollars has declined to 45 percent from a peak of 49 percent. Though Schick has followed with a variation of the flexible-blade idea, called the Tracer, no rival has yet reproduced the Sensor design—in part because the manufacturing equipment needed to make it is so expensive and complicated.

What's next? Gillette has a Sensor II in development that company officials vow will "supersede" Sensor. "That's one of the successes of the Japanese: They always have their next play in hand when making their current play," says Scott Roberts, the Gillette vice president.

And in another move from the Japanese playbook, the next generation razor isn't likely to be introduced first in the United States, says Mr. Zeien, the chairman. "This is what the auto companies learned from the Japanese," he says. "If you want to be a leader on a global basis, you can't just be a leader in your home market."

Source: Lawrence Ingrassia, "Keeping Sharp: Gillette Holds Its Edge by Endlessly Searching for a Better Shave," *The Wall Street Journal,* December 10, 1992, pp. A1 and A5.

CASE 2–4 Gap, Inc.

The nation's merchants, many as glum as the Grinch this Christmas, are struggling to get through a retail recession by ballyhooing bargains, gift give-aways and even exotic vacations.

But not Gap Inc.

It's bright white Gap stores are oddly devoid of holiday hype. The company isn't displaying gimmicky merchandise to lure crowds. Its shelves are stocked with simple, all-cotton, no-frills clothing.

Nevertheless, the 21-year-old apparel chain is booming. It is benefiting from a sudden cachet with a wide spectrum of consumers—from teen-agers to celebrities. The current issue of *Gap Rap,* an in-house magazine, brags about the sighting of Jacqueline Onassis at a Manhattan Gap and reports recent purchases by Kathleen Turner, Arnold Schwarzenegger, and the Duchess of Kent.

The Gap has become hip as consumers, discarding their 1980s excesses, turn back to a "basics" frame of mind. Keds are popular, while Dove Bars and imported beers are passé. "It's a return to an earlier kind of Americana, when things weren't quite so complicated," say Mona Doyle, a consumer researcher.

The Gap brand of men's, women's and kids' clothes, the company contends, is now the third-largest-selling label in America—after Levi Strauss and Liz Claiborne sportswear. While competitors are struggling to match 1989 receipts, Gap's same-store sales have surged 15 percent this year. Its annual profit is expected to jump 35 percent (Exhibit 1). And Gap's results are even more impressive if its one struggling unit, Banana Republic, isn't included.

Gap is taking advantage of its good fortune—and the industry's bad times. Recession or not, Gap is plunging ahead with an ambitious, albeit risky, five-year expansion plan. It is bent on doubling sales—to nearly $4 billion by 1995—and its floor space. Next year alone, it plans to spend about $220 million, financed mostly from cash flow, and add as many as 165 new stores to its roster of 1,100 Gap, GapKids, and Banana Republic outlets.

"This is an opportunity to take market share," declares Donald Fisher, Gap's 62-year-old chairman and founder. He figures that Gap can woo discouraged customers away from weak, debt-laden chains that can't afford to keep stores looking sharp.

Gap isn't the only retailer prospering. Discounters Wal-Mart Stores Inc. and the Target unit of Dayton Hudson Corp. are faring well and see the economy's slide more as an opportunity than a threat. Target is even testing fashion ads aimed at department-store customers who might be trading down. One touts Target's $19.99 stirrup pants as "what to wear with a $175 Adrienne Vittadini sweater."

In a recession, Gap's basic clothes seem likely to retain their appeal. Its strategy of changing the colors of its stock every two months or so could keep Gap stores looking fresher than competitors—while many of the competitors are trimming orders for new goods, leaving a jumble of old and new shades on their sales floors.

Furthermore, Gap's strategy could attract more bargain hunters: To move out slow-selling items quickly, the chain typically slashes prices by a third.

"The two things they offer—quality and value—are the things people put a premium on in tight times," says Thomas Flexner, a New York real-estate executive and Gap shopper.

Like other retailers, Gap expects slower sales growth through at least next year's first half. But it is predicting a still-healthy increase in roughly the 5 to 8 percent range at stores open at least a year.

A common item such as Gap's pocket T-shirt illustrates why. When consumers first began tightening their purse strings last summer, Gap already had positioned it as a stylish but inexpensive fashion statement. Singer Ricki Lee Jones and Twin Peaks heartthrob James Marshall wore it in Gap ads. The all-cotton shirt was available in a dozen colors, including trendy "chili" red as well as basic black and white. And Gap priced it at just

EXHIBIT 1 The Gap: Reaping the Rewards of Success

Earnings have jumped . . .
Annual net income, in millions

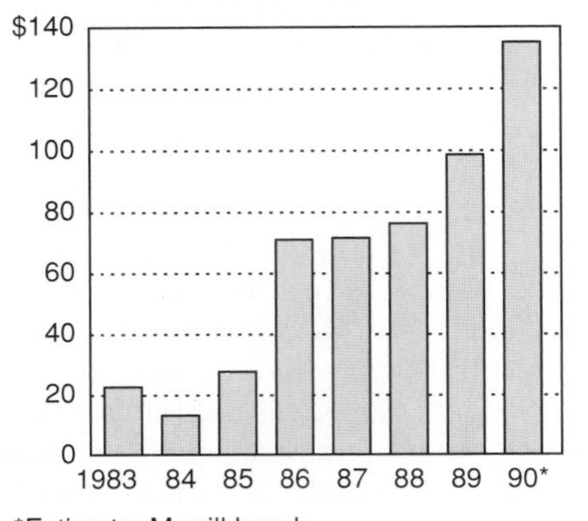

*Estimate: Merrill Lynch

And stores proliferate . . .
Number of stores at year end

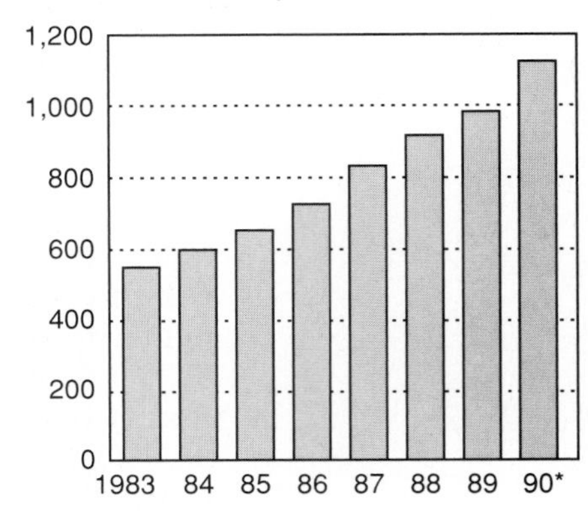

As it outpaces competitors . . .
Year-to-date same-store sales, in percent

	Percent change
Gap	**+ 15.0 %**
Dillard Dept. Stores*	+ 11.0
Burlington Coat*	+ 10.0
Dayton Hudson*	+ 6.8
Limited	+ 5.0
Charming Shoppes	+ 4.0
TJX*	+ 2.0
May Dept. Stores*	+ 1.4
Nordstrom*	+ 0.7
Carter Hawley Hale	– 1.0

*Estimate: Seidler Amdec Securities
Source: Seidler Amdec Securities

Benefiting investors.
Comparison of Gap stock vs. DJ Apparel Retailers index, Dec. 29, 1989 = 100

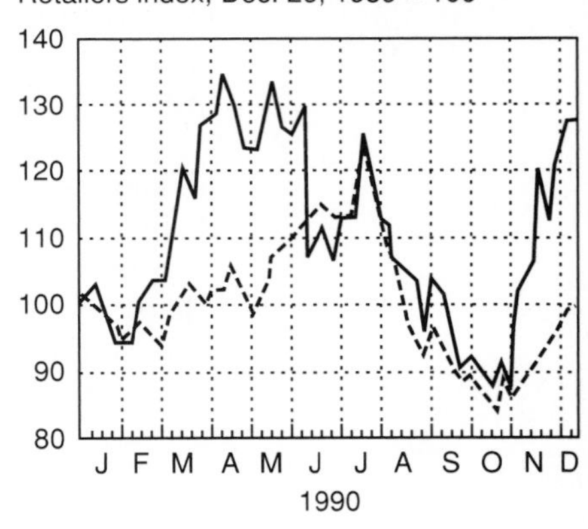

$10.50—about 15 percent less than competitors were charging. Gap sold nearly a million.

In the fickle world of fashion, Gap could trip, of course. It has before. In 1987, it stumbled by sticking too long with such styles as shaker-knit sweaters and buffalo plaid shirts. In the fall of 1989, it introduced pastel-colored clothes that bombed. Its attempt to launch an upscale clothing chain called

Hemisphere was a washout, triggering an after-tax charge of $6.5 million last year to close the nine shops.

But Gap's biggest swamp has been its 129-store Banana Republic chain. In the mid-1980s, the chain expanded rapidly on the strength of its safari look, which was popular when Indiana Jones action films and *Out of Africa* were hot. But the safari craze fizzled in 1987, and the Banana Republic chain struggled for two years with losses and declining same-store sales. Lately, the unit has staged a turnaround, posting three consecutive quarters of what Gap officials call "modest" profits. They add that they still see room for improvement—especially in Banana Republic's women's business.

"We're always trying things that don't work," acknowledges Millard "Mickey" Drexler, Gap's 46-year-old president. At the moment, he has doubts about a new $325 leather jacket that may be too expensive for Gap shoppers. He also worries that Gap managers may have overreacted to his call for simplicity and eliminated too many prints from the richly colored holiday assortment.

Gap didn't carry any clout when, in 1969, Mr. Fisher set out to sell a wide selection of Levi's. A real-estate executive then, Mr. Fisher hit on the idea of a jeans shop after failing to find Levi's in his common size at department stores. Initially, he also sold discounted records and tapes to draw shoppers into his first San Francisco store, but he quickly quit the music business because of losses to thieves.

His wife, Doris, coined the store's name after a cocktail party at which "the generation gap" was a hot topic. By the early 1980s, however, The Gap was having an identity crisis of its own. Levi's could be purchased almost everywhere; Sears sold them, and jean shops were sprouting like weeds. Discounting was rampant—even at The Gap—and Mr. Fisher was worried.

So, in 1983, he recruited Mr. Drexler, who already had transformed the unprofitable Ann Taylor chain into a healthy, chic specialty store for working women. Previously, Mr. Drexler, the son of a New York garment-district worker, had worked at Bloomingdale's, Macy's and Abraham & Straus department stores.

Although the two executives initially considered starting a new chain, Mr. Drexler figured that he could do more for The Gap. He believed the company was squandering a good name by emphasizing low prices instead of fashion. He saw a market for casual clothes with "good style, good taste and good value."

Mr. Drexler made that point in his first day on the job by waving pictures ripped from magazines. One showed Fiat mogul Giovanni Agnelli in a Levi's chambray shirt; in another, designer Ralph Lauren posed in Levi's jeans and a jean jacket. "Good taste doesn't have to be more expensive," Mr. Drexler kept asserting.

Soon, Mr. Drexler discarded a dozen clothing labels, retaining only Levi's and The Gap brand he intended to build. He spruced up Gap stores. He also hired a team of seasoned Seventh Avenue designers—now numbering about 30—to study the world fashion scene and develop distinctive Gap collections.

Alan Millstein, publisher of the *Fashion Network Report* newsletter, contends that Gap designers "blaze no new trails" and "aren't the Lewis and Clark of retailing." But, he adds, there's nothing wrong with that. He had just snapped up four long-sleeve Gap polo shirts that, at $30 each, cost about half of what department stores charge for a similar Ralph Lauren shirt.

Mr. Drexler also brought in Magdalene Gross, an Ann Taylor marketing expert, who changed Gap's image by advertising in places such as the *New York Times Magazine* and *Rolling Stone* instead of on television. She dreamed up the award-winning black-and-white "Individuals of Style" campaign showing actress Winona Ryder and other personalities in basic Gap T-shirts and jeans.

The results, at least initially, were disastrous. Net income slid 43 percent in 1984—a year the intense Mr. Drexler says he wouldn't want to relive. By 1985, however, profit was back on track: up 127 percent on a 25 percent sales rise. Mr. Drexler was rewarded handsomely. He received one million shares of restricted stock, some of which he cashed in earlier this year for $20.3 million. He still holds a 3 percent stake in Gap. Mr. Fisher's family owns 42 percent.

Except for 1987, when profit was flat, Mr. Drexler's record is impressive. Between 1984 and 1989, net income grew eightfold to $97.6 million on sales that tripled to $1.6 billion.

Still, the fast-talking Mr. Drexler isn't content. He spends most of his time at headquarters in product meetings or simply wandering around. His cavernous corner office is so barren it echoes when he talks. By contrast, the hallways and nearby offices are decorated with Lichtensteins, Calders, and other pieces from Mr. Fisher's modern-art collection.

Now, Mr. Drexler is pushing Gap's private-label jeans. They are priced a few dollars below Levi's but bring in bigger profits. And it is no coincidence that Gap's net income has ballooned as its sales of Levi's have shrunk; this year, Levi's will account for less than 5 percent of company sales, down from 23 percent in 1984.

At the stores, the emphasis is clearly on the house label. A large Gap store in San Francisco displays the line prominently on its first floor and relegates Levi's to a small area upstairs. A new store in Chicago doesn't carry Levi's at all. From time to time, Gap salespeople are paid extra for selling Gap jeans. A Levi Strauss marketing official says his company is "happy that they continue to carry Levi's products in whatever amounts."

Although Gap sometimes tests new styles—this spring, it will introduce a woman's sleeveless T-shirt that sold well at 35 stores in the South—Mr. Drexler operates largely on gut instinct. The four-year-old GapKids line was conceived at a meeting where he and other Gap executives shared frustrations about the difficulty of finding all-cotton clothes for their children. They tested the idea by displaying colorful sweatshirts in children's sizes in a Gap store in San Francisco. Despite inconclusive results, Mr. Drexler opened the first GapKids store anyway. "We loved what the clothes looked like," he says.

With 167 stores, GapKids is now the company's fastest growing unit. A new babyGap line was added in February. Even though the tiny jean jackets go for $32 and pint-sized jeans and shaker-knit sweaters for $28 each, parents, many of them baby boomers, aren't balking at the prices. "Kids can wear them and wear them," says 34-year-old Linda Kirkendall of Warsaw, Ind., who stops at GapKids whenever she makes the two-hour drive to Chicago or Indianapolis.

On a recent afternoon, Mr. Drexler dropped in on a GapKids manager who was sitting on the floor and peering at sock designs with striped patterns. Mr. Drexler took a look.

"I think you'll do business on stripes," he announced, "but not on those stripes." He has trouble explaining why, saying finally that the colors are too dull. Gap clothes, he declares, should be "clean, all-American, simple good taste."

Source: Francine Schwadel, "Simple Success," *The Wall Street Journal,* December 12, 1990, pp. A1, 6. Reprinted by permission of The *Wall Street Journal,*

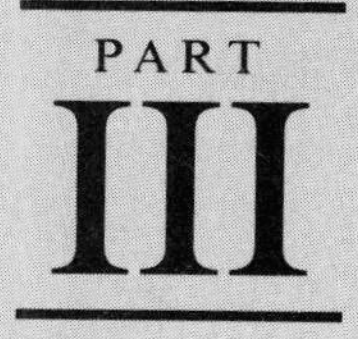

DESIGNING MARKETING STRATEGY

CHAPTER

9

Market Targeting and Positioning Strategies

Deciding which product-market(s) to serve is a crucial business strategy decision. These strategic choices are implemented by management's decisions on how to compete in each product-market of interest to the business. Strategic marketing decisions select which buyers to target in each product-market and how to position the firm's products for each target.

Market targeting and positioning are key factors in Pier 1 Imports' strong sales and profit performance during the last decade.[1] Pier 1 is North America's largest and fastest-growing specialty retailer of decorative home furnishings, gifts and related items. Sales in 1992 were $587 million, compared to $147 million in 1984. During this same period, net income grew at a 24 percent annual compounded rate to $26 million in 1992. Pier 1 Imports is positioned to take advantage of changing demographics, baby boomer lifestyles, and buyers' escalating demands for value and uniqueness. Pier 1's global supply networks, retailing systems, and operating strengths are major competitive advantages. The retailer's strong market position and brand identity in major metromarkets create difficult entry barriers for potential competitors.

In analyzing the corporate and marketing strategies of successful companies like Pier 1 Imports, one feature stands out. Each has a market target and positioning strategy that is a major factor in gaining a strong market position for the firm, although the strategies of each company are often quite different. Examples of effective targeting and positioning strategies are found in all kinds and sizes of businesses, including those marketing industrial and consumer goods and services. We begin the chapter by examining market-targeting strategies and discussing how market targets are selected. Next, we consider the choice of a positioning concept and describe the available methods for use in positioning analysis. The chapter concludes by discussing the selection and management of the positioning strategy.

MARKET TARGET STRATEGY

The market target decision identifies the people or organizations in a product-market toward which an organization directs its positioning strategy. Selecting a good market target strategy is one of management's most demanding challenges. For example, should the organization attempt to serve all people who are willing and able to buy a particular product or service, or instead selectively focus on one or more subgroups? Study of the product-market, its buyers, and the structure of competition are necessary in order to make this decision. The chapters in Part II provide important supporting analyses for the targeting decision.

Targeting Strategies

A *segmentation strategy* includes: (1) identifying and analyzing the segments in a product-market, (2) deciding which segment(s) to target, and (3) designing and implementing a marketing program positioning strategy for each targeted segment. Thus, a complete segmentation strategy involves more than just subgroup identification.

Targeting Practices. Companies typically appeal to only some of the people or organizations in a product-market, regardless of the market target strategy used. Management may identify one or more segments for its firm to serve. Alternatively, although a specific segment strategy is not formulated, the marketing program selected by the firm positions the brand (or company) in a product-market, so that it appeals to a particular subgroup within the market. The former situation is obviously preferred. Finding a segment by chance does not give management the opportunity to evaluate different segments in terms of the revenue, cost, and profit implications associated with each. At the other extreme, the task of selecting the very best market target is often impossible because of the product-market complexity, research and analysis costs, and the difficulty of estimating the market segment response to a marketing effort. When a segmentation strategy is employed, it should be by design, and the underlying analyses should lead to the selection of a good target opportunity.

Segmentation can be carried to an extreme, which results in segments too small to provide economically feasible targets. The most disaggregated form of segmentation occurs when *each* buyer is a segment. In large consumer markets this is not possible. In industrial markets, targeting of individual organizations may be effective because of their high buying potential. It is necessary to evaluate the value and cost of different degrees of segmentation in choosing an optimal targeting strategy.

Most companies use some form of market segmentation. During the last decade, buyers have become increasingly differentiated as to their needs and wants. Microsegmentation is becoming popular, aided by effective segmentation methods such as database marketing. We shall assume that the product-market is segmented on some basis. Emerging markets may require rather broad macrosegmentation, resulting in a few segments, whereas more mature markets can be divided into several microsegments. It may be necessary for a new market to advance to the growth stage before meaningful segmentation can occur. We consider this issue further in Chapter 10.

Targeting Alternatives. The targeting decision indicates whether to go after most of the segments, only a few, or a single segment. A major company may decide to serve more than a single segment. It may select a few segments or it may go after intensive coverage of the product-market by targeting all or most of the segments. A specific marketing effort (positioning strategy) is directed toward each segment that management decides to serve. Anheuser-Busch Companies, Inc., the leading U.S. brewer, with its multiple offering of beer brands, targets several major population groups within the total product-market. Some of the targets are quite large, and some people buy more than one of the Anheuser-Busch brands. The firm's market target strategy is a segmentation approach, since different brands, prices, distribution, and promotional programs are involved.

In some large product-markets organizations may select market target strategies that offer buyers a variety of products. On the surface this appears to be a segmentation strategy, with each product offering a different appeal. Yet these *variety* strategies are designed to give buyers brand alternatives. When a buyer desires a brand change, a switch can be made to another brand or product version offered by the same firm. It may be difficult to distinguish whether a firm is using a segmentation or a variety strategy, and there may be some elements of both strategies present. For example, the firm may offer variety to buyers in a particular market segment. Providing customers different flavors or varieties of food products are illustrations of variety strategies. The variety strategy is popular in food and beverage product markets.

Targeting a Single Segment. This targeting strategy helps an organization to focus its efforts on one group of buyers with similar needs. Targeting a single segment is appropriate for a small firm with limited resources. It can direct its total effort toward the buyers in the segment. Single-segment targeting may gain competitive advantage more easily than trying to simultaneously target multiple segments. The disadvantage of a single target is the dependence on one customer group. Often, market attractiveness and competition vary across market segments. Single-segment targeting should pursue a segment with promising attractiveness and an opportunity for the organization to gain sustainable competitive advantage. The organization should try to dominate the segment.

Convex Computer targets the market for mini-supercomputers. Its sales for 1989 totaled $160 million, a 50 percent increase over the previous year.[2] Profits were about double the $6 million of the previous year. Competing in this segment avoids head-on competition with supercomputer developers like Cray Research, Inc. Convex markets a less expensive version of the supercomputer that is air-cooled and does not require refrigerants or plumbing. The design is very adaptable to programs written for Cray computers. Convex provides complete systems designed to meet the specific needs of customers. Examples include modeling underground terrain for oil companies and simulation models for aircraft design. Marketing Convex computers globally helps the firm to avoid large sales fluctuations that occur in serving a single domestic market. Half of Convex Computer's sales are outside the United States. In the early 1990s Convex experienced new competition from other computer makers.

Selective Targeting. This strategy extends beyond a single segment to include a few targets. Multiple targets expand market opportunities and eliminate dependence on a single market target. Selective targeting is an attractive strategy when some of the positioning components can be used for more than a single target. For example, A. T. Cross, in writing instruments, uses a similar line of products to target upscale individual consumers and to target business incentive and employee recognition organizational buyers. Forschner Group, Inc., the U.S. distributor of the Victorinox Swiss Army Knife, has a similar targeting strategy. Selective targeting enables an organization to select targets where its competitive advantages are best.

Extensive Targeting. A major competitor may decide to appeal to all or most of the buyers in a product-market to gain a dominant market position. When pursuing this objective, the variability in buyers' needs and preferences in many product-markets requires an extensive targeting strategy. Unless specific marketing mix appeals are developed for each segment, buyers' needs will not be met and the organization's sales are likely to be unsatisfactory. Examples of extensive targeting include General Motors in automobiles, American Airlines in air travel, Anheuser-Busch in beer, and Hartmarx in men's suits.

Factors Influencing Targeting Decisions Strategy

The segmentation information discussed in Chapter 6 helps to rank the overall attractiveness of the segments under consideration as market targets. These evaluations include analysis of customers, competitor positioning, and the financial and market attractiveness of the segments under consideration. The information is used to evaluate both existing and potential market targets.

Two questions need to be answered in deciding the targeting strategy to be used: (1) Are there opportunities for multiple targeting? (2) Should the organization target a single segment, selectively target a few segments, or target all or most of the segments in the product-market? The factors that influence the choice of the targeting strategy include:

- Stage of product-market maturity
- Extent of buyer diversity
- Company position in the product-market
- Structure and intensity of competition
- Corporate resources and capabilities
- Economy of scale considerations

It is necessary to examine each factor to assess its influence on the market target. The relative importance of each factor often varies by company situation. The objective is to consider how each factor affects the market target strategy.

Stage of Product-Market Maturity. Finding and targeting segments is most critical at the maturity stage of the product-market, although segmentation should be considered at all stages. At the introductory stage there are few, if any, direct competitors, though competition may occur among alternative product types. Substitute products, such as filmless electronic camera and a conventional 35mm camera, may appeal to different segments. For example, the electronic filmless camera was targeted initially to newspaper photographers and for other business-use situations.

If there are no product-type substitutes, broad targeting may be appropriate at the introductory stage of the life cycle. This can be done by identifying a profile of promising buyers. As the product-market moves toward maturity, the opportunity (and need) for segmentation increases. The nature and intensity of competition at each stage are important in guiding market targeting decisions. Segmentation strategies are often essential at the maturity stage because buyers' needs are different.

Extent of Diversity of Buyers' Needs and Wants. When buyers' needs and wants are similar across the product-market, the opportunity for extensive segmentation is limited. A product-market made up of a relatively small number of end-users also suggests a broad targeting strategy, particularly if the value of purchases per buyer is small. The more complex the product-market structure as to competing firms, variety of product offerings, variation in user needs and wants, and other factors that contribute to complexity, the more likely it is that a useful segmentation scheme can be found. Consider, for example, the U.S. Surgical Corporation. When it entered the new product-market for surgical staplers, a broad market target strategy was a logical choice in view of the similarity of users' needs and the size and lack of complexity of the market. There was no apparent way to make major distinctions among surgeons' needs; the number of users was small in any particular location; and U.S. Surgical had no direct competitors other than the companies supplying needles and thread. The primary targeting issue was to identify surgeons that could benefit most from using the new procedure and would be willing to try a new method of closure.

Market Position. A firm's market share is an important factor in deciding what market target strategy to use. Low-market-share firms can often strengthen their position against the competition by finding a segment where they have a differential advantage. Strategy guidelines for low-market-share firms are described below:

> A low-share company must compete in the segments where its own strengths will be most highly valued and where its large competitors will be most unlikely to compete. Whether that strength is in the type and range of products offered, the method by which the product is produced, the cost and speed of distribution, or the credit and service arrangements is irrelevant. The important thing is that management spend its time identifying and exploiting unique segments rather than making broad assaults on entire industries.[3]

Pasquale Food Company illustrates how a small firm in a very competitive market can gain a marketing edge through perceptive market targeting. Management repositioned the small pizza chain into a new market segment by performing a new role in the distribution channel.[4] Pasquale sells tomato sauce, pizza crust, and sausage meat to deli sections of 5,000 supermarkets, including Kroger and Safeway. Through creative market targeting, management has avoided the intensive competition of brands in the supermarket freezer section by using a new marketing strategy. Pasquale's staff trains supermarket personnel to make and sell fresh pizza. The firm's sales increased from $11 million in 1980 to $80 million in 1989.

Structure and Intensity of Competition. When several firms are competing in an industry, selective targeting is often an appropriate market target strategy. Selectivity may be essential for small firms in fragmented, transitional, and global industries. Large firms may find extensive targeting profitable. This is illustrated by Du Pont's market target strategy for Kevlar, the fiber that is stronger, yet lighter, than steel.[5] The applications for Kevlar include uses by aircraft designers, plant engineers, and commercial fishermen. These customers have different use criteria that they are trying to satisfy. While the product is the same, aircraft designers are interested in Kevlar's high strength and low weight, plant engineers need the fiber strength and durability, and commercial fishermen require the overall performance offered by the material. Du Pont designed its promotional efforts to appeal to each target group's preferences concerning Kevlar's characteristics.

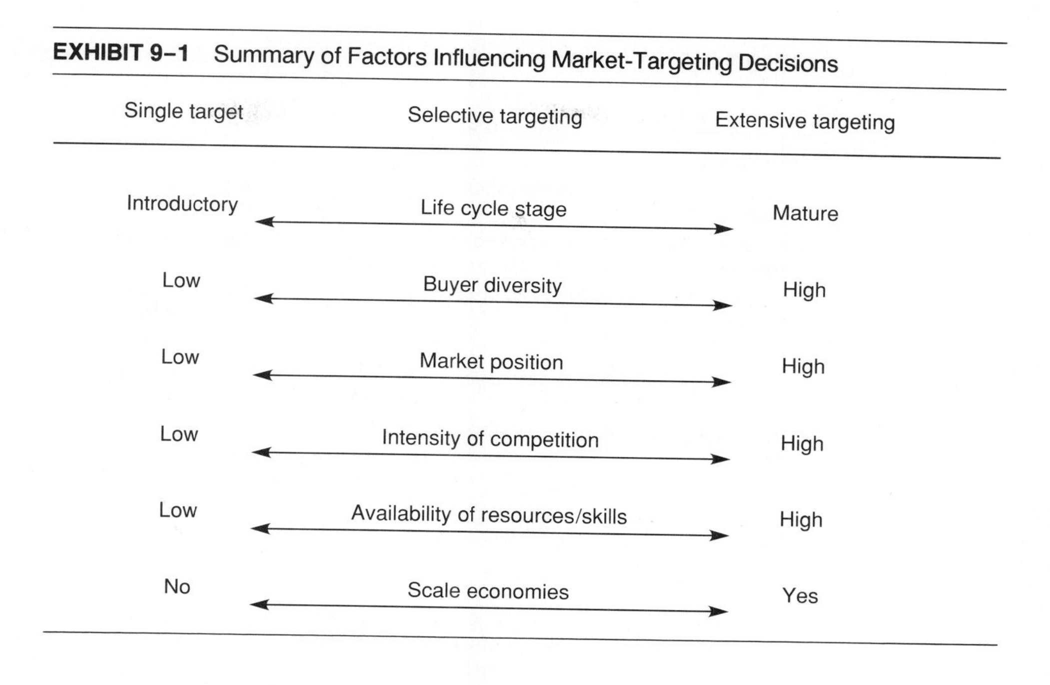

EXHIBIT 9–1 Summary of Factors Influencing Market-Targeting Decisions

Other Targeting Issues. Having adequate resources may create an opportunity for an organization to consider a range of market target alternatives. In contrast, limited resources may require a company to adopt a single segment targeting strategy. Market analysis capabilities may also offer advantages to particular firms, particularly when segmentation is complex. Having both resources and market analysis capabilities offers important flexibilities in choosing market targets.

Finally, production and marketing scale economies may influence management in choosing a strategy. For example, the production process may require a large-scale output to achieve necessary cost advantages. The same may be true for marketing and distribution programs. If so, an extensive market coverage strategy may be necessary to gain the sales volume necessary to support large-volume production and distribution.

Selecting a Targeting Strategy

The various factors that influence market-targeting decisions are summarized in Exhibit 9–1. It is useful to consider market characteristics, the competitive situation, and the organization's skills and resources when selecting a market-targeting strategy. Targeting choices involve deciding how extensive targeting will be and recognizing the close ties between targeting and positioning.

EXHIBIT 9–2 Advantages and Limitations of Selective and Extensive Market Targeting

	Selective Targeting	*Extensive Targeting*
Advantages	• Requires much less resources than extensive targeting	• Opportunity to develop strong market position
	• Builds competitive advantage through specialization	• Major opportunity for expanding sales
	• Opportunity to target the most promising buyers	• Market knowledge extensive due to breadth of market scope
Limitations	• Potentially vulnerable to competition from large firms	• Major resource and marketing expertise requirements
	• Affected by major change in segment market demand	• Complexity in selecting favorable segment portfolio strategies
		• Possibility of diluting competitive advantage due to scope of market involvement

Selective versus Extensive Targeting. This decision is influenced by management's assessment of the attractiveness of the opportunity, evaluation of existing and potential competitive advantage, and consideration of management's objectives. Selective targeting is a good strategy for small firms with segment-specific competitive advantages in mature product-markets dominated by large firms. For example, Autodesk, Inc., the software firm specializing in computer-aided design (CAD) programs, uses a very selective targeting strategy. The company commands a 72 percent share in its market segment (see Case 1–1). In contrast, extensive targeting is a feasible strategy for market domination by large companies with substantial resources. The major advantages and limitations of the targeting approaches are shown in Exhibit 9–2.

Targeting and Positioning Relationships. Not surprisingly, these strategies are very interrelated. Selecting one or more market targets is based, in part, on the feasibility of designing and implementing an effective positioning strategy to meet the target's needs. Each positioning strategy used for a target may be unique from the strategy used for other targets, or instead the strategies used for different targets may share certain features. For example, the same product is marketed to all segments in the case of Du Pont's Kevlar fiber. The same airline services are used to appeal to business, special travel groups, and pleasure travelers, although different advertising and sales efforts are aimed at each segment and fare prices may vary across segments.

Pier 1's marketing strategy shows the close relationship between market targeting and positioning. Pier 1 Import's primary target customers are college-educated women in the 25–44 age group with incomes over $35,000 a year. As many as four out of five of these women are working, although not all full time. Importantly, these baby boomers' tastes, preferences, and priorities are changing as they grow older. "The signs are clear: in the 1990s America's largest consumer group will place less emphasis on money and more on meaning."[6] Time is important to these experienced shoppers, and they want favorable experiences in their relentless pursuit of quality and value.

Pier 1 has defined the business and positioned itself to respond to the requirements of the large and attractive customer group.[7] The specialty retailer offers buyers an opportunity to satisfy their demands for individualism and uniqueness. The continuing flow of exciting new merchandise into the stores from China, Taiwan, and India meets the diversity of buyers' wants. Pier 1's experienced buyers enable the firm to offer high value at competitive prices.

SELECTING THE POSITIONING CONCEPT

Johnson & Johnson's strategy for positioning its successful Tylenol brand is described in the accompanying Strategy Feature. Positioning strategy is examined in the rest of the chapter. First, we overview the positioning process, beginning with the selection of the positioning concept. Next, we discuss the choice of the positioning strategy and how the positioning components are combined. Finally, we look at how the position of a brand is determined and how positioning effectiveness is assessed.

The Positioning Process

The major steps in the positioning process are shown and described in Exhibit 9–3. The market target establishes the focus of the positioning strategy. The *positioning concept* management selects is the product (brand) meaning derived from the needs of the buyers in the market target.[8] For example, the positioning concept used by Pier 1 Imports is to offer buyers an unusual and unique shopping experience. Selecting the positioning concept requires an understanding of buyers' needs, wants and perceptions of competing brands. The *positioning strategy* is the combination of marketing actions used to portray the positioning concept to targeted buyers. This strategy includes the physical product, supporting services, distribution channels, price, and promotion activities. The *position* of the brand is determined by the buyer's perceptions of the firm's positioning strategy (and the perceptions of competitors' strategies). Positioning may focus on an entire company, a mix of products, a specific line of products, or a particular brand, although positioning is often centered at the brand level. *Positioning effectiveness* considers how well management's positioning objectives are achieved in the market target.

STRATEGY FEATURE Positioning Tylenol with Doctors and Consumers

Tylenol's success in gaining and keeping its dominant brand position in the pain relief market is due to a brilliantly executed marketing strategy that simultaneously targets doctors, hospitals, and consumers with effective, complementary positioning programs. Tylenol's sustained competitive advantage is particularly impressive in view of the devastating product tampering problems in the early 1980s and strong competitive challenges by several competitors going after Tylenol's $600 million in sales.

- A core element in Tylenol's strategy is its strong association with doctors and hospitals.
- Using a micromarketing strategy for the Tylenol line, Johnson & Johnson targets its professional and consumer segments using different product mixes, separate sales organizations, and specific communications programs.
- Tylenol with codeine is a prescription product that is available from physicians, enabling the brand to sustain a strong loyalty with physicians.
- Consumer advertising positions the Tylenol brand featuring its doctor and hospital heritage.
- All of the Tylenol advertising is focused on Extra-Strength Tylenol which supports the regular-strength product and creates name awareness for other advertised line extensions in related categories.
- Competitors describe Tylenol's powerful brand image as being "in a class by itself."

Source: D. John Loden, *Megabrands* (Homewood, Ill.: Business One Irwin, 1992), pp. 141–42.

Selecting the Positioning Concept

The positioning concept portrays the perception or association that management wants target market buyers to have concerning the firm or its products. Aaker and Shansby comment on the importance of this decision:

> The position can be central to customers' perception and choice decisions. Further, since all elements of the marketing program can potentially affect the position, it is usually necessary to use a positioning strategy as a focus for the development of the marketing program. A clear positioning strategy can ensure that the elements of the marketing program are consistent and supportive.[9]

Choosing the positioning concept is an important first step in positioning a brand. The positioning concept is "the general meaning that is understood by customers in terms of its relevance to their needs and preferences."[10] The positioning strategy is the combination of marketing mix actions that implement the product (brand) concept into a specific position with targeted buyers.

Positioning Concepts.[11] The positioning concept should be linked to buyers' needs and wants. The concept may be *functional, symbolic,* or *experiential.* The *functional* concept applies to products that solve consumption-related problems for externally generated consumption needs. Examples of brands using this basis of positioning include Crest toothpaste (cavity pre-

EXHIBIT 9–3 The Positioning Process

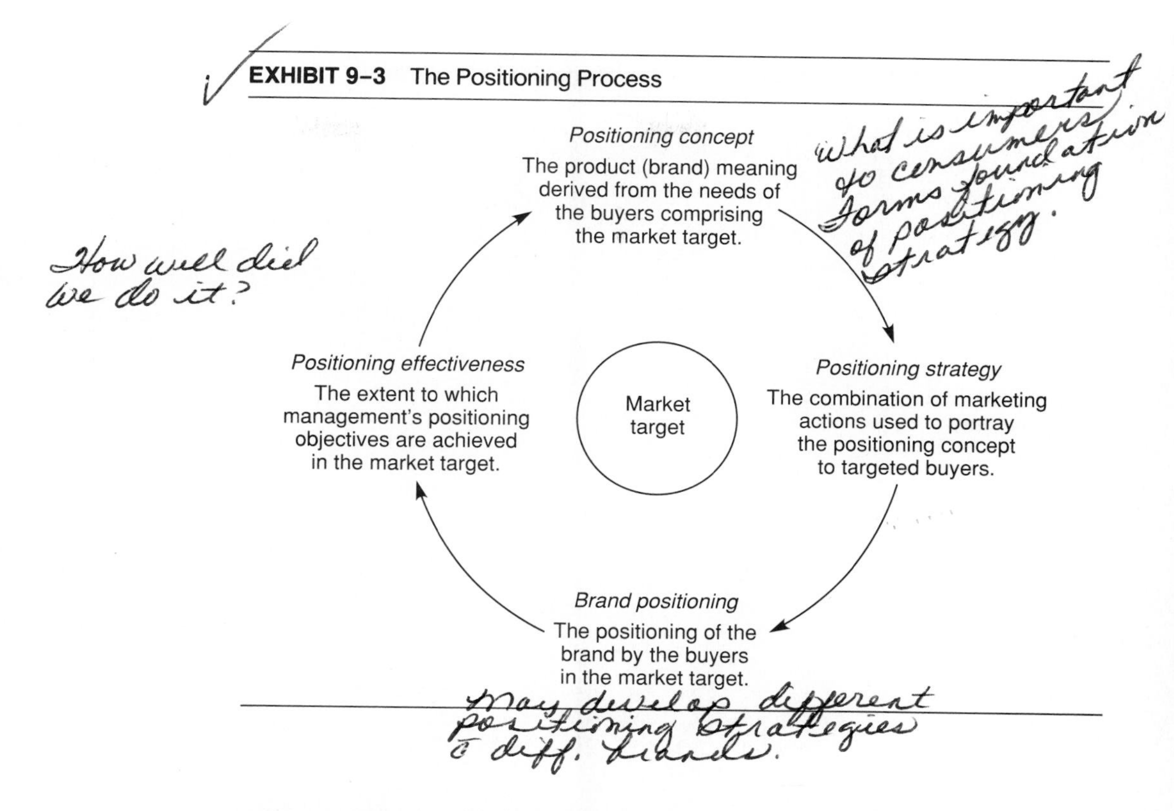
Positioning concept
The product (brand) meaning derived from the needs of the buyers comprising the market target.
Positioning strategy
The combination of marketing actions used to portray the positioning concept to targeted buyers.
Brand positioning
The positioning of the brand by the buyers in the market target.
Positioning effectiveness
The extent to which management's positioning objectives are achieved in the market target.
Market target

vention), Clorox liquid cleaner (effective cleaning), and a checking account with ABC Bank (convenient services). The *symbolic* concept relates to the buyer's internally generated needs for self-enhancement, role position, group membership, or ego-identification. Examples of symbolic positioning are Charlie perfume (life-style) and the Signature line of Cross pens (prestige), as illustrated by the accompanying advertisement. Finally, the *experiential* concept is used to position products that provide sensory pleasure, variety, and/or cognitive stimulation. Pier 1 Imports is positioned using an experiential concept that emphasizes the shopping experience.

A company brand is often the focus of positioning strategy. Three aspects of brand concept selection are important.[12] First, the concept applies to a specific brand rather than all of the competing brands that compose a product classification such as toothpaste. Second, the concept is used to guide positioning decisions over the life of the brand, recognizing that the brand's specific position may change. Third, if two or more concepts, for example, functional and experiential are used to guide positioning strategy, the multiple concepts are likely to confuse buyers and perhaps weaken the effectiveness of positioning actions. Of course, the specific concept selected may not fall clearly into one of the three classifications.

Symbolic Positioning of the Signature Line of Pens

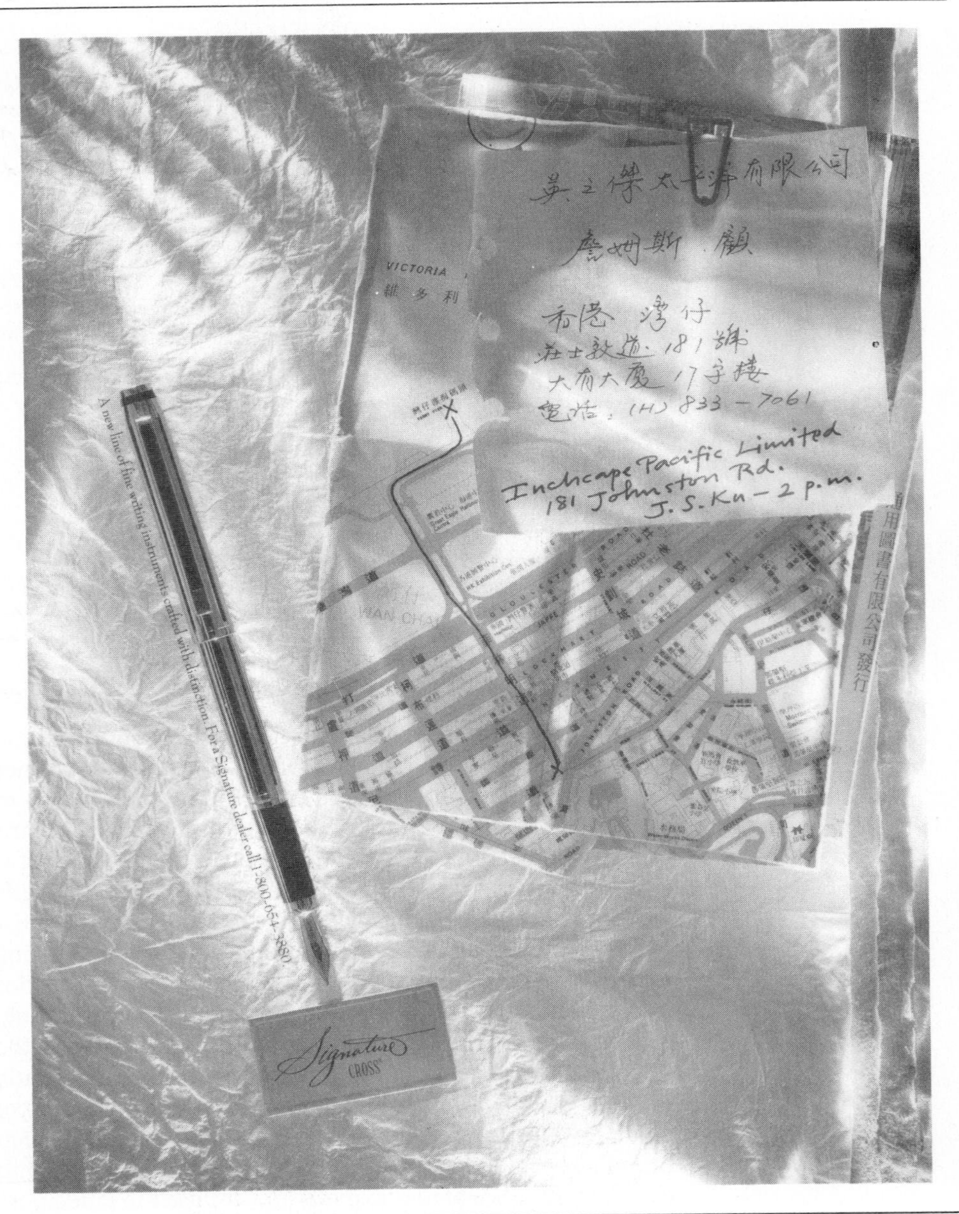

Courtesy of Hill, Holiday, Connors, Cosmopulos, Inc.

Positioning Examples. Often the competition is the frame of reference for the positioning concept. These are examples of positioning approaches:[13]

Attribute Use of one or more attributes, product features, or customer benefits associated with the firm's product brand. Singapore Airlines features its impressive in-flight services in advertising.

Price/Quality Various positions on the price/quality scale may be selected depending upon management's positioning objective. Examples range from Neiman-Marcus at the high end to Toys "R" Us at the low end.

Use or Application This strategy positions the brand according to how the product is used or applied. The positioning of the Hewlett Packard HP 95 LX palmtop PC stresses its functions and small size. Application positioning is used for various industrial products.

Product User This positioning approach focuses on the person using the product. Revlon's Charlie cosmetic line was introduced using a life-style positioning strategy.

Product Class This positioning approach involves association with a product class, such as freeze-dried coffee compared to regular and instant coffee.

Competitor This strategy directly positions a brand against its competition. Datril used this approach when entering the nonaspirin market against Tylenol.

Each positioning concept offers certain features and possible limitations. For example, direct positioning against a competitor is very visible but may encourage the competitor to take aggressive actions. Both concept evaluation and testing may be necessary to fully assess a proposed positioning concept.

Selecting the Positioning Concept. The positioning concept indicates how management wants to position the brand relative to the competition. It may be necessary to study the positioning of competing brands using attributes that are important to existing and potential buyers of the competing brands. The objective is to find the preferred (or ideal) position for the buyers in each market segment of interest and to compare this preferred position with the actual positions of competing brands.

Determining the existing position of a brand and deciding whether it satisfies management's positioning objectives are considered later in the chapter. First, we discuss the choice of the positioning strategy, then examine several resource allocation guidelines for combining the positioning components.

CHOOSING THE POSITIONING STRATEGY

The positioning strategy places the marketing mix components into a coordinated set of actions designed to achieve the positioning objective(s). This strategy: (1) selects the total amount of resources to be used for the marketing program; (2) indicates how to allocate these resources among the marketing mix components of product, distribution, price, advertising, personal selling, and sales promotion; and (3) allocates the resources within each program component. Two generalizations about these decisions can be made.

- These decisions are interrelated, with the first constraining the second and the second constraining the third.
- Many alternatives are available depending on the amount, deployment, and use of resources.

The positioning strategy is determined by a combination of management judgment and experience, trial and error, some experimentation (e.g., test marketing), and sometimes field research. First, we look at the factors that affect positioning strategy. Next, several considerations about targeting and supporting activities are discussed. Deciding how much to spend for the positioning strategy and allocating the resources to the marketing program components are considered in the next section.

Factors Affecting the Positioning Strategy

The choice of a positioning strategy is influenced by the factors shown in Exhibit 9–4. The starting point is the target market. Market opportunity analysis supplies information about the characteristics and the people and organizations in the target market. The objective is to estimate the responsiveness of the target market to alternative positioning strategies while taking into account the competition, management's performance priorities (e.g., sales, market share, profit contribution), and available resources. These same factors are considered in making the market target decision. The issue is finding the best fit between the market target, the positioning concept, and the positioning strategy.

Target Market. The positioning concept management selects is guided by customer needs. The characteristics and needs of the target market indicate the nature of the marketing program necessary to gain a favorable response from the target market. For example, if the people in the target market want a high-quality product, then meeting their expectations requires a marketing mix that they perceive to be high quality. The market target also helps to identify existing key competitors. Similarly, the choice of the market target will establish the market potential and market share that is feasible. Finally, the selection of the target market must take into account the firm's resource capabilities for serving the target market.

EXHIBIT 9–4 Factors Influencing the Choice of a Marketing Program Positioning Strategy

Product Life Cycle Stage. The stage of the product-market life cycle often affects the role and importance of the different marketing program components. In moving through the introductory, growth, maturity, and decline stages, the roles of the mix elements are adjusted to respond to changing conditions. Price, for example, typically declines as the product-market matures. Advertising is initially used to create awareness of a new product and to interest potential buyers in the offering. At later stages, advertising may stress the advantages of one brand over competing brands.

Management's Priorities. The performance criteria set for the market target also influence the positioning strategy selected. Management's priorities may be placed on expanding market share, holding position and generating profits, reducing the firm's commitment, or actually leaving the product-market. Thus, positioning strategy is tied to the strategic business unit (SBU) strategy. Expanding share versus holding a position call for different marketing programs. Moreover, if marketing management is designing a major growth program while the SBU management favors a stabilizing position, conflict is inevitable. What top management wants to do in an SBU must match the selected positioning strategy. (See Chapter 2 for discussion of develop, stabilize, turnaround, and harvest strategies.)

Resource and Competitive Influences. Available resources constrain management's actions concerning program design. For example, small companies are limited in how much they can spend on advertising and the media that can be used. Competitors' existing programs (and future actions) must also be evaluated in strategy design and program changes. This requires continually monitoring competitors' product, distribution, price, and promotion strategies.

Positioning Application

Consider the positioning strategy used by Maker's Mark Distillery, the producer of a premium-priced bourbon with the cap sealed with a distinguishing hand-dipped red wax.[14] The bourbon was first marketed in 1958. Management has built an impressive growth and performance record. Meeting the needs of bourbon drinkers who desire a superior product with a mellow flavor is the crux of the firm's business purpose. The distilling formula substitutes more expensive wheat for rye to give a smoother taste. The positioning strategy consists of a high-quality brand with a pleasant taste placed in a distinctive package and given a prestigious brand name. The product is marketed through distributors to retailers and is backed by a highly effective sales effort managed by the president and two other top executives. The firm has no field sales force. Revenues were around $15 million in 1991 with advertising expenditures at $300,000.[15] Advertising is targeted at billboards and magazines such as *The New Yorker, Texas Monthly,* and *L.A. Style.* The brand commands a premium price that is even higher than Jack Daniel's. The brand's steady increases in annual sales for several years are even more significant, given the steady decline in bourbon sales during the last 20 years. In 1990, an industry total of 16 million cases was shipped, compared to 36 million in 1970. Some industry observers believe that Maker's Mark sales can be expanded even faster than the current growth rate. Instead, management wants to grow at a slow but steady rate. This shows the influence of management's performance criteria on the marketing program design.

Considerations about Targeting/Supporting Activities

A positioning strategy is usually centered on a single brand (microwave ovens) or a line of related products (kitchen appliances) for a specific market target. Whether the strategy is brand specific or broader in scope depends on such factors as the size of the product-market, characteristics of the product or service, the number of products involved, and product interrelationships in the consumers' use situation. For example, the marketing programs of Procter & Gamble, Johnson & Johnson, and Chesebrough-Pond position their different brands, whereas firms such as General Electric Company, Caterpillar, and IBM use the corporate name to position the product-line or product-portfolio. When serving several market targets, an umbrella strategy covering multiple targets may be used for some of the marketing program components. For example, advertising can be designed to appeal to more than a single target, or the same product targeted to different buyers through different distribution channels.

COMBINING THE POSITIONING COMPONENTS

Several decisions are made in combining the positioning components into the positioning strategy. As discussed earlier, it is necessary to determine the amount of resources to be used in the positioning strategy, then allocate the resources to program components. We describe these decisions and discuss the relationship between marketing effort and target market response.

Marketing Program Decisions

A look at Pier 1 Imports' positioning strategy shows how the retailer combines marketing mix components into a coordinated strategy.[16] Its positioning strategy includes unique merchandise, strategically located stores, outstanding customer service, and modern retail systems.

Product Strategy. Pier 1's array of merchandise includes decorative home furnishings, gifts, and related items. The assortment is unique and ever changing, imported from 44 countries around the world. The objective is to create a casual, sensory store environment. The merchandise offers customers an opportunity to satisfy their desire for diversity.

Distribution Strategy. The retailer markets through a vertical marketing system (Chapter 13), integrating its global supply network with its strategically located retail stores. Management has an objective of increasing its nearly 600 stores in 42 states to 1,000 before the year 2000. Pier 1 avoids mall locations, instead using free-standing and strip retail sites that are more quickly and conveniently accessed by customers. Store layouts and exteriors are attractively designed. Information systems are installed throughout company operations to provide real-time information to manage the business. Seven regional distribution centers supply merchandise to the retail store networks.

Pricing Strategy. Pier 1's global supply network and purchasing experience result in merchandise costs that enable the company to sell quality merchandise at attractive prices. Information systems target slow-moving merchandise for possible pricing actions. The pricing strategy emphasizes the value and uniqueness of the merchandise.

Promotion Strategy. The retailer uses an effective combination of advertising, sales promotion, personal selling, and public relations to communicate with customers. It's aggressive advertising strategy positions Pier 1 as

"The Place to Discover." Attractive color ads encourage people to visit the stores. Experienced store managers and sales associates share the corporate culture of a customer-driven company. The customer service policy states, "The customer is always right."

Competitive Advantage. Pier 1 Imports' advantage is a combination of value and uniqueness of merchandise that is competitively priced. The slowdown in household relocation during the 1990s will encourage spending on accent pieces and decorative home furnishings. Furniture sales declined during the early 1990s because of the recession. These pressures forced many small retailers to close, strengthening Pier 1's market position. Management's continual investment in market research studies keeps the retailer's strategy focused on customers' needs and wants.

Pier 1's products are positioned to appeal to the women in its target market. While there are many other specific activities involved in the positioning strategy for Pier 1 Imports, the illustration provides important insights into strategy development.

An overview of the various decisions that are made in developing a positioning strategy is shown in Exhibit 9–5. Several of these actions are described in the Pier 1 illustration. Each positioning strategy component is examined in detail in Part IV. The present objective is to show how they fit into the positioning strategy. The positioning concept is the core focus for designing the integrated strategy. The positioning strategy indicates how (and why) the product mix, line, or brand is to be positioned in the target market. This strategy indicates:

- The overview of product strategy including how the product(s) will be positioned against the competition in the product-market.
- The distribution strategy and approach to be used.
- The pricing strategy including the role and positioning of price relative to competition.
- The advertising and sales promotion strategy and the objectives these promotion components are expected to achieve.
- The sales force strategy indicating how personal selling is used in the positioning strategy.

Positioning Strategy Design. First, it is necessary to establish the major strategy guidelines for every marketing program component. For example, what type of channel of distribution should be developed? Recall Pier 1's use of a vertical marketing system for the distribution of its products. Second, management strategies for each of the program components need to be implemented. For example, distribution management in Pier 1's case involves informing store managers about new merchandise, providing logistical support to the stores, and making necessary changes in the strategy over time.

EXHIBIT 9–5 Positioning Strategy Overview

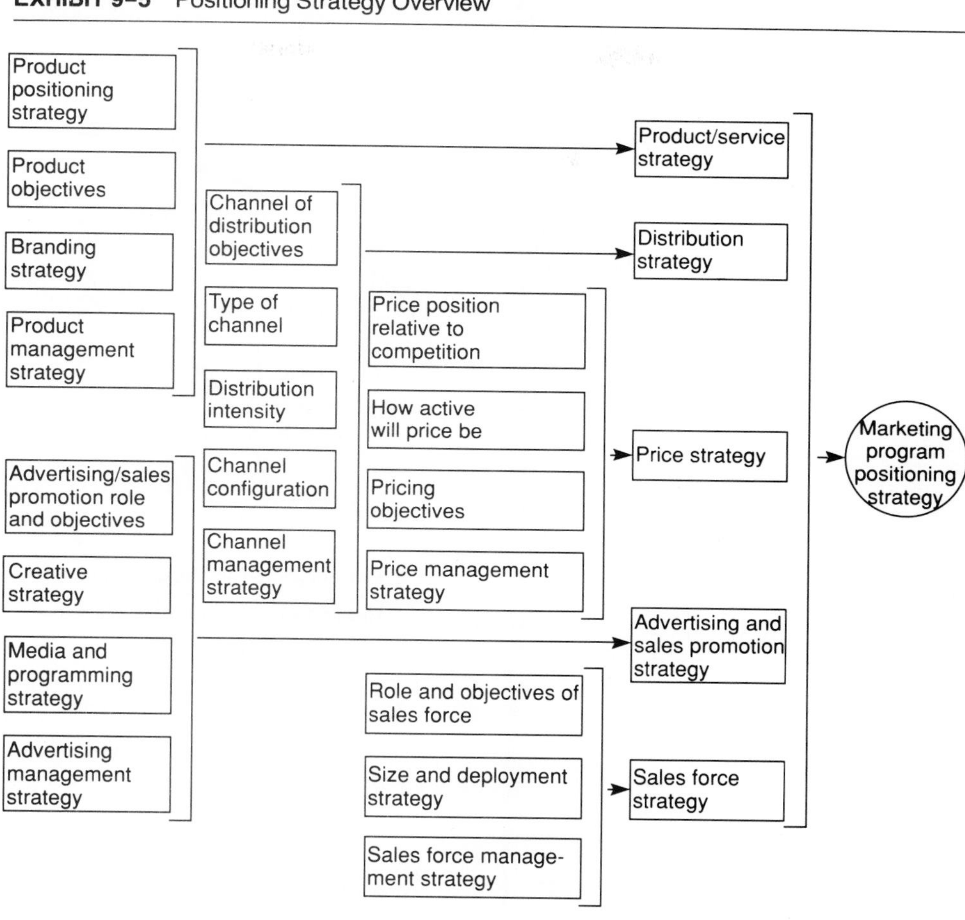

Functional Relationships. Responsibilities for the positioning strategy components (product, distribution, price, and promotion) are often assigned to various functional units within a company or business unit. These functions are typically not combined into an integrated marketing strategy budget. This separation of responsibilities (and budgets) highlights the importance of coordinating the positioning strategy. An executive should be responsible for managing all aspects of the positioning strategy. Some companies use strategy teams for this purpose. For example, Rubbermaid uses teams of people from different business functions to plan new products (see Strategy Feature in Chapter 11).

EXHIBIT 9–6 Effort-to-Response Example

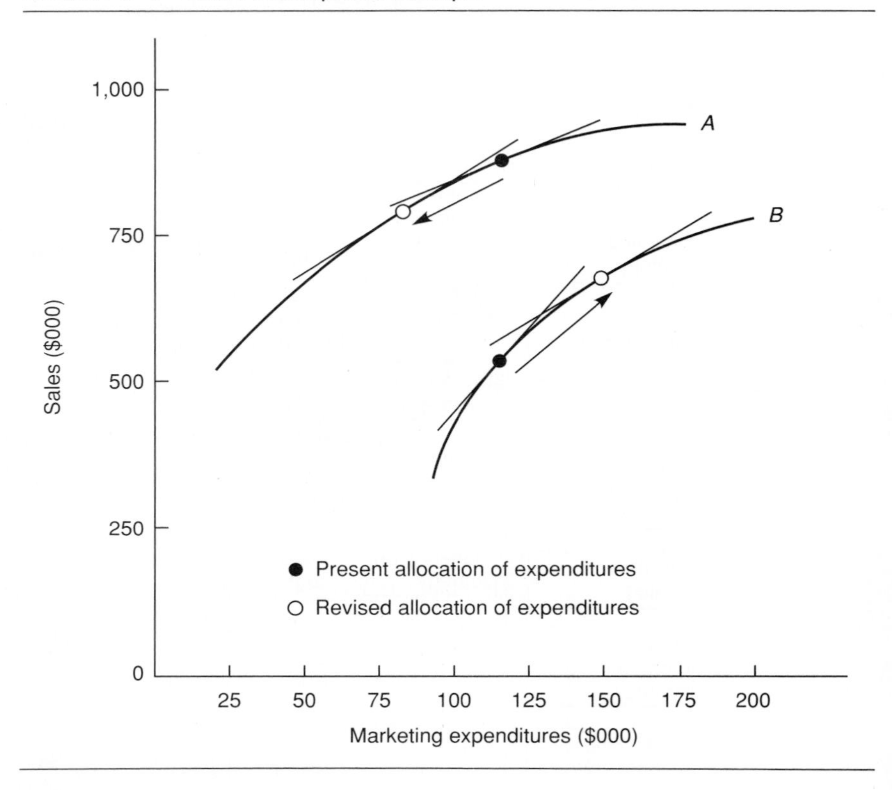

Effort-to-Response Relationship

A key factor in selecting the positioning strategy is estimating how the market target will respond to a proposed marketing program. Response is often measured by sales. Other response measures include brand awareness, market share, and size of purchase. Effort is measured by the expenditures for the program. The objective is to evaluate the relationship between marketing effort and sales response.

An example shows how effort and response are analyzed. The sales-to-marketing-effort relationships for two marketing program strategies are shown in Exhibit 9–6. The solid circles are the present allocations of expenditures in markets A and B. Assume that it is profitable for the company to compete in markets A and B and that the margins over direct costs are the same in both markets. By shifting expenditures in A and B as shown, sales are increased at no total increase in marketing expenditures. This type of analysis of revenues and costs is central to making marketing resource allocation decisions. While Exhibit 9–6 is oversimplified, it demonstrates the nature of the marketing programming task.

The next section discusses and illustrates several methods of analyzing the relationship between effort and response.

DETERMINING POSITION

Positioning analysis is concerned with identifying the competitors serving a target market; determining how they are perceived, evaluated, and positioned by buyers; and analyzing customer needs and preferences.[17] "Positioning helps customers know the real differences among competing products so that they can choose the one that is of most value to them."[18] Positioning shows how a company or brand is distinguished from its competitors. Buyers position companies or brands using specific attributes or dimensions about products or corporate values. The objective is to gain a preferred position for the company or brand. Finding out the actual position a company or brand occupies helps decide what future actions should be regarding positioning strategy.

Several methods are available to analyze marketing program positioning strategy and positioning results, including customer and competitor research, market testing of proposed strategies, and the use of analytical models.

Customer and Competitor Research

Research studies generate useful buyer and competitor information for designing positioning strategies. Several of the research methods discussed in Part II help to determine the position of a brand. For example, research about the product and brand positioning can be helpful in formulating a marketing program strategy by mapping customer preferences for various competing brands.

Methods are available for considering the effects of several marketing program components on sales response. For example, a screening experiment can be used to identify important causal factors affecting market response.[19] A medical equipment firm identified seven factors as possible influences on the sales of a new product for use by surgeons in the operating room. The factors are: (1) special training of salespeople; (2) monetary incentives for salespeople; (3) vacation incentives for salespeople; (4) mailing product information to physicians; (5) mailing product information to operating room supervisors; (6) letter from the president of the firm about the product; and (7) a customized surgical product (in contrast to a standardized product). The effect of each factor was measured by using field tests to vary the amount of the factor exposed to targeted buyers. For example, the high level of factor 1 consisted of training whereas the low-level treatment was no training. A fractional factorial experimental design was used to evaluate the effects of the seven factors. Different factor combinations were tested. One factor combination included no training, a monetary incentive, no vacation incentive, no mailing to physicians, mailing to operating room supervisors, a letter from the president, and a standard product. A sample of 64 salespeople was randomly selected, and groups of 8 were randomly assigned to each of the eight treatment combinations. The eight treatment combinations were designed to enable testing the effects of each factor plus the influence of various combinations of factors.

One useful finding was that several of the factors had no impact on sales. A key finding from the screening experiment was that the customized product did not sell as well as the standard product. This result saved the firm an estimated $1 million in expenses by eliminating the need to offer customized product designs. Before conducting the experiment, management had planned to customize the product for surgeons' use. The other results of the screening experiment were useful in designing the marketing strategy for the product. Interestingly, of all of the factors, the vacation incentive had the largest effect on sales, surpassing even the money incentive.

Test Marketing

Market testing supplies information about the commercial feasibility of a promising new product or about new positioning strategies for new products. The decision to test the market depends on the following factors:

1. How much risk and investment are associated with the venture? When both are low, launching the product without a test market may be appropriate.
2. How much of a difference is there between the manufacturing investment required for the test versus the national launch? A large difference would favor a test market.
3. What are the likelihood and speed of the competitive response to the product offering?
4. How do the marketing costs and risks vary with the scale of the launch?[20]

While usually costing less than a national introduction, test marketing is nevertheless expensive. The competitive risks of revealing one's plans must also be weighed against the value of test market information. The major returns from testing are risk reduction through better demand forecasts and the opportunity to fine-tune a marketing program strategy. Market tests of packaged consumer products are expensive, often costing $2 million or more depending on the scope of the tests and locations involved.[21] Experienced testers are admittedly uneasy about using market test results from only one city to project the national performance of a new product.

Test marketing provides market (sales) forecasts and information on the effectiveness of alternative marketing program strategies. Both are highly dependent on how well results from one or a few test markets provide accurate projections of the national market or regional market. Model-based analysis is an approach designed to help overcome problems associated with idiosyncrasies of test cities by using a detailed behavioral model of the consumer to analyze test-market measurements and develop forecasts that can be made for the effect of modified marketing strategies.[22] Test marketing of new products is discussed in Chapter 11.

Positioning Models

Obtaining useful information about customers and prospects, analyzing it, and then developing strategies based on information and management judgment is the crux of positioning analysis. Some promising results have been achieved by incorporating research data into formal models of decision analysis. For example, ADVISOR is a comprehensive marketing mix budgeting model developed for industrial products.[23] It sets a marketing budget, then splits it into budgets for personal and impersonal (e.g., advertising) communications. ADVISOR is a multiple regression-type model that has several predictor variables, including the number of users, customer concentration, fraction of sales made to order, attitude differences, proportion of direct sales, life-cycle stage, product plans, and product complexity. The model is similar in concept and approach to the PIMS model described in Chapter 2, although ADVISOR concentrates on the marketing budget and its components rather than offering complete strategies for business units or products. Comprehensive discussion of marketing modeling is available from other sources.[24]

POSITIONING EFFECTIVENESS

How do you know if you have a good positioning strategy? The important issue is deciding if it yields the expected results concerning sales, market share, profit contribution, growth rates, customer satisfaction, and other competitive advantage outcomes. Gauging the effectiveness of a marketing program strategy using specific criteria such as market share and profitability is more straightforward than evaluating competitive advantage. Yet developing a marketing program strategy that cannot be easily copied is an essential consideration. For example, a competitor would need considerable resources—not to mention a long time period—to duplicate the powerful SABRE information system developed by American Airlines. In contrast, an airline can respond immediately with a price cut to meet the price offered by a competitor. A strong information systems advantage is more difficult for a competitor to copy than a price cut.

Companies do not alter their positioning strategies frequently, although adjustments are made at different stages of product-market maturity and in response to environmental, market, and competitive forces. Even though frequent changes are not made, a successful positioning strategy should be evaluated on a regular basis to identify shifting buyer preferences and changes in competitor strategies.

First, we look at the strategic brand concept as a guide to making positioning effective. Next, we emphasize how targeting and positioning work together to obtain strategy effectiveness. Finally, it is necessary to evaluate if the strategy is feasible.

Strategic Brand Concept

The "strategic brand" concept is a useful framework for brand concept management. It portrays the life of the brand in four stages: brand concept selection, introduction, elaboration, and fortification.[25] The positioning concept selected for the target market guides initial strategy selected and implementation. The introduction stage is intended to establish the brand image/position with the market target during market entry. This position should be capable of being extended during subsequent stages. During the introduction stage, the marketing mix must communicate the desired brand image and perform essential operating activities (e.g., making the brand available in retail outlets).

Positioning strategies during the elaboration stage are concerned with "enhancing the value of the brand's image so that its perceived superiority in relation to competitors can be established or maintained."[26] Without this enhancement buyers may find it difficult to discriminate among brands. Also, experience may affect their needs and preferences. The objective is to *elaborate* the positioning concept rather than to reposition the brand. Expanding the uses of the brand (e.g., Crest with tartar protection) is an illustrative elaboration action.

The goal of fortification "is to link an elaborated brand image to the image of other products produced by the firm in different product classes" (e.g., linking Swiss Army watches with knives).[27] Note that elaboration continues during the life of the brand. Fortification is an option that can be used concurrently.

The positioning strategy that is adopted depends on the positioning concept selected by management and the stage in the life of the brand. For example, during introduction, positioning according to the functional concept emphasizes problem solving, the symbolic concept emphasizes reference group/ego enhancement associations, and the experiential concept focuses on cognitive/sensory stimulation of targeted buyers.[28] Positioning strategies are adjusted to respond to the objectives of the other brand concept stages.

Positioning and Segmentation Strategies

Recognizing the interrelationship between market target and positioning strategies is important:

> Positioning usually means that an overt decision is being made to concentrate only on certain segments. Such an approach requires commitment and discipline because it's not easy to turn your back on potential buyers. Yet the effect of generating a distinct, meaningful position is to focus on the target segments and not be constrained by the reaction of other segments.[29]

Positioning becomes particularly challenging when management decides to target several segments. The objective is to develop an effective positioning strategy for each segment. The use of a different brand for each targeted segment is one way of focusing a positioning strategy.

Determining Positioning Feasibility

"It is tempting but naive—and usually fatal—to decide on a positioning strategy that exploits a market need or opportunity but assumes that your product is something it is not."[30] In selecting a positioning strategy, management must realistically evaluate the feasibility of the strategy, taking into consideration the product's strengths, the positions of competing brands, and the probable reactions of buyers to the strategy.

Cherry Coke, which was introduced nationally in 1985, surprised many industry observers with its strong sales performance at the same time that New Coke and Classic Coke were in the limelight.[31] Network TV and radio spots positioned Cherry Coke as an "out and outrageous" alternative to the other Cokes. The new brand was launched with a $50 million budget, which generated a surprisingly strong and fast payback. Positioning was in terms of the flavor of the soft drink, thus using an experiential positioning concept.

SUMMARY

Choosing the right market target strategy can affect the performance of the enterprise. This decision is critical to properly positioning a firm in the marketplace. Sometimes a single target cannot be selected for an entire SBU when it contains different product-markets. Moreover, locating the firm's best competitive advantage may first require a detailed analysis of several segments. Market target decisions integrate strategic planning and marketing strategy. Targeting decisions establish key guidelines to design the marketing program.

The targeting options include a single segment, selective segments, or extensive segments. Choosing among these options involves consideration of the product life cycle stage, buyer diversity, the market position of the firm, intensity of competition, available resources and skills, and economies of scale.

Developing the positioning strategy requires the blending of the product, distribution, price, and promotion strategies to focus them on a market target. The result is an integrated strategy designed to achieve management's positioning objectives while gaining the largest possible competitive advantage. Shaping this bundle of strategies is a major challenge to marketing decision makers. Since the strategies span different functional areas and responsibilities, they require close coordination.

Building on an understanding of the market target and the objectives to be accomplished by the marketing program, positioning strategy matches the firm's capabilities to buyers' needs. These programming decisions include selecting the amount of expenditure, deciding how to allocate these resources to the marketing program components, and making the most effective use of resources within each mix component. The factors that affect program strategy include the market target, the competition, resource constraints, management's priorities, and the product life cycle. The positioning statement describes the desired positioning relative to the competition.

Central to the positioning decision is examining the relationship between the marketing effort and the market response. Positioning analysis is useful in estimating the market response as well as in evaluating competition and buyer preferences. The analysis methods include customer/competitor research, market testing, and positioning models. Analysis information, combined with management judgment and experience, is the basis for selecting a positioning strategy. The close tie between positioning and segmentation strategies requires the coordination of these strategies.

Finally, management is concerned with moving the positioning strategy for the product through the stages of the product-market life cycle. The strategic brand concept is a useful framework for concept design, elaboration, and fortification. It emphasizes the importance of selecting a good positioning concept and managing it properly during the life of the brand.

QUESTIONS FOR REVIEW AND DISCUSSION

1. Discuss why it may be necessary for an organization to alter its targeting strategy over time.
2. What factors are important in selecting a market target?
3. Discuss the considerations that should be evaluated in targeting a macromarket segment whose buyers' needs vary versus targeting three microsegments within the macrosegment.
4. How might a medium-sized bank determine the major market targets served by the bank?
5. Select a product and discuss how the size and composition of the marketing program might require adjustment as the product moves through its life cycle.
6. Suggest an approach that can be used by a regional family restaurant chain to

determine the firm's strengths over its competitors.

7. Select and discuss a strategy that corresponds to each of these positioning approaches: attribute, price/quality, competition, application, product users, and product class.
8. Discuss some of the more important reasons why test market results may *not* be a good gauge of how well a new product will perform when it is launched in the national market.
9. "Evaluating marketing performance by using return-on-investment (ROI) measures is not appropriate because marketing is only one of several influences upon ROI." Develop an argument against this statement.
10. Two factors complicate the problem of making future projections as to the financial performance of marketing programs. First, the flow of revenues and costs is likely to be uneven over the planning horizon. Second, sales may not develop as forecasted. How should we handle these factors in financial projections?
11. Discuss the relationship between the positioning concept and positioning strategy.
12. Select a product-type product-market (e.g., ice cream). Discuss the use of functional, symbolic, and experiential positioning concepts in this product category.

NOTES

1. This illustration is based on *Pier 1 Imports 1992 Annual Report,* April 30, 1992.
2. Andy Zipser, "Convex Computer Looks to Big Future in Tiny Niche," *The Wall Street Journal,* July 24, 1989, p. B1.
3. R. G. Hammermesh, M. J. Anderson, Jr., and J. E. Harris, "Strategies for Low Market Share Businesses," *Harvard Business Review,* May–June 1978, p. 98.
4. Toni Mack, "Pizza Power," *Forbes,* September 23, 1985, pp. 106–7.
5. Robert E. Linneman and John L. Stanton, Jr. "Mining for Niches," *Business Horizons,* May–June 1992, pp. 47–48.
6. Brad Edmondsom, "Burned-Out Boomers Flee to Families," *American Demographics,* December 1991, p. 17.
7. *Pier 1 Imports 1992 Annual Report,* pp. 12–13.
8. C. Whan Park, Bernard J. Jaworski, and Deborah J. Macinnis, "Strategic Brand Concept-Image Management," *Journal of Marketing,* October 1986, pp. 135–45.
9. David A. Aaker and J. Gary Shansby, "Positioning Your Product," *Business Horizons,* May–June 1982, pp. 56–62.
10. C. W. Park and Gerald Zaltman, *Marketing Management* (Hinsdale, Ill.: Dryden Press, 1987), p. 248.
11. This discussion is based on Park, Jaworski, and Macinnis, "Strategic Brand Concept-Image Management," pp. 136–37.
12. Ibid., pp. 135–45.
13. Aaker and Shansby, "Position Your Product," p. 56.
14. This illustration is based upon the article by David P. Garino, "Maker's Mark Goes against the Grain to Make Its Mark," *The Wall Street Journal,* August 1, 1980, pp. 1, 4.
15. Gretchen Morgenson, "Whiskey in His Veins," *Forbes,* November 25, 1991, pp. 186–87, 189.
16. This illustration is drawn from *Pier 1 Imports 1992 Annual Report* and discussions with management.
17. Aaker and Shansby, "Positioning Your Product," p. 60.

18. Edward D. Mingo, "The Fine Art of Positioning," *Journal of Business Strategy,* March/April 1988, p. 34.
19. David W. Cravens, Charles H. Holland, Charles W. Lamb, Jr., and William C. Moncrief III, "Marketing's Role in Product and Service Quality," *Industrial Marketing Management,* November 1988, p. 301.
20. N. D. Cadbury, "When, Where, and How to Test Market," *Harvard Business Review,* May–June 1975, pp. 97–98.
21. Glen L. Urban and John R. Hauser, *Design and Marketing of New Products* (Englewood Cliffs, N.J.: Prentice Hall, 1980), p. 419.
22. Ibid.; see Chapter 15 for a discussion of alternative methods for analyzing test markets.
23. Gary L. Lilien, "Advisor Z: Modeling the Marketing Mix Decision for Industrial Products," *Management Science,* February 1979, pp. 191–204.
24. See, for example, Gary L. Lilien and Philip Kotler, *Marketing Decision Making* (New York: Harper & Row, 1983).
25. The following discussion is based on Park, Jaworski, and Macinnis, "Strategic Brand Concept-Image Management," pp. 135–45.
26. Ibid., p. 138.
27. Ibid., pp. 138–39.
28. Ibid., p. 137.
29. Aaker and Shansby, "Positioning Your Products," p. 61.
30. Ibid., p. 62.
31. Julie Franz, "Cherry Coke Takes the Fizz out of Sister Brands," *Advertising Age,* October 28, 1985, p. 4.

CHAPTER

10

Marketing Strategies for Different Market and Competitive Environments

The rate of growth of a product-market, the diversity in the needs and wants of buyers, the structure of competition, the organization's competitive advantage, and other situational factors influence the selection of a marketing strategy. These factors are evaluated in selecting market targeting and positioning strategies.

When asked to name the first fast-food company, most people mention McDonald's. However, White Castle System was the market pioneer, entering the market over 70 years ago in Wichita, Kansas.[1] The restaurants look like small white castles. The menu has always been square burgers, fries, and onion rings. White Castle's $319 million sales in 1990 represented a tiny fraction of McDonald's, but the small chain's sales per unit (250 domestic units) place White Castle second-highest in the industry. The chain dominates a small segment in the giant fast-food market. Its loyal customer base keeps coming back for the 38-cent hamburgers. Sixty years ago you could get five burgers for 10 cents.

Companies like White Castle have several strategy options, which include deciding whether to compete in a product-market, and, if so, selecting the segments in which to compete, deciding when to compete, and choosing how to compete. The family-owned White Castle chain has experienced slow but steady growth and performance in line with management's objectives. In this chapter we discuss how marketing strategies are influenced by various situational factors. First, we identify several considerations in strategy selection, then look at strategies for competing in new markets. Next, we consider strategies for growth markets, mature markets, and declining markets. Finally, we discuss marketing strategies for competing in global markets, highlighting several important issues in competing beyond domestic boundaries.

CONSIDERATIONS IN STRATEGY SELECTION

Deciding how to look at the market is important in guiding strategy decisions. An industrywide focus may be too broad, particularly in mature markets where industry members compete in several markets with many different products. Similarly, looking only at head-on competitors may be too narrow in scope to identify the competitive structure. The product-type (class) product-market often provides a favorable trade-off between a very narrow and very broad scope:

> The product class reflects the aggregate effects of interbrand rivalry and of extensions brought about through the emergence of new or improved product forms. The product class also corresponds most closely to the business unit level where competition between firms occurs most directly.[2]

Examples of product type (class) include apartments, soft drinks, cereals, and automobiles (Chapter 5). The product-type product-market is used as the central focus for strategy analysis in this and subsequent chapters. We first present an approach to strategy selection, then discuss several market-entry barriers. The section concludes with an examination of strategy choice criteria.

Approach to Strategy Selection

Strategy selection may involve: (1) developing a new marketing strategy, or (2) changing an existing strategy. An approach for selecting strategies for different market and competitive situations is shown in Exhibit 10–1. The steps in the approach integrate the analysis and strategy choice material discussed in Chapters 1–9. A summary of the important issues to be considered at each step and the major actions/decisions that are required are also shown in Exhibit 10–1. The exhibit is a useful checklist for strategy analysis. It can also serve as a guide for case analysis.

The starting point in selecting a strategy is defining and analyzing the product-market. Next, market segmentation describes and evaluates segments. Assuming that the segments exist, one or more of them is targeted. Segment identification also provides a basis for analyzing the competitive structure and determining the existing and/or potential competitive advantages of the organization in each segment of interest. In the third step we define and analyze industry structure. This is followed by an in-depth anal-

EXHIBIT 10–1 Selecting Strategies for Different Market and Competitive Situations

	Important Issues	*Major Actions/Decisions*
Product-market definition and analysis ▽	• Evaluating the complexity of the product-market structure. • Establishing product-market boundaries	• Defining product-market structure • Customer profiles • Industry/distribution/competitor analysis • Market size estimation
Market segmentation ▽	• Deciding which level of the product-market to segment. • Determining how to segment the market.	• Select the basis of segmentation • Form segments • Analyze segments
Define and analyze industry structure ▽	• Defining the competitive area • Understanding competitive structure • Anticipating changes in industry structure	• Sources of competition • Industry structure • Strategic group analysis
Competitive Advantage ▽	• Deciding when, where, and how to compete	• Finding opportunity gaps • Cost/differentiation strategy/focus • Good/better/best brand positioning strategy
Market targeting and positioning strategies	• Deciding market scope • Good/better/best brand positioning strategy	• Selecting targets • Positioning for each target • Positioning concept • Marketing mix integration

ysis of each key competitor, and the choice of a competitive advantage strategy, indicating when, where, and how to compete in the segment(s) of interest to the organization. Finally, the targeting and positioning strategies indicate the specific customer targets and positioning strategy for each target.

Market Entry Barriers

The firms actively competing in a market often have an advantage over a company planning to enter the market.[3] This competitive edge is created by the market-entry barriers that the new entrant will encounter. The entry barriers to the product-market are important in deciding whether to enter the market. Entry-barrier analysis involves: (1) identifying the specific barriers that are present and their relative importance, and (2) estimating the effect of the barriers on entry at different stages of product-market maturity.

Entry Barriers. Six barriers are the major sources of influence on market entry decisions.[4] These are shown and described in Exhibit 10–2. The descriptions in Exhibit 10–2 suggest several specific factors that contribute to each entry barrier. For example, cost advantage may be gained through volume production, design efficiency, or experience.

EXHIBIT 10–2 Market Entry Barriers

Concept	*Definition*
Cost advantages of incumbents	The advantages include the decline in unit cost of a product as the absolute volume of production per period increases as well as the reduction in unit cost resulting from product know-how, design characteristics, favorable access to raw materials, favorable locations, government subsidies, and learning or experience curve.
Product differentiation of incumbents	Established firms have brand identification and customer loyalties stemming from past advertising, customer service, product differences, or simply being first into the market.
Capital requirements	The need to invest large financial resources to enter a market and compete in that market.
Customer switching costs	One-time costs to the buyer due to switching from one supplier to another (i.e., employee retraining costs, cost of new ancillary equipment, need for new technical help, product redesign, etc.).
Access to distribution channels	The extent to which logical distribution channels for a product are already served by the established firms in the market.
Government policy	The extent to which government limits or forecloses entry into industries with such controls as licensing requirements and limits access to raw materials (i.e., regulated industries and Environmental Protection Agency laws).

Source: Fahri Karakaya and Michael J. Stahl, "Barriers to Entry and Market Entry Decisions in Consumer and Industrial Goods Markets," *Journal of Marketing,* April 1989, p. 85.

Entry barriers are more significant in some product-markets than in others. A sample of Fortune 500 executives placed in a simulated environment indicated that all of the barriers in Exhibit 10–2 were relevant.[5] Cost advantages were perceived as the most important entry barrier, with capital requirements second and product differentiation third. No clear pattern of relative importance was found among the respondents for the remaining three factors.

Early versus Late Market Entry. The experiences of market pioneers (first to enter) suggest that they often gain a sustainable competitive advantage over subsequent firms entering the market.[6] However, early entry must be combined with good strategy choices in order to achieve this advantage. Simply being first is not enough. Entering the market first does not assure the pioneer of a favorable market and profit position. While initial entry offers an opportunity for rewards, it is also risky. The successful pioneer must select and implement strategies for sustaining competitive advantage.

Entry Barriers in Different Product-Markets. Some variation exists in the importance of the six entry barriers in consumer and industrial markets.[7] One study found all of the barriers except capital requirements to be different for industrial and consumer markets. Product differentiation and access to distribution channels are more influential in early entry for consumer markets.

Strategy Choice Criteria

Several factors influence the choice of a particular marketing strategy. There are major benefits in evaluating each strategy alternative using a set of choice criteria.[8] Evaluation of the criteria provides answers to these questions: (1) Is the strategy sound? (2) Can we implement the strategy? (3) Is the strategy worth pursuing?

Is the Strategy Sound? Answering this question requires examining the assumptions for the proposed strategy, assessing its cohesiveness, and considering the flexibility/adaptability of the strategy to changing conditions. The assumptions on which a proposed strategy is based must be sound. Realism is important in forecasting the revenues and costs of a proposed strategy, taking into account how competition is likely to respond. Critical review of the assumptions is essential when entering new markets or competing in rapidly changing markets.

The widespread turbulence in the business environment in the 1990s highlights the critical importance of selecting strategies that are adaptable to changes in the environment. The use of global supply networks by apparel firms like The Limited, Liz Claiborne, and Benetton is an example of a flexible strategy. Claiborne contracts much of its apparel production to producers in the Far East. The company has an overseas staff that monitors product quality and distribution.

Can We Implement the Strategy? This question focuses on the ability of the organization to develop and implement the strategy and the commitment of the operating managers toward achieving a successful strategy. A small organization deciding to enter an established product-market must realistically evaluate the skills and resources needed to successfully enter the market. Even a large firm with substantial resources may lack the necessary skills to compete when entering a product-market that is new to the firm. The willingness of the management team to favorably support the strategy is also very important.

Potential risk is an important aspect of implementation. Two factors are important in assessing risk: (1) the importance of the risk factor to the strategy choice, and (2) how much control the organization has over the risk factor.[9] The more important the risk factor and the less control the organization exercises over it, the more vulnerable the strategy is to the risk.

Is the Strategy Worthwhile? Does the proposed strategy offer an opportunity to gain an advantage that is sustainable? Will it lead to favorable outcomes (profits, market share, customer satisfaction)? For example, the strategy for late market entry should be carefully evaluated as to its competitive advantage. An important issue is evaluating the attractiveness of the market opportunity targeted by the strategy. An example of a strategy that provided sustainable competitive advantage is Domino's Pizza's. The founder targeted and positioned Domino's to meet the needs of buyers seeking rapid and reliable home delivery of pizza. No major competitor was satisfying this need when Domino's entered the market.

Answering the three questions helps to screen the marketing strategies under consideration by management. The discussion now turns to strategies appropriate at different stages of market maturity.

STRATEGIES FOR ENTERING NEW PRODUCT-MARKETS

A new or existing company considering entry into a new product-market needs a market entry strategy. The discussion follows the steps shown in Exhibit 10–1, beginning with product-market definition and analysis.

Market Definition and Analysis

> Emerging industries are newly formed or re-formed industries that have been created by technological innovations, shifts in relative cost relationships, emergence of new consumer needs, or other economic and sociological changes that elevate a new product or service to the level of a potentially viable business opportunity.[10]

A new product-market is at the introductory stage of its life cycle. Buyers' needs are not well defined, and there is no established history of market behavior. A new product-market develops for one of two reasons. The most common reason is a product innovation that offers an alternative technology for meeting an existing need in the marketplace. It may be a substitute for a product in an existing product-market, or a substitute technology that can meet the needs of buyers in two or more product-markets. An example of the former is the surgical stapler as an alternative to needle and suture. The latter is illustrated by fax machines, which provide an alternative to overnight mail, telephone communication, and telegrams. The second reason for a new product-market to emerge is an innovation that satisfies an unmet need. An example is a new drug that can cure a previously incurable disease. The human heart transplant from donor to recipient created a new-to-the-world product market.

"The most pervasive feature of emerging markets is uncertainty about customer acceptance and the eventual size of the market, which process and product technology will be dominant, whether cost declines will be realized, and the identity, structure, and actions of competitors."[11] Market definition and analysis are rather general in the early stages of product-market development. Buyers' needs are not highly differentiated because they do not have experience with the product. Determining the future scope and direction of product-market development may be difficult. Forecasting the size of market growth is also difficult. There is often a tendency to overestimate the speed and magnitude of market growth. For example, estimates of the market size for artificial intelligence software made in the mid-1980s for 1990 were six to eight times larger than the actual size of the market.[12]

Market Segmentation

The similarity of buyers' needs in the new product-market often limits segmentation efforts. It may be possible to identify a few broad segments. For example, heavy, medium, and low product usage can be used to segment a new product-market where usage varies across buyers. In some instances segmentation may not be feasible. An alternative is to define and describe an average or typical user, then target marketing efforts toward these potential users.

A segment of an existing product-market may emerge to form a new product-market variant. The segment category becomes large enough to start a new product-market. The market for laptop computers is illustrative. This market developed so rapidly that it became a distinct product-market within the personal computer market.

Segmenting the new product-market into broad user groups may be feasible using judgmental rather than analytical methods. One approach for the market pioneer is to identify the most promising user group(s) and to focus marketing efforts on one or a few segments that display the primary opportunity for sales. For example, the market for microwave cookware in the early 1980s was initially determined by microwave oven ownership coupled with factors influencing heavy usage (e.g., two working spouses, large family, and so on).

Industry Structure and Competition

There is no industry structure at the time the market pioneer enters the market, unless it emerges from an existing segment of a product-market. The rate of industry development depends on the attractiveness of the market and entry barriers. "The emerging phase of the industry is usually accompanied by the presence of the greatest proportion of newly formed companies (to be contrasted with newly formed units of established firms) that the industry will ever experience."[13]

Study of the characteristics of market pioneers indicates that new enterprises are more likely to enter a new product-market than are large, well-established companies. The exception is the availability of a major innovation in a large company coupled with strong entry barriers. The pioneers developing a new product-market "are typically small new organizations set up specifically to exploit first-mover advantages in the new resource space."[14] These entrepreneurs often have limited access to resources and must focus on product-market opportunities that require low levels of investment and simple organizational designs.

Industry development is influenced by various factors, including the rate of acceptance of the product by buyers, entry barriers, the performance of firms serving the market, and future expectations. The pioneer's proprietary technology may make entry by others impossible until they can gain access to the technology. Xerox with its copying process and Polaroid with its instant film held monopoly positions for several years. In contrast, the availability of standard components and ease of design enabled many firms to enter the personal computer market in the 1980s.

The emerging industry may develop along various lines, depending on how various factors affect industry structure. Porter identifies several problems that may constrain industry development:[15]

Inability of firms to obtain raw materials and components and/or rapid escalation of supply prices.

Absence of an established distribution network, support services, and other infrastructure inadequacies.

Lack of product standardization and erratic product quality.

Customers' confusion because of lack of experience and perceptions of possible obsolescence of the product.

High costs resulting from supply constraints and learning costs.

Financial and regulatory constraints.

The initial period of development may include many changes in industry structure, creating both high risks and high rewards for the firms that enter. Major change during the initial years is a common feature of emerging industries.

Strategy for Competitive Advantage

A firm entering a new product-market is more likely to achieve competitive advantage by offering buyers unique benefits rather than lower prices for equivalent benefits. (See Chapter 2's discussion of competitive advantage.) However, cost may be the basis of superior value when the new product is a lower-cost alternate technology to an existing product. For example, fax transmission of letters and brief reports is both faster and less expensive than overnight delivery services.

Research concerning the order of market entry indicates that the pioneer has a distinct advantage over subsequent firms entering the market. These studies estimate that the second firm entering the market will obtain 60 to 70 percent of the share of the pioneer.[16] The pioneer can develop entry barriers, making it more difficult and costly for others to enter. The advantage of an early follower is the opportunity to evaluate the pioneer's performance and thus reduce the risk of entry failure. Entry timing may also depend on the firm's resources and skills.

In selecting a strategy for competitive advantage in an emerging industry, companies often adopt a wide variety of strategies.[17] The uncertainty about how buyers will respond to marketing programs causes differences in managers' product designs, positioning concepts, distribution strategies, and supporting activities. Competing products often do not have the same standards. Sony introduced the Betamax videocassette recorder/player as the market pioneer. Ultimately, the competing VHS system captured the market. Similar differences in personal computer operating systems occurred in early stages of this product-market, which caused different computer brands to be incompatible.

Targeting and Positioning Strategies

Despite the uncertainties in an emerging industry, some evidence indicates "that more successful or longer-living firms engage in less change than firms which fail."[18] Instead these firms select and follow a consistent strategy on a continuing basis. If this behavior is characteristic of a broad range of successful new ventures, then choosing the entry strategy is very important. The essential objective is achieving a good strategic fit between the organization's strategy and the conditions of the environment. Targeting and positioning strategies are designed to take into account the requirements of each market-entry situation.

Targeting. Illustrative new product-market entry situations are shown in Exhibit 10–3. In situation A, the customer target is the potential user of a product that meets a need not previously satisfied. A cure for the AIDS virus is an example. The targeting strategy for this type of entry should include a substantial portion of potential buyers who are both willing and able to buy the product. The price of the product, how well it satisfies buyers' needs and wants, and other factors may restrict the size of the potential market.

Entry situation B requires a more focused strategy than A. Identifying potential users in the surgery closure product-market, where surgical stapling offers an advantage over conventional closure methods, is a logical targeting strategy. U.S. Surgical's market penetration strategy has successfully expanded its sales. The company is the world market leader for surgical stapling equipment (see Case 3–2).

Situation C involves targeting two or more segments in the product-markets where the new product offers a promising substitute solution to buyers' needs and wants. As mentioned earlier, fax communication technology is a substitute for other communications alternatives. For example, one segment for fax machines is made up of large- and medium-sized businesses that have been using overnight delivery services for letters and short

Exam: Develop strategy for one of the market level maturities

EXHIBIT 10–3 Illustrative Market-Entry Situations for New Products

Targeting Strategy	*New Market*	*Existing Market*
Single Target	A. Targeting a new product-market (new drug for incurable disease)	B. Targeting existing product-market (surgical staplers for surgery closure)
Multiple Targets	D. Targeting a few broad segments	C. Targeting several substitute markets (fax machines for overnight delivery and other substitutes)

reports. Another related segment is within-city delivery of letters and reports.

Situation D may occur when there is some opportunity for buyer need differentiation and the entering firm wants to establish a dominate position in the new market. If the initial targeting is too narrow, the firm may fail to develop its capabilities in meeting customer needs for more than one group of users.

If 1st one there, can focus on name you can trust.

Cos. that come in later will have to offer more value, a better product.

Positioning. A new enterprise targeting a new product-market develops a positioning concept and a new marketing mix. This situation is indicated in Exhibit 10–3 (A and D). The effectiveness of the mix components is unknown. Major changes in product design, distribution, and promotion are likely during the early years of market development. Nevertheless, positioning decisions should consider the long-term management of individual products and services when following the framework of the strategic brand concept (Chapter 9):

> It addresses the need to determine, prior to market entry, how positioning strategies at each stage should proceed. This advanced planning enables the firm to develop the appropriate resources at each stage so that a positioning strategy at the next stage can be better implemented.[19]

Decisions concerning positioning and mix composition are influenced by whether the firm is the first to enter or, instead, is a later entrant. The primary guidelines available to the pioneer are the needs of the customer targets and knowledge about any existing products that satisfy the same needs targeted by the new entry. Later entrants have the benefit of assessing the targeting and positioning actions and results of earlier entrants. If two or more segments are targeted, positioning strategies are needed for each target (Exhibit 10–3 C and D). To implement a segment strategy, the firm needs information on the buyers and the competition in the markets it is entering. Knowledge of customers' needs and competitors' positioning strategies (situation C) can be evaluated in designing the market-entry strategy.

EXHIBIT 10–4 Life Cycle Stages of the Personal Computer Market

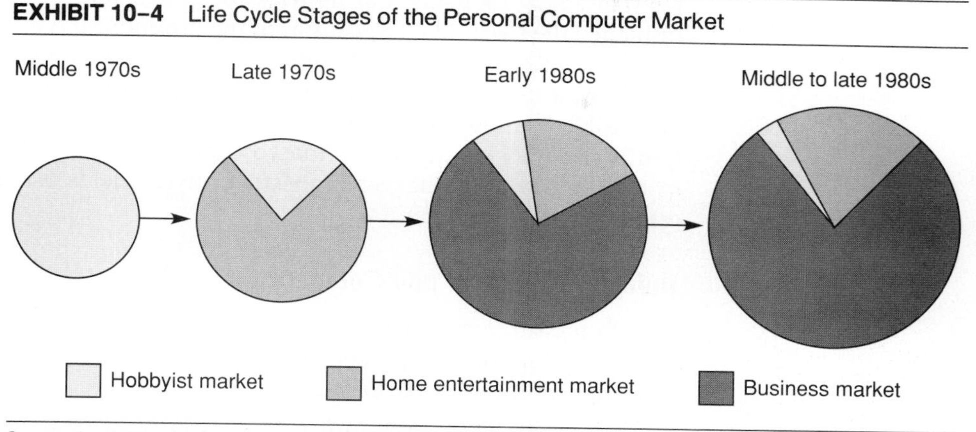

Source: David W. Cravens and Robert B. Woodruff, *Marketing* (Reading, Mass.: Addison-Wesley, 1986), p. 102.

STRATEGIES FOR GROWTH MARKETS

The emerging industry eventually expands into the growth stage. The following discussion assumes a rapid growth rate, although various rates of growth may occur. We examine several important strategy issues for growth markets.

Market Definition and Analysis

During the growth stage, buyers have experience with the product, and sales response patterns develop. Further changes are likely, as illustrated by the personal computer market (see Exhibit 10–4). Yet, the growth stage is better defined and has less uncertainty than is present in the emerging stage.

Knowing what factors influence market trends is important in evaluating the market's current and future attractiveness. Business and marketing planning require close coordination to select the most promising growth opportunities. The "market drivers" may vary across the segments in the product-market.

Market Segmentation

If not already developed in the emerging market, segments should occur in the growth stage. Identifying customer groups with similar needs improves targeting, and "experience with the product, process, and materials technologies leads to greater efficiency and increased standardization."[20] The market environment moves from highly uncertain to moderately uncertain.

Further change is likely, but information is available about the forces that influence the size and composition of the product-market.

Patterns of use can be identified, and the characteristics of buyers and their use patterns can be determined. Segmentation by type of industry may be feasible in industrial markets. Characteristics such as age, income, and family size may identify broad macrosegments for consumer products such as food and drugs. Analysis of existing buyers yields useful guidelines for estimating market potential.

Industry Structure and Competition

We often assume that high-growth markets are very attractive and that early entry offers important competitive advantages. Nevertheless, there are some warnings for industry participants:

> First, a visible growth market can attract too many competitors—the market and its distribution channel cannot support them. The intensity of competition is accentuated when growth fails to match expectations or eventually slows. Second, the early entrant is unable to cope when key success factors or technologies change, in part because it lacks the financial skills or organizational skills.[21]

Industry structure generalizations in growth markets are difficult. There is some evidence that large, established firms are more likely to enter growth markets rather than emerging markets. This is because they may not be able to move as quickly as the small specialist firms can in exploiting the opportunities in the emerging product-market.[22] The established companies have skills and resource advantages for achieving market leadership. These powerful firms can overcome the timing advantages of the market pioneers. These later entrants also have the advantage of evaluating the attractiveness of the product-market during its initial development.

Strategy for Competitive Advantage

A framework for strategic analysis of the different stages of market evolution is shown in Exhibit 10–5. The "developing" market category corresponds to the growth stage under discussion. Analysis of past performance of successful strategies suggests that the "K-generalists" are often the best performers in developing markets. These firms are early followers with established businesses in related markets. Examples of large firms entering a new market at the growth stage include IBM in personal computers and Johnson & Johnson (Ethicon) in surgical staplers.

Survival analysis of firms in the minicomputer industry highlights two performance characteristics in the rapid growth stage of the product-market: (1) survival rates are much higher for aggressive firms competing on a broad market scope compared to conservative firms competing on the same basis and (2) survival rates are high (about three quarters) for both aggressive and conservative specialists.[23] This research suggests that survival requires

EXHIBIT 10–5 Competition and Selection in Developing Markets: Strategies for Success[a]

Niche Configuration	*Embryonic*	*Developing*	*Maturing*
Population density	Low	Increasing	High
Size and rate of environmental change	High	Reducing	Low
Predominant organization form	r-specialists	K-generalists	K-generalists
Other forms	r-generalists	Polymorphists	K-specialists
Best performers	r-specialists	K-generalists	K-generalists

[a]r-specialists are small-scale pioneers and r-generalists are large-scale pioneers. K-generalists are early followers with established businesses in related markets. Polymorphists are early followers with widely diversified portfolios. K-specialists are small-scale late entrants occupying narrow market segments.

Source: Mary Lambkin and George S. Day, "Evolutionary Processes in Competitive Markets: Beyond the Product Life Cycle," *Journal of Marketing*, July 1989, p. 12.

aggressive action by firms that seek large market positions in the total market. Other competitors are likely to be more successful by targeting one or a few market segments.

Targeting and Positioning Strategies

The targeting strategy for a growth market is influenced by several factors: (1) the capabilities and resources of the organization; (2) the competitive environment; (3) the extent to which the product-market can be segmented; (4) the future potential of the market; and (5) the market-entry barriers confronting potential competitors. Exhibit 10–5 highlights three possible targeting strategies: extensive market coverage by firms with established businesses in related markets (these are the K-generalists); selective targeting by firms with diversified product portfolios (polymorphists); and market niche strategies by small organizations serving one or a few market segments.

Narrow Market Scope. This targeting strategy is feasible when buyers' needs are differentiated or when products are differentiated. The segments that are not served by large competitors provide an opportunity for the small firm to gain competitive advantage. The market leader(s) may not find small segments attractive enough to seek a position in the segment. If the buyers in the market have similar needs, a small organization may gain advantage through product specialization. This strategy would concentrate on a specific product or component.

Dell Computer is an interesting example of a company that competed successfully in the growth stage of the personal computer market. The company used standard components to assemble computers marketed through mail-order channels. Dell's computers offer speed and price advantages over competing units. The company's phone contact with customers provides direct feedback from the marketplace. Dell eventually expanded its channel

EXHIBIT 10–6 Illustrative Positioning Strategies in Growth Markets

	Narrow Market Scope	*Broad Market Scope*
Product	Product designed for a segment or focused on a specific product or component in nonsegmented market.	Broad product line designed to meet multiple needs of a wide range of buyers.
Channel	Typically a single channel using intermediary or direct contact with end-users.	Multiple channels or extensive single channel network.
Price	Price determined on value provided by product. Margins should be relatively high.	Pricing strategies likely to vary between market targets. Intensity of competition may impose price pressures.
Promotion	Advertising targeted for cost effectiveness. Personal selling may target middlemen or end-users.	Advertising may be broad in scope or focused depending on targets. Personal selling varies according to targets and role in marketing program.

strategy to include direct selling to large corporations and selling through retail dealers. These changes placed Dell in more direct competition with industry giants like IBM and Compaq Computers.

Broad Market Scope. The objective of this targeting strategy is to cover a large portion of the buyers in the product-market. The number of specific targets depends on the segments that exist in the market. During the growth stage of the business market for personal computers, the three major segments are small, medium, and large companies. Segments in the growth stage are likely to be few and identified by one or a few general characteristics (e.g., size of business). When segments are not apparent, extensive targeting is guided by a general profile of buyers. This profile becomes the target.

Positioning Strategy. This strategy will vary according to the targeting strategy that is selected by the organization. Several general characteristics of positioning strategy for selective targeting and extensive targeting are shown in Exhibit 10–6. These guidelines are illustrative, since many factors may influence the choice of a particular strategy. For example, major differences often occur in the use of positioning components in different markets. Personal selling is important when business firms are targeted because the number of buyers is small (compared to consumer markets) and the size of purchase is large. Advertising consumes much more of the marketing budget than personal selling in many consumer products firms.

The Market Feature describes the growth market for nicotine patches in 1992. It shows the difficulty in predicting how buyers will respond to a new product that offers substantial benefits over existing products. This market moved from the emerging stage to the growth stage in less than 12 months. The core issue is whether the high levels of demand will be sustained. New users must continue to enter the market to replace users who quit smoking and those who do not respond to the treatment. Market growth really slowed

MARKET FEATURE Coping with the Perils of a Growth Market

The market for nicotine patches exploded in 1992, with sales estimated to top $1 billion. This was over double the industry estimate made in late 1991 when the product was introduced. The market leader is Ciba-Geigy–Habitrol, with over double the share of Marion Merrell Dow–Nicoderm. The remaining competition, American Cyanamid–ProStep, has about one-half the share held by Nicoderm. The treatment takes six to eight weeks.

- The three companies flooded smokers with advertising announcing a new and better way to stop smoking, and the response was overwhelming.
- Buyers are being turned away by pharmacies because of patch shortages.
- The big loser is Nicoderm, which rapidly gained over a 40 percent market share, then lost over one third of the share because of shortages.
- American Cyanamid's ProStep, the late entrant, gained most of Nicoderm's lost share, moving from 1 percent to 13 percent of the market.
- Frequent brand switching and the equivalence of brands is jeopardizing the brand loyalty opportunities for all three brands. Creating independent brand identities will be difficult.
- The medical community is concerned that patch users will become discouraged and start smoking again, or not properly use the patches.
- Warner Lambert Co. entered the market in late 1992 with its Nicotrol patch.
- New prescriptions declined 65 percent between April and August of 1992 because of reduced promotion.

Source: Suein L. Hwang and Lourdes Lee Valeriano, "Marketers and Consumers Get the Jitters over Severe Shortage of Nicotine Patches," *The Wall Street Journal,* May 22, 1992, pp. B1 and B6; and Elyse Tanouye, "Nicotine Patch Promotion Blitz Draws Scrutiny," *The Wall Street Journal,* October 19, 1992, pp. B1 and B8.

down in late 1992, causing observers to reevaluate their optimistic sales forecasts. Apparently, some patch users experienced heart attacks while continuing to smoke, although conclusive evidence of the linkage was not found.

STRATEGIES FOR MATURE AND DECLINING MARKETS

Not all firms that enter the emerging and growth stages of the market survive during the maturity stage. The needs and characteristics of buyers also change over time. Consider, for example, the changes in the size and composition of the personal computer market during different life-cycle stages shown in Exhibit 10–4. Market entry at the maturity stage is less likely than in previous life-cycle stages.

Market Analysis and Segmentation

Segmentation is advisable at the maturity stage of the life cycle. At this stage, the product-market is clearly defined, indicating buyers' needs and preferences and the competitive structure. The factors that drive market growth are often apparent. The market is not likely to expand or decline rapidly.

Eventual decline is probable unless actions are taken to extend the product life cycle through product innovation and development of new product applications.

Identification and evaluation of market segments are necessary to select targets that offer each firm a competitive advantage. Experience should be available concerning how buyers respond to the marketing efforts of the firms competing in the product-market. Knowledge of the competitive and environmental influences on the segments in the market helps to obtain accurate forecasts. Marketing research information is useful to identify the existing (and potential) buyers, growth trends, gaps in customer satisfaction, and competitor strengths and weaknesses. Database marketing information is an illustrative source (Chapter 8). Standardized information services are available for large mature markets such as food and drugs, pharmaceuticals, automobiles, and computers. These services provide marketing research data on a subscription basis to participating companies.

Since the maturity of the product-market may reduce its attractiveness to the companies serving the market, actions may be taken in developing alternative strategies: (1) scanning the external environment for new opportunities that are consistent with organization's skills and resources; (2) identifying potential competitor threats to the current technologies for meeting customer needs; and (3) identifying opportunities within specific segments for new and improved products.

The buyers in mature markets are experienced and often demanding. They are familiar with competing brands and often display preferences for particular brands. The key marketing issue is developing and sustaining brand preference, since buyers are aware of the product type and its features. An interesting comparison of the leading brands for several U.S. consumer products is shown in Exhibit 10–7. Most of the top brands have kept their leading positions for more than half a century. This example highlights the importance of obtaining and protecting a lead position at an early stage in the development of a market.

Industry Structure and Competition

The characteristics of mature industries include intense competition for market share, emphasis on cost and service, slowdown in new-product flows, international competition, pressures on profits, and increases in the power of channel organizations that link manufacturers with end-users.[24] Deciding how to compete successfully in the mature product-market is a demanding challenge.

The typical industry structure consists of a few companies that dominate the industry and several others that pursue market selectivity strategies. The larger firms may include a market leader and two or three competitors with relatively large market positions. Entry into the mature product-market is often difficult because of major barriers and because of intense competition for sales and profits. Those that enter follow market or product

EXHIBIT 10–7 The Leading Brands: 1925 and 1985

	Leading Brand 1925	*Current Position 1985*
Bacon	Swift	Leader
Batteries	Eveready	Leader
Biscuits	Nabisco	Leader
Breakfast cereal	Kellogg	Leader
Cameras	Kodak	Leader
Canned fruit	Del Monte	Leader
Chewing gum	Wrigley	Leader
Chocolates	Hershey	No. 2
Flour	Gold Medal	Leader
Mint candies	Life Savers	Leader
Paint	Sherwin-Williams	Leader
Pipe tobacco	Prince Albert	Leader
Razors	Gillette	Leader
Sewing machines	Singer	Leader
Shirts	Manhattan	No. 5
Shortening	Crisco	Leader
Soap	Ivory	Leader
Soft drinks	Coca-Cola	Leader
Soup	Campbell's	Leader
Tea	Lipton	Leader
Tires	Goodyear	Leader
Toothpaste	Colgate	No. 2

Source: D. John Loden, *Megabrands* (Homewood, Ill.: Business One Irwin, 1992), p. 10.

selectivity strategies. Acquisition is often the best way of market entry rather than trying to develop products and marketing capabilities. Mature industries are increasingly experiencing pressures for global consolidation. Examples include automobile tires, foods, household appliances, and consumer electronics.

Strategy for Competitive Advantage

The strategies of companies competing in mature product-markets may be to *stabilize, turn around,* or *harvest* the business (Chapter 2). The stabilize objective is pursued through cost reduction, selective targeting, or product differentiation. Restructuring the corporation is undertaken to try to improve financial performance. Harvesting is the decision not to compete.

Market Position Advantage. In markets where production volume and experience lower costs, a few large firms tend to dominate the market. For example, the tire-making industry leaders are Michelin (France), Goodyear, and Bridgestone (Japan). Tire producers consolidated through mergers, acquisitions, and restructuring during the 1980s. The three giants are battling for market domination. The competitive advantage of the market leaders includes scale economies, brand position, experience, and resources.

The organizations at a disadvantage in the mature market are the small-scale subunits of large diversified companies and small specialists who entered the market at the growth stage and are unable to develop a competitive advantage.[25] Shakeouts of these companies are typical during product-market maturity. The companies with small market positions must have differentiated products and/or competitive advantages in certain market segments.

Specialization. Competing among the giants in a mature product-market requires market focus by small competitors. Opportunities are available because the market leader(s) may dominate the market while not satisfying the needs of all buyers:

> Typically, a generalist strategy appeals to some common denominator across all areas of the markets in order to maximize economies of scale. The cost advantage of such a strategy, however, may be offset by an inability to cater to segments of the market that have heterogeneous requirements.[26]

Examples of successful specialization strategies in mature markets include Cooper Tire in automobile tires, WD-40 Company in spray lubricants, and Convex Computer in mini-supercomputers. Cooper targets the replacement tire segment, WD-40's spray cans are in three fourths of U.S. households, and Convex targets scientists and engineers with applications requiring extensive numerical calculations.

Targeting and Positioning Strategies

Both targeting and positioning strategies may change in moving from the growth to maturity stages of the product-market. Targeting may be altered to reflect changes in priorities among market targets. Positioning within a targeted market may be adjusted to improve customer satisfaction and operating performance. When the product-market reaches maturity, management is likely to place heavy emphasis on efficiency. For example, during the early 1990s AT&T invested heavily to automate field sales operations using laptops and communications networks. Since the market opportunity is growing slowly and competition is heavy, the challenge is to manage each market target for performance.

Targeting. Targeting segments is appropriate for all firms competing in the mature product-market. The strategic issue is deciding which segments to serve. Market maturity may create new opportunities and threats in the firm's market target(s). Firms pursuing extensive targeting strategies may decide not to compete in certain segments. Those targets retained in the portfolio are prioritized to help guide product research and development, channel management, pricing strategy, advertising expenditures, and selling effort allocations. Elimination of targets and shifts in targeting priorities by large competitors may create new opportunities for the smaller competitors that use selective targeting strategies.

Positioning. During the maturity stage of the product-market life cycle, management often puts more emphasis on control than on planning. At this stage there should be well-established operating guidelines concerning the effectiveness of all components of the marketing mix. Adjustments in these positioning components are typically small unless operating results are unsatisfactory. Regular audits of marketing effectiveness are essential to fine-tune performance and identify problem areas.

Restructuring in Mature Markets

When major problems develop, restructuring may lead to big changes in marketing mix components such as advertising and personal selling. Changes in customer requirements, intensity of competition, poor performance, unfavorable market trends, and other pressures may require restructuring actions. Since we look at environmental turbulence and business restructuring in Chapter 2, the present discussion considers the effects of restructuring on marketing strategy.

Organizational restructuring often requires major changes in targeting and positioning strategies. Exhibit 10–8 illustrates its effects on market targeting and positioning. Any change in business strategy will have some effect on marketing strategy. Operating strategies are developed to implement the desired restructuring actions.

The restaurant market is experiencing a form of restructuring. The escalating popularity of takeout service is causing traditional on-premises operators to alter their services.[27] Many restaurant owners who resisted these services are installing takeout, drive-through, and delivery services. Off-premises sales in 1991 were 35 percent of the $130 billion industry sales. Takeout is about 61 percent of off-premises sales, and drive-through another 31 percent. The change is significant, and industry observers do not expect it to go away. During the five-year period ending in 1991, off-premises dining rose at a much greater rate than on-premises sales. The major drivers of these changes are two-career couples who do not want to cook or dress to eat out and employees who want to save money and be seen eating in the office. One problem is designing the takeout services so that they do not interfere with customers eating inside the restaurant.

Changing Strategic Leverage

The discussion so far considers the marketing strategy implications resulting from industry structure, a firm's market position, and the stage of evolution of the market. Several possible actions may improve a company's strategic

EXHIBIT 10–8 Illustrative Impacts of Business Restructuring on Targeting and Positioning Strategies

Changes in Business Strategy	*Market Targeting Impact*	*Positioning Impact*
Rapid growth/ Retrenchment	Market target(s) may not change although scope may be increased or reduced.	Substantial changes in resource allocation (e.g., advertising expenditures), organizational design, and sales force size.
Changing the product mix	No change is necessary unless increase in product scope creates opportunities in new segments.	Changes in product strategy, methods of distribution, and promotional strategies may be necessary.
Altering market focus	Targeting is likely to change to include new targets.	Positioning strategy must be developed for each new target.
Repositioning	Should not have a major effect on targeting strategy.	Product, distribution, price, and promotion strategies may be affected.
Distribution channel integration	Should have no effect on targeting strategy.	Primary impact on channel, pricing, and promotion strategies.
Diversification	Targeting strategies must be selected in new business areas.	Positioning strategies must be developed (or acquired) for the new business areas.
Strategic alliance	Targeting strategy may be affected based on the nature and scope of the alliance.	Operating relationships and assignment of responsibilities must be established.

leverage. These actions include acquiring other firms, establishing strategic alliances, introducing new technology, and intensifying price competition.[28] Lele proposes two change agendas: (1) changing the rules; (2) changing the game itself.

Changing the Rules. The items on this agenda include:[29]

- *Attacking the pricing gaps* by finding a price sector where competitive offerings are not available. (Mazda used this strategy successfully with its RX-7 and Miata cars.)
- *Changing channels of distribution or channel roles,* as illustrated by Dell Computer's entry into the personal computer market using the direct-mail channel.
- *Raising the intensity of competition* by accelerating new-product introductions, advertising, and sales promotion. (Rubbermaid's high volume of new-product introductions is illustrative.)
- *Altering the value/price ratio,* as did Toyota with the Lexus 400 by offering comparable value at lower prices for European-style luxury automobiles.

Changing the Game. This approach to gaining strategic leverage seeks to alter the basic structure of the industry by:[30]

- *Introducing new technology,* as illustrated by American Airlines' SABRE reservation system and frequent flyer program innovations.
- *Consolidating distribution channels,* such as Vallen Corporation's consolidation of industrial safety equipment wholesale distribution channels.
- *Consolidating the industry,* as illustrated by SuperValue's consolidation strategy by acquisitions in the food wholesalers industry.

The focus of changing strategic leverage is to overcome the influences of external or internal constraints on the organization's strategic options.

Strategies for Declining Markets

A mature market may grow slowly or not change for several years. Eventually, the market may decline, as measured by annual sales. An important issue is deciding how to compete in a declining market. Factors that affect the decision include the speed and rate of decline, the firm's position in the market, the opportunities for future profits, and the anticipated actions of competitors. If the conditions are severe, one or more of the competitors may decide to exit the market. If not, a strategy for competing must be selected and implemented.

Walker, Boyd, and Larréché propose four ways to compete in declining markets: harvest, maintenance, survivor, and niche strategies.[31] Harvesting involves generating cash as rapidly as possible. The maintenance strategy consists of holding a strong market position by continuing the prior strategy. The profitable survivor strategy is an aggressive action designed to increase an already strong position. The niche strategy is intended to capitalize on one or more segments that are more attractive than the overall market. Each strategy is described in Exhibit 10–9.

COMPETING IN GLOBAL MARKETS

Many business firms are competing outside national boundaries in pursuing market opportunities throughout the world. For example, the Campbell Soup Company is expanding rapidly into international markets.[32] The company began its global emphasis in the early 1980s. Campbell's international sales doubled from 1985 to 1989 as shown in Exhibit 10–10. Several of Campbell's international brands are also listed. Management's objective is to increase international sales to 40 percent of total sales by the early 1990s. By 1992, foreign sales were approaching 30 percent of Campbell's total sales. Some industry critics indicate that Campbell is trying to expand too rapidly and may have problems in competing with more experienced global food

EXHIBIT 10–9 Situational Determinants of Appropriate Marketing Objectives and Strategies for Declining Markets

	Strategies for Declining Markets			
Situational Variables	*Harvesting*	*Maintenance*	*Profitable Survivor*	*Niche*
Primary objective	Maximize short-term cash flow; maintain or increase margins even at expense of a slow decline in market share.	Maintain share in short term as market declines, even if margins must be sacrificed.	Increase share of the declining market with an eye to future profits; encourage weaker competitors to exit.	Focus on strengthening position in one or a few relatively substantial segments with potential for future profits.
Market characteristics	Future market decline is certain, but likely to occur at a slow and steady rate.	Market has experienced recent declines, but future direction and attractiveness are currently hard to predict.	Future market decline is certain, but likely to occur at a slow and steady rate; substantial pockets of demand will continue to exist.	Overall market may decline quickly, but one or more segments will remain as demand pockets or decay slowly.
Competitor characteristics	Few strong competitors; low exit barriers; future rivalry not likely to be intense.	Few strong competitors, but intensity of future rivalry is hard to predict.	Few strong competitors; exit barriers are low or can be reduced by firm's intervention.	One or more stronger competitors in mass market, but not in the target segment.
Firm's characteristics	Has a leading share position; has a substantial proportion of loyal customers who are likely to continue buying brand even if marketing support is reduced.	Has a leading share of the market and a relatively strong competitive position.	Has a leading share of the market and a strong competitive position; has superior resources or competencies necessary to encourage competitors to exit or to acquire them.	Has a sustainable competitive advantage in target segment, but overall resources may be limited.

Source: Orville C. Walker, Jr., Harper W. Boyd, Jr., and Jean-Claude Larréché, *Marketing Strategy* (Homewood, Ill.: Richard D. Irwin, 1992), p. 330.

EXHIBIT 10–10 Campbell Soup Expands into International Markets

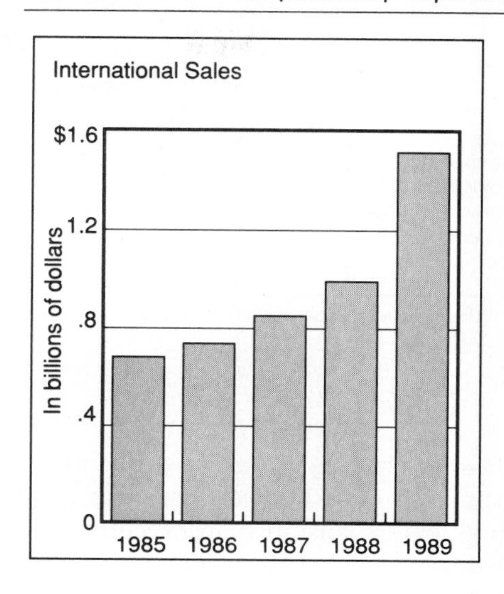

Key Brands Abroad

Name Product Line	*Country*
Biscuits Delacre Biscuits and cookies	Belgium
Continental Foods Condiments, soups and sweets	Belgium
Eugen Lacroix Premium soups and sauces	West Germany
Freshbake Foods Frozen meals and vegetables	United Kingdom
Groko Frozen vegetables	Netherlands
Lamy-Lutti Chocolates, candy and gum	France
Lassaroni & Co. Biscuits and seasonal cakes	Italy
Theodor Kattus Pasta, condiments and sauces	West Germany

Source: Vindu P. Goel, "Campbell Soup Seeks to Broaden International Presence," *The Wall Street Journal*, September 20, 1989, p. A6.

processors such as CPC International, Inc. and H. J. Heinz Company in the United States, Nestlé S. A. of Switzerland, and the British-Dutch Unilever Group. Nevertheless, Campbell Soup's international expansion demonstrates the escalating importance of global markets to the survival and success of many corporations.

We look at competing in global markets to identify several considerations in developing competitive strategies. Then we examine important aspects of global competition to illustrate the scope of the global marketplace. Next, we consider global marketing strategy alternatives. A discussion of international market entry strategies follows.

Aspects of Global Competition

Chief executives in a wide range of industries recognize that competing internationally is essential in the interlinked global economy. Several factors highlight the importance of expanding into international markets, as shown

EXHIBIT 10–11 Chief Executives' Reasons for Global Expansion

	CEOs From:			
	U.S.	*Europe*	*Japan*	*Pacific Rim*
Increase revenue	38%	52%	58%	46%
Increase profitability	27	53	53	40
Achieve technological leadership	20	30	44	34
Diversify into new businesses	23	35	53	27
Lower business costs	19	39	55	34
Improve product quality	19	35	34	37

Source: George Anders, "Going Global: Vision vs. Reality," *The Wall Street Journal,* September 22, 1989, pp. R20–21.

in Exhibit 10–11. These opinions were obtained from 433 chief executives on three continents. The United States executives appear to be less concerned with global expansion than executives in Europe, Japan, and the Pacific Rim, although U.S. concerns about global competitiveness increased significantly by the early 1990s.

Understanding global markets is important regardless of where an organization decides to complete, since domestic markets often include international competitors. The increasingly smaller world linked by instant communications capabilities, global supply networks, and international financial markets mandates evaluating global opportunities and threats. When firms select strategies for global markets, Day recommends consideration of: (1) the advantages of global reach and standardization; and (2) the advantages of local adaption.[33]

Global Reach and Standardization. This factor considers the extent to which standardized products and other strategy elements can be designed to compete on a global basis. The world is the market arena and buyers are targeted without regard to national boundaries and regional preferences. Global strategy products are not commodities. Instead they are differentiated but standardized across nations. The objective is to identify market segments that span global markets and to serve these needs with global positioning strategies. Examples include large commercial aircraft, construction equipment, computers, and expensive watches.

Local Adaption Requirements. In some markets domestic customers must be targeted and positioning strategies designed to consider the requirements of domestic buyers. For example, food companies competing in the European Community market consolidation (EC-92) must recognize national and regional preferences for foods and beverages. As an illustration, beer brand preferences are very localized even within one country such as Germany.

Differences in Buyers. A wide variety of social, political, cultural, economic, and language differences among countries affects buyers' needs and preferences. These variations must be recognized in targeting and positioning strategies. Consider, for example, the comparisons of food markets and habits shown in Exhibit 10–12. Note the differences in cereal consumption, frozen-food consumption, and microwave availability in homes. These variations may offer market opportunities. Low consumption rates may also indicate the purchasing resistance of buyers. For example, instant coffee is popular in Britain but not in France.

A global market perspective takes into account differences among buyers in the countries targeted by a firm. Experienced international competitors recognize the importance of satisfying buyers' needs and preferences:

> The key to successful international marketing is adaptation to the environmental differences from one market to another. Adaptation is a conscious effort on the part of the international marketer to anticipate the influences of both the foreign and domestic uncontrollable environments on a marketing mix and then to adjust the marketing mix to minimize the effects.[34]

Some products are global in their appeal to buyers. Many others must be designed to meet the needs of buyers in each country targeted. Economic unifications among countries, such as Europe in 1992, will not immediately transform the countries into a unified market.

Industry Structure and Competition

Industry structure and competition are changing throughout the world as companies seek to improve their competitive advantage in the rapidly shrinking global marketplace. Industry scope needs to be examined using a global perspective, since many competitive boundaries extend beyond national borders. Corporate actions include restructuring, acquisition, merger, and strategic alliances. For example, General Mills has a strategic alliance with Nestlé to market General Mills' products in Europe, offering a major opportunity for General Mills to increase sales of cereal products (Exhibit 10–12). Nestlé has the experience and distribution network needed to tap the cereal market. Kellogg, a key competitor, is already serving European markets.

Several factors affect the nature and scope of global competition, including:

- *Market consolidation.* Market unification through the elimination of trade barriers helps to consolidate intercountry markets. Firms competing in a single country must alter their past strategies or risk loss of their market position.
- *Competitive pressures.* The competitive threats of Japanese and U.S. companies were major influences on the unification of Europe and the restructuring of European companies.

EXHIBIT 10–12 Food Markets and Habits

Food Markets and Habits

The Major Players

1988 European food companies, ranked by sales, in billions of dollars*

Company	Nationality	1988 sales,* in billions of dollars
Nestle	Swiss	$ 8.76
Unilever	Britain/Neth.	5.98
BSN	French	3.46
Eridania	Italy	3.33
Hillstown Holdings	Britain	2.56
General Foods-Europe**	Britain	2.52
Jacobs Suchard	Swiss	2.48
Daigety	Britain	2.01
Associated British Food	Britain	1.88
United Biscuits	Britain	1.88

*Based on exchange rate of December 30, 1988
**Excludes acquisition of Kraft at end of 1988

Source: UBS Philips and Drew Ltd.

Breakfast of Choice

1988 per-capita cereal consumption, in pounds

Ireland	15.4
Britain	12.8
Australia	12.3
U.S.	9.8
Canada	8.7
Denmark	4.6
West Germany	2.0
France	1.1
Spain	0.4

Source: UBS Philips and Drew Ltd.

Where Convenience Rules

1988 per-capita frozen-food consumption, in pounds

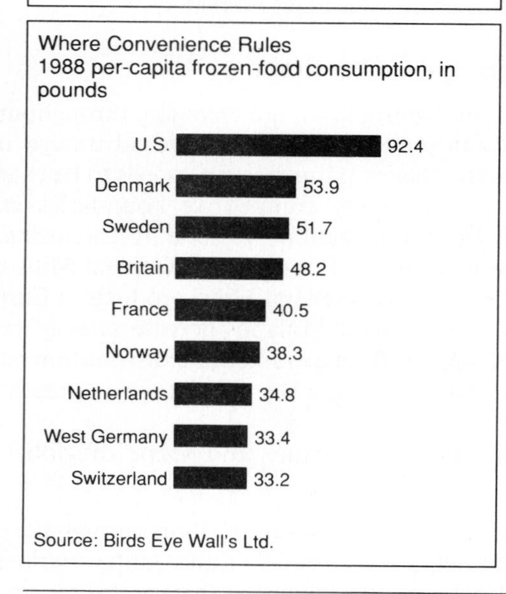

Source: Birds Eye Wall's Ltd.

Fast Cooking

Percentage of homes with microwave ovens

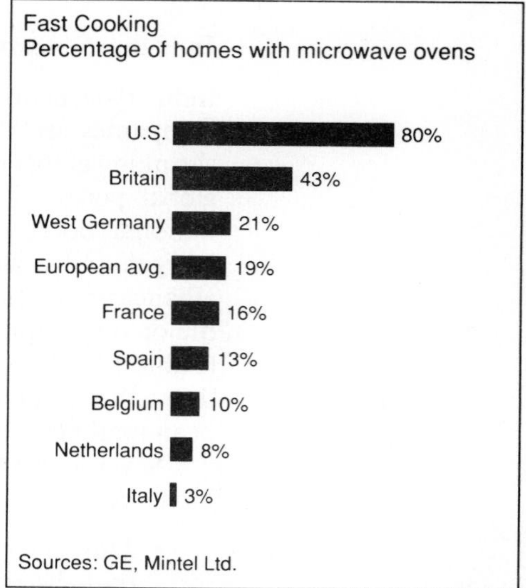

Sources: GE, Mintel Ltd.

Source: Joann S. Lublin, "Slim Pickings: U.S. Food Firms Find Europe's Huge Market Hardly a Piece of Cake," *The Wall Street Journal,* May 15, 1990, p. A18.

- *Similarity of buyers' needs.* The acceptance of standardized products affects industry structure by encouraging consolidation. Examples include automobile tires, consumer electronics, and industrial chemicals.
- *Government regulatory actions.* Various actions of governments influence industry structure and competition. Many companies outside of Europe are establishing ties with EC firms to avoid possible market-entry barriers created by government actions.
- *Communications technology.* The instant access to world markets and suppliers through communications technology encourages the establishment of networks of organizations aligned together from suppliers to end-users.

These influences suggest the broad scope of changes occurring in the global business environment. Corporate and national responses cause modifications of industry structure and competition to take advantage of opportunities and to avoid potential threats.

Global Marketing Strategy Alternatives

Strategies for competing in international markets range from targeting a single country, multinational targeting, or competing on a global basis. The strategic issue is deciding whether to compete internationally and, if so, how to compete. Also, the choice of a domestic focus requires an understanding of relevant global influences on the domestic strategy.

The differences between the multinational and global corporation indicate different strategic perspectives. The global corporation considers the entire world as the competitive arena. It may be located anywhere, and it uses its resources and capabilities in a worldwide network of manufacturing and marketing operations.[35] This strategy is appropriate when there are advantages to using a global strategy and no requirements for local adaptation. In contrast, the multinational corporation develops its strategy for each of the countries targeted rather than using a coordinated strategy for competing in global markets.

The global and the domestic strategies represent the extremes between global reach/standardization and local adaptation.[36] If there are no advantages to either standardization or local adaptation, there may be advantages in applying a domestic strategy that is successful in other countries with similar needs and market conditions. When both standardization and local adaptation are important, Day recommends a composite strategy using decentralized marketing and a reasonably standard product with selected options.

A key issue is selecting a good future strategy by the multinational company. Buzzell and Quelch identify three strategic options that may be considered by a multinational threatened by global competition.[37] One possibility is to convert to a global strategy. The strategies used by Boeing and IBM are examples of global strategies. A second option is to establish a strategic alliance with one or more companies that provide market access and other global benefits (see Chapter 3). A third option is to target a market segment that the organization can dominate and build entry barriers against global competitors. The segment strategy may be domestic or international in scope. Producers of expensive Swiss watches follow this strategy. Millipore in water treatment equipment also follows this strategy.

Market-Entry Strategies

There are several methods for entering international markets depending on desired market scope, company resources and capabilities, entry barriers, and other specific considerations. We look at the major market-entry strategies to indicate the major features of each.

Exporting. This strategy consists of shipping products from the producer's country to the targeted country, with marketing and distribution functions performed by an independent distributor or importer or by a marketing subsidiary owned by the producer. The use of independent intermediaries is a popular entry strategy for firms that do not have international experience and whose resources are limited. The company-owned marketing organization requires more investment, but it has greater control over operations.

Licensing. In selecting this strategy "a company assigns the right to a *patent* (which protects a product, technology, or a process) or a *trademark* (which protects a product name) to another company for a fee or royalty."[38] This strategy is used by Löwenbräu AG to market its beer worldwide. The Miller Brewing Company is licensed in the United States to produce the Löwenbräu brand. Licensing agreements include fee arrangements and other marketing requirements such as advertising support provided by both parties. The major advantages of the strategy are low resource requirements and market access through the licenses established network.

Joint Ventures. This strategy is used by a company that decides to share management with one or more collaborating foreign firms.[39] This strategy, like licensing, greatly limits the political and economic risks of the company entering the market. Certain countries require joint venture establishment as a condition of market entry. The strategy is used by U.S. and foreign automobile manufacturers.

Strategic Alliance. This strategy is similar to the joint venture but normally does not involve the creation of a new organization with a local partner. Instead, the alliance is a cooperative arrangement between two independent corporations, which may involve ownership. Recall our discussion of joint ventures and strategic alliances in Chapter 3. Drucker describes the nature and scope of the strategic alliance:

> Alliances of all kinds are becoming increasingly common, especially in international business: joint ventures; minority holdings (particularly cross-holdings, in which each partner owns the same percentage of the other); research and marketing compacts; cross-licensing and exchange-of-knowledge agreements; syndicates, and so on. The trend is likely to accelerate. Marketing, technology and people needs all push it.[40]

The successful performance of the alliance depends on how well the participating organizations can work together.

Complete Ownership by the Entering Company. This strategy consists of creating a wholly owned manufacturing and marketing subsidiary in the targeted country. This requires a major investment and is subject to the environmental threats of the country. The subsidiary may involve establishing a new entity or, instead, acquiring an existing company.

International Planning Process

The major phases of planning for a multinational firm operating in several countries is shown in Exhibit 10–13.[41] The first step in the planning process is the market opportunity analysis. This may represent a major activity for a company that is entering a foreign market for the first time. Because of the risks and uncertainties in international markets, the market assessment is very important for both new market entrants and experienced firms.

Phase 1 determines which targets to pursue and establishes relative priorities for resource allocation. Phase 2 fits the positioning strategy to each target market. The objective is to match the mix requirements to the needs identified and the positioning concept management selects. Phase 3 consists of the preparation of the marketing plan. Included are the situation assessment, objectives, strategy and tactics, budgets and forecasts, and action programs. Finally in Phase 4, the plan is implemented and managed. Results are evaluated and strategies adjusted when necessary to improve results. Although, the international market planning process is similar to planning domestic marketing strategies, the environment is far more complex and uncertain in international markets.

SUMMARY

Situational factors affect marketing strategy selection in various ways. Strategy choice begins with product-market definition and analysis, followed by market segment identification and analysis of industry structure and competition. Next, competitive advantage is evaluated for each market target

EXHIBIT 10–13 International Planning Process

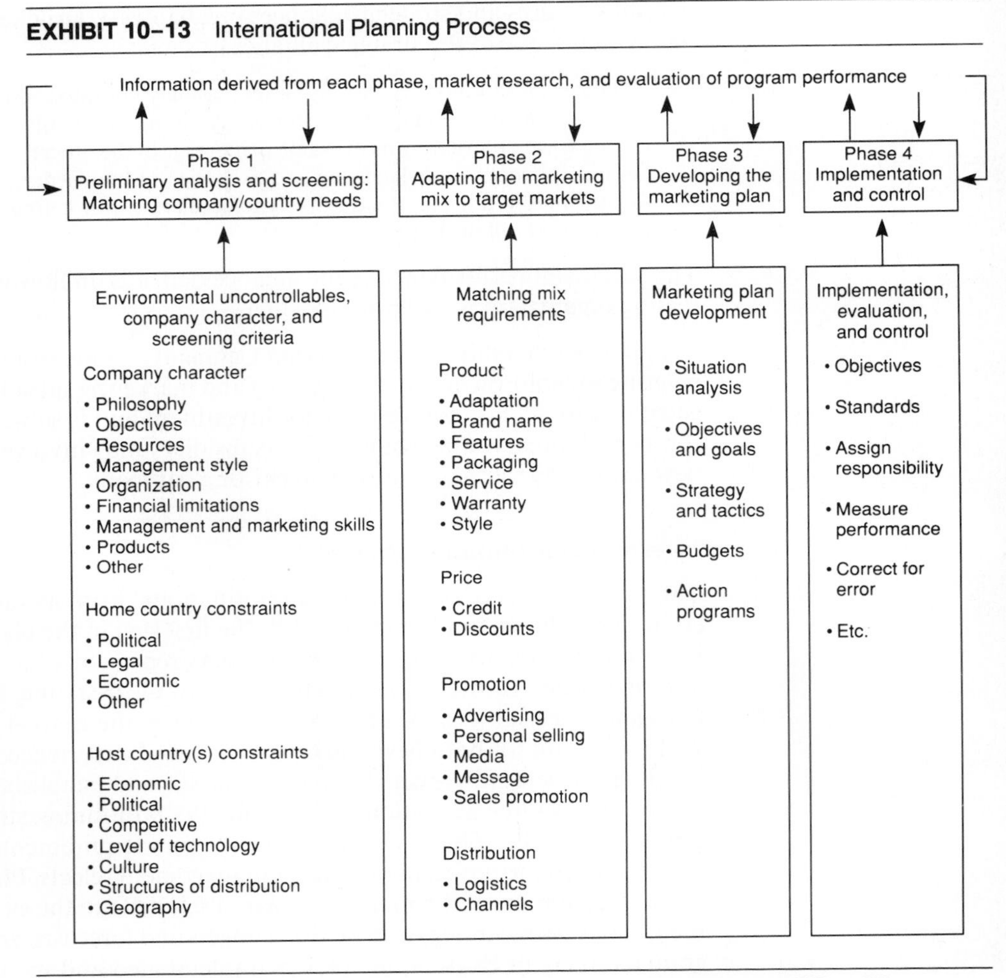

Source: Philip R. Cateora, *International Marketing*, 7th ed. (Homewood, Ill.: Richard D. Irwin, 1990), p. 351.

(segment) under consideration. Finally, market targeting and positioning strategies are selected, taking into account the situational variables that may influence the strategies that are implemented.

This strategy choice process can be used to analyze how any set of situational factors affect a proposed strategy. Evaluation of entry barriers is important in market entry and in protecting an existing market position against competitive threats. The effects of barriers vary across different product-markets. Looking at the advantages and limitations of early versus late market entry is important. Also, evaluation of several criteria is useful in strategy selection. The relevant criteria include sustainable competitive advantage; the premises used in strategy analysis; the skills, resources, and management commitment of the organization; the cohesiveness of the strategy; the evaluation of potential risks and contingencies if the strategy is implemented; the flexibility/adaptability of the strategy to changing conditions; and the value added by the strategy.

The chapter highlights how marketing strategy is affected by various situational factors. This is illustrated by considering the kinds of strategies for entering new, growth, and mature product-markets. Restructuring actions in mature markets are also examined and strategies are discussed. Finally, the several aspects of competing in international markets are considered and strategies for competing in global markets are examined.

QUESTIONS FOR REVIEW AND DISCUSSION

1. Discuss the similarities and differences in the barriers to market entry for the automobile and restaurant industries.
2. Suppose you have been asked to advise a wealthy entrepreneur concerning possible entry into the soft-drink industry. What are your recommendations?
3. De Beers has a virtual world monopoly on the distribution of diamonds. The company distributes an estimated 85 percent of all diamonds produced. Discuss the feasibility of another company actively competing with De Beers.
4. Discuss the advantages and limitations of being the market pioneer in a new market. Why is it possible for a firm like Compaq to successfully enter the personal computer market subsequent to the entry of Apple, Tandy, and other PC producers?
5. Compare and contrast market-entry conditions during the emerging and growth stages of product-market development.
6. Using Exhibit 10–1 as a guide, discuss the development of a marketing strategy by Pier 1 Imports for competing in the 1990s. (See Chapter 9 discussion of Pier 1.)
7. Discuss the conditions that might enable a new competitor to enter a mature product-market.
8. Competing in the mature market for air travel promises to be a demanding challenge in the 1990s. Discuss the marketing strategy issues facing Delta Airlines during the next decade.
9. By 1990, microwave oven household penetration was approaching 80 percent in the United States. Discuss the competitive impact of the use of microwave food preparation on the fast-food market.
10. Competing in global markets presents several complex strategic issues. Discuss the market-entry alternatives available to a small producer of electronic control equipment currently operating in the United States.

NOTES

1. Matthew Grimm, "White Castle at 70: Still the Value King," *AdWeek's Marketing Week,* January 28, 1991, p. 24.
2. Mary Lambkin and George S. Day, "Evolutionary Processes in Competitive Markets: Beyond the Product Life

Cycle," *Journal of Marketing,* July 1989, p. 4.
3. Michael Porter, "Industry Structure and Competitive Strategy: Keys to Profitability," *Financial Analysis Journal,* July–August 1980, pp. 30–41.
4. Fahri Karakaya and Michael J. Stahl, "Barriers to Entry and Market Entry Decisions in Consumer and Industrial Goods Markets," *Journal of Marketing,* April 1989, pp. 80–91.
5. Ibid.
6. See, for example, ibid., and William T. Robinson, "Sources of Market Pioneer Advantages: The Case of Industrial Goods Industries," *Journal of Marketing Research,* February 1988, pp. 87–94.
7. Karakaya and Stahl, "Barriers to Entry," pp. 80–91.
8. These criteria are suggested by George S. Day, "Tough Questions for Developing Strategies," *Journal of Business Strategy,* Winter 1986, pp. 60–68.
9. Ibid., pp. 66–67.
10. Michael E. Porter, *Competitive Strategy* (New York: The Free Press, 1980), p. 215.
11. Lambkin and Day, "Evolutionary Processes in Competitive Markets," p. 9.
12. "Slow Growth for Artificial Intelligence," *The Wall Street Journal,* July 5, 1990, pp. B1 and B4.
13. Porter, *Competitive Strategy,* p. 218.
14. Lambkin and Day, "Evolutionary Processes in Competitive Markets," p. 13.
15. Porter, *Competitive Strategy,* pp. 221–25.
16. See, for example, William T. Robinson and Claes Fornell, "Sources of Market Pioneer Advantages in Consumer Goods Industries," *Journal of Marketing Research,* August 1985, pp. 305–15; and Glen L. Urban, Theresa Carter, Steven Gaskin, and Zofia Mucha, "Market Share Rewards to Pioneering Brands: An Empirical Analysis and Strategic Implications," *Management Science,* June 1986, pp. 645–59.
17. Porter, *Competitive Strategy,* p. 217.
18. Elaine Romanelli, "New Venture Strategies in the Minicomputer Industry," *California Management Review,* Fall 1987, p. 161.
19. C. W. Park and Gerald Zaltman, *Marketing Management* (Hinsdale, Ill.: Dryden Press, 1987), p. 249.
20. Lambkin and Day, "Evolutionary Processes in Competitive Markets," p. 14.
21. David A. Aaker and George S. Day, "The Perils of High-Growth Markets," *Strategic Management Journal* 7 (1986), p. 419.
22. Lambkin and Day, "Evolutionary Processes in Competitive Markets," p. 11.
23. Romanelli, "New Venture Strategies," pp. 170–72.
24. Porter, *Competitive Strategy,* pp. 238–40.
25. Lambkin and Day, "Evolutionary Processes in Competitive Markets," p. 15.
26. Ibid., p. 14.
27. Kevin Heliker, "Forget Candlelight, Flowers, and Tips: More Restaurants Tout Takeout Service," *The Wall Street Journal,* June 18, 1992, pp. B1, B5.
28. Milind M. Lele, "Selecting Strategies That Exploit Leverage," *Planning Review,* January/February 1992, p. 21.
29. Ibid.
30. Ibid.
31. Orville C. Walker, Jr., Harper W. Boyd, Jr., and Jean-Claude Larréché, *Marketing Strategy* (Homewood, Ill.: Richard D. Irwin, 1992), pp. 329–33.
32. Vindu P. Goel, "Campbell Soup Seeks to Broaden International Presence," *The Wall Street Journal,* September 20, 1989, p. A6.
33. George S. Day, *Market-Driven Strategy* (New York: The Free Press, 1990), pp. 266–70.
34. Philip R. Cateora, *International Marketing,* 7th ed. (Homewood, Ill.: Richard D. Irwin, 1990).
35. Jeremy Main, "How to Go Global—and Why," *Fortune,* August 28, 1989, pp. 266–70.

36. Day, *Market-Driven Strategy,* pp. 266–70.
37. Robert D. Buzzell and John A. Quelch, *Multinational Marketing Management,* Reading, Mass.: Addison-Wesley, 1988, pp. 7–8.
38. Jean-Pierre Jeannet and Hubert D. Hennessey, *International Marketing Management* (Boston: Houghton-Mifflin, 1988), p. 279.
39. Cateora, *International Marketing,* pp. 343–46.
40. Peter F. Drucker, "From Dangerous Liaisons to Alliances for Progress," *The Wall Street Journal,* September 8, 1989, p. A8.
41. The following discussion is based on Cateora, *International Marketing,* pp. 351–57.

CHAPTER

11

Planning for New Products

New products are the center of attention in most companies because of their obvious contribution to the survival and prosperity of the enterprise. Planning for new products is an essential and demanding strategic activity. New products, when matched to customer needs, help an organization strengthen its position in existing product-markets and move into new product-markets.

New-product planning is a top priority at United States Surgical Corporation, the market leader in the manufacture of surgical stapling instruments. U.S. Surgical's (USS) 1992 sales were over $1.5 billion, 10 times 1983 sales. The company was founded in the 1960s to produce and market staplers for use in skin closure and other surgical applications. It has generated a continuing stream of successful new products that contribute to impressive sales and profit growth. The close working relationship of USS sales representatives with surgeons in operating rooms gives USS a critical competitive advantage.[1] For example, a salesperson perceptively identified a new-product opportunity by observing early experiments in laparoscopy (see Case 3–2). Using this procedure, the surgeon inserts a tiny TV camera into the body with very thin surgical instruments. USS responded quickly to this need by designing and introducing a basic laparoscopic stapler in early 1990. The product is used in gallbladder removal and other internal surgical applications. These instruments contributed $315 million to USS's 1991 sales.

New products are critically important to the financial performance of U.S. Surgical. Its close ties to users of its product and rapid new-product development enabled the firm to gain an important competitive edge over its primary competitor, Johnson & Johnson's Ethicon Endo-Surgery Division.[2] Ethicon countered the competitive threat by restructuring management and strengthening its sales force. J&J's management announced that it would be the market leader in laparoscopic instruments by 1995. Regardless of the outcome of this competitive battle, it shows the importance of new-product planning in these companies.

We examine the planning of new products, beginning with a discussion of customer needs analysis. Next, we discuss the steps in new product planning, including generating ideas, screening and evaluating the ideas, business analysis, development and testing, designing the marketing strategy, market testing, and new product introduction. The chapter concludes with a discussion of several product planning issues.

PRODUCT PLANNING AS A CUSTOMER SATISFACTION PROCESS

New-product introductions are classified according to two factors: (1) newness to the market and (2) newness to the company. Six categories of new products are defined as follows:

1. *New-to-the-world products:* new products that create an entirely new market (10 percent of total new introductions).
2. *New product lines:* new products that, for the first time, allow a company to enter an established market (20 percent of total).
3. *Additions to existing product lines:* new products that supplement a company's established product lines (26 percent of total).
4. *Improvements in/revisions to existing products:* new products that provide improved performance or greater perceived value and replace existing products (26 percent of total).
5. *Repositioning:* existing products that are targeted to new markets or market segments (7 percent of total).
6. *Cost reductions:* new products that provide similar performance at lower cost (11 percent of total).[3]

Typically, a company's new-product program includes items in several of the six categories. Totally new products account for only 10 percent of all new-product introductions. The planning process we discuss in this chapter applies to any of the six categories and is used in planning for new services as well as tangible products.

New-product planning is guided by customer needs analysis. Even new-to-the-world product ideas should have some relationship to needs that are not being met by existing products. For example, U.S. Surgical's development of the surgical stapler considered the skin closure needs of operating room surgeons.

Corporate and Business Strategies

The business mission, objectives, and strategies identify the product-market areas that are of interest to management. Business purpose and scope set important guidelines for new-product planning. The entire management team considers product-market opportunities and establishes priorities to guide product planning. Customer needs yield important information for determining where competitive advantage can be gained by developing new products.

Market segment identification and evaluation help determine which segments offer new-product opportunities to the organization. Extensive analysis of existing and potential customers and competition are vital to effective new-product planning. For example, U.S. Surgical's market focus consists of equipment and supplies to meet the needs of surgeons and operating room staff.

Finding Customer Satisfaction Opportunities

Customer satisfaction monitoring seeks to identify gaps in satisfaction that may offer opportunities for product innovation. As we discussed in Chapter 6, the gaps are determined by comparing the customer's expectations about the product and supporting services with the actual performance of the product and supporting services.

Customer satisfaction analysis finds opportunities for (1) new products, (2) improvements in existing products, (3) improvements in production processes, and (4) improvements in supporting services. The product planning process that we look at in this chapter also is used in product and process improvement planning, and improvement in supporting services. Many of the new-product activities of companies do not involve totally new products. We discuss product portfolio management in Chapter 12. The entire organization is involved in customer satisfaction analysis. This market-driven approach to product planning helps to avoid a mismatch between technologies and customer needs.

Customer satisfaction analysis has a product-market frame of reference and may include examining the generic, product-type, and product-variant product-market levels. Market segment analyses are often necessary to identify specific customer needs and competitive opportunities. The objective is to find gaps between buyers' expectations and the extent to which they are being satisfied. As shown by Exhibit 11–1 a large gap may offer a new product opportunity. For example, U.S. Surgical's sales representative saw the

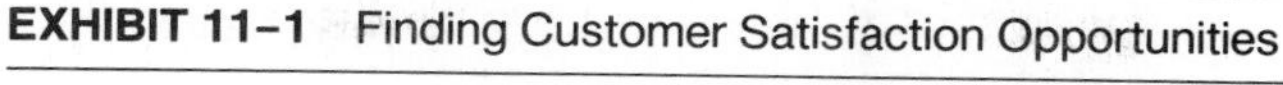

EXHIBIT 11–1 Finding Customer Satisfaction Opportunities

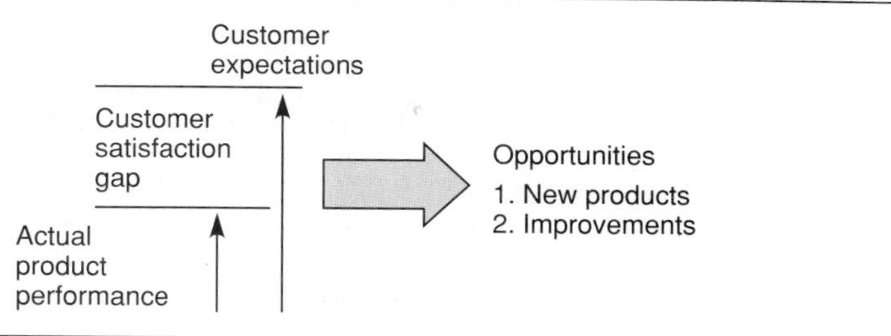

trend toward laparoscopy surgery, a gap not satisfied with the available surgical equipment.

Buyers' satisfaction with existing products and brands is evaluated using various product/service attributes to express buyers' preferences and comparisons of competing brands. These comparisons may include preference mapping and the other analyses discussed in Chapters 5, 6, and 7. The objective of these techniques for existing products is to identify the important preferences for the buyers in specific market segments. Opportunities for new and improved products are highlighted by the existence of major preference gaps for attributes that are important to buyers in the product category (e.g., internal surgery equipment) of interest to the organization.

Quality Function Deployment

Quality function deployment (QFD) is used to find customer satisfaction opportunities. It is a management system for new-product planning that assures that customer needs drive product design and production processes.[4] Developed in Japan in the early 1970s, QFD offers several potential benefits in guiding new-product planning:

- Product objectives based on customer requirements are not misinterpreted at subsequent stages.
- Particular marketing strategies or "sales points" do not become lost or blurred during the translation process from marketing through planning and on to execution.
- Important production control points are not overlooked—everything necessary to achieve the desired outcome is understood and in place.
- Tremendous efficiency is achieved because misinterpretation of program objectives, marketing strategy, and critical control points—and need for change—are minimized.[5]

EXHIBIT 11–2 Illustrative QFD Planning Matrix

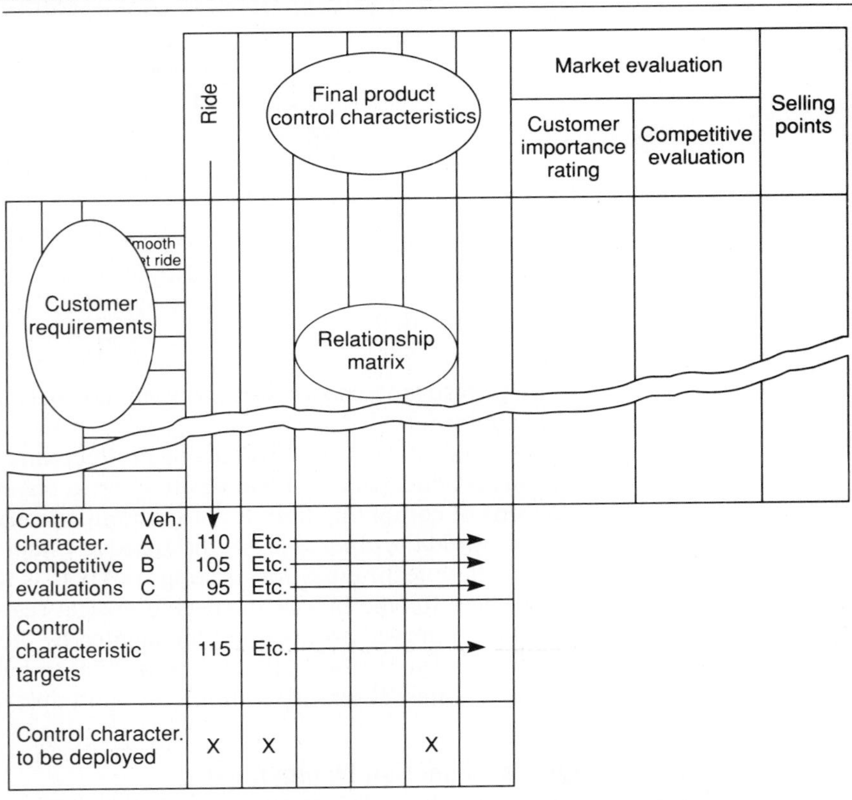

Source: L. P. Sullivan, "Quality Function Deployment," *Quality Progress,* June 1986, p. 46.

QFD is a comprehensive analysis and planning process centered on customer needs. The objective is to translate customer requirements into important final product control characteristics that guide the organization's design, production, and marketing process.[6] QFD involves the use of a two-way matrix relating customer requirements and product characteristics. One of the matrices used in planning a new automobile design is shown in Exhibit 11–2. Several matrices are employed in the overall process:

> The number of phases (or translations) needed to move from general customer requirements to highly specific production process controls varies with the product's complexity. As with much of QFD, there are no absolute rules—use as much or as little as necessary to ensure that key customer requirements will be met every time.[7]

EXHIBIT 11–3 Factors Contributing to the Success of New Products

Percentage of responses

0 10 20 30 40 50 60 70 80 90 100

Product fit with market needs

Product fit with internal functional strengths

Technological superiority of product

Top management support

Use of new product process

Favorable competitive environment

Structure of new product organization

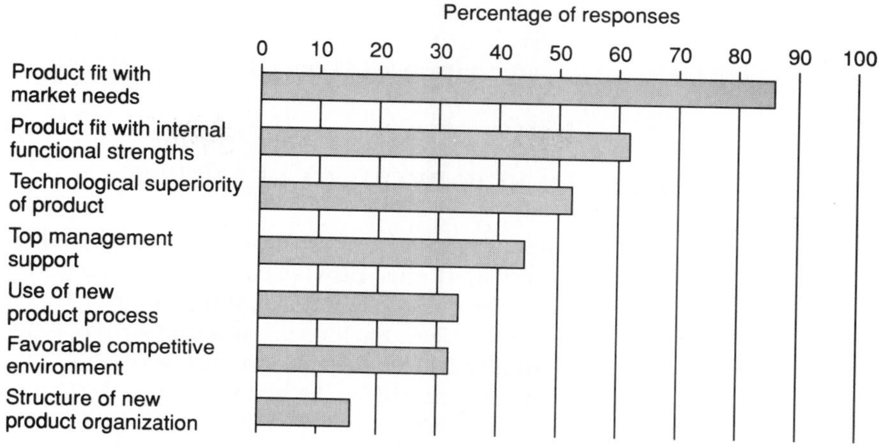

Source: *New Products Management for the 1980s* (New York: Booz, Allen & Hamilton, 1982), p. 16.

Success Criteria

Exhibit 11–3 highlights the factors that contribute to the success of new products, based on responses obtained from more than 700 U.S. manufacturers of over 13,000 new products introduced during a five-year period. The study found some differences between industrial and consumer products firms, as well as across different industries. Technological superiority is considered more important by industrial products firms, while top management support is a greater concern for consumer durable and nondurable companies. The study also found that the importance of these factors varies by the type of new product being developed.

Booz, Allen & Hamilton compare companies that successfully launched new products to those who were unsuccessful. The successful companies have the following characteristics:[8]

Operating philosophy These companies are committed to growth through internally developed new products and follow a formal new-product planning process. Tight idea-screening practices are used.

Organization structures The formal new-product planning structure is located in the research and development or engineering functional area but provides for close cooperation between marketing and R&D functions.

The experience effect With increased new-product experience, companies improve new-product profitability by reducing the cost per introduction. The more new products introduced, the better companies are at developing new products.

Management styles There is an effective matching of management style to new-product development needs. Management is willing to adjust its style to keep up with changing conditions.

STEPS IN NEW-PRODUCT PLANNING

A new product does not have to be a high-technology breakthrough to be successful. It must provide customer satisfaction. Post-it Notes is a big winner for Minnesota Mining & Manufacturing Co.[9] The notepaper pads come in various sizes. Each page has a thin strip of adhesive on the back and can be attached to reports, telephones, walls, and other places. The idea came from a 3M employee (he had used slips of paper to mark songs in his hymn book, but the paper kept falling out). Interestingly, office-supply vendors saw no market for the sticky-back notepaper. The 3M company used extensive sampling to show users the value of the product. Using the name of the 3M chairman's secretary, samples were sent to executive secretaries at all Fortune 500 companies. After using the samples, they wanted more. Today, the product is indispensable in both offices and homes.

Deciding Which Customer Needs to Target

New products help companies achieve corporate and business unit objectives. To define the scope of new products to consider, businesses often formulate guidelines for new-product planning. Management decides the product-markets and market segments in which to compete. These decisions become important guidelines for the new-product planning process. Customer satisfaction analyses determine opportunities for new products and processes.

Consider, for example, the new-product planning activities of companies competing in unified Europe. Meeting the needs of consumers in the 12 nations of the European Community is a complex product planning challenge. Trade restrictions have been reduced, banking regulations altered, and other actions taken to create a unified market. However, the EC is divided by important differences in consumer tastes and national preferences, as shown in this example:

> Pillsbury did extensive research in preparation for a new-product rollout in the United Kingdom last fall. Taste tests in London revealed that the English like their baked goods flaky and dry rather than moist and chewy, and they abhor strong flavors. Pillsbury changed recipes and, because U.K. consumers associate plastic tubes with cheap sausage, repacked its cookie-dough products in plastic tubs.[10]

EXHIBIT 11–4 New-Product Planning Process

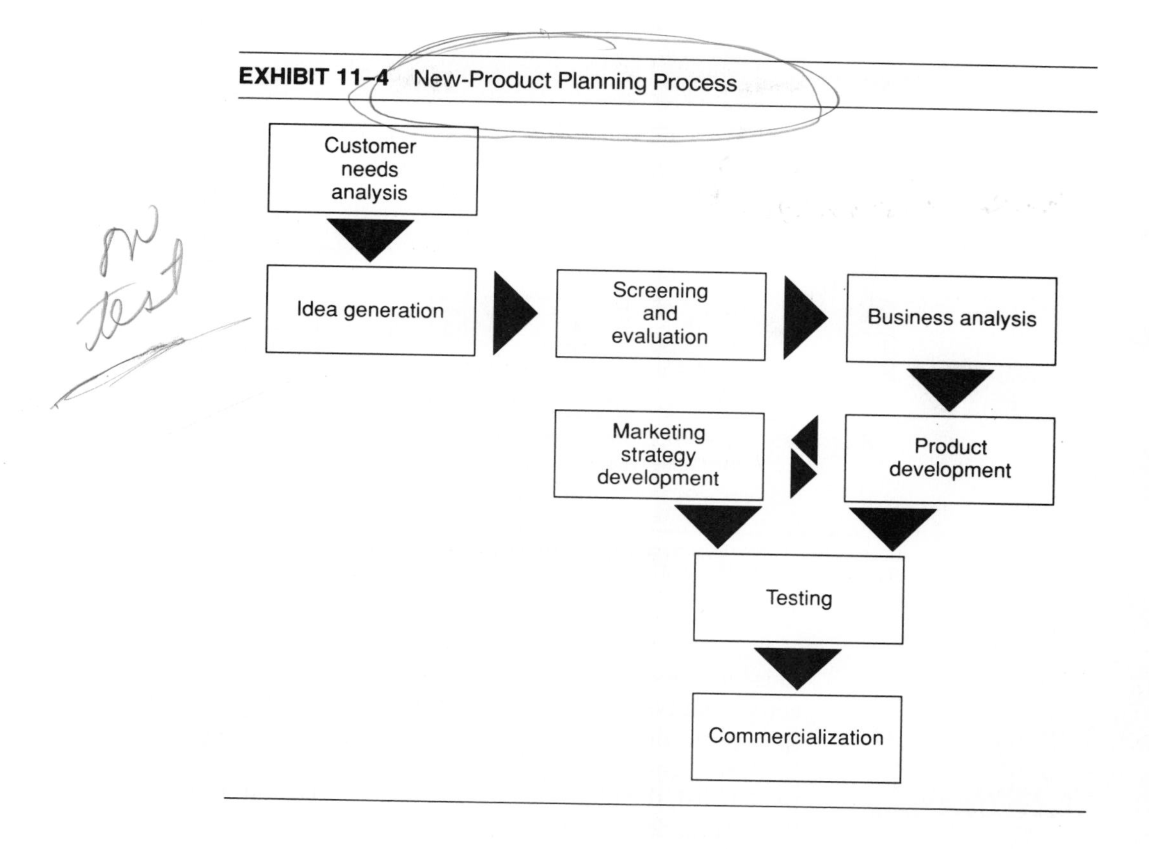

Companies must adapt to local attitudes and buying habits when developing new products and positioning existing products.

New-Product Planning Process

Making new products like 3M Post-it Notes successful requires systematic planning to coordinate the many decisions, activities, and functions necessary to move a new-product idea to commercial success. The major stages in the planning process are shown in Exhibit 11–4. We examine each stage to see what is involved, how the stages depend on each other, and the importance of a coordinated program of new-product planning. There are two key considerations in new-product planning: (1) generating a stream of new-product ideas that will satisfy management's requirements for new products and (2) establishing procedures and methods for evaluating new-product ideas as they move through the planning stages.[11] Customer needs analysis drives the planning process.

Four aspects of the planning process are important in effectively applying it to develop and introduce new products. First, the process involves var-

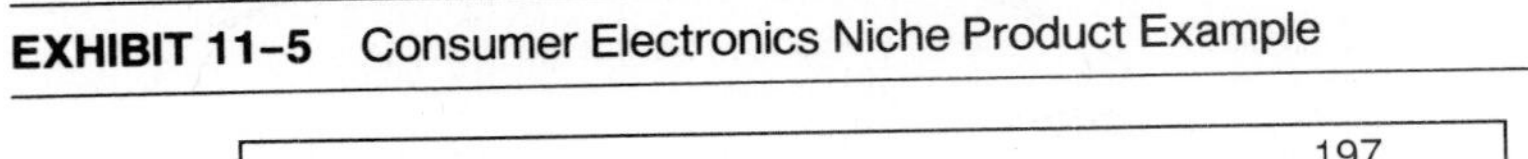

EXHIBIT 11–5 Consumer Electronics Niche Product Example

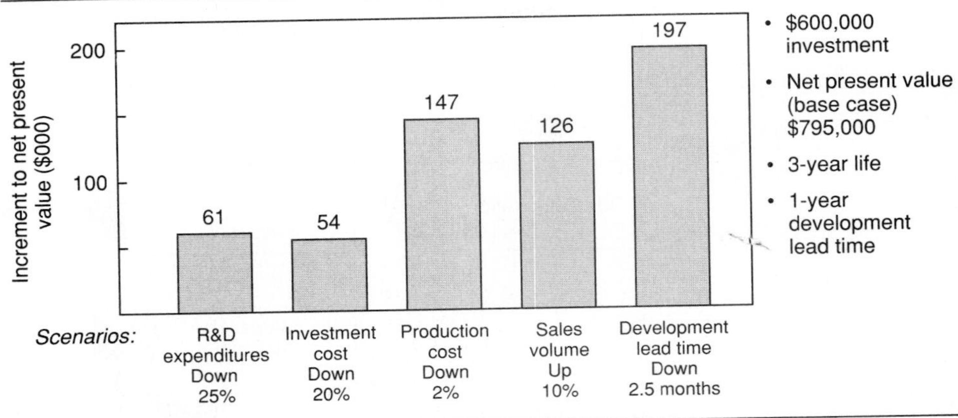

Source: Jean-Phillipe Deschamps and P. Ranganath Nayak, "Competing through Products," *Columbia Journal of World Business*, Summer 1992, p. 41.

ious business functions, so it is essential to develop ways of coordinating the activities involved in the planning process. Second, compressing the time span of product development creates an important competitive advantage. U.S. Surgical's quick response to laparoscopy equipment needs is illustrative. Third, the planning process is expensive and must be managed so that the results deliver high levels of customer satisfaction at acceptable costs. Finally, the planning process is used for new service development as well as for physical products. Certain differences in new service planning are highlighted as we discuss the planning stages.

An evaluation of the financial impact of several different scenarios on the net present value of a consumer electronics niche product is shown in Exhibit 11–5.[12] Reducing the time for developing the new product has a higher financial return than reducing R&D expenditures, investment cost, or production costs. Reducing lead time also has a higher financial return than a 10 percent sales increase. This example shows why many companies are placing a high priority on reducing the time needed to develop new products.

IDEA GENERATION

Finding promising new ideas is the starting point in the new-product development process. Idea generation ranges from incremental improvements to existing products to new-to-the-world products. An example of an incremental improvement is a glaucoma drug comparable to an existing glaucoma drug, but having fewer side effects. An example of a totally new product is a drug that will cure AIDS. Many new-product ideas are incremental improvements.

Sources of Ideas

New-product ideas come from many sources. Limiting the search for new-product ideas to internal research and development activities is far too narrow an approach for most firms. Sources of new-product ideas include company personnel, customers, competitors, outside inventors, acquisition, and channel members. Both solicited and spontaneous ideas may emerge from these sources, and some even occur by accident. Procter & Gamble's Ivory soap, for example, was the result of an accident; overmixing in the manufacturing process created air bubbles in the soap, causing it to float.

The objective is to establish an idea-generation and evaluation program that meets the needs of the enterprise. Answering several questions is helpful in developing an idea generation program:

- Should idea search activities be targeted or open-ended? Should the search for new-product ideas be restricted to ideas that correspond to corporate mission, business segment, and SBU strategies?
- How extensive and aggressive should new-product idea search activities be? Should search be an active or passive function within the firm?
- What specific sources are best for generating a regular flow of new-product ideas?
- How can new ideas be obtained from customers?
- Where will responsibility for new-product idea search be placed? How will new-product planning activities be directed and coordinated?

Research findings indicate that financial performance in high-technology companies is higher for those firms that develop distinctive competence in a core technology.[13] Companies that focus their product strategy performed much better over a long time span than those that did not focus their new-product strategies. These findings came from a study of 236 products across 26 small- and medium-sized companies.

For most firms, the idea search program should probably be targeted within a range of product and market involvement that is consistent with corporate mission and objectives and business unit strategy. While some far-out new-product idea may occasionally change the future of a company, more often open-ended idea search dissipates resources and misdirects efforts.

The favorable performance of several companies argues strongly for pursuing an aggressive and continuing effort of finding and developing new-product ideas. Companies like 3M, Johnson & Johnson, Hewlett-Packard,

NEW-PRODUCT FEATURE How Rubbermaid, Inc. Is Successful with 90 Percent of Its New Products

Rubbermaid introduced over 365 new products in 1992. Sales and earnings grew at an average rate of 15 percent yearly in the past decade. These are the core examples of Rubbermaid's new-product planning:

- The company has an impressive record of spotting trends and bringing innovative products to market.
- Entrepreneurial teams made up of a product manager, research and manufacturing engineers, and financial, sales and marketing executives conceive new-product ideas and move them from the design stage to the marketplace.
- The innovations are incremental product improvements such as a new mailbox that is large enough for magazines, doesn't leak when opened, is rustproof, and shows a flag when the mail is delivered.
- Rubbermaid's differentiated products are premium priced to reflect their good value and quality. The design team is responsible for pricing.
- The company's strong relationships with retailers like Wal-Mart and Kmart help to move new products through the distribution channels.
- Product designs incorporate the needs of retailers (e.g., easy stacking on shelves) as well as end-users.
- The design teams relentlessly work on the details that improve products like brooms, mops, or lunchboxes.

Source: Valerie Reitman, "Rubbermaid Turns Up Plenty of Profit in the Mundane," *The Wall Street Journal,* March 27, 1992, p. B3.

Rubbermaid, and U.S. Surgical develop a continuing flow of new products. The New-Product Feature describes Rubbermaid's use of new-product teams to develop successful products.

It is difficult to generalize about the best idea sources and how to manage new-product planning, since these issues depend on many such factors as the size and type of firm, technologies involved, new-product needs, resources, management's preferences, and corporate capabilities. Management needs to consider these questions and develop a plan for idea generation that will satisfy the firm's requirements.

Many new-product ideas originate with the users of products and services. Lead user analyses offer promising potential for the development of new industrial products.[14] Lead users are companies whose existing needs and requirements identify broad marketplace trends that will develop in the future. The approach is to try to identify these market leaders and to study their needs to improve the productivity of new-product development in product-markets that change rapidly. The objective is to satisfy the lead users' needs, thus accelerating new-product planning.

Methods of Generating Ideas

We examine several ways of obtaining ideas for new products. Typically, a company uses more than one of these options.

Search. Monitoring several information sources may be helpful in identifying new-product ideas. New-product idea publications are available from companies that wish to sell or license ideas they do not wish to commercialize. New technology information is available through commercial and government computerized search services. News sources may also yield information about the new-product activities of competitors. Many trade publications contain new-product announcements. Companies need to identify the relevant search areas and assign responsibility for search to an individual or group.

Marketing Research. Surveys of product end-users identify needs that can be satisfied by new products. One particularly useful technique to identify and evaluate new-product concepts is the focus group, which can be used for both consumer and industrial products. A small group of 8 to 12 people is invited to meet with an experienced moderator to discuss new-product ideas. Idea generation may start with a discussion of the production requirements for a particular product-use situation. Later focus group sessions are used to evaluate product concepts formulated to satisfy the needs identified in the initial session. More than one focus group can be used at each stage in the process. Focus groups can be conducted using channel members and company personnel as well as customers. Several uses of focus groups are described in Exhibit 11–6.

Another consumer research technique used to generate new-product ideas is the advisory panel. These groups are selected to represent the firm's target market. For example, a producer of mechanics' hand tools would include mechanics on the panel. Customer advisory groups are used by companies in various industries, including telecommunications and pharmaceuticals. These groups provide insights and evaluations to new and existing products.

Internal and External Development. Companies' research and development laboratories generate many new-product ideas. For example, AT&T's Bell Laboratories has a world-renowned reputation for state-of-the-art technology.[15] As a result of deregulation, AT&T is placing more emphasis on identifying new-product ideas with commercial potential. A vice president who heads a management group at Bell Laboratories called Venture Technologies is responsible for identifying and evaluating ideas. When the group was first formed, letters were sent to 150 laboratory directors asking for promising ideas outside of AT&T's traditional telephone markets. The directors responded with 800 proposals for new products.

New-product ideas may also originate from development efforts outside the firm. Sources include inventors, private laboratories, and small high-technology firms. Strategic alliances between companies (Chapter 3) may result in identifying new-product ideas as well as sharing responsibility for other activities in new-product planning.

EXHIBIT 11–6 Uses of Focus Groups

Generating New Creative Ideas

Listening to consumers talk about how they use a product or what they like or dislike about a product can provide input for creative teams in developing advertising copy. Advertising agencies often use focus group interviews for this reason.

Uncovering Basic Consumer Needs and Attitudes

In talking about a product or product category, consumers often express basic needs and attitudes that can be useful in generating hypotheses about what may or may not be accepted and about the factors responsible for the perceived similarity or dissimilarity among a set of brands.

Establishing New-Product Concepts

Focus group interviews are particularly useful in providing information on the major strengths and weaknesses of a new-product idea. In addition, the focus group interview can be effective in judging whether strategy-supporting promises of end-benefits have been communicated clearly.

Generating New Ideas about Established Markets

Listening to consumers talk about how they discovered ways to put a product to alternative use can stimulate marketing executives to recognize new uses for old products.

Interpreting Previously Obtained Quantitative Data

In some instances focus group interviews are used as the last step in the research process to probe for detailed reasons behind quantitative test results obtained in earlier marketing research studies.

Source: William R. Dillon, Thomas J. Madden, and Neil H. Firtle, *Marketing Research in a Marketing Environment,* 2nd ed. (Homewood, Ill.: Richard D. Irwin, 1990), p. 160.

Other Idea-Generation Methods. Incentives may be useful to get new product ideas from employees, marketing middlemen, and customers. The amount of the incentive should be high enough to encourage submission. Management should also guard against employees leaving the company and developing a promising idea elsewhere. For this reason many firms require employees to sign secrecy agreements.

Finally, acquiring another firm offers a way to obtain new-product ideas. This strategy may be more cost-effective than internal development and can substantially reduce the lead time required for new-product planning. General Motors' acquisition of Electronic Data Systems (computer systems) is an example.

Idea generation identifies one or more product concepts, which are screened and evaluated. An idea for a new product must be transformed into a defined product concept. A complete product concept is "A statement about selected anticipated product attributes that shows how they will yield selected benefits relative to other products or problem solutions already available."[16] For example, the pump toothpaste dispenser (attribute) offers a simple and quick alternative (benefit) to the traditional tube.

SCREENING, EVALUATING, AND BUSINESS ANALYSIS

Evaluating new ideas is an important part of new-product planning. A successful new product is one that will satisfy management's criteria for commercial success (e.g., sales, profit contribution, market share). Moving too many ideas too far into development and testing is expensive. Management needs a screening and evaluation procedure that will kill unpromising ideas as soon as possible while keeping the risks of rejecting good ideas at acceptable levels. Expenditures build up from the idea stage to the commercialization stage, whereas the risks of developing a bad new product fall as more and more information is obtained about the product and the market. The objective is to eliminate the least promising ideas before too much time and money are invested in them. The tighter the screening procedure, the higher the risk of rejecting a good idea. Based on the specific factors involved, a company should establish a level of risk that is acceptable.

Evaluation occurs regularly as an idea moves through the new-product planning stages. Ideas may be rejected at any stage, even though the objective is to eliminate the poor risks as early as possible in the planning process. The evaluation techniques used at each stage in the planning process are matched to the evaluation task. We illustrate them as the stages in new-product planning are discussed.

Screening

A new-product idea receives an initial screening to determine its strategic fit in the company or business unit. Two questions need to be answered: (1) Is the idea compatible with the organization's mission and objectives? (2) Is the venture commercially feasible? The compatibility of the idea considers factors such as internal capabilities (e.g., development, production, marketing), financial needs, and competitive factors. Commercial feasibility considers market attractiveness, technical feasibility, and social and environmental concerns.

Screening eliminates ideas that are not compatible or feasible for the business. These assessments are often subjective, since management must establish how narrow or wide the screening boundaries should be. For example, managers from two otherwise similar firms may have very different missions and objectives as well as different propensities toward risk. An idea may be strategically compatible in one firm and not in another: "The dimensions on which management evaluates ideas/concepts/products encompass all key management areas and in particular should reflect the corporate idiosyncrasies and unique situational factors."[17]

Some firms use various scoring and rating techniques for the factors considered in the screening process. The result is a score for each idea being screened. Management can set ranges for passing and rejecting. The effectiveness of these methods is highly dependent on gaining agreement on the relative importance of the screening factors from the managers involved.

Evaluation

The boundaries between idea screening, evaluation, and business analysis are not clearly drawn. Some firms combine these evaluation stages. Nevertheless, the distinction is useful. After completing initial screening, each idea that survives receives more comprehensive evaluation. Several of the same factors used in screening may be evaluated in greater depth, including buyers' reactions to the proposed concept.

Concept tests are useful in evaluation and refinement of new-product ideas. The purpose of concept testing is to obtain a reaction to the new-product concept from a sample of potential buyers before the product is developed. Concept tests can be used at various stages in the new-product planning process. The technique supplies important information for reshaping, redefining, and coalescing new-product ideas.[18] Concept tests help to evaluate the relative appeal of ideas or alternative product positionings, supply information for developing the product and marketing strategy, and identify potential market segments. A proposal to conduct a concept test for evaluating alternative investment products is described in Exhibit 11–7.

The concept test is a very useful way to evaluate a product idea very early in the development process. The costs of these tests are reasonable, given the information that can be obtained. Nevertheless, there are some important cautions. The test is a very rough gauge of commercial success. Since an actual product and a commercial setting are not present, the test is somewhat artificial.

The concept test is probably most useful in signaling very favorable or unfavorable product concepts. It also offers a basis for comparing two or more concepts. An important requirement of concept testing is that the product can be expressed as a concept and that the participant has the experience and capability to evaluate the concept.

Business Analysis

Business analysis estimates the commercial performance of the proposed product. Obtaining an accurate financial projection depends on the quality of the revenue and cost forecasts. Business analysis is normally accomplished at several stages in the new-product planning process. The first assessment occurs before the product concept moves into the development stage. Financial projections are refined at later stages.

Revenue Forecasting. The newness of the product, the size of the market, and the competing products all influence the accuracy of revenue projections. In the case of an established market such as breakfast cereals, estimates of total market size can usually be obtained from industry informa-

EXHIBIT 11–7 Project Proposal: New Product Concept Screening Test

Brand:	New products.
Project:	Concept screening.
Background and Objectives:	The New York banking group has developed 12 new-product ideas for investment products (services). The objectives of this research are to assess consumer interest in the concepts and to establish priorities for further development.
Research Method:	Concept testing will be conducted in four geographically dispersed, central location facilities within the New York metropolitan area. Each of the 12 concepts plus 1 retest control concept will be evaluated by a total of 100 men and 100 women with household incomes of $25,000. The following age quotas will be used for both male and female groups within the sample: 18–34 = 50 percent 35–49 = 25 percent 50 & over = 25 percent Each respondent will evaluate a maximum of eight concepts. Order of presentation will be rotated throughout to avoid position bias. Because some of the concepts are in low incidence product categories, user groups will be defined both broadly and narrowly in an attempt to assess potential among target audiences.
Information to Be Obtained:	This study will provide the following information to assist in concept evaluation: Investment ownership. Purchase interest (likelihood of subscription). Uniqueness of new service. Believability. Importance of main point. Demographics.
Action Standard:	In order to identify concepts warranting further development, top-box purchase intent scores will be compared to the top-box purchase intent scores achieved by the top 10 percent of the concepts tested in earlier concept screening studies. Rank order of purchase intent scores on the uniqueness, believability, and importance ratings will also be considered in the evaluation and prioritization of concepts for further development.
Material Requirements:	Fifty copies of each concept.
Cost:	The cost of this research will be $15,000 ± 10 percent.
Timing:	This research will adhere to the following schedule: Field work 1 week Top-line 2 weeks Final report 3 weeks
Supplier:	Burke Marketing Research.

Source: William R. Dillon, Thomas J. Madden, and Neil H. Firtle, *Marketing Research in a Marketing Environment,* 2nd ed. (Homewood, Ill.: Richard D. Irwin, 1990), pp. 642–43.

tion. Several industry associations publish industry forecasts. The more difficult task is estimating the market share that is feasible for a new-product entry. For example, the size of the ready-to-eat (RTE) cereal market can be projected accurately, but estimating the market share of a new cereal brand is far more difficult. A range of feasible share positions can be indicated at the concept stage and used as a basis for preliminary financial projections. Established markets also may have success norms. For example, a 1 percent market share is considered a successful entry for a new RTE cereal. A norm provides a basis for estimating the possibility of reaching a successful level of sales. Accurate forecasts of market acceptance require some type of acceptance test such as a market test.

Preliminary Marketing Plan. An initial marketing strategy is often developed as a part of business analysis. Included are market target(s), positioning concepts, and marketing mix plans. While this plan is preliminary, it encourages strategy development and coordination with marketing, production, and other business functions early in the planning process. The choice of the marketing strategy is necessary in developing the revenue forecast.

Cost Estimation. Several different costs are encountered in the planning and commercialization of new products. One way to categorize the costs is to estimate them for each stage in the new-product planning process (Exhibit 11–4). The costs increase rapidly as the product concept moves through the process. The costs for each planning stage can be further divided into functional categories (e.g., marketing, research and development, and manufacturing).

Profit Projections. Several types of profit projections are used to gauge a new product's financial performance. Illustrative financial analysis techniques are examined in the appendix to Chapter 4. Those appropriate for new-product business analysis include break-even computation, cash flow, return on investment, and profit contribution. Break-even analysis is particularly useful to show how many units of the new product must be sold before it begins to make a profit. Management can use the break-even level to examine the feasibility of the project.

Management needs to determine the appropriate length of time for projecting sales, costs, and profits. For example, the product may be required to recoup all costs within a certain time period. Business analysis estimates should take into consideration the estimated flow of revenues and costs over the time span used in the analysis. Typically, new products incur heavy costs before they start to generate revenues.

Other Considerations. Several issues are considered in the business analysis of a new-product concept. First, management often has guidelines for the financial performance of new products. These can be used to accept, reject, or further analyze the product concept. Another issue is assessing the amount of risk. This factor should be included either in the financial projections or as an additional consideration beyond the financial estimates. Finally, the possible cannibalization of sales by the new product from existing products needs to be considered. New products that are substitutes for existing products often cannibalize sales. For example, a major premise in Gillette's business analysis of the Sensor razor was that its superior shaving effectiveness would attract substantial sales from disposable razors rather than resulting in a major cannibalization of Atra and Trac II sales. Sensor's sales in the first year of introduction (1990) were 25 million razors, compared to a forecast of 10 million.[19] The new razor obtained a higher portion of total sales than was forecast from users of disposable razors shifting to Sensor. It was profitable in the first year of introduction, even with research and development, engineering, and marketing costs totaling $300 million. (See Case 2–3.)

DEVELOPMENT AND TESTING

After successfully completing the business analysis stage, product planning moves to development and testing. During this stage the concept is transformed into one or more prototypes. The prototype is the actual product, but it is produced by research and development (R&D) rather than with an established manufacturing process. The development and testing stage includes manufacturing development as well as product development.

Our earlier discussion of customer-guided new-product design and manufacturing emphasizes the importance of transferring customer preferences into internal guidelines for new-product planning. The methods of quality function deployment are illustrative. Technical people recognize that product design decisions needs to be guided by customer preferences and analysis of competitor advantages and weaknesses. Importantly, the design requirements and costs of design are evaluated in the development stage. Product development should involve the entire new-product planning team.

Product Development

A description of product, package, and service design is shown in Exhibit 11–8. The constraints and guidelines that affect product design are indicated. Since product development is largely a technical activity, our discussion considers the input information to R&D and the output of development and testing.

Product Specifications. R&D needs guidelines in order to develop the product. These specifications describe what the product will do rather than how it should be designed. Product specifications indicate product planners' expectations regarding benefits, including essential physical and operating

EXHIBIT 11–8 Product, Package, and Service Design and Its Determinants

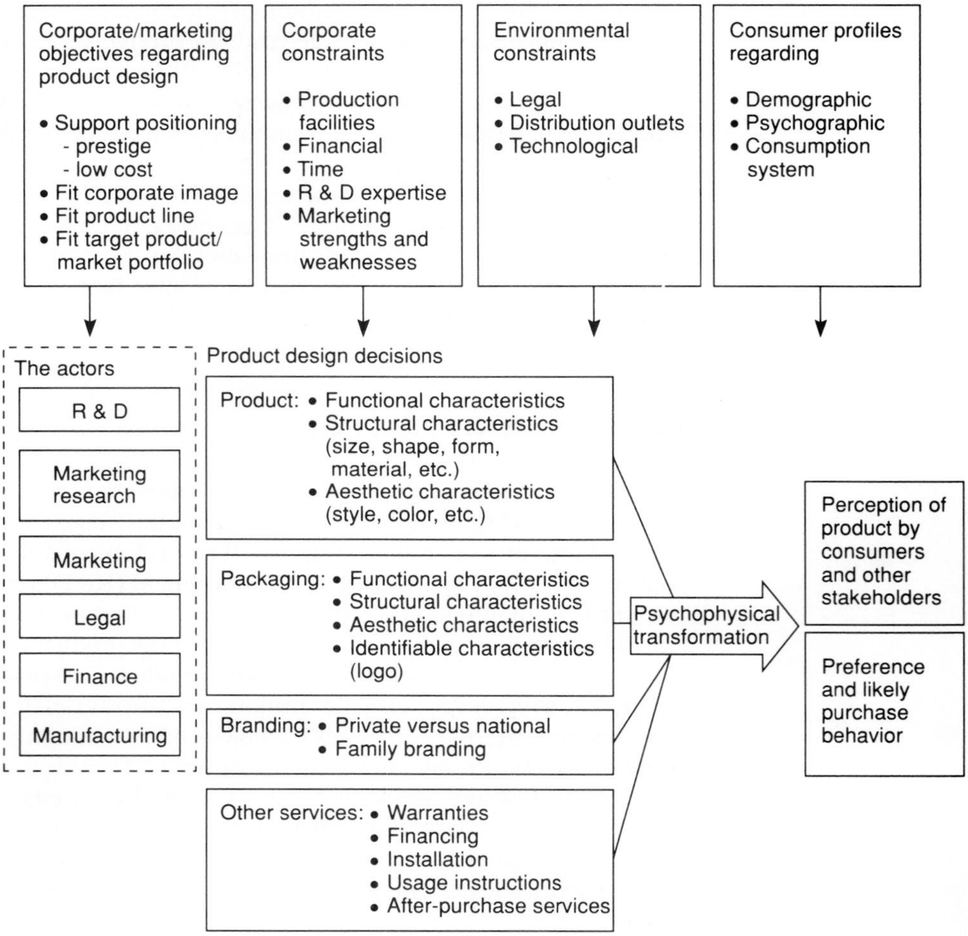

Corporate/marketing objectives regarding product design
- Support positioning
  - prestige
  - low cost
- Fit corporate image
- Fit product line
- Fit target product/market portfolio

Corporate constraints
- Production facilities
- Financial
- Time
- R & D expertise
- Marketing strengths and weaknesses

Environmental constraints
- Legal
- Distribution outlets
- Technological

Consumer profiles regarding
- Demographic
- Psychographic
- Consumption system

The actors
- R & D
- Marketing research
- Marketing
- Legal
- Finance
- Manufacturing

Product design decisions

Product:
- Functional characteristics
- Structural characteristics (size, shape, form, material, etc.)
- Aesthetic characteristics (style, color, etc.)

Packaging:
- Functional characteristics
- Structural characteristics
- Aesthetic characteristics
- Identifiable characteristics (logo)

Branding:
- Private versus national
- Family branding

Other services:
- Warranties
- Financing
- Installation
- Usage instructions
- After-purchase services

Psychophysical transformation

Perception of product by consumers and other stakeholders

Preference and likely purchase behavior

Source: Yoram J. Wind, *Product Policy: Concepts, Methods, and Strategy* (Reading, Mass.: Addison-Wesley, 1982), p. 340.

characteristics.[20] This allows R&D to determine the best physical structure for delivering the benefits.

Recall the earlier discussion of U.S. Surgical's development of laparoscopy equipment. Illustrative specifications for developing this type of product include equipment size, features (e.g., ease of operation), functions to be performed (visual view of inside the patient's body via TV camera), types of material, and cleaning requirements. The more complete the specifications for the product, the better the designers can incorporate the requirements into the design.

Prototype. R&D uses the product specifications to create one or more physical products. At this stage the product is called a prototype, since it is not ready for commercial production and marketing. It is a custom version. Many of the parts may be custom built, and materials, packaging, and other details may differ from the commercial version. Nevertheless, the prototype needs to be able to deliver the benefits spelled out in the specifications. Scale models are used in some kinds of products, such as commercial aircraft. Models can be tested in wind tunnels to evaluate their performance characteristics.

Use Tests. The prototype may be tested in a use situation. If use testing is feasible, designers can obtain important feedback from users concerning how well the product meets the needs included in the product specifications. A standard approach to use testing is to distribute the product to a sample of users, asking them to try the product. Follow-up occurs after each test participant has had enough time to evaluate the product. The design of new industrial products may include the active involvement of users in testing and evaluating the product at various stages in the process. The relatively small number of users in industrial markets compared to consumer markets makes use testing very feasible. Use tests are also popular for gaining user reactions to new consumer products such as foods, drinks, and health and beauty aids.

An example of a proposed use test for a new soup flavor is described in Exhibit 11–9. Unlike a market test, the use test does not identify the brand name of the product or the company name. While the use test is not as indicative of market success as the market test, the use test information yields important information such as preferences, ratings, likes/dislikes, advantages/limitations, unique features, usage and users, and comparisons with competing products.[21]

Manufacturing Development. A company must develop a process for producing the product in commercial quantities. Manufacturing the product at an acceptable cost is a critical determinant of profitability. The new product may be feasible to produce in the laboratory but not in a manufacturing plant because of costs, production rates, and other considerations. Initial production delays can also jeopardize the success of a new product.

The success of the Japanese in penetrating U.S. and European markets with high-quality, value-priced products mandates quality improvement as a top priority throughout U.S. industry. One consequence of improved product quality is that production costs are reduced.[22] By considering quality improvement throughout the design process, the high costs of scrapping and reworking products are avoided. A close working relationship between all business functions is essential to producing high-quality products and services.

EXHIBIT 11–9 Project Proposal: Product Test

Brand:	New product: Hardy Soup.
Project:	Campbell's versus new Hardy Soup blind product test.
Background and Objectives:	R&D has developed a new Hardy Soup in two different flavors (chicken noodle and mushroom). Additionally, each flavor has been developed at two different flavor strengths. The brand groups have requested that research be conducted to determine (1) whether this product should be considered for introduction, (2) if so, if one or both flavors should be introduced, and (3) which flavor variation(s) would be preferred most by the consumer. The objective of this research will be to determine consumers' preferences for each flavor variation of the new product relative to Campbell's Chunky products.
Method:	There will be four cells. In each cell, a blind paired-product test will be conducted between a different flavor variation of the new product and the currently marketed Campbell's product, as follows • Campbell's Chunky Chicken Noodle versus Hardy's Chicken Noodle 1. • Campbell's Chunky Chicken Noodle versus Hardy's Chicken Noodle 2. • Campbell's Chunky Mushroom versus Hardy's Mushroom 1. • Campbell's Chunky Mushroom versus Hardy's Mushroom 2. In each cell, there will be 200 past-30-day ready-to-serve soup user/purchasers. Respondents will be interviewed in a shopping mall and given both products to take home and try. Additionally, respondents must be positively disposed toward chicken noodle or mushroom flavors in order to be used in the test. Order of product trial will be rotated to minimize position bias. Telephone callbacks will be made after one week period.
Action Standard:	Each new soup flavor will be considered for introduction if one or more of its flavor variations achieves at least absolute parity with its Campbell's Chunky control. If for either flavor alternative more than one flavor level variation meets the action standard, the one that is preferred over Campbell's at the highest level of confidence will be recommended to be considered for introduction. A single sample *t*-test for paired comparison data (two-tail) will be used to test for significance.
Cost and Timing:	The cost of this study will be $32,000 ± 10 percent. The following schedule will be established: Field work 2 weeks Top-line 2 weeks Final report 4 weeks
Research Firm:	Burke Marketing Research.

Source: William R. Dillon, Thomas J. Madden, and Neil H. Firtle, *Marketing Research in a Marketing Environment,* 2nd ed. (Homewood, Ill.: Richard D. Irwin, 1990), pp. 664–65.

Japanese new-product designers have modified the planning process (Exhibit 11–4) by determining a target cost based on the price the market is likely to accept for a new product *before* design is initiated.[23] The target cost is an integral part of the planning process. Cost engineers with experience in purchasing, design, and other functions such as sales participate in the planning process to assure that the product meets the desired target cost. This eliminates the need to redesign products whose costs are too high. This planning approach also helps to reduce product development time.

Collaborative Design and Manufacturing. Collaborative research and development partnerships are used to increase the competitive advantage of a single company and reduce the time required to develop and market new products. These relationships may be strategic alliances or supplier-producer collaborations (Chapter 3). The development of Hewlett-Packard's (HP) HP FAX-300 is the result of an alliance between HP and Matsushita, a leading Japanese producer of fax machines.[24] HP applied the technology from its very successful DeskJet printer. Matsushita contributed the fax technology. HP gained important copier cost savings by producing the fax in the same plant as the DeskJet. The result was a plain paper fax at a price competitive with thermal fax machines and far below laser machines.

MARKETING STRATEGY AND TEST MARKETING

Regardless of how new the product actually is, examining the product's entire marketing strategy helps to avoid problems and identify opportunities. Guidelines for marketing strategy depend largely on the new product being developed. A totally new product requires complete targeting and positioning strategies. A product improvement may only need a revised promotion strategy to convey to target buyers information on the benefits the improved product offers.

Marketing Decisions

Product evaluation efforts (e.g., use tests) conducted during product development supply information for designing the marketing strategy. Examples of useful planning guidelines include user characteristics, product features, advantages over competing products, use situations, feasible price range, and buyer information.

The design of the marketing strategy begins as soon as possible in new product planning, since several activities need to be completed and shortening the time to market introduction is an important competitive advantage. Marketing strategy planning can be initiated during product development. Activities such as packaging, environmental considerations, product information, colors, materials, and product safety must also be decided between engineering, manufacturing, and marketing.

Market Targeting. Selection of the market target(s) for the new product range from offering a new product to an existing target to identifying an entirely new group of potential users. A totally new product requires a new targeting strategy (see Chapter 9). Examining the prior marketing research for the new product may yield useful insights as to targeting opportunities.

It may also be necessary to conduct additional research before finalizing the market targeting strategy.

Positioning Strategy. Several positioning decisions are resolved during the marketing strategy development stage. Product strategy regarding packaging, name selection, sizes, and other aspects of the product must be decided. A channel strategy is needed to access new channels of distribution. It is also necessary to formulate a price strategy and to develop an advertising and sales promotion strategy. Testing of advertisements may occur at this stage. Finally, sales management must design a personal selling strategy including deciding about sales force training and allocation of selling effort to the new product.

Market Testing Options

Market testing can be considered after the product is fully developed and if the product is suitable for market testing. Market tests are used to gauge buyer response to the new product and evaluate one or more positioning strategies. Test marketing is used for many consumer products such as foods, beverages, and health and beauty aids. In addition to conventional test marketing, less-expensive alternatives are available. The costs of test marketing are out of reach for many companies.

Simulated Test Marketing. This test method is implemented by recruiting potential buyers while they are shopping:

> The prototypical procedure involves intercepting shoppers at a high-traffic location, sometimes prescreening them for category use, exposing the selected individuals to a commercial (or concept) for a proposed new product, giving them an opportunity to buy the new product in a real life or laboratory setting, and interviewing those who purchased the new product at a later date to ascertain their reaction and repeat-purchase intentions.[25]

These tests offer several advantages, including speed (12 to 16 weeks), low cost ($40,000 to $85,000 compared to an excess of $1 million for full-scale market tests), and relatively accurate forecasts of market response.[26] They also eliminate the risk in conventional testing that competitors will jam the test.

Scanner-Based Test Marketing. This method is less artificial than simulated testing and is less expensive than the conventional market test. Information Resources Inc.'s BehaviorScan system pioneered the use of cable television and a computerized database to track new products. The system uses information and responses from 2,500 panel members in each test city. Each member has an identification card to show to participating store cashiers. Purchases are electronically recorded and transmitted to a central data bank. Cable television enables this system to use controlled advertisement testing.

Firms can use scanner testing to evaluate various aspects of marketing strategy, including what kind of advertising attracts different people. BehaviorScan was useful in determining that the audience for TV's "General Hospital" buys 25 percent more granola bars than the average viewer.[27] BehaviorScan tests take about 12 months and costs over $250,000, which is still one quarter or less than conventional testing.

Conventional Test Marketing. Market testing puts the product under actual market conditions in one or more test cities. It is used for frequently purchased consumer products. Test marketing uses a complete marketing program including advertising and personal selling. Product sampling is often an important factor in launching the new product in the test market. The product is marketed on a commercial basis in the test cities, and test results are then projected to the national or regional target market. Because of its high cost, conventional test marketing represents the final evaluation before full-scale market introduction. Firms sometimes decide not to test market in order to avoid competitor awareness and high testing costs and to accelerate introduction.

Testing Industrial Products. Market testing can be used for various industrial products. Selection of test sites may need to extend beyond one or two cities to include sufficient market coverage. The test firm has substantial control of an industrial products test since it can use direct mail and personal selling. The relatively small number of customers also aids targeting of marketing efforts. The product should have the characteristics necessary for testing: It should be producible in test quantities, relatively inexpensive, and not subject to extensive buying center influences throughout the organization.

Factors in Test Marketing. Many factors are important in testing, such as selecting good test sites, determining the length of the test, controlling for external influences on the test (such as competition), and interpreting results. A. C. Nielsen's experience indicates that about 75 percent of products that are test marketed are successful, compared to an 80 percent failure rate for new products that are not fully tested.[28]

Selecting Test Sites. Test sites should have the buyer and environmental characteristics of the commercial market target. Since no site is perfect, the objective is to find a reasonable match between the test and commercial market. Each test city should be isolated from other cities, contain people generally comparable to the market target profile, have a representative media mix, offer research and audit services, provide a diversified socioeconomic cross-section of people, and show no unusual environmental characteristics.[29]

America's best metropolitan test markets are profiled in Exhibit 11–10. These areas are ranked according to an "index of dissimilarity."[30] The index takes into account age, race, and housing value (proxy for income). Detroit has the lowest cumulative index value of the 20 best metropolitan areas. An

EXHIBIT 11–10 America's Best Test Markets

Rank	*Metropolitan Area*	*1990 Population*	*Cumulative Index*	*Housing-Value Index*	*Age Index*	*Race Index*
1	Detroit, MI	4,382,000	22.8	11.8	1.5	9.5
2	St. Louis, MO-IL	2,444,000	22.8	15.1	1.6	6.2
3	Charlotte-Gastonia-Rock Hill, NC-SC	1,162,000	24.1	13.5	2.7	7.9
4	Fort Worth-Arlington, TX	1,332,000	25.0	17.0	5.9	2.2
5	Kansas City, MO-KS	1,566,000	25.4	17.9	2.7	4.8
6	Indianapolis, IN	1,250,000	25.5	16.7	2.4	6.3
7	Philadelphia, PA-NJ	4,857,000	26.7	18.0	1.7	7.1
8	Wilmington, NC	120,000	27.2	15.1	4.1	8.0
9	Cincinnati, OH-KY-IN	1,453,000	27.2	19.1	1.6	6.6
10	Nashville, TN	985,000	27.6	18.5	2.9	6.2
11	Dayton-Springfield, OH	951,000	27.6	19.5	1.9	6.2
12	Jacksonville, FL	907,000	27.6	17.2	2.5	7.9
13	Toledo, OH	614,000	27.8	20.0	2.4	5.5
14	Greensboro-Winston-Salem-High Point, NC	942,000	27.8	17.6	2.9	7.3
15	Columbus, OH	1,377,000	28.4	19.0	3.8	5.7
16	Charlottesville, VA	131,000	28.5	16.9	6.3	5.2
17	Panama City, FL	127,000	28.6	20.1	2.6	6.0
18	Pensacola, FL	344,000	28.7	21.8	2.2	4.7
19	Milwaukee, WI	1,432,000	28.8	23.4	1.4	4.1
20	Cleveland, OH	1,831,000	28.9	18.2	3.4	7.4

Note: An index of zero indicates that the area's demographics match the United States perfectly.
Source: Judith Waldrop, "All-American Markets," *American Demographics,* January 1992, p. 26.

index of zero is a perfect match to overall U.S. demographics. Detroit's 23 is a very good score.

Length of the Test. The length of the test affects the test results. A. C. Nielsen's analyses of more than 100 market tests of new-brand introductions indicate that the predictability of national results from test market data increases significantly with time.[31] After 4 months of testing, 37 percent of the predictions were correct; after 18 months, the figure was 100 percent. Manufacturers need 10 months to be reasonably sure that market share data are representative. Market tests of more than a year are common.

External Influences. Probably the most troublesome external factor that may affect test market results is competition that does not operate on a normal basis. Competitors may attempt to drive test market results awry by increasing or decreasing their marketing efforts and making other changes in their marketing actions. It is also important to monitor the test market environment to identify other unusual influences during the test period. For example, unusual economic conditions may affect test results for some products.

New-Product Models

New-product models are useful in analyzing test market data and predicting commercial market success. Some of the newer models also consider the effects of marketing mix components. Product newness and repurchasability are useful for classifying the models.[32] They fall into two categories: (1) first-purchase models designed to predict the cumulative number of new-product tries over time, and (2) models designed to predict the repeat purchase rate of those buyers who have tried the product. The latter type combines a first-purchase model with a repeat-purchase model. A brief overview of the consumer adoption process for new products sets the stage for our look at the two types of models.

Consumer Adoption Process. Research concerning the adoption of innovations indicates that (1) new-product adopters follow a sequence of stages in their adoption process; (2) their characteristics vary according to how soon they adopt the product after introduction; and (3) adoption findings may be of value in new-product planning. The adoption stages are awareness, interest, evaluation, trial, and adoption.[33] By finding and targeting such "early adopters," firms may be able to accelerate a new product's adoption. Rogers has found early adopters to be younger, of generally higher socioeconomic status, and more in contact with impersonal and cosmopolitan sources of information than later adopters.[34] The early adopter also uses a variety of information sources and is more cosmopolitan than the later adopters.

First-Purchase Models. These models are based on the diffusion of the new product into the market. The models generate a life-cycle sales curve using a mathematical model that contains a small number of parameters.[35] The parameters are estimated based on the experiences of similar products, consumer pretests, or early sales results. The models range from simple exponential curve fitting using market potential and rate of penetration as parameters, to more complex, multistage models. Mahajan and Peterson have developed a comprehensive critique and comparative assessment of first-purchase diffusion models of new-product acceptance.[36]

Repeat-Purchase Models. Many consumer and industrial new products are nondurables that are repurchased on a regular basis. Models are available for projecting sales of these products and for evaluating marketing program positioning strategy combinations. The ASSESSOR model illustrates this group of models.[37] It evaluates the new product before test marketing but after decisions have been made regarding positioning strategy. Management can use this information in combination with direct behavior and attitude data obtained from laboratory and usage tests to make market share predictions and diagnostic information. Trial/repeat and attitude models are built into the structure of ASSESSOR. The model uses two parallel approaches (trial/repeat and preference models) to estimate the brand's market share. This is a key feature. The use of a laboratory facility and a simulated shopping experiment is also innovative. Applications typically use samples of 300 people.

New-product models such as ASSESSOR are very data-dependent and complex. Their validity has not been fully tested, although for certain kinds of applications the results have been promising. Strengths of such models include their capacity to analyze interrelationships among several variables and to generate outputs based on input data. Applications appear most appropriate for frequently purchased nondurable products that are not totally new, so that purchasers have some experience with the product category. Model applications like ASSESSOR are expensive, but their cost is a small fraction of that of market tests or full-scale commercializations.[38] Considering the stakes involved in the introduction of new products, the use of modeling to reduce risks is likely to expand in the future.

COMMERCIALIZATION

Introducing new products into the market includes finalizing the marketing plan, coordinating introduction activities with business functions, implementing the marketing strategy, and monitoring and controlling the product launch. Commercialization of the Hewlett-Packard palmtop personal computer was very effective. It is targeted to business users who want a very small computer with built-in software. Its impressive capabilities and sound marketing plan resulted in a very successful market entry for the HP95LX palmtop PC (see the accompanying advertisement for product description).

The Marketing Plan

The commercialization stage requires a complete marketing strategy. It should be coordinated with the various people responsible for the introduction, including salespeople, sales managers, and managers in other functional areas such as production, distribution, finance, and human resources. Responsibility for the new-product launch is normally assigned to the marketing manager or product manager. Companies may form product planning and market introduction teams, as illustrated by Rubbermaid in the New-Product Feature.

The timing and geographical scope of the launch are important decisions. The options range from a national market introduction to an area-by-area rollout. In some instances the scope of the introduction may extend to

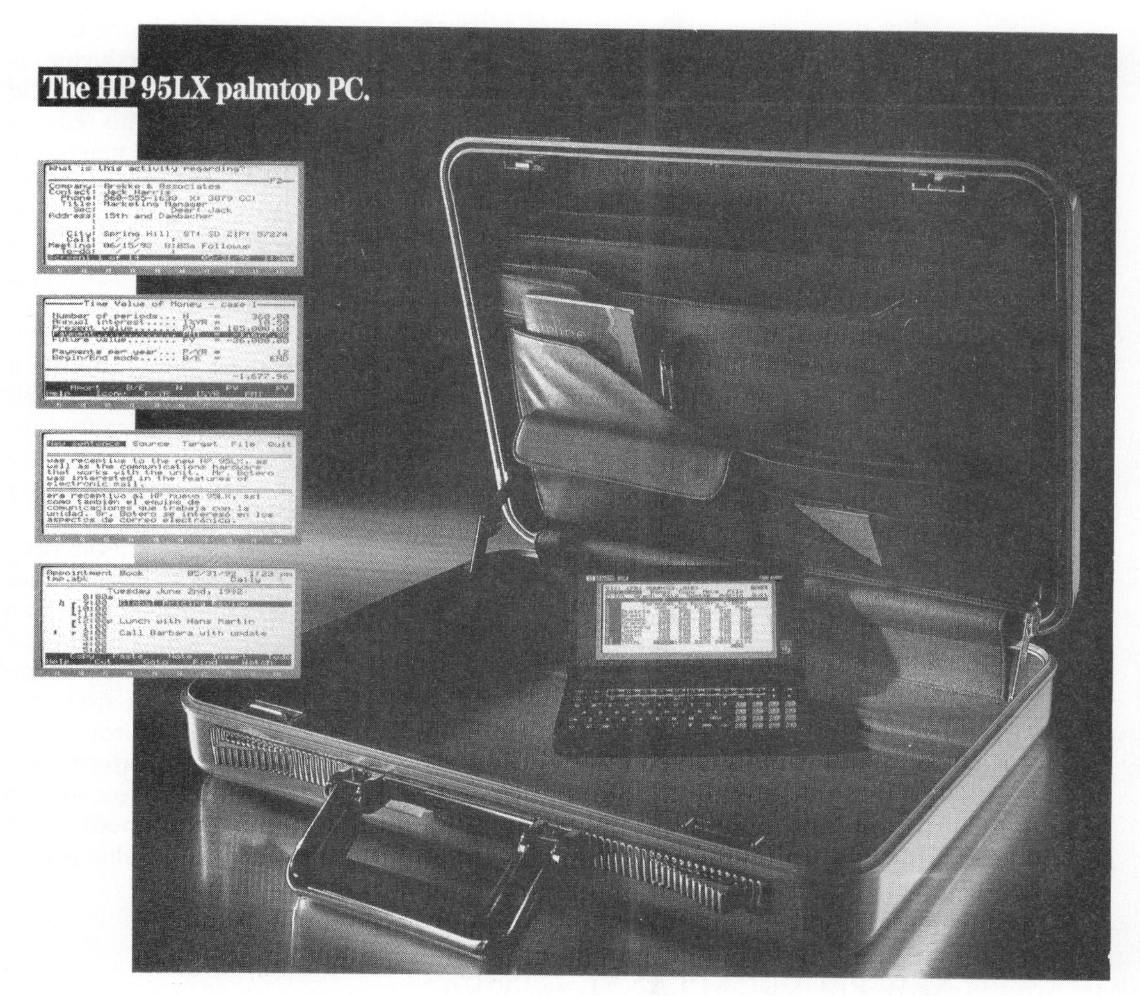
The HP 95LX palmtop PC.

Don't forget to pack your office.

Just because you're out of the office doesn't mean you have to be away from your critical business information. Now you can transfer your files and take them with you. With the HP 95LX. An MS-DOS® based computer that measures just 6.3" x 3.4" x 1" (closed).

The HP 95LX is packed with built-in software. Lotus® 1-2-3® lets you take your spreadsheets with you. Do "what ifs." And attend meetings with all the latest figures. Phone Book allows you to instantly access names, phone numbers and addresses. Appointment Book lets you monitor your schedule. There's even Memo Editor. And, of course, a powerful HP financial calculator.

Dozens of optional applications are also available. For example, SkyStream receives messages wirelessly. Money Manager tracks monthly expenses. ACT! manages client data. Globalink translates languages. And IntelliLink interacts with Microsoft® Windows.

The HP 95LX applications reside in the 1-Mbyte ROM. There's up to 1-Mbyte RAM for *your* files. And with the plug-in slot, plenty of software and memory can be added.

Call 800-443-1254, Dept. 26 for details and U.S. retailer locations. In Canada, call 800-387-3867. After all, you're going places.

HEWLETT
PACKARD

Courtesy of Hewlett-Packard; photography by Robert Mizono

international markets. For example, Kodak's new Ektar 35-millimeter film was introduced throughout the world in 1989. The national introduction is a major endeavor, requiring a comprehensive implementation effort. Some firms prefer to introduce the product on a stage-by-stage basis. This reduces the scope of the introduction and enables management to adjust marketing strategy based on experience gained in the early stages of the launch. One limitation of the rollout approach is that, like market testing, rollout gives the competition more time to react.

Monitoring and Control

Real-time tracking of new-product performance at the commercialization stage is extremely important. Standardized information services are available for monitoring sales of products such as foods, health and beauty aids, and prescription drugs. Information is collected through store audits, consumer diary panels, and scanner services. Special studies may be necessary for products that are not included in standardized information services.

It is important to include product performance standards in the new-product plan to evaluate how well the product is performing. Performance targets often include profit contribution, sales, market share, and return on investment objectives—including the time horizon for reaching objectives. It is also important to establish values for objectives that indicate unacceptable performance. For example, market share threshold levels are sometimes used to gauge new-product performance. Regular measures of customer satisfaction are also important measures of market performance. Management can designate zones for new-product performance, such as very good, acceptable, poor, and unacceptable. Management needs to be prepared to drop a new product if it is apparent that unacceptable performance will continue.

NEW-PRODUCT PLANNING ISSUES

We conclude the chapter with a discussion of several issues that influence developing and marketing new products. These include applying the planning process to services, encouraging interfunctional teamwork, standardization of products in international markets, and the environmental and ethical aspects of new products.

Product Planning for Services

The selection of new service ideas for development and commercialization generally follows the same new-product planning phases as do physical products. Since services are intangible, when applying the planning process intangibility must be taken into account. Several implications also result because services cannot be produced and stocked for consumption.

Service ideas can be evaluated through concept tests. The potential user can be given a description of the new service idea using various attributes of the service. Exhibit 11–7 describes a concept test for a new financial service. Potential buyers should have no difficulty evaluating this concept.

In developing a service firms may need people with experience that is different from the experience of scientists and engineers who design physical products. Customer involvement in the process may be necessary to evaluate the features of alternative designs. Test marketing of new services may be more feasible than testing physical products, particularly if extensive facilities and equipment are not necessary to provide the service. A new banking service may be relatively inexpensive to test market. Alternatively, market testing a new hotel design requires constructing and operating the facility.

Interfunctional Teamwork

Finding new-product ideas and moving them to the marketplace involves several business functions, including accounting, finance, information systems, human resources, marketing, purchasing, manufacturing, research and development, and general management. Companies that are successful in their new-product planning are increasingly assigning multifunctional teams the responsibility (and authority) to move new-product ideas through the planning process.

Companies are also involving their customers and suppliers in new-product planning. Boeing's planning of its new 777 commercial airliner is an example of a customer-driven planning process:

> Boeing invited eight airlines to participate in design discussions more than two and a half years before the project officially got off the ground. The result is a collaborative relationship that extends from Boeing's top management to the design-build teams that include design professionals from United, the 777's first customer.[39]

Boeing's subcontractors are also employing cross-functional approaches, using teams to integrate design and manufacturing processes.

Globalization and Product Standardization

Global competition in many markets creates product standardization challenges. Buyers want diversity in their choices. Producers want scale economies to lower costs. These requirements may be resolved through the process of mass customization. Firms that are capable of flexible manufacturing are better able to adapt to customer needs, program production processes, and create competitive products that are customized. This illustration shows how mass customization works:

> The National Bicycle Industrial Company in Kokuby, Japan, builds made-to-order bicycles on an assembly line. Bicycles, fitted to each customer's measurements, are delivered within two weeks of the order—and the company offers 11,231,862 variations on its models, at prices only 10 percent higher than ready-made models.[40]

Environmental and Ethical Concerns

Environmental contamination and the depletion of natural resources can be addressed on a proactive basis by incorporating these concerns into new-product planning analysis and decisions. Many ethical issues are also created by new products. The importance of environmental and ethical concerns is escalating in the 1990s. These complex issues create challenges in designing, packaging, using, and disposing of products.

Rubbermaid, Inc. responded to ecological concerns in its design of the successful "Litterless Lunch Box."[41] The container is designed to eliminate drink boxes, aluminum foil, and plastic wrap. This concept of eco-eating began in Canada. One of Rubbermaid's retailers, Canadian Tire, asked the company to develop the lunch box. The product is a major success in Canada and the United States. In addition to an effective functional design, the box helps kids to be actively involved in solving environmental problems.

SUMMARY

New-product planning is a vital activity in every company. It applies to services as well as physical products. Companies that are successful in new-product planning follow a formal process of new-product planning combined with effective organization structures for managing new products. Experience helps these firms to improve product planning over time. The corporate cultures of companies like Rubbermaid are responsive to the demands of new-product planning.

The steps in new-product planning include customer needs analysis, idea generation, screening and evaluation, business analysis, product development, marketing strategy development, market testing, and commercialization (Exhibit 11–4).

Idea generation starts the process of planning for a new product. The idea is evaluated as it moves through the process and the costs of new-product planning accumulate. There are various internal and external sources of new-product ideas. Ideas are generated by information search, marketing research, research and development, incentives, and acquisition. Screening, evaluation, and business analysis help determine if the new-product concept is sufficiently attractive to justify proceeding with development.

Development and testing transform the product from a concept to a prototype. Product development creates one or more prototypes. Use testing gains user reaction to the prototype. Manufacturing development determines how to produce the product in commercial quantities at costs that will enable the firm to price the product at a level attractive to buyers. Marketing strategy development begins early in the product planning process. A complete marketing strategy is needed for a totally new product. Product line additions, modifications, and other changes require a less-extensive development of marketing strategy.

Completion of the product design and marketing strategy moves the process to the market testing stage. At this point management often wants some form of user reaction to the new product. Testing options include simulated test marketing, scanner-based test marketing, and conventional test marketing. Industrial products are not tested as much as consumer products, although frequently purchased nondurables can be tested. Instead, use tests of product prototypes are more typical for industrial products. Commercialization completes the planning process, moving the product toward sales and profit performance objectives.

Several product planning issues need to be considered. The process can be used to plan new services as well as physical products. Interfunctional new-product teams are being used by several successful firms like Boeing, Hewlett-Packard, and Rubbermaid. Flexible manufacturing processes enable companies to customize their products while producing them at competitive costs. Finally, environmental and ethical concerns should be included in companies' new-product planning. There is an opportunity to respond to these concerns during the planning process rather than after the product is in the marketplace.

QUESTIONS FOR REVIEW AND DISCUSSION

1. Discuss the relationship between customer satisfaction and quality function deployment.
2. In many consumer products companies, marketing executives seem to play the lead role in new-product planning, whereas research and development executives occupy this position in firms with very complex products such as electronics. Why do these differences exist? Do you agree that such differences should occur?
3. Discuss the features and limitations of focus group interviews for use in new product planning.
4. Identify and discuss the important issues in selecting an organizational approach for new-product planning.
5. Discuss the issues and trade-offs of using tight evaluation versus loose evaluation procedures as a product concept moves through the planning process to the commercialization stage.
6. What factors affect the length of the new-product planning process?
7. Compare and contrast the use of scanner tests and conventional market tests.
8. Is the use of a single city test market appropriate? Discuss.

9. What is the relationship of new-product strategy to corporate and marketing strategies?
10. Do you believe the strategic importance of new products will increase or decrease during the next decade? Support your argument.

NOTES

1. "Getting Hot Ideas from Customers," *Fortune,* May 18, 1992, pp. 86–87.
2. Ibid.
3. *New Products Management for the 1980s* (New York: Booz, Allen & Hamilton, 1982), p. 8.
4. L. P. Sullivan, "Quality Function Deployment," *Quality Progress,* June 1986, pp. 39–50.
5. Ibid., p. 40.
6. Sullivan, "Quality Function Deployment," pp. 39–50.
7. Ronald M. Fortuna, "Quality of Design," in *Total Quality: An Executive's Guide for the 1990s* (Homewood, Ill.: Business One Irwin, 1990), p. 119.
8. *New Products Management for the 1980s,* pp. 17–18.
9. Lawrence Ingrassia, "By Improving Scratch Paper, 3M Gets New-Product Winner," *The Wall Street Journal,* March 31, 1983, p. 27.2.
10. Phil Davies, "Europe Unbound," *Express,* Spring 1992, p. 19.
11. *New Products Management for the 1980s,* p. 11.
12. Jean-Phillipe Deschamps and P. Ranganath Nayak, "Competing through Products," *Columbia Journal of World Business,* Summer 1992, pp. 40–41.
13. Marc H. Meyer and Edward B. Roberts, "Focusing Product Technology for Corporate Growth," *Sloan Management Review,* Summer 1988, pp. 8–16.
14. Glen L. Urban and Eric von Hippel, "Lead User Analyses for the Development of New Industrial Products," *Management Science,* May 1988, pp. 569–82.
15. Janet Guyon and Charles W. Stevens, "AT&T's Bell Labs Adjusts to Competitive Era," *The Wall Street Journal,* August 13, 1985, p. 6.
16. Crawford, *New Products Management,* pp. 352–53.
17. Yoram J. Wind, *Product Policy: Concepts, Methods, and Strategy* (Reading, Mass.: Addison-Wesley, 1982), pp. 303–4.
18. William R. Dillon, Thomas J. Madden, and Neil H. Firtle, *Market Research in a Marketing Environment,* 2nd ed. (Homewood, Ill.: Richard D. Irwin, 1990), p. 639.
19. Subrata N. Chakravarty, "We Had to Change the Playing Field," *Forbes,* February 4, 1991, p. 83.
20. C. Merle Crawford, *New Products Management* (Homewood, Ill.: Richard D. Irwin, 1983), pp. 352–53.
21. Dillon, Madden, and Firtle, *Marketing Research,* p. 667.
22. W. Edwards Deming, *Out of the Crisis* (Cambridge, Mass.: Massachusetts Institute of Technology, Center for Advanced Engineering Study, 1986).
23. Ford S. Worthy, "Japan's Smart Secret Weapon," *Fortune,* August 12, 1991, pp. 72–75.
24. "Hewlett-Packard's Generation Gap," *AdWeek's Marketing Week,* November 4, 1991, pp. 34–35.
25. Dillon, Madden, and Firtle, *Marketing Research,* p. 732.
26. Ibid.
27. Eleanor Johnson Tracy, "Testing Time for Test Marketing," *Fortune,* October 29, 1984, p. 76.
28. Lee Adler, "Test Marketing—And Its Pitfalls," *Sales & Marketing Management,* March 15, 1982, p. 78.
29. "S&MM's Special Test Marketing Sec-

tion," *Sales & Marketing Management,* March 15, 1982, p. 76.

30. Judith Waldrop, "All-American Markets," *American Demographics,* January 1992, pp. 24–28.
31. "The True Test of Test Marketing Is Time," *Sales & Marketing Management,* March 15, 1982, p. 76.
32. Gary L. Lilien and Philip Kotler, *Marketing Decision Making* (New York: Harper & Row, 1983), Chapter 19.
33. Everett M. Rogers, *Diffusion of Innovations* (New York: Free Press, 1962).
34. Ibid.
35. Lilien and Kotler, *Marketing Decision Making,* p. 706.
36. Vijay Mahajan and Robert A. Peterson, "First-Purchase Diffusion Models of New-Product Acceptance," *Technological Forecasting and Social Change* 15 (1979), pp. 127–46.
37. Glen L. Urban and John R. Hauser, *Decision and Marketing of New Products* (Englewood Cliffs, N.J.: Prentice-Hall, 1980), pp. 397–405.
38. Ibid., p. 387.
39. "Timing Is Everything in Product Development Strategy," *Focus,* National Center for Manufacturing Sciences, October 1991, p. 3.
40. Regis McKenna, "Marketing Is Everything," *Harvard Business Review,* January–February 1991, p. 72.
41. Jon Berry, "Rubbermaid Packs an Ecological Lunch," *AdWeek's Marketing Week,* September 9, 1991, p. 10.

Cases for Part III

CASE 3–1 Intuit Corporation

This past February, on the day postal rates jumped from a quarter to 29 cents, I visited my local post office. So did a lot of other people. Not that anything was different there. The clerks had still opened only one window out of a possible three, thus creating a line that was 10 deep. And the one guy on duty had run out of 4 cent stamps.

OK, so the post office hasn't yet discovered customer service. But every other organization seems to have gone nuts over it. Hotels virtually beg you to fill out those little cards telling them where they messed up. Retailers trumpet their money-back guarantees, manufacturers their toll-free numbers (Questions? Complaints? Call 1-800-WELOVE-U). Banks—banks!—stay open later and promise no-hassle loan applications. Or at least they did before they quit lending money.

Most companies, of course, stop right there. They want customers to feel fawned over, but they rarely seem to care whether those same customers actually go away happy. My health club, for example, uses the ubiquitous tell-us-how-we-can-do-better cards. But do the people who run it really need me to tell them the rowing machines are busted half the time? And if they cared about customer satisfaction, as opposed to the semblance of customer service, wouldn't they just fix the damn machines?

The fact is, the icons of customer service—800 numbers, guarantees, suggestion cards, and surveys—have become no more than a ticket of admission to today's marketplace. They no longer confer a competitive advantage; indeed, they may even be liabilities. (Customers who get curt responses from that toll-free line will be madder than if they had never called.) They cost money, and they don't deliver commensurate benefits.

And yet, as long as we're on the subject of customer service, let your imagination run wild. Suppose your company could *really* satisfy its customers. Suppose you could provide a product or service that was better than they expected, for less money than anybody else charged. Suppose that every time you brought out something new it was just what buyers wanted. Suppose your after-sale service was so good that customers with problems went away feeling better than before.

What would happen? Easy—you'd own your marketplace. People would buy from you over and over again, would relish the experience, would never even dream about doing business with anybody else. They would proselytize on your behalf, telling their friends and associates to buy from you. You'd hardly need salespeople.

Impossible, you say. Farfetched. Then again, you haven't met Scott Cook, and you probably don't know much about his company, Intuit Inc. All those statements apply to Intuit. Better yet, Cook has figured out how to build that kind of customer orientation into the organizational bricks and mortar of his company.

"Operating without a safety net," the 38-year-old president calls it. Or "the Toyota approach." Or simply "getting it right." Whatever—it's partly a matter of management techniques, partly a matter of fundamental philosophy. And it's what sets Cook's company way, way apart from the competition.

Intuit makes microcomputer software. Its flagship product is Quicken, a program that allows consumers and small businesses to write checks and keep track of their finances on a personal computer. Owning the marketplace? Quicken is probably the most successful personal-finance program ever written, holding a market share estimated at 60 percent. "It has become the brand-name product in what would otherwise be a commodity business," says Jeffrey Tarter, editor of the industry publication *Softletter*. "It's the Kleenex or Xerox of its market." Intuit, accordingly, has been exploding. It ranked #15 on the 1990 *Inc.* 500. Revenues last year hit $33 million, up from $19 million the year before. After-tax earnings were into double digits.

Granted, the software industry has always been populated by hotshot fast-growth companies. But Intuit doesn't fit the conventional mold. Unlike, say, Lotus, it started without venture capital or other early advantages. (See box, "Wager: One Company.") Unlike VisiCorp or Wordstar, it has dominated its marketplace through several generations of software, beating back waves of would-be competitors. Consumers yank Quicken off the shelves

WAGER: ONE COMPANY

Scott Cook's Year of Living Dangerously

May 1, 1985. Almost six years later, Scott Cook still remembers the date. "It was the worst day of my life," he says.

Who would disagree? His company, Intuit, was less than two years old. And he had to tell his seven employees he could no longer pay their salaries.

Cook knew he had a promising product, an easy-to-use check-writing program for personal computers. What he didn't have was money.

The dozens of venture capitalists he had approached scarcely gave him a second glance. The $350,000 he himself had sunk into Intuit, a sum pieced together from life savings and home-equity credit, from credit cards and loans from his father, was nearly gone. Without money, he had no distribution channels and no customers. What computer store would carry an unknown software product—unsupported by advertising?

Intuit's sales so far had been a kind of good-news-bad-news joke. The good news: Cook had persuaded a few banks to sell the program in their lobbies. Each one ordered several hundred copies for inventory when it signed up, generating a little cash. The bad news: banks were lousy at selling software, so reorders were slim. Knowing he had to get the program into computer stores, he scrambled to sell to just a few more banks.

By the summer of 1986 Cook's efforts had just barely paid off. The little company had $125,000, enough to start an ad campaign. By rights he and his colleagues should have done some tests. But there was no time, not if they wanted to catch the Christmas selling season. So early in the fall they took the $125,000—all of it—and spent it on one make-or-break ad campaign. Cook wrote the ad himself. If it didn't work . . . nah, better not to think too hard about that.

Well, Lady Luck was smiling that fall. Or maybe Cook's extraordinary efforts to create a product that would truly satisfy its buyers were on the money. Whatever the reason, the ad launched Intuit's program on what turned out to be a brilliant career.

"The company," says Cook, now president of a $33-million business, "grew a bunch."

virtually unbidden. Intuit sold close to a million units in 1990. Its product is carried by retailers all over the country, by Target stores and Wal-Marts as well as computer chains. Yet the company's sales force numbers exactly two.

So what moves the goods? Asked that question, founder and president Scott Cook peers mock-earnestly through his thick glasses, allowing only the hint of a grin to cross his face. "Really," he says innocently, "we have hundreds of thousands of salespeople. They're our customers." Suddenly missionary-sober, he adds that he wants his customers to be "apostles" for Quicken. Intuit's mission is to "make the customer feel so good about the product they'll go and tell five friends to buy it."

And as to what would make a customer feel that good, which is to say better than most customers feel about *any* product or service—well, the only way to understand it may be to watch Cook and his company at work.

The year is 1984; the place Palo Alto, Calif., not far from Intuit's current hometown of Menlo Park. Cook and three colleagues are in a room with a bunch of computers and several well-dressed women. The women—members of the Palo Alto Junior League—are not what you'd call computer nuts; some have never even touched one of the machines before. But today, after croissants and orange juice, they are sitting at the keyboards, trying to use the computers to write checks. Cook and his colleagues watch but don't help.

Cook—a Harvard MBA, a Proctor & Gamble–trained marketer—is a bit on edge. In a way, his fledgling company depends on what he learns here.

His epiphany, a year or so earlier, was simplicity itself. More and more consumers and small businesses were buying PCs. All those computer buyers wrote checks and kept financial records. Outfitted with the right software, a computer should be able to automate such tasks. The only rub: a few dozen check-writing programs were already on the market, and Cook had no money to elbow them aside. If he wanted to start a software company—and he did—he would have to offer customers something his competitors didn't.

Wondering what that something might be, he and a newly hired assistant began placing telephone calls to middle- and upper-middle-income households. They didn't stop until the calls numbered in the hundreds—and until they began hearing the same responses over and over.

The vast majority of respondents said they did financial work every month, they didn't like spending so much time on it, and they would consider using a computer to do the work. But they couldn't be bothered with learning a complex program, and they certainly didn't want to spend more time on the chore than they were spending now. Curious, Cook assembled a panel of computer buffs to test the most popular programs then available, writing checks and keeping records first by computer and then by hand. Sure enough—in every case, the computer was slower.

Conclusion: there was a market out there, already big and undoubtedly growing bigger, a market capable of appealing to Cook's P&G-honed aspirations. But if he wanted to reach that potential mass market, his program had better be fast, cheap, hassle free, and above all easy to use, so easy that anyone could sit down at the computer and start writing checks.

So, now he's watching very intently as the Junior Leaguers stare at the unfamiliar keys. He and his chief programmer, a recent Stanford graduate named Tom Proulx (rhymes with true), have developed a prototype, and today's trial is one of many to see how well they've done. If the women flunk, so does the program.

For a while the test goes swimmingly. The women hunt and peck, but they don't have much trouble selecting "write checks" from a menu on the screen. The outline of a check appears, and the cursor jumps neatly from date to payee to amount. Anyone who has ever written a paper check, they discover, can write one with this new software. And the computer's check register looks just like an ordinary checkbook.

Then, alas, they go to print the checks they've written. Cook and the others have loaded up the printers with specially prepared checks, and the testers find "print checks" on the menu. But the first check prints too high, or maybe too low. To a woman they fumble with the printers; to a woman they make the problem worse. *What's the matter with this computer? The checks just won't line up right.*

Cook cringes. So does Proulx; so does Tom LeFevre, another colleague present at the creation.

"We knew one thing," recalls Proulx, now the company's vice president of product development. "If people had that much trouble the first time they used the program, they'd never use it again."

"Scott looked at Tom and me," adds LeFevre, also a vice president. "He said, 'You guys figure out a way to solve that problem.' His tone said, And don't come back until you do."

Jump cut: 1990. Proulx and LeFevre have long since resolved the alignment problem, developing a fancy bit of programming (patented and still unique in the industry) that makes the computer line the checks up automatically. And Quicken has long since been released, upgraded, and released again. It has climbed to the top of the best-seller charts; it has won industry awards. Intuit is making a lot of money selling not only the programs but upgrades, special checks, and other supplies.

Yet now Alex Young, a product-development manager for the next release of Quicken, is sitting in the home of a man he doesn't know, watching him open a shrink-wrapped box.

Maybe it was the P&G training, maybe the lesson of the Junior Leaguers, maybe just the impact of the original market research. Whatever the reason, figuring out how to satisfy customers has become Cook's, and Intuit's, obsession. The company runs an annual customer survey, asking which of Quicken's features buyers use and don't use, like and don't like. It polls dealers anonymously, asking what personal-finance programs they recommend and why. It compiles data from customers who call in with problems or write in with suggestions. It runs focus groups, usually consisting of people who aren't Quicken customers but (according to Intuit) ought to be. Information from all those sources flows directly to product-development teams (working on the next version of Quicken), to the documentation department (which regularly updates the manual), and to marketing.

The company also tests its programs relentlessly. And not just the so-called alpha and beta testing commonly practiced by most software companies—tests that are designed primarily to locate bugs in the programming—but tests at a much earlier stage of product development. Get in some experienced Quicken users—see if this new version is going to confuse them in any way. Get in some Junior League–style novices. What's their reaction to a certain screen? "You watch their eyebrows, where they hesitate, where they have a quizzical look," says Cook. "Every glitch, every momentary hesitation is our fault."

Enough, you might think. That'll do it, you might think. Not that all the research costs so much—only the big sample surveys represent much of a cash outlay, in the neighborhood of $150,000 a year. But surely Intuit has been finding out all it possibly can about its customers' experiences with the product?

Nope. "There's still a group of people we were missing," says product manager Mari Latterell. "People just setting the program up. In fact, we didn't really know how easy it was to get started with Quicken. When you survey customers, they've been using it for six months or a year and won't remember. When you bring in testers you have then in an artificial situation. They aren't entering their own data in their own homes."

Which is why Latterell, imbued with Cook's market-research mission, proposed the Follow-Me-Home program, in which Quicken buyers from local stores are asked to let an Intuit representative observe them when they first use Quicken. And why Alex Young, who volunteered to participate, is now watching his new acquaintance unwrap the shrink-wrapped Quicken box.

Today Young will spend five hours with his subject, longer than any of the dozen or so other employees who have so far followed customers home. Sitting behind the customer, he watches and listens. Customer confronts the program's main menu. (Confusion, notes Young: he thinks the word *register,* meaning the check register, has something to do with the product-registration card.) Customer begins to enter data from his checkbook. (Problem: he tries to enter a balance manually. You can't do that; once the opening balance is entered, the program calculates the balances automatically.) Customer tries to print checks. (He prints more samples than he needs to.) Finally, the day is done, and the customer is happy. As part of the deal, Young is now allowed to offer a little help and advice.

Young and Intuit, for their part, have their payoff: a thick sheaf of notes on the myriad ways that the next incarnation of Quicken, already the most popular program on the market, might be made just a tiny bit easier for first-time users.

"If people don't use the product," observes Tom LeFevre, "they won't tell their friends to use it, either."

Suna Kneisley, senior customer support specialist, can't quite believe the fax. A customer she has just spoken with wants to know how to put his various records onto Quicken and has just faxed her nine pages' worth of data. It's a Friday; no way she can go through it all today. Oh, well. She calls the customer and leaves a message; she'll take it home with her over the weekend and get back to him Monday. Monday, she has the answers he wants.

Technical-support reps such as Kneisley are Intuit's front-line employees, like waiters in a restaurant or reservation clerks at an airline. There are 40 of them, almost a quarter of the company's 175-person work force. You've just bought a new printer, and you can't get it to work with Quicken? Call tech support. You've damaged a disk and lost some data? Call tech support. The response you get, of course, will define your attitude toward Quicken and Intuit, probably forever.

So ask yourself: How much is it worth to the company when a customer gets a response like Kneisley's—not only that she'll answer a request going well beyond the ordinary, but that she'll take it home and work on it *over the weekend?*

Kneisley, 24, has been at Intuit only five months when this particular request comes in. No matter—she has already absorbed the messages that Cook has somehow built into the very structure of his company. *Intuit stands or falls with what happens in tech support. Do whatever you need to do to satisfy the customer.* The messages are hammered home in several different ways:

- Thank-you letters from customers are read aloud, circulated throughout the company, and then framed and posted on the wall. Kneisley's colleague Debbie Peak gets a letter because she faxed a customer some printer information, then thought to call the next day to make sure it had arrived safely. Kneisley herself gets one from a woman who damaged four years' worth of data; working at home with a special data-recovery program, Kneisley salvaged it.
- Virtually everyone in the company, from Cook on down, spends a few hours each month working the customer service lines, underscoring by example the importance of what the department does. "I was hired in September," recalls Victor Gee, who started as a rep and is now a supervisor in tech support. "That same month Scott came by and started taking calls, too. I thought, What other company would have the president do the same thing I'm doing?" Every few months, moreover, each employee is taken to lunch by a top manager. Lunch with a Dork, employees have christened the program—but its message is not lost. "My last one was with Scott," says customer support specialist Dwight Joseph. "He had his notebook with him, and he writes down what you say, any ideas you might have. It's pretty gratifying."
- A torrent of statistics—daily write-ups, weekly summaries, hand-lettered charts covering a whole quarter—tracks the tech-support department's performance for all to see. How many callers have to wait longer than 60 seconds? How many give up? At the company's Monday morning meetings, says Cook, "the first four numbers we go through have to do with customer service. Even before we get to revenues. It creates real peer pressure to improve service—people see how we're doing each week."

At a lot of companies, pressure to improve customer service creates a white-collar sweatshop: harried managers brow-beat supervisors; supervisors keep an iron grip on employees. Intuit, by contrast, is structured to encourage cooperation and to make improvements through innovation rather than through tighter controls. Greg Ceniceroz, recently promoted from tech-support rep to product specialist, is assigned the job of figuring out how to cut down on the average time spent with each customer. His first step toward a solution: a big loose-leaf reference binder containing answers to customers' most frequent questions, for every rep's desk. He encourages reps to submit questions and answers for inclusion in the binder and makes sure those who do get a public thank-you.

Kneisley, meanwhile, notices that management is looking for a volunteer to chair a group dubbed the Innovative Ideas Committee, which has been charged with collating and following up on every product-improvement idea emanating from the tech-support department and from Quicken users. She writes a four-page proposal about what she thinks the group ought to do, and gets the job. "We worked with her to set the committee's objectives," says Tom LeFevre, "since she had been here only a few months. But she was *very* interested. And the more interested someone is, the better job they'll do."

Involvement of that sort, of course, translates into a sense of ownership more valuable and more productive than any amount of iron-grip supervision. "Most of us work at least 50 hours a week," says Kneisley. "We don't get any extra compensation. But we do have a profit-sharing plan, and if Intuit does well, we will, too."

Scott Cook is showing me Intuit's latest ad campaign. I'm a little incredulous, but there it is: Send for a copy of Quicken. Pay only an $8 shipping-and-handling charge. If you don't think you're doing useful work within a few minutes, don't pay for the product. No, not "send it back for a refund." *Keep it.* Just don't pay for it.

Why would a company do this?

"It's like the Japanese," Cook says.

"Oh," I answer, trying to think of the last time a Japanese company offered me something virtually free. Fortunately, Cook elaborates.

"It's like the Japanese assembly lines, where they have only two hours' worth of inventory. There's no margin for error—they have to have super-reliability from their suppliers." Cook goes to his bookshelf, pulling out a copy of *The Machine That Changed the World,* the new book about Toyota's "lean production" system. "What we're doing is the Toyota approach. We take away the safety net. If you do that, you have to get it right."

The more Cook talks, the more the scenes I have observed at Inuit begin to fall into place.

Tech support, for example. Here are 40 people answering all kinds of crazy questions—for free. Here is a $500,000 state-of-the-art telephone system, installed in late 1989 just so callers won't have to wait so long. This isn't normal: nearly all of Intuit's competitors put a limit on tech support, some charging for it and some curtailing it so many months after purchase. And nearly every company with an after-sale call-in line doesn't mind keeping customers waiting for a few minutes.

But then, those companies have a safety net. "Most software companies would go broke if they didn't charge for tech support," argues Cook. "We said, We're not going to charge. If our customers have problems, we pay. That makes us get the product right the first time."

Take the product itself. For $50 or less—sometimes as low as $20 on store-sponsored special sales—you can buy a copy of Quicken. In its latest form, you get a program capable not only of writing checks but of tracking investments, generating profit-and-loss statements, and doing a dozen other chores a small-business owner or financially sophisticated consumer might want to do on a computer. You also get a 460-page manual, the right to regular upgrades at modest cost, and access to unlimited help. Once again: abnormal. Quicken's chief competitor lists for three and a half times as much as Quicken, and Quicken's price could probably double before Intuit noticed much of a sales decline.

But that would be a safety net. "We sell an inexpensive product, and we offer free customer support," says Alex Young. "We have to make sure it's right when it goes out the door." Suddenly, refinements like the Follow-Me-Home program make perfect sense.

And finally, look at Intuit's marketing. The no-pay ad, for example. "We heard from our focus groups that people really didn't believe the product could be so easy to use," recalls Mari Latterell. "After all, software never is. So we did this big advertising campaign—'You'll be using Quicken in six minutes or it's free.' The goal was to put our money where our mouth is." Even the company's tiny sales force—two people—begins to seem comprehensible. Outside salespeople could maybe push more product into stores. But depending on pull-through marketing means the company can't survive without satisfying its customers. "When someone comes in and thanks a clerk for selling him Quicken," says marketing vice president John Monson, "there's nothing a salesperson could do that would come close to being as powerful a recommendation."

Funny that Monson should conjure up that image. When I return from my visit to Intuit, I call up the manager of the local Egghead Discount Software store and ask him about the product. "People love it," he says. "Someone actually came in here and thanked me for selling it to him. That doesn't happen too often."

By some reckonings, Intuit's approach to customer satisfaction is costly.

Technical support and other departments that have customer contact (the one taking orders for checks, for example) cost the company about 10 percent of revenues, or upward of $3 million a year. The testing, surveys, fancy telephone systems, focus groups, and other stay-close-to-the-customer expenses add another $1 million to $2 million. Imagine yourself a corporate raider concerned only with the next quarter's earnings; you'd buy up Intuit, cut back on all such expenditures, and boost profits anywhere from 50 percent to 100 percent.

"That," says Scott Cook, "is the advantage of owning the company. When you own the company, you take the long view."

In that long view, the payoff of the Intuit approach is far higher than the immediate cost. Quicken is likely to continue its utter domination of the market. Other products introduced by Intuit will be launched with a running start. Even now, fully one third of Quicken customers say they bought the product because it was recommended by a friend. As they say in the trade, that's advertising money can't buy.

So is this: As I am working on this article, my friend Bruce stops by. "I hear you're writing about Intuit," he says. "I just bought its program, Quicken."

Bruce doesn't buy much software. A copy of Lotus 1-2-3 given to him by his sister-in-law sits on the shelf unopened. He uses his computer mostly for writing. But he bought Quicken because two different people urged him to. "You've got to get this program," they told him.

Now he has become an apostle himself. The reason: one day, while working on some financial records, he left the room. His two-and-a-half-year-old daughter, Emma, waltzed in and cheerfully turned off the computer. In panic, Bruce turned it back on and booted up Quicken. "Don't worry!" the screen cheerfully informed him. Quicken had saved all but the last little bits of data.

Somewhere, at some point, Scott Cook's engineers had put that capability and its comforting message into the program. Intuit, they knew, was depending on its customers to sell the product.

And customers, they knew, don't really want money-back guarantees or complaint forms or even 800 numbers. What they want is the product to be right.

Source: John Case, "Customer Service: The Last Word," *INC.*, April 1991, pp. 89–93.

CASE 3–2 U.S. Surgical Corporation

Leon Hirsch, the chairman of U.S. Surgical Corp., sold 100,000 of his company's shares last August at $45 apiece. He sold too soon. The stock now fetches $122.50.

But Mr. Hirsch isn't looking back. Riding his company's growing reputation for innovative technology and its soaring sales, he is declaring war on Johnson & Johnson, the king of surgical supplies.

At a big meeting of nurses in Atlanta last week, U.S. Surgical unveiled its first line of sutures. J&J's Ethicon division makes more than 80 percent of the sutures sold in the United States and claims two thirds of the $1.3 billion business worldwide, but Mr. Hirsch isn't daunted. "Our sutures come out of the package straight and smooth," he says. "Theirs come out kinked and rough."

Nearly a decade of research went into developing the new sutures, and Mr. Hirsch is betting that a lot of surgeons will switch to his line. But Ethicon, acknowledging the kink problem, countered by rolling out its own kink-free sutures at the nurses' meeting.

The showdown involves a lot more than stitching. For the first time, U.S. Surgical can go head-to-head against Ethicon in three major segments of the surgery business. It dominates the other two: staplers, used for closing incisions and other tasks, and so-called endoscopic instruments used in a fast-growing technique in which doctors do gallbladder and other surgery through small holes instead of wide gashes in the abdomen.

The U.S. market for the three segments could triple to $3 billion by 1995, and some analysts think that by then U.S. Surgical will overtake Ethicon as the top supplier to the nation's surgeons. But as the new, minimally invasive procedures grow from 70,000 last year to an expected two million or more a year by the mid-1990s, the real prize will be leadership in the technological changes transforming surgery.

Reflecting U.S. Surgical's dominant status in endoscopy equipment—by far the fastest-growing segment of the surgery market—the company is expected to report today that its first-quarter earnings soared more than 60 percent from a year earlier. For all of last year, earnings climbed 50 percent to $46 million and revenue 49 percent to $514.1 million. Some analysts expect U.S. Surgical to be a $1 billion company by next year (see Exhibit 1).

Caught flat-footed at first by the pace of change, Ethicon currently runs a distant second in instruments for endoscopic surgery (often called laparoscopy). But it recently pledged a major offensive to close the gap; among other moves, it plans to quadruple its engineering staff from 1989 levels to 230 this year, and a slew of new products are starting to hit the market.

"Our effort will be as focused, intense, and ambitious as any we have ever embarked upon," vows Ralph S. Larsen, J&J's chairman and chief executive. "We are prepared to do whatever it takes to assure success."

Doctors and buyers for hospitals hail the rivalry as a spur to innovation and quality and a potential check on price. Both companies are "very hungry," says Jonathan Sackier, director of surgical endoscopy at Cedars Sinai Medical Center in Los Angeles. "They're pushing out extremely good new products at an amazing rate."

EXHIBIT 1 U.S. Surgical: Trying to Sew Up a Market

To Keep Profit Rising . . .

Annual net income, in millions

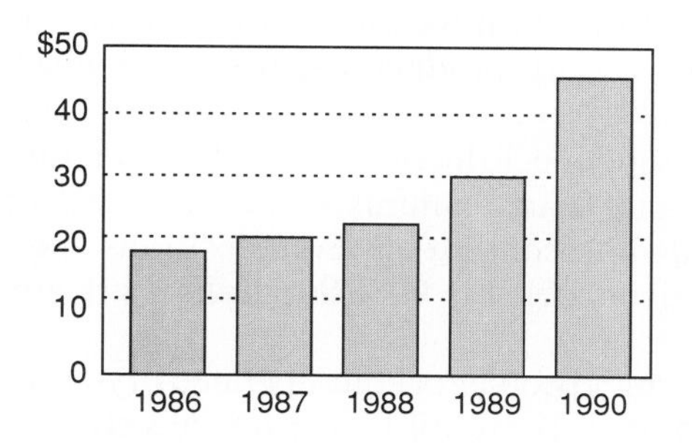

In a Competitive Market . . .

Domestic surgical supply market share, in percent

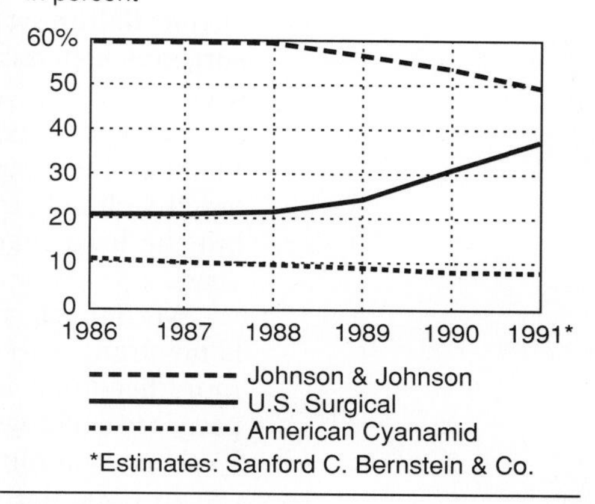

*Estimates: Sanford C. Bernstein & Co.

It Goes After Sutures . . .

Estimated 1991 domestic suture market, in percent

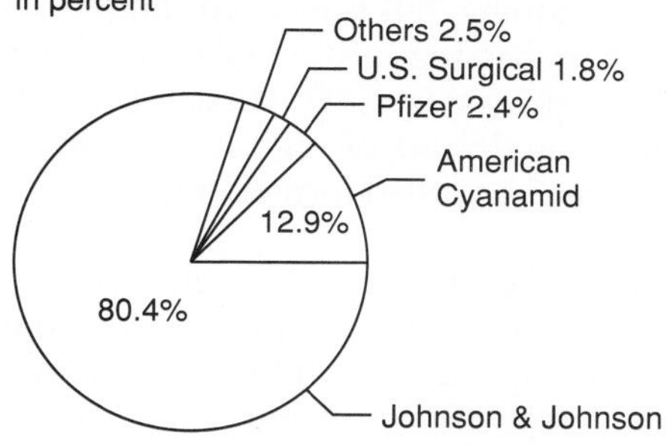

*Estimates: Sanford C. Bernstein & Co.

Tries to Make Investors Happy.

Monthly closing price of U.S. Surgical's stock

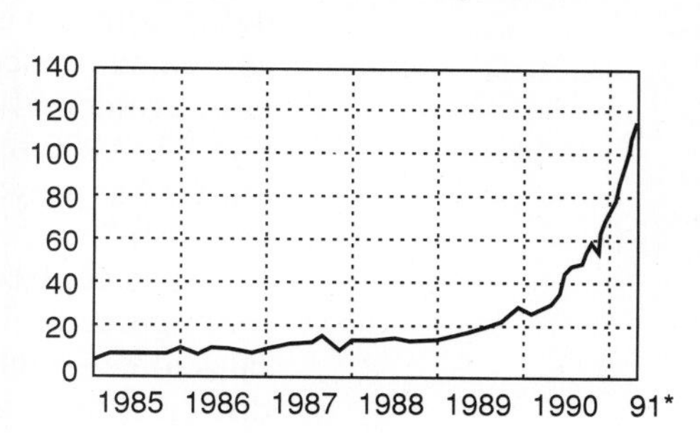

Although other companies are also scrambling for this business, the main event will be between J&J and Mr. Hirsch, whom Kurt Kruger, a Hambrecht & Quist securities analyst, calls "the pit bull of the wound-closure business." As each company takes aim at the other's strength, the combat has intensified to surgery's version of the cola wars.

The University of California at Davis has to run an "Ethicon Day" and a "U.S. Surgical Day" in its courses that train doctors in new surgical techniques because Mr. Hirsch, like an incumbent ahead in the polls, won't share a platform with Ethicon. "We're happy to go head-to-head," says David Murray, Ethicon's vice president for marketing.

When administrators at Johns Hopkins Hospitals signed a contract with Ethicon for staplers a couple of years ago, U.S. Surgical salespeople complained to doctors, who, in turn, complained to Mr. Hirsch. He then traveled to Baltimore to dress down the institution's purchasing officials. "The surgeons kept asking for our product and they were given Ethicon's," he says.

To defend its suture line, Ethicon contested every request U.S. Surgical made to the Food and Drug Administration to exempt its sutures from lengthy clinical trials. Ethicon lost all seven decisions and several appeals, but the legal maneuvers delayed U.S. Surgical's marketing plans by two years.

Mr. Hirsch, a former peddler of coin-operated dry-cleaning equipment, is no stranger to conflict. But until U.S. Surgical's stock surged, he made more headlines in tussles with animal rights groups opposed to the company's use of dogs in research and sales training and with the Securities and Exchange Commission than with competitors.

In 1984, the SEC charged the company with overstating earnings by falsifying purchase orders, shipping unordered products to hospitals while booking them as sales, and other securities-law violations. The company didn't admit to any wrongdoing, but it restated three years of earnings and consented to a court order barring future violations. By settling, the company avoided $10 million in legal fees, Mr. Hirsch says, but the incident cost him $317,000 in bonuses and years of respect on Wall Street. He says the matter was provoked by a disgruntled former employee and "was just plain hogwash."

Such controversies, however, didn't distract the company from relentlessly pursuing its most important constituency: surgeons. Its 650-person sales force—including 375 in the United States—has taught thousands of doctors how to use staplers, which it invented more than 20 years ago and has developed into a business running $400 million a year and growing 20 percent annually. Its salespeople spend much of the workweek in surgery, providing what Mr. Hirsch calls "technical assistance" to doctors using the company's products.

Sometimes, says Bruce Wolfe, chief of gastrointestinal surgery at UC Davis, the salespeople "are a little too forward in telling doctors how to do their surgery." But Dr. Wolfe adds: "They've been highly trained in how to use their equipment, and surgeons in these parts respect them."

That respect has paid huge dividends to U.S. Surgical as doctors begin to switch to minimally invasive surgery for gallbladder patients. Most of the 15,000 doctors who learned the operation last year did so at courses supported by U.S. Surgical and staffed by sales representatives demonstrating its products.

Among those products are trocars, sharp-pointed tubes that serve as ports of entry into the abdominal cavity for surgical instruments and a tiny camera that displays a patient's innards on a monitor. The doctor watches the monitor while manipulating the instruments. The typical gallbladder procedure requires four keyhole-sized slits, not the traditional six- to eight-inch incision.

Last year, 70,000 patients underwent the procedure, and most of the 600,000 people who have gallbladder surgery each year are considered candidates for it.

In addition, some doctors use the technique for appendectomies, hysterectomies, and treatments for hernia, ulcers, and other ills. It's possible that, in a few years, trocars could be used in two million cases annually. Trocars, as well as many trocar-compatible instruments on the market or under development, are used just once and discarded. Both U.S. Surgical and Ethicon sell disposable gallbladder kits that include most of the required accessories, and they plan similar packages for other procedures.

And, seeking to develop new instruments, they are working closely with physicians they consider leaders in various fields. For example, Ethicon engineers are working with Thierry Vancaillie, who with colleagues at the Texas Endoscopy Institute in San Antonio has started using endoscopy for colon surgery.

Ethicon is stepping up its support of physician training courses, and it expects to benefit from the clout of its parent, J&J. For instance, an antiadhesion compound already on the market for other uses and a wound-healing agent under development in another division may be included in the kits for various endoscopic procedures. J&J even makes a surgical drape especially designed for the operation.

In a market so new, the company insists, an early lead means little. "In the long run," says David Clapper, Ethicon's vice president for product management, "the endoscopy explosion is the best thing that's happened to Ethicon."

U.S. Surgical, however, currently claims about 90 percent of the endoscopic business. Its clip applier, used to seal off ducts and vessels, is preferred by doctors because it holds several clips; Ethicon's must be removed from the abdomen and reloaded after each use.

While the endoscopic business is expected to grow 40 percent a year, sutures plod along, with sales rising only about 5 percent annually. Sutures involve a broad range of special technologies ranging from microneedles used in eye surgery to the wire thread used to close chests after bypass operations. Bought in bulk, they are more price-sensitive than other U.S. Surgical products. Kaiser Permanente, the big Oakland, California, health-maintenance organization, puts price tags on sutures in surgical supply rooms to encourage doctors to avoid a $12 stitch if a $2 one will do.

But thanks to sutures, Ethicon's domestic sales last year exceeded $1.5 million per salesperson, compared with less than $1 million at U.S. Surgical. Moreover, Ethicon often ties discounts on sutures to purchases of its staplers and trocars, an attractive deal for hospitals seeking to cut costs and control inventories.

With its own sutures, U.S. Surgical can blunt that advantage. Its sutures are packaged in a mazelike circular channel, and as a nurse pulls one out, it hangs straight. By contrast, Ethicon's absorbable Vicryl sutures used to come in a figure-eight package that caused the thread, when pulled out, to kink up like an accordion.

Mr. Hirsch claims other advantages: a smoother, stronger thread that passes easily through tissue and a needle that is sharper and readily accessible when the package is opened. A comparison of the products staged by sales reps at U.S. Surgical headquarters last month appeared to convince a small group of doctors.

But the doctors didn't see Ethicon's improved line. Needles made with a new, proprietary alloy are sharper, and some have grooves on the inside of the shaft to provide a firmer grip. The absorbable suture retains 40 percent of its strength in the body after three weeks, against 20 percent previously. And its new "relay" package gives nurses easy access to the needles and replaces the figure-eight with an "oval wind" that practically eliminates kinks.

In the early 1980s, when Ethicon had about 30 percent of the U.S. suture market against the then-dominant Davis & Geck division of American Cyanamid Co., Ethicon launched a new, coated version of Vicryl. Its salespeople prowled hospital corridors, wads of string dangling from their pockets, to buttonhole doctors, and they propelled Ethicon to its current dominance in sutures. Says Mr. Clapper: "You go to the ultimate customer—the surgeon—and sell, sell, sell."

Mr. Hirsch couldn't have said it better.

Source: Ron Winslow, "Major Operation," *The Wall Street Journal,* April 16, 1991, pp. A1, A4. Reprinted by permission of *The Wall Street Journal,* © 1991 Dow Jones & Company, Inc. All Rights Reserved Worldwide.

CASE 3–3 Stop N Go

As he takes a visitor on a whirlwind tour of the convenience-store business, V. H. "Pete" Van Horn passes a boarded-up Circle K store, a vivid symbol of the industry's past follies. With their archaic marketing techniques and crazy-quilt expansion, he says, his anger rising, "Circle K and 7-Eleven have created the impression that the industry is doomed."

The chief executive of National Convenience Stores Inc. is quickly pacified, however, by the sight of one of his own Stop N Go stores, which he brassily calls "the convenience store of the future." He marches through the store's wide aisles, extolling its virtues: bright lights and decorative wooden shelves stuffed with trendy products such as fresh pasta, expensive wines, Bart Simpson T-shirts and deli items. The store is a far cry from the industry's traditional shoe-box stands where beer, cigarettes and soda pop make up more than half of sales. "We're reinventing the business," Mr. Van Horn boasts.

The business could use some reinventing. Convenience stores once were little cash machines for their owners, where harried consumers were willing to pay more to pick up a few essentials without the hassle of wading through a supermarket. But that was before the spread of gas station mini-marts and before supermarkets fought back with express lanes and 24-hour operation. It was also before the industry's biggest chains, Circle K Corp. and Southland Corporation's 7-Eleven, unwisely loaded up on debt and ended up in bankruptcy proceedings.

Now the two industry leaders have shed hundreds of stores. The total number of convenience stores in the United States, after growing explosively for years, leveled off in the late-1980s at 83,000. And industry profits plummeted 75 percent in 1989 from the year before, spurring much doomsday forecasting. "The convenience-store concept of offering less for more is outdated," says John Roscoe, a longtime industry consultant who predicts that "only small chains with stores in great locations will survive."

Mr. Van Horn will have none of that. The problem, he insists, is that convenience store executives have been lousy marketers. "In an age of health-consciousness, customers walking into convenience stores are still greeted by racks of cigarettes, snuff, beer and beef jerky," he says. Another problem, he adds, is that operators continue to plop down cookie-cutter stores. "In ethnic neighborhoods, we've never had products or signage indicating we recognize that most of our customers are, say, Hispanic," he says.

So Mr. Van Horn is overhauling merchandise and remodeling his 1,071-store chain—the seventh largest—and designing store prototypes for three kinds of neighborhoods: mainstream, upscale, and Hispanic. He is tracking product performance store by store with a sophisticated point-of-sale scanning system, pretty advanced stuff for what has been a doggedly low-tech business. And in joint ventures with companies including Pizza Hut, NCS is about to install fast-food eateries in Stop N Go stores.

The industry is watching closely to see if Stop N Go can lure enough minorities and working women to replace the industry's shrinking traditional customer base: blue-collar men, especially blue-collar white men. At the handful of stores that have received complete overhauls, Mr. Van Horn says, sales are up about 20 percent and sales from women up nearly 100 percent. After operating losses in three of the last four years—attributable partly to huge investments required to redefine and redesign the chain—NCS expects to post a large enough operating profit this year to break even after paying a $3.2 million preferred-stock dividend. It had sales last fiscal year of $1.06 billion.

But the effort is expensive, risky and hasn't always gone smoothly. Some of Mr. Van Horn's previous ideas, such as selling television sets and bicycles at a few stores, have flopped. His ethnic-targeted stores have been criticized for stereotyping. The immediate results of some of the changes have been disappointing.

Varying the product mix from store to store could dilute the chain's buying power. And higher-class inventory costs a lot more to carry if sales languish. Fresh sandwiches and produce will introduce significant new spoilage costs. "A can of Coke isn't as difficult to manage as a piece of fruit, and it has a longer shelf life and national advertising behind it," says Coney Elliot, an industry consultant.

Moreover, many still doubt that the stores can overcome their blue-collar image. "I spent a whole day looking at stores with Pete," says Mr. Roscoe, the consultant. "When a guy walked out of Stop N Go in a suit and tie, Pete yelled, 'That's our new market!' Hell, it was the only guy in a suit and tie we saw all day."

The reaction of professional women like Kim Kindred illustrates the problem. As the 24-year-old Houston restaurant-company manager waits in line at an Apple Tree grocery here with pasta and wine, she's told she could get the same things at the Stop N Go next door—without the wait. "Convenience stores are glorified gas stations," she responds. "I don't buy my dinner at gas stations."

There are other problems, too. Oil companies still have thousands of stations they can convert into stores, and, like Stop N Go, they are beginning to experiment with larger units that offer more nontraditional merchandise such as deli food. "In four or five years, oil companies will be the giants of the convenience-store industry," predicts David Glass, chief executive of Wal-Mart Stores Inc., which recently bought the nation's largest convenience-store supplier, McLane Co.

Officials of Ito-Yokado Co., the Japanese franchiser of 7-Eleven stores that is seeking to assume control of Southland, has indicated that it, too, will introduce new products and install point-of-sale systems to discern customer habits. "Changing life-styles and the aging of the baby-boom generation mean that our product mix has to change, and it will," says Southland spokeswoman Cecilia Norward, adding that 7-Eleven will begin downplaying cigarettes and emphasizing healthier items.

And some say that whole strategy is wrong anyway. Circle K officials, in fact, say it was their attempt to add new products and services that—along with heavy debt taken on in an unsuccessful expansion—helped land the company in bankruptcy proceedings. "By getting into movie rentals, lottery tickets, ATM machines, fast food and a bunch of other sexy new products, the company took its eye off the ball," says Karen Simon, the new senior vice president of marketing. Circle K's reorganization plan calls for the company to return its focus to what it calls the "power categories"—beer, cigarettes, and soda pop. As for Mr. Van Horn's strategy, Ms. Simon laughs and says, "All I can say is, 'Good luck, Pete.'"

Mr. Van Horn who is 52 years old, says luck has nothing to do with it. Reared by a rich oil man who refused to share his wealth with the kids, believing they should earn their own success, Mr. Van Horn worked his way through school delivering newspapers and pumping gas, then abandoned a planned career in oil to join NCS in 1966 as a store manager. He rose through district manager, Southwest division manager and vice president of stores before becoming CEO in 1975. Since then, he says, he has invested "virtually all" of his net worth in NCS stock, of which he now owns a 2 percent stake (worth about $2 million). "My life and career are invested in this," he says. "Not to mention my ego."

Until 1985, his ego was doing just fine. Profits rose every quarter, and the company's stock, adjusted for splits and stock dividends, rose 2,138 percent from 1975 to 1984. But the 80s oil bust devastated Houston, the company's largest market, at the same time that oil companies starting using that market to launch an aggressive expansion of their mini-mart program. As a result, long before hard times hit the rest of the industry, profits disappeared at NCS and its stock plummeted from nearly $20 a share in 1984 to $4.75 yesterday.

At the same time, Karl Eller, then chief of Circle K, was considering a takeover attempt, Mr. Van Horn says, but backed off after Cincinnati financier Carl Lindner—the largest shareholder of both NCS and Circle K—declined to back him without Mr. Van Horn's approval. Mr. Van Horn took advantage of Circle K's seemingly insatiable appetite for growth, selling the Phoenix-based company 186 stores in nine cities as part of his effort to concentrate on fewer markets. "I sold Karl Eller a bunch of crap," he says. (Mr. Eller and Mr. Lindner didn't return calls seeking comment for this article.)

At the same time, Mr. Van Horn bought all of Southland's 7-Eleven stores in Houston and San Antonio, giving Stop N Go a dominant market share in those cities.

When the dust settled, NCS was operating nearly the same number of stores in eight markets that it operated in 21 five years before, Mr. Van Horn then quadrupled his advertising budget to $12 million a year to saturate those markets. Still, the trimmed-down Stop N Go didn't take off.

In 1988, some retail repositioning specialists took Mr. Van Horn on a cross-country tour of successful businesses such as Nordstrom's, the Walt Disney Store chain, and Simon David, a Dallas gourmet grocery. Intoxicated by their fancy offerings, he came back to Houston determined to lure the affluent away from supermarket express lanes. "The average person in a supermarket express lane has 10 items, and 7 of them are available in the typical convenience store," he says. "It's the other three that's always killed us."

From lists showing household income by zip code, he and other company officials identified 200 Stop N Go stores serving affluent neighborhoods in Houston. Using the point-of-sale scanners, the company was able to identify 200 slow-selling items to clear out, including *Guns & Ammo* magazine, Sugar Pops cereal, and Hamburger Helper. Next, they drew up a fancier list: rich cheeses, gourmet pastries, *The New Yorker* magazine.

The expected flood of yuppies failed to materialize. For one thing, company marketing managers, feeling pressures from Mr. Van Horn to increase sales, were spending ad dollars promoting cigarettes, soda pop, and beer, items they knew they could move.

After four months, even after that problem was corrected, sales in many stores declined.

Recalling his tour of one of the Walt Disney stores, with its video screens, bright colors and creative shelves, Mr. Van Horn decided the problem was visual. "Our idea of presentation was stacking up 20 cases of Coca-Cola and putting a sign on top," he says. Back at the drawing board, company officials sketched in potted plants, wooden shelves, fancy display tables and a reading area beside magazine racks, as well as improved signs and lighting outside. They also devised an employee dress code of white shirts, bow ties, and green aprons.

The first unit boasting those changes opened here last April, and sales immediately shot up 20 percent over the same month a year earlier, a trend that has continued. Leaving the store recently with some fruit and a bagel, Julie Jeffers, a college student majoring in dietetics, says, "It's nice not to have to go into a big grocery store for these items."

Meantime, company officials last summer studied the Hispanic market. Internal data showed that ice cream and beverage sales were 30 percent higher in Hispanic-area Stop N Go stores than elsewhere—crucial information in determining how to stock an expressly-for-Hispanics stores. A design firm hired by Mr. Van Horn gave the store its logo: a Mayan welcome sign painted outside. The first Hispanic store opened here in late September. Since then, sales are up more than 20 percent, led by Mexican-made products such as Gamesa Iced Wheelies (a cookie) and some U.S. brands that have long been sold in Mexico.

The company's ethnic strategy could also backfire because it calls for loading up the stores with fatty foods and salty snacks. Even store manager Roy Enriquez, a big admirer of his Hispanic prototype store, says that its merchandise is based on "a bit of a misconception that Hispanics aren't as health-conscious as other people."

Mr. Van Horn says the Hispanic store mix is based on statistics rather than stereotypes, and he says that in certain categories Hispanics are in fact more health-conscious consumers. For instance, they buy fewer cigarettes, he says, so cigarettes aren't emphasized in the Hispanic prototype.

Mr. Van Horn junked the idea of a black-oriented store after concluding from his point-of-sale data that blacks' buying habits didn't differ significantly from those of blue-collar whites. To serve both groups, he is planning to unveil a mainstream prototype in March that he says will feature products from both the Hispanic and "upscale" prototypes. While continuing to emphasize traditional products such as beer and cigarettes, the mainstream store will carry fresher and more fashionable items. Already, all Houston Stop N Go stores offer sandwiches made fresh daily.

Despite the fatter margins produced by the made-over stores, Mr. Van Horn says he won't be rolling out new ones quickly. Conversions cost tens of thousands of dollars per store, a considerable burden for a company that already has long-term debt of nearly $190 million. The company estimates that fewer than 150 stores will have been repositioned by midyear.

Repositioning customer attitudes could take even longer. Mr. Van Horn goes quickly from elation to deflation one day as he watches two men in ties and sports coats deliberate over Stop N Go's new fresh-daily $3.50 sandwiches, then opt instead for an old standby: 99-cent hot dogs. "The industry has been offering stale products so long," he says, "the customer isn't trained to buy anything else."

Source: Kevin Hellider, "Off the Shelf," *The Wall Street Journal,* February 16, 1991, pp. A1, A10. Reprinted by permission of *The Wall Street Journal,*

CASE 3–4 Apex Chemical Company

The Executive Committee of Apex Chemical Company—a medium-sized chemical manufacturer with annual sales of $60 million—is trying to determine which of two new compounds the company should market. The two products were expected to have the same gross margin percentage. The following conversation takes place among the vice president for research, Ralph Rogovin; the vice president for marketing, Miles Mumford; and the president, Paul Prendigast.

VP-Research: Compound A-115, a new electrolysis agent, is the one; there just isn't any doubt about it. Why, for precipitating a synergistic reaction in silver electrolysis, it has a distinct advantage over anything now on the market.

President: That makes sense, Ralph. Apex has always tried to avoid "me too" products, and if this one is that much better . . . what do you think, Miles?

VP-Marketing: Well, I favor the idea of Compound B-227, the plastic oxidizer. We have some reputation in that field; we're already known for our plastic oxidizers.

VP-Research: Yes, Miles, but this one isn't really better than the ones we already have. It belongs to the beta-prednigone group, and they just aren't as good as the stigones are. We *do* have the best stigone in the field.

President: Just the same, Ralph, the beta-prednigones are cutting into our stigone sales. The board of directors has been giving me a going over on that one.

VP-Marketing: Yes, Ralph, maybe they're not as good scientists as we are—or think we are—but the buyers in the market seem to insist on buying beta-prednigones. How do you explain that? The betas have 60 percent of the market now.

VP-Research: That's your job, not mine, Miles. If we can't sell the best product—and I can prove it *is* the best, as you've seen from my data and computations—then there's something wrong with Apex's marketing effort.

President: What do you say to that, Miles? What *is* the explanation?

VP-Marketing: Well, it's a very tricky field—the process in which these compounds are used is always touch-and-go; everyone is always trying something new.

VP-Research: All the more reason to put our effort behind Compound A-115, in the electrolysis field. Here we know that we have a real technical breakthrough. I agree with Paul that that's our strength.

President: What about that, Miles? Why not stay out of the dogfight represented by Compound B-227, if the plastic oxidizer market is as tricky as you say?

VP-Marketing: I don't feel just right about it, Paul. I understand that the electrolysis market is pretty satisfied with the present products. We did a survery, and 95 percent said they were satisfied with the Hamfield Company's product.

President: It's a big market, too, isn't it, Miles?

VP-Marketing: Yes, about $10 million a year total.

President: And only one strongly entrenched company—Hamfield?

VP-Marketing: Yes, I must admit it's not like the plastic oxidizer situation—where there are three strong competitors and about a half-dozen who are selling off-brands. On the other hand, oxidizers are a $40 million market—four times as big.

President: That's true, Ralph. Furthermore our oxidizer sales represent 25 percent of our total sales.

VP-Research: But we've been losing ground the past year. Our oxidizer sales dropped 10 percent, didn't they, Ralph? While the total oxidizer market was growing, didn't you say?

VP-Marketing: Well, the electrolysis field is certainly more stable. Total sales are holding level, and as I said before, Hamfield's share is pretty constant, too.

President: What about the technical requirements in the electrolysis field? With a really improved product we ought to be able . . .

VP-Marketing: Well, to tell you the truth, I don't know very much about the kind of people who use it and how they . . . you see, it's really a different industry.

President: What about it, Ralph?

VP-Research: It's almost a different branch of chemistry, too. But I have plenty of confidence in our laboratory men. I can't see any reason why we should run into trouble. . . . It really does have a plus-three-point superiority on a scale of 100—here, the chart shows it crystal clear, Miles.

VP-Marketing: But aren't we spreading ourselves pretty thin—instead of concentrating where our greatest know-how . . . You've always said, Paul, that . . .

President: Yes, I know, but maybe we ought to diversify, too. You know, all our eggs in one basket.

VP-Marketing: But if it's a good basket . . .

VP-Research: Nonsense, Miles, it's the kind of eggs you've got in the basket that counts—and Compound A-115, the electrolysis agent, is scientifically the better one.

VP-Marketing: Yes, but what about taking eggs to the market? Maybe people don't want to buy that particular egg from us, but they would buy Compound B-227—the plastic oxidizer.

President: Eggs, eggs, eggs—I'm saying to both of you, let's just be sure we don't lay any!

Source: Edward C. Bursk and Stephen A. Greyser, *Cases in Marketing Management,* 2nd ed., 1975, pp. 204–7, 208–10. Reprinted by permission of Prentice Hall, Englewood Cliffs, N.J.

MARKETING PROGRAM DEVELOPMENT

CHAPTER

12

Product, Branding, and Customer-Service Strategies

The decisions organizations make about the products to offer have an important impact on the company's performance. Few business decisions have such widespread influence as do choices about new products and product improvements. These decisions cut across every functional area and affect all levels of the organization.

Hewlett-Packard (HP) has a successful product strategy in the very competitive computer market. The computer maker keeps its customers satisfied with high-quality innovative products, continues to enhance its strong brand image, and effectively manages its lines of work stations, mini-computers, and printers and supplies. HP's performance is particularly impressive considering the intense competition and price cutting found in the industry in the early 1990s. Management relentlessly pursues a product strategy that offers both value and cost advantages to customers.[1] HP is the first big computer maker to implement a successful strategy for competing in the new computer environment of the 1990s. The company's comeback in the printer market is particularly impressive, given the loss of that market to the Japanese in the 1980s. The DeskJet 500 was the best selling printer in 1991, contributing to HP's first position in global sales of printers. Management follows the dual strategies of introducing product improvements and lowering costs through economies of scale.

Developing and implementing product strategies require a variety of decisions like those confronting Hewlett-Packard. First we examine product quality and competitive advantage, then discuss product portfolio analysis and strategy selection. Next, we consider how to identify the brand. We conclude the chapter with a discussion of customer-service strategy.

PRODUCT QUALITY AND COMPETITIVE ADVANTAGE

"A product is anything that is potentially valued by a target market for the benefits or satisfactions it provides, including objects, services, organizations, places, people, and ideas."[2] This view of the product covers a wide range of situations, including both tangible goods and intangible services. Thus, political candidates are products, as are travel services, medical services, refrigerators, gas turbines, and computers.

Services differ from physical products in several ways. A service is intangible.[3] It cannot be placed in inventory; the service is consumed at the time it is produced. There is often variability in the consistency of services rendered. Services are often linked to the people who produce the service. Establishing a brand image for a service requires association with the tangible components that produce the service or are somehow related to the service. The use of well-known personalities in the advertisements of the American Express Card is illustrative.

First, we look at the relationship between product quality and cost, then at the elements that make up a quality improvement strategy. A discussion follows of how other decisions affect product success. Finally, we examine marketing's role in product strategy.

Product Quality and Cost Relationship

Improving product and service quality is a critical competitive challenge facing companies competing in the global marketplace.[4] Product quality improvement reduces cost and increases competitive advantage. The successful adoption of a customer-driven organizational strategy is essential for improving product quality.

The experience of the Japanese shows that high product quality creates a sustainable competitive advantage, providing there is a continuing organizational commitment to quality improvement. W. Edward Deming, a leading product quality authority, indicates that improving all processes of the business increases the uniformity of the products produced, reduces rework and mistakes, and reduces waste of manpower, machine-time, and materials usage.[5] These improvements lead to productivity gains, lower costs, better competitive position, and job satisfaction. The benefits of improving product quality contradict the widely held view in the United States during the 1970s and 1980s that high quality requires higher costs. The traditional and total quality management (TQM) views of quality are compared in Exhibit 12–1.

EXHIBIT 12–1 Two Views of Quality

Traditional View

- Productivity and quality are conflicting goals.
- Quality is defined as conformance to specifications or standards.
- Quality is measured by degree of nonconformance.
- Quality is achieved through inspection.
- Some defects are allowed if the product meets minimum quality standards.
- Quality is a separate function and focused on evaluating production.
- Workers are blamed for poor quality.
- Supplier relationships are short-term and cost-oriented.

Total Quality Management View

- Productivity gains are achieved through quality improvements.
- Quality is conformance to correctly defined requirements satisfying user needs.
- Quality is measured by continuous process/product improvement and user satisfaction.
- Quality is determined by product design and is achieved by effective process controls.
- Defects are prevented through process-control techniques.
- Quality is part of every function in all phases of the product life cycle.
- Management is responsible for quality.
- Supplier relationships are long-term and quality-oriented.

Source: V. Daniel Hunt, *Quality in America* (Homewood, Ill.: Business One Irwin, 1992), p. 76.

Executives generally agree that quality improvement is essential to competing in global markets. The success of the Japanese in penetrating world markets has created a need to reduce major quality gaps confronting U.S. and European manufacturers. Increasingly, companies are implementing total business strategies to increase quality, productivity, and customer-perceived value.

Quality Improvement Strategy

Quality Culture. Analysis of successful business strategies for improving product and service quality indicates that a corporate culture committed to product quality and a participative management philosophy involving everyone in the organization are essential success factors. Quality improvement is an organizational responsibility. Essential managerial style and leadership characteristics in developing a quality-oriented culture include attention to detail, complete planning, problem monitoring, high personal standards, ongoing commitment to quality improvement, responsive and participative management style, and trustworthiness.[6]

Process View of the Business. In addition to a favorable corporate culture, the various processes of the organization (e.g., new-product planning) need to encourage teamwork. The quality improvement approach to business operations defines and analyzes the various processes that create business results. Processes manufacture products, create new product designs, market products, and provide customer service and other results essential to the functioning of the business. Thus, the focus of the organization shifts from specialized functions to team-oriented multifunctional processes.

As an illustration, consider the process that produces a small kitchen appliance. Several factors contribute to the quality of the final product, including the production equipment, workers, product design, materials, and supervision. The objective is to define the overall process and various subprocesses that produce, distribute, and service products. Once it is clear how the process works, attention is directed to improving it.

Statistical Methods. The last part of the product quality improvement strategy is the use of statistical quality control concepts and methods to analyze, control, and improve the business's processes. Control charts and other methods are used to analyze the processes of the business, identifying process changes that will improve product quality. The experience of quality improvement professionals indicates that much of the potential for improvement comes from changing the processes of the business rather than trying to improve the outputs of a given process. Many of the opportunities for improvement do not require the installation of expensive new equipment.

Product Success Depends on Other Decisions

Products are essential to execute a business strategy, but they do not guarantee successful performance. It is necessary to match the firm's products with market needs. Consider, for example, the difference in the sales performance of the Plymouth Laser and the Mitsubishi Eclipse sports coupes. These cars are identical in design. Both are produced by Diamond Star Motors (equal partnership between Chrysler and Mitsubishi).[7] In 1990 Laser sales averaged 13 cars per dealer compared to 100 cars per Eclipse dealer. Perhaps the Japanese quality image was the reason for Eclipse's high sales. Mitsubishi also used a more effective marketing strategy. Both brands targeted women but were positioned differently. Mitsubishi launched an earlier and more focused advertising program. The Eclipse was positioned as a woman's car, using a symbolic positioning concept—the "in" car to own. Contests were used to encourage aerobics students to take test drives. This experience shows that a high-quality product alone cannot achieve management's performance goals and must be matched with other key business and marketing strategies.

Competitive pressures and the changing needs and wants of buyers help to explain why many companies devote a lot of attention to planning the product portfolio. Product strategies are often a key component in top management's plans for improving the performance of a business. Actions may include modifying products, introducing new products, and eliminating products. Several examples of product decisions are shown in Exhibit 12–2.

EXHIBIT 12–2 Illustrative Product Decisions and the Strategy Implications

Decision	*Strategic Implications of the Decision*
Coca-Cola's withdrawal of Classic (old) Coke from the market.	Coca-Cola's market share was threatened by Pepsi. On the basis of extensive favorable taste tests of a new sweeter formula, old Coke was replaced by new Coke. Loyal old Coke consumers revolted and management reintroduced old Coke as Classic Coke. By late 1985 the old formulation was outselling new Coke by a substantial margin.
Minolta's introduction in 1985 of the Maxxum 35-mm SLR camera.	This completely automated state-of-the-art camera enabled Minolta to strengthen its market position in the highly competitive camera market, challenging Canon, the market leader.
International Harvester's 1985 sale of its farm equipment division.	This product elimination decision was one of several strategic actions intended to keep International Harvester from financial failure. Low farm prices had caused major reductions in farm equipment purchases.
The Beef Industry Council's marketing strategy to promote beef consumption.	Responding to declining per capita consumption of beef, advertising, public relations, and product development activities were launched during the 1980s to increase the demand for beef.

Marketing's Role in Product Strategy

Marketing management has three major responsibilities in the organization's product strategy. First, market analysis is needed at all stages of product planning, providing information for matching new-product ideas with consumer needs and wants. The knowledge, experience, and marketing research methods of marketing professionals are essential in product strategy development. Customer information is needed in finding and describing unmet needs, in evaluating products as they are developed and introduced, and in monitoring the performance of existing products. Several methods of product evaluation and testing are available in the marketing professional's portfolio of techniques. They are discussed in this and the previous chapter.

Marketing's second contribution to product strategy concerns product specifications. Increasingly, top management is looking to marketing executives in identifying the characteristics and performance features of products. Information about customers' needs and wants is translated into specifications for the product. The cornerstone of TQM is the customer. Matching customer needs with product capabilities is essential in designing and implementing successful product strategies. Quality function development discusssed in Chapter 11 offers one approach for translating customer requirements into product design guidelines.

The third contribution of marketing to product strategy is deciding target-market and program-positioning strategies. Marketing management looks for the best strategy for targeting and marketing the product. These decisions are often critical to the success of both new and existing products. Since the choice of product specifications and positioning are very much interrelated, product positioning needs to be considered at an early stage in the marketing planning process. Positioning decisions may include a single product or brand, a line of products, or a mix of product lines within a strategic business unit.

Product decisions affect all businesses, including wholesalers, distributors, and retailers. While many of these decisions involve the evaluation, selection, and dropping of products that are developed by manufacturers, intermediaries may also develop new products and services. For example, financial institutions are more like intermediaries than producers. Yet many service innovations have been developed, tested, and offered commercially during the past several years.

THE STRATEGIC ANALYSIS OF EXISTING PRODUCTS

The combinations of products that make up the product portfolio for a company may range from a single product to a product line to a mix of product lines. We assume that product decisions are being made for a strategic business unit (SBU). The product composition of the SBU is determined by one or more product lines and by the specific product(s) that make up each line. The SBU may have a single product or single line or various lines and specific products within each line.

Evaluating the performance of the product portfolio helps management guide strategies for new products, product modification, and product elimination. Consider, for example, the marketing battle for the leading position in the $1 billion U.S. toothpaste market. Procter & Gamble's Crest brand, the market leader, was attacked in 1980 with sweet-tasting gels and pump dispensers.[8] Crest's share declined from double Colgate's market share to only 3 percent above Colgate's 28 percent in 1985. Colgate's strategy was to overtake Crest with Dentagard, launched in 1985 with a $30 million marketing budget. Colgate's introduction of a gel form of toothpaste, ahead of P&G, also helped narrow the share gap between the two brands. P&G should have reacted earlier to competitive threats from gels and pumps. P&G countered with an aggressive product and advertising strategy. Crest's market share in 1992 was about 31 percent compared to Colgate's 22 percent. Colgate lost market share to the new market entrant, the Arm & Hammer brand, which held the third largest share position.

Analysis Objectives

The analysis of existing products requires tracking the performance of the various products in the portfolio, as shown in Exhibit 12–3. It is necessary to first state the criteria and levels of performance for gauging product per-

EXHIBIT 12–3 Tracking Product Performance

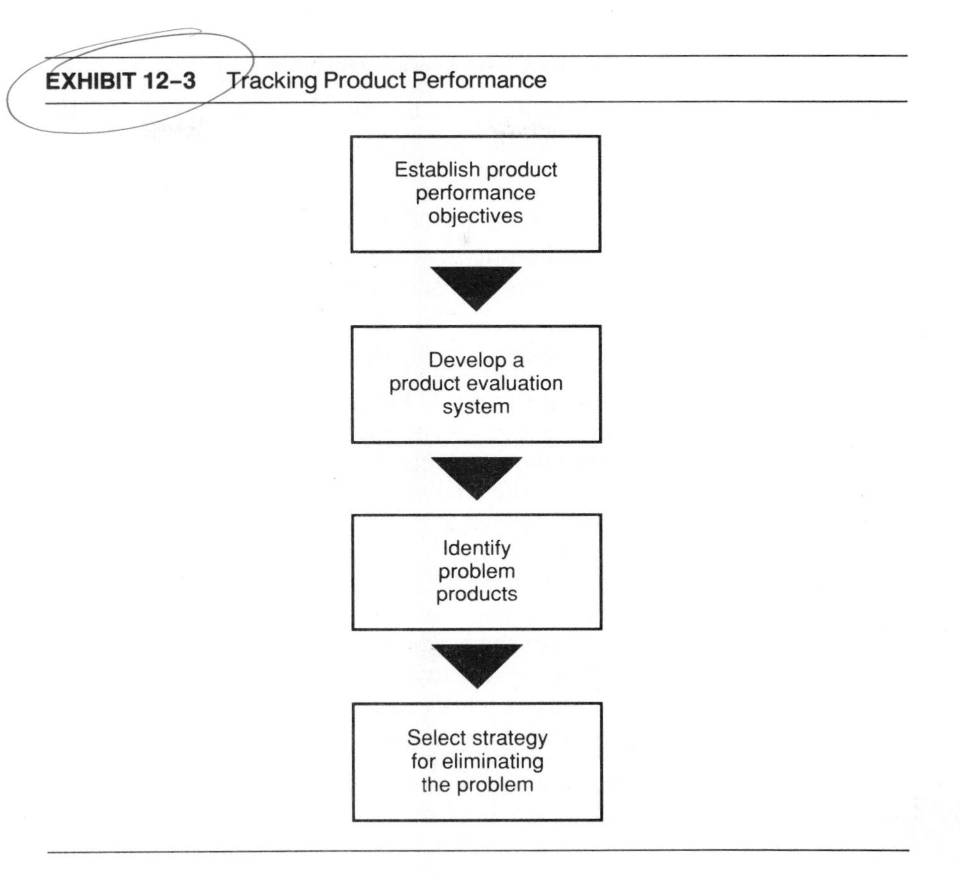

formance. These may include both financial and nonfinancial factors. Because of the demand and cost interrelationships among products, an information system may be needed to show how well a particular product is doing. The purpose of the tracking system is to maintain a product review process that will spot problem products. The diagnosis also helps management decide how to eliminate the problem.

An interesting application of portfolio analysis is the pricing and yield management system American Airlines uses to evaluate route performance and service strategies. Each route (e.g., Los Angeles to Dallas–Ft. Worth) is an item in the route portfolio. Based on performance, forecasts of demand, competition, and other strategic and tactical considerations, the airline makes decisions to expand, contract, or terminate service throughout the route network.

We look at product life cycle analysis, product portfolio analysis, and positioning analysis to illustrate diagnosing product performance and identifying product strategy alternatives.

Product Life Cycle Analysis

In Chapter 7 we describe the major stages of the product life cyle (PLC): introduction, growth, maturity, and decline. Some of the issues in PLC analysis include:

- Determining the length and rate of change of the product life cycle.
- Identifying the current PLC stage and selecting the product strategy that corresponds to that stage.
- Anticipating threats and finding opportunities for altering and extending the PLC.

Rate of Change. Product life cycles are becoming shorter for many products.[9] There are, of course, wide variations in the length of PLC stages for particular products. A clothing style may last only one season, whereas a new commercial aircraft may be produced for many years. Determining the rate of change of the PLC is important because the firm must adjust its marketing strategy to correspond to the changing conditions. A short and rapidly changing PLC requires modifying marketing strategy in a dynamic environment. The short PLC of the personal computer is illustrative; in a few years the product moved from its introduction into the growth stage and is now moving toward maturity. Fast movement through the PLC also creates the need to alter the life cycle (e.g., product improvements) and/or introduce new products.

Stage and Strategy Identification. The PLC stage of the product has important implications regarding all aspects of targeting and positioning (see Chapter 10). Four strategy phases are encountered in moving through the PLC, as shown in Exhibit 12–4. These guidelines illustrate the changing focus of marketing strategy over the PLC. In the first stage the objective is to establish the brand in the market through brand development activities such as advertising. In the growth stage the brand is reinforced through marketing efforts. During the maturity stage, product repositioning efforts may occur by adjusting size, color, and packaging to appeal to different market segments. Finally, during the decline stage the features of the product may be modified.

Analysis of the growth rate, sales trends, time since introduction, intensity of competition, pricing practices, and competitor entry/exit information are useful in PLC position analysis. Identifying when the product has moved from growth to maturity is more difficult than determining other stage positions. Analysis of industry structure and competition (see Chapter 7) helps in estimating when the product has reached maturity.

PLC Planning Model. Some progress has been made in predicting the sales volume of a product class and identifying the factors that influence the shape and amplitude of the volume projections.[10] A PLC model has been developed for short- and long-range planning for housewares and consumer elec-

EXHIBIT 12–4 Illustrative Product Strategy at Each PLC Stage

Marketing strategy considerations	**Types of brand strategies**			
Type	Brand development	Brand reinforcement	Brand repositioning	Brand modification
Objectives	Establish market position	Expand target market	Seek new market segments	Prepare for re-entry
Product strategy	Assure high quality	Identify weaknesses	Adjust size, color, package	Modify features
Advertising objectives	Build brand awareness	Provide information	Use imagery to differentiate from competitors	Educate on changes
Distribution	Build distribution network	Solidify distribution relationships	Maintain distribution	Re-establish and deliver new version
Price	Skimming or penetration strategy	Meet competition	Use price deals	Maintain price
Phase in life cycle	**Introduction**	**Growth**	**Maturity**	**Decline**

Source: Adapted from Ben M. Enis, Raymond La Grace, and Arthur E. Press, "Extending the Product Life Cycle," *Business Horizons* 20 (June 1977), p. 53. Copyright 1977 by the Foundation for the School of Business at Indiana University. Reprinted by permission.

tronics goods. While the model was designed for evaluating new-product development projects, the approach can be used to predict the PLC of an existing product. Estimating the timing and magnitude of turning points of a successful product introduction is one application of the model.

The planning model determines sales volume by combining estimates of original purchases and replacements.[11] Original purchases are estimated using three predictor variables: (1) consumer needs and wants, (2) number of competitors, and (3) amount of advertising and promotional effort (industry total). Replacement estimates are a function of the product's useful life, the percent of owners who will replace it, the trade-off of repair versus replacement, and the level of the initial purchases. The validity tests of model predictions against actual PLCs show a close correspondence between PLC shapes.

Product Portfolio Analysis

Product portfolio analysis considers whether each product is measuring up to management's minimum performance criteria and assesses the strengths and weaknesses of the product relative to other products in the portfolio. The comparative analysis of products can be performed by using the grid method for SBU evaluation (Chapter 2). These grids highlight differences among products. After identifying the relative attractiveness and business strength of the products in the portfolio, analysis of specific performance factors may also be useful, including: profit contribution; barriers to entry; sales fluctuations; extent of capacity utilization; responsiveness of sales to prices, promotional activities, and service levels; technology (maturity, volatility, and complexity); alternative production and process opportunities; and environmental considerations.[12]

The grid analysis can also compare competing brands when they are targeting different market segments. Otherwise, the market attractiveness will be constant across all brands targeting the same market.

Positioning Brands

Perceptual maps are useful for comparing brands. These methods are discussed in Chapters 5, 6, and 7. The map is developed by obtaining preference information on a set of competing brands or firms from a sample of buyers. Various product attributes are used, and the results are summarized by the preference map.

Competitive mapping analysis offers useful guidelines for strategic product positioning. The analyses can relate buyer preferences to different brands and indicate possible brand repositioning options. New-product opportunities may also be identified through the analysis of preference maps. These are shown by preferences that are not satisfied by the existing brands. Positioning studies over time can measure the impact of repositioning strategies.

Other Product Analysis Methods

The financial analysis tools in the appendix to Chapter 4 are used to evaluate product financial performance. Other product analysis methods include research studies that show the relative importance of product attributes to buyers and rate brands against these attributes. This information indicates brand strengths and weaknesses. Many of the standardized information services provided by marketing research firms, such as Information Resources, Inc. and A. C. Nielsen Company, help in monitoring the market performance of competing brands of food and drug products. Industry trade publications also publish market share and other brand performance data.

A major consideration when introducing new products that meet similar needs to a firm's existing brands is estimating how much sales volume the new product will attract from one or more existing brands. Such cannibalization may reduce the contribution of the new product to the overall performance of the product portfolio. Gillette's Sensor razor offered a possible cannibalization threat to Atra and Trac II sales.[13] The plan was to target disposable users, recognizing that some cannibalization would occur. Also, the Sensor blades were priced about 25 percent higher than Atra. Since both Atra and Trac II were in the mature stages of their life cycles, the new brand was needed to hold Gillette's position in the market. The Sensor performed even better than the sales and profit forecasts made by Gillette's management (see Case 2–3). The Sensor for Women, introduced in 1992, gained the leading market position in women's razors.

DEVELOPING PRODUCT STRATEGIES

The portfolio analysis determines how well existing product strategies are performing. The information helps management to identify new product needs and where existing product strategies should be altered.

Brands that have been successful over a long time period offer useful insights about product strategies. While many new products fail, established brands like Coca-Cola, Levi's, Budweiser, and Hershey continue to build strong market positions. These good performance records are the result of (1) marketing skills, (2) product quality, and (3) strong brand preference developed by years of successful advertising.[14] The financial value (brand equity) of the well-respected brand names of RJR Nabisco, Kraft, and Pillsbury made these firms very attractive takeover candidates in the 1980s. Kohlberg Kravis Roberts & Co. paid $25 billion in 1989 to acquire RJR Nabisco. The brand equity that has been developed for the company's many famous brands is a valuable asset. A common characteristic of many enduring brands is that the targeting and positioning strategy initially selected has generally been followed during the life of each brand. "These brands haven't strayed much from the basic marketing strategies that made them stars."[15] We discuss brand equity in the next section.

Selecting and implementing good product strategies pays off. Research findings suggest that the leading brands are 50 percent more profitable than their nearest competitors.[16] Product strategies include decisions for each product, product line, and the product mix, as shown in Exhibit 12–5. Product line actions may include adding a new product, reducing cost, improving the product, altering market strategy, and dropping a product. The product mix strategy may involve adding a product line, deleting a line, or changing the priority of a line (e.g., increasing the marketing budget for one line and cutting the budget for another line). We examine the nature and scope of these decisions.

EXHIBIT 12–5 Product Strategies

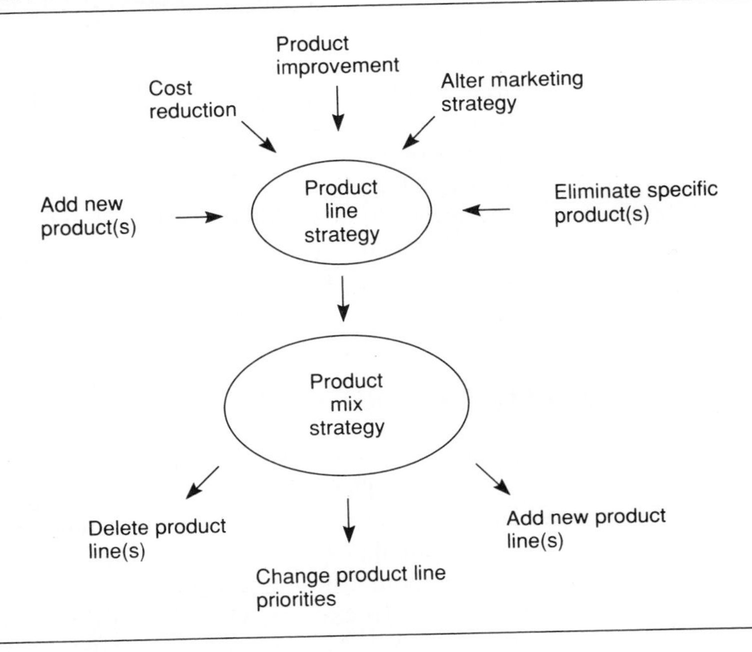

Setting Priorities

Priorities concerning product lines and individual products are useful in guiding resource allocation and management attention. In instances where multiple products or lines make up an SBU, it helps to indicate the strategic priorities for all product categories within the SBU. These priorities guide product-planning activities for the SBU, showing where to allocate resources for product development and improvement.

Exhibit 12–6 shows how the management of an industrial equipment SBU evaluates each product line according to business strength (internal) and market (external) factors. The factors are evaluated to obtain the product line positioning shown in Exhibit 12–6. They include competition, required resources, profit contribution, company strengths, industry potential, and other factors. The positioning of lines A–J is a composite of these factors. High resource priorities are shown for product lines A–E. The guidelines are shown for product groups I, II, and III. Exhibit 12–6 illustrates how management can assign priorities among various products in the mix. These decisions lead to specific product-planning activities and resource allocations.

EXHIBIT 12–6 Establishing Product Line Priorities and Strategic Guides for an Industrial Equipment SBU

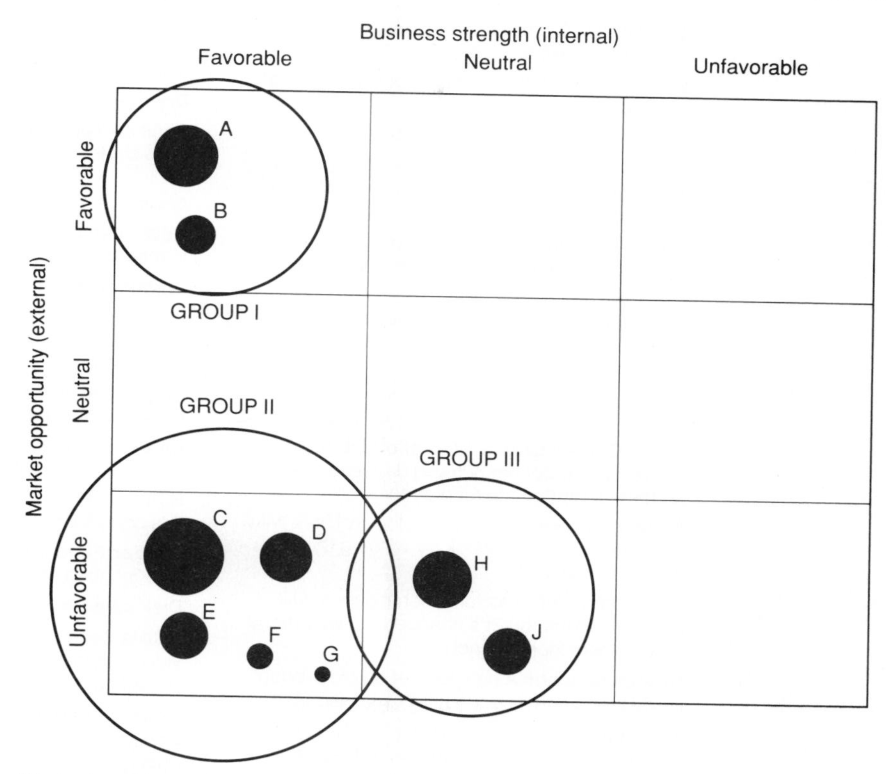

Strategic guides:
Group I: Increase product development/improvement and sales development effort to expand market share.
Group II: Increase profit contribution by reducing costs and selective sales development.
Group III: Reduce assets and reduce costs.
Product Lines A, B, C, D, and E to receive 80 percent of SBU effort.

Note: Diameters of circles indicate relative size of product line based on sales in dollars.

Strategies for Existing Products

Several examples of consumer product innovation successes and failures are shown in Exhibit 12–7. Many of the new products are actually modifications of existing products. The impact of the microwave oven on tastes and preferences has changed food preparation practices for many existing foods such as vegetables, meats, and liquids. Some of the products listed in Exhibit

EXHIBIT 12–7 Marketing Milestones of the Decade

Hits

IBM PC Big Blue claimed the power to set industry standards.

Microwave food It's changing our definition of good food.

Diet Coke Brilliant brand extension.

Lean Cuisine Pricey diet entrees launched at the height of the recession. Caught the fit-but-fast wave.

Macintosh computer Apple computer's new design changed the way people use these machines.

Super-premium ice cream Haagen-Dazs, Ben & Jerry's, Dove Bar, the perfect end to low-calorie meals.

Chrysler minivans These station wagons of the 80s created a new category of cars.

Tartar Control Crest P&G's efforts to teach consumers about nasty tooth deposits helped restore its toothpaste market share.

Athletic footwear After stumbling in 1986, Nike slam-dunked rival Reebok by winning the favor of big-city kids.

USA Today The colorful national daily is still mired in red ink, but it's changed the way many newspapers look and act.

Swatch watches A new look at an old product made watches into hot fashion accessories.

Nintendo video games Games like Super Mario Brothers continue so strong they're zapping the rest of the toy business.

SPF sunscreens Do you need SPF 5 or SPF 15? High-tech sunscreens sell well to aging baby boomers.

Flashes

Oat bran With oat bran snacks and oat bran beer on the market, this one's got to be peaking.

Corona beer Who ever really wanted lime in beer anyway?

Cabbage Patch Kids They're still around, although sales have crashed. Maker Coleco wasn't so lucky.

Miniskirts They're in. They're out. Or are they?

Granola bars In the mid-1980s, nearly a score of companies battled to be "health" snack king, while consumers snuck back to salty favorites.

Dry beer Why is it called "Dry" again?

Wine coolers They're sweet as ever, but sales have cooled.

Misses

New Coke Fixed what wasn't broken; customers immediately clamored for the original.

Premier cigarette "Smokeless" cigarette couldn't be lit with matches.

IBM PCjr A problematic keyboard contributed to its demise.

Yugo Yugoslavian minicar was billed as cheapest new car in America, and it showed.

LA Beer Despite the New Sobriety, the market for reduced alcohol beer has little fizz.

Home banking Consumers weren't ready for this complicated "service."

Pontiac Fiero Looked great, but was discontinued after problems with engine fires.

Disk camera Kodak's Edsel.

RCA's SelectaVision Bad timing for the videodisk player once lauded as RCA's premier product of the 80s.

Generic products An 80s flop, if not an 80s innovation; consumers felt queasy about their quality.

Fab 1 Shot Colgate-Palmolive Co.'s premeasured laundry detergent means consumers can't use just enough for a small load.

Holly Farms roasted chickens Consumers liked these fully cooked birds, but retailers balked at their short shelf life.

Source: Kathleen Deveny, "Lesson of the '80s: Emphasize Health, Eliminate Hassles," *The Wall Street Journal,* November 28, 1989, p. B1.

12–7 promise to be long-term successes, while others may experience short life spans.

Once the need for changing the strategy of an existing product is identified, there are several options for responding to the situation, as shown earlier in Exhibit 12–5. We discuss each strategy to indicate the issues and scope of the action.

Cost Reduction. Low costs give a company a major advantage over the competition. As an illustration, Nabisco's Ritz Cracker was introduced in 1934 and is still the best-selling cracker in the world.[17] Nearly 16 billion crackers are sold each year, generating $150 million in sales. The original ingredients are essentially the same today as they were 60 years ago. In addition to a flavor that has wide appeal, Ritz's low price compared to other types of crackers gives it a major competitive advantage. Ritz's high-volume production helps to keep costs low. Product costs may be reduced by changes in the engineering design, manufacturing improvements, supply costs, and increases in marketing productivity.

Products are often improved by changing their features, quality, and styling. Automobile features and styles are modified on a continuing basis. Many companies allocate substantial resources to the regular improvement of their products. Compared to a decade ago, today's products, such as disposable diapers, cameras, computers, and consumer electronics, show vast improvements in their performance and features.

Features. One way to differentiate a brand against competition is with unique features. For example, the Hewlett-Packard Company Series 10 line of hand-held calculators is targeted to professionals in science and engineering and financial services. Special programmed features simplify calculations such as present value determination. Another option is to let the buyer select the features desired in a product. Optional features offer the buyer more flexibility in selecting a brand. This strategy is used by automobile manufacturers. The capability to produce products with varied features that appeal to market diversity is an important competitive advantage. Japanese automobile manufacturers have plants that can economically produce smaller unit volumes than U.S. producers. This advantage can be used to meet the specific needs of the different market segments targeted by the firm.

Quality. An important strategy for increasing competitive advantage is quality improvement. As discussed earlier in the chapter, companies are adopting total quality management as a basic business strategy. For example, an international study of quality management practices conducted by Ernst & Young and the American Quality Foundation found that "virtually every organization in the sample believes that quality is a critical factor in its strategic performance."[18] The sample included more than 500 businesses in Canada, Germany, Japan, and the United States.

Style. Despite the probable greater importance of product quality, style may offer an important competitive edge for certain products. Moreover, style may serve as a proxy for quality in some product categories. Seiko has very effectively used style (and other features) to make its watches attractive to buyers. The many different styles offered by Seiko allow consumers a wide range of choice. Other examples of product style strategies include Ethan Allen in furniture, Lexus in automobiles, and Escada in women's clothing. Ethan Allen concentrates on one style, traditional American furniture. Lexus has created a strong customer preference for its European-style luxury autos. Escada A.G. offers a variety of high priced women's apparel using its different labels.

Marketing Strategy Alteration. Some changes in market targeting and positioning are often necessary as a product moves through its life cycle. Problems or opportunities may point to adjusting marketing strategy during a PLC stage. Consider, for example, New England Apple Products Company Inc., a small wholesaler selling juice products under private labels to stores and supermarkets.[19] A new logo and new packaging transformed a commodity product into a marketing success. The small firm was able to establish its brand identity in a market comprising two giant brands—Tree Top and Mott's—and many small firms. The label shows a partially eaten apple in red and green colors and the brand name, Very Fine. The wrap-around foam label helps insulate the 10-ounce single-serving bottle. The brand is distributed in 35 states. The company has expanded its juice offering to include several other fruit drinks. New England Apple's marketing strategy benefited from the natural food trend that expanded rapidly in the 1980s.

Product Elimination. Dropping a problem product may be necessary when cost reduction, product improvement, or marketing mix alteration strategies are not feasible. In deciding to drop a product, management may consider a variety of performance criteria in addition to the product's sales and profit contribution. Elimination may occur at any PLC stage, although it is more likely to be considered in either the introduction or decline stages. Management may decide to halt production and sell off its existing inventory, or to try to sell the product(s) to another company. Sales of entire lines to other companies occurred during the 1980s: Black & Decker purchased General Electric's small household appliance lines, and a French computer firm purchased Zenith's computer business.

Product Mix Modifications

The modification of a company's product mix is a major product strategy change. The motivation for changing the product mix may be to:

- Increase the growth rate of the business.
- Offer a complete range of products to wholesalers and retailers.

- Gain marketing strength and economies in distribution, advertising, and personal selling.
- Capitalize on an existing brand position.
- Diversify to avoid dependence on one product area.

The product mix is expanded through internal development or by purchase of an entire company or a line of products. Purchase was a popular option in the 1980s as a result of low stock market prices compared to the costs of internal development. Acquisition also offers a faster means of expanding the product mix. Strategic alliances among competitors are used for gaining access to new markets and expanding product lines. These collaborative relationships promise to escalate in importance during the 1990s (see Chapter 3).

Product mix modification is normally a corporate or business unit decision. Chapter 2 considers product and market strategies. Restructuring actions may affect the mix of products a company offers. One interesting trend of the 1980s was the expanded amount of product acquisitions and divestments on a global scope. Examples include IBM's sale of Rolm (office telephone switches) to Siemens AG, the European telecommunications company; and the purchase of Combustion Engineering, Inc. (a U.S. power-generation equipment company) by the Swedish-Swiss electric engineering firm, AAB Asea Brown Boveri Ltd.

Who Manages Products?

Responsibility for product strategy extends to several organizational levels. We examine three product management levels that often exist in companies that have strategic business units, different product lines, and specific brands within lines.

Product/Brand Management. This activity consists of planning, managing, and coordinating strategy for a specific product or brand. Responsibilities at this management level include market analysis, targeting, positioning strategy, product analysis and strategy, identification of new product needs, and management and coordination of product/brand marketing activities. Marketing plans for specific products or brands are often prepared at this level. Product or brand managers typically do not have authority over all product management activities. Nevertheless, they have product responsibility. These managers are sponsors or advocates of their products, negotiating on behalf of their products with the sales force, research and development, marketing research, and advertising managers.

Product Group/Marketing Management. A business with several products or brands may assign responsibility for managing its product or brand managers to a product director, group manager, or marketing manager. This person coordinates the activities and approves the recommendations of a group of product or brand managers. The nature and scope of the group responsibilities are similar to those of product/brand managers. Additionally, the product group manager coordinates product management activities and decisions with the SBU management.

Product Mix Management. This responsibility is normally assigned to the chief executive at the SBU or corporate level of an organization or to a team of top executives. Illustrative decisions include product acquisitions, research and development priorities, new-product decisions, and resource allocation. Evaluation of product portfolio performance is also centered at this level. In a corporation with two or more SBUs, top management may coordinate and establish product management guidelines for the SBU management. We look at the organization of all aspects of marketing activities in Chapter 16.

Environmental Effects of Products. Environmental issues about product labeling, packaging, use, and disposal are considered in the marketing strategies of most companies. Protection of the environment involves a complex set of trade-offs among social, economic, political, and technology factors. Companies like McDonald's, Procter & Gamble, Rubbermaid, and many others incorporate environmental considerations into their product strategies. Moreover, these environmental concerns are global in scope.

Many of the environmental issues are very complex, and may require consumers to change their use and disposal behavior. Even the technical authorities do not always agree on the extent to which environmental problems exist or how to solve the problems. Nevertheless, many companies, governments, and special-interest groups are proactively working toward reducing environmental contamination. For example, P&G's environmental strategy regarding disposable diapers is described in the Environment Feature.

BRANDING STRATEGY

A strong brand image offers an organization several important advantages. The brand name distinguishes a product from competitors' products. A powerful brand identity creates a major competitive advantage. A brand that is recognized by buyers encourages repeat purchases. Consider this assessment by a Korean executive of the importance of brand recognition in the consumer-electronics market:

> "We are producing almost the same quality as the Japanese manufacturers," says Mr. Kim, president of Gold Star Electronics International Inc., the U.S. sales subsidiary. "The only reason our products are cheaper is because the Gold Star name isn't known to the American consumer. Our main strategy is to increase our brand image and awareness among American consumers."
>
> Gold Star is discarding a long-successful strategy for selling in the United

ENVIRONMENT FEATURE P&G's Environmental Strategy

Before the heightened awareness of a product's impact on the environment, Procter & Gamble's products met four basic consumer needs: They were safe, high performing, convenient and a good value. Now, however, we have identified a fifth consumer need: Product and packaging must be *environmentally acceptable*. . . .

One of Procter & Gamble's greatest challenges has been its diaper brands—Luvs and Pampers. Disposable diapers have become a symbol of a disposable society (though they represent less than 2 percent of total landfill volume). Through the use of new technology—absorbent gelling material—Pampers has been able to reduce the volume of its product by 50 percent. A change from bulky cardboard packaging to a poly film reduced packaging volume by 80 percent. And the company recently made a twofold announcement. First, it will begin testing a new diaper with a compostable backsheet in 1991. The change will make the entire diaper compostable. Second, P&G allocated $20 million for projects that will advance municipal solid-waste composting worldwide. The single largest untapped opportunity to reduce municipal solid waste is accelerated composting. Composting in conjunction with other forms of recycling is the best chance we have to reduce municipal solid waste in landfills.

Source: James K. Goodwin, "Environmental Strategies—A Competitive Weapon," in *Marketing: What's New, What's Next?* (New York: The Conference Board, Inc., 1991), pp. 27, 28.

States in favor of one whose outcome is far from certain. It is forsaking its profitable, but low-profile, position in the lower end of the consumer-electronics market to try to capture a more visible position among the well-known brand names at the upper end.

There is some doubt whether dealers will go along. "We don't want Gold Star to become a Panasonic or a Sony," says Lorin Bardele, a merchandise manager for the 34-outlet Kohl's Department Stores of Brookfield, Wis. "We need Gold Star to continue being our promotional brand. We're trying to make sure we—and they—don't price Gold Star [products] out of what I feel is their strongest niche."[20]

One of several brand strategy options may be appropriate for a company. We look at the features of each strategy, then highlight the strategic advantages of brand identity.

Branding Strategies

The major branding alternatives are shown in Exhibit 12–8. Branding applies to services as well as physical products. There are many examples of strong brand images for services including American Express, American Airlines, CitiBank, Marriott, and United Parcel Service.

No Brand Identity. Many small and medium-sized manufacturers do not have an established brand identity, even though the company name is printed on the package or item. The lack of financial resources and marketing capabilities make it difficult for a small firm with an unknown brand to

EXHIBIT 12–8 Alternative Branding Strategies

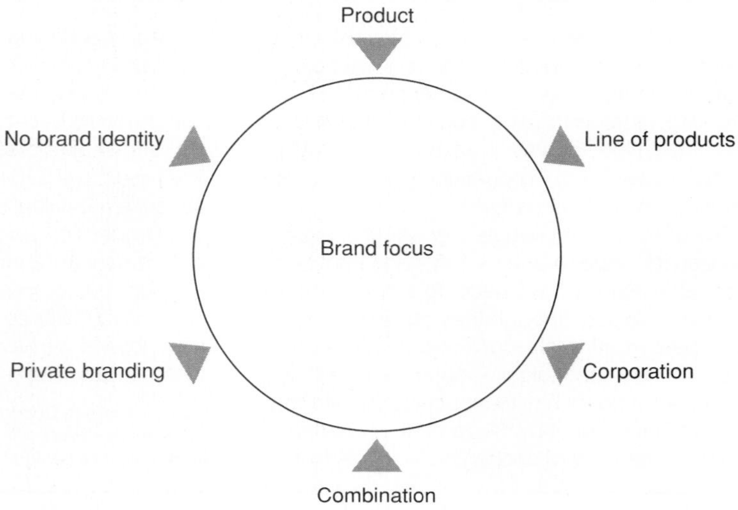

build buyer awareness in the marketplace. Major expenditures are required to introduce and promote the brand. A firm in this situation often relies on wholesalers or retailers to encourage buyers to purchase its brand. Buyers associate the unknown brand to the intermediaries that carry the brand. Typically, the producer of an unknown brand concentrates its marketing efforts on wholesalers and retailers rather than end-users. These products may develop consumer loyalty over time if the users' experiences with the product are favorable and if it is purchased frequently. Even if a firm does not have the resources to aggressively promote a brand, it should use a brand name for the product, particularly if the item is repurchased on a continuing basis. Favorable use experience and word-of-mouth promotion with friends will help to build the brand's reputation with buyers.

Private Branding. Retailers with established brand names, such as The Limited, Target, and Wal-Mart Stores, Inc., contract with producers to place the retailers' brands on the products manufactured. This practice is called private branding. The major advantage to the producer is eliminating the costs of marketing to end-users, although a private-label arrangement makes the manufacturer dependent on the firm using the private brand. Producing private-label merchandise for a single company is risky since the arrangement may be terminated by the buyer. Nevertheless, the arrangement can yield benefits to both the producer and middleman. The sales volume of the producer is expanded rapidly. The retailer uses its private brand to build store loyalty, since the private brand is associated with the retailer's stores. Private brands are often profitable for retailers. For example, the profit margins of the private brands carried by supermarkets typically run 10 percent to 15 percent higher than other brands.[21] Private brands account for about 13 percent of total sales in supermarkets.

Corporate Branding. This strategy builds brand identity using the corporate name to identify the entire product offering. Examples include IBM in computers, AT&T in communications, and Detroit Diesel in truck engines. Corporate branding has the advantage of using one advertising and sales promotion program to support all of the firm's products. It also simplifies the promotion of new products. The shortcomings of corporate branding include a lack of focus on specific products and the adverse effects on the entire product portfolio if the company encounters negative publicity. For example, the publicity in 1992 concerning the alleged unnecessary repairs in Sears auto shops created negative impressions about Sears retail stores. Using corporate branding as a primary approach to branding is appropriate when it is not feasible to establish specific brand identity and when the product offering is relatively narrow.

Product-Line Branding. This strategy places the brand name on a line of related products. Hartmarx, the men's apparel producer, has several brands of men's suits, such as Austin Reed. Product-line branding provides more focus than corporate branding and is cost effective by promoting the entire line rather than each product. This strategy is effective when a firm has one or more lines, each of which represents an interrelated offering of product items. London Fog outer wear, for example, is marketed as a line of apparel rather than establishing a brand identity for each item in the line.

Specific Product Branding. The strategy of assigning a brand name to a specific product is used by various producers of frequently purchased items, such as Procter & Gamble's Crest toothpaste, Pampers diapers, and Ivory soap. The brand name on a product gives it a unique identification in the marketplace. A successful brand develops a strong customer loyalty over time. Products that are low-involvement purchases benefit from a popular brand name. The major limitation of using brand names on individual products is the high expense of building and supporting each brand through advertising and sales promotion. One danger is that the brand name may be so popular that it becomes a generic term that people use to describe the product type. Companies work aggressively to avoid this and other misuses of their popular brand names. The annual advertising expenditures for several brands are shown in Exhibit 12–9. Building a new brand name through advertising initially can cost over $50 million, plus the expense of maintaining the brand identity in the market place.

Combination Branding. A company may use a combination of the branding strategies shown in Exhibit 12–8. Sears, for example, uses both product-

EXHIBIT 12–9 Annual Advertising Expenditures for Various Brands ($ millions)

Brand	
American Express	$107
CitiBank	89
Healthy Choice	24
Huggies	30
Pert Plus	21
Plax	21
Tylenol	134

Source: "Superbrands 1991," *AdWeeks Marketing Week.*

line and corporate branding. (e.g., the Kenmore appliance and Craftsman tool lines). The Rolex brand name identifies the line of watches while each item in the line also has a name (e.g., the Rolex Daytona). Combination branding benefits from the buyer's association of the corporate name with the product or line brand name. However, corporate advertising may not be cost-effective for inexpensive, frequently purchased consumer brands. For example, companies like Procter & Gamble and Chesebrough-Ponds (Vaseline, Q-Tips) do not actively promote the corporate identity.

Brand Equity

Recognizing the value (equity) of a brand name and managing the name to gain maximum competitive advantage for the owner of the name are very important. "Brand equity is a set of brand assets and liabilities linked to a brand, its name and symbol, that add to or subtract from the value provided by a product or service to a firm and/or to that firm's customers."[22] The assets and liabilities that impact brand equity include brand loyalty, name awareness, perceived quality and other brand associations, and proprietary brand assets (e.g., patents).

The possible inclusion of brand equity values on balance sheets has been the subject of considerable debate. The objective is to show a brand's financial worth. Several methods for valuation are proposed. One method is momentum accounting, which considers how the earning power of the brand changes over its life cycle because of the revenues and expenses associated with the brand:

> Momentum accounting uses functions similar to depreciation curves in conventional accounting to monitor the sources of change in brand value over time. Momentum accounting tries to capture managers' intuition about the reasons

for momentum change in terms of "impulses"—the marketing, competitive, and environmental events that affect a brand's value.[23]

The concept of brand equity is clearly established. How to measure equity and whether or not to include its value on the balance sheet continue to be discussed. Nevertheless, the attention given to brand equity has increased executives' recognition of the power and value of brand names and the importance of managing brand equity over the life cycle of the brand.

Gaining Strategic Advantage through Brand Identity

Established brand names may be useful in introducing other products by linking the new product to an existing brand name. A brand name that is familiar to many buyers can be used to identify other products in a company's portfolio. The primary advantage is immediate name recognition for the new product. Two methods of capitalizing on an existing brand name are brand extension and licensing.

Brand Extension. This approach uses consumers' familiarity with an existing brand name to launch a new product line of a different product type. The new line may or may not be closely related to the brand from which it is being extended. Examples of related extensions include Ivory shampoo and conditioner, Hershey chocolate milk, and Swiss Army watches.

Critics of brand and line extensions indicate that extensions often do not succeed and may damage the mother product.[24] They argue that a brand name is weakened when it stands for two things. Some observers have questioned Procter & Gamble's use of the Duncan Hines brand image to launch its bagged cookies, because some ads encourage using bake mixes while others promote purchase of ready-made cookies.

Regardless of the possible dangers of brand extension, it continues to be used. Two considerations are important. First, there should be a logical tie between the core brand and the extension. It may be a different product type while having some relationship to the core brand. For example, the Swiss Army knife brand was used to introduce Swiss Army watches and sunglasses. Second, the extension needs to be carefully evaluated as to any negative impact on the brand equity of the core brand.

Licensing. Another method of using the core brand name is licensing. The sale of a firm's brand name to another company for use on a noncompeting product is a major business activity. Total retail sales of licensed products were estimated at $75 billion in 1990.[25] Apparel and accessories account for 38 percent of licensed products followed by 19 percent of toys and games, 12 percent of publishing and stationery, and 11 percent of gifts and novelties. The firm granting the license obtains additional revenue with only lim-

EXHIBIT 12–10 Brand Loyalty by Product Category

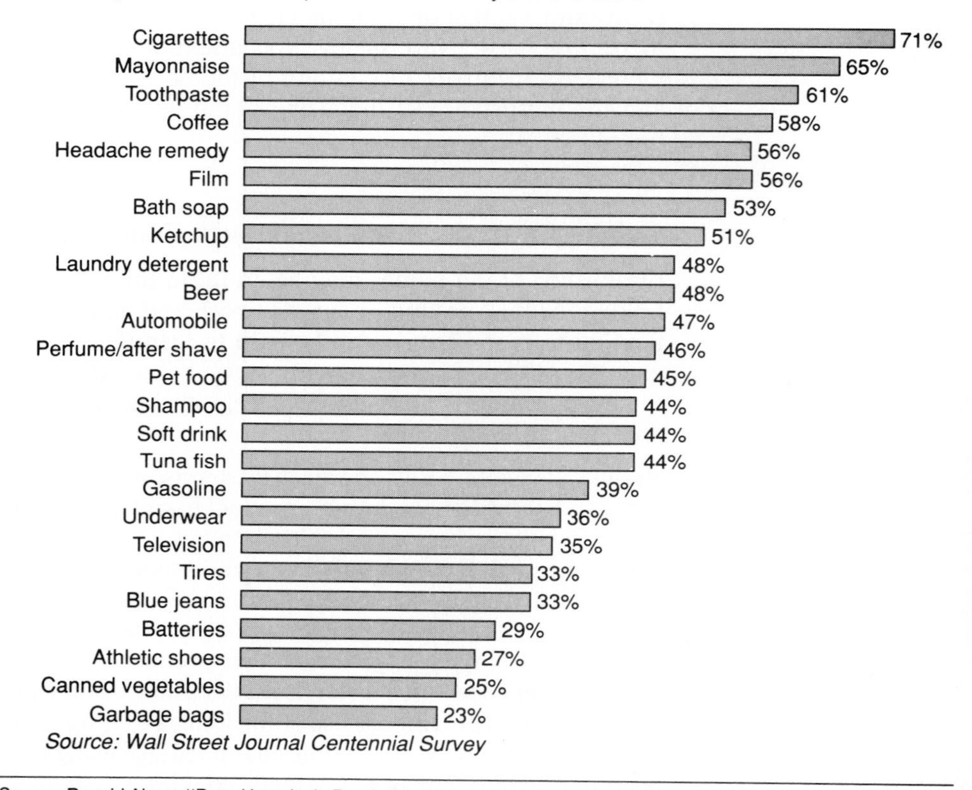

Source: Ronald Alsop, "Brand Loyalty Is Rarely Blind Loyalty," *The Wall Street Journal,* October 19, 1989, p. B1.

ited costs. It also gains free publicity for the core brand name. The main limitation is that the licensee may create an unfavorable image for the brand. Licensing may be used for corporate, product line, or specific brands. Anheuser-Busch Companies, Inc. (Budweiser beer) is one of the largest corporate licensers.

Variations in Brand Loyalty. Brand loyalty varies by type of consumer product, as shown in Exhibit 12–10. Loyalty to brands is stronger for products that have distinctive flavors.[26] Some erosion of brand loyalty may have occurred during the 1980s. Heavy promotional programs, bargain prices, and nutritional and environmental concerns caused consumers to shift brands. *The Wall Street Journal*'s survey of 2,000 consumers in 1989 found that over 12 percent are not brand loyal for *any* of the products shown in

EXHIBIT 12–11 Customer Service Involves Most Functions in an Organization

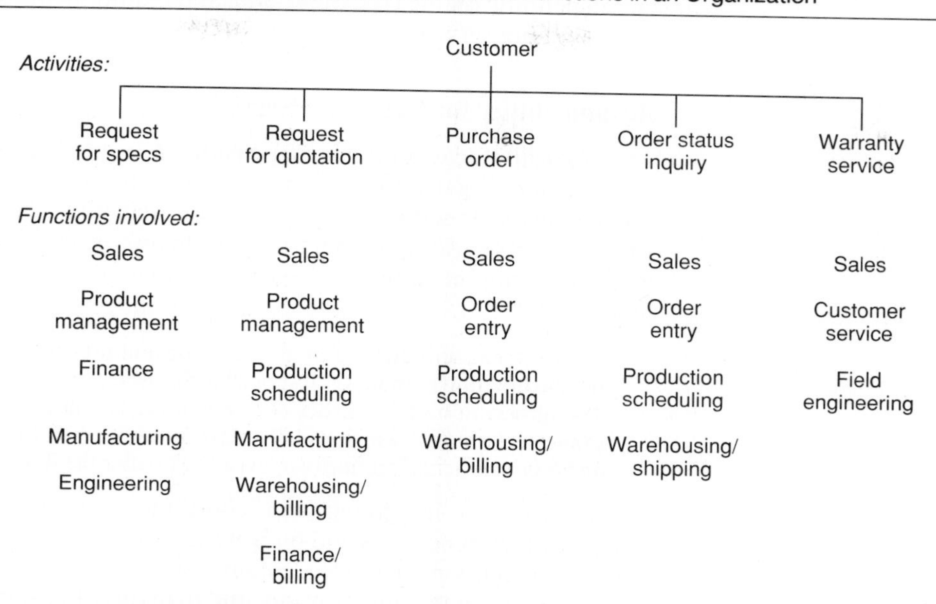

Reprinted from *Business Horizons*, March-April. Copyright © 1992 by the Foundation of the School of Business at Indiana University. Used with permission.

Exhibit 12–10. Nearly half of them are loyal for one to five of the categories. Brand loyalty varies by age. Apparently older buyers display stronger preferences toward specific brands.

CUSTOMER-SERVICE STRATEGY

Customer service is an important and sometimes neglected part of product strategy. We define customer service and discuss the responsibility for this product function in the organization.

Defining Customer Service

The activities included in customer service are requests for product specifications such as performance data, requests for quotation, purchase order processing, order status inquiries, and warranty service.[27] As shown in Exhibit 12–11, customer service involves many functions in the organization. A major problem in providing effective services is coordinating the activities of the various functions shown in Exhibit 12–11. This array of product and supporting services must be managed to achieve high levels of customer satisfaction. Various attributes of customer service may be important depending on the type of product and requirements of specific customers. Customer services enhance the value of product to the customer.

Responsibility for Customer Service

An important factor in managing customer service is viewing it as a major part of marketing strategy. It is necessary to define the internal processes that impact customer service, establish service objectives, develop and manage strategies for providing services, and assign responsibilities for customer service. The fragmentation of service activities in many companies is described:

> The different activities required to develop and process an order typically have no one function or manager responsible for overseeing all the required activities. The closest thing to an order overseer in many companies is the formal customer-service staff, which usually plays a reactive role to customer complaints and has little actual authority to expedite or alter the flow of an order.[28]

Creating an integrated and coordinated customer-service strategy requires developing plans and budgets, measuring performance, and assigning responsibility for service. Customer service needs to be part of the marketing strategy of the organization, and to involve the various business functions whose activities impact customers.

Customer-service responsibility is often assigned to the sales force or to a marketing staff unit that processes customer inquiries and complaints. A better approach is to develop strategies (and priorities) for service, assigning responsibility to the various functions involved in providing service. Customer service is a process of activities that add value to the buyer-seller relationship. The process must be defined, analyzed, and managed with the objective of improving customer satisfaction.

SUMMARY

Product strategy, which sets the stage for selecting strategies for each of the remaining components of the positioning strategy, forms the leading edge of the marketing program. Product strategy is matched to the right distribution, pricing, and promotion strategies. Product decisions shape both corporate and marketing strategies, and are made within the guidelines of the corporate mission and objectives. The major product decisions for a strategic business unit include selecting the mix of products to be offered, deciding how to position an SBU's product offering, developing and implementing strategies for the products in the portfolio, selecting the brand strategy for each product, and planning and implementing customer-service strategies.

The importance of product quality to competing in global markets requires the development of an organizational philosophy and management process for improving quality. Quality is the responsibility of everyone in the organization. Competitive advantage in the 1990s depends on the success of the company's product quality improvement and cost reduction. Quality improvement involves developing a philosophy toward product quality, implementing quality improvement programs, and applying statistical methods to improve business processes.

Evaluating the existing products helps to establish priorities and guidelines for managing the product portfolio. These methods include the analysis of the product life cycle, portfolio screening, positioning analysis, and financial analysis. It is necessary to decide for each product if: (1) a new product should be developed to replace or complement the product; (2) the product should be improved (and, if so, how); or (3) the product should be eliminated. Product strategy alternatives for the existing products include cost reduction, product alteration, marketing strategy changes, and product elimination. Product mix modification may also occur.

Most successful corporations have found that an individual or organizational unit should be assigned responsibility for product planning. The approaches that are used range from a committee to a product planning department. Product managers for planning and coordinating product activities are used by many companies.

Branding strategy involves deciding among private branding, corporate branding, product-line branding, specific product branding, and combination branding. Brand equity is an important asset. Brand identification in the market place offers a firm an opportunity to gain a strategic advantage through brand extension and licensing.

Finally, the influence of customer service on the buyer-seller relationship must be recognized. It is often neglected or treated in a fragmented manner in many organizations. Customer service is a process; it involves most of the functions in an organization. Competitive advantage is gained by developing an integrated and coordinated customer-service strategy, assigning responsibility for the activities, and involving the various functions in providing services.

QUESTIONS FOR REVIEW AND DISCUSSION

1. Eli Lilly & Company manufactures a broad line of pharmaceuticals with strong brand positions in the marketplace. Lilly is also a manufacturer of generic drug products. Is this combination branding strategy a logical one? If so, why?
2. Discuss the advantages and limitations of following a branding strategy of using brand names for specific products.
3. In 1985 Philip Morris Incorporated acquired General Foods Company. Discuss the advantages and limitations of

acquiring a company in order to obtain its established brand names.

4. To what extent are the SBU strategy and the product strategy interrelated?
5. Referring to Exhibit 10–6, do you see any benefit in separately analyzing the specific products within each of the product lines A–J?
6. Suppose that a top administrator of a university wants to establish a product-management function covering both new and existing services. Develop a plan for establishing a product planning program.
7. Many products like Jell-O reach maturity. Discuss several ways to give mature products new vigor. How can management determine whether it is worthwhile to attempt to salvage products that are performing poorly?
8. How does improving product quality lower the cost of producing a product?
9. Why do some products experience long successful lives while others have very short life cycles?
10. Discuss why it is important to coordinate the organization's customer service functions.

NOTES

1. This illustration is based on Steven Kreider Yoder, "Hewlett-Packard Is Too Busy to Notice Industry Slump," *The Wall Street Journal,* May 11, 1992, p. B3.
2. David W. Cravens, Gerald E. Hills, and Robert B. Woodruff, *Marketing Management* (Homewood, Ill.: Richard D. Irwin, 1987), p. 375.
3. Leonard Berry, "Services Marketing is Different," *Business,* May–June 1980, pp. 24–30.
4. The following discussion is based on David W. Cravens, Charles W. Holland, Charles W. Lamb, Jr., and William C. Moncrief III, "Marketing's Role in Product Service/Quality," *Industrial Marketing Management,* November 1988 pp. 285–303.
5. W. Edwards Deming, *Quality, Productivity, and Competitive Position* (Cambridge, Mass.: Massachusetts Institute of Technology, Center for Advanced Engineering Study, 1982).
6. Frank S. Leonard and W. Earl Sasser, "The Incline of Quality," *Harvard Business Review,* September–October 1982, pp. 163–71.
7. John Harris, "Advantage, Mitsubishi," *Forbes,* March 18, 1991, pp. 100, 104.
8. Kathleen Deveny, "Colgate Puts the Squeeze on Crest," *Business Week,* August 19, 1985, pp. 40 and 41; and "Toothpaste Makers Tout New Packaging," *The Wall Street Journal,* November 10, 1992, pp. B1, B10.
9. William Qualls, Richard W. Olshavsky, and Ronald E. Michaels, "Shortening of the PLC: An Empirical Test," *Journal of Marketing,* Fall 1981, p. 77.
10. Steven G. Harrell and Elmer D. Taylor, "Modeling the Product Life Cycle for Consumer Durables," *Journal of Marketing,* Fall 1981, pp. 68–75.
11. Ibid., pp. 70–71.
12. George S. Day, "Diagnosing the Product Portfolio," *Journal of Marketing,* April 1977, p. 37.
13. Lawrence Ingrassia, "Face-Off: A Recovering Gillette Hopes for Vindication in a High-Tech Razor," *The Wall Street Journal,* September 29, 1989, pp. A1, A4.
14. Ronald Alsop, "Enduring Brands Hold Their Allure by Sticking Close to Their Roots," *The Wall Street Journal,* Centennial Edition, pp. B4–B5.
15. Ibid.
16. Ibid.
17. "If It's Not Broken, Don't Fix It," *Forbes,* May 7, 1984, p. 132.
18. American Quality Foundation and

Ernst & Young, *International Quality Study,* 1991, p. 4.

19. Jeffrey A. Trachtenberg, "Small Is Beautiful," *Forbes,* December 31, 1984, pp. 112–13.
20. Steven P. Galante, "Korea's Gold Star Is Banking on Quality to Build an Image in the U.S. TV Market," *The Asian Wall Street Journal,* November 26, 1984, p. 12.
21. Alix M. Freedman, "Supermarkets Push Private-Label Lines," *The Wall Street Journal,* November 15, 1988, p. B1.
22. David A. Aaker, *Managing Brand Equity* (New York: The Free Press, 1991), p. 15.
23. Peter H. Farquhar, Julie Y. Han, and Yuji Iiri, "Brands on the Balance Sheet," *Marketing Management,* Winter 1992, p. 19.
24. Ronald Alsop, "Firms Unveil More Products Associated with Brand Names," *The Wall Street Journal,* December 13, 1984, p. 31.
25. Joanne Y. Cleaver, "Licensing: Starring on Marketing Team," *Advertising Age,* June 6, 1985, pp. 15–16.
26. Ronald Alsop, "Brand Loyalty Is Rarely Blind Loyalty," *The Wall Street Journal,* October 19, 1989, p. B1.
27. Frank V. Cespedes, "Once More: How Do You Improve Customer Service?" *Business Horizons,* March–April 1992, pp. 61–62.
28. Ibid., p. 62.

CHAPTER

13

Distribution Strategy

The channel of distribution connects suppliers and producers with the end-users of goods or services. An effective and efficient distribution channel provides the member organizations with an important strategic edge over competing channels. Distribution strategy concerns how a company reaches its market targets. While some producers market their products directly to the end-users of goods and services, many others move their products through one or more channels of distribution. Various independent channel intermediaries (e.g., wholesalers, retailers) perform the necessary distribution functions.

Escada A.G. is a leading producer of high-fashion women's apparel.[1] The German company experienced rapid growth during the 1980s and had 1992 sales of over $800 million. Aggressive distribution combined with stylish designs are important contributors to Escada's success in the marketplace. It is vertically integrated from manufacturing to retailing. Escada's designs offer far more variety than its competitors', but the colors of the clothing do not change so that customers can add to their wardrobes each year. Escada's 40 automated factories in Bavaria produce 6 million items of clothing each year at very short lead times. Satisfied customers cite high quality workmanship and attention to detail as key features of Escada garments. Escada distributed its products initially in the United States through department stores and boutique retailers. The company's current retail strategy of its own stores, department stores and boutiques, and Escada factory outlets is a major concern with its independent retailers. For example, in New York an Escada boutique is located in the same block with Bergdorf-Goodman and Saks Fifth Avenue, which have Escada departments. These and other retailers helped to build the Escada brand name. Management has major plans to open company-owned stores in the United States and around the world. More than 40 Escada stores were opened in the United States from 1990 to 1992.

While some manufacturers distribute direct to consumer or organizational end-users using a company sales force, many producers use marketing intermediaries to perform all or part of the distribution functions. A good distribution strategy requires a penetrating analysis of the available alternatives in order to select the most appropriate channel network. Channel-of-distribution decisions are important to organizations in a wide range of industries. A company's channel strategy may involve: (1) developing and managing the channel; or (2) gaining entry into a particular channel by a producer, wholesaler, or retailer.

We first look at the role of distribution channels in marketing strategy and discuss several channel strategy issues. Next, we examine the process of selecting the type of channel, determining the intensity of distribution, and choosing the channel configuration of organizations. A discussion of managing the distribution channel follows. Next, we look at distributing through international channels. Finally, some important trends in distribution strategy in the 1990s are highlighted.

STRATEGIC ROLE OF DISTRIBUTION

A good distribution network creates a strong competitive advantage for an organization. The Limited (apparel), Deere & Company (farm equipment), and Snap-On Tools, Inc. (mechanics' hand tools) have one common feature in their marketing strategies: Each has a well-developed distribution channel that is a major contributing factor to the firm's performance. The Limited manages the entire value-added system from its global network of garment manufacturers to its company-owned retail stores. Deere has a strong worldwide group of farm equipment dealers. Snap-On Tools' independent dealers in vans provide a close link with customers, supply feedback to guide product improvement, assist customers in tool selection, and expand sales every year.

First, we describe the distribution functions in the channel, then discuss the key role of physical distribution in the channel. Finally, we examine several factors affecting the choice of whether to use distribution channels.

Distribution Functions

The *channel of distribution* is a network of organizations performing functions that connect the producer to the end-users. The distribution channel consists of *interdependent* and *interrelated* institutions and agencies, functioning as a system or network, who cooperate in their efforts to produce and distribute a product to end-users. Thus, hospitals, ambulance services, physicians, test laboratories, insurance companies, and drugstores make up a channel of distribution for health care services.[2] Examples of channels of distribution for consumer and industrial products are shown in Exhibit 13–1. In addition to the intermediaries that are shown, many facilitating organizations perform services. These specialists include financial institutions, transportation firms, advertising agencies, and insurance firms.

Several functions are necessary in moving products from producers to end-users. *Buying and selling* activities by marketing intermediaries reduce the number of transactions for producers and end-users. *Assembly* of products into inventory helps to meet buyers' time-of-purchase and variety preferences. *Transportation* eliminates the locational gap between buyers and sellers, thus accomplishing the physical distribution function. *Financing* facilitates the exchange function. *Processing and storage* of goods involves breaking large quantities into individual orders, maintaining inventory, and assembling orders for shipment. *Advertising and sales promotion* communicate product availability, location, and features. *Pricing* sets the basis of exchange between buyer and seller. *Reduction of risk* is accomplished through mechanisms such as insurance, return policies, and futures trading. *Communications* between buyers and sellers include personal selling contacts, written orders and confirmations, and other information flows. Finally, *servicing and repairs* are essential for many types of products.

Major factors in channel strategy are deciding the functions that are needed and which organizations will be responsible for each function. Middlemen offer important cost and time advantages in the distribution of a wide range of products. Steel service centers illustrate functional specialization.[3] These firms buy steel coil or bar in bulk from steel producers. They cut and shape the steel at lower costs than the producers, and the centers can react more quickly than steel mills to customer needs. This responsiveness helps reduce the buyer's inventory. These cost-effective middlemen are expected to continue to take over more processing of bulk steel from producers.

When first selecting a channel of distribution for a new product, the pricing strategy and desired positioning of the product may influence the choice of the channel. For example, the decision to use a premium price and a symbolic positioning concept calls for retail stores that buyers will associate with this image. Escada's entry into the U.S. high-fashion women's apparel market was enhanced by selecting department stores and specialty retailers with prestigious images.

Once the channel-of-distribution design is complete and responsibilities for performing the various marketing functions are assigned, these decisions establish guidelines for pricing, advertising, and personal selling strategies. For example, the manufacturers' prices must take into account the requirements and functions of middlemen as well as pricing practices in the chan-

EXHIBIT 13–1 Basic Channels of Distribution

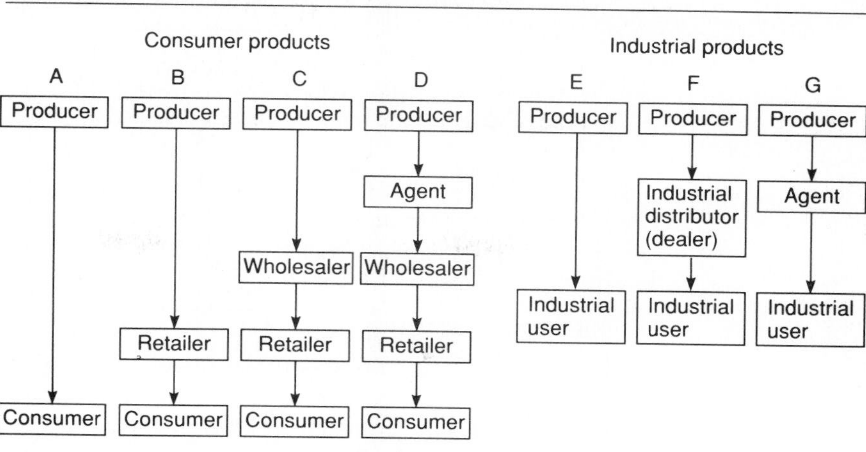

Source: Paul S. Busch and Michael J. Houston, *Marketing* (Homewood, Ill.: Richard D. Irwin, 1985), pp. 458–59.

nel. Likewise, promotional efforts must be matched to the various channel participants' requirements and capabilities. Consumer-products manufacturers often direct advertising to consumers to help *pull* products through distribution channels. Alternatively, promotion may be concentrated on middlemen to *push* the product through the channel. Intermediaries may also need help in planning their marketing efforts and other supporting activities.

Physical Distribution

Physical distribution strategy has received considerable attention in recent years from logistics, marketing, manufacturing, and transportation professionals. The objective is improving the distribution of supplies, goods in process, and finished products. The decision to integrate physical distribution with other channel functions or to manage it separately is a question that must be resolved by a particular organization. There are instances when either approach may be appropriate. Physical distribution is a key channel function and thus an important part of channel strategy and management. Management needs to first select the appropriate channel strategy, considering the physical distribution function and other essential channel activities. Once the strategy is selected, physical distribution management alternatives can be examined for the channel network.

One approach for integrating marketing and logistics activities is outlined in Exhibit 13–2. The basis of integrating the two groups of activities is customer service. Recall our discussion of integrating business functions to

EXHIBIT 13–2 Cost Trade-Offs Required in Marketing and Logistics

Product

Price

Promotion

Marketing

Place customer service levels

Inventory carrying costs

Transportation costs

Logistics

Lot quantity costs

Warehousing costs (throughout costs not storage)

Order processing and information costs

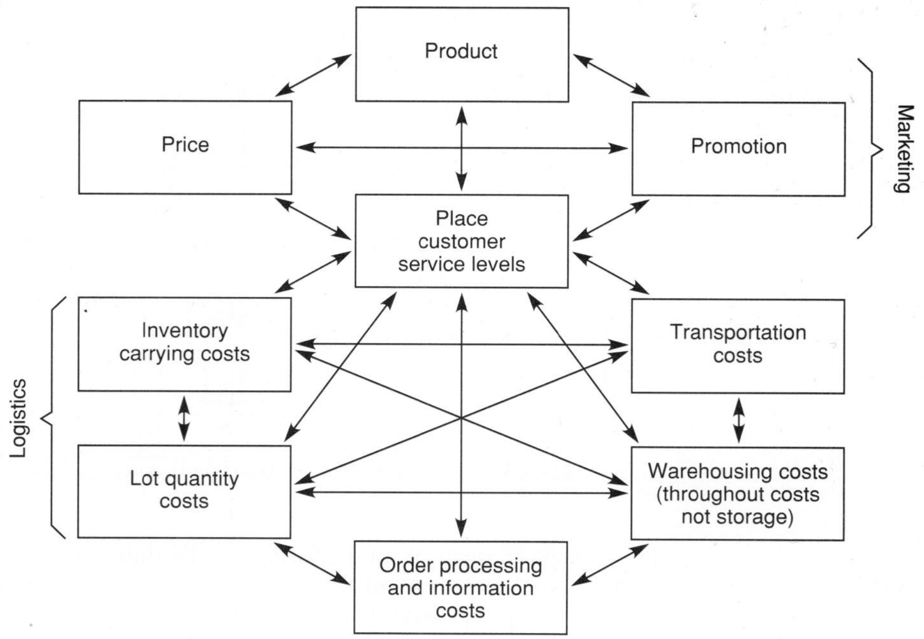

Marketing objective: Allocate resources to the marketing mix to maximize the long-run profitability of the firm.

Logistics objective: Minimize total costs given the customer service objective. (Total costs = transportation costs + Warehousing costs + Order processing and information costs + Lot quantity costs + Inventory carrying costs)

Source: James R. Stock and Douglas M. Lambert, *Strategic Logistics Management,* 2nd ed. (Homewood, Ill.: Richard D. Irwin, 1987), p. 42.

improve customer service in Chapter 12. The cost trade-offs are shown by Exhibit 13–2. Illustrative objectives of marketing and logistics are also indicated. The integration task is to give customers the services that meet their needs while satisfying the organization's performance objectives.

Direct Distribution by Manufacturers

We look at distribution strategy from a manufacturer's point of view, although many of the strategic issues apply to firms at any level in the distribution channel—wholesale or retail. Manufacturers are unique because they have the option of going directly to end-users through a company sales force or serving end-users through marketing intermediaries. Manufacturers have three distribution alternatives: (1) direct distribution; (2) use of intermediaries; or (3) situations in which both (1) and (2) are feasible. The factors that influence the distribution decision include buyer considerations, product characteristics, and financial and control factors.

Buyer Considerations. Manufacturers look at the amount and frequency of purchases by buyers as well as the margins over manufacturing costs that are available to pay for direct selling costs. Customers' needs for product information and applications assistance may determine whether a company sales force or independent marketing intermediaries can best satisfy buyers' needs. Substantial differences in the size and the requirements of the end-user buyers may suggest using two or more distribution channels.

The personal computer (PC) industry is an interesting illustration of the role of distribution in gaining access to end-users. Tandy's Radio Shack retail distribution network gave the firm an early competitive edge when the PC market was first developing. Selling to consumers and small business users required retail outlets. IBM had to create a distribution network for its successful PC line, introduced in 1981. An industry shakeout began in early 1984, when IBM's production of PCs caught up with demand and the company started broadening its distribution channels.[4] IBM also uses its salespeople to push the computers through channels and to make direct contact with large corporate buyers. Several retail chains developed to meet the distribution needs of PC producers. By the end of the decade competition was intense at both the manufacturing and retail levels of PC channels. Retailers were going after business buyers to survive. This required developing sales forces to make calls on large and medium-sized business firms.

Product Characteristics. Manufacturers often consider product characteristics in deciding whether to use a direct or distribution-channel strategy. Complex products and services often require close contact between customers and the producer, who may have to provide application assistance, service, and other supporting activities. For example, chemical-processing equipment, mainframe computer systems, pollution-control equipment, and engineering-design services are often marketed directly to end-users via company sales forces. (See Case 1–1, Autodesk Inc.) Another factor is the range of products offered by the manufacturer. A complete line may make company distribution economically feasible, whereas the cost of direct sales for a single product may be prohibitive. High-volume purchases may make direct distribution feasible for a single product. Companies whose product designs change because of rapidly changing technology often adopt direct sales approaches. And qualified marketing intermediaries may not be available, given the complexity of the product and the requirements of the customer. Direct contact with the end-user provides feedback to the manufacturer about new product needs, problem areas, and other concerns.

Financial and Control Considerations. Some producers do not have the financial resources to market direct to their end-users. Others are unwilling to make the large investments in field sales forces and service facilities. It is necessary to decide if resources are available and, if they are, whether selling direct to end-users is the best use of the resources. Both the costs and benefits need to be evaluated. Direct distribution gives the manufacturer control over distribution, since independent organizations cannot be managed in the same manner as company employees. This may be an important factor to the manufacturer.

An example shows how problems may develop with channel members when the producer changes its marketing strategy. Procter & Gamble launched a new strategy in 1991 intended to "reshape the supermarket pricing system and wean Americans off bargain bonanzas and rich coupons."[5] Rather than discounting a product at different times during the year, P&G is offering constant list prices that are 8 to 25 percent lower than in the past. Wholesalers and retailers did not like the change. The outcome will either change the way these middlemen do business or, if they are able to exert enough power, they will force P&G to change back to its former use of incentive discount pricing. Apparently, P&G implemented the new strategy without holding discussions with its major channel customers. The former trade discounts were significant. Industrywide, the discounts totaled more than $36 billion in 1991, exceeding advertising spending (see Case 4–3).

Exhibit 13–3 highlights several factors favoring distribution by the manufacturer. A firm's financial resources and capabilities may also be impor-considerations. The producers of business and industrial products are more likely than producers of consumer products to utilize company distribution to end-users. This is achieved by a network of company sales offices and a field sales force or by a vertically integrated distribution system (distribution centers and retail outlets) owned by the manufacturer. The producer may use independent middlemen to avoid consuming extensive financial resources and to gain the benefits of the experience and skills of the channel organizations.

CHANNEL-OF-DISTRIBUTION STRATEGY

Channel strategy includes selecting the type of channel, determining the intensity of distribution, and designing the channel configuration (Exhibit 13–4).

Type of Channel

There are two major types of distribution channels. The conventional channel is a group of vertically linked independent organizations, each trying to look out for itself, with little concern about the total performance of the

EXHIBIT 13–3 Factors Favoring Distribution by the Manufacturer

Opportunity for competitive advantage
Profit margins adequate to support distribution organization
Rapidly changing market environment
Complete line of products
Early stages of product life cycle
Distribution by the manufacturer
Purchases are large and infrequent
Complex product/ application
Small number of geographically concentrated buyers
Supporting services are required
Extensive purchasing process

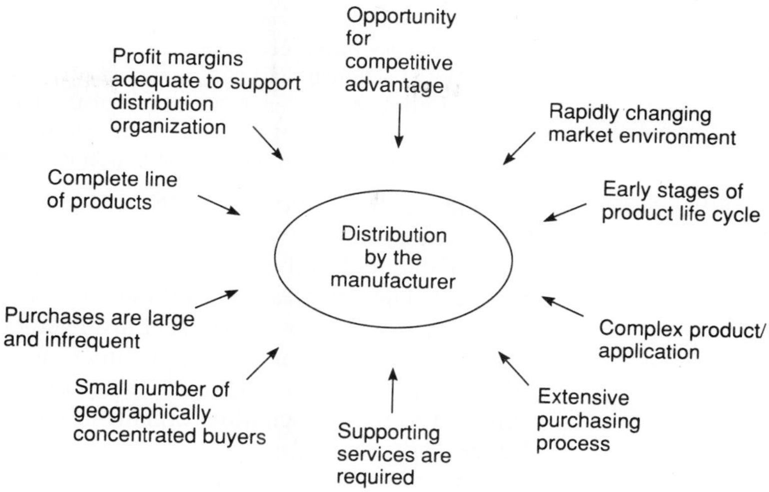

EXHIBIT 13–4 Channel of Distribution Strategy

Type of channel
Channel configuration
Distribution intensity

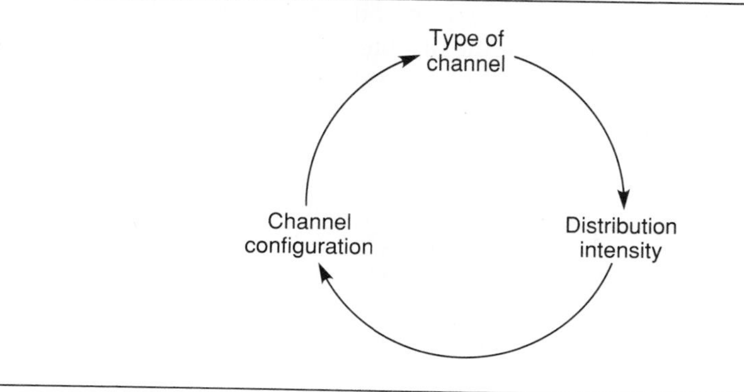

channel. The ties between the channel participants are rather informal, and the members are not closely aligned with each other.

The alternative type of distribution channel is the vertical marketing system (VMS). Marketing executives in an increasing number of firms realize the advantages to be gained by managing the channel as a coordinated or programmed system of participating organizations. These vertical marketing systems dominate the retailing sector and are significant factors in the business and industrial products and services sectors. Vertical marketing systems are:

> professionally managed and centrally programmed networks preengineered to achieve operating economies and maximum market impact. Stated alternatively . . . vertical marketing systems are rationalized and capital-intensive networks designed to achieve technological, managerial, and promotional economies through the integration, coordination, and synchronization of marketing flows from points of production to points of ultimate use.[6]

The characteristics of a VMS include management (or coordination) of the distribution channel by one organization. Programming and coordination of channel activities are directed by the firm that is the channel manager. The organizations in the channel are linked together through ownership by one firm, a contractual arrangement, or an administrative relationship. Operating rules and guidelines indicate the functions and responsibilities of each participant. Management assistance and services are supplied to the participating organizations by the firm that is the channel leader.

There are three types of vertical marketing systems: *ownership, contractual,* and *administered.* A single firm in the channel may own all of the participating organizations in the channel. Alternatively, the contractual VMS establishes formal operating arrangements between channel participants. Finally, in an administered channel, one firm manages the channel by exerting power and influence rather than by ownership or contractual ties. Often, the administrator is the producer, and its product line(s) comprises only a portion of the products moving through intermediaries. For example, Procter & Gamble is the channel administrator for many of its brands.

Examples of companies using vertical marketing systems are shown in Exhibit 13–5. The firm managing the channel is not always the manufacturer. Wal-Mart exerts considerable influence on its suppliers. A company may also use a combination arrangement (e.g., ownership and contractual). The administered channel is difficult to identify because there is often no formal administered relationship. The difference between it and a conventional channel is more one of degree than of kind. One distinction is that the administered channel relationship is more collaborative than the conventional channel relationship.

The contractual form of the VMS may include various formal arrangements between channel participants, including franchising and voluntary chains of independent retailers. Franchising is popular in fast foods, lodging, and many other retail lines. Automobile dealerships are another example of a contractual VMS. Wholesaler-sponsored retail chains are used by food and drug wholesalers to establish networks of independent retailers. Contractual programs may be initiated by manufacturers, wholesalers, and retailers.

The administered VMS exists because a channel member has one or

EXHIBIT 13–5 Illustrative Vertical Marketing Systems*

	Product/Service	
	Consumer	*Industrial*
Ownership	The Bombay Co. (furniture) The Limited, Inc. (retail)	Vallen Corp. (Industrial safety equipment
Contractual	Ethan Allen, Inc. (furniture) Wendy's International, Inc. (fast foods)	Snap-On Tools, Inc. (mechanics' tools) Deere & Company (farm equipment)
Administered	Procter & Gamble (health and beauty aids) Wal-Mart (discount goods)	Butler Manufacturing Co. (metal buildings) Loctite Corp. (industrial adhesives)

*Several of the companies fall into more than one of the categories below.

more bases of power. The capacity to influence other channel members and, thus, administer the operation of the channel may be the result of financial strengths, brand image, specialized skills (e.g., marketing, product innovation), and assistance and support to channel members.

The economic performance of vertical marketing systems should be higher than that in conventional channels if the channel network is properly designed and managed. However, the participating firms in the channel must make certain concessions. There are rules to be followed, control is exercised in various ways, and generally there is less flexibility for the channel members. Also, some of the requirements of the total VMS may not be in the best interests of a particular participant. Recall the earlier discussion of P&G's new pricing strategy and the potential loss of promotion pricing benefits by wholesalers and retailers. On the other hand, competing in a conventional distribution channel against a VMS is a major competitive challenge. The competition is fierce, and, without some special advantage, financial performance may be affected.

Distribution Intensity

Distribution intensity is best examined in reference to how many retail stores carry a particular brand in a geographical area. If a company decides to distribute its product in many of the retail outlets in a trading area that might normally carry such a product, it is using an *intensive* distribution approach. For example, Kodak film is widely available in the United States and throughout the world. A trading area may be a portion of a city, the entire metropolitan area, or a larger geographical area. If one retailer or dealer in the trading area distributes the product, then management is following an *exclusive* distribution strategy. Examples include Lexus automobiles and Caterpillar equipment. Different degrees of distribution intensity can be implemented. *Selective* distribution falls between the two extremes. Rolex watches and Coach leather goods are distributed on a selective basis.

Choosing the appropriate distribution intensity depends on management's targeting and positioning strategies and the product and market characteristics. The major steps in deciding distribution intensity are:

- Identifying which distribution intensities are feasible, taking into account the size and characteristics of the market target, the product, and the requirements likely to be imposed by prospective intermediaries (e.g., they may want exclusive sales territories).
- Selecting the alternatives that are compatible with the proposed market target and marketing program positioning strategy.
- Choosing the alternative that (1) offers the best strategic fit, (2) meets management's financial performance expectations, and (3) is attractive enough to intermediaries so that they will properly perform their assigned functions.

The characteristics of the product and the market target to be served often suggest a particular distribution intensity. For example, an expensive product, such as a Toyota Lexus luxury automobile, does not require intensive distribution to make contact with potential buyers. Moreover, several dealers in a trading area could not achieve adequate sales and profits because of the car's limited sales potential. Similarly, Escada's management, in choosing to serve the middle to upper price-quality segment of the apparel market, essentially preempted consideration of an intensive distribution strategy. In contrast, Kodak film needs to be widely available in the marketplace.

The distribution intensity should fit the marketing strategy management selects. For example, Estée Lauder distributes cosmetics through selected department stores that carry quality products. Management decided not to meet Revlon head-on in the marketplace, and instead concentrates its efforts on a small number of retail outlets. In doing this, Estée Lauder avoids huge national advertising expenditures and instead uses promotional pricing to help attract its customers to retail outlets. Buyers are offered free items when purchasing other specified items.

Strategic requirements, management's preferences, and other constraints help determine which intensity level offers the best strategic fit and performance potential. The requirements of intermediaries are considered, along with management's desire to control and motivate them. For example, exclusive distribution is a powerful incentive to intermediaries and it also simplifies management and control for the channel leader. But if the exclusive agent is unable (or unwilling) to fully serve the needs of target customers, the manufacturer will not achieve the sales and profit opportunities that are obtained by using more intermediaries.

Channel Configuration

The next step in selecting the distribution strategy is deciding how many levels of organizations to include in the vertical channel and the types of intermediaries to be selected at each level. The channel levels are shown in Exhibit 13–6. The type of channel (conventional or VMS) and the distribution intensity selected provide guidelines for deciding how many channel levels to use and what types of intermediaries to select. We discuss several factors that may influence the channel configuration.

End-User Considerations. A key issue is determining *where* the targeted end-users purchase the products of interest. The intermediaries that are selected should be contacting the market segment(s) targeted by the producer. Analysis of buyer characteristics and preferences provides important information for retailer selection. This, in turn, guides decisions concerning additional channel levels, such as the middlemen selling to the retailers that contact the market target customers.

Product Characteristics. The complexity of the product, special application requirements, and servicing needs are useful in guiding the choice of intermediaries. Looking at how competing products are distributed may suggest possible types of intermediaries. The breadth and depth of the products to be distributed are also important considerations. Some intermediaries may want full lines of products.

Manufacturer's Capabilities and Resources. Large producers with extensive capabilities and resources have a lot of flexibility in choosing intermediaries. These producers also have a great deal of bargaining power with the middlemen. Also, the producer may be able (and willing) to perform certain of the distribution functions. These choices are more limited for producers with capability and resource constraints.

Required Functions. Our earlier discussion of the functions that are performed in moving products from producer to end-user identifies the various channel activities such as storage, servicing, and transportation. Studying these functions is useful in choosing the types of intermediaries that are appropriate for a particular product or service. For example, if the producer is primarily concerned with the direct-selling function, then independent manufacturers' agents may be the right middlemen to use.

Availability and Skills of Intermediaries. The intermediaries that the producer wants may not be willing to distribute the producer's lines. For example, some types of middlemen will not distribute competing products. The evaluation of the experience, capabilities, and motivation of the intermediaries under consideration is also important. The firms within the same industry vary in skills and experience.

A channel with only one level between the producer and end-user simplifies the coordination and management of the channel. The more complex the channel network, the more challenging it is to complete various distri-

EXHIBIT 13–6 Distribution Alternatives from a Manufacturer's Point of View

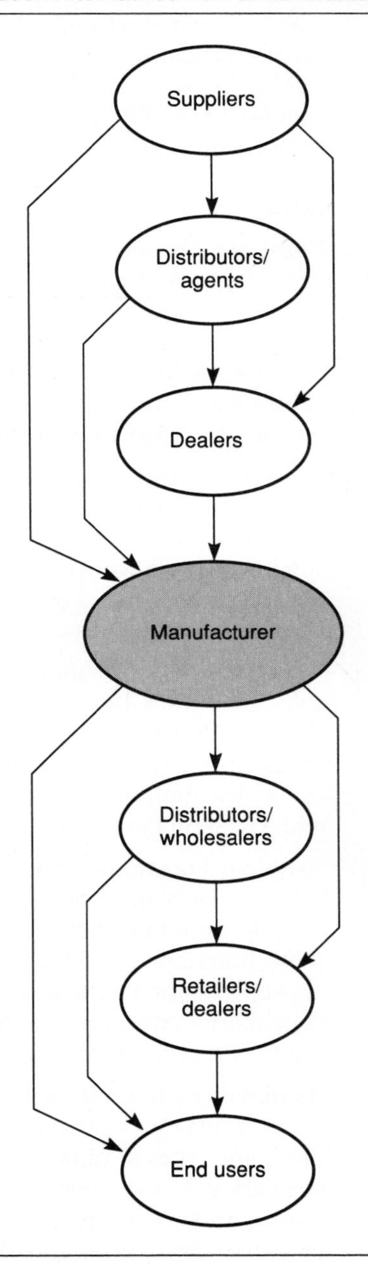

EXHIBIT 13–7 Steps in Channel Strategy Selection

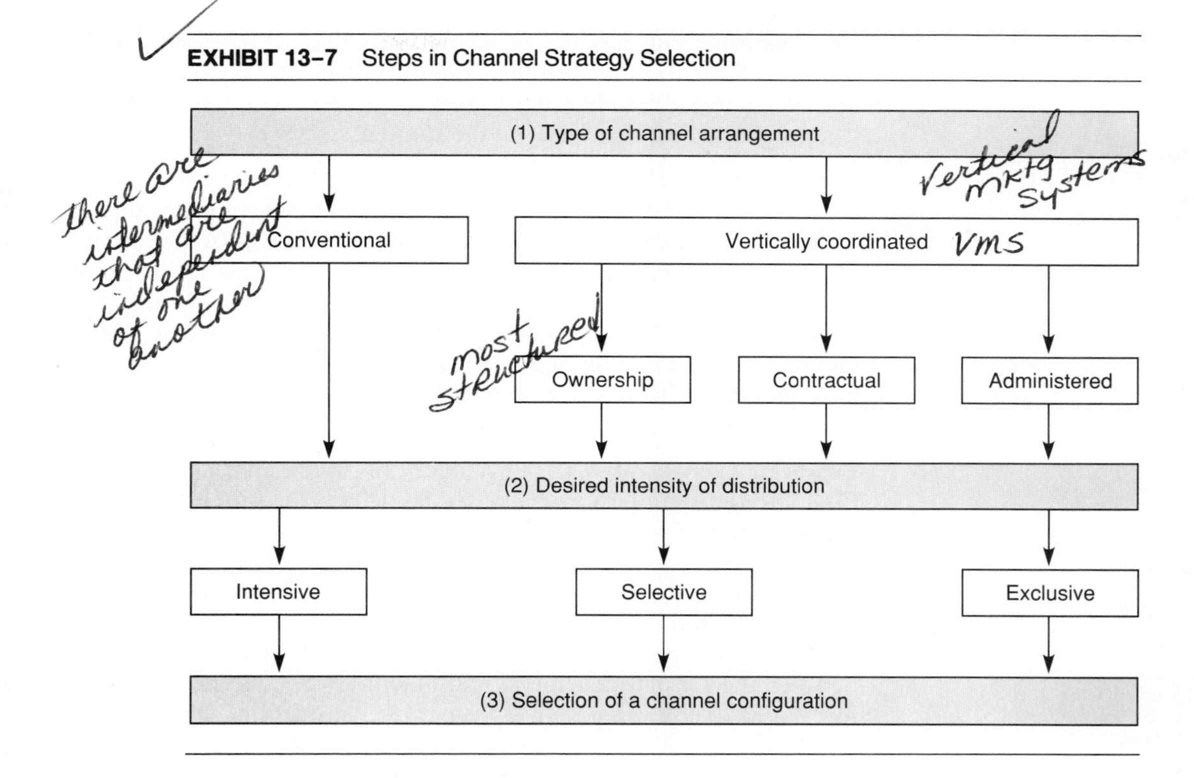

bution functions. Nevertheless, allocating functions to various channel specialists (e.g., brokers, wholesalers, dealers, financial institutions, transporters) may offer substantial economies of scale through the specialization of functions. The channel configuration that is selected takes into account several important trade-offs. As an example, manufacturers' agents (independent sales representatives) may give the producer greater channel control than will full-service wholesalers. However, the agents require the manufacturer to perform several functions, such as inventory stocking, invoicing, and service.

Selecting the Channel Strategy

Channel-strategy selection is summarized in Exhibit 13–7. Management: (1) chooses the type of channel arrangement to be used, (2) determines the desired intensity of distribution, and (3) selects the channel configuration. One of the first isues is deciding whether to manage the channel or instead to be a participant. This choice often rests on the bargaining power a company can exert in negotiating with other organizations in the channel system. Management may decide to manage or coordinate operations in the channel of distribution, become a member of a vertically coordinated channel, or become a member of a conventional channel system. The following factors often affect the choice of the channel strategy.

Access to Market Target. The choice of a market target needs to be closely coordinated with channel strategy, since the channel connects suppliers and end-users. The market target decision is not finalized until the channel strategy is selected. Information about the customers in the market target can help eliminate unsuitable channel-strategy alternatives. Multiple market targets may require more than a single channel of distribution. One advantage of the use of middlemen by the manufacturer is that the intermediaries have an established customer base. When this customer base matches the producer's market target(s), market access is achieved very rapidly.

Financial Considerations. Two financial issues affect channel strategy. First, are the resources available for launching the proposed strategy? For example, a small producer may not have the money to build a distribution network. Second, the revenue-cost impact of alternative channel strategies needs to be evaluated. These analyses include cash flow, income, return on investment, and operating capital requirements (see Appendix to Chapter 4). For example, suppose a producer of industrial controls must decide between the use of independent manufacturers' agents and a company sales force. A sales commission of 8 percent is required by each agent. At annual sales of $1.25 million, commissions total $100,000. This is the approximate cost of the compensation and expenses for one company salesperson. Unless each salesperson assigned to a field territory can develop sales greater than $1.25 million, the use of independent agents may be more cost-effective.

Flexibility and Control Considerations. Management should decide how much flexibility it wants in the channel network and then how much control it would like to have over other channel participants. An example of flexibility is how easily channel members can be added (or eliminated). A conventional channel offers little opportunity for control by a member firm, yet there is a lot of flexibility in entering and exiting from the channel. Legal and regulatory constraints also affect channel strategies in such areas as pricing, exclusive dealing, and allocation of market coverage.

Analyzing Existing Distribution Systems. The restructuring of many companies during the 1980s created a need to review channel options. Changes in distribution may improve both customer satisfaction and productivity. Companies with direct sales forces may consider using indirect channels (wholesalers, distributors, dealers, and retailers) to serve part of the customer base. Manufacturers are also using other customer contact methods such as telephone sales, computer ordering, and catalog sales.

Strategies at Different Channel Levels

We have examined distribution largely from the producer's viewpoint. Wholesalers and retailers are also concerned with channel strategies, and in some instances they may exercise primary control over channel operations. The Limited is a powerful force in its channels. Large food wholesalers and retailers are major factors in their channels of distribution. Moreover, decisions by wholesalers, distributors, brokers, and retailers about which manufacturers' products to carry often affect the performance of all channel participants.

Channel strategy can be examined from any level in the distribution network. The major distinction lies in the point of view (retailer, wholesaler, producer) used to develop the strategy. Intermediaries may have fewer alternatives to consider than producers and, thus, less flexibility in channel strategy. Nevertheless, their approach to channel strategy is often active rather than passive.

MANAGING THE CHANNEL

After deciding on the channel design, the actual channel participants are identified, evaluated, and recruited. Finding competent and motivated intermediaries is critical to successfully implementing the channel strategy. The choice of channel type, distribution intensity, and channel configuration establish many specific channel-management activities.

Channel-management activities include choosing how to assist and support intermediaries, developing operating policies, providing incentives, selecting promotional programs, and evaluating channel results. These activities consume much of management's time, since the channel design is not modified frequently. Changes in channel design may have serious consequences for the members. Consider, for example, Goodyear Tire & Rubber Company's decision in 1992 to include Sears, Roebuck & Company in its distribution network. The decision was very unpopular with Goodyear's 2,500 independent dealers.[7] Hundreds of the dealers have taken on competing tire brands. Goodyear's motivation for the channel strategy change was the market share growth in tire sales of 30 percent in the past five years by less-expensive chain stores, department stores, and warehouse clubs compared to a 4 percent share decline by tire dealerships. The dealers are concerned that Goodyear will make further additions to its distribution network by adding Kmart and the warehouse clubs.

To gain a better insight into channel management, we examine channel leadership, channel relationships, conflict resolution, performance, and legal and ethical considerations.

Channel Leadership

Gaining a leadership role in the channel is an important management issue. Some form of interorganization management is needed to assure that the channel has satisfactory performance as a competitive entity.[8] One firm may gain power over other channel organizations because of its specific characteristics (e.g., size), experience, and environment factors, and its ability to capitalize on such factors. Thus, the channel leader's power depends on its competitive advantages and its environment.[9] Gaining this advantage is more feasible in a VMS than in a conventional channel.

Performing the leadership role may also lead to conflicts arising from differences in the objectives and priorities of channel members. The conflicts with retailers created by the channel strategy changes of Goodyear and Procter & Gamble discussed earlier are illustrative. The organization with the most power may make decisions that are not considered favorable by other channel members. The conflict created by manufacturers competing with their retailers is described in the Strategy Feature.

Management Structure and Systems

Channel coordination and management are often the responsibility of the sales organization (Chapter 15). For example, a manufacturer's salespeople develop buyer-seller relationships with wholesalers and/or retailers. The management structure and systems may vary from informal arrangements to highly structured operating systems. Conventional channel management is more informal, whereas the management of VMS is more structured and programmed. The VMS management systems may include operating policies and procedures, information-system linkages, various supporting services to channel participants, and setting performance targets.

Channel Relationships

Chapter 3 considers the relationships between organizations, examining the degree of collaboration between companies, the extent of commitment of the participating organizations, and the power and dependence ties between the organizations. We now look at these concepts as they relate to channel relationships.

Degree of Collaboration. Channel relationships are more transactional in conventional channels but more collaborative in VMSs. The extent of collaboration is influenced by the complexity of the product, the potential benefits of collaboration, and the willingness of channel members to work together as partners. Just-in-Time inventory programs and other total quality management activities encourage collaboration between suppliers and producers.

STRATEGY FEATURE Factory Outlets Anger Retailers

The operation of retail factory outlets by manufacturers is a major threat to other retailers. The charts highlight the rapid growth in these outlets. The items offered are discounted 25 to 70 percent. The brand names include Eddie Bauer, Bass, Coach, Esprit, and many others. The merchandise is first quality. Producers try to appease retailers by using store locations outside cities, and the items stocked are often a season behind. Nevertheless, retailers are unhappy. Some are considering dropping the brands of the producers that operate outlets.

Source: Kevin Helliker, "Thriving Factory Outlets Anger Retailers as Store Suppliers Turn into Competitors," *The Wall Street Journal*, October 8, 1991, pp. B1 and B6.

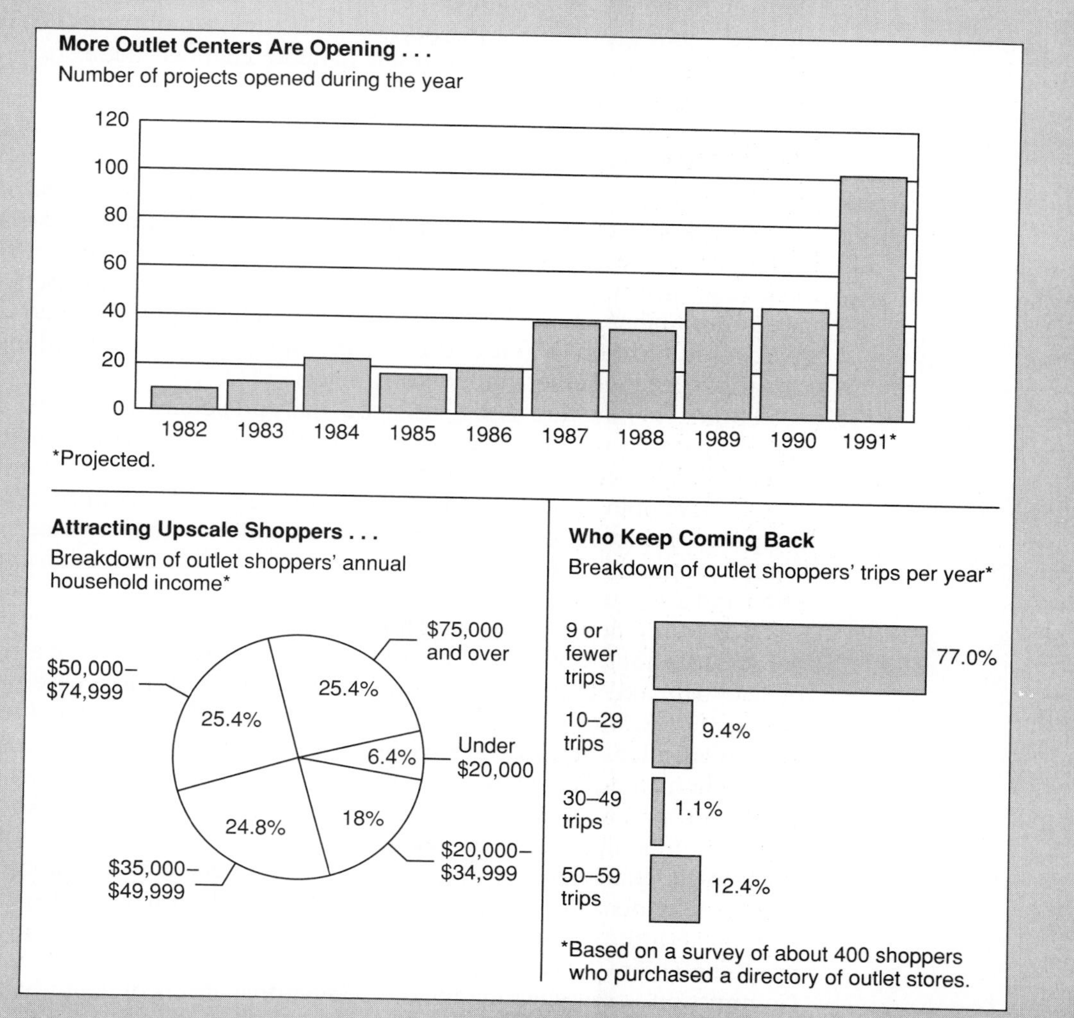

Commitment of the Channel Members. The commitment of channel organizations is likely to be higher in VMSs compared to conventional channels. For example, a contractual arrangement (e.g., franchise agreement) is a commitment to work together. Nevertheless, the strength of the commitment may vary depending on the contract terms. For example, contracts between manufacturers and their independent representatives or agents typically allow either party to terminate the relationship with a 30-day notification.

Power and Dependence. In VMSs power is concentrated in one organization and the other channel members are dependent on the channel manager. Power in conventional channels is less concentrated than in VMSs, and channel members are less dependent on each other. Conventional channel relationships may, nevertheless, result in some channel members having more bargaining power than others.

Conflict Resolution

Conflicts are certain to occur between the channel members because of differences in objectives, priorities, and corporate cultures. Looking at a proposed channel relationship by each participating organization may identify areas (e.g., incompatible objectives) that may lead to major conflicts. In such situations, management may decide to seek another channel partner. Effective communications before and after establishing the channel relationships can also help to eliminate or reduce conflicts.

Several methods are used to resolve actual and potential conflicts.[10] One useful approach is to involve channel members in the decisions that will affect the members. Another helpful method of resolving or reducing conflict is developing effective communications channels between channel members. Pursuing objectives important to all channel members also reduces conflict. Finally, it may be necessary to establish methods for mediation and arbitration.

The coffin industry illustrates how channel power is exercised by member organizations. Coffin producers market their products through a system of 22,000 funeral homes.[11] At the wholesale level sales of coffins exceed $800 million a year, with retail prices three to four times the wholesale prices. A few independent retailers are trying to compete against the established funeral home network by offering discount prices. However, channel entry barriers exist. Both the coffin manufacturers and funeral homes make channel entry difficult for the new retailer. Large producers limit their sales to licensed funeral directors. High coffin-handling charges are imposed by funeral directors when the coffin is not included in the funeral package. Boycott threats against coffin producers have also been used to discourage them in selling coffins to independent third-party retailers. The Federal Trade Commission is investigating the anticompetitive effects of coffin-handling fees.

Channel Performance

The performance of the channel is important from two points of view. First, each member is interested in how well the channel is meeting the member's objectives. Second, the organization that is managing or coordinating the channel is concerned with the overall performance of the channel.

Tracking performance for the individual channel members includes various financial and market measures such as profit contribution, revenues, costs, market share, customer satisfaction, and rate of growth. Several criteria for evaluating the overall performance of the channel are shown in Exhibit 13–8. These aspects of channel performance include product availability, promotional effort, customer service, market information, and cost effectiveness.

Legal and Ethical Considerations

Various legal and ethical considerations may impact channel relationships. Legal concerns by the federal government include arrangements between channel members that substantially lessen competition, restrictive contracts concerning products and/or geographical coverage, promotional allowances and incentives, and pricing practices.[12] State and local laws and regulations may also impact channel members.

The importance of ethics in corporate America is shown by a research survey of Fortune 1000 companies indicating that 40 percent of the responding companies hold ethics workshops and seminars and one third have ethics committees.[13] Ethical issues are heavily influenced by corporate policies and practices. Corporate pressures on performance may create ethical situations. Deciding whether a practice is ethical is sometimes complex. Channel decisions that impact other channel members may create ethical dilemmas. Many companies have established internal standards on how business should be conducted. Written statements of working relationships among channel members may also include such statements.

INTERNATIONAL CHANNELS

The distribution channels available in international operations are not totally different from the channels in a particular country such as the United States. Uniqueness is less a function of structural alternatives and more related to the vast range of operational and market variables that influence channel strategy.[14] Several channel-of-distribution alternatives are shown in Exhibit 13–9. The arrows display many possible channel networks linking producers, middlemen, and end-users. The objective is to manage domestic and international distribution activities so that customer satisfaction is achieved.

EXHIBIT 13–8 Distribution Channel Objectives and Measurement Criteria

Performance Objective	*Possible Measures*	*Applicable Product and Channel Level*
Product Availability		
• Coverage of relevant retailers	• Percent of effective distribution	• Consumer products (particularly convenience goods) at retail level
• In-store positioning	• Percent of shelf-facings or display space gained by product, weighted by importance of store	• Consumer products at retail level
• Coverage of geographic markets	• Frequency of sales calls by customer type; average delivery time	• Industrial products; consumer goods at wholesale level
Promotional Effort		
• Effective point-of-purchase (P-O-P) promotion	• Percent of stores using special displays and P-O-P materials, weighted by importance of store	• Consumer products at retail level
• Effective personal selling support	• Percent of salespeoples' time devoted to product; number of salespeople receiving training on product's characteristics and applications	• Industrial products; consumer durables at all channel levels; consumer convenience goods at wholesale level
Customer Service		
• Installation, training, repair	• Number of service technicians receiving technical training; monitoring of customer complaints	• Industrial products, particularly those involving high technology; consumer durables at retail level
Market Information		
• Monitoring sales trends, inventory levels, competitors' actions	• Quality and timeliness of information obtained	• All levels of distribution
Cost-Effectiveness		
• Cost of channel functions relative to sales volume	• Middlemen margins and marketing costs as percent of sales	• All levels of distribution

Source: Harper W. Boyd, Jr., and Orville C. Walker, Jr., *Marketing Management* (Homewood, Ill., Richard D. Irwin, 1990), p. 519.

Analyzing International Distribution Patterns

While the basic channel structure (e.g., agents, wholesalers, retailer) is similar across countries, there are many important differences in distribution patterns among countries. Several of the factors that create variations in world distribution practices include:[15]

EXHIBIT 13–9 International Channel-of-Distribution Alternatives

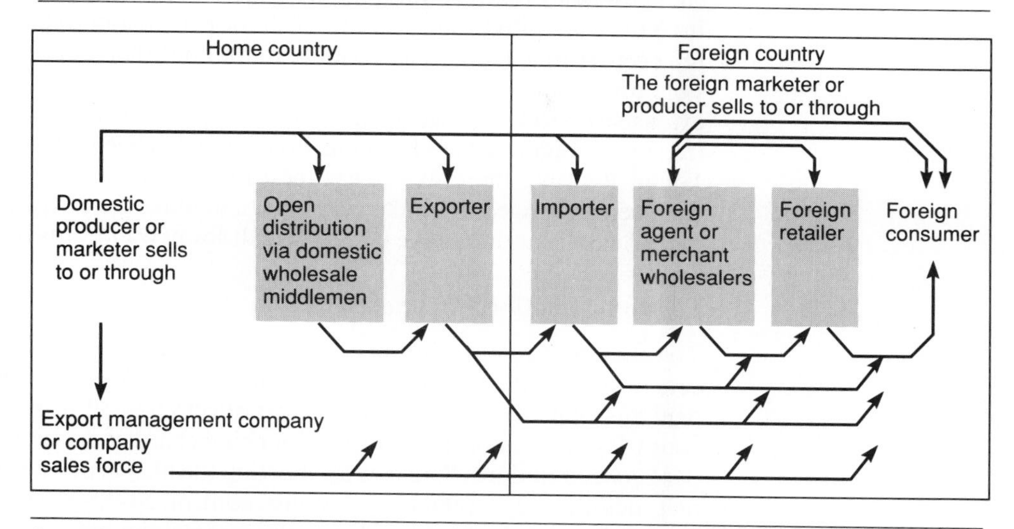

Source: Philip R. Cateora, *International Marketing,* 7th ed. (Homewood, Ill.: Richard D. Irwin, 1990), p. 572.

- The stage of economic development of the nation.
- The role of the government in distribution practices.
- The influence of competition, trade associations, and cartels in limiting access to distribution channels and affecting operating practices.
- The national patterns of product assortment, cost and margins, channel length, and distribution intensity.
- The structure and practices of wholesaling and retailing in the country of interest.

Generalization about distribution practices throughout the world is obviously not possible. Studying the distribution patterns in the nation(s) of interest is important in obtaining guidelines for distribution strategy. Various global trends such as satellite communications, regional cooperative arrangements (e.g., Europe 1992), and transportation networks (e.g., intermodal services) impact distribution systems in various ways. Global market turbulence and corporate restructuring create additional influences on distribution strategies and practices.

An interesting example of differences in distribution patterns between countries are the laws influencing retailing in Japan.[16] About 83 percent of Japan's 1.6 million retailers employ fewer than five people. Japan's so called Large Store Retail Law requires retail organizations building or operating large new stores to apply to the government for permission to (1) build a store, (2) expand an existing store, (3) stay open later in the evening, or (4) change the days of the month the store is closed. One large Japanese retailer, Ito Yokado, waited from 1981 to 1988 for permission to build a new shopping center in a Tokyo suburb, only to find out that a decision was impossible until more information was provided. Japan's small businesses have extensive collective power over retail decisions. Consumers are often penalized by the retailing laws by being forced to patronize high-markup stores in Japan. By 1992 there were clear indications that Japan's tight retail laws were being changed to benefit consumers, to make the distribution structure more flexible, and to make it less difficult for new entrants to gain access.

Factors Affecting Channel Selection

The channel-strategy analysis and selection process presented in the chapter can be used for developing or evaluating international channel strategy, recognizing that many situational factors affect channel decisions in specific countries. Several of the factors influencing channel decisions are also similar between nations. The factors affecting the choice of international channels include cost, capital requirements, control, coverage, strategic product-market fit, and the likelihood that the middlemen will remain in business over a reasonable time horizon.[17] The political and economic stability of the country is, of course, very important. Stability needs to be evaluated early in the decision to enter the country.

Strategic Alliances

A strategic alliance between an organization that wants to enter an international market and a firm already serving the market may provide the advantage of existing distribution channels for the foreign firm and a new product for the domestic firm. For example, several American companies are seeking cooperative arrangements with firms serving the European common market. Such an agreement between General Mills Inc. and Nestlé S.A. provides entry into Nestlé's vast sales and distribution network and its factories in Europe.[18] General Mills contributes the cereals to stock the shelves of food stores. Implementation of the alliance will require several years. Many of the cereal eaters around the world are located in English-speaking countries. The development of cereal preference in other countries could provide a huge growth market. Europe has the potential by the year 2000 of being equal in size to the current $6.5 billion U.S. cereal market. Sales of cereals in Europe are about $1.6 billion.

STRATEGIC TRENDS IN DISTRIBUTION

Several trends in distribution are creating opportunities and threats for channel participants. Both channel institutions and methods of distribution are experiencing shorter and shorter life cycles. It is necessary to appraise channel strategy regularly to maintain performance and to avoid problems caused by changing external conditions. We examine several distribution trends that are affecting distribution strategies in the 1990s.

New Retailing Concepts

The new retailing concepts that emerged in the 1980s include superstores, warehouse buying clubs, and specialty retailers. The success of the warehouse buying clubs that cater to small businesses and job-related groups (e.g., government employees) shows how new distribution concepts affect existing channels. The Price Company, founded in 1976, is now the leading firm in this industry, with fiscal 1993 sales estimated at over $8 billion. The Price Club's explosive growth in sales and profits attracted a dozen competitors, including Wal-Mart and Pay 'n Save.[19] Buying clubs operate in many of the 100 largest markets in the United States. The typical Price Club store has 100,000 square feet and stocks 4,000 items—one tenth the items in a Kmart store. Limited selection, low overhead, and membership fees enable the warehouse clubs to operate on 10 percent gross margins. Business customers typically represent half of total purchases.

Industry dynamics are creating intense competition in retailing. Survival in the 1990s requires effective information systems, focused targeting and positioning strategies, flexible marketing to different customer needs, and responsive services.[20] Industry authorities predict a shakeout during the 1990s, with Sears and Kmart losing competitive position to J. C. Penny and Wal-Mart. Other strong retailers placing pressure on their competitors include Dillard Department Stores, The Gap, The Limited, R. H. Macy, and Nordstrom. The 1990s will undoubtedly reveal some new retailing concepts.

Vertical marketing systems for services is another new retailing concept. Moving into previously fragmented industries, corporate and contractual chains have emerged in medical and dental services, lawn care (ChemLawn), travel services (American Express), real estate brokerage, and office supplies (Office Depot). These strong and efficient vertical marketing systems are affecting the performance of small independent retailers. Similar consolidations have occurred in public accounting and marketing research services.

Expanding Importance of Channel Power

Gillette is one of several companies using channel-driven strategies. These firms are developing and acquiring products that can be marketed through their existing channels. Gillette paid $190 million in cash to acquire toothbrush maker Oral-B Laboratories from Cooper Laboratories.[21] Oral-B is the market leader in the United States and is also strong in international markets. This product-line addition shows Gillette's interest in expanding its mix of consumer nondurables that can be distributed through its current channels to mass merchants and food and drug retailers. Blades and razors continue to be the primary thrust of Gillette's product strategy. The company has also eliminated unprofitable lines such as its Cricket disposable lighter business, which was sold to Swedish Match AB in 1985. Toiletries and cosmetics represent Gillette's second largest segment. (See Case 2–3.)

Channel-Driven Product Strategies. Consumer product firms' corporate and marketing decisions, as illustrated by Gillette, are influenced by distribution-channel considerations for several reasons. A wider range of products moving through the same channel network enhances bargaining power with middlemen. Operating efficiencies can be gained in sales and distribution costs. Market trends are easier to spot through close contact with customers. And channels that are moving a wide range of successful existing products also help new-product introductions.

Multiplex Distribution. Another important trend in distribution is the use of multiple channels to gain access to end-user consumers. For example, Dayton-Hudson markets through its traditional department stores, through its discount retailers (Target and Mervyn's), and through specialty stores. The unifying component of Dayton-Hudson's strategy is merchandising and the merchant orientation of top management.[22] In the mid-1960s, Dayton-Hudson recognized the mass-merchandising trend and moved into discount retailing through Target and more recently Mervyn's to promote the latest fashion and the best deal.

Direct Marketing

The explosive growth of direct marketing during the last decade represents an important trend in distribution. Customer contact is made by mail or phone. These channels include catalog retailers such as Lands' End and L. L. Bean, phone and media retailers, and electronic shopping. These direct-marketing companies take business away from conventional retailers. Convenience buying is stimulated by today's life-styles (two-income families, limited leisure time, high incomes), the ease of shopping via catalogs, toll-free phone numbers, and effective marketing by the firms involved.

Using an existing customer list facilitates entry into direct marketing. American Express has been very successful in using its credit card membership list. Database marketing provides access to buyers for direct-marketing programs (see Chapter 8). An existing customer base must be willing to purchase by mail.

Improving Distribution Productivity

Marketing intermediaries gain a strategic advantage by improving distribution productivity. Reducing distribution costs and the time in moving products to end-users are high-priority action areas in many companies.

These costs may account for one third or more of total product costs. Consider these examples:[23]

- Helene Curtis reduced distribution costs 40 percent by replacing six older warehouses with a new distribution center that uses computer-controlled forklifts and automated order processing and shipment.
- Mervyn's has reduced the average time merchandise is in the pipeline from vendor to retail store from 14 days to fewer than 9.
- Sun MicroSystems' distribution is handled by a specialist, the Federal Express Business Logistics Services unit, that moves Sun's machines from the factory floor to customers.

Monitoring the changes that are taking place in distribution and incorporating distribution-strategy considerations into the strategic-planning process are essential strategic-marketing activities. Market turbulence, global competition, and information technology create a rapidly changing distribution environment.

SUMMARY

The channel of distribution connects the producer with the end-users of goods and services. One or more levels of organizations may operate between the user and producer. A strong channel network is an important way to gain competitive advantage. Distribution channels provide access to market targets. The choice between company distribution to end-users and the use of intermediaries is guided by end-user needs and characteristics, product characteristics, and financial and control considerations.

Manufacturers select the type of channel to be used, determine distribution intensity, design the channel configuration, and manage various aspects of channel operations. These channels are either conventional or vertical marketing systems (VMS). The VMS, the dominant channel for consumer products, is increasing in importance for business and industrial products. In a VMS, one firm owns all organizations in the channel, a contractual arrangement exists between organizations, or one channel member is in charge of channel administration. Channel decisions also include deciding on intensity of distribution and the channel configuration. Channel management includes implementing the channel strategy, coordinating channel operations, and tracking the performance of the channel.

The choice of a channel strategy begins when management decides whether to manage the channel or to assume a participant role. Strategic analysis identifies and evaluates the channel alternatives. Several factors are evaluated, including access to the market target, channel functions to be performed, financial considerations, and legal and control constraints. The channel strategy adopted establishes several guidelines for price and promotion strategies.

International channels of distribution are similar in structure to those found in the United States and other developed countries. Nevertheless, important variations exist in the channels of different countries because of the stage of economic development, government influence, and industry practices. Strategic alliances offer a way to gain market access to the existing channels of a company operating in a country of interest to the firm.

Several strategic trends in distribution channels are creating both opportunities and threats for participants. These include the emergence of new distribution concepts, the expanding importance of channel power, the explosive growth of direct-marketing channels, and the escalating importance of distribution productivity.

QUESTIONS FOR REVIEW AND DISCUSSION

1. Using the examples of Tandy Corporation (Radio Shack) and IBM in personal computers, discuss how product branding and distribution strategies are closely related.
2. Distribution analysts indicate that costs for supermarkets equal about 98 percent of sales. What influence does this high break-even level have on supermarkets' diversification into delis, cheese shops, seafood shops, and nonfood areas?
3. Why do some large, financially strong manufacturers choose not to own their dealers but instead establish contractual relationships with them?
4. What are the advantages and limitations of the use of multiple channels of distribution by a manufacturer?
5. Discuss some likely trends in the distribution of automobiles during the 1990s, including the shift away from exclusive distribution arrangements.
6. During the 1980s, Radio Shack began opening retail computer stores rather than depending on its existing electronics stores to serve the small-computer market. Discuss the logic of this strategy, pointing out its strengths and shortcomings.
7. Identify and discuss some of the factors that should increase the trend toward vertical marketing systems.
8. Why might a manufacturer choose to enter a conventional channel of distribution?
9. Suppose the management of a raw material supplier is interested in performing a financial analysis of a distribution channel comprising manufacturers, distributors, and retailers. Outline an approach for doing the analysis.
10. Discuss some of the important strategic issues facing a drug manufacturer in deciding whether to distribute veterinary prescriptions and over-the-counter products through veterinarians or distributors.

NOTES

1. Teri Agins, "Bright and Bold: Despite the Recession High-Fashion Escada Expands Worldwide," *The Wall Street Journal,* April 15, 1992, pp. A1, A60.
2. Louis W. Stern, Adel I. El-Ansary, and James R. Brown, *Management in Marketing Channels* (Englewood Cliffs, N.J.: Prentice Hall, 1989), p. 4.

3. Elizabeth Sangler, "Proving Their Mettle," *Barron's,* July 9, 1984, pp. 13 and 20.
4. John Marcom, Jr., "Consumers Are Taking a Back Seat as Computer Stores Court Business," *The Wall Street Journal,* July 26, 1985, p. 21.
5. Valerie Reitman, "Retail Resistance: Eliminated Discounts on P&G Goods Annoy Many Who Sell Them," *The Wall Street Journal,* August 11, 1992, p. A1.
6. Bert C. McCammon, Jr., "Perspectives for Distribution Programming," in *Vertical Marketing Systems,* ed. Louis P. Bucklin (Glenview, Ill.: Scott, Foresman, 1970), p. 43.
7. Dana Milbank, "Independent Goodyear Dealers Rebel," *The Wall Street Journal,* July 8, 1992, p. B2.
8. For a complete discussion of channel management see Stern, El-Ansary, and Brown, *Management in Marketing Channels.*
9. Michael Etgar, "Channel Environment and Channel Leadership," *Journal of Marketing Research,* February 1977, p. 70.
10. James A. Narus and James C. Anderson, "Turn Your Industrial Distributors into Partners," *Harvard Business Review,* March–April 1986, pp. 66–71.
11. John R. Emshwiller, "Independent Coffin Sellers Fight Established Industry," *The Wall Street Journal,* July 5, 1989, pp. B1 and B2.
12. An expanded discussion of these issues is available in Louis W. Stern and Adel I. El-Ansary, *Marketing Channels,* 3rd ed. (Englewood Cliffs, N.J.: Prentice Hall 1988), Chapter 6.
13. Kenneth Labich, "The New Crisis in Business Ethics," *Fortune,* April 20, 1992, p. 168.
14. Philip R. Cateora, *International Marketing,* 5th ed. (Homewood, Ill.: Richard D. Irwin, 1983), Chapter 18.
15. Ibid., pp. 616–32.
16. This example is based on Robert E. Weigand, "So You Think Our Retailing Laws Are Tough," *The Wall Street Journal,* November 13, 1989, p. A10.
17. Cateora, *International Marketing,* pp. 632–36.
18. Richard Gibson, "General Mills Would Like to Be Champion of Breakfasts in Europe," *The Wall Street Journal,* December 1, 1989, p. B5.
19. "Boom Times in a Bargain-Hunter's Paradise," *Business Week,* March 11, 1985, pp. 116 and 120.
20. Bill Saporito, "Retailing's Winners and Losers," *Fortune,* December 18, 1989, pp. 69–78.
21. Frank Campanella, "Looking Sharp," *Barron's,* April 29, 1985, pp. 41–42.
22. M. Howard Gelfand, "Dayton-Hudson Keeps Its Vision," *Advertising Age,* July 9, 1984, pp. 4, 46–47.
23. Rita Koselka, "Distribution Revolution," *Forbes,* May 25, 1992, pp. 54, 58, 60, 62.

CHAPTER

14

Pricing Strategy

The pricing of goods and services performs a key strategic role in many firms as a consequence of deregulation, intense global competition, slow growth in many markets, and the opportunity for firms to strengthen market position. Price impacts financial performance and is an important influence on buyers' perceptions and positioning of brands. Price becomes a proxy measure for product quality when buyers experience difficulty in evaluating complex products.

The aggressive pricing strategies of air passenger carriers illustrate the importance of pricing decisions in business performance. Discounted pricing and high operating costs resulted in industry losses of $6 billion for the two years ending in mid-1992. Robert Crandall, chief executive officer of American Airlines, proposed the conditions necessary to move the industry back to profitability:[1] (1) adopt a simplified value-pricing structure that can be administered at low cost; (2) use pricing policies that charge according to the cost of the service provided to each customer; (3) reduce airline operating costs by at least 10 percent; and (4) persuade the U.S. government to implement policies that do not punish successful airlines or favor foreign over U.S. companies.

Pricing decisions may have explosive and far-reaching consequences. Once implemented, it may be difficult to alter a price strategy—particularly if the change calls for a significant increase. Pricing actions that violate laws can land executives in jail. Price has many possible uses as a strategic instrument in corporate and marketing strategy. Price often performs an active role in the strategies and tactics of retailers. Changes in pricing practices have led to more flexible strategies and tactics by both producers and retailers. The realities of the pricing environment are apparent.[2] Price wars occur frequently in a wide range of markets for both goods and services. The motivation for these wars includes attempts to use production capacity, survival actions by companies operating under Chapter 11 bankruptcy provisions, and competitive pressures on market-share position. Producers have money invested in fixed assets that they are unable or unwilling to liquidate. The companies and products affected by price wars range from potato chips to computers. One of the dangers of these price wars is losing brand equity. Reducing costs is mandatory if the pricing environment is ongoing, unless an organization can dominate one or more segments less sensitive to intense price competition.

First, we examine the strategic role of price in marketing positioning strategy and discuss several pricing situations. Following a step-by-step approach to pricing strategy, we describe and illustrate the steps. We then present an approach to situation analysis for pricing decisions, and several applications highlight the nature and scope of analysis activities. Next, the choice of a pricing strategy is considered. Finally, we discuss determining specific policies and examine several special pricing issues.

STRATEGIC ROLE OF PRICE

Several factors influence management's decisions about how price will be used in marketing strategy. An important concern is estimating how buyers will respond to alternative prices for a product or service. The relationship between demand and price affects pricing decisions. The cost of producing and distributing a product sets lower boundaries on the pricing decision. Costs affect an organization's ability to compete. The existing and potential competition in the market segments targeted by management constrains the flexibility in selecting prices. Finally, legal and ethical constraints also create pressures on decision makers.

The pricing of the life-prolonging AIDS drug AZT by the Burroughs-Wellcome Company shows the effect of price on profits and public opinion.[3] The company's profits doubled during a three-year period. AZT was priced at about $8,000 for a one-year supply. At this price, analysts estimated AZT sales could increase to $1 billion by 1992, with about half of this amount resulting in net profit. Not surprisingly, Burroughs-Wellcome received widespread criticism from patients and their advocates about the pricing of AZT. Unknown to many critics, the company was 75 percent owned by a charitable organization until 1992, when some of its stock was sold to investors. About one fourth of Burroughs-Wellcome's earnings is distributed in dividends; the rest is spent on research and development of experimental drugs for a wide range of diseases. The criticism continued, and the company announced a 20 percent price reduction in September of 1989. Critics argued that further cuts should be made because of the drug's huge market potential and the opportunity to lower costs and recover development costs. These pressures eventually forced additional price reductions.

Price in the Marketing Mix

The role of price in marketing strategy depends on the target market, the product, and the distribution strategies management selects. Strategic choices about products and distribution set guidelines for both price and promotion strategies. Product quality and features, type of distribution channel, end-users served, and intermediaries' functions all help establish a price range. When an organization establishes a new distribution network, selection of the channel and intermediaries may be driven by price strategy. Thus, the influence of one mix component on another may vary in different strategy situations.

Responsibility for pricing decisions varies among organizations. Marketing executives are responsible for price strategy in many companies. Pricing decisions may be made by the chief executive officer in some firms such as aircraft producers and construction firms. Manufacturing and engineering executives may be assigned price responsibility in companies that produce customer-designed industrial equipment. In general, marketing executives are likely to have pricing responsibility for consumer products and services. Price determination for very large purchases may involve the chief executive officer and other members of the top management group. Industrial-product companies are more likely to assign pricing responsibility to nonmarketing executives.

Marketing strategy may be fragmented if pricing is not part of the chief marketing executive's responsibilities. Pricing decisions must be coordinated with other decisions in the marketing program. Operations, engineering, and finance executives should, of course, participate in strategic pricing decisions, regardless of where responsibility is assigned. Coordination of strategic and tactical pricing decisions with other aspects of marketing strategy is critical because of the interrelationships involved.

Product Strategy. When one product is involved, the price decision is simplified. Yet, in many instances, a line or mix of products must be priced. Consider a situation involving a product and consumable supplies for the product. One popular strategy is to price the product at competitive levels and set higher margins for supplies. Examples include film for cameras, parts for automobiles, and refills for pens. Also, the prices for products in a line do not necessarily correspond to the cost of each item. Prices in supermarkets are based on a total mix strategy rather than individual item pricing. Understanding the composition of the mix and the interrelationships among products is important in determining pricing strategy, particularly when the branding strategy is built around a line or mix of products rather than on a brand-by-brand basis. Product quality and features affect price strategy. A high-quality product may require a high price to help establish a prestige position in the marketplace and to satisfy management's profit-performance requirements. Alternatively, a manufacturer supplying private-branded products to a retailer like Wal-Mart or Kmart must price competitively to obtain sales. Pricing executives analyze the product mix, branding strategy, and product quality and features to determine the effects of these factors on price strategy.

Distribution Strategy. Type of channel, distribution intensity, and channel configuration also influence price strategy. The needs and motivation of intermediaries are considered in setting prices. Firms need margins to pay for middleman functions and to offer sufficient incentives to obtain their cooperation. Pricing is equally important when distribution is performed by the manufacturer. Pricing in vertically coordinated channels reflects total channel considerations more so than in coventional channels. Intensive distribution is likely to call for more competitive pricing than selective or exclusive distribution.

An important consideration in pricing strategy is the role and influence of various channel members. A particular firm may be very active or passive, depending on its role and power in the channel network. A firm that manages the channel usually plays a key role in pricing for the entire channel, subject to legal constraints and restrictions.

Pricing Situations

The pricing strategy of an organization requires continuous attention because of changing external conditions, the actions of competitors, and the opportunities for gaining a competitive edge through pricing actions. Pricing situations include:

- Deciding how to price a new product. Often, considerable flexibility exists in the selection of a price.
- Evaluating the need to adjust price because of external forces and changes in the product life cycle.
- Changing a positioning strategy that requires modifying the current price strategy.
- Responding to the pressures of a price war and other competitive threats.

Decisions about price for existing products may include increasing, decreasing, or holding prices at current levels. The competitive situation is an important factor in deciding if and when to alter prices. Demand and cost estimates are strong influences on new-product pricing. Deciding how to price a new product also requires considering competing substitutes, since few new products occupy the unique position held by the AZT drug.

American Telephone & Telegraph Company (AT&T) illustrates the effects on pricing decisions when the business environment changes. Deregulation of the telecommunications industry created a new competitive situation for AT&T. The former monopolist experienced aggressive competition in the late 1980s, forcing AT&T to become more customer oriented and to offer lower prices on long distance services.[4] AT&T lost major customers to MCI Communications Corporation and U.S. Sprint Communications Company. Lower prices was a major reason for deregulating the telecommunications industry and this is happening. AT&T's market share in wide-area telecommunications service (WATS) was 60 percent in 1989, 17 percent lower than in 1987. Nevertheless, the giant holds a very strong market position. AT&T's sales force is much more responsive to customers than in the past. Large numbers of staff personnel have been moved to the field to make direct contact with customers. Promotional pricing discounts are being used. Some industry experts suggest that AT&T's new marketing strengths are helping the company regain its monopoly power. Long distance service contributes 90 percent of AT&T's profits.

Uses of Price-Positioning Strategy

Price is used in various ways in the marketing-program positioning strategy—as a signal to the buyer, an instrument of competition, a means to improve financial performance, and a way to perform other marketing-mix functions (e.g., promotional pricing).

Signal to the Buyer. Price offers an immediate way of communicating with the buyer. The price is visible to the buyer and provides a basis of comparison between brands. Price may be used to position the brand as a high-quality product or, instead, to pursue head-on competition with another brand. When the product cannot be evaluated, price is a proxy for value.

Instrument of Competition. Price offers a way to quickly attack competitors or, alternatively, to position a firm away from direct competition. Off-price retailers use a low-price strategy against department stores and other retailers. Price strategy is always related to competition whether firms use a higher, lower, or equal price.

Improving Financial Performance. Price and costs determine financial performance. Pricing strategies are assessed as to their estimated impact on the firm's financial statements, both in the short and long run. Historically, financial considerations have been major factors in the pricing strategies of large firms in mature industries such as oil, steel, rubber, automobiles, and chemicals. These industries have used target-return methods for pricing; that is, they set a desired profit return and then compute the price necessary

EXHIBIT 14–1 Pricing Strategy for New and Existing Products

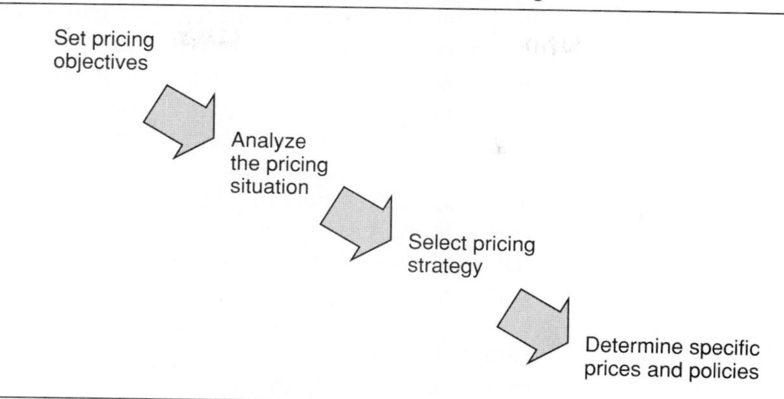

to achieve this return. Global competition has forced many firms to adopt pricing approaches that are more demand-oriented. AT&T's market-driven strategy for long distance services is illustrative. Pricing objectives may include pricing for short-term recovery of investment, long-term profitability, or market penetration on a break-even basis. The issue is the nature and extent to which management uses financial considerations to establish the role of price.

Marketing-Mix Considerations. Price may serve as a substitute for selling effort, advertising, and product quality. Alternatively, price may be used to reinforce these activities in the marketing program. The role of price often depends on how other variables in the marketing mix are used. For example, price can be used as an incentive to channel members and company salespeople, as the focus of promotional strategy, and as a signal of value. In deciding the role of price in marketing strategy, management evaluates the importance of price to competitive positioning, the buyer, financial requirements, and interrelationships in the marketing mix.

Pricing Strategy

The major steps in selecting a pricing strategy for a new product or altering an existing strategy are shown in Exhibit 14–1. Setting one or more pricing objectives provides a frame of reference for strategy development. Next, it is important to analyze the pricing situation, taking into account demand, cost, competition, and legal and ethical forces. The analysis shows how much flexibility there is in setting or changing a price. Based on this and the price objectives, the pricing strategy is selected. Finally, specific prices and policies are determined to implement the strategy.

Pricing Objectives

Companies use their price strategies to achieve several objectives. They may price for results (sales, market share, profit), for market penetration or position, for achieving certain functions (e.g., promotional pricing), or to avoid government intervention. More than one objective is usually involved, and objectives may conflict with each other. If so, limits may need to be imposed on one of the conflicting objectives. For example, if the pricing objective is to increase market share by 20 percent while another is to price to break even on sales, management must decide if both objectives are feasible. If not, one must be adjusted. Objectives establish essential guidelines for price strategy.

Pricing objectives vary according to the situational factors present and management's preferences. A low price may be intended to gain market position, discourage new competition, or attract new buyers. Several examples of pricing objectives follow:

- **Gain market position** The use of low prices to gain sales and market share is illustrative. Limitations include encouraging price wars and reduction (or elimination) of profit contributions.
- **Achieve financial performance** Prices are selected to contribute to financial objectives such as profit contribution and cash flow. Prices that are too high may not be acceptable to buyers.
- **Product positioning** Prices may be used to enhance product image, promote the use of the product, create awareness, and other positioning objectives. The visibility of price (high or low) may reduce the effectiveness of other positioning components such as advertising.
- **Stimulate demand** Price is used to encourage buyers to try a new product or to purchase existing brands during periods when sales slow down (e.g., recessions). A potential problem is that buyers may balk at purchasing when prices return to normal levels.
- **Influence competition** The objective of pricing actions may be to influence existing or potential competitors. Management may want to discourage market entry or price cutting by current competitors. A price leader may want to encourage industry members to raise prices. One problem is that competitors may not respond as predicted.

The purpose of a major price war in 1989 was to gain market share for photo film in the United States.[5] Photographic companies reduced prices to 30 percent below list and offered further discounts through mail-in rebates. Film producers spent nearly one half of their annual advertising budgets in December, which accounts for about 30 percent of the $2.5 billion (manufacturers' sales) annual sales of film in the United States. Eastman Kodak Company's 80 percent market share had been eroded by Fuji Photo Film Company and other film producers in recent years. Fuji's 1989 advertising budget was 65 percent higher than the previous year. Other companies seeking a market position include Polaroid (35-millimeter One Film) and Konica. Kodak offered special incentives and promotions to retailers to protect its market position.

ANALYZING THE PRICING SITUATION

Pricing analysis is important in evaluating new-product ideas, in developing test marketing strategy, and in selecting a national introduction strategy. Analysis also is necessary for existing products because of changes in the market and competitive environment, unsatisfactory performance of products, and modifications in marketing strategy over the product's life cycle. Analyzing the pricing situation includes: (1) estimating the product-market's responsiveness to price; (2) determining product costs; (3) analyzing competition; and (4) assessing legal and ethical constraints.

Product-Market Responsiveness to Price

One of the challenges of pricing in a new industry is estimating how buyers will respond to alternative prices. The pricing of software for personal computers illustrates this situation. Buyers have difficulty evaluating the applicability and cost benefits of these products. Many new programs are introduced. One software manufacturer offered a new program at $395 and supported it with an aggressive advertising campaign.[6] Designed to compete with Lotus's Symphony and Aston-Tate's Framework, both listing at $695, the program did not move off the shelves. Experimenting with alternative prices and no advertising, management eventually selected a price of $89.95 after encountering buyer resistance above $100. Since software is apparently sold on the basis of features and performance, buyers did not consider the program competitive with Symphony and Framework.

Product-market analysis with respect to price should answer the following questions:

1. How large is the product-market in terms of buying potential?
2. What segments exist in the product-market and what market target strategy is to be used?
3. How sensitive is demand in the segment(s) of interest to changes in price?
4. How important are nonprice factors, such as features and performance?
5. What are the estimated sales at different price levels?

Since forecasting product-market size, segmentation, and targeting are discussed in Chapters 5, 6, and 9, the last three questions are now considered.

EXHIBIT 14–2 Demand Curves with Differing Price Elasticity

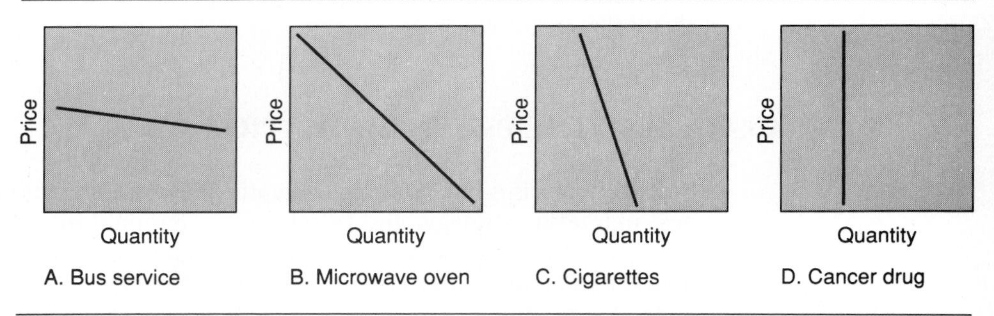

Source: David W. Cravens and Robert B. Woodruff, *Marketing* (Reading, Mass.: Addison-Wesley, 1986), p. 443.

Price Elasticity. Price elasticity is the percentage change in the quantity demanded when price changes divided by the percentage change in price. Elasticity is measured for changes in price from some specific price level and is not necessarily constant over the range of prices under consideration. Surprisingly, research indicates that people will sometimes buy more of certain products at *higher* prices, thus establishing a price-quantity relationship that slopes upward to the right. In these instances, people seem to be using price as a measure of quality because they are unable to evaluate the product. Estimating the exact shape of the demand curve (price-quantity relationship) is probably impossible in most instances. Even so, there are ways to estimate the sensitivity of sales to alternative prices. Test marketing can be used for this purpose. Analysis of historical price and quantity data may be helpful. End-user research studies, such as consumer evaluations of price, are also used. These approaches, coupled with management judgment, indicate the sensitivity of sales to price in the range of prices that is under consideration.

Demand curves for several products are shown in Exhibit 14–2. Elasticity varies for different products because buyers' responsiveness to price differs from one product to another.

Nonprice Factors. Various factors in addition to price may be important in analyzing buying situations. Buyers may be willing to pay a premium price to gain other advantages or, instead, be willing to forgo certain advantages for lower prices. Factors other than price that may be important are quality, uniqueness, availability, service, and warranty. In an attempt to recover from intense price competition, fast-food chains are marketing value menus of higher-priced items.[7] These value strategies include the quality of the food, user-friendly service, and attractive dining facilities. For example, McDonald's advertising message, "What you want is what you get," emphasizes the concept of value.

Certain purchasing situations may reduce the importance of price in the buyer's choice process. The price of the product may be a minor factor when the amount is relatively small compared to the importance of the use situation. Examples include infrequently purchased electric parts for home entertainment equipment, batteries for appliances, and health and beauty aids during a vacation. The need for important but relatively inexpensive parts for industrial equipment is another situation that reduces the role of price in the buyer's purchase decision. Quick Metal, an adhesive produced by Loctite Corporation, is used by maintenance personnel to repair production equipment. At less than $20 a tube, the price is not a major concern since one tube will keep an expensive production line operating until a new part is installed.

Other examples of nonprice factors that affect the buying situation include: (1) purchases of products that are essential to physical health, such as the AZT drug; (2) choice between brands of complex products that are difficult to evaluate, such as stereo equipment (a high price may be used as a gauge of quality); and (3) image-enhancement situations such as serving prestige brands of drinks to socially important guests.

Forecasts. Forecasts of sales are needed for the range of prices that management is considering. These forecasts, when combined with cost estimates, indicate the financial impact of different price strategies. The objective is to estimate sales in units for each product (or brand) at the prices under consideration.

Elasticity estimates can be used to develop sales projections, assuming all other marketing-program influences remain constant. This method of forecasting is illustrated in Exhibit 14–3. The parity price (Step 1) corresponds to an index value of 100. This indicates that the firm's price is equal to the average for the product category in which it competes. In Steps 2 and 3, the effects of price changes are estimated. Using these relative measures of elasticity, forecasts can be made from test-market data, or historical sales data in the case of existing products. Other methods of forecasting are discussed in the appendix to Chapter 5.

There are many forecasting situations when all other marketing-program influences are not constant. In these instances, the effects of other factors must be included in the analysis. Controlled tests are used for this purpose. For example, a fast-food chain can evaluate the effects of different prices on demand through tests in a sample of stores. Experimental designs measure or control the effects of factors other than price. Methods for analyzing the effects of positioning strategy components and positioning results are considered in Chapter 9.

Cost Analysis

Cost information is vital in making pricing decisions. A guide to cost analysis is shown in Exhibit 14–4. First, we analyze the structure of the cost of producing and distributing the product (Step A). This involves determining

EXHIBIT 14–3 Demand Elasticity to Price Change

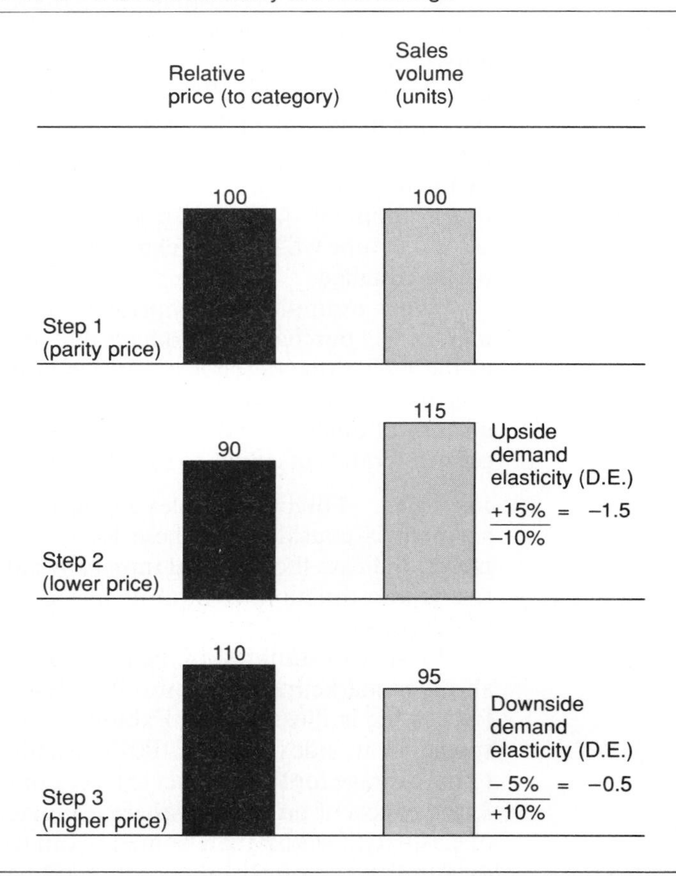

Source: Earl L. Bailey, ed., *Pricing Practices and Strategies* (New York: The Conference Board, Inc., 1978), p. 8.

fixed and variable components of cost. Also, it is necessary to find the portion of product cost accounted for by purchases from suppliers. A large portion of the cost of a personal computer comprises components produced by suppliers. It is useful to separate the cost components into labor, materials, and capital categories when studying cost structure.

Volume Effect on Cost. Step B of cost analysis examines cost and volume relationships. How do costs vary at different levels of production or quantities purchased? Can economies of scale be gained over the volume range under consideration, given the target market and program positioning strategy? At what volumes are significant cost reductions possible? The main task in this part of the analysis is to determine the extent to which the volume

EXHIBIT 14–4 Guide to Cost Analysis

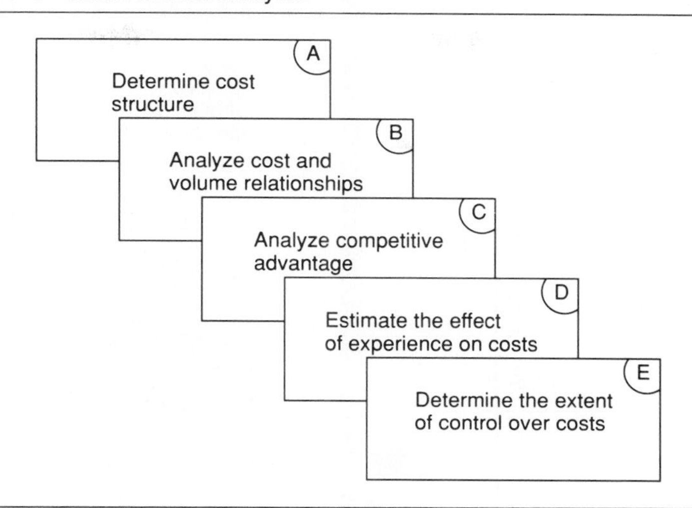

produced or distributed should be taken into account in selecting the pricing strategy.

Competitive Advantage. Step C analyzes competitive advantage. Comparing key competitors' costs is often valuable. Are their costs higher, lower, or about the same? Although such information is sometimes difficult to obtain, experienced managers can often make accurate estimates. The important consideration is placing key competitors into relative product cost categories (e.g., higher, lower, same). In some situations analysts can estimate competitive cost information from a knowledge of wage rates, material costs, production facilities, and related information. Exhibit 14–5 illustrates the concept of competitive cost advantage. The basis of comparison is the power output of a commercial equipment product. Notice how price advantage changes at different power outputs for companies X and Y. Company X, which is smaller than Y, the industry leader, has important cost advantages over Y in two zones of power output because of the technical differences in their products. Thus, cost advantage depends on the power output required by buyers. Company X has an advantage for some applications, Y in others.

Experience Effect. Step D of cost analysis estimates the effect of experience on costs. Experience or learning-curve analysis (using historical data) indicates that costs and prices for various products decline by a given amount each time the number of units produced doubles. Price declines may be uneven because of competitive influences. When unit costs (vertical axis) are plotted against total accumulated volume (horizontal axis), costs

EXHIBIT 14–5 Zones of Competitive Advantage for Competing Products

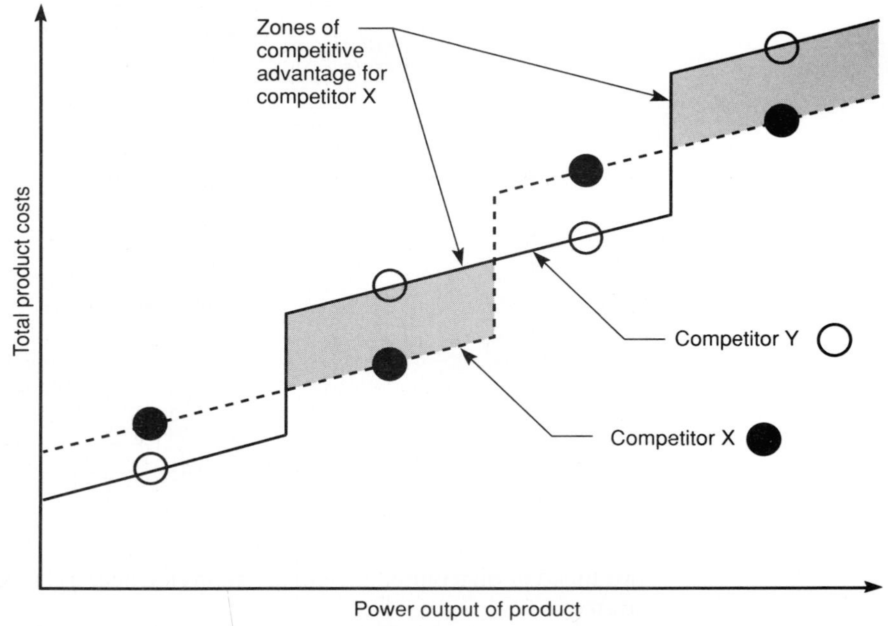

Source: Earl L. Bailey, ed., *Pricing Practices and Strategies* (New York: The Conference Board, Inc.,1978), p. 52.

decline with volume. This effect occurs when experience increases the efficiency of production operations. The experience-curve effect needs to be examined on an industry and company basis since the effect is not the same across all product categories. There are several issues to be evaluated in experience-curve estimation including the effect of aggregation of product data, errors in variables, functional form of the relationship, and measurement.[8] The experience curve can be estimated using the total direct costs required to produce the first unit (or a later unit) and the improvement rate resulting from experience.[9] The cumulative total direct cost at any point will be equal to the cost of the first unit times the number of units raised to the power equal to 1 minus the improvement rate. The improvement rate ranges from 0 to 1, and the equation for cumulative cost is:

$$(\text{Unit 1 cost}) \times (\text{Number of units})^{1 - \text{Improvement rate}}$$

Control over Costs. Finally, in Step E it is useful to determine how much influence the firm may have over costs in the future. To what extent can research and development, bargaining power with suppliers, process innovation, and other factors be expected to reduce costs over the planning horizon? These considerations are interrelated with the experience-curve analysis, yet may operate over a shorter time range. The bargaining power of an organization in its channels of distribution, for example, can have a major effect on costs, and the effects can be immediate.

Competitor Analysis

Each competitor's price strategy is evaluated to determine: (1) which firms represent the most direct competition (actual and potential) for the market targets under consideration; (2) how competing firms are positioned on a relative price basis and the extent to which price is used as an active part of their marketing strategies; (3) how successful each firm's price strategy has been; and (4) what the key competitors' probable responses to alternative price strategies will be.

The discussion in Chapter 7 considers methods for competitor identification. It is important to determine both potential and current competitors. Sears adopted a new "everyday-low" pricing strategy in 1989, which changed both buyers' perceptions and the retailers with which Sears competes most directly. The new strategy placed Sears in direct competition with retailers actively promoting low prices. Some retailing authorities question Sears's choice of the new price strategy.[10] Regardless of its impact on Sears, the low price strategy forced many competing retailers to adopt defensive strategies.

The success of a competitor's price strategy is usually gauged by financial performance, as illustrated by the poor short-term results Sears's retail operations achieved after implementing the new price strategy. The problem with this measure is accounting for other influences on profits. For example, retail authorities indicate that poor services and limited merchandise assortments adversely affect Sears's patronage by buyers.

The most difficult of the four questions about competition is predicting what they will do in response to alternative price actions. No changes are likely unless one firm's price is viewed as threatening (low) or greedy (high). Competitive pressures, actual and potential, often narrow the range of feasible prices and rule out the use of extremely high or low prices relative to competition. In new-product markets, competitive factors may be insignificant, except that very high prices may attract potential competitors.

Legal and Ethical Considerations

The last step in analyzing the pricing situation is identifying legal and ethical factors that may affect the choice of a price strategy. A wide variety of laws and regulations affect pricing actions. The following legal factors apply to the United States. Legal constraints are important influences on the pricing of goods and services in many different national and cooperative regional trade environments. Pricing practices that have received the most attention from government include:

Horizontal price fixing Price collusion between competitors. Products with narrow profit margins are more likely to lead to price fixing. The Sherman Act and the Federal Trade Commission Act prohibit price fixing between companies at the same level in the channel.

Price discrimination Charging different customers different prices without an underlying cost basis for discrimination. The Clayton Act and the Robinson-Patman Act prohibit price discrimination if it lessens or injures the competition.

Price fixing in channels of distribution Specifying the prices of distributors. The Consumer Goods Pricing Act places vertical price fixing under the jurisdiction of the antitrust laws.

Price information Violating requirements concerning the form and the availability of price information for consumers. Unit pricing and consumer credit requirements are examples. For example, the Consumer Credit Protection Act requires full disclosure of annual interest rates and other financial charges.[11]

Ethical issues in pricing are more subjective and difficult to evaluate than legal factors. The difficulties encountered by Burroughs-Wellcome in pricing AZT are illustrative. Some companies include ethical guidelines in their pricing policies. Deciding what is or is not ethical is often difficult. For example, the strategy used in pricing AZT was similar to that used for other new drugs. The important consideration is to include evaluation of possible ethical issues when developing a pricing strategy.

SELECTING THE PRICING STRATEGY

Analysis of the pricing situation provides useful information for selecting a pricing strategy. Additional considerations include: (1) determining price flexibility; (2) deciding how to position price relative to cost and deciding how visible to make the price of the product; and (3) selecting the competitive strategy and positioning. The Strategy Feature describes how the hypermarket retailing concept of low prices and one-stop shopping has not performed well in the United States.

How Much Flexibility Exists?

Demand and cost factors determine the extent of price flexibility. Within these upper and lower boundaries, competition and legal and ethical considerations also influence the choice of a specific price strategy. Exhibit 14–

STRATEGY FEATURE A Successful European Retailing Concept Doesn't Work in the United States

The hypermarket concept worked in Europe, in part because shopping malls and large discount stores were not readily available to shoppers when the new stores were introduced. The idea is to offer shoppers low prices and a complete range of groceries, electronics, clothing, furniture, financial services, and other merchandise under one roof. These large shopping facilities are not performing well in the United States. They entered a very competitive retail market which offers shoppers many attractive alternatives.

The data compare different store types. The hypermarket has to attract as many as four times the number of customers that shop at a regular discount department store to be profitable. And the purchase total would need to be double the discount store average. Buyers did not respond in enough numbers to successfully launch the hypermarket. Wal-Mart, SuperValue, and Kmart opened stores. Most of these ventures never moved beyond the experimental stage.

Buyers apparently don't enjoy working their way through these huge stores. Also, the assortment of specific products is more limited than in other stores. Attractive prices are not enough to persuade buyers to change their shopping habits and preferences.

Source: Laurie M. Grossman, "Hypermarkets: A Sure-Fire Hit Bombs," *The Wall Street Journal,* June 25, 1992, p. B1.

	Discount Store	*Super Center*	*Hypermarket*
Average size* (in square feet)	70,000	150,000	230,000
Employees**	200–300	300–350	400–600
Annual sales per store** (in millions)	$10–$20	$20–$50	$75–$100
Gross profit margins***	18%–19%	15%–16%	7%–8%
Stock-keeping units* (number of different kinds of items stocked)	60,000–80,000	100,000	60,000–70,000

**Management Horizons, source; **Peter E. Monash & Associates; ***Barnard's Retail Consulting Group*

6 illustrates how these factors determine flexibility. The price band between demand and cost may be narrow or wide. A narrow gap simplifies the decision; a wide gap suggests a greater range of feasible strategies. Choice of the price strategy within the gap is influenced by competition strategies, present and future, and by legal and ethical considerations. Management must determine where to price within the gap shown in Exhibit 14–6. In competitive markets the feasibility range may be very narrow. New markets or emerging market segments in established markets may allow a firm a lot of flexibility in strategy selection.

Bristol-Myers's entry into the AIDS drug market is an interesting case study of price-flexibility analysis and strategy design and implementation.[12] The strategy that was selected benefited from management's analysis of the mistakes made by Burroughs-Wellcome in marketing AZT. DDI, named Videx, was given to 30,000 AIDS patients at no charge before it was

EXHIBIT 14–6 How Much Flexibility in Price Strategy?

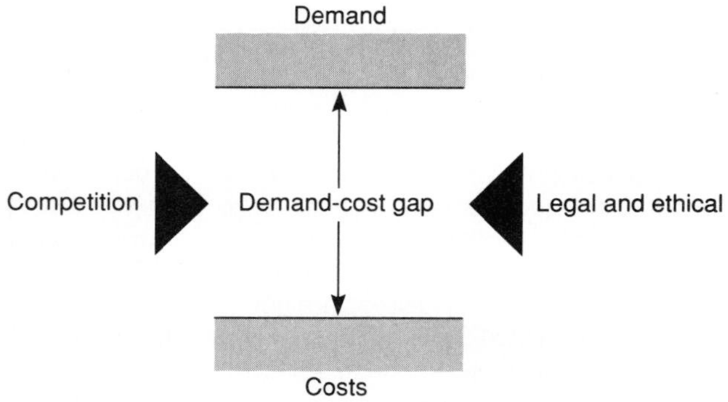

approved for sale by the U.S. Food and Drug Administration. Deciding where to position the price in the price gap (Exhibit 14–6) was complex. Negative reaction was likely if the price was perceived to be too high. If too low, the millions of dollars spent in developing the drug would not be recovered. The price selected was $1,745 for a year's supply of Videx. Industry analysts considered this price about one third lower than their estimates of an appropriate price using conventional pharmaceutical pricing guidelines.

Potential adverse reaction from AIDS groups and U.S. government pressures about reasonable pricing of new drugs apparently influenced the pricing of Videx. Competitive pricing was not a critical influence on the decision, since Videx can be taken by patients intolerant of AZT. Interestingly, some doctors and patients consider $1,745 too high. This price should generate annual sales of $50 million for Bristol-Meyers.

Price Positioning and Visibility

A key decision is how high to price a new product within the flexibility brand. Firms can charge a relatively low entry price with the objective of building volume and market position, or management can set a high price to generate large margins. The former is a "penetration" strategy, whereas the latter is a "skimming" strategy. Lack of knowledge about previous market response to the new product complicates the pricing decision. Several factors may affect the choice of a pricing approach for a new product, including the cost and life span of the product, the estimated responsiveness of buyers to alternative prices, and assessment of competitive reaction.

A decision should also be made about how visible price will be in the promotion of the new product. The use of a low entry price requires active promotion of the price to gain market position. When firms use a high price relative to cost, price often assumes a passive role in the marketing of the

EXHIBIT 14–7 Illustrative Price Strategies

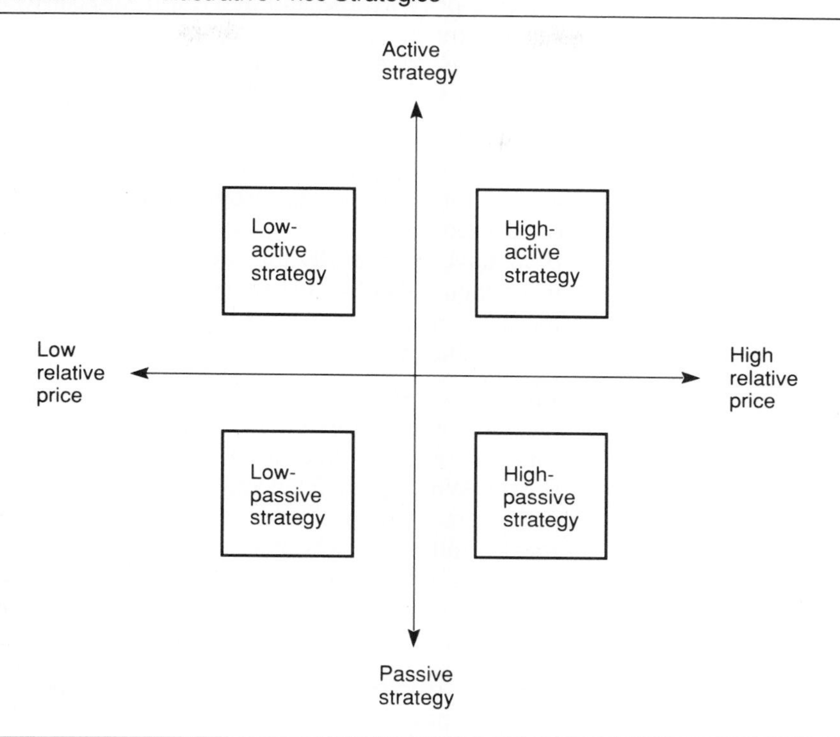

new product. Instead, the performance and other attributes of the product are stressed in the marketing-program positioning strategy.

Competitive Strategy and Positioning

The choice of a price strategy depends on how management decides to price the product relative to competition and whether price performs an active or passive role in the marketing program. The use of price as an active or passive factor refers to whether price is discussed in advertising, personal selling, and other promotional efforts. The strategies shown in Exhibit 14–7 indicate the range of price strategies companies can use. Many firms choose to price at or near the prices of key competitors and emphasize nonprice factors in their marketing strategies.

High-Active Strategy. This strategy is sometimes used for prestige brands seeking an affluence image. When the buyer cannot easily evaluate the quality of a product, price can serve as a signal of value. High prices may be essential to gain the margins necessary to serve small target markets, produce high-quality products, or pay for the development of new products. Making price visible and active can appeal to the buyer's perceptions of quality, image, and dependability of products and services. A firm using a high-price strategy is also less subject to retaliation by competitors, particularly if its products are differentiated from other brands.

High-Passive Strategy. High-priced items are often marketed by featuring nonprice factors rather than using high-active strategies. Product features and performance can be stressed when the people in the target market are concerned with product quality and performance. BMW and Mercedes-Benz have successfully followed this strategy for many years. Rubbermaid in kitchen aids (e.g., plastic containers) competes effectively against commodity-type competition using a high-passive strategy through innovation and product differentiation.

Low-Active Strategy. Several retailers use this strategy, including Home Depot (home improvement), Dollar General Stores (apparel), Office Depot (office supplies), Toys "R" Us (toys), and Pic 'N Pay Shoe Stores (family shoes). When price is an important factor in the buyer's decision, a low-active price strategy is very effective, as indicated by the rapid growth of these retailers. However, this strategy may start a price war. It is a more attractive option when the competition for the market target is not heavy or when a company has cost advantages and a strong position in the product-market.

Low-Passive Strategy. This strategy may be used by manufacturers whose products have lower-cost features than other suppliers. By not emphasizing a low price, the firm runs less danger that potential buyers will assume the product quality is inferior to other brands. Some firms participating in conventional channels may not spend much on marketing their products and, thus, may offer low prices because of lower costs. Other firms that have actual cost advantages for comparable competing products may decide to stress value rather than price, even though they are offering prices lower than those of competing brands.

DETERMINING SPECIFIC PRICES AND POLICIES

The last step in developing the pricing strategy (Exhibit 14–1) is selecting specific prices and policies to help manage the pricing strategy. Pricing methods are first examined, followed by a discussion of pricing policy. The chapter concludes by examining several special pricing considerations.

Determining Specific Prices

It is necessary to either assign a specific price to each product item or to provide a method for computing price for a particular buyer-seller transaction. Many methods and techniques are available for calculating price.

Price determination is based on cost, demand, competition, or a combination of these factors. Cost-oriented methods use the cost of producing and marketing the product as the basis for determining price. Demand-oriented pricing methods consider estimated market response to alternative prices. The most profitable price and market response level is selected. Competition-oriented methods use competitors' prices as a reference point in setting prices. The price selected may be above, below, or equal to competitors' prices. Typically, one method (cost, demand, or competition) provides the basis for pricing, although the other factors may have some influence.

Cost-Oriented Approaches. Break-even pricing is a cost-oriented approach to determining prices. The initial computation is as follows:

$$\text{Break-even (units)} = \frac{\text{Total fixed costs}}{\text{Unit price} - \text{Unit variable cost}}.$$

When using this method, price analysts select a price and calculate the number of units that must be sold at that price to cover all fixed and variable costs. Next, they assess the feasibility of exceeding the break-even value and, thus, generating a profit. One or more possible prices may be evaluated in the analysis. This form of analysis was no doubt included in Bristol-Meyers's pricing strategy formulation for Videx. Break-even analysis is not a complete basis for determining price, since both demand and competition are important considerations in the pricing decision. With break-even price as a frame of reference, demand and competition can be evaluated. The price selected is typically at some level higher than the break-even price.

Another popular pricing method is cost-plus pricing. This technique uses cost as the basis of calculating the selling price. A percentage amount of the cost is added to cost to determine price. A similar method, markup pricing, calculates markups as a percentage of the selling price. With markup pricing, this formula determines the selling price.

$$\text{Price} = \frac{\text{Average unit cost}}{1 - \text{markup percent*}}.$$

*Percent expressed in decimal form.

Competition-Oriented Approaches. Pricing decisions are always affected by the actions of competitors. Pricing methods that use competitors' prices in calculating actual prices include setting prices equal to or at some specified percentage above or below the competition's. In industries such as air travel, one of the firms may be viewed by others as the price leader. When the leader changes its prices, other firms follow with similar prices. American Airlines has attempted to perform such a leadership role in the United States, although its pricing changes are not always adopted by competing airlines. Another form of competition-oriented pricing is competitive bidding, where firms submit sealed bids to the purchaser. This method is used in the purchase of various industrial products and supplies.

Demand-Oriented Approaches. The buyer is the frame of reference for these methods. One popular method is estimating the value of the product to the buyer. The objective is to determine how much the buyer is willing to pay for the product based on its contribution to the buyer's needs or wants. This approach is used for both consumer and business products. Information on demand and price relationships is needed in guiding demand-oriented pricing decisions.

Many pricing methods are in use, so it is important to select specific prices within the guidelines provided by price strategy and to incorporate demand, cost, and competition considerations.[13]

Establishing Pricing Policy and Structure

Determining price flexibility, positioning price against competition, and deciding how active a component it will be in the marketing program do not establish the operating guidelines necessary for implementing a pricing strategy. It is helpful to also determine policy to guide pricing decisions and pricing structure.

Pricing Policy. An illustration shows how pricing decisions are guided by policies. Toys "R" Us is an exciting example of the success of specialty retailing. It is the largest retailer of toys in the United States, and company sales were nearly $5 billion in 1989, compared to $1 billion in 1982. With over 350 stores, the rapid growth of Toys "R" Us should continue in the 1990s. The company's European stores provide access to the unified market after 1992. The firm is unique in that its stores handle toys only in large barnlike outlets averaging 43,000 square feet. These are the major elements of the company's strategy:[14]

- Low prices are the keystone of the firm's corporate and marketing strategies, with additional volume generated by aggressive expansion of stores.
- A tight rein is kept on inventories using a computer control system.
- Management prides itself on never running a sale, and to keep customers coming back, it prices its goods accordingly.
- Stores provide fast service and keep customers happy.

Price is the focal point of this firm's positioning strategy. The growth and financial performance of the firm have been impressive. Notice how the price strategy is clearly established and how objectives (e.g., profit performance) depend significantly on the success of the strategy. Considering the range of toy prices and the variety of playthings from dolls to electronic games, the need for pricing policy and structure is clear.

A pricing policy may include consideration of discounts, allowances, returns, and other operating guidelines. The policy serves as the basis for implementing and managing the pricing strategy. The policy may be in written form, although many companies operate without formal pricing policies.

Pricing Structure. Anytime more than one product is involved, a firm must determine product mix and line-pricing interrelationships in order to establish price structure. For example, a strategy of low prices does not automatically provide management of Toys "R" Us with specific prices for each item the firm offers. And when more than one market target is involved, what relationship exists between the products offered in each? Assuming differences in products, should price be based on cost, demand, or competition?

Price structure concerns how individual items in the line are priced in relation to one another: The items may be aimed at the same market target or different end-user groups. For example, department stores often offer economy and premium product categories. In the case of a single product market, price differences between products typically reflect more than variations in costs. Large supermarket chains price for total profitability of the product offering rather than for performance of individual items. These retailers have developed computer analysis and pricing procedures to achieve sales, market-share, and profit objectives.

The pricing of the 1992 Toyota Camry and the Lexus ES 300 is an interesting example of pricing products in relation to each other. The ES 300 is targeted to the semiluxury market.[15] The ES 300 has essentially the same body as the Camry, but the Lexus sells for some $14,000 more than the Camry. The Lexus has several unique features (e.g., leather seats), but some of the price difference has to be image rather than substance. Both cars sold well in 1992. There was a waiting list for the ES 300 in Australia.

Once product relationships are established, some basis for determining price structure must be selected. Many firms base price structure on market and competitive factors as well as differences in the costs of producing each item. Some use multiple criteria for determining price structure and have sophisticated computer models to examine alternate pricing schemes. Others use rules of thumb developed from experience. The following guidelines are useful in pricing a line of products.

1. Price each product in relation to all others; noticeable differences in products should be equivalent to perceived value differences.
2. The top and bottom prices in the line should be priced so as to facilitate desired buyer perceptions.
3. Price differences between products should become larger as price increases over the line.[16]

Most approaches include not only cost considerations, but also demand and competitive concerns. For example, industrial-equipment manufacturers sometimes price new products at or close to cost and depend on sales of high-margin items such as supplies, parts, and replacement items to generate profits. The important consideration is to price the entire mix and line of products to achieve pricing objectives.

Special Pricing Considerations

Several special pricing situations may occur in particular industries, markets, and competitive environments.

Price Segmentation. Price is used in several markets to appeal to different market segments. For example, airline prices vary depending on the conditions of purchase. Different versions of the same basic product may be offered at different prices to reflect differences in materials and product features. Industrial-products firms may use quantity discounts to respond to differences in the quantities customers purchase. Price elasticity differences make it feasible to appeal to different segments.

Distribution-Channel Pricing. The pricing strategies of manufacturers using marketing middlemen include consideration of the pricing needs of channel members. The strategy adopted by the producer should allow the flexibility and incentives necessary to achieve sales objectives. These decisions require analysis of cost and pricing at all channel levels. If producer prices to intermediaries are too high, inadequate margins may discourage intermediaries from actively promoting the producer's brand. Margins vary based on the nature and importance of the functions that intermediaries in the channel are expected to perform. For example, margins between costs and selling prices must be large enough to compensate a wholesaler for carrying a complete stock of replacement parts.

Price Flexibility. Another special consideration is deciding how flexible prices will be. Will prices be firm, or will they be negotiated between buyer and seller? Toys "R" Us uses low yet firm prices and avoids special sales, but management does adjust prices over time. Perhaps most important, firms should make price flexibility a policy decision rather than a tactical response. Some companies' price lists are very rigid, while others have list prices that give no indication of actual selling prices. It is also important to recognize the legal issues in pricing products when using flexible pricing policies.

Product-Life-Cycle Pricing. Some firms have policies to guide pricing decisions over the life cycle of the product. Depending on its stage in the product life cycle, the price of a particular product or an entire line may be based on market share, profitability, cash flow, or other objectives. In many product-markets, price declines (in constant dollars) as the product moves through its life cycle. Because of life-cycle considerations, different objectives and policies may apply to particular products within a mix or line. Price becomes a more active element of strategy as products move through the life cycle and competitive pressures build, costs decline, and volume increases. Life-cycle pricing strategy should correspond to the overall marketing program positioning strategy used.

The intense competition present in the computer industry indicates the downward pressures on prices that often occur at mature stages of the product life cycle. In late 1989 IBM announced major write-offs and a cut of 10,000 jobs, responding to the pressures on profits of the pricing war affecting even the giant market leader.[17] Discounts granted by IBM were estimated to range from 15 percent to as high as 40 percent for mainframe computer purchases. IBM's share of the worldwide IBM-compatible mainframe market was expected to fall to 76 percent by 1991 compared to 88 percent in 1987. Personal computer pricing in the early 1990s was also very competitive.

SUMMARY

Pricing strategy gains considerable direction from the decisions management makes about the product mix, branding strategy, and product quality. Distribution strategy also influences the choice of how price will work in combination with advertising and sales force strategies. Pricing strategy also influences other marketing-mix decisions. Price, like other marketing program components, is a means of generating market response.

Two important trends are apparent in the use of price as a strategic variable. First, companies are designing far more flexibility into their strategies in order to cope with the rapid changes and uncertainties in the turbulent business environment. Second, price is more often used as an active rather than passive element of corporate and marketing strategies. This trend is particularly apparent in the retail sector, where aggressive low-price strategies are used by firms such as Wal-Mart, Office Depot, and Home Depot. Assigning an active role to price does not necessarily lead to low prices relative to competition—companies may use relatively high prices.

Product, distribution, price, and promotion strategies must fit together into an integrated strategy of program positioning. Pricing strategy for new and existing products includes (1) setting pricing objectives, (2) analyzing the pricing situation, (3) selecting (or revising) the pricing strategy, and (4) determining specific prices and policies. Companies use their pricing strategies to achieve one or more of several possible objectives. These include gaining market position, achieving financial performance, positioning the product, stimulating demand, and influencing competition.

Analyzing the pricing situation is necessary to develop a pricing strategy for a mix or line of products or to select a pricing strategy for a new product or brand. Underlying strategy formulation are several important activities, including analysis of the product market, cost, competition, and legal and ethical considerations. These analyses indicate the extent of pricing flexibility. The choice of a pricing strategy includes consideration of price positioning and visibility. Price strategies are classified according to the firm's price relative to the competition and how active the promotion of price will be in the marketing program. Pricing approaches for products include high-active, high-passive, low-active, and low-passive strategies. Variations within the four categories occur. In many industries market leaders establish prices that are followed by other firms in the industry.

The determination of specific prices may be based on costs, competition, and/or demand influences. Implementing and managing the pricing strategy also includes establishing pricing policy and structure. Finally, several special pricing considerations include price segmentation, distribution channel pricing, product life cycle pricing, and price and quality relationships.

QUESTIONS FOR REVIEW AND DISCUSSION

1. Discuss the role of price in the marketing strategy for Rolex watches. Contrast Timex's price strategy with Rolex's strategy.
2. In 1992, Toyota introduced two new automobiles. The redesigned Camry and the Lexus ES 300 were very similar but the ES 300 was priced substantially higher than the Camry. Discuss the features and limitations of this pricing strategy.
3. Indicate how a fast-food chain can estimate the price elasticity of a proposed new product such as a chicken sandwich.
4. Real estate brokers typically charge a fixed percentage of a home's sales price. Advertising agencies follow a similar price strategy. Discuss why this may be sound price strategy. What are the arguments against it from the buyer's point of view?
5. Cite examples of businesses to which the experience-curve effect is not applicable. What influence may this have on price determination?
6. In some industries prices are set low, subsidies are provided, and other price-reducing mechanisms are used to establish a long-term relationship with the buyer. Utilities, for example, sometimes use incentives to encourage contractors to install electric- or gas-powered appliances. Manufacturers may price equipment low, then depend on service and parts for profit contribution. What are the advantages and limitations of this pricing strategy?
7. Some private clubs exclude prices from their menus. Analyze and evaluate this price strategy.
8. Discuss some of the ways that estimates of the costs of competitors' products can be determined.
9. Discuss how a pricing strategy should be developed by a new firm to price its business-analysis software line.
10. Suppose a firm is considering changing from a low-active price strategy to a high-active strategy. Discuss the implications for this proposed change.
11. Describe and evaluate the price strategy used for the Toyota Lexus 400 European-style luxury sedan.

NOTES

1. This illustration is based on Dan Reed, "Straighten Up and Fly Right," *Fort Worth Star Telegram,* September 16, 1992, pp. B1, B3.
2. Bill Saporito, "Why the Price Wars Never End," *Fortune,* March 23, 1992, pp. 68–71, 74, 78.
3. This illustration is based on Marilyn Chase, "Pricing Battle: Burroughs-Wellcome Reaps Profits, Outrage from Its AIDS Drug," *The Wall Street Journal,* September 15, 1989, pp. A1 and A4.
4. Janet Guyon, "Stung by Rivals, AT&T Is Fighting Back," *The Wall Street Journal,* June 30, 1989, p. B1.
5. Peter Pae, "Holidays Become War Days for Makers of Photo Film," *The Wall Street Journal,* December 13, 1989, pp. B1 and B6.
6. "Software Economics 101," *Forbes,* January 28, 1985, p. 88.
7. Richard Gibson and Laurie M. Grossman, "Fast-Food Chains Hope Diners Swallow New 'Value' Menu of Higher-Priced Items," *The Wall Street Journal,* March 13, 1992, pp. B1 and B3.
8. David B. Montgomery and George S. Day, "Experience Curves: Evidence, Empirical Issues, and Applications," in *Strategic Marketing and Management,* ed. H. Thomas and D. Gardner (Chichester, U.K.: John Wiley & Sons, 1985). pp. 213–38.
9. A guide to determine experience curves is provided in Kent B. Monroe, *Pricing: Making Profitable Decisions* (New York: McGraw-Hill, 1979), pp. 115–19.
10. Francine Schwadel, "Troubles Deepen at Sears as the Christmas Season Nears," *The Wall Street Journal,* October 25, 1989, p. B1.
11. These and other aspects of marketing and the law are discussed in David W. Cravens, Gerald E. Hills, and Robert B. Woodruff, *Marketing Management* (Homewood, Ill.: Richard D. Irwin, 1987), Chapter 24.
12. This illustration is based on Marilyn Chase, "Deft Distribution: Bristol-Meyers Guides AIDS Drug through a Marketing Minefield," *The Wall Street Journal,* October 10, 1991, pp. A1, A6.
13. See, for example, Thomas T. Nagle, *The Strategy and Tactics of Pricing* (Englewood Cliffs, N.J.: Prentice Hall, 1987).
14. "Up and Down Wall Street," *Barron's,* October 27, 1980, pp. 1 and 35.
15. Jerry Flint,"Alfred Sloan Spoken Here," *Forbes,* November 11, 1991, pp. 96, 101.
16. For a discussion of product-line pricing, see Monroe, *Pricing,* Chapter 10.
17. Paul B. Carroll, "Big Blues: Hurt by a Pricing War, IBM Plans Write-Off and Cut of 10,000 Jobs," *The Wall Street Journal,* December 6, 1989, pp. A1 and A8.

CHAPTER

15

Promotion Strategy

Promotion strategy combines advertising, personal selling, sales promotion, and publicity into a coordinated program for communicating with buyers and others who affect purchasing decisions. Promotion activities are important influences on the sales achieved by companies. Billions are spent every week in the United States and other nations around the world on promotion. Effective management of these expensive resources is essential to gain the optimum return from the promotion expenditures.

The changing composition of promotion budgets for packaged-goods manufacturers during the last decade highlights the role of promotion in the marketing strategies of these companies. During the decade ending in 1991, advertising (as a percent of all promotion except personal selling) declined from 44 percent to 25 percent, coupons and consumer promotion increased only 3 percent to 25 percent, while trade deals and discounts surged from 33 percent to 50 percent.[1] These changes in promotion expenditures encouraged retailers and wholesalers to stock excess products. The trade deals and discounts loaded the distribution channels, and middlemen became very dependent on the profits made possible by stockpiling inventory. In the early 1990s manufacturers like Procter & Gamble announced changes in their promotion policies. The trade discounts and incentives were eliminated with the objectives of: (1) lowering costs, (2) decreasing the time in moving goods from factory to the supermarket shelf, and (3) reducing prices to consumers. Before the change, the average grocery product took nearly three months to move through the distribution network. As we saw in Chapter 13, channel members are not reacting favorably to the changes, since the discounts are a major source of their profits (see also Case 4–3).

Promotion is used to inform people about products and persuade buyers in a firm's market targets, channel organizations, and the public at large to purchase its brands. Increasingly, marketing management is finding it profitable to combine the promotion components into an integrated strategy for communicating with buyers and others who influence purchasing decisions. Since each form of promotion has strengths and shortcomings, the integrated strategy incorporates the advantages of each component in designing a cost-effective promotion mix.

We begin the chapter with an overview of promotion strategy and examine several considerations in selecting the strategy. Next, we discuss the major decisions that lead to an advertising strategy and the factors affecting these decisions. The following section considers the design and implementation of personal selling strategies. Finally, sales-promotion strategy is overviewed.

PROMOTION STRATEGY

Promotion strategy is the planning, implementing, and controlling of the communications from an organization to its customers and other target audiences. The function of promotion in the marketing mix is to achieve various communications objectives with each audience. The components of the promotion mix include advertising, personal selling, sales promotion, and public relations. An important marketing responsibility is planning and coordinating an integrated promotion strategy and selecting strategies for the promotion components. The marketing manager has little or no control over word-of-mouth communications or the communications of other organizations. Nevertheless these communications also influence the firm's target audience(s).

The Components of Promotion Strategy

Advertising. "Advertising is any paid form of nonpersonal presentation and promotion of ideas, goods, or services by an identified sponsor."[2] Advertising expenditures in the United States were $126 billion in 1991, compared to $88 billion in 1984.[3] From 1989 to 1991 annual advertising expenditures were constant. Major advertising expenditures are necessary to launch and maintain consumer products. Burger King spent $30 million in just eight weeks to announce a 6-ounce increase in the size of its Whopper sandwich.[4] (The campaign was not particularly effective in increasing consumer awareness of Burger King, perhaps because consumers thought the message was not very significant.) The same year, Procter & Gamble and Colgate-Palmolive each spent over $10 million promoting the new Crest Tartar Control Formula and the new Dentagard plaque-remover toothpastes, respectively.

Among the advantages of using advertising to communicate with buyers are the low cost per exposure, the variety of media (newspapers, magazines, television, radio, direct mail, and outdoor advertising), control of exposure, consistent message content, and the opportunity for creative message design. In addition, appeal and message can be adjusted when communications objectives change. Advertising also has some disadvantages. It cannot interact with the buyer and may not be able to hold viewers' attention. Moreover, the message is fixed for the duration of an exposure.

Personal Selling. "Personal selling is the oral presentation in a conversation with one or more prospective purchasers for the purpose of making a sale."[5] Annual expenditures on personal selling are substantially larger than advertising, perhaps twice as much. However, both promotion components share some common features, including creating awareness of the product, transmitting information, and persuading people to buy. Personal selling is expensive. For industrial products the cost per field sales call is more than $250 compared to less than $10 per 1,000 exposures for national television advertising. Personal selling has several unique strengths: Salespeople can interact with buyers to answer questions and overcome objections, they can target buyers, and they have the capacity to accumulate market knowledge and provide feedback. Top management often participates in selling by calling on key customers.

Sales Promotion. Sales promotion consists of various promotional activities including trade shows, contests, samples, point-of-purchase displays, trade incentives, and coupons. Sales-promotion expenditures are substantially greater than the amount spent on advertising. This array of special communications techniques and incentives offers several advantages: Promotion can be used to target buyers, respond to special occasions, and create an incentive for purchase. One of the more successful sales-promotion concepts is the frequent-flyer incentive program. American Airlines launched the innovative AAdvantage program in 1981. It was initially developed with a core customer group of 250,000 frequent flyers.[6] AAdvantage now has 15 million members, and 200,000 join each month. American's SABRE reservation system enables the company to track mileage and efficiently manage the program. American's costs per member per year for communications and administration are less than $5.

Publicity. "Publicity is nonpersonal stimulation of demand for a product, service, or idea by means of commercially significant news planted in the mass media and not paid for directly by a sponsor."[7] Public-relations activities can make an important contribution to promotion strategy if the activity is planned and implemented to achieve specific promotion objectives. (Public relations is also used for other organizational purposes such as com-

EXHIBIT 15–1 Developing a Promotion Strategy

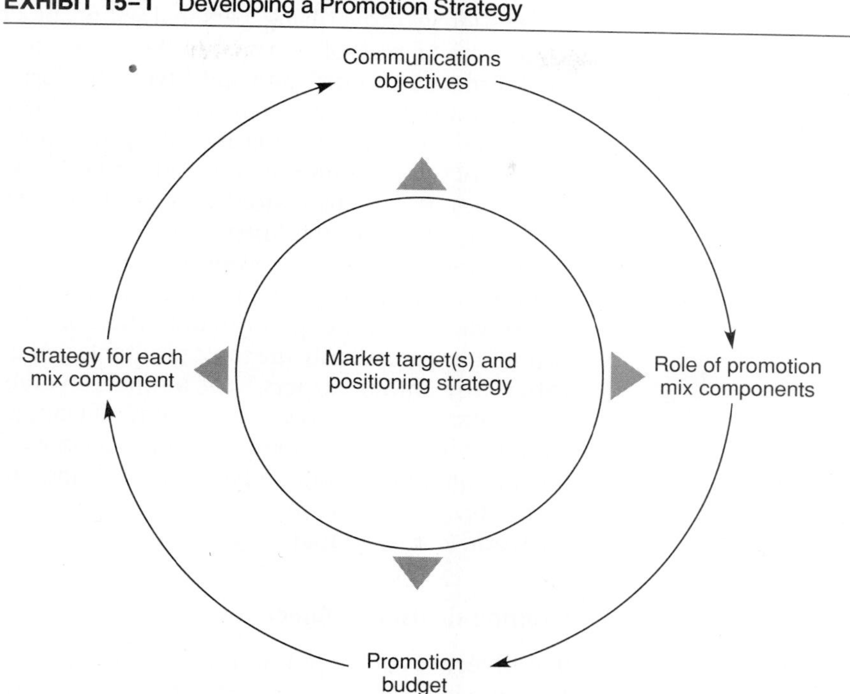

municating with financial analysts.) Publicity can be negative as well as positive and cannot be controlled to the same extent as other promotion components. Since the organization does not purchase the media coverage, publicity is a cost-effective method of communication. The media are usually willing to cover topics of public interest.

Developing the Promotion Strategy

Market targets and positioning strategy guide promotion decisions. Promotion strategy includes deciding: (1) communications objectives, (2) the role of the components that make up the promotion mix, (3) the promotion budget, and (4) a strategy for each mix component (Exhibit 15–1). Strategies are selected for advertising, personal selling, sales promotion, and public relations.

Market targets and product, distribution, and price decisions guide: (1) deciding the role of promotion strategy in the total marketing program and (2) identifying the specific communications tasks of the promotion activities. One important question is deciding the role promotion will play in marketing strategy. Advertising, personal selling, or a combination of the two is often a major part of a firm's marketing strategy. In consumer package-goods firms, sales promotion and advertising form the major part of the promotional mix. In industrial firms, personal selling often dominates the promotion mix, with advertising and sales promotion playing a supporting role. The use of sales promotion and public relations varies considerably among companies. When promotion is not an important part of an organization's marketing program, the function is usually handled by other firms in the distribution channel. For example, producers of private-label brands of clothing rely on retailers to promote the brands to end-users.

Singapore Airlines plays an important promotion role in marketing the nation. It is consistently the most profitable global airline, although ranking 15th in size among carriers.[8] The airline's favorable image helps to position the country to executives, government officials, and tourists who are familiar with Singapore Airline's renowned services. The tiny city-state with a population under 3 million has a strong brand image, the result in no small part of the airline's reputation with customers and competitors throughout the world (see accompanying advertisement).

Communications Objectives

The objectives of the promotion-mix components are interrelated. An illustration will show how these objectives are closely linked together. Suppose that health-care Brand A is perceived by buyers in a target segment as being gentle to use but less effective than competing Brand B. In fact, A is equivalent to B regarding effectiveness. Therefore, an important positioning objective is to convince buyers in the target segment that Brand A is both effective and gentle. The communications objective is to communicate to the target segment that A is gentle yet effective. The advertising objective is to communicate this message to the target segment via the appropriate media. The sales force must convey a similar message in direct sales contacts.

Communications objectives help determine how advertising, personal selling, and sales promotion are used in the marketing program. A look at the stages of a buyer's decision process suggest the range of communications objectives possible.

Need Recognition. One communications objective, typical for new-product introductions, is to trigger a need. Need recognition may also be important for existing products and services, particularly when the buyer can postpone purchasing or choose not to purchase (life insurance is a good example). For example, De Beers diamond advertisements often highlight a need to purchase jewelry. The company controls over 80 percent of the world's supply of uncut diamonds. A major objective of De Beers's communications is to encourage the purchase of diamond jewelry. One adver-

ON OUR DAILY NONSTOP MEGATOP 747 TO HONG KONG
WE'VE NEVER FORGOTTEN THE LITTLE THINGS.

It might be an extra pillow. Or the up-to-date reading material that you'll find on every flight. Maybe it's the Independent Television News beamed daily via satellite from London. All little things. But on our daily nonstop Megatop™ 747 from San Francisco to Hong Kong, we've never forgotten how important those little things can be. En route, enjoy inflight service even other airlines talk about.

A great way to fly
SINGAPORE AIRLINES

Courtesy of Singapore Airlines

tising approach is to emphasize different events, such as a couple's 10th anniversary.

Gathering Information. Promotion can aid a buyer's search for information. One of the objectives of new-product promotional activities is to help buyers learn about the product. Prescription drug companies advertise to the public to make people aware of diseases and brand names;[9] in the past, they targeted only doctors through ads in medical journals and contacts by salespeople. A U.S. Food and Drug Administration market-research study found that consumers want more information on prescription drugs, and drug companies are finding that advertising is an effective way to provide it. Advertising is often a more cost-effective way to disseminate information than personal selling, particularly when the information can be supplied by electronic or printed media.

Evaluation of Alternatives. Promotion helps buyers evaluate alternative products or brands. Both comparative advertising and personal selling are effective in demonstrating a brand's strengths over competing brands. An example of this form of advertising is to analyze the competing brands of a product, showing a favorable comparison for the brand of the firm placing the ad. Specific product attributes (e.g., effectiveness) may be used for the comparison. Salespeople seek to identify buyers' needs and present the features of their brand that correspond to the needs.

Decision to Purchase. Personal selling is often used to obtain a purchase commitment from the buyers of consumer durable goods and industrial products. Door-to-door selling organizations such as Avon use highly programmed selling approaches to encourage buyers to purchase their products. Communications objectives in these firms include making a target number of contacts each day. Point-of-purchase sales promotions, such as displays in retail stores, are intended to influence the purchase decision, as are samples and coupons. One of the advantages of personal selling over advertising is its flexibility in responding to the buyer's objectives and questions at the time the decision to purchase is being made.

Product Use. Communicating with buyers after they purchase a product is an important promotional activity. Follow-up by salespeople, advertisements stressing a firm's service capabilities, and toll-free numbers placed on packages to encourage users to seek information or report problems are illustrations of postpurchase communications. Hotels leave questionnaires in rooms for occupants to use in evaluating hotel services.

Various communications objectives may be assigned to promotion strategy. The uses of promotion vary according to the type of purchase, the stage of the buyer's decision process, the maturity of the product-market, and the role of promotion in the marketing program. Communications models are available to guide management in analyzing and selecting promotion objectives and strategies. Two examples are the AIDA model (attention, interest, desire, action) and the hierarchy-of-effects model. The steps in both models move from the awareness to action stages of the purchasing process.[10]

Objectives are selected for the entire promotional program and for each promotion component. Certain objectives, such as sales and market-share targets, are shared with other marketing-program components. Illustrative promotion objectives include:

- Creating or increasing buyers' awareness of a product or brand.
- Influencing buyers' attitudes toward a company, product, or brand.
- Increasing the level of brand preference of the buyers in a targeted segment.
- Achieving sales and market-share increases for specific customer or prospect targets.
- Generating repeat purchases of a brand.
- Encouraging trial of a new product.
- Attracting new customers.

The following sections discuss and provide examples of objectives for each promotion component.

Role of the Promotion-Mix Components

Promotion objectives can be linked to the specific role of each component in the promotion mix. For example, the role of the sales force may be to obtain sales or, instead, to inform channel-of-distribution organizations about product features and applications. Advertising may play a major or minor role in the promotion strategy. Sales promotion (e.g., trade shows) may be used to achieve various objectives in the promotion mix.

Early in developing the promotion strategy, it is useful to set some guidelines for the promotion-mix components. These guidelines help determine the strategy for each promotion component. It is necessary to decide which communications objective(s) will be the responsibility of each component. For example, advertising may be responsible for creating awareness of a new product. Sales promotion (e.g., coupons and samples) may encourage trial of the new product. Personal selling may be assigned responsibility for getting retailers to stock the new product. It is also important to decide how large the contribution of each promotion component will be. Indicating the relative contribution of each component will help to determine the promotion budget.

Budgeting Approaches

Not surprisingly, achieving an optimal balance between revenues and promotion expenditures is difficult because factors other than promotion also influence sales. Isolating the effects of promotion may require complex analysis. Because of this, more practical budgeting techniques are normally used. These methods include (1) objective and task, (2) percent of sales, (3) competitive parity, (4) all you can afford, and (5) budgeting models. Similar approaches are also used to determine advertising and sales-promotion budgets. The personal-selling budget is set by the number of people in the sales force and their qualifications.

The promotion budget may be based only on the planned expenditures for advertising and sales promotion. Companies typically develop separate budgets for the sales organization. Public-relations budgeting also may be separate from promotion budgeting. Nevertheless, it is important to consider the size and allocation of total promotion expenses when formulating the promotion strategy. Unless this is done, the integration of the components is likely to be fragmented.

An example of a promotion budget (excluding sales force and public relations) for a pharmaceutical product is shown in Exhibit 15–2. Note the relative size of advertising and sales-promotion expenditures. Advertising accounts for only 28 percent of the total budget. The sampling of drugs to doctors by salespeople is often a sizable amount of the promotion budget.

Objective and Task. This logical and cost-effective method is probably the most widely used budgeting approach. Management sets communications objectives, determines the tasks necessary to achieve the objectives, and adds up costs. This method also establishes the mix of promotion components by selecting the component(s) appropriate for attaining each objective. Marketing management must carefully evaluate how the promotion objectives are to be achieved and choose the most cost-effective promotion components. The effectiveness of the objective and task method depends on the judgment and experience of the chief marketing executive and staff. The budget shown in Exhibit 15–2 was determined using the objective and task method.

Percent of Sales. Using this method, the budget is calculated as a percent of sales and is, therefore, quite arbitrary. The percentage figure is often based on past expenditure patterns. The fundamental problem with the method is that it fails to recognize that promotion efforts and results are related. For example, a 10 percent-of-sales budget may be too much or not enough promotion expenditure to achieve forecasted sales. This procedure can also lead to too much spending on promotion when sales are high and too little when sales are low. In a cyclical industry, where sales follow up-and-down trends, a strategy of increasing promotion expeditures during low sales periods may be more appropriate.

Competitive Parity. Promotion expenditures for this budgeting method are guided by how much competitors spend. A major shortcoming of the method is that differences in marketing strategy between competing firms

EXHIBIT 15–2 Illustrative Promotion Budget for a Pharmaceutical Product

Promotional Activity	*1995 Budget*
Promotional material	$100,000
Samples	200,000
Direct mail	150,000
Journal advertising	175,000
Total budget	$625,000

may require different promotion strategies. For example, Revlon uses an intensive distribution strategy, while Estée Lauder targets buyers by distributing through selected department stores. A comparison of promotional strategies of these firms is not very meaningful, since their market targets and promotion objectives are different.

All You Can Afford. Since budget limits are a reality in many companies, this method is used in these instances. Top management may specify how much can be spent on promotion. For example, the guideline may be to reduce the budget to 75 percent of last year's actual promotion expenditures. The objective and task method can be combined with the "all-you-can-afford" method by setting task priorities and allocating the budget to the higher priority tasks.

Budgeting Models. This method sets the budget using a mathematical model, often developed from analysis of historical data. The basic concern in using the model for budget determination is establishing the validity of the model and its stability over time. Advisor 2, a comprehensive model for budgeting the marketing mix for industrial products, determines a marketing budget and allocates expenditures for personal and impersonal (e.g., advertising) communications.[11] Advisor 2 is a multiple regression-type model that utilizes several predictor variables, including number of users, customer concentration, fraction of sales made to order, attitude difference, proportion of direct sales, life-cycle stage, product plans, and product complexity. The model is similar in concept and approach to the Profit Impact of Marketing Strategy (PIMS) model, although Advisor 2 sets the marketing budget and its components rather than offering complete strategies for business units or products.

Integrating Promotion Strategies

Several factors may affect a firm's promotion mix, as shown by Exhibit 15–3. Advertising, publicity, personal selling, and sales-promotion strategies are often fragmented because they are assigned to different organizational units. There are differences in priorities, and evaluating the produc-

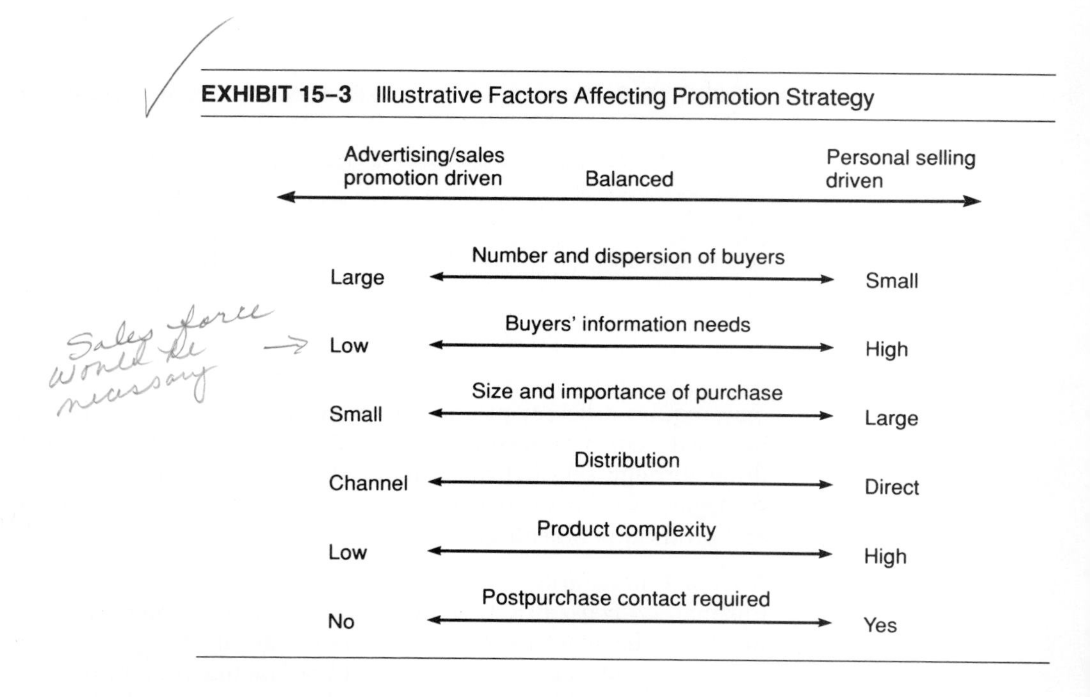

tivity of the components is complex. The lack of coordination between selling and advertising often occurs in firms marketing to industrial buyers. These firms tend to follow personal-selling-driven promotion strategies. The same separation of selling and advertising strategies prevails in a variety of consumer-products firms.

Integrated marketing communications (IMC) strategies are replacing fragmented advertising, publicity, and sales programs. These approaches differ from traditional promotion strategies in several ways:

1. IMC programs are comprehensive. Advertising, personal selling, retail atmospherics, behavioral-modification programs, public relations, investor-relations programs, employee communications, and other forms are all considered in the planning of an IMC.
2. IMC programs are unified. The messages delivered by all media, including such diverse influences as employee recruiting and the atmospherics of retailers upon which the marketer primarily relies, are the same or supportive of a unified theme.
3. IMC programs are targeted. The public relations program, advertising programs and dealer/distributor programs all have the same or related target markets.
4. IMC programs have coordinated execution of all the communications components of the organization.

5. IMC programs emphasize productivity in reaching the designated targets when selecting communication channels and allocating resources to marketing media.[12]

The Limited, the women's apparel retailer, has been unusually successful in implementing an integrated marketing-communications program; Byerly's in Minneapolis uses atmospherics to communicate that the supermarket is the place to be seen by trendy people.[13] The upscale Nordstrom department store chain is another example of a firm using a coordinated promotion program. The retail sales force is the focus of Nordstrom's promotion strategy.

Advertising, personal selling, and sales-promotion strategies are examined in the remainder of the chapter to illustrate how these strategies are developed. Public relations is also a very important promotion component. Since these activities vary widely in scope and are similar in certain ways to advertising, they are not included in the discussion.

ADVERTISING STRATEGY

Advertising strategy development begins by identifying and describing the target audience. Next, it is important to establish the role and scope of advertising, decide on the advertising budget, and set specific objectives. The selection of the creative strategy follows. It determines how the objectives will be accomplished. Advertising media and programming schedules are used to implement the creative strategy. The final step is implementing the advertising strategy and evaluating its effectiveness. We examine each of these activities, highlighting important features and strategy issues.

Advertising's Role in Promotion Strategy

Estimating advertising's impact on buyers helps management to decide advertising's role and scope in the marketing program and to choose specific objectives. Management's perception of what advertising can contribute to promotion objectives has an important influence in deciding advertising's role. The Strategy Feature describes how Gillette positions its new line of toiletries using advertising to link the line with the successful Sensor razor. Advertising plays a key role in this marketing strategy. Recall our discussion of product-line extension in Chapter 12.

A study using the PIMS data bank identifies factors that determine advertising's role in marketing strategy. The PIMS program is described in Chapter 2. The research provides support for several of the factors shown earlier in Exhibit 15–3. Using a sample of 789 businesses that spend at least 0.01 percent of sales on advertising and promotion, Farris and Buzzell found

STRATEGY FEATURE Using Sensor's Success to Launch the Gillette Series Line of Toiletries

The positioning concept for Gillette's new line of toiletries is "The Best a Man Can Get." This theme helped launch the highly successful Sensor razor. The chart shows the market position of the major competitors before the new line was introduced. Gillette's joint advertising budget for Sensor and the Gillette series totaled $60 million for the first year. The objective is to create a megabrand under the Gillette name. The toiletries line is priced 10 to 20 percent higher than existing products. A new fragrance, Cool Wave, spans the line. The key challenge is convincing buyers that the toiletries are better than competing brands. Unlike razors, Gillette is not the leader in the medicine chest (see chart). Gillette's product tests for the new line were very favorable. One-minute TV commercials will feature the new line of shaving cream and after-shave with Sensor. Gillette chose not to place the Sensor name on the new line.

Source: Laurence Ingrassia, "Gillette Ties New Toiletries to Hot Razor," *The Wall Street Journal,* September 18, 1992, pp. B1, B6.

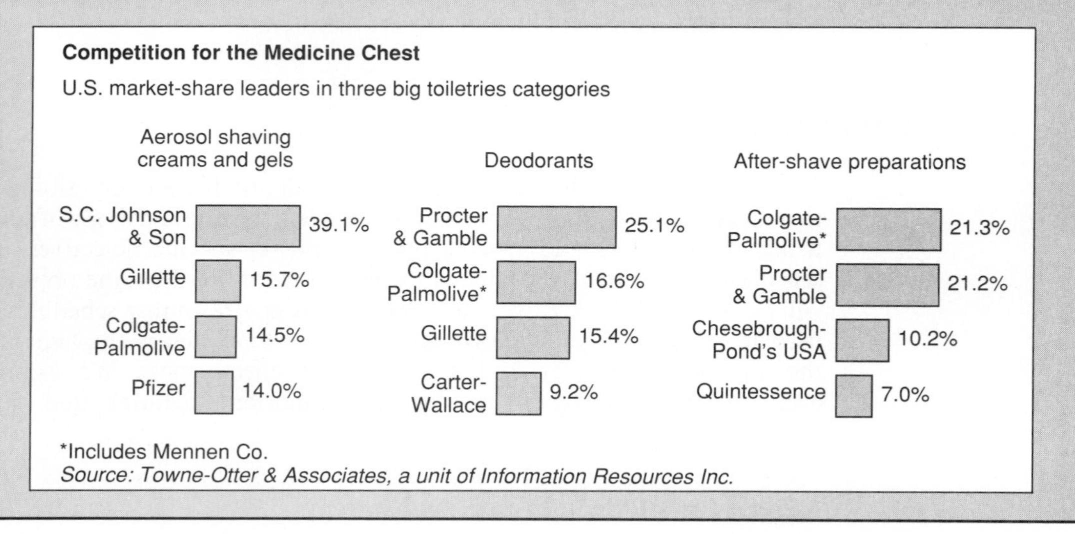

that firms with higher ratios of advertising and promotion to sales displayed the following characteristics:

Standardized products.

Many end-users.

Typical purchase amount small.

Auxiliary services important.

Sales through channel organizations.

Premium-priced product.

Manufacturer's contribution margin high.

Relatively small market share and/or surplus production capacity.

High proportion of sales from new products.[14]

EXHIBIT 15–4 Alternative Levels for Setting Advertising Objectives

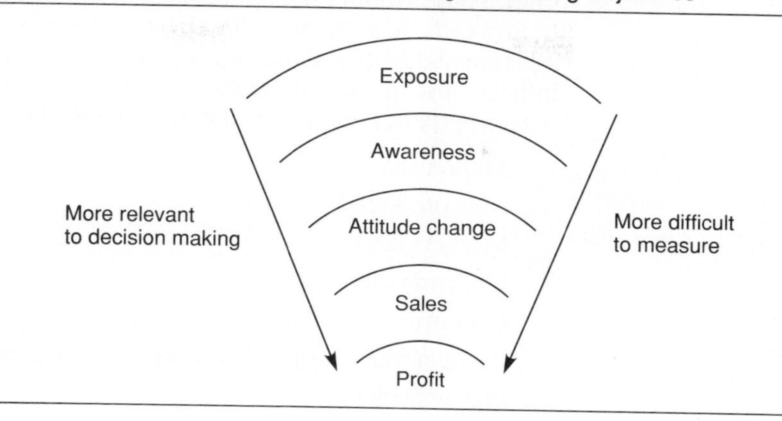

The study describes existing relationships rather than indicating what they should be. Nonetheless, the analysis includes a large cross section of firms. The factors that are related to high advertising and promotion expenditures offer useful guides for examining the role and scope of advertising.

Setting Advertising Objectives and Budgeting

Advertising Objectives. Exhibit 15–4 shows alternative levels for setting advertising objectives. In moving from the most general level (exposure) toward the most specific level (profit contribution) the objectives are increasingly closer to the purchase decision. For example, knowing that advertising causes a measurable increase in sales is much more useful to the decision maker than saying that advertising exposed a specific number of people to an advertising message. The key issue is whether the objectives at the general levels in Exhibit 15–4 are linked to purchase behavior. For example, how much will awareness increase the chances that people will purchase a product? Achievement of very general and mid-level objectives often can be measured, whereas the sales and profit impact of advertising is very difficult to measure.

Research indicates that brand awareness leads to increased market share and, in turn, to greater profits. A study conducted by the Strategic Planning Institute involving 73 industrial-products businesses supports the relationship between brand awareness, sales, and profits.[15] Exposure measures of advertising effectiveness are subject to much more debate. These measures are more useful in guiding media-allocation decisions than in gauging the value of advertising to a firm.

Budget Determination. The budgeting methods for promotion discussed earlier in the chapter are also used in advertising budgeting. The PIMS program of the Strategic Planning Institute offers more specific budgeting guidelines. The Farris and Buzzell PIMS research identified several characteristics of firms whose advertising and promotion expenditures as a percentage of sales are higher than those of other firms. Additionally, budgeting guidelines indicate how the following factors are related to advertising and sales-promotion expenditures for the firms in the PIMS sample.[16]

Market share
New products
Market growth
Utilization of plant capacity
Unit price of product
Product purchases as a percentage of total purchases
Product pricing
Product quality
Breadth of product line
Standard versus custom (made-to-order) products

Illustrations of four of the factors are shown in Exhibit 15–5. The Cahners Publishing Company and the Strategic Planning Institute have developed a guide for estimating the budget.[17] For example, the media advertising budget based on a firm's market share of 12 percent (between 10 percent and 17 percent on chart A of Exhibit 15–5) and annual sales of $100 million is:

$$0.7 \times \frac{100{,}000{,}000}{1{,}000} = \$70{,}000.$$

By repeating this computation for each factor, the results can be averaged to calculate the budget. Weighing can be used to take into account the importance of each factor to a particular firm.

The PIMS budgeting approach is a useful diagnostic tool for comparing a firm's current advertising and sales-promotion budget with the PIMS guidelines. When used in conjunction with management's experience, the guide can indicate that a budget may be too high or too low compared to PIMS norms.

Creative Strategy. The creative strategy guides the advertising campaign. Two considerations affect the strategy selection: (1) whether the campaign is intended to maintain or to change market conditions, and (2) whether the campaign will communicate information or imagery and symbolism.[18] Maintenance and reinforcement strategies are used to support an established brand. A strategy to change market conditions may reposition a brand, expand the market for a brand, or launch a new product. Information messages communicate product benefits, whereas image messages seek to either reinforce or create change using symbolism and imagery.

The creative strategy is guided by the positioning concept selected for

EXHIBIT 15–5 Guidelines for Advertising and Sales-Promotion Expenditure

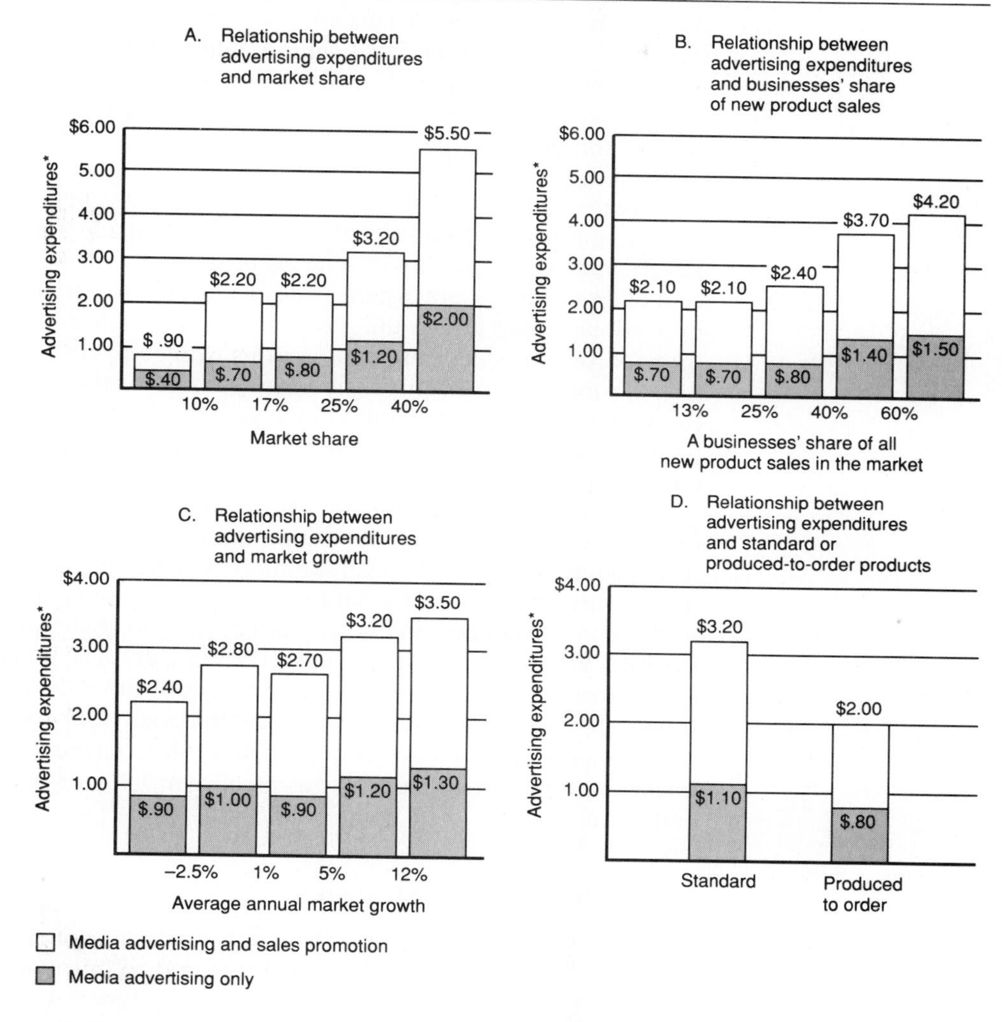

*Advertising expenditures: media advertising and sales promotion expenditures per $1000 market sales.

Source: Valerie Kijewski, "Advertising and Promotion: How Much Should You Spend?" pamphlet prepared by the Strategic Planning Institute, June 1983, pp. 4, 5, 6, and 11.

the product or brand. Chapter 9 discusses positioning according to the *functions* performed by the brand, the *symbol* to be conveyed by the brand, or the *experience* provided by the product. The creative theme seeks to effectively communicate the positioning concept to buyers and others who influence the purchase of the brand.

The Wall Street Journal asked several of the advertising industry's top executives their opinions on the best and the worst advertisements of the

1980s.[19] Included in the best categories were the American Express "portrait" series of celebrity "card members," and Nike's "Just Do It" campaign. Among the poor ad campaigns cited were Burger King's disastrous "Herb the Nerd" series and the 1989 Infinity automobile series of Zen-inspired nature scenes featuring pussy willows and rocks. Interestingly, some of the highest-rated and lowest-rated ads were created by the same agency. Television dominated the high ratings, but a print and a billboard campaign also received top ratings.

Creative advertising designs enhance the effectiveness of advertising by providing a unifying concept that binds together the various parts of an advertising campaign. Advertising agencies, who typically receive 15 percent of gross billings, are experts in designing creative strategies. The agency professionals may design unique themes to position a product or firm in some particular way or use comparisons with competition to enhance the firm's brands. Choosing the right creative theme for the marketing situation can make a major contribution to the success of a program. While tests are used to evaluate creative approaches, the task is more of an art than a science. Perhaps the best guide to creativity is an agency's track record.

The creative strategy used for Murphy's Oil Soap shows the importance of a segment focus and brand positioning through creative advertising. For nearly a hundred years the soap was marketed in a single region of the country.[20] Fourteen years after a national rollout program starting in 1976, the brand gained sixth position in its product category. Sales in 1990 increased to over $30 million, eight times more than in 1980. The brand is positioned as an effective wood cleaner. Its "Great Houses" advertising campaign portrays impressive old homes that highlight the beauty of wood and the special requirements of a wood-cleaning product. More recently, advertising and sales promotion position the soap as effective in "cleaning wood surfaces . . . and more."

Media/Programming Strategy

A company's advertising agency normally guides media and programming decisions. The agency has the experience and technical ability to match media and programming to the target audience specified by the firm. The media, timing, and programming decisions are influenced largely by two factors: (1) access to the target audience(s), and (2) the costs of reaching the target group(s). Suppose a product manager is interested in advertising to business executives through printed media. Possible publications and approximate costs for one-page, four-color advertisements are:

Fortune (monthly)	$53,600
Forbes (52 issues)	48,200
Harvard Business Review (6 per year)	15,000

Source: *Standard Rates and Data Services,* July 24, 1991.

Standard Rates and Data Services publishes advertising costs for various media. The costs are determined by circulation levels and the type of publication. In deciding which medium to use, it is useful to evaluate the cost per exposure and the characteristics of the subscribers.

Media models are available to analyze allocations and decide which media mix best achieves one or more objectives.[21] These models typically use an exposure measure (Exhibit 15–4) as the basis for media allocation. For example, cost per thousand of exposure can be used to consider alternative media. The models also consider audience characteristics (e.g., age-group composition) and other factors. The models are useful in selecting media when many advertising programs and a wide range of media are used.

Implementing the Advertising Strategy and Measuring Its Effectiveness

Before the advertising strategy is implemented, it is important to establish criteria for measuring its effectiveness. Advertising expenditures are wasted if firms spend too much or allocate expenditures improperly. Measuring effectiveness provides useful feedback for future advertising decisions. The quality of advertising can be as critical to getting results as the amount of advertising.

Tracking Advertising Performance. Advertising's impact on sales is difficult to measure because other factors also influence sales and profits. Most efforts to measure effectiveness consider objectives such as attitude change, awareness, or exposure (Exhibit 15–4). Comparing objectives and results helps firms decide when to stop or alter advertising campaigns. Services such as TV's Nielsen ratings are available for the major media. In recent years Nielsen's long-standing domination of TV ratings has been questioned by rivals.[22] These ratings have a critical impact on the allocation of advertising dollars. Recent research findings question the accuracy of the ratings. One major concern is the possible biased representation of the public's viewing. These concerns have resulted in several changes in the rating process.

Methods of Measuring Effectiveness. Several methods are used to evaluate advertising results. Analysis of historical data identifies relationships between advertising expenditures and sales statistical techniques such as regression analysis. Recall tests measure consumers' awareness of specific ads and campaigns by asking questions to determine if a sample of people remember an ad. Longitudinal studies track advertising expenditures and sales results before, during, and after an advertising campaign. Controlled tests are a form of longitudinal study in which extraneous effects are measured and/or controlled during the test. Test marketing is used to evaluate advertising effectiveness. Effort/results models use empirical data to build a mathematical relationship between sales and advertising effort.

A particularly promising method for measuring advertising effectiveness is the use of consumer panels in cities with cable TV. The panel is a

EXHIBIT 15–6 IBM's Advertising Campaign Research Measurement Model

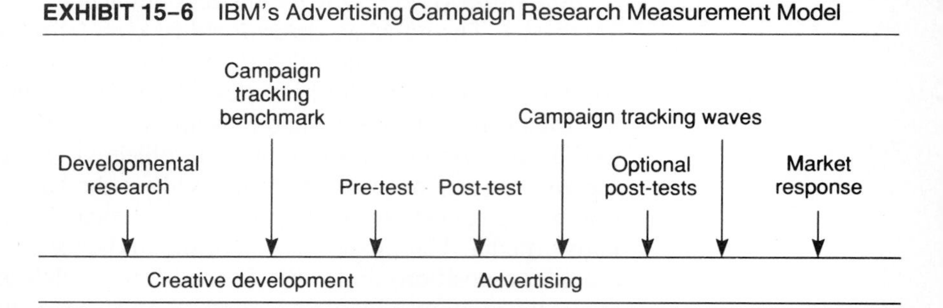

Source: Byron G. Quann, "How IBM Assesses Its Business-to-Business Advertising," *Business Marketing,* January 1985, p. 108.

group of consumers who agree to provide information about their purchases on a continuing basis. Cash-register scanning of the purchases of panel members provides data on brands purchased, prices, and other information. Samples of consumers can be split into groups that are exposed or not exposed to advertising on cable television. With equivalent samples, the influence on sales of factors other than advertising can be controlled. The difference in sales between the control and the experimental (exposed) groups over the test period measures the effect of advertising. This technique is appropriate for certain types of frequently purchased consumer products such as food items and health and beauty aids.

Advertising research is used for more than just measuring the effectiveness of advertising. Research can be used for various activities in advertising strategy development, including generating and evaluating creative ideas and concepts and pretesting concepts, ideas, and specific ads.

Effectiveness Illustration. The approach that IBM uses to assess its business-to-business advertising is described in Exhibit 15–6. Because of the difficulty in evaluating an individual ad's effectiveness, IBM concentrates on assessing campaigns in particular business applications. Use of the model starts with the creative development process. Effectiveness research involves pretests and postintroduction tests, standardized information services, tracking studies, buyer-impression studies, and focus groups. Note the early determination of the campaign tracking benchmark and the pretesting of advertising concepts.

DEVELOPING AND IMPLEMENTING SALES FORCE STRATEGY

The design of the sales force strategy includes six major steps. First, the role of the sales force in the promotion mix is determined. This requires deciding what personal selling is expected to do in the marketing program. Second, the selling process is defined, indicating how selling will be accomplished with targeted customers. Third, in selecting sales channels, it is necessary to decide how field selling, major account management, telemarketing, and electronic channels will contribute to the selling process. Fourth, the design of the sales organization is determined, or its adequacy evaluated in an existing organization. Fifth, the sales force is recruited, trained, and managed. Finally, the results of the selling strategy are evaluated, and adjustments are made to narrow the gap between actual and desired results.

The Role of Selling in Promotion Strategy

The role of personal selling varies in different companies. Salespeople may serve primarily as order takers or instead fulfill major responsibilities as consultants to customers. While marketing management has some flexibility in choosing the role and objectives of the sales force in the marketing mix, several factors often shape the role of selling in a firm's marketing strategy. These factors are shown in Exhibit 15–7. The selling effort needs to be integrated into the overall communications program. It is also useful to indicate how the other promotion-mix components, such as advertising, support and relate to the sales force. Sales management needs to be aware of the marketing plans and activities of the other promotion components.

The objectives assigned to salespeople often include management's expected sales results. Sales quotas are used to state these expectations. Companies may give incentives to salespeople who achieve their quotas. Team selling incentives may also be used. Objectives other than sales are also important in many organizations. These include increasing the number of new accounts, providing services to customers and channel organizations, selecting and evaluating middlemen, and obtaining market information. The objectives selected need to be consistent with marketing strategy and promotion objectives and measurable so that sales performance can be evaluated.

Illustrative Roles for the Sales Force

The possible roles for the sales force include new business, trade selling, missionary selling, and consultative/technical selling.[24]

New Business Strategy. This selling role involves obtaining sales from new buyers. The buyers may be one-time purchasers or repeat buyers. For example, the first-time sale of sheet steel by a steel producer to a container manufacturer may lead to further purchases. Alternatively, the selling strategy may be concerned with obtaining new buyers on a continuing basis. Insurance and real estate sales firms use this strategy.

EXHIBIT 15–7 Factors Influencing the Role of Personal Selling in a Firm's Marketing Strategy

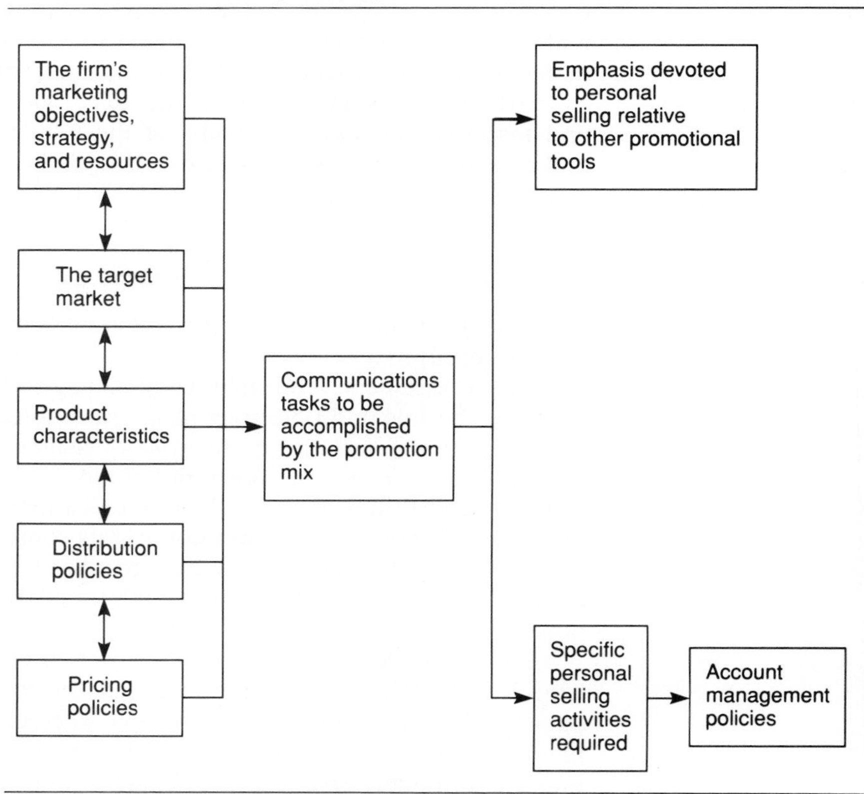

Source: Gilbert A. Churchill, Jr., Neil M. Ford, and Orville C. Walker, Jr., *Sales Force Management,* 4th ed. (Homewood, Ill.: Richard D. Irwin, 1993), p. 121.

Trade Selling Strategy. This form of selling provides assistance and support to middlemen rather than obtaining sales. A manufacturer marketing through wholesalers, retailers, or other intermediaries may provide merchandising, logistical, promotional, and product information assistance. Grocery wholesalers' salespeople assist retailers in merchandising and provide other support activities.

Missionary Selling Strategy. A strategy similar to trade selling is missionary selling. A manufacturer's salespeople work with the customers of a channel member to encourage them to purchase the manufacturer's product from the channel member. For example, pharmaceutical sales representatives contact physicians, providing them with product information and samples and encouraging the doctors to prescribe the producer's drugs.

Consultative/Technical Selling Strategy. Firms that use this strategy sell to an existing customer base, and provide technical and application assistance. IBM's strategy for selling mainframe computers direct to business customers is illustrative, as is the sale of architectural services to commercial building developers. Understanding and responding to customer needs is essential to the success of this strategy.

An organization may use more than one of the above selling strategies. For example, a transportation services company might use a new business strategy for expanding its customer base and a missionary selling strategy for servicing existing customers. The skills needed by the salesperson vary according to the selling strategy used.

Defining the Selling Process

Several activities are involved in moving from identifying a buyer's needs to completing the sale and the postsale relationships between buyer and seller. This selling process includes: (1) prospecting for customers, (2) opening the relationship, (3) qualifying the prospect, (4) presenting the sales message, (5) closing the sale, and (6) servicing the account.[25] The process may be very simple, consisting of a routine set of actions designed to close the sale. Alternatively, the process may extend over a long time period, with many contacts and interactions between the buyer, other people influencing the purchase, the salesperson assigned to the account, and technical specialists in the seller's organization.

Sales management defines the selling process by indicating the customer and prospects the firm is targeting and the guidelines for developing customer relationships and obtaining sales results. This process is management's strategy for achieving the sales force objectives in the organization's selling environment. Salespeople implement the process, following the guidelines set by management, such as the relative emphasis on different products, customer targeting and priorities, and the desired selling activities and outcomes.

The selling process is managed by the salesperson who has responsibility for each customer account. Account management includes planning and executing the selling activities between the salesperson and the customer or prospect. Some organizations analyze this process and set guidelines salespeople use to guide their selling activities. Process analysis may result in programmed selling steps or, instead, may lead to highly customized selling approaches the salesperson develops for each account. A company may also use team selling (e.g., product specialists and salesperson), major account management, telemarketing, and electronic support systems (e.g., computer ordering).

The selling process guides sales force recruiting, training, allocation of effort, organizational design, and the use of selling-support activities such as telemarketing. Understanding the process is essential in coordinating all elements of the marketing mix.

Sales Channels

Studies conducted by The Conference Board, Inc. show that companies are responding to the pressure of costs and competition in three major directions: (1) field sales forces are being restructured to provide greater specialization by types of users or products (product specialists, major account management); (2) companies are shifting toward greater use of indirect reseller channels; and (3) companies are adopting supplemental sales support channels such as telemarketing and computer-to-computer ordering.[26]

The choice of a particular sales channel is influenced by the buying power of customers, the selling channel threshold levels, and the complexity of buyer-seller relationships.[27] Consideration of customer contact requirements illustrates the strengths and limitations of alternative sales channels.

Customer Buying Power. The purchasing potential of customers and prospects often places them into different importance categories. The "major" or "national" account represents the most important customer category. The major account: (1) purchases a significant volume on an absolute dollar basis and as a percent of a supplier's total sales, and (2) purchases (or influences the purchase) from a central or headquarters location for several geographically dispersed organizational units.[28] The buying power of a supplier's total customer base may range from several major accounts to a large number of very low-volume purchasers. Customers and prospects are classified into major accounts, other customers requiring face-to-face contact, and accounts whose purchases (or potential) do not justify regular contact by field salespeople.

Threshold Levels. The number of customers in each buying-power category influences the selection of selling channels. The value of using more than one selling channel should be determined. For example, the amount of telemarketing effort that is needed determines if establishing a telemarketing support unit should be considered. Similarly, enough major accounts should exist in order to develop and implement a major-account program. If the customer base does not display substantial differences in purchasing power and servicing requirements, then the use of a single selling channel may be appropriate.

Complexity of the Customer Relationship. The account management relationship is also a key factor in deciding what type of sales channel is appropriate. For example, a customer who: (1) has several people involved in the buying process; (2) seeks a long-term, cooperative relationship with the supplier; and (3) requires a specialized attention and service creates a complex buyer-seller relationship.[29] Such a relationship coupled with sufficient buying power suggests the use of a major-account management channel. In contrast, a simple, routinized buying situation suggests telemarketing or electronic buyer-seller linkages. The field-selling channel corresponds best to customer relationships that fall between very complex and highly routinized.

Designing the Sales Organization

Designing the sales organization includes selecting an organizational structure and deciding the size and deployment of the sales force.

Organizational Structure. The organizational approach should support the firm's sales force strategy. As companies adjust their selling strategies, organizational structure may also require changes.

Important influences on organizational design are the customer base, the product, and the geographic location of buyers. Thus, organizational designs for a sales force are driven by market, product, geography, or a combination of these factors. The answers to several questions guide the choice of an organizational design.

1. What is the selling job? What functions are to be performed by salespeople?
2. Is specialization of selling effort necessary according to type of customer, different products, or salesperson activities (e.g., sales and service)?
3. Are channel-of-distribution relationships important in the organizational design?
4. How many and what kinds of sales management levels are needed to provide the proper amount of supervision, assistance, and control?
5. How and to what extent will sales channels other than the field sales force be used?

The organizational design that is selected should be compatible with the selling strategy and other marketing-mix strategies. The major types of organization designs are shown in Exhibit 15–8. These designs take into account the extent of product diversity and differences in customer needs. Whenever the customer base is widely dispersed, geography is likely to be included in the organizational design. The assigned area and accounts that are the responsibility of the salesperson make up the sales territory.

Sales Force Deployment. The sales manager must decide how many salespeople are needed and how to deploy them to customers and prospects. Several factors outside the salesperson's control often affect his or her sales results. These influences include market potential, the number and location of customers, the intensity of competition, and the market position of the company. Productivity analysis considers both salesperson factors and the uncontrollable factors.

Several methods can be used for analyzing sales force size and the deployment of selling effort, including: (1) revenue/cost analysis, (2) single-factor models, (3) sales and effort response models, and (4) portfolio deployment models. Normally, sales and/or costs are the basis for determining sales force size and allocation.

Revenue/cost analysis techniques require information on each saleper-

EXHIBIT 15–8 Sales Organization Designs

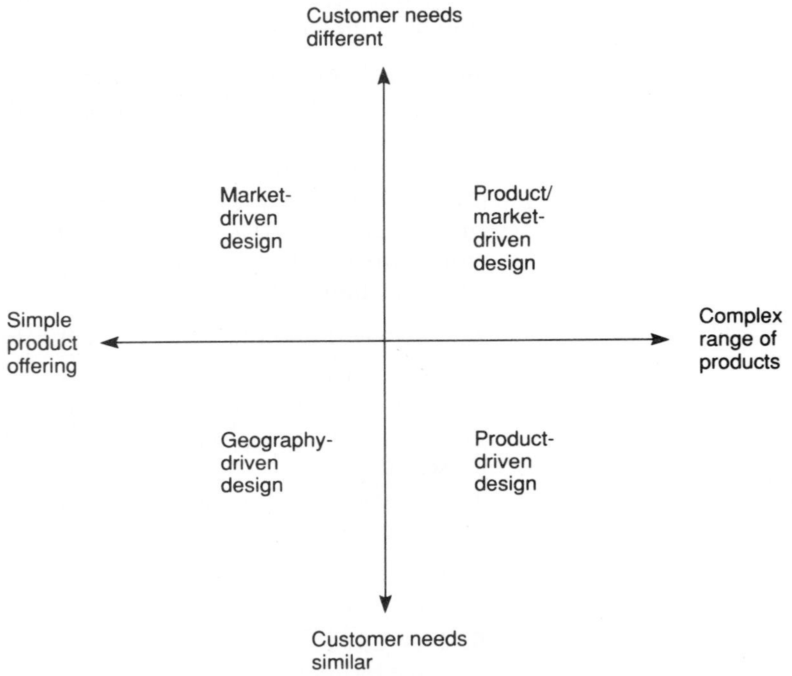

Customer needs different

Market-driven design

Product/market-driven design

Simple product offering

Complex range of products

Geography-driven design

Product-driven design

Customer needs similar

son's sales and/or costs. One approach compares each salesperson to an average break-even sales level, thus helping management to spot unprofitable territories. Another approach analyzes the profit performance of accounts or trading areas to estimate the profit impact of adding more salespeople or to determine how many people a new sales organization needs. These techniques are very useful in locating high- and low-performance territories.

Single-factor models assume that size and/or deployment are determined by one factor, such as market potential, workload (e.g., number of calls required), or others whose values can be used to determine required selling effort. Suppose there are two territories, X and Y. Territory X has double the market potential (opportunity for business) of territory Y. If selling effort is deployed according to market potential, X should get double the selling effort of Y.

Consideration of multiple influences (e.g., intensity of competition) on market response can improve deployment decisions. Several promising *sales and effort response models* aid size and deployment decisions.[30] Exhibit 15–9 shows the output provided by these models. The analysis indicates that

EXHIBIT 15–9 Sales Force Decision Model Output for Jones's and Smith's Territories

	Trading Area†	Present Effort (percent)	Recommended Effort (percent)	Estimated Sales*	
				Present Effort	Recommended Effort
Jones:					
	1	10	4	19	13
	2	60	20	153	120
	3	15	7	57	50
	4	5	2	10	7
	5	10	3	21	16
	Total	100	36	260	206
Smith:					
	1	18	81	370	520
	2	7	21	100	130
	3	5	11	55	65
	4	35	35	225	225
	5	5	11	60	70
	6	30	77	400	500
	Total	100	236	1,210	1,510

*In $000.

†Each territory is made up of several trading areas.

Jones's territory requires only about 0.36 percent of a person whereas Smith's territory can support about 2.36 people. The allocations are determined by increasing selling effort in high-response areas and reducing effort where sales response is low. Note that Exhibit 15–9 includes only two territories of a large sales organization. Sales response is determined from an empirically derived effort-to-sales relationship.

A *portfolio deployment strategy model* uses a version of the market attractiveness–business strength grid for business unit and product strategic analysis (Chapter 2). Promising accounts receive effort allocation based on their position on the grid.[31] An account which has a high market opportunity and where the firm has a strong competitive position receives more effort than an account with less opportunity where the firm's market position is not strong. One major advantage of this technique is that it is easily understood by management and salespeople.

Managing the Sales Force

Salespeople display differences in ability, motivation, and performance. Managing them involves the activities of supervising, selecting, training, motivating, and evaluating. A brief look at each activity shows the responsibilities and functions of a sales manager.

Finding and Selecting Salespeople. A major study of the chief sales executives in 107 firms asked them to indicate on a 1 to 10 scale how important 29 salesperson characteristics are to the success of their salespeople.[32] The executives consistently agreed that the three most significant success characteristics are (1) being customer driven and highly committed to the job; (2) accepting direction and cooperating as a team player; and (3) and being motivated by one's peers, financial incentives, and oneself.

Exhibit 15–10 shows several characteristics that are often important for different types of selling situations. The characteristics vary based on the type of selling strategy, so we must first define the job that is to be performed. Managers may use application forms, personal interviews, rating forms, reference checks, physical examinations, and various kinds of tests to assist them in making hiring decisions. The personal interview is widely cited as the most important part of the selection process.

Training. Some firms use formal programs to train their salespeople; others use informal on-the-job training. Factors that affect the type and duration of training include the size of the firm, type of sales job, product complexity, experience of new salespeople, and management's satisfaction with past training efforts. Training topics may include selling concepts and techniques, product knowledge, territory management, and company policies and operating procedures.

In training salespeople, companies may seek to (1) increase productivity, (2) improve morale, (3) lower turnover, (4) improve customer relations, and (5) produce better management of time and territory.[33] Each of these objectives is concerned with increasing results from the salesperson's effort and/or reducing selling costs. Sales training should be evaluated concerning benefits and costs. Evaluations may include before-and-after training results, participant critiques, and comparison of salespeople receiving training to those that have not been trained. Product knowledge training is probably more widespread than any other type of training.

Supervising and Motivating Salespeople. The manager that supervises salespeople has a key role in implementing a firm's selling strategy. He or she faces several important management issues. Coordinating the activities of a field sales force is difficult because of lack of regular contact. Compensation incentives are often used to encourage salespeople to sell. Also, as discussed earlier, sales executives want salespeople who are customer driven and committed to the company and to team relationships.

In the 1980s, many firms returned to using incentives for salespeople instead of fixed salaries.[34] The most widely used compensation plan is a combination of salary and incentive (80 percent salary and 20 percent incentive pay is a typical arrangement). The compensation plan should be fair to all participants and create an appropriate incentive. Salespeople also respond favorably to recognition programs and special promotions such as vacation travel awards.

Managers assist and encourage salespeople, and incentives highlight the

EXHIBIT 15–10 Characteristics Related to Sales Performance in Different Types of Sales Jobs

Type Sales Job	*Characteristics that Are Relatively Important*	*Characteristics that Are Relatively Less Important*
Trade selling	Age, maturity, empathy, knowledge of customer needs and business methods	Aggressiveness, technical ability, product knowledge, persuasiveness
Missionary selling	Youth, high energy and stamina, verbal skill, persuasiveness	Empathy, knowledge of customers, maturity, previous sales experience
Technical selling	Education, product and customer knowledge—usually gained through training, intelligence	Empathy, persuasiveness, aggressiveness, age
New business selling	Experience, age and maturity, aggressiveness, persuasiveness, persistence	Customer knowledge, product knowledge, education, empathy

Source: Gilbert A. Churchill, Jr., Neil M. Ford, and Orville C. Walker, Jr., *Sales Force Management,* 3rd ed. (Homewood, Ill.: Richard D. Irwin, 1990), p. 404.

importance of results, but the salesperson is the driving force in selling situations. Sales management must match promising selling opportunities with competent and self-motivated professional salespeople while providing the proper company environment and leadership. Although most sales management professionals consider financial compensation the most important motivating force, recent research indicates that personal characteristics, environmental conditions, and company policies and procedures are also important motivating factors.[35]

Sales Force Evaluation and Control

Sales management is continually working to improve the productivity of selling efforts. During the 1980s personal selling costs increased much faster than advertising costs. The evaluation of sales force performance considers sales results, costs, and salesperson behavior and outcome performance. Several issues are important in evaluation, including the unit(s) of analysis, measures of performance, performance standards, and factors that the sales organization and individual salespeople cannot control.

Unit of Analysis. Evaluation extends beyond the salesperson to include other organizational units such as districts and branches. Selling teams are used in some types of selling. These companies focus evaluations on team results. Product-performance evaluation by geographical area and across organization units is relevant in the firms that sell more than one product. Individual account sales and cost analyses are useful for customers such as national accounts and accounts assigned to salespeople.

Performance Measures. Management needs yardsticks for measuring salesperson performance. For example, the sales force of a regional food processor that distributes through grocery wholesalers and large retail chains devotes most of its selling effort to calling on retailers. Since the firm does not have information on sales of its products by individual retail outlet, evaluations are based on the activities of salespeople rather than sales outcomes. This type of control system focuses on "behavior" rather than "outcomes."

Sales managers may use both activity (behavior) and outcome measures of salesperson performance. Research indicates that measures of both activities and outcomes are used in performance evaluation.[36] The areas include expense control, sales presentation, technical knowledge, information feedback, and sales results. Achievement of the sales quota is a widely used outcome measure of sales performance. Other outcome measures include new business generated, market share gains, new-product sales, and profit contributions.

Setting Performance Standards. Although internal comparisons of performance are frequently used, they are not very helpful if the performance of the entire sales force is unacceptable. A major problem in setting sales performance standards is determining how to adjust them for factors beyond the salesperson's control (i.e., market potential, intensity of competition, differences in customer needs, and quality of supervision). A competent salesperson may not appear to be performing well if assigned to a poor sales territory. These differences need to be included in the evaluation process, since territories often are not equal in terms of opportunity and other uncontrollable factors.

Evaluating performance is one of sales management's more difficult tasks. Typically, performance tracking involves looking at a combination of outcome and behavioral factors. In compensation plans other than straight commission, performance evaluation affects the salesperson's pay, so obtaining a fair evaluation is important.

By evaluating the organization's personal selling strategy, management may identify problems requiring corrective action. The problems may be linked to individual salespeople or to decisions that impact the entire organization (e.g., size of the sales force). A well-designed information system helps in the diagnosis of performance and guides corrective actions when necessary. Information management and evaluation and control are discussed in Chapters 8 and 17.

SALES PROMOTION STRATEGY

Sales promotion expenditures increased more rapidly than advertising in many companies during the 1980s.[37] Both promotion components are receiving major attention by companies in their attempts to boost productivity and reduce costs. When marketing expenditures account for one third or more of total sales, the bottom-line impact of improving the effectiveness of promotion expenditures and/or lowering costs is substantial. The chapter lead-in example profiles the changes under way in the promotion budgets of packaged-goods manufacturers.

We look at the nature and scope of sales promotion, the types of sales promotion activities, the advantages and limitations of sales promotion, and the decisions that make up sales promotion strategy.

Nature and Scope of Sales Promotion

The responsibility for sales promotion strategy is often fragmented among marketing functions, such as advertising, merchandising, product planning, and sales. For example, a sales contest for salespeople is typically designed and administered by sales managers and the costs of the contest are included in the sales department budget. Similarly, planning and coordinating a coupon refund program may be assigned to a brand manager. Point-of-purchase promotion displays in retail stores may be handled by the advertising department.

Total expenditures for sales promotion by business and industry are much larger than the total spent on advertising. The complete scope of sales promotion is often difficult to identify because the activities are included in various departments and budgets. There are several similarities between sales promotion and advertising, but there are some important differences as well.

An important issue is how to manage the various sales-promotion functions. While these activities are often used to support advertising, pricing, channel of distribution, and personal selling strategies, the size and scope of sales promotion suggest that the responsibility for managing the program should be assigned to one executive. Some proponents argue for the establishment of a department of sales promotion. At minimum, the chief marketing executive should coordinate and evaluate sales-promotion activities.

Sales-Promotion Activities

A variety of activities may fit into the total promotion program, including trade shows, specialty advertising (e.g., imprinted calendars), contests, point-of-purchase displays, coupons, recognition programs (e.g., awards to middlemen), and free samples. Expenditures for sales promotion may be very substantial. For example, Gaines Foods Inc. distributed more than 50 million 50-cent coupons as part of a $20 million advertising, trade, and consumer promotion campaign for its Gaines Burgers, Top Choice, and Puppy Choice brands.[38] At the average coupon redemption rate of 1 in 25, about 2.2 million of the 50-cent coupons were redeemed.

Companies may aim their sales-promotion activities at consumer buyers, industrial buyers, middlemen, and salespeople, as shown in Exhibit 15–11.

EXHIBIT 15–11 Sales Promotion Activities Targeted to Various Groups

Sales Promotion Activity	*Targeted To:* Consumer Buyers	*Industrial Buyers*	*Middlemen*	*Salespeople*
Incentives				
Contests	X	X	X	X
Trips	X	X	X	X
Bonuses			X	X
Prizes	X	X	X	X
Advertising support			X	
Free items	X	X		
Recognition			X	X
Promotional Pricing				
Coupons	X			
Allowances		X	X	
Rebates	X	X	X	
Cash	X			
Informational Activities				
Direct mail	X	X	X	
Displays	X			
Demonstrations	X	X	X	
Selling aids			X	X
Catalogs	X	X	X	X
Specialty advertising (e.g., pens)	X	X	X	
Trade shows	X	X	X	

Promotion to Consumer Targets. This form of promotion includes a wide variety of activities, as shown in Exhibit 15–11. Sales promotion is often used in the marketing of many consumer products and services. A key management concern is evaluating the effectiveness of promotions such as coupons, rebates, contests, and other awards. The large expenditures necessary to support these programs requires that the results and costs be objectively assessed.

Information technology offers penetrating insights into the productivity of promotion programs.[39] For example, sophisticated checkout scanner data analyses indicate trade and consumer promotions that lose money. This information helps in shifting promotion spending to more productive programs, customer groups, and product categories. Promotion programs can be evaluated on a financial basis by combining customer-response data with cost information.

Promotion to Industrial Targets. Many of the sales-promotion methods that are used for consumer products also apply to industrial products, although the role and scope of the methods may vary. For example, trade shows perform a key role in small and medium-sized companies' marketing strategies. The advantage of the trade show is the heavy concentration of potential buyers at one location during a very short time. The cost per contact is much less than calling on prospects at their offices. While people attending trade shows also spend their time viewing competitor's products, salespeople, product managers, and other company personnel have a unique opportunity to hold the prospects' attention.

Sales promotion to industrial buyers may consume a greater portion of the marketing budget than advertising. Promotional activities support direct-selling strategies. They include catalogs, brochures, product information reports, samples, trade shows, application guides, and promotional items such as calendars, pens, and calculators.

Promotion to Middlemen. Sales promotion is an important part of manufacturers' marketing efforts to wholesalers and retailers for such products as foods, beverages, and appliances. Catalogs and other product information are essential promotional components for many lines. Promotional pricing is often used to push new products through channels of distribution. Various incentives are popular in marketing to middlemen. Specialty advertising items such as calendars and memo pads are used in maintaining buyer awareness of brands and company names.

Promotion to the Sales Force. Incentives and informational activities are the primary forms of promotion used to assist and motivate company sales forces. Sales contests and prizes are popular. Companies also make wide use of recognition programs like the "salesperson of the year." Promotional information is vital to salespeople. Presentation kits help salespeople describe new products and the features of existing products. Electronic aids such as videotapes, slides, and disc players are becoming increasingly important in helping salespeople communicate product information. Portable computers offer impressive presentation and display capabilities.

Advantages and Limitations of Sales Promotion

Because of its wide array of incentive, pricing, and communication capabilities, sales promotion has the flexibility to contribute to various marketing objectives. A product manager can target buyers, intermediaries, and salespeople and can measure the sales response of the sales promotion activities to determine their effectiveness. For example, a company can track its coupon redemption or rebate success. Many of the incentive and price promotion techniques trigger the purchase of other products.

Sales promotion is not without its disadvantages, however. In most instances, rather than substituting for advertising and personal selling, sales promotion supports other promotional efforts. Control is essential to prevent some people from taking advantage of free offers, coupons, and other incentives. The problems concerning manufacturers' trade discounts discussed in the chapter introduction are illustrative. Incentives and price-promotional activities need to be monitored. An effective advertisement can be run thousands of times, but promotional campaigns are usually not reusable. Thus, the costs of development must be evaluated in advance.

Sales-Promotion Strategy

The steps in developing the sales-promotion strategy are similar to the design of advertising strategy. It is necessary to first define the communications task(s) that the sales-promotion program is expected to accomplish. Next, specific promotion objectives are set regarding awareness levels and purchase intentions. It is important to evaluate the relative cost-effectiveness of feasible sales-promotion methods and to select those that offer the best results/cost combinations. Both the content of the sales promotion and its timing should be coordinated with other promotion activities. Finally, the program is implemented and evaluated on a continuing basis. Evaluation measures the extent to which objectives are achieved. For example, trade show results can be evaluated to determine how many show contacts are converted to purchases.

SUMMARY

Promotion strategy is a vital part of the positioning strategy. The components—advertising, sales promotion, publicity, and personal selling—offer an impressive array of capabilities for communicating with market targets and other relevant audiences. However, promotion activities are expensive. Management must decide the size of the promotion budget and allocate it to the communications components. Each promotion activity offers certain unique advantages and also shares several characteristics with the other components. The major budgeting methods are objective and task, percent of sales, competitive parity, all you can afford, and budgeting models. Several product and market factors affect whether the promotion strategy will emphasize advertising, sales promotion, personal selling, or a balance between the forms of promotion. The integration of communications mixes is a major challenge for many firms today.

The steps in developing advertising strategy include identifying the target audience, deciding the role of advertising in the promotional mix, indicating advertising objectives and budget size, selecting the creative strategy, determining the media and programming schedule, and implementing the program and measuring its effectiveness. Advertising objectives may range from audience exposure to profit contribution targets. Advertising agencies offer specialized services for developing creative strategies, designing messages, and selecting media and programming strategies.

Management analyzes the firm's marketing strategy, the target market, product characteristics, distribution strategy, and pricing strategy to identify the role of personal selling in the promotion mix. New-business, trade selling, missionary selling, and consultative/technical selling strategies illustrate the possible roles that may be assigned to selling in various firms. The selling process indicates the selling activities necessary to move the buyer from need awareness to a purchase decision. Various sales channels are used in conjunction with the field sales force to accomplish the selling process activities.

Sales force organizational design decisions include the type of organizational structure to be used, the size of the sales force, and the allocation of selling effort. Deployment involves decisions regarding sales force size and effort allocation. Managing the sales force includes recruiting, training, supervising, and motivating salespeople. Evaluation and control determine the extent to which objectives are achieved and determine where adjustments are needed in selling strategy and tactics.

The discussion of sales promotion highlights several methods available for use in a total communications program. Typically, firms use sales-promotion activities in conjunction with advertising and personal selling rather than as a primary component of promotion strategy. Sales-promotion strategy should be based on the correct selection of methods to provide the best results/cost combination for achieving the communications objectives desired.

QUESTIONS FOR REVIEW AND DISCUSSION

1. Compare and contrast the role of promotion in an international public accounting firm with promotion by American Airlines.
2. Identify and discuss the factors that are important in determining the promotional mix for the following products:
   a. Video tape recorder/player.
   b. Personal computer.
   c. Boeing 757 commercial aircraft.
   d. Residential homes.
3. What are the important considerations in determining a promotion budget?
4. Under what conditions is a firm's promotion strategy more likely to be advertising/sales-promotion-driven?
5. Discuss the advantages and limitations of using awareness as an advertising objective. When might this objective be appropriate?
6. Identify and discuss the important differences between advertising and public relations strategies in the marketing promotion strategy.
7. What information does management need to analyze the selling situation?
8. Suppose an analysis of sales force size and selling effort deployment indicates that a company has a sales force of the right size but that the allocation of selling effort requires substantial adjustment in several territories. How should such deployment changes be implemented?
9. What questions would you want answered if you were trying to evaluate the effectiveness of a business unit's sales force strategy?
10. Discuss some of the advantages and limitations of recruiting salespeople by hiring the employees of companies with excellent training programs.

11. Is incentive compensation more important for salespeople than for product managers? Why?

12. Select a company and discuss how sales management should define the selling process.

13. Coordination of advertising and selling strategies is a major challenge in large companies. Suggest a plan for integrating these strategies.

14. Discuss the role of sales-promotion methods in the promotion strategy of a major airline.

NOTES

1. Trade loading is discussed in Patricia Sellers, "The Dumbest Marketing Ploy," *Forbes,* October 5, 1992, pp. 88–90, 92, 94.
2. Committee on Definitions, *Marketing Definitions: A Glossary of Marketing Terms* (Chicago: American Marketing Association, 1960).
3. Robert J. Coen, "How Bad a Year for Ads was '91? At Most the Worst," *Advertising Age,* May 4, 1992, pp. 3, 51; and Joanne Lipman, "Advertising," *The Wall Street Journal,* June 15, 1989, p. B5.
4. "Forecast and Review," *Advertising Age,* December 30, 1985, p. 14.
5. Committee on Definitions, *Marketing Definitions.*
6. "Exclusive Interview: Mike Gunn of American Airlines," *Colloquy* 3, no. 2, (1992), pp. 8–10.
7. Committee on Definitions, *Marketing Definitions.*
8. "Singapore Airlines: Flying Beauty," *The Economist,* December 14, 1991, p. 74.
9. "Going to the Public with Ads for Prescription Drugs," *Business Week,* May 21, 1984, pp. 77, 81.
10. For an in-depth discussion of these models, see David A. Aaker and John G. Myers, *Advertising Management,* 2nd ed. (Englewood Cliffs, N.J.: Prentice Hall, 1982), Chapter 4; and James F. Engel, Martin R. Warshaw, and Thomas C. Kinnear, *Promotional Strategy,* 5th ed. (Homewood, Ill.: Richard D. Irwin, 1983), Chapter 10.
11. Gary L. Lilien, "Advisor 2: Modeling the Marketing Mix Decision for Industrial Products," *Management Science,* February 1979, pp. 191–204.
12. Roger D. Blackwell, "Integrated Marketing Communications," presented at the Stellner Symposium, University of Illinois, 1985, pp. 2–3.
13. Ibid., p. 9.
14. Paul W. Farris and Robert D. Buzzell, "Why Advertising and Promotional Costs Vary: Some Cross-Sectional Analyses," *Journal of Marketing,* Fall 1979, p. 120.
15. "Brand Awareness Increases Market Share, Profits: Study," *Marketing News,* November 28, 1980, p. 5.
16. Valerie Kijewski, "Advertising and Promotion: How Much Should You Spend?" (Cambridge, Mass.: Strategic Planning Institute, June 1983).
17. *Work Book for Estimating Your Advertising Budget* (Boston: Cahners Publishing).
18. Henry Assael, *Marketing Management: Strategy and Action* (Boston: PWS–Kent Publishing, 1985). p. 392.
19. Joanne Lipman, "Ads of the '80s: The Loved and the Losers," *The Wall Street Journal,* December 28, 1989, pp. B1 and B4.
20. D. John Loden, *Megabrands* (Homewood, Ill.: Business One Irwin, 1992), pp. 188–90.

21. Roland T. Rust, *Advertising Media Models* (Lexington, Mass.: D. C. Heath, 1986).
22. See, for example, Dennis Kneale, "Fuzzy Picture: TV's Nielsen Ratings, Long Questioned, Face Tough Challenges," *The Wall Street Journal,* July 19, 1990, pp. A1, A12.
23. Byron G. Quann, "How IBM Assesses its Business-to-Business Advertising," *Business Marketing,* January 1985, pp. 106, 108, 110, 112.
24. Gilbert A. Churchill, Jr., Neil M. Ford, and Orville C. Walker, Jr., *Sales Force Management,* 3rd ed. (Homewood, Ill.: Richard D. Irwin, 1990), pp. 3–7.
25. Ibid., pp. 99–106.
26. Howard Sutton, *Rethinking Company's Selling and Distribution Channels,* Report No. 885 (New York: The Conference Board, Inc., 1986).
27. The following discussion is drawn from Raymond W. LaForge, David W. Cravens, and Thomas N. Ingram, "Evaluating Multiple Sales Channel Strategies," *Journal of Business and Industrial Marketing,* Summer/Fall 1991, pp. 37–48.
28. Jerome A. Colletti and Gary S. Tubridy, "Effective Major Account Management," *Journal of Personal Selling and Sales Management,* August 1987, pp. 1–10.
29. Ibid.
30. For an expanded discussion of sales force decision models, see David W. Cravens, "Sales Force Decision Models: A Comparative Assessment," in *Sales Management: New Developments from Behavioral and Decision Model Research,* ed. Richard P. Bagozzi (Cambridge, Mass.: Marketing Science Institute, 1979), pp. 310–24.
31. Raymond W. LaForge, David W. Cravens, and Clifford E. Young, "Improving Salesforce Productivity," *Business Horizons,* September/October 1985, pp. 50–59.
32. David W. Cravens, Thomas M. Ingram, Raymond W. LaForge, and Clifford E. Young, "Hallmarks of Effective Sales Organizations," *Marketing Management,* Winter 1992, pp. 56–67.
33. Churchill, Ford, and Walker, *Sales Force Management,* p. 400.
34. John A. Byrne, "Motivating Willy Loman," *Forbes,* January 30, 1984, p. 91.
35. Churchill, Ford, and Walker, *Sales Force Management,* Chapter 13.
36. David W. Cravens, Thomas M. Ingram, Raymond W. LaForge, and Clifford E. Young, "Behavior-Based and Outcome-Based Sales Force Control Systems," *Journal of Marketing,* forthcoming October 1993.
37. Andrew J. Parsons, "Focus and Squeeze: Consumer Marketing in the '90s," *Marketing Management,* Winter 1992, pp. 51–55.
38. Kevin Higgins, "Couponing's Growth Is Easy to Understand: It Works," *Marketing News,* September 28, 1985, p. 12.
39. Parsons, "Focus and Squeeze."

Cases for Part IV

CASE 4–1 Du Pont Company

From the creation of nylon during the Depression to the latest studies of exotic carbon molecules, Du Pont Company has long been at the forefront of basic corporate research. It led the nation's chemical companies last year in U.S. patents applied for and granted.

But good science hasn't always been good for Du Pont shareholders. Despite spending more than $13 billion on chemical and related research over the past 10 years, Du Pont's 5,000 scientists and engineers were a technological black hole: They sucked in money but, company officials concede, didn't turn out a single all-new blockbuster product or even many major innovations. And only about 5 percent of Du Pont's own managers surveyed recently rate the company among the best U.S. or Japanese corporations in introducing new products.

"They've been like the space program: The technology is great, but where's the payoff?" says John Garcia, an industry analyst at Wertheim Schroder & Co.

But now Du Pont, one of the nation's most prolific inventors, is trying to reinvent itself. It is striving to create a new culture driven by profits, not just research prowess. It is betting that radical improvements in the way it develops new products, as well as the way it makes nylon and other mainstays, can yield huge savings. At the same time, it is trying to restructure a bloated bureaucracy.

Du Pont needs a top-to-bottom overhaul, says Edgar S. Woolard, Jr., its chief executive officer since 1989. He ticks off its shortcomings: The company takes too long to "convert research into products that can benefit our customers," he says. In major established products, it has lost ground to rivals that spend more on improving manufacturing (it was forced out of the Orlon fiber business for that reason). And years of paternalistic employment practices have made Du Pont a secure place to work, but "we have too much bureaucracy running these businesses," Mr. Woolard complains.

The deceptively soft-spoken, 58-year-old North Carolina native is forcing change on a corporate culture widely considered about as agile as one of the company's lumbering Conoco supertankers. Du Ponters were shocked out of their complacency last summer when Mr. Woolard announced a plan to slash annual costs by $1 billion within two years. The company also aims to increase pretax profit by another $2 billion within five years, mainly by improving its manufacturing efficiency and reducing its plants' turnaround time between processing runs.

Wilmington is still shaking from the initial jolt: 5,500 Du Pont employees here have already taken early retirement, and more cutbacks are expected. Du Pont has about 20,000 employees in the area and 133,000 worldwide.

Perhaps shielded by his Southern-gentleman manners, Mr. Woolard hasn't been blamed for Du Pont's problems, even though he has been part of top management since being named an executive vice president in 1983. Wall Street applauds the steps he is taking, but some complain that he is taking too long.

Mr. Woolard says he is moving as fast as he can. He says he wants to avoid short-term moves, such as being too quick to sell or close weak operations, that might someday damage the company.

If anything can scorch Mr. Woolard's Teflon coating, it may be the recession's effect on Du Pont's earnings. Last year, net income dropped nearly 40 percent to $1.4 billion. That plunge partly reflected lower oil revenues at Du Pont's Conoco unit as oil prices dropped after Operation Desert Storm ended quickly. Sales last year slipped 3 percent to $38.7 billion. Over the past 12 months, Du Pont's stock has traded between the mid-30s and 50½; it closed yesterday at $47.25, up 25 cents in New York Stock Exchange trading.

But even after the recovery kicks in, the heat isn't going to be off Du Pont or many other U.S. corporate giants. Companies ranging from Du Pont to International Business Machines Corporation and American Telephone & Telegraph Company are being forced by mounting competition to deliver both new and existing products faster and more efficiently. And a history of dominating an industry doesn't provide much of a competitive edge. In fact, it can be a hindrance, if, as at Du Pont, it spawned a somewhat sluggish and backward-looking culture.

Du Pont isn't used to such pressure. After diversifying away from its gunpowder and munitions businesses after World War I, it became, for decades, one of America's most innovative companies. It introduced synthetic fibers and rubber, new plastics and polymers. After World War II, with European and Japanese rivals leveled, Du Pont and other U.S. chemical makers reigned supreme in many areas for another 20 years.

But, obsessed with finding the next big breakthrough, many Du Pont scientists slighted minor advances, customer needs—and profitability. Joseph Miller, director of polymers research, notes a "mind-set that research's responsibility was to find another nylon." And the pursuit of what he calls "Big Bangs" led to some spectacular new-product busts. Among them:

- Kevlar, pound for pound stronger than steel, was the Superman of synthetic fibers when introduced in 1972. But it began to resemble Clark Kent when tire makers instead went for cheaper steel-belted radials. After nearly 20 years and $600 million of development and marketing costs, Kevlar recently turned a profit, having found niche markets such as bulletproof vests and army helmets.
- Synthetic silk is a product Du Pont would like to forget. Qiana, as it was known, cost about $200 million to develop and market. After a brief fling with high-fashion designers in the late 1960s and early 1970s, it was abandoned for natural fibers and died barely a decade later.
- Electronic-imaging businesses have cost Du Pont more than $600 million since the mid-1980s. The technological potential of things such as digital printing may seem dazzling, but all Du Pont has got out of it so far is a river of red ink.
- And pharmaceuticals, Du Pont officials admit after 10 years and $1 billion, take longer and cost more to bring to market than they anticipated. In 1990, Merck & Company was brought in as a partner in a joint venture to add marketing muscle.

With new-product development faltering, Du Pont has relied on "tweaking" existing products into slightly improved versions. Its Lycra spandex fiber, which was introduced more than 30 years ago to replace rubber in girdles, has expanded via modifications to dominate the active-wear market. And low-dose herbicides, invented in the mid-1970s, are selling well.

To focus "more intensity on customer needs," Mr. Woolard says Du Pont has shifted about 30 percent of its research budget, or more than $400 million a year, toward speeding new products to customers.

In the past, customers wanting to make changes in high-strength Zytel nylon-resin products used to have to wait as long as six months to get an answer out of Du Pont, says John Jack, Zytel global product manager. By that time, the customer, often an auto maker or one of its suppliers, may have taken the business elsewhere.

In response, Du Pont salespeople created an informal "skunkworks" with the aid of frustrated in-house researchers to go outside channels and push their pet projects. But those projects often didn't produce much profit, Mr. Jack says, and they may not have even been in the customer's best long-term interests.

A skunkworks antidote is being tried by several Du Pont departments and is supposed to be adopted throughout the company. To speed the new-product process, the departments have created small, interdisciplinary teams to field all new-product ideas. These teams, including research, manufacturing and sales representatives, get just two weeks to make a decision. If they decide to go ahead with the idea, they have two more weeks to form another team to carry it out. The elapsed time for a new, still-secret auto-safety product, from the idea to a prototype product, was just two months, Mr. Jack says.

Du Pont is also working more closely with customers. Fluorware Inc., a supplier to the semiconductor industry, wanted Du Pont to make a purer version of a Teflon basket that Fluorware uses to hold silicon wafers during production. The companies formed a joint team to find a solution, even though Fluorware's annual sales total only about $60 million. Last year, Du Pont brought out a commercial version of the product for sale to other companies. The Fluorware–Du Pont team now holds regular meetings, "which we hope will lead to breakthroughs in materials science," says John Goodman, the Minnesota company's senior director for corporate technology.

Another problem at Du Pont: bugs. Some divisions spend about three times as much money and effort on debugging new products—ironing out problems after the product is launched—than the top new-product development companies in the U.S. That can send costs through the roof. Substantially cutting debugging time companywide could lift profit by more than $200 million a year, officials estimate.

"We need to shift the emphasis from investment in product development to improving our understanding of the processes used to manufacture our products," says Uma Chowdhry, an efficiency expert in Du Pont's microcircuits and component-materials business.

Some scientists studying nylon in the lab are doing just that. It might seem that Du Pont couldn't learn much more about nylon after making it for more than 50 years. Yet in recent months the scientists have, for the first time, devised a way to break down nylon into its raw materials without creating waste by-products.

"This is one of our high-risk, big-impact activities," says James Meyer, the project leader. The company could eventually recycle nylon and save tens of millions of dollars in raw materials if the process works on a commercial scale. It also would eliminate the cost of handling the waste byproduct—and perhaps a big environmental headache.

The potential profits from improving manufacturing at Du Pont's more than 100 plants world-wide are huge. Reducing the down time between the dozens of processes at polymer plants is expected to raise profits by as much

EXHIBIT 1

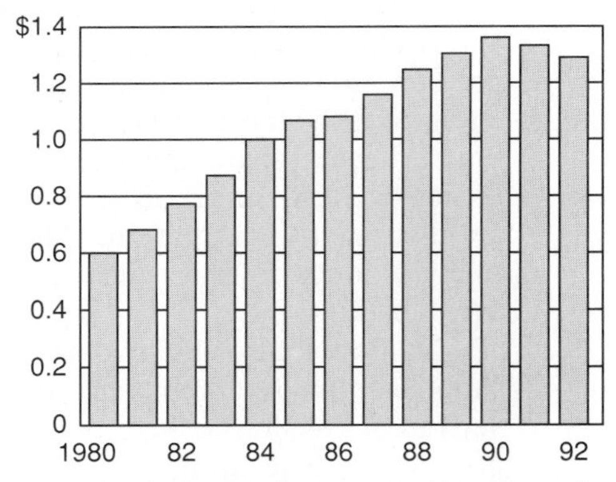

as $200 million a year within a few years, says Mr. Miller, the head of polymers research. With so much money at stake, it's no surprise that the polymers division now spends 60 percent of its research budget on improving its processing and only 40 percent on products. A few years ago, 70 percent of the budget went to products and only 30 percent to processing.

One of Du Pont's most efficient plants sits along the Delaware River not far from company headquarters in downtown Wilmington. Fixed costs to produce titanium dioxide, an opaque pigment used in paper and paint, have been flat since 1989 while productivity has jumped sharply, says Jack Kane, the plant manager. The efficiency gains came from shutting down one production line and reducing down time between processing runs on the remaining line. The plant is running 22 hours a day, up from 18 hours just a few years ago.

Mr. Kane says many of the plant's productivity gains came from involving workers in the process. When he started working at the plant in 1956, he says, a supervisor answered one of his questions by saying, "You don't need to know that." Mr. Kane says that to get workers to think for themselves and identify with the company's goals, he "gives cost figures on any of our operations down to the newest guy on a maintenance team."

In a program started last year, plant management has paid about $18,000 to workers for actions that ended up saving Du Pont a multiple of that amount, says Cindy Coker, the assistant plant manager. Walt Zerbe, an employee, got a bonus of more than $1,000, for example; he rejected a contractor's bid to paint the plant's buildings and equipment, and the contractor came back a few days later with a bid 20 percent lower. "That wouldn't have happened even two years ago," Ms. Coker says.

Meanwhile, Mr. Woolard's back-to-basics sermon has led to inevitable strains between applied research directed at processing and fundamental research. Research managers say they think a lot harder before approving projects without an obvious payoff.

"The trickiest thing is to strike that balance between 'buckyballs' [a new form of pure carbon] and process technology," says Richard Quisenberry, head of central research. Buckyballs are being studied by a highly respected group of nearly 20 Du Pont scientists even though practical applications are probably years off.

Senior management's commitment to fundamental research remains strong, Mr. Quisenberry insists, despite all the talk about profits. He adds: "I still get notes from people written across the top of research proposals that say, 'This looks pretty applied. Are you sure we're taking care of our long-term interests?'"

Source: Scott McMurray, "Changing a Culture: Du Pont Tries to Make Its Research Wizardry Serve the Bottom Line," *The Wall Street Journal,* March 27, 1992, pp. A1, A4. Reprinted by permission of *The Wall Street Journal.*

CASE 4–2 Cincinnati Milacron Inc.

Workers in Cincinnati Milacron Inc.'s robotics plant gathered one bright morning a year ago to say good-bye to the future.

Executives from headquarters had flown down to the Greenwood, S.C., factory to announce what many of the 200 workers waiting on the shop floor had suspected all along. Milacron, the last big American robot maker, was getting out of the business.

A decade earlier, Milacron had touted robots and other high-tech diversifications as its salvation at a time when its traditional machine-tool business was fast losing ground to the Japanese. But Milacron soon found itself out of its league with the glitzy new robots, lasers and semiconductor wafers: Customers bolted, profits dried up and morale sagged. "It didn't take a rocket scientist to know that we were in trouble," says Floyd DeMoss, former robotics manufacturing manager.

Hit by the same problems that are hurting U.S. automakers, consumer-electronics companies and construction-equipment giants, Milacron embarked on a bold bid to save itself. After years of drifting and soul-searching, it decided that the answer to foreign competition might not lie in high-end niches. It abandoned its high-tech businesses and returned with new fervor to the basic machine-tool business it had all but fled a decade earlier. Now, it hopes to restore the qualities that made its nuts-and-bolts business work in the first place: low costs, rapid product development and devotion to small customers.

"We took our eye off the target," says Daniel J. Meyer, Milacron's chief executive officer. "We just didn't pay attention to being the world-class competitor we had been in standard products."

Now, Milacron has a clear vision—but it also has a lot of catching up to do. Even though voluntary restraint agreements have been limiting imports, foreign-made machine tools have seized half the U.S. market, and foreign companies are increasing production in the U.S. as well.

In reaction, some major American producers have found strategic niches where the Japanese and Taiwanese don't compete. Chief among these is the new industry leader, Giddings & Lewis Inc., which switched away from the standard tools, such as lathes and other machines that cut and form metal parts, that Milacron hopes to recapture. Giddings now makes large, integrated systems that haven't attracted much foreign interest. "We're not going into competition with the Japanese," vows Giddings Chairman William J. Fife Jr.

In effect, Milacron's return to standard machinery represents the last stand of the traditional American tool industry, an industry it pioneered. If Milacron wins, it will serve as a model for beleaguered U.S. manufacturers; if it fails, another vital domestic industry could be lost.

Milacron says that it has slashed its manufacturing costs as much as 40 percent, and that now 20 percent of its standard machine-tool lines can match foreign prices and quality. It has also signed on 30 distributors, many of whom dropped Japanese lines, to recapture orders from small job shops. To funnel capital into standard tools, it halved its dividend last month and announced a $90 million charge to move some machine-tool production to more modern plants and sell assets unrelated to its core businesses.

The risk is that Milacron, weighed down by debt and chronic losses, could be too out of shape to run the course it has set. Yesterday, Moody's Investors Service joined Standard & Poor's in downgrading Milacron's debt; S&P cited a debt level of 55 percent to 60 percent of total capital and a bleak financial outlook due in part to Milacron's "corrective actions."

Says David Sutliff, an S.G. Warburg & Company analyst: "I give them credit for giving it the old college try, but I don't think it's too smart. They're going into the most competitive sector again, where the Japanese sell tools like cookies."

That's what made Milacron flee the business in the first place. In the capital-investment boom of the early 1980s, the company found it had all the business it could handle building specialty machines for the defense, aerospace and auto industries. It let the Japanese provide cheaper tools for small machining shops. When the investment boom ended, Milacron couldn't match the price or quality of standard Japanese tools.

"The board decided we were beating a dead horse with machine tools, so the decision was made to more or less abdicate the standard line," recalls Donald G. Shively, former executive vice president for operations. Indeed, that's why Mr. Shively, a machine-tool man, was passed over for the top job in favor of Mr. Meyer, who pushed diversification. "Don only knew machine tools," says James A.D. Geier, the previous Milacron CEO.

While its machine tools withered, Milacron invested tens of millions of dollars to diversify into semiconductor wafers, lasers, specialty chemicals, robots and plastics machinery. Of all these, only plastics machinery, which is closely related to machine tools, remains.

An examination of Milacron's affair with robots shows why. When the company began selling robots in 1977, its machines were the envy of the industry. Competitors—even the Japanese—licensed Milacron's sophisticated systems. Pundits forecast that the domestic robot market would reach $4 billion a year by 1990. Wall Street relabeled the toolmaker a robot company and sent its stock to a 30-year high of $52 a share. By 1981, its robot revenue pushed toward $100 million, and the line occasionally made a profit.

But while Milacron celebrated, Japan, fearing a domestic labor shortage, began subsidizing robots. Robot manufacturing exploded in Japan, and the then-high dollar allowed cheap robots to spill over to the U.S. Milacron wasn't handicapped by technological glitches, unlike its American robot rivals, but it couldn't match Japanese production efficiency. It suffered from a rigid assembly line that led to duplicative efforts and from thickly layered management. Customers were amazed that Milacron couldn't employ robots in its own robot plant.

Then, in early 1982, Mr. Geier got a troubling phone call from a friend at General Motors Corp. GM, hoping to become a big robot maker itself, was talking with Japan's Fujitsu Fanuc Ltd. about a joint venture. Milacron soon lost some $50 million a year in business from GM, its biggest customer.

Moreover, the American robot market was shriveling. Because U.S. employers didn't face a labor shortage, they wanted robots only for isolated tasks and had little need for Milacron's broad line of complex machines. It became clear the U.S. market would reach only 10 percent of previous forecasts. By 1985, with Milacron's robot sales dropping and the line leaking red ink, the company sought help. Messrs. Geier and Meyer sought a partnership with a Swedish-Swiss robot maker, Asea Brown Boveri AG, but the talks failed.

Faced with disasters in both robots and standard machine tools, Milacron was adrift by 1987. Mr. Meyer held a series of turbulent meetings with top executives. They eventually agreed on a new course: Milacron would leave the robot business and devote itself to standard machine tools. "Machine tools weren't the wrong business," says a changed Mr. Meyer. "They were the right business, but we were doing them in the wrong way."

The company removed the lasers and robots from its headquarters building lobby, giving more prominence to an 1884-vintage milling machine. It also returned to Asea Brown Boveri in April 1990 and this time sold its whole robot line.

And so Milacron rededicated itself to its old business—resolving to do it with shorter development and production cycles, better quality, lower costs and more attention to customer needs. Milacron's rebirth partly reflected a lower dollar and a market more promising for machine tools than robots. But more important, Mr. Geier says, "We had more confidence in machine tools."

Already, Milacron says its "Wolfpack" engineering program (consisting of a rapid, concentrated attack on problems by teams of engineers, hourly workers and salesmen working together) has revamped 20 percent of its products so that they are competitive with the Japanese. All the resulting products claim cost savings of 30 percent or more. Milacron reduces costs by making some tools with half as many parts, reducing warranty, labor and installation costs. It also uses more standard, off-the-shelf parts and buys 60 percent of them from outside suppliers, up from 40 percent before.

The company also has quadrupled the sales force and signed on 30 distributors to help service small accounts. Distributors like York-Penn, a Pennsylvania firm that dropped its Japanese line. "Some of my compatriots think I'm nuts for taking this risk," says York-Penn's president, Tom Cassidy. But he figures that Milacron's "Made in USA" label will give it the edge if its prices are competitive. John McDonald, U.S. sales manager for Mori Seiki Company, a Japanese toolmaker, concurs. "We see them as an increasing threat," he says.

Others, however, think the industry's wisest course is to avoid the Japanese. Giddings & Lewis, which will overtake Milacron and Litton Industries Inc. as the largest U.S. toolmaker when it completes its acquisition of Cross & Trecker Corporation this fall, is successful partly because it *doesn't* compete in standard machine tools. In the past four years, Giddings has gone from losses to big profits by finding a high-margin niche business. It sells machine tools in flexible, integrated manufacturing systems that cost up to $30 million.

Giddings vows to remove Cross & Trecker's lines from foreign competition by using its standard tools in Giddings' large systems. "The Japanese move low-end machine tools by the truckload," says Giddings' Mr. Fife. "We're going to stay away from truckload sales."

Milacron's new efforts, by contrast, target the $100,000 tools. But many of its new machines aren't compatible with each other, and customers can't link them in a multifunction manufacturing system like Giddings' custom-made lines.

Milacron, meantime, finds inspiration in its plastics-machinery operations, which since 1987 have shrunk the Japanese market share in the U.S. to 50 percent from 62 percent. Its Vista line cut prices 25 percent, winning the business of Toyota Motor Corporation's U.S. operations and regaining GM's.

And Milacron has clearly had some success with machine tools as well. At its "incubator" plant in Cincinnati, the company has already turned out more than 50 new Talons, computer-controlled turning centers that make bearings and other round parts. The plant looks like a how-to model for modern manufacturing. It uses just-in-time inventory, has only 16 vendors and makes a product with 60 percent fewer parts. Workers, who don't punch time clocks, sign their finished products. Managers dress in work clothes just like the rank and file. The result: a product that costs 40 percent less to make and outperforms earlier models.

But Milacron still has far to go.

C. William Murray, Milacron's division manager for standard machine-tool products, says it may take five years before these advanced manufacturing notions travel beyond this 19-worker plant and reach Milacron's 8,000 employees. And because Milacron hasn't increased its engineering staff, it may have trouble spreading the new gospel.

The company also faces resistance from some middle managers, who fear the changes will put them out of jobs or out on plant floors. Competitors report phone calls and piles of resumes from Milacron managers seeking jobs. "They've got the basic technology and capability, but they have had a problem in that it's very difficult to change the culture and direction of that kind of organization," says Richard C. Messinger, who was Milacron's chief technical officer before retiring this year.

Nor do Milacron's efforts prove a resurgence in American manufacturing. Seven of Milacron's 27 "Wolfpack" projects are made outside the U.S. and imported, and even many U.S.-made tools use almost 50 percent foreign parts. "They're importing just like the Japanese, and what they're importing are not good machines," says Jack Addy of Addy Morrand Machine Tools in Detroit, which was wooed by Milacron as a distributor but chose to stay with its Japanese line instead.

Money's another problem. Milacron posted losses of $24.3 million after charges last year and of $10.4 million in the 1991 first half. It spent only 4.1 percent of sales on research and development last year, and 3.6 percent of machine-tool sales on capital expenditures; Giddings & Lewis, by contrast, spent 10 percent on R&D and 8.2 percent on capital outlays. Milacron has already backed off its promise to distributors to spend $250 million on machine tools over five years.

Even if Milacron succeeds in its new tack, cheap Asian tools will keep profit margins low, especially if the current U.S. restrictions on imports of foreign machinery aren't renewed at year end. And with the machine-tool market likely to contract as new materials and manufacturing methods are introduced, some people wonder why Milacron wants so badly to re-enter the fray.

But Milacron is confident. "We have a 107-year reputation in manufacturing, and the opportunity for success is still there, based on the history we have," Mr. Meyer says. "We're not going to lose."

EXHIBIT 1

Erratic Earnings . . .

Annual net income or loss, in millions

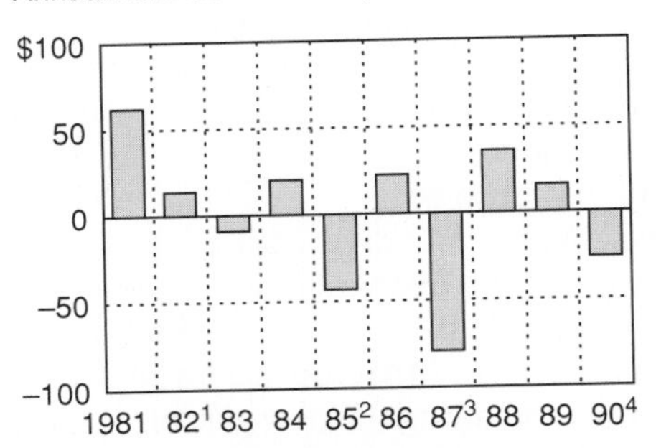

[1]Includes a one-time charge of $10 million.
[2]Includes a one-time charge of $30 million.
[3]Includes a one-time charge of $69 million.
[4]Includes a one-time charge of $31 million.

Prompt a Return to Tools . . .

Annual sales of machine tools and industrial products (including robots), in millions

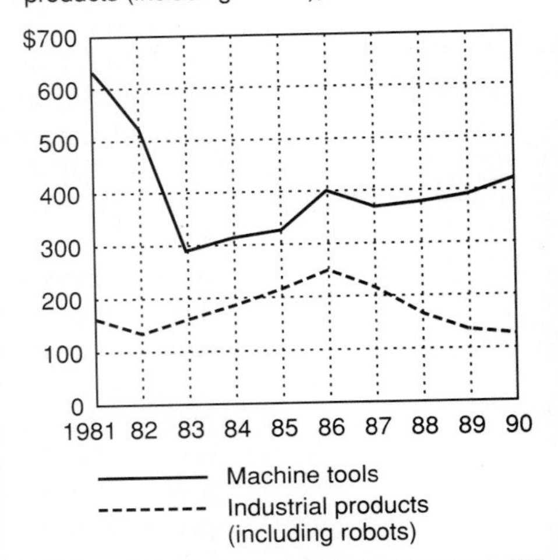

As Outlays Rise . . .

Machine tool capital expenditures (in millions)

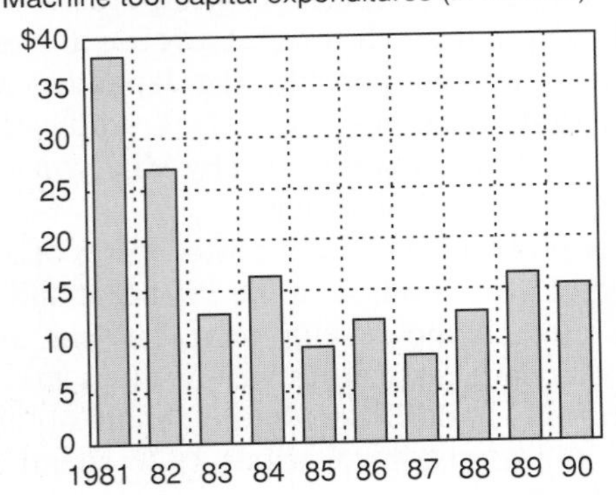

But the Stock Stays Low

Monthly closing stock price

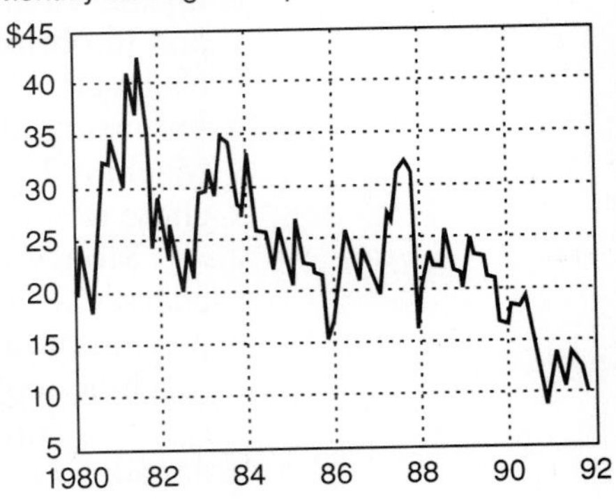

Source: Dana Milbank, "Grinding It Out: After a Flop in Robots, Cincinnati Milacron Is Back to Machine Tools," *The Wall Street Journal,* October 4, 1991, pp. A1, A4. Reprinted by permission of *The Wall Street Journal.*

CASE 4–3 Procter & Gamble Company

Procter & Gamble Company, the giant consumer-products maker, has never gotten along splendidly with the nation's grocery chains and wholesalers. But listen to how some of them are talking about P&G these days.

"We think [P&G] will end up where most dictators end up—in trouble," fumes Lewis G. Schaeneman Jr., the chairman of Stop & Shop Companies, a chain of 119 groceries in the Northeast.

Hundreds of miles away, Brad Olson is plotting an attack. "We should drop their top dogs—like half the sizes of Tide—and say, 'Now see who put you on the shelf and who'll take you off of it,'" says the assistant maanger of Paulbeck's Super Valu in International Falls, Minnesota.

What this furor is all about is a sweeping new pricing strategy that Procter & Gamble introduced last fall. P&G says it will phase out virtually all deep discounts and offer the same price every day. Instead of selling wholesalers and distributors a case of, say, cake mix for $10 one week and offering it on sale for $7 the next, it will charge $8 every week. No more wild fluctuations.

The new strategy, applied so far to only half of P&G's many products, is designed to reduce high-cost promotions, eliminate binge-buying of discounted products and boost the manufacturer's sluggish earnings. Just Monday, P&G reported flat operating earnings—sluggishness that analysts attributed in part to promotional expenses and discounts. P&G and its competitors "are beating each other's brains out in markets that aren't growing," says analyst Gabe Lowy of Gruntal & Company.

But P&G's solution to these problems is infuriating many retailers and wholesalers. Part of it is fairness: They contend that P&G continues to cut special deals for really big customers like Wal-Mart, a charge that P&G denies.

Of greater concern, discounts are the bread and butter of many retailers and wholesalers. Products purchased from P&G at special low prices can be used for weekly sales to lure value-minded consumers into supermarkets or stores. In other cases, retailers and wholesalers buy products at the discounts—meant to be passed along to consumers—and then profit by selling some of the low-cost products at normal prices later. Suddenly altering this system "is like giving a unicycle to somebody used to riding a bicycle—the center of gravity has changed," said Boyd George, president of North American Wholesale Grocers, a trade group.

P&G executives declined to be interviewed for this article, but in a prepared statement, P&G said: "The great majority of our trade customers have been very supportive of our move. This is a big change, so it's not surprising that some customers have had questions or concerns."

P&G's initiative is bold, if for no other reason than it has alienated some of the very businesses that sells its wares to the public. It also attempts to reshape the supermarket pricing system and wean Americans off bargain bonanzas and rich coupons. The outcome will be pivotal: The new program stands either to empower P&G and overhaul the way most wholesalers and retailers do business—or to damage P&G's market share and force it to retreat.

P&G, which had $29.4 billion in sales for the fiscal year ended June 30, is counting on its enormous clout. Retailers can ill-afford, the company hopes, to eliminate heavily advertised powerhouse brands such as Tide detergent, Crest toothpaste, Folgers coffee, Pert shampoo and Ivory soap.

But size, and even power, may not be enough. Other giants have failed to impose such broad changes because they underestimated the strength of their competitors and the will of their customers. And when rivals start cutting prices on such important products as disposable diapers, P&G may have to buckle to discounts.

"P&G, like IBM, thinks that because it's the biggest and the best, people are going to fall in line," asserts Roger Strom, owner of Roger & Marv's Super Valu market in Kenosha, Wisconsin. "They're not going to do it anymore. It's the same thing that happened to IBM" when clones eventually stole much of its PC market.

Pruning Shelves

Already, some chains with thousands of stores, such as Rite-Aid drugstores, A&P and Safeway, are pruning their variety of P&G sizes or eliminating marginal brands such as Prell and Gleem. Super Valu, the nation's largest wholesaler, which also runs some stores, is adding surcharges to some P&G products and paring back orders, to compensate for profits it says it's losing under the new pricing system. Meanwhile, Certified Grocers, a Midwestern wholesaler, has dropped about 50 of the 300 P&G varieties it stocked.

And numerous chains are considering moving P&G brands from prime, eye-level space to less visible shelves. In P&G's place: more profitable private-label brands and competitors' varieties.

P&G tried to head off the opposition with a preemptive strike. Earlier this month, it disclosed plans to eliminate up to 25 percent of the marginal and less profitable product sizes it sells.

Though P&G executives wouldn't be interviewed, a P&G executive vice president, Durk Jager, acknowledged in talking recently with trade publication Supermarket News, "This whole process won't be cost-free to us." In the fourth quarter, domestic unit volumes fell 2 percent.

Retailers might have been less rebellious if not for P&G's rather poor bedside manner. Instead of meeting with its major customers to discuss how to smooth out pricing variations, the company dictated almost overnight the new pricing policy. "In less than six months, they eliminated 10 years of work" devoted to correcting perceptions of the company as arrogant, says

Mr. George, chairman of Merchants Distributors Inc., a Hickory, N.C., wholesaler and supermarket chain.

Furthermore, P&G seemed to show little sensitivity to their situation by launching a profit-squeezing program in the middle of a recession. Supermarkets make only about a cent on every dollar they take in, and wholesalers even less. With ferocious competition from mass merchandisers and deep-discounters, promotions are among the few ways to lure frugal spenders into stores.

The discounting system evolved over the past two decades as consumer-goods companies frenetically pumped out new products and brands in multiple shapes, colors and sizes. They gave wholesalers and retailers price breaks in return for sales and other promotions. Indeed, P&G is trying to slay the dragon that it and its competitors created. "Manufacturers relied on short-term, price-oriented trade promotions to build short-term market share," says Frank Blod, of New England Consulting Group.

Wholesalers and large retail chains with their own warehousing operations became conditioned to wait for goodies. They would load up with products only when deals were offered, selling some at a discount to retailers and the remaining goods at a full price later.

A buyer at Super Valu says he would buy three months' worth of Prell shampoo, getting 30 cents off the $2.65 price. He would sell Prell for $2.35 for about a month, and raise prices back for the next two months. Such practices generated an estimated 70 percent of a wholesaler's profits and 40 percent for supermarkets.

Under the new system, Prell will cost him less—$1.89—but he won't get such fat profits because he can't charge his customers much more than his own price. "Any P&G items that are fringe, I'm gonna throw out," the buyer says, replacing them with others, such as private-label goods, that can offer higher profits.

Tumbling Prices

Under the new pricing program, which began last fall and is intended eventually to apply to all P&G products, list prices have dropped 8 percent to 25 percent on items like Mr. Clean floor cleaner, Jif peanut butter and Pert shampoo.

P&G says the new policy rewards "loyal consumers" who are consistent buyers who don't wait for sales. Those P&G diehards paid, on average, almost $2 more on Folgers than "disloyal consumers, who shopped brand to brand and store to store in search of the deal of the week." P&G contends that coffee sales have increased since prices have steadied. And although coupon values are being reduced by one-third, the company also notes that retailers will still receive some promotional money and consumers some specials.

"This is what consumers say they've wanted for a long time: 'Cut the price, cut the coupons—we'll still buy,'" says Mona Doyle, president of the Consumers Network. "Is it true? It's anybody's guess. It will probably be true until they get bored with the new prices."

Joyce Kane, a Blue Ash, Ohio, homemaker, says she would certainly prefer consistently reasonable prices for her favorite brands such as P&G's Dawn, Tide and Duncan Hines. But, she concedes, if she has a valuable coupon or sees a big sale, she'll settle for rival brands Palmolive, Fab or Betty Crocker.

And competitors certainly aren't slowing down their promotions. A Colgate-Palmolive Company spokesman says his company continues to offer large discounts to wholesalers and "will deal with [customers] as they wish to be dealt with."

But P&G says it's not about to flinch, insisting that price fluctuations and promotions had gotten out of hand. Trade discounts more than tripled in the past decade to $36.5 billion in 1991, according to Nielsen Marketing Research. In fact, for the first time last year, those discounts surpassed advertising spending.

At P&G, a bottle of Dawn dishwashing liquid had been selling at retail for anywhere from 99 cents to $1.99, and at the high end P&G says it was losing market share to discounted competitors' products. But now, with P&G selling Dawn for between $1.29 and $1.49, the company says the gap between Dawn and competing products is never large, enabling it to establish consumer loyalty.

Moreover, with mounting promotions and discounts, P&G had been losing control of its costs. When the company offered a special promotion, its factories would have to work round the clock. Meanwhile, products such as coffee bought on special deal could grow stale sitting around in a warehouse for 10 months.

The new policy "smoothes out manufacturing cycles and costs," says Mr. Lowy, the Gruntal analyst. "Plus they [P&G] get a better track on exactly what and how products are selling and can match production cycles to meet customer demand."

P&G says that many of its largest retailers love the new system and in fact inspired it. The boosters are primarily mass merchandisers, which account for an estimated 25 percent of P&G revenue, and not surprisingly include Wal-Mart.

"While my warehouse doesn't like it, it's actually easier to do business this way," says Paul Butera, of the 13-store Butera Finer Foods in Chicago. He says he'll just have to go back to doing business as he did 30 years ago: by offering loss leaders and smart merchandising. His only concern is that P&G treat everyone the same.

Many retailers are quietly cheering P&G from the sidelines, hoping that some order is restored to prices and promotions. "The competition is using P&G as the blocking back, letting them blow open a hole and follow quietly behind," figures Jeffrey Hill, cofounder of Meridian Consulting Group, of Westport, Connecticut.

Still, there's a lot to trip P&G up. The perceived integrity of its same-price-everywhere-everyday program could be undermined by a single retailer's deciding to sell a P&G product at a loss in order to stir business. And competitors, even those in favor of more consistent pricing in the industry, will undoubtedly take advantage of P&G's ban on promotions and highlight their own specials.

That idea appeals to Beth Martini, a 28-year-old Cincinnati teacher, and savvy shopper, who has come to enjoy the wild price swings. "I like big sales," she says. "If it's on sale now, I stock up and by the time I run out, it's on sale again."

Source: Valerie Reitman, "Retail Resistance: Eliminated Discounts on P&G Goods Annoy Many Who Sell Them," *The Wall Street Journal,* August 11, 1992, pp. A1, A6. Reprinted by permission of *The Wall Street Journal,* © 1992. Dow Jones & Company, Inc. All Rights Reserved Worldwide.

CASE 4–4 Hampton Inns

What would happen if a big hotel chain took its basic product, then threw out the parts that didn't make much money?

The result would be a Hampton Inn, one of the hottest chains in an otherwise tepid market. A subsidiary of Promus Companies of Memphis, Tennessee, Hampton is part of the growing limited-service sector. Its success shows that a lot of travelers can live without lofty glass atriums, liveried bellmen, room service and other fripperies if they receive a clean, comfortable room in a good location—and free breakfast. And at an average national rate of $48.50, Hampton usually charges at least 20 percent less than its full-service competitors.

Since opening the first Hampton Inn in Memphis in 1984, president and chief executive Raymond E. Schultz has overseen the chain's growth to 317 properties in 43 states. "Our chain has done considerably better than the rest of the industry," he says. In 1991, when the industry's occupancy rate slid to a 20-year low of 60.8 percent, Hampton's rate was seven percentage points higher, Mr. Schultz says, "and if you take out properties that were open less than a year, it would have been 70 percent chainwide."

Hampton and its brethren, such as Marriott Corp.'s Fairfield Inns and Choice Hotels International Inc.'s Sleep Inns, have largely avoided the industry doldrums by being the right product at the right time. They're higher-quality successors to the cheap highway motels built in the 1950s and 1960s. With more privacy, better furnishings and some attention to security, they have shaken much of the orange-bedspread-and-Astroturf stigma that many business travelers attached to economy lodging.

The typical Hampton stands along an interstate highway or other well-traveled area, and usually is within a stone's throw of a full-service restaurant. The lobby, filled with sofas and chairs, doubles as the breakfast area, where visitors can grab a free continental breakfast before hitting the road.

All properties offer some facilities for handicapped travelers, and areas that double as sites for small-business meetings and social functions or guest rooms. The rooms, though simple, offer such extras as free in-room movies and local phone calls. And for the inevitable disgruntled guest, Hampton guarantees a full refund to make amends for any shortcomings.

Hampton's growth stems in part from building in secondary markets that are less overbuilt than big urban centers. Recently, Hampton developed a modified inn for communities of about 75,000 that can only support hotels of 50 to 80 rooms, which is about half the size of the standard Hampton.

Conversion of existing properties will add to the chain's expansion. Overall, Hampton expects to open 40 new properties this year, with more planned for 1993.

Financing, while scarce, can still be secured in some markets. The basic Hampton costs about $31,000 a room to develop, excluding land, while the scaled-down version runs about $26,000 a room. A standard full-service business hotel would cost $80,000 or more a room, if any banker could be found to finance one.

Hamptons and other limited-service inns keep construction simple, which in turn keeps costs down. They don't waste real estate on sweeping lobbies and public areas, manicured grounds, tennis courts or other extras that don't translate directly into revenue. Nor are they architecturally complex, to put it charitably.

They are cheap to operate. The biggest cost, labor, is held to a minimum—a staff of about 20 to 24 can run a typical Hampton, with the mini-Hampton requiring the equivalent of 12 full-time employees, from desk clerks to maids.

Hampton still has a ways to go to put its flag in some important markets, and it has plenty of competition. "How big that segment can get remains to be seen," says John Rohs, a hotel analyst with Wertheim Schroder & Company. And as the hotels age, they will doubtless lose some of their appeal.

But for now, most hotel executives would love to be worried about managing growth instead of low occupancy rates and spiraling costs. Mr. Schultz's biggest fear is sacrificing quality for size. "It's the bad-apple-in-the-crate routine," he says. "That's where I spend a majority of my time."

Source: "Limited-Service Chains Offer Enough to Thrive," *The Wall Street Journal,* July 27, 1992, p. B1. Reprinted by permission of *The Wall Street Journal,*

EXHIBIT 1

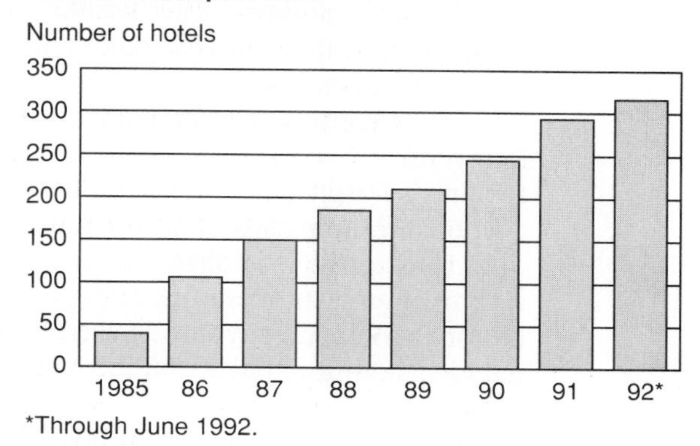

*Through June 1992.

Industry Trends

If you could knock on the doors of all 3.3 million hotel rooms in the U.S. on any given night, you probably wouldn't get a response 40 percent of the time. Though business this time of year is better in, say, Orlando, Florida, than in New York, the lodging industry remains stuck in one of its worst slumps ever, and the nation's innkeepers don't expect much improvement anytime soon.

The industry lost $2.7 billion last year, according to a survey by Arthur Andersen & Company and Smith Travel Research, on the heels of an eye-popping $5.5 billion loss in 1990—perhaps the worst year in the last quarter-century. Nearly every part of the business, from bare-bones economy motels to lush resorts, had losses last year, and most will again this year as cautious consumers and businesses limit their travel expenses.

But there are signs of life amid the wreckage as both hotels and travelers adapt to new ways of doing business. Bargain airline fares and hotel promotions are luring summer vacationers, pushing demand for rooms well above last year's levels. Marriott Corporation, Hyatt Corporation and ITT Corporation's Sheraton chain offer discounts of 25 percent to 50 percent for those willing to book in advance, and many other chains are giving discounts, free meals, goodies for kids and other bonuses.

Moreover, since banks several years ago lost their huge appetite for financing hotels, the construction of new rooms has plunged to 35,000 this year from a peak of 110,000 in 1988, Smith Travel says. So while the industry remains overbuilt, new competition for established hotels and motels no longer is spreading as fast.

Many operators, in fact, expect 1993 to bring modest but steady gains in the industry's occupancy rate, which last year fell to a 20-year low of 60.8 percent, and perhaps even a slight boost in room prices if the economy doesn't unravel again. The industry tends to lag behind the economy by about six months, and any stalling of the fragile recovery could prolong the industry's convalescence.

"We expect to see continuing improvement in 1992, and modest gains in revenues," says David A. Berins, an Arthur Andersen director who heads the firm's hospitality practice. "There's a good prospect that the industry as a whole will approach break-even in 1993."

Hoteliers have slashed operating costs, Mr. Berins says, producing big improvements in operating margins. The industry cut labor costs by $1.08 billion in 1991, mostly through layoffs. Refinancings and lower interest rates pared an additional $1.27 billion, the Arthur Andersen/Smith Travel survey found.

Sheraton is saving about $100,000 per property by installing hotel voice-mail systems in place of message operators. It also put coffeemakers in each room, a popular extra that saves guests money and saves Sheraton the added room-service expense.

Cost-cutting alone isn't enough to cure a business devastated by overbuilding, consumer skittishness and the collapse of the real-estate market, which left many hotels burdened by more debt than their revenues and diminished property values could justify. Some 60 percent of all U.S. hotels are running in the red, according to consultants Coopers & Lybrand.

But at least one small slice of the beleaguered business may produce profits this year. That segment is limited service, which, as its name implies, does without sit-down restaurants, convention space or bellmen. They do offer fresh rooms, convenient locations and a price-conscious alternative—generally $50 or less a night—to the full-service hotels that are the cornerstone of Hilton Hotels Corporation, Hyatt, Marriott, Sheraton and other major chains.

The limited-service brands, such as Marriott's Fairfield Inns or Promus Companies' Hampton Inns, "will be the mass-market lodging product of the 1990s," says Bjorn Hanson, Coopers & Lybrand's national hospitality industry chairman.

Another segment, extended-stay hotels, also may see growth over the next few years. These properties have narrower appeal than limited-service hotels; they are designed for customers, mainly business types, who need lodging for weeks or months at a time.

At the other end of the spectrum, luxury hotels and resorts, charging $180 and up a night, haven't been hurt as badly as most other segments and should rebound quickly as the economy gains strength. But full-service business hotels, the backbone of the industry, are faring worse and will continue to struggle as the rest of the industry crawls out of its hole.

"The vast middle market is vulnerable," says John Rohs, a hotel analyst with Wertheim, Schroder & Company who thinks the full-service chains will continue to be eroded by both the new limited-service hotels and luxury properties. Much of the full-service room base is aging, giving an advantage to newer properties, and they are more expensive to run than the limited-service inns. Full-service hotels spent an average of $43.12 per occupied room night on labor last year, compared with only $13.61 for limited-service hotels, Smith Travel found.

While the lodging industry is in turmoil, customers are having a field day. Discounting and special rates have become so pervasive that few customers ever pay the "rack rate," or full price—and those who do feel as if they're being taken for a ride. Instead, rack rates and corporate rates for businesses have become more like theoretical bench marks at which to start haggling.

"The rack rate has become fiction, because as a concept it's not flexible enough to keep up with the times," says Michael Ribero, Hilton's head of marketing, who adds that the business is increasingly influenced by the constantly changing fares and discounts of the airline industry. Mr. Ribero espouses using more realistic bench marks than the rack rate and stressing service and other quality issues. But he concedes that, at least for now, "price may continue to be the weapon of choice."

Hotel scion J.W. Marriott, chairman of Marriott, says many customers have come to expect a good bargaining session before agreeing on a price. "But the industry can't continue in a bazaar mentality," he says.

Marriott has more reason than most to hope for an end to rampant discounting. Among the hardest hit by the collapse in real estate, the company expanded by building hotels and selling them to limited partnerships as tax shelters, retaining the management contracts. But tax-law changes in 1986 and a glut of hotel rooms left Marriott in a fix. The company has earmarked $1.1 billion of its real estate for sale and hopes to sell as much as $500 million in assets by year's end. Still, Mr. Marriott expects better times by 1994 or 1995, as demand outstrips supply and the company's cost-cutting efforts pay off.

A few are even more bullish. If cheap has become chic, Robert Hazard, Jr., and Gerald Petitt say, their Choice Hotels International Inc. will benefit. As the two top executives at Choice, they oversee a franchised empire of 2,800 properties worldwide, and say they have 25 percent of the domestic market for hotels priced at less than $60 a night. "If you sniff the wind, there's growth in the air," Mr. Hazard says.

The Choice brands, which include Comfort Inns, Quality Inns, Clarion, Sleep Inns, Rodeway Inns and Econo Lodge, have particular appeal for young families and seniors. At a Sleep Inn, children under 18 can stay free with parents or grandparents, and seniors can knock 10 percent to 30 percent off the regular rate of $30 to $40. Customers get new rooms with amenities such as an oversized shower and telephones with data ports.

Mr. Hazard argues that the recession has pushed countless business travelers into Choice properties instead of aging full-service hotels. He says the company will continue to add about 300 properties a year, as its parent

EXHIBIT 1

Trends in the U.S. Hotel Industry

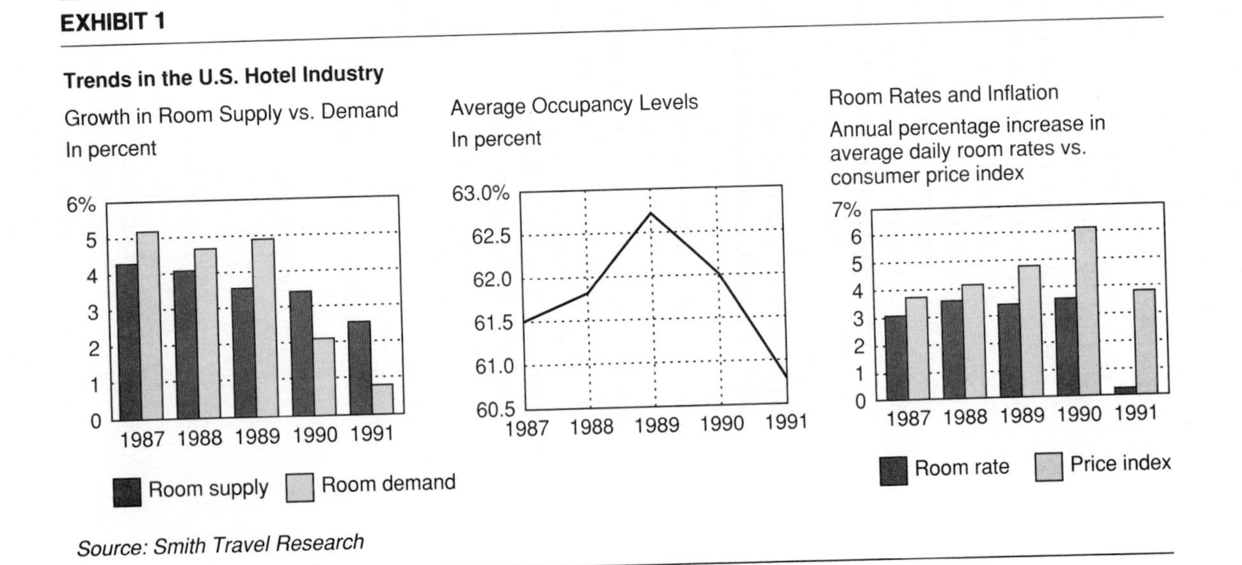

Source: Smith Travel Research

company, Manor Care Inc., a nursing-home operator based in Silver Spring, Maryland, generates cash to buy other chains.

No matter how soon business and leisure travel revive, the current slump is likely to leave a lasting impact on the industry. Mr. Rohs of Wertheim Schroder predicts the ranks of independent hotels will dwindle as marketing muscle and big reservation systems become more important. Independent hotels, which accounted for 45 percent of all hotels rooms in 1980, saw their share drop to 36 percent last year and will account for only 29 percent by 1996, he says.

New hotels will have to be financed the old-fashioned way—with lots of equity from the developer—rather than with the 90 percent or 100 percent financing dished out during the boom years. Growth for big hotel chains will come mainly through conversion of existing properties rather than new construction.

Though buyers have their pick of distressed hotel properties, not all hostelries are bargains waiting to be snapped up. Hotel sales remain sluggish at best, and financing remains hard to come by. Mortgage holders are loath to foreclose on a hotel, since a shuttered inn instantly loses much of its value, so sales are expected to be gradual.

Stephen W. Brener, a New York real estate broker who specializes in hotels, warns that many properties on the market were built for tax shelters, not operating profits. "This is an excellent time to buy a hotel, provided you know what a hotel is," he says. "It's not a fixed rate of return, but a going business."

Source: Pauline Yoshihashi, "Hotel Recovery Will Be a Late Arrival," *The Wall Street Journal*, July 27, 1992, pp. B1, B8. Reprinted by permission of *The Wall Street Journal*.

PART

V

MARKETING ORGANIZATION AND CONTROL

CHAPTER

16

Designing Effective Marketing Organizations

"In outfits as diverse as Eastman Kodak, Hallmark Cards, and General Electric—even the San Diego Zoo—the search for the organization perfectly designed for the 21st century is going ahead with the urgency of a scavenger hunt."[1] Several influences are impacting the design of organizations, including (1) the implementation of self-managing teams and other employee empowerment methods, (2) emphasis on managing and improving business processes using the concepts and methods of total quality management, and (3) the application of an array of impressive information technology. Organizational effectiveness is particularly important in marketing operations because of marketing's interaction with the external environment and its coordination between the various business functions.

The last decade was an unprecedented period of organizational change. Companies realigned their organizations to establish closer contact with customers, improve customer service, reduce unnecessary layers of management, decrease the time span between decisions and results, and improve organizational effectiveness in other ways. Organizational changes include the use of information systems to reduce organizational layers and response times, the use of multifunctional teams to design and produce new products, and creation of flexible organizational units to compete in turbulent business environments.

We begin by examining several organization design issues, then consider alternative designs and the features and limitations of each in different situational settings. A discussion of selecting an organization design follows. Finally, several global dimensions of organizations are considered.

CONSIDERATIONS IN ORGANIZATION DESIGN

Several factors influence the design of marketing organizations. These include (1) using independent organizations to perform certain marketing activities, (2) determining the vertical structure of the organization, (3) establishing horizontal relationships, (4) improving response time between decisions and results, and (5) understanding and managing the operating environment.

Internal and External Organizations

Marketing organization design should include consideration of the trade-offs between performing marketing functions within the organization and having external organizations perform the functions. The discussion of channel-of-distribution design in Chapter 13 examines the use of intermediaries to perform various distribution functions. For example, independent manufacturers' agents may conduct the sales function for producers. Contractual arrangements are often made for advertising and sales promotion services, marketing research, and telemarketing. Services are also available to perform marketing functions in international markets (see Chapter 10).

Internal units provide more control of activities, easier access to other departments, and greater familiarity with company operations. The commitment of the people to the organization is often higher, since they are part of the corporate culture. The limitations of internal units include difficulty in quickly expanding or contracting size, lack of experience in other business environments, and limited skills in specialized areas such as advertising and marketing research.

External organizations offer specialized skills, experience, and flexibility in adapting to changing conditions. These firms may have lower costs than an organization that performs the function(s) internally. Obtaining services outside the firm also has limitations, including loss of control, longer execution time, greater coordination requirements, and lack of familiarity with the organization's products and markets. Coordination of relationships, defining operating responsibilities, and establishing good communications are essential to gaining effective use of external organizations.

Vertical Structure

The vertical dimension of the organization structure is shown by the organization chart. Vertical design issues include determining reporting relationships, establishing departmental groupings, and creating vertical information linkages.[2] Reporting relationships indicate who reports to whom in the organizational hierarchy. Departmental grouping considers how sets of employees are assigned responsibilities. Groupings may be according to function, geography, product, market, or combinations of these factors. Vertical information linkages are necessary to aid communications among organizational participants. Various techniques help to move information through the organization, including approval of proposed actions, rules and procedures, plans and schedules, creation of additional levels or positions, and information systems.

The organization of the future will have fewer levels than traditional organizations and will be organized around processes such as order processing, new product planning, and customer services. One estimate is that the typical large business in 2010 will have fewer than half the levels of management of its counterpart today.[3] These flat organizations will have no more than one third the number of managers of today and will be information-based. Information storage, processing, and decision-support technology will move information swiftly up and down and across the organization (see Chapter 8). Levels of management can be eliminated, since people at those levels function primarily as information relays rather than as decision makers and leaders. In many organizations, management is under pressure to reduce operating costs. Eliminating organizational levels and increasing the number of people supervised help to reduce staff size.

The span of control (number of people supervised) will be much greater in the future. For example, the use of an innovative information system enables Mrs. Fields Cookies to operate with a much larger span of control than McDonald's. Mrs. Fields retail store managers have direct access to top management through the information system.

Horizontal Relationships

The traditional focus in organization design has been the vertical structure. Horizontal relationships are also very important to achieving organizational objectives.[4] The use of horizontal multifunction teams for new-product planning and other projects requires close working relationships. Coordination between organizational units such as research and development, finance, manufacturing, human resources, and marketing is accomplished in various ways, including written communications, direct contact, liaison roles, task forces, full-time integrators (e.g., product managers), and teams (permanent task forces).

A major concern in horizontal relationships is improving relationships with customers in the field. Many companies have restructured their sales and marketing organizations to move closer to their customers:

> An electrical products manufacturer, previously organized on a functional basis, has set up four separate operating divisions, each with its own sales and engineering units.

A packaging company, following the successful revamping of its sales force along industry lines, is now reorganizing its warehousing and customer service activities on a geographic basis, so as to ensure more familiarity with customer by area.

A manufacturer serving industrial markets has formed a special marketing group solely for support of its distribution network.[5]

These actions indicate marketing executives' continuing concern about organizational effectiveness. Organizational change will occur more frequently in the future as businesses respond to market turbulence and competitive pressures.

Multifunctional teamwork is critical to improving product and supporting-service quality. Union Pacific Railroad (UP) found that nearly one fifth of its invoices contained errors.[6] Management formed a special team to analyze the problem. Statistical analysis identified 20 specific causes of the billing errors originating from several departments. A quality-improvement team was formed with the objective of reducing the errors to one half the current level within a year for each of the 20 causes.

Speed of Response

The design of an organization affects its ability (and willingness) to respond quickly. The advantage of doing things faster than the competition is clearly established in various kinds of business. The Limited's skill in moving women's apparel from design to the store in weeks instead of months enables the retailer to market new designs ahead of its competition. Organizations that can do things faster are more competitive. General Electric reduced the time between order receipt and delivery for custom-made industrial circuit-breaker boxes from three weeks to three days.[7] The company formed a team of manufacturing, design, and marketing experts with the responsibility of changing the manufacturing process.

Managing the Operating Environment

The environment influences an organization in several ways.[8] For example, as environmental complexity increases, management may expand the number of positions and departments to cope with the complexity. Uncertainties in the external environment are created by instability, variability, dispersion, turbulence, and resource constraints. Rapidly changing customer needs and wants require organizations to adapt to customers' requirements. One organization form may be more adaptable than another.

Environmental complexity and risk create new organizational challenges. Flexibility and adaptability in an organization are important capabilities. Responses to environmental uncertainty may include: (1) creating additional positions and departments; (2) performing buffering and boundary-spanning roles by units that work with environmental elements (for example, placing a salesperson in the facilities of a key customer); (3) performance of specialized functions within departments and intensified integration between departments; (4) adoption of looser, free-flowing, and adaptive internal organizations; (5) selection of structures, management processes, and strategies used by other industry members; and (6) expanded planning and environmental forecasting activities.[9]

Environmental complexity and skill and resource gaps may cause an organization to establish a collaborative relationship with another partner (Chapter 3). The strategic alliance, for example, may be used to overcome these problems. The collaborative nature of these interorganizational forms involves sharing of people, responsibilities, and knowledge. Unlike the joint venture, the alliance is not a separate organization. Instead, it involves informal ties between the partners.

ORGANIZATIONAL DESIGN OPTIONS

Functional specialization is often one consideration in selecting an organizational design. Emphasis on functions may be less appropriate when trying to direct activities toward market targets, products, and field sales operations. Market targets and product scope also influence organizational design. When two or more targets and/or a mix of products are involved, companies often depart from the functional organizational designs that place advertising, selling, research, and other supporting services into functional units (e.g., sales department). Similarly, distribution channels and sales force considerations may influence the organizational structure a firm adopts. For example, the marketing of home entertainment products targeted to business buyers of employee incentives and promotional gifts might be done by a unit separate from the unit marketing to consumer end-users. Geographical factors have a heavy influence on organization design because of the need to make the field supervisory structure correspond to how the sales force is assigned to customers.

In this discussion we assume that the marketing organization is part of a strategic business unit. Companies with two or more business units may have corporate marketing organizations as well as business unit marketing organizations. Corporate involvement may range from a coordinating role to one in which the corporate staff has considerable influence on business unit marketing operations. Also, the chief marketing executive and staff may participate in varying degrees in strategic planning for the enterprise and the business unit.

We first look at several traditional approaches to organizing marketing activities and assigning responsibilities, and we examine the role of corporate marketing. This is followed by a discussion of some new concepts in marketing organization design.

Traditional Designs

The major forms of marketing organizational designs are *functional, product, market,* and *matrix* designs.

Functional Organizational Design. This design assigns departments, groups, or individuals the responsibility for specific activities, such as advertising and sales promotion, pricing, sales, marketing research, and marketing planning and services. Depending on the size and scope of its operations, the marketing organization may include some or all of these activities. The functional approach is often used when a single product or a closely related line is marketed to one market target.

Product Organizational Design. The product mix may need to be given special attention in the organizational design. New products may not receive the attention they need unless specific responsibility is assigned for planning and coordinating the new-product activities. This problem may also occur with existing products when a business unit has several products and each involves technical and/or application differences. Organizational schemes for managing products can be categorized according to whether they are temporary or permanent and whether the people involved are assigned full-time or part-time.[16] Approaches to product management are shown in Exhibit 16–1. We examine several of the approaches to organizing using a product focus.

The *new-products committee* is widely used because it involves the various functional interests in new-product planning without creating an organizational unit.[11] It is quite flexible and can be used either as a coordinating mechanism for a particular project or on a continuing basis. Committees may be formed at the top management level for decision-making purposes or at operating levels for coordination or special-purpose assignments, such as screening new-product proposals.

By using the committee system, companies avoid creating a permanent, full-time organizational unit—a major advantage. Limitations of the committee include lack of authority, coordination difficulties, and lack of full-time monitoring. Key factors in the success of a new-product committee are the chairperson and the choice of members.

The *product/brand manager,* sometimes assisted by one or a few additional people, is responsible for planning and coordinating various business functions for the assigned products. Typically, the product manager does not have authority over all product-planning activities but may coordinate various product-related activities. The manager usually has background and experience in research and development, engineering, or marketing and is normally assigned to one of these departments. Product managers' titles and responsibilities vary widely across companies.

The *product department* places product-planning responsibility in a formal department. Two versions may be found: (1) a separate department to

EXHIBIT 16–1 Organizational Approaches for Managing New and Existing Products

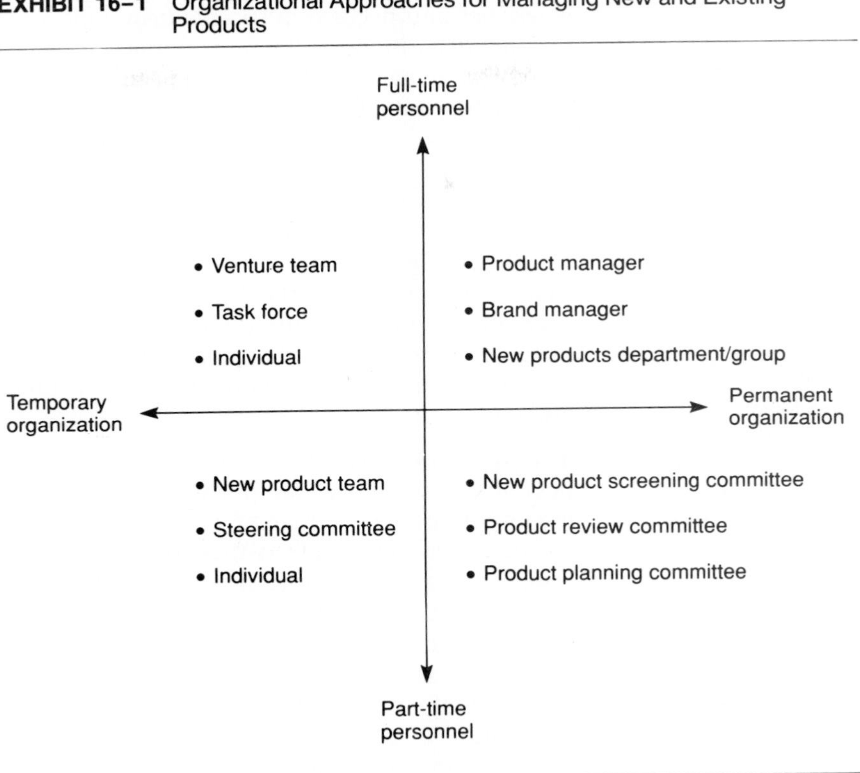

give new products attention, push, focus, and drive, as would occur if the chief operating executive were managing the product; and (2) the product manager cluster, in which a manager is responsible for two or more product managers.[12] The departmental approach provides a strong base of support for new-product planning, but the separate department may also create internal frictions with other functional areas.

The *venture team* requires the creation of an organizational unit to perform some or all of the new-product-planning functions. This unit may be a separate division or company created specifically for new product or new business ideas and initiatives.[13] Examples of successful products planned by venture units include the Boeing 757 aircraft, the IBM personal computer line, and Xerox products other than photocopiers. Venture teams offer several advantages, including flexibility and quick response. They provide functional involvement and full-time commitment, and they can be disbanded when appropriate. Team members are motivated to participate on a project that offers possible job advancement opportunities.

Selecting a good product organization must take into account the characteristics and needs of a specific firm. One study of 267 firms found the product department is the most popular organizational form, followed by the brand manager and the new-product committee.[14]

Factors that often influence the choice of a product organization design are the kinds and scope of products offered, the amount of new-product development, the extent of coordination necessary among functional areas, and the management and technical problems previously encountered with new products and existing products. For example, a firm with an existing functional organizational structure may create a temporary task force to manage and coordinate the development of a major new product. Before or soon after commercial introduction, the firm will shift responsibility for the product to the functional organization. The task force's purpose is to allocate initial direction and effort to the new product so that it is properly launched.

The Market Organizational Design. This approach is used when a business unit serves more than one market target and customer considerations are important in the design of the marketing organization. For example, the customer base often affects the structuring of the field sales organization. Some firms appoint market managers and have a field sales force that is specialized by type of customer. The market manager operates much like a product manager, with responsibility for market planning, research, advertising, and sales force coordination. Market-oriented field organizations may be deployed according to industry, customer size, and type of product application to achieve specialization by end-user groups. Conditions that suggest a market-oriented design are: (1) multiple market targets being served within a strategic business unit, (2) substantial differences in the customer requirements in a given target market, and/or (3) each customer or prospect purchases the product in large volume or dollar amounts.

Combination or Matrix Design. This design is a cross-classification approach to emphasize two different factors, such as products and marketing functions (Exhibit 16–2). Field sales coverage is determined by geography, whereas product emphasis is obtained using product managers. In addition to working with salespeople, the product managers coordinate with the other marketing functions such as advertising and marketing research. Other matrix schemes are possible. For example, within the sales regions shown in Exhibit 16–2, salespeople may be organized by product type or customer group. Also, the marketing functions may be broken down by product category, such as appointing an advertising supervisor for Product II.

The combination approaches are effective in responding to different influences on the organization and offer more flexibility than the other traditional approaches. A major difficulty with these designs is establishing lines of responsibility and authority. Product and market managers fre-

EXHIBIT 16–2 A Marketing Organization Based on a Combination of Functions and Products

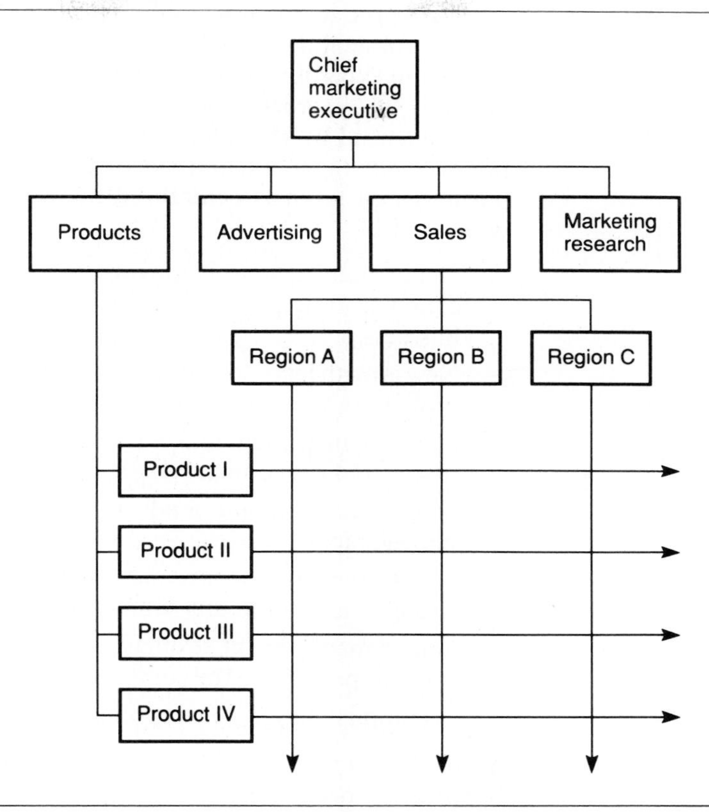

quently complain that they lack control over all marketing functions even though they are held accountable for results. Nevertheless, the matrix approaches are popular, so their operational advantages must exceed their limitations.

Marketing's Corporate Role. An important organizational issue in firms with two or more operating units is deciding whether a corporate marketing function is needed, and if so, what its role and scope should be. The Conference Board identifies three possible roles of corporate marketing:

1. Performing services for the company and/or its operating units.
2. Controlling or monitoring the performance of operating unit marketing activities.
3. Providing an advisory or consulting service to corporate management and/or operating units.[15]

Services may include media purchases, marketing research, planning assistance, and other supporting activities. Control may cover pricing policies, new-product planning, sales force compensation, and other monitoring/control actions. Advisory or consulting services provide professional marketing expertise, such as market segmentation analyses, new-product planning, and marketing strategy.

Influenced by the trend toward decentralized management, corporations are moving marketing functions away from the corporate level to the business unit level. Decentralized marketing activities are more likely to occur when:

Senior management is moving the company toward further diversification into areas having little or no relation to its present array of businesses.

New growth leads to added organizational complexities and to a further proliferation of the company's operating components.

Senior management makes no attempt to integrate newly acquired businesses into the company's existing corporate structure.

Senior management tends to focus on financial results and asset management.

Areas other than marketing are the principle sources of a company's strength, efficiency, and momentum.

Senior management strongly prefers decentralizing as much responsibility as possible to the company's operating units.

A company has to cut corporate staff to reduce costs.[16]

Thus, the corporate role of marketing is influenced by top management's approach to organizing the corporation as well as by the nature and complexity of business operations. Marketing strategy decisions are typically centered at the business-unit and product-market levels. Nevertheless, it is very important for the top management team to include strategic marketing professionals. The market-driven nature of business strategy requires the active participation of marketing professionals.

New Forms of Marketing Organizations

As we discussed early in the chapter, the use of self-managing employee teams, the emphasis on business processes rather than activities, and the application of information technology are creating major changes in organization design. First, we explore how these influences are altering the traditional vertical organization. Then, we look at some new marketing organization designs.

Transforming Vertical into Horizontal Organizations. Total quality management (TQM) is changing how organizations are structured. This transformation involves defining the business as a group of interrelated processes rather than as separate functions of research and development, manufacturing, marketing, and finance. Since most business processes involve several business functions, the basis of organization becomes the process rather than the function. Consider, for example, the process of "order generation and fulfillment."[17] The process owners are manufacturing and marketing. The process team responsible for defining, analyzing, and continually improving the process includes the workers that perform the various activities necessary to create the process outputs (completed orders delivered to customers).

The process concept of managing a business is a major departure from traditional, functional organizational designs. The use of matrix and the team-oriented designs provides some experience in coordinating the activities of multifunctional teams. For example, a large industrial products company uses teams to develop and implement its marketing plans. Team members include product managers, research and development managers, manufacturing managers, sales management, finance executives, and top management. Nonetheless, making the transition to the true process-driven organization requires a major alteration in how the organization is designed and how it functions.

New Organization Forms. An example of one new concept of how to design an organization is the marketing coalition company shown in Exhibit 16–3.[18] This horizontally aligned organization is the control center for organizing a division of functions using several specialist firms. The core of this organization is a functionally specialized marketing capability that coordinates a network of independent functional units. They perform such functions as product technology, engineering, and manufacturing.

No pure forms of the marketing coalition company are known to exist. However, companies such as IBM and General Electric appear to be moving toward this organization form. Several Japanese companies have certain of the characteristics of the coalition company. One U.S. retail chain, the Bombay Company, is organized in a form similar to the coalition design in its supplier network. Bombay has a global network of specialized suppliers of its home furnishings. Specific components (e.g., legs, top) of a table are produced by different manufacturers, shipped to Bombay's product-assembly faculty, and deployed through a national distribution system to Bombay's company-owned retail stores. While the Bombay design is not identical to the design shown in Exhibit 16–3, there are striking similarities.

SELECTING AN ORGANIZATION DESIGN

The design of the marketing organization is influenced by market and environmental factors, the characteristics of the organization, and the marketing strategy followed by the firm. A sound organizational scheme has several characteristics:

EXHIBIT 16–3 The Marketing Coalition Company

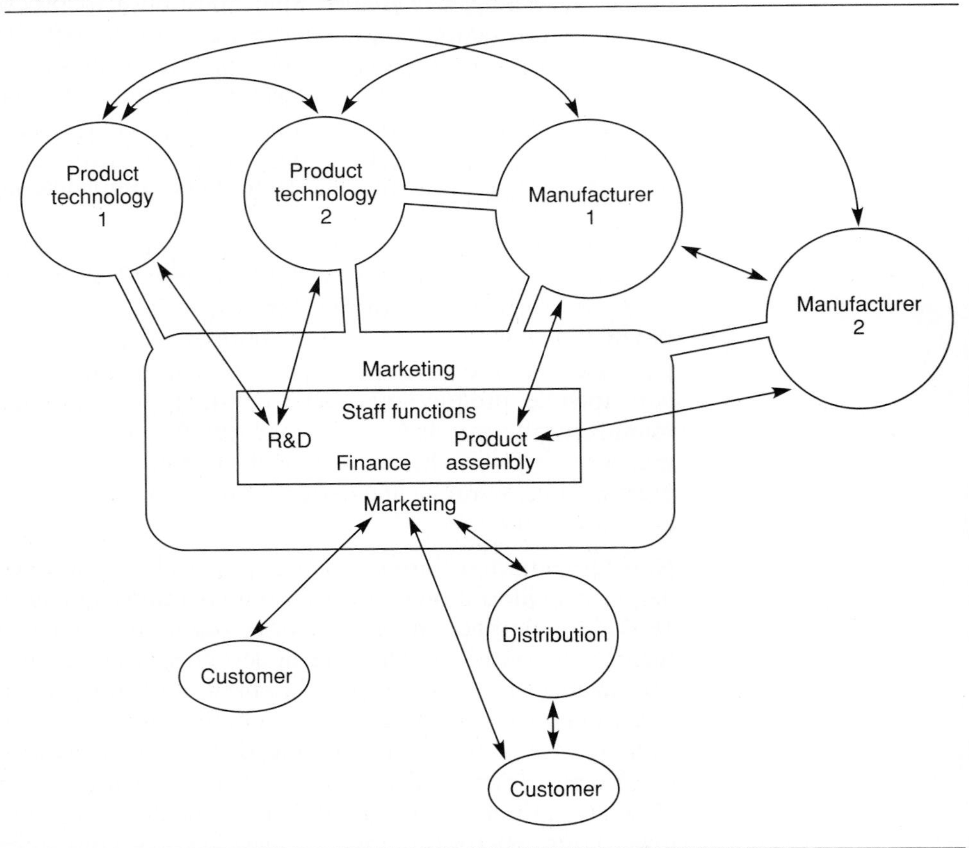

Source: Ravi S. Achrol, "Evolution of the Marketing Organization: New Forms for Turbulent Environments," *Journal of Marketing,* October 1991, p. 88.

The organization should correspond to the strategic marketing plan. For example, if the plan is structured around markets or products, then the marketing organizational structure should reflect this same emphasis.

Coordination of activities is essential to successful implementation of plans, both within the marketing function and with other company and business unit functions. The more highly specialized marketing functions become, the more likely coordination and communications will be hampered.

Specialization of marketing activities leads to greater efficiency in performing the functions. As an illustration, a central advertising department may be more cost-efficient than establishing an advertising unit for each product category. Specialization can also provide technical depth. For example, product or application specialization in a field sales force will enable salespeople to provide consultative-type assistance to customers.

The organization should be structured so that responsibility for results will correspond to a manager's influence on results. While this objective is often difficult to fully achieve, it is an important consideration in designing the marketing organization.

Finally, one of the real dangers in a highly structured organization is the loss of flexibility. The organization should be adaptable to changing conditions.

Of course, some of these characteristics conflict with others. Because of this, organizational design requires looking at priorities and balancing conflicting consequences.

Structure-Environment Match

Matching the organization design to its markets and competitive environment should contribute to organizational effectiveness. A framework for analyzing the structure-environment match is shown in Exhibit 16–4. It utilizes the dimensions of market/environmental complexity, interconnectedness, and predictability, and indicates organizational designs for each contingency.[19] Interconnectedness refers to the degree to which the organization, intermediaries, and markets function as an organized and integrated system. Thus, a vertical marketing channel system has this characteristic. A predictable environment is one that does not change rapidly, marketing relationships with buyers are routinized, and the organization is in direct contact with the environment.

High environmental complexity coupled with a predictable environment suggest the use of a decentralized organization to gain organizational effectiveness (Cell I):

> Decentralization offers many benefits for coping with a complex multiproduct-market environment. The unit managers can focus their entire efforts on a specific set of products and/or markets. They are task oriented versus function oriented. All of the resources to perform the marketing function are possessed by each decentralized unit. Thus, the need to compete for shared resources is eliminated. The unit managers in a decentralized organization assume some of the decision-making and coordination roles concentrated in the marketing manager of a functional organization. Thus, decisions are made more quickly. In effect, a complex environment has been divided up into a subset of simpler environments that can be effectively dealt with by the simple functional organizational form.
>
> The increase in effectiveness gained through decentralization is not costless. There is duplication of functional services across units and thus these specialized

EXHIBIT 16–4 Structure-Environment Match of the Marketing Organization

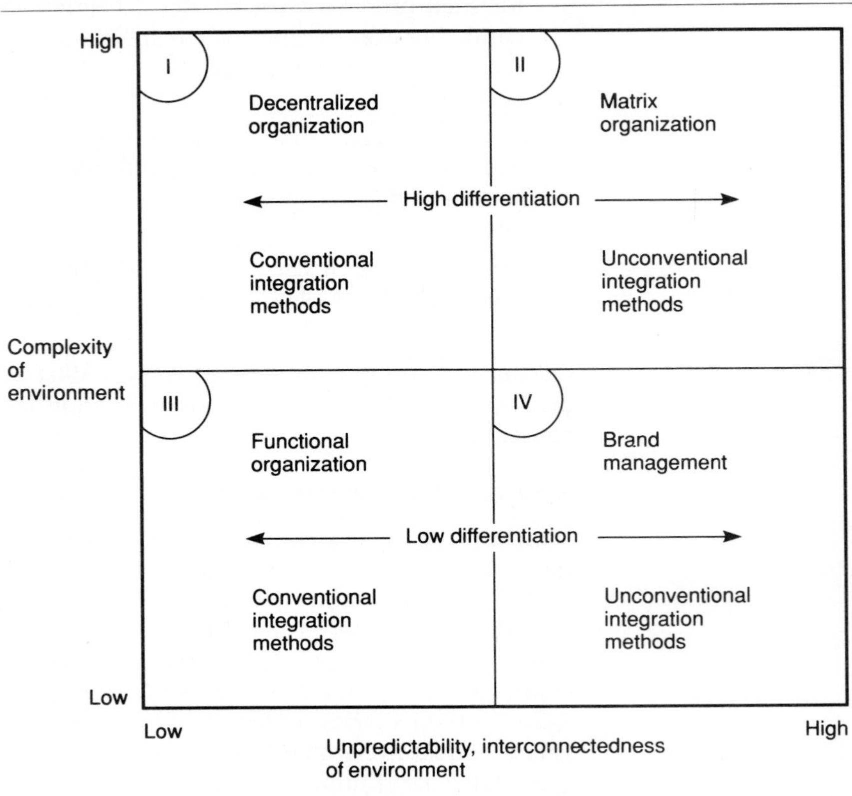

Source: Barton Weitz and Erin Anderson, "Organizing the Marketing Function," in *Review of Marketing 1981,* ed. Ben M. Enis and Kenneth J. Roering (Chicago: American Marketing Association, 1981), p. 137.

> services may not be used to their full capacity. This duplication and potential under-utilization may lead to a deterioration of in-depth competence. It may be difficult, for example, to attract an advertising specialist to work in a product group as opposed to an advertising department.[20]

A decentralized marketing organization reduces the problems created by a large organization as well as by environmental complexity. Management's challenge is to coordinate and integrate the activities of the units. Organizational units (e.g., market, product) that have independent marketing activities are appropriate for a decentralized organizational design.[21]

Choosing the best design for each of the situations shown in Exhibit 16–4 involves trade-offs. Exhibit 16–4 is a useful framework for analysis. When considered with other influences, such as corporate culture, available staff, and cost-benefits, the framework helps to select an effective organizational design.

Organizing Concepts

How marketing activities are organized affects strategy implementation. Consider, for example, the four organizational forms in Exhibit 16–5. Note the usage context and performance characteristics of each structure. Since implementation may involve a usage context that combines two of the structures, trade-offs are involved. The organization structure adopted may facilitate the implementation of certain activities and tasks. For example, the bureaucratic form should facilitate the implementation of repetitive activities such as telephone processing of air travel reservations and ticketing. Once management analyzes the task(s) to be performed and the environment in which they will be done, it must determine its priorities. Is the objective performance and short-run efficiency or adaptability and longer-term effectiveness?

> Activities in different categories should be structured differently whenever feasible. Some firms appear to be moving in this direction, as shown by reports of cuts in corporate staff departments, the shifting of more planning and decision-making authority to individual business unit and product-market managers, and the increased use of ad hoc task forces to deal with specific markets or problems—all of which indicate a shift toward more decentralized and flexible structures.[22]

The corporate culture may also have an important influence on implementation. For example, implementing new strategies may be more difficult in highly structured, bureaucratic organizations. General Motors' difficulty in responding to the global competitive pressures during the last decade is illustrative. Management should consider its own management style, accepted practices, specific performance of executives, and other unique characteristics in deciding how to design the organization.

Organizing the Sales Force

In many companies, the sales force comprises most of the marketing organization. Because of this, organizing the sales force is often a central part of the marketing organization design. We discuss the design of the sales organization in Chapter 15. Designs that correspond to variations in product offering and customer needs are presented (see Exhibit 15–8). Additional aspects of organizing the sales force are now examined.

Organizing Multiple Sales Channels. Expanding the sales organization beyond the field sales force to include major-account programs, telemarketing, and/or electronic sales programs requires consideration as to how to organize the channel network. A key issue is whether to establish separate organizational units or instead to combine two or more channels into one unit. For example, should the national account salespeople be placed in a separate organizational unit or instead assigned to field sales units (e.g., regions or districts)?

EXHIBIT 16–5 Four Archetypal Organizational Forms

		Market versus Hierarchical Organization	
		Internal Organization of Activity	*External Organization of Activity*
Structural Characteristics	Centralized Formalized Nonspecialized	**Bureaucratic Form** *Appropriate usage context* • conditions of market failure • low environmental uncertainty • tasks which are repetitive, easily assessed, requiring specialized assets *Performance characteristics* • highly effective and efficient • less adaptive *Examples in marketing* • functional organization • company or division sales force • corporate research staffs	**Transactional Form** *Appropriate usage context* • under competitive market conditions • low environmental uncertainty • tasks which are repetitive, easily assessed, with no specialized investment *Performance characteristics* • most efficient form • highly effective for appropriate tasks • less adaptive *Examples in marketing* • contract purchase of advertising space • contract purchase of transportation of product • contract purchase of research field work
	Decentralized Nonformalized Specialized	**Organic Form** *Appropriate usage context* • conditions of market failure • high environmental uncertainty • tasks which are infrequent, difficult to assess, requiring highly specialized investment *Performance characteristics* • highly adaptive • highly effective for nonroutine, specialized tasks • less efficient *Examples in marketing* • product management organization • specialized sales force organization • research staffs organized by product groups	**Relational Form** *Appropriate usage context* • under competitive market conditions • high environmental uncertainty • tasks which are nonroutine, difficult to assess, requiring little specialized investment *Performance characteristics* • highly adaptive • highly effective for nonroutine, specialized tasks • less efficient *Examples in marketing* • long-term retainer contract with advertising agency • ongoing relationship with consulting firm

Source: Robert W. Ruekert, Orville C. Walker, Jr., and Kenneth J. Roering, "The Organization of Marketing Activities: A Contingency Theory of Structure and Performance," *Journal of Marketing*, Winter 1985, p. 20.

When sales channel activities are relatively independent of the field sales force, a separate channel organization is appropriate. This occurs when major-account managers or telemarketing salespeople provide all contacts with assigned accounts. An example is the assignment of low-sales-volume accounts to telemarketing salespeople. A more likely situation is when contacts are made by both field personnel and other channels. These contacts require coordination between salespeople. The creation of independent sales-channel organizations complicates the coordination of selling activities.

Coordinating Major-Account Relationships. A look at the alternatives for coordinating key account relationships highlights several multiple-channel issues. A major-account program requires assignment of account responsibility to account managers. When the customer has several purchasing locations, coordination of selling and service activities is necessary. Several alternatives are available including (1) assigning key accounts to top sales executives (e.g., sales vice president), (2) creating a separate corporate division, or (3) establishing a separate major-accounts sales force.[23] Factors that influence the choice of an alternative include the number of major accounts served by the organization, the number of different geographical contacts with an account, the organizational level of contact (e.g., vice president versus maintenance supervisor), and the customer sales and service functions to be performed.

Marketing's Links to Other Functional Units

Marketing professionals often coordinate their activities with other functional areas of the business. Examples include new-product planning, distribution-channel coordination, and pricing analysis. Ruekert and Walker offer guidelines regarding these interactions resulting from their research.[24]

> Effectiveness is improved by developing organizational structures and processes to move resources faster across departments with strong resource dependencies.
>
> Promising coordination mechanisms are formalized operating rules and procedures and horizontal resolution of conflicts. However, resolving conflicts may decrease efficiency.
>
> Communications between functions appear to be enhanced by similarity in departmental tasks and objectives, and when formal operating rules and procedures are used.
>
> There is mixed support for the proposition that higher conflict occurs when higher levels of interaction or resource flows exist between marketing and other functional areas.

These research findings offer useful insights into marketing's horizontal organizational relationships. Additional research is needed to determine how applicable these preliminary findings are in different internal and external organizational environments.

GLOBAL DIMENSIONS OF ORGANIZATIONS

Implementing the global strategies of companies creates several important marketing organizational issues. The president of The Conference Board, Inc. comments on managing in a competitive global environment:

> Finding that critical point where regional differentiation can give way to product standardization will spell success. In many instances your core product will be essentially the same in every market, but marketing will differ widely according to local tastes.[25]

Several issues in organizing global marketing strategies are examined followed by a discussion of organizational concepts that are used to manage global marketing activities. Much of the earlier material in the chapter applies to international operations. This discussion highlights several additional considerations.

Issues in Organizing Global Marketing Strategies

The important distinction in marketing throughout the world is that buyers differ in their needs, preferences, and priorities. Since such differences exist *within* a national market, the variations between countries are likely to be greater. "What success would Swedish car makers or Italian pasta manufacturers have in the United States if they went after the same solid consumer of their home markets instead of appealing to affluent, trendy consumers of their products in this country?"[26] Global market targeting and positioning strategies create several marketing organizational issues.

Variations in Business Functions. Global decisions concerning products, finance, and research and development are often more feasible than making the marketing decisions that span these markets. Marketing strategies require sensitivity to cultural and linguistic differences. Foreign currencies, government regulations, and different product standards further complicate buyer-seller relationships. The important issue is recognizing when standardized marketing strategies can be used and when they must be modified. There is probably no better global marketer than Coca-Cola:

> It is far more patient than most companies. It spent 15 years and several million dollars in China before it began turning a profit there a few years ago.
>
> And Coke deftly uses the same tricks abroad that have worked in the United States. Aiming to be ubiquitous, it is a staple at sporting events. The red and white logo shows up a bullfights in Spain, camel races in Australia, and sheep-shearing contests in New Zealand. . . .
>
> Coke does adjust a bit from country to country. In Spain, it is used heavily as a mixer—even for wine. In Italy, it is increasingly drunk with meals in place

EXHIBIT 16–6 Marketing Organization Plan Combining Product, Geographic, and Functional Approaches

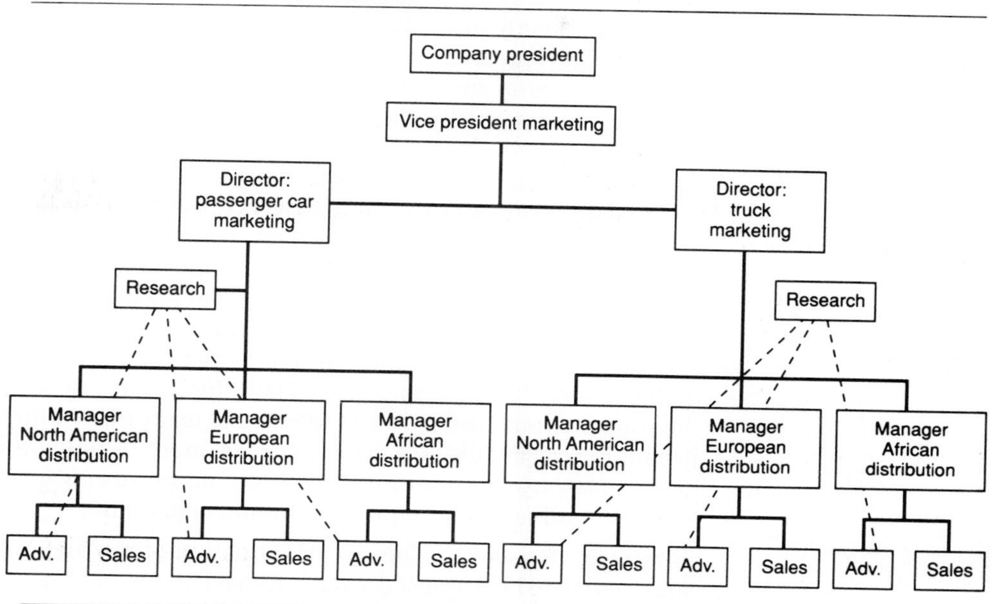

Source: Philip R. Cateora, *International Marketing,* 7th ed. (Homewood, Ill.: Richard D. Irwin, 1990), p. 360.

of wine or cappuccino. In China, it is a luxury item, served on silver trays at government functions.[27]

Organizational Considerations. The marketing organization selected for competing in national markets is influenced by the market *scope* (e.g., single-country, multinational, or global strategy), and by the market *entry strategy* (export, licensing, joint venture, strategic alliance, or complete ownership). Recall the discussion of marketing strategies in global markets in Chapter 10. The adoption of a global strategy using joint ventures, alliances, and/or complete ownership presents the most complex organizational challenge.

The marketing organization design in international operations may consist of one of three possible forms: (1) a global product division; (2) geographical divisions, each with product and functional responsibilities; or (3) a matrix design incorporating (1) or (2) in combination with centralized functional support, or instead a combination of area operations and global product management.[28] The global form corresponds to rapid growth situations for firms that have a broad product portfolio. The geographic form is used to obtain a close relationship with national and local governments. The matrix form is used by companies reorganizing for global competition. An example of a combination organization design is shown in Exhibit 16–6.

Coordination and Communication

Organizing marketing activities to serve international markets creates important coordination and communication requirements. Language and distance barriers complicate organizational relationships. Beech Aircraft Corporation uses an international team-marketing approach to respond faster to market opportunities, manage budgets more effectively, and coordinate goals and objectives.[29] The world is divided into three geographic landmasses, with a marketing team assigned to each area. Previously, Beech used 10 independent regional managers to cover the world. The new teams are responsible for analyzing markets, planning strategy, presenting their recommendations to top management, and executing the strategy. The three teams make quarterly presentations to the president.

"Global teamwork approaches are now being tested by companies with vastly different organizational structures and varying levels of international involvement."[30] The Conference Board, Inc.'s study of 30 major U.S. multinational companies indicates that global teamwork improves market and technological intelligence, contributes to more flexible business planning, leads to stronger commitment to corporate worldwide goals, and achieves closer coordination in implementing strategic actions.

Strategic Alliances. The rate of formation of international strategic alliances escalated in the last decade.[31] Expanded use of alliances is expected in the 1990s. IBM has 40 active alliances, including major partnerships with Japan. The alliance relationship presents major interorganizational coordination and strategy implementation requirements. Peter Drucker offers several guidelines for improving strategic alliances:

> Before the alliance is completed, all parties must think through their objectives and the objectives of the "child."
>
> Equally important is advance agreement on how the joint enterprise should be run.
>
> Next, there has to be careful thinking about who will manage the alliance.
>
> Each partner needs to make provision in its own structure for the relationship to the joint enterprise and the other partners.
>
> Finally, there has to be prior agreement on how to resolve disagreements.[32]

The effectiveness of the alliance depends on how well operating relationships are established and managed on an ongoing basis and how well the partners can work together.

Executive Qualifications. International experience will increasingly be required for executive advancement in the 1990s. (See Global Feature.) Managing international marketing operations requires knowledge of finance, distribution, manufacturing, and other business functions. The trend toward flat organizations with wide spans of control will make on-the-

GLOBAL FEATURE Developing Global Managers

Several companies are offering fast-track managers global management training. The core objective is to develop an internationally experienced cadre of executives. The programs are offered to managers early in their careers. Japanese and European companies are ahead of U.S. firms in implementing these programs. The training includes conducting business in foreign cultures and understanding differences in global customers' needs. Several programs are described in the chart. The typical participant in the Colgate-Palmolive Company's 24-month global marketing management program has an M.B.A. degree, speaks a foreign language, and has strong computer skills and prior business experience. They become associate product managers in the United States or abroad after completing the program. One fourth are foreign nationals. More than 15,000 people apply for 15 positions in the program every year.

Learning the Ways of the World

Company	*Program*
American Express Co.'s Travel Related Services unit	Gives American business-school students summer jobs in which they work outside the United States for up to 10 weeks. Also transfers junior managers with at least two years' experience to other countries
Colgate-Palmolive Co.	Trains about 15 recent college graduates each year for 15 to 24 months prior to multiple overseas job stints
General Electric Co.'s aircraft-engine unit	Will expose selected midlevel engineers and managers to foreign language and cross-cultural training even though not all will live abroad
Honda of America Manufacturing Inc.	Has sent about 42 U.S. supervisors and managers to the parent company in Tokyo for up to three years, after preparing them with six months of Japanese language lessons, cultural training, and life-style orientation during work hours
PepsiCo Inc.'s international beverage division	Brings about 25 young foreign managers a year to the United States for one-year assignments in bottling plants
Raychem Corp.	Assigns relatively inexperienced Asian employees (from clerks through middle managers) to the United States for six months to two years

Source: Joan L. Lublin, "Younger Managers Learn Global Skills," *The Wall Street Journal,* March 31, 1992, p. B1.

job executive development more difficult. Similarly, the qualifications for the chief executive's job will require experience in several areas. With creative financing techniques that turn financial decisions into marketing questions, manufacturing processes that are driven by computer technology, and product designs that depend on rapid market feedback, the chief executive will instead need a varied background.[33]

SUMMARY

The rapidly changing business environment requires change in marketing organizations. Differences in environmental situations create unique organization design requirements. The design and adaptation of organizations to their environments involves consideration of several important issues for marketing organization design, including decisions regarding the use of internal and external organizations, designing the vertical structure, coordinating horizontal relationships, increasing speed of response, and analyzing environmental complexity and the forces of change.

Several traditional marketing organization designs may be used. The options include functional, product, market, and combination designs. Increasingly, market considerations are included in organization designs. The role and scope of corporate marketing is changing in many firms with multibusiness operations. The importance of corporate marketing appears to be declining in many firms, with marketing strategy emphasis instead being focused at the SBU level.

During the 1990s new forms of marketing organizations will develop, driven by the use of multifunction teams in organizations that manage business processes rather than functions, and by the use of powerful information technology. These influences are transforming vertical organizations into horizontal ones. An example is the marketing coalition company.

The choice of an organization design involves finding a good structure-environmental match. The match is influenced by the complexity of the environment and by the unpredictability and interconnectedness of the environment. The design also involves selecting the best organizational form based on structural characteristics and the internal versus external orientation of marketing operations. The key role of the sales force in many organizations makes it a central part of marketing organization design. Marketing's interactions with other functional units is an important factor in organization design.

Finally, the global strategies of companies highlight several marketing organizational issues. These include recognizing the differences in business functions in international operations and the increased coordination and communication requirements in international markets. Strategic alliances, an expanding area of global activity, present complex management and coordination situations. Executive qualifications in marketing and other business functions increasingly include international experience.

QUESTIONS FOR REVIEW AND DISCUSSION

1. The chief executive of a manufacturer of fibers for use in carpets is interested in establishing a marketing organization in the firm. Sales to carpet tufters are handled by a manufacturer's agent, and advertising is planned and executed by an advertising agency. Other than the CEO, no one inside the firm is responsible for the marketing function. What factors should the CEO consider in designing a marketing organization?

2. Of the various approaches to marketing organization design, which one(s) offers the most flexibility in responding to changing conditions? Discuss.

3. Discuss the conditions where a matrix-type marketing organization is appropri-

ate, indicating important considerations and potential problems in using this organizational form.

4. Assume that you have been asked by the president of a major transportation services firm to recommend a marketing organizational design. What factors should you consider in selecting the design?
5. Discuss some of the important issues related to integrating marketing into an organization such as a regional women's clothing chain compared to accomplishing the same task in The Limited Inc.
6. What are possible internal and external factors that may require changing the marketing organization design?
7. Is a trend toward more organic organizational forms likely during the 1990s?
8. How will the expanded use of information and decision-support systems contribute to organizational effectiveness?
9. Discuss the important issues in establishing an effective strategic alliance between organizations.
10. What are the major approaches to organizing the marketing function for international operations? Discuss the factors that may affect the choice of a particular organization design.

NOTES

1. Thomas A. Stewart, "The Search for the Organization of Tomorrow," *Fortune.* May 18, 1992, pp. 93–98.
2. Richard L. Daft, *Organization Theory and Design,* 3rd ed. (St. Paul, Minn.: West Publishing, 1989), pp. 212–17.
3. Peter F. Drucker, "The Coming of the New Organization," *Harvard Business Review,* January–February 1988, pp. 45–53.
4. Daft, *Organization Theory and Design,* pp. 218–24.
5. Earl L. Bailey, *Getting Closer to the Customer,* Research Bulletin No. 229 (New York: The Conference Board, Inc., 1989), p. 5.
6. Brian Dumaine, "What the Leaders of Tomorrow See," *Fortune,* July 3, 1989, p. 51.
7. Brian Dumaine, "How Managers Can Succeed Through Speed," *Fortune,* February 13, 1989, pp. 54–59.
8. Daft, *Organization Theory and Design,* p. 55.
9. Ibid., pp. 55–62.
10. George Benson and Joseph Chasin, *The Structure of New Product Organization* (New York: AMACOM, 1976), p. 10.
11. C. Merle Crawford, *New Products Management* (Homewood, Ill.: Richard D. Irwin, 1983), pp. 169–70.
12. Crawford, *New Products Management,* pp. 174–75.
13. Christopher K. Bart, "New Venture Units: Use Them Wisely to Manage Innovation," *Sloan Management Review,* Summer 1988, p. 35.
14. Benson and Chasin, *The Structure of New Product Organization,* p. 21.
15. David S. Hopkins and Earl L. Bailey, *Organizing Corporate Marketing* (New York: The Conference Board, Inc., 1984), p. 23.
16. Ibid., p. 40.
17. Stewart, "The Search for the Organization of Tomorrow," p. 94.
18. Ravi S. Achrol, "Evolution of the Marketing Organization: New Forms for Turbulent Environments," *Journal of Marketing,* October 1991, pp. 77–93.

19. The following discussion is based on Barton Weitz and Erin Anderson, "Organizing the Marketing Function," in *Review of Marketing 1981,* ed. Ben M. Enis and Kenneth J. Roering (Chicago: American Marketing Association, 1981), pp. 134–42.
20. Ibid., p. 138.
21. Ibid., p. 139.
22. Quote from Robert W. Ruekert, Orville C. Walker, Jr., and Kenneth J. Roering, "The Organization of Marketing Activities: A Contingency Theory of Structure and Performance," *Journal of Marketing,* Winter 1985, pp. 23–24. See also Hopkins and Bailey, *Organizing Corporate Marketing,* and "A New Era for Management," *Business Week,* April 25, 1983, pp. 50–67.
23. For an expanded discussion of this and other sales force organizational design issues, see Gilbert A. Churchill, Jr., Neil M. Ford, and Orville C. Walker, Jr. *Sales Force Management,* 3rd ed. (Homewood, Ill.: Richard D. Irwin, 1990), Chapter 4.
24. Robert W. Ruekert and Orville C. Walker, Jr., "Marketing's Interaction with Other Functional Units: A Conceptual Framework and Empirical Evidence," *Journal of Marketing,* January 1987, pp. 1–10.
25. *The Conference Board's Management Briefing: Marketing,* December 1989/January 1990, p. 5.
26. Ibid.
27. Michael J. McCarthy, "The Real Thing: Its a Global Marketer, Coke Excels by Being Tough and Consistent," *The Wall Street Journal,* December 19, 1989, pp. A1, A6.
28. This discussion is based on Philip R. Cateora, *International Marketing,* 7th ed. (Homewood, Ill.: Richard D. Irwin, 1990), pp. 359–62.
29. *The Conference Board's Management Briefing: Marketing,* February/March, 1989, pp. 1–2.
30. Ibid., p. 2.
31. Jeremy Main, "The Winning Organization," *Fortune,* September 26, 1988, p. 52.
32. Peter F. Drucker, "From Dangerous Liaisons to Alliances for Progress," *The Wall Street Journal,* September 8, 1989, p. A8.
33. Amanda Bennett, "Going Global: The Chief Executives in Year 2000 Will Be Experienced," *The Wall Street Journal,* February 27, 1989, p. A1.

CHAPTER

17

Marketing Strategy Implementation and Control

The ultimate performance of market targeting and positioning decisions rests on how well the marketing strategy is implemented and managed on a continuing basis. Placing the strategy into action and adjusting it to eliminate performance gaps are essential success factors.

One of Japan's more impressive business capabilities is the effective implementation of marketing strategies. Consider Japan's domination of the Chinese market even though anti-Japanese sentiment is strong and widespread in China.[1] Although the local reception of Japanese traders is often unfavorable, Japan has twice the U.S. market share. Japan holds a strong market position by using an extensive network of sales offices in China. The marketing strategy Japanese companies use includes selling initially at low prices to gain market position, later raising prices and making money on spare parts and services. A Japanese trading company adds value to the trading relationship by coordinating an entire project. Japanese traders understand and adapt to China's culture and customs, benefiting from a close location and cultural affinity. The Japanese understand and use the Chinese system called *guanxi*—a complex set of relationships whereby Chinese people become obligated to each other. Gifts help Japanese traders gain access to the system. The gifts are viewed as tokens of esteem rather than bribes. The Japanese government supports trade relations with China through loans.

The Japanese are skilled in moving from marketing planning to implementation. Implementation, a critical part of marketing strategy, ultimately spells the success of the strategic plan. We begin with an overview of the marketing plan, followed by a discussion of implementing the plan. Next, developing a strategic evaluation and control program is overviewed. Finally, the major evaluation activities are discussed and illustrated. These include conducting the strategic marketing audit, selecting performance criteria and measures, determining information needs and analysis, evaluating performance, and taking needed actions to keep performance on track.

THE MARKETING PLAN

The marketing plan guides implementation and control, indicating marketing objectives and the strategy and tactics for accomplishing the objectives. Since Chapter 4 presents a step-by-step planning process, we briefly consider several planning issues and offer examples of marketing planning activities.

How the Marketing Plan Guides Implementation

The relationships between marketing strategy and the annual plan are shown in Exhibit 17–1. The planning cycle is continuous. Plans are developed, implemented, evaluated, and adjusted to keep the marketing strategy on target. Since a strategy typically extends beyond one year, the annual plan is used to guide short-term marketing activities. The planning process is a series of annual plans guided by the marketing strategy. An annual planning period is necessary, since several of the activities shown require action within 12 months or less. Budgeting also requires annual planning information. Longer-range strategic decisions look beyond one year.

A look at the marketing planning process used by a large pharmaceutical company illustrates how planning is done. Product managers are responsible for coordinating the preparation of plans. A planning workshop is conducted mid-year as the kickoff for the next year's plans. The workshop is attended by top management and product, research, sales, and finance managers. The firm's advertising agency also participates in the workshop. The current year's plans are reviewed, and each product manager presents the marketing plan for next year. The workshop members critique each plan and suggest changes. The same group comes together 90 days later and the revised plans are reviewed. At this meeting the plans are finalized and approved for implementation. Each product manager is responsible for coordinating and implementing the plan. Progress is reviewed throughout the plan year.

Contents of the Marketing Plan

An outline for developing the marketing plan is presented in Chapter 4. Many plans follow this general format. An executive summary can be used to provide top management and other executives not closely involved in

EXHIBIT 17–1 Marketing Planning Relationships

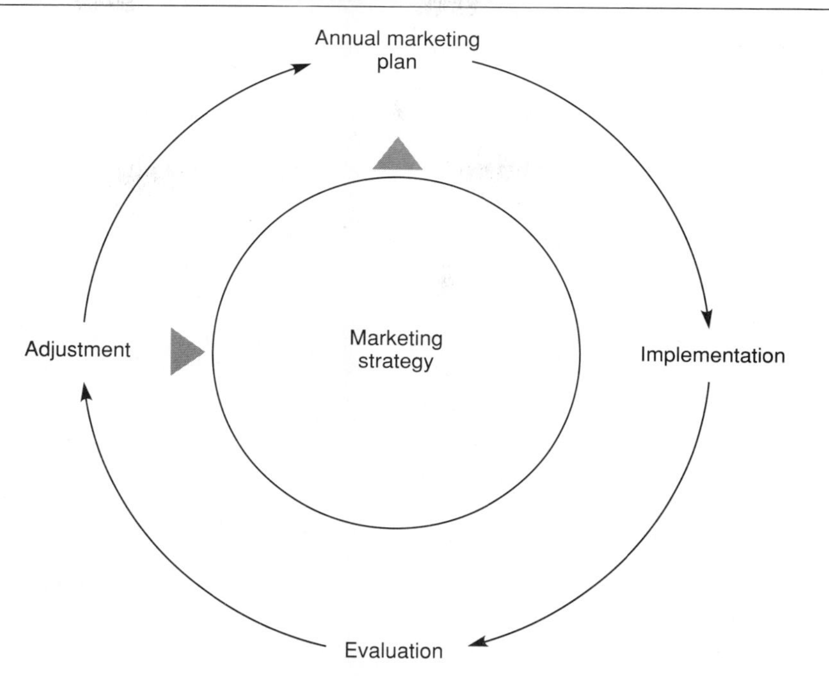

implementation with an overview. The summary outlines the current situation, indicates marketing objectives, summarizes strategies, outlines action programs, and indicates financial expectations.[2]

The steps in the planning sequence are shown in Exhibit 17–2. The activities include making the situation assessment, setting objectives, developing targeting and positioning strategies, deciding action programs for the marketing-mix components, and preparing supporting financial statements (budgets and profit-and-loss projections).

The typical planning process in a company that has an effective planning approach involves quite a bit of coordination and interaction among functional areas. Team planning approaches like the pharmaceutical company's planning workshop are illustrative. Successful implementation of the marketing plan requires a broad consensus among various functional areas.[3] For example, a consensus is essential between product managers and sales management. Product managers must obtain a commitment from the sales department to provide sales effort for their products. Multiple products require negotiation in reaching agreement on the amount of sales force time devoted to various products. The Planning Feature provides a CEO's view of how plans are coordinated by a consumer-products manufacturer.

EXHIBIT 17–2 Marketing Planning Sequence

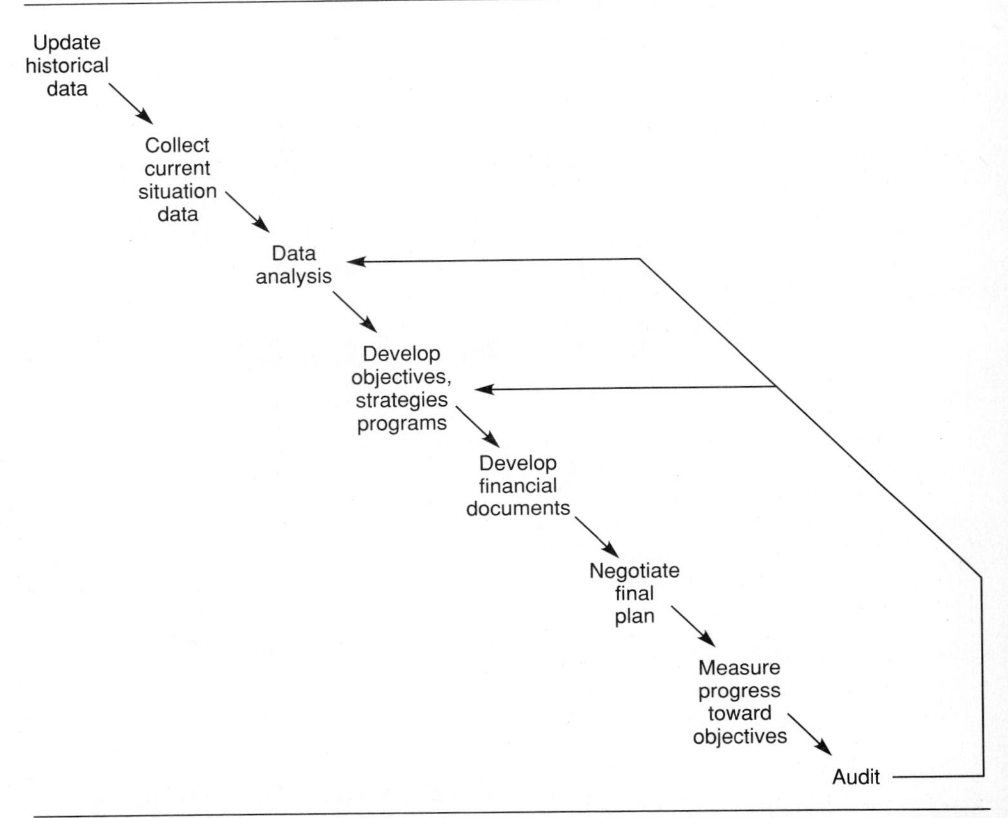

Source: Donald R. Lehmann and Russell S. Winer, *Analysis for Marketing Planning,* 2nd ed. (Homewood, Ill.: Richard D. Irwin, 1991), p. 8.

IMPLEMENTING THE PLAN

Implementation determines the outcome of the marketing planning. Responding to implementation pressures, Procter & Gamble in 1985 began making changes in its long-established brand manager system so it could implement marketing strategies better and shorten the time from planning to action.[4] One change is the "talk sheet," an informal memo that helps several levels of management quickly refine a proposal through conversation instead of just written communications. P&G's top management delegates decision making to lower organizational levels. Interdivisional project teams are getting results, such as moving Ivory shampoo into national distribution in 4 months rather than the normal 18 months. Nevertheless, this huge bureaucratic corporation faces a major challenge in implementing market-

PLANNING FEATURE Integrating Marketing Plans with Business Strategy

Our planning process begins with a half-day meeting to discuss strategic issues. The meeting includes just three people—the president of the division (me), the chairman of the board, and the president of the corporation. I have about three sheets of paper, maybe four, that talk about these things: What are the issues? What are the market dynamics, as I see them today and what do I see in the next three years? What should we be spending in terms of protecting our market share? Where is the market going, from a demographic standpoint?

This is a high-level strategic discussion. We just sit and talk about my business—not a lot of slides, not a lot of pictures, more informal than formal—to get a frame around what I think the strategic issues in the division are. I want to get agreement from them, the chairman and the president, that, yes, those are the issues they're concerned about as well, and that we need to develop plans around those issues.

What we agree to is that there are five or six strategic imperatives. In each case, we agree that a particular objective has to be successfully achieved or the division will not succeed in its business efforts, and we have a three-year horizon. The objectives might have to do with share, or new-product technologies, or management development, or organizational issues that need to be addressed.

Then I draw up a two-page response. It says, here's what we talked about, here's what we agreed to do. Then I go back to the division with this document in my hand. I say, "OK, here's what we're headed for, here's where we got strategic agreement from the corporation." Then we start developing a plan around that direction.

There isn't an awful lot of planning that goes into that first meeting. I mean, we get bunches of numbers, and we look at the most strategic spots, such as share, such as technology. But it's really an opportunity for one time during the year for the three of us to sit down and just talk. That's much better than having a bunch of people in the room, presenting and showing what they want us to see. The next step is to come back to the division and put together a team to prepare a plan based on the strategic plan. This book, which we call a marketing strategic plan, deals with marketing and the whole focus on what we're going to do, and what we're going to do different.

The preparation is typically done by the marketing department, supervised by the manager or director of marketing services and planning. He sort of heads up the committee that puts the book together. Then, once the book is done, we have a meeting at corporate headquarters. We go over very specific areas, with a 35- to 50-page report. That's basically the way it ends up. That seems to be a basic Marketing 101 kind of process, but it's amazing how much disagreement there can be. You have one idea of what your job is, and other people in the organization may have a different idea. I think the key is to get agreement on the mission: what are we really trying to accomplish?

—President of a division of a manufacturer of consumer products

Source: Howard Sutton, *The Marketing Plan in the 1990s* (New York: The Conference Board, Inc., 1990), p. 20.

ing plans. Its many organizational layers and large numbers of people complicate implementation.

The Implementation Process

A good implementation plan shows the activities to be implemented, who is responsible for implementation, the time and location of implementation, and how implementation will be achieved (Exhibit 17–3). Consider the following statement from a product manager's marketing plan:

EXHIBIT 17–3 The Implementation Process

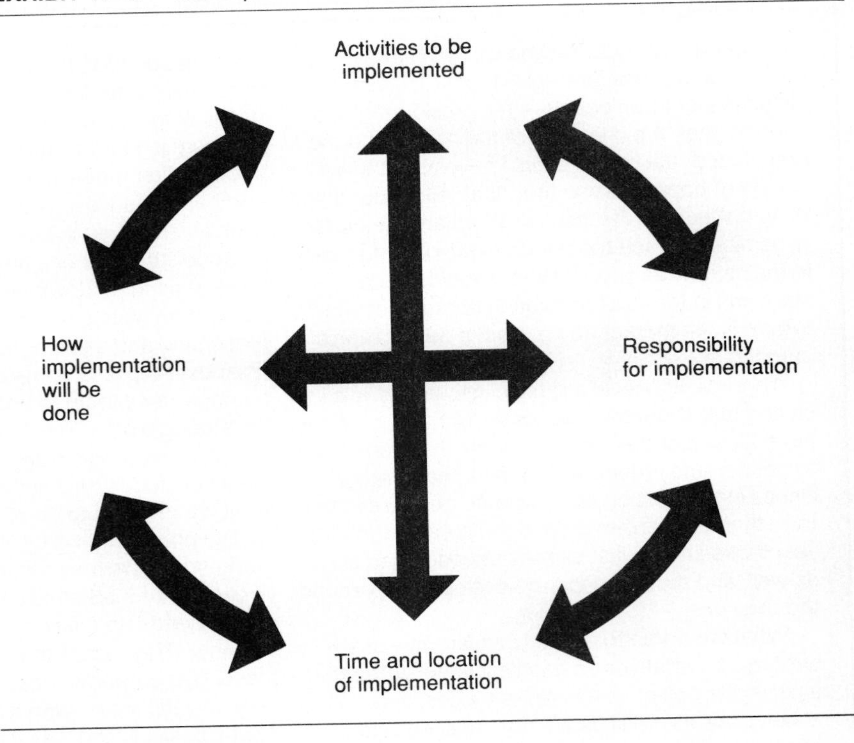

> Sales representatives should target all accounts now using a competitive product. A plan should be developed to convert 5 percent of these accounts to the company brand during the year. Account listings will be prepared and distributed by product management.

In this instance, the sales force is charged with implementation. An objective (5 percent conversion) is specified, but very little information is provided as to *how* the accounts will be converted. A strategy is needed to penetrate the competitor's customer base. The sales force plan must translate the proposed actions and objective (5 percent conversion) into assigned salesperson responsibility (quotas), a timetable, and selling strategy guidelines. Training may be necessary to show the product advantages—and the competitors' product limitations—that will be useful in convincing the buyer to purchase the firm's brand.

The marketing plan can be used to identify the organizational units and managers that are responsible for implementing the various activities in the plan. Deadlines indicate the time available for implementation. In the case of the plan above, the sales manager is responsible for implementation through the sales force.

Improving Implementation

Managers are important facilitators in the implementation process. Some executives are more effective implementers than others. Good planners and implementers often have different strengths and weaknesses. An effective planner may not be good at implementing plans. Desirable implementation skills include:

- The ability to understand how others feel, and good bargaining skills.
- The strength to be tough and fair in putting people and resources where they will be most effective.
- Effectiveness in focusing on the critical aspects of performance in managing marketing activities.
- The ability to create a necessary informal organization or network to match each problem with which they are confronted.[5]

In addition to people, several implementation methods facilitate the process. These include *organizational design, incentives,* and *effective communications.* The features of each method are highlighted.

Organizational Design. Certain organizational forms aid implementation. For example, product managers and multifunctional coordination teams are useful implementation methods. Management may create implementation teams consisting of representatives from the business functions and/or marketing activities involved. The flat, flexible organization designs discussed in Chapter 16 offer several advantages in implementation, since they encourage interfunctional cooperation and communication. These designs are responsive to changing conditions.

Incentives. Various rewards may help achieve successful implementation. For example, special incentives such as contests, recognition, and extra compensation are used to encourage salespeople to push a new product. Since implementation often involves teams of people, creation of team incentives may be necessary. Performance standards must be fair, and incentives should encourage something more than normal performance.

Communications. Rapid and accurate movement of information through the organization is essential in implementation. Both vertical and horizontal communications are needed in linking together the people and activities involved in implementation. Meetings, status reports, and informal discussions help to transmit information throughout the organization. Computerized information and decision-support systems help to improve communication speed and effectiveness.

Difficulties often occur during implementation and affect how fast and how well plans are put into action. Examples include competitors' actions, internal resistance between departments, loss of key personnel, delays affecting product availability (e.g., supply, production, and distribution problems), and changes in the business environment. Corrective actions may require appointing a person or team for troubleshooting the problem, increasing or shifting resources, or changing the original plan. Consider, for example, Gillette's experience in moving the Sensor razor to market in early 1990. Production and distribution were unable to meet the initial demand for the new product. Management corrected the problem by speeding up production and delaying the introduction of Sensor in Europe.

Internal Strategy-Structure Fit

It is important that the organization's competitive and marketing strategy be compatible with the internal structure of the business and its policies, procedures, and resources.[6] Several internal factors that may impact the implementation of marketing strategy are shown in Exhibit 17–4. These factors include higher-level corporate and business strategies, SBU and corporate relationships (e.g., extent of autonomy), the SBU's internal organization structure and coordination mechanisms, and the specific actions programmed in the marketing plan.

Coping with the influence of these factors on marketing strategy implementation requires close coordination of the strategies at the four levels shown in Exhibit 17–4. The marketing plans must be compatible with this internal structure. Otherwise, implementation and performance are constrained. For example, a major objective of the marketing-planning process of the pharmaceutical company discussed earlier is to communicate and respond to issues and concerns at these four levels. Similarly, the earlier Planning Feature highlights a CEO's methods of achieving a good strategy-structure fit.

Integrating Marketing throughout the Organization

Encouraging and facilitating a marketing orientation throughout the business is an important responsibility of marketing management. The chief executive officer of a large transportation services company states that the marketing and operations functions are the customer-service components of the firm, and that the role of accounting, finance, human resources, and information systems is to support the two operating components of the business. He emphasizes that the supporting functions are evaluated on the basis of how effectively they meet the needs of marketing and operations. Since the entire organization is concerned with delivering customer satisfaction, this CEO's operating philosophy encourages (and rewards) a customer-driven approach throughout the organization.

EXHIBIT 17–4 Factors Affecting the Implementation of Business and Marketing Strategies

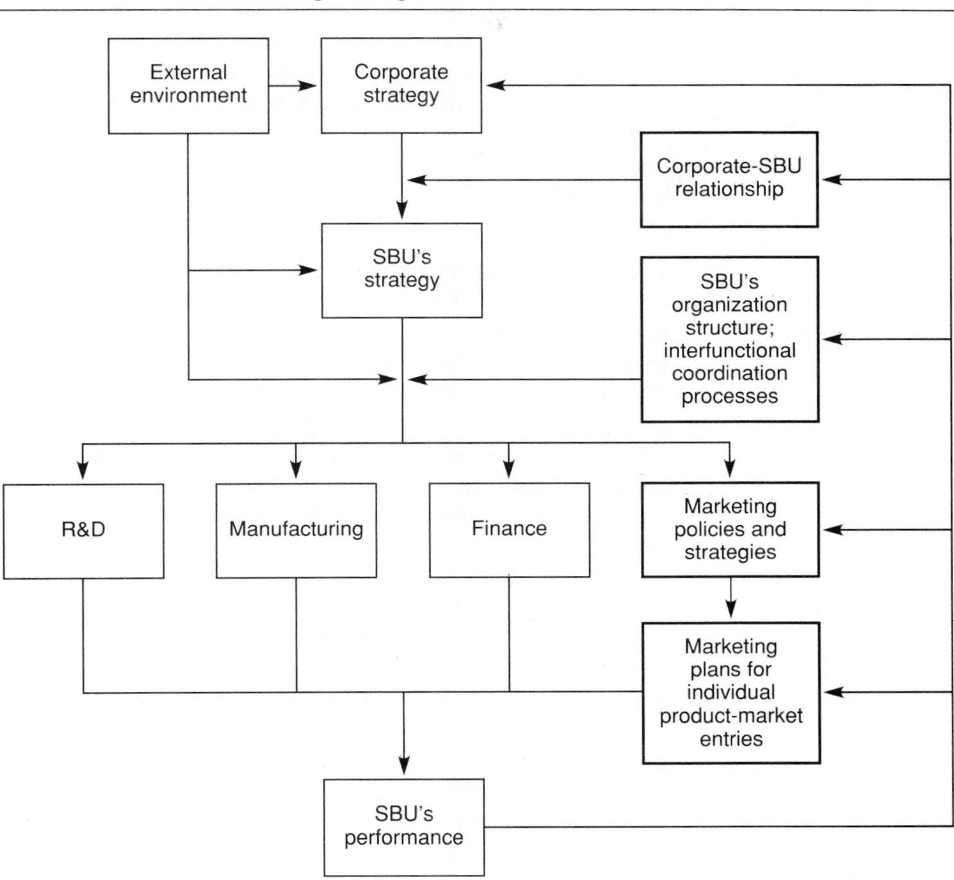

Source: Harper W. Boyd, Jr., and Orville C. Walker, Jr., *Marketing Management* (Homewood, Ill.: Richard D. Irwin, 1990), p. 826.

The Customer Is First. A key issue in developing a marketing perspective throughout an organization is convincing every employee that customer satisfaction is his or her responsibility. Training programs are used to achieve this objective. The starting point is getting the entire management team to recognize its role and responsibility for market-oriented leadership. Customer advisory groups are sometimes used in developing an internal awareness about the importance of the marketplace. Multifunctional (e.g., finance, marketing, operations) task forces may also be helpful integrating methods.

The characteristics and culture of an organization effect developing a marketing orientation in the business. Small companies achieve this integration more easily than large, multilayered corporations. The corporate culture may aid or constrain marketing integration. Managers of nonmarketing functions must be encouraged to recognize the importance of meeting customer needs through their activities. A strong commitment and active participation by the chief executive officer are essential to integrate marketing into the thinking and actions of everyone in the firm. Lee Iacocca has played an active role in integrating marketing into Chrysler's organizational units.

The Role of External Organizations. The implementation of marketing strategy is affected by external organizations such as marketing research firms, marketing consultants, advertising and public relations firms, channel members, and other organizations participating in the marketing effort. These outside organizations present a major coordination challenge when they actively participate in marketing activites. Their efforts should be identified in the marketing plan and their roles and responsibilities clearly established and communicated. There is a potential danger in not informing outside groups of planned actions, deadlines, and other implementation requirements. For example, the organization's advertising agency account executive and other agency staff members need to be familiar with all aspects of promotion strategy as well as with the major aspects of marketing strategy (e.g., market targets, positioning strategy, and marketing-mix component strategies). Withholding information from participating firms hampers their efforts in strategy planning and implementation.

The development of collaborative relationships between suppliers and producers improves implementation. Total quality improvement programs encourage reducing the number of suppliers and building strong relationships (see Chapter 3). Companies that are effective in working with other organizations are likely to also do a good job with implementation inside the organization, since they have skills in developing effective working relationships. Total quality programs also encourage internal teamwork among functions.

STRATEGIC EVALUATION AND CONTROL

Marketing strategy has to be responsive to changing conditions. After it is implemented, evaluation and control keep the strategy on target and show when adjustments are needed. The competitive pressures on Japan Air Lines (JAL) highlight the importance of control.[7] JAL lost over 13 billion yen in fiscal 1992. Intense price competition and high operating costs squeezed out profits. JAL has the highest operating costs of all Asian airlines, and on a global basis JAL's costs are near the top. Staff reductions are used by other airlines to lower costs, but JAL's six powerful unions and Japan's stable employment culture make layoffs difficult. JAL's chairman believes that the U.S. carriers are too powerful, and this places JAL at a competitive disadvantage. Nevertheless, JAL faces major pressures for lowering costs and developing strategies for competing in the 1990s. Other carriers, including American Airlines, KLM Royal Dutch Airlines, British Airways, and Iberia Airlines of Spain, have made substantial staff reductions, as well as establishing stragetic alliances with other airlines. The relentless pursuit of cost reductions through strategy adjustments is a reality for competing in the 1990s.

Strategic evaluation requires information for gauging performance and then taking the actions necessary to keep results on track. Marketing executives need to continually monitor performance and, when necessary, revise their strategies because of changing conditions. Strategic evaluation, the last stage in the marketing strategy process, is really the starting point. Strategic marketing planning requires information from ongoing monitoring and performance evaluation. We delayed discussion of strategic evaluation until now in order to first consider the strategic areas that require evaluation and to identify the kinds of information needed for assessing marketing performance. Thus, the first 16 chapters offer an essential foundation for building the strategic evaluation program.

Overview of Evaluation Activities

Evaluation of marketing activities and results is essential to keeping performance in line with objectives. Evaluation consumes a high proportion of marketing executives' time and energy. Evaluation may seek to (1) find new opportunities or avoid threats, (2) keep performance in line with management's expectations, and/or (3) solve specific problems. Areas of evaluation include environmental scanning, product-market analysis, marketing program evaluation, and gauging the effectiveness of specific marketing-mix components such as advertising.

These are illustrations of the three types of evaluation. An example of a threat identified via product-market analysis is the shift away from wearing suits and more formal business attire toward sporty clothing. These changes in preferences are major threats for companies like Hartmarx, which produces several brands of men's suits. The Japan Air Lines example shows the importance of keeping performance on track. Evaluating the effectiveness of alternative TV commercials is an example of problem solving in decision making.

The major steps in establishing the strategic evaluation program are shown in Exhibit 17–5. Strategic and short-term marketing plans set the direction and guidelines for the evaluation and control process. A strategic marketing audit is often conducted when setting up an evaluation program. Next, performance standards, measures, and information needs are

EXHIBIT 17–5 The Strategic Marketing Evaluation and Control Process

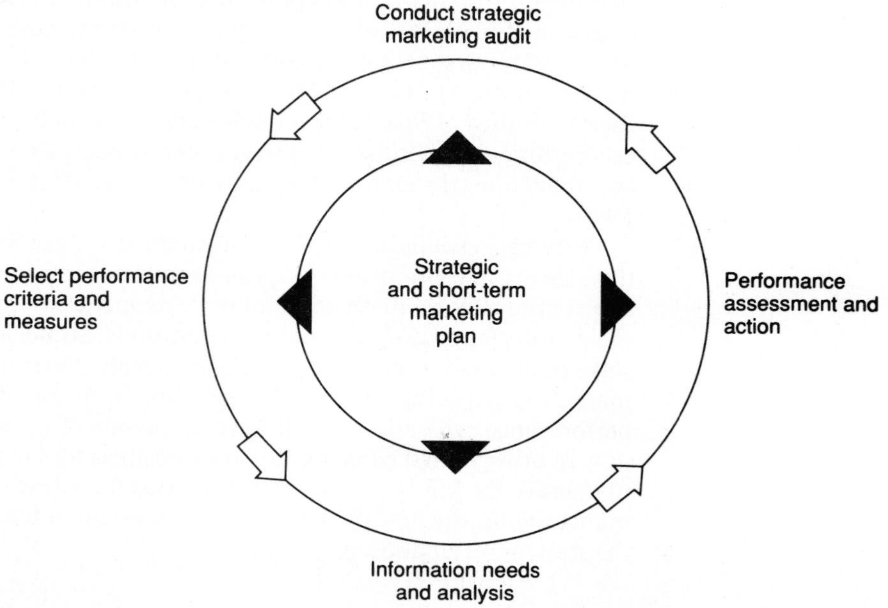

determined, followed by analysis of evaluation-and-control information and performance-gap identification. Actions are initiated to pursue opportunities or avoid threats, keep performance on track, or solve a particular decision-making problem.

Supermarket monitoring of buyers' purchases is an important information source for evaluating the marketing program effectiveness of food and health and beauty products. For example, sales data indicate that displays pay off for grocery marketers.[8] The use of frozen dinner displays increased sales by 245 percent during the 13 weeks ending in September 1992 (according to Information Resources Inc.'s InfoScan service). Other products benefiting from display promotion include laundry detergent, snack foods, and soft drinks. The companies with large percentages of volume sold on display in 1992 are shown in Exhibit 17–6.

The Strategic Marketing Audit

A marketing audit is useful when initiating a strategic evaluation program. Since evaluation compares results with expectations, it is necessary to lay some groundwork before setting up a tracking program. This complete

EXHIBIT 17–6 Manufacturers' Supermarket Volume Sold on Display (percentage of total unit sales during 52 weeks ending September 13, 1992)

	Percentage of Manufacturer's Volume Sold on Display
Pepsi-Cola	61.6%
Dr Pepper/Seven-Up	48.8
Frito-Lay	36.8
Eagle Snacks	33.8
Keebler	32.6
Ft. Howard Paper	32.0
Nabisco Biscuit	30.1
Georgia-Pacific	29.7
Tetley	29.7
Ocean Spray Cranberries	28.2
Anheuser-Busch	27.8
Sunshine Biscuits	27.8
Miller Brewing	26.8
Coca-Cola	25.0
Mars	25.0

Source: Kathleen Devency, "Market Scam," *The Wall Street Journal,* October 15, 1992, pp. B1, B5; from Information Resources Inc.

review and assessment of marketing operations is similar to the situation analysis discussed in Part II. However, the marketing audit goes beyond customer and competitive analysis to include all aspects of marketing operations. The audit is larger in scope than the situation analysis and is a more complete review of marketing strategy and performance. The audit can be used to initiate a formal strategic marketing planning program; it then may be repeated on a periodic basis. Normally, the situation analysis is part of the annual updating of marketing plans. The marketing audit is conducted less frequently. Auditing intervals may span three to five years.

A guide to conducting the strategic marketing audit is shown in Exhibit 17–7. It can be adapted to meet the needs of a particular firm. For example, if a company or business unit does not use indirect channels of distribution, this section of the audit guide will require adjustment. Likewise, if the sales force is the major part of a marketing program, then we expand this section to include other aspects of sales force strategy. The items included in the audit correspond to the strategic marketing plan because the main purpose of the audit is to appraise the effectiveness of strategic marketing operations. The audit guide includes several questions about marketing performance. The answers to these questions are incorporated into the design of the strategic tracking program.

Beyond deciding what should be audited, other aspects of conducting the audit are important.[9]

Conducting the audit. Some authorities advocate use of company personnel, while others suggest outside consultants. A combination

EXHIBIT 17–7 Guide to Conducting the Strategic Marketing Audit

I. CORPORATE MISSION AND OBJECTIVES
- A. Does the mission statement offer a clear guide to the product-markets of interest to the firm?
- B. Have objectives been established for the corporation?
- C. Is information available for the review of corporate progress toward objectives, and are the reviews conducted on a regular (quarterly, monthly, etc.) basis?
- D. Has corporate strategy been successful in meeting objectives?
- E. Are opportunities or problems pending that may require altering marketing strategy?
- F. What are the responsibilities of the chief marketing executive in corporate strategic planning?

II. BUSINESS COMPOSITION AND STRATEGIES
- A. What is the composition of the business (business segments, strategic planning units, and specific product-markets)?
- B. Have business strength and product-market attractiveness analyses been conducted for each planning unit? What are the results of the analyses?
- C. What is the corporate strategy for each planning unit (e.g., develop, stabilize, turnaround, or harvest)?
- D. What objectives are assigned to each planning unit?
- E. Does each unit have a strategic plan?
- F. For each unit what objectives and responsibilities have been assigned to marketing?

III. MARKETING STRATEGY (FOR EACH PLANNING UNIT)
- A. Strategic planning and marketing:
  1. Is marketing's role and responsibility in corporate strategic planning clearly specified?
  2. Are responsibility and authority for marketing strategy assigned to one executive?
  3. How well is the firm's marketing strategy working?
  4. Are changes likely to occur in the corporate/marketing environment that may affect the firm's marketing strategy?
  5. Are there major contingencies that should be included in the strategic marketing plan?
- B. Marketing planning and organizational structure:
  1. Are annual and longer range strategic marketing plans developed, and are they being used?
  2. Are the responsibilities of the various units in the marketing organization clearly specified?
  3. What are the strengths and limitations of the key members of the marketing organization? What is being done to develop people? What gaps in experience and capabilities exist on the marketing staff?
  4. Is the organizational structure for marketing effective for implementing marketing plans?
- C. Market target strategy:
  1. Has each market target been clearly defined and its importance to the firm established?
  2. Have demand, industry, and competition in each market target been analyzed and key trends, opportunities, and threats identified?
  3. Has the proper market target strategy been adopted?
  4. Should repositioning or exit from any product-market be considered?
- D. Objectives:
  1. Are objectives established for each market target, and are these consistent with planning unit objectives and the available resources? Are the objectives realistic?
  2. Are sales, cost, and other performance information available for monitoring the progress of planned performance against actual results?
  3. Are regular appraisals made of marketing performance?
  4. Where do gaps exist between planned and actual results? What are the probable causes of the performance gaps?
- E. Marketing program positioning strategy:
  1. Does the firm have an integrated positioning strategy made up of product, channel, price, advertising, and sales force strategies? Is the role selected for each mix element consistent with the overall program objectives, and does it properly complement other mix elements?
  2. Are adequate resources available to carry out the marketing program? Are resources committed to market targets according to the importance of each?
  3. Are allocations to the various marketing mix components too low, too high, or about right in terms of what each is expected to accomplish?
  4. Is the effectiveness of the marketing program appraised on a regular basis?

EXHIBIT 17–7 Concluded

IV. MARKETING PROGRAM ACTIVITIES

A. Product strategy:
   1. Is the product mix geared to the needs and preferences that the firm wants to meet in each product-market?
   2. What branding strategy is beins used?
   3. Are products properly positioned against competing brands?
   4. Does the firm have a sound approach to product planning and management, and is marketing involved in product decisions?
   5. Are additions to, modifications of, or deletions from the product mix needed to make the firm more competitive in the marketplace?
   6. Is the performance of each product evaluated on a regular basis?

B. Channel of distribution strategy:
   1. Has the firm selected the type (conventional or vertically coordinated) and intensity of distribution appropriate for each of its product-markets?
   2. How well does each channel access its market target? Is an effective channel configuration being used?
   3. Are channel organizations carrying out their assigned functions properly?
   4. How is the channel of distribution being managed? What improvements are needed?
   5. Are desired customer service levels being reached, and are the costs of doing this acceptable?

C. Price strategy:
   1. How responsive is each market target to price variations?
   2. What role and objectives does price have in the marketing mix?
   3. Should price play an active or passive role in program positioning strategy?
   4. How do the firm's price strategy and tactics compare to those of competition?
   5. Is a logical approach used to establish prices?
   6. Are there indications that changes may be needed in price strategy or tactics?

D. Advertising and sales promotion strategies:
   1. Have a role and objectives been established for advertising and sales promotion in the marketing mix?
   2. Is the creative strategy consistent with the positioning strategy that is being used?
   3. Is the budget adequate to carry out the objectives assigned to advertising and sales promotion?
   4. Do the media and programming strategies represent the most cost-effective means of communicating with market targets?
   5. Do advertising copy and content effectively communicate the intended messages?
   6. How well does the advertising program measure up in meeting its objectives?

E. Sales force strategy:
   1. Are the role and objectives of personal selling in the marketing program positioning strategy clearly specified and understood by the sales organization?
   2. Do the qualifications of salespeople correspond to their assigned roles?
   3. Is the sales force of the proper size to carry out its function, and is it efficiently deployed?
   4. Are sales force results in line with management's expectations?
   5. Is each salesperson assigned performance targets, and are incentives offered to reward performance?
   6. Are compensation levels and ranges competitive?

V. IMPLEMENTATION AND MANAGEMENT

A. Have the causes of all performance gaps been identified?

B. Is implementation of planned actions taking place as intended? Is implementation being hampered by marketing or other functional areas of the firm (e.g., operations, finance)?

C. Has the strategic audit revealed areas requiring additional study before action is taken?

approach offers the advantages of both company and external experience, capabilities, and perspectives. Objectivity and professional expertise are two key prerequisites in selecting an individual or team to plan and conduct the audit.

Planning the audit. Depending on the size and scope of the business unit, attention needs to be given to planning the areas to be audited, defining the scope of audit operations, scheduling activities, coordinating participation, and indicating desired results. Auditing costs and expected benefits should be estimated and priorities set regarding various aspects of the audit program.

Using the findings. The results of the audit should help improve strategic performance. Opportunities and problems that are identified should be incorporated into strategic plans. If nothing happens as a result of the audit, it may not have been needed.

There are other reasons for conducting a strategic marketing audit. Corporate restructuring may bring about a complete review of strategic marketing operations. Major shifts in business activities such as entry into new product and market areas or acquisitions may require strategic marketing audits.

PERFORMANCE CRITERIA AND INFORMATION NEEDS

The next two stages in the evaluation and control process (Exhibit 17–5) are (1) selecting the performance criteria and the measures to be used for monitoring performance and (2) identifying the information management needs to perform various marketing control activities.

Selecting Performance Criteria and Measures

As the marketing plans are developed, performance criteria are selected to monitor performance. Specifying the information needed for marketing decision making is important and requires management's concentrated attention. In the past, marketing executives could develop and manage successful marketing strategies by relying on intuition, judgment, and experience. Successful executives of the 1990s are using judgment and experience with information and decision support systems (Chapter 8). These information systems are becoming increasingly important in gaining a strategic edge in industries such as airline services, direct marketing, packaged foods, wholesaling, retailing, and financial services.

Objectives state the results that management is seeking and also serve as the basis for evaluating the strategy's success. Objectives set standards of performance. Progress toward the objectives in the strategic and short-term plans is monitored on a continuing basis. In addition to information on objectives, management requires other kinds of feedback for use in performance evaluation. Some of this information is incorporated into regular tracking activities (e.g., the effectiveness of advertising expenditures). Other information is obtained as the need arises, such as a special study of consumer preferences about different liquid-diet brands.

A study of sales organization effectiveness illustrates several measures of performance.[10] A comparison of over 100 sales organizations is shown in Exhibit 17–8. The companies are divided into those that are more and less effective, based on subjective ratings by the chief sales executive in each company. The comparisons show several differences in effectiveness between the two groups of companies. The hallmarks of the more effective sales organizations found in the study include: (1) building long-term relationships with customers; (2) creating right-sized sales organizations (proper size and effort allocation); (3) effective coaching of salespeople by field managers; (4) agreeing on the success characteristics of salespeople; (5) compensating salespeople with the proper blend of salary and incentives; and (6) achieving high sales force performance on sales results, sales presentations, and product knowledge.

Examples of performance criteria are discussed in several chapters. They should be selected for the total plan and its important components. Illustrative criteria for total performance include sales, market share, profit, expense, and customer satisfaction targets (Exhibit 17–8). Brand-positioning analyses may also be useful in tracking position relative to key competitors. These measures can be used to gauge overall performance and for specific market targets. Performance criteria are also needed for the marketing-mix components. For example, new-customer and lost-customer tracking is often included in sales force performance monitoring. Pricing performance monitoring may include comparisons of actual to list prices, extent of discounting, and profit contribution. Many possible performance criteria can be selected. Management must identify the key measures that will show how the firm's marketing strategy is performing in its competitive environment and where changes are needed.

Determining Information Needs

The costs of acquiring, processing, and analyzing information are high, so the potential benefits of needed information must be compared to costs. Normally, information falls into two categories: (1) information regularly supplied to marketing management from internal and external sources, and (2) information obtained as needed for a particular problem or situation. Examples of the former are sales and cost analyses, market share measurements, and customer satisfaction surveys. Information from the latter category includes new-product concept tests, brand-preference studies, and studies of advertising effectiveness.

Several types of information are needed by management (see Chapter 8).

EXHIBIT 17–8 Sales Organization Effectiveness Comparisons

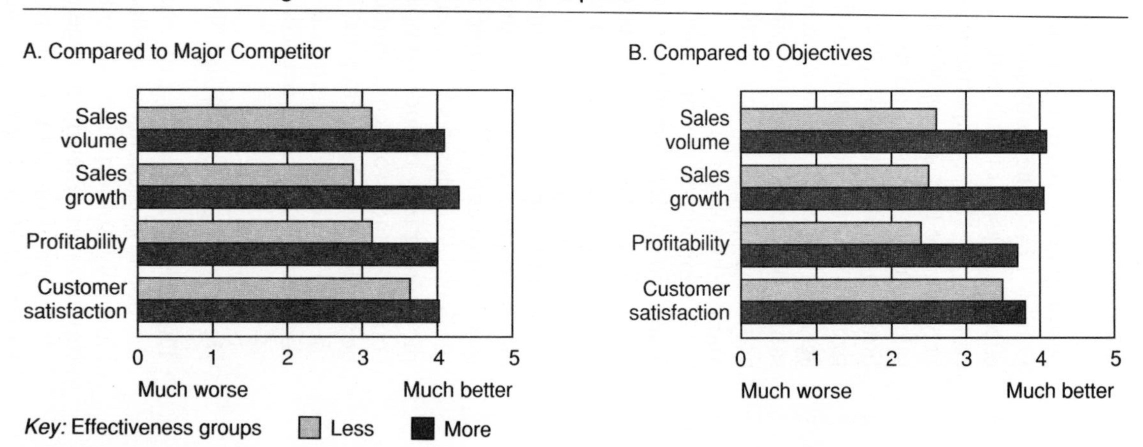

Source: David W. Cravens, Thomas M. Ingram, Raymond W. LaForge, and Clifford E. Young, "Hallmarks of Effective Sales Organizations," *Marketing Management,* Winter 1992, p. 59.

EXHIBIT 17–9 Shrinking Liquid-Diet Brands sales and market shares in supermarkets, drugstores and mass-merchandise outlets for the 13-week period ended September 20, 1992)

	Sales ($ million)	*% Change vs. Year Earlier*	*Current Market Share*
Ultra Slim-Fast	51.6	−45%	70.5%
Slim-Fast	9.6	−54	13.2
Ultra Slim-Fast Plus*	5.4	—	7.4
DynaTrim	2.8	−65	3.8
Figurine 100	1.4	−23	1.9
Carnation Slender	1.1	−28	1.6
Sego	0.6	−25	0.9
Total	73.3	−44%	100.0%

*New brand

Source: Kathleen Deveny, "Market Scam," *The Wall Street Journal,* October 13, 1992, pp. B1, B10; from Information Resources Inc.

Information for strategic planning and evaluation can be obtained as part of the following information-acquisition activities:

1. The *internal information system* is the backbone of any strategic evaluation program. These systems range from primarily sales and cost reports to highly sophisticated computerized marketing information systems.
2. *Standardized information services* are available by subscription or on a one-time basis, often at a fraction of the cost of preparing such information for a single firm. Nevertheless, these services are expensive. Standardized services are available in both printed form and in data files for computer analysis. Nielsen's TV rating data service is an example.
3. Marketing managers may require *special research studies.* A study of distributor opinions concerning a manufacturer's services is an example.
4. The firm's *strategic intelligence system* is concerned with monitoring and forecasting external, uncontrollable factors that influence the firm's product-markets. These efforts range from formal information activities to informal surveillance of the marketing environment. (See Chapter 7.)

Standardized data services are important information sources in several product categories such as foods, drugs, and other packaged goods. Information Resources, Inc. is one of the leading suppliers of this information. An example of IRI's InfoScan service is shown in Exhibit 17–9. Interestingly, the sales of most liquid-diet brands declined significantly in 1992.[11]

Dieters apparently became disillusioned with liquid meals, perhaps due to alternative foods for weight loss. For example, diet microwave food sales increased during the same period. In 1990 liquid diets were the top seller in weight control. Services like InfoScan track sales, market share, customer demographics, and other information on a regular basis during the year. IRI's information is obtained from 2,700 supermarkets, 500 drugstores, and 250 mass-merchandise outlets, selected to represent the national marketplace. Transactions are recorded by universal product code with scanners connected to cash registers. IRI monitors 45 million transactions each week.

PERFORMANCE ASSESSMENT AND ACTION

The last stage in the marketing evaluation and control process is determining how the actual results compare with planned results. When performance gaps are too large, corrective actions are taken. For example, the large decline in liquid-diet sales (Exhibit 17–9) triggered pricing cuts and advertising increases by the companies competing in this market.

Opportunities and Performance Gaps

Strategic evaluation activities seek to (1) identify opportunities or performance gaps and (2) initiate actions to take advantage of the opportunities or to correct existing and pending problems. Strategic intelligence, internal reporting and analysis activities, standardized information services, and research studies supply the information needed by marketing decision makers.

The real test of the value of the marketing information system is whether it helps marketing management to identify problems. In monitoring, there are two critical factors to take into account:

Problem/opportunity definition. Strategic analysis should lead to a clear explanation of an opportunity or problem, since this will be needed to guide whatever strategic action may be taken. Often it is easy to confuse problem symptoms with problem causes.

Interpreting information. Management must also separate normal variations in performance from significant gaps in performance, since the latter are the ones that require strategic action. For example, how much of a drop in market share is necessary to signal a performance problem? Limits need to be set on the acceptable range of strategic performance.

No matter how extensive the information system may be, it cannot interpret the strategic importance of the information. This is the responsibility of management.

EXHIBIT 17–10 Planning Guidelines, Metropolitan Life Insurance Company

COMPARING THE PERFORMANCE WITH THE PLAN

Each person, to do a satisfactory job, must achieve his or her portion of the plan. And this is where the concept of control fits in. This section discusses:

1. The general principles underlying the process of management control.
2. The Performance Reports we use to implement control.

THE PROCESS OF MANAGEMENT CONTROL

Simply defined, the process of management control consists of seeing that everything is being carried out in accordance with the plans that have been adopted. From this definition, it follows that the primary purpose of the control process is to isolate *variances* from plan so that they can be analyzed, to determine their significance, and to take corrective action as needed.

This does not mean that *variances* from plan are necessarily bad. It simply means that *variances* should be the basis for analysis to determine: (1) whether the *variance* should be accepted as a sound and desirable departure from our plan, (2) whether the *variance* is unavoidable and therefore should serve to sharpen future planning, or (3) whether a different course of action should be taken, such as refocusing of effort or increasing the amount of effort.

The three primary control tools

Control is exercised in a variety of ways, but there are three basic tools or mechanisms which underlie the process.

1. *Pre-approval of proposed courses of action.* This form of control is implemented by the use of our marketing plan procedure. For example, one of the items we plan is the creation and abolishment of districts in various areas. The effect of such planning is to establish control over changes that will actually be made in the number and location of our districts.
2. *Direct observation.* This is the basic day-to-day control technique used at the district level. It takes the form of the face-to-face supervision and guidance that district management provides the field force.
3. *Analysis of formal performance reports and taking required action.* The key control tool of management is the set of performance reports that each manager receives indicating his/her subordinates' performance versus plan. These reports provide the basis for identifying and analyzing *variances* and for taking corrective action as required.

Performance reports

The primary purpose of performance reports are:

1. To show the *net effect* of many day-to-day decisions and developments.
2. To provide a check on the adequacy of front-line controls.
3. To provide a means of continuously motivating down-the-line personnel to take objectives and action programs seriously.
4. To serve as a further stimulus to continuous sharpening of the planning process.

From all of the above, it follows that performance reports by themselves represent only one aspect of the total control process. Nevertheless, they are an indispensable aspect of the control system, since they provide the basis for evaluating and planning management action.

Source: David S. Hopkins, *The Marketing Plan,* Report No. 801 (New York: The Conference Board, Inc., 1981), p. 127.

Exhibit 17–10 describes how the Metropolitan Life Insurance Company links the control function to planning. Management recognizes that gaps occur between desired and actual results. The guidelines emphasize looking at the causes of variances. The description of the three primary control tools highlights what information is used for comparing performance with the plan. Finally, the role of performance reporting in the company's overall planning and control process is indicated.

Determining Normal and Abnormal Variability

Variability is inherent in everything that occurs in the world. Operating results such as sales, market share, profits, order-processing time, and customer satisfaction display normal up-and-down fluctuations. The issue is determining whether these variations represent random variation or instead are the result of special causes. For example, if a salesperson's sales over time remain within a normal band of variation, then the results are acceptable under the present operating conditions. Random high and low variations do not indicate unusually high or low performance. If this range of performance is *not* acceptable to management, then the system must be changed. This may require salesperson training, redesign of the territory, improvement in sales support, or other changes in the salesperson's operating system.

Statistical process-control concepts and methods are useful in determining when operating results are fluctuating normally or instead are out of control.[12] Quality-control charts can be used to analyze and improve results in marketing performance measures such as the number of orders processed, customer complaints, and territory sales. Control-chart analysis indicates when the process is experiencing normal variation and when the process is out of control.

The basic approach to control-chart analysis is to establish average and upper and lower control limits for the measure being evaluated. Examples of measures include order-processing time, district sales, customer complaints, and market share. Control boundaries are set using historical data. Future measures are plotted on the chart to determine whether the results are under control or instead fall outside the acceptable performance band determined by the upper and lower control limits. The objective is continually improving the process that determines the results.

Deciding What Actions to Take

Many corrective actions are possible, depending on the situation. One objective of this book is to provide a process for selecting strategic actions based upon the opportunity or problem at hand. Management's actions may include exiting from a product-market, new-product planning, changing the target-market strategy, adjusting marketing strategy, or improving efficiency.

An illustration shows how evaluation and control guide corrective action. Deere & Company, the giant farm equipment producer, had a strong performance record during the agricultural slump of the 1980s.[13] Management invested in product and process research, reduced employment, and cut costs. Monitoring of performance indicated the need to take further corrective action in 1989. The industry shakeout of the 1980s weakened farmers' brand loyalty and created two strong competitors. Deere was losing customers that had been buying the popular green farm equipment for three generations. The nation's 2.2 million farmers were making money and buying equipment, but Deere purchases had been drastically curtailed during the early 1980s.

The J. I. Case unit of Tenneco is the number two firm in the U.S. market, strengthened by acquisitions of International Harvester and Steiger Tractor. Case had 1989 global farm equipment sales of $2.9 billion, compared to Deere's $4.1 billion. The number three competitor is the Ford Motor Company with sales of $2.3 billion. Both firms are fighting Deere for top position in the $8 billion-a-year domestic market. Farmers' purchases are heavily influenced by equipment quality, price, and dealer service. Competitors are beginning to penetrate Deere's loyal customer base with high-quality equipment, aggressive selling, and dealer support.

Deere has a reputation for high-quality products. Its greatest edge is its 1,700-dealer U.S. network. To strengthen its advantage, Deere's factory employees are phoning or visiting farmers who have purchased Deere products. Service teams are deployed to the field for troubleshooting during heavy equipment-usage periods such as harvesting. Continued investment in new and improved products is planned for the 1990s. Competitors are challenging Deere with requests for equipment comparisons. This battle for position in farm equipment promises to be an interesting marketing challenge in the decade ahead.

Managing in a changing environment is what strategic marketing is all about. Keeping up with and even anticipating change is the essence of marketing evaluation and control. Executives develop innovative marketing strategies and monitor their effectiveness, altering the strategies as a result of changing conditions.

SUMMARY

Marketing strategy implementation and control are vital links in a series of strategic marketing activities. These actions emphasize the continuing process of planning, implementing, evaluating, and adjusting marketing strategies. Strategic evaluation of marketing performance is the first step in strategic marketing planning and the last step after launching a strategy. The objective is to develop an approach to strategic evaluation, building on the concepts, processes, and methods discussed in Chapters 1 through 16. Strategic evaluation is one of marketing management's most demanding and time-consuming responsibilities. While the activity lacks the glamour and excitement of new strategy development, perceptive evaluation often separates the winners from the losers. The management of successful companies anticipate and respond effectively to changing conditions and pressures. Regular strategic evaluation processes guide these responses.

Marketing strategy implementation and control are guided by the marketing plan and budget (Exhibit 17–1). The plan indicates the activities to be accomplished, how this is to be done, and the costs. The planning process moves into action through the annual marketing plan. It shows the activities to be implemented, responsibilities, deadlines, and expectations. Implementation (Exhibit 17–3) makes the plan happen.

Much of the actual work of managing involves strategic and tactical evaluation of marketing options. Yet performing this function depends greatly on management's understanding of the planning process and the decisions that form plans. Strategic evaluation is a continuing cycle of making plans, launching them, tracking performance, identifying performance gaps, and initiating problem-solving actions. In accomplishing strategic evaluation, management must select performance criteria and measures and then set up a tracking program to obtain the information needed to guide evaluation activities. As an initial step in the strategic evaluation program (and periodically thereafter), the strategic marketing audit provides a useful basis for developing the program.

It is so easy for practicing managers to become preoccupied with day-to-day activities, neglecting to step back and review overall operations. Regular audits and continuous monitoring of the market and competitive environment can prevent sudden shocks and can alert management to new opportunities. Building on findings from the strategic marketing audit, the chapter examines the major steps in acquiring and using information for strategic analysis. While the execution of the steps varies by situation, they offer a useful framework for guiding a strategic evaluation program in any type of firm. An important part of this process is setting standards for gauging marketing performance. These standards help determine what information is needed to monitor performance.

QUESTIONS FOR REVIEW AND DISCUSSION

1. Discuss the similarities and differences between strategic marketing *planning* and *evaluation.*

2. Establishing a strategic evaluation program involves a series of activities. Beginning with selecting performance criteria and measures, indicate which executives (type of position) and marketing specialists should be responsible for each step.

3. Selecting the proper performance criteria for use in tracking results is a key part of a strategic evaluation program. Suggest performance criteria for use by a fast-food retail chain to monitor strategic marketing performance.

4. What justification is there for conducting a marketing audit in a business unit whose marketing performance has been very good? Discuss.

5. Examination of the various areas of a strategic marketing audit shown in Exhibit 17–7 would be quite expensive and time-consuming. Are there any ways to limit the scope of the audit?

6. Several kinds of information are collected for a strategic marketing evaluation. Develop a list of information that would be useful for a strategic evaluation in a life insurance company.

7. One of the more difficult management control issues is determining whether a process is experiencing normal variation or is actually out of control. Discuss how management can resolve this issue.

8. How frequently should a marketing manager evaluate the market share of the firm's brands to determine if the brands are performing well against competition? Discuss.

NOTES

1. This account is based on Barry Kramer, "Master Merchants: Japanese Dominate the Chinese Market with Savvy Trading," *The Wall Street Journal,* November 18, 1985, pp. 1 and 10.
2. Donald R. Lehmann and Russell S. Winer, *Analysis for Marketing Planning,* 2nd ed. (Homewood, Ill.: Richard D. Irwin, 1991), pp. 10–13.
3. Ibid., pp. 4–7.
4. "Cultural Change: Pressed by Its Rivals, Procter & Gamble Co. Is Altering Its Ways," *The Wall Street Journal,* May 20, 1985, pp. 1 and 16.
5. Thomas V. Bonoma, "Making Your Marketing Strategy Work," *Harvard Business Review,* March–April 1984, p. 75.
6. This discussion is based on Harper W. Boyd, Jr., and Orville C. Walker, Jr., *Marketing Management* (Homewood, Ill.: Richard D. Irwin, 1990), pp. 824–25.
7. Yumiko Ono and Susan Carey, "Japan Air Lines Is Struggling to Come Down to Earth," *The Wall Street Journal,* September 22, 1992, p. B4.
8. Kathleen Deveny, "Market Scam," *The Wall Street Journal,* October 15, 1992, pp. B1, B5.
9. See, for example, Dr. Ernst A. Tirmann, "Should Your Marketing Be Audited?" *European Business,* Autumn 1971, pp. 49–56.
10. David W. Cravens, Thomas M. Ingram, Raymond W. LaForge, and Clifford E. Young, "Hallmarks of Effective Sales Organizations," *Marketing Management,* Winter 1992, pp. 56–67.
11. Deveny, "Market Scam," pp. B1, B10.
12. Kaori Ishikawa, *Guide to Quality Control* (Tokyo: Asian Productivity Organization, 1982).
13. This account is based on Robert L. Rose, "Tougher Row: Deere Faces Challenge Just When Farmers Are Shopping Again," *The Wall Street Journal,* February 8, 1990, pp. A1 and A6.

Cases for Part V

CASE 5–1 Lee Co.

For more than 50 years, the five-pocket blue jeans made by Lee Co. of Merriam, Kan., were the uniform of cowboys and farmhands.

Lee did a good, steady business, and that was enough to satisfy the dry-goods merchant Henry David Lee, who owned the company. But the once-stable jeans business has become extremely volatile, and the Lee brand has fallen on hard times. Today it is trying for a comeback.

In the 1960s of Bob Dylan and Vietnam, and even more so in the late '70s of designer jeans, Lee was riding high. The cotton denims, suddenly fashionable among women as well as men, crashed the gates of every American institution from high school to Studio 54.

Lee couldn't make pants fast enough. The company, which was acquired by VF Corp. in 1969, added new automated sewing plants and, in the '80s, laundries for stonewashing dungarees. The way Lee saw it, jeans were a permanent fixture, and the Lee name was spun gold.

But its vision proved myopic. In the early 1980s, the shrinking population of young people (age 12 to 24), the spreading body shapes of the older generation and the new popularity of sweat pants, warmup suits and khakis ended the boom. In 1989, only 387 million pairs of jeans were sold in the United States, down from 502 million in the peak year of 1981. After 1987, Lee experienced a two-year decline in U.S. jeans sales totaling 23 percent. VF had let inertia, not demand, steer the business.

Today, VF finally is aggressively trying to solve its Lee jeans problems, but the brand still is reeling.

Boom and bust left Lee with too many factories and too much unsold stock. In the past two years it has closed 10 plants while working down its inventory. To attract more retail business, Lee this year has also cut wholesale prices 5 to 9 percent.

The brand now must recapture luster lost to neglect, while such parvenus as Gitano, Guess, and private-label imports sold by Gap Inc. and other big retailers were cutting into the market. Lee is counting on the success of a new collection of casual pants, which are to be introduced in the fall—four long years after Lee's privately held rival, Levi Strauss Associates Inc., introduced its enormously successful Dockers brand. Lee also has to catch up in the thriving jeans markets overseas, where Levi, the inventor of blue jeans and ever the leader, has a beachhead.

Fourth quarter net income at Levi Strauss jumped 51.2 percent, to $75.3 million, boosted by international sales and strong demand for Dockers, which had 1990 sales of about $500 million.

While Lee continues to be a major force in the $6.3 billion U.S. jeans industry, second only to Levi, the brand's market share has slipped to about 10 percent. Fred Rowan, chief executive since 1989, figures it will take Lee two more years to accomplish "an architectural redesign" of its operations. "You can't get rid of your sins in six months," he says. All top executives in marketing, operations, and manufacturing have been replaced since 1989.

Meanwhile, Lee's parent, VF, is leaning on its other operations to keep shareholders happy. FV owns Wrangler, Rustler, and Girbaud jeanswear, all of which are in better shape than Lee; Vanity Fair lingerie; Jantzen sportswear, Red Kap uniforms; Bassett-Walker fleecewear (sweatshirts and such); and Health-Tex children's clothes.

On Feb. 12 VF announced a fourth-quarter net loss of $9.9 million, the result of, among other things, an $11.5 million restructuring charge from the Lee division and a $21 million provision for excess inventories at Lee. VF's jeanswear brands contributed some $1.4 billion of the $2.6 billion in sales. (Analysts estimate that Lee's sales account for about $600 million.)

Over the past two years, Lee's problems have cost VF some $100 million in profit, estimates Deborah Bronston, an analyst who follows the apparel stocks at Prudential Securities Inc.

In December, Standard and Poor's lowered VF's long-term debt ratings, cautioning that the extent of its progress on its turnaround "is still uncertain." S&P also cited softness in both retailing and the jeans market.

Just about everybody involved—stores, competitors, insiders—blames Lee's problems partly on VF and partly on the management of Lee. Critics say that VF ordered Lee to bolster corporate earnings by squeezing as much as it could from its basic jeans business while doing no long-term planning. Others say the Lee division itself was heavy with managers who had a "commodity mentality," meaning they would fill the retail pipeline with basic jeans and let retailers worry about how to sell them. "We had a management problem at Lee," says Lawrence Pugh, VF's chairman.

VF was just a lingerie company with annual sales of $69 million when it bought Lee in 1969, a year in which Lee had $87.5 million in sales. Lee could boast that it had outfitted World War I doughboys, dressed the actors on "Gunsmoke" and "The Beverly Hillbillies," and supplied the rodeo circuit. Then in 1972 Lee realized something that seemingly hadn't dawned on other big jeans makers: Women wanted jeans made for women, jeans that fit. Lee developed the Ms. Lee brand, and Lee today remains America's best-selling women's jeans. Its total jeans sales, men's and women's, doubled from 1972 to 1978 and grew another 70 percent between 1981 and 1985, even as the jeans industry overall was declining.

When jeans were the rage, Lee apparently gave little thought to anything other than boosting production. Lee jeans were in such demand that they sometimes were rationed to retail stores. But the company had a reputation for not servicing its retail accounts, of refusing, for example, to participate in cooperative ad campaigns with some stores.

"The managers at Lee were very conservative, they didn't encourage creativity, they wanted a safe output," says Kathy Ferguson, a former Lee vice president who left for Levi Strauss after 13 years.

As other jeans makers branched out into different styles, Lee clung to its basic Lee Rider, which Lee felt transcended faddishness. In 1978, Colonel Days, a chain of 34 midwestern jeans stores with headquarters in St. Louis, did 80 percent of its business in four different styles and three different brands—all in dark indigo, the traditional color of blue jeans. "As long as you could procure product, it was a 'no-brainer' when it came to selling," says Gary Krosch, the chain's president.

Today the chain carries eight brands and 40 styles (including baggy jeans that everybody calls "anti-fit") in a range of colors from black and white to every conceivable shade of blue down to the ultrapale "ice washed" denim.

As jeans sales flattened in the early 1980s, Lee made the tactical blunder of broadening its distribution to mass-market chains such as Bradlees and Target. Discounters at the same time were intent on replacing most of their private-label jeans with brand-name goods.

In a way, Lee's decision made sense. Mass merchants and discounters now sell more than a third of all jeans—more than specialty stores and department stores combined. Selling through discounters would, it was assumed, guarantee Lee an outlet. But the decision had unwanted effects.

"They figured they could grow their way out of the slump through production instead of trying to find ways to market fashion," says a former Lee sales executive.

Selling to discounters threw Lee into the hurly-burly competition with low-cost jeans importers like Gitano, which had a strong brand name and did a lot of advertising. Lee jeans were priced as much as 35 percent higher than other brands sold in discount stores, so, to move the merchandise, stores would mark down the jeans, at the expense of the stores' profit margins.

In a survey of discount-store shoppers by Leo J. Shapiro Associates, the top-selling brands in 1990 were Gitano, Sasson, Jordache, Hanes, and Chic. Lee, which had been the most popular brand in the same survey in 1989, fell to No. 21, as stores cut back on their orders of Lee jeans because the profit margins were slimmer.

When Lee started selling to discount chains, some department stores decided Lee was déclassé and dropped their pants in favor of higher priced and more popular brands, including Girbaud jeans, now also a VF brand. (Lee continues to do much of its business with J. C. Penney, Sears, and Montgomery Ward.) Meanwhile, Levi's jeans, priced higher and sold both by department stores and chains like The Gap, maintained their status.

"When the demand is down, everybody gets pickier, and a product with an OK image and an OK price will get squeezed out," says Robert Gregory, who was president of Lee in 1982 and 1983, then president of the parent, VF, from 1983 to 1990.

VF hit on another way as well to attempt to build market share, with its 1986 acquisition of Blue Bell Holdings Inc., the maker of Wrangler, Rustler, and Girbaud brand jeans. In buying Blue Bell, VF increased its domesitc jeans market share to about 27 percent, compared with Levi Strauss's 22 percent, according to MRCA Services Inc., apparel marketing consultants.

The acquisitions should have been good for Lee. Wrangler was a popular brand with adult men; Rustler was popular with budget retailers—Kmart and Wal-Mart, which Lee doesn't deign to sell to; Girbaud is aimed at people with deeper pockets. Wall Street analysts believed VF would benefit from the merger by combining operations, but it didn't do that. Instead, VF continued to operate Wrangler and Lee separately. "They were killing all of this with the duplicate staffs," recalls Josie Esquivel, an apparel-industry analyst at Shearson Lehman Brothers Inc.

While Lee was preoccupied with trying to reinvigorate jeans sales, it failed to notice an emerging trend. More older consumers—the so-called "broad-butt market"—preferred other types of trousers.

Christine Rogers, a 38-year-old computer programmer from Fort Lee, N.J., says that she didn't buy jeans last year. She prefers now to wear sweatpants and leggings. "Jeans just aren't a big deal for me anymore," she says.

VF actually had a head start in casual clothes when, in 1984, it acquired Troutman Industries Inc., the maker of Skeets casual pants. But making the pants cost too much to sell them at a profit, VF concluded, so it closed Troutman in 1986. VF's chairman, Mr. Pugh, now thinks the move may have been a mistake. "In retrospect, [the product] was right," he says. "Perhaps we didn't give it enough time."

In 1986, Levi Strauss introduced its Dockers casual pants—tailored styles with a more generous cut in the legs and hips. Retailers ordered so

EXHIBIT 1 VF Corp.: A Blue Jeans Market

Earnings Have Been Hurt . . .
Annual net income, in millions

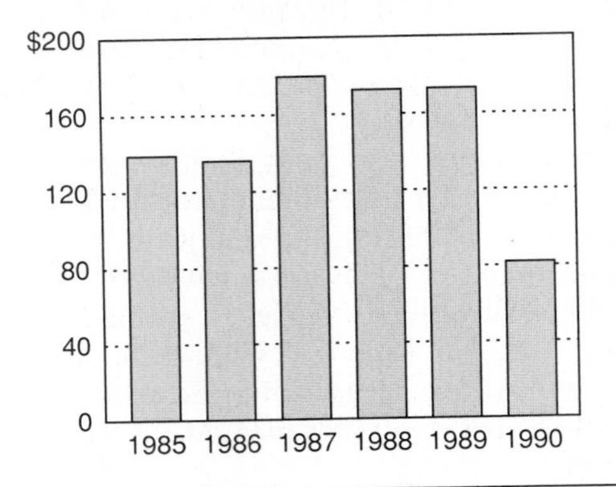

While Business Struggles . . .
Lines of business as a percent of 1990 revenue

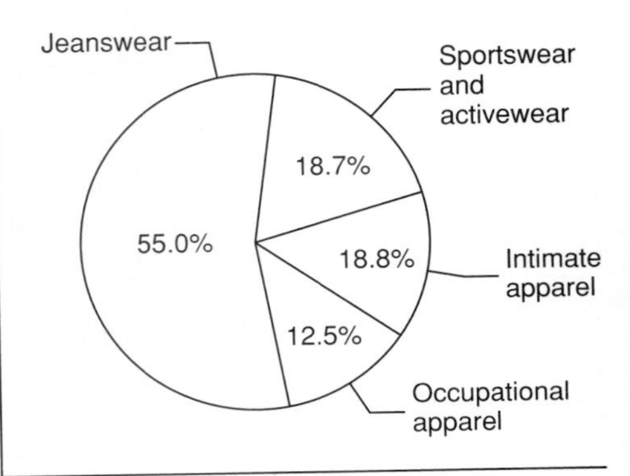

In a Fierce Market . . .
1990 U.S. market share of leading jeans brands, in percent

Levi Strauss	22.0
Lee*	10.0
Rustler*	9.5
Wrangler*	5.5
Gitano	3.7
Chic	2.5
Other	46.9

*Owned by VF Corp.
Source: Prudential Securities Inc. estimates

And the Stock Lags.
Comparison of VF Corp. stock and DJ Textile and Apparel index, Dec. 29, 1989 = 100

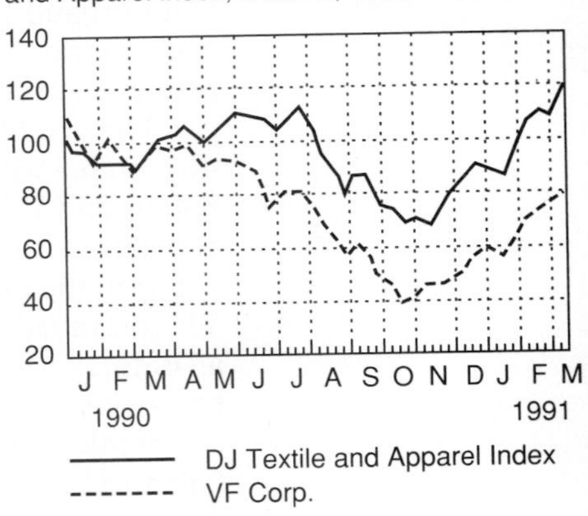

much of the stuff that Dockers at first couldn't deliver the goods. Store buyers urged Lee's sales force to come out with competing products.

"You could have driven a Mack Truck through the opportunity we missed by not following Dockers," says a former Lee sales vice president, who says one Lee executive wore Dockers to work every day for a week to rub in the point.

"The last pair of jeans I bought was four years ago," says Mark Plummer, 30 years old, a part-time graduate student who works at Stephens Inc., a securities firm in Little Rock, Ark.

About "once every two weeks," he wears his old jeans, he says. "But when I want to be casual and I'm going out to eat, I'd rather wear Dockers or Haggar," cotton slacks that "are kind of loose and baggy and more comfortable."

This year, both Lee and Wrangler will introduce casual-pants collections. Wrangler's Timber Creek line will be out in the spring, and Lee says it will introduce its line, yet to be named, in the fall. But Dockers is already an entrenched, $500-million business.

As jeans sales fell, Lee started tinkering with its image, which had become as dowdy as its age-old ad slogan: "Lee, the brand that fits." For years Lee had eschewed close-up photos of rear ends in its ads. Finally it realized what Madison Avenue long knew: Sex sells. And, with advice from the ad agency Fallon McElligott, it changed its advertising to appeal to younger customers.

Inspired by the gritty, urban appeal of Levi's 501 button-fly jeans, Lee ran black and white ads on TV and in magazines showing kids in convertibles and at the laundromat wearing Lee jeans. The ad agency won prizes, but customers didn't seem to get the message. VF chairman Mr. Pugh shudders at the very thought of that campaign: "Wrong, wrong, a big mistake," he says.

Lee's assault on youth exposed a number of its weaknesses. The brand added a number of fancier jeans to its repertoire—jeans with cargo pockets, jeans with embroidered detail. But Lee's factories—despite all their unused capacity—would have had to be retooled to make them. So Lee started using overseas contractors that were late and erratic in their deliveries. In the back-to-school selling season of 1989, just half of Lee's jeans shipments got to stores on time. As a result, orders were canceled. Hundreds of thousands of jeans were returned.

Today, VF is concentrating on integrating its businesses. With sweatpants outselling jeans at many stores, both Lee and Wrangler (a big supplier of desert fatigues to the Pentagon) are selling fleecewear manufactured by VF's Bassett-Walker division. Lee and Wrangler are retooling their factories to be more flexible. Wrangler now can product some styles for VF's Girbaud brand that had been made by contractors.

Still, Lee has a long way to go. It is easy enough for VF to set goals for improving manufacturing operations, but it is harder to predict when, if ever, in a shrinking market consumers will again think that Lee jeans are hot.

Source: Teri Agins, "Bottom Line," *The Wall Street Journal,* March 7, 1991, pp. A1, A4.

CASE 5–2 Wm. Wrigley Jr. Co.

Each year, Wm. Wrigley Jr. Co. makes more than 14,000 tons of a rubbery compound with ingredients found also in paint, underwear-elastic, and petrochemicals. Machines roll out blobs of the stuff, slice it into thin sticks, and sheathe it in foil wrap.

Chewing gum is a lucrative business, Wrigley's only business. Indeed, Wrigley dominates the world of chewing gum more thoroughly than Coca-Cola Co. looms over soft drinks. Wrigley has a 48 percent share of a $2.4 billion U.S. retail market, nearly twice that of Warner-Lambert Co., its biggest competitor (Trident, Dentyne). And it soundly beats back the competitive threat from consumer-goods powerhouse RJR Nabisco Inc. (Beech-Nut, Care Free).

"We get a lot of letters about brands that we don't even make because people assume we make all chewing gum," says William Piet, Wrigley's corporate secretary.

Yet in selling gum, Wrigley is a throwback to the time before micromarketing. It continues to run television advertising campaigns with themes that have been around since Eisenhower. It seldom resorts to sweepstakes or other gimmicks to promote its brands. Even so, Doublemint remains paramount among gum buyers worldwide, and Juicy Fruit, Spearmint, Extra, Freedent, Big Red, and Hubba Bubba are holding their own.

"The advertising community badmouths Wrigley," says Al Reis, a marketing consultant in Greenwich, Conn. "But what Wrigley does is very successful."

Wrigley is flourishing in the recession. In the first quarter, its net earnings rose 6 percent, to $31.7 million, thanks to a "modest" rise in shipments of chewing gum. Gum sales rarely are hurt by problems in the wider world.

Atypically, Wrigley almost always maintains or increases ad spending in tough times. One reason: gum is such an impulse purchase that Wrigley figures it can't afford to become less visible. Last year, it spent about $158 million on advertising, up from $134 million in 1989. Sales figures for Doublemint, first sold in 1914, aren't available because the company doesn't break down sales by brand.

Says one company director: "The only thing [Wrigley] would consider as a new venture is something else in the gum business."

Single-mindedness has paid off for the Wrigley family and the now-public company it founded. The business is run from a wedding cake-shaped headquarters—the famous Wrigley Bulding— overlooking the fur and jewelry boutiques of Chicago's Michigan Avenue.

The current president and chief executive officer is William Wrigley, 58 years old and the grandson of the company's founder. His son, William Wrigley Jr., 27, is being groomed to succeed him. Recently, young Mr. Wrigley was elected by the board to the dual posts of vice president and assistant to the president, doubling his pleasure no doubt.

The Wrigley family owns 37 percent of the company's stock. William Wrigley, who is said to be worth more than $500 million, also owns a stable of Arabian horses. The Wrigleys have an estate where they can get away from it all called Wychwood, in Lake Geneva, Wis., and another on Santa Catalina Island, off the California coast.

The Wrigleys don't care for publicity, in part perhaps because of the decades of press criticism they endured as owners of the Chicago Cubs baseball franchise. After they sold the perennially losing Cubs and Wrigley Field to Tribune Co. in 1981, *Chicago* magazine commented that selling the Cubs was the biggest contribution the Wrigleys had ever made to the city.

But in gum, Wrigley plays to win, and it isn't shy. It has been a fierce competitor ever since founder William Wrigley Jr. refused to join the so-called chewing gum trust—a merger of the industry's six largest companies in 1899—and decided to compete on his own. The company was one of the first to offer premiums—razors, lamps, and such—to merchants as an inducement to sell Wrigley's. In 1915, it mailed a stick of gum to everyone listed in U.S. phone books.

Wrigley hit a bad patch in the late 1970s, when its market share declined 35 percent over a four-year period as competitors began promoting sugar-free gums, but it made a comeback with Extra, introduced in 1984 and pushed extra hard.

"We had a very late start, and the key was formulating what we felt was a superior product," says Ronald Cox, Wrigley's group vice president for marketing. The more than $30 million Wrigley spent launching Extra was the most it had ever spent on a new brand. By 1989, Extra had become the industry's best-selling sugarless gum.

Wrigley has also prospered from making something of a science of the relationship between retail price and the number of sticks in a pack. Its PlenTpak of 17 sticks makes up the bulk of Wrigley sales, but little things mean a lot. After a 25-cent pack of five sticks was reintroduced in 1987 (following two years of study and 15 years of not offering a five-stick pack), Wrigley's single-pack sales increased, and market share rose about 4 percent. Older gum chewers will recall when the five-stick pack cost a nickel, which it did for more than 60 years, until 1960.

Wrigley also has the industry's most effective distribution network, capable of shipping more than a million pounds of chewing gum a day. And to stay ubiquitous, Wrigley has its telephone sales people contact most wholesalers at least once a week. That way, nobody ever runs out of Juicy Fruit.

But the Wrigley style is still ridiculed. Madison Avenue hooted in the '50s when the Doublemint twins made the scene. They were a hokey concept, people said, but in their fourth decade, they continue to move the merchandise.

"The twins mnemonic still evokes a response from consumers," says Eric Harkna, president of BBDO-Chicago, Wrigley's ad agency. (The agency recently surprised Madison Avenue with a new campaign to encourage smokers to chew gum where smoking is prohibited.)

Wrigley is determined to maintain a conservative and wholesome image. Accordingly, it won't advertise on TV shows it thinks are "risqué or offensive."

There was one misstep.

In 1989, Wrigley was inundated with letters from angry nurses when one of its commercials appeared on a short-lived ABC show called "Nightingales," a series criticized by some as demeaning and sexist. In response, William Wrigley sent a personal note to everyone who wrote in, promising to never advertise on the show again.

Mr. Wrigley answers his own phone, but he declined to be interviewed for this story. He has avoided the limelight ever since his scandalous divorce from his second wife. In 1976, according to press accounts, his wife, Joan, sued to invalidate a prenuptial agreement; he in turn filed for an annulment of the marriage; and she then sued for divorce. The case dragged on for six years and included 12 lawsuits altogether, in two states. The back and forth played like a soap opera in the Chicago papers, with charges of gold-digging against her, adultery against him, and with words from Mrs. Wrigley about how much she hated living in a house where everything was monogrammed W. The marriage ultimately was annulled after Mr. Wrigley's attorneys discovered in Alabama that Joan Wrigley had two previous quickie divorces and was still legally married to her second husband. So it wasn't just the Chicago Cubs that made Mr. Wrigley publicity shy.

Mr. Wrigley, who studied psychology at Yale, oversees a paternalistic corporate culture (Wirgley's 5,700 workers get a cash bonus each year of up to 15 percent of their gross pay) and a secretive manufacturing operation. Wrigley's sprawling red-brick compound in southwest Chicago, one of the 13 gum factories it operates throughout the world, is guarded by security cameras and tall barbed-wire gates. Were it not for a small, brass nameplate and the smell of mint hanging in the air, the factory would be a complete mystery in a mixed-use neighborhood of warehouses and modest old houses. Uniformed security guards patrol the compound in Jeeps. Their "GUM" license plates are another clue to what goes on here.

Chewing gum is whipped up like a big batch of bread, in giant mixers that hold a ton of ingredients. Then it is rolled into sheets, chilled, and cut into slices. In the past five years, Wrigley says, it has upgraded its equipment. Thanks to faster wrapper machines and such, it has increased productivity more than 30 percent over competitors. But it won't show its new gizmos to people who don't work there. And it is so worried about its secrets that it doesn't get patents for innovations that others might copy. It is best that nobody else knows anything about them at all, Wrigley figures.

The major ingredient in chewing gum is always identified on the pack simply as gum base and can include any of about 45 natural and synthetic flavors, softeners, and other stuff. It was once made primarily from sap taken from chicle trees in the Yucatan peninsula. But as that process became too expensive during World War II, gum makers developed synthetic materials, with ingredients that include butadiene-styrene rubber, a hydrocarbon refined from crude oil; polyvinyl acetate, used as an adhesive in some paints; and petroleum wax.

As unappetizing as some of those things might sound, they all have been approved as safe by the Food and Drug Administration. Wrigley also uses natural latexes such as sorva and jelutong, which still are transported out of jungle areas of Central and South America by canoe.

Over the years, Wrigley has shied away from overt assaults on the biggest impediment to gum sales: social stigma. It isn't just schoolteachers and pedestrians who hate chewing gum. "People in certain social groups see it as a symbol of people they find repulsive," says Lynn Kahle, a psychologist and chairman of the marketing department at the University of Oregon.

In the latest edition of *Etiquette,* now written by Emily Post's granddaughter-in-law, Elizabeth, a short section on gum chewing begins: "It is hard to understand why so many otherwise attractive people totally destroy their appearance by chewing gum like a cow chewing cud." The columnist Miss Manners advises that "Gum may be chewed in the presence of others only when it is safe to assume that they will not be offended. It is only safe to assume that others will not be offended if they are also chewing gum."

Convincing people that it is all right to chew gum is a "hard thing to deal with," says Mr. Cox, the Wrigley marketing executive. The company tried, albeit obliquely, in its recent "Piece of America" campaign, which showed otherwise respectable people chewing gum in public. Wrigley thinks it eased minds.

Wrigley says chewing gum aids digestion, sweetens breath, keeps the chewer alert and even helps clean teeth, despite what dentists used to tell patients.

Sociologists say gum also makes people feel tough. Chewing and popping are a major statement in some circles, says Michael Solomon, a lifestyles expert at Rutgers University. "People chew gum and, in an inexpensive and harmless way, they become a James Dean kind of rebel."

No such boasts make it into Wrigley's ad copy. "The truth is they don't have all that much to sell," says Leo Shapiro, a Chicago-based marketing consultant. "The key to their advertising is to refresh their name in the mind of consumers without saying anything."

Source: Brett Pulley, "Impulse Item: Wrigley Is Thriving, Despite the Recession, in a Resilient Business," *The Wall Street Journal,* May 29, 1991, pp. A1, A8. Reprinted by permission of The Wall Street Journal,

CASE 5–3 Digital Equipment Corporation

Two of the computer industry's most powerful figures, Apple Computer Inc. chairman John Sculley and Digital Equipment Corp. president Kenneth H. Olsen, met in secret last spring in Washington, D.C., at Mr. Sculley's request. His question: Would an alliance make sense?

Apple needed a partner for a new generation of chip designs. And Digital, which makes large office computers, needed a bigger presence in the surging business of personal computers. But the talks, which were never disclosed, went nowhere. Instead, Apple stunned the industry with a sweeping technology-sharing agreement with its arch-foe, International Business Machines.

Thus was another opportunity apparently lost to Digital and Mr. Olsen, whose longstanding skepticism about the PC—he used to call it a "toy"—hobbled the nation's second largest computer maker as PCs reshaped the market. Mr. Olsen also long resisted two other major industry trends of the last decade: the moves to so-called "open" systems that use standard operating software, and to a new generation of simpler, more potent chips.

This legacy now haunts Digital and its 66-year-old founder as they face the danger of being left behind by the industry they did so much to create. The $14 billion company that has been Mr. Olsen's singular passion for 35 years is mired in huge losses on declining sales. Despite vast resources spent on research and engineering, its latest products have largely failed to ignite growth. Repeated restructurings have sapped morale. Key employees and executives have departed following run-ins with Mr. Olsen. The company's shares now trade at one fourth their 1987 peak, closing at $45.25 on the Big Board yesterday.

And it isn't clear Mr. Olsen knows what to do next. Even though DEC has made some deft moves recently, such as an alliance with software powerhouse Microsoft Corp., there is no quick relief in sight. The depth of the latest loss ($294.1 million in the quarter ended March 28) "caught us by surprise," Mr. Olsen says. "When we laid out our restructuring last summer, we thought we'd have more time." One of Mr. Olsen's first moves after the loss was to disband much of the organizational structure he had created only weeks earlier, sidelining a key executive and leaving an impression of management in disarray.

The troubles inevitably raise anew the difficult question of succession at Digital, which has been dominated by Mr. Olsen's towering presence for so long that few leaders have emerged and remained. "He's at a defining moment in his extraordinary career, where he can be remembered as a titan who built this great company, or the founder who couldn't let go," says Jeffrey Sonnenfeld, author of *The Hero's Farewell,* a study of corporate succession.

But as Digital's difficulties have deepened, so too has Mr. Olsen's determination to solve them. "No way am I going to leave now," he says. "I only want the job as long as I'm the best. But there's a clear mission to accomplish now. I'm not a quitter."

For now, Digital's directors are behind him; no one expects a General Motors-style board revolt. But in a secret, seven-hour meeting recently, the long-compliant board pressed Mr. Olsen as never before. Directors insisted that restructuring efforts be stepped up and that strong outsiders be brought into senior executive ranks, beginning with the chief financial officer's post, which has been empty since James M. Osterhoff resigned last year.

The board's new aggressiveness is being led by former Ford Motor Co. president Philip Caldwell, insiders say. He has the support of Thomas L. Phillips, retired chairman of Raytheon Co., who has long been viewed as an Olsen ally, someone who'd attended a local monthly prayer breakfast with Mr. Olsen for more than a decade. Also supporting Mr. Caldwell were Robert Everett, former president of Mitre Corp., and Colby Chandler, Eastman Kodak Co.'s former chairman, say Digital insiders. None of the directors would comment for this article.

Mr. Olsen, the only Digital executive on the nine-member board, won't discuss the reaction of directors either. But he says the unexpectedly steep loss "certainly got their attention," and the board "wants a clear plan" for faster restructuring.

Mr. Olsen says he supports reaching outside for new talent: "Over the years, we haven't brought enough new blood and new ideas into the company."

A new urgency was apparent the day after the board meeting. On April 24 senior vice president John F. Smith said Digital will record a charge that may reach $1 billion and will cut more jobs—perhaps 10,000 to 15,000—in the year beginning July 1. That's on top of $1.65 billion in charges already taken and 10,000 previous dismissals (employees currently number about 116,000). And Mr. Smith did nothing to dispel expectations of at least three more losing quarters, nor did he predict when revenue would pick up. In the latest quarter, sales fell 7.6 percent to $3.25 billion.

Some former managers say Mr. Olsen must take the blame. Digital "has everything it needs to turn around—good people, good products, and great service—but it won't happen while he's still in charge," argues John Rose, who resigned last month as manager of the company's PC unit.

Mr. Olsen rejects criticism of his leadership. "The real question is whether I have allowed too much freedom," he says. And he had, indeed, rescued Digital from hard times in the past and managed each time to ignite new growth. In the early 1980s, in particular, Digital was written off and Mr. Olsen sharply criticized—old and in the way, analysts said—only to roar back with the strongest growth of any major computer maker of the time.

Moreover, the Maynard, Mass.-based concern still has a strong balance sheet, with no debt. And, though long overdue, it has a powerful new computer design that could fuel a comeback in 1993. Based on RISC chip technology (reduced-instruction-set computing), its new Alpha computers aren't limited to Digital's proprietary operating software but can also use Unix and Microsoft's Windows NT.

"They're doing a lot of the right things, playing off their technological strengths with foresight about the way the industry is headed," says John Levinson, a Goldman, Sachs & Co. analyst. "The problem is, they still have a ridiculous amount of baggage left over from the successes of the past."

Most people can't imagine Digital without Mr. Olsen. "No matter what changes, there's one constant, and that's Ken," says David Smith, a former Digital software analyst. "He's a living legend."

But many Digital executives contend that Mr. Olsen, who shows no sign of retiring, has become increasingly isolated and irascible. His convoluted, rambling speeches, long a staple of company lore, have become even more difficult to follow, and the pearls of wisdom that once rewarded the careful listener seem more scarce.

At a manager's meeting April 16, Mr. Olsen's presentation left many in the audience confused, participants say. The speech meandered from topic to topic and went on for an hour and a half. Some managers stared down at their cold chicken lunches and others rolled their eyes or shook their heads.

At one point, Mr. Olsen made an attempt at black humor. "You know, someone just came up to me in the hall and said, 'Ken, I'd been considering taking early retirement but decided to stay because working here is so much fun,' " he told the group. "There was an embarrassed silence," one manager says. The atmosphere in the crowded room, he says, "was like a wake."

"He's the Fidel Castro of the computer industry," contends Gordon Bell, a one-time star computer designer at Digital, who resigned in 1983 after a run-in with Mr. Olsen. Mr. Bell charges that "he's out of touch, and anyone who disagrees with him is sent into exile."

A recurring criticism of Mr. Olsen's stewardship is that his dominance of decision making tends to drive out good people. The most recent casualty is William Strecker, Digital's chief engineer, whose product-development group was abruptly disbanded by Mr. Olsen three weeks ago. The group had been created only weeks earlier, and Mr. Strecker had been promoted to oversee all development. Mr. Strecker remains at Digital, which said he wasn't available for comment.

Colleagues of Mr. Strecker say he had repeatedly crossed Mr. Olsen, including opposing a mainframe project that had Mr. Olsen's personal backing but has so far proved a costly failure.

Mr. Strecker's demotion dismayed some longtime Olsen loyalists. "It's a criminal shame, because Bill Strecker was really the only one capable of charting a coherent product strategy in the inner circle" of senior executives, says Don McInnis, a former Digital manager now a vice president at Prime Computer Inc.

Another key talent was lost when Mr. Olsen pulled the plug in 1989 on Prism, a RISC computer design headed by David Cutler, a highly regarded software engineer. Instead, Digital bought a stake in MIPS Computer Systems Inc. and designed a line of workstations around its RISC chips. Mr. Cutler resigned and went to Microsoft. Mr. Strecker also opposed the Prism cancellation and the alliance with MIPS.

When it began to appear that Digital's MIPS-based machines weren't going to be a big hit, Digital recharged its internal RISC project. Ironically, Mr. Cutler became the designer of Microsoft's Windows NT software, which Digital now hopes will boost future Alpha sales.

And just when Digital most needs an experienced hand overseeing finances, the chief financial officer's job remains unfilled, nearly a year after Mr. Osterhoff quit following a disagreement with Mr. Olsen. "He went to the mat" against Mr. Olsen, opposing acquisition of two European companies without more research, an associate says. Mr. Osterhoff's concern was well placed: Digital last year paid a total of $390 million for the computer units of Philips Electronics N.V. and Mannesmann AG, but so far their weak performance hasn't helped results, while adding 10,000 people to the payroll. Mr. Osterhoff won't discuss his departure.

There are signs, too, of stress within Mr. Olsen's core management group. Mr. Smith, his second-in-command, appears to have lost some authority in the latest reorganization. Colleagues say Mr. Smith, fiercely loyal to Digital, seems increasingly exasperated. Mr. Smith says he continues to have a close working relationship with Mr. Olsen, adding: "It shouldn't come as a surprise that the level of frustration inside the company right now is sky high."

The management problems are worrisome, critics say, because Mr. Olsen's vision of the computer industry has proved to be lacking of late. From PCs to standard software, the choices he has made have left the company at a disadvantage in a fast-changing market.

As a result, his critics say, he didn't grasp the significance of a possible alliance with Apple, in which Apple might have used Digital's Alpha RISC chip. That could have established Alpha instantly in a market segment where Digital was weak. The apparent lost opportunity still leaves some current and former Digital executives bitter.

Within the small circle of Digital's senior staff aware of the Olsen-Sculley meeting a year ago, Mr. Olsen gets the blame for its going nowhere. Digital executives and Apple's Roger Heinen, senior vice president, confirm that the meeting took place. Mr. Heinen asserts that Mr. Olsen's "lack of interest and understanding of the role of the personal computer industry" was indeed an obstacle. Mr. Heinen, himself a former Digital executive, says the companies "continue to have a close relationship."

Mr. Olsen dismisses the talks with Apple. "It just never came to fruition. It wasn't that important to me." He notes that Apple talked to other companies, too, before settling on an alliance with IBM, and that such alliances are decided on a whole range of factors.

But at Mr. Olsen's direction, Digital has tried to make up for lost time in PCs. In the past six months, it has brought out a line of aggressively priced IBM-compatible PCs sold by mail order, which are going strong. Though the late start makes it unlikely Digital will be a major player anytime soon, PC hardware sales should hit $500 million this year.

One of Mr. Olsen's most costly decisions has been backing the ill-fated VAX 9000 mainframe computer, which cost $1 billion to bring to market but attracted few buyers. "It wasn't a mistake, because we needed a high-end machine," says Dorothy Terrell, a former Digital manager now at Sun Microsystems Inc. "But it was late, too complicated and costly to build, and the sales force wasn't selling it effectively." Mr. Olsen repeatedly resurrected its funding after others tried to kill it, she adds.

Mr. Olsen concedes that the project "took longer and cost us more than it should have." But, he says, "we belong in that business." Before long, Digital is expected to introduce a redesigned mainframe based on simpler technology.

While such hugely expensive projects have gone forward, management's efforts to cut other costs often have focused on items such as water coolers and magazine subscriptions. In January, a memo circulated at a Digital office in Acton, Mass., identifying the building as a test site for lower-cost toilet tissue, "a project being driven by Win Hindle, corporate staff senior vice president."

Mr. Hindle, who has been acting chief financial officer since Mr. Osterhoff's departure, says, "I can see how that might look silly. But if a new national paper-supply contract can save something like $300,000 a year, well, every little bit helps."

Source: John R. Wilke, "On the Spot: At Digital Equipment, Ken Olsen Is Under Pressure to Produce," *The Wall Street Journal,* May 13, 1992, pp. A1, A8. Reprinted by permission of The Wall Street Journal,

CASE 5–4 Deprenyl Research Ltd.

Twice a day, Edward Greenberg of Brooklyn, N.Y., gives his wife, Ann, an experimental drug called Alzene. Mr. Greenberg is convinced that the pills, a mixture of two purified vegetable oils, are slowing her relentless mental deterioration from Alzheimer's disease.

Many Alzheimer's researchers doubt that Alzene, which hasn't been approved for sale in the U.S., helps the dozens of U.S. families such as the Greenbergs who buy it by mail through a crack in U.S. import laws. But nobody doubts the promotional prowess of two young drug companies, a flamboyant Canadian entrepreneur, and an obscure Israeli inventor that are touting the drug and investments in its prospects.

The Alzene story—its development and marketing—typifies the hope and hype that richochet among desperate people with incurable illnesses such as Alzheimer's disease, AIDS, and some cancers.

"The families of people with Alzheimer's are so susceptible to claims of effectiveness, no matter what the source or the evidence," says Miriam Aronson, a gerontologist at New York's Jewish Guild for the Blind. "I know many people taking all variety of unapproved drugs, traveling overseas to get them. Do they work? I just haven't seen the proof."

Proof may be coming, Alzene's promoters say, from two preliminary clinical trials currently testing the drug on 20 Americans. Although that's a small study by scientific standards, researchers consider it large enough to uncover even the slimmest evidence that Alzene is useful. Meanwhile, most users buy the pills on faith from Deprenyl Research Ltd., a small Toronto drug company. Alzene "is expensive as hell, but there's nothing else," says the 81-year-old Mr. Greenberg, who pays $120 a month for the pills.

No Alzheimer's drug is approved for sale in the U.S., though many are being tested, including half a dozen from major pharmaceutical companies. The potential market is huge; Alzheimer's is a leading cause of death among older Americans, and more than $3 billion is spent annually on care of the nation's four million Alzheimer's patients. A licensed drug against the disease, or one that just sounds as if it works, would be a potent moneymaker.

Thus Alzene is gold waiting to be mined to Shlomo Yehuda, an Israeli psychologist who formulated Alzene five years ago and holds a U.S. patent on it; to Ivax Corp., a fledgling Miami company with U.S. rights to develop and sell it; and to Deprenyl Research, which last year acquired Canadian marketing rights from Ivax.

Shares of Ivax have soared 42 percent and those of Deprenyl Research are up 50 percent since early 1991 as company officials and securities underwriters promote Alzene to doctors, investors, and the media with a quirky publicity campaign. In American Stock Exchange composite trading, Ivax closed yesterday at $28.625 a share, down 75 cents, and in over-the-counter trading, Deprenyl Research ended at $7.50 a share, down 50 cents.

Much of the drumbeat for Ivax, which is developing several experimental drugs, comes from Wall Streeters such as Ronald Nordmann, a respected drug-industry analyst at PaineWebber Inc. He calls Alzene's potential "extraordinary" and predicts annual sales of $350 million by 1995.

PaineWebber helped underwrite Ivax's $55 million public offering in early 1991 and was co-underwriter for a $110.5 million private placement last November. Mr. Nordmann says he didn't begin recommending Ivax until after the public offering. Among other analysts, only Ronad Stern of

Tucker Anthony Inc. follows Ivax, and he also recommends it. Tucker Anthony was the other underwriter of Ivax's offerings.

Deprenyl Research, formed five years ago to sell a drug against Parkinson's disease in Canada, also is banking on Alzene. Its founder and co-chairman is a wealthy physician and former politician and Toronto coroner, Morton Shulman.

In those roles, Dr. Shulman, who is widely known as "Morty," always made his presence felt. As coroner, he lobbied against sloppy operating-room practices and even sampled LSD in order to testify at an inquest into a drug-related death. As a socialist member of Ontario's Parliament, he liked to photograph colleagues slumbering during sessions. He also sold copies of *The Happy Hooker* from his office after Toronto's morals squad pulled it from bookstores—and he gave fellow legislators a 10 percent discount on the porn classic.

Quitting politics, Dr. Shulman attracted a cult following as a contributor to an investment newsletter. His bestseller, *How to Make a Million Dollars,* made him a millionaire.

"A person with strong convictions that has no time for unbelievers" is how Dr. Shulman has been described by Andrew Sarlos, a Toronto investor who has worked with him in selling investment funds to the public.

Now, Dr. Shulman is selling Alzene to Americans under a four-year-old U.S. regulation allowing patients to import unapproved medicines for life-threatening diseases such as Alzheimer's or AIDS if they get a doctor's prescription.

Last January, Dr. Shulman decided he needed to "get the word out fast" concerning Alzene because, he told *The Wall Street Journal,* he had only a few years in which he could sell the drug here. Once Ivax receives approval from the Food and Drug Administration, Deprenyl Research would be blocked under its licensing agreement from selling Alzene in the U.S., he said. Dr. Shulman then wrote to many American neurologists notifying them of the drug's availability. In one set of letters, he said "overwhelming demand" for the drug had caused a shortage.

"As far as I'm concerned, the letter violates the law prohibiting the marketing of an unapproved drug," says Leon Thal, a researcher at the Veterans Administration Medical Center in San Diego. Learning of the mailings in February, the FDA ordered Deprenyl Research to stop promoting Alzene and now, a spokeswoman says, is "looking into" its marketing tactics.

About the same time, Deprenyl Research upset Canadian regulators with a press release announcing that it had received an "emergency go-ahead" from the Health Protection Branch, Canada's FDA, to provide Alzene to Canadians whose doctors request it. But the Canadian agency says Dr. Shulman's publicity release overstated the government's action.

"Any unapproved drug for a life-threatening illness that doesn't pose a safety risk can be provided if a doctor requests it," says a Health Protection Branch spokeswoman. "Alzene received no special approval." The agency also is investigating Deprenyl Research's marketing efforts.

Dr. Shulman denies he is exaggerating claims or going beyond the law. He says he ceased the U.S. mailings after the FDA reprimand. "I have done nothing more than inform my shareholders of events that might affect the stock," he says. Moreover, Dr. Shulman says he is making Alzene merely as a humanitarian gesture, with all proceeds going to a charitable foundation he created.

Deprenyl Research's publicity campaign seems to be working. To support his contention that the drug is in great demand, Dr. Shulman produces an Alzene sales list showing that in mid-June the company was shipping more than a hundred 120-pill bottles a day to American doctors and patients. More than 70 patients or doctors are listed as receiving the drug during a five-day period. Daily sales were running at more than $12,000.

Dr. Shulman says each $2 Alzene pill costs him about 50 cents, half of which goes to royalties to Ivax. Ivax officials say they are unaware of his marketing program.

The Alzene affair isn't Dr. Shulman's only foray into merchandising himself, stocks, and drugs. He formed his company after he developed Parkinson's disease and got hold of a drug developed in Hungary but not then available in North America. When the drug, deprenyl, proved remarkably helpful to Dr. Shulman, he decided to buy the Canadian rights to it. He set up Deprenyl Research in 1987 to sell the drug under the brand name Eldepryl.

For about a year before Eldepryl was approved for sale in the U.S., Deprenyl Research sold it through the mail to American patients. Analysts say Deprenyl Research makes an 80 percent pretax profit on each $2.10 capsule of Eldepryl.

For 1991, Deprenyl Research reported sales of C$13.9 million, most of which was from Eldepryl, and profit of C$6.6 million, or 41 Canadian cents a share. The company says its pharmaceutical operations earned C$4 million pretax, but it got an additional C$6.3 million in pretax profit from investment income and sale of shares in new companies that it spun off.

Recently, Dr. Shulman has been promoting the shares of its Deprenyl USA unit, which owns the rights to an experimental cancer treatment called ALA-Photodynamic Therapy. The drug, in cream form, involves a chemical that is activated when exposed to light and has shown some benefit against skin cancers.

In June, Dr. Shulman called the Toronto Stock Exchange asking that it halt the trading of shares of Deprenyl USA because a major study of the drug's effectiveness was going to gain media attention, as it was being reported in a scientific journal. But because the journal is relatively unknown, Deprenyl Research made certain the press knew of the study by having a New York public-relations firm mail it to reporters in a glossy press kit and then follow up with phone calls.

The exchange declined to halt trading, and few publications carried details of the report. (During an interview, Dr. Shulman blithely offered to give a reporter's family shares of another Deprenyl Research subsidiary,

Deprenyl Bone Health, which is to be spun off from the parent next month in the form of warrants. The offer was turned down.)

To recruit subjects for an Alzene-related test at the University of Toronto, and to attract publicity, Dr. Shulman asked shareholders at Deprenyl Research's 1991 annual meeting to volunteer. More than 100 people sought entry into the test, which is expected to be finished sometime this year.

But it is the U.S. sales of Alzene that seem especially promising. A Pittsburgh neurologist, Richard Kasdan, says he regularly provides a prescription for imported Alzene for a 70-year-old patient. Dr. Kasdan says the woman's family read an article in *The Jewish Press,* a weekly newspaper published in Brooklyn, reporting "very encouraging" results in a human study of the drug in Israel.

"The children desperately want to do something to help their mother," Dr. Kasdan says, noting he checked to ensure that the drug wasn't dangerous. "It hasn't hurt her, but it isn't helping her, either."

Many Alzheimer's disease scientists and doctors are either unaware of Alzene or regard it as one of many unproved therapies tried by patients' families. "There's no scientific reason to expect Alzene to work," says Dr. Thal of the San Diego VA. "That's not to say by some miracle it won't help. It's just awfully darn premature, and unfair, to promise someone it does." Dr. Shulman says he warns people that the drug is experimental.

Numerous other U.S. families and doctors acknowledge getting the drug from Deprenyl Research, but most decline to speak for attribution. One 79-year-old woman in Delaware says her son, an investment analyst, buys the drug for her. "I want to remember things better. I think it is helping," she says.

In fact, the science underlying Alzene isn't easy to fathom. Dr. Yehuda, a professor at Bar-Ilan University in Israel, created Alzene when, he says, he discovered he could sharpen the memory of laboratory rodents by giving them a special combination of alpha-linolenic and linoleic acids, two fats commonly found in vegetable oils such as soybean and safflower oil. Dr. Yehuda says highly purified forms of the fats enter the brain and nourish the weakened membranes of nerve cells destroyed by Alzheimer's disease.

However, William Connor, who studies the effects of fatty acids on eye nerve cells at Oregon Health Sciences University in Portland, terms such claims questionable. He says the two fats blended in Alzene "aren't active in the membranes of brain nerve cells and wouldn't seem to be very helpful to them." He adds that purifying the fatty acids isn't necessary because the body naturally purifies fats in certain vegetables before making use of them. "The drug is a very expensive way to get these fatty acids," he observes.

Officials at Deprenyl and Ivax, as well as PaineWebber's Mr. Nordmann, say they have reviewed a 141-patient study conducted by Dr. Yehuda. They say the test, which compared Alzene with a placebo, produced a significant improvement in mental functioning for many of those receiving the drug for just three weeks. But because neither that study nor the animal tests have been published, an independent review of the study is impossible.

Dr. Yehuda says he hasn't published any of his numerous animal and human studies because Ivax asked him to keep the research private until patents were issued. But many researchers hold up publication of discoveries until after a patent application is filed, not until it is issued. In any case, Ivax received a U.S. patent in 1989 and one in Europe in 1991.

Dr. Yehuda says he considers his drug experimental and is awaiting results of the small U.S. study. While he doesn't suggest people should be taking Alzene, he says the drug appears to have stopped the deterioration in memory of about 15 of his research subjects who have continued taking the drug for more than two years. "I think for some people Alzene appears to be remarkably beneficial," he says. "But my results certainly need to be confirmed."

Dr. Yehuda says he has received no money from Ivax or Deprenyl Research but only the promise that the drug would be tested in the U.S. and, if it's approved for sale, an undisclosed royalty payment.

Stephen Ferris, a noted Alzheimer's researcher at New York University Medical Center who also has seen the Israeli study, says, "The magnitude of reported effect is much higher than anything you'd expect." Dr. Ferris says the study isn't considered an independent test since it was overseen by the drug's inventor.

The NYU center is one of two places in the U.S. running a small test of Alzene; the other is a nursing facility in Miami. Dr. Ferris says his center is doing so "because of all the interest in it and because of the dramatic claims made in the Israeli test." His results should be out later this year. "We're not advising that anyone take the drug right now," Dr. Ferris says.

—Suzanne McGee in Toronto contributed to this article.

Source: Michael Waldholz, "Problematic Pills: An Unapproved Drug for Alzheimer's Gets a Big Marketing Push," *The Wall Street Journal,* August 25, 1992, pp. A1, A8.

COMPREHENSIVE CASES

CASE 6–1 Jaguar Cars Inc.

Have you driven a Ford lately? Before long, the answer might be yes even if your car is a Jaguar or, perhaps, a Saab.

Ford Motor Co. yesterday jolted the automotive world—and Britain—by disclosing that it wants to buy a stake of up to 15 percent of Britain's leading luxury-car maker, Jaguar PLC. The announcement came just two weeks after Ford said it was negotiating "closer cooperation" with Sweden's Saab Scania AB.

Other European auto makers including Group Lotus PLC, Aston Martin Lagonda Ltd., Automobili Lamborghini S.p.A. and Alfa Romeo S.p.A.—have surrendered their independence in recent years, but now the trend, driven by growing competition, may be shifting into high gear. Though Ford's overtures to Jaguar and Saab haven't produced any firm deals yet, auto-industry watchers are already wondering who's next. Prime candidates for an alliance, they suggest, are Britain's Vickers PLC, which makes Rolls-Royce and Bentley cars, and West Germany's Porsche AG. Some even suggest that Germany's Bayerische Motoren Werke AG, or BMW, might one day need a partner.

All are gilded marques that confer instant status on their owners, especially in the U.S., where sales of European luxury cars boomed in the early 1980s. But in the last few years, their U.S. sales have plunged, thanks to a lower dollar that made all imports more expensive and to an onslaught of new competition from Japanese luxury cars. Now, many of Europe's best-known small auto makers—BMW being the notable exception—are struggling financially, and unable to spend the huge sums needed to develop and market innovative new models in an increasingly competitive world.

"The European little guys were already losing out as independent competitors before the Japanese came on the [luxury-car] scene," says James Womack, research director of the International Motor Vehicle Program at the Massachusetts Institute of Technology. "I basically think all the little guys are going to become subsidiaries of the big guys."

Such a shakeout promises to be shaped by individual corporate strategies, executive egos and, not least, by national pride. Ford's bold bid to buy Italy's Alfa Romeo a couple of years ago got squashed when Fiat S.p.A. came on the scene, and argued that Alfa should be kept in Italian hands. Likewise, when General Motors Corp. tried to buy the Land Rover and Leyland subsidiaries of state-owned BL PLC three years ago, British politicians howled at the thought of foreigners owning a national institution. GM backed off.

It isn't clear how British pride might affect Ford's move on Jaguar, but the U.S. auto maker clearly will have to deal with Jaguar's corporate pride first. Ford's terse announcement was made at around 4 P.M. London time and 11 A.M. EDT in Detroit. "We believe there are substantial benefits for both companies in a holding that could lay the foundation for a long-term association between Ford and Jaguar," L. Lindsey Halstead, chairman of Ford of Europe, said. He praised Jaguar as "an outstanding British company with a distinctive product range," and promised that if Ford should eventually gain control, it would keep Jaguar "as a separate and autonomous entity."

Those diplomatic words notwithstanding, the announcement caught Jaguar executives flat-footed. Though rumors of a possible Ford overture had been circulating since last spring, the executives had no warning of Ford's decision beyond a phone call from the auto maker just before the announcement yesterday.

"I think we are going to remain independent," declared Sir John Egan, the tough-minded Jaguar chairman who was dubbed "England's Lee Iacocca" for rescuing his company from the brink of bankruptcy in 1986. "I would remind you of the 'golden share' provisions."

The "golden share" is a strong antitakeover measure. When the British government sold its stake in Jaguar in 1984, it retained one share that prevents any outside investor, British or foreign, from buying more than 15 percent of Jaguar without the government's permission. The golden share expires on December 31, 1990.

It isn't clear how the British government might view Ford's move, but the spate of British acquisitions in the U.S. in recent years might head off outright opposition. "We look silly if we don't allow Americans to buy here," says David Willetts, director of a London-based think tank with close ties to Prime Minister Margaret Thatcher. "The last thing you want is to give the economic nationalists in Congress an excuse to be obstructive about British takeovers.

But it is clear that, beneath Sir John's stern words and the golden-share protection, Jaguar's fortunes are slipping badly. The company recently reported a precipitous decline in pretax profit for the first half of this year to £1.4 million ($2.2 million) from £22.5 million. In recent months, Sir John has talked to virtually every major car maker about a possible partnership, but found nothing to his liking yet. Jaguar's problems, and those of Saab as well, illustrate the woes afflicting virtually every one of Europe's small auto makers—a situation that contrasts starkly with their huge prosperity earlier in the decade.

Then, a strong dollar made imported goods of all kinds inexpensive to Americans. The Reagan years—with their robust stock market and recovery from recession—made upscale consumption fashionable. European makes became the cars of choice for a generation of Americans who suddenly had money, but wanted no part of their father's Oldsmobile, Cadillac, or Lincoln.

Jaguar's U.S. sales jumped 55 percent between 1983 and 1986. During the same period, BMW's American sales surged 63 percent, Mercedes-Benz's 35 percent, Porsche's 40 percent, and Saab's 83 percent (Exhibit 1).

European automakers got so bullish on America they expanded their plants. In early 1984, for example, Saab could produce 105,000 cars a year. Over the years it kept enlarging its factories, to the point that now it has the capacity to build 180,000 cars annually. Saab had assumed its sales in the U.S. would continue to grow. But the world was changing.

In 1985, with the U.S. trade deficit burgeoning, governments of the major industrial nations agreed to drive down the value of the dollar. The U.S. currency nearly halved in value compared with other major currencies, and suddenly, European cars weren't so affordable any more.

The base sticker price of Saab's 900 four-door sedan in the U.S., for example, has soared 38 percent in the last four years to $17,515. The Mercedes 190D with a 2.5-liter engine has jumped in price more than 27 percent since 1986.

Making matters worse, Japanese auto makers invaded the luxury-car market. Honda Motor Co. led the way with its Acura division, which sold nearly 53,000 cars in its inaugural year, 1986. Last year Acura sold more than 128,000 cars, and many were purchased by people who once owned European cars.

One is George Pendergast, who lives in suburban Boston and markets financial services. Just last month he traded in his 1986 Saab turbo for a new Acura Legend, which carries a sticker price of nearly $27,000. "One of the things I miss is having that 'ugly' Saab around," says Mr. Pendergast, who concedes he grew fond of the Swedish car's quirky shape. But he says he found the Acura far more comfortable, with a much smoother ride.

The Japanese threat to the Europeans is only getting worse. Last month Toyota Motor Corp. launched its luxury Lexus line in the U.S., and in November Nissan Motor Co. is unveiling its Infiniti models. The Japanese offer technologically advanced cars that get completely reengineered every four to five years. The big change on European models, in contrast, tends to be their price tags; the Europeans often make only minor physical changes in their cars for the better part of a decade.

Jaguar's 1988 model XJ6 luxury sedan, for example, is the only car the automaker completely reengineered during the 1980s. This year, to boost lagging U.S. sales, the company is introducing a stripped-down variation of the car, which will come without a sun roof, fancy suspension system, and full-scale walnut interor trim. The price is $39,700, compared with the regular XJ6's $44,000. But even the "bargain" Jaguar costs more than the top-of-the-line Lexus and Infiniti models.

The Europeans' problem: the huge sums it takes to develop new cars and bring them to market. Small automakers must spread those development costs—which can run in the billions—over a thin sales base. For years, the small European companies assumed they never had to bother with frequent make-overs of their products. Now they know better, but simply don't have the money.

Access to cash, and to technical talent, is what Ford is dangling before

Exhibit 1 Hard Times for European Luxury Cars in U.S. (U.S. car sales of selected European auto makers in thousands)

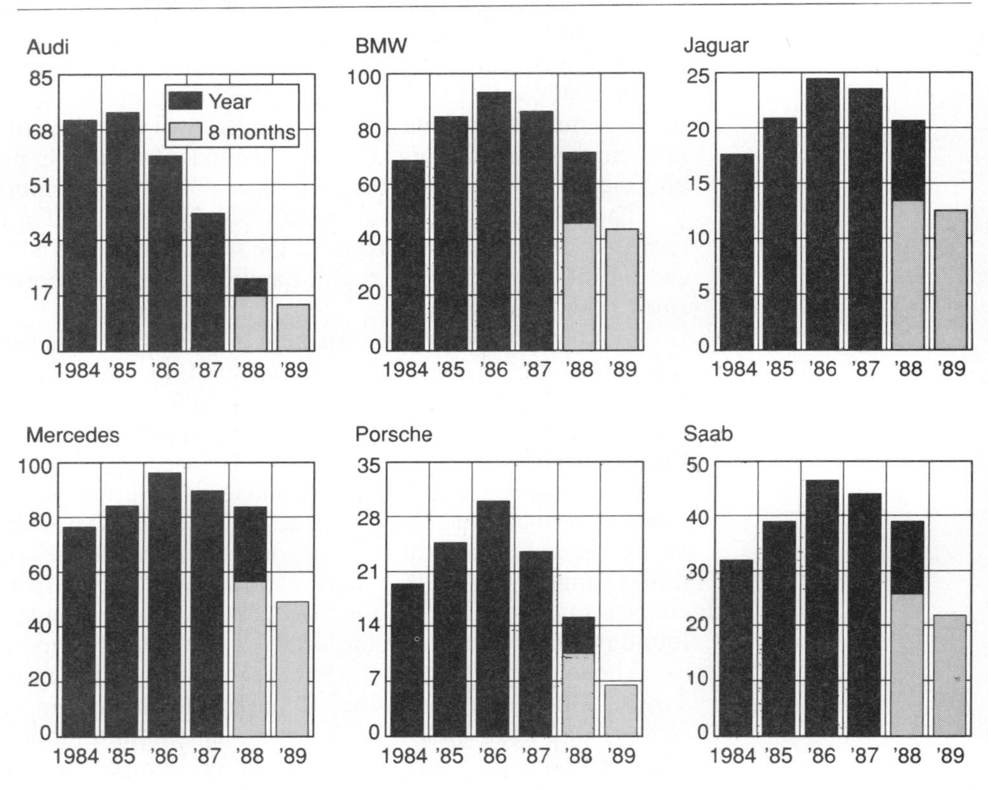

Jaguar. "We could help strengthen Jaguar in areas like advanced technological design and development, manufacturing processes, and worldwide marketing," said Ford's Mr. Halstead, "by offering full access to our technical and financial resources in Britain and around the world."

What Ford appears to want in return from Jaguar and Saab is snob appeal. Ford has a distinctly middle-brow image, both in the U.S. and Europe. Its effort to ship some of its European-made Fords into the U.S. and sell them under the pricey Merkur label has bombed.

"Ford hasn't got any $40,000 to $50,000 cars in the U.S.," says David Healy, auto analyst with Drexel Burnham Lambert. "This is an easy way to associate themselves with a luxury-car producer that can broaden their product mix."

Ford's risk, though, is in possibly buying a couple of losers. "I don't see sales turning around for the Eruopeans," says Edward J. Sullivan, who tracks the auto industry for the WEFA Group, a consulting firm in Bala Cynwyd, Pennsylvania. "I don't see what Ford is going to gain. They would be throwing [Jaguar] right into the teeth of Lexus and Infiniti."

It's uncertain how the battle for Jaguar will play out, or even if there's to be a battle. Ford is already bracing for political repercussions in Britain, where Jaguar is a national symbol. At a news briefing, Ford executives wrapped themselves in the British flag as a preemptive move. "We are the biggest British carmaker," said Derek Barron, a native Londoner and chairman of Ford's U.K. subsidiary.

After breaking their news to Jaguar's Sir John in a phone call yesterday, Ford officials instructed their investment bankers to start buying Jaguar stock. Ford's purchases didn't exceed $15 million, says Bruce Blythe, vice president of business strategy for Ford's European operations. That's enough to buy just over 1 percent of Jaguar.

Jaguar shares surged after the Ford announcement Tuesday in very heavy volume on London's Stock Exchange. Some 8 percent of the company's shares changed hands, and the price closed at 467 pence ($7.33), up 62 pence (97 cents). Jaguar could command a total price of about $1.4 billion, said Andrew Chambers, an analyst at Nomura Research Institute in London, a securities firm.

Under U.S. law, Ford can't buy more than $15 million worth of Jaguar stock for the next 30 days, Mr. Blythe explained. But after that, Ford could raise its stake to 15 percent. Jaguar's board, meanwhile, is expected to meet this week to map strategy. The company so far is keeping its options open. "Let's get our breath back," said a Jaguar spokesman yesterday. "We only got [word of] this this afternoon."

Source: "Rule of the Road: Europe's Luxury Cars Face Pressure to Join with Big U.S. Makers," *The Wall Street Journal,* September 20, 1989, pp. A1, A9.

EPILOGUE

Struggling Jaguar Cars Inc. is promising to take a smaller bite out of your wallet.

When Jaguar unveils its 1993 models here today, it will spotlight a car whose price has been slashed by a whopping $10,750, or 18 percent.

The unusual pricing action illustrates Jaguar's attempt to pump up sales by going a bit "down market" within the ultracompetitive luxury-car segment. The British auto maker, owned by Ford Motor Company, is dogged by a poor-quality image and tough competition from Germany, Japan, and a resurgent Detroit. Jaguar has seen its U.S. sales plunge 64.1 percent since 1986, their peak year.

Even at a time when luxury-car makers are restraining price increases, offering rebates, and offering sweet lease deals, Jaguar's price cut is especially aggressive. The base price of the 1993 XJS is now $49,750, compared with $60,500 a year ago.

Along with the lower price comes something that consumers might find rather less attractive: a smaller engine. Jaguar is equipping the new XJS couple with six-cylinder, four-liter engines rated at 219 horsepower. Previously, the cars were powered by a monstrous 5.3 liter V-12 engine with 260 horsepower.

Jaguar said the price of the XJS offered in the U.S. is now in line with the price of that model in England and other parts of the world. The car's base price was cheaper outside the U.S., because Jaguar already offered those markets a six-cylinder version of the car.

Jaguar, acquired by Ford in 1989, desperately needs to bolster its arsenal against Japanese and European luxury-car makers, which have turned up the pressure by restraining price increases.

Mercedes-Benz, a unit of Daimler-Benz AG, for example, raised the prices on some of its 1993 models by less than 1 percent and held prices on other models. Meanwhile, the U.S. sales arm of Bayerische Motoren Werke AG is raising the price of its 1993 model 740i by just 1.9 percent, even though it has a new V-8 engine and passenger-side airbag. BMW's steepest price increase comes on the 325is, which is rising by 6.3 percent or $1,850.

Meanwhile, Audi of America, Volkswagen AG's U.S. luxury-car unit, has set the base price of its 1993-model 90 S sedan with automatic transmission at $26,650, the same as the 1991 model. Audi didn't offer the 90 sedan in the 1992 model year.

Jaguar, or course, isn't the only luxury-car maker that has languished recently. The European companies all have been hammered in the U.S. by the weak dollar, the luxury and gas-guzzler taxes, the recession, and an onslaught of new Japanese competitors—notably Toyota Motor Company's Lexus and Nissan Motor Company's Infiniti.

Even Honda Motor Company's Acura division, the first Japanese luxury-car brand, is feeling the pinch. While Lexus and Infiniti sales are up, Acura's sales have fallen 13.4 percent to 94,676 cars through the first nine months of this year. Acura hopes for a boost next summer, when it launches a revamped Integra model.

But as Jaguar has continued to flounder, many of its rivals are bouncing back by offering deep discounts on their cars. "Jaguar has been faced with a great deal of price competition," says Christopher Cedergren, an auto analyst with AutoPacific Group Inc. "Jaguar hasn't been able to compete with what Mercedes and some other luxury-car makers are offering."

That's especially because Jaguar's problems are more fundamental than

Waning Jaguar Sales (number of Jaguars sold in the U.S., in thousands)

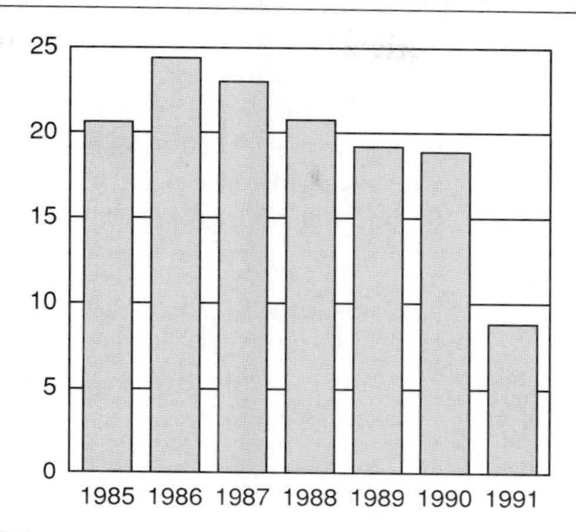

pricing. Jaguar scores high marks for the muscular grace of its styling, but has fallen short in technological and safety innovations. Also, Jaguar has been slow to bring new products to market. The company last introduced a completely new car in the U.S. in 1987, and won't offer another one until 1995.

"The current sedan has been in the market for several years, and there hasn't been much change in the styling or technology," says John Casesa, an auto analyst at Wertheim Schroder & Co. "Jaguar's most direct competitors offer state-of-the-art technology."

Jaguar also continues to suffer from its image, even though defects have dropped 80 percent under Ford's quality-control system. "Ford is doing a good job in terms of getting the cars right," says Herschel White, a Jaguar salesman at Hennessy Cadillac-Jaguar in Atlanta. "They've got a way to go, but every year the cars improve."

Despite quality improvements, Jaguar's sales haven't picked up. So far this year, Jaguar has sold just 7,143 cars in the U.S., down 10.7 percent from a year earlier. So Jaguar is trying a new approach.

For starters, the automaker expects a boost from the repositioned XJS. Jaguar has also added more standard equipment to the 1993 model XJ6, previously called the Sovereign. The car now comes with such standard gear as a driver's-side airbag and a chlorofluorocarbon-free air conditioning system.

But the XJ6 sedan will cost $5,250 more than the least expensive car offered by Jaguar a year ago. That model, which cost $44,500, is no longer available.

Jaguar is aiming to sell its vehicles with the help of some unusual advertisements, developed by its new ad agency, WPP Group PLC's Ogilvy & Mather in New York. The goal: to highlight the Jaguar heritage, something that newer luxury brands, for all their advantages, don't have.

In the two-page ad a fictitious woman talks about her experiences and feelings while test driving a 1993 model XJ6. The woman talks about her "well-thought-out design to own a Jaguar by the time I reached the age of 40" and her "obsessive love of the Jaguar."

Source: Krystal Miller, "Jaguar Pulls in Its Car-Pricing Claws," *The Wall Street Journal,* October 14, 1992, pp. B1, B8.

CASE 6–2 Lands' End, Inc.

Lands' End, Inc. (LEI) was founded in 1963 by Gary C. Comer, an avid sailor and an award-winning copywriter with the advertising agency of Young & Rubican. LEI was founded to sell equipment to racing sailors by direct mail. Its unique name was the result of a mistake in its first printed mailing piece. Lands' End was meant to be Land's End, the name of a famous English seaport. The error was left uncorrected and the firm was off and running. Mr. Comer has said, "For me, Lands' End is a dream that came true. I always wanted to create a company of my own and here it is."

From its founding until 1976, LEI emphasized the sales of sailing gear while gradually adding related traditional recreational clothing and soft luggage to its product line. The clothing and luggage became so popular among the firm's upscale clientele that by 1976, LEI shifted its focus entirely to these more popular items. In 1979, having outgrown its Chicago location, LEI moved to its current headquarters in Dodgeville, Wisconsin. The Chicago facility which once housed the whole firm was retained as the location of its marketing creative staff of thirty-five people.

In its first 25 years, Lands' End has grown to sales of over $335 million, making it one of the nation's largest merchants selling entirely through the medium of the direct mail catalog. In the five years between 1982 and 1987, LEI's sales more than tripled and the firm set a goal of doubling fiscal 1986 sales by 1991. LEI went public in October 1986, achieving listing on the New

---

This case was prepared by Peter G. Goulet, professor of management, and Lynda L. Goulet, instructor, both of the University of Northern Iowa and is intended to be used as a basis for class discussion rather than to illustrate either effective or ineffective handling of an administrative situation. The authors thank Julie Coppock, a UNI graduate student, and Stephen Ashley of Blunt, Ellis, and Loewi for their help in the preparation of this case.

Presented to and accepted by the refereed Midwest Society for Case Research.

EXHIBIT 1 Lands' End Customer Analysis

	Median Household Income	*Women, Percent Employed*	*Percentage 25–49*	*Growth 25–49 >$30K**	*Percent Employed Professional*
LEI	$46,000	75%	69%	3.2%	70%
U.S.	24,500	<50	50	<1.0	<25

*Annual growth expected from 1985–95 for population group with incomes over $30,000 ages between 25–49.

York Stock Exchange in late 1987. LEI's 20,040,000 shares had a market value of $560 million in September 1988. For the fiscal year ending in January 1989, Lands' End is expected to circulate 72 million catalogs, achieve sales of $388,000,000, and earn profits of $26,000,000, or $1.30 per share.[1] Further financial information is presented in Exhibits 3 through 5.

Business and Customers

Lands' End is a clothing retailer serving the market by direct mail through its extensive catalog of traditional clothing and related items. The main types of products sold include men's dress shirts, slacks, ties, and accessories, as well as sport clothes such as sweaters, shoes, jogging suits and sweats, and a myriad of styles of knit shirts. The women's line includes similar sport clothing, as well as traditional natural fiber shirts, skirts, slacks, shoes, and accessories. The firm also offers a limited but growing line of children's clothing in styles similar to the adult lines. Finally, the firm manufactures and sells a line of soft luggage products and has recently introduced a line of linens and bedding.

The Lands' End customer is reasonably affluent. Sixty percent have incomes in excess of $35,000. Most have been to college and are employed in professional or managerial jobs. Exhibit 1 compares the typical Lands' End customer to its counterpart in the population as a whole. In 1986, LEI estimated that there were 23 million households in the U.S. that met its typical customer characteristics. Moreover, this group was growing more than three times as fast as the population as a whole. Further, it typically spends a larger proportion of its income on apparel than the average for the population.

The Direct Marketing Association (DMA) estimated that 10.1 percent of the total female population and 5.4 percent of the male population ordered at least one item of clothing from a catalog or other direct mail merchant in 1986. On average, between 9 percent and 10 percent of all the

[1]All financial data in this case come from Lands' End annual reports and analytical reports prepared by Stephen Ashley of Blunt, Ellis, and Loewi, Inc. (August 4, 1987 and November 23, 1987).

EXHIBIT 2 Retail Sales Data ($ billions)

	1985	*1986*	*1987E*	*1988E*	*Growth Rate†*
Retail sales	1,374.0	1,454.0	1,541.0	1,633.0	5.9%
Retail apparel	74.0	81.0	86.7	92.8	7.8
Catalog sales*	26.0	27.5	29.7	32.1	7.3
Catalog apparel*	7.5	8.2	8.9	9.5	8.6
Lands' End	.23	.26	.34	.39	19.2
Share catalog apparel	3.1%	3.1%	3.8%	4.1%	

*Estimated.

†Average annual growth 1985–88.

Source: U.S. Commerce Department.

people with incomes over $30,000 made a direct-mail clothing purchase. In addition, DMA has estimated that 10.7 percent of the college graduates and 10.5 percent of the professional/managerial households made such a purchase. Overall, it would appear that about 10 percent of the group Lands' End considers to be its prime customers can be expected to make a direct mail clothing purchase from some firm in a given year. Out of the base of 23 million customers this would imply an average of 2.3 million active customers per year. In fact, LEI estimates that in the 36 months preceding February 1988, it had made at least one sale to 3.4 million different persons.

Industry Environment

Lands' End is part of the catalog apparel industry which accounts for approximately 10 percent of all apparel sales. Recent data for these markets is shown in Exhibit 2. In 1988, the firm held about a 4 percent share of the catalog apparel market, making it the seventh largest direct market or catalog apparel retailer (see Exhibit 6 for a list of selected competitors). This market has enjoyed recent growth at 8.6 percent per year and is expected to continue to grow at 10 percent per year through 1991. Lands' End has grown roughly two to three times as fast as the market since calendar 1985.

Though catalog retailing is expected to grow faster than retailing in general in the next three to five years, there are some clouds on the horizon. The prospects for growth have caused a sharp increase in the number of catalogs directed to the buying public. In 1985, a total of 10 billion catalogs were mailed, rising to 11.8 billion in 1987.[2] In addition, poor service on the part of some catalog merchants may help create a negative image for the segment in general. *Consumer Reports* has recently published ratings of catalog retailers to help consumers determine the relative service quality of many of

[2]A. Hagedorn, "Tis the Season for Catalog Firms," *The Wall Street Journal* (November 24, 1987), p. 6.

the larger firms, including Lands' End. Lands' End was beaten only by L. L. Bean in these initial consumer ratings.

Another threat to catalog retailers is the rising cost of shipping goods and mailing catalogs. Early in 1988, the postal service raised postage rates for catalogs 25 percent and UPS raised surface shipping costs as well. In addition, catalog production costs are also rising, as are catalog sizes. The typical cost for a catalog the size and quality of that published by Lands' End can run as high as $750–$800 per thousand, exclusive of mailing and handling costs. A typical 64-page catalog in two or four colors costs around $350–$400 per thousand. To partially offset these rising costs, some catalog retailers such as Bloomingdale's, for example, have begun to sell their catalogs in major-chain bookstores and sell advertising space in the catalogs.

Finally, most states do not require catalog retailers to charge sales tax on catalog sales outside of the states in which the firm operates. Recently, however, states are beginning to view this practice as a significant source of lost revenue. In 1988, Iowa was added to a small but growing list of states which will require catalog firms to remit sales tax on all purchases made from catalogs by residents of the state, regardless of where the catalog firm is located. If all states move to this type of policy, it will reduce one of the key advantages to catalog retailers and could create significant overhead expenses for keeping the records required to satisfy each state.

A segment of the direct market retailing industry outside of the catalog segment may also pose a threat to the catalog retailers. Home shopping directed through cable television was expected to generate an estimated $1.75 billion in sales in 1987. The companies in this segment, of which the largest is the Home Shopping Network, Inc., were estimated to have reached over 40 million households in that year. Further, though some view the cable shopping phenomenon as a fad, DMA estimates that by 1992 this industry segment could be generating $5.6 billion in sales and be reaching nearly 80 million households. If this is true, it represents a 26 percent average annual growth rate for the period. Given the growth of retail sales in general and forecasts for direct marketing retailing, this would seem to be growth that could easily come at the expense of other direct marketers.

Though entry into direct marketing does not require the same level of investment required to generate similar sales in the normal retail market, the costs may still be significant. To provide sufficient service requires expertise and may involve a large equipment investment. To develop a mailing list is also important and expensive. Name rental may run anywhere from $60–$100 per thousand names annually, or upward of $100,000 for a million quality, proven names. As the established firms such as Lands' End and L. L. Bean become large, economies of scale and learning curve effects may make it difficult for new firms to enter the business in all but small niche markets.

Pure catalog retailers have a number of significant advantages over conventional retailers. The most obvious of these is that they have no stores to operate and have, therefore, lower costs. Passing on some of these cost savings can create a competitive advantage. In spite of this inherent advantage, however, several of the major catalog competitors do operate store locations in addition to their catalog operation, thus offsetting the advantage. What these firms have attempted to do is improve their performance as traditional retailers by using higher profit catalog sales as an adjunct to normal store-based selling. The Limited, Eddie Bauer, Talbots, J. C. Penney, and Sears, for example, operate anywhere from several dozen to several hundred stores each.

In addition to having lower costs and prices, catalog retailers give the customer the advantage of convenience. Being able to shop through a catalog and call in an order even in the middle of the night may be of great benefit to households where both spouses are working outside the home, for example. Further, using a catalog means the consumer may think about the purchase and compare alternative sources without costly transportation and sales pressure. Finally, catalog shopping is also a convenience for people who live in smaller communities where a variety of upscale goods, especially, is typically not available and obtaining such goods from a conventional store would be even more inconvenient than purchasing through a catalog.

The biggest weaknesses of catalog shopping involve the inability to see an item before buying it and the cost and inconvenience of having to return an unsatisfactory purchase. In spite of these issues, however, a Gallup poll reported by the DMA in 1987 shows that two thirds of the population would consider making a direct/catalog purchases even if the item were available in conventional stores.

Lands' End's Strategy

Catalog retailers must adhere to most of the principles that govern traditional store-based retailers. Merchandise must be fresh, varied, and of satisfactory quality. By maintaining itself as a retailer of traditional clothing, Lands' End does not have the concerns with fad and fashion faced by such combination in-store and direct-mail retailers as The Limited and Bloomingdales, for example. However, the firm does have to offer new merchandise regularly. Its most recent introductions have been its line of children's clothing and linens. Other featured items include its knit shirts and rugby shirts, the latter having been chosen by the U.S. National Rugby Team as their official jersey.

All Lands' End merchandise carries the firm's own private label. All catalog items except luggage are produced by outside vendors. The luggage is manufactured by the firm at its plant in West Union, Iowa. Product quality is assured by frequent inspections of goods, both at the manufacturer's facility and at the company. The firm even maintains a Lear jet to fly its staff of quality assurance personnel to the factories of domestic manufacturers to direct production according to Lands' End specifications. Further, 10 percent of every shipment received at Dodgeville is inspected to assure continuing quality. Critical products are purchased from more than one vendor and consistency between them is maintained by strict specifications. To further assure quality and service from vendors, officers of these companies are regularly brought to Dodgeville to see the Lands' End operation.

Lands' End understands that catalog retailing is a difficult business in which to create a competitive advantage. Its catalogs, therefore, are produced with what the firm calls an *editorial* approach. Goods are not merely described in short, dry descriptions. Rather, key product lines are given large half- or full-page descriptions which are designed to be interesting, appealing, and original. In addition, the catalog often contains several pages devoted to editorials, essays, and witty commentary dealing with a variety of subjects of interest to the firm's clientele. Two pages in the April 1988 issue described glass blowing. This kind of content is not unique to Lands' End. The catalog issued by the trendy Banana Republic also employs a similar approach. However, because different writers and subjects are involved in each catalog, Lands' End's catalogs can still be differentiated and are difficult to copy.

In addition, the quality and presentation of the Lands' End catalog is tightly controlled and merchandise is presented in life-style settings designed to appeal to the firm's clientele. Merchandise is grouped in *programs* to promote multiple item sales. This *magazine style* approach is further supported by the use of product teams. New items are studied by a team consisting of a writer, an artist, and a buyer to make certain that each item is presented properly in the catalog.

To interest prospective customers, Lands' End utilizes print advertising. The cost of this national campaign in selected upscale publications such as *The Wall Street Journal* and *The New Yorker* is approximately 1 percent of sales. The campaign is designed to be compatible with the firm's editorial catalog structure and contains copy in a similar style.

Lands' End considers itself a *direct merchant* and summarizes its marketing and operations strategy as:

1. Establishing a strong, unique consumer brand image.
2. Placing an emphasis on product quality and value.
3. Identifying and expanding an active customer base.
4. Creating a continuous relationship with active customers.
5. Building customer confidence and convenience through service.

Service

At least part of the success of Lands' End has been attributed to its customer-oriented marketing philosophy. This customer orientation is reflected in a number of ways. Prompt service is supported by rapid response and personal attention. The firm claims its 24-hour-a-day 800 number, which is the source of 73 percent of all incoming orders, rarely requires more than two rings before it is answered. In addition, 99 percent of its orders are shipped within 24 hours of receipt. This level of service is facilitated by a dedicated staff, a sophisticated computerized operating system, and a distribution center just doubled in size to 275,000 square feet. The DMA reports in its 1987 survey of customer attitudes that 83 percent of all direct-mail customers have some sort of complaint about direct-mail purchasing. Though the most common complaints center on the inability to tell what one is likely to receive or that one will have been deceived by the merchandise, a significant percentage either object to poor service (20%) or inconvenience of some kind (16%). In addition, over half of consumers surveyed by DMA say they would buy more from direct marketers who provide prompt delivery.

Lands' End deals with customer complaints with the same commitment they have to customers placing orders. This is essential if the firm is to retain its strong group of dedicated customers. The DMA reports that though a high proportion of customers may have some complaint with mail order, 73 percent will remain as repeat customers if the complaint is satisfactorily handled, compared to 17 percent if it is not.

Lands' End sums up its marketing and service philosophy through its "Principles of Doing Business." These principles have been published in the catalog, annual reports, and advertising copy produced by the company.

> *Principle 1:* We do everything we can to make our products better. We improve material and add back features and construction details that others have taken out over the years. We never reduce the quality of a product to make it cheaper.
>
> *Principle 2:* We price our products fairly and honestly. We do not, have not, and will not participate in the common retail practice of inflating markups to set up a future phony "sale."
>
> *Principle 3:* We accept any return, for any reason, at any time. Our products are guaranteed. No fine print. No arguments. We mean exactly what we say: GUARANTEED. PERIOD.
>
> *Principle 4:* We ship faster than anyone we know of. We ship items in stock the day we receive the order. At the height of the last Christmas season, the longest time an order was in the house was thirty-six hours, excepting monograms which took another twelve hours.
>
> *Principle 5:* We believe that what is best for our customers is best for all of us. Everyone here understands that concept. Our sales and service people are trained to know our products, and to be friendly and helpful. They are urged to take all the time necessary to take care of you. We even pay for your call, for whatever reason you call.
>
> *Principle 6:* We are able to sell at lower prices because we have eliminated middlemen; because we don't buy branded merchandise with high protected markups; and because we have placed our contracts with manufacturers who have proved they are cost conscious and efficient.

Principle 7: We are able to sell at lower prices because we operate efficiently. Our people are hard-working, intelligent, and share in the success of the company.

Principle 8: We are able to sell at lower prices because we support no fancy emporiums with their high overhead. Our main location is in the middle of a forty-acre cornfield in rural Wisconsin. We still operate our first location in Chicago's Near North tannery district.

Operations

The heart of any catalog retailing operation is, of course, the catalog itself. Lands' End currently mails thirteen 140 page (average) catalogs a year to its proven customers. In all, the firm circulated a total of 50 million catalogs in fiscal 1987. That number is expected to rise to 63.5 million in 1988 and is expected to reach 72 million in 1989, up from 18 million in 1984, the firm's most productive year in terms of sales per catalog mailed.

Another key to effective catalog retailing is the mailing list. Firms the size of Lands' End commonly maintain lists of 5 million or more names. The firm itself maintains a proprietary list of 7.8 million names. Although many catalog retailers obtain names from mailing list brokers and even competitors, Lands' End has attempted to build its list internally as much as possible as a source of competitive advantage. It has also reduced its participation in the mailing list rental market.

Catalog retailing also depends on order fulfillment and service. Merchandise is stored in and distributed from the firm's 275,000-square-foot distribution center. In spite of the size of this facility, however, it is only expected to be able to satisfy the firm's needs through 1989 when another 250,000 square foot addition is expected to be completed. Through its center, Lands' End processed approximately 31,000 orders per day in 1987 with a high of 75,000 orders on its peak day. The center has the capacity to process 35,000 orders per nine-hour shift.

To facilitate the function of the distribution center, manage inventories, and minimize shipping costs, the firm utilizes an optical scanning sorting system. Orders are processed through the firm's mainframe computer system based on three very large Series 3090 computers by IBM. Through this computer system management can obtain real-time information on any part of its current operation status. In addition, during 1987, the firm installed a new computer-controlled garment-moving system and inseaming system as part of $6 million in capital expenditures. Finally, an automated receiving system installed during 1987 has increased the firm's receiving capacity to 10,000 boxes per day from 4,000.

Phone service is maintained through company phone centers. This service was recently enlarged by the addition of an auxillary center designed to handle seasonal overload traffic. This phone system now operates on a fiber-optic cable system to increase communication quality. Through the computer system, each operator has access to customer records and past sales

EXHIBIT 3 Lands' End Income Statements for the Fiscal Years Ended January 31, (thousands of dollars)

	1988	*Percent*	*1987*	*Percent*	*1986*	*Percent*	*1985*	*Percent*
Net sales	$336,291	100.0%	$265,058	100.0%	$227,160	100.0%	$172,241	100.0%
Cost of sales	190,348	56.6	152,959	57.7	135,678	59.7	101,800	59.1
Gross profit	$145,943	43.4%	$112,099	42.3%	$ 91,482	40.3%	$ 70,441	40.9%
Operating expense	104,514	31.0	80,878	30.5	67,781	29.9	55,431	32.2
Depreciation	3,185	1.0	2,576	1.0	1,867	.8	1,435	.8
Operating income	$ 38,244	11.4%	$ 28,645	10.8%	$ 21,834	9.6%	$ 13,575	7.9%
Interest expense	(1,357)	−0.4	(1,488)	−0.6	(1,579)	−0.7	(1,697)	−1.0
Other income	1,441	0.4	1,329	0.5	1,329	0.6	938	0.5
Income before tax	$ 38,328	11.4%	$ 28,486	10.7%	$ 21,584	9.5%	$ 12,816	7.4%
Income tax[1]	15,523	4.6	13,881	5.2	10,314	4.5	6,076	3.5
Net income	$ 22,805	6.8%	$ 14,605	5.5%	$ 11,270	5.0%	$ 6,740	3.9%
Per share[2]	$ 1.14*		$ 0.73		$ 0.56			
Catalogs mailed	63.5 mil.		50.0 mil.		44.0 mil.		29.0 mil.	

Quarterly Percents	*Sales*	*Gross Percent*	*Sales*	*Gross Percent*	*Sales*	*Gross Percent*
February–April	18.0%	17.6%	17.8%	16.7%	19.1%	19.5%
May–July	19.0	18.8	19.9	18.7	19.4	18.1
August–October	23.8	24.1	24.5	25.3	23.7	24.4
November–January	39.1	39.4	37.8	39.3	37.8	38.0

Lands' End was a Subchapter S Corporation through part of 1987. Therefore:
[1]Income taxes from 1985–87 are estimated to reflect a normal corporate structure.
[2]Earnings per share are estimated based on shares outstanding in 1988.

history as well as a fact file on each catalog item. It is not unusual for this system to handle 75 calls at a time, around the clock, in normal times, with a much higher load in the Christmas season.

Though 95 percent of all sales are through the catalog and Lands' End operates no retail stores, it does maintain nine outlet stores at various locations in Chicago and Wisconsin. The firm also utilizes a Lands' End Outlet section in its catalog to help dispose of overstocks.

As the firm has grown, so has the number of employees. The firm now employs more than 2,200 people, with as many as 1,200 more added to handle the extra load during the busy fourth quarter. Both the founder and the current president have extensive advertising experience as well as considerable experience with the company. New additions to the list of top managers

EXHIBIT 4 Lands' End Statements of Changes in Working Capital for the Fiscal Years Ended (thousands of dollars)

	1988	1987	1986	1985
Sources:				
Operations[1]	$25,668	$21,804	$23,451	$14,251
Long-term debt		264	316	
Sale of stock		22,584		520
Fixed assets—net	776	38	243	205
Total sources	$26,444	$44,690	$24,010	$14,976
Uses:				
Dividends[2]	$ 4,008	$28,000	$13,775	$11,755
Fixed assets	5,862	9,595	6,631	2,658
Reduce long-term debt	1,918			478
Other		40	24	
Total uses	$11,788	$37,635	$20,430	$14,891
Net increase with changes	$14,656	$ 7,055	$ 3,580	$ 85

[1]Cash flow from operations consists of net income, depreciation, and additions to deferred taxes.

[2]Lands' End was a Subchapter S Corporation through part of 1987. Therefore, dividends from 1985–87 are Subchapter S distributions.

include experts in catalog merchandising, quality assurance, and other related specialties.

Lands' End realizes the importance of a quality work force. It has worked with the University of Wisconsin, Platteville, to set up an extension in Dodgeville to help workers increase their skills at company expense. Part-time workers earn full-time benefits after they work 1,040 hours in a year. All workers receive the right to an employee discount on the firm's products and share in the firm's profits. The firm also plans to provide a $5 million employee fitness center in 1988. Overall, wage levels in this industry average approximately $5.75 per hour.

Competitors

There are dozens of catalog retailers selling apparel, even in the market dominated by Lands' End. However, in its specific target market, LEI has apparently become the market leader. LEI's competitors may be classified into several basic categories. There are firms such as the J. Crew unit of Popular Services, Inc. (men's clothing); Talbots (women's clothing), formerly owned by General Mills; and The Company Store (linens), who compete directly with a product segment served by Lands' End. Other firms, such as Hanover House, produce multiple catalogs serving a wide variety of customer product and demographic segments. Some of these segments may overlap with those served by LEI. Major retailers such as Sears, J. C. Penney, and Spiegel produce large, seasonal, full-line catalogs selling a wide variety of

EXHIBIT 5 Lands' End Balance Sheets for the Fiscal Years Ended January 31 (thousands of dollars)

	1988	*1987*	*1986*
Current assets:			
Cash and marketable securities	$ 28,175	$16,032	$ 3,578
Receivables	274	238	319
Inventories	46,444	40,091	31,057
Other	3,363	1,299	733
Total current	$ 78,256	$57,660	$35,687
Plant and equipment:			
Land and buildings	$ 15,114	$13,809	$ 9,499
Equipment	21,974	19,667	13,266
Leasehold improvement	908	661	584
Other	674		1,250
Total	$ 38,670	$34,137	$24,599
Depreciation	9,947	7,315	4,758
Net fixed assets	$ 28,723	$26,822	$19,841
Total assets	$106,979	$84,482	$55,528
Current liabilities:			
Current portion long-term debt	$ 1,918	$ 321	$ 193
Accounts payable	21,223	16,791	13,927
Order advances	453	449	193
Accruals	7,226	4,394	2,589
Profit sharing	2,646	1,707	830
Taxes payable	5,394	9,258	
Total current	$ 38,860	$32,920	$18,002
Long-term debt	8,667	10,585	10,321
Deferred income taxes	2,776	3,100	
	$ 50,305	$46,605	$28,323
Stockholders' equity:			
Common stock	$ 200	$ 100	$ 95
Paid-in-capital	22,308	22,408	73
Retained earnings	34,166	15,369	27,037
Total equity	$ 56,674	$37,877	$27,205
Total debt and owners' equity	$106,979	$84,482	$55,528

merchandise, of which apparel is only a part. These large firms, as well as other small catalog retailers who also operate retail stores, tend to compete more closely with traditional retailers. Exhibit 6 identifies a number of major catalog retailers and competitors for LEI. Exhibit 7 describes and contrasts several operating characteristics of LEI's closest competitors.

Performance

Since 1984, when Lands' End achieved sales of $123.4 million and net profits of $7.3 million, the firm's sales and profits have grown at 22.2 percent and 25.6 percent annually, respectively. Sales and profit growth in the first

EXHIBIT 6 Direct/Catalog Sales, 1985 (largest direct mail/catalog apparel firms)

Firm	*Direct/Catalog Total 1985 Sales ($ millions)*
Fingerhut Corp/Cos	$1,485
Spiegel	847
Sears	695
The Limited/Brylane	612
J. C. Penney	510
New Process	330
Combined international	227
Lands' End	227
L. L. Bean	220
Hanover House	212
Avon Direct Response	205
Bear Creek	130
General Mills	104
CML Group	55
Popular Services	40

Source: *Inside the Leading Mail Order Houses,* 3rd ed. (Colorado Springs: Maxwell Scroge Publishing, 1987).

EXHIBIT 7 Lands' End Competitor Characteristics, 1985

Company	*Catalog Sales ($ millions)*	*Catalogs Mailed (millions)*	*Sales per Catalog*	*Active Buyers (millions)*	*Stores and/or Notes*
Lands' End	$227	44	$5.16	3.43	9 outlets
Hanover House	212	250	0.85	4.00	20 catalogs
L. L. Bean	221	68	3.25	2.15	1 store
Popular Services:					
J. Crew	30	7	4.29	.45	
Cliff & Wills	10	2	5.00	.20	
CML Group	55	25	2.20	.49	5 catalogs
General Mills—1985:					
Talbots	47	38	1.25	.47	59 stores
E. Bauer	57	25	2.28	.72	39 stores
General Mills—1987:					
Talbots	84	60+	<1.40	65+	109 stores
E. Bauer	76	N/A	N/A	1.00	39 stores

half of fiscal 1989 were 33.7 percent and 64.6 percent higher than the same period in 1988, respectively. Gross margins have improved steadily and may be compared to a level of approximately 42.5 percent typical for apparel retailers in general. Net profit margins have also improved and may be compared to a recent level of about 3.5 percent for large retailers. The percentage of debt to equity has declined steadily throughout the period. The net profit to total assets measure of return on investment has averaged 21 percent over the last five years, compared to 4.4 percent for the nation's 33 largest value retail firms (including LEI) in 1988 and approximately 7.5 percent for all retail establishments. LEI's return on stockholder's equity has averaged 40.4 percent since 1984, having earned 40.2 percent in 1988, compared to 15.4 percent for the largest firms. Financial results for Lands' End are presented in Exhibits 3 through 5.

Although Lands' End's recent performance is spectacular and far exceeds industry standards, it remains to be seen how long their growth and margins can be maintained. As the catalog market becomes increasingly competitive, new products and marketing methods will have to be developed. In spite of the prospect of future pressures, the sale of General Mills' catalog operations in 1988 brought the firm $585 million or about 19 times the pretax operating earnings of this unit.

REFERENCES

Major sources of information included:

1987 Supplement to the Fact Book, Direct Marketing Association (New York, 1987).

Inside the Leading Mail Order Houses, 3rd ed., Colorado Springs: Maxwell Sroge Publishing, 1987.

Lands' End Annual Reports—1987 and 1988.

1988 Industrial Outlook, U.S. Department of Commerce.

CASE 6–3 Playboy Enterprises, Inc.

The approach to doing business at Playboy Enterprises, Inc. (hereafter referred to as PEI), was recently characterized by Christie Hefner, chairman and chief executive officer (CEO) of PEI, as "a commitment to think globally and act locally." That statement truly represents the essence of PEI's business strategy toward the year 2000. Emphasis will be placed on global expansion to take advantage of Playboy's name recognition and the demise of communism worldwide. However, PEI's net income fell 16 percent in fiscal 1991. The number of U.S. households subscribing monthly to the Play-

This case was written by James W. Fenton, Jr., and Fred R. David, Francis Marion University.

boy Service on television also declined, from 428,000 in 1989 to 358,000 in 1990 and to 314,000 in 1991, respectively. Improvements are needed in PEI's operations.

PEI was organized in 1953 to publish *Playboy* magazine. Since its inception, PEI has expanded its publishing operations and has engaged in other businesses related to the life-style developed and promoted in *Playboy*. PEI's businesses are grouped into three divisions: publishing, entertainment, and product marketing. PEI's trademarks include Playboy, Playmate, Sarah Coventry, and the Rabbit Head design. Christie Hefner succeeded her father, Hugh M. Hefner, as chairman of the board and CEO in 1988. Hugh Hefner owns 71 percent of Playboy's stock. As of September 1991, PEI employed 586 full-time employees, of whom 279 worked in the publishing segment. A year earlier, PEI employed 561 full-time employees with 263 in publishing.

Publishing

The publishing segment of PEI includes the publication of *Playboy* magazine, the publication of newsstand specials and calendars, the licensing of foreign editions of *Playboy* magazine, 900-number telephone services, the licensing of artwork owned by the firm, and the publishing of direct-mail catalogues. This division accounted for 54 percent of company operating profits in 1991 and 81 percent of revenues. Exhibit 1 gives the position of *Playboy* magazine among the top 20 consumer magazines for the first six months of 1991.

Playboy magazine is the world's best-selling magazine aimed at the adult male audience and is the major project of the publishing segment. The magazine is sold principally in the United States by subscriptions delivered through the mail and on a single-copy basis at newsstands. The data in Exhibit 2 show the average net paid circulation per issue (single-copy sales and subscriptions) for the first and second six months of 1988 through 1991.

Net circulation revenues from the U.S. edition of *Playboy* for the fiscal years ended June 30, 1991, 1990, 1989, and 1988 were $65,832,000, $65,247,000, $66,022,000, and $69,124,000, respectively. PEI publishes the U.S. edition of *Playboy* in several U.S. geographic editions that have the same editorial material but different advertising copy. In May 1991 a Czechoslovakian edition of *Playboy* magazine was launched. Thirteen other foreign editions of *Playboy* are published in Argentina, Australia, Brazil, Germany, Greece, Hong Kong, Hungary, Italy, Mexico, the Netherlands, Spain, Taiwan, and Turkey. The three largest-selling editions—Germany, Brazil, and Japan—account for 63 percent of total royalty income from foreign countries. The average monthly circulation for all foreign editions is 1.3 million copies.

Net advertising revenues for the U.S. edition of *Playboy* during 1991 and 1990 were $32,682,000 and $31,407,000, respectively. This increase

EXHIBIT 1 Number of Copies of Leading Consumer Magazines Sold during the First Six Months of Year (in millions)

Magazine	*1989*	*1990*	*1991*
1. *Reader's Digest*	16.3	16.4	16.3
2. *TV Guide*	15.4	15.8	15.4
3. *National Geographic*	9.9	10.2	9.9
4. *Better Homes and Gardens*	8.0	8.0	8.0
5. *Family Circle*	5.2	5.2	5.2
6. *Good Housekeeping*	5.0	5.1	5.0
7. *McCall's*	5.0	5.0	5.0
8. *Ladies' Home Journal*	5.0	5.0	5.0
9. *Woman's Day*	4.8	4.6	4.8
10. *Time*	4.4	4.3	4.2
11. *Redbook*	3.8	3.9	3.8
12. *National Enquirer*	3.7	4.0	3.7
13. *Playboy*	3.5	3.4	3.5
14. *Sports Illustrated*	3.4	3.5	3.4
15. *Newsweek*	3.4	3.2	3.4
16. *People*	3.2	3.2	3.2
17. *Star*	3.2	3.6	3.2
18. *Prevention*	3.1	3.0	3.1
19. *Cosmopolitan*	2.7	2.7	2.7
20. *First for Women*	2.4	2.8	2.4

Source: Audit Bureau of Circulations.

EXHIBIT 2 Playboy Magazine's Average Net Paid Circulation per Issue

			Approximate Percentage of Circulation from	
Calendar Year	*First 6 Months*	*Second 6 Months*	*Single-Copy Sales*	*Subscriptions*
1991	3,500,000	3,500,000	23	77
1990	3,400,000	3,400,000	25	75
1989	3,600,000	3,700,000	27	73
1988	3,700,000	3,400,000	31	69

occurred at a time when magazine circulation across the country was declining due to the slumping economy. This decline naturally has had a negative impact on ad pages sold and advertising revenues of most magazines. New advertisers in key growth categories enhanced advertising revenue results in 1991. Examples of these growth categories were the apparel and fragrance industries. Some of the new accounts included Timberlane Fashions, Giorgio Red for Men, Perry Ellis for Men, and Guess Perfumes for Men.

Paper is the major raw material necessary to the publishing business.

Purchase of paper by PEI is done through a number of suppliers, and the firm has not experienced any problems acquiring paper. PEI conducts all print operations and typesetting in-house for its entire line of publications.

PEI is also engaged in the production and sale of newsstand specials and calendars. The specials include Playboy-style photography and cartoons. Both wall and desk calendars feature photographs of Playboy playmates. A 1991 calendar featured women in lingerie and sold 200,000 copies worldwide. Due to its popularity, a second lingerie calendar will be published in 1992 as well as a new Women of Canada calendar for distribution in Canada only. PEI increased the number of specials published in 1991 to 14 from 13 the prior two years.

The March 1990 issue of *Playboy* started a new business that PEI calls audiotext. Using a 900-toll-call telephone line, callers telephone what is dubbed the Playboy "Hotline" and receive an expanded version of the Playboy editorial view. The hotline was successful in its first year of operation. As a follow-up to the hotline success, PEI introduced the Playboy Wake-Mate in February 1991. This 900-series telephone service allows customers to schedule wake-up calls recorded by Playmates. In addition, PEI recently introduced Coast to Coast, a 900-series phone service through which toll callers speak live with a different Playmate each weeknight.

Recent Acquistions. PEI owns a 20 percent interest in DuPont Publishing Inc., publisher of the *DuPont Registry,* a magazine that advertises classic, luxury, and exotic automobiles. *DuPont Registry* sales increased 80 percent in 1990, with accompanying advertising levels climbing accordingly. The *Registry* saw moderate growth in revenues in 1991, with operating income reported to be $250,000.

An additional publishing-related acquisition was announced in 1991 when PEI entered into a joint agreement with Spectradyne, Inc., to publish *SV Entertainment,* a monthly guide to in-hotal television programming and general entertainment editorial. Initial circulation was 500,000 copies. The first issue premiered in October 1991 and offered PEI a vehicle to attract upscale advertisers.

Playboy Artwork. A wholly owned subsidiary of PEI, Special Editions, Ltd. (SEL) licenses and sells artwork owned by the company. PEI reproduces and markets limited editions of original *Playboy* artwork in fine-art galleries in Asia, Europe, and North America and prints and posters of selected *Playboy* artwork through joint-venture arrangements. In addition, SEL sold 161 paintings by LeRoy Neiman that were originally done for Playboy clubs and hotels. The agreement gives PEI an ongoing interest both in the future sales by the purchaser of such paintings and in licensing royalties from reproduction of the paintings. SEL has additional partnerships and joint ventures to reproduce and market artwork of Keith Haring, Patrick Nagel, Frank Gallo, Pater Sato, Brad Holland, Elizabeth Bennett,

Michael Knigin, and Kinuko Kraft. Revenues of SEL were $1,173,000, $2,310,000, and $64,000 in fiscal 1990, 1989, and 1988, respectively. Beginning in fiscal 1992, SEL operations will be reported in the product marketing segment.

Retail Mail-Order Catalogue. PEI publishes a retail mail-order catalogue biannually to market the Playboy and Playmate product line and Playboy videocassettes. Other items also offered in the catalogue include Playboy collectibles (e.g., calendars and back issues of *Playboy*), gift and specialty items, jewelry, video movies, and special-interest cassettes. PEI owns 80 percent of the common stock of Critics' Choice Video, Inc., and publishes a videocassette catalogue under the Critics' Choice name. Video Search Line, a 900 telephone number, was introduced in 1991 to provide information on and access to 35,000 videos not listed in the catalogue.

In 1991 PEI entered into its first overseas direct-marketing venture, an agreement with 7-Eleven Japan Company Ltd. to sell selected reproductions of Playboy-owned art to Japanese consumers through the *Shop America* catalogue. Playboy's strategy is to provide outstanding customer service, including 24-hour toll-free ordering, quick and efficient delivery, and hassle-free returns. PEI has a biannual retail mail-order catalogue that highlights the Sarah Coventry products. Revenues from catalogue operations have shown dramatic growth, being $18.1 million in 1991, $12.5 million in 1990, and $5.9 million in 1989. The publishing division of PEI reported operating income of $12.1 million in 1991 versus $10.3 million and $10.2 million in 1990 and 1989, respectively; revenues increased to $141 million from $133 million in 1990 and $138 million in 1989.

Entertainment

PEI is involved in the development, production, and distribution of programming principally for domestic and international pay television (including pay-per-view, monthly subscription pay cable, direct broadcast satellite dish, and hotel/motel distribution) and of home videos for both domestic and international markets and syndicated television. Television programming is generally composed of original programs 30 or 60 minutes in length and of licensed, independently produced feature-length movies 90 minutes or more in length. This division accounted for 15 percent of company profits in 1991. The company invested $15.9 million in the entertainment division in 1991, up from $11.4 million in 1990 and $6.1 million in 1989.

The Playboy Channel Relaunched as Pay-per-View. The Playboy Channel was launched in November 1982 with approximately 300,000 monthly subscribers. As of June 30, 1991, the channel had approximately 314,000 monthly subscribing households, down from 428,000 in 1989. The number of pay-per-view purchasers of the Playboy Service were 2,112,000, 1,051,000, and 580,000 in fiscal 1991, 1990, and 1989, respectively.

Pay-per-view services are available from cable systems equipped with the hardware that offers cable subscribers two-way addressability, or the capacity to "call up" specific programs. Playboy programming has been available since 1987 as a pay-per-view service, although it has been programmed primarily for the monthly subscriber. On June 30, 1991, Playboy programming was available to approximately 4.7 million households, up from 3.2 million in 1990. Revenues from pay-per-view purchases of the channel were $1,908,000 and $1,182,000 in fiscal 1990 and 1989, respectively.

In fiscal 1990, PEI launched an international television series called "Playboy Late Night." The first 26 episodes of this series were successful, so an additional 26 episodes are being developed. "Playboy Late Night" was sold in nine countries at the end of fiscal 1991 and had been renewed in seven. PEI also has a similar series, called "Inside/Out," that is sold in 12 countries.

PEI's television business depends on obtaining and maintaining distribution contracts with affiliates to carry Playboy programming. Multiple-system cable operators (MSOs) may control several affiliates that offer the channel, and each affiliate has a certain Playboy Channel subscriber base. On June 30, 1991, the video segments' top three MSOs supplied the channel to 60 of the 380 affiliates, and those affiliates supplied the service to approximately 115,000 of the 314,000 subscribers of the channel. There were 401 affiliates and 126,000 subscribers in 1990. PEI's revenues from television programming declined in 1991 to $24,426,000 from $25,518,000 in 1990; revenues were $21,638,000 in 1989.

PEI has an agreement with cataloguer and retailer Sharper Image to develop and market Playboy videos geared to couples. The agreement calls for an exclusive distribution arrangement in which all jointly produced videos premiere in *Playboy* and *Sharper Image* catalogues for six months and subsequently roll to national distribution through video retailers and direct marketing distribution. PEI released three of these videos in 1991, up from one in 1990. PEI has released a total of 24 videos at retail, all of which were distributed by HBO.

Effective August 1991, Playboy's North American home video distribution will be handled by Uni Distribution and MCA Entertainment Group Company. Uni's strength is in both audio and video markets and offers more growth opportunities for Playboy in selling its products in combination (video and audio) outlets.

The annual Playboy Jazz Festival is considered a business of the entertainment segment. Each year the Playboy Jazz Festival is held at the Hollywood Bowl in Los Angeles, California. It is always a popular outdoor event and an international attraction. PEI came to an agreement with a Japanese firm, Tokyo Dome Company, for the production of Playboy Jazz Festival events in Tokyo and Fukuoka, Japan. Tickets revenues and merchandise sales in 1990 amounted to $2.1 million.

Revenue from the entertainment group for 1991 declined to $26.7 million from $28.1 million in 1990. The entertainment group reported that overall earnings for 1991 were $3.1 million, compared to $2.98 million in 1990 and an operating loss in 1989 of $900,000.

Product Marketing

Product marketing, which includes all activities related to licensing the Playboy name, licenses the manufacture, sale, and distribution of a significant number of consumer products worldwide. Playboy products are currently sold in more than 60 countries and account for more than $250 million in retail sales. All of these products carry some form of brand identification via one or more of the Playboy or other trademarks.

The Playboy and Playmate product line consists primarily of men's and women's apparel items (including active wear, underwear, loungewear, and intimate apparel), footwear, watches, jewelry, fragrances, sunglasses, luggage and other leather goods, automotive accessories, and home fashions. The Sarah Coventry line consists of women's fashion jewelry and accessories. The lines are sold through mass merchants and other retail outlets. Additionally, the Playboy and Playmate line is sold through the company's biannual retail mail-order catalogue. PEI's art subsidiary, SEL, is being moved from the publishing division to product marketing in fiscal 1992.

On October 30, 1987, a newly formed subsidiary of the company, Licensing Unlimited, Inc., acquired licensing and trademark assets of Sarah Coventry, Inc. Two Sarah Coventry catalogues were launched in fiscal 1990. The sale and distribution of these products are accomplished through exclusive license agreements that include manufacturing as well as selling and distribution; however, the design and quality specifications are controlled by the company.

Licensing the Playboy brand expanded globally in 1991 as Chaifa Investment Ltd. launched a comprehensive Playboy men's apparel program in Hong Kong and mainland China. The Munsin Garment Corporation established a Playboy apparel program in Taiwan, and Joya Marketing introduced a comparable line in Singapore and Malaysia. In Japan P & B, a PEI licensee, introduced a new line of men's contemporary sportswear. PEI also has licensees in Germany, the Netherlands, Czechoslovakia, and Hungary. In fiscal 1991, about 41 percent of licensing royalties were derived from the United States, 42 percent from the Far East, and the remainder from Europe, Australia, and Canada.

Product marketing revenues were $6.4 million, $6.3 million, and $6.2 million in fiscal 1991, 1990, and 1989, respectively. In fiscal 1991 the product marketing division reported earnings of $3.4 million and accounted for 15.5 percent of company operating profits and 3.8 percent of revenues.

Legal Issues

Proceedings in which it has been contended that *Playboy* magazine is obscene and cannot be sold or otherwise distributed have commenced from time to time in local jurisdictions in the United States. The last time this occurred was in 1977. No obscenity ruling has ever been upheld against *Playboy* magazine at a federal or state level; however, an adverse determination could have a negative impact on PEI's revenues and profits, depending on the market involved and the nature of any such decision.

Playboy magazine is sometimes the target of fundamentalist pressure groups who contend that the magazine is obscene. In February 1986 the Attorney General's Commission on Pornography sent a threatening letter to several major convenience and drugstore chains that sold *Playboy* and other adult magazines. PEI subsequently filed a lawsuit and won a preliminary court injunction ordering a retraction letter and forbidding the government from printing a "blacklist" of outlets that sell adult magazines or taking any other action that interferes with the distribution of constitutionally protected materials. The commission's final report, issued in July 1986, clearly indicated that *Playboy* was not at fault. However, despite the outcome of the lawsuit and the commission's final report, the threatening letter caused the loss of a significant number of retail outlets selling *Playboy.* This event prompted increased display restrictions in a number of stores, which adversely affected *Playboy*'s newsstand sales that year.

Finance

Information on PEI's top executives is given in Exhibit 3. PEI's income statement, balance sheet, statement of changes in shareholders' equity, and segment information are given in Exhibits 4, 5, 6, 7, and 8, respectively. PEI's net income declined in 1991 to $4.5 million compared to $6.2 million in 1990.

Public Affairs

Preserving and enhancing civil liberties and social justice for all Americans continues to be the focus and commitment of Playboy's public affairs activities and programs. PEI's philanthropic arm, the Playboy Foundation, awarded $333,000 in grants, contributions, and gifts in kind, including *Playboy* advertising space, to a variety of social change organizations in fiscal 1991.

The Playboy Foundation supports not-for-profit organizations and public interest projects that seek to foster and encourage freedom of speech and expression, human rights, civil liberties, and social justice programs. In addition, PEI encourages its employees to participate in not-for-profit organizations within their communities through its Neighborhood Relations

EXHIBIT 3 Playboy Enterprises, Inc. Executive Officers

Name	*Age*	*Position*
Hugh M. Hefner	65	Chairman emeritus and editor-in-chief
Christie Hefner	38	Chairman of the board and CEO
Howard Shapiro	44	Executive vice president–law and administration, and general counsel
Richard S. Rosenzweig	56	Executive vice president
Michael S. Perlis	38	President, publishing group, and publisher, *Playboy* magazine
Robert J. Friedman	35	President, Playboy Entertainment Group, Inc.
Dale C. Gordon	43	Vice president, secretary, and associate general counsel
Rebecca S. Maskey	43	Vice president–financial services, and treasurer
Michael R. Nott	36	Assistant corporate controller

Source: Playboy Enterprises, Inc., Form 10K, 1990.

Boards and Employee Matching Gift and Time Match programs. From time to time, the company also has contributed funds to the HMH Foundation, a tax-exempt charitable foundation, which donates funds to various community social service, cultural, and medical projects.

In fiscal 1991 the foundation gave special considerations to proposals to protect women's reproductive rights and free expression. Financial awards were issued to Cincinnati's Contemporary Arts Center to help defray expenses incurred in defending the museum and its director against obscenity charges for the display of an exhibit of Robert Mapplethorpe's photography. Other recipients included the Planned Parenthood Federation of America for research on reproductive technologies, National Family Planning and Reproductive Health Association to educate the public concerning family planning issues, People for the American Way in its defense of free expression, and the Student Press Law Center in its defense of First Amendment rights.

Future Plans

PEI would like to capitalize on the trends in Europe and Asia toward democracy and freedom. Which new countries worldwide should be targeted by PEI for entry? Which of PEI's three divisions should receive the greatest emphasis and resources in the early 1990s? Should the company focus more on publishing, licensing, television, telephone, videos, or artwork? How can PEI improve its corporate image among critics who contend that its business is obscene and unethical?

EXHIBIT 4 Playboy Enterprises, Inc. Consolidated Statements of Operations for the Years Ended June 30 (in thousands, except per share amounts)

	1991	*1990**	*1989**
Net revenues	$174,042	$167,697	$166,174
Cost and expenses:			
Cost of sales and operating expenses	(144,196)	(140,854)	(145,101)
Selling and administrative expenses	(27,556)	(26,578)	(27,682)
Total costs and expenses	(171,752)	(167,432)	(172,783)
Operating income (loss)	2,290	265	(6,609)
Nonoperating income (expense):			
Investment income	3,522	2,745	2,937
Interest expense	(298)	(335)	(433)
Gain on sale of Boarts International, Inc.	—	4,806	—
Recapitalization expense	—	(928)	—
Gain on sale of *Games* magazine	—	—	672
Other, net	376	426	18
Total nonoperating income	3,600	6,714	3,194
Income (loss) from continuing operations before income taxes and extraordinary item	5,890	6,979	(3,415)
Income tax expense	(3,479)	(3,383)	(541)
Income (loss) from continuing operations before extraordinary item	2,411	3,596	(3,956)
Discontinued operations:			
Gain (loss) on disposal	(120)	—	126
Income (loss) before extraordinary item	2,291	3,596	(3,830)
Extraordinary item—tax benefit resulting from utilization of loss carryforwards	2,219	2,632	—
Net income (loss)	$ 4,510	$ 6,228	$ (3,830)
Weighted average number of common shares outstanding	18,563	18,813	18,814
Income (loss) per common share:			
Income (loss) before extraordinary item:			
From continuing operations	$ .13	$ .19	$ (.21)
From discontinued operations	(.01)	—	.01
Total	.12	.19	(.20)
Extraordinary item applicable to continuing operations	.12	.14	—
Net income (loss)	$ .24	$ .33	$ (.20)

*Per-share amounts and weighted number of common shares outstanding have been adjusted to reflect the June 7, 1990, recapitalization on a retroactive basis. The accompanying notes are an integral part of these consolidated financial statements.

Source: Playboy Enterprises, Inc., *Annual Report,* 1991.

Should PEI consider making a major acquisition in fiscal 1992 to begin publishing magazines directed toward women, such as *Cosmopolitan, Woman's Day, Ladies' Home Journal,* and *First for Women?* Which of these magazines could feasibly be acquired? What should be PEI's offering price?

EXHIBIT 5 Playboy Enterprises, Inc. Consolidated Statements of Financial Position as of June 30 (in thousands, except share data)

	1991	*1990*
Assets		
Cash and cash equivalents	$ 16,247	$ 16,368
Short-term investments	50	1,504
Receivables, less allowances for doubtful accounts of $4,389, and $3,663 respectively	13,882	17,127
Inventories	16,239	16,517
Film production costs	11,302	5,507
Other current assets	5,733	5,081
Total current assets	63,453	62,104
Property and equipment:		
Land	343	343
Buildings and improvements	8,676	8,421
Furniture and equipment	18,046	16,542
Leasehold improvements	7,140	6,859
Total property and equipment	34,205	32,165
Accumulated depreciation	(19,868)	(17,804)
Property and equipment, net	14,337	14,361
Long-term investments	13,263	12,181
Deferred subscription acquisition costs	9,864	9,780
Film production costs—noncurrent	4,853	2,703
Trademarks and other assets	9,694	8,989
Total assets	$115,464	$110,118
Liabilities		
Current financing obligations	$ 313	$ 310
Accounts payable	8,464	7,389
Accrued salaries, wages and employee benefits	4,531	4,015
Net liabilities of and reserves for losses on disposals of discontinued business	1,188	650
Income taxes payable	314	547
Accrued retail display allowance	2,419	2,992
Other liabilities and accrued expenses	6,949	5,919
Total current liabilities	24,178	21,822
Long-term financing obligations	1,987	2,300
Deferred revenues	42,141	43,111
Other noncurrent liabilities	7,570	6,655
Commitments and contingencies (Notes C, P, and U)		
Shareholders' equity		
Common stock, $.01 par value		
Class A—7,500,000 shares authorized; 5,042,381 issued	50	50
Class B—30,000,000 shares authorized; 15,127,143 issued	151	151
Capital in excess of par value	24,613	24,613
Retained earnings	23,526	19,016
Cost of 345,827 Class A common shares, and 1,314,052 and 1,037,445 Class B common shares, in treasury, respectively	(8,752)	(7,600)
Total shareholders' equity	39,588	36,230
Total liabilities and shareholders' equity	$115,464	$110,118

Source: Playboy Enterprises, Inc., *Annual Report,* 1991.

EXHIBIT 6 Playboy Enterprises, Inc. Financial Information Relating to Industry Segments for the Years Ended June 30 (in thousands)

	1991	*1990*	*1989*
Net Revenues[1],[2]			
Publishing			
Playboy magazine	$100,295	$ 98,232	$100,462
Playboy-related	22,530	20,928	21,060
Catalogs	18,135	12,584	6,191
Boarts	—	1,535	10,249
Total publishing	140,960	133,279	137,962
Entertainment	26,691	28,104	21,948
Product marketing[3]	6,391	6,314	6,264
Total	$174,042	$167,697	$166,174
Income (Loss) from Continuing Operations Before Income Taxes and Extraordinary Item[2]			
Publishing	$ 12,116	$ 10,313	$ 10,157
Entertainment	3,127	2,980	(926)
Product marketing[3]	3,448	3,367	3,245
Corporate administration and promotion	(16,401)	(16,395)	(19,085)
Investment income	3,522	2,745	2,937
Interest expense	(298)	(335)	(433)
Gain on sale of Boarts International, Inc.	—	4,806	—
Recapitalization expense	—	(928)	—
Other, net	376	426	690
Total	$ 5,890	$ 6,979	$ (3,415)
Identifiable Assets			
Publishing	$ 41,663	$ 43,118	$ 37,460
Entertainment	23,899	15,213	12,622
Product marketing[3]	4,349	4,654	3,691
Corporate administration and promotion[4]	45,553	47,133	50,887
Total	$115,464	$110,118	$104,660
Depreciation and Amortization[5]			
Publishing	$ 842	$ 653	$ 574
Entertainment	187	120	163
Product marketing[3]	163	218	267
Corporate administration and promotion	1,528	1,421	1,320
Total	$ 2,720	$ 2,412	$ 2,324
Capital Expenditures[6]			
Publishing	$ 832	$ 3,005	$ 568
Entertainment	316	326	96
Product marketing[3]	39	257	53
Corporate administration and promotion	926	2,666	1,818
Total	$ 2,113	$ 6,254	$ 2,535

The accompanying notes are an integral part of these tables.

Notes to Financial Information Relating to Industry Segments

[1]Net revenues include export sales of $20,157,000, $20,894,000, and $26,958,000 in fiscal 1991, 1990, and 1989, respectively.

[2]Intercompany transactions, which are immaterial, have been eliminated.

[3]The product marketing segment was formerly called product licensing.

[4]Corporate assets consist principally of cash and cash equivalents, short-term investments, property and equipment and long-term investments.

[5]Amounts include depreciation of property and equipment and amortization of intangible assets. Amortization and market value adjustment of film production costs of $7,931,000, $10,239,000, and $11,171,000 in fiscal 1991, 1990, and 1989, respectively, are not included in these amounts.

[6]Capital expenditures for fiscal 1990 were higher for all segments due to the relocation of the company's corporate headquarters in October 1989 under the terms of a 15-year lease. Included in corporate administration and promotion capital expenditures for fiscal 1989 were construction and related costs incurred in preparation for such relocation.

Source: Playboy Enterprises, Inc., *Annual Report,* 1991.

EXHIBIT 7 Playboy Enterprises, Inc. Consolidated Statements of Changes in Shareholders' Equity for the Years Ended June 30, 1991, 1990, and 1989 (in thousands of dollars)

	Class A Common Stock	*Class B Common Stock*	*Capital in Excess of Par Value*	*Retained Earnings*	*Treasury Stock*
Balance at June 30, 1988	$10,100	$ —	$14,904	$16,618	$(7,619)
Net loss	—	—	—	(3,830)	—
Issuance of 1,175* common shares to employees as service awards	—	—	4	—	13
Balance at June 30, 1989	10,100	—	14,908	12,788	(7,606)
Net income	—	—	—	6,228	—
One-for-two reverse common stock split	(5,040)	—	5,040	—	—
Reserve for purchase of fractional shares	(20)	—	(233)	—	—
Reduction in par value from $1.00 to $.01	(4,990)	—	4,990	—	—
Three-for-one Class B common stock dividend	—	151	(151)	—	—
Issuance of 2,458 and 7,374 shares of Class A and Class B common stock, respectively	—	—	58	—	—
Issuance of 522* common shares and 36 Class B common shares to employees as service awards	—	—	1	—	6
Balance at June 30, 1990	50	151	24,613	19,016	(7,600)
Net income	—	—	—	4,510	—
Issuance of 1,393 Class B common shares to employees as service awards	—	—	—	—	7
Purchase of 278,000 Class B common shares	—	—	—	—	(1,159)
Balance at June 30, 1991	$ 50	$151	$24,613	$23,526	$(8,752)

*Represent common shares prior to recapitalization on June 7, 1990.

Source: Playboy Enterprises, Inc., *Annual Report,* 1991.

EXHIBIT 8 Playboy Enterprises, Inc., Consolidated Statements of Cash Flows for the Years Ended June 30 (in thousands)

	1991	*1990*	*1989*
Cash Flows from Operating Activities			
Income (loss) from continuing operations	$ 4,741	$ 6,228	$ (3,956)
Adjustments to reconcile income (loss) from continuing operations to net cash provided by (used for) operating activities:			
Depreciation of property and equipment	2,127	1,833	1,748
Amortization and market value adjustment of film production costs	7,931	10,239	11,171
Gain on sale of Boarts International, Inc.	—	(4,806)	—
Gain on sale of *Games* magazine	—	—	(672)
(Gain) loss on disposals of property and equipment	(4)	(6)	378
Additions to film production costs	(15,876)	(11,411)	(6,109)
Changes in current assets and liabilities:			
Accounts receivable	3,350	(2,086)	788
Inventories	278	(594)	(1,046)
Other current assets	(652)	809	(1,635)
Accounts payable	1,064	(1,516)	(1,339)
Income taxes payable	104	6	34
Other liabilities and accrued expenses	993	(782)	4,554
Increase in trademarks and other assets	(623)	(983)	(95)
Increase (decrease) in deferred revenues, net of deferred subscription acquisition costs	(1,059)	2,440	3,336
Increase in other noncurrent liabilities	1,203	643	18
Net cash provided by (used for) discontinued operations	(27)	(43)	76
Other, net	(344)	(523)	(299)
Net cash provided by (used for) operating activities	3,206	(552)	6,952
Cash Flows from Investing Activities			
Purchases of short-term investments	(1,050)	(978)	(3,754)
Sales and maturities of short-term investments	2,500	5,500	7,186
Net increase in long-term investments	(1,082)	(949)	(803)
Receipts from (advances to and investment in) duPont Publishing, Inc.	250	(200)	(842)
Additions to property and equipment	(2,113)	(6,254)	(2,535)
Proceeds from disposals of property and equipment	14	47	185
Proceeds from sale of Boarts International, Inc.	—	483	—
Collection of note receivable from sale of *Games* magazine	—	—	650
Proceeds from sale of assets of discontinued operation	—	—	132
Other, net	(317)	(207)	(109)
Net cash provided by (used for) investing activities	(1,798)	(2,558)	110
Cash Flows from Financing Activities			
Repurchase of common stock	(1,159)	—	—
Repayment of debt	(350)	(350)	(1,850)
Purchase of fractional shares resulting from recapitalization	(20)	(2)	—
Proceeds from issuance of common stock	—	58	—
Net cash used for financing activities	(1,529)	(294)	(1,850)
Net increase (decrease) in cash and cash equivalents	(121)	(3,404)	5,212
Cash and cash equivalents at beginning of year	16,368	19,772	14,560
Cash and cash equivalents at end of year	$16,247	$16,368	$19,772

Source: Playboy Enterprises, Inc., *Annual Report,* 1991.

There are rumors that PEI itself could be acquired in the early 1990s. How much is the company worth today? What would be your recommendations to Christie Hefner to reverse the company's declining profitability and to grow internationally? Develop a comprehensive strategic plan for PEI.

CASE 6–4 Pier 1 Imports Inc.

In many places, Pier 1 Imports Inc. still conjures up the image of psychedelic pillows, scented candles, beaded curtains, and other cheap furnishings for counterculture digs.

But yesterday's Sgt. Pepper generation has grown up and, after a time, so has Pier 1. Now its stores are piled to the rafters with pricey wicker settees, French stemware, and decorative Italian tables that appeal to the stores' new customers—college-educated women between the ages of 25 and 44 who earn more than $35,000 a year. With nearly 400 stores in 37 states, the Fort Worth, Texas-based chain is the only specialty home-furnishing outfit that can claim national status.

To remake its image, Pier 1 has turned itself inside out, remodeling its stores, sprucing up its advertising, and bringing in tough, corporate management. "They had to wrench themselves into the '80s and they spent the whole '70s doing it," says Chris LaBastille, a growth-company analyst for Shearson Lehman Hutton Inc.

The company is now so Establishment, in fact, that last week the industry was thick with rumors that such All-American retailing giants as Sears, Roebuck and Company, J. C. Penney Company, and K mart Corporation might seek to acquire Pier 1, which racked up about $327 million in sales last year.

Pier 1's stock soared to $11.25 a share from $8.75 in composite trading on the New York Stock Exchange last week after the company announced an unsolicited inquiry from an unnamed retailer seeking to buy it. Pier 1 immediately hired Drexel Burnham Lambert to help it weigh offers. Yesterday, Pier 1 closed at $10.75, up 12.5 cents, giving the company an indicated value of $326.8 million based on 30.4 million shares outstanding.

Pier 1 has approval from its major owner, Intermark Inc., to sell the company, but only if the price is "substantially" above its current market price, says Charles Scott, Intermark's president and chief executive. An offer of $13 "wouldn't even pique our interest," he says.

Sears and other retailers won't discuss any plans they might have to acquire Pier 1. But last year Sears created a specialty stores division and recently acquired several specialty retailers. A Sears spokesman says the company "is committed to expanding" into specialty retailing, and Sears has compelling reasons to do so. Like most other big retailers, it is finding it tough to increase earnings internally; profit for its merchandise group peaked in 1984 and has slipped since. Pier 1, in contrast, is expected to grow at a heady 25 percent a year clip for at least five years.

"The big retailers don't have that kind of growth out in front of them," says Bo Cheadle, a specialty retailing analyst for Montgomery Securities in San Francisco. "They're all reaching out and looking for some segment of retailing that they can grow in."

In recent months, Sears bought a small chain of women's clothing stores, a Texas-based eye-care company, and is wrapping up its purchase of the Western Auto automotive parts chain. Penney also has ventured into specialty stores, buying a 20 percent stake in the Alcott & Andrews women's apparel outlets.

There's plenty of reason why Pier 1 is suddenly attracting attention. Since new management took over three years ago, sales have climbed 23 percent and profits 40 percent. Pier 1's gross profit margins, a measure of just how high a retailer can mark up its goods, reached an enviable 57.3 percent in fiscal 1988. And the company is expanding by leaps and bounds, having opened 179 new stores under its new management. Pier 1 plans another 87 new stores this year and expects to have 500 stores across the United States and Canada by 1990. And as an importer, it has buying and manufacturing capabilities in about 60 countries that competitors would be hard pressed to duplicate (see Exhibit 1).

Pier 1 also dominates a niche it created—exotic imported furniture and housewares that, experts predict, will continue to enjoy rapid growth as baby boomers reach their peak home-furnishing years.

Yesterday's "flower children" are still flocking to Pier 1 because its stores offer the unique and the exotic. The difference is that Pier 1's patrons today own their own homes and have the money to fix them up. "Pier 1 appeals to the innate snobbishness of the group for uniqueness," says Carl Steidtman, chief economist at Management Horizon, a retail consulting unit of Price Waterhouse.

Charles Tandy, founder of Tandy Corporation, opened the first Pier 1 in 1962 as an outlet for a little-known San Francisco importer of Far Eastern pottery and housewares. Soon, the stores blossomed as the flower children of the sixties flocked to Pier 1 in search of "far-out" furnishings that reflected their distaste for tradition. By the end of the decade, Pier 1 was the recognized outfitter of college dorms and hippie pads—the Ralph Lauren of the bead-and-incense set.

But as its former customers left college, cut their hair, and climbed the corporate ladder, the company began to flounder. From 1971 to 1980, the number of sales dropped by half. In desperation, stores tried to win back shoppers with art supplies, wine and spirits—even tropical fish. All of these retailing experiments failed miserably.

EXHIBIT 1 Growth at Pier 1

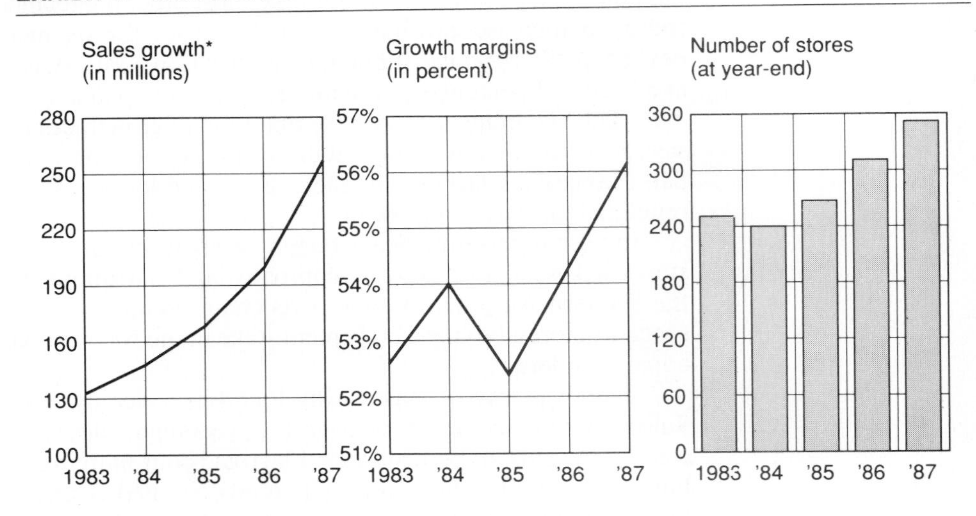

*Fiscal year ending in February.

Pier 1's unconventional style extended even to its annual reports. Its 1984 report resembled a National Geographic magazine which informed shareholders of the company's "gypsy team" that scoured such exotic places as Java and Bali in search of ethnic clothing and accessories.

Pier 1 badly needed a new sense of direction—and quickly. Clark A. Johnson, a former president of Wickes Furniture—a company battered by the severe recession in the 1970s—was brought in to turn Pier 1 around. Mr. Johnson instilled a market-driven, by-the-numbers approach to the business, and pushed Pier 1 to upgrade its merchandise and quadruple its size by the end of the century. "We wanted to hurry up and increase our stores so that the company was positioned to take advantage of that growth," says Mr. Johnson.

That was an ambitious undertaking for a company that, like love beads and Day-Glo posters, had become passé. Pier 1's shoppers, if they remembered Pier 1 at all, recalled dingy stores reeking of incense and crowded with college-dorm furnishings. "It was like visiting a poorly lit bazaar in some Third World country," says Stan Richards of Richards Group, Pier 1's outside advertising agency.

To shed its Third World image, floors were painted red and store layouts were redone to a less-cluttered look. Fluorescent fixtures gave way to focused spots that highlighted merchandise. And candles and incense were relegated to corners of the stores.

In changing its image, however, Pier 1 didn't completely reject its past. The large Japanese paper lanterns still hang prominently from the ceilings, and rattan emperor chairs, albeit with higher price tags, are still popular. Such items "really defined the company in a way that we hoped people would recognize," explains Thomas Christopher, Pier 1's senior vice president for operations.

Pier 1's "new image" advertising highlights merchandise with brightly colored photos of umbrellas, pillows, and kitchenware. Black-and-white newspaper advertisements that simply stated "Sale $29.99," were replaced by eye-catching color ads in Sunday supplements that promised "the best swiveling rocker since Elvis."

All the company's efforts aren't lost on former customers who are finding their way back. Joe Crews, a Dallas attorney who used to buy his window shades and bedspreads at the store while in college, now shops for end tables and lampshades while his wife buys cotton clothing.

On a recent visit, they were looking at bedspreads for a new king-size bed. "When I first came back (a few years ago), I had the impression it was cheaper and poorer-quality stuff," Mr. Crews recalls as he browses through some bedspreads priced at about $70 at one of Pier 1's Dallas emporiums. In the old days, the bedding selection would have been largely limited to India print spreads that sold for about $5.

Mr. Crews, like a lot of Pier 1 shoppers who used to shop there during his college days, seemed impressed. "I've seen it go from a lot of little baskets and candles to better-quality furniture," he says. "The styles are substantially different."

Source: Michael Totty, "For Pier 1, the Days of the Counterculture Are Gone," *The Wall Street Journal,* April 27, 1988, p. 6.

Epilogue

Two years after the recession surprised Pier 1 Imports, forcing it to cut costs and delay new store openings, the home furnishing retailer is beginning to see what its executives hope will be a sustained boost in sales.

The Fort Worth company's stock has shot up in price in the past few months, as investors have increasingly viewed the shares as undervalued and a good play with an impending national recovery.

Heading into the holidays, the company's executives are optimistic that they will reap the benefits of their belt-tightening and of a $20 million inventory system designed to allow management more immediate access to sales information.

And Pier 1 plans to begin accelerating store openings in the next fiscal year.

"We're seeing a measurable pickup in our business that is occurring everywhere in the United States," Pier 1 Chairman and Chief Executive Clark Johnson says.

President Marvin Girouard says: "The war is over, the elections are over. We just want people to get back to living better."

Evidence of a recovery in Pier 1's sales became evident in September and October, executives say. Same-store sales, those in stores open at least a year, posted a mere 0.3-percent increase for the quarter that ended Aug. 29. But they climbed 5 percent in September and 12 percent to 13 percent in October.

That came atop weak comparisons, 8 percent and 5 percent declines, respectively, for the same months last year.

But the numbers were still encouraging, executives say. Johnson is predicting at least a 5 percent same-store sales gain this holiday season, compared with a 1 percent gain for the same period last year.

"We're not going against killer numbers," Girouard says of Pier 1's same-store comparisons in October. "But they're still double-digit gains, and that is what we've been looking for."

Investors have pushed up the price of Pier 1's stock in recent months, as the company's profits and sales have improved. In the past week, the stock has traded at more than $9—and has neared $10. The shares were trading at less than $7 in late June.

But even at the increased price, Pier 1 shares are still trading at a multiple of 14 times earnings—low compared with a high-flying retailer such as The Bombay Co., whose shares trade today at 36 times earnings. Consequently, most analysts are rating Pier 1 shares an attractive buy as the economy recovers.

"They've done a good job" of managing the business during the recession, says Dennis Telzrow, a retail analyst with The Principal/Eppler Guerin & Turner investment firm in Dallas. "And the stock has started to move."

Although Pier 1's sales results have been inconsistent through the company's two-year slowdown, its tight controls have steadily improved profitability since a dramatic downturn in fiscal year 1991, which ended in February.

Pier 1 posted a $15.5 million net profit through the fiscal year's first six months, ending in August, compared with $17 million for the same period the prior year.

The drop was the result of a change in Pier 1's accounting of its 49.5 percent ownership interest in Fort Worth–based Sunbelt Nursery Group. Sunbelt's bad-weather year thus far has also been a factor.

Sunbelt aside, Pier 1 posted $13.9 million in income from its Pier 1 stores through the year's first six months, compared with $11.2 million for the same period the year before.

An Impressive Performance

More Stores

The company has cut back on openings, but still expects to have 28 new sites by end of fiscal 1993. (Figures in parentheses are number of stores opened.)

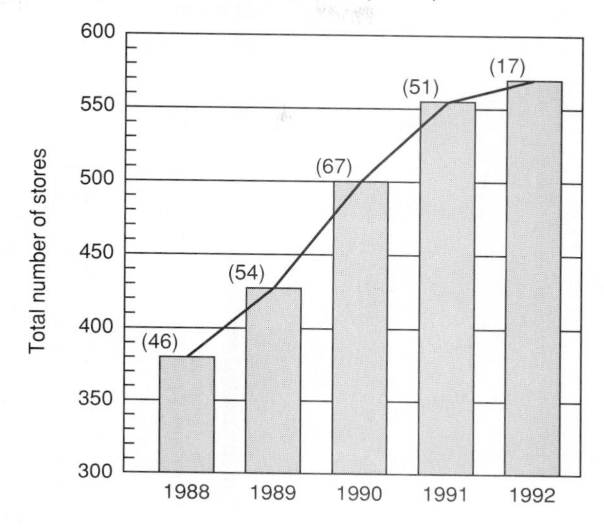

Sales

Figures in parentheses are actual sales amounts.

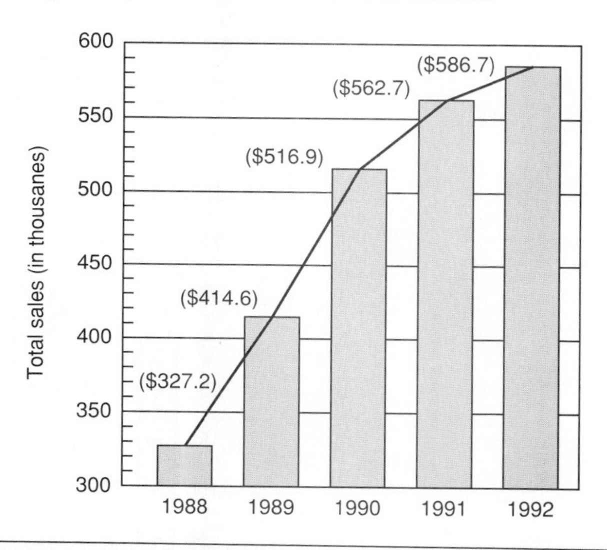

By cutting back on stores openings and other expenses, Pier 1 was able to remain profitable through the recession. For fiscal 1993, which ends next February, the company plans to open 28 new stores, and also is expecting to have strong Christmas sales.

Pier 1 actually recorded $608 million in sales for the 1991 fiscal year, including results from its wholly owned Sunbelt Nursery Group subsidiary. The restated figures Sunbelt's 1991 results, after spinning off the company.

Net Profit

Figures in parentheses are actual amounts.

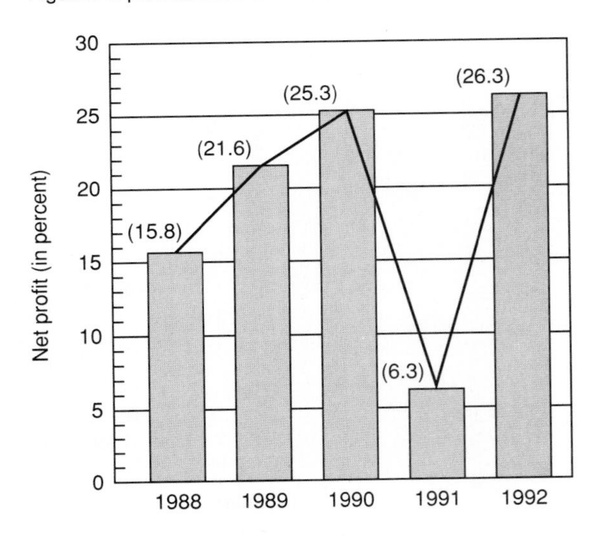

. . . And More Space

Selling space also has to increase (figures in parentheses indicate growth by percentage).

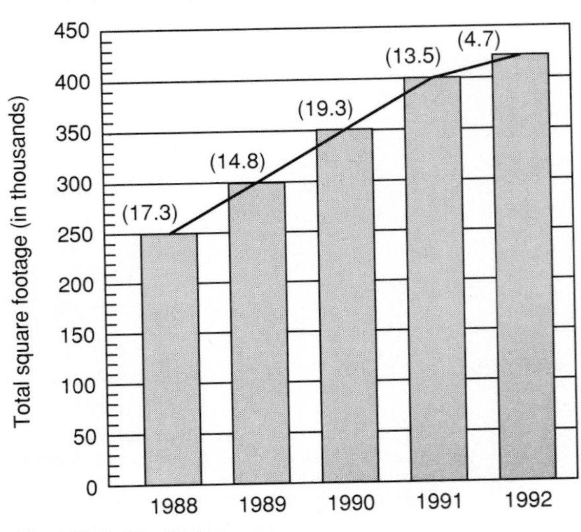

Fort Worth Star-Telegram

"For reasons wrong or right, the market has focused on same-store sales" as the chief measure of retailers' progress, Johnson says, attributing Pier 1's lower stock price until recently to sluggish sales. "For a year and a half, we managed this company from the bottom line up—not the sales line down."

The past 2½ years for Pier 1 have belied the turnaround the company enjoyed during the latter half of the 1980s consumer boom. Under a five-year plan designed and implemented by Johnson and Girouard, Pier 1 doubled its stores to 517 by 1990. Johnson promptly announced that the company's next goal was 1,000 stores and $1 billion in sales by the end of the decade.

But the Persian Gulf War and national recession hit, dampening retail sales. And in January 1991, Pier 1 initiated plans to scale back and intensively manage its store base.

The company reined in expenses, laying off 29 corporate-office employees and trimming stores' payrolls. Today, Pier 1 carries 16 percent fewer employees than it did two years ago—even with 50 new stores added since then.

The company, which hit a peak of 74 new stores in 1990 at the end of its growth boom, cut back to 17 last year and is opening 28 this year. Johnson now talks about reaching a market saturation of "900-plus" Pier 1 stores by the end of the decade, or early in the 21st century. The company now has more than 600 stores.

Pier 1 also pared back debt, paying down $80 million last year and reducing its debt-equity ratio substantially to 37.6 percent from 47.3 percent.

The company also maintains that it has better control of its inventories, having completed the installation of a sophisticated system that allows managers better access to sales information. The company will enter the holidays this year with $165 million in inventory, $8 million less than last year.

That inventory level will be adequate to cover the holidays and should assure that the company won't have overstocks that must be marked down after the season, Girouard says.

"We haven't scrimped on Christmas," he says, but the company's new management system "is giving us good controls over buying better, buying less merchandise over the same productivity."

Adds Johnson: "We have gotten our act together as far as systems."

With that optimism in hand, Pier 1 plans to accelerate store openings to 40 to 45 during the next fiscal year, which begins in March. Pier 1 wants to open 60 stores a year until it reaches its goal of more than 900, Johnson says.

After concentrating on major markets during its growth boom, Pier 1 is focusing on smaller cities that could handle just one Pier 1 store, Johnson says. He says he expects the retail industry consolidation of the past few years to continue at least for the next five, creating more prospective retail sites for Pier 1.

New developments continue to be hard to come by because of the dearth of shopping center financing, he says.

"There's going to be some second-use space available after Christmas this year," he says.

In addition to the company's cost-cutting, improved inventory controls, strengthened balance sheet, and optimistic economic outlook, analysts also say the nation's demographic trends favor home furnishings retailers such as Pier 1 and The Bombay Company.

Housing starts are expected to continue recovering as the nation's economy emerges from its slowdown. The bulk of the country's largest population segment—72 million postwar baby boomers born between 1945 and 1964—is entering its 40s and peak earning power. Another large segment is nearing retirement age and opening another market niche.

The home furnishings industry continues to consolidate, leaving more room for what experts say will be survivors such as Pier 1 and Bombay. The end of the baby boom in the mid-1960s resulted in a slowdown in family formation in the late 1980s, causing home furnishings expenditures to drop.

There were 25,000 furniture outlets nationally in 1978 but fewer than 14,000 in 1990, industry data show.

But even with declining competition, it will be a challenge for survivors to encourage consumers to spend money on home furnishings, experts say.

Management Horizons, the retail consulting arm of Price Waterhouse, says consumers are less settled, more prone to divorce, and perhaps as likely to spend their discretionary dollars today on recreational purchases as they are on home furnishings.

When they do spend money on home furnishings, they are more likely to spend it on less expensive decorative accessories such as the kind customers can find in a Pier 1 or Bombay store, Management Horizons says.

"There'll be plenty of money available," Al Meyers, a vice president in Management Horizons' Dallas office, says of consumer discretionary dollars in the future. "The question is whether the people will be willing to spend it on furniture."

Meyers says retailers such as Pier 1, Bombay, and Crate & Barrel should continue to flourish. Traditional home furnishings stores must dramatically improve customer service and reconfigure their distribution strategies to survive into the next century, he says.

He views the current practices of many traditional furniture retailers, in which customers have to wait days or weeks for their purchase to be delivered, as antiquated and contrary to an increasing desire for instant gratification among consumers.

"It's an industry ripe for change, with a lot of antiquated practices still in place," Meyers says.

Johnson says Pier 1's mix of less-expensive housewares and accessories, in addition to its hard lines, will help the retailer take advantage of the industry's demographic and competitive trends.

"We're ideally positioned," he says.

Source: Scott Nishimura, "Poised for a Comeback," *Tarrant Business,* November 9–15, 1992, pp. 16–17.

CASE 6–5 Highlights for Children, Inc.*

Elmer C. Meider, president of Highlights for Children, Inc., had just completed a lengthy meeting involving several of his managers. Each manager had been assigned the task of preparing recommendations that would allow Highlights for Children to more effectively utilize the three marketing channels currently being used. Meider felt that the company had not been taking full advantage of the capabilities of direct mail, telemarketing, and direct sales in terms of prospecting, lead distribution, current and new product sales, and overall profitability. Moreover, Meider contends that Highlights for Children needs to capitalize on the continuity of direct mail, the rapid follow-up possible via telemarketing, and the value of face-to-face customer contact available through direct sales.

Although Meider knew he had the authority to eliminate the direct sales force operation, he felt this would not be in the best interests of Highlights. Rumors were abundant about possible legal restrictions on telemarketing programs. In fact, several states were considering legislation that would greatly restrict when telephone calls could be made for sales purposes. One such law would limit telephone calls to specified times and no later than 7:00 P.M. Meider knew that such a limit would sharply curtail Highlights's successful telemarketing program. Moreover, the threat of increases in postal rates caused Meider concern about the future of Highlights's successful direct-mail program. These possible environmental changes provided support for Meider's position to keep the direct sales arm intact. Company experience revealed that the direct sales force was in a better position to learn about and resolve customer problems and concerns than either telemarketing or direct mail.

Managers from each of the three distribution methods had been asked to prepare recommendations concerning changes they would implement to improve the overall sales and profitability picture. Meider's task would be to

---

review the various recommendations and prepare a final report to present to Garry C. Myers III, chief executive officer, who was present at the meeting. Also present at the meeting were Richard H. Bell, chairman of the board; Lynn Wearsch, national rep sales service manager; Chuck Rout, vice president—telemarketing; and Gayle Ruwe, mail marketing manager.

Of the various recommendations, the one that provoked the most discussion was that Highlights for Children rely exclusively on telemarketing and direct-mail distribution and that the company eliminate the direct sales force. Richard Bell, responding to this suggestion, pointed out that it was the direct sales force that got the company started, and would keep the company going well into the future. He commented, "Highlights for Children might as well close its doors if the direct sales force is eliminated." One manager's response to Bell's defense of the direct sales force consisted of referring to the relative sales contributions from each source and how telemarketing and direct mail have grown faster. This manager noted the following:

> Telemarketing and direct sales are in a competitive position from a lead utilization standpoint. Profitability is greatly enhanced when leads are sent directly to telemarketing rather than to the direct sales force. Sure, representatives can sell a bigger package and a longer-term subscription than the other marketing arms, but the reps rely solely on company-generated leads and are not using referrals generated from customers, nor are they doing any local prospecting. The resources assigned to the direct sales force could be more profitably used by telemarketing and direct mail. Our opportunity costs, or losses, have been rising as a result of sending leads to the direct sales group. They cannot handle all of the leads, and by the time telemarketing receives them they are stale and of little value.

Bell agreed in part with these observations but was quick to note that the size of the direct sales force had dropped from an all-time high of 750 to the current level of 265 independent sales reps, which includes 65 area managers. "We need to be more effective recruiting new sales reps. Just doubling the direct sales force would produce significant benefits," noted Bell in his rejoinder. After this interchange, Garry Myers suggested that Elmer would take all proposals into consideration and attempt to arrive at a recommendation that would combine the best of everything.

The Company

General Information. Begun in 1946 as a children's publication, Highlights for Children, Inc. has become a multidivisional company, selling not only magazines but also textbooks, newsletters, criterion referenced tests, and other materials. The consumers include children, parents, and teachers.

The Mission Statement of Highlights for Children states:

> Highlights for Children, Inc.'s mission is to create, publish, produce, or distribute on a profitable basis quality products and services uniquely designed for the

educational development of children, their parents and teachers, and others with specific educational needs.

Each of the current divisions or subsidiaries operates within these guidelines.

Highlights emphasizes the fair and courteous treatment of its customers. Promotional offers are closely reviewed to ensure prospective customers are not being misled. Highlights is committed to maintaining a "pure" image in the marketplace in terms of marketing efforts as well as quality of its product.

Highlights for Children magazine is circulated to approximately 2 million subscribers. It is marketed through direct selling (via independent contractors), telephone marketing, and direct mail. Parents, teachers, doctors, and gift donors are targeted by the different marketing arms. In addition, Highlights sells various educational products that have been promoted through the introductory-offer school programs.

History. Dr. Garry C. Myers, Jr., and Caroline C. Myers founded Highlights for Children, Inc. in 1946 in Honesdale, Pennsylvania. Based on the belief that learning must begin early in order to fully develop a child's learning ability, the magazine was geared to challenge children's creative thinking and abilities. Today, the editorial offices are still in Honesdale, although the corporate headquarters are located in Columbus, Ohio, and the magazine is printed in Nashville, Tennessee.

At the time *Highlights for Children* was founded, magazines were sold almost exclusively by door-to-door salesmen. *Highlights for Children* followed suit. Today, Highlights continues to use direct selling in conjunction with telephone marketing and direct mail to market the magazine.

In 1955, Myers hit upon the idea of putting *Highlights for Children* in doctors' offices with lead cards. At about the same time, his wife came up with the introductory-offer program to be marketed to parents through the schools. This was the beginning of marketing *Highlights for Children* by mail. Both programs met with immediate and resounding success.

Magazine Content

Highlights for Children targets and services a diverse age group from 2 to 12. The material in the magazine ranges from easy to advanced. This conforms to the philosophy of challenging children: Rather than having material graded and directed to a particular age child, children are allowed to work at their own rate and are "encouraged" to achieve and understand more.

The tag line of *Highlights for Children* is "Fun with a Purpose." The *purpose* of the magazine is to educate and instruct, not merely entertain. The magazine is positioned as supplemental material to be used in the home, rather than in the classroom.

Highlights for Children likes to maintain the image of an educational magazine. No cutouts or markups are included in the magazine content, enhancing the idea of *lasting* quality. There is no paid advertising in *Highlights for Children,* which is in line with the educational image. Throughout the years, advertising has been considered at various times. Management continues to feel the magazine is more salable as an educational supplement without advertising. Highlights also believes that children are already subjected to more than enough advertising pressure through other sources, much of which is resented by parents and teachers. Recently, President Elmer Meider raised the advertising issue and suggested that advertising revenues might be a way to improve *Highlights*'s profit performance.

The Marketing Program

Highlights for Children uses three different marketing arms to sell its products: direct selling, telephone marketing, and mail marketing. Each type is discussed in following sections. Exhibit 1 shows the current organization.

Direct Selling. The direct selling organization has two kinds of representatives: the school representatives and regular representatives. Almost all reps receive company-generated leads; however, school reps make most of their sales from self-generated "school drop" leads.

School Representatives. Reps make their initial presentation to a school principal or superintendent. The object of the presentation is to gain permission to leave sample copies of *Highlights for Children* in grades K–4. If the school agrees to participate, a sample copy, along with a lead card, is sent home with each child. The child is instructed to return the card to the school if the parents are interested in ordering *Highlights.* Reps then pick up the lead cards from the schools. A school rep usually visits a particular school once every two to three years. Currently *Highlights for Children* has about 70 school reps.

Regular Reps. Regular reps contact the following company-generated leads:

1. *Parent inquiries (PI)* and *doctor inquiries (DI).* These people have not had a subscription but have sent in a card indicating interest.
2. *Introductory-offer renewals (IO).* These people have been sold the 6-month introductory offer through the school and are now up for renewal.
3. *Regular renewals (RR).* These people have had a regular subscription (11 issues or more) and are up for renewal.
4. *Donor renewals (DR).* These people have given a gift subscription (11 issues or more) and are up for renewal.

A rep has a set amount of time to work the leads (depending on the type). At the end of that time period, the lead automatically goes to either phone or mail for follow-up. Reps send back the leads marked "no contact"

EXHIBIT 1 Highlights for Children, Inc., Organization Chart

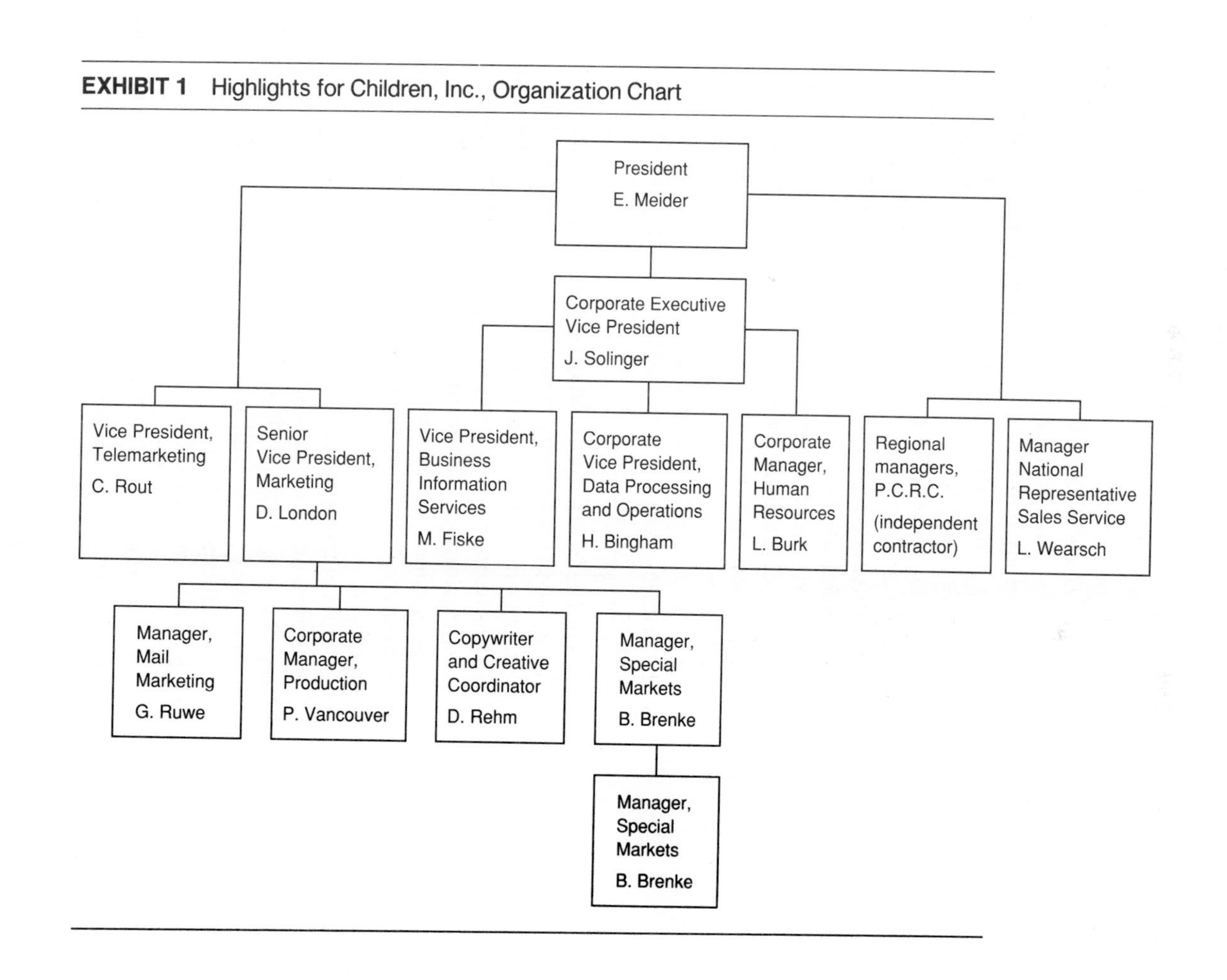

or "no sale" once they have been worked, so the other departments can follow up quickly.

Reps call on parents at home. The increasing number of women working and higher gasoline prices have made the rep's job more difficult over the years. When reps do find someone at home, their presentation hits mainly on what *Highlights for Children* is, how to use it, and its educational value. The rep sells, on average, a 2.8-year term subscription.

There is a management structure in the regular rep program. Not all reps are under a manager; none reports directly to the home office. Managers receive an override on all area sales (personal and representative's sales).

The current rep structure is composed of about 265 active reps, of which about 65 are managers. The Columbus, Ohio, office has seven employees who are assigned to the direct-selling arm. Reps are independent contractors and as such are not paid a salary, but rather they earn a commission on their sales. Their commission is calculated by commission level times sales units. Units are determined by term sold: five-year subscription = 1.4 units; three-year subscription = 1.0 unit; two-year subscription = .7 unit; and one-year subscription = .3 unit. *Highlights for Children* subscription rates are $49.94 for 33 issues (three years) and $79.95 for 55 issues (five years). For example, the commission for a three-year subscription is $24.97 (1.0 unit = .50; $49.95 × .50 = $24.97).

Telephone Marketing. Started over 10 years ago in response to the energy crisis and the possibility of the greatly reduced mobility of the representative selling arm, telephone marketing has grown and flourished from a staff of 3 to 190 telemarketing reps, all paid on a commission basis. Telemarketing commissions are about one half (23 percent) of direct-sales commissions. Commissions are not paid for sales that are canceled or never paid by the customers. These reps are located in Columbus along with 25 staff employees.

Telemarketing receives basically three types of leads: parent and doctor inquiries, introductory-offer renewals, and regular renewals. Telemarketing reps have a specified time period in which to contact and sell their leads before they go to mail marketing for follow-up. They attempt to contact leads, all types, 10 times before giving up. In one day's time, they can make up to four attempts. On average, telemarketing sells a 2.3-year-term.

Mail Marketing. The Mail Marketing Department consists of three primary areas: creative, production/analysis, and list rental. Currently, 10 employees work in the mail marketing department. Major responsibilities, in addition to list rental, include acquiring *new customers* (through efforts such as the Christmas mailing and school teacher introductory-offer mailing), acquiring *new leads* (through the doctors' offices, doctor inquiries, and parent inquiries mailings), and converting leads (these leads may be new or renewals) to customers (typically after regular reps and/or phone reps have tried to convert). All activities are conducted through direct mail.

More specifically, all promotion packages (to acquire either a lead or a customer), space ads, package inserts, billing stuffers, preprinted computer forms, and so forth are created and produced through the efforts of this department. The actual mail production (merge/purge, lettershop, etc.) is also coordinated here. Finally, the analysis of the results is performed here as well.

Christmas Program. The Christmas program is a multimedia effort to acquire one-year subscriptions targeting a donor. The mail program consists of over 5 million names, mailed from mid-September to mid-October.

Additionally, the Christmas program includes card inserts in the October, November, and December issues of *Highlights for Children* magazine, statement stuffers, approximately two million package inserts in outside packages (*Drawing Board, Current,* etc.) and space ads (*The Wall Street Journal, The New York Times, Christian Science Monitor,* etc.).

Introductory-Offer Program. A mailing is made to teachers who hand out "take-home" slips on which the parents can subscribe. The subscription offer to the parents is for six months of *Highlights for Children,* an "introductory offer."

Parent Inquiry/Doctor Inquiry Program. Several times a year, *Highlights for Children* purchases doctor lists for an outside mailing to produce doctor inquiries. General practitioners, pediatricians, dentists, any doctors who have children, and/or parents visiting their offices and waiting rooms are targeted. Doctors who subscribe are especially valuable because they provide a vehicle to reach parents, and the primary purpose of the doctor mailing is to eventually reach parents. Highlights for Children can send the magazine, complete with parent inquiry cards, into a doctor subscriber's office on a *monthly* basis, potentially reaching many parents.

Marketing Arm Effectiveness

Background information revealed that mail marketing produced the most revenue for the last seven years. In 1983, telemarketing surpassed direct marketing in terms of revenue. Exhibit 2 shows sales by marketing arm since 1976. Order-per-lead ratios by marketing arm are as follows:

Telemarketing: over 30 percent.

Direct sales: over 20 percent.

Mail: over 5 percent.

Normally, order-per-lead ratios are higher for direct sales. In fact, for a given number of leads, say 50, the direct sales group will produce more orders than the telemarketing group. However, since the reps are asking for more leads than they can possibly handle, many end up wasted and are not viable by the time they are received by telemarketing and direct mail.

EXHIBIT 2 Highlights for Children, Inc. Annual Gross Sales by Source, 1976–1985 ($000)

	Reps	*Telephone*	*Mail*
1976	11,400	860	10,700
1977	11,800	1,500	11,300
1978	12,100	2,300	12,100
1979	10,300	3,300	14,400
1980	10,400	6,400	16,300
1981	11,100	8,400	16,400
1982	12,400	9,000	21,400
1983	12,300	13,400	28,000
1984	10,800	20,400	36,000
1985	10,200	23,800	46,000

The decline in the number of independent contractors has been of some concern for several years. Various programs have been initiated over the years to increase the number of reps. These programs have not met with much success as evidenced by the size of the direct sales force. Selling low-ticket items, however, limits how much a regular rep can earn. About one half of the regular reps worked part-time. Earnings range from as low as $1,000 a year for some reps to as high as six figures for those reps who are managers. Managers earn overrides on the sales of those reps that they have recruited into the sales organization, a common practice in direct selling programs. Exhibit 3 is typical of the literature used by Highlights to recruit new reps.

Meider and others are aware that this is a problem that others in direct selling have faced. Giants in the direct-selling industry such as Avon, Tupperware, Mary Kay, Amway, and so forth have all confronted this problem and have adopted various techniques to alleviate the negative impact that fewer reps have had on sales. A major contributing factor has been the dramatic increase in the number of working mothers who are no longer home during the day.

The ability of people in direct selling to earn a reasonable level of income has been inhibited due to these trends. Many companies have adopted party plan selling programs in an attempt to increase the income earning opportunities of the reps. Other companies have expanded their product lines in order to provide their direct sales reps with more commission opportunities. Exhibit 4, a fact sheet published by the Direct Selling Association, provides a summary of the direct selling industry.

Meider, on the other hand, feels that despite these trends the direct sales reps are not working as hard as they should and are not following prescribed

EXHIBIT 3 Sales Opportunity Fact Sheet

Highlights for Children is an educational magazine for children ages 2 through 12. There are 11 issues published each year, and the December issue includes an annual Resource Index, which turns that year's books into a home reference library for the whole family.

Highlights is available by enrollment only. It is not sold in any newsstand, contains no advertising, and is created primarily for family use. The vast majority of its subscribers are parents. *Highlights* contains a wide range of fiction, nonfiction, thinking and reasoning features, contributions from readers, and things to make and do. The high interest articles include humor, mystery, sports, folk tales, science, history, arts, animal stories, crafts, quizzes, recipes, action rhymes, poems, and riddles.

Dr. Garry Cleveland Myers and Caroline Clark Myers founded *Highlights for Children* in 1946 as the outcome of years of professional work in child psychology, family life, education, and publishing for children. *Highlights* has grown from a first issue circulation of 22,000 to over 1,500,000 in 1982 and is the world's most honored book for children.

Noted educator, psychologist, and author Dr. Walter B. Barbe is the editor-in-chief of *Highlights*. Dr. Barbe's books and professional publications have made him nationally renowned in education and in demand as an international speaker. The ongoing production of each issue is coordinated by a talented staff of educators, most of whom are parents. The editorial offices are located in Honesdale, Pennsylvania. The marketing arm for *Highlights for Children* is Parent and Child Resource Center, Inc., and the administrative offices are centered in Columbus, Ohio, where a dedicated representative sales staff plans and directs the business of selling and delivering *Highlights* all around the world.

Highlights for Children is sold nationally by authorized independent representatives directly to families, teachers, preschools, daycare centers, doctors' offices, and to any other person or place interested in the welfare and development of children. This is a direct, person-to-person sales opportunity.

As an independent contractor selling *Highlights'* products, you are free to work the hours you want and earn as much commission as possible. You are in business for yourself with exclusive leads and virtually no product competition. There is no investment required, and you are provided with the information and instruction you need to grow in skill, experience, and earnings. Your business will grow in proportion to the time, skill, and resourcefulness you use in presenting the values of *Highlights* to families, individuals, or groups in your community. Your job is to visit with prospective customers, show them how *Highlights* will benefit their children, and write up the order. Statistics show that one out of three contacts will enroll.

You will find that selling *Highlights'* products is enjoyable, pleasant, and profitable. The only qualifications necessary are that you enjoy meeting people and have a sincere interest in children.

There is no limit to your earnings. Every home with children ages 2 through 12 is a potential customer. You retain a liberal commission on every enrollment at the time of the sale, plus additional commissions as your sales record grows. You receive bonuses for the quantity of sales you report, bonuses for the quality of the sale you make, and bonuses for recommending others as representatives. Your sales can also make you eligible to win incentive contests with case and/or merchandise prizes.

If you are interested in a sales career, complete the enclosed Confidential Information form and mail it today!

and proven methods of selling. Reps are supposed to ask customers who have ordered a subscription to *Highlights for Children* for the names of others who might be interested in subscribing. Since the reps knew that they could secure company-generated leads free, there was no financial incentive for them to ask for referrals. This referral process has been the mainstay method of direct selling not only for *Highlights for Children* but other direct selling companies as well. Reps are expected to engage in local prospecting, which involves locating residential areas occupied by parents of young

EXHIBIT 4 Fact Sheet

Summary: 1985 Direct Selling Industry Survey

Total retail sales: $8,360,000

Percent of sales by major product group:	
Personal care products	34.8%
Home/family care products	50.0%
Leisure/educational products	9.4%
Services/other	5.8%
Sales approach (method used to generate sales reported as a percent of sales dollars).	
One-on-one contact	81.0%
Group sales/party plan	19.0%
In a home	77.0%
In a workplace	11.8%
At a public event*	2.5%
Over the phone	6.9%
Other	1.8%
Total salespeople: 2,967,887	
Demographics of salespeople:	
Independent	97.9%
Employed	2.1%
Full-time (30+ hours per week)	11.7%
Part-time	88.3%
Male	22.0%
Female	78.0%

*Such as a fair, exhibition, shopping mall, theme park, et cetera.

Source: Direct Selling Association, Washington, D.C.

children. These activities have been neglected, and reps today rely solely on company-generated leads.

Sales reps continually ask for more leads than they can process, resulting in lost opportunities. By the time the leads are sent back to Columbus, they are of limited value. Meider was particularly distressed to learn that several reps had established their own telemarketing operations to enhance their earnings opportunities. As a result of this practice, Highlights was paying the reps a commission that was twice the amount normally paid for telemarketing sales. A report prepared by Marilyn Fiske, vice president of business information services, added further to Meider's concern. Her report contained the following points:

- Telemarketing sales in general are for the magazine only; sales of other products are very limited.
- Telemarketing sales do not involve a down payment, hence there are more cancellations.
- Recruiting of additional direct-sales reps has declined, especially in those situations where the reps, with the assistance or blessing of their managers, have started their own telemarketing operations.

Meider's reaction to Fisk's report solidified his decision that changes were needed. He could understand why the managers would favor telemarketing conducted by their direct reps. Each subscription netted a $4 override for the manager regardless of how it was secured, although suggestions had been made that the $4 override was not adequate. And, the direct reps received their usual commission. He had attempted at an earlier date to persuade the former national sales manager to do something about this practice only to be told that the direct reps were independent and would view this as interference. Besides, as the national sales manager indicated, "The reps view the annual Christmas mailing as a direct threat and want the program to be eliminated or at least share in the commissions on sales from their territories."

Sometime later, the national sales manager left Highlights for Children due to a reorganization that eliminated the position. Meider hired two regional sales managers who work in the field and can provide closer supervision of the direct sales reps and their managers. Meider divided the United States into two regions: east and west. This move greatly reduced the span of control problems experienced by the former national sales manager.

Meider discussed these problems with Garry Myers III and asked for his reactions. Myers noted that it should not be surprising that reps rely totally on company-generated leads. As Myers stated, "Our reps want to make the most sales, and the best avenue is to call on people who have taken the effort to complete a card and mail it in to Highlights. Reps know that these leads are more likely to produce sales than what they are likely to obtain using the referral process." Myers likened the referral process to "cold-call selling" and company-generated leads as "warm-call selling." Regardless, Highlights for Children is losing profits as a result of these practices, and Myers hoped that Meider's report would be available soon.

Meider indicated that his initial report would contain a series of alternative recommendations that would be used to generate discussion. For example, Meider suggested that one alternative would be to eliminate company-generated leads. Another possibility, suggested by Meider, would place a limit on the number of company-generated leads that a rep could receive each month. The number received might be a function of previous referral sales or some other factor. Meider also suggested charging the managers and/or the reps for each company-generated lead. To offset these additional charges, one likely counter-suggestion would be to increase commissions paid to the reps. The Fisk reported prompted another option: reducing the commission paid to reps for orders received without a down payment. This might curtail the use of telemarketing by the reps, a practice Meider wanted to stop. Finally, one manager suggested that the school reps be charged a small fee for all of the sample copies that are left at schools for K–4 distribution. The manager said, "'If the regular reps are wasteful of the excessive leads that they receive, then the school reps may be just as guilty when they give away too many free samples."

Eliminating the independent reps is one alternative, as is increasing the number of reps. Meider did not agree with Bell that more reps was the best solution, although he did think that it was an alternative to consider. Expanding the product line to give the reps more items to sell and more commission opportunities was another alternative suggested to Meider. Currently, a three-year subscription at $49.95 produces a commission of $24.97. Meider knew that no one would suggest replacing the direct sales force with a company sales force. Such a move would increase overhead expenses by at least 15 percent to cover fringe benefits costs plus staff additions needed for purposes of governmental reporting. Eliminating the direct selling arm would be a better solution than creating a company sales force.

Myers thought that Meider's suggestions would indeed produce much discussion among his management team. At this juncture, he felt that Meider should narrow the alternatives down to a final set of recommendations.

CASE 6–6 The North Face

The North Face was a privately owned company which designed, manufactured, and sold high-quality outdoor equipment and clothing. It began as a specialty mountain shop in San Francisco in 1966, and started manufacturing in Berkeley in 1968. Since that time, the company had emphasized quality backpacking and mountaineering equipment featuring state-of-the-art design and functional detail. The North Face soon dominated this market and became the market leader in three of the four product categories it manufactured—tents, sleeping bags, backpacks, and clothing. Sales in 1980 were in excess of $20 million (see Exhibits 1 and 2 for historical financial statements). All items were produced domestically at the company's manufacturing facility in Berkeley. In the early 1980s The North Face operated five well-located retail stores and two factory outlets in the San Francisco Bay area and Seattle. In addition, it employed 14 independent sales representatives who covered 10 sales territories in the United States. Its dealer structure consisted of about 700 specialty shops throughout the United States as well as representation in 20 foreign countries.

The company's desire for continued growth in the face of a maturing backpacking market prompted Hap Klopp, president of The North Face and the driving force behind its success to date, to investigate expansion into new products related to the current backpacking business. One avenue of growth which appeared to have significant potential was that of Alpine (downhill) ski clothing. This opportunity was pursued, with the result that

This case was written by Gary Mezzatesta and Valorie Cook, Stanford Graduate School of Business, under the supervision of Professor Robert T. Davis.

EXHIBIT 1 Profit and Loss Comparisons (in 000's)

	1977	*1978*	*1979*	*1980*
Sales				
Manufacturing	$11,437	$13,273	$15,153	$17,827
Retail	2,254	2,570	2,879	3,358
Total	$13,691	$15,843	$18,032	$21,195
Cost of Sales	9,337	11,188	12,443	13,964
Gross Margin	4,354	4,655	5,589	7,231
Selling and operating expense	2,186	2,320	2,646	3,306
Contributing to overhead	2,168	2,335	2,943	3,925
Corporate G&A expense	686	685	777	924
Interest expense	242	268	438	658
Incentive compensation and ESOP	235	204	253	330
Total	$ 1,163	$ 1,157	$ 1,468	$ 1,912
Total pretax profits	$ 1,005	$ 1,178	$ 1,475	$ 2,013
Total after-tax profits	$ 498	$ 609	$ 776	$ 1,019

EXHIBIT 2 Comparative Balance Sheets (year ended September 30—in 000's)

	1977	*1978*	*1979*	*1980*
Assets				
Current				
Cash	$ 110	$ 149	$ 201	$ 370
Accounts receivable	2,765	3,765	3,910	4,573
Inventories	4,496	4,494	4,452	5,947
Other	319	329	229	196
Long term	803	1,012	1,256	1,437
Other assets	65	68	100	104
Total assets	$8,558	$9,817	$10,148	$12,627
Liabilities				
Current				
Notes payable to bank	$2,624	$3,180	$ 2,563	$ 2,613
Accounts payable	2,019	2,186	2,109	2,231
Accrued liabilities	693	589	627	783
Income taxes payable	318	339	360	568
Current portion LT debt	141	159	222	316
Other				
Long-term debt	351	302	360	1,103
Deferred income taxes	33	73	143	230
Stockholders' equity				
Common stock—A	1,687	1,687	1,687	1,687
Common stock—B	0	2	2	2
Retained earnings	692	1,300	2,075	3,094
Total liabilities	$8,558	$9,817	$10,148	$12,627

The North Face Skiwear Line was being readied for formal introduction in fall 1981.

The uppermost question in management minds at this point was what was the most effective way to distribute the new skiwear line?

Early History

Hap Klopp, 39-year-old president of The North Face and a graduate of the Stanford MBA program, purchased the original company in 1968, following a brief period as manager of another backpacking retail outlet in the San Francisco Bay area. At that time the operation consisted of three retail stores and a small mail-order business. The firm sold a line of private-label backpacking and brand-name downhill ski equipment. Klopp closed two stores, brought in equity, and opened a small manufacturing facility for the production of down-filled sleeping bags in the back of the main store in Berkeley, California. Sales in 1969 were just under $500,000.

Prior to 1971, most of the retail sales were in Alpine (downhill) ski equipment, where competition had depressed the margins. To gain relief, management decided to concentrate on the backpacking and ski touring (cross country) markets, where margins were higher and such adverse influences as seasonality, fashion cycles, and weather conditions were less damaging.

The North Face Products

The North Face manufactured four key lines for the backpacking market: sleeping bags, packs, outdoor clothing, and tents. All products stressed quality, design, and durability and were priced for the high-end of the market. All products carried a full lifetime warranty.

Sleeping Bags. The North Face sleeping bags ranged from "expeditionary" models (designed to provide protection to −40° F) to bags offering various combinations of lightness and warmth (aimed at satisfying the needs of the vacationing, leisure-oriented backpacker). The North Face bags were considered superior to competitive products in construction and durability and offered the optimal trade-off between warmth and weight. As the company grew, TNF expanded the variety of sleeping bags offered to meet virtually every environmental condition that a backpacker could expect in the United States. The quality of down used, the nylon fabric thread count, the unique coil zippers, and the stitching were key points of differentiation. Goose-down bags retailed from $162 to $400, with the price escalating as the warmth of the bag increased. Initially, the bags were only down-filled, but in recent years, a complete line of synthetic-filled models were introduced. Synthetic fills were preferred by some for damp weather environments and where weight and compressibility were of lesser importance. Synthetic bags ranged in retail price from $75 to $205—also the top end of the competitive market.

From the start, the company had manufactured only two sizes of sleeping bags instead of the usual three found in the industry. This policy not only simplified production but also reduced retailers' stocking needs and retail stock-outs. When TNF began, sleeping bags had been the fastest growing segment of the backpacking industry, but this growth had begun to slow during the early 1970s.

Parkas and Other Outdoor Clothing. Parkas and functional outerwear were the growth leaders for The North Face in 1981. Their line included a range of parkas designed to appeal to the serious backpacker. Design stressed maximum comfort over a wide temperature range and contained convenient adjustments for ventilation control. Other features such as pocket design, snap-closed flaps over zippers, and large overstuffed collars further enhanced the line. As the industry grew and fashion became more of an element, a much wider range of colors and surface fabrics were incorporated into the line. Materials such as Gore-Tex (a breathable yet waterproof material) had been introduced, which offered a functional advantage over existing products on the market. Two types of parkas were offered: those which afforded primary protection from cold, damp conditions (generally of synthetic material); and those which were intended to withstand cold, dry conditions (primarily of down). As in fabrics, a number of new, strongly promoted synthetics, such as Thinsulate, Polarguard, and Hollofill, had been incorporated into the line to meet expanding customer base and desires. Parkas varied in price from approximately $50 for a synthetic-filled, multipurpose vest to $265 for a deluxe expeditionary model. The company was in the process of trying to sell a system of clothing called "Layering," which utilized multiple layers of clothing combined in a variety of ways to meet climatic conditions.

Tents. In 1981, The North Face had revolutionized the world market for lightweight backpacking tents with its geodesic designs. With assistance from well-known design engineer R. Buckminster Fuller, the company's employees had created and patented geodesic tents. These tents provided the greatest volume of internal space with the least material and the highest strength to weight ratio of any tent design. They also had more headroom, better use of floor space, and better weather shedding. Because geodesics are free-standing, they also required less anchoring to the earth. Competitors throughout the world were beginning to copy the products; but to date, the company had not legally pursued its patent production. Other special tent features included reinforced seams and polymer-coated waterproof fabric that management believed provided three times the tear strength and superior performance at subfreezing temperatures. The company had helped develop unique tent poles that were available nowhere else in the world. The North Face still carried two A-frame tents for the purpose of price and continuity of line at $200 and $240 price points while the geodesic line had eight tents ranging from $220 to $600. As with the other North Face products, these were at the high end of the price spectrum; but management was convinced that consumers were getting very good value for their money.

The market for tents had accelerated recently with the introduction of the geodesics, which met new customers' needs better than did A-frame tents. Management felt that two to four years of rapid growth in geodesic tent sales would continue while A-frames were becoming obsolete, and then the market would return to its former modest levels of growth.

Backpacks. The North Face divided the pack market into three segments:

Soft Packs/Day Packs
Internal Frame Packs
External Frame Packs

The North Face introduced the first domestically made internal frame pack, which created a market niche and produced extremely good sales for the company. Retail price ranges from $45 to $115 were at the high end of the scale, but management was sure that the quality details (including extra strength nylon, bartack stitching, extra loops and straps, high-strength aluminum, etc.) made these good values for the money.

In the soft-pack area, there were fewer features to distinguish the company's products from its competitors'. Price competition—with competitors' prices from $16 to $37—was much more noticeable.

In the external frame market, historically dominated by Kelty, the company had introduced a remarkably different, patented product called the Back Magic. It was an articulated pack with independent shoulder and hip suspension, which placed the weight of the pack closer to the backpacker's center of gravity than other packs had done. Although offering an expensive product ($150 to $160) and encountering some bothersome contractor delays, the company was significantly increasing its market share in this category.

Additionally, to expand this category of the company's sales and to open up a whole new market for its dealers, The North Face introduced a complete line of soft luggage in 1981. The company was attempting to capitalize upon the peripatetic nature of its customers and its belief that customers wanted the much higher quality traditionally found in luggage shops. Features such as binding in all seams, leather handles on nylon webbing, shoulder straps with leather handles, and numerous zippered internal pockets were incorporated. Prices ranged from $40 to $65.

Marketing Philosophy

The North Face promoted more than just a product, it fostered a way of life. Throughout the ranks of management one found a cadre of outdoor enthusiasts.

It is important to note how Hap Klopp viewed his company's business:

> (The North Face) may be selling bags, tents, packs, boots, or parkas, but I suggest that people are buying better health, social contact, sunshine, adventure, self-confidence, youth, exercise, romance, a change of pace, or a chance to blow off steam and escape from the urban degeneration of pollution, economic collapse, and congestion.

One central theme served as the foundation for The North Face's corporate strategy. It was best summarized by Hap Klopp: "Make the best product possible, price it at the level needed to earn a fair return, and guarantee it forever." Hap contended that profits were not made from the first sale to a customer. After all, it took considerable effort and money to attract that purchase in the first place. Rather, the customer had to be treated well once he had been attracted. Repeat sales were the key to this business' profitability. Hence, there was the need to provide a product that would always satisfy.

A key conceptual tool that The North Face used to analyze the backpacking market and similar specialty markets is what Klopp called "the pyramid of influence":

EXHIBIT 3 Market Pyramid of Influence

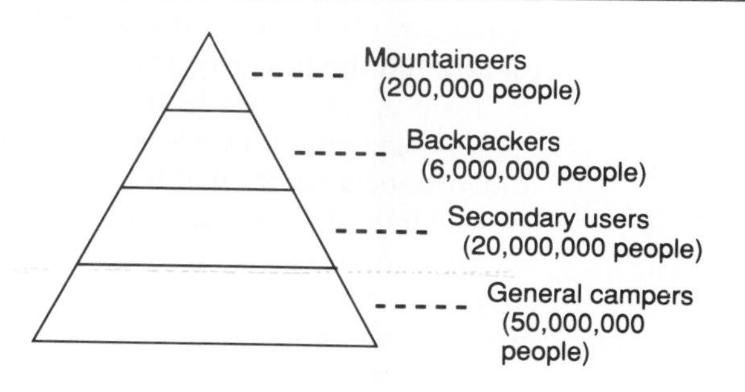

Within this hierarchy, management believed that word-of-mouth communication flowed down a chain of expertise from the mountaineer, to the backpacker, to the secondary user, and finally to the general camping public. Those at the high end of the chain, the "technocrats," tended to influence the buying decisions of the average outdoorsman, who relied upon recommendations and brand image rather than his own research. The North Face characterized the market pyramid as follows:

Segment	*Use*	*Price*	*Preferred Product Characteristics*
Mountaineer	Frequent, hard	No object	Durable, functional, perfect workmanship
Backpacker	Frequent, careful	Value conscious	Lightweight, repairable, comfortable, brand more important
Secondary user	Inconsistent, careful	Value conscious	Durable, multipurpose, comfortable, brand name
General camper	Inconsistent, careless	Price sensitive	Simple, sturdy, multipurpose, brand name

The company believed that a number of its competitors had made serious marketing blunders in changing their distribution and products to meet the needs of the larger, lower strata, thereby ignoring the pattern of influence of the pyramid and the foundation of the business. This led to the erosion of their name and franchise in all of the strata. In contrast, The North Face's long-term strategy was to maintain an orientation toward the top of the pyramid and quietly broaden the line so that its existing dealers would be able to meet the needs of both the peak of the pyramid and the emerging customers.

The North Face adamantly declared that the pattern of influence in specialty markets only worked one way—downward. By designing and selling high-quality, functional items focused at the top of the pyramid, a firm could systematically build a strong market image hinging on credibility. Klopp discounted the integrity and wisdom of the switch from a "top down" to a "bottom up" strategy. Many companies shortsightedly looked at the financials associated with each segment and changed their distribution network and products to meet the larger, lower strata. This process, he claimed, eventually led to failure, since ignoring the foundations of the business eventually caused a "franchise erosion" at all levels of the pyramid. In short, lowering the quality of product and service to maintain sales growth was a no-win game which would inevitably lead to erosion of market and image and to the advancement of someone who was at the top of the cone. If a company wanted to maintain its commitment to a market and customer group for the long term, it had to stick to the "top down" approach.

Because of its strict adherence to this philosophy, The North Face approached the marketplace with the following strategy: enter specialty markets; nurture them carefully; focus R&D at the top of the pyramid; use specialty shops to skim the market; target promo efforts for trendsetters. Once a dominant position in a market was established growth was sought via two paths:

1. Finding new geographical or new use markets.
2. Introducing new quality products.

The company led the backpacking industry with the following market shares (estimated from available data) in 1980:

	Market Share	*Industry Ranking*
Outerwear/Clothing	47%	1
Sleeping bags	48	1
Tents	28	1
Packs	20	3

The North Face accounted for 21.9 percent of the sales of backpacking products to specialty stores in 1980, while its closest competitor achieved a 13.5 percent market share. In summary, the company's distinctive competence, which distinguished it from its competition, was the manufacture of high-quality, functional products of classic design, which sold at a premium price and carried a lifetime warranty. The key success factors were thought to be the company's reputation as a specialty supplier of quality products, its strong relationship with its distribution network, and its high-caliber management team. The North Face was generally recognized as having the best management team in the industry, due to its depth of industry knowledge and length of time in the business.

While the backpacking industry had enjoyed substantial growth over the past decade, from total U.S. industry specialty store sales of $15,400,000 in 1971 to $81,700,000 in 1980, the backpacking market appeared to be maturing, with total sales forecasted to grow to $95,100,000 by 1985. (See Exhibit 4 for historical and projected market size.) Klopp believed that the industry was out of the high-growth stage of the product life cycle, heading toward the maturity stages; the increasing difficulty the company reported in achieving product differentiation seemed to validate this observation.

Channels of Distribution

The North Face's reliance on the "pyramid of influence" also dictated its handling of distribution channels. Since they were in specialized markets, The North Face preferred to build its brand name carefully by using specialty stores as a foundation. Once this foundation was established, The North Face attempted to nurture it carefully by providing the dealers with new products and techniques (via training classes) to attract new customers. The company only used the more general sporting goods stores (e.g., Herman's, EMS) when it needed geographic coverage in a particular area, and

EXHIBIT 4 U.S. Industry Specialty Store Sales* of Backpacking Products (wholesale prices—in 000's)

	Total Sales
1971	$15,400
1972	21,600
1973	27,400
1974	40,700
1975	44,800
1976	57,050
1977	65,850
1978	70,400
1979	77,500
1980	81,700
1981 (est.)	84,300
1982 (est.)	86,900
1983 (est.)	90,100
1984 (est.)	92,400
1985 (est.)	95,100

*Domestic only

even then tried to limit distribution to certain outlets of the chain. The firm avoided mass merchandising stores as much as possible. TNF felt that specialty shops developed brand awareness and consumer franchise for their products, while general shops exploited their brand name. Thus, it relied heavily upon the prosperity of these specialty outlets. Careful control of the channels lay at the cornerstone of The North Face's marketing strategy.

Wholesaling. Backpacking industry sales were distributed among retail stores in the following proportions:

	Dollar Value	*Number of Outlets*
Backpacking specialty stores	50%	40%
Sports specialty stores	25	30
General sporting goods stores	10	5
Ski shops, department stores, etc.	15	25

Sales were fairly evenly distributed among the Pacific, North Central, and Northeast regions of the United States, with lesser proportions falling in the Mountain and Southern states.

The North Face sold primarily to approximately 700 retail stores, 75 percent of which specialize in backpacking and mountaineering equipment and the rest in general sporting goods. Wholesale distribution by The North Face was handled by 14 independent sales representatives who carried hiking, mountaineering, and cross-country skiing lines. These representatives covered 10 sales territories in the United States and were paid on commission. The North Face products were their major source of income. Management felt that this network was especially valuable as a conduit for information about market conditions, product knowledge, retail management programs, and competition. It was estimated that 55–60 percent of all consumer purchases resulted from word-of-mouth endorsement from a satisfied friend or from a sales presentation in the store. Thus, the primary marketing thrust of The North Face was to (1) sell dealers on the company's products and markets; and (2) provide information and point-of-sale aids to help floor salespeople.

The representatives were crucial to this effort and all were carefully chosen by the sales and marketing vice president and cofounder, Jack Gilbert. As a group, the reps had an average of seven to eight years' experience in the industry, were avid backpackers and lovers of the outdoors, and had been with The North Face since its inception. The reps were highly successful and had been well-treated by the company through the years. Over that time, the nature of their responsibilities had evolved from pioneering or prospecting for new accounts to training existing accounts in industry and management techniques, having established The North Face as the authority in the backpacking field.

The company long pursued a policy of building stable, ongoing relationships with carefully selected dealers. It followed a limited distribution policy, seeking to maintain a balance of dealers and market demand in any geographic area. The company individually reviewed and approved all potential dealer locations, including new locations of existing accounts, and was committed to maintaining and strengthening its dealers. In seeking new product areas in which to expand, it was considered important for The North Face to evaluate the potential of its current dealers to sell the products under consideration.

Retailing. The North Face's retailing objective was to use its own retail stores to attain its desired market share and profit objectives only where wholesaling was unable to achieve satisfactory market penetration and where the policy had no adverse impact on wholesale distribution. To meet this objective, the strategy was to expand existing outlets and introduce new outlets in an orderly fashion, locating only where conflict with the wholesale division was minimized. This strategy was reinforced in the following policy statement:

> The Retail Division will continue to examine expansion possibilities on a local basis. The Retail Division will not expand into any domestic geographic area which will have a significant adverse effect on the wholesale sales of The North Face. The focus of expansion efforts will only be around those areas where The North Face presently has established stores.

The North Face currently owned and operated five well-located retail stores and two factory outlets in the San Francisco Bay area and Seattle. In 1980, the mail order operation was closed down due both to its lack of profitability and its perceived conflict with the wholesaling operations. In recent years, the Retail Division had enjoyed considerable increases in sales and profits, significantly above the industry average:

Company Stores (in 000's)				
	1977	*1978*	*1979*	*1980*
Sales	$2,189	$2,574	$2,884	$3,368
Gross margins	N/A	974	1,156	1,446
Profits/contribution	N/A	104	220	364
Inventory turns	1.6X	1.7X	2.1X	2.1X
Transfers to stores (sales from company wholesale to company retail)	$ 918	$ 908	$ 770	$1,120

It should be noted that the "transfer" figures represent sales from company wholesale to company retail. Management felt that not all of these sales would have gone to independents if the company stores did not exist. This is important to consider in looking at The North Face's total profitability. The significance of these figures was underscored by the comparison that the average North Face store bought $200,000 from wholesaling while the average wholesale account bought slightly over $30,000 annually. Additionally, the Retail Division test-marketed some promotional programs and products and, through its factory outlets, took nearly $500,000 of seconds—which otherwise would have created image problems if sold through wholesale channels—as well as products that were made out of overstocked materials supplies. While the exact impact on corporate profit of these activities was hard, if not impossible, to calculate, it was thought to be considerable.

Conflict between Retailing and Wholesaling

A continual conflict existed between retail and wholesale because of the feeling that retail might expand into an area which was beyond its domain. In part to alleviate this problem, The Retail Division closed down its mail-order operation. The retail expansion into Seattle caused the loss of some wholesale business and was used as a lever by some competitive reps; but since The North Face did not terminate any existing dealers, the issue died. Although there were a number of good wholesale accounts left, The North Face did not sell to them because of the geographical protection it had granted it dealers. The company felt it received increased loyalty and purchases because of this protection and would lose them if its accounts were increased randomly.

Differing opinions on the subject of further retail expansion existed even at the highest levels of the company. At one point, at least, Klopp felt that retail expansion was the most effective means of generating market share and promoting brand-name allegiance, while Jack Gilbert, the sales and marketing vice president, had serious reservations in three areas:

1. *The Impact on the Dealers.* Gilbert felt that retailers in this industry were "very paranoid" that manufacturers would expand their retail operations. Indeed, competitive reps in the industry were known to advise dealers not to "give too much of your business to The North Face because they are out there gathering information about your market area in order to expand their retail operation." He believed that a North Face retail expansion would damage the company's excellent relationship with its dealers.
2. *The Profit Implications.* While the going margin at retail was 40 percent compared to a target margin at wholesale of 30 percent, entry into expanded retail operations was not a profitable strategy in the short run. The initial investment for a store was $40,000 in fixtures and capital improvements, plus $100,000 of inventory at retail prices. It took three years for an individual store to make the contribution management wanted—12 percent contribution to overhead and 8 percent to pretax profits.
3. *Growth.* Finally, Gilbert was concerned about whether The North Face could meet its growth objectives by going both the wholesale and retail routes, particularly given the company's limited financial resources.

Additional concerns regarding inventory control and the development of capable store managers via a training program were voiced by John McLaughlin, financial vice president for The North Face.

Outlook toward Growth

Maintaining a healthy rate of growth was also a major goal of management. The style of the company was aggressive and entrepreneurial. Hap and his management team did not want to risk frustrating the young, energetic staff they had gathered. As mentioned earlier, the backpacking industry seemed to be entering the maturity phase of the product life cycle. Over the past few years, the total market was growing only at a 5 percent compound annual growth rate. The North Face had grown at a faster rate than the overall market, consistently gaining market share, but it was evident that this situation would not last forever, especially given the company's reliance on the "pyramid of influence" theory.

In evaluating potential new markets, management looked for opportunities that could fulfill the following objectives:

- An overlap with current customer base.
- A product compatible with current machinery capabilities.

- A line that would complement seasonal production peaks.
- A market in which "top down" strategy would work.
- A line which matched with the interests and expertise of the existing management team.
- A line that would maintain and strengthen The North Face's current dealer network.
- A line that would not threaten or cannibalize the base business.

TNF's decision-making style added further complexity to the situation. The firm espoused a collaborative style of strategy formation and implementation. Employee input and consensus were essential. Hap fostered this environment by utilizing a paternalistic management style. In fact, each individual felt as if he or she had influence on the direction of TNF. In the context of the approaching decision, this meant that marketing needed to receive a general approval before entering a new business.

The Skiwear Line

The company's desire for continued growth in the face of this maturation of the backpacking market spurred management to investigate expansion into new products. In looking at manufacturing and marketing growth opportunities, the company analyzed its own sales, those of its dealers, and the markets highlighted, to see what opportunities were not being completely exploited. Interestingly, the company found that, although it never manufactured or marketed its products specifically for skiing, it held nearly 2 percent of the skiwear market; in some categories, such as down vests, it had nearly 5 percent. It was also discovered that over two thirds of all dealers handling The North Face products also sold skiwear. Most appealing was the fact that the market appeared to be highly fragmented. As pointed out in an industry study published in May 1980: "Most skiwear categories have one or two market leaders, but in all areas no one brand dominates the market. In fact, in all categories studied, it required between 9 and 12 brands to make up 70 percent of the market share in dollars."

Market Size (1980—in 000's)	
Adult down parkas/vests	$ 30,000
Adult non-down parkas/vests	54,000
Adult bibs and pants	21,000
Shell pants	1,600
X-Country ski clothing	2,600
	$109,200

(Exhibits 5 and 6 contain details on the skiwear market.)

EXHIBIT 5 Skiwear* Market Sales 1979–1980 (in millions)

	Dollars	*Market Share*
1. White Stag	$ 27.0	12.5%
2. Roffee	19.0	8.8
3. Skyr	13.5	6.3
4. Head Ski & Sportswear	13.0	6.0
5. Aspen	12.5	5.8
6. Gerry	12.0	5.5
7. Swing West (Raven)	10.0	4.6
8. Alpine Designs	9.0	4.2
9. Obermeyer	8.0	3.7
10. Sportscaster	7.5	3.5
11. Beconta	7.0	3.3
12. Bogner America	7.0	3.3
13. C. B. Sports	6.0	2.8
14. Serac	5.0	2.3
15. Profile	5.0	2.3
16. Demetre	5.0	2.3
17. Woolrich	4.5	2.0
18. The North Face	4.0	1.9
19. Other	41.0	18.9%
	$216.0	100.0%

*Excluding underwear.

These factors, coupled with an increasing number of requests for uniforms "which work" (i.e., functional, durable, and warm) from ski instructors, ski patrollers, and other professional users thought to influence the market, led The North Face to introduce its skiwear line. The company's strategy in skiwear was predicated on the same strategy as its backpacking business—functionally designed, classically styled clothing. The skiwear was targeted to the "professional skier" (not the racer), since management felt that a Trendsetter and Uniform Program targeted to ski patrollers and lift operators would serve to trigger sales in the same manner that using mountaineers impacted the backpacking pyramid of influence.

Issues with Skiwear

The decision to introduce skiwear was also not without some problems. Although a majority of the dealers carried skiwear, some did not. The latter might oppose The North Face trade name going into another local store, even if it was part of a product line they did not carry. Further, the current

EXHIBIT 6 Estimated Market Share by Segments of Skiwear Market

Down Parkas				*NonDown Parkas*				*Bibs*			
Men's		Women's		Men's		Women's		Men's		Women's	
1. Gerry	21.7%	1. Gerry	15.0%	1. Roffee	14.6%	1. Roffee	12.4%	1. Skyr	13.7%	1. Roffee	15.0%
2. Roffee	8.6%	2. Slalom	9.8%	2. White Stag	8.7%	2. White Stag	12.3%	2. Roffee	12.4%	2. Skyr	14.6%
3. Alpine Designs	7.4%	3. Roffee	8.7%	3. Skyr	8.0%	3. Skyr	10.6%	3. White Stag	11.0%	3. White Stag	9.1%
4. Powderhorn	5.4%	4. Head	7.8%	4. Head	7.7%	4. Head	10.2%	4. Head	7.2%	4. Head	6.6%
5. Head	5.3%	5. Mountain Goat*	6.1%	5. C. B. Sports	7.2%	5. Slalom	6.2%	5. Beconta	5.2%	5. Slalom	6.5%
6. White Stag	4.7%	6. White Stag	4.7%	6. Serac	5.9%	6. Swing West	5.0%	6. Swing West	4.9%	6. Swing West	4.6%
7. Mountain Goat*	3.6%	7. Tempco	4.2%	7. Cevas	4.6%	7. Bogner	4.4%	7. Gerry	4.1%	7. No. 1 Sun†	4.6%
8. C. B. Sports	3.3%	8. Sportscaster	3.9%	8. Slalom	4.2%	8. Cevas	3.2%	8. Slalom	3.9%	8. Beconta	4.4%
9. Obermeyer	3.1%	9. No. 1 Sun†	3.4%	9. Swing West	4.2%	9. No. 1 Sun†	3.0%	9. No. 1 Sun†	3.8%	9. Gerry	3.8%
10. Sportscaster	3.1%	10. C. B. Sports	2.8%	10. No. 1 Sun†	3.8%	10. C. B. Sports	2.6%	10. Alpine Designs	3.7%	10. Bogner	3.1%
11. All other	33.8%	11. All other	33.6%	11. All other	31.1%	11. All other	30.1%	11. All other	30.1%	11. All other	27.7%

*Second brand name of White Stag.

†Second brand name of Head.

dealers were not always the most influential top end shops required to build a market, and their ski departments might not take The North Face's ski-oriented products as seriously as they did the company's backpacking offerings. Similarly, some of the best ski shops which influenced the entire market were not presently The North Face outlets. Out of a total market size of over 3,000 Alpine ski dealers, only about 475 were currently carrying The North Face products. Moreover, the sales reps already had a very extensive line and it was a concern of management that they might have difficulty pushing the ski items during the critical start-up phase. Further, this expansion into a new area in effect required the established sales reps to "start over" again with prospecting for new accounts, a task which might tax their capabilities and desires.

Different complications arose in each of TNF's markets. The following example from a metropolitan center in California highlights some critical issues.

At the time of the skiwear decision, TNF distributed its backpacking products primarily through one large, specialty backpacking/skiing shop in the city. Suburban neighborhood stores were utilized for additional coverage. The city store ranked among the top 20 percent of TNF dealers. In the past, TNF had rewarded this supplier by withholding merchandise from direct competitors.

TNF serviced this account with regular visits of the local sales representative, frequent visits by sales managers, an annual dealer seminar, and periodic information-gathering visits by top management. The store's annual sales topped $1 million, with 65–70 percent of this deriving from backpacking products. Sales of TNF items accounted for the majority of backpacking revenue. TNF management felt that this shop, as the largest specialty shop in the area, "made" the area backpacking market. TNF developed consumer awareness via close association with this outlet and by regular co-op advertisements. In short, if a serious local backpacker needed equipment, he would most likely shop at this store.

In backpacking, this shop had little formidable competition. Some second-tier specialty shops existed, but they offered less ease of access and a narrower product range. A wide variety of general sporting goods shops also competed in the territory. These stores each had backpacking sections but did not emphasize service. TNF did not associate with these stores.

Unfortunately, the skiing market was much more fragmented in this territory. Although TNF's key backpacking account also sold skiing products, it did not have a dominant position. The store was one of the handful of large dealers that handled skiwear. It did not "make the market." Instead, it often reacted to the environment in setting pricing, merchandising, and product selection policies. In addition, five comparably sized ski specialty shops (no backpacking gear at all) competed in this territory. Each shop carried roughly the same product line frequently featuring loss leadership on hardware (Rossignol, Nodica, Lange, etc.). Soft goods were the primary profit maker. The offerings emphasized aesthetics and functionality.

EXHIBIT 7 Partial Organization Chart

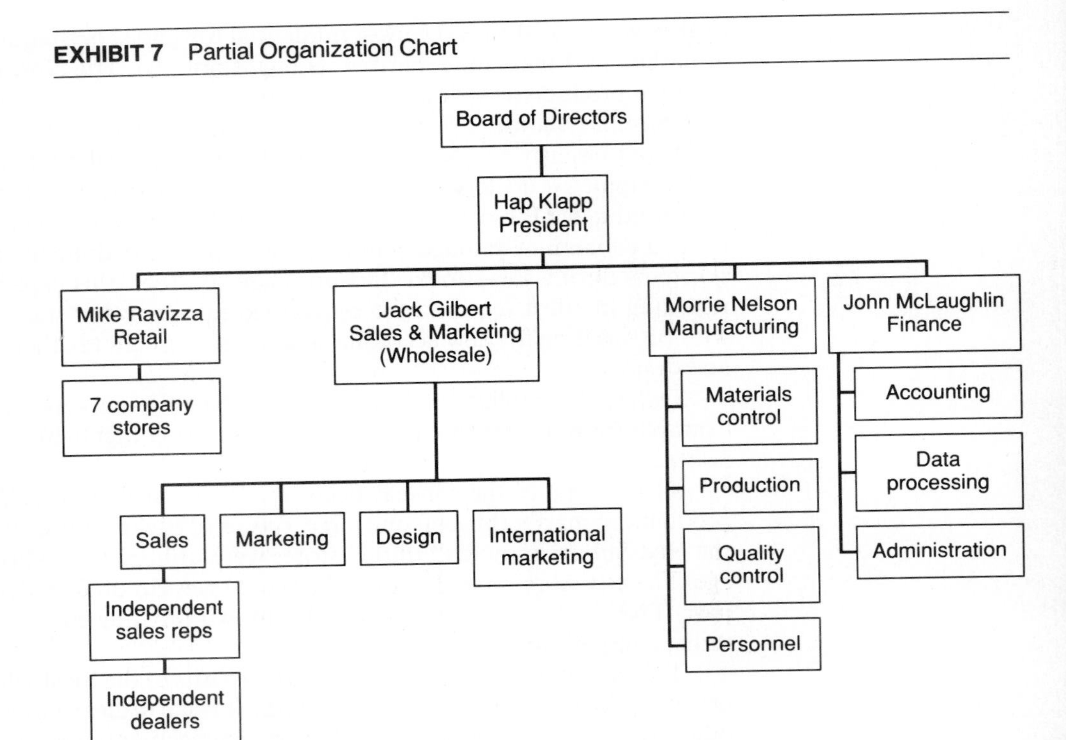

Backgrounds
Mike Ravizza, Retail—Joined The North Face in 1969; Stanford undergraduate.
Jack Gilbert, Sales & Marketing—Co-founder of the North Face in 1968; Stanford undergraduate.
Morrie Nelson, Manufacturing—Joined The North Face in 1975; University of Washington undergraduate, Santa Clara MBA.
John McLaughlin, Finance—Joined The North Face in 1970; Dartmouth undergraduate, Stanford MBA.

TNF management obviously faced a serious problem in introducing the skiwear line in this market. On the one hand, they owed special consideration to their key backpacking account. But they also realized that this account alone would not develop sufficient brand awareness as a pioneer for the skiwear line. The key account's owner was concerned about losing backpacking sales if TNF decided to offer its products to other area shops. In this territory, as in others, TNF needed to act quickly and carefully.

CASE 6–7 Food Lion, Inc.

In 1957 three former Winn-Dixie employees opened their first supermarket in Salisbury, North Carolina, under the name Food Town. Cofounders Ralph Ketner, Brown Ketner, and Wilson Smith all had considerable retail experience in the grocery industry; however, Food Town struggled in its early years. Various marketing gimmicks were implemented (the company gave away trading stamps and even free automobiles), but the stores failed to win the loyalty of customers. In fact, Ralph Ketner had to close 9 of the 16 stores during the first 10 years of operation. He blamed much of this failure on the underpricing techniques of Winn-Dixie. By 1966, only seven Food Town stores remained.

In response to the problem, Ketner decided to slash prices on all items sold in the stores. He realized that a drastic increase in volume would be necessary to make this approach work and keep the company afloat. The company theme of LFPINC or "Lowest Food Prices in North Carolina" became popular as both customers and sales increased greatly. Sales rose 54 percent to $8.9 million, and profits rose 165 percent to $95,000 in the first year under the new pricing strategy.[1]

In 1970 the company went public. Establissements Delhaize Freres et Cie, a Belgium grocery chain, purchased 47.6 percent of the stock in 1974. Today, Delhaize controls 50.6 percent of the voting stock and has 5 of the 10 seats on the board of directors.[2] The company changed its name to Food Lion in 1983 to avoid confusion with another similarly named chain. Also, the company began implementing its expansion program.

Today, Food Lion operates in eight states, from Delaware to Florida, and is considered to be one of the fastest growing retail grocers in the country. (See Exhibit 1.) Food Lion President and CEO Tom E. Smith explains, "Our goal is to bring extra low grocery prices to as many people in the Southeast as possible."[3]

Food Lion has 27,000 employees, and continues to operate conventional size stores (21,000–29,000 square feet) and to offer discount prices. The company remains committed to expansion throughout the Southeast and has avoided moving into the sale of general merchandise in its stores. A food consultant's comments highlight the company's success in the aforementioned areas. He states that Food Lion is "probably the best example of commitment to a format and operating style in the industry today. And although it is a conventional store operator, it also stands as an excellent

---

Prepared by Janet L. Caswell under the direction of Professor Neil H. Snyder, both of the University of Virginia.

[1]Richard Anderson, "That Roar You Hear Is Food Lion," *Business Week,* August 24, 1987, p. 66.

[2]Ibid.

[3]*1987 Food Lion, Inc. Annual Report,* p. 1.

EXHIBIT 1 Store Distribution

Location	*Stores*	*Percent of Total*
North Carolina	233	49.1%
Virginia	112	23.5
South Carolina	74	15.6
Tennessee	29	6.1
Georgia	19	4.0
Florida	6	1.3
Delaware	1	0.2
Maryland	1	0.2
Total	475	100.0%

Source: *Standard & Poor's Stock Report,* p. 3905.

practitioner of niche marketing. The stores aren't fancy, but beat everyone on price, and the company doesn't make many mistakes."[4]

Ralph Ketner. Since cofounding Food Lion, Ralph Ketner has continued to be a force behind its success. In 1968 it was his idea to adopt the strategy of discount pricing and his LFPINC theme which promoted the company. He acted as chief executive officer until 1986, when he passed the reins to President Tom Smith. Despite giving up his CEO title, Ketner still exerts considerable influence over the operation of Food Lion. He remains chairman of the board of directors, and plans to retain this position until 1991. In addition, Delhaize signed an agreement in 1974 to vote with Ketner for 10 years. This agreement was later extended and was in effect until 1989.[5]

Tom E. Smith. President and CEO Tom E. Smith is very much responsible for Food Lion's growth and success. This is largely attributed to his involvement with the company since his youth. At age 17, Smith began as a bag boy at Food Lion's first store. He attended night school at Catawba College and graduated in 1964 with a degree in business administration. He spent the next six years working for Del Monte, when he was hired as Food Lion's sole buyer. Smith developed the successful strategy of stocking fewer brands and sizes than his competitors. He also took advantage of wholesaler specials by purchasing large volumes at discount prices. He was named vice president for distribution in 1974, and later became executive vice president in 1977. His continued success in these areas led to his promotion to president in 1981, at the age of 39. In 1986 he was named CEO.

[4]Richard DeSanta, "Formats: Growing Apart, Coming Together," *Progressive Grocer,* January 1987, p. 37.

[5]Ketner Gives Up Food Lion Reins," *Supermarket News,* January 6, 1986, p. 18.

Smith views himself as a planner who carefully molds the company's growth while keeping a close eye on the operations. This style has enabled him to react to and resolve any problems quickly and effectively. He has been a primary reason for Food Lion's constant commitment to its overall strategy of discount pricing and cost reduction. Smith has also become well-known through his participation in over 50 percent of the Food Lion commercials. This media exposure has brought him recognition not only in the Southeast, but as far away as San Francisco and even Scotland from visiting customers.[6] These commercials portray Smith as a hard-working and very trustworthy manager.

Food Lion's Attitude toward Social Responsibility

Food Lion is recognized as a corporate neighbor, and it takes pride in performing charitable acts. In 1986 the company received the Martin Luther King, Jr., Award in recognition of its humanitarian efforts. Food Lion received the award for its role in donating trucks to aid southeastern farmers during a prolonged drought; the trucks enabled the farmers to transport hay from Indiana. Also, the company was cited for providing equal opportunity employment and establishing express lanes for handicapped customers.[7]

The Supermarket Industry

Several trends in the supermarket industry were of concern to many retail grocers. During 1987 there was a decline in the percentage of disposable income spent for food at home. After discounting for inflation, real sales did not increase from 1986. As Exhibit 2 shows, food-at-home spending accounted for more retail sales than any other category in 1983. However, slow growth caused a reduction in this percentage, leaving food stores in second place behind auto dealers. The percentage of retail sales for eating and drinking establishments during this same period trended upward.

The grocery industry is also experiencing competition from other types of stores. Discount department and drug stores are starting to sell more packaged foods. Many fast-food restaurants continue to sell a larger variety of prepared foods for takeout. Sales from specialty shops, which concentrate on one particular type of food, have increased as well. Wholesale clubs have also been of concern to retail grocers. These clubs have been effective at luring many customers away from conventional supermarkets. Those supermarkets stressing discount prices have been hurt most by the emergence of the wholesale clubs.

In response to the trends, most grocery chains are stressing the idea of one-stop shopping. New store formats and product offerings are abundant.

[6] Anderson, "That Roar You Hear Is Food Lion," p. 65.

[7] *1986 Food Lion, Inc. Annual Report,* p. 4.

EXHIBIT 2 Percentage of U.S. Retail Sales by Type of Establishment

Type of Establishment	*1983*	*1984*	*1985*	*1986*	*1987**
Food stores	22.0%	21.1%	20.6%	20.4%	20.3%
Eating and drinking	9.9	9.6	9.7	10.0	10.1
Drug and proprietary	3.5	3.4	3.4	3.4	3.6
General merchandise	11.1	11.0	10.9	10.7	11.0
Furniture and appliance	4.6	4.8	5.0	5.4	5.5
Auto dealers	19.8	21.6	22.6	22.9	22.2
Hardware and lumber	4.4	4.7	4.8	5.2	4.7
Clothing	5.3	5.3	5.4	5.5	5.8
Gas stations	8.5	7.8	7.3	6.1	5.7
All others	10.9	10.7	10.4	10.4	11.2

*First six months.

Source: Bureau of the Census (revised), 1987.

These ideas are an attempt to obtain a product mix that stresses higher margin items and services, as well as creating an atmosphere causing consumers to view the supermarket as more than a place to buy groceries. Items such as flowers, greeting cards, videocassettes, and pharmacy items are appearing more frequently in many supermarkets. There has also been a greater emphasis on stocking perishables.

However, the biggest trend in the industry is the shift to bigger stores. Several experts believe that increased size is necessary to provide the variety that many consumers desire. One chain president expressed this sentiment: "Customer satisfaction starts with the store design: one-stop shopping, complete service departments, and integrating a drugstore and pharmacy into the store."[8] Much of the one-stop shopping trend is a result of increases in the numbers of working women, dual-income families, single parents, and singles living alone. Time and convenience are two characteristics that consumers fitting into these groups often desire.

The one-stop shopping concept has resulted in several new store formats. Combination stores offer consumers a variety of nonfood items. These stores can be as large as 35,000 square feet, and 25 percent of the space is devoted to nonfood and pharmacy items. Superstores are similar to the combination stores in that they offer a wide selection of general merchandise items. These stores are all greater than 40,000 square feet, and are thought to be the strongest format for the near future. Exhibit 3 shows chain executives' views on the prospects for the various formats that exist today.

The newest and largest of the formats is the hypermarket. Currently, 55

[8]"Retail Operations: The New Basics," *Progressive Grocer,* September 1987, p. 56.

EXHIBIT 3 Chain Executives' Opinions on Prospects for New Formats

	Percent		
	Excellent	*Good*	*Fair/Poor*
Superstores	56%	36%	8%
Combination	38	53	9
Convenience stores	26	39	35
Super warehouse	22	39	39
Hypermarkets	10	33	57
Specialty	8	37	55
Wholesale clubs	6	30	62
Conventional	4	35	59
Warehouse stores	1	17	79

Source: *Progressive Grocer,* April 1988.

of these stores exist in the United States. The typical hypermarket ranges in size from 125,000 to 330,000 square feet and requires $25 to $50 million in sales per year just to break even.[9] Normally, 40 percent of the floor space in hypermarkets is devoted to grocery items and the remaining 60 percent is used for general merchandise. Freeway access, population density, and visibility are all key variables contributing to a hypermarket's success. A majority of the stores are run by companies which are not U.S. food retailers. For example, Wal-Mart has opened several stores under the Hypermarket USA name. Also, Bruno's, a retail grocery chain, is teaming up with Kmart to build a store in Atlanta.[10]

Because of the trend to expand store size, the number of stores declined for the first time in years. However, the larger store sizes resulted in an increase in actual square footage. Many small units have been closed due to the openings of larger stores. In many market areas, there continue to be too many stores and too few customers to support them. This is going to be an even bigger concern given the advent of the combination stores and hypermarkets, since they tend to attract customers from a wider area than the conventional stores.

Although the majority of retailers believe that the bigger stores are necessary to be successful in the future, there is a large group that believes the industry is going overboard in its attempt to provide one-stop shopping. Chain executive Carole Bitter believes that the emphasis on size is unfounded. "There has been an ego problem in the industry that has led to

[9]David Rogers, "Hypermarkets Need Something Special to Succeed," *Supermarket Business,* May 1988, p. 26.

[10]Ibid.

EXHIBIT 4 Store Attributes Desired by Consumers

Rank	*Characteristic*
1	Cleanliness
2	All prices labeled
3	Low prices
4	Good produce department
5	Accurate, pleasant clerks
6	Freshness date marked on products
7	Good meat department
8	Shelves kept well stocked
9	Short wait for checkout
10	Convenient store location

Source: *Progressive Grocer,* April 1988.

overbuilding and has driven up store sizes and has increased the number of formats."[11] Proponents of conventionals claim that the larger stores are too impersonal to be attractive to everyone. They also believe that many consumers desire the conventional type of store, and that this format will continue to be successful. Although many consumers claim that they want more service departments, studies have shown that the shoppers are not willing to pay enough for such departments to make them profitable. Exhibit 4 reveals what the average shopper desires. One-stop shopping capabilities rate only 26th on the list.

Competition

In recent years, competition in the Southeast has become quite intense. Previously, this area was characterized by predominantly conventional stores. Combination and superstores were scarce. However, many retailers realized that the Southeast was a prime location for the newer formats. In 1984 Cub Foods opened three large, modern stores in the Atlanta area in an attempt to challenge Kroger's dominance in the Southeast. This move marked the beginning of several competitive shakeups in the South.

Kroger. Kroger operates 1,317 supermarkets and 889 convenience stores in the South and Midwest. In 1987 sales were nearly $18 billion. More than 95 percent of the floor space is either new or has been remodeled during the past 10 years.[12] This is a result of the chain's move to larger combination and superstore formats. Kroger has not been as successful as it would like. The

[11] "Retail Operations: The New Basics," p. 62.

[12] *Standard & Poor's Standard Stock Reports,* p. 1318.

company realizes a net profit margin of approximately 1 percent. This is partly due to its new outlets cannibalizing its existing stores and has caused same-store sales comparisons to be relatively flat.[13]

In response to the disappointing profit margins, Kroger is planning to decrease its capital spending plans by about $300 million. It is hoped that this will reduce interest costs as well as keep start-up expenses down. Also, the firm is cutting corporate overhead 20 percent. As for future store designs, Kroger is considering the curtailment of the new super-warehouse stores. These stores combine low grocery prices with high-priced service departments and have not appealed to a large segment of the market. Furthermore, the company is planning to reduce store remodeling in mature market areas.[14]

Winn-Dixie. Winn-Dixie is the fourth largest food retailer in the country with sales of nearly $9 billion. The chain operates 1,271 stores in the Sunbelt area, with the heaviest concentration of stores located in Florida, North Carolina, and Georgia. During the past few years, Winn-Dixie has been hurt by the influx of competition in the Southeast. As a result, profit margins have dipped to just over 1 percent. Net income also declined in 1987. Management points to a lack of investment in new stores and a rather slow response to competitors' underpricing methods as the main reasons for the decline in profits.[15]

Management has adopted several new strategies to combat the competition. Foremost is the move to larger store formats. In the past, the chain operated mostly conventional stores and depended on operating efficiencies to realize sizable profits. However, management believes that it is now necessary to alter the stores in response to changing consumer needs. At the end of 1987, the averge supermarket was 27,700 square feet. There are approximately 250 new stores in the 35,000–45,000-square-feet range, and they are expected to account for nearly half of all sales in the next five years.[16] The units in the 35,000-square-feet category are combination stores operated under the Winn-Dixie name. The 45,000-square-feet stores employ the superstore format and use the name Marketplace. Emphasis is being placed on service departments as well as price-sensitivity.

Other changes involve management. Last year, the company eliminated a layer of management that resulted in 60 layoffs. The firm is also adopting a decentralized strategy which divides the company into 12 operating units. Each division is allowed to develop its own procedures and image. It is hoped that this will help the stores cater to the consumers in each market area more effectively.

[13] *Value Line Investment Survey,* 1987, p. 1511.

[14] Ibid.

[15] *Standard & Poor's,* p. 2491.

[16] "Winn-Dixie Strategy," *Supermarket News,* March 3, 1987, p. 12.

Lucky Stores. Lucky operates nearly 500 supermarkets throughout the country. The majority of these are located in California; however, the chain does operate 90 stores in Florida. In 1986 Lucky began a major restructuring. This resulted in the sale of all the nonfood businesses. Also, the company has concentrated on increasing the store size to enable the sale of more service and nonfood items. The average size of the stores at the end of 1986 was 31,000 square feet.[17]

At the end of the year, there was much speculation that American Stores Company would begin to pursue an unsolicited tender offer for all outstanding shares of Lucky common stock. American is a leading retailer in the country and operates mostly combination food and drug stores.

Bruno's. Bruno's operates approximately 100 supermarkets and combination food and drug stores in the Southeast. This chain pursues a strategy of high-volume sales at low prices. Another strategy involves the use of four different formats under various names. Consumer Warehouse Foods stores are relatively small warehouse stores which emphasize lower prices and reduced operating costs. Food World stores are large supermarkets which offer a variety of supermarket items at low prices. Bruno's Food and Pharmacy stores promote the idea of one-stop shopping through the combination store format. Finally, FoodMax stores are superwarehouses which offer generic and bulk foods in addition to the national labels.[18]

The company is also well-known for its innovative forward buying program. Bruno's is able to purchase goods at low prices because of its 900,000-square-feet distribution center which houses excess inventory. This strategy has been very successful as the company boasts high operating and net profit margins.[19] Exhibit 5 presents comparative statistics for Food Lion and its four major competitors.

Expansion at Food Lion

Food Lion has continued to grow and expand in the Southeast. During 1987 the chain opened 95 new stores while closing only 8, bringing the total to 475. With the exception of four supermarkets, Food Lion operates its stores under various leasing arrangements. The number of stores has grown at a 10-year compound rate of 24.1 percent.[20] With this expansion has come a 29.7 percent compound growth rate in sales and a 30.9 percent compound growth rate in earnings (Exhibit 6).[21]

The existence and further development of distribution centers serve as

[17] *Standard & Poor's,* p. 1387.

[18] Ibid., p. 3358M.

[19] John Liscio, "Beefing Up Profits," *Barron's,* May 25, 1987, p. 18.

[20] *1987 Food Lion, Inc. Annual Report,* p. 9.

[21] Ibid.

EXHIBIT 5 Selected Statistics for Major Southeastern Supermarket Chains, 1987

	Kroger	*Lucky*	*Winn-Dixie*	*Bruno's*	*Food Lion*
Stores	2,206	481	1,271	111	475
Employees	170,000	44,000	80,000	10,655	27,033
Sales ($ million)	$17,660	$6,925	$8,804	$1,143	$2,954
Sales/employee	103,881	157,386	110,049	107,265	109,267
Net profit ($ million)	$246.6	$151	$105.4	$31	$85.8
Net profit margin	1.4%	2.2%	1.2%	2.7%	2.9%
Gross margin	22.4	25	22	20.8	19.2
Current ratio	1.1	.83	1.65	1.63	1.41
Return on equity	24.5	46.3	15.2	15.4	25.3
Return on assets	5.5	11.8	7.9	10.3	10.6
Long-term debt/equity	.69	.38	.03	.04	.26
Earnings per share	$3.14	$3.92	$2.72	$.79	$.27
Average price/earnings ratio	15.1	10.2	13.9	23.1	35.3

Source: *Standard & Poor's.*

EXHIBIT 6 Food Lion's Growth and Expansion (in thousands)

Year	*Stores*	*Sales*	*Net Income*
1987	475	$2,953,807	$85,802
1986	388	2,406,582	61,823
1985	317	1,865,632	47,585
1984	251	1,469,564	37,305
1983	226	1,172,459	27,718
1982	182	947,074	21,855
1981	141	666,848	19,317
1980	106	543,883	15,287
1979	85	415,974	13,171
1978	69	299,267	9,418

Source: Food Lion, Inc. annual reports.

The existence and further development of distribution centers serve as the core for continued expansion. At the end of 1987, four such centers had been completed. These are located in Salisbury and Dunn, North Carolina; Orangeburg County, South Carolina; and Prince George County, Virginia. Two additional centers are planned for Tennessee and Jacksonville, Florida. These distribution centers enable Food Lion to pursue expansion using its "ink blot" formula. Using this strategy, new stores are added to an existing market area in order to saturate the market. "If anyone wants to go to a competitor, they'll have to drive by one of our stores," explains CFO Brian Woolf.[22] Despite the emergence of new stores, cannibalization has not been a problem. In fact, same-store sales increase approximately 8 percent annually. When Food Lion enters a new area, the strategy of underpricing the competitors is employed. Such a strategy has caused average food prices to decline 10–20 percent in some parts of the country.[23] Every new store is constructed no further than 200 miles from a distribution center. With continued expansion, new distribution centers whose radiuses overlap an existing distribution territory are erected to keep warehouse and transportation costs down.

Moreover, Food Lion continues to employ a cookie-cutter approach to its new stores. Rather than purchase existing stores, the firm much prefers to build new ones from scratch. All the stores fall into the conventional store category. The majority are 25,000 square feet and cost only $650,000 to complete. These stores emphasize the fruit and vegetable departments. Approximately 40 percent of the new stores are 29,000 square feet and contain a bakery/delicatessen. These are placed after careful consideration is given to the demographics and psychographics of the area. Normally, new stores turn a profit within the first six months of operation. In comparison, most competitors construct slightly larger stores which cost over $1 million to complete.[24]

The standard size of the stores has allowed the company to keep costs down while sticking to basics. Aside from the bakery departments, Food Lion has stayed away from service departments such as seafood counters and flower shops. Such departments are often costly due to the increase in required labor. Also, Food Lion has remained a retail grocery chain, shunning the idea of moving into the general merchandise area.

With the steady increase in stores over the past 10 years comes an increase in the need for quality employees. In an interview last March, Smith expressed concern over the high dropout rate of high school students.[25] Food Lion relies heavily on recent graduates, and the current trend may signal a decline in the quality of the average worker. Food Lion has responded to the labor problem by setting up an extensive training program for its 27,000 employees. These programs range from in-store training at the operational level to comprehensive training programs for potential managers. In addition, the firm continues to offer programs at headquarters to upgrade the work of the upper staff. Management is also attempting to increase the use of computers within the company. More specifically, Smith is hoping to utilize computer systems to handle much of the financial reporting aspects in the individual stores in an attempt to lessen the need for more employees.

[22] Liscio, "Beefing Up Profits," p. 19.

[23] "Food Lion's Roar Changes Marketplace," *Tampa Tribune,* April 5, 1988, p. 1.

[24] Anderson, "That Roar You Hear Is Food Lion," p. 65.

[25] "Food Lion, Inc." *The Wall Street Transcript,* March 28, 1988, p. 88890.

Advertising

Rather than employ costly advertising gimmicks, such as double coupon offers, Food Lion's advertising strategy combines cost-saving techniques with an awareness of consumer sentiment. Smith is the company's main spokesman, appearing in over half of the television commercials. Not only has this method kept advertising expenses down, but it has also made the public aware of both Smith and his discount pricing policy. By producing most of the ads in-house and using only a few paid actors, the cost of an average TV spot is only $6,000. Also, the company policy of keeping newspaper ads relatively small results in annual savings of $8 million. Food Lion's advertising costs are a mere 0.5 percent of sales, one fourth of the industry average.[26]

The content of the ads is another reason for Food Lion's success. Many of the TV spots feature some of the cost-cutting techniques used by the firm. One often-mentioned theme at the end of ads is "When we save, you save." Another commonly used theme states, "Food Lion is coming to town, and food prices will be coming down." Before moving into the Jacksonville, Florida, area, Food Lion launched a nine-month advertising campaign. Many of these ads focused on innovative management methods which permit lower prices to be offered in the stores. For example, one ad demonstrates how a central computer is used to help control freezer temperatures. Other ads attempt to characterize Food Lion as a responsible community member. One such spot describes the importance that management places on preventive maintenance for its forklifts and tractor trailers.

Smith has also used the media to react to potential problems. For instance, Winn-Dixie launched an advertising attack against Food Lion reminding customers how competitors have come and gone. The company countered with an ad featuring Tom Smith in his office reassuring consumers: "Winn-Dixie would have you believe that Food Lion's low prices are going to crumble and blow away. Let me assure you that as long as you keep shopping at Food Lion, our lower prices are going to stay right where they belong—in Jacksonville."[27] Smith also reacted quickly to a possible conflict in eastern Tennessee in 1984. Several rumors circulated which linked the Food Lion logo to Satanic worship. In response, Smith hired Grand Ole Opry star Minnie Pearl to appear in the Tennessee advertisements until the stories disappeared.[28]

Innovations

The grocery industry is characterized by razor-thin margins. While most retail grocery chains have failed to introduce new innovations in the indus-

[26] Anderson, "That Roar You Hear Is Food Lion," p. 65.

[27] "Food Lion, Winn-Dixie in Animated Squabble," *Supermarket News,* September 14, 1987, p. 9.

[28] Anderson, "That Roar You Hear Is Food Lion," p. 66.

try, Food Lion has employed several techniques which enable the firm to offer greater discounts on nearly all its products. These innovations help Food Lion to realize a profit margin of nearly 2.9 percent, twice the industry average. The company's credo is doing "1,000 things 1 percent better."[29] Such a philosophy has resulted in keeping expenses at 14 percent of sales as compared to the industry average of 20 percent.

Examples of the company's cost-cutting ideas are abundant. Rather than purchase expensive plastic bins to store cosmetics, Food Lion recycles old banana crates. These banana boxes are also used for storing groceries in warehouses. These innovations save the company approximately $200,000 a year.[30] Furthermore, the firm utilizes waste heat from the refrigerator units to warm part of the stores. Also, motion sensors automatically turn off lights in unoccupied rooms. Costs are further reduced by Food Lion's practice of repairing old grocery carts rather than purchasing new, more expensive models. Perhaps the greatest savings can be attributed to the carefully planned distribution system. This system allows management to take advantage of wholesalers' specials. The centralized buyout-and-distribution technique allows products for all stores to be purchased at one volume price.

Moreover, labor costs remain lower than those of many competitors. Smith is vehemently opposed to the use of unionized labor. Despite protests from the United Food and Commercial Workers International Union claiming that Food Lion's wages are well below union standards, management has continued to please its workers and avoid unionization. In fact, Smith believes its employee-benefit package is unequaled in the industry. A profit-sharing plan linking an employee's efforts in making Food Lion profitable with wealth accumulation for the future is already in use. Plans to improve long-term disability insurance benefits are under way.[31] In contrast, several other chains have experienced problems solving labor union problems. For example, a month-long strike by Kroger's Denver-area employees resulted in concessions on wages, benefits, and work rules. Safeway employees were also given quick concessions after threatening to close down several stores.[32]

Other innovations are designed to increase sales. Food Lion often sells popular items such as pet food and cereal at cost in an attempt to draw more customers into the stores. The company makes $1 million a year selling fertilizer made from discarded ground-up bones and fat. Lower prices are also feasible due to the policy of offering fewer brands and sizes than competitors. The company has increased its private label stock, which now includes at least one unit in every category. These two methods allow the company to price its national brand products below many competitors' private brands.

[29] Ibid., p. 65.

[30] "Ad Series Heralds First Florida Food Lion," *Supermarket News,* March 2, 1987, p. 12.

[31] *1986 Food Lion, Inc. Annual Report.*

[32] *Value Line Investment Survey,* August 28, 1987, p. 1501.

EXHIBIT 7 Selected Financial Ratios for Food Lion, 1978–1987

Year	*Operating Margin*	*Net Profit Margin*	*Return on Assets*	*Return on Equity*	*Long-Term Debt as a Percent of Capital*
1987	6.8%	2.9%	14.2%	32.4%	26.0%
1986	6.9	2.6	14.1	29.8	24.0
1985	6.3	2.6	14.4	29.1	20.5
1984	6.3	2.5	13.6	30.2	22.8
1983	5.9	2.4	13.0	28.3	25.9
1982	5.6	2.3	15.7	28.1	18.0
1981	6.7	2.9	18.1	32.3	12.4
1980	5.9	2.8	17.7	33.4	15.5
1979	6.7	3.2	20.0	39.0	19.0
1978	6.9	3.2	19.5	38.3	22.8

Source: *1987 Food Lion, Inc. Annual Report.*

As mentioned earlier, the smaller store size and sale of mostly food items have contributed to the high profit margin realized by the company.

Finance

Food Lion has been able to expand without becoming overextended or burdened with heavy debt repayments. The firm's capital structure consists of 26 percent long-term debt and 74 percent equity. The majority of growth has been financed through internally generated funds. The company does not want to grow at the expense of profits. Exhibit 7 presents selected financial ratios for the company.

The growth in Food Lion's stock price also reflects the sound financial position of the company. This growth illustrates the continued confidence of investors in the future productivity of the firm. In response to the rapid rise of Food Lion's stock price, management has declared two stock splits since late 1983, when the two separate classes of stock were formed from the previous single class. These splits are designed to keep the price of the stock low enough to be attractive and affordable to all investors. The price/earnings ratio indicates how much investors are willing to pay for a dollar of the company's earnings. In 1987 Food Lion's P/E ratio was the 83rd highest of all the companies listed in the Value Line Investment Survey.

Future

Next week, Tom Smith is meeting with the board of directors to discuss and present his ideas for the next few years. Given the recent troublesome trends in the grocery industry as well as the increasing competition in the Southeast, he is reviewing the future strategy of Food Lion. Foremost in his mind is the extent to which Food Lion should continue to expand operations of its conventional stores in this area. He is also pondering movement into other market areas. Smith wants to be sure that the company will be able to finance future growth without greatly changing its current capital structure. Although the current success of Food Lion is quite impressive, Smith realizes that other grocery chains have experienced problems by not responding to the changing environment. He wants to be certain that this does not happen to Food Lion.

CASE 6–8 Barro Stickney, Inc.

Introduction

With four people and sales of $5.5 million, Barro Stickney, Inc. (BSI) had become a successful and profitable manufacturers' representative firm. It enjoyed a reputation for outstanding sales results and friendly, thorough service to both its customers and principals. In addition, BSI was considered a great place to work. The office was comfortable and the atmosphere relaxed but professional. All members of the group had come to value the close, friendly working relationships that had grown with the organization.

Success had brought with it increased profits as well as the inevitable decision regarding further growth. Recent requests from two principals, Franklin Key Electronics and R. D. Ocean, had forced BSI to focus its attention on the question of expansion. It was not to be an easy decision, for expansion offered both risk and opportunity.

Company Background

John Barro and Bill Stickney established their small manufacturers' representative agency, Barro Stickney, Inc., 10 years ago. Both men were close friends who left different manufacturers' representative firms to join as partners in their own "rep" agency. The two worked very well together, and their talents complemented each other.

John Barro was energetic and gregarious. He enjoyed meeting new people and taking on new challenges. It was mainly through John's efforts that many of BSI's eight principals had signed on with BSI. Even after producing

This case was written by Tony Langan, B. Jane Stewart, and Lawrence M. Stratton, Jr., under the supervision of Professor Erin Anderson of the Wharton School, University of Pennsylvania. The writing of the case was sponsored by the Manufacturers' Representatives Educational Research Foundation. The cooperation of the Mid-Atlantic Chapter of the Electronic Representatives Association (ERA) is greatly appreciated.

$1.75 million in sales this past year, John still made an effort to contribute much of his free time to community organizations in addition to perfecting his golf score.

Bill Stickney liked to think of himself as someone a person could count on. He was thoughtful and thorough. He liked to figure how things could get done, and how they could be better. Much of the administrative work of the agency, such as resource allocation and territory assignments, was handled by Bill. In addition to his contribution of $1.5 million to total company sales, Bill also had a Boy Scout troop and was interested in gourmet cooking. In fact, he often prepared specialties to share with his fellow workers.

A few years later, as the business grew, J. Todd Smith (J.T.) joined as an additional salesperson. J.T. had worked for a nationally known corporation, and he brought his experience dealing with large customers with him. He and his family loved the Harrisburg area, and J.T. was very happy when he was asked to join BSI just as his firm was ready to transfer him to Chicago. John and Bill had worked with J.T. in connection with a hospital fund-raising project, and they were impressed with his tenacity and enthusiasm. Because he had produced sales of over $2 million this past year, J.T. was now considered eligible to buy a partnership share of BSI.

Soon after J.T. joined BSI, Elizabeth Lee, a school friend of John's older sister, was hired as office manager. She was cheerful and put as much effort into her work as she did coaching the local swim team. The three salespeople knew they could rely on her to keep track of orders and schedules, and she was very helpful when customers and principals called in with requests or problems.

Most principals in the industry assigned their reps exclusive territories, and BSI's ranged over the Pennsylvania, New Jersey, and Delaware area. The partners purchased a small house and converted it into their present office located in Camp Hill, a suburb of Harrisburg, the state capitol of Pennsylvania. The converted home contributed to the familylike atmosphere and attitude that was promoted and prevalent throughout the agency.

Over the years, in addition to local interests, BSI and its people had made an effort to participate in and support the efforts of the Electronics Representative Association (ERA). A wall of the company library was covered with awards and letters of appreciation. BSI had made many friends and important contacts through the organization. Just last year BSI received a recommendation from Chuck Goodman, a Chicago manufacturers' rep who knew a principal in need of representation in the Philadelphia area. The principal's line worked well with BSI's existing portfolio, and customer response had been quite favorable. BSI planned to continue active participation in the ERA.

Each week BSI held a 5:00 o'clock meeting in the office library where all members of the company shared their experiences of the week. It was a time when new ideas were encouraged and everyone was brought up to date. For example, many customer problems were solved here, and principals' and members' suggestions were discussed. An established agenda enabled members to prepare. Most meetings took about 60–90 minutes, with emphasis placed on group consensus. It was during this group meeting that BSI would discuss the future of the company.

Opportunities for Expansion

R. D. Ocean was BSI's largest principal, and it accounted for 32 percent of BSI's revenues. Ocean had just promoted James Innve as new sales manager, and he felt an additional salesperson was needed in order for BSI to achieve the new sales projections. Innve expressed the opinion that BSI's large commission checks justified the additional effort, and he further commented that J. T.'s expensive new car was proof that BSI could afford it.

BSI was not sure an additional salesperson was necessary, but it did not want to lose the goodwill of R. D. Ocean or their business. Also, while it was customary for all principals to meet and tacitly approve new representatives, BSI wanted to be very sure that any new salesperson would fit into the close-knit BSI organization.

Franklin Key Electronics was BSI's initial principal and had remained a consistent contributor of approximately 15 percent of BSI's revenues. BSI felt its customer base was well suited to the Franklin line, and it had worked hard to establish the Franklin Key name with these customers. As a consequence, BSI now considered Franklin Key relatively easy to sell.

A few days previously, Mark Heil, Franklin's representative from Virginia, perished when his private plane crashed, leaving Franklin Key without representation in its D.C./Virginia territory. Franklin did not want to jeopardize its sales of over $800,000 and was desperate to replace Heil before its customers found other sources. Franklin offered the territory to BSI and was anxious to hear the decision within one week.

BSI was not familiar with the territory, but it did understand that there were a great number of military accounts. This meant there was a potential for sizable orders, although a different and specialized sales approach would be required. Military customers are known to have their own unique approach to purchase decisions.

Because of the distance and the size of the territory, serious consideration was needed as to whether a branch office would be necessary. A branch office would mean less interaction with and a greater independence from the main BSI office. None of the current BSI members seemed anxious to move there, but it might be possible to hire someone who was familiar with the territory. There was, of course, always the risk that any successful salesperson might leave and start his or her own rep firm.

In addition to possibilities of expanding its territory and its sales force, BSI also wanted to consider whether it should increase or maintain its number of principals. BSI's established customer base and its valued reputation put them in a strong position to approach potential principals. If, however, BSI had too many principals, it might not be able to offer them all the attention and service they might require.

Preparation for the Meeting

Each member received an agenda and supporting data for the upcoming meeting asking them to consider the issue of expansion. They would be asked whether BSI should or should not expand its territory, its sales force, and/or its number of principals. In preparation, they were each asked to take a good hard look at the current BSI portfolio and to consider all possibilities for growth, including the effect any changes would have on the company's profits, its reputation, and its work environment.

It was an ambitious agenda: one that would determine the future of the company. It would take even more time than usual to discuss everything and reach consensus. Consequently, this week's meeting was set to take place over the weekend at Bill Stickney's vacation lodge in the Pocanos starting with a gourmet dinner served at 7:00 P.M. sharp.

Before the meeting, Bill Stickney examined the sources of BSI's revenue and the firm's income for the previous year. He also estimated the future prospects for each of BSI's lines, considering each line's market potential and BSI's level of saturation in each market. Finally, he estimated the costs of hiring a new employee both in the current sales territory and in the Washington/Virginia area. Immediately before the meeting, Elizabeth finished compiling Bill's data into four exhibits.

Exhibit 1 evaluates the amount of sales effort (difficulty in selling) necessary to achieve a certain percentage of sales in BSI's portfolio (return). Difficulty in selling is measured by the level of marketing investment required for growth. Stickney's estimate is shown on the vertical axis. Return for this investment is measured by the relative sales commissions as a percent of BSI's portfolio shown on the horizontal axis. If BSI's time were evenly divided among its eight principals, each would receive 12.5 percent of the agency's time. The X-axis shows each principal's time allocation as a proportion of 12.5 percent of the "par" time allocation. The area of each ellipse reflects each principal's share of BSI's commission revenue.

Bill Stickney presented the following additional comments as a result of his research:

1. Swanson's products are being replaced by the competition's computerized electronic equipment, a product category the firm has ignored. As a result, the company is losing its once prominent market position.

EXHIBIT 1 Return versus Difficulty in Selling

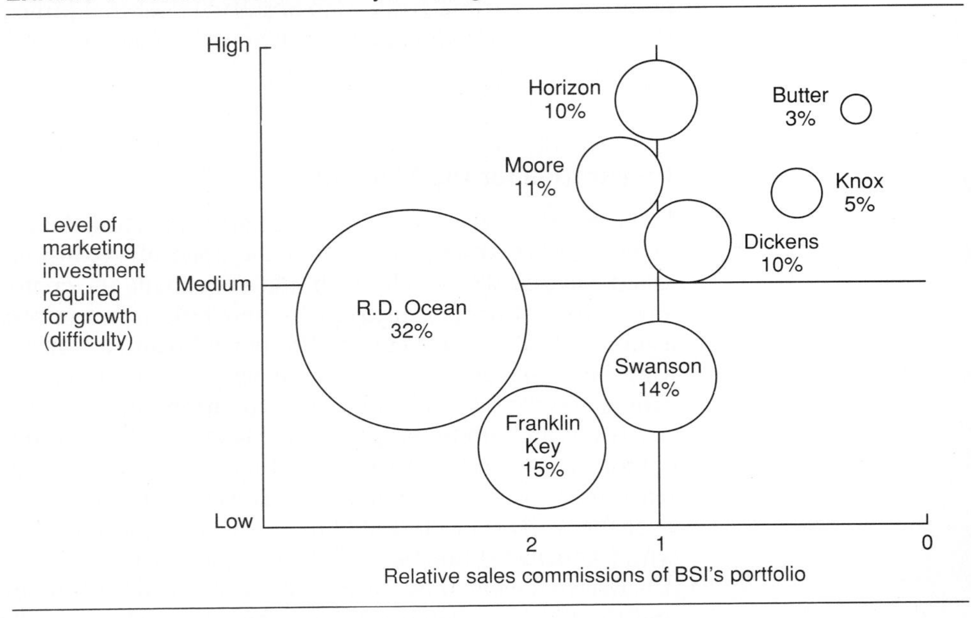

2. Although small amounts of effort are required to promote Ocean's product line to customers in the current sales territory, Ocean is extremely demanding of both BSI and other manufacturer's representative firms.

3. According to a seminar at the last ERA meeting, the maximum safe proportion of a rep firm's commissions from a single principal should be 25–30 percent. Also, at the meeting, one speaker indicated that if a firm commands 80 percent of a market, it should focus on another product or expand its territory rather than attempt to obtain the remainder of the market.

4. The revenue for investment for the manufacturer's representative firm comes from one or more of several sources. These sources include reduced forthcoming commission income, retained previous income, and borrowed money from a financial institution. Most successful firms expand their sales force or sales territory when they experience income growth and use of the investment as a tax write-off.

EXHIBIT 2 Barro Stickney, Inc., Estimation of Cost of Additional Sales Representative

Compensation Costs for New Sales Representative:

Depending on the new sales representative's level of experience, BSI would pay a base salary of $15,000–$25,000 with the following bonus schedule:

0% firm's commission revenue up to $500,000 in sales

20% firm's commission revenue first $.5 million in sales over $500,000

25% firm's commission revenue for the next $.5 million in sales

30% firm's commission for the next $.5 million in sales

40% firm's commission sales above $2 million

Estimate of Support Costs[1] for New Representative:[2]

Search applicant pool, psychological testing, hiring, training,[3] flying final choice to principals for approval.[4]	$28,000
Automobile expenses, telephone costs, business cards, entertainment promotion.	$22,000
Insurance, payroll taxes (social security, unemployment compensation)	$16,000
Total expenses	$66,000

Incremental Expenses for New Territory

Transportation (additional mileage from Camp Hill to Virginia)	$ 2,000
Office equipment and rent (same regardless of headquarter's location)	$ 4,000
Cost of hiring office manager[5]	$18,000
Total increment expenses	$24,000

[1]Rounded to the nearest thousand.
[2]In current territory.
[3]Excludes the lost revenue from selling instead of engaging in this activity (opportunity cost).
[4]Although rep agencies are not legally required to show prospective employees to principals, it is generally held to be good business practice.
[5]Discretionary.

EXHIBIT 3 Barro Stickney, Inc., Statement of Revenue (total sales revenue 1988, $5.5 million)

Principal	*Estimated Market Saturation*	*Product Type*	*Sales/ Commission Rate*	*Share of BSI's Portfolio*	*Commission Revenue*
R. D. Ocean	High	Components	5%	32%	$96,756
Franklin Key	High	Components	5	15	45,354
Butler	Low	Technical/computer	12	3	9,070
Dickens	Low	Components	5	10	30,236
Horizon	Medium	Components	5.5	10	30,237
Swanson	High	Components	5.25	14	42,331
Moore	Medium	Consumer/electronics	5.25	11	33,260
Knox	Low	Technical/communications	8.5	5	15,118

EXHIBIT 4 Barro Stickney, Inc. Statement of Income (for the year ending December 31, 1988)

Revenue	
Commission income	$302,362
Expenses	
Salaries for sales and bonuses (includes Barro Stickney)	130,250
Office manager's salary	20,000
Total nonpersonnel expenses[1]	128,279
Total expenses	$278,529
Net Income[2]	**$ 23,833 (7.9% of revenue)**

[1]Includes travel, advertising, taxes, office supplies, retirement, automobile expenses, communications, office equipment, and miscellaneous expenses.
[2]Currently held in negotiable certificates of deposits in a Harrisburg bank.

CASE 6–9 Norsk Kjem A/S

In the summer of 1984, Mr. Johan Sunde, product manager at Norsk Kjem A/S, commented, "Although Nick, Per, and I spend many weeks visiting distributors and customers around the world, it is difficult to feel that we really know what is going on in the promotion and the many different applications of our products. It is difficult to make our distributors put any effort behind our products as we have very little control over what they do. However, our product group broke even for the first time last year and we would like to start making our 20 percent target return."

Norsk Kjem A/S (NK) was an integrated chemical company situated in Larvik, Norway. The company had been in business for 25 years and it had an excellent reputation throughout the world. The company was organized into three major divisions as shown in Exhibit 1. The NK Chemicals Division marketed more than 100 different chemicals and each chemical had many different applications. The division was organized into five product groups according to basic input chemicals such as polymers, alcohols, and sulphates.

Sulphates

In 1978, NK had taken out a license from an American company on a process for converting a by-product from one of the main processes into a sal-

The case was prepared by Professor Kenneth G. Hardy of the Western Business School. The author thanks the North European Management Institute for its cooperation.

EXHIBIT 1 Simplified Organization Chart

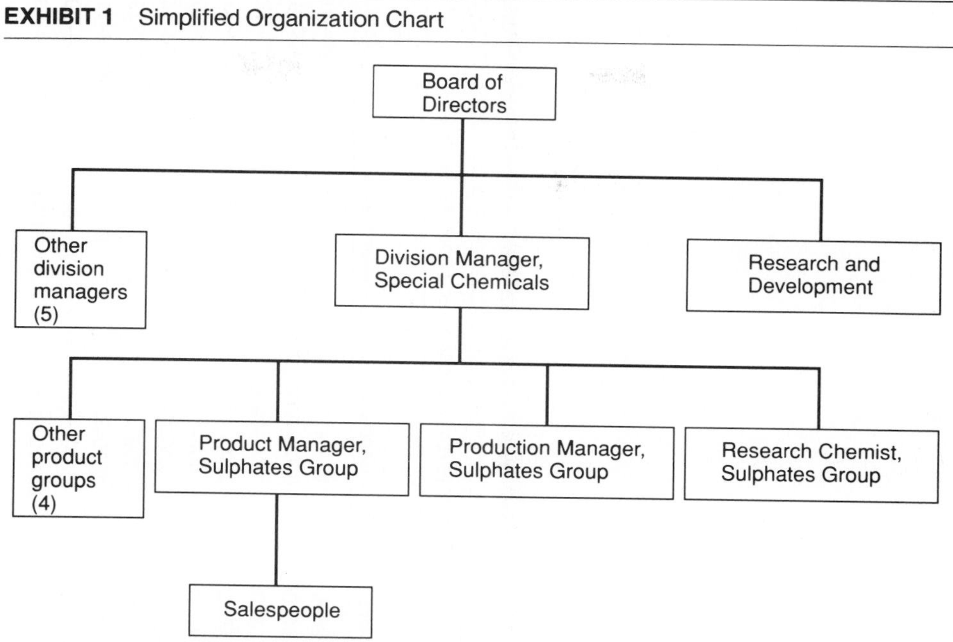

able chemical usually employed as a wetting agent. A wetting agent is used in many processes to promote the retention and even distribution of liquids.

Prior to taking out the 1978 license and investing in the necessary plant and equipment, the market for wetting agents had been thoroughly researched by Mr. Nick Deveny. Mr. Deveny had visited many applicators in Europe and they had said, "give us a product equal to what we get from the United States and we will be interested." Mr. Deveny's estimates of demand by industry and country are shown in Exhibit 2.

In 1978, a product manager and two technical salespeople had been hired to launch the wetting agents. Mr. Nick Deveny, who had made the original market survey, was one of the two salespeople employed. All three people held university degrees in chemistry or engineering. Together, they named the original product and subsequent offshoots, prepared technical literature, designed packages, and established a distribution system.

In setting up distributors, the product manager and his salespeople used the following criteria of (1) establish only one distributor per country, (2) use established chemical distributors owned by nationals, and (3) try to get distributors that serve the concrete, dyeing, and pesticide industries because these end-users seemed to have the largest potential. Subsequent to establishing the distributors, the product manager discovered that the Norwegian products had to have demonstrable advantages before end-users would risk

EXHIBIT 2 Norsk Kjem A/S Estimated Potential as of 1976 for Chemical Products (by application and country; in tons)

Country	*Textile Dyestuff*	*Carbon Back and Pigments*	*Pesticides*	*Concrete*	*Plasterboard*	*Total*
Benelux	200–360	0–100	1000–2000	1200–1600	0	2400–4060
England	1600–3000	240–320	4000–6000	6000–7000	0	11,840–16,320
France	2200–3000	100–300	4000–6000	4000–8000	100–600	10,300–16,900
Italy	800–1600	200–400	4000–8000	2000–4000	20–100	7020–15,100
Israel	0	0	200–1000	400–1000	0	600–2000
Scandinavia	0	100–200	200–400	200–600	100–200	600–1400
Spain	100–300	100–200	200–400	200–400	0	600–1300
Switzerland	3000–6000	100–200	200–1000	1000–4000	0	4300–11,200
Germany	4000–6000	500–1000	2000–6000	2000–6000	600–1000	9100–20,000
Total	11,900–20,200	1400–2800	15,800–30,800	17,000–32,600	800–1900	46,760–135,100

a switch to a new ingredient. From 1976 to 1980, sales of the two major products were very disappointing.

The original product manager in the Sulphates Group had established distributors on many different arrangements. Some carried inventory and others did not, some took title to the product and others left the transaction between NK and the end-user. For example, the German distributor was wholly owned by NK. The United Kingdom distributor kept inventory, whereas Holland was handled by direct shipments. Distributor margins ranged from 5 to 8 percent of their selling price.

In the establishment of the distributors the original product manager had considered the "hungry" versus the "established" and had gone with the established special chemical distributors because of a bad experience with an overeager distributor and because he felt that a distributor would have to invest three or four years of market development with NK sulphates before he could expect a reasonable financial return.

Most of the distributors were old family-owned companies and all of them carried many other lines, but none that were directly competitive with Sulphates Group products. The margins and required selling effort were the same for NK sulphate products as they were for other manufacturers' products. Special chemical distributors usually had some technical expertise but the wide variety of applications taxed their abilities. The distributors employed from 2 to 100 salespeople and in Mr. Sunde's judgment, all of them needed technical service and backup.

In 1980, NK underwent a major reorganization. A new product manager, Mr. Sunde, was appointed and he reported to Mr. Andreas Hoxmark, general manager for the Chemicals Divisions. Mr. Hoxmark had been one of the two corporate planners at Norsk Kjem and he had excellent education and experience in chemistry.

Just before the reorganization, the previous product manager had decided to buy a second license from the United States company which had sold the rights to the first process. A new series of light-colored wetting agents was launched and the plant was expanded at a cost of $800,000. The new wetting agents were tailor-made for three specific applications: pesticides, concrete, and textile dyestuffs.

Shortly after his appointment, Mr. Sunde decided that he should tell all his customers and potential customers about the many applications of the three new agents as well as the original products. To do this, he prepared a master brochure which showed all five wetting agents and where they applied in 10 different major applications. Then a detailed brochure was prepared for each of the 10 applications and the appropriate brochures were sent to the customers who had been coded according to their current applications. A response card and a letter from Mr. Sunde were sent out with the brochures. The distributors received quantities of all literature in the appropriate language. Mr. Sunde commented, "The response was only fair. The

EXHIBIT 3 Norsk Kjem A/S Sales, Products, Commission Structure, and Inventory of Exclusive Distributors in Each Country in 1983 ($000)

	Sales					
Country	*Tons*	*$ Value‡*	*Commission*	*Inventory*	*Industries Served*	*Notes*
Switzerland*	2,000	$ 450	5% fab	Yes	Textile dyestuff	Small company, manager looks after sulphates, good connections in textile dyestuff
Holland	100	400	n.a.	No	Pesticides	
Germany*	2,200	400	3% fob	No	Textile dyestuff, carbon black, concrete and plasterboard	Norsk Kjem sales company, Norwegian chemist sells sulphates
U.K.*	800	320	7% cif	Yes	Textile dyestuff, carbon black, pesticides	2 people buy in 20-ton lots
France†	400	160	5% fob	Yes	Pesticides, plasterboard	Large dealer, 100 employees and 8 offices
Japan	300	160	n.a.	No	Textile dyestuff	
Italy†	100	160	n.a.	Yes	Concrete	Medium-sized dealer
Eastern Europe	4,400	128	n.a.	No	Animal feed	
Scandinavia	4,246	120	n.a.	Yes	Animal feed, concrete	
Spain†	600	120	n.a.	Yes	Concrete, plaster	Small- to medium-sized dealer
Australia	1,200	90	n.a.	No	Pesticides, concrete	
Belgium	1,200	60	n.a.	No	Pesticides	
Kuwait	300	60	n.a.	No	Concrete, plasterboard	
Israel	270	54	n.a.	No	Concrete, plasterboard	
Others	2,000	160	n.a.	No	Miscellaneous	
Total	20,116	$2,834				

*Dependent on Sulphates Group or Norsk Kjem for accounts or financing.
†Mr. Sunde was dissatisfied with the performance of these distributors.
‡Norwegian kroner have been converted to American dollars at the prevailing rate of exchange.
n.a. = Not available.

EXHIBIT 4 Norsk Kjem A/S Sales, Costs, and Contribution for 1982 and 1983 ($000)*

	1982		1983	
Sales		$1,852		$2,834
Variable cost		746		1,058
Contribution		1,106		1,776
Fixed manufacturing costs	$914		$1,180	
Promotion costs	212		262	
Corporate and division overhead	104	1,230	150	1,592
Net profit before tax		$ (124)		$ 184

*Norwegian kroner have been converted to American dollars at the prevailing rate of exchange.

big seller turned out to be one of the new products but mainly to two accounts in Switzerland and Germany, a contract which was arranged even before we bought the license to make the new products."

Between 1980 and 1983, Mr. Sunde and his two salesmen, Mr. Deveny and Mr. Per Wiencke, spent a great deal of time traveling with distributors in order to meet customers and to give out samples. Mr. Sunde called on distributors in Switzerland, France, and Denmark, while Mr. Deveny took Germany, Eastern Europe, Finland, Israel, and Italy. The second salesman, Mr. Wiencke, called on distributors in the United Kingdom, Benelux, Spain, Norway, Sweden, and all others. Exhibit 3 shows the sales volume and arrangement with each distributor in 1983.

In September 1983, Mr. Sunde took a leave in order to study industrial marketing but he kept in touch with his colleagues at NK. When he returned in the summer of 1984, the research people had redeveloped the product line so that it was more than completely competitive in terms of quality. Exhibit 4 shows sales, costs, and contribution for 1982 and 1983.

Customers

In making any first purchase of a new wetting agent, the technical people in a client company would require samples for testing. In large companies, their recommendation would go to a purchasing agent and production manager, but in small companies, the owner/manager would make the final decision. Mr. Hoxmark considered that it was very important to develop a close rapport with customers. He encouraged contact between customers and R&D people in the Chemicals Division in order that R&D personnel could hear customer wants at first hand. He observed that small companies often

EXHIBIT 5 Norsk Kjem A/S Ton Volume per Customer (by application, 1983)

Applications	*Total Number of Customers*	*Tons per Customer*						*Total Sales (Tons)*
		<10	*10–19*	*20–49*	*50–99*	*100–499*	*>500*	
Textile dyestuff	17	7	—	6	—	3	1	5,160
Carbon black and pigments	14	8	3	2	1	—	1	480
Pesticides	18	7	2	5	3	1	—	1,176
Concrete	5	1	1	—	1	1	1	2,088
Plasterboard	8	1	2	4	1	—	—	516
Industrial cleaning	2	2	—	—	—	—	—	16
Animal feed	9	1	—	4	—	1	3	9,744
Miscellaneous	37	17	13	7	—	—	—	936
Total	110	44	21	28	6	6	5	20,116

preferred small suppliers regardless of nationality. Most customers kept open two sources of supply because delivery was just as important as technical support.

There were 110 end-users buying from Sulphates Group distributors. Nearly 80 percent of the Sulphates Group volume was taken by 20 percent of the distributor's customers. Exhibit 5 shows the customers and their annual volume by application for 1983.

Small companies were numerous but not easily identified as potential customers. Compared to larger organizations, small companies tended to have more first-time applications, less information on competitive offerings, less technical expertise, less sensitivity to price, and smaller order quantities. Switching chemicals posed a substantial production risk, especially for large companies.

Differences by Industry. There were some differences in purchasing criteria by industry. The *textile dyestuff* manufacturing industry was dominated by large multinational corporations which used a wide variety of auxiliary chemicals. The distributor's salesperson first called on lab and production personnel in the user companies in order to have the NK products tested. If lab and production people approved the products, the distributor's salesperson would discuss price, delivery time, and packaging with the purchasing agent. NK products were priced competitively. The entire process of first visit, discussing test results, and arranging an order could take from six months to more than one year.

The buying procedure in the pesticide and herbicide manufacturing industries was similar to the textile dyestuff industry. However, the manufacture of pesticides and herbicides called for some additional physical criteria of the product. Moreover, multinationals and small formulators were prevalent in these manufacturing industries.

The *industrial cleaning* market was particularly price competitive. The same products were used in the *plasterboard* market where a good wetting agent could reduce water requirements and drying costs. Multinational corporations dominated the manufacture of plasterboard.

In making *concrete,* a good wetting agent could provide better distribution of all particles which would lead to increased compression strength. Small- and medium-sized companies were prevalent in the manufacture of concrete.

Distributor Policies. North Carolina Chemical was Mr. Sunde's toughest competition. Despite having only one distributor for all of Europe, North Carolina Chemical had tied up almost all the big dye houses. As one example of their promotional methods, North Carolina sponsored a technical conference for all the people involved in the textile dyestuff industry.

Mr. Deveny told the casewriter, "We have to support the distributor heavily in the introduction period when a customer is trying our product. After that, there is little maintenance required. Our total sales depend heavily on our marketing effort because we can do research in each market and tell the distributors what to do. We are trying now to work on key users with good volume and fair prices. We are a long way from saturating the market but almost none of our distributors are scanning customers for new end-users. Furthermore, there are a lot of sample requests as a result of our advertising but there is little follow-up from the distributors. We inform them of the sample request and some call on the customer, some do not."

Mr. Sunde had tried to institute a system of field reports from the distributors but they did not fill in the reports. As a result, Mr. Sunde and his salespeople relied on their own observations during their periodic field trips. In each country their itinerary was set up by the local distributor. Mr. Sunde would visit France, for example, two weeks a year and see 20 end customers in each of those weeks.

Mr. Sunde talked about some experiments with their distributors. First of all, the German subsidiary was developing sales faster than any other distributor. Mr. Sunde ascribed this to the large German market, the German technical sophistication and willingness to try new products, and "the fact that we have a good man there working only with our products." Mr. Sunde had just fired the United Kingdom distributor and shifted the business to two of the distributor's former salespeople. In France, the distributor had hired a product manager, who grouped customers, established potentials and sales goals for salespeople, and helped the salesperson look for new possibilities and pushed them. The result was a big increase in sales for the French distributor. Mr. Sunde had tried to woo the French pesticide industry with price concessions, but the French distributor would only partly go along with the plan. The distributor would have been obliged to take a small reduction in his margin.

Marketing Options. The first option which Mr. Sunde had considered was to drop all the distributors and replace them with either a Norwegian-based sales force or one NK salesperson located in each major market. One field office would cost $100,000 per year for a salesperson's salary, travel expenses, secretarial and other expenses. The extra travel and communication expense from Norway would bring the cost of a Norwegian-based force up to the same cost of $100,000 per person.

The second major option was to help the distributors. In major markets, Mr. Sunde would share 50 percent of the cost of a distributor's salesperson if the salesperson would spend half his time on NK sulphates. Most distributor salespeople earned about $50,000 in salary and commissions. In smaller markets, an NK man might do missionary work for part of the year on a split (50–50) commission basis.

Another option would be to delineate selling tasks such as identifying prospects, developing the application, selling the customer, maintaining inventory, and after-sale servicing. Possibly the tasks could be divided between NK and the distributors. To compensate for the performance of these tasks, some sort of commission points or fee structure could be developed.

A fourth option was to assign additional NK salesmen to train the distributor's salespeople. It would take at least a month for one NK salesperson to thoroughly train one of the distributor's people. The likely sales response would vary considerably, depending on the market potential and the skill of the distributor's salespeople.

A fifth option was to work with the distributors, using existing resources. Some sort of management-by-objectives system might serve to motivate and guide the distributors. Mr. Sunde was well aware that the difficult part of a management-by-objectives system was the implementation of the system. The distributor reaction could range from enthusiastic cooperation to rejection of the NK sulphate line. Mr. Sunde had considered hiring more than one distributor per country, but generally he felt that the sulphate business was too narrow to support more than one distributor.

In order to get more effort from his distributors, Mr. Sunde had considered the alternative of raising margins from the 5 to 8 percent range up to approximately 15 percent. But he was not sure that this would evoke sufficient extra effort to reach profit targets, given the competitive prices offered by the company.

However, before he could make any of these decisions, Mr. Sunde felt there was a more basic decision of target customers and priority of country/application. He was not sure that Mr. Deveny's 1976 survey of potential sales still held for his products. However, Mr. Hoxmark had asked for a report on distribution strategy and policy by the end of the month.

CASE 6–10 Knowles Products

In early 1989, Clive Langdon, group vice president—pharmaceutical products of Knowles Products, was reviewing a specially commissioned report on his division's brand management system. Knowles, a major marketer of a well-known brand of analgesic and a number of personal care products and owner of a southern U.S. chain of franchised drug stores, had used a brand management system for more than a decade. This system had worked well for Knowles; however, it seemed to Langdon that a review of this system was appropriate. Consequently, in September he had asked Leslie Nome, a well-regarded marketing consultant, to conduct such a review. After some discussion, Langdon and Nome agreed that the first stage of the project should be to document the way that brand management system operated at Knowles. Langdon was reviewing that report in anticipation of a meeting the next morning with Nome.

Company Background

In the early 1900s Jason Knowles, a pharmacist by training and traveling salesman by profession, developed a patent medicine that he claimed was beneficial for relieving a variety of ills. Over time, the claims moderated but Knowles' product, sold primarily in tablet form, gained popularity as a headache remedy. Descendants of the original family maintained control of the company until the late 1970s, when the stock was first publicly offered.

Product Line

Prior to going public in 1978, the firm had essentially been a one-product company. Although Knowles analgesic was sold in liquid and tablet form and combined with other ingredients to produce such products as cough syrups and cold remedies, the focus was always on Knowles pills and their promised relief from headaches. Some other brands had been introduced but none had ever accounted for more than 10 percent of corporate sales.

In the late 1970s, Knowles management had begun to plan a major expansion of its product line. In 1980, the company announced a program for growth marked by expansion in four major directions:

1. Health-related products.
2. Personal care products.
3. Franchised drug stores.
4. International markets.

This case was written by Charles B. Weinberg of the University of British Columbia.

EXHIBIT 1 Knowles Products: Corporate Performance (by line of business; $ millions)

	1988	*1987*	*1986*	*1985*	*1984*	*1983*
Net sales:						
Consumer products						
Pharmaceuticals	513	461	399	338	339	251
Personal care	110	94	86	67	39	31
Subtotal	623	555	485	405	378	282
Drugstores	690	678	596	403	240	—
Total	1313	1233	1,081	808	618	282
Net income:						
Consumer products	53	49	41	39	32	29
Drugstores	20	18	16	10	7	—
Total	73	67	57	49	39	29

In the immediately ensuing years, Knowles acquired three companies, each with a major well-known brand name of health-related product (an
a muscle relaxant, and a treatment for athlete's foot). In addition, Knowles also acquired several small companies that marketed specialty personal care products, such as a dandruff shampoo and a denture cleaner. In the six years ending in 1986, Knowles acquired companies with a total of 15 significant brand names and introduced 3 new internally developed brands as well. Although selling a variety of pharmaceutical and personal care products, the majority of the company's sales was made through supermarkets. In 1986, senior management decided to cease acquiring new companies and concentrate on internal development.

In 1984, Knowles acquired a chain of drugstores, named Southern Star, located in Florida and Georgia. About half of Southern Star's outlets were franchised; the rest were wholly owned. Although some additional smaller acquisitions were made, expansion of the Southern Star was accomplished primarily through opening new outlets and increasing sales per store.

Knowles analgesics had been sold in Western Europe for almost 30 years. Several of the new brands were also manufactured in Europe or Asia, but most overseas markets were served through export sales.

Overall corporate sales had increased by more than tenfold in the past decade to $1.3 billion in 1988. However, profits had not kept pace. Exhibit 1 summarizes corporate performance by line of business. An abridged organization chart for Knowles products is given in Exhibit 2.

The Brand Management System

Knowles had been organized on a product management system, particularly in the pharmaceutical products division as shown in Exhibit 3. There were

EXHIBIT 2 Partial Organization Diagram for Knowles Products

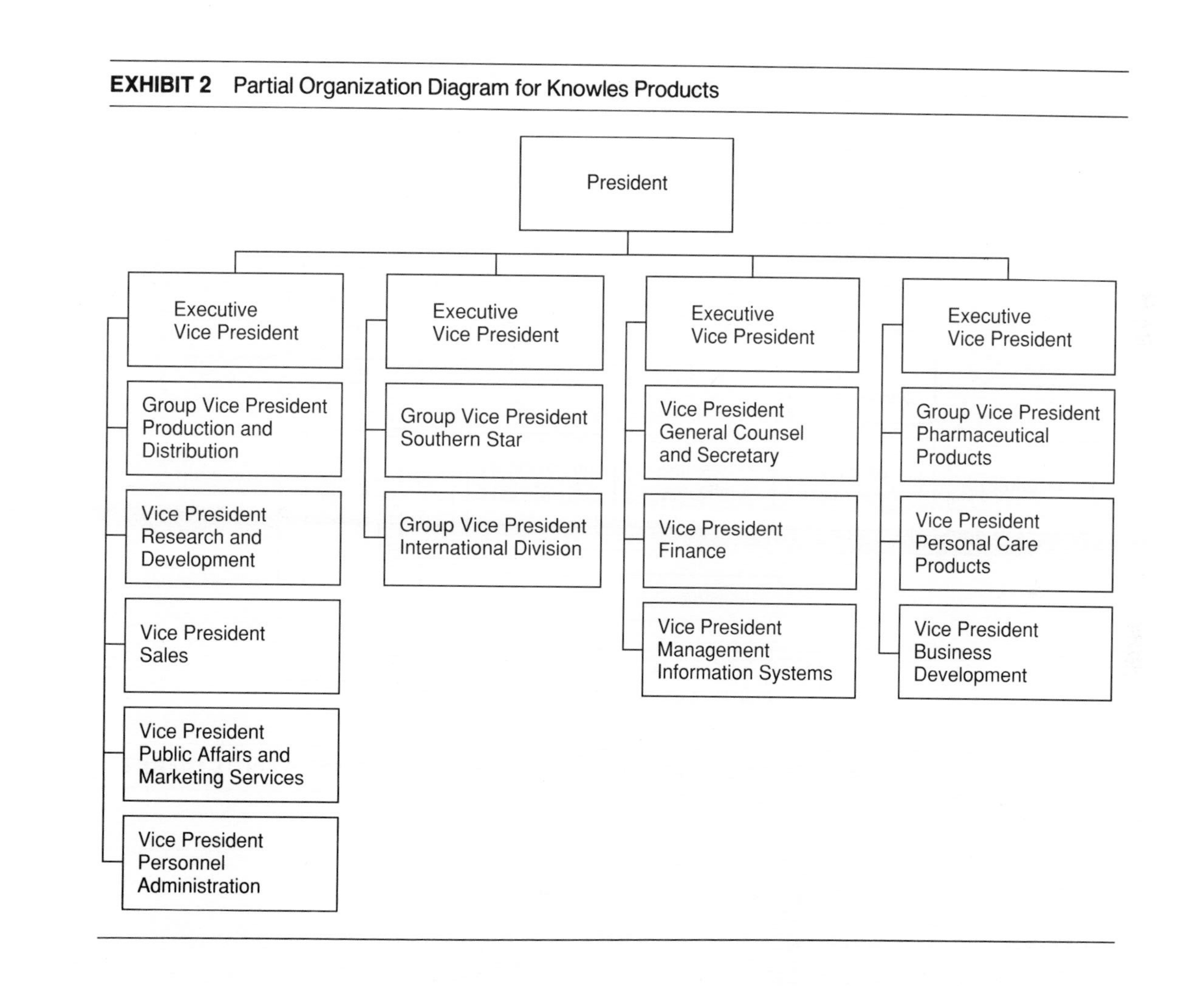

EXHIBIT 3 Knowles Marketing Organization, Pharmaceutical Products Division

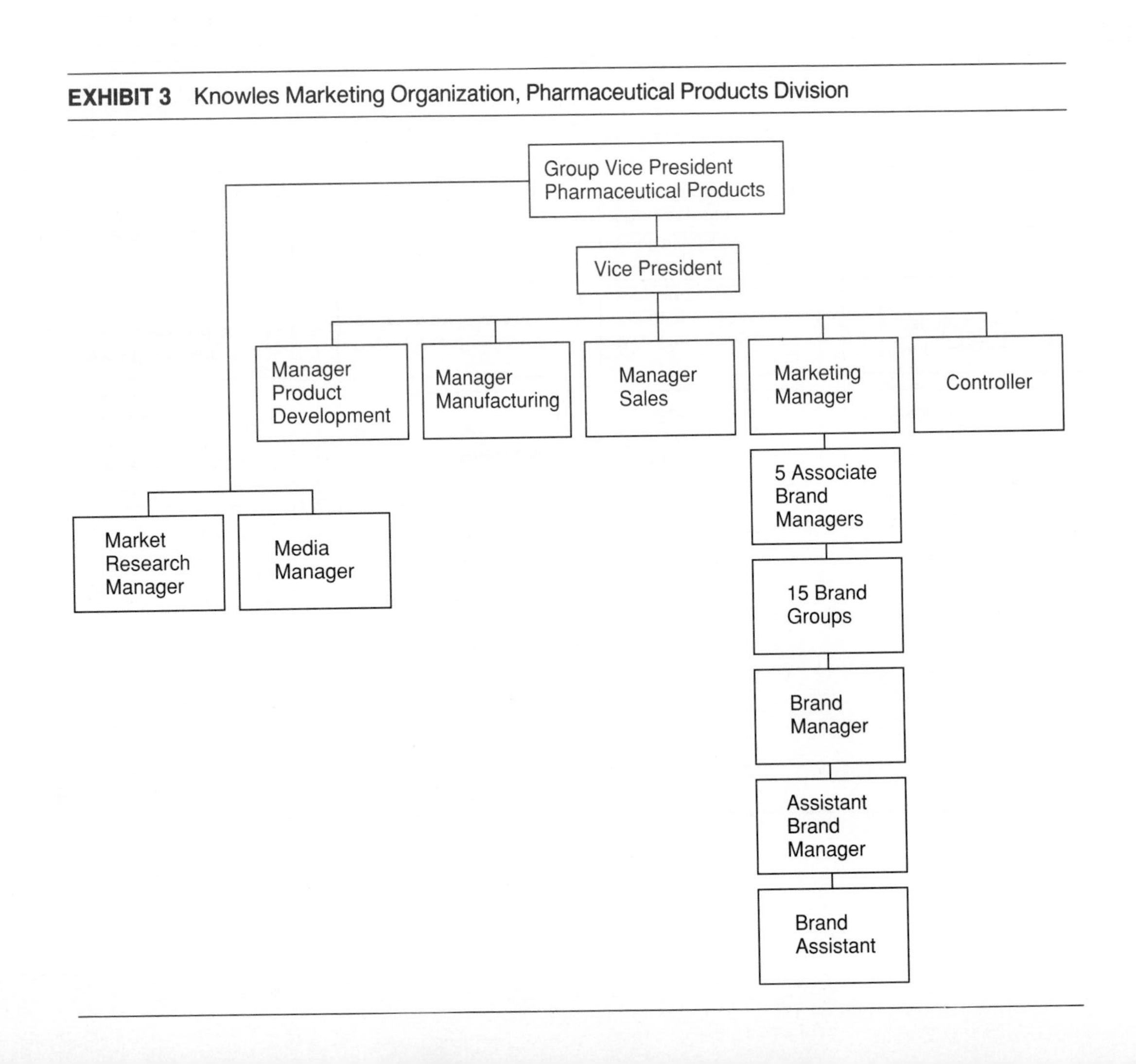

EXHIBIT 4 Job Description–Brand Manager

Function: *To contribute to the overall growth of Knowles through development, recommendation, and implementation of effective marketing programs capable of building brand volume, share, and profit for assigned brands. The brand manager is charged to:*

1. Provide management with relevant data regarding the state of the business, serving as management's antennae in the category to identify problems and opportunities.
2. Develop recommendations which are designed to stimulate brand growth.
3. See that all programs are coordinated and run properly, serving as the focal point for all brand-related activity.
4. Ensure that brand personnel learn the skills to handle multifaceted responsibilities of the job.

The brand manager's specific marketing responsibilities are as follows:

1. *Product.* Ensure that the product and package are superior to competition within cost constraints demanded by the marketplace and profit considerations. Requires consumer usage/attitude and product research, establishment of product improvement objectives, and periodic review of progress toward these objectives.
2. *Positioning.* Position the product to maximize volume within the existing consumer and competitive environments. Periodically review marketing strategy in light of changing consumer needs, wants, and attitudes and competitive product positionings and sales. Develop and test alternative copy and promotion strategies attuned to the marketing strategy to improve the brand's overall positioning.
3. *Copy.* Ensure that copy provides the optimum selling power. Demands an ongoing effort in development and testing of new copy pools, different executional formats, and alternative copy strategies.
4. *Media.* Ensure that media plans are designed to deliver advertising in the most effective and efficient manner against the brand's target audience. Requires periodic review of target audience criterion and testing of alternative mixes of media vehicles within budget constraints, as well as testing of different media weights.
5. *Promotion.* Plan, execute, and evaluate, with the assistance of the sales department, consumer and trade promotions which are cost-effective in increasing brand volume. Demands testing of a variety of promotions each fiscal year and testing, on a periodic basis, alternative annual promotion levels and/or alternative consumer/trade promotion splits within existing budgets.
6. *Volume/Control.* Make adjustments as necessary in fiscal year plans to deliver volume base.

The brand manager's specific management information responsibilities are to identify, analyze, and recommend actions in response to significant developments in the following areas:

1. Realized volume versus budgeted level.
2. Competitive developments.
3. Product and package problems.
4. Problem markets.
5. Implementation delays and cost overruns.
6. Legislative and regulatory activities.

five job levels in the brand system; brand assistant (BA), assistant brand manager (ABM), brand manager (BM), associate marketing manager (AMM), and marketing manager (MM). The focus of Nome's initial report was on the brand manager and lower levels, that is, assistant brand manager and brand assistant. (See Exhibits 4, 5, and 6, for relevant job descriptions.)

Although Nome's report did not deal extensively with the MM and AMM levels of management, these managers played a critical role in brand management. The MM managed all aspects of marketing, except sales execution, for the division. This manager's key objectives were not only achievement of short-term volume and profit goals but also development, testing, and expansion of new products, improved products, and line

EXHIBIT 5 Job Description—Assistant Brand Manager

Marketing Responsibilities:

1. *Business Building Plans.* Develop, recommend, and execute those key projects which, long term, will have a major effect on the shipments and consumption of the brand. Examples of these are the introduction of new sizes/products, major distribution building programs, or major trial generating promotions.
2. *Copy.* Work with the brand manager in providing direction to the advertising agency in the development of new executional formats (based on current strategy) and the testing of new copy strategies/executions. Also, work with technical and legal to obtain copy clearance/claim support.
3. *Media.* In conjunction with the brand manager, provide the agency with direction on new ways to more efficiently reach the brand's target audience. This may take the form of media mix tests or testing of different media levels.
4. *Product.* Ensure that a product which fulfills consumer needs and wants is marketed within cost constraints.
5. *Market Research Planning and Analysis.* Initiate and analyze those market research projects which will yield information upon which the brand may act to improve current market position or correct an ongoing problem.
6. *Package Design.* Ensure that the package in the marketplace is appealing, eyecatching, and connotes those attributes of the product most important to consumers.

Management Information:

1. *Market Research.* Analyze research and recommend next steps to correct any problems or capitalize on any opportunities.
2. *Media.* Analyze results of media testing and recommend action to be taken.
3. *Schedule Changes.* Inform brand manager of delays in the progress of key projects in order that management may be apprised of the delay and the reason why.

extensions. These latter goals were emphasized by top management to ensure continued corporate growth. The AMMs largely served coordinating, controlling, training, and strategic overview roles between the AM and BMs. They also had final decision-making authority on promotion activities within existing budgets, and handled many of the administrative jobs in the advertising department.

The entry-level job was that of BA. The BA was primarily responsible for monitoring the product budget, developing sales promotions, and analyzing marketing information (e.g., sales data from the company's management information system, consumption data from the A. C. Nielsen Company, and additional data from other outside market research services). New projects were added as competence was gained until the BA was sent out for sales training, a 12-week field sales assignment.

Promotion to ABM followed this selling experience. Emphasis was placed upon learning advertising copy and media, developing long-term business-building programs, and assisting and helping train the BA in the area of sales promotion. ABM was a transition job which could last from one to two and a half years, depending on the capabilities of the person and the needs of the company.

When the ABM was promoted to BM, he or she was given overall mar-

EXHIBIT 6 Job Description—Brand Assistant

Marketing Responsibilities:

1. *Sales Promotion.* Plan, in consultation with other brand group members and the sales department, national and test promotions. Write promotion recommendations and issue related feasibility requests and production orders. Implement consumer-oriented portions of promotions (e.g., coupon copy and media, sample drops, etc.) and oversee and/or cooperate with sales department in implementing trade-oriented portions of promotions. Budget and evaluate promotions.

2. *Budget Administration and Control.* Review and code invoices. Reconcile the budget with accounting on quarterly basis. Close out budget with accounting at the end of the fiscal year.

3. *Market Analysis.* Analyze Nielsen data and write bimonthly Nielsen reports. Audit other sources of market information (monthly shipment reports, SAMIs, etc.) and write analytical reports as necessary.

4. *Shipment Estimates.* Prepare monthly shipment estimate which forecasts next three months' shipments with supporting rationale.

5. *Competitive Activity.* Monitor competitive activity reported by sales (promotion and pricing activity), agency (competitive and media spending), and other sources (periodicals, etc.). Write reports on significant developments.

6. *Public Relations.* Cooperate with consumer services in handling special consumer-oriented problems which fall outside normal consumer services activities. Work with research services (home economists) and public affairs on brand-related consumer information projects.

Other areas where brand assistant may contribute, depending upon individual brand assignments, include package design and business-building tests.

Management Information:

Report to brand manager on:

1. *Competitive Activity.* Significant competitive developments.
2. *Budget Variance.* Any variations from budget forecasts.
3. *Promotion Problems.* Any problems with implementation of promotions.
4. *Consumer Relations.* Any product problems which threaten volume.

keting responsibility for one or more products, including planning, forecasting, and controlling volume and spending for these products. He or she also supervised ABMs and BAs. Due to rotation and normal turnover, not all brand groups were fully staffed with a BA and ABM.

In terms of day-by-day operations, the brand management group considered the other functions as "staff" to them. Nonetheless, brand management had no direct authority over sales, manufacturing, market research, and product development. But it did have the responsibility to obtain from staff the inputs necessary for successful marketing. Each functional group, for this purpose, had a representative designated to deal with the brand manager. An integral part of this system of "responsibility without direct authority" was the fact that brand management controlled budgets for areas such as market research and package design and represented the staff's channel to top management. For example, a departmental request for information or specific action was typically directed to the brand manager who not only had to concur but was the interface with top management. (See Exhibit 7.)

Excerpts from interviews with several brand managers are given in the appendix at the end of the case.

EXHIBIT 7 Interface Matrix

Brand manager responsibilities	*Work with these departments*	*Brand role*
Product or package improvement	Sales, R&D market research, manufacturing, and controller	a. Develop objectives for product or package development. b. Approve aesthetics. c. Develop consumer research objectives, fund research, and summarize results. d. Determine unit profit potential and return on investment. e. Recommend test market to management. f. Write manufacturing production orders for test market production of product. g. Analyze test market results and recommend national expansion.
Positioning	Advertising agency, market research, and legal	a. Develop alternative positionings. b. Develop consumer research objectives and fund research. c. Analyze research results and recommend test market. d. Analyze test market results and recommend national expansion.
Copy	Advertising agency, market research, and legal	a. Review agency copy submissions and select copy to be presented to management. b. Approve final production for on-air copy testing. c. Analyze copy test results. d. Recommend national airing of copy.
Media	Advertising agency and media services	a. Review agency media objectives and strategies and recommend alternatives. b. Review and modify agency media plans with help of media services. c. Forward agency media plan to management. d. With help of media services monitor implementation of media plan.
Sales promotion	Sales, manufacturing, promotion development, and legal	a. Develop national promotion plan with help of sales department. b. Recommend loan to management. c. Write manufacturing production order for production of sales promotion product. d. Implement consumer portion of promotion (i.e., coupons, samples, etc.) and fund all trade allowances and consumer promotions.
Volume control	Sales	a. Monitor shipments. b. If undershipment of objectives seems possible, recommend remedial marketing efforts.

Corporate Atmosphere

Nome considered Knowles to be an almost classic example of brand management. Brand managers played a "line management" role within the marketing function at Knowles. The reasoning for this was that the BM had direct responsibility for the most critical marketing factor—advertising—and had the broadest exposure to the operations of the company and the best overall perspective on his product and markets.

Brand managers were able to accomplish their goals through other people by using their control over the product budget, their position as coordinator of all information, and their interpersonal skills. They had to be successful "at getting others to do the job."

But there was even more to the essential nature of the brand manager's job, a perspective that can only be expressed by senior management. These people looked upon brand managers as individuals who could be expected to ask the type of questions a top manager might ask, gather the facts necessary to make a decision, and then recommend a course of action in a very succinct memo. The net effect was that top management's job of managing the marketing of a large number of diverse brands in diverse categories became easier and more effective. The system assured that all brands, even those with small sales, were given attention and that a variety of marketing approaches designed to stimulate growth would at least be explored and recommended.

The power of the brand managers rested largely in their authority to ask questions anywhere in the company and demand carefully thought out, responsible answers, as long as the questions and answers were limited to matters which either directly affected the consumer of their product or affected their brand's contribution margin (revenue less manufacturing and shipping costs and brokerage commission). In addition, successful brand managers had informal authority arising from their superior knowledge, as compared to that of a functional specialist's, of all consumer aspects of their product, and they had the power to discuss their recommendations (in writing, usually) with top management.

Selection and Screening

Typically, brand assistants were recent MBAs from leading business schools with minimum work experience (See Exhibit 8 for a sample recruitment ad.) In recent years, Knowles had hired some graduates with advertising experience as well as some transferees from other company departments, but these were exceptions. Brand managers were almost always promoted from within. In initial hiring, Knowles sought individuals who were intelligent, trainable, competitive, aggressive, and hardworking. Ideal candidates had qualities which were generalized as: analytical ability; communications

EXHIBIT 8 Sample Recruiting Advertisement

Marketing Careers with
One of the Nation's
Leading Companies

Knowles Corporation manufactures and markets over 15 major consumer brands. Many are among the country's market leaders.

A limited number of entry level positions are available as BRAND ASSISTANT, working within a Brand Group which has responsibility for one or more individual products and is the driving force behind them.

As a Brand Assistant, you will be assigned to a specific product. Your Brand Manager will give you immediate responsibility for a variety of projects and then look to you for leadership, ideas, and results. Some examples of your assignments will be: planning, executing, and evaluating promotions; analyzing business performance; planning and executing a sales presentation for a new market initiative; developing new packaging; and helping to manage your brand's budget.

In addition to individual projects, you will be broadly exposed to all aspects of brand management. As you contribute to the management of your brand and demonstrate your ability to handle additional responsibility, you will be assigned more complex and important projects. Your Brand Manager is responsible for your training and will work very hard to accelerate your personal development. The emphasis, however, is always on you . . . your thinking, your ideas, your contributions. Management career development is excellent. At Knowles, promotion is always from within, and based upon individual performance and contribution.

If you are about to obtain an MBA degree or equivalent and are just starting your career, if you have a background of achievement and can exhibit good analytical and communication skills, and if you are interested in talking further with us, send your resume to:

CORPORATE RECRUITING MANAGER
KNOWLES CORPORATION

skills; the ability to plan, organize, and follow through; the ability to work well with others; leadership, resourcefulness, and ingenuity; decision-making skill; drive and determination; and maturity.

Training

The introduction for the new brand assistant was strenuous. Although the initial jobs might range from planning promotions to writing market research summaries, there was a lot of arduous number crunching. Hours were long, often including weekends. There were no shortcuts or special courses and readings that could bypass this breaking-in period. Nor was there much sympathy for the neophyte. Everyone in brand management had been through the same experience, recognized its necessity, and knew the work could be done. "Help" was mainly in the form of providing initial direction, pointing out errors, and suggesting new projects as competence increased. The newer projects were invariably more interesting and challenging, which provided additional incentive to master the earlier tasks. And as new BAs were hired, the more mundane jobs could be passed down.

The purpose of this training was to internalize certain "first principles" which were considered necessary to maintain the brand management system:

1. *All information could be derived from numerical data:* Brand people had minimal contact with either customers or suppliers. Customers were normally represented by market research findings and sales results. Suppliers were represented by specific liaison people. Thus there always had to be an analytic justification for a project or program. Results needed to be summarized in terms of cases of product and net revenue (minus all costs except advertising).

2. *Concern for mistakes:* Brand people were trained to be detail-oriented and concerned about not making errors. No mistake, particularly in a memo, was too small to be noticed. The feedback was intense, since memos were commented on in writing as they were passed up and down the distribution chain. If anyone found a mistake, then everyone who missed it was embarrassed.

3. *Brand manager's budget as a control system:* This principle was a bit deceptive, however. While some staff groups—market research, sales merchandising, and package design—were dependent upon brand management for funding of projects, brand management did not use the budgets as a club. The range of interrelationships between brand management and staff was too involved to be reduced to the single level of money control.

4. *Career success required "the Knowles style":* The Knowles style contributed to the climate and mystique which made brand management successful. This style included memo format, job concept, and attitude. Memos conformed to a particular writing style and format and were not supposed to exceed two pages without an attached summary. Brand people had to be the resident experts on everything affecting their products. Brand managers thought of themselves as the general managers of a very small company. Nonetheless, brand people had to maintain their aggressive, competitive attitude without hurting their relations with staff. The BA might achieve a basic competence in one or two years. The competence was recognized by the addition of more complex assignments. As the BA's credibility and influence increased with the staff, he or she conformed more and more to the corporate style. BMs estimate that they spent as much as 25 percent of their time training BAs and ABMs. In fact, the entire brand management system was a training program. There was no such thing as an old BM; there was no place for the person who didn't want to be promoted.

Management Information Systems

The BM used current data almost exclusively, even though comprehensive historical files were maintained. Meetings were usually frequent and short. Memos were passed through for comment and review by the BM. Magazines might be scanned for ideas but were seldom read. For many BMs, only the Nielsen chart books, the product fact book, and project folders were kept within easy reach.

Tests were used extensively to determine the accuracy of the information routinely received so that results could be optimized and problems avoided. Brand people went out into the field infrequently, yet they had a strong perception about what was happening through their tests and the management information system.

Emphasis had to be placed on the management information system because the BM changed products about every two years and thus lost personal contacts in the agency and staff groups who tended to remain with the products.

Relationship with the Big Five

The five groups which brand management dealt with regularly were the advertising agency, sales, market research, manufacturing, and product development. With each group, there were conflicts which the BM had to resolve. These conflicts might include work priorities, differences of opinion about strategy or objectives, or disagreements over project timing. Brand managers sometimes argued that they had the responsibility for volume and spending without explicit authority to force staff compliance. These other departments, however, saw brand management as more in control due to its final authority to make recommendations to top management as well as its role in setting initial objectives. The other departments would have preferred a better understanding (by brand management) of their role and problems, yet essentially believed in the brand system as the best way to run the company.

Rotation and Promotion

Brand people were expected to shift products about every two years. Due to attrition, new hires, and promotions, the time could vary but seldom exceeded three years. It took a BM several months to become familiar with a new assignment and perhaps a year to implement a major strategy. Thus, the typical BM was working on a predecessor's strategy for much of his or her tenure.

Performance was judged on a number of bases:

1. Did the BM prepare a sound annual marketing plan and was he or she able to sell it to management?
2. How well did the product perform against the volume objective in the marketplace (regardless of who prepared the budget)?
3. What sort of major improvements or line extensions were proposed (though not necessarily implemented)?
4. How well did he or she train others?

In addition, part of a BM's evaluation was based on such factors as: communication, analysis, thoroughness, prioritization, productivity, organization, leadership, work with others, responsibility, ability to accept criticism, motivation, maturity, capacity, judgment, and attitude.

Summary

Brand management at Knowles was a total system. The selection, training, and promotion all tended to encourage the best and brightest people to dedicate themselves to making a product successful.

The people were supported by a management information system and organized structure that allowed them to be trained on the job and rotate from product to product at frequent intervals. The products were all marketed in a similar enough way, for example, advertising, sales promotions, supermarkets, and retail drug outlets, that the system and organization were the same for each.

The strength of the system lay in the fact that each product had a "champion" who attempted to achieve volume and share objectives, as predicted in an annual plan. The short term was not sacrificed for the long term since the long term generally represented the incumbent's proposed strategy and ongoing business-building tests, and the short term represented a predecessor's strategy. In addition, a pool of potential general management talent was being established and utilized as experienced managers were promoted and new employees added.

APPENDIX

Selected Portions of Interviews with Brand Managers

Question 1: You typically hire business school graduates with a small amount of work experience. What do you look for and how would you describe their jobs as BAs?

Brand Manager No. 1: I find it takes several months for a BA to become acclimated. New people are usually too theoretically oriented; at this level, pragmatic application of judgment to problems is more important. The most important thing for a BA to learn is to pay attention to detail. Even typos have a dollar impact. The BA should learn to think things through comprehensively.

The BA begins working about 10 hours per day plus homework, but the time goes down as the job is learned. All marketers are pretty much alike—aggressive, detail-minded—and that's what we look for here.

BM No. 2: The biggest problem a new BA has is to learn how to juggle projects and determine priorities. Business schools teach sequential problem solving but "Brand" requires juggling 15 trivial things and 1 major one. The BA's initial problem is establishing credibility. Brand management requires a mixture of talents but no one specific personality is appropriate. Some brand people do consider themselves prima donnas.

BM No. 3: The BA's problem is simply a lack of experience with our system. The system relies on numbers, and the numbers come from the BA. The BA is constantly calculating and must think in analytic terms. The BA must work very hard, develop rapidly, and learn what brand management is all about. It takes two to six months for the BA to have a good grasp of the job and become acclimated to the system. All training is on the job.

Question No. 2: What is the relationship between brand management and the other departments?

BM No. 1: Brand managers are considered with respect by the advertising agency but brand managers are committed to the agency because the BM cannot fire the agency. Most of the people in other departments do not want to move as fast as brand management. It is a problem conveying the urgency and importance of timing. The BM is responsible for planning, and the other departments for advice and/or execution.

Knowledge is power and the BM is the resident expert on his or her products.

BM No. 2: Brand management is more a line than a staff function.

Brand management has responsibility for achieving volume objectives and keeping profit/case close to target level, but brand management has no direct authority over many other departments which impact on the ability to achieve objectives.

Senior management recognizes that sometimes performance is beyond the control of brand managers.

BM No. 3: Brand managers control the money. Many other departments must rely upon brand management for direction and project funding. The advertising agency has account executives who deal with brand people and the agency's creative and media departments. The agency presents a national media plan once a year. Since the marketing budget is mainly advertising, brand and agency personnnel write the request. Sales promotions are originated by brand management and proposed to the sales department.

Brand management recommends and analyzes market research and test markets. The purpose of these is to avoid national blunders although the risk is relatively small with ongoing products.

Question 3: How do brand managers spend their time?

BM No. 1: Daily activities are coordination, fielding short questions with answers on the telephone, and commenting on memos passing through. Wide variation exists, but a day might have one hour for thinking and strategy, one hour for standard reports, one hour for the In/Out basket, two hours on the phone, one hour with subordinates, and two hours in meetings.

Dealings are mainly with the "big five"; the account executive at the advertising agency; sales; the manufacturing coordinator; market research; and the product development specialists.

On the average, the BM travels to the field once every three months. Brand management's job is to study the product, determine what is needed, and prioritize projects. The budget for this is set once a year.

BM No. 2: The most important job of a brand manager is the budget request and appropriation. Once each year, a two- to three-hour meeting is held which lays out how and why money is to be spent for the next year. During the period preceding this meeting, much of a BM's time may be spent with the agency. During the remainder of the year, the time falls off with the time spent in once-a-week meetings and telephone calls.

The second major job is the Brand Improvement Objectives meeting which is also held once a year. Brand works with R&D to develop both short-term and long-term product development plans.

Brand strategies require 1½ to 2 years to implement. Long-range planning is important because few changes can be made in the short term due to long lead times in production and media planning.

Most of the BM's time is spent on specific projects.

Heavy use is made of the telephone and many short meetings are held, usually with six people or less.

Brand management has a meeting with the Product Development Center every two weeks.

Question 4: How often does a brand manager change brands?

BM No. 1: All brand people are interchangeable, although it takes about two to four months to become the most knowledgeable. You spend one to two years on a brand.

BM No. 2: Rotation is caused by promotions and departures and occurs every 1½ to 2 years. Continuity is provided by the staggered rotation of BAs, ABMs, and BMs. Once you rotate, you usually do not have time to find out how your old product is doing.

CASE 6–11 Ryan's Family Steak Houses, Inc.

Ryan's Family Steak Houses, Inc. had experienced tremendous success since beginning operations in 1978. The management of the firm had guided Ryan's to an enviable position as an operator of steak house restaurants for the family trade. Much of the success was credited to tight managerial control over expansion and a desire to serve a quality product for a reasonable price. The reputation of the company within its segment of the overall restaurant business was outstanding, and the favorable financial performance of the firm was reflected in the compound growth in revenue of 96 percent and net earnings of 90 percent since the first year of operations.

The managers of the firm were aware that its success was based on concentrating operations in the growing economy of the southeastern portion of the United States. However, the region not only provided a favorable business climate for a firm admired for its steady growth, it also held the largest number of family steak house restaurants. Competition in the area was strong, but in spite of this the managers of Ryan's consistently had been able to open the new units planned each year. In 1985, it planned to open 14 new company-owned units and 3 franchised units, and the firm was on schedule as it reached the mid-year mark.

This case was prepared by Kenneth Gardner and Alan Bauerschmidt, University of South Carolina.

The reputation of family steak houses in other areas of the country was far below that enjoyed by firms operating in the Southeast. This difference in customer perception was also characteristic of cafeterias such as those operated under the familiar names of Morrison's, Piccadilly, and Luby's. As a region, the Southeast also held the largest concentration of cafeterias. The reason for these differences in the level of acceptance by consumers in the various regions of the country were difficult to understand, especially when it is obvious that cafeterias can cater to regional tastes and preferences.

Ryan's had established its position in the southeastern market by gradually expanding outside its initial base in Greenville, South Carolina. New units had been opened in smaller cities throughout the state until 1982, when company officials decided to test larger metropolitan areas. Atlanta was selected as the starting point for this expansion; by the end of 1984 Ryan's was operating in eight states extending south from Kentucky to Florida and west to Alabama.

Investors in this expansion of the firm were obviously pleased by the growth in the number of restaurants operated by the firm as well as by the gains in earnings per share. Ryan's went public in 1982, and has traded over the counter at a price earnings ratio well above the norm for the restaurant industry throughout its period of public ownership. Earnings have been reinvested in the business, rather than paid out in dividends. Thus, the investors look to the continued expansion in the number of restaurants owned or operated by Ryan's as the basis for the value of the firm. At this juncture, the managers of the firm must consider further extension of operations outside the Southeast to meet this expectation.

History

Ryan's Family Steak House opened its first restaurant in Greenville in 1978. Alvin McCall founded the new company on the relatively simple concept that success could be attained by providing customers with a quality product for a reasonable price. Superior service and overall good customer relations were also stressed as a way to distinguish Ryan's from other restaurants emphasizing budget steak operations. The company philosophy was probably best stated by T. Mark McCall, Alvin McCall's 27-year-old son and vice president of operations, when he said that:

> We make less per customer than other restaurants, but we feed more customers. We serve the highest quality product—USDA, grain-fed steak from Colorado. We're built around doing the best in every area—we don't cut quality. We swallow losses if we have to, but we put out the best no matter what it costs. Ultimately, it all flows to the bottom line.

From the beginning of operations until 1982, Ryan's expanded every year by opening new restaurants in South Carolina. In 1982, the elder Mr. McCall realized that the firm could not continue to expand unless additional

EXHIBIT 1 Ryan's Family Steak Houses Income Statement (in thousands)

	1978	*1979*	*1980*	*1981*	*1982*	*1983*	*1984*
Revenues							
Sales by company-owned restaurants	$563	$3,476	$5,344	$7,937	$9,434	$19,153	$31,995
Revenues from franchised restaurants	—	15	—	16	124	299	436
Interest and other income	5	20	66	95	231	390	443
Total revenues	568	3,511	5,410	8,048	9,789	19,842	32,874
Cost and Expenses							
Company-owned restaurants							
Food and beverage	244	1,715	2,633	3,847	4,528	9,081	15,039
Payroll and benefits	118	694	1,089	1,564	1,876	3,786	6,525
Depreciation and amortization	18	84	126	175	222	477	902
Other operating expenses	67	311	497	647	792	1,710	2,878
General and administrative expenses	35	161	262	392	515	889	1,539
Interest expense	11	61	106	160	144	81	—
Total costs and expenses	493	3,026	4,713	6,785	8,077	16,024	26,883
Earnings before income taxes	75	485	697	1,263	1,712	3,818	5,991
Income taxes	5	194	299	602	738	1,695	2,646
Net earnings	70	291	398	661	974	2,123	3,345
Net earnings per common share	.01	.04	.05	.08	.10	.15	.23

capital was obtained from external sources. At this time, each new unit cost approximately $900,000, including $185,000 for the basic equipment required for operations. To obtain the additional funding required for expansion, the company offered the public 500,000 shares of common stock at $25.25 per share; this netted the firm $7 million in needed funds. As described in the prospectus connected with the public offering, the newly raised capital was to be put to use in the expansion of the company, primarily outside the state of South Carolina. This growth plan outlined in the offering has continued to attract the attention of outside investors and the additional capital provided has allowed the continued expansion of the firm. From 1982 through 1984, Ryan's opened exactly the number of units that had been planned, and the firm was on target for new openings during 1985. During this period, revenue grew from $9,789,000 to $32,874,000, while net income increased from $974,000 to $3,345,000. Financial statements are shown in Exhibits 1, 2, and 3.

EXHIBIT 2 Ryan's Family Steak Houses Balance Sheet (in thousands)

	1982	1983	1984
Assets			
Current assets			
Cash and cash equivalents	$3,192	$ 7,086	$ 2,220
Receivables	18	55	126
Inventories	152	237	389
Prepaid expenses	17	20	7
Total current assets	3,379	7,398	2,742
Property and equipment			
Land and improvements	1,128	2,060	3,985
Buildings	3,133	5,801	9,284
Equipment	1,621	2,886	6,939
Construction in progress	32	960	2,378
Total property and equipment	5,914	11,707	22,586
Less accumulated depreciation	600	1,060	1,929
Net property and equipment	5,314	10,647	20,657
Other assets, principally deferred charge	102	246	500
Total assets	$8,795	$18,291	$23,899
Liabilities and shareholders' equity			
Current liabilities			
Accounts payable	$ 645	$ 597	$ 1,446
Income taxes	238	86	86
Accrued liabilities	96	168	287
Current maturity of long-term debt	28	24	27
Total current liabilities	1,097	875	1,846
Long-term debt	1,302	829	802
Deferred franchise fees	30	38	22
Deferred income taxes	218	520	1,055
Shareholders' equity			
Common stock at $1.00 par	1,262	4,116	4,320
Additional paid-in capital	3,896	8,800	9,396
Retained earnings	990	3,113	6,458
Total shareholders' equity	6,148	16,029	20,174
Total liabilities and equity	$8,795	$18,291	$23,899

Operations

A typical Ryan's unit is a 7,500-square-foot structure with simple decor which has remained relatively unchanged since the opening of the first unit in 1978. The buildings are all freestanding and the newer units seat approximately 345 people. Management is in the process of expanding the seating of the previously built units from the current size of 250 to approximate the

EXHIBIT 3 Ryan's Family Steak Houses Statement of Changes in Financial Position (in thousands)

	1981	*1982*	*1983*	*1984*
Sources of Working Capital				
Net earnings	$ 661	$ 974	$ 2,123	$ 3,345
Items not affecting working capital:				
Depreciation and amortization	176	229	495	951
Deferred income taxes	—	128	302	535
Funds provided by operations	837	1,331	2,920	4,831
Proceeds from issuance of common stock	—	3,729	7,758	524
Increase in deferred franchise fees	30	—	8	—
Disposals of property and equipment	—	1	—	—
Tax benefit from exercise of nonqualified stock options	—	—	—	276
Income tax expense, pro forma	600	—	—	—
Total sources of working capital	1,467	5,061	10,686	5,631
Uses of Working Capital				
Additions to property and equipment	21	3,037	5,793	10,879
Increases in other assets	—	59	179	336
Reduction of long-term debt	5	27	473	27
Decrease in deferred franchise fees	—	—	—	16
Distribution to partners	1,483	—	—	—
Provision for costs of exchange offer	10	—	—	—
Total uses of working capital	1,519	3,123	6,445	11,258
Increase (decrease) in working capital	$ (52)	$1,938	$ 4,241	$(5,627)

size of the newer restaurants. Tables and chairs are arranged in one large room with a salad bar acting as the main focal point.

The highest quality USDA grain-fed steak is the primary menu item and major emphasis is placed on the quality of this entrée. Less than 4 percent of the budget is spent on advertising—well below industry norms—and food costs are typically 45 percent of total costs. This figure is seven percentage points above the industry average; however, Ryan's management has no intention of lowering the amount spent on food. The company does not run specials or promotions and primarily relies on word-of-mouth advertising.

Customers place orders for entrées, which range in price from $1.29 for a hamburger to $6.99 for a prime-rib dinner, on a cafeteria-style line. The average check is $4.50. Food orders are brought to the tables and waitresses refresh coffee and beverage orders, but tables turn every 35 minutes on average. The average restaurant in the chain has gross revenues of close to $1.5 million annually and serves 6,500 customers a week, figures indicative of a volume-oriented operation.

At year-end 1984, the company was operating in eight states including franchised operations in four states. The managers of Ryan's intended to limit any future expansion of franchising to the state of Florida. This decision was based on the desire of management to maintain the image of a food product of high quality upon which the company was founded.

The expansion outside of South Carolina was best described as "slow and steady." McCall believed the poor reputation of his competitors in the family steak house business hurt the overall industry. This was an obvious concern to management since expansion had become a central feature of the plans for the company. The general perception of the public in many regions of the country was that the quality and selection of food at budget steak houses was inferior to that of traditional restaurants and cafeterias.

New site location was based on strict demographic studies and took existing real estate prices into account. Typically a selected site would have 50,000 or more people within a three-mile radius. The dinner business is directed toward the low-middle and middle-income groups with the realization that families with the head-of-household holding down a blue-collar position are the primary clientele and a staple element in Ryan's success. Ryan's has consciously avoided locations that are situated within a city's "restaurant row." A major reason for this policy is the cost of real estate for such sites and the potential for rivalry that can develop when competitors are located beside one another. It may be surprising that this unusual site location strategy did not require offsetting advertising expenditures, but this had been Ryan's experience in its successful introduction of new restaurants.

McCall has made a great offer to instill pride in the 2,000 employees involved in the operation of the company-owned units. All employees are given full health coverage which includes dental, travel accident, and life insurance. Paid vacations are also enjoyed by every worker. The compensation of the managers of the various company-owned units consists of a base salary plus bonuses that reflect unit sales. The bonus often makes up 50 percent of the overall compensation of managers which McCall feels is an excellent way to motivate superior performance. In addition, options on stock purchases are granted to managers and higher-level executives, and McCall is considering the institution of a stock purchase plan that will be available to all employees. He believes such a plan will encourage managers to feel that they are in business for themselves, and McCall hopes that all employees will adopt this philosophy.

Industry Review

During 1984, the number of restaurants in the United States increased by almost 3 percent. The Department of Agriculture estimated that by the end of the year there were 253,854 separate commercial eating places in operation. These provided a wide selection in respect to menu, location, and other features that cater to consumer circumstances, tastes, and preferences.

Among this number of eating places were 124,433 restaurants and lunch rooms, 123,769 fast-food outlets, and 5,640 cafeterias, accounting for sales of approximately $100 billion out of a total $159 billion expended on food services away from home. The number of commercial eating places accounting for the $100 billion in sales has grown by an average of 1.5 percent over the last seven years, although the volume of sales by these establishments grew by an average of approximately 16 percent during the same period.

The pattern of growth in the number of the various establishments and their sales differed: the number of restaurants and lunch rooms increased by an average of less than 1 percent, while the number of fast-food outlets increased by over 3 percent; during the same period of time the number of cafeterias decreased by an average of a little less than 3 percent. Sales of each of these three types of establishments increased over the seven years, with restaurants and lunch rooms increasing by somewhat less than an average 14 percent, fast-food outlets by an average 19 percent, and cafeterias by an average of approximately 9.5 percent. Estimates of the growth in the number of meals served and the value of those meals in dollar terms would not be quite as dramatic because of price level increases during this seven-year period.

It might also be noted that the number of restaurants catering to certain types of food segments grew at a faster pace than others. For example, the fastest growing types of restaurants in 1984 included those that served Oriental food and higher-priced full-service menu items. Both types of operations showed a 10 percent increase over the previous year, a year in which the rate of growth in restaurant establishments increased by just less than 3 percent. Restaurants that emphasized chicken items on their menus and pizza restaurants also grew well above the average, increasing their numbers by 7 and 6 percent, respectively. Those restaurants serving seafood, steak, barbecue, and Italian food items all grew at a rate less than the overall average.

The most common specialty restaurant serves pizza, although the 31,000 of these establishments is somewhat less than the 39,000 generic sandwich shops. The other popular specialty restaurants include 8,500 seafood restaurants, 11,900 Mexican restaurants, 12,500 Chinese restaurants, 4,000 Italian restaurants, and 1,300 French restaurants. There were approximately 7,700 restaurants serving a steak menu in 1984; these included 840 higher-priced steak houses and 3,600 family steak houses. The remaining steak houses were unclassified in respect to their type. An additional 12,300 restaurants catered to the family trade with a full menu, while an additional 1,700 restaurants provided a full menu at upscale prices.

An examination of growth in particular regions of the country reveals the influences of population migration and local taste preferences. During 1984, no region experienced a decline in growth in the number of restaurants. The slowest growing regions increased 1 percent. The fastest growing regions in 1984 included the South Atlantic states (5.4%), the Pacific region

(4.3%), and the states in the region of the Rocky Mountains (3.5%). The quicker rate of growth in the South Atlantic was attributed primarily to an increase in the number of hamburger and pizza restaurants. Hamburger restaurants account for 9.5 percent of all restaurants in the region while pizza restaurants accounted for 9 percent. The South Atlantic region also had the largest number of seafood restaurants of any region, and these made up almost 5 percent of the total restaurants in this area of the country.

Steak restaurants comprised approximately 2.6 percent of the total restaurants in the United States in 1984; however, these were distributed unequally among the various regions of the country. The highest concentration of steak restaurants was in the East South Central region, where approximately 3.9 percent of the total restaurants had a steak menu. The South Atlantic and West North Central regions contained the next largest concentrations of steak restaurants, with 3.5 and 3.4 percent, respectively. The New England, Middle Atlantic, and Pacific states held the lowest proportionate number of steak houses, with such restaurants making up 1.8 percent of the total number in these regions.

Family steak houses made up the largest proportion of all steak restaurants in those states that had the largest number of steak restaurants. The states of Alabama, Kentucky, Mississippi, and Tennessee that made up the East South Central region of the country had 62 percent of these restaurants classified as family-type steak restaurants. The next largest proportion—57 percent—was found in the South Atlantic states, followed by the states of Illinois, Indiana, Michigan, Ohio, and Wisconsin that made up the East North Central region of the country. The proportion of the steak restaurants in the family category made up 51 percent of the total number. The lowest proportion of steak restaurants in the family category—33 percent—existed in the New England states, followed by the Middle Atlantic, West North Central, and Pacific states, each with 36 percent of the steak restaurants in the family steak house category.

Many observers believe that the United States is close to a saturation point in the number and capacity of restaurants. It has been noted that a new restaurant is more likely to draw customers away from existing establishments, rather than creating its own new demand. Under these circumstances success depends upon operating strategies that clearly distinguish the restaurant from others in the field, providing the customer with choices among restaurants, improving productivity to glean greater profits from fewer sales, and consolidating the restaurant's position in its market. The most recent growth in the overall restaurant industry is largely the product of restaurant chains catering to the mass of consumers with specialty operations. These chains have greater opportunity to effect the operating strategies that can cope with market saturation.

In today's market, restaurants are less frequently the destination of their patrons, so the chains compete with one another by pre-empting convenient locations that capture customers engaged in other activities. Another factor that seems to be shaping the nature of the restaurant business is the recent trend to more home entertainment and consequently eating at home. Firms operating restaurant chains have become quite imaginative under these circumstances, making their locations more attractive to the casual customer. New restaurant concepts abound, and more recent trends include catering to tastes in lighter, fresher food items; pleasant experiences in more informal settings that borrow from European motifs and earlier days of the American experience; and more casual dining that has come to be described as grazing on appetizer-styled food items in larger variety.

These trends in the conduct of restaurant business have produced only minor changes in the basic structure of the industry. The essentially fragmented nature of the business, brought about by the need to locate in proximity to a targeted clientele, can be only partially offset by chain operations that permit some consolidation of activities. Therefore, restaurants still compete in a fashion that fits the model of monopolistic competition and suits niche strategies, although some economies of scale can be attained in supporting activities. What chain operation has permitted is the deployment to wider markets of distinctive competencies and proprietary advantages held by corporations, overcoming the limitations of time and space in respect to the variety of eating-out experiences that can be enjoyed by the American public.

The raw materials and supplies essential to restaurant operations have remained in the hands of traditional suppliers. Some firms entering the restaurant business as chain operators have principal lines of business that are related to some of these raw materials. In most cases, however, these items make up only a small part of overall requirements.

Franchising of restaurants has played an important part in the overall industry, and it is a typical aspect of chain restaurant operation. A U.S. Department of Commerce report on the impact of franchising in those segments of the industry where this is a practice states that sales of company-owned restaurant operations will total $17.9 billion in 1985, while sales from franchised operations will reach $30.9 billion by year-end. According to this report, franchising has become a powerful force partly because economic factors have made growth through company-owned units difficult for many businesses. With rising costs of construction and training, and with franchising enlarging its share of retail receipts, the Commerce Department predicted an increased trend toward multiunit ownership by franchisees and the increased granting of rights to develop large regional areas to such licensees.

Consumer Trends and Competition

Ryan's Family Steak House has suffered the consequences and reaped the benefits of many of the features of the changing restaurant business during its existence. These included the change in consumer preference for food items during the six years of Ryan's existence. The health-conscious attitude of the public had carried over to the diet that many Americans were adopting. The concern over consumption of large amounts of red meat had prompted many restaurants, fast-food varieties included, to offer "lighter" menu options. The introduction of salad bars in restaurants was an indication that owners were aware of the trend and had taken action to increase the appeal of their outlets. Manifestation of this change was evident in the creation of new chain operations, such as D'Lites of America, which emphasized the fact that all menu items carried less caloric and fat content. D'Lites, based in Atlanta, had embarked on an aggressive franchising plan and by mid-1985 had better than 50 units operating, while only being in business for three years. Ponderosa Steak Houses, Inc. had taken what management had termed a new direction in 1983 with the installation of a $20,000 salad bar unit with heating and cooling capabilities. This move was expected to allow the company more flexibility in the entrées offered. Specials such as country fried steak and meat loaf could be utilized to increase the appeal to customers. The Ponderosa management believed this move was consistent with the nutritional concerns of the public and would serve to set Ponderosa apart from other chains that offered a standard salad bar.

Large corporations were also becoming involved in the trend to open new restaurants featuring a more nutritional appeal. General Mills Corporation started a new chain, The Good Earth, which emphasized salads and pita bread sandwiches. Along similar lines, R. J. Reynolds opened an alternative to heavier menu items, the Fresher Cooker, in the past two years. The biggest question facing firms opening operations centered around the soup, salad, and sandwich idea was how large a market was available. Although the estimates varied, there were many who felt the market for such restaurants was as large as the fast-food hamburger market.

As indicated previously, the chain operation of restaurants is the dominant feature of the changing industry. The portion of market share taken by these operations has grown over the years; in 1970 the portion of market share of the top 100 chain companies was 24 percent; by 1982 this had grown to 47.7 percent. Any list of major chain restaurants would be dominated by those in the fast-food categories, but this is not the exclusive realm of the chain operator. One list (with many intermediate exclusions) includes the firms in Exhibit 4.

Many of the listed firms compete either directly or indirectly with Ryan's. All compete with one another in providing an opportunity for individuals and families to enjoy a meal prepared away from home, depending upon the immediate tastes and preferences of customers at a particularly limited location. If the particular restaurant of a firm at a given location offers a specialty menu, it may not compete with the restaurant of another firm offering a different menu, in spite of the close proximity of the two operations. Two restaurants that would otherwise be close substitutes in respect to taste and preferences of customers would be noncompetitive if located in different cities. In this same respect, the restaurants of the same firm with

EXHIBIT 4 Selected Restaurant Operations

Firm (representative businesses)	*1984 sales (in millions)*
McDonald's	$3,366
PepsiCo (Taco Bell, Pizza Hut)	2,002
Pillsbury (Burger King, Steak & Ale)	1,877
Transworld (Hardee's, Quincy's)	1,341
General Mills (Red Lobster, York Steak)	1,288
W. R. Grace (Restaurant Group)	1,076
Wendy's International (Wendy's, Sisters)	939
Marriott (Big Boy, Roy Rogers)	635
Morrison	476
Sizzler's Restaurants International	451
Ponderosa (Steakhouse, Casa Lupita)	422
USACafes (Bonanza, Culpepper's, Shakey's)	421
Luby's Cafeterias	175
Ryan's Family Steak Houses	32

identical menus do not compete because of the separation of locations. Some firms that more directly compete with Ryan's Family Steak House are discussed in more detail below.

Ponderosa, Inc. This Dayton, Ohio, firm is mainly involved in the operation and franchise of a chain of steak houses in the United States, and it remains among the largest of these chains. It also has been developing Casa Lupita Mexican restaurants and overseas steak house operations, with the long-range goal of expanding its franchising base in order to even out earnings. In 1984, the firm operated 444 restaurants and franchised an additional 220; this number was down somewhat from the previous year when the company owned and operated 450 restaurants and franchised 243. The steak house portion of the business is significantly concentrated in Ohio, Pennsylvania, New York, Illinois, and Michigan. It features steak, prime rib, hamburgers, chicken, and seafood entrées, an all-you-can-eat salad bar, hot soups, beverages, desserts, and breakfast. The ESI Meats unit of the firm processes and distributes meat and related products throughout the United States. These latter products include salad dressings, steak sauce, and baked goods.

In 1982, the firm opened the first of its international steak houses in Watford, England. The firm intends to expand its international operations to other overseas locations in competition with the York Steak house operations of General Mills, as well as with the European chain operations of Berni Steak House, Beefeater Steak Restaurants, and Cavalier Steak Bar in the United Kingdom. Other chain steak house operations on the European continent include the well-known Churrasco Steak Houses and the French operations of Hippopotamus and Couste-Paille and the German Maredo and Block House. Elsewhere in the world, steak is a menu item in many small, owner-operated establishments.

USACafes. This Dallas, Texas, company is the most recent phenomena in the family steak house business. It was created in August 1983 as a subsidiary of Bonanza International to operate the franchised Bonanza Restaurants, and later in the same year it was spun off as an independent entity. More recently the firm has declared its intention to become a multiconcept franchiser and it has become an aggressive acquirer of restaurants that fit that bill.

As far as steak house operations are concerned the firm has attempted to reshape the image of its restaurants. It is moving from its previous emphasis on a budget, Western-theme steak house attractive to a blue-collar clientele, toward a more diverse menu that would be attractive to the broader middle class. This had involved the remodeling of the restaurants and changing menus to include broiled fish, broiled chicken, and fresh vegetables offered on a salad bar that the firm has called Freshtastics. As a result, the average weeky sales of a Bonanza unit went from $14,117 in 1983 to $14,934 in 1984, with weekly sales in the first quarter of 1985 averaging $16,500.

USACafes operates its Bonanza steak houses in 43 of the United States, Puerto Rico, Canada, and Australia. All are franchised, except for two in Dallas and one in Oklahoma that are retained as sites for employee training and test-marketing of new services and products. The major markets that the firm hopes to penetrate more fully in its repositioned configuration include the northwestern portion of the United States, Canada, Pennsylvania, New York, Kentucky, Tennessee, Wisconsin, and Minnesota.

The attempt to diversify the restaurant operations of the firm included the acquisition of a small Colorado-based barbecue chain called Culpepper's, which USACafes hopes to expand as a delivery and drive-through chain in other portions of the country. These "Ribby" outlets would deliver ribs, beef, and chicken with assorted vegetables to make up an entire meal. The cost to build one of these outlets is $175,000, in contrast to the $800,000 to $900,000 cost of a Bonanza restaurant.

Still another development activity involved signing an option in 1984 to purchase a franchise to operate Primo Delicafes, Jan Drakes's Garden Cafes, and several other quick service outlets designed for shopping mall operation. The same year saw the purchase of a 36 percent interest in Shakey's Pizza and an attempt to take over the Ponderosa corporation. USACafes acquired somewhat less than 5 percent of the shares of Ponderosa at about $12 a share and sold it recently for approximately $19.25, when this plan to rapidly expand steak house operations failed.

Sizzler Restaurants International. Sizzler Restaurants International, after being spun off from Collins Foods in 1982, instituted a renovation plan designed to enlarge seating capacity and give the units a more open garden-like atmosphere. In May 1983, Sizzler acquired 17 Rustler Steak House units from the Marriott Corporation. The revenues and profits for the Rustler units have shown a steady increase from 1983 through the end of the 1985 fiscal year, ended April 30, 1985. In June 1985, Sizzler purchased privately owned Tenly Enterprises of Rockville, Maryland. Tenly operated a chain of 85 restaurants, comprised of the remainder of the Rustler chain exclusive of the 17 Western units previously purchased by Sizzler. Tenly had recorded modest profits with the operation on sales of $65 million. Renovation of the cafeteria-style Rustler restaurants would not be completed until late 1985. The Tenly acquisition expanded Sizzler's operations in New York, New Jersey, Pennsylvania, Maryland, and the District of Columbia. At fiscal year-end 1985, 45 percent of the company's revenues were from California with no other state accounting for more than 10 percent. The acquisition of Tenly created net interest expense of $500,000 for the 1986 fiscal year and created $8 million of long-term debt for the previously debt-free firm.

Morrison's. Owners of cafeteria operations such as Morrison's were seeing similar changes in trends of food choices by customers as those experienced by operators of steak houses. Morrison's operations were concentrated in the Southeast with one third of the units located in Florida. Menu changes had included the addition of Mexican dishes as well as more expensive items like steak and lobster.

Along with menu changes, Morrison's was offering a take-out option to its customers. This tactic was being used primarily in newly constructed units and it had experienced only mixed success. The percentage of take-out sales to total unit sales varied from 10 percent to 25 percent among the company stores. The management at Morrison's felt that in order for this part of the business to run effectively it was necessary to limit the number of menu items and provide separate parking facilities for take-out customers.

The need to provide a separate parking area for a take-out operation was impossible in the Morrison's restaurants located in shopping malls. However, the slowdown in shopping mall construction forced the company to begin developing freestanding units. This meant the firm was now having to compete for the same real estate as family steak houses and other chain operations.

Realizing the need to expand the geographic scope of operations from the Southeast, Morrison's management test-marketed in Ohio, Illinois, and Oklahoma in 1984. The results of the test indicated that cafeterias were generally viewed negatively and these types of operations had a problem of identity in the mind of the consumer. These negative opinions were coupled with the fact that numerous menu changes had to be instituted for the different regions to suit local tastes. Management assessment of the test effort was generally unfavorable. Morrison's had opened only 6 new units in each of the last two years but management predicted the company would be opening 12 new units in each of the forthcoming years.

Luby's Cafeterias. Another regional cafeteria operation, Luby's, Inc., operates exclusively in the Southwest with 82 out of 94 units being located in Texas. The company earned a net income of $17.4 million on its sales of $175 million in 1984. The management of the firm was becoming increasingly aware of the strong regional reputation of the company, which led it to develop plans for expansion. The firm has not performed any test-marketing in other regions. However, with such a large concentration of restaurants in the oil-dependent state of Texas, management was anxious to expand the geographical scope of its operations.

Conclusion

Mr. McCall realized that growth was an essential component in the success of Ryan's up to the present time. The southeastern market, especially the markets in South Carolina and Georgia, had supported the largest share of restaurant units for Ryan's, and he did not doubt that the firm and its business had a strong regional association. The family steak house segment of the restaurant industry was not as welcomed by the population in other regions. This concerned Mr. McCall and the other managers of the firm. They felt that the existing units could support faster customer turnover and enlarged seating capacity to accommodate 325 to 350 patrons as one way to expand revenue.

Although Ryan's had included a soup and salad bar in all of the current units, a new idea had been proposed. To augment the traditional, beef-dominated menu the management had developed a plan to install a much larger hot and cold bar. The new addition would offer several different meats and vegetables as well as desserts and fresh bread. An initial examination of this proposal indicated that it would cost $55,000 to install such a new super bar in a typical Ryan's operation. Management's desire to maintain uniformity among the units would require installations in each existing restaurant. With 41 company-owned restaurants expected to be in operation by the end of 1985, the more than $2 million cost of such a project was something to be examined closely.

Company officials realized the cost of food, which Ryan's spent more on by a large margin than competitors, would present a problem if inflation in food prices should suddenly occur. If this happened at the same time as the $2 million capital outlay for the new super bars, the profit margin of the firm would be squeezed and the gains made by the firm in the first six years would be frustrated.

The notion of operating a nationwide chain of restaurants is an obvious attraction to Mr. McCall and the investors in the business. This is not quite as easy to accomplish in the family steak house business as it is with the chain operation of hamburger, pizza, or chicken outlets. Franchising has been the key element in each of these three types of business. Mr. McCall's views on franchising had been stated previously, and he will not be easily swayed from this opinion.

The ability to maintain an aggressive expansion of company-owned units is the principal ingredient in the growth strategy of the firm. Alvin McCall had been an integral part of a similar growth situation during his association with the Quincy's steak house chain. Quincy's was also based in South Carolina and had expanded rapidly during the six years of Mr. McCall's involvement. He sold his interest in Quincy's in 1977. As one of the founding partners, the normal agreement to eschew participation in a similar business for a stipulated period was avoided in this sale, and Mr. McCall made it clear in the agreement that he reserved the privilege to start what became Ryan's Family Steak House during the following year.

Mr. McCall's experience with Quincy's chain undoubtedly would be invaluable at this point in the growth-life of the Ryan's chain as the firm faces decisions critical to its future. Ryan's has been in operation for approximately seven years, one year longer than the number of years Mr. McCall was associated with Quincy's. He will need to draw on the experience from each of those years as the firm shapes its strategy for the near future.

CASE 6–12 TenderCare Disposable Diapers

Tom Cagan watched as his secretary poured six ounces of water onto each of two disposable diapers lying on his desk. The diaper on the left was a new, improved Pampers, introduced in the summer of 1985 by Procter & Gamble. The new, improved design was supposed to be drier than the preceding Pampers. It was the most recent development in a sequence of designs that traced back to the original Pampers, introduced to the market in 1965. The diaper on his right was a TenderCare® diaper, manufactured by a potential supplier for testing and approval by Cagan's company, Rocky Mountain Medical Corporation (RMM). The outward appearance of both diapers was identical.

Yet the TenderCare diaper was different. Just under its liner (the surface next to the baby's skin) was a wicking fabric that drew moisture from the

---

This case was written by Professor James E. Nelson, University of Colorado. © 1986 by the Business Research Division.

surface around a soft, waterproof shield to an absorbent reservoir of filler. Pampers and all other disposable diapers on the market kept moisture nearer to the liner and, consequently, the baby's skin. A patent attorney had examined the TenderCare design, concluding that the wicking fabric and shield arrangement should be granted a patent. However, it would be many months before results of the patent application process could be known.

As soon as the empty beakers were placed back on the desk, Cagan and his secretary touched the liners of both diapers. They agreed that there was no noticeable difference, and Cagan noted the time. They repeated their "touch test" after one minute and again noted no difference. However, after two minutes, both thought the TenderCare diaper to be drier. At three minutes, they were certain. By five minutes, the TenderCare diaper surface seemed almost dry to the touch, even when a finger was pressed deep into the diaper. In contrast, the Pampers diaper showed little improvement in dryness from three to five minutes and tended to produce a puddle when pressed.

These results were not unexpected. Over the past three months, Cagan and other RMM executives had compared TenderCare's performance with 10 brands of disposable diapers available in the Denver market. TenderCare diapers had always felt drier within a two- to four-minute interval after wetting. However, these results were considered tentative because all tests had used TenderCare diapers made by RMM personnel by hand. Today's test was the first made with diapers produced by a supplier under mass manufacturing conditions.

Rocky Mountain Medical Corporation

RMM was incorporated in Denver, Colorado, in late 1982 by Robert Morrison, M.D. Sales had grown from about $400,000 in 1983 to $2.4 million in 1984 and were expected to reach $3.4 million in 1985. The firm would show a small profit for 1985, as it had each previous year.

Management personnel as of September 1985 included six executives. Cagan served as president and director, positions held since joining RMM in April 1984. Prior to that time he had worked for several high-technology companies in the areas of product design and development, production management, sales management, and general management. His undergraduate studies were in engineering and psychology; he took an MBA in 1981. Dr. Morrison currently served as chairman of the board and vice president for research and development. He had completed his M.D. in 1976 and was board certified to practice pediatrics in the state of Colorado since 1978. John Bosch served as vice president of manufacturing, a position held since joining RMM in late 1983. Lawrence Bennett was vice president of marketing, having primary responsibilities for marketing TenderCare and RMM's two lines of phototherapy products since joining the firm in 1984. Bennett's background included an MBA received in 1981 and three years' experience in groceries product management at General Mills. Two other executives had also joined RMM in 1984. One served as vice president of personnel; the other as controller.

Phototherapy Products. RMM's two lines of phototherapy products were used to treat infant jaundice, a condition experienced by some 5 to 10 percent of all newborn babies. One line was marketed to hospitals under the trademark Alpha-Lite. Bennett felt that the Alpha-Lite phototherapy unit was superior to competing products because it gave the baby 360-degree exposure to the therapeutic light. Competing products gave less complete exposure, with the result that the Alpha-Lite unit treated more severe cases and produced quicker recoveries. Apart from the Alpha-Lite unit itself, the hospital line of phototherapy products included a light meter, a photo-mask that protected the baby's eyes while undergoing treatment, and a "baby bikini" that diapered the baby and yet facilitated exposure to the light.

The home phototherapy line of products was marketed under the trademark Baby-Lite.® The phototherapy unit was portable, weighing about 40 pounds, and was foldable for easy transport. The unit when assembled was 33 inches long, 20 inches wide, and 24 inches high. The line also included photo-masks, a thermometer, and a short booklet telling parents about home phototherapy. Parents could rent the unit and purchase related products from a local pharmacy or a durable-medical-equipment dealer for about $75 per day. This was considerably less than the cost of hospital treatment. Another company, Acquitron, Inc., had entered the home phototherapy market in early 1985 and was expected to offer stiff competition. A third competitor was rumored to be entering the market in 1986.

Bennett's responsibilities for all phototherapy products included developing marketing plans and making final decisions about product design, promotion, pricing, and distribution. He directly supervised two product managers, one responsible for Alpha-Lite and the other for Baby-Lite. He occasionally made sales calls with the product managers, visiting hospitals, health maintenance organizations, and insurers.

TenderCare Marketing. Right now most of Bennett's time was spent on TenderCare. Bennett recognized that TenderCare would be marketed much differently than the phototherapy products. TenderCare would be sold to wholesalers, who in turn would sell to supermarkets, drugstores, and mass merchandisers. TenderCare would compete either directly or indirectly with two giant consumer-goods manufacturers, Procter & Gamble and Kimberly-Clark. TenderCare represented considerable risk to RMM.

Because of the uncertainty surrounding the marketing of TenderCare, Bennett and Cagan had recently sought the advice of several marketing consultants. They reached formal agreement with one, a Los Angeles consultant named Alan Anderson. Anderson had extensive experience in advertising at J. Walter Thompson. He had also had responsibility for marketing and sales at Mattel and Teledyne, specifically for the marketing of such products as

IntelliVision,® the Shower Massage,® and the Water Pik.® Anderson currently worked as an independent marketing consultant to several firms. His contract with RMM specified that he would devote 25 percent of his time to TenderCare the first year and about 12 percent the following two years. During this time, RMM would hire, train, and place its own marketing personnel. One of these people would be a product manager for TenderCare.

Bennett and Cagan also could employ the services of a local marketing consultant who served on RMM's advisory board. (The board consisted of 12 business and medical experts who were available to answer questions and provide direction.) This consultant had spent over 25 years in marketing consumer products at several large corporations. His specialty was developing and launching new products, particularly health and beauty aids. He had worked closely with RMM in selecting the name TenderCare, and had done a great deal of work summarizing market characteristics and analyzing competitors.

Market Characteristics

The market for babies' disposable diapers could be identified as children, primarily below age 3, who use the diapers, and their mothers, primarily between ages of 18 and 49, who decide on the brand and usually make the purchase. Bennett estimated there were about 11 million such children in 1985, living in about 9 million households. The average number of disposable diapers consumed in these households was thought to range from zero to 15 per day and to average about 7.

The consumption of disposable diapers is tied closely to birth rates and populations. However, two prominent trends also influence consumption. One is the disposable diaper's steadily increasing share of total diaper usage by babies. Bennett estimated that disposable diapers would increase their share of total diaper usage from 75 percent currently to 90 percent by 1990. The other trend is toward the purchase of higher-quality disposable diapers. Bennett thought the average retail price of disposable diapers would rise about twice as fast as the price of materials used in their construction. Total dollar sales of disposable diapers at retail in 1985 were expected to be about $3 billion, or about 15 billion units. Growth rates were thought to be about 14 percent per year for dollar sales and about 8 percent for units.

Foreign markets for disposable diapers would add to these figures. Canada, for example, currently consumed about $0.25 billion at retail, with an expected growth rate of 20 percent per year until 1990. The U.K. market was about twice this size and growing at the same rate.

The U.S. market for disposable diapers was clearly quite large and growing. However, Bennett felt that domestic growth rates could not be maintained much longer because fewer and fewer consumers were available to switch from cloth to disposable diapers. In fact, by 1995, growth rates for disposable diapers would begin to approach growth rates for births, and unit sales of disposable diapers would become directly proportional to numbers of infants using diapers. A consequence of this pronounced slowing of growth would be increased competition.

Competition

Competition between manufacturers of disposable diapers was already intense. Two well-managed giants—Procter & Gamble and Kimberly-Clark—accounted for about 80 percent of the market in 1984 and 1985. Bennett had estimated market shares at:

	1984	*1985*
Pampers	32%	28%
Huggies	24	28
Luvs	20	20
Other brands	24	24
	100%	100%

Procter & Gamble was clearly the dominant competitor with its Pampers and Luvs brands. However, Procter & Gamble's market share had been declining, from 70 percent in 1981 to about 50 percent today. The company had introduced its thicker Blue Ribbon® Pampers recently in an effort to halt the share decline. It had invested over $500 million in new equipment to produce the product. Procter & Gamble spent approximately $40 million to advertise its two brands in 1984. Kimberly-Clark spent about $19 million to advertise Huggies in 1984.

The 24 percent market share held by other brands was up by some 3 percentage points from 1983. Weyerhaeuser and Johnson & Johnson manufactured most of these diapers, supplying private-label brands for Wards, J. C. Penney, Target, Kmart, and other retailers. Generic disposable diapers and private brands were also included here, as well as a number of very small, specialized brands that were distributed only to local markets. Some of these brands positioned themselves as low-cost alternatives to national brands; others occupied premium ("designer") niches with premium prices. As examples, Universal Converter entered the northern Wisconsin market in 1984 with two brands priced at 78 and 87 percent of Pampers' case price. Riegel Textile Corporation's Cabbage Patch® diapers illustrated the premium end, with higher prices and attractive print designs. Riegel spent $1 million to introduce Cabbage Patch diapers to the market in late 1984.

Additional evidence of intense competition in the disposable diaper industry was the major change of strategy by Johnson & Johnson in 1981. The company took its own brand off the U.S. market, opting instead to produce private-label diapers for major retailers. The company had held about 8 percent of the national market at the time and decided that this simply was not enough to compete effectively. Johnson & Johnson's disposable diaper was the first to be positioned in the industry as a premium product. Sales at one point totaled about 12 percent of the market but began to fall when Luvs and Huggies (with similar premium features) were introduced. Johnson & Johnson's advertising expenditures for disposable diapers in 1980 were about $8 million. The company still competed with its own brand in the international market.

Marketing Strategies for TenderCare

Over the past month, Bennett and his consultants had spent considerable time formulating potential marketing strategies for TenderCare. One strategy that already had been discarded was simply licensing the design to another firm. Under a license agreement, RMM would receive a negotiated royalty based on the licensee's sales of RMM's diaper. However, this strategy was unattractive on several grounds. RMM would have no control over resources devoted to the marketing of TenderCare: the licensee would decide on levels of sales and advertising support, prices, and distribution. The licensee would control advertising content, packaging, and even the choice of brand name. Licensing also meant that RMM would develop little marketing expertise, no image or even awareness among consumers, and no experience in dealing with packaged-goods channels of distribution. The net result would be that RMM would be hitching its future with respect to TenderCare (and any related products) to that of the licensee. Three other strategies seemed more appropriate.

The "Diaper Rash" Strategy. The first strategy involved positioning the product as an aid in the treatment of diaper rash. Diaper rash is a common ailment, thought to affect most infants at some point in their diapered lives. The affliction usually lasted two to three weeks before being cured. Some infants are more disposed to diaper rash than others. The ailment is caused by "a reaction to prolonged contact with urine and feces, retained soaps and topical preparations, and friction and maceration" (Nelson's *Text of Pediatrics,* 1979, p. 1884). Recommended treatment includes careful washing of the affected areas with warm water and without irritating soaps. Treatment also includes the application of protective ointments and powders (sold either by prescription or over the counter).

The diaper rash strategy would target physicians and nurses in either family or general practice and physicians and nurses specializing either in pediatrics or dermatology. Bennett's estimates of the numbers of general or family practitioners in 1985 was approximately 65,000. He thought that about 45,000 pediatricians and dermatologists were practicing in 1985. The numbers of nurses attending all these physicians was estimated at about 290,000. All 400,000 individuals would be the eventual focus of TenderCare marketing efforts. However, the diaper rash strategy would begin (like the other two strategies) where approximately 11 percent of the target market was located—California. Bennett and his consultants agreed that RMM lacked resources sufficient to begin in any larger market. California would provide a good test for TenderCare because the state often set consumption trends for the rest of the U.S. market. California also showed fairly typical levels of competitive activity.

Promotion activities would emphasize either direct mail and free samples or in-office demonstrations to the target market. Mailing lists of most physicians and some nurses in the target market could be purchased at a cost of about $60 per 1,000 names. The cost to print and mail a brochure, cover letter, and return postcard was about $250 per 1,000. To include a single TenderCare disposable diaper would add another $400 per thousand. In-office demonstrations would use registered nurses (employed on a part-time basis) to show TenderCare's superior dryness. The nurses could be quickly trained and compensated on a per-demonstration basis. The typical demonstration would be given to groups of two or three physicians and nurses and would cost RMM about $6. The California market could be used to investigate the relative performance of direct mail versus demonstrations.

RMM would also advertise in trade journals such as the *Journal of Family Practice, Journal of Pediatrics,* and *Pediatrics Digest.* However, a problem with such advertisements was waste coverage because none of the trade journals published regional editions. A half-page advertisement (one insertion) would cost about $1,000 for each journal. This cost would be reduced to about $700 if RMM placed several advertisements in the same journal during a one-year period. RMM would also promote TenderCare at local and state medical conventions in California. Costs per convention were thought to be about $3,000. The entire promotion budget as well as amounts allocated to direct mail, free samples, advertisements, and medical conventions had yet to be decided.

Prices were planned to produce a retail price per package of 12 TenderCare diapers at around $3.80. This was some 8 to 10 percent higher than the price for a package of 18 Huggies or Luvs. Bennett thought that consumers would pay the premium price because of TenderCare's position: the pennies-per-day differential simply would not matter if a physician prescribed or recommended TenderCare as part of a treatment for diaper rash. "Besides," he noted, "in-store shelf placement of TenderCare under this strategy would be among diaper rash products, not with standard diapers. This will make price comparisons by consumers even more unlikely." The $3.80 package price for 12 TenderCare diapers would produce a contribution margin for RMM of about 9 cents per diaper. It would give retailers a per-diaper margin some 30 percent higher than that for Huggies or Luvs.

The Special-Occasions Strategy. The second strategy centered around a "special-occasions" position that emphasized TenderCare's use in situations where changing the baby would be difficult. One such situation was whenever diapered infants traveled for any length of time. Another occurred daily at some 100,000 day-care centers that accepted infants wearing diapers. Yet another came every evening in each of the 9 million market households when babies were diapered at bedtime.

The special-occasions strategy would target mothers in these 9 million households. Initially, of course, the target would be only the estimated 1 million mothers living in California. Promotion would aim particularly at first-time mothers, using such magazines as *American Baby* and *Baby Talk.* Per-issue insertion costs for one full-color, half-page advertisement in such magazines would average about $20,000. However, most baby magazines published regional editions where single insertion costs averaged about half that amount. Black-and-white advertisements could also be considered; their costs would be about 75 percent of the full-color rates. Inserting several ads per year in the same magazine would allow quantity discounts and reduce the average insertion cost by about one third.

Lately, Bennett had begun to wonder if direct-mail promotion could instead be used to reach mothers of recently born babies. Mailing lists of some 1 to 3 million names could be obtained at a cost of around $50 per 1,000. Other costs to produce and mail promotional materials would be the same as those for physicians and nurses. "I suppose the real issue is, just how much more effective is direct mail over advertising? We'd spend at least $250,000 in baby magazines to cover California while the cost of direct mail would probably be between $300,000 and $700,000, depending on whether or not we gave away a diaper." Regardless of Bennett's decision on consumer promotion, he knew RMM would also direct some promotion activities toward physicians and nurses as part of the special-occasions strategy. Budget details were yet to be worked out.

Distribution under the special-occasions strategy would have TenderCare stocked on store shelves along with competing diapers. Still at issue was whether the package should contain 12 or 18 diapers (like Huggies and Luvs) and how much of a premium price TenderCare could command. Bennett considered the packaging and pricing decisions interrelated. A package of 12 TenderCare diapers with per-unit retail prices some 40 percent higher than Huggies or Luvs might work just fine. Such a packaging/pricing strategy would produce a contribution margin to RMM of about 6 cents per diaper. However, the same pricing strategy for a package of 18 diapers would probably not work. "Still," he thought, "good things often come in small packages, and most mothers probably associate higher quality with higher price. One thing is for sure—whichever way we go, we'll need a superior package." Physical dimensions for a TenderCare package of either 12 or 18 diapers could be made similar to the size of the Huggies or Luvs package of 18.

The Head-On Strategy. The third strategy under consideration met major competitors in a direct, frontal attack. The strategy would position TenderCare as a noticeably drier diaper that any mother would prefer to use anytime her baby needed changing. Promotion activities would stress mass advertising to mothers, using television and magazines. However, at least two magazines would include a dollar-off coupon to stimulate trial of a package of TenderCare diapers during the product's first three months on the market. Some in-store demonstrations to mothers using "touch tests" might also be employed. Although no budget for California had yet been set, Bennett thought the allocation would be roughly 60:30:10 for television, magazines, and other promotion activities, respectively.

Pricing under this strategy would be competitive with Luvs and Huggies, with the per-diaper price for TenderCare expected to be some 9 percent higher at retail. This differential was needed to cover additional manufacturing costs associated with TenderCare's design. TenderCare's package could contain only 16 diapers and show a lower price than either Huggies or Luvs with their 18-count packages. Alternatively, the package could contain 18 diapers and carry the 9 percent higher price. Bennett wondered if he really wasn't putting too fine a point on the pricing/packaging relationship. "After all," he had said to Anderson, "we've no assurance that retailers or wholesalers would pass along any price advantage TenderCare might have due to a smaller package. Either one or both might instead price TenderCare near the package price for our competitors and simply pocket the increased margin!" The only thing that was reasonably certain was TenderCare's package price to the wholesaler. That price was planned to produce about a 3-cent contribution margin to RMM per diaper, regardless of package count.

Summary of the Three Strategies. When viewed together, the three strategies seemed so complex and so diverse as to defy analysis. Partly the problem was one of developing criteria against which the strategies could be compared. Risk was obviously one such criterion; so were company fit and competitive reaction. However, Bennett felt that some additional thought on his part would produce more criteria against which the strategies could be compared. He hoped this effort would produce no more strategies; three were plenty.

The other part of the problem was simply uncertainty. Strengths, weaknesses, and implications of each strategy had yet to be given much thought. Moreover, each strategy seemed likely to have associated with it some surprises. An example illustrating the problem was the recent realization that the Food and Drug Administration (FDA) must approve any direct claims RMM might make about TenderCare's efficacy in treating diaper rash. The chance of receiving this federal agency's approval was thought to be reasonably high; yet it was unclear just what sort of testing and what results were needed. The worst-case scenario would have the FDA requiring lengthy consumer tests that eventually would produce inconclusive results. The best case would have the FDA giving permission based on TenderCare's superior dryness and on results of a small-scale field test recently completed by Dr. Morrison. It would be probably a month before the FDA's position could be known.

"The delay was unfortunate—and unnecessary," Bennett thought, "especially if we eventually settle on either of the other two strategies." In fact, FDA approval was not even needed for the diaper rash strategy if RMM simply claimed (1) that TenderCare diapers were drier than competing diapers and (2) that dryness helps treat diaper rash. Still, a single-statement, direct-claim position was thought to be more effective with mothers and more difficult to copy by any other manufacturer. And yet Bennett did want to move quickly on TenderCare. Every month of delay meant deferred revenue and other postponed benefits that would derive from a successful introduction. Delay also meant the chance that an existing (or other) competitor might develop its own drier diaper and effectively block RMM from reaping the fruits of its development efforts. Speed was of the essence.

Financial Implications

Bennett recognized that each marketing strategy held immediate as well as long-term financial implications. He was particularly concerned with finance requirements for start-up costs associated with the California entry. Cagan and the other RMM executives had agreed that a stock issue represented the best option to meet these requirements. Accordingly, RMM had begun preparation for a sale of common stock through a brokerage firm that would underwrite and market the issue. Management at the firm felt that RMM could generate between $1 and $3 million, depending on the offering price per share and the number of shares issued.

Proceeds from the sale of stock had to be sufficient to fund the California entry and leave a comfortable margin remaining for contingencies. Proceeds would be used for marketing and other operating expenses as well as for investments in cash, inventory, and accounts receivable assets. It was hoped that TenderCare would generate a profit by the end of the first year in the California market and show a strong contribution to the bottom line thereafter. California profits would contribute to expenses associated with entering additional markets and to the success of any additional stock offerings.

Operating profits and proceeds from the sale of equity would fund additional research and development activities that would extend RMM's diaper technology to other markets. Dr. Morrison and Bennett saw almost immediate application of the technology to the adult incontinent diaper market, currently estimated at about $300 million per year at retail. Underpads for beds constituted at least another $50 million annual market. However, both of these uses were greatly dwarfed by another application, the sanitary napkin market. Finally, the technology could almost certainly be applied to numerous industrial products and processes, many of which promised great potential. All these opportunities made the TenderCare situation that much more crucial to the firm; making a major mistake here would affect the firm for years.

CASE 6–13 W. L. Gore & Associates, Inc.

On July 26, 1976, Jack Dougherty, a newly minted MBA from the College of William and Mary, bursting with resolve and dressed in a dark blue suit, reported to his first day at W. L. Gore & Associates. He presented himself to Bill Gore, shook hands firmly, looked him in the eye, and said he was ready for anything.

What happened next was one thing for which Dougherty was not ready. Gore replied, "That's fine, Jack, fine. Why don't you look around and find something you'd like to do." Three frustrating weeks later he found that something, dressed in jeans, loading fabric into the mouth of a machine that laminates the company's patented GORE-TEX[1] membrane to fabric. By 1982, Dougherty had become responsible for all advertising and marketing in the fabrics group.

This story is part of the folklore that is heard over and over about W. L. Gore. Today the process is slightly more structured. New Associates[2] take a journey through the business before settling into their own positions, regardless of the specific position for which they are hired. A new sales Associate in the Fabric Division may spend six weeks rotating through different areas before beginning to concentrate on sales and marketing. Among other things he or she may learn is how GORE-TEX fabric is made; what it can and cannot do; how Gore handles customer complaints; and how it makes its investment decisions.

Anita McBride related her early experience at W. L. Gore & Associates this way:

> Before I came to Gore, I had worked for a structured organization and I came here, and for the first month it was fairly structured because I was going through training, and this is what we do and this is how Gore is and all of that, and I went to Flagstaff for that training. After a month, I came down to Phoenix and my sponsor said, "Well, here's your office"—it's a wonderful office—and "Here's your desk" and walked away. And I thought, Now what do I do, you know? I was waiting for a memo or something, or a job description. Finally after another month I was so frustrated, I felt what have I gotten myself into, and so I went to my sponsor and I said, "What the heck do you want from me? I need something from you," and he said, "If you don't know what you're supposed to do, examine your commitment and opportunities."

Frank Shipper, Salisbury State University, and Charles Manz, Arizona State University.

[1]GORE-TEX is a registered trademark of W. L. Gore & Associates.

[2]In this case the word *Associate* is used and capitalized because in W. L. Gore & Associates' literature the word is always used instead of *employees* and is capitalized. In fact, the case writers were told that Gore "never had 'employees'—always 'Associates.'"

Background

W. L. Gore & Associates is a company that evolved from the late Wilbert L. Gore's experiences personally, organizationally, and technically. Gore was born in Meridian, Idaho, near Boise, in 1912. By age six, he claimed that he had become an avid hiker in the Wasatch Mountain Range in Utah. In those mountains, at a church camp, he met Genevieve, his future wife. She is called Vieve by everyone. In 1935 they got married—in their eyes, a partnership. He would make breakfast, and she would make lunch. The partnership lasted a lifetime.

Gore received both a bachelor of science degree in chemical engineering in 1933 and a masters of science in chemistry in 1935 from the University of Utah. He began his professional career at American Smelting and Refining in 1936. He moved to Remington Arms Company in 1941. He moved once again, to E. I. du Pont de Nemours in 1945, where he was research supervisor and head of operations research. While at Du Pont he worked on a team to develop applications for polytetrafluoroethylene, frequently referred to as PTFE in the scientific community and known as "Teflon" by Du Pont's consumers (it is known by consumers under other names from other companies). On this team Gore felt a sense of excited commitment, personal fulfillment, and self-direction. He followed the development of computers and transistors and felt that PTFE had the ideal insulating characteristics for use with such equipment.

He tried a number of ways to make a PTFE-coated ribbon cable, but without success. A breakthrough came in his home basement laboratory. He was explaining the problem to his son, Bob. Bob saw some PTFE sealant tape made by 3M and asked his father, "Why don't you try this tape?" His father then explained to his son that everyone knows you cannot bond PTFE to itself. Bob went on to bed.

Gore remained in his basement lab and proceeded to try what everyone knew would not work. At about 4:00 A.M., he woke up his son waving a small piece of cable around, saying excitedly, "It works, it works!" The following night father and son returned to the basement lab to make ribbon cable coated with PTFE.

By this time in his career, Gore knew some of the decision makers at Du Pont. For the next four months, he tried to persuade Du Pont to make a new product—PTFE-coated ribbon cable. It became clear after talking to several people that Du Pont wanted to remain a supplier of raw materials and not a fabricator.

Gore began to discuss with Vieve the possibility of starting their own insulated wire and cable business. On January 1, 1958, their wedding anniversary, they founded W. L. Gore & Associates. The basement of their home served as their first facility. After finishing dinner on their anniversary, Vieve said, "Well, let's clear up the dishes, go downstairs, and get to work." They viewed this as another partnership.

Gore was 45 years old with five children to support when he left

Du Pont. He left behind a career of 17 years and a good, secure salary. To finance the first two years of the business, the Gores mortgaged their house and took $4,000 from savings. All of their friends told them not to do it.

The first few years were rough. In lieu of salary, some of their Associates accepted room and board in the Gore home. At one point 11 Associates were living and working under one roof. The order that was almost lost and that put the company on a profitable footing came from Denver's water department. One afternoon, Vieve answered a phone call while sifting PTFE powder. The caller indicated that he was interested in the ribbon cable but wanted to ask some technical questions. Gore was out running some errands. The caller asked for the product manager. Vieve explained that he was out at the moment. Next he asked for the sales manager and finally, the president. Vieve said that they were also out. The caller became outraged and hollered, "What kind of company is this anyway?" With a little diplomacy, the Gores were able eventually to secure an order for $100,000. This order put the company over the hump, and it began to take off.

W. L. Gore & Associates has continued to grow and develop new products primarily derived from PTFE, including its best known product, GORE-TEX fabric. In 1986 Gore died while backpacking in the Wind River Mountains of Wyoming. Before he died he had become chairman and his son Bob, president, a position he continues to occupy. Vieve remains as the only other officer, secretary-treasurer.

The Operating Company

W. L. Gore & Associates is a company without titles, hierarchy, or any of the conventional structures associated with enterprises of its size. The titles of president and secretary-treasurer are used only because they are required by the laws of incorporation. In addition, Gore does not have a corporate-wide mission or code of ethics statement, although Gore does not require or prohibit business units from developing such statements for themselves. Thus, the Associates of some business units who have felt a need for such statements have developed them for themselves. The majority of business units within Gore do not have such statements. When questioned about this issue, one Associate stated, "The company belief is that (1) its four basic operating principles cover ethical practices required of people in business; and (2) it will not tolerate illegal practices." Gore's management style has been referred to as un-management. The organization has been guided by Gore's experiences on teams at Du Pont and has evolved as needed.

For example, in 1965 W. L. Gore & Associates was a thriving and growing company with a facility on Paper Mill Road in Newark, Delaware, with about 200 Associates. One warm Monday morning in the summer, Gore was taking his usual walk through the plant when he realized that he did not know everyone in the plant. The team had become too big. As a result, the company has a policy that no facility will have over 200 Associates. Thus was born the expansion policy of "Get big by staying small." The purpose of maintaining small plants is to accentuate a close-knit and interpersonal atmosphere.

Today, W. L. Gore & Associates consists of 44 plants worldwide with over 5,300 Associates. In some cities the plants are clustered together on the same site, as in Flagstaff, Arizona, with four plants on the same site. Twenty-seven of those plants are in the United States, and 17 are overseas. The company's overseas plants are located in Scotland, Germany, France, and Japan, manufacturing electronics, medical, industrial, and fabric products.

Gore electronic products are found in unconventional places where conventional products will not do—in space shuttles, for example, where Gore wire and cable assemblies withstood the heat of ignition and the cold of space. In addition, they are found in fast computers, transmitting signals at up to 93 percent of the speed of light. Gore cables are even underground, in oil-drilling operations, and undersea, on submarines that require superior microwave signal equipment and no-fail cables that can survive high pressure. The Gore Electronic Products Division has a history of anticipating future customer needs with innovative products. Gore electronic products are well known in industry for their ability to last under adverse conditions.

In the medical arena, GORE-TEX-expanded PTFE is considered an ideal replacement for human tissue in many situations. In patients suffering from cardiovascular disease, the diseased portion of arteries are often replaced by tubes of expanded PTFE that are strong, biocompatible, and able to carry blood at arterial pressures. Gore has a dominant share in this market. Other Gore medical products include patches that can literally mend broken hearts by patching holes and repairing aneurysms, a synthetic knee ligament that provides stability by replacing the natural anterior cruciate ligament, and sutures that allow for tissue attachment and offer the surgeon silklike handling coupled with extreme strength. In 1985 Gore won Britain's Prince Philip Award for Polymers in the Service of Mankind. The award recognized especially the life-saving achievements of the Gore medical products team.

The Industrial Products Division produces a number of products including sealants, filter bags, cartridges, clothes, and coatings. These products tend to have specialized and critical applications. Gore's reputation for quality appears to influence the industrial purchasers of these products.

The Gore Fabrics Division, which is the largest division, supplies laminates to manufacturers of foul-weather gear, ski wear, running suits, footwear, gloves, and hunting and fishing garments. Firefighters and U.S. Navy pilots wear GORE-TEX fabric gear, as do some Olympic athletes. And the U.S. Army has adopted a total garment system built around a GORE-TEX fabric component.

GORE-TEX membrane has 9 billion pores randomly dotting each square inch and is feather light. Each pore is 700 times larger than a water vapor molecule yet thousands of times smaller than a water droplet. Wind and water cannot penetrate the pores, but perspiration can escape. As a result, fabrics bonded with GORE-TEX membrane are waterproof, windproof, and breathable. The laminated fabrics bring protection from the elements to a variety of products—from survival gear to high-fashion rain wear. Recently, other manufacturers including 3M have brought out products to compete with GORE-TEX fabrics. Gore, however, continues to have a commanding share of this market.

Gore wanted to avoid smothering the company in thick layers of formal "management." He felt that they stifled individual creativity. As the company grew, he knew that a way had to be devised to assist new people to get started and to follow their progress. This was seen as particularly important when it came to compensation. Gore has developed what they call their "sponsor" program to meet these needs. When people apply to Gore, they are initially screened by personnel specialists as in most companies. For those who meet the basic criteria, there are interviews with other Associates. Before anyone is hired, an Associate must agree to be their sponsor. The sponsor is both a coach and an advocate who takes a personal interest in the new Associate's contributions, problems, and goals. He or she tracks the new Associate's progress, helping and encouraging, dealing with weaknesses and concentrating on strengths. Sponsoring is not a short-term commitment. All Associates have sponsors, and many have more than one. When individuals are hired initially, they will have a sponsor in their immediate work area. If they move to another area, they will have a sponsor in that work area. As Associates' responsibilities grow, they may acquire additional sponsors.

Because the sponsoring program looks beyond conventional views of what makes a good Associate, some anomalies occur in the hiring practices. Gore has proudly told the story of "a very young man" of 84 who walked in, applied, and spent five very good years with the company. The individual had 30 years of experience in the industry before joining Gore. His other Associates had no problems accepting him, but the personnel computer did. It insisted that his age was 48. The individual success stories at Gore come from diverse backgrounds.

An internal memo by Gore described three kinds of sponsorship expected and how they might work as follows:

1. The sponsor who helps a new Associate *get started* on his job. Also, the sponsor who helps a present Associate get started on a new job (starting sponsor).
2. The sponsor who sees to it the Associate being sponsored *gets credit* and recognition for contributions and accomplishments (advocate sponsor).
3. The sponsor who sees to it that the Associate being sponsored is *fairly paid* for contributions to the success of the enterprise (compensation sponsor).

A single sponsor can perform any one or all three kinds of sponsorship. A sponsor is a friend and an Associate. All the supportive aspects of the friendship are also present. Often (perhaps usually) two Associates sponsor each other as advocates.

In addition to the sponsor program, Gore Associates are asked to follow four guiding principles:

1. Try to be fair.
2. Use your freedom to grow.
3. Make your own commitments, and keep them.
4. Consult with other Associates prior to any action that may adversely effect the reputation or financial stability of the company.

The four principles are often referred to as fairness, freedom, commitment, and waterline. The waterline terminology is drawn from an analogy to ships. If someone pokes a hole in a boat above the waterline, the boat will be in relatively little real danger. If someone pokes a hole below the waterline, however, the boat is in immediate danger of sinking.

The company's operating principles were put to a test in 1978. By this time, the word about the qualities of GORE-TEX fabric were being spread throughout the recreational and outdoor markets. Production and shipment had begun in volume. At first a few complaints were heard, then some of the clothing started coming back. Finally, much of the clothing was being returned. The trouble was that the GORE-TEX fabric was leaking. Waterproofness was one of the two major properties responsible for GORE-TEX fabric's success. The company's reputation and credibility were on the line. Peter W. Gilson, who led Gore's Fabrics Division said, "It was an incredible crisis for us at that point. We were really starting to attract attention; we were taking off—and then this." Gilson and a number of his Associates in the next few months made many of those below-the-waterline decisions.

First, the researchers determined that oils in human sweat were responsible for clogging the pores in the GORE-TEX fabric and altering the surface tension of the membrane. Thus, water could pass through. They also discovered that a good washing could restore the waterproof property. At first this solution, known as the "Ivory Snow Solution," was accepted.

A single letter from "Butch," a mountain guide in the Sierras, changed the company's position. Butch wrote that he had been leading a group and, "My parka leaked and my life was in danger." As Gilson said, "That scared the hell out of us. Clearly our solution was no solution at all to someone on a mountaintop." All of the products were recalled. "We bought back, at our own expense, a fortune in pipeline material—anything that was in the stores, at the manufacturers, or anywhere else in the pipeline," Gilson said.

In the meantime, Gore and other Associates set out to develop a permanent fix. One month later, a second-generation GORE-TEX fabric had been developed. Gilson, furthermore, told dealers that if at any time a customer returned a leaky parka, they should replace it and bill the company. The replacement program alone cost Gore roughly $4 million.

EXHIBIT 1 W. L. Gore's Lattice Structure

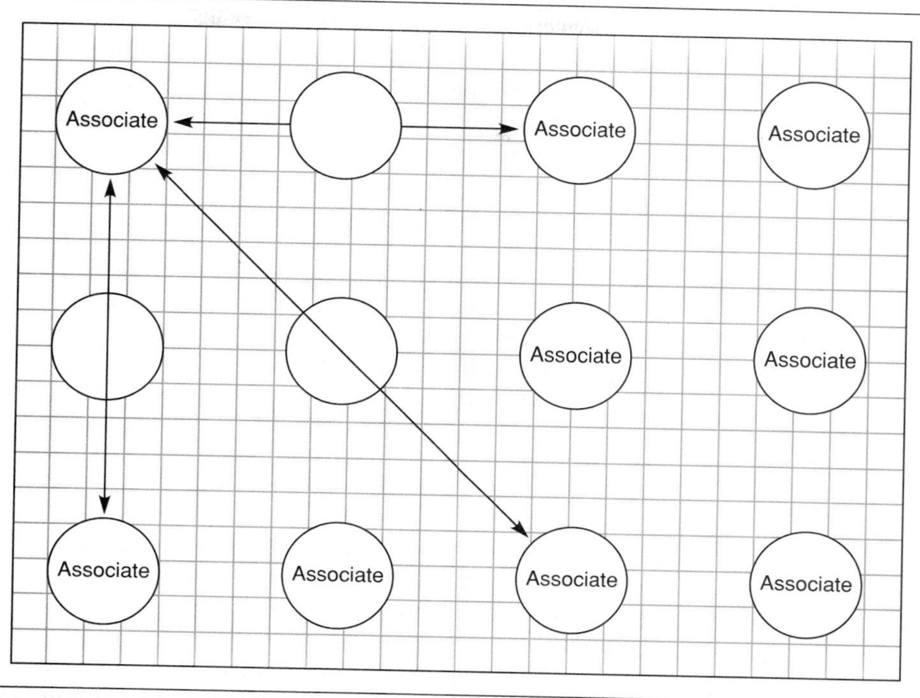

Source: W. L. Gore & Associates, Inc.

Organizational Structure

W. L. Gore & Associates has not only been described as un-managed but also as un-structured. Gore referred to the structure as a lattice organization. A lattice structure is portrayed in Exhibit 1 and has the following characteristics:

1. Direct lines of communication are direct, person to person, with no intermediary.
2. No fixed or assigned authority.
3. Sponsors, not bosses.
4. Natural leadership defined by followership.
5. Objectives set by those who must "make them happen."
6. Tasks and functions organized through commitments.

The structure within the lattice is described by the people at Gore as complex and evolves from interpersonal interactions, self-commitment to group-known responsibilities, natural leadership, and group-imposed discipline. Gore once explained this structure by saying, "Every successful organization has an underground lattice. It's where the news spreads like lightning, where people can go around the organization to get things done." Another description of what is occurring within the lattice structure is constant cross-area teams—the equivalent of quality circles going on all the time. When a puzzled interviewer told Gore that he was having trouble understanding how planning and accountability worked, Gore replied with a grin, "So am I. You ask me how it works—every which way."

The lattice structure does have some similarities to traditional management structures. For instance, a group of 30 to 40 Associates who make up an advisory group meets every six months to review marketing, sales, and production plans. As Gore conceded, "The abdication of titles and rankings can never be 100 percent."

One thing that might strike an outsider in the meetings and the other places in Gore's organization is the informality and amount of humor. Meetings tend to be only as long as necessary. As Trish Hearn, an Associate in Newark, Delaware, said, "No one feels a need to pontificate." Words such as *responsibilities* and *commitments* are, however, commonly heard. This is an organization that seems to take what it does very seriously, but its members do not take themselves too seriously.

Gore, for a company of its size, may have the shortest organizational pyramid. The pyramid consists of Bob Gore, the late Bill Gore's son, as president, and Vieve, Gore's widow, as secretary-treasurer. All the other members of the Gore organization are referred to as Associates. Words such as *employees, subordinates,* and *managers* are taboo in the Gore culture.

Gore does not have any managers, but it does have many leaders. Gore described in an internal memo the kinds of leadership and the role of leadership as follows:

1. The Associate is recognized by a team as having a special knowledge, or experience (for example, this could be a chemist, computer expert, machine operator, salesman, engineer, lawyer). This kind of leader gives the team *guidance in a special area.*
2. The team looks to the Associate for coordination of individual activities in order to achieve the agreed upon objectives of the team. The role of this leader is to persuade team members to *make the commitments* necessary for success (commitment seeker).
3. The Associate proposes necessary objectives and activities and seeks agreement and team *consensus on objectives.* This leader is perceived by the team members as having a good grasp of how the objectives of the team fit in with the broad objective of the enterprise. This kind of leader is often also the "commitment seeking" leader in 2. above.
4. The leader evaluates relative contribution of team members (in consultation with other sponsors), and reports these contribution evaluations to a compensation committee. This leader may also participate in the

compensation committee on relative contribution and pay and *reports changes in compensation* to individual Associates. This leader is then also a compensation sponsor.

5. The leader coordinates the research, manufacturing, and marketing of one product type within a business, interactive with team leaders and individual Associates who have commitments regarding the product type. These leaders are usually called *product specialists*. They are respected for their knowledge and dedication to their products.
6. *Plant leaders* help coordinate activities of people within a plant.
7. *Business leaders* help coordinate activities of people in a business.
8. *Functional leaders* help coordinate activities of people in a "functional" area.
9. *Corporate leaders* help coordinate activities of people in different businesses and functions and try to promote communication and cooperation among all Associates.
10. *Intrapreneuring Associates organize new teams* for new businesses, new products, new processes, new devices, new marketing efforts, new or better methods of all kinds. These leaders invite other Associates to "sign up" for their project.

Leaders are not authoritarians, managers of people, or supervisors who tell us what to do or forbid us doing things, nor are they "parents" to whom we transfer our own self-responsibility. However, they do often advise us of the consequences of actions we have done or propose to do. Our actions result in contributions, or lack of contribution, to the success of our enterprise. Our pay depends on the magnitude of our contributions. This is the basic discipline of our lattice organization.

Many other aspects of Gore's operations are arranged along egalitarian lines. The parking lot does not have any reserved parking spaces except for customers and the handicapped. There is only one area in each plant in which to eat. The lunchroom in each new plant is designed to be a focal point for Associate interaction. Dave McCarter of Phoenix explained, "The design is no accident. The lunchroom in Flagstaff has a fireplace in the middle. We want people to like to be here." The location of the plant is also no accident. Sites are selected based on transportation access, a nearby university, beautiful surroundings, and climate appeal. Land cost is never a primary consideration. McCarter justified the selection by stating, "Expanding is not costly in the long run. The loss of money is what you make happen by stymieing people into a box."

Not all people function well under such a system, especially initially. For those accustomed to a more structured work environment, there are adjustment problems. As Gore said, "All our lives, most of us have been told what to do, and some people don't know how to respond when asked to do something—and have the very real option of saying no—on their job. It's the new Associate's responsibility to find out what he or she can do for the good of the operation." The vast majority of the new Associates, after some initial floundering, adapt quickly.

For those who require more structured working conditions and cannot adapt, Gore's flexible workplace is not for them. According to Gore, for those few "it's an unhappy situation, both for the Associate and the sponsor. If there is no contribution, there is no paycheck." Anita McBride, an Associate in Phoenix, said, "It's not for everybody. People ask me do we have turnover, and yes we do have turnover. What you're seeing looks like utopia, but it also looks extreme. If you finally figure the system, it can be real exciting. If you can't handle it, you gotta go. Probably by your own choice, because you're going to be so frustrated."

In rare cases an Associate "is trying to be unfair," in Gore's own words. In one case the problem was chronic absenteeism, and in another the individual was caught stealing. "When that happens, all hell breaks loose," said Gore. "We can get damned authoritarian when we have to."

Over the years, Gore has faced a number of unionization drives. The company neither tries to dissuade an Associate from attending an organizational meeting nor retaliates when flyers are passed out. Each attempt has been unsuccessful. None of the plants have been organized to date. Gore believed that no need exists for third-party representation under the lattice structure: "Why would Associates join a union when they own the company? It seems rather absurd."

Overall, the Associates appear to have responded positively to the Gore system of un-management and un-structure. Gore estimated the year before he died that "the profit per Associate is double" that of Du Pont. However, the lattice structure is not without its critics. As Gore stated, "I'm told from time to time that a lattice organization can't meet a crisis well because it takes too long to reach a consensus when there are no bosses. But this isn't true. Actually, a lattice, by its very nature, works particularly well in a crisis. A lot of useless effort is avoided because there is no rigid management hierarchy to conquer before you can attack a problem."

The lattice has been put to the test on a number of occasions. For example, in 1975 Dr. Charles Campbell, the University of Pittsburgh's senior resident, reported that a GORE-TEX arterial graft had developed an aneurysm. An aneurysm is a bubblelike protrusion that is life-threatening. If it continues to expand, it will explode. Obviously, this kind of problem has to be solved quickly and permanently.

Within only a few days of Dr. Campbell's first report, he flew to Newark to present his findings to Bill and Bob Gore and a few other Associates. The meeting lasted two hours. Dan Hubis, a former policeman who had joined Gore to develop new production methods, had an idea before the meeting was over. He returned to his work area to try some different production techniques. After only three hours and 12 tries, he had developed a permanent solution; in other words, a potentially damaging problem to both patients and the company was resolved. Furthermore, Hubis's redesigned graft has gone on to win widespread acceptance in the medical community.

Other critics have been outsiders who had problems with the idea of no titles. Sarah Clifton, an Associate at the Flagstaff facility, was being pressed by some outsiders as to what her title was. She made one up and had it printed on some business cards: SUPREME COMMANDER. When Gore learned what she did, he loved it and recounted the story to others.

Another critic, Eric Reynolds, founder of Marmot Mountain Works Ltd. of Grand Junction, Colorado, and major Gore customer, said "I think the lattice has its problems with the day-to-day nitty-gritty of getting things done on time and out the door. I don't think Bill realizes how the lattice system affects customers. I mean, after you've established a relationship with someone about product quality, you can call up one day and suddenly find that someone new to you is handling your problem. It's frustrating to find a lack of continuity." He went on to say, "But I have to admit that I've personally seen at Gore remarkable examples of people coming out of nowhere and excelling."

Gore was asked a number of times if the lattice structure could be used by other companies. His answer was "No. For example, established companies would find it very difficult to use the lattice. Too many hierarchies would be destroyed. When you remove titles and positions and allow people to follow who they want, it may very well be someone other than the person who has been in charge. The lattice works for us, but it's always evolving. You have to expect problems." He maintained that the lattice system works best when put in place in start-up companies by dynamic entrepreneurs.

Research and Development

Research and development like everything else at Gore are unstructured. There is no formal research and development department. Yet the company holds many patents, although most inventions are held as proprietary or trade secrets. Any Associate can ask for a piece of raw PTFE, known as a silly worm, with which to experiment. Gore believed that all people had it within themselves to be creative.

The best way to understand how research and development works is to see how inventiveness has previously occurred at Gore. By 1969, the wire and cable division was facing increased competition. Gore began to look for a way to straighten out the PTFE molecules. As he said, "I figured out that if we ever unfold those molecules, get them to stretch out straight, we'd have a tremendous new kind of material." He thought that if PTFE could be stretched, air could be introduced into its molecular structure. The result would be greater volume per pound of raw material without affecting performance. Thus, fabricating costs would be reduced and the profit margins would be increased. Going about this search scientifically with his son, Bob, Gore heated rods of PTFE to various temperatures and then slowly stretched them. Regardless of the temperature or how carefully they stretched them, the rods broke.

Working alone late one night after countless failures, Bob in frustration yanked at one of the rods violently. To his surprise, it did not break. He tried it again and again with the same results. The next morning Bob demonstrated his breakthrough to his father, but not without some drama. As Gore recalled, "Bob wanted to surprise me so he took a rod and stretched it slowly. Naturally, it broke. Then he pretended to get mad. He grabbed another rod and said, 'Oh the hell with this' and gave it a pull. It didn't break—he'd done it." The new arrangement of molecules changed not only the wire and cable division but led to the development of GORE-TEX fabric and what is now the largest division at Gore plus a host of other products.

Initial field-testing of GORE-TEX fabric was conducted by Gore and Vieve in the summer of 1970. Vieve made a hand-sewn tent out of patches of GORE-TEX fabric. They took it on their annual camping trip to the Wind River Mountains in Wyoming. The very first night in the wilderness, they encountered a hailstorm. The hail tore holes in the top of the tent, but the bottom filled up like a bathtub from the rain. As Gore stated, "At least we knew from all the water that the tent was waterproof. We just need to make it stronger, so it could withstand hail."

The second largest division began on the ski slopes of Colorado. Gore was skiing with his friend Dr. Ben Eiseman of the Denver General Hospital. As Gore told the story, "We were just to start a run when I absentmindedly pulled a small tubular section of GORE-TEX out of my pocket and looked at it. 'What is that stuff?' Ben asked. So I told him about its properties. 'Feels great,' he said. 'What do you use it for?' 'Got no idea,' I said. 'Well give it to me,' he said, 'and I'll try it in a vascular graft on a pig.' Two weeks later, he called me up. Ben was pretty excited. 'Bill,' he said, 'I put it in a pig and it works. What do I do now?' I told him to get together with Pete Cooper in our Flagstaff plant and let them figure it out." Now hundreds of thousands of people throughout the world walk around with GORE-TEX vascular grafts.

Every Associate is encouraged to think, experiment, and follow a potentially profitable idea to its conclusion. For example, at a plant in Newark, Delaware, a machine that wraps thousands of feet of wire a day was designed by Fred L. Eldreth, an Associate with a third-grade education. The design was done over a weekend. Many other Associates have contributed their ideas through both product and process breakthroughs. Without a research and development department, innovations and creativity work very well at Gore. The year before he died, Gore claimed, "The creativity, the number of patent applications and innovative products is triple" that of Du Pont.

Associate Development

Ron Hill, an Associate in Newark, said, Gore "will work with Associates who want to advance themselves." Associates are offered many in-house training opportunities. They do tend to be technical and engineering focused because of the type of organization Gore is, but it also offers in-house programs in leadership development. In addition, the company has cooperative programs with their Associates to obtain training through universities and other outside providers. Gore will pick up most of the costs for the Associates. The emphasis in Associate development as in many parts of Gore is that the Associate must take the initiative.

Products

The products that Gore makes are arranged into four divisions—electronics, medical, industrial, and fabrics. The Electronic Products Division produces wire and cable for various demanding applications in aerospace, defense, computers, and telecommunications. The wire and cable products have earned a reputation for unequaled reliability. Most of the wire and cable is used where conventional cables cannot operate. For example, Gore wire and cable assemblies were used in the space shuttle *Columbia* because they would stand the heat of ignition and the cold of space. Gore wire was used in the moon vehicle shuttle that scooped up samples of moon rocks, and Gore's microwave coaxial assemblies have opened new horizons in microwave technology. Back on earth, the electrical wire products help make the world's fastest computers possible because electrical signals can travel through them at up to 90 percent of the speed of light. Because of the physical properties of the GORE-TEX material used in their construction, the electronic products are used extensively in defense systems, electronic switching for telephone systems, scientific and industrial instrumentation, microwave communications, and industrial robotics. Reliability is a watchword for all Gore products.

In medical products, reliability is literally a matter of life and death. GORE-TEX expanded PTFE is an ideal material used to combat cardiovascular disease. When human arteries are seriously damaged or plugged with deposits that interrupt the flow of blood, the diseased portions can often be replaced with GORE-TEX artificial arteries. GORE-TEX arteries and patches are not rejected by the body because the patient's own tissues grow into the graft's open porous spaces. GORE-TEX vascular grafts come in many sizes to restore circulation to all areas of the body. They have saved limbs from amputation and saved lives. Some of the tiniest grafts relieve pulmonary problems in newborns. GORE-TEX-expanded PTFE is also used to help people with kidney disease. Associates are developing a variety of surgical reinforcing membranes, known as GORE-TEX cardiovascular patches, which can literally mend broken hearts, by patching holes and repairing aneurysms.

Through the Fabrics Division, Gore technology has traveled to the roof of the world on the backs of renowned mountaineers. GORE-TEX fabric is waterproof and windproof yet breathable. Those features have qualified GORE-TEX fabric as essential gear for mountaineers and adventurers facing extremely harsh environments. The PTFE membrane blocks wind and water but allows sweat to escape, which makes GORE-TEX fabric ideal for anyone who works or plays hard in foul weather. Backpackers have discovered that a single lightweight GORE-TEX fabric shell will replace a poplin jacket and a rain suit and dramatically outperform both. Skiers, sailors, runners, bicyclists, hunters, fishermen, and other outdoor enthusiasts have also become big customers of garments made of GORE-TEX fabric. General sportswear, as well as women's fashion footwear and handwear of GORE-TEX fabric, are as functional as they are beautiful. Boots and gloves, both for work and recreation, are waterproof thanks to GORE-TEX liners. GORE-TEX garments are even becoming standard items issued to many military personnel. Wetsuits, parkas, pants, headgear, gloves, and boots keep the troops warm and dry in foul-weather missions. Other demanding jobs also require the protection of GORE-TEX fabric because of its unique combination of chemical and physical properties.

The GORE-TEX fibers products, like the fabrics, end up in some pretty tough places. The outer protective layer of NASA's spacesuit is woven from GORE-TEX fibers. GORE-TEX fibers are in many ways the ultimate in synthetic fibers. They are impervious to sunlight, chemicals, heat, and cold. They are strong and uniquely resistant to abrasion.

The Industrial Products Division produces joint sealant, a flexible cord of porous PTFE that can be applied as a gasket to the most complex shapes, sealing them to prevent leakage of corrosive chemicals even at extreme temperature and pressure. Steam valves packed with GORE-TEX valve-stem packing are guaranteed for the life of the valve when used properly. Industrial filtration products, such as GORE-TEX filter bags, reduce air pollution and recover valuable solids from gases and liquids more completely than alternatives; they also do it more economically. They could make coal-burning plants completely smoke free, contributing to a cleaner environment.

The coatings division applies layers of PTFE to steel castings and other metal articles by a patented process. Called Fluroshield[3] protective coatings, this fluorocarbon polymer protects processing vessels in the production of corrosive chemicals.

GORE-TEX microfiltration products are used in medical devices, pharmaceutical manufacturing, and chemical processing. These membranes remove bacteria and other microorganisms from air or liquids making them sterile and bacteria free.

Compensation

Compensation at Gore takes three forms: salary, profit sharing, and an Associates' Stock Ownership Program (ASOP).[4] Entry-level salary is in the middle for comparable jobs. According to Sally Gore, daughter-in-law of the

[3]Fluroshield is a registered trademark of W. L. Gore & Associates.

[4]Gore's ASOP is similar legally to an ESOP (Employee Stock Ownership Plan). Gore simply does not use the word *employee* in any of its documentation.

founder, "We do not feel we need to be the highest paid. We never try to steal people away from other companies with salary. We want them to come here because of the opportunities for growth and the unique work environment." Associates' salaries are reviewed at least once a year and more commonly twice a year. The reviews are conducted by a compensation team for most workers in the facility in which they work. The sponsors for all Associates act as their advocate during this review process. Prior to meeting with the compensation committee, the sponsor checks with customers or whoever uses the results of the person's work to find out what contribution has been made. In addition, the evaluation team will consider the Associate's leadership ability, his or her willingness to help others to develop to their fullest.

Besides salaries, Gore has profit-sharing and ASOP plans for all Associates. Profit sharing typically occurs twice a year but is dependent on profitability. The amount also depends on time in service and annual rate of pay. In addition, the firm buys company stock equivalent to 15 percent of the Associates' annual income and places it in an ASOP retirement fund. Thus, an Associate becomes a stockholder after being at Gore for one year. Gore wanted every Associate to feel that they themselves are the owners.

The principle of commitment is seen as a two-way street. Gore tries to avoid layoffs. Instead of cutting pay, which is seen at Gore as disastrous to morale, the company has used a system of temporary transfers within a plant or cluster of plants and voluntary layoffs.

Marketing Strategy

Gore's marketing strategy is based on making the determination that it can offer the best-valued products to a marketplace, that people in that marketplace appreciate what it manufactures, and that Gore can become a leader in that area of expertise. The operating procedures used to implement the strategy follow the same principles as other functions at Gore.

First, the marketing of a product revolves around a leader who is referred to as a "product champion." According to Dave McCarter, "You've got to marry your technology with the interests of your champions, as you've got to have champions for all these things no matter what. And that's the key element within our company. Without a product champion you can't do much anyway, so it is individually driven. If you get a person interested in a particular market or a particular product for the marketplace, then there is no stopping them."

Second, a product champion is responsible for marketing the product through commitments with sales representatives. "We have no quota system," said McCarter. "Our marketing and our salespeople make their own commitments as to what their forecasts are. There is no person sitting around telling them that that is not high enough, you have to increase it by 10 percent, or whatever somebody feels is necessary. You are expected to meet your commitment, which is your forecast, but nobody is going to tell you to change it. . . . There is no order of command, no chain involved. These are groups of independent people who come together to make unified commitments to do something and sometimes when they can't make those agreements. . . . You may pass up a market place, . . . but that's OK because there's much more advantage when the team decides to do something."

Third, the sales representatives are on salary. They are not on commission. They participate in the profit-sharing and ASOP plans in which all other Associates participate.

As in other areas of Gore, individual success stories come from diverse backgrounds. McCarter related one of these success stories as follows:

> I interviewed Sam one day. I didn't even know why I was interviewing him actually. Sam was retired from AT&T. After twenty-five years, he took the golden parachute and went down to Sun Lakes to play golf. He played golf a few months and got tired of that. He was selling life insurance.
>
> I sat reading the application; his technical background interested me. . . . He had managed an engineering department with 600 people. He'd managed manufacturing plants for AT&T and had a great wealth of experience at AT&T. He said, "I'm retired. I like to play golf but I just can't do it every day, so I want to do something else. Do you have something around here I can do?" I was thinking to myself, This is one of these guys I would sure like to hire, but I don't know what I would do with him. The thing that triggered me was the fact that he said he sold insurance, and here is a guy with a high degree of technical background selling insurance. He had marketing experience, international marketing experience. So, the bell went off in my head that we were trying to introduce a new product into the marketplace that was a hydrocarbon leak protection cable. You can bury it in the ground, and in a matter of seconds it could detect a hydrocarbon (gasoline, etc.). I had a couple of other guys working on it who hadn't been very successful with marketing it. We were having a hard time finding a customer. Well, I thought that kind of a product would be like selling insurance. If you think about it, why should you protect your tanks? It's an insurance policy that things are not leaking into the environment. That has implications, big-time monetary. So, actually, I said, "Why don't you come back Monday? I have just the thing for you." So he did. We hired him; he went to work, a very energetic guy. Certainly a champion of the product, he picked right up on it, ran with it single-handed. . . . Now it's a growing business. It certainly is a valuable one, too, for the environment.

In the implementation of its marketing strategy, Gore relies on cooperative and word-of-mouth advertising. Cooperative advertising is especially used to promote GORE-TEX fabric products. Those products are sold through a number of clothing manufacturers and distributors, including Apparel Technologies, Lands' End, Austin Reed, Timberland, Woolrich, The North Face, Grandoe, and Michelle Jaffe. Gore engages in cooperative advertising because the Associates believe positive experiences with any one product will carry over to purchases of other and more GORE-TEX fabric products.

The power of informal marketing techniques extends beyond consumer products. According to McCarter, "In the technical end of the business, company reputation probably is most important. You have to have a good reputation with your company." He went on to say that without a good reputation, a company's products would not be considered seriously by many industrial customers. In other words, the sale is often made before the representative calls. Using its marketing strategies, Gore has been very successful in securing a market leadership position in a number of areas ranging from waterproof outdoor clothing to vascular grafts.

Financial Information

Gore is a closely held private corporation. Financial information is as closely guarded as proprietary information on products and processes. About 90 percent of the stock is owned by Associates who work at Gore. According to Shanti Mehta, an Associate, Gore's return on assets and sales rank it among the top 10 percent of the Fortune 500 companies. According to another source, Gore is working just fine by any financial measure. It has had 31 straight years of profitability and positive return on equity. The compounded growth rate for revenues at Gore from 1969 to 1989 was over 18 percent discounted for inflation. In comparison, only 11 of the 200 largest companies in the Fortune 500 have had positive return on equity each year from 1970 to 1988, and only two other companies missed only one year. The revenue growth rate for these 13 companies was 5.4 percent compared to 2.5 percent for the entire Fortune 500. Moreover, in 1969 Gore's total sales were about $6 million and in 1990, $660 million. This growth has been financed without debt.

Conclusion

Some analysts are beginning to question whether a large, multinational organization such as Gore can prosper in the 1990s without formal strategic planning and with such an unstructured, unusual management style. Do you feel the analysts' concerns are legitimate, or would you conclude from the case that Gore's strategic management process, or lack thereof, is effective? In the event that Gore's top management decides to institute strategic planning, prepare a document that gives an overview of the benefits and potential problems of the process in light of Gore's unorthodox operating principles. Which principles, if any, would need changing? Outline a plan of action for Gore to implement strategic management.[5]

[5]A number of sources were especially helpful in providing background material for this case. The most important sources of all were the W. L. Gore Associates who generously shared their time and viewpoints about the company. We especially appreciate the input received from Anita McBride, who spent hours with us sharing her personal experiences as well as providing many resources including internal documents and videotapes. In addition, Trish Hearn and Dave McCarter also added much to this case through sharing their personal experiences as well as ensuring that the case accurately reflected the Gore company and culture.

BIBLIOGRAPHY

Aburdene, Patricia, and John Nasbitt. *Re-inventing the Corporation.* New York: Warner Books, 1985.

Angrist, S. W. "Classless Capitalists." *Forbes,* May 9, 1983, pp. 123–24.

Franlesca, L. "Dry and Cool." *Forbes,* August 27, 1984, p. 126.

"The Future Workplace." *Management Review,* July 1986, pp. 22–23.

Hoerr, J. "A Company Where Everybody Is the Boss." *Business Week,* April 15, 1985, p. 98.

McKendrick, Joseph. "The Employees as Entrepreneur." *Management World,* January 1985, pp. 12–13.

Milne, M. J. "The Gorey Details." *Management Review,* March 1985, pp. 16–17.

Posner, B. G. "The First Day on the Job." *Inc.,* June 1986, pp. 73–75.

Price, Kathy. "Firm Thrives without Boss." *AZ Republic,* February 2, 1986.

Rhodes, Lucien, "The Un-manager." *Inc.,* August 1982, p. 34.

Simmons, J. "People Managing Themselves: Un-management at W. L. Gore Inc." *Journal for Quality and Participation,* December 1987, pp. 14–19.

Trachtenberg, J. A. "Give Them Stormy Weather." *Forbes,* March 24, 1986, pp. 172–74.

Ward, Alex. "An All-Weather Idea." *The New York Times Magazine,* November 10, 1985, sec. 6.

Weber, Joseph. "No Bosses. And Even 'Leaders' Can't Give Orders." *Business Week,* December 10, 1990, pp. 196–97.

"Wilbert L. Gore." *Industry Week,* October 17, 1983, pp. 48–49.

CASE 6–14 Makhteshim Chemical Works

"To say that we are unhappy with our progress to date would be an understatement," admitted Mr. Ilan Leviteh, vice president of Makhteshim Chemical Works, a small Israeli specialty chemicals company. In 1987, Makhteshim faced a key decision: "Our penetration of the U.S. market has not gone well, and we have to decide what to do about it. We have to be here," he emphasized. "The U.S. market is just too important."

For the last three years, M&T Chemicals (M&T), a U.S. company, had marketed the F–2000 Series of brominated polymeric flame retardants for

---

This case was prepared by Patricia P. McDougall of Georgia Institute of Technology, Earl H. Levith of Edlon Products, Inc., and Kendall J. Roth of the University of South Carolina. Mr. Levith served as the 1985–86 director of the Fire Retardant Association. The authors wish to thank Dr. William R. Sandberg for his helpful comments.

EXHIBIT 1 Organizational Structure

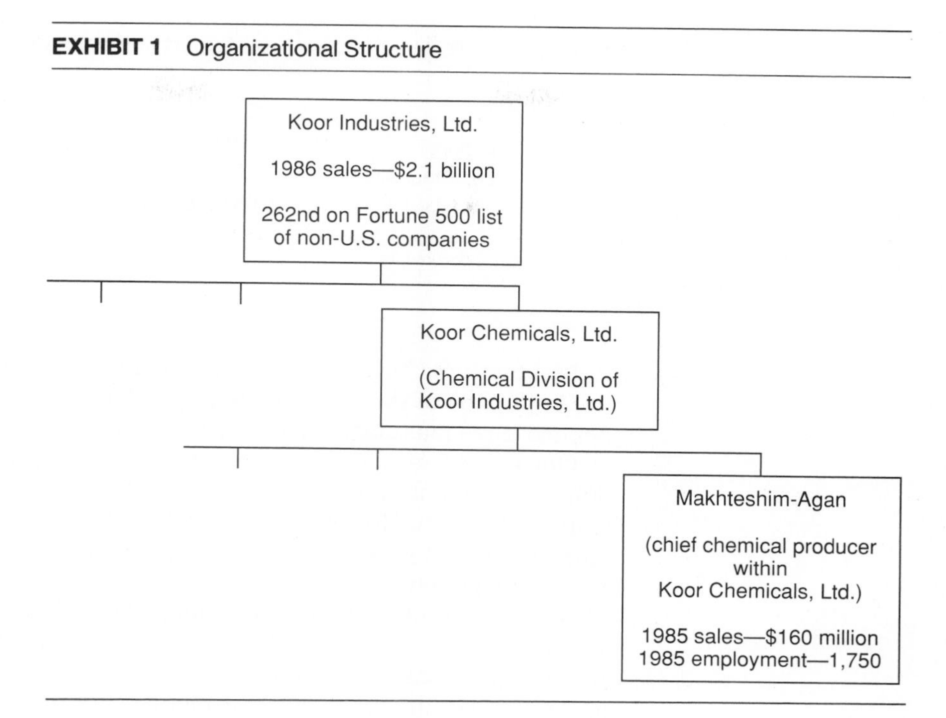

Makhteshim. If Makhteshim wanted to exercise its cancellation option in its contract with M&T for the sale of it flame-retardant product line in the United States, it had to do so soon. Another major U.S. flame retardant company has asked Makhteshim to produce a generic product for them. Determined to be in what they regarded as a vital market, Makhteshim's management was reassessing its entry strategy.

Makhteshim Chemical Works

Makhteshim Chemical Works was established in Israel in 1952. Makhteshim was the majority shareholder of Agan Chemical Manufacturers in 1987. When combined, the two companies operated as Makhteshim-Agan. Makhteshim-Agan was the chief chemical producer within Koor Chemicals, Ltd., the chemical division of Koor Industries, Ltd.

Koor Industries, Ltd. was Israel's largest industrial manufacturing firm. Koor Industries, Ltd. had worldwide sales of over $2.1 billion in 1986, and ranked 262nd on the Fortune 500 list of non-U.S. companies. It had over 100 manufacturing facilities, and over 180 marketing, financial, and commercial companies within the group. An organizational structure diagram is presented in Exhibit 1.

EXHIBIT 2 1985 Makhteshim-Agan Export Percentages

	Sales Dollars	*Production*
Export	$112,000,000 (70%)	90%
Local Markets	48,000,000 (30)	10
Total sales	$160,000,000	

Source: Company documents.

Makhteshim Chemical Works and Agan Chemical Manufacturers, Ltd. were both parts of the chemical branch of Koors Industries. Together they operated three manufacturing facilities in Israel and had 1,750 employees.

Outside of Israel, Makhteshim and Agan operated somewhat as a joint company—Makhteshim-Agan—sharing offices, staffs, and communication facilities. The agricultural chemicals sales and marketing forces of the two companies were joined in the United States; however, they were not joined for the nonagricultural chemicals in the United States.

Makhteshim-Agan had three regional sales offices which were located in Europe, the United States, and Brazil. The company had attained distribution of its products in 65 countries through more than 40 distribution centers on five continents. Sales in Israel accounted for only 10 percent of Makhteshim-Agan's production. Sales in 1985 were $160 million, with export sales accounting for 70 percent of the sales dollars (Exhibit 2). The distribution of sales among the company's main product groups is shown in Exhibit 3.

In Israel, Makhteshim Chemical Works and Agan were run as basically two different companies, each with separate headquarters and staffs. They competed with each other and other Koors subsidiaries for the resources from the parent company. Agan dealt primarily in agricultural chemicals and household pesticides. Makhteshim, on the other hand, produced agricultural chemicals, fine chemicals,[1] flame retardants, polymer intermediates, and other industrial chemicals. A diagram of their operating structure within Israel is presented as Exhibit 4.

Because of their different product focuses, the marketing approaches and operating philosophies of these two organizations were different. The agricultural chemical business tended to be more tightly focused, with fewer suppliers competing in a relatively homogeneous marketplace for chemicals. The number of customers tended to be smaller and more stable, and

[1]Fine chemicals are specialty chemicals made in very small volumes. They are usually used in complex reactions, have high profit margins, and are extremely expensive. For example, a fine chemical may be made in a 50 gallon batch and sell for $20 per pound, while a commodity chemical would be made in a continuous process and may sell for $20 per ton.

EXHIBIT 3 Makhteshim-Agan 1987 Main Product Groups

Product	*Percentage of Revenues*
Agrochemicals and household pesticides	88.0%
Fine chemicals and intermediates	5.0
Polyester and flame retardants	3.0
Photographic chemicals	2.0
Industrial chemicals	2.0
Total	100.0%

Source: Company documents.

EXHIBIT 4 Operating Structure within Israel

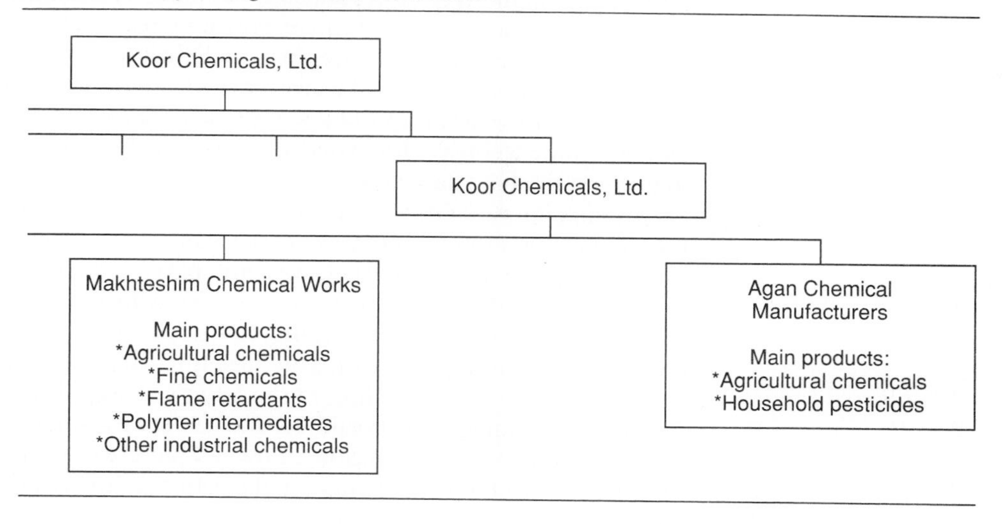

ongoing relationships could be built up on the business side of customer companies. Agan sold primarily chemical compounds of known technology and enjoyed widespread recognition for providing quality products. There was little interaction between Agan's R&D staffs and the customers' technical people. In most parts of the world, Agan's technical people generally limited their contacts to demonstrating the application of herbicides and pesticides, along with general agronomic techniques. Thus, Agan had developed a marketing approach that did not require great technical sales expertise, but relied on price. This strategy had been successful for Agan.

Makhteshim, on the other hand, sold a diverse product line in many markets. One common element in these markets was their strong technological orientation. Makhteshim's management believed the company enjoyed a strong technological position based primarily on its work in bromine and phosgene chemistry. They considered Makhteshim's technical staff to be of excellent quality and its laboratory facilities to be "world class." They had backed these resources with an $80 million capital investment program begun in 1986 and were confident that Makhteshim did fine technical work when it was aware of a problem or issue confronting a customer industry. Makhteshim had been successful in its European and Far East markets using a low-cost strategy. Makhteshim had used Israeli nationals in these markets.

A second common element in Makhteshim's markets was the incorporation of chemicals, such as flame retardants, into the customer's end product. In this environment the customer's technical staff (who specify the components of the end product) played a key role in the purchasing decision. In the flame-retardant industry, suppliers typically hired technically trained salespeople, as competitive pressures required that salespeople be familiar with the product technology and various issues facing the customer's industry. Knowledge of a customer's technology and the nature of its end product were also important since rival sellers of flame retardants often used alternate technologies to perform the same function. Additional information on the U.S. flame retardant industry is provided in the appendix.

In the opinion of its management, Makhteshim operated at a disadvantage in its ability to incorporate chemicals into the customer's end product. The company's technical staff was not part of its marketing program. Instead, they remained in their laboratories with limited interaction with customers or industry peers, tending toward isolation from industry issues and trends. Their contacts with Makhteshim's sales force were limited, generally consisting of responding to the latter's request for specific technical information. Management believed that this state of affairs made it difficult for the technical staff to develop an overall picture of industry trends or an understanding of how they might make better commercial use of their technical skills.

Some elements of Makhteshim's management believed the company had failed to recognize opportunities and to obtain the resources required to implement its own strategy because many of its overseas activities were combined with Agan. Instead, Makhteshim had been forced to adopt a low-cost strategy that limited the resources committed to its technical sales function and to the regulatory and political conflicts that surrounded some of its products. Sometimes this had meant bringing new products to market with limited technical support.

In entering the U.S. market, Makhteshim had attempted to overcome this shortcoming by arranging for M&T to market its F–2000 flame retardant product line. Flame-retardant products comprised less than 5 percent of Makhteshim's sales. The flame retardant products were very profitable.

While M&T was not considered by industry sources to be one of the strongest players in the flame retardant marketplace, it was considered to have a good technical staff that called regularly on customers and would easily be able to handle the F–2000 line. M&T was a specialty chemicals company. Industry sources described their technical department as "competent" and "credible," but lacking technological leadership. M&T's good cost position was viewed as its primary competitive advantage, with its products marketed primarily on the basis of price. One industry expert referred to M&T's product line as "copycat products," and noted that the deal with Makhteshim afforded M&T the opportunity to buy into a high-tech line. M&T manufactured its own product line, which included Thermoguard. In some respects Thermoguard was competitive with Makhteshim's F–2000 flame-retardant product line. M&T simply added the F–2000 product line to its own narrow flame-retardant product line and tried to sell it as an additional product. No major emphasis was given to the F–2000 line.

Makhteshim had expected to gain a significant (>15 percent) market share of the U.S. flame-retardant market within its first two years, but the product had thus far not been incorporated into a major customer's end product. M&T's position was that Makhteshim expected too much too soon. M&T pointed to a recent major customer order as a breakthrough in the marketing program. Although the initial order was small, M&T attested that the fact the customer had developed a new product line based on Makhteshim's product offered the potential of continuing sales for a long time.

While Makhteshim was committed to the U.S. flame-retardant market, the Israelis were increasingly concerned about the style and cost of doing business in the U.S. marketplace. They were unfamiliar with a large sales force. They were not accustomed to large bills for dinners, tended to stay in less expensive hotels, and controlled entertainment expenses tightly.

As the deadline for exercising its cancellation option in M&T's contract approached, Makhteshim's management was reassessing its basic strategy in the U.S. flame-retardant market. In particular, some now doubted the efficacy of distributor marketing when it was not backed with knowledge of the market and strong support from their own manufacturing operations. All recognized that any request for more resources would undergo intense scrutiny by Koor management, and would be questioned vigorously by other groups within Koor, who were all competing for the same limited resources. A clear consensus was at present not available.

Appendix: U.S. Flame-Retardant Industry Note

In 1987, the flame-retardants industry in the United States was an $850 million dollar business growing at annual rates in excess of 15 percent per year (see Exhibits A–1 and A–2). Gross profit margins were about 40 percent. In comparison to the U.S. market, the profitability of other world markets was about 75 percent of the U.S.

EXHIBIT A–1 U.S. Sales of Flame-Retardant Substances, 1986

	Pounds (millions)	*Sales (millions, $)*
Organic		
Chlorinated	100	$ 70
Brominated	150	260
Inorganic		
Aluminum trihydrate	400	80
Antimony oxide	40	60
Other	350	350
Total	1040	$850

Source: Interviews with industry experts.

EXHIBIT A–2 Flame-Retardant End-Use, 1987 (U.S. Market Growth Rates)

	Percent
Carpet backing	(5)
Wire/cable	>15
Unsaturated polyester	8–10
Thermoplastics	6–10
Flexible PVC	>10
New applications/polymers	>20

Source: Interviews with industry experts.

levels. Major competitors in the industry included Occidental Chemical, Ethyl-Saytex, and Great Lakes Chemical.

The purpose of flame retardants was to slow down the development and spread of a fire, allowing sufficient time for people to react to the fire situation. Flame retardants were used in a multitude of end-use applications, from electrical wire insulation, connectors, and circuit boards to carpet backing, children's clothing, plywood paneling, and plastic plumbing. With the continuing increase in the use of new materials, and new applications for existing materials, industry experts predicted that the U.S. flame-retardant chemical industry would grow to over $2 billion by the year 2000.

U.S. FLAME-RETARDANT INDUSTRY CHARACTERISTICS

The flame-retardant industry was a high-profit, value-added industry, and had three major characteristics. It was (1) created by regulation, (2) driven by technology, and (3) sustained by supplier commitment.

The flame-retardant industry was *regulation created.* Few consumers of flame retardants would use them if they were not required to do so. Flame retardants added cost to the end product, changed and degraded properties of the base polymer, and were generally inconvenient to work with. However, with the increasing rash of highly publicized fires taking their toll in both lives and property, and the increasing use of polymers in critical applications, flame and fire retardants were increasingly demanded by building codes, insurance regulators, the military, large consumers, and government bodies at all levels.

Standards had been set by Underwriters Laboratories, the U.S. military, the states of California and New York, Factory Mutual, the EEC, and a multitude of countries around the world. For example, laws had been passed in California regulating mattresses sold in the state. In 1987, New York passed laws requiring testing and registration of plastic products containing flame retardants used in New York. The upholstered furniture industry had accepted standards governing their products. The VIC (Verband Chemische Industrie, Germany's principal industry trade group) had announced that its members would stop further development of plastics containing polybrominated diphenyl oxides[2] until a toxicity issue was resolved.

While Israel had been successful negotiating a free trade agreement with the United States, a notable exception to this success was in the area of bromine chemicals and flame retardant chemicals. Industry sources had described Israeli testimony and efforts as "surprisingly" poor.

Most industry analysts foresaw increasing regulation as a certainty, with more and more governmental entities concerning themselves with the issues of smoke emissions and toxic gasses from plastics in fires. It had been estimated that the cost of compliance with current and proposed regulations in the United States alone, would be in the amount of hundreds of millions of dollars. As a consequence of this governmental involvement, political issues had overwhelmed technology, creating a severe threat to some products and technologies, and a golden opportunity for others.

The flame-retardant industry was *technology driven.* The customers for flame retardants had a single objective—to meet a specific flame-retardant performance requirement at the lowest possible cost, giving them a competitive advantage in a specific application. They were relatively indifferent to the product or technology which gave them this level of flame-retardant performance. However, the flame-retardant user had a variety of performance requirements which they were attempting to satisfy simultaneously. Thus, a product that gave them flame retardancy alone, but degraded other performance characteristics they were trying to achieve, was unacceptable. For example, aluminum trihydrate (ATH) was an inexpensive flame retardant for wire insulation. However, to reach a high level of flame retardancy, so much ATH had to be used in the wire that the wire became stiff and difficult to bend. Unless this could be overcome with other additives, ATH would not be the product of choice in wire insulation, no matter how well it performed as a flame retardant.

The flame-retardant manufacturers had to be aware of and be able to address the properties of the total polymer system. They had to know the effects of their products on the polymer, the interaction of their products with other additives and modifiers, and the total system cost and performance characteristics. This usually resulted in a close working relationship between the flame-retardant manufacturer and the customer. The technical people of the customer, those actually developing new prod-

[2]Makhteshim's F–2000 series had received full clearance on toxicology and would not be affected by this action.

EXHIBIT A–3 Flame-Retardant Producers' Distribution Chain

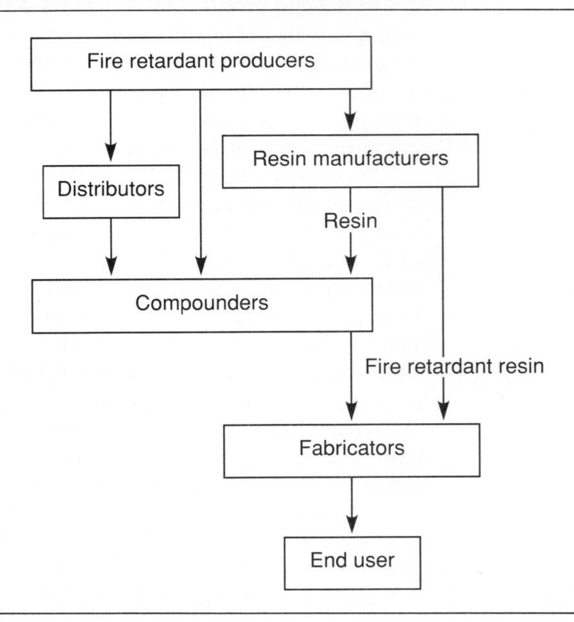

ucts for the marketplace, had to feel comfortable that the flame-retardant supplier understood his problems and could help solve them. The flame-retardant supplier was expected to be able to give technical assistance to the customer on the application of his products. The marketing and business people of the flame-retardant supplier were expected to know the end-users of the products and the characteristics of the industry being served by their customers. They also had to be sufficiently knowledgeable of the industry technology to understand and deal with the technical issues. An example of the distribution chain can be found in Exhibit A–3.

The third major characteristic of successful flame-retardant businesses was the importance of the customer's perception of a long-term *commitment* from the supplier. A customer's new products could require years of research to develop. They were highly proprietary, and rarely patentable. It could take at least a year and easily over $200,000 to get the necessary UL or MILSPEC certifications before the product could be sold for a specific application. Often, a flame-retardant supplier would run many of the tests for his customer before the customer would submit them for official testing. Once the official testing was completed (usually a UL test was required), it could take an additional year or more before the customer certified the product and incorporated it into its product line. A customer would not likely undertake the development of a new product with a supplier that the customer felt lacked either the commitment or staying power to assure the new product's continued availability.

EXHIBIT A–4 Flame Retardant Product Pricing, 1986

Type	*$/Lb.*
Flourine compounds	15.00–20.00
Chlorine/bromine compounds	.50– 3.05
Phosphorus compounds	1.10– 1.80
Antimony	1.50– 1.90
Aluminum trihydrate	.10– .30

Source: Interviews with industry experts.

FLAME-RETARDANT INDUSTRY SITUATION

Marketing

The flame-retardant industry was a specialty chemicals business which sold a performance characteristic rather than a chemical product. Sales of products for flame-retardant purposes to the polymers industry in the United States in 1986 were on the order of $850 million, with an industry growth rate in excess of 15 percent. Pricing levels ranged from a low of $.15 per pound in aluminum trihydrate to specialty fluoropolymers costing $15 to 20 per pound. Halogen flame retardants (chlorine or bromine based) were typical in the wire/cable markets, and were priced in the $2.25–2.75 per pound range. Synergists (e.g., antimony oxide) cost around $1.90 (see Exhibit A–4). Operating profit in the flame retardant specialty additives business was high, typically running 20–40 percent on sales.

A key point to understand, however, was that there was no universal flame retardant for all polymer systems. Each flame-retardant system had performance advantages and disadvantages in any particular polymer system. For example, halogenated systems (bromine or chlorine in combination with antimony oxide as a synergist) had been the primary flame-retardant systems in polypropylene, polyethylene, and nylon in the United States due to their ability to withstand the high processing temperatures required. Phosphorus systems had served a similar market in Europe along with bromine and chlorine. Aluminum trihydrate had been used primarily in carpet backing and some wire/cable applications due to its low cost relative to halogens and its acceptable performance characteristics. Opportunity in the flame-retardant industry depended on the performance of the given technology in a particular application.

Key Marketing Trends

There were currently three trends which were radically changing the character of the industry and redefining the opportunities available to the participants. These were:

- Increasing politicization.
- Industry consolidation.
- Technological change.

There was *increasing politicization* of the regulatory standards in which the flame-retardants industry must function. Toxic gas and smoke emissions in a fire environment were becoming critical to the nontechnical community due to the rather spectacularly publicized deaths in recent hotel fires. The MGM Grand Hotel in Reno, Nevada, in 1981, and the Du Pont Hotel fire in Puerto Rico in 1986 were particularly vivid examples of publicized horror. The public was demanding a "safe" fire environment, and was demanding that technology provide a solution. Some flame-retardant systems would probably be regulated out of existence, not on the scientific merits of their products, but on the political issues at hand. Primarily at risk were some brominated products which were also under attack in Germany as dioxin creators. All halogen-based systems were at risk due to their high smoke levels and their evolution of acid gases.

The second major trend was that of recent industry consolidation. Major players were consolidating their strengths.

Finally, the issue of market obsolescence due to technological change would have a profound effect on certain market segments. Ten years ago, Occidental Chemical had sold several million pounds of their product, Dechlorane® Plus to the polypropelyne market. In 1987, less than one tenth of that amount was sold in that segment. This was due to new polymers being used in the previous applications and to engineering redesigns to remove the need of flame retardancy altogether. A similar situation was occurring in carpet backing, as major carpet manufacturers were conducting research and development to make the carpet fiber itself flame retardant.

Technology

Technology, brought to play in the marketplace, was considered by most industry experts to be the single most important factor of success in the flame-retardant business. New regulations for smoke and toxic gas emissions required technological improvements in existing products. The acid gasses (HCl, HBr) that developed during a fire not only posed a threat to lives, but could do considerable damage to expensive electronic equipment. When a New York City telephone switching station burned, over $50 million of equipment was destroyed, not by flames, but by the acid gases released in the fire. Also, because halogens acted primarily in the vapor phase, large amounts of smoke were generated, hampering escape from the fire. For these two primary reasons, regulators and consumers were driving the flame-retardant industry away from halogen systems. Aluminum trihydrate was the main beneficiary of this effect, as its primary mechanism was that of a heat sink in the early stage, later decomposing into innocuous water vapor.

New polymers were constantly being brought to market, replacing other construction materials (wood, metal), as well as other polymers. With these new polymers came increasing challenges for flame retardancy. Some of these challenges were higher processing temperatures, polymer and copolymer compatibility, and smaller particle size for thinner sections.

The flame-retardant companies were addressing these technology issues with significant research programs in surface modifications and coating, fine particle grinding technology, encapsulation techniques, concentrates, and chemical/matrix modifications. Industry associations such as the Fire Retardant Chemical Association (FRCA) and the Society of Plastics Industry (SPI), as well as groups of individual producers, were addressing the questions of regulation and toxicity.

Manufacturing

Manufacturing plants for fire retardant chemicals tended to be small (annual capacities of 10–50 million pounds) and flexible. Several products were made using the same equipment. Their $5–$20 million capital cost was considered low by chemical industry standards. The plants often required specialized equipment, and production was usually campaigned, resulting in significant inventory levels. In campaigned production, plants made up to about a six months' supply of a specific chemical before changing the equipment over to make a different chemical. This allowed the plant to take advantage of long production runs and reduced the set-up cost and the cost of the extensive cleaning of the equipment that was necessary to avoid cross-contamination. A plant's location was usually not a factor in competition because transportation costs, even from overseas, were small relative to value added. For example, Occidental's Dechlorane® Plus sold for approximately $2.60 per pound. Transportation, duty, and handling costs to most parts of the world rarely exceeded $.05 per pound. Product quality and consistency, however, were critical. Raw materials tended to be a small part of the overall cost of the products (15–25 percent). While a strong raw materials base might be a competitive advantage, it was not a requirement for success.

Other Key Points

Several other key points must be made in order to understand the industry situation. First, the flame-retardants business was a *worldwide business,* both in terms of markets and producers. Companies based in West Germany, Israel, and Japan had established strong marketing presences in the United States, just as U.S. companies have done overseas. Applications technology was the name of the game, and technology transfers were rapid and efficient.

Second, while the industry was large in dollar terms, it was a *very small industry* in people and organizational terms. Everyone in the industry knew everyone else, what they were doing, and with whom they were doing it. There were very few secrets for very long. This required that market participants have strong leadership, with clearly defined plans and objectives, as execution of plans had to be clean and sure. False starts or hesitation in execution could cause the loss of an opportunity or of a competitive position.

Finally, the *rapid change* of the rules by which the industry had lived for the last 30 years had thrown the industry into confusion. Managers who were used to dealing with technical performance issues were somewhat at a loss in dealing with political regulatory bodies. Newer managers seemed to face these issues more effectively. However, industry management was currently in a generational transition and remained for the most part ill-equipped to deal in this new arena. Thus, companies that could deal with the public policymakers had an opportunity to influence regulation in the direction most beneficial to their products and technologies.

CASE 6–15 Ohmeda Monitoring Systems

Looking out his office window at the magnificent Front Range of the Colorado Rockies, Joseph W. Pepper, general manager of Ohmeda Monitoring Systems, was deep in thought concerning the future of Finapres®, a relatively new Ohmeda product. Introduced in 1987, the product had not lived up to its expectations. Now, in mid-June 1990, Pepper was considering a number of options. His choice, he knew, would have a significant impact on Ohmeda Monitoring Systems.

Background

Finapres (the name was derived from its use of finger arterial pressure) was the product on the market providing *continuous noninvasive blood pressure monitoring* (CNIBP). As such, it was the only unique product that Ohmeda could offer in 1990.

Originally introduced to the market in 1987, initial results had been disappointing. Its introduction in the United States had been generally unsuccessful. Results in Europe, and internationally, had been somewhat better but still had failed to meet the firm's expectations. Concerns about the product had led Ohmeda to stop shipments on May 1, 1990, pending a review of product problems and the overall situation.

At an all-day meeting on May 23, 1990, marketing research, field sales, and R&D had presented information on the status of Finapres. In particular, R&D had given its assessment as to the likelihood that proposed product changes and improvements would solve some of the product's shortcomings.

The specter of the disappointing initial introduction, and the uncertainty that R&D could improve the product sufficiently to satisfy all the concerns, hung over the decision to commit more funds to the product. An unsuccessful reintroduction would further hurt Ohmeda's credibility, both with customers and with the field sales force. On the other hand, successful reintroduction of Finapres would ensure a strong, and possibly dominant, position in the noninvasive blood pressure monitoring market, plus the possibility of increased sales of other monitoring products, as Finapres was combined with other Ohmeda products into packaged systems.

Subsequently, Pepper had many discussions with his key managers regarding their views of Finapres. In early June he visited a number of Ohmeda customers and distributors in Japan, many of whom were very

---

This case was prepared by Professor H. Michael Hayes and Research Assistant Brice Henderson as a basis for class discussion, rather than to illustrate either effective or ineffective handling of an administrative situation.

interested in Finapres. Although there were several unanswered questions, it was up to Pepper to make the key decisions concerning Finapres.

BOC/Ohmeda

Ohmeda Monitoring Systems was a business unit of The BOC Group, a multinational firm, headquartered in Windlesham, Surrey, England. The Group had an international portfolio of what it described as "world-competitive" businesses, principally industrial gases, health care products and services, and high-vacuum technology. The Group operated in some 60 countries and employed nearly 40,000 people.

Health care products and services were provided by BOC Health Care for critical care in the hospital and in the home. Their equipment, therapies, and pharmaceuticals were used in operating rooms (OR), recovery rooms (PACU), intensive care (ICU), and cardiac care (CCU) units throughout the world. Divisions of BOC Health Care were organized around *pharmaceuticals, home health care, intravascular devices,* and *equipment and systems.*

Ohmeda Health Care, providing equipment and systems, was an autonomous division of BOC Health Care. It was made up of five major business units, plus a field operations unit. The five business units manufactured products for *suction therapy, infant care, respiratory therapy, anesthesia,* and *monitoring systems.* Field operations provided field sales and sales support, worldwide, on a pooled basis to all the business units. (See Exhibit 1 for a partial organization chart of Field Operations.)

A 1985 reorganization had put all business decisions in the hands of the business general managers, and established profit of the business unit as a major performance measure. In 1990, the managers of the business units, and the manager of field operations, reported to the president of Ohmeda Health Care, Richard Leazer, who, in turn, reported to the managing director of BOC Health Care, W. Dekle Rountree.

Ohmeda Monitoring Systems. Ohmeda Monitoring Systems (headquartered in Louisville, Colorado) designed, manufactured, and sold (through the field operations unit) monitoring equipment for a number of segments of the health care industry. It focused its business activities on three classes of products:

- Oximetry products, used to measure oxygen content in arterial blood.
- Gas analysis products, used to measure a patient's respiratory gas levels.
- Noninvasive blood pressure measurement products.

Applications for these products were found in a wide variety of departments within hospitals and other health care facilities. Products were usually sold to the health care facility, either directly by the field sales force or by a

EXHIBIT 1 Ohmeda Monitoring Systems Partial Organization Chart—Field Operations

- Vice President, Field Operations (Worldwide), John C. Carr
  - Vice President, FOI, Mark Halpert
    - Regional Director, Southern Europe, René Bernava
      - Direct Sales: Spain, Italy, France
    - Regional Director, Latin America, Eastern and Western Europe
      - Direct Sales: Sweden, Luxembourg, Netherlands, Switzerland, Austria
      - Distributor Sales: Belgium, Greece, Turkey, Cyprus, Ireland, Portugal, Yugoslavia, Israel, Hungary, South Africa, Middle East, Egypt
    - Regional Director, United Kingdom, Germany, International Accounts
  - Vice President, AFO, James D. Valenta
  - Vice President, NAFO

distributor. Some products, however, were also sold to equipment manufacturers (OEMs) for incorporation in a larger measurement package.

Most Ohmeda oximetry and Finapres products consisted of a "box," containing the hardware, software, and a display unit, and a probe, or cuff, to allow a noninvasive way to measure the parameter of interest. These were of two types, disposable or reusable, and were designed to be attached to the patient's toe, foot, finger, hand, or ear, depending on the application.

Ohmeda had access to Finapres technology by virtue of a worldwide exclusive license, obtained from Research Unit Biomedical Instrumentation TNO (Amsterdam, the Netherlands). Many other technologies had also been acquired, either by license or outright purchase.

Ohmeda estimated the noninvasive monitoring market was $1.2 billion worldwide, with 60 percent of the market in the United States. Overall, its market share was some 15 percent of those segments it served. In selected categories, however, its market share was considerably higher. With considerable variation by country and specific product, Ohmeda estimated the growth rate of its served market at 5–10 percent per year.

The competitive picture for Ohmeda was complex. Its main competitors were U.S.-based firms. Many of its products, however, faced strong competition from European firms. In oximetry there were an estimated 25 competitors, although only 4 had significant shares. Major competitors and estimated market shares were:

Nellcor (U.S.)	50%
Ohmeda (U.S.)	30%
Criticare (U.S.)	10%
Novametrix (U.S.)	8%

In respiratory gases there were an estimated 12 competitors. Major competitors and estimated market shares were:

Datex (Finland)	16%
Ohmeda	15%
Siemens (West Germany)	14%
Hewlett-Packard (U.S.)	12%

In blood pressure measurement only five companies competed. With an 80 percent share, Critikon (U.S.) dominated the noninvasive market with its oscillometric, or noncontinuous, product. Ohmeda's sales of its noninvasive products represented just 2 percent of this market.[1]

Based on pretax operating profits in 1989, Ohmeda's financial situation appeared to be very healthy. There were concerns, however. As Pepper observed:

> We tend to be more financially driven than market driven. Also, we have not been investing heavily in R&D. As a result, our product line is relatively mature and I don't know how much longer we can count on present products for high contribution margins.
>
> Finapres is the only major new product that is close to ready to go. Perfecting Finapres, and successfully reintroducing it, would not only produce direct sales but its uniqueness could also benefit our other monitoring businesses, through integrated packages that included a technology available nowhere else. The sales force in Europe, and also in Asia, is very excited about the product, even with its present deficiencies, and believes that with reasonable improvement it could become a major contributor to sales and profits. In the U.S. there is not the same excitement. There is agreement that if all the product deficiencies could be corrected we would have a real winner, but R&D can't give us any guarantees.

Field Operations. Following the 1985 reorganization of Ohmeda Health Care from a functional organization to the five therapy units, the firm had considered how to organize its field sales operations. Given the complexity of the five product lines, and some desire on the part of the therapy unit managers to have more direct control over the sales forces that represented them, there was considerable support to establish specialized sales forces. There was also support for direct sales, as opposed to extensive use of

[1]Market shares were for the U.S. market.

distributors or dealers. Selling anesthesia equipment, it was argued, was very different than selling patient monitors and other Ohmeda products, both because of product differences and customer buying procedures. Many of Ohmeda's competitors (e.g., Siemens and Hewlett-Packard) relied heavily on direct sales, feeling that distributors or dealers could not provide the required level of technical knowledge and service.

Arguing against specialized selling was the belief that it was far more efficient, in terms of time, travel expense, and customer knowledge, to have one salesperson calling on a hospital, rather than three, as was contemplated in one proposed form of organization. Still further, there was great concern about the consequences of terminating distributors or dealers, some of whom had been associated with Ohmeda (or its predecessor companies) for over 70 years. Finally, Ohmeda was aware that Baxter-Travenol, the largest medical supplies and equipment company in the world, had specialized its sale force in 1981 but had subsequently gone back to a general sales organization.

After extensive study, it was decided to continue with a pooled form of sales organization, together with pooled product service, customer service, and finance, all reporting to the vice president of Field Operations. As of early 1990 Field Operations had three principal regional components: NAFO, responsible for sales and service in North America (the U.S. and Canada); FOI, responsible for sales and service in Europe, the Middle East, and Latin America; and AFO, responsible for sales and service in Asia, including Japan. Depending on the particular country, sales were all direct, a combination of direct and dealer, or totally through dealers.

Ohmeda recognized the need for making specialized product knowledge, beyond the expertise of the local salesperson, available quickly to the customer. In NAFO it was assumed that such specialized knowledge could be provided by specialists from manufacturing locations. In FOI and AFO it was deemed impractical for specialists to travel from the United States, and product champions were appointed in the major countries. Paid principally on salary (as opposed to the salespeople who were paid on a salary and commission basis), the product champions supported the sales force for their assigned products in a variety of ways. They were available to call on customers with the salespeople. They held product seminars, either for salespeople or for customer groups. In some instances they acted as missionary salespeople, soliciting orders from new customers. In all instances, they provided a focused communication channel between the field and headquarters marketing. It was Ohmeda's view that the product champions had played a major role in assisting the introduction of Finapres in Europe. There was also some concern that not enough manpower was available from headquarters to provide similar support to the field sales force in the United States and Canada.

Health Care Markets

The health care industry was one of the largest, and most rapidly growing, segments of the world economy. While growth was occurring worldwide, the potential for Ohmeda products was greatest in the United States, Europe, Japan, and, generally, in the developed countries of the world. With certain exceptions, the United States tended to lead the world in the development and use of technologically sophisticated health care products. U.S. manufacturers of such products generally felt that the rest of the world followed the U.S. lead in acceptance and use, with countries in Europe following in as little as six months but with longer delays in other parts of the world.

Hospitals were the principal buyers of Ohmeda products. With some variation, due mainly to government regulations, purchasing practices were very similar in the developed countries of the world. All purchases of medical equipment required budgetary approval of the hospital administration. Their purchasing influence, however, was generally inversely related to the complexity of the item. Purchase decisions of disposable supplies and gases, for instance, were generally made solely by the hospital purchasing agent, based on the lowest price. By contrast, capital equipment was invariably selected by the hospital's medical specialists and clinical area end-users. Because any machine malfunction was potentially life-threatening, medical specialists were especially concerned with precision, reliability, and safety. In addition, both the sophistication of clinical procedures and the technical expertise and interest of medical specialists were increasing. As a result, the product and clinical knowledge required to sell medical equipment was also increasing.

Ohmeda segmented its market by hospital department or application, as follows:

OR/PACU (Operating Room/Post Anesthetic Care Unit, or Recovery Room)

ICU/NICU/CCU (Intensive Care Unit/Neonatal Intensive Care Unit/ Coronary Care Unit)

L&D (Labor and Delivery)

Floors (Basically patients' rooms in hospital wards)

Nonhospital (The growing nonhospital segment, which included ambulances, surgicenters, physicians' offices, dental and home care, for oximetry and blood pressure products.)

Sales potential varied substantially, depending on the particular segment and the product, as shown in Exhibit 2. Segments outside the United States generally had lower saturation levels than in the United States. As was pointed out, however, saturation levels were not always the best indicator of

EXHIBIT 2 Ohmeda Monitoring Systems U.S. Market Size (sales potential in units, 1990–1992)

Segment	*Potential Sites**	*Oximetry*	*Gas Analysis*	*Blood Pressure*	*Saturation*
OR/PACU	60,000	26,000	31,000	15,000	HI
ICU/NICU/CCU	78,000	20,000	15,500	9,750	HI
L&D	57,000	10,000	0	4,000	MED
Floors	800,000	15,000	0	2,000	LO
Nonhospital	65,000	10,500	0	200	MED

*Number of physical locations.

sales potential. In many instances the replacement markets offered high potential as well.

In the operating room the physician (generally the anesthetist) was the key buying influence for all products. In all other segments decision making was a shared responsibility, as indicated in Exhibit 3. Key buying influences were thought to be influenced by different factors, in order of importance as indicated below:

Physician	**Nurse**	**Technician**
Technology	Ergonomics	Serviceability
Ergonomics	Relationship	Technology
Relationship	In-service	
Price/Value	Technology	

Administrator	**Financial Officer**	**Material (Purchasing)**
Company reputation	Leasing options	Price/Value
Price/Value	Total package cost	Total package cost
Revenue generation	Reimbursement	Serviceability

Personal contact with key buying influences by direct sales representatives or distributors was an essential ingredient to securing an order. Key to success, however, were favorable results from experimental trials, particularly of new products, as reported in medical journals. Manufacturers worked closely with the medical community worldwide to identify opinion leaders interested in equipment who were willing to experiment with it and then publish their results in scholarly journals. Most such experiments were reported in English language journals, but these were widely read in non-English-speaking countries.

EXHIBIT 3 Ohmeda Monitoring Systems Buying Influences

	OR	*ICU*	*NICU*	*PACU*	*CCU*	*Floors*	*L&D*
Probes	P	NTM	NT	NT	NTM	NTM	NT
Blood pressure	P	PNM	PN	PN	PNM	PNM	PN
Gas analysis	P	PTM	PT	PT	—	—	PT
Oximetry	P	NTM	NT	NT	NTM	PNTM	NT

Legend:
P = Physician
N = Nurse
T = Technician
A = Administrator
F = Financial officer
M = Materials (purchasing)

OR = Operating room
ICU = Intensive Care Unit
NICU = Neonatal Intensive Care Unit
PACU = Post Anesthetic Care Unit
CCU = Coronary Care Unit
L&D = Labor and Delivery

Finapres®

Modern medicine viewed measurement of arterial blood pressure as essential in the monitoring of patients, both during and after surgery. Traditional monitoring techniques have included both invasive and noninvasive methods. Arterial line monitoring provided continuous measurement but invasion (meaning surgical insertion of a long, small-bore catheter into the radial or femoral arteries) involved the risk of thrombosis, embolism, infections, and nerve injuries. These risks were acceptable when arterial blood samples had to be taken regularly but otherwise were to be avoided.

An oscillometric monitor, such as Criticon's Dinamap, was noninvasive. As commonly used, such a device provided readings automatically every three to five minutes, or on demand. It could provide readings more frequently, but this involved considerable patient pain or discomfort. As normally used, therefore, it could miss vital data due to the time lag of the readings. (Ohmeda sold a noninvasive blood pressure monitor of this type, manufactured for them, but had not promoted it heavily.) Manual methods were noninvasive but were highly dependent on the skill of the clinician and the application of the correct size arm cuff and involved even more time lag.

Finapres Technology. In 1967 a Czech physiologist, Dr. Jan Peñaz, patented a method with which it was possible to measure finger arterial pressure noninvasively. (See Exhibit 4 for a detailed description of the method.) In 1973 the device was demonstrated at the 10th International Conference on Medical and Biological Engineering at Dresden. Subsequently, a group of engineers at the Research Unit Biomedical Instrumentation TNO in the Netherlands became interested in the technology and constructed, first, a laboratory model, and then a model that they felt was clinically and experimentally useful and commercially viable. In 1983 Ohmeda acquired an exclusive license for the Finapres technology.

EXHIBIT 4 Ohmeda Monitoring Systems Principles of Operation

Arteries transport blood under high pressure to the tissues. The artery walls are strong and elastic; that is, they stretch during systole (when blood is forced onward by contraction of the heart) and recoil during diastole (dilation of the heart when its chambers are filling with blood). This prevents arterial pressure from rising or falling to extremes during the cardiac cycle, thus maintaining a continuous uninterrupted flow of blood to the tissues. The volume of blood inside the artery increases when it expands and decreases when it contracts. This change in volume is the key phenomenon on which the Peñaz/Finapres technology was based.

In the Finapres system, a cuff with an inflatable bladder was wrapped around the finger (see diagram below). A light source (LED) was directed through the finger and monitored by a detector on the other side. This light was absorbed by the internal structures according their various densities. The emitted light was an indication of blood volume in the artery. Through a complex servomechanism system, the cuff was inflated, or deflated, to maintain the artery size at a constant level. Thus, cuff pressure constantly equaled arterial pressure and was displayed on the monitor as an arterial waveform and also digitally.

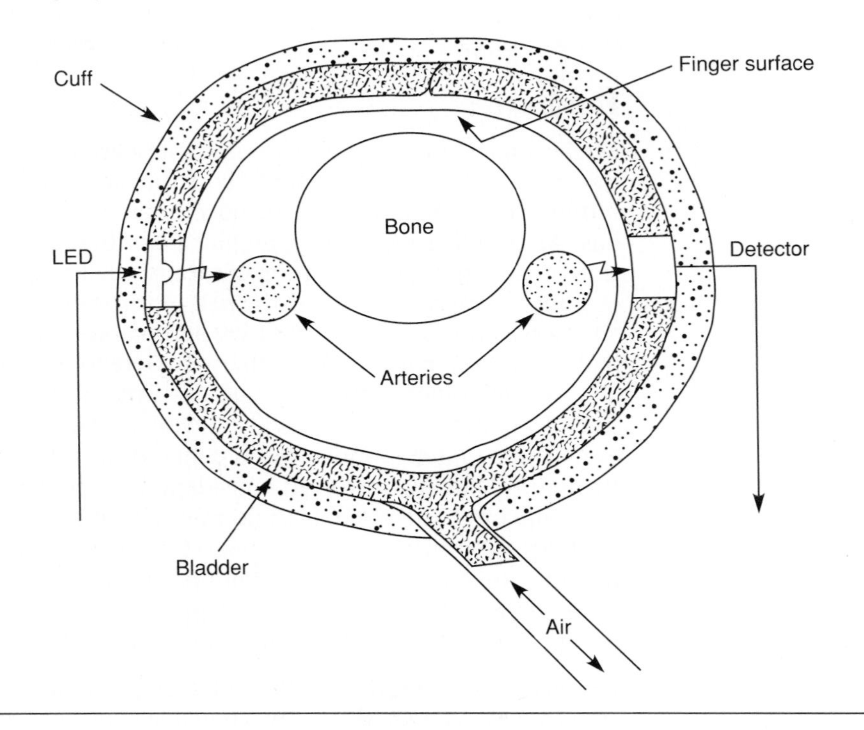

Finapres and Ohmeda. Although TNO had produced a working model of Finapres, Ohmeda had invested between two and three million dollars in R&D in order to develop a manufacturable box and cuff and to recode the software to conform to Ohmeda protocols. The resultant design could be built largely on existing equipment, although some $100,000 was required for tooling the cuff. Prior to commercial introduction, extensive work was done with opinion leaders to establish the credibility of the product. Favorable test results of clinical studies of Finapres were reported in medical journals, and were widely distributed to the medical profession. Cost of this work, and other market development expenditures, was roughly equivalent to the cost of R&D.

Ohmeda introduced a commercial design of Finapres in 1987 in the United States and in 1988 in Europe and other world markets. The initial offering consisted of a box, a patient interface module that attached to the patient's hand, and three reusable cuffs. It was positioned to compete against invasive measuring products. Although it was expected it would ultimately be offered to the OEM market it was originally introduced directly to the OR market. Priced at approximately $9,500 it was expected to return a contribution margin in excess of 70 percent (generally typical for new and unique products in the health equipment industry). Some price resistance was experienced and the U.S. price was reduced to $8,500, six months after introduction. Disappointingly, U.S. sales through 1989 totaled only 200 units.

In 1988 the product was introduced internationally, at a U.S. equivalent price of $9,600. In contrast to the U.S. introduction, the product was targeted, for direct sale, at a number of segments in hospitals. As in the United States, price resistance was encountered and by 1989 the price had been reduced to approximately the U.S. equivalent of $5,000.

To some extent low sales in the United States were blamed on tactical marketing errors, such as the positioning and price of the product at introduction. There were also some technical problems with the system. Some were cosmetic in nature and easily fixed. Others were more serious, both for the clinicians using the equipment and for Ohmeda. Major problems were the difficulty in applying the cuff properly in order to get an accurate reading, and drift in readings that occurred after several hours of continuous use, a particularly serious problem in OR. Another problem was the inability of the equipment to accurately monitor patients with poor blood circulation.

Results were more promising in Europe. The European medical community had been anxious to get access to Finapres. Much had been written about the Peñaz methodology and the system developed by TNO in the European medical press. The noninvasive aspect of Finapres was particularly attractive. European doctors were less comfortable with arterial line methodology than were their American counterparts. In addition, they tended to be more willing to invest time and effort to learn new technologies and there was less preoccupation with patient throughput than in the United States.

News of the problems experienced in the ORs in the United States had made penetration of the OR segment in Europe difficult. With its broader contacts, the sales force was able to introduce the product to other segments, particularly in CCU and physiology in teaching hospitals, where stability over long periods of time was either not as critical as in OR or where continuous blood pressure monitoring was of paramount importance. With this approach, supported by the willingness of the sales force to train medical personnel in application of the cuff, the company experienced much greater success, selling a total of 700 units in these markets through 1989.

Commenting on results through 1989, Melvyn Dickinson, international marketing manager observed:

> There are significant differences between the hospital markets in the United States and Europe, and in how our sales forces sell to them. In the United States, for example, anesthetic machines, made by one of our sister therapy units, are sold by the same field sales force that sells our monitoring equipment. The U.S. machines are made to more stringent requirements and are much more expensive than those sold in Europe. In addition, they tend to be replaced on a 5-year cycle, compared to 10–15 years in, say, Italy. As a result, our sales force in the United States tends to really concentrate on the OR market, whereas in Europe the sales force takes a broader approach.
>
> It's also important to recognize that the key influence for OR purchases is an anesthesiologist, for whom blood pressure is just one of many concerns. In other segments of the hospital, the situation is very different. In the CCU, or the cardiac operating theater, blood pressure is of paramount importance. Not all procedures are lengthy, and even where they are many cardiologists saw value in CNIBP, even though there was drift. For physiological measurements in research hospitals, or in hypertension units, there were even fewer drawbacks, plus the clinicians in these situations were much more inclined to take extra care with application of the cuff.
>
> Beyond these differences, we misread the market in general. It had been our assumption that arterial lines (the term for invasive systems) were the major competitors for Finapres. We priced and positioned Finapres accordingly. Unfortunately, our promotion didn't get this position established in the minds of our customers. As it turned out, many customers viewed the oscillometric machines as our major competitor. For these customers, our original price involved too large a premium, versus the less expensive oscillometric machines. Now there is some real question about going back to the original positioning strategy.

The two years following the introduction of Finapres were characterized by indecision about its future and lack of significant support for the product. Once introduced, Ohmeda required it to be self-supporting, with product improvements made on an ongoing basis financed out of current revenues. When the sales force began to report complaints from the clinicians in the field, it was felt that the major problems were cosmetic, concerning the size of the box and the readability of the screen. Complaints regarding inaccurate readings were thought to result from misapplication of the cuff. Despite some modifications, complaints continued and sales declined. As 1990 began, it was apparent that decisions as to the future of Finapres needed to be made.

Reassessment. Reassessment of Finapres had started with the development of the five year plan for Ohmeda Monitoring Systems. Subsequently, concerns on the part of the sales force about the commitment to Finapres indicated the desirability of a meeting involving sales force management, product management, and R&D. On May 23, 1990, Joe Pepper convened a meeting of representatives of all three groups, as well as headquarters marketing. The main points that emerged from the meeting were as follows:

- There was general agreement that the market potential for CNIBP was large. There was, however, considerable disagreement as to its exact size. Some estimates of the U.S. market were as large as 7,740 units per year. International estimates were considerably lower. There was general agreement that the largest market segments for Finapres were OR and ICU/CCU. It was the view of Ohmeda's product managers, however, that the focus of the NAFO sales force on the OR market made selling to the ICU/CCU segment difficult.
- It was emphasized that the diffusion of innovation in many instances took a long time. Acceptance of some currently standard medical equipment came only after a number of years. Oximetry, for example, took 14 years, echocardiography took 10 years and, as it was emphasized, capnometry (CO_2 gas analysis) took 40 years to become accepted. However, if Finapres was to ultimately succeed, investment was necessary not only in technological development, but in market development as well.
- The following reasons for lack of success to date were identified:
    - *Drift in readings over time.*
    - *Not accurate for average clinician.*
    - *Not easy to use.*
    - *Inadequate alert for misapplied cuff.*
    - *No alerts for problems with poor circulation.*
    - *No toe/pediatric/neonatal thumb cuffs.*
- Concerns were expressed about:
    - *Lack of a research culture.*
    - *Bottom line/short-term focus.*
    - *R&D research shortage.*
- R&D gave its assessment of time and cost to develop fixes and their likelihood of success:
    - *The cause of drift was not certain, but there was a high probability that the problem could be fixed with changes in software, probably in 1990. If this fix worked the cost would be relatively modest.*
    - *Assessing the present cuff as offering 30 percent of ideal requirements, currently contemplated modifications could be expected to improve performance to 40 percent by January 1991, again with relatively modest cost. With a more substantial effort it was expected performance could be improved to 80 percent in two years.*

- Noninvasive oscillometric blood pressure machines were not likely to be "thrown out" in favor of Finapres. It was more likely they would be replaced on a normal schedule.
- On the positive side a number of strengths were identified:
  - *Patents lasting past the year 2000 (except U.K. and Germany).*
  - *Strong distribution, particularly in OR.*
  - *Technical expertise.*
  - *Head start over competition.*

Following extensive discussion, four options were presented:

1. Stay on the present course. Make sufficient modifications to make it possible to carefully reintroduce the product in selected markets. This approach was estimated to cost $307,000 in R&D expense, generate sales of 820 units through 1994, and have a net present value of $30,000.
2. Stop the project. Taking into account writing off current inventory costs and possible return costs, this approach was estimated to have a negative NPV of $160,000.
3. Make a significant investment in R&D and marketing (including going forward with a mini-Fini, a much smaller version of Finapres that would be targeted at the OEM market). This contemplated a 50 percent penetration of the OR market by 1995, a 50 percent penetration of the ICU market by 1998, and significant penetration of the OEM market. Cumulative sales estimates for this approach were 7,700 units in the US and 4,000 internationally (through 1995). With projected revenues of $40 million, investment in R&D of $2 million, investment in marketing of $1.2 million, the net present value of this approach through 1995 was estimated to be $2,200,000.
4. Sell the business. There was considerable discussion of this option but the general view was that it was not likely Ohmeda could find a buyer willing to pay any significant amount for the business. In any event, it was unlikely that top management at BOC would approve such a step.

Management Views. Subsequent to the May 23 meeting a number of views were expressed by Ohmeda managers. As John Carr, vice president of Field Operations saw it:

> The international experience with Finapres was more successful for a variety of reasons. The original technology was developed by a European company (TNO) so the European medical community was familiar with the concept. The sales force is more balanced in its approach to the market. Hence, it was able to exploit niche markets where the device worked very well. The initial sales built confidence. The real key was the use of product champions. The product was given support and attention that it did not receive in the States.

Finapres represented a once-in-5-to-10-years type of opportunity. It was a significant new technology which didn't seem to fit Ohmeda's culture or annual financial cycle. If the initial effort had been followed by product enhancements, Finapres would have been successful. From here, the only two decisions I see are sell or go.

Similar views were expressed by James Valenta, vice president for Asia (AFO):

Finapres is a great product, which, from my view in the Asian markets, has significant customer appeal. It seems that things were stacked against the product from the beginning. Soon after Finapres was purchased, Ohmeda reorganized. The individual who had pushed to buy the technology moved on to other assignments, which resulted in some lost momentum. Finapres never really had a home, which compounded the problems with the system itself. Had there been a quicker response to feedback from the international sales force, most of what was discussed at the meeting today, the drift issue and the cuff, could have been resolved some time ago. Ohmeda had trouble accepting the fact that there was a problem. The feedback domestically was focused more on cosmetic rather than substantive issues. Changes were made without knowledge of the impact to other parts of the system.

Japan is more technologically oriented, they grasped the idea of the system quickly and easily. Maybe it's just that invasive technology isn't as advanced overseas as in the United States. The doctors in Japan seem more interested in learning about new technology than in the States.

If Ohmeda doesn't want to continue with Finapres, I'll buy it and produce it. I believe in the product that much.

A somewhat different perspective was given by René Bernava, regional director for Southern Europe:

Europe was ready for Finapres. The medical community, especially in Germany, was excited about the studies and papers written about the product. As a whole, European doctors were much less comfortable with arterial monitoring than their American counterparts. Finapres should have been a dazzling success in Europe, but there were problems, both with the product and the way it was marketed.

The technology for Finapres was purchased but not improved. The early version did not work. The project had software problems and lacked leadership. The original plan was to make an inexpensive disposable cuff. With this focus, a cuff that really worked regardless of cost was never developed. Also, the product was introduced at a premium price. That philosophy did not work.

The international sales force felt we had the top technology and wanted to go ahead. The meeting today occurred because we were the most vocal. I went to Dekle (President Dekle Rountree) some time ago and asked him to investigate the product, renew agreements with TNO, and put some money into the project. Some money was forthcoming but it wasn't a continuing process.

As Mark Halpert, vice president for FOI, saw the situation:

There are several reasons Finapres was more successful in Europe and overseas than in the United States. The sales force in Europe sells many products whereas in the United States the sales force only sells Ohmeda products. With the large product line, we developed customer expertise. We know what the customer wants, and we use technical support to help conclude the transactions.

The organization or the medical community in Europe is different also. Anesthesia and monitoring are the same customer. In the United States there are more specialists. The sales force, with its broader coverage and experience, went after other niches rather than anesthesia, where the product had failed in the United States.

The key difference internationally was the product champion. Internationally, the product champion was part of the sales force, thus closer to the customers. In the United States, management served this role. Europe is still enthusiastic about the product. In Germany, just with the 1991 cuff, the product will be a success.

Bonnie Queram was manager of Sales Programs and Administration in NAFO and reported to the vice president of Sales. As she recalled:

Everyone was enthusiastic when Finapres was introduced. It looked easy to sell, although the box was big and clunky. Initially there was a high level of sales activity and orders. Unfortunately, when problems surfaced we tended to focus on cosmetic fixes and sales tapered off in the United States. In contrast, sales held up well in Europe. I developed a questionnaire to find out why. The responses indicated there is a major difference in clinical practice between the United States and Europe. The physicians, for instance, are more down-to-earth there. In contrast to the United States, they are very patient and want to work with the manufacturer, particularly on a new product. The anesthesiologists will spend lots of time in pre-op making sure things like the cuff are OK, whereas in the United States they are very impatient. For these reasons, and a number of others, I concluded that the European experience wouldn't transfer to the United States. Our normal assumption is that we can develop our products for the U.S. market, and then go abroad with the same strategy. This is the one case in a hundred where this assumption doesn't apply.

Bill Belew, a senior product manager in Louisville, had a somewhat different view. According to Belew:

The product problems in Europe and the United States are identical. The only difference is the sales approach. What we need is a complete fix. That will cost in the neighborhood of $2 million, but once we have it we can go after the OR/ICU markets anywhere in the world.

He went on to say:

The May 23 meeting was both good and bad. The potential for the product was reiterated, and we heard the product would not be killed. On the other hand, it didn't sound as if we were going to make the kind of commitment the potential justified. And this was despite information that Nellcor might introduce a CNIBP product in September.

The enthusiasm for Finapres was shared by Lloyd Fishman, director of marketing. He had a number of concerns, however:

I've been watching Finapres evolve since joining Ohmeda 2½ years ago. I think the product has potential to represent as much as 10% of our sales, but I was concerned that there was no sense of purpose, no vision, about the product. We were doing lots of little "fixits" without any real sense of our markets or what the product should be. I called the May 23 meeting to see if we couldn't develop such a sense of purpose or vision.

There's no question that we face a complex situation. The markets in the United States and international are very different. The financial orientation of the doctors in the United States rubs off on our sales force and they're much less inclined to sell concept products than in Europe, where the doctors like to work with us on new developments.

Ray Jones had recently joined Ohmeda as R&D group manager and was responsible for the Finapres R&D effort. As he put it:

I think Finapres has lots of potential, but we need to resolve a number of critical issues. For instance, we use finger pressure as a measure of central blood pressure, but we're not sure how closely finger pressure simulates central pressure or how accurately we're measuring finger pressure.

Management would like us to give some performance guarantees, but that's not the nature of R&D. We can, however, identify the key technical and physiological issues and identify milestones with the expectation that we can get data to indicate if the issue is resolvable.

One of the things that would really help would be for marketing to give us some better performance criteria.

Finally, Joe Pepper reflected on his thoughts subsequent to the May 23 meeting, his various discussions with his managers, and his visit to Japan:

I know the people in the organization feel we don't spend enough on R&D. But its a question of balance. We have been spending over 6 percent of sales on R&D, plus the corporation has a major research facility at Murray Hill, New Jersey, where we do the riskier, blue sky, R&D. In the past our competitors have spent a higher percent of sales on R&D. We estimate that Nellcor, for instance, spent over 10 percent during the last four years. However, we also estimate that they will reduce this in the next four years.

The May 23 meeting was valuable and we got a lot of opinions on the table. One option that was not looked at, however, was to go exclusively with OEMs.

In Japan the product is selling well. The physicians appear more willing to fiddle with the product to make it work. Based on what's going on in Japan, and what is going on in Europe, I wonder if we might not be able to bootstrap their experience back into the U.S. market.

Part of our problem is our whole development process. We've hired some new people, Ray Jones as product development manager and Nick Jensen as a research scientist, but it's going to take them some time to sort out the problems and establish better procedures.

I know John Carr wants us to go with a product that will sell in the United States. Part of the question, though, is how much faith do I put in the numbers?

Name Index

Subject Index